WAYS OF BEING RELIGIOUS

WAYS OF BEING RELIGIOUS

Gary E. Kessler

California State University, Bakersfield

Mayfield Publishing Company
Mountain View, California
London • Ontario

Library of Congress Cataloging-in-Publication Data

Ways of being religious / [compiled by] Gary E. Kessler.
   p.   cm.
  Includes bibliographical references.
  ISBN 0-7674-0089-5
  1. Religions. I. Kessler, Gary E.
  BL80.2.W38   2000
  200—dc21   99-051379

Manufactured in the United States of America

10   9   8   7   6   5   4   3   2   1

Mayfield Publishing Company
1280 Villa Street
Mountain View, California 94041

Sponsoring editor, Kenneth King; *production editor,* Carla White Kirschenbaum; *manuscript editor,* Margaret Moore; *text and cover designer,* Linda Robertson; *design manager,* Glenda King; *manufacturing manager,* Randy Hurst. The text was set in 9.5/11.5 Janson by G&S Typesetters, Inc. and printed on 45 # Chromatone Matte by Banta Book Group.

Cover image: Andrew Hall/Tony Stone Images

To Lucia and Caleb, may you live in a peaceful world.

Contents

Preface xv

PART 1 • INTRODUCTION 1

CHAPTER 1 A Challenge 3

1.1 Spiritual Regret 6
Lee H. Yearley, NEW RELIGIOUS VIRTUES AND
THE STUDY OF RELIGION 7

Key Terms and Concepts 15
Suggestions for Further Reading 15
Research Projects 15

CHAPTER 2 What Is Religion? 17

2.1 Defining Religion 20
Rem B. Edwards, THE SEARCH FOR FAMILY
RESEMBLANCES OF RELIGION 21

Key Terms and Concepts 24
Suggestions for Further Reading 24
Research Projects 24

CHAPTER 3 How Should We Study
Religion? 25

3.1 Comparing Religions 29
William E. Paden, COMPARATIVE
PERSPECTIVES 29

3.2 Explaining Religion 31
Wayne Proudfoot, EXPLANATION 32

Key Terms and Concepts 35
Suggestions for Further Reading 35
Research Projects 36

PART 2 • WAYS OF BEING RELIGIOUS
ORIGINATING IN AFRICA AND NORTH
AMERICA 37

CHAPTER 4 Ways of Being Religious in
Africa 39

INTRODUCTION 39

4.1 An Overview 39
Benjamin C. Ray, AFRICAN RELIGIONS: AN
OVERVIEW 41

SOURCES 50

4.2 Creation 50
Recorded by *Marcel Griaule,* CONVERSATIONS
WITH OGOTEMMÊLI 51

4.3 God the Eternal 53
PYGMY HYMN ON GOD 53

4.4 The First Man/King and Death 53
KINTU—A STORY OF THE GANDA 54

4.5 Sacrifice 56
E. E. Evans-Pritchard, NUER SACRIFICE 56

4.6 Healing 59
Recorded by *Marjorie Shostak,* NISA—A WOMAN
HEALER 59

CONTEMPORARY SCHOLARSHIP 61

4.7 African Religion and Philosophy 61
Kwasi Wiredu, AFRICAN RELIGIONS FROM A
PHILOSOPHICAL POINT OF VIEW 62

Key Terms and Concepts 67
Suggestions for Further Reading 67
Research Projects 68

CHAPTER 5 Ways of Being Religious Among
    Native North Americans 69

INTRODUCTION 69

5.1 An Overview 70
Åke Hultkrantz, NATIVE NORTH AMERICAN
    RELIGIONS 70

SOURCES 78

5.2 Creation 78
Recorded by *Frank Waters*, SPIDER WOMAN AND
    CREATION 79
Tsimshian, RAVEN AND THE LIGHT 81

5.3 The Divine 82
Sword, Recorded by *J. R. Walker*, WAKAN
    TANKA 83

5.4 The Origin of Death 83
COYOTE AND THE ORIGIN OF DEATH 83

5.5 Ritual Dancing and Singing 84
Thomas Tyon, THE SUN DANCE 85

5.6 Visions 87
Black Elk, THE GREAT VISION 87

5.7 Shamans and Feminine Power 89
Inuit, SEDNA 90

CONTEMPORARY SCHOLARSHIP 90

5.8 Land Ethic and Language 91
N. Scott Momaday, THE MAN MADE OF WORDS 91

5.9 Spiritual Values 94
Joseph Epes Brown, BECOMING PART OF IT 94

Key Terms and Concepts 98
Suggestions for Further Reading 99
Research Projects 99

PART 3 • WAYS OF BEING RELIGIOUS
ORIGINATING IN ASIA 101

CHAPTER 6 Hindu Ways of Being Religious
    103

INTRODUCTION 103

6.1 An Overview 103
David R. Kinsley, HINDUISM 105

SOURCES 115

6.2 The Vedic Period 115

6.2.1 *Rig Veda* 116
    HYMNS FROM THE RIG VEDA 117
    I PRAY TO AGNI 117

WE HAVE DRUNK THE SOMA 117
PURUṢA-SŪKTA, or THE HYMN OF
    MAN 118
CREATION HYMN (NĀSADĪYA) 118

6.2.2 *Upanishads* 119
    BRIHADARANYAKA 119
    CHANDOGYA 121

6.3 The Classical Period 122

6.3.1 Laws of Manu 123

6.3.2 Sita and Rama 126
Valmiki, RAMAYANA 127

6.3.3 *Bhagavad Gita* 131
    BHAGAVAD GITA (Books 2 and 12) 132

6.3.4 Yoga Sutra 136
    YOGA SUTRA (2.1–55, 3.1–8) 137

6.4 Medieval Period 140

6.4.1 Mirabai 140
Mira, SONGS 141

6.4.2 Birth of Kali 141
    DEVI-MAHATMYA 142

6.4.3 Vedanta 143
Shankara, CREST-JEWEL OF DISCRIMINATION
    (VIVEKA-CHUDAMANI) 144
Ramanuja, VEDANTA SUTRA COMMENTARY
    (SHRI-BHASHYA) 145

6.4.4 Tantra of the Great Liberation 146
    MAHANIRVANA TANTRA 147

6.5 Modern Period 148

6.5.1 Adherence to Truth 149
Gandhi, EXPERIMENTS WITH TRUTH 149

6.5.2 Religion and Politics 150
Katherine K. Young, THE CASE OF UMA
    BHARATI 150

CONTEMPORARY SCHOLARSHIP 152

6.6 Puranic Accounts of Creation 152
Tracy Pintchman, GENDER COMPLEMENTARITY
    AND HIERARCHY 153

6.7 Darsan 156
Diana L. Eck, SEEING THE DIVINE 157

Pronunciation Guide 160
Key Terms and Concepts 160
Suggestions for Further Reading 162
Research Projects 162

CHAPTER 7 **Buddhist Ways of Being Religious** 163

INTRODUCTION 163

7.1 An Overview 163
Donald S. Lopez Jr., BUDDHISM: AN OVERVIEW 164

SOURCES 176

7.2 Enlightenment 177
Ashvaghosha, ENLIGHTENMENT (*Buddhacarita*) 177

7.3 Nikaya or Hinayana Buddhism 180

7.3.1 The Evolution of the World 180
SUTRA ON KNOWING THE BEGINNING (*AGGANNA SUTTA*) 181

7.3.2 The Three Marks of Existence 182
SUFFERING, CO-DEPENDENT ORIGINATION, IMPERMANENCE, AND NO-SELF (*SAMYUTTA-NIKAYA* AND *ANITYATASUTRA*) 183

7.3.3 The Path to Enlightenment 184
MORAL CONDUCT AND MEDITATION 185

7.3.4 The Goal 186
NIRVANA 187
THE CESSATION OF SUFFERING 187
THE JOY OF RELEASE 187

7.4 Mahayana Buddhism 187

7.4.1 Parable of the Lost Son 188
THE LOST SON 188

7.4.2 Perfection of Wisdom 190
HEART SUTRA 191

7.4.3 Mahayana Philosophy 192
Nagarjuna and Vasubandhu, NIRVANA AND CONSCIOUSNESS-ONLY 193

7.4.4 The Bodhisattva Vow 195
Shantideva, ENTERING THE PATH (*Bodhicaryavatara*) 196

7.4.5 Savior *Bodhisattvas* and Buddhas 197
AVALOKITESHVARA, TARA, AND AMITABHA 198

7.5 Mahayana Buddhism in China and Japan 200

7.5.1 The Goddess 200
THE GODDESS 201

7.5.2 Buddha Nature 202
Tsung-mi, AN INQUIRY ON MAN 202

7.5.3 Ch'an Buddhism 203
Hui-neng, PLATFORM SUTRA 204

7.5.4 Zen Buddhism 205
Dogen, EYE AND TREASURE OF THE TRUE LAW 206

7.5.5 Nichiren Buddhism 207
Nichiren, RIGHTEOUSNESS AND SECURITY 208

7.6 Vajrayana or Tantric Buddhism in Tibet 209

7.6.1 The Tibetan Book of the Dead 210
BARDO THODAL 210

7.6.2 Pilgrimage to Mount Kailasa 212
Kazuhiko Tamamura, SEIZAN JUNREI 212

7.6.3 The White Lotus 213
The Dalai Lama, FREEDOM IN EXILE 214

CONTEMPORARY SCHOLARSHIP 218

7.7 Satori 218
D. T. Suzuki, THE ESSENCE OF ZEN 219

7.8 Gender and Emptiness 220
Rita M. Gross, FEMINIST COMMENTS ON THE MAHAYANA 220

Key Terms and Concepts 223
Suggestions for Further Reading 225
Research Projects 225

CHAPTER 8 **Confucian Ways of Being Religious** 227

INTRODUCTION 227

8.1 An Overview 228
Julia Ching, CONFUCIANISM AS RELIGIOUS HUMANISM 228

SOURCES 239

8.2 The Classical Period (ca. 700–221 B.C.E.) 239

8.2.1 Book of Rites 239
THE PRINCIPLES OF SACRIFICE 240
THE MEAN 242
THE GREAT LEARNING 243

8.2.2 Analects 244
Confucius, SELECTED SAYINGS 244

8.2.3 Is Human Nature Good or Evil? 248
Mencius, HUMAN NATURE IS GOOD 249
Hsün Tzu, HUMAN NATURE IS EVIL 251

8.3 Han Orthodoxy (206 B.C.E.–220 C.E.) 253

8.3.1 Correlative Thinking 253
Tung Chung-shu, LUXURIANT GEMS 254

8.3.2 The Perfect Confucian Woman 256
Pan Chao, LESSONS FOR WOMEN 256

8.4 The Defense of the Confucian Way (220–907) 260

8.4.1 The True Way 260
Han Yü, MEMORIAL ON THE BONE OF THE BUDDHA AND WHAT IS THE TRUE WAY? 261

8.5 Neo-Confucianism (960–1644) 264

8.5.1 The Great Ultimate 264
Chou Tun-i, EXPLANATION OF THE DIAGRAM OF THE GREAT ULTIMATE AND PENETRATING THE BOOK OF CHANGES 265

8.5.2 Spiritual Beings 267
Chu Hsi, SPIRITUAL BEINGS AND FORCES 268

8.5.3 Why Does Great Learning Manifest Clear Character? 269
Wang Yang-Ming, INQUIRY ON THE GREAT LEARNING 269

8.6 Ch'ing Confucianism (1644–1911) 272

8.6.1 The Harmony of Nature 272
Wang Fu-chih, THE PRINCIPLE OF NATURE AND HUMAN DESIRES 272

8.7 New Confucianism (1911–present) 273

8.7.1 Does Confucianism Have a Religious Element? 273
Tu Wei-ming, ON CONFUCIAN RELIGIOUSNESS 274

CONTEMPORARY SCHOLARSHIP 276

8.8 The Secular as Sacred 276
Herbert Fingarette, HUMAN COMMUNITY AS HOLY RITE 277

8.9 Confucian Women 281
Theresa Kelleher, CONFUCIANISM 281

Pronunciation Guide 289
Key Terms and Concepts 289
Suggestions for Further Reading 290
Research Projects 290

CHAPTER 9 Taoist Ways of Being Religious 291

INTRODUCTION 291

9.1 An Overview 291
Laurence G. Thompson, THE TAOIST TRADITION 292

SOURCES 299

9.2 The Early Foundations 299

9.2.1 The Way and Its Power 300
Lao Tzu, TAO TE CHING (1, 2, 4, 6, 8, 11, 14, 16, 22, 25, 34, 37, 42) 300

9.2.2 Mystical Tales 303
Chuang Tzu, CHUANG TZU 303

9.2.3 Ecstatic Travel 306
FAR-OFF JOURNEY 306

9.3 Taoism Expands 308

9.3.1 Commenting on the Tao 308
Celestial Master, HSIANG-ERH COMMENTARY 309

9.3.2 Immortality, Alchemy, and Merit 311
Ko Hung, THE PHILOSOPHER WHO EMBRACES SIMPLICITY 311

9.3.3 Immortal Ladies 315
THE LADY OF GREAT MYSTERY 315

9.4 Taoism Flourishes 316

9.4.1 The Path 316
THE MASTER OF HEAVENLY SECLUSION 316

9.4.2 Gods and Goddesses 319
Tu Kuangtin, THE QUEEN MOTHER OF THE WEST 319

9.4.3 Ascension 321
Tu Kuangtin, THE FLOWER MAIDEN 321

9.5 Taoism Abides 321

9.5.1 Floating with the Tao 322
Wang Ch'ung-yang, FIFTEEN TEACHINGS 322

9.5.2 The Great Tao Has No Form 324
SCRIPTURE OF PURITY AND TRANQUILITY 325

9.5.3 Taoist Breathing Techniques 326
Jiang Weiqiao, QUIET SITTING WITH MASTER YINSHI 326

CONTEMPORARY SCHOLARSHIP 329

9.6 Women and Taoism 329
Barbara E. Reed, WOMEN IN TAOISM 329

9.7 Religion on the Ground 336
Daniel L. Overmyer, POPULAR RELIGION 337

Key Terms and Concepts 338
Suggestions for Further Reading 339
Research Projects 339

PART 4 • WAYS OF BEING RELIGIOUS ORIGINATING IN THE NEAR EAST 341

CHAPTER 10 Jewish Ways of Being Religious 343

INTRODUCTION 343

10.1 An Overview 344
Jacob Neusner, THE FOUR PERIODS IN THE HISTORY OF JUDAISM *345*

SOURCES 351

10.2 The First Age of Diversity (ca. 586 B.C.E.–70 C.E.) 352

10.2.1 Torah 352
From Genesis
CREATION (Genesis 1–3) 353
COVENANT WITH ABRAHAM (Genesis 17) 356
From Exodus
PASSOVER AND EXODUS (Exodus 12:29–42, 14) 356
MOSAIC COVENANT (Exodus 19, 20) 358
From Leviticus
HOLINESS CODE (Leviticus 19) 359

10.2.2 Nevi'im (Prophets) 360
FROM ISAIAH (1:1–28, 6) 360

10.2.3 Ketuvim (Writings) 362
FROM PSALMS (8, 23, 51, 137) 363
FROM ESTHER (3–5:5a, 7) 364

10.3 The Age of Definition (ca. 70–640) 366

10.3.1 Creation of the Intelligible World 366
Philo of Alexandria, ON THE INTELLIGIBLE WORLD 367

10.3.2 Dead Sea Scrolls 368
COMMUNITY RULE 369

10.3.3 Wisdom of the Fathers 370
MISHNAH (*Abot* Chapter 1) 371
TALMUD (*Baba Mezia* 59a–59b) 371
TALMUD (*Yebamot* 61b–64a) 371

10.4 The Age of Cogency (ca. 640–1800) 373

10.4.1 Principles of Faith 374
Moses ben Maimon, THE THIRTEEN PRINCIPLES 374

10.4.2 Mystical Visions 375
Moses de Leon, THE ZOHAR 375

10.4.3 Spiritual Tales 378
Nahman of Bratslav, THE LOSS OF THE PRINCESS 379

10.5 The Second Age of Diversity (ca. 1800–present) 381

10.5.1 Reform and Conservative Judaism 382
THE PITTSBURGH PLATFORM 382
Solomon Schechter, THE CHARTER OF THE SEMINARY 383

10.5.2 Zionism 385
Theodor Herzl, THE JEWISH STATE 385

10.5.3 Judaism as a Life of Dialogue 388
Martin Buber, THE DIALOGUE BETWEEN HEAVEN AND EARTH 388

CONTEMPORARY SCHOLARSHIP 392

10.6 After Auschwitz 392
Elie Wiesel, TO BE A JEW 393

10.7 Dilemmas of a Jewish Feminist 397
Judith Plaskow, THE WIFE/SISTER STORIES 397
Key Terms and Concepts 401
Suggestions for Further Reading 402
Research Projects 402

CHAPTER 11 Christian Ways of Being Religious 403

INTRODUCTION 403

11.1 An Overview 403
Lawrence S. Cunningham, CHRISTIANITY 403

SOURCES 410

11.2 Early Christian Writings 410

11.2.1 New Testament Letters 410
From PAUL'S LETTER TO THE GALATIANS (1–2) 411
From PAUL'S LETTER TO THE I CORINTHIANS (15:12–28, 35–57) 413
From PAUL'S LETTER TO THE ROMANS (3:9–28) 414

11.2.2 Synoptic Gospels 414
THE BIRTH OF JESUS (Mt 1:18–25, 2:1–15; Lk 2:1–21) 415
SERMONS ON THE MOUNT (Mt 5–7, Lk 6:17–49) 417
THE PRODIGAL SON (Lk 15:11–32) 420

THE LAST SUPPER (Mk 14:1–25;
Mt 26:20–29; Lk 22:7–38) 420
CRUCIFIXION AND RESURRECTION
(Mk 15:21–16:8; Mt 27:32–28:20;
Lk 23:26–24:11) 422

11.2.3 The Gospel of John 425
THE WORD MADE FLESH (Jn 1:1–18) 425
THE RESURRECTION OF LAZARUS
(Jn 11:17–44) 426

11.2.4 The Gospel of Mary (Magdalene) 426
MARY MAGDALENE TEACHES PETER 427

11.2.5 The Martyrdom of Perpetua 428
Perpetua, PERPETUA'S VISION 429

11.2.6 The Council of Nicaea 430
NICENE CREED 431

11.3 Christianity in the Middle Ages 431

11.3.1 A Tale of Two Cities 431
Augustine of Hippo, THE CITY OF GOD (Book
14:4, 25–28) 432

11.3.2 Spiritual Stillness 435
Hesychios of Sinai, THE JESUS PRAYER 436

11.3.3 Nature, Grace, and the Sacraments 437
Thomas Aquinas, SUMMA THEOLOGICA (Q. 110,
Art. 2; Q. 112, Art. 1; Q. 114, Art. 2) 438

11.4 Reforming Christianity 440

11.4.1 Attacking the Roman Defense 441
Martin Luther, THE THREE WALLS 441

11.4.2 Spiritual Marriage 444
Teresa of Avila, THE INTERIOR CASTLE (7.2) 445

11.5 Some Christian Currents in Nineteenth- and
Twentieth-Century America 447

11.5.1 New Revelations 447
THE BOOK OF MORMON ("Mormon,"
Chapter 9) 448

11.5.2 Christian Science 450
Mary Baker Eddy, SCIENCE AND HEALTH WITH
KEY TO THE SCRIPTURES 451

11.5.3 Battles Over the Bible 454
Benjamin B. Warfield, THE INSPIRATION OF
SCRIPTURE 454

11.5.4 Contemplation 455
Thomas Merton, NEW SEEDS OF CONTEMPLA-
TION 455

CONTEMPORARY SCHOLARSHIP 459
11.6 The Orthodox Church 459
Ernst Benz, THE GREATNESS AND WEAKNESS OF
ORTHODOXY 459

11.7 African American Women and Christian
Redemption 464
Delores S. Williams, BLACK WOMEN'S SURROGACY
EXPERIENCE 464

Key Terms and Concepts 471
Suggestions for Further Reading 472
Research Projects 473

CHAPTER 12 Islamic Ways of Being Religious
475

INTRODUCTION 475

12.1 An Overview 476
Richard C. Martin, ISLAM 477

SOURCES 483

12.2 The Formative Period 483

12.2.1 Qur'an 483
THE OPENING (surah 1) 485
CREATION (surah 15:1–48, 2:28–39) 485
ALLAH REVEALS HIMSELF (surahs 2:255–
257, 112:1–4) 486
EVILS OF IDOLATRY (surah 10:26–38) 487
PEOPLE OF THE BOOK (surah 5:44–51,
65–78) 487
ETHICS (surah 17:21–37) 488
LAWS ON MARRIAGE (surah 4:13–25, 34–
35, 128–135) 489
PILLARS OF ISLAM AND JIHAD (surah 2:
144–150, 183–200, 216–218) 490
THE RESURRECTION (surah 75) 492

12.2.2 Hadith 492
THE NIGHT JOURNEY (Sahih al-Bukhari,
5:227) 493
RECITING THE QUR'AN (Sahih al-Bukhari,
6:514) 494
THE DEATH OF MUHAMMAD (Sahih al-
Bukhari, 5:727, 730, 736) 494
THE DEFINITIVE QUR'AN (Sahih al-
Bukhari 6:510) 495

12.3 Medieval Developments 495

12.3.1 Law (Shari'a) 495
Al-Shafi'i, CONSENSUS AND ANALOGY 496
Al-Quayrawani, RITUAL PRAYER 497

Al-Marghinani, **MARRIAGE AND DIVORCE** 499
Al-Mawardi, **CALIPHATE** 500

12.3.1 Theology (*Kalam*) 501
Al-Maturidi, **GOD AND THE WORLD** 502
Al-Ashari, **WHATEVER GOD WILLS IS RIGHT** 503
Al-Hilli, **TWELVER SHI'ITE THEOLOGY** 504

12.3.3 Sufism 505
Rabi'a, **LOVE OF GOD** 506
Al-Ghazali, **DELIVERANCE FROM ERROR** 507
Attar, **THE CONFERENCE OF THE BIRDS** 508
Rumi, **UNION AND SEPARATION** 511

12.4 Islam in the Modern Age 511

12.4.1 Pan-Islam 512
Al-Afghani, **ISLAMIC SOLIDARITY** 512

12.4.2 Authentic Islam 514
Naguib Mahfouz, **PREPARING FOR HAJJ** (*Midaq Alley*) 515

CONTEMPORARY SCHOLARSHIP 517

12.5 Islamic Revival 517
Khurshid Ahmad, **THE NATURE OF ISLAMIC RESURGENCE** 517

12.6 Women and Islam 523
Fatima Mernissi, **FEMININITY AS SUBVERSION** 524

Pronunciation Guide 530
Key Terms and Concepts 530
Suggestions for Further Reading 531
Research Projects 531

Appendix: Religion on the Web 533

Preface

Ways of Being Religious provides both primary source material and secondary interpretative studies for students who wish to learn about different religions. Instructors can use this book alone or in conjunction with a standard textbook on world religions. My intention is to provide material useful for lower-division world religion courses or introductory religious studies courses. The material gathered here can also serve as background reading for courses in philosophy of religion, sociology of religion, and psychology of religion.

Most collections of sources now available for use in world religion courses concentrate on scriptural texts and exclude secondary interpretations. *Ways of Being Religious* provides source material from various historical periods to give students some sense of how a religious tradition has developed along with introductory overviews and scholarly studies of specific issues. The first three chapters pay more attention than most textbooks to how one goes about studying religion in an academic setting and to the problems associated with defining religion. In addition, this text pays more attention to issues relating to women and religion than is usual in survey textbooks.

I wrote this text to provide students and instructors with sources for interpreting religion and with examples of scholarly approaches to the study of religion. The scholarly studies model for students how one goes about utilizing sources for enhancing one's understanding of a religious tradition. The interplay between primary sources and secondary interpretations show students how to approach the interpretation of religious sources in a scholarly and responsible way.

Coverage

A glance at the contents for *Ways of Being Religious* indicates the different religious traditions that are represented. Space prevents the inclusion of more traditions, but those found here have had, at different times and in different places, a great deal of influence on the development of human society. Instructors using the combined textbook will find some of the religious traditions from different cultural groups in Africa and from Native peoples of North America included along with all of the material found in both volumes one and two. *Eastern Ways of Being Religious* focuses on ways of being religious originating in Asia (Hinduism, Buddhism, Confucianism, Taoism), and *Western Ways of Being Religious* focuses on ways of being religious originating in the Middle East (Judaism, Christianity, and Islam). Both of these volumes also include the introductory chapters dealing with how to best define and study religion.

Organization

Each chapter, after the first three, has an introductory essay providing an overview of a specific religious tradition. These general essays give students a macro-view of the tradition before they plunge into more specific information.

A section titled Sources follows the introductory overview. Here students will find a selection of some of the most influential formative scriptural texts or oral traditions and important later commentaries along with texts representing other developments in belief and practice. I have chosen these sources not only because of their importance to the tradition in question but also to represent such various dimensions of each tradition as the experiential, mythic, ritual, doctrinal, ethical, and social dimensions. Apart from the chapters on African and North American Native traditions, the material is not organized explicitly according to these dimensions because many of the selections embody more than one in a unified narrative. Thus, I have judged it best not to cut up unified narratives in brief selections in order to fit these preconceived categories. Selections dealing with women have also been included because this is frequently a neglected topic in the study of world religions (although the situation is, I am happy to say, improving rapidly).

The final section of each chapter dealing with a religious tradition is titled Contemporary Scholarship. Here I include recent interpretative essays that model different approaches to the study of religion—from the philosophical and historical to the theological and sociological.

Pedagogical Features

As I wrote this book, I kept in mind student needs as well as the pedagogical problems instructors in religious studies encounter while teaching about different ways of being religious, and I have tried to meet these needs and solve these problems in a variety of ways. The following list highlights some of the pedagogical features found in *Ways of Being Religious*:

- reading questions that help students interpret the selections
- introductions that supply students with background information and an interpretative context
- emphasis on developing comparative and interpretative skills
- suggestions for further readings at the end of each chapter
- pronunciation guides
- information on internet resources for studying religion
- maps to aid students' grasp of religious geography

Special Features

I have also incorporated a number of special features that not only make *Ways of Being Religious* different from most other textbooks on the market but also enhance student learning. These include:

- a unique organization (overview, sources, scholarly essays)
- combining primary sources with secondary interpretative articles
- providing both "outsider" and "insider" perspectives

- providing Gospel parallels for New Testament selections
- modeling different scholarly approaches (historical, anthropological, philosophical, phenomenological, sociological, and theological)
- providing discussions of problems involved in defining religion, a description of the field of religious studies, and methods for studying religion

Acknowledgments

California State University, Bakersfield provided a sabbatical and the Centre for Studies in Religion and Society at the University of Victoria provided a fellowship that enabled me to get this project started. I particularly wish to thank the Centre's director, Harold Coward and his staff for their kind help and support. Ken King, the religion editor at Mayfield, gave encouragement and creative ideas and the helpful staff at Mayfield saw to the production details. Margaret Moore cleaned up my prose and made the book more readable. Katy Kessler did research, listened patiently to my ideas, and offered constructive advice. Barbara McNaughton and Mona Aguilar helped with the permissions and duplicating tasks. I also wish to thank Wendell Charles Beane, University of Wisconsin at Oshkosh; Katherine Carlitz, University of Pittsburgh; Dell deChant, University of South Florida; Kai-Wing Chow, University of Illinois; Frederick M. Denny, University of Colorado at Boulder; John Grimes, Michigan State University; Rita M. Gross, University of Wisconsin at Eau Claire; Stephen L. Harris, California State University at Sacramento; Howard L. Harrod, Vanderbilt University; Russell T. McCutcheon, Southwest Missouri State University; Michael Molloy, Kapiolani Community College; Professor Robert Platzner, California State University at Sacramento; Gerald Michael Schnabel, Bemidji State University; James S. Thayer, Oklahoma State University; Dr. Dan Vaillancourt, Loyola University Chicago, John Whittaker, Louisiana State University, and Mark R. Woodward, Arizona State University. I find it regrettable that I could not incorporate all of their thoughtful suggestions. Whatever errors and limitations remain are of my own doing.

I invite students and instructors alike who use this book to provide me with their thoughts and ideas.

My goal is to provide useful material for understanding some of the ways humans express their religiosity. No one person can ever hope to master the vast amount of literature available on religion. We need to pool our knowledge and experience. Your advice can help make this book better should a need for a new edition arise.

Gary E. Kessler, California State University, Bakersfield, e-mail: gkessler@csubak.edu

PART 1

INTRODUCTION

1

A Challenge

It is 10 A.M. on a Sunday morning in British Columbia, Canada. A girl is beginning her Sunday school lesson. On Saturday, some Jewish boys in Italy were studying commentaries on Genesis at a synagogue. In Philadelphia, Islamic students gathered at a mosque on Friday to pray and to study the Qur'an. In Bangkok, Thailand, a thirteen-year-old boy is studying the Buddhist Sutras in preparation for taking monastic vows.

INSIDER'S AND OUTSIDER'S PERSPECTIVES

Like the people I have just described, those of you who have studied religion in Sunday school, Synagogue school (*beth midrash*, or house of study), or Bible study classes or have studied the Qur'an in a mosque have studied from an insider's point of view. The **insider's** view is that of someone who participates in a particular religious tradition. This sort of study presupposes religious commitment and promotes an understanding that will lead to greater commitment. It promotes the interests and furthers the causes of a specific religious organization.

The academic study of religion is different from the insider's study. In the academic study, the student stands outside all religious traditions and studies religions from the viewpoint of the methods and standards associated with the secular academy. The **outsider's** viewpoint does not presuppose any kind of religious commitment, although it does presuppose a commitment to the standards of the academy. Its goal is neither to increase nor to decrease an individual's religious faith, although it may have profound effects on that faith.

For the insider, the study of religion is itself a religious activity. For the outsider, it is not, at least not in a sectarian sense. The difference between the two ways of studying religion is like the difference between speaking a language and studying how a language is spoken. The latter is a **meta,** or second-order, activity because it stands outside the actual **first-order** practice it seeks to understand. The academic study of religion is a second-order activity that involves observing those who worship.

The controversial ruling of the U.S. Supreme Court on prayer in public schools noted the difference between the insider's and outsider's perspectives by distinguishing between the teaching *of* religion and the teaching *about* religion. The teaching *of* involves sectarian instruction while teaching *about* does not. According to the Court, nothing in the ruling prohibiting prayer in public schools should be understood to forbid teaching *about* religion in public schools.

If I were to ask you to list the advantages and disadvantages of each of these viewpoints, it would not take you long to create a list. On the one hand, the outsider's viewpoint presents a greater hope for achieving objectivity, which is particularly valuable when studying many different religions. On the other hand, the insider's viewpoint presents a greater hope for sympathetic understanding of one particular religious tradition. It can appreciate nuances and feelings that the observer can easily miss.

The situation is like the relationship between you and a psychological counselor. You know yourself from the inside and hence have a unique advantage when it comes to self-knowledge. However, your very intimacy can lead to self-deception, distortions, and blind spots that an outside, trained observer like a counselor can detect almost immediately.

There can be considerable conflict between the insider's view and the outsider's view. The values that each hold appear opposed. The outsider appeals to such values as critical reason, disinterested and unemotional judgment, impersonal observation, and detached analysis. The insider's approach certainly involves the use of reason, but it is tempered by a personal, passionate, and involved pursuit of faith as well as knowledge. At its worst the outsider's approach can lead to a radical depersonalization of the subject matter, taking the vitality out of religions by reducing them to causal factors far removed from the living reality. For example, some scholars claim that religion originates in fear of higher powers—that religious faith is just another form of fear. This hardly seems plausible given the richness and diversity of religions, even if some fear does play a role in religions.

At its worst the insider's approach can become so defensive and prejudicial that it ceases to be honest, distorting facts and ignoring or suppressing evidence. For example, some insiders regard all religions other than their own as the "work of Satan"—that all other religions have the devil as their father! This kind of attitude reduces the comparative study of religion to a combination of **apologetics** and polemics. It reveals nothing about the ways in which "others" understand themselves.

I have identified the academic study of religions with the outsider's viewpoint in contrast to the insider's viewpoint. However, the picture I have painted is distorted. None of us are completely inside or outside in our viewpoints. Even if we practice no religion, religious traditions and values have so permeated our cultures and societies that, like fish, we live in a sea already containing religious currents. There is no view totally outside everything and no view totally inside. These extremes are "ideal types" that characterize the very ends of a continuum. The real situation is more complex. The outsider can be as prejudiced as the insider, although in a different direction, and one might make a plausible case that the outsider is as much committed to promoting the interests of the academic "church of reason" as the insider is committed to promoting the interests of her or his church.

You probably are beginning to see how challenging the academic study of religion can be. It requires a scrupulous self-consciousness about how fairly you are treating others who may have very different values and beliefs from your own. The "other" is always threatening to some extent, and the "religious other" can be very threatening because often it is a good person who believes in her or his way of life as sincerely as you believe in your own. It is difficult in such a situation to sustain the belief that other people are totally wrong religiously.

The academic study of religion challenges you to develop the qualities of openness, honesty, critical intelligence, careful reading and listening, and critical tolerance. We will examine each of these qualities in turn.

OPENNESS

To be open in the academic study of religions is to be always ready to be surprised. It is a constant willingness to regard tentatively the categories, classification systems, labels, and names with which we pigeonhole religious phenomena. We must realize that they are revisable and incomplete. It is not a refusal to draw conclusions nor is it a noncommittal willingness to entertain anything and everything. To be open is to recognize that however helpful classification systems, explanations, and theories can be, they may be wrong and in need of revision as additional evidence comes to light. As a student of religion, you should welcome, as does the student of physical science, evidence that you might be wrong, because if you are wrong and it can be shown, you have learned something new and thereby come that much closer to understanding.

HONESTY

Honesty involves responsibility to yourself, others, and your subject matter. By responsibility I mean the ability to respond in a nonprejudicial way to what you learn. To be prejudiced is different than being biased (although the words are often used interchangeably). Prejudice means prejudgment. Bias means a particular slant, outlook, or perspective. Even the honest person is biased because human beings see, of necessity, what they take to be real from a certain viewpoint. There cannot be a view from nowhere just as there cannot be a view from everywhere. However, the honest person understands his or her biases and constantly is mindful of them, thereby attempting to overcome whatever limitations the biases might impose. Using again our analogy with studying a language, we might characterize honesty in terms of the ability to responsibly study the "language" of religion and at the same time to be aware of the perspective embedded in the meta-language we use to describe religion.

CRITICAL INTELLIGENCE

Critical intelligence is a formidable phrase smacking of abstractions, destructive intentions, and obscure theories. True, critical inquiry may be destructive of some cherished beliefs and deep-seated prejudices. However, its goal is not destruction for the sake of destruction. Its goal is construction. If critical inquiry tears down, it does so in the hope of building up.

To be critical involves a number of intellectual skills including both analysis and synthesis. In analysis we seek to take things apart, to break wholes into basic elements. Just as you may have taken a clock apart in order to see what makes it tick, engaging in the academic study of religion challenges you to take apart religious rituals and beliefs to see what makes them work. However, synthesis—putting things back together—is also required. We must be ever alert for the discovery of previously unseen relationships and for the sudden insight that what we took to be contradictions are reconciliated in a greater harmony. Our task as academic students of religion is not only to analyze religion but also to synthesize its various parts so that the underlying and often unexpected convergences come to light.

At the heart of critical intelligence is the pursuit of truth. Although we live in an age of relativism when phrases like "the pursuit of truth" sound outdated, such a pursuit cannot be given up even when we are uncertain there is any truth to be found. To look for truth in our studies of religions necessitates criteria regarding what is going to count as truth. The task of articulating such criteria is by no means easy and is also an ongoing task. However, there are generally acceptable standards available for what is to count as truth, and the student of religion ought to employ them and seek to improve them.

Arguments supporting a particular conclusion must be carefully examined to see if the premises are true and whether the conclusion follows from the premises. Consistency in theory and its application is a hallmark of the pursuit of truth. Evidence must be carefully examined for reliability and checked out. If I claim that the essence of religion is fear and present evidence to support that claim, then I must also check for counterevidence and counterexamples. If there are none, so much the better for my claim. However, if there are some, I must be prepared to modify my claim. I also need to check to see if my terms are defined precisely enough to be useful. For example, I do not know if the admonition of some religions to "fear God" counts as evidence for my claim or not unless I know that the fear I am talking about and the fear they are talking about mean the same thing.

Crucial to the search for truth is the ability to question. Most of us are too easily satisfied with superficial answers and stop questioning too soon. The willingness to continue to raise questions even when you think you understand and to pursue alternative answers is an indispensable tool in the quest for truth. Moreover, there is an art to questioning that involves carefully examining your questions, seeking to find out whether they are correctly formulated and lead in useful directions. The student of religions is challenged to remind herself or himself that questioning is not an end in itself; rather, its purpose is to lead the way to answers.

CAREFUL READING AND LISTENING

Careful reading and listening is a deceptively simple phrase. Doesn't every student read and listen? My experience has been that while I think I am reading or listening, I am not always doing so. As a teacher, I am used to students asking questions. The more I teach the more I become accustomed to certain questions. This has sometimes lulled me into not listening fully. The student may be in the midst of a question or comment, and I find myself already formulating a reply in my mind. I become so preoccupied with formulating my reply that I cease to listen. Also, comments, questions, and textual materials are often deceptive in that the words say one thing, but the person behind the words may be saying something else. We need to listen and to read for hidden meanings. This is especially important when dealing with religious texts such as sacred writings, which contain many different levels of meaning. The student of religions needs to become sensitive to as many different levels of meaning as possible. There is great joy in studying religions when you are surprised by a new level of meaning in some familiar saying or ritual action. Religious rituals and experiences contain a symbolic richness that will unfold for the student who reads and listens carefully.

Careful reading and listening requires sympathetic imagination. Imagination is one of the student's greatest assets. Through it we can project ourselves, at least partially, into the worldview of a shaman doing magical healing, a yogi in meditation, a prophet proclaiming a judgment she or he hopes will never come true, and a Christian or a Muslim at prayer.

The ability to imagine is the ability to play, to make-believe. Such an ability is invaluable to the student of religions as he or she struggles to comprehend cultures, beliefs, practices, and experiences that seem very different and strange. Sympathetic imagination requires projecting oneself into the viewpoint of another.

Such projection, of course, can easily lead to distortion and deception. We project ourselves into the shoes of another, and insofar as we all share in a common humanity and a common world, such a projection is possible and valuable. However, insofar as the other is truly alien to us and utterly strange, imagination must acknowledge its limits and beware of manufacturing false similarities at the expense of real differences.

CRITICAL TOLERANCE

Sympathetic imagination is indispensable in studying religion, but it must be balanced by critical intelligence, honesty, and openness. The student of religion must learn to cultivate all of these qualities in such a way that they complement one another. Sympathetic imagination and openness promotes tolerance for those who are different, and critical intelligence promotes a tolerance tempered by critical evaluation. We can and should come to understand religious tragedies such as Jonestown or Heaven's Gate, but we cannot condone mass suicide and violence.

Sometimes it is easy to know where to draw the line between understanding and tolerance. At other times it is more difficult. We can understand why some religions sacrificed humans and thought it was right to do so, and we have no difficulty condemning such a practice should it occur today. However, what should we say about the sacrifice of animals, which still takes place in religious settings? Should it be tolerated? What should be done about the repressive treatment of women in Afghanistan? Should we tolerate fundamentalist sects that advocate beating children?

As these questions indicate, there is no simple way to balance sympathetic understanding and critical intelligence in all situations, but it is a challenge worth meeting. The study of religions can be as difficult and as exciting as learning to understand and appreciate another human being, another culture, another way of life. At its best, the study of religions can show you how to see what the world is like through the eyes of another. It can disclose the depths of human suffering and the heights of human joy, and can challenge you to examine the limits of toleration. The simple act of praying, making a sacrifice, lighting incense, or eating a humble meal can reveal symbolic richness, a sense of proportion and grace, a feeling of awe and mystery that enlarges your soul.

1.1 SPIRITUAL REGRET

The qualities of openness, honesty, critical intelligence, and reading/listening with sympathetic imagination that need to be cultivated by the student of religions might be termed virtues in the sense of excellences. People who have these qualities we generally admire more than people who are closed-minded, dishonest, uncritical, and careless in their reading and listening.

In the study of religions, we frequently find religions other than our own that attract us. For example, I was raised a Christian in the Lutheran Church, but I have been very attracted to Zen Buddhism (among other religions) and even spent some time practicing meditation in a Zen monastery. As you study the religions represented in this book, you may find yourself in a similar situation. How should you best respond? One option is to convert. However, perhaps you have good reasons for not converting such as still being deeply committed to your own tradition or to a nonreligious perspective. Such situations, argues Lee H. Yearley (the author of the following lecture), call for the development of *new* religious virtues, in particular, the virtue he calls **spiritual regret.**

You are probably aware of traditional religious virtues such as faith and hope but may be less aware that various virtues and vices have been added to that list in response to particular historical circumstances. For example, the Walloon Synod of Leydon (seventeenth century), which was mostly made up of French Protestants (Huguenots) who had been persecuted by Roman Catholics, condemned religious toleration (especially toward Roman Catholics) as a vice and a heresy. To them, tolerance meant a lax complacency toward evil. Religious intolerance became, for the Huguenots, a religious virtue. Since then, religious tolerance, at least in some circles, has once again become a virtue and intolerance a vice. Yearley thinks today's circumstances require the development of other religious virtues besides toleration. The times require us, he argues, to recognize new religious virtues such as spiritual regret. He acknowledges objections to his position but still maintains that spiritual regret is a better response to religious pluralism (the existence of many different religions) than either complacency or parochialism (the denial of the need to learn about other religions sympathetically).

Lee H. Yearley is the Walter Y. Evans-Wentz Professor of Religion at Stanford University. He delivered this lecture as part of the University Lecture Series in Religion at Arizona State University in 1994.

As you read his lecture, write brief answers to the following reading questions. They will help you catch key ideas and clarify your own thoughts about Yearley's arguments.

LEE H. YEARLEY

New Religious Virtues and the Study of Religion

READING QUESTIONS

1. As you read, make a list of all the words and ideas you do not understand or are uncertain about. Discuss them with a classmate, look them up in a dictionary, or bring them up in class for discussion and clarification.
2. What is Yearley's subject, and what will he argue?
3. Describe in your own words the four ways of "solving" the problem of religious plurality. Does any of these four ways characterize your own view? If so, which one? If none, what is your own view, and how does it differ from these four?

From Lee H. Yearley, *New Religious Virtues and the Study of Religion* (Arizona State University, Department of Religious Studies, 1994, pp. 1–10, 12–17, 19–22. Reprinted by permission of the author. Endnotes deleted.

4. What does Yearley mean by "articulation of the implicit," and what role does this play in recognizing a new virtue?
5. According to Yearley, what are the characteristics of someone who is modern? Do you consider yourself modern in Yearley's sense? Why or why not?
6. Why do the new virtues like spiritual regret produce both joy and sadness? Do you think the word *regret* is the best word to use in order to describe this virtue?
7. How would you, in your own words, characterize the virtue of spiritual regret? If you have ever felt spiritual regret, describe the situation.
8. Why, according to Yearley, is imagination important for studying comparative religions?
9. What are "sophisticated complacency" and "sophisticated parochialism"? Why does Yearley reject these two types of "principled opposition to imaginative religious voyaging"?

I. INTRODUCTION

Teaching about religion produces numerous situations that set us back on our heels no matter how seasoned we may think we are. Three examples, all with undergraduates: A knowledgeable, reflective Irish-Catholic appears at my door and with evident perplexity and some pain tells me how the Taoist work we just finished makes more sense to her than do those Catholic works that have underpinned her understanding of life. Weeks later, a highly intelligent East Asian Buddhist talks with me at length about how best to understand Aquinas's ideas about sin, ideas she finds compelling but that seem to have no evident place in the religious world she inhabits.

Third, several weeks of lecturing on the Confucian tradition to a large required course leads several Asian American students to tell me, an aging white male, that I had articulated for them ideas that they live from but had barely understood much less evaluated. Indeed, they speak about how they had always felt odd, so different were many of their basic inclinations about say proper attitudes to parents, but now they see those attitudes as manifesting, however confusedly, a long and deep tradition.

Much can, of course, be said about each example and the general situation they illustrate. I want here, however, to discuss how they highlight what I believe is a new and crucial demand on us both as teachers of religion and as people interested in religious positions or committed to them. It involves meeting the teaching challenges and constructive challenges presented by a new understanding of not just religious diversity but of religious goods that are integral but alien. My subject, then, is how best to respond not just to what is often called today the religious "Other" but to the religious "Other" that attracts us.

My focus is not on how we ought as a matter of public policy deal with religious diversity. I do think what I will say is relevant to those issues; I sometimes even think we will not be able to work out the public problems until we work out the private ones. My topic today, however, is what we should do when facing or teaching about alien but tempting religions.

I believe the best way to talk about these situations is to use a language that relies on ideas about virtues. Ideas about virtue, and what they imply, generate understandable suspicions in many people. There are, however, rich traditions—in the West and elsewhere—that have argued a language that employs ideas about virtue provides us with the best way to talk about crucial features of our lives, and I hope to persuade you this approach has much merit. In these traditions virtues are human excellences, aspects of what we call character. Put more abstractly, they are those characteristic patterns of feeling and motivation that reflect a life plan the fulfillment of which is thought to be all important.

If we think in terms of other people's perceptions, virtues are those admirable characteristics that a significant number of people in a society think reflect instances of human excellences. This formulation, however, points up a perplexing feature of my enterprise. I will argue that we need to manifest new virtues, especially new religious or spiritual virtues. These virtues are not generally recognized; they are, at best, only implicit in people's ideas about human excellence.

These new virtues appear when we face what is implied by the diversity of integral religious goods. My example of such a new religious virtue will be the virtue of spiritual regret. That virtue deals with the recognition that various, legitimate ideals of religious flourishing exist and that although some of them move you deeply you cannot manifest them, indeed may not even want to manifest them.

Cultivating such new virtues involves, I believe, acquiring skills that are intimately involved with the disciplined study of diverse religions. That study can occur, of course, in many places, but it surely does have a place in higher education, and I want to talk about how best to cultivate it. Finally, I will end by examining, if briefly, my understanding of what will in the future be, I believe, a most serious debate. The debate is between those who accept some version of the position I describe here and those who would accept much of what is said here but are in principle opposed to the new virtues described—indeed might even call them vices.

Much to do then; let us begin by discussing how apparent religious differences have been treated.

II. How Apparently Alien Religions Have Been Treated

Basic to the idea I will be examining is the notion that genuine goods, especially religious goods, can differ substantially enough to present a person with sharply divergent life plans, plans which are both legitimate and appealing. This is, I believe, a novel idea. Divergences and conflicts among apparent goods surely have been recognized. Nevertheless, the notion that the conflicting goods are truly legitimate ones is not found, I think, in the Western tradition or in those non-Western traditions with which I am familiar. In all those earlier traditions a central claim, one that underlies all other claims, is that there is a single goal. That is, there is either a single, limited form of ideal human excellence or a harmony among somewhat different forms.

People who adhered to a tradition have, needless to say, recognized that other traditions seemed to pursue different goals. But they "solved" the seemingly irreducible plurality among religious ideals in one of four ways. Allow me to use labels for the proponents of each position in order to give a brief typological account: the first sees the adherents of another religious position as simply "in error"; the second sees them as "less developed"; the third sees them as "more developed"; and the fourth sees them as "only apparently different."

Each of these positions vis-à-vis apparent plurality required that its adherents manifest specific virtues— for example the virtue of righteous indignation or the virtue of tolerance. That is, the ideas contained in the positions were supposed to inform one's character. They were to be incarnated in a personal excellence that appeared when one faced divergent religious goods.

The first approach is to see the religiously alien as in error, as "heretics," as mistaken versions of one's own truth. One brings them into the structure of one's own tradition and places them as unorthodox or aberrant members. (A variant of this is to make the religiously different part of a larger cosmological scheme in which it represents some version of the forces of evil.) Those who differ may then be candidates for conversion, extinction, or possibly benign neglect.

A second approach is to employ a developmental scheme in which the religiously alien is seen as a lower stage of development. That stage may have integrity, may even have represented an appropriate response in some contexts. But the hierarchy of developmental stages is clear and the adherent's religion is of a higher sort than is the alien religion.

A third approach uses similar presuppositions about the final state but claims that another tradition represents that to which the home tradition aspires. One's own tradition represents imperfectly what is more fully seen elsewhere. A final approach has been to argue that the differences between oneself and the other are probably only apparent. A lack of information and physical or psychological distance from the religious other means little thought need be given to the issue of differences in religious fulfillment.

These four approaches continue, I believe, to underlie most contemporary Western and non-Western theological attempts to relate religions to one another. They also, therefore, underlie the picture of what virtues are needed when dealing with other religions. That situation says much about the grip of basic paradigms; it underlines for instance how fundamental has been the idea that there is finally a single goal. It also, I think, says much about people's failure to take sophisticated comparative work seriously enough to grapple with the challenges and possibilities it presents.

Some things have, of course, changed. Thankfully, in much of the modern West the inclination to convert the religiously alien or to destroy them if conversion fails has died or at least abated. (Tragically this is far less true in other areas of the world where sophisticated religious accounts are still used to justify terrible acts.) Variants of the last three responses are, however, alive and well today. That is, contemporary approaches reflect features of the traditional strategies for dealing with the religious alien. One approach is to deny that any real differences are present or that all apparent differences can be explained developmentally. This can take the form, for instance, of finding abstract similarities among religions or incorporating into one's own religion features of other religious views. Another strategy is simply to view other religions as one would view exhibits in a museum or specimens in a zoo. They then can be admired as unchallenging but different, be looked on as odd but interesting instances or even mutants of a single species. These approaches all can appear in woefully unsophisticated or even downright foolish forms. But they also appear in elaborate academic garb—which we will presume for the moment is not foolish.

The perseverance of these traditional ways of dealing with religious diversity is, however, far from the whole tale. In various ways and with various people, both inside and outside the academy, awareness grows that something is amiss in these ways of formulating matters. Yet just what is amiss usually remains unclear and new approaches, much less solutions, seem even more murky. Most important to us, no clear idea exists of what new human virtues are called for by this unease about traditional solutions and virtues. In fact, it is even unclear if we can make sense of the idea of truly new virtues.

III. ARTICULATING THE IMPLICIT: THE THEORETICAL BASIS OF NEW RELIGIOUS VIRTUES

The whole idea of new virtues seems to be questionable, to require not only explanation but defense. This problem has various facets and we will examine some of them only when treating my example of a new religious virtue: spiritual regret. That example can also give texture, concrete density, to our initial more abstract discussion. For now, however, let us turn to the most fundamental of the theoretical questions.

Virtues are qualities that, as I put it earlier, most people in a society think reflect admirable qualities. With a new virtue, however, most people will not *explicitly* affirm that a quality is admirable. Nevertheless, I believe they have a general perspective that allows for or even produces an *implicit* affirmation of the quality's admirableness. Therefore they can be persuaded that a quality is a new virtue because it gathers up or focuses attention on discrete and valuable but heretofore inchoate features of their overall perspective. To move from an implicit affirmation of something to an explicit affirmation is for people to become more articulate about the important ideas and attitudes they possess but have no adequate vocabulary for expressing. This "articulation of the implicit," this making explicit what was inchoate, underlies the idea of new virtues.

The idea that nuanced language about virtues enables people to understand themselves in fuller and more subtle ways than they otherwise could, and therefore also to live better lives, has been a standard defense of the significance of virtue theory. It is a defense which rests on controversial but to my mind compelling ideas: that, for example, we often are strangers to ourselves and we find it exceedingly difficult to think well, using ordinary language, about those things that matter most to us. Conventional virtue theory moves from this view to urge closer analysis and better understandings of traditional virtues. I am here arguing that it provides the grounding for new virtues as well.

I believe, then, that people's general perspective implicitly contains or allows for the idea that virtues, like spiritual regret, which manifest different ways of responding to alternative religious views are new virtues. I realize that many people might not initially think they refer to admirable qualities. I aim, however, to show that these qualities deserve to be defined as virtuous and hope thereby to make explicit for people what is implicit in their perspectives. Nevertheless, I also realize that such an inquiry is always a "two-way street." It involves the risk that the persuader can be persuaded. People can have principled objections, as we will see, to labeling a quality like spiritual regret a virtue. They can even see it as a vice, a human deformation. And they may convince me I am wrong.

In fact, unlike some believers in articulation, I think the process may produce not just significant agreements but also deep disagreements. If the disagreements turn out to be shallow so much the better but I think it a mistake to predict they will. Even if deep disagreements result, however, the process of articulation is still very important. The ability to formulate clearly and thereby to discuss well what may be deep disagreements is extremely important to a society like the one we inhabit. Such formulations and discussions are also critical to us personally as the disagreements may well reflect unresolved conflicts between different parts of our views about life. The key point in both cases is that we need to be able to talk about these issues. We need to have, if you will, a "what is X" discussion of the kind that was the staple of many classical Western analyses of various matters, notably the character of virtues like courage or moderation.

The new "what is X" discussion that is needed aims to make explicit the new religious virtues that appear when we think out the implications of three specifically modern emphases or themes and the reactions they generate. Academics who dare to utter the word "modern" can subject themselves, I know, to a barrage of questions or at least quizzical glances, but allow me to proceed.

First is an emphasis on the significance of autonomy, on the importance either of having chosen to be a person of a certain sort or of having consciously affirmed that you choose to be as you have been determined to be by various external forces. Put simply, moderns want to be able to say "It is my life." . . . Second is a valuing of that understanding of self which arises from introspection and retrospection, from reflecting upon one's present self and history. People should feel obligated to grasp as well as they can who they are and what they have been.

These two notions underlie the modern presumption that the "integrity" or "authenticity" of an individual is of crucial value. They also, in turn, generate the modern concern with hypocrisy or insincerity. Whatever

may be the problems associated with these ideas (and those problems can be substantial), features of this perspective remain compelling to most people and for good reason. Possessing integrity can, for example, rightly be called a virtue or excellence that ranks with being just or benevolent.

The third modern theme is an understanding of the diversity of possible forms of human actualization, religious or non-religious, that are present in the world. It arises from ideas that are probably less widely shared than the valuing of individual integrity. One is the idea that all our lives are inevitably embedded in specific cultures and are shaped by commitments that are underdetermined by the reasons that support them. We live in ways that we cannot fully justify by the reasons that we have for living that way. This notion rests, in turn, on the belief that our way of life is only one among many.

These ideas form or reinforce the notion that people cannot legitimately appeal to authoritative supports that they might well have invoked before. People, then, must be conscious of the real conflicts that are present about what is the best way to live. That is, I believe, a very difficult thing to do, or at least to do consistently. It involves, at its core, the dual recognitions that many legitimate goods exist and that whatever goods you pursue, they are but one among many possible sets of goods.

Understanding this will always present some problems. But it poses a specific problem for people who wish to be autonomous and reflective about themselves, a problem that underlies the need for new virtues. That a person who desires to possess integrity affirms only one among the different kinds of human excellence he or she could affirm is the notion that lies at the center of the notion that new virtues, like spiritual regret, are needed.

The peculiar character and weight of these virtues arises from the state that follows from this situation, a state where joy and sadness interact. That is, at the heart of the character of these new virtues is the idea that to encounter any real good is to be drawn by it, to find it attractive, and thus to enjoy it. Enjoyment or joy, then, becomes the mark of having recognized a good. This joy remains even if that good must also remain unavailable, unavailable just because of the integrity of the self that meets the alien good. That situation, in turn, must produce sadness because the good cannot be fully realized. People must, then, both encounter goods that draw them and encounter their own integrity, an integrity that makes impossible a full acceptance of the alternative good. That circumstance, a circumstance which defines these virtues, produces both joy and sadness. To feel only sadness would signal that one had not fully encountered the good. But to feel only joy would signal a failure to encounter fully the good of one's own integrity. . . .

IV. INTERLUDE: THE IDEA OF VIRTUE

Although I think the best way to talk about the full encounter with other religious goods involves ideas about virtues, I realize that for many today the word "virtue" has an archaic ring. It often seems to be associated with problematic ideas like priggish scrupulosity; or to be restricted to narrow areas like sexual activity, or to reflect fixed unjust social hierarchies like that found in virtually all traditional societies.

Given that, let me say something about what I mean by the idea of a virtue, drawing my examples from the realm of ethical virtues. For me a virtue is a human excellence or example of human flourishing. It is a permanent addition to the self, part of what makes people who they are, a feature of what we call character. One of my friends, for example, possesses or even exemplifies the virtue of generosity. If she sees a troubled person, she is immediately inclined to give her time or money to that person. I, on the other hand, see a troubled person and often think of other things, for example how much work I have to do or what helping the person will cost me psychologically and financially. I then probably also get tangled up in the question of whether being generous will, in the long term, be good for the troubled person. I might finally do generous things but I am not a generous person in the sense my friend is; she possesses the virtue and I have at best a semblance of it.

Virtues, then, display some characteristic pattern of desire and motivation. They are not simple thoughts that occur and pass: I do not manifest a virtue if I think how compassionate it would be to invite that lonely person to dinner as I walk on past them. Nor are they emotional states that pass quickly: I am not virtuous if I feel very strongly that I should at least talk to my lonely acquaintance but realize the movie is about to start and move on. . . .

V. AN EXAMPLE: SPIRITUAL REGRET AS A NEW, CORRECTIVE VIRTUE

Spiritual regret is one of those virtues that concerns the appropriate response to the recognition that extremely varied, legitimate religious ideals exist and that no person can possibly manifest all of them. Like all virtues it is corrective of a corresponding human weakness, in this case the tendency to overlook the challenge produced by the presence of other integral and even tempting religious goods. It is also new in that it both responds to challenges that were not fully understood before and develops capacities that were previously undeveloped.

Before examining just how it is both "new" and "corrective," a word more about its general character. Spiritual regret, it needs to be underlined, is a virtue and not simply an emotional reaction or even a passing thought or attitude. All those characteristics of virtue mentioned earlier are present: for instance, it is a part of one's character and manifests a general picture of what you think a good life is. Some legitimate uses of the word "regret" do refer to passing emotional perturbations and therefore one can easily think of spiritual regret as a simple emotion. But I want to talk about it as a virtue, one aspect of which often is the presence of a specific emotion —or more accurately the propensity to feel that emotion in appropriate ways in specific situations. The important and complicated virtue of regret has a similar structure.

Spiritual regret arises when we recognize three things. First, that various, legitimate ideas of religious flourishing exist. Second, that conflict among them means that no single person can come close to exhibiting all of them. Third, that those ideals or states which one can pursue or possess will usually be largely determined by forces either beyond one's immediate control or beyond anyone's control. This regret can arise in different forms at different times in one's life. It seems, however, normally to be linked to maturity, to a well understood fund of experience.

Examples of spiritual regret are, I think, myriad. They range from reading texts, most notably for me classical Confucian and Taoist texts, to personal encounters with extraordinary people from other traditions, most notably for me five days of meetings, with five other people, with the Dalai Lama. The most striking example I know occurred when I spent two hours very early one morning in Korea on a cliff high above the East Sea looking at the Sokkurum Buddha. A large granite statue of the Buddha in meditation carved in the 8th century C.E. and flanked by wall carvings of disciples and guardians, it sits in a recessed grotto. One of East Asia's greatest statues, the figure draws one's attention, or at least drew mine, with a magnetic power and generates a mysterious kind of peace or at least stillness. The spiritual vision presented there was as powerful and as tempting as I have ever seen. Yet I wanted it neither for myself nor for those about whom I care most. I wanted the religious goods expressed in the Sokkurum Buddha to exist, and even to be incarnated by many people, and yet did not want the people I cared about most to possess them.

Of the various reasons for that judgment, the one which most haunts me concerns my response to the transcendence of normal human pain and turmoil that I saw. This was true even though the statue was not completely "self-enclosed"; it manifested a calmness and luminosity that involved contact with the world. Statues which expressed that "self-enclosed" kind of perfection, one which would be disturbed by any contact with the world, could be seen within miles of the Sokkurum Buddha in the now largely deserted surrounding hills. They generated in me, at best, a muted admiration. In contrast, the poise, self-possession, and equanimity I saw in the Sokkurum Buddha contained a compassion aimed toward a world the pain and frustration of which was well understood. Nevertheless, that world was distant in a way I found both compelling and disturbing.

The experience was one about which much can be said, ranging from comments about my own possible lack of understanding, or even self-deception, to theoretical issues about the relationship of the mystical and ethical aspects of religion. Most important here, the experience exemplifies many features that contribute to a virtue like spiritual regret, and it can help us understand the virtue's character and newness.

The notion that this or any virtue can be new requires, as noted, both explanation and defense. At least it does for those people who believe ideas about virtue only make sense when coupled with ideas about a constant human nature, all of whose capacities are evident at any time. "Newness" implies that specific historical and cultural complexes, particular chronological features, can be relevant to the identification of a virtue or can even determine it. It means that virtues can be called "era specific." They can be seen as excellences at one age or period but at another they will be unidentified or seen as indifferent qualities or even vices.

In defending the idea that virtues can be new, let me start with the relatively benign notion that specific virtues can be said to have histories that determine their form and value both in people and in civilizations. That is, the character of a virtue changes over time, even though its structural form stays steady enough that we can identify its various manifestations as belonging to the same general category. This kind of change in a specific virtue is perhaps especially evident when dealing with personal histories. Innocence differs significantly for a five-year-old, a thirty-year-old, and a fifty-year-old. An attitude toward odd people or events that is appropriate and even charming in a five-year-old is suspect in a thirty-year-old and positively problematic in a fifty-year-old.

We see a similar phenomenon in civilizations. Courage in Homer, in Aristotle, and in Aquinas is still courage; an identifiable structure is there. But courage's paradigmatic actions have changed from a warrior's defeat of a dangerous enemy to a saint's acceptance of death in martyrdom. The primary instances of courageous dispositions and actions thus appear to be fundamentally different. A new, important, and perhaps even crucial attribute of human goodness has surfaced. (The significance of such changes and difficulties in identifying them are other reasons, incidentally, why attention to comparative method is crucial, even when dealing with the history of one's own tradition.)

The situation with spiritual regret resembles that which we find with the example of courage. As we discussed, people have often recognized the divergences and conflicts among religious goods, and identifiable structures for thinking about the issue and acting well were present. Spiritual regret, however, responds to that situation in a new way. It arises from the sense, however implicit, that the traditional ways of dealing with distinctions among religions are deficient, that they fail to meet adequately the specific demands the modern situation produces. Therefore the virtues that manifest those traditional ways, virtues like toleration or righteous indignation, are also in error or incomplete.

Like all virtues, spiritual regret can productively be thought of as being *corrective*. That is, ideas about this and other virtues rest on a picture of human weakness and need. Virtues correct some difficulty thought to be natural to human beings, some temptation that needs to be resisted or some motivation that needs to be made good. Courage, for example, corrects the inclination to be dissuaded by fear from doing what should be done. Similarly, normal regret can be said to correct the tendency to self-deception and the inclination to forgo painful or nuanced accounts of one's past.

What the virtue of spiritual regret corrects most generally is the human propensity to overlook differences among legitimate goods. It corrects the inclination to subsume different goods under one's own or to deny that different goods are really goods. More specifically, spiritual regret corrects the common human unwillingness to face fully what is involved in a plurality of religious goods. It therefore also corrects the propensity to kinds of idolatry or envy; to see diverse spiritual goods only in one's own image or to feel antipathy toward spiritual goods that one does not possess. The virtue deals, then, with the new need to face fully fundamentally different religious ideals. Moreover, it also deals with the weaknesses present in those basically flawed or overly simple ways of conceiving and responding to those differences that we examined earlier.

This correction can occur, however, only if people understand both what needs correction and why it must be corrected. That is they must, first, be able to grasp the character of genuine religious differences and, second, they must also believe that a virtue is needed to deal with that new recognition. The grasping of differences involves, I believe, the acquisition of a skill—the skill that appears in the activity of accurate and imaginative comparisons between religious phenomena. The accepting that a new virtue is necessary involves a normative judgment about how best to deal with the situation—and that judgment is one that has principled opponents. Let us end by examining these two subjects.

VI. Training of the Academic Religious Imagination

The correction which spiritual regret produces can appear only if the skill of comparison is well developed. That can occur only if one not only has the imagination to enter into other religious visions but also educates that imagination, and believes one should exercise that imagination. The crucial points, then, about what is involved in dealing with powerful but alien religions all revolve around the idea of imagination. The first concerns the role of imagination in understanding; the second concerns the need to educate it; and the third concerns the belief it should be used.

To focus on the imagination may seem odd. But I would argue that the capacity to imagine is as important as the capacity to deliberate when the subject is how best to live and therefore what are the virtues we should pursue. Moreover, the capacity to imagine underlies, I think, all significant comparative work whether it involves our subject, the understanding of different religions, or even related subjects such as understanding more fully people we may think we know well.

I believe all people have the capacity to enter imaginatively into other religious visions. Like virtually all capacities or potentialities that can generate skills, however, it can be actualized only if it is trained. That training can be hard to come by. Travel, reading, temperament, and sustained attention to the people around one can surely help. Moreover, portions of the media, especially television, often do present foreign religious perspectives and more than occasionally do so in very striking ways. Nevertheless, the training to understand and appreciate those perspectives is for many people available only in educational institutions. They are one of the few places, and I am often tempted to say only places, it can occur. Indeed, I would even argue that media presentations and many kinds of travel usually foster the kind of tourist mentality that leads people away from rather than toward complex understandings.

Obviously a position like mine can carry the rancid odor of self-justification or even self-aggrandizement. Such suspicions are surely understandable, whether they arise from observers within or outside of the profession, but several comments may alleviate them. First, the general purposes of education often differ dramatically from what higher education can accomplish. I do believe the purpose of education, when defined most generally, is to develop all those human excellences a culture thinks are important. But few American institutions of higher education either have the time or possess the ethos to develop most ethical or religious virtues. Indeed, it would be self-deceiving and probably silly to believe that such institutions can fundamentally change the ethical and religious dispositions that have been formed by the powerful forces of family and culture.

That does not mean, however, that education cannot develop skills. These skills, in turn, will inform virtues in ways we discussed earlier. Given higher education's character many of the virtues it informs will be intellectual ones, and the contribution of the acquired skills will be direct and basic. Other virtues, however, will be ethical or religious ones, and the contribution of both the acquired skills and the resultant intellectual virtues will be less direct and basic. I think the disciplined and imaginative understanding of other religious perspectives is one skill that can be developed in higher education. Moreover, the development of this skill is not only valuable in itself but it also contributes much to the growth of other virtues—intellectual, ethical, and religious. We can help train people's imagination in this area, then, and therefore aid in the development of virtues such as spiritual regret. . . .

VII. Encountering the Principled Opposition

Presuming needed development of the imagination has occurred we are still left with our third question, the question of whether full human flourishing demands that the power should be exercised. This question involves dealing with many daunting issues, and here I will just sketch out the competing positions and what are, I think, the major issues separating them.

People have and surely can argue that the imaginative

voyaging I recommend is unnecessary or even destructive. They may see it, for example, as a kind of voyeurism or self-torture. Opposing positions have many variants, but they all fit into two groups, groups that represent, to my mind, the different major alternatives. Both are integral views and have powerful spokespeople; both can even provide opportunities for virtues like spiritual regret.

The first response is avowedly secularist; it is areligious or antireligious if we employ any conventional notion of being religious. Most in this category share what has been called the modern ideal of the affirmation of ordinary life and therefore will distrust the heroic. They will also embrace at least some kind of pluralism and remain suspicious of grand claims. At the core of this position is, I believe, a kind of *sophisticated complacency*, especially a complacency about the need to respond to the kinds of questions religions deal with. The aim, then, is to help people overcome their fears about the importance of the answers they give to religious questions.

This position can easily produce a debilitatingly banal vision of human fulfillment. But it can also produce a powerful view where pride of place is always given to moral not religious questions and to realistic, practical solutions. Moreover, it can share the spiritual ideal of disciplined detachment from many normal human concerns which underlies the notion of human excellence. . . . It can, then, represent a powerful spiritual alternative to what I have been arguing for; it may, for example, hold to the dramatic notion that regret of any sort ought not be part of a well-lived life.

The second response includes people who would claim to be religious however conventionally or unconventionally they take that term. For them imaginative voyaging and the virtues like spiritual regret that it aims to produce represent at best a problematic ideal, at worst a significant vice or religious deformation. They could, for example, classify spiritual regret as a virulent case of primordial pride, a violation of humility, an attempt to encompass all possible goods and to become "god-like."

Most important for these people are the implications to be drawn from human finitude. Especially important are the limits that must be observed if a full religious life is to be lived. Proponents of this position argue that imaginative voyaging undercuts the only possible basis for active, and perhaps saving, participation in a religious community. Such participation, it is said, requires one to limit the sorts of religious questions one entertains. It may even require, on religious grounds, that one treat the claims of fundamentally different religious perspectives with ironic distance or cultivated neglect rather than with intense attention. They argue, then, for a kind of *sophisticated parochialism*, an intentional and reasoned closing off of perspectives.

Any full response to these two principled opponents involves, as noted, dealing with questions I cannot examine fully here. However, let me sketch out the most crucial features of the rationale for my position. I think imaginative voyaging, and what it produces, is necessary for three related reasons. We need it, first, if we are to meet fully both the demands and the possibilities our current religious situation places before us. That is, we face a situation which requires new responses from us if any religious ideas are to meet the criteria of appropriateness and plausibility. That in turn presents striking new opportunities to rethink what we are committed to and why. We also need it if we are to see the new kinds of spiritual discipline the current situation makes possible. That is, the particular asceticism which characterizes scholarly inquiry into different religions—for instance, the cultivation of thinking without assenting—can be seen as part of a discipline the spiritual implications of which extend beyond scholarship, at least as it is narrowly defined. Finally, we need it if we are to operate well and perhaps even survive in the present world. That is, our contact with diverse religious ideas and practices grows at a pace that places striking new demands on us about how best to understand and to judge them.

I want, then, to defend the significance of virtues like spiritual regret. Nevertheless, I also agree with some features of the positions presented by the principled opposition. Most important, I agree there are areas where such virtues are inappropriate and can, at times, even be called vices. Indeed, seeing where virtues like spiritual regret ought not function is an extremely important part of this kind of analysis, just as courage is best understood in the context of foolhardiness and timidity. Separating out areas where they are appropriate from areas where they are not is critical for seeing both what the virtues are and what their deformations are. Let me end with a few brief comments on this subject.

Some confrontations that might seem to be occasions for, say, spiritual regret are not. They are not appropriate occasions because one cannot accept the option presented and still remain oneself in any meaningful sense. In one such area, really entertaining the option is impossible because of either the *theoretical* or the *ethical* webs of belief a person has. Those two webs of belief differ in important ways but either can make impossible a full encounter. For example, my web of theoretical beliefs would have to be surrendered if I embraced the religious ideals presented by a Korean shaman and my web of ethical beliefs if I embraced the religious ideals presented by a pre-Ch'in Taoist. In either case I would cease to be me.

Another more complex area involves cases where the fundamental choices a person has made within his or her general webs of theoretical and ethical beliefs have established enduring patterns that have basically changed the person. (Decisions to marry, have children, or commit to a profession can all be examples of such choices.) That is, I differ enough from what I would have become had another choice been made that I cannot really spiritually regret an option. In considering the alternative religious option, I am involved in a relationship that is not to myself but rather is to someone who closely resembles me, someone like an intimate friend.

Failures to see the inappropriateness of virtues like spiritual regret in either of these areas can be the result of intellectual mistakes. They can also, and more usually do, reflect the grip of vices like sentimentality or nostalgia. At worst the people involved manifest truly distorted human states. Unhappily, examples of this are all too evident both in people who have dabbled with powerful but alien religions and those who have ardently embraced them. At best these states manifest the counterfeits or perhaps semblances of the full virtue. Their state has only a few of the qualities the full virtue displays, and it is mixed with naive or even pathetic features.

Despite all this, there is also a range of other cases in which people face more subtle confrontations, and these are the places where virtues like spiritual regret ought to function. . . .

KEY TERMS AND CONCEPTS

apologetics The activity of offering a defense of one's religion.

insider's vs. outsider's perspectives Two different viewpoints from which the study of religion can be conducted. The insider's view is that of a religious participant who seeks understanding in order to increase faith. The outsider's perspective refers to the academic study of religion, which seeks understanding from a nonsectarian point of view.

meta, or second order, vs. first order *First order* refers to engagement in some primary activity like speaking a language or practicing a religion. *Second order* (meta) refers to reflection on some first-order activity. The academic study of religion is here characterized as a second-order activity.

spiritual regret According to Yearley, this is a new religious virtue appropriate for the study of religion in our age of religious pluralism that involves both joy at discovering a new spiritual view that attracts you and sadness that you cannot fully adopt such a view.

SUGGESTIONS FOR FURTHER READING

Carman, J., and S. Hopkins, eds. *Tracing Common Themes: Comparative Courses in the Study of Religion.* Atlanta, Ga.: Scholars Press, 1991. Essays on the value and importance of the academic study of religion.

Creel, Richard E. *Religion and Doubt: Toward a Faith of Your Own.* 2nd ed. Englewood Cliffs, N.J.: Prentice-Hall, 1991. Creel's first chapter addresses the issue of why one should study religion, and his fifth chapter details what he thinks are the traits of a healthy religious faith.

McCutcheon, Russell T., ed. *The Insider/Outsider Problem in the Study of Religion: A Reader.* London: Cassell, 1999. A useful collection of writings on issues relating to the academic study of religion.

Plantinga, Alvin. "A Defense of Religious Exclusivism." In *Philosophy of Religion: An Anthology*, 3rd ed., edited by Louis P. Pojman, pp. 517–530. Belmont, Calif.: Wadsworth, 1994. Plantinga argues that even in a pluralistic situation, religious exclusivism is neither morally wrong nor unreasonable—some exclusivism in belief is inevitable. However, he does believe we should seek knowledge of other religions, even if we risk lessening our own assurance.

Porter, Jean. "Virtue Ethics." In *A Companion to Philosophy of Religion*, edited by Phillip L. Quinn and Charles Taliaferro, pp. 466–472. Oxford: Blackwell, 1997. Provides a clear overview of recent developments in the thinking about virtue.

Reynolds, F., and S. Burkhalter, eds. *Beyond the Classics? Essays on Religious Studies and Liberal Education.* Atlanta, Ga.: Scholars Press, 1990. These essays take the reader deeper into the issues of how the study of religion relates to liberal education.

RESEARCH PROJECTS

1. Write a paper focusing on the insider/outsider distinction, and investigate whether the distinction is useful and whether it can be clearly articulated.

2. Write a paper on Yearley's notion of spiritual regret and investigate whether it truly is a virtue. This would involve pursuing the objections of sophisticated complacency and sophisticated parochialism in greater depth.

3. Consider this statement by Bruce Lincoln: "Reverence is a religious, and not a scholarly, virtue. When good manners and good conscience cannot be reconciled, the demands of the latter ought to prevail" ("Theses on Method," *Method and Theory in the Study of Religion* 1996). Write a brief paper exploring what you think Lincoln may mean, provide concrete examples, and evaluate Lincoln's thesis.

2

What Is Religion?

The question "What is religion?" is deceptively simple. Most people think they know what religion is. If I asked you to write a one-sentence definition, you could do so after a little thought. So, what is the problem with defining religion?

There are many problems for the student of religions, because not any sort of definition will do. In order to engage in the academic study of religion, we need a definition that is analytically useful. That means it should *be useful for the purposes at hand, be as precise as possible without being too narrow in scope, and be as free from bias as possible.*

USEFULNESS

Definitions are not true or false, but more or less useful. They tell us how to use words effectively depending on the situation and what we are trying to communicate. Historians who wish to study religious beliefs and practices that characterize people in China two thousand years ago may find one kind of definition useful for their purposes, but a sociologist who wishes to describe social influences on religious practices in contemporary England may find another kind of definition useful. Definitions are heuristic devices—they are an aid that stimulates further investigation and thought. Hence different academic disciplines (e.g., history, sociology, psychology, anthropology, literature, philosophy) find different definitions more or less useful, depending on the perspective of their discipline. Given these circumstances, the quest for one universal definition of religion that is useful for all academic disciplines seems hopeless.

You might be thinking that what I have just said does not sound quite right. What if the definition the historian uses and the definition the sociologist uses are totally different? How could we be sure that they

were both studying religion rather than two very different phenomena?

PRECISION

That question leads directly into a discussion of precision. The purpose of definitions is to *draw boundaries* and thereby limit the field of study. If everything fell under the category of religion, then the study of religion would become the study of everything and thereby become impossible to manage. When drawing boundaries, however, we can be too precise and draw them so narrowly that we exclude some things that ought to be included. For example, if I defined religion as "belief in God," I would be leaving out too much of importance, such as religious practices. Religions are more than belief systems; they involve ritual practices, moral codes, various types of social organizations, and much more. Also, what about polytheistic religions that believe there is more than one god, religions that deny ultimate reality is divine (some types of Buddhism), or those that believe in totems and spirits? Is it reasonable to exclude them by definition?

The other side of the coin of drawing the boundaries too narrowly is drawing them too broadly. Some scholars have favored definitions that involve the use of words like *ultimate concern* or *sacred*. Unless carefully specified, these words are so vague that it seems practically anything can fit within their boundaries. Is the capitalist who devotes his life to the pursuit of wealth religious because money and the power it brings have become his ultimate concern? Is the socialist who devotes her life to the pursuit of social justice through the equal or near-equal distribution of wealth religious because economic justice is a sacred cause for the socialist?

The questions and problems associated with precision are closely tied to two very different theories of the nature of definition. For scholars who hold to a theory of essentialism, the purpose of definitions is to state the essence of something. The **essence** is a universal quality or set of qualities that make something *what it is* and *not something else.* For example, the fact that I have gray hair is not an essential quality. I could have black hair and still be who I am. However, it is hard to imagine me being who I am if I did not have the quality of being a human being. Being human seems to be more essential to who I am than my hair color.

However, an essence must be a quality or characteristic that not only makes something what it is but also makes it not something else. This means an essence must consist of both **necessary** and **sufficient** traits or characteristics. A quality might be necessary without being sufficient. I am human and that is necessary to my identity, but it is not sufficient to make me who I am because all other humans have that quality as well. A quality might also be sufficient, but not necessary. For example, a baseball striking a window is sufficient to break it, but it is not necessary since many other things besides baseballs break windows.

If you think good definitions must be **essential definitions,** then you need to find characteristics of religion that are both necessary and sufficient. This involves correctly identifying the genus and species. A **genus** is a class divisible into a smaller class called a **species.** For example, Aristotle's famous definition of a human being as a rational animal states the genus (animal) and within that genus a smaller class (rational beings). The smaller class or species is discovered by stating the differences (referred to as *differentia*) that distinguish one type of animal from another. This gives the definition greater precision because while all humans are animal, not all animals are human. There are other kinds of animals (like frogs), and what makes them different, if we follow Aristotle, is that they are not rational while humans are rational. If we take the two qualities (animal and rational) together, we have, if Aristotle is right, the necessary and sufficient characteristics of human beings.

Those who pursue essential definitions of religion usually favor either a **substantive definition** that states what religion is or a **functional definition** that states what religion does. Defining religion as belief in the supernatural is an example of a substantive type of essential definition. Defining religion as a be-

lief system that gives meaning and purpose to human life is an example of a functional type of essential definition. Both definitions identify the genus of religion as belief. The substantive example (belief in the supernatural) differentiates religious beliefs from other types of belief by stating what it is a belief in, namely, the supernatural. The functional example differentiates religious beliefs by stating what they do (provide meaning and purpose to human life).

Both of these types, substantive and functional, are problematic. Substantive types often turn out to be too narrow because of the vast diversity of religious beliefs and practices, and functional types often turn out to be too broad because different things can often function in the same way. For example, various types of political beliefs as well as religious beliefs can give meaning and purpose to human life.

A very different theory of definition rejects the idea of essences. According to this theory, we should look for a cluster of characteristics that makes something part of a certain family. **Cluster definitions** are based on an analogy with families. Families are made up of many members who have many different traits or qualities. Yet, despite these differences, they are all members of the same family. There may be no set of traits that are both necessary and sufficient, but there are traits that allow us to group them into the same family.

Perhaps religion is like a family. There are many members with many different characteristics but no set of characteristics that capture some essence. Those who favor cluster definitions of religion readily acknowledge that the boundaries between religion and other things are fuzzy. There is no sharp line of demarcation, but a kind of fading away until the cluster of qualities has become so thin that we best start talking about a different family.

BIAS

We said at the outset that good definitions of religion should be as free from bias as possible. As I said in the first chapter, none of us can totally escape our biases since we must necessarily study from various perspectives, but we can become aware of them. This awareness allows us to correct for bias when we formulate definitions. One common bias is what we might call the Western bias. It is very subtle (as many biases are), and to unmask it will take careful analysis.

The English word *religion* comes from the Latin word **religio**. Latin scholars are not certain whether *religio* comes from the Latin *relegere*, which refers to people who are careful in their ritual actions rather than neglectful, or *religare*, which means "to bind," that is, to be under an obligation. Early Latin Christians used the word *religio* to distinguish true religion from false. For them *religio* did not refer to the world religions as it does today, but rather to genuine or true worship. In the Middle Ages, *religio* was not widely used, but when it was, it often referred to "the religious," that is, those who choose the monastic life. Hence, *religio* distinguished the monastic life from the life of the laity.

With the dawn of the modern age, when knowledge of and encounters with religions different from Christianity increased, people began using the word *religion* to refer to the various religious traditions of the world. Today, *religion* and its cognates are also used to refer to different historical traditions with different beliefs and practices. In addition, the adjective form is used to refer to personal piety as in "She is a very religious person." Sometimes, *religion* is used in an ideal sense to refer to something that is desirable or valuable as in "Religion is a good thing." In the singular, the word can refer to religion in general.

Given this history, it is not surprising that some scholars have proposed dropping the use of the word *religion* for scholarly purposes because it is hopelessly abstract and tied too deeply to Western biases. Benson Saler, an anthropologist, summarizes this view when he writes, "The practitioners of a mostly Western profession (anthropology) employ a Western category (religion), conceptualized as a component of a larger Western category (culture), to achieve their professional goal of coming to understand what is meaningful and important for non-Western peoples" (*Conceptualizing Religion*, 1993:9).

Complicating this ethnocentric bias that seems to be built into the very word *religion* is a value bias. Definitions reflect how the people creating them value religion. If their attitude is positive, the definition will be positive. If their attitude is negative, the definition will be negative, and if their attitude is mixed or uncertain, their definition will reflect that too. For example, if I defined religion as "an illusory hope for a better future," you would immediately detect a negative attitude in my definition. We can check our value biases by adding qualifying words such as *allegedly*, *presumably*, or *maybe*. So I might revise my

definition of religion to "the hope for a better future, a hope that may or may not prove to be an illusion."

Correcting for the very ethnicity of the word *religion* is much harder. If we do not use *religion*, what word should we use? Are *faith* or *tradition* any more free from a Western bias? Probably the best we can do is recognize that some ethnocentric words are starting points (we have to start from our own culture), but ethnocentrism should not be a stopping point. If it is, it shows we have not learned anything about our biases.

Every definition of religion is part of a more general theory of religion. It is "theory-laden" to use the technical term. Behind every definition is some theory about what religion means and how it functions. This is not a bad thing; indeed, it is unavoidable. However, one needs to be aware of the ways theory influences definition. For example, some theories hold that there is something irreducibly "religious" about religions—that religions are unique and can be understood only on their own ground. Other theories claim that religions are like any other human phenomenon and can be understood in cultural, historical, sociological, or psychological terms. According to these theories, there is nothing that is uniquely religious about religions. These two divergent types of theories generate very different definitions.

Still another subtle bias that slips into both theory and definition is gender bias. Since religions historically have been largely dominated by males, and since females often have been relegated to the back pews, so to speak, when we think about religion we often take as our implicit model traditional patriarchal religions. Our theories and definitions are then built up under the influence of these models and gender bias is the result. Even the word *God* implies for many a male figure. People may be inclined to define religion as "belief in God or gods," rather than "belief in gods and goddesses."

Another bias that slips into definitions is the confusion between spirituality and religion. Consider these two statements:

1. A person can belong to a religion and not be religious.
2. A person can be religious and not belong to a religion.

The key term is *belong to*. If *belong to* means being an official member of some organization, then the first statement seems obviously true. The term *religious hypocrite* would have little meaning if someone could not formally belong to a religious organization and fail to personally embody spirituality. The second statement is more problematic because one could make the case that the truly spiritual person will seek membership in some religious organization because religious organizations try to foster spirituality and provide an opportunity for spiritual fellowship. It is undoubtedly true that religious organizations present themselves as a path or way that fosters growth in spirituality, but there seems to be no good reason why someone could not foster spiritual growth in ways other than belonging to some religious organization.

Crucial to this debate about the relationship between **spirituality** and **religion** is a clear distinction between the two. Defining spirituality is even harder than defining religion. This is complicated by the fact that we sometimes use the adjective *religious* interchangeably with *spiritual.* To be spiritual is to be deeply and genuinely religious. But how can one be religious without religion?

There have, of course, been various attempts to define spirituality. The psychologist of religion William James (1842–1910) suggested that spirituality is a quest for a transformation from a state of perceived wrongness to a state of perceived rightness by making contact with some higher power or powers. The contemporary philosopher John Hick thinks of spirituality as a transformation from a selfish and egocentric state to an unselfish and caring state. However, all of these terms are vague and notoriously different to make precise. Nevertheless, it is important to not confuse religion and spirituality. When we do, we are tempted to transfer whatever negative qualities we may find in religious organizations to people who sincerely seek to make a better life for themselves and others.

The two statements I asked you to consider earlier presuppose that spirituality or religiosity is best thought of as a personal quality—a characteristic or set of characteristics that some people have. They also presuppose that religion refers to an organized group of people. This organized group presents itself as an effective way to nurture the personal quality of spirituality, but it is always possible that it fails to do so or, at least, fails to satisfy the spiritual desires of those who join. The problem of how religion and spirituality are related is itself a product of how we conceptualize religion.

I have discussed some of the many problems involved in the deceptively simple task of defining religion. Finding a useful definition that is analytically precise and free from bias is no easy task. There is another problem as well: Should we define religion before we study religions or only afterward? Some argue it is not fair to define one's subject matter before looking and seeing what is there. Others argue that without some idea of where to look (and a definition gives us an idea of where to look), we will be looking in vain. This is a variation of the chicken and the egg problem. But rather than being a problem about which came first (obviously, religion did), which *should* come first—definition or observation? I think this problem is not a real problem. Instead, definition and observation must go hand in hand. We need to start with working definitions that tell us where to look, and as we look we need to revise and refine our definitions.

2.1 DEFINING RELIGION

We discussed the differences between the concepts of essential definition and cluster definition earlier. Here we examine in greater detail the notion of a cluster definition and how it might be usefully applied to the problem of defining religion.

Rem B. Edwards, a professor of philosophy at the University of Tennessee, explores, in the following selection, the possibility of a cluster definition of religion. He discovers that the meaning of the English word *religion* is so influenced by Western theistic religions and Western culture that its cross-cultural usefulness is questionable. His discussion not only illuminates the notion of cluster definition but also illustrates how one might construct such a definition of religion. Edwards's analysis of the traits frequently associated with religion reveals some significant features of the way many of us think about religion.

REM B. EDWARDS

The Search for Family Resemblances of Religion

READING QUESTIONS

1. As you read, make a list of all the words and ideas you do not understand or are uncertain about. Discuss them with a classmate, look them up in a dictionary, or bring them up in class for discussion and clarification. (You should continue doing this for every selection in this book.)
2. What makes finding the essence of religion difficult?
3. All superior beings are not supernatural beings. Why?
4. Which family traits appear to be common or nearly common to all family members? What does this imply about the influence of Western religions on the search for family traits?
5. Edwards thinks that many of the family traits are sufficient, yet none of them is necessary. Do you agree? Why or why not?

The influential twentieth-century philosopher Ludwig Wittgenstein thought that there are many perfectly meaningful, useful words in our language that have no "common essence" of connotation. These words are not used to name some characteristic or set of characteristics common to and distinctive of all the objects to which we normally apply such words. Wittgenstein thought that the common-sense assumption that there has to be a common essence where there is a common name is exceedingly naive, and he recommended that instead of making this assumption uncritically we should "look and see" if it is so. He believed that we would not always find a common essence for many perfectly useful words, such as *game*, *language*, *knowledge*, and so on. That he was correct with respect to *all* the words he used to illustrate his point may be questioned, but his general idea that some words have only "family resemblances" instead of "common essences" is a very fruitful one to explore, especially in its application to the word *religion*. Wittgenstein him-

self did not apply it to *religion*, but others who have been influenced by him have made preliminary studies of its possible application in this area. We shall first discuss briefly what is meant by "the search for family resemblances," and then we shall see if the search throws any light on our understanding of *religion*.

Not all objects called by a common name have a common essence, but they are frequently related to one another by "a complicated network of similarities overlapping and criss-crossing: sometimes overall similarities, sometimes similarities of detail," according to Wittgenstein. He compared this web of resemblances to the complicated way in which members of a human family resemble one another and are recognizable as members of the same family. Suppose that there are five brothers and sisters who are easily recognizable as members of the same family, but among whom there is not a single family trait that each has in common with *all* the others, as illustrated by the following diagram. Their resemblance to one another may depend not on a common essence, but on a complicated web of traits shared with one or more, but not with all, of the other members of the family. (In the diagram, the presence of a family trait is indicated by P and the absence by A.)

FAMILY TRAITS	FAMILY MEMBERS				
	Alex	Bill	Cathy	Dave	Enid
Over 6 feet tall	P	P	P	P	A
Blue eyes	P	P	P	A	P
Blond hair	P	P	A	P	P
Pug nose	P	A	P	P	P
Irritability	A	P	P	P	P

The obvious weakness of the family resemblance comparison is that if we were to add one additional family trait to our diagram, namely "Having the same parents," we would have a characteristic that was both common to and distinctive of each member of the family. But even this trait would not necessarily be common to all; suppose that Enid resembles all her brothers and sisters in all the respects indicated and yet is an adopted child! Nevertheless, there is always the possibility that such an additional family trait has been overlooked and will later turn up in any attempt to explore the meaning of a word in terms of family resemblances. When such a trait is discovered, this would seem to mean that our search for family resemblances has turned up a common essence as well and that the two approaches complement rather

From Rem B. Edwards, *Reason and Religion*, pp. 14–18, 37–38. Copyright © 1979 by University Press of America. Used by permission. Endnotes deleted.

than conflict with each other. Perhaps this will turn out to be the case with the concept of "religion."

FAMILY TRAITS OF RELIGION

Many college students in the Western world who register for their first course in World Religions or Comparative Religions have some weird misconceptions about the non-Christian religions. They may think, for example, that in most of the non-Christian religions it is really the supernatural Christian God who is known and worshiped, but he is called by some other name such as the Buddha, the Brahman, or Allah, and that this knowledge is somewhat perversely distorted, since the devotees of these religions have not received all the benefits of the Christian revelation. Many students assume that most of the world religions teach that the individual human "soul" is created by God and is destined to everlasting existence in some place of reward or punishment, and that a program of "salvation" from the latter and for the former is invariably provided. Many students further assume that all world religions include a moral program —again somewhat distorted, of course—which contains the essentials of the Ten Commandments and the Sermon on the Mount and which is derived from and sanctioned by the Supreme Being. In short, it is typical for Westerners to assume at the outset of a study of the concept of "religion" or the phenomena of the world religions that the field of inquiry is considerably less diversified than it in fact turns out to be. Yet it is precisely this diversity that makes it so difficult to discover some common essence for "religion" and that has suggested that the search for family resemblances might be a more fruitful approach to the concept of "religion." Let us see how such a search can be conducted.

We shall now look at a selected list of family traits and family members for the concept of "religion." In the chart, . . . the family traits listed in the column on the left are all prominent characteristics of at least some of the things that we call religions, and the list of family members is a partial list of some of the things to which we apply the word with some degree of regularity. Neither list is in any way complete, especially the list of family members, and you can add to each list as you see fit. This chart and the discussion that follows are *not* to be construed as a survey of the field of comparative religion. The family members that are included were selected mainly because they permit us to introduce a preliminary discussion of the difficulties involved in discovering a common essence. The exercise as a whole is valuable because it allows us to make a place for the richness and concreteness of meaning that *religion* normally has. . . .

GENERAL CONCLUSIONS OF "THE SEARCH FOR FAMILY RESEMBLANCES"

1. The only family members in our chart that clearly exhibit all the family traits are Christianity, Judaism, and Islam, though Hinduism comes very close. This suggests that these Western religions have had a definitive influence on our very conception of religion. We do in fact take them as paradigms for the application of the concept, since they exhibit *all* the important traits that we ascribe to a "religion." We might conjecture that if we were making an ordinary-language analysis of religion in Ceylon we would have set up our list of family traits in such a way as to get a P in each case for Hinayana Buddhism, or in India a clear-cut P in each case for Hinduism—and in the languages of these countries it would be the Western religions that would be found wanting! If this is the case, then *religion* in English is only an approximate translation of any corresponding words in these other languages.

2. The family members on the chart are arranged in such a way that fewer and fewer P's appear as we move to the right in the direction of success, wealth, golf, and fishing, and get further and further away from our paradigms of Christianity, Judaism, and Islam. This suggests that as we Westerners become acquainted with other cultures and new developments in our own cultures, we are willing to extend the application of *religion* to those phenomena that bear some significant similarities to our own standard religions. It further suggests that as these similarities become fewer and fewer in particular cases, we come to have more and more reservations about the legitimacy of extending *religion* to cover these cases. This explains why we are uneasy about calling success, wealth, golf, and fishing religions—they are like Christianity *only* in that they involve deep, intense concern. We say that such "religions" are only "borderline cases," or that in speaking of them as religions we are only speaking metaphorically.

3. In deciding whether to call something a religion, it is not merely the *number* of respects in which it resembles our paradigms that guides us, it is also the *importance* of these traits. Other traits besides deep, intense concern, such as a complex world view interpreting the significance of human life or an account of the nature of, origin of, and cure for evil, are nearly universal in the religions, and this may be one clue that guides us in as-

SELECTED FAMILY TRAITS OF SOME RELIGIONS

FAMILY TRAITS	Christianity, Judaism, Islam	Vedanta Hindu Pantheism	Early Buddhism and Hinayana Buddhism	Early Greek Olympian Polytheism	Aristotle's Concept of Unmoved Mover	Communism	Moral Naturalistic Humanism	Spinozistic Pantheism	Success, Wealth, Golf, Fishing, etc.
1. Belief in a *supernatural* intelligent being or beings	P	A?	A	A	P	A	A	A	A
2. Belief in a *superior* intelligent being or beings	P	P	A	P	P	A	A	A?	A
3. Complex world view interpreting the significance of human life	P	P	P	P	P	P	P	P	A
4. Belief in experience after death	P	P	P	P?	A	A	A	A	A
5. Moral code	P	P	P	A	P	P	P	A	A
6. Belief that the moral code is sanctioned by a *superior* intelligent being or beings	P	P	A	A	A	A	A	A	A
7. An account of the nature of, origin of, and cure for evil	P	P	P	P?	P	P	P	P	A
8. Theodicy	P	P?	A	A	A	A	A	A	A
9. Prayer and ritual	P	P	P	P	A	P?	A	A?	A
10. Sacred objects and places	P	P	P	P	A	P	A	A	A?
11. Revealed truths or interpretations of revelatory events	P	P	P?	P	A	A	A	A	A
12. Religious experience—awe, mystical experience, revelations	P	P	P	P	A	A	A	A	P
13. Deep, intense concern	P	P	P	P	P?	P	P	P	P
14. Institutionalized social sharing of some of traits 1–13	P	P	P	P	A?	P	A?	A?	A?
15.									
16.									
17.									

Key: P = Present, A = Absent, ? = Unclear.

sessing their importance. What other traits are of crucial importance? To us Westerners belief in God and in experience after death weigh heavily, though even these are not deemed absolutely necessary. A typical Western atheist who passionately denies God and immortality, who never indulges in anything resembling prayer, ritual, or mysticism, and whose principles we regard as less than moral would not be called a religious man; but a dedicated Hinayana Buddhist who fails to affirm God and immortality and yet does engage in something resembling prayer, ritual, mysticism, and morality is called a religious man, mainly because his situation does exhibit a significant number of important resemblances to our paradigmatic religions.

4. The traits provide the differentia of "religion." We are willing to call a religion only a finite set of beliefs and practices through which we express our ultimate concerns. . . . The list of family traits on our chart represents the hard core of the traits that the "religions" must manifest, and although it is by no means complete, it nevertheless could not be indefinitely extended. Neither could the list of family members be indefinitely extended. There are many sufficient but no necessary conditions for calling something a religion if the Wittgensteinian approach is correct. So long as there are family resemblances, it is not necessary that there be common essences in order for there to be limits on the correct application of a concept and rules to guide us in

making those applications. However, is the contention that there are *only* family resemblances completely correct? What shall we say about the several nearly universal traits of religion that we have discovered? Would we call something a religion that completely failed to involve deep concern, answers to questions about the significance of human life, and perhaps even some account of the origin of, nature of, and cure for evil? Is the search for family resemblances completely at odds with the search for common essences? In looking to see, have we not found? In being nearly if not completely universal, these traits come as close to being necessary conditions for calling something a religion as we could expect to find for such a complex ordinary-language concept.

KEY TERMS AND CONCEPTS

cluster vs. essential definitions Cluster definitions list a set of family traits found in many members of the "family" religion. Essential definitions attempt to state the essence of religion.

essence That quality or qualities that make something what it is and not something else.

genus and species Genus is a class to which something belongs, and species is a subclass of the genus that distinguishes a particular member of the genus from other members.

necessary and sufficient qualities A necessary quality is any quality that X must have in order to be X, while a sufficient quality is any quality that X may have whose presence is enough to make X occur, but X could occur in its absence. Qualities may be necessary and not sufficient, or sufficient and not necessary, or both. A person searching for an essential definition seeks qualities that are both necessary and sufficient because these constitute the essences of the *diffiendum* (thing to be defined).

religio Latin word for religion that means either taking care in practicing rites like sacrifice or being under an obligation to practice rites. Combining both meanings, we get "the obligation to practice rites carefully."

spirituality vs. religion The development of spirituality is the goal of many religions, but it is not necessary to belong to a religious organization in order to pursue spiritual development.

substance vs. functional definitions Both are different types of essential definitions. The first focuses on the "what," or content, of religion; the second focuses on what religion *does*, that is, how it functions.

SUGGESTIONS FOR FURTHER READING

King, Winston L. "Religion." In *The Encyclopedia of Religion*, edited by Mircea Eliade, vol. 12, pp. 282–293. New York: Macmillan, 1987. A discussion of different definitions and some of the problems associated with defining religion along with different categories useful in comparing religions such as sacred actions, sacred times and places, sacred objects, myths, and symbols.

Smart, Ninian. *Worldviews: Crosscultural Explorations of Human Beliefs.* 2nd ed. Englewood Cliffs, N.J.: Prentice-Hall, 1995. Smart argues that we should subsume the category of religion under the even broader category of worldviews and that we should think of and compare worldviews in terms of six dimensions: doctrinal or philosophical, mythic or narrative, ethical or legal, ritual or practical, experiential or emotional, social or institutional.

Streng, Frederick J. *Understanding Religious Life.* 3rd ed. Belmont, Calif.: Wadsworth, 1985. The first chapter, "The Nature and Study of Religion," insightfully treats some of the themes and topics I have discussed in this chapter and in chapter 1.

RESEARCH PROJECTS

1. By yourself or with a study group of students, research some of the most influential definitions of religion in the past fifty years (your instructor can guide you). Then pick one definition and defend it as better than one or two other definitions you have selected.

2. Construct your own definition of religion and show how it is analytically useful (useful for the purpose at hand, as precise as possible without being too narrow in scope, and as free from bias as possible) for the comparative study of religions.

3. Write a one- or two-page critical précis of the selection by Edwards that consists of four elements: (1) a one-sentence statement of the thesis or main point of the reading; (2) a summary of the argument and evidence the author uses to establish the thesis; (3) a critique of the thesis *and* argument (critiques can be positive, negative, or a mixture of both); and (4) a statement of your own position with respect to the topic.

How Should We Study Religion?

The first chapter discussed some of the personal qualities useful in the study of religion: openness, honesty, critical intelligence, and careful reading and listening. This chapter is slightly more technical because we explore issues of methodology. How do we engage in the academic study of religion? That is, what are some of the methods we can employ?

THE FIELD OF RELIGIOUS STUDIES

Before I discuss method directly, let's look at a brief disciplinary outline of the field of religious studies as it is presently practiced in many colleges and universities in the United States and elsewhere:

I. History of religions
  A. Developmental studies
  B. Comparative studies
II. Social scientific study of religions
  A. Anthropology
  B. Sociology
  C. Psychology
III. Philosophical study of religions
  A. Analytical
  B. Critical

This outline is incomplete because there are areas that cut across these divisions such as feminist studies, literary studies, biblical studies, and much more. However, it will do as a starting point.

Historical studies employ the theories and methods of history to study how a religion, religions, or part of a religion has developed through time. All religions change because nothing that survives can do so without adapting to its changing environment. Religions that are living traditions have changed and are changing. Those that have ceased to change are dead religions (although parts may have survived in other religious forms such as Easter and Christmas). The developmental historian is interested in how religions have changed and what factors are at work that cause change. A basic assumption of this approach is that religions are complex dynamic historical processes.

Comparative studies primarily focus on comparing different religious traditions. The concern is less with the changes religions undergo (although one could do a comparative study of changes) and more with structures or types. The comparativist often arrests time by taking snapshots, as it were, of different religious phenomena and then comparing them. The comparativist may select one of the many dimensions of religion such as ritual and do a comparative study of, for example, certain types of ritual activities in Islam and Judaism during the nineteenth century in Poland and Turkey. One basic assumption of comparative studies is that there are certain analytical categories (belief, ritual, morality, and so on) that are useful for cross-cultural comparison. Ideally the comparativist should be balanced in her or his description of similarities and differences, but this is sometimes difficult to do. Often, differences get submerged or overlooked in the rush to find similarities.

Social scientists use the current methods and theories of their fields to understand and explain religion within a larger setting. A basic assumption for social scientists is that insofar as religion is a human activity, it can be explained by cultural, social, or psychological factors just as any human phenomenon can. The anthropologist sees religion as an expression of and part of a wider culture. Religion is treated as a subclass of culture. For sociologists, the operative category is society: What are the social functions of religion? How do societies influence religions, and how do religions influence societies? Psychologists are usually more individually oriented than sociologists: How might religion express unconscious structures? How does religion affect character development? Does religious commitment have any bearing on deviant behavior, mental illness, or moral development?

I divide philosophy of religion into two categories: analytic and critical. However, this is somewhat artificial because in practice the categories are often combined. Elsewhere I have defined *philosophy of religion* as "the rational attempt to formulate, understand, and answer fundamental questions about religious matters" (*Philosophy of Religion: Toward a Global Perspective*, 1999:3). That definition requires quite a bit of detailed unpacking, but I will note here only that the philosophical quest for formulating, understanding, and answering fundamental questions demands both careful analysis of religious belief and action and a critical response (negative or positive) whose goal is a deeper rational understanding of religious matters. Exactly what is rational and what are fundamental questions are subjects of intense debate. A basic assumption of this field is that if there is such a thing as religious truth, careful philosophical criticism and analysis should be able to uncover it. So, philosophy of religion is characteristically concerned with arguments for God's existence, arguments for life after death, whether or not religious experiences provide evidence of some religious reality, and so on. Historians and social scientists usually refrain from offering judgments about the truth or falsity of the religious beliefs and actions they study, but philosophers often boldly go where others fear to tread. Philosophers want to know if religions are bearers of truth.

UNDERSTANDING AND EXPLANATION

As you might imagine, there is considerable professional rivalry among these various areas of religious studies and considerable debate about what is appropriate and what is not. One major debate centers on a distinction between understanding and explanation. These terms are vague and are often used in different ways (understanding can even be thought of as one type of explanation), but in this debate understanding usually means reconstructing meanings from the "agent's point of view." This is equivalent to a type of interpretation. Explanation amounts to a casual account that subsumes religion under a theory in the social sciences and treats it just like any other social phenomenon.

According to the camp (called **phenomenology of religion**) that seeks only understanding, religion is *sui generis*, which means that it is based on something irreducibly religious and hence cannot be explained in nonreligious terms. The phenomenologists (so called because they claim to focus on only what appears, or phenomena) maintain that the academic study of religion is properly made up of only one discipline, a discipline appropriate to the study of the *sui generis* nature of religion, sometimes referred to as "the sacred." The good student of religion is to describe and interpret what appears (religious phenomena), but should not explain or evaluate it by standards foreign to religion. Phenomenologists sometimes call what they do history of religions or comparative religions (remember, I said the terminology is vague and confusing). They shun social scientists as hopelessly prejudiced because they project their own nonreligious theories into religious phenomena. Phenomenologists accuse social scientists of being "reductionistic" because they explain religion in terms of social causes—economic, cultural, or psychological.

Social scientists and philosophers generally see the field of religious studies as multidisciplinary and multimethodological. There are many different ways of studying religion, and each has something of value to offer. There is no good reason to exclude nonreligious causes of religious events if in fact they were causes of that event, and, at least for the philosophers, there is no good reason to refrain from asking whether what some religions claim is true is in fact true.

Let us assume for now that the goal of religious studies, be it historical, social scientific, or philosophical, is very much like the general goal of all academic disciplines, namely, to describe, interpret, explain, and evaluate certain phenomena. Given the preceding discussion, it is clear that phenomenologists would disagree with the last two (explaining and evaluating), but having noted this, let us move on to distinguish these activities and say something about how they are done.

DESCRIPTION

There is no such thing as pure **description** because every description is already an interpretation, but if we might artificially isolate it for a minute, we can characterize it as gathering and stating the facts of the case. Much like in a court of law, a case cannot proceed without knowing the facts, so the study of religion cannot proceed with knowing the data. In the field of religious studies, there is an enormous amount of data in a variety of different languages and cultures ranging from archaeological artifacts, pictures, coins, statues, and the like to sacred scriptures, commentaries on sacred scriptures, and other writings. The range is great, and I have not yet mentioned rituals, rites, oral traditions, and extraordinary experiences of transformation and revelation. No one can hope to master all of this data, and this book includes only a very small amount of mostly textual data such as scriptures, commentaries, and interpretations.

Gathering the data requires mastering a variety of technical skills, and presenting the data fairly and accurately is sometimes quite difficult. Mistakes can easily creep in, especially when dealing with gestures, customs, games, and rites from a culture very different from one's own. In order to facilitate the collection and presentation of data, students of religion often resort to classification schemes. These schemes can be very general, often referring to religious traditions as a whole (e.g., Buddhism, Islam, Christianity, or they can be more specific, referring to aspects of different religious traditions (e.g., beliefs, myths, symbols, sacred scriptures, experiences, morality, rituals, organization). Whatever classification scheme is used, it is created by scholars based on reflection on data and then used to organize and interpret further data. That is one reason why I said pure description is not possible. It simply is not possible to describe without classifying, and every classification scheme reflects an interpretation.

INTERPRETATION

What do the described data mean? That is the central problem for **interpretation.** The first obvious question is "mean to whom?" If we are talking about meaning for the insider, then that meaning is part of the descriptive data. If we are talking about meaning for the outside observer, then that meaning reflects the best understanding an outsider can come to given the data, the methods of interpretation employed, and the theories available.

Methods of interpretation are often called hermeneutical. **Hermeneutics** is the "science of interpretation," although the word *science* is used here in a very broad sense. Theoretically, hermeneutical studies can focus on any aspect of religion (beliefs, rituals, or experiences), but I will focus on the interpretation of written texts. The first rule of hermeneutics

is that meaning is context dependent; that is, what a text means depends on a variety of contexts both immediate and remote. Just as words have different meanings in different contexts (the work bank can mean the shore beside a river, stream, or lake; a place where money is stored; a rebound off the side of a pool table; and so on), texts have different meanings in different contexts. If I said, "I am going to the bank," you would not know the exact meaning of the word *bank* until I went on to specify, "in order to fish." The context of fishing rather than the context of cashing a check lets you know what I mean. One way to get at the context is to discover what the Germans call the **Sitz im Leben** (situation in life) of a text. Where and when was it written? By whom and to whom was it written? What is its purpose or function? Knowing the situation in life will tell you much about the meaning of a text.

There are also certain formal features of a text that will tell you much about its meaning. These include what type of writing it is (a letter, poem, narrative, sacred scripture, commentary) and what its surface structure (organization, style, themes) is. There is also a deep structure that is more difficult to discern. Deep structures are the hidden rules governing what is said much like the structure of language is determined by the hidden rules of grammar. In order to get at this hidden structure, scholars often distinguish between the text (what the author writes) and the subtext (either explicit asides by the author about what he or she writes or indirect meanings such as irony). Scholars look at what is included in a text, but they must also be aware of what is excluded. Social rules about inclusion and exclusion determine, in part, what is said. For example, there are certain words I have excluded in my account of hermeneutics because they are deemed inappropriate in textbook writing or I have judged them to be misleading.

Fair **comparison** is an indispensable tool in determining meaning. The remote context of a religious phenomenon can be uncovered by comparing different examples and discerning their similarities and differences. Comparison is implicit in the activities of determining the type of text (or ritual or moral code or whatever) and in determining structure and function. A story of a saint in Christianity can be illuminated by comparison with a story of a saint in Buddhism even if the stories are very different and unrelated culturally and historically. F. Max Müller (1823–1900), an influential linguist and historian of religions, liked to apply to the study of religion what

Goethe applied to the study of language. "He who knows one . . . knows none" (*Lectures on the Science of Religion*, 1872:10–11).

No attempt should be made to determine if one example is "better than" another in the sense of truer or morally superior (the Christian saint is really a saint and the Buddhist saint is a fraud). One example might be judged more typical or less typical of the type under discussion (stories about saints), but even that judgment is tricky. As you can readily see, prejudice and unconscious bias can enter the selection process. Why is this story rather than "that" selected as "typical"? In fact, as the historian of religions Jonathan Z. Smith reminds us, the scholar's "primary skill is concentrated" in his or her choice of examples. Smith goes on to claim that three conditions are implicit in the scholar's effort to articulate her or his choices:

> First, that the exemplum [chosen example] has been well and fully understood. That requires a mastery of both the relevant primary material and the history and tradition of its interpretation. Second, that the exemplum be displayed in the service of some important theory, some paradigm, some fundamental question, some central element in the academic imagination of religion. Third, that there be some method for explicitly relating the exemplum to the theory, paradigm, or question and some method for evaluating each in terms of the other.
>
> *Imagining Religion: From Babylon to Jonestown*, 1982:xi–xii

EXPLANATION

Smith's mention of theory leads us directly to **explanation.** The study of religion seeks not only to collect and describe data and to interpret it by employing classificational, hermeneutical, and comparative methods, but also to explain what is going on. Phenomenologists, as I noted earlier, would insist the task is done once the data are described and understood, but other scholars would insist the most important work is yet to be done, namely, explanation.

The word *explanation* can mean several different things in the field of religious studies. Some mean by it no more than an understanding gained by discovering the meaning of religious phenomena. In other words, interpretation is one type of explanation. To others, explanation means finding and describing the cause(s) of some religious phenomenon. To do this, one must directly and explicitly appeal to some theory. Description and interpretation are influenced by theory, but explanation is more clearly theory-laden because it is by subsuming some activity under a theory that a causal explanation is found. In physics the event of a falling apple is explained by subsuming it (along with many other examples of falling things) under the theory of gravity. So, a religious event like a sacrifice might be explained by subsuming it under a general theory about violence and the role substitute victims play in bringing cycles of violent vengeance to a close (see René Girard's *Violence and the Sacred*, 1977).

EVALUATION

For an explanation to make sense, the theory that gives rise to it must be right. How can we find that out? Physical scientists can check their theories by conducting controlled experiments in a laboratory, but in religious studies such checking procedures are seldom possible. What is possible is to check the usefulness of a theory by measuring it against many different examples to see if it makes sense of all or most of them. Does a detailed and careful study of fifty examples of sacrifices selected at random from the world's religions make more sense when viewed from the violence theory rather than from some other theory?

Evaluation is difficult because there are so many different levels of it. You might be evaluating the accuracy of a description by checking it against your own reading of the original data, or evaluating an interpretation by checking on how rigorously the hermeneutical method was employed, or evaluating a theory and hence a causal explanation by checking its general fruitfulness against other possible theories. In this sense of evaluation, one scholar is evaluating the work of another against such criteria as logical consistency, strength of evidence and argument, compelling counterexamples, and alternative explanations.

What about evaluating religious claims themselves? Can this be done? Should it be done? Many scholars openly acknowledge that the methods of history, the social sciences, and philosophy are limited to natural explanations—that there is no human way to evaluate supernatural claims. Was Jesus truly the son of God, or did he and others just think so? That he made that claim or did not make it, that others made it, that it meant thus and so—these are things that are possible to check provided enough information survives. But the theological claim that Jesus is the son of God—how could we check that?

Some philosophers and theologians might think we can check this claim just like we check other metaphysical claims—that is, is it logically consistent with everything we know about all kinds of things? Given what we know about history, the physical universe, human behavior, other religions, and about the effects of believing Jesus is God's son on people's lives, is it plausible that Jesus is truly the son of God? You can imagine the arguments on both sides and also arguments claiming such questions fall outside the range of questions that can be asked (let alone answered) in the academic study of religion.

SUMMARY

The academic study of religion seeks to describe, interpret, explain, and evaluate religious data. It draws on the specific methods of different disciplines—history, social science, and philosophy—in order to do this. Some very general methods involve collecting and classifying data, applying hermeneutical tools, and using techniques of comparison. Phenomenologists generally want to limit religious studies to description and understanding the agent's interpretation because they think anything else involves projecting the bias of the scholar into the phenomena. They also believe that religion is *sui generis* and that its uniqueness will be overlooked if we treat it as we would any other human phenomenon. Other scholars claim explanation and/or evaluation are legitimate activities of the scholar. Whatever else it may be, religion is at least a human phenomenon and, like any other human phenomenon, understandable by the application of the normal methods of history, social science, and philosophy.

3.1 COMPARING RELIGIONS

William E. Paden, author of the next selection, teaches religious studies at the University of Vermont. He is particularly concerned with how best to do comparative studies of religion and with developing the concept of a plurality of worlds in order to better understand religion. He believes there is a uniquely "religious language," which he calls the "language of 'the sacred,'" and that the task of the student of religion is to learn how to understand that language.

Answer the reading questions and see whether Paden can convince you.

❧❧

WILLIAM E. PADEN

Comparative Perspectives

READING QUESTIONS

1. As you read, make a list of all the words and ideas you do not understand or are uncertain about. Discuss them with a classmate, look them up in a dictionary, or bring them up in class for discussion and clarification.
2. What are the characteristics of what Paden calls the "comparative perspective"?
3. How does the comparative perspective differ from the activity of describing different religions?

In its elementary sense, comparative religion involves the study of the many religious traditions of the world. Such knowledge about "others" is deprovincializing. But it is one of the purposes of this book to show that the study of religion is not just limited to the description of various religious traditions, as if these were so many belief systems that posed alternatives to one's own or so many objects of intrinsic curiosity. Full comparative perspective involves more than simply describing side by side or serially the religions of the world, as though one were just sampling or judging various claims to truth.

There is also a second dimension of comparative investigation in religion: the study not just of different *religions* but of the structures of *religion*. What do we learn from the many species of religion about the genus itself? Religions do have things in common. They are in-

From *Religious Worlds* by William E. Paden, pp. 1–5. © 1988, 1994 by William E. Paden. Reprinted by permission of Beacon Press, Boston. References deleted.

stances of a human activity that has typical, expressive forms of its own. These religious structures constitute a subject matter in their own right. Like the study of music, which is not limited to examining a sequence of composers but also considers the special world of musical categories such as rhythm and harmony, so the study of religion is not limited to analyzing historical traditions such as Buddhism, Judaism, and Christianity but also investigates the religious "language" common to all traditions, the language of myth, gods, ritual, and sacrifice —in short, the language of "the sacred."

The general categories of religious behavior and the framework they provide for understanding particular religious systems are the primary subject matter of this book. This study therefore addresses the need to go beyond interpreting other religions simply in terms of their relationship to one's own.

Dissatisfied with the imposition of European and biblical classifications onto the interpretation of non-Western religious cultures, and eschewing grand, evolutionary hypotheses that simply reflected Western values, modern anthropology understandably abandoned attempts to find overarching patterns in religion and instead devoted itself to in-depth studies of individual cultures. Comparative typologies and concepts are still perceived by many scholars as a dangerously antihistorical endeavor that overlooks the important contexts and particularity of religious symbols and behavior. Certainly comparison has served as a vehicle for all kinds of distortions and apologetics.

Comparison has also been used as a polemical weapon by religions themselves to show the inferiority of other traditions and the superiority of one's own. It has been used to show that all religions are really the same. It has been used to show that all religions are false. Many people sense that the absoluteness of their own beliefs is threatened by the existence of parallels elsewhere. So there is a kind of politics of comparison.

In some ways comparison is simply unavoidable. We all employ comparison every day, and thinking itself is in large measure based on it. It is built into language and perception. What a thing "is" is determined by its similarity and difference with other things like or unlike it. Science would be impossible without it, and without it the realm of metaphor would vanish. The analogical process is part of the way every cultural system classifies its world.

Comparison can create error and distortion as well as insight and knowledge, and this is noticeably so in the area of religion. Religious phenomena have been compared for centuries, but not necessarily in the pursuit of fair description or accurate understanding. Comparison is most often a function of self-interest. It gets

used to illustrate one's own ideology. It easily becomes an instrument of judgment, a device for approval or condemnation.

We all tend naturally to reduce areas of life to certain themes that fit our own worldview. As we thematize our world so we thematize religion. Everyone has summarizing ideas, usually positive or negative in connotation, about religion, and religious phenomena become occasions for all manner of precritical impressionistic generalizations. Thus, all religion is "about" love, money, God, social repression, escapism. All sects become "systems of brainwashing," oriental religions are "navel gazing." These approaches reduce religious phenomena to imagined stereotypes and ignore all evidence inconsistent with the type. It is as if the mind innately needs to reduce and typify experience in order to avoid the confusion and contradiction that might come with confronting religious diversity. The issue, then, is not *whether* to generalize and thematize about religion, but *how* to do so in appropriate and accurate ways.

In spite of the potential dangers of misuse, comparative perspective is a necessity for any field of study, and without it no real understanding of religion is possible. In this book I have tried to lay out a conceptual framework that avoids some of the past difficulties with comparative biases while still resolutely maintaining the importance and application of cross-cultural categories. Let us consider at the outset a summary of how the concept "comparative perspective" will be used.

1. First and most broadly, comparative perspective is not just a matter of juxtaposing one religion with another, but is the process of understanding any continuities and differences in the history of all types of religious phenomena. Comparative perspective is the knowledge of the whole in relation to the part, which are mutually informative. Every field of knowledge has its equivalent framework. Comparative literature, for example, studies not just writings other than English but themes, genres, and topics common to the whole history of literature as a human enterprise.

2. Comparative perspective is derived inductively from historical knowledge, not deductively from one's own philosophy. Comparative study presupposes history. It is not an alternative to historical perspective but an enrichment of it. Every religious expression has its own unique context of meaning, its own distinctive configuration that is different in some ways from others. Historical facts keep typologies honest, testing and challenging comparative generalizations at every point.

3. Comparative perspective involves different levels of specificity, different levels of part-to-whole relation-

ship. One can compare what a pilgrimage means to different people at one time and place, or one can compare that pilgrimage with all others within the same religion, or one can study pilgrimage as a theme that is manifest in all times and religions. Although this particular book makes a point of focusing on transcultural religious forms of the broadest generic scope, many "types" of religious expression—such as saviors, priests, or temples—are not found universally but within certain regions, periods, or types of religion. Much specific comparative work is best limited to studies of variations within a single religious culture or cluster of cultures. Each kind of phenomenon researched will have its own justifiable scope of comparative data and analysis.

4. Where comparative analysis deals with similarity, it deals with analogy rather than with identity, in which things, otherwise unlike, are similar in some respects. It is not just a matter of identifying what is "the same" everywhere. The *significance* of the analogies or parallels is a matter of judgment.

5. Comparative work is not only a process of establishing similarities or analogies. It is also the fundamental instrument for discerning differences. The point needs stressing because this double function has not been fully appreciated. Many people fear that comparative approaches lose sight of the richness of cultural diversity. But the study of continuity (or parallels) and the study of individuality cannot be separated. Only by seeing what is common between things can one see what is different or innovative about any one of them. A Christian or Jewish theology cannot fully understand its own uniqueness and its nuances, without knowing which of its features belong to religion in general and which are distinctively its own.

6. Finally, comparison is not an end in itself. It yields comparative *perspective*, the process by which overarching themes on the one hand and historical particulars on the other get enriched by the way they illumine each other. Because it is the central purpose of this book to illustrate this larger process, let us consider it a little further here.

There is a creative interplay between theme and example that enriches understanding of both. The variations develop, reveal, "work" the theme, as does a set of musical variations. Or, shifting the analogy, the species add to our understanding of the genus, just as the genus calls attention to common patterns present in a species. Many different creatures—such as fish, birds, mammals—amplify the theme "vertebrate." Dolphins, giraffes, armadillos, and humans are interestingly different versions of what a mammal can be. One could say the same

of any subject: bicycles and jets show what transportation can be, pianos and flutes demonstrate what musical instruments can be, Gandhi and Napoleon embody what leadership can be.

It is exactly the same with religious forms. Our understanding of what religious language and practice "can be" is diminished if we do not have the most complete awareness of its possible variations. By looking at all the gods in religious history, we see more fully what a god is. The variations make the theme stronger and more interesting. By seeing all the different things observed in various rites, we see more fully what ritual can be.

The Kaaba, the Muslim shrine at Mecca, the symbolic connecting point of heaven and earth for the Islamic world, is more fully comprehensible if we are familiar with the generic theme of "world centers." Without a sense of that theme and its prevalence, the Kaaba symbolism might be viewed merely as an odd or unintelligible belief. By the same token, the profound centering role of the Kaaba in the lives of Muslims provides an extraordinary living illustration and amplification of the world center motif.

The comparative process does not prejudge religious phenomena, as though they are there to be pinned and tagged like helpless specimens that must be made to conform by all means to our favorite taxonomies. Rather, religious expressions are facts—often living and articulate—that can continually instruct and illuminate our categories. In these ways, comparative perspective is a larger educational and interpretive process than any simple, straightforward act of describing or comparing different religions. . . .

3.2 EXPLAINING RELIGION

Wayne Proudfoot teaches religious studies at Columbia University. He is particularly interested in the psychology and philosophy of religion and has made important contributions to methodology. In the selection that follows, he considers the problems of **reductionism** and explanation, using some accounts of religious experiences as his primary examples. He argues that it is important to distinguish between descriptive and explanatory reduction. The first is inappropriate, but the second is both appropriate and essential for the student of religions. Note the ways in which the hermeneutical principle of context informs his readings of these accounts and the way he sees interaction between theory and explanation.

WAYNE PROUDFOOT

Explanation

READING QUESTIONS

1. As you read, make a list of all the words and ideas you do not understand or are uncertain about. Discuss them with a classmate, look them up in a dictionary, or bring them up in class for discussion and clarification.
2. According to Proudfoot's account of Mircea Eliade's views, what does Eliade think is wrong with reductionism?
3. What is **first-person privilege,** and how does it differ from the explanation offered by the analyst?
4. What is the difference between "descriptive reduction" and "explanatory reduction," and why is this distinction important?

Reductionism has become a derogatory epithet in the history and philosophy of religion. Scholars whose work is in other respects quite diverse have concurred in advocating approaches to the study of religion which are oriented around campaigns against reductionism. These campaigns are often linked to a defense of the autonomy of the study of religion. The distinctive subject matter of that study, it is argued, requires a distinctive method. In particular, religious experience cannot properly be studied by a method that reduces it to a cluster of phenomena that can be explained in historical, psychological, or sociological terms. Although it is difficult to establish exactly what is meant by the term, the label "reductionist" is deemed sufficient to warrant dismissal of any account of religious phenomena.

Questions have been raised about this wholesale rejection of reductive accounts and about the theological motivations that sometimes underlie it, but the issues in the discussion have not been sufficiently clarified. Penner and Yonan . . . , for example, take the problem to be crucial for the study of religion, survey the meaning of *reduction* in empiricist philosophy of science, and deplore the negative connotations that have been attached to the term. But they admit that they have found the issue difficult. They show no appreciation of why the at-

tack on reductionism has such an appeal, and thus they are unable to elucidate the discussion. The warnings against reductionism derive from a genuine insight, but that insight is often misconstrued to serve an apologetic purpose. I shall try to clarify the confusion surrounding the term *reduction* as it is applied to accounts of religious experience and to distinguish between the insight and misapplications that result in protective strategies. A recent essay in the philosophy of religion devoted to the exposure and critique of reductionism will serve to illustrate those misapplications and strategies.

THE PROBLEM

One of the most influential critics of reductionism in the study of religion has been Mircea Eliade. He has argued that the task of the historian of religion is a distinctive one and has contrasted it with what he takes to be the reductionist methods of the social sciences. . . . According to Eliade, a historical or sociological approach fails to grasp the meaning of religious phenomena. Like the literary critic interpreting a text, the historian of religion must attempt to understand religious data "on their own plane of reference." He or she should adopt a hermeneutic method. Just as literary works cannot be reduced to their origins, religious phenomena ought not to be reduced to their social, psychological, or historical origins or functions. Eliade . . . contends that "a religious datum reveals its deeper meaning when it is considered on its plane of reference, and not when it is reduced to one of its secondary aspects or its contexts." He cites Durkheim and Freud as examples of those who have adopted reductionist methods for the study of religion.

Two points are worthy of note: (1) Eliade thinks that what is lost by reductive approaches is the *meaning* of religious phenomena. He praises van der Leeuw for respecting the peculiar intentionality of religious data and thus the irreducibility of religious representations . . .; (2) his examples of reductionist approaches are drawn almost exclusively from history and the social sciences. Theories that purport to account for religious phenomena in terms of their origins or the functions they serve in a particular social context are *ipso facto* reductionist.

Eliade holds further that religious data represent the expression of religious experiences. Religion is "first of all, an experience *sui generis*, incited by man's encounter with the sacred . . . ." In order to understand religious data on their own plane of reference, the scholar must "'relive' a multitude of existential situations. . . ." Only through such a procedure can the meaning of the data be grasped. To reduce those data to their origins or social functions is to fail to understand them as expressions of

From Wayne Proudfoot, *Religious Experience* (Berkeley: University of California Press, 1985). Excerpts from chapter 5. Copyright © 1985 by The Regents of the University of California. Used by permission. References deleted.

religious experience. That understanding can come only from acquaintance. Since Eliade regards religious experience as experience of the sacred, he can summarize his antireductionist position by reference to "the irreducibility of the sacred."

Religious experience is the experience of something. It is intentional in that it cannot be described without reference to a grammatical object. Just as fear is always fear of something, and a perceptual act can only be described by reference to its object, a religious experience must be identified under a certain description, and that description must include a reference to the object of the experience. Eliade employs the term *sacred* to characterize the object of all religious experience. The notorious obscurity of that term need not concern us here, nor need we accept the suggestion that all religious experiences have the same object. The point is that when Eliade refers to the irreducibility of the sacred, he is claiming that it is the intentional object of the religious experience which must not be reduced. To do so is to lose the experience, or to attend to something else altogether.

This point is well taken. If someone is afraid of a bear, his fear cannot be accurately described without mentioning the bear. This remains true regardless of whether or not the bear actually exists outside his mind. He may mistakenly perceive a fallen tree trunk on the trail ahead of him as a bear, but his fear is properly described as fear of a bear. To describe it as fear of a log would be to misidentify his emotion and reduce it to something other than it is. In identifying the experience, emotion, or practice of another, I must restrict myself to concepts and beliefs that have informed his experience. I cannot ascribe to him concepts he would not recognize or beliefs he would not acknowledge. Though historical evidence might turn up to show that Socrates was dying of cancer, no evidence could show that he was afraid of dying of cancer. No such fear could be ascribed to him because he didn't possess the concept of cancer which is presupposed by that emotion.

Consider two examples cited by William James. The first is an experience reported by Stephen Bradley. . . .

I thought I saw the Saviour, by faith, in human shape, for about one second in the room, with arms extended, appearing to say to me, Come. The next day I rejoiced with trembling; soon after my happiness was so great that I said that I wanted to die; this world had no place in my affections, as I knew of, and every day appeared to me as the Sabbath. I had an ardent desire that all mankind might feel as I did; I wanted to have them all love God supremely. . . .

The second is from Mrs. Jonathan Edwards.

Part of the night I lay awake, sometimes asleep, and sometimes between sleeping and waking. But all night I continued in a constant, clear, and lively sense of the heavenly sweetness of Christ's excellent love, of his nearness to me, and of my dearness to him. I seemed to myself to perceive a glow of divine love come down from the heart of Christ in heaven into my heart in a constant stream, like a stream or pencil of sweet light. At the same time my heart and soul all flowed out in love to Christ, so that there seemed to be a constant flowing and reflowing of heavenly love, and I appeared to myself to float or swim, in these bright, sweet beams, like the motes swimming in the beams of the sun, or the streams of his light which come in at the window. . . .

Bradley tells of a vision in human shape, and Edwards reports a lively sense of Christ's love, which seemed to glow like a stream or pencil of light. Each of these experiences can only be properly described by reference to Christ and to Christian beliefs. One might try to separate the description of the core experience from its interpretation and to argue that only the interpretation is specifically Christian. But if the references to the Savior, the Sabbath, and God are eliminated from Bradley's report, we are left with something other than his experience. After deleting references to Christian concepts, we have a vision of a human shape with arms extended saying, "Come." Is this any less informed by Christian beliefs and doctrines than was the original experience? Surely the vision of a person with outstretched arms is not some universal archetype onto which Bradley has added an interpretation in Christian terms. Nor can his experience of comfort and salvation be abstracted from his Christian beliefs. Sarah Edwards's experience is not a vision, but it would be inaccurate to describe it exclusively in general terms and to characterize it only as a lively sense of sweetness, accompanied by the sensation of floating in streams of bright light. Her report cannot be purged of references to Christ and Christian beliefs and still remain an accurate description of the experience.

An emotion, practice, or experience must be described in terms that can plausibly be attributed to the subject on the basis of the available evidence. The subject's self-ascription is normative for describing the experience. This is a kind of first-person privilege that has nothing at all to do with immediate intuitive access to mental states versus mediated inferential reasoning. It is strictly a matter of intentionality. It is like the distinction between the words of a speaker and those of one who reports what he says. The speaker's meaning, and his choice of words to express that meaning, are normative for the reporter. The latter may choose to paraphrase or elaborate, but the words uttered by the speaker are authoritative for determining the message. Where it is the subject's experience which is the object of study, that experience must be identified under a description that can plausibly be attributed to him. In the cases cited above, the subject's own words constitute the description. If, however, an observer or analyst describes the experience of another, he must formulate it in terms that would be familiar to, incorporating beliefs that would be acknowledged by, the subject. If challenged, he must offer reasons in support of his ascription of those concepts and beliefs to the subject. He is not responsible for reasons offered in support of those beliefs.

The explanation the analyst offers of that same experience is another matter altogether. It need not be couched in terms familiar or acceptable to the subject. It must be an explanation of the experience as identified under the subject's description, but the subject's approval of the explanation is not required. Bradley's experience might be explained in terms of the conflicts of early adolescence and that of Sarah Edwards as a consequence of her life with Mr. Edwards. No reference need be made to God or Christ in the construction of these explanations. If the explanation is challenged, the one who proposed it is responsible for providing reasons to support it and for showing how it accounts for the evidence better than any of its rivals does. . . .

In the study of religion, considerable confusion has resulted from the failure to distinguish the requisite conditions for the identification of an experience under a certain description from those for explaining the experience. The analyst must cite, but need not endorse, the concepts, beliefs, and judgments that enter into the subject's identification of his experience. He must be prepared to give reasons for his ascription of those beliefs and judgments to the subject, but he need not defend the beliefs and judgments themselves. If he proposes an explanatory hypothesis to account for the experience, he need not restrict himself to the subject's concepts and beliefs, but he must be prepared to give reasons in support of his explanation.

DESCRIPTIVE AND
EXPLANATORY REDUCTION

We are now in a position to distinguish two different kinds of reduction. *Descriptive reduction* is the failure to identify an emotion, practice, or experience under the description by which the subject identifies it. This is indeed unacceptable. To describe an experience in non-

religious terms when the subject himself describes it in religious terms is to misidentify the experience, or to attend to another experience altogether. To describe Bradley's experience as simply a vision of a human shape, and that of Mrs. Edwards as a lively warm sense that seemed to glow like a pencil of light, is to lose the identifying characteristics of those experiences. To describe the experience of a mystic by reference only to alpha waves, altered heart rate, and changes in bodily temperature is to misdescribe it. To characterize the experience of a Hindu mystic in terms drawn from the Christian tradition is to misidentify it. In each of these instances, the subject's identifying experience has been reduced to something other than that experienced by the subject. This might properly be called reductionism. In any case, it precludes an accurate identification of the subject's experience.

Explanatory reduction consists in offering an explanation of an experience in terms that are not those of the subject and that might not meet with his approval. This is perfectly justifiable and is, in fact, normal procedure. The explanandum is set in a new context, whether that be one of covering laws and initial conditions, narrative structure, or some other explanatory model. The terms of the explanation need not be familiar or acceptable to the subject. Historians offer explanations of past events by employing such concepts as socialization, ideology, means of production, and feudal economy. Seldom can these concepts properly be ascribed to the people whose behavior is the object of the historian's study. But that poses no problem. The explanation stands or falls according to how well it can account for all the available evidence.

Failure to distinguish between these two kinds of reduction leads to the claim that any account of religious emotions, practices, or experience must be restricted to the perspective of the subject and must employ only terms, beliefs, and judgments that would meet with his approval. This claim derives its plausibility from examples of descriptive reduction but is then extended to preclude explanatory reduction. When so extended, it becomes a protective strategy. The subject's identifying description becomes normative for purposes of explanation, and inquiry is blocked to insure that the subject's own explanation of his experience is not contested. On this view, to entertain naturalistic explanations of the experiences of Bradley and Edwards is reductionist because these explanations conflict with the convictions of the subjects that their experiences were the result of divine activity in their lives.

Many of the warnings against reductionism in the study of religion conflate descriptive and explanatory reduction. Eliade exhorts the historian of religion to understand religious data on their own plane of reference and contrasts this understanding with the reductive accounts offered by social scientists. Wilfred Cantwell Smith . . . contends that a necessary requirement of the validity of any statement about a religion is that it be acknowledged and accepted by adherents of that religious tradition. This is appropriate if addressed to the problem of providing identifying descriptions of experiences in different traditions, but it is inappropriate if extended to include all statements about religion.

For some years Smith has waged a campaign against the use of the term *religion* in the study of what he calls faith and the historical traditions . . .. In criticizing this use of the term, he brings forth abundant evidence to show that it is of rather recent and parochial origin. According to his research, there is no concept in most of the world's cultures and traditions which can accurately be translated by our term *religion*. In other words, there is no evidence to support the ascription of that concept to people outside the modern West. From this evidence Smith concludes that the term ought to be avoided by scholars of the faiths of mankind. Even if the results of his philological researches were granted, however, there would be no more reason to reject *religion* than to reject *culture* and *economy*. The fact that it cannot accurately be ascribed to people in many societies does not require that it be excluded from the accounts we give of those societies. Smith's conclusion follows from his evidence only with the addition of the premise that any account of the religious life, including explanatory accounts, must be couched in terms that are familiar and acceptable to participants in that life. Smith accepts this premise and regards it as a requirement of the comparative study of religion, but we have seen that explanatory accounts are not subject to this restriction. . . .

first-person privilege The notion that the explanation offered by the subject is normative for anyone who wishes to accurately describe the phenomenon.

hermeneutics A method for interpreting data, particularly textual data, that pays close attention to the context and structure of the data or text.

interpretation A statement of what the data mean.

phenomenology of religion Sometimes used as equivalent to history of religions, but better thought of as a particular theory and comparative method that assumes religion and its history as the manifestations of the sacred and opposes all "reductionism" or causal explanations by social scientists on the grounds that religion is *sui generis* (literally, "of its own kind").

reductionism Often used by phenomenologists in a pejorative sense to refer to what they see as inappropriate explanations of religious phenomena. According to Proudfoot, there are two kinds: descriptive reduction, which results in a failure to accurately describe a situation by using ideas unacceptable to the subject; and explanatory reduction, which consists in offering a causal account of some phenomenon that is accurately described from the subject's viewpoint in terms that may not be acceptable to the subject but are acceptable to the analyst and are supported by good evidence and argument.

Sitz im Leben German, meaning "situation or place in life." Technically it refers to the establishment of the context of a text (where, when, by whom, to whom it was written, and its purpose or function) for purposes of interpretation.

KEY TERMS AND CONCEPTS

comparison A balanced description of the similarities and differences among examples of phenomena.

description A statement of facts of a case as objectively as possible. These facts can then serve as data for interpretation.

evaluation A value judgment about the quality of some description, interpretation, or explanation. It can also refer to a value judgment about the interpretation of the religious subject.

explanation Either an interpretation that deepens our understanding or a statement of a cause(s) that makes sense given some theory.

SUGGESTIONS FOR FURTHER READING

Benson, Thomas L. "Religious Studies as an Academic Discipline." In *The Encyclopedia of Religion*, edited by Mircea Eliade, vol. 14, pp. 88–92. New York: Macmillan, 1987. A brief history of the development of religious studies in the academy.

Capps, Walter H. *Ways of Understanding Religion*. New York: Macmillan, 1972. A somewhat dated but still useful collection of essays from a variety of disciplines (anthropology, history, psychology, philosophy, and others) on theories and methods.

Connolly, Peter, ed. *Approaches to the Study of Religion*. London: Cassell, 1999. A collection of essays discussing different ways of studying religions ranging from anthropological to theological approaches.

Penner, Hans H. "The Study of Religion." In *The HarperCollins Dictionary of Religion*, edited by Jonathan Z. Smith and William Scott Green, pp. 909–917. New York: HarperCollins, 1995. A clear and concise account of the nature of theory and basic approaches (sociological, phenomenological, psychological, historical, etc.) to the study of religion along with a critical discussion of functional theories and other types of theories.

Sharpe, Eric J. "Methodological Issues." In *The Encyclopedia of Religion*, edited by Mircea Eliade, vol. 14, pp. 83–88. New York: Macmillan, 1987. A discussion of different methodological issues such as value judgments, vocabulary translation, insider's and outsider's perspectives, and the like.

RESEARCH PROJECTS

1. Create a debate either in class between groups of students or in writing in which you present a position paper in favor of or against reductionism in the study of religions. If you write it, present a brief position paper on *both* sides of the issue.

2. Look at William James's *Varieties of Religious Experience: A Study in Human Nature* and select one of the first-person accounts of religious experience that James records. Describe the experience and then interpret it by applying the hermeneutical tools described in this chapter. (James's *Varieties* is available in many different editions but was first published in 1902 by Longmans, Green of New York.)

PART 2

WAYS OF BEING RELIGIOUS ORIGINATING IN AFRICA AND NORTH AMERICA

4

Ways of Being Religious in Africa

INTRODUCTION

The term *African religions* is ambiguous in a variety of ways. Does it refer to precolonial, colonial, or post-colonial religions? There are many different religions in Africa, which is the second largest continent and, given present evidence, the birthplace of the human race. The more than three thousand ethnic groups speak almost as many languages and have similar, but different, religious ways. They practice numerous varieties of Christianity, Judaism, Islam, Hinduism, and other religions. Sometimes the term *traditional religion* is used for the practices associated with pre-colonial times. If the term *traditional* has any validity, then somewhere between thirty and forty percent of the African population practices traditional religion. But many Muslims and Christians also incorporate some traditional practices and, if we include them, then perhaps as much as seventy percent of the population might be called "traditional" in some sense.

Is there one traditional African religion or many? Some scholars support the view that the similarities among the African religions are so great, we can legitimately speak of a pan-African traditional religion. Others focus on the differences and argue that we must speak of **traditional African religions** in the plural.

The word *traditional* is in itself problematic. Some scholars maintain that within the religious worlds of Africa, there is no such term. It is, they contend, an invention of Europeans who colonized Africa. At first Europeans used *heathen, savage,* and *primitive*—then, less perjoratively, *pre-literate, nonliterate,* or, more positively, *exclusively oral* to designate the fact that many religious traditions were passed on orally rather than in writing (although they were also passed on in art, crafts, and ritual practices). Today the word *tra-*

ditional is in widespread use, but none of these terms is satisfactory and all are misleading (although some more than others) because their meaning depends on a contrast between *us* and *them* that places emphasis on something *we* have (civilization, Christianity, writing, texts, scriptures, literature, modernism) that *they* lack. That they lack such things may be (and often is) viewed negatively since what we have is good, superior, or more advanced. Or this situation may be viewed positively and romantically as a more pristine, untainted, and innocent religious piety that our modern, secular world has lost.

Even the term *religion* is problematic. Some scholars debate whether there is an equivalent word in indigenous African languages. It is, they say, an imported word, a term Europeans and Arabs brought with them to Africa and used to talk about certain ideas and practices. The term brings with it, just like *Africa* and *traditional*, a host of associations and feelings that sometimes do more to cloud than clarify the problem of accurate terminology.

There are no easy solutions to the problems of terminology. In one way or another, all words constitute interpretations that reflect the point of view of the observer. Perhaps the best we can do is to be careful of the ways we speak and realize that words not only describe but also interpret and come with all kinds of ambiguities, vagueness, biases, and frequently unintended connotations. As I pointed out in the previous chapter, there is no such thing as a pure description totally devoid of all interpretation.

4.1 AN OVERVIEW

Given the diversity of African religion and the difficulties involved in the way the words we use distort what we wish to know about, it is not easy to

MAP OF MAJOR ETHNIC GROUPS OF AFRICA

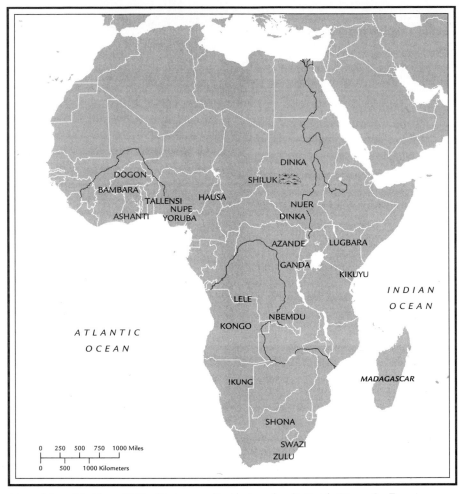

Adapted from *The HarperCollins Dictionary*, edited by Jonathan Z. Smith (HarperSanFrancisco, 1995), p. 15. Copyright © 1995 by the American Academy of Religion. Reprinted by permission of HarperCollins Publishers, Inc.

give a descriptive overview of the ways Africans are religious. In the following selection, Benjamin C. Ray tries, despite the difficulties, to do just that. In order to manage the material, he focuses on the similarities among traditional religions south of the Sahara.

Professor Ray studied the history of religions at the University of Chicago and is a specialist in African religions. He teaches at the University of Virginia. He has written widely on the topic of African religions, and in 1976 Prentice-Hall published his *African Religions: Symbol, Ritual, and Community*.

BENJAMIN C. RAY

African Religions: An Overview

READING QUESTIONS

1. As you read, make a list of all the words and ideas you do not understand or are uncertain about. Discuss them with a classmate, look them up in a dictionary, or bring them up in class for discussion and clarification.
2. Why does Ray think that cults of affliction and an emphasis on a supreme being developed in sub-Saharan Africa from the seventeenth to the early nineteenth centuries?
3. Of the general characteristics of African religions that the author describes, which ones strike you as most like and most different from other religions you know about?
4. What do you think is the social significance of those myths that attribute the origin of death to a woman?
5. Do you agree with Ray's claim that the "value of divination lies not in the precision of prediction but in the decision-making process that it offers to the client"? Why or why not?
6. Are there any similarities between the fivefold structure of sacrificial rites and the threefold pattern of rites of passage? If so, what are they? If none, why not?
7. Why is the term *ancestor worship* misleading when applied to African religion?
8. Why is witchcraft socially useful?
9. Why do you think "patience" is regarded as a "feminine" virtue and not a "masculine" virtue? What does this gender designation say about the relationship among art, religion, and society?

Prior to the coming of Christianity and Islam to Africa, the peoples south of the Sahara developed their own religious systems, and these formed the basis of much of their social and cultural life. Today, the indigenous religions, modified by colonial and postcolonial experience, continue to exist alongside Christianity and Islam and to play an important role in daily existence.

From Benjamin C. Ray, "African Religions: An Overview," in *The Encyclopedia of Religion*, editor in chief, Mircea Eliade, vol. 1 (New York: Macmillan Publishing Company), pp. 60–69. © 1987 by Macmillan Publishing Company. Reprinted by permission. Bibliography omitted.

African traditional religions are closely tied to ethnic groups. Hence it may be said that there are as many different "religions" as there are ethnic language groups, which number over seven hundred south of the Sahara. There are, however, many similarities among the religious ideas and practices of major cultural and linguistic areas (e.g., Guinea Coast, central Bantu, Nilotes), and certain fundamental features are common to almost all African religions. Although these features are not unique to Africa, taken together they constitute a distinctively African pattern of religious thought and action.

HISTORICAL BACKGROUND

Except for the most recent colonial and precolonial past, there is little evidence concerning the early history of African religions, especially from the remote Paleolithic period. Because of the conditions of climate and habitation, archaeological remains, such as pottery, stone implements, bronze and stone figures, earthworks, and rock paintings, have been discovered at only a few places in eastern, western, and southern Africa, and the cultural contexts of these finds are largely unknown. It was once supposed that the various contemporary hunting-gathering, agricultural, and pastoral societies in Africa developed from a few basic cultural systems, or civilizations, each with its own set of linguistic, racial, religious, economic, and material cultural characteristics. Thus the early cultural and religious history of African societies was seen in terms of the interaction and intermixture of these hypothetical cultural systems, producing the more complex cultural and religious patterns of today. But it is now recognized that elements of language, race, religion, economics, and material culture are not so closely related as was assumed and that the early cultural systems were too speculatively defined. Hence historical reconstruction on these grounds has been abandoned.

Nevertheless, recent research has been able to bring to light important evidence concerning the early phases of religion in certain areas. The rock paintings of southern Africa, which date mostly from the nineteenth century but also from 2000 and 6000 and 26,000 B.P., appear to represent a continuous tradition of shamanism practiced by the San hunters and their ancestors. Nineteenth-century and contemporary San ethnography suggest that shamanistic trance states, induced by dancing, are the subject matter of much southern African rock art. In trance states, San men experience the presence of a sacred power in their bodies, a power that also exists in certain animals, especially the eland, a large antelope. When this power enters the dancing men, they fall into a state of deep trance, or "half-death," as the !Kung San call it. Trance enables the men to perform three kinds of acts: the luring of large game animals to the hunters, the curing of illness, and the causing of rain by killing of special "rain animals." The rock art painted by the San and their ancestors shows men performing each of these tasks. The visual signs of trance that appear in the art are bleeding from the nose, perspiration, dancing, lines piercing (or extending from) the head, the wearing of caps with antelope ears, and the partial transformation of men into animals, especially antelopes. While manifesting these signs of trance, men are shown bending over people and drawing out illness, shooting rain animals, and luring game by ritual means. There is no indication that the art itself was regarded as magical; instead, the paintings depict the ritual acts and visionary experiences by which the shamans governed the relationships between human beings, animals, and the spirits of the dead. These relationships lay at the core of San society, and the rock paintings may well record practices that date from the earliest times in southern Africa. . . .

When agriculture began to spread south of the Sahara around 1500 B.C.E, an important religious development accompanied the gradual change from hunting-gathering to agricultural economies. This was the emergence of territorial cults, organized around local shrines and priests related to the land, crop production, and rain. These autochthonous [indigenous] cults provided political and religious leadership at the local level and also at the clan and tribal level. In central Africa the oral tradition and known history of some territorial cults date back five or six centuries and have been the key to historical reconstruction of religion in this area.

When ironworking penetrated sub-Saharan Africa in 400–500 C.E., it gave rise to a number of myths, rites, and symbolic forms. Ironworking was said to have been brought by a mythic culture hero, blacksmiths were regarded as a special caste subject to ritual prohibitions, and the blacksmith's forge was sometimes regarded as a sanctuary. Iron itself was thought to have sacred properties. Throughout West Africa ironmaking, hunting, and sometimes warfare formed a sacred complex of rites and symbols under the tutelage of a culture hero or deity.

In northern Nigeria over 150 terra-cotta figures have been found dating from at least 500 B.C.E. to 200 C.E., the earliest known terra-cotta sculpture in sub-Saharan Africa. This sculpture, known as Nok sculpture after the site at which it was first found, consists of both human and animal figures. Although it is likely that these pieces had religious significance, either as grave goods or as ritual objects (or both), their meaning at present is entirely unknown.

The famous bronze heads of Ife, Nigeria, date from the twelfth to fifteenth centuries and may be distantly related to Nok sculpture. The sixteen naturalistic Ife heads were found in the ground near the royal palace at Ife. The heads have holes to which beards and crowns were attached. Each head may have represented one of the founders of the sixteen city-states that owed allegiance to Ife, and each may have carried one of the sixteen crowns. Among the Yoruba, the "head" (*ori*) is the bearer of a person's destiny, and the "head" or destiny of a king was to wear the crown. The crown was the symbol of the sacred *aṣe*, or power, of the king that the crown or the head itself may have contained. Bronze heads were also made in the kingdom of Benin, an offshoot of Ife located to the southeast, where they served as shrines for deceased Bini kings.

In southern Africa the wall ruins of Great Zimbabwe in present-day Zimbabwe belong to a cultural complex that evolved in the early twelfth century. Great Zimbabwe was the political capital of the Shona kings for two hundred years, until 1450. The ancestors of the kingship seem to have been represented by large, eaglelike sculptures with human characteristics, and these are thought to have been the focus of the royal ancestor cult.

Wherever kingship arose in Africa during the thirteenth to fifteenth centuries, it became a dominant part of the religious system. The rulers, whether sacred or secular, generally attained total or partial control of the preexisting territorial cults above the local level. Oral tradition usually records the encounter between the conquering kings and the autochthonous cults, which sometimes put up resistance. This encounter was often memorialized in the form of annual rites that recalled the initial conquest and subsequent accommodation between the king and the autochthonous cults whose powers over the land were necessary for the welfare of the state. For example, at Ife there is an annual ceremonial enactment of the defeat and return of the indigenous creator god Ọbatala (also known as Orisa-nla), and the restoration of his cult in the city. In other cases, the local cults were taken over and grafted onto the royal cult. Thus the Lundu kings took over the preroyal cults of the supreme being in Malawi, Zimbabwe, and Mozambique and incorporated their priests and prophets into the royal sphere.

Most kings were regarded as gods or as the descendants of gods and were spiritually related to the fertility of the land and to the welfare of the people. Even in Buganda in central Uganda, where they did not have such mystical powers, the kings were regarded as sacred personages. It is now recognized that the institution of sacred kingship, which was once thought to be derived from ancient Egypt because of some general similarities with sub-Saharan kingships, was independently invented in various places in the African continent, not only in Egypt. . . .

From the seventeenth to early nineteenth centuries, there is evidence of two types of development: an increase in spirit possession and healing cults, generally known as cults of affliction, and an emphasis upon the concept of the supreme being. The emergence of popular healing cults seems to have been linked to a breakdown in local political institutions and to contact with outside forces and new diseases. The well-documented Lemba cult in western Zaire, which dates from the seventeenth century to the early twentieth century, was but one of many *ngoma* ("drum") therapies that were, and still are, characteristic of the religions of the Bantu-speaking peoples of central and southern Africa. During the same period, the growing importance of the concept of supreme being appears to have been linked to the enlargement of political scale and to the need to explain widespread social and political changes at the most universal level.

GENERAL CHARACTERISTICS

Common to most African religions is the notion of the imperfect nature of the human condition. Almost every society has a creation myth that tells about the origins of human life and death. According to this myth, the first human beings were immortal; there was no suffering, sickness, or death. This situation came to an end because of an accident or act of disobedience. Whatever the cause, the myth explains why sickness, toil, suffering, and death are fundamental to human existence.

The counterpart to this idea is the notion that the problems of human life may be alleviated through ritual action. African religions are systems of explanation and control of immediate experience. They do not promise personal salvation in the afterlife or the salvation of the world at some future time. The promise of African religions is the renewal of human affairs here and now, a this-worldly form of salvation. Through ritual action misfortunes may be overcome, sicknesses removed, and death put off. In general, bad situations may be changed into good ones, at least temporarily. The assumption is that human beings are largely responsible for their own misfortunes and that they also possess the ritual means to overcome them. The sources of suffering lie in people's misdeeds, or sins, which offend the gods and ancestors,

and in the social tensions and conflicts that can cause illness. The remedy involves the consultation of a priest or priestess who discovers the sin or the social problem and prescribes the solution, for example, an offering to appease an offended deity or a ritual to settle social tensions. Belief in the perfectibility of human beings is not a part of African traditional religions. Instead, such religions provide the means for correcting certain social and spiritual relationships that are understood to be the causes of misfortune and suffering, even death. They assume that the traditional moral and social values, which the gods and ancestors uphold, are the guidelines for the good life and emphasize these rules and values in ritual performances in order to renew people's commitment to them.

At the theological level, African religions contain both monotheistic and polytheistic principles. The concept of a supreme god is widely known in tropical Africa and existed before the coming of Christianity and Islam. The idea of a supreme god expresses the element of ultimacy, fate, and destiny, which is part of most African religions. As the ultimate principle behind things, the supreme god usually has no cult, images, temples, or priesthood. These are unnecessary because he stands above reciprocal relationships with human beings, on which the lesser gods depend.

In contrast to the invisibility and remoteness of the supreme god, the lesser gods and the ancestor spirits, which often serve as the supreme being's intermediaries, are constantly involved in daily affairs. Their many shrines, images, and priesthoods make them highly visible and important features of traditional life. They are sources of both protection and harm, depending upon how faithfully they are served. People regularly attend their shrines to pray, receive advice, and make offerings, usually in the form of animal sacrifice. Thus African religions are both polytheistic and monotheistic, depending upon the context. In matters concerning the ultimate destiny and fate of individuals and groups, the supreme god may be directly involved. In matters concerning everyday affairs, the lesser gods and ancestors are more immediately involved.

From the point of view of African religions, a human being consists of social, moral, spiritual, and physical components united together; the individual is viewed as a composite totality. That is why social conflicts can make people physically ill and why moral misdeeds can cause spiritual misfortunes. Rituals that are aimed at restoring social and spiritual relationships are therefore deemed to affect people's physical health and well-being. A person's life is also seen to pass through several stages. One of the important tasks of traditional religion is to move people successfully through the major stages of life: birth, puberty, marriage, elderhood, death, ancestorhood. Each phase has its duties, and rites of passage make sure that people know their responsibilities. In this way people's lives are given shape and pattern. Important traditional offices, such as kingship, chieftaincy, and priesthood, are also maintained by rites of passage. Other rituals divide the year into seasons and give the annual cycle its form and rhythm.

Ritual authorities, such as diviners, prophets, priests, and sacred kings, serve a common religious purpose: the communication between the human world and the sacred world. Shrines and temples facilitate this process by linking together the two worlds around an altar. The priest's job is to perform prayers and sacrifices that carry people's desires to the spiritual world; the priest, in turn, communicates the will of the spiritual beings to the people.

MYTHOLOGY: CREATION, HEROES, AND TRICKSTERS

African myths deal primarily with the origin of mankind and with the origin of social and ritual institutions. They explain both the structure of the world and the social and moral conditions of human life. Most creation myths posit an original state of cosmic order and unity, and they tell of a separation or division that arose between divinity and humanity, sky and earth, order and disorder, which resulted in human mortality. These myths explain why human beings are mortal by telling how they became mortal. Thus they presuppose that humanity was originally immortal and passed into a state of mortality. The myths usually say that mortality was the result of a deliberate or accidental misdeed committed by a human being, often a woman, or an animal. Although questions of human responsibility are sometimes involved, the underlying meaning is generally that death was a necessary, indeed, a natural, outcome; otherwise, human beings would not be truly human and humanity and divinity would not be properly separated.

Some myths explain the origins and significance of death by showing that it is essentially linked to the agents of human fertility and reproduction: women, food, sexuality, and marriage. The Dinka of the southern Sudan say that the first woman disobeyed the creator god who told her to plant or pound only one grain of millet a day, lest she strike the low-hanging sky with her hoe or tall pestle. When she lifted her pole to cultivate (or pound) more millet, she struck the sky, causing the sky and God to withdraw. Thenceforth, human beings suffered sick-

ness and death and had to toil for their food. In this myth it is a woman's desire for plenty (life), which the Dinka view indulgently, that overcame the original restrictive proximity between humanity and God. The Nuer, who live near the Dinka, say that in the beginning a young girl descended from the sky with her companions to get food and that she fell in love with a young man whom she met on earth. When she told her companions that she wished to stay on earth, they ascended to the sky and spitefully cut the rope leading to the ground, thus severing the means for immortality. The myth reflects the choice that every Nuer woman must make in marriage when she leaves her childhood home and friends and goes to live with her husband. According to the Ganda of central Uganda, the first woman disobeyed her father, the sky god, which caused her brother, Death, to come into the world and kill some of her children. In Buganda a girl's brother is the traditional agent of marriage and has a temporary claim to one of his sister's children. The myth implies that death is viewed as a necessary counterpart to life, as the mother's brother is a necessary counterpart to marriage and a claimant to one of his sister's children. . . .

Another widely known myth among Bantu-speaking peoples explains the origin of death in terms of a message that failed. In the beginning the creator god gave the message of life to a slow-moving animal (e.g., chameleon, sheep). Later, he grew impatient and gave the message of death to a faster animal (e.g., lizard, goat). The faster animal arrived first and delivered his message, and death became the lot of mankind. In this myth the natural slowness and quickness of the two animals determine the outcome, making death a natural and inevitable result. Other myths emphasize the similarity between death and sleep and the inability of human beings to avoid either. According to this myth, the creator god told the people to stay awake until he returned. When he came back they had fallen asleep and failed to hear his message of immortality. When they woke up he gave them the message of death.

Hero myths tell how important cultural discoveries, such as agriculture and ironmaking, originated and how major social and ritual institutions, such as marriage, village organization, kingship, priesthood, and cult groups, came into existence. Often the founding deeds of the hero are reenacted in ritual with creative and transforming effect. The hero may continue to live among the people in spiritual form through a priest or prophet and become manifest on important ritual occasions. Many African deities are said to have been heroes who died and returned in spiritual form to serve as guardians and protectors of the people. In Africa myth and history often overlap, and together they form a unified explanation of the world since the time of the beginning.

Another type of myth is the trickster story. **Trickster** stories range from fablelike satirical tales to accounts of world creation. The trickster may exist only as a character in stories or as an active deity. Whatever his particular form, the trickster image expresses the fundamental ambiguities of human life. He is both fooler and fooled, wily and stupid, maker and unmade. A seemingly misguided culture hero, the trickster introduces both order and disorder, confusion and wisdom into the world. His comic adventures convey a widely recognized African principle: life achieves its wholeness through the balance of opposites. The trickster's acts of disorder prepare the way for new order; death gives way to birth. According to the Dogon of central Mali, the trickster god Ogo destroyed the original perfection of the creator god's plan and could only partly restore it. Yet the trickster also helps human beings to discover the hidden dangers of life through divination. Among the Yoruba of western Nigeria, the god Eṣu is both the agent of social conflict and the peacekeeper of the marketplace, as well as the confuser of humans and the messenger of the gods. His two-sided nature brings together the gods and human beings in a cooperative manner through divination and sacrifice, which he supervises. The Akan-Ashanti tales about Ananse the Spider in southern Ghana and the tales about the Hare in eastern and southern Africa express profound and ironic insights into the foibles and possibilities of human nature. In general, African trickster mythology expresses optimism about the paradoxes and anomalies of life, showing that cleverness and humor may prevail in a fundamentally imperfect world. . . .

MONOTHEISM AND POLYTHEISM

African religions combine principles of unity and multiplicity, transcendence and immanence, into a single system; thus they generally contain both monotheistic and polytheistic aspects. Often there is also the concept of an impersonal power, such as the Yoruba concept of *aṣẹ*, by which all things have their being. In different contexts each of these principles may come to the fore as the primary focus of religious thought and action, although each is part of the larger whole.

As ultimate principles, many supreme gods are like African sacred kings: they reign but do not rule. They occupy the structural center of the system but are rarely seen or heard, and when they are it is only indirectly. For this reason the supreme gods belong more to the dimension of myth than to that of ritual. However, the world would cease to exist without them, as would a kingdom without the king. Thus, in many instances the supreme god is the one, omniscient, omnipotent, transcendent, creator, father, and judge. From the time of the first contact with Muslims and Christians, Africans recognized their supreme gods to be the same as the God of Christianity and Islam. It is not known whether African religions were more or less monotheistic than they are today, although it is certain that African concepts of God have changed over time.

DIVINITY AND EXPERIENCE

Unlike the supreme beings, which remain in the background of religious life, the lesser divinities and spirits are bound up with everyday experience. These powers are immanent, and their relation to human beings is reciprocal and interdependent. Hence they require many shrines, temples, priests, cult groups, images, rituals, and offerings to facilitate their constant interactions with people.

The gods and spirits are known through personal encounter as living agents who directly affect people's lives. Often associated with elements of nature, such as lightning, rain, rivers, wild animals, and forests, they may be understood as images or symbols of collective psychological and social realities that resemble these natural phenomena in their powerful, dangerous, and beneficial aspects. The most common form of encounter between the human and the divine is spirit possession, the temporary presence of a deity or spirit in the consciousness of a person. Spirit possession may occur in a formal ritual context or in the normal course of everyday life. In Africa, as elsewhere, possession behavior is culturally stylized and highly symbolic. It is neither extremely pathological nor physiologically uncontrollable. It is an integral part of religion and has a well-defined role within it. In some societies possession is regarded as an affliction, and the aim is to expel the intruding god or spirit so that the suffering person may resume a normal life. Once the god or spirit has made the reasons for its appearance known through the voice of the afflicted person or through divination, offerings are made and the spirit departs. Usually the cause is some misdeed or sin that must be redressed through ritual action. In other societies possession is a more desirable phenomenon. People may regularly seek to come closer to their gods, even to identify personally with them, through possession-inducing dances that have beneficial psychological and social effects.

MEDIUMS, DIVINERS, AND PROPHETS

Sometimes a divinity may wish to form a special relationship with an individual. The god usually makes his desire known through an illness. Indeed, sickness is sometimes seen as a sacred calling that is manifested in the form of a possession. The cure will take the form of apprenticeship and initiation into the service of the deity, and it will place the person in lasting debt to society. Henceforth, the chosen man or woman becomes professionally established at a shrine and becomes the god's medium, devoted to the healing of afflicted people. He or she treats illnesses and social problems through mediumship séances. Treatment begins with a payment of money and with the questioning of the client by the spirit speaking through the medium. The interrogation is skillful and focuses upon the client's social situation. The remedy usually involves moral advice, herbal prescriptions, ritual actions, and sometimes membership in a special cult group, as among the central Bantu-speaking peoples. The client himself may already have thought of the diagnosis and of the remedies that the medium proposes, or the séance may reveal new insights and procedures. In either case, the client departs from the consultation knowing that his problem has been expertly investigated and that he has received authoritative advice. . . .

In Africa the distinction between mediums, diviners, priests, and prophets is a fluid one, and transition from one to the other is made easily. Generally, diviners and mediums are spiritual consultants, whereas prophets are leaders of men. Prophets may go directly to the people with programs for action and initiate religious and political movements. For this reason prophets are often sources of religious and political change. In circumstances of widespread political unrest, priestly mediums may develop prophetic powers and initiate socioreligious change. This occurred during colonial times in East Africa: traditional prophets became leaders of political resistance in parts of Sudan, Uganda, Tanzania, and Zimbabwe. In Kenya, the Mau Mau resistance movement was also significantly implemented and sustained by traditional ritual procedures.

A more indirect form of spiritual communication involves the use of **divination** equipment, such as cowrie shells, leather tablets, animal entrails, palm nuts, a winnowing basket, small animal bones, and animal tracks. After careful interrogation of the client, the diviner manipulates and interprets his material in order to reach a diagnosis. Such systems work according to a basic typology of human problems, aspirations, and causal factors. The diviner applies this framework to his client's case by manipulating his divination apparatus.

The most complex system of divination in Africa is Ifa. It is practiced by the Yoruba of southern Nigeria and in various forms by the Igbo, Igala, and Nupe of Nigeria, the Ewe of Togo, and the Fon of Benin. It consists of a large number of poems that are related to a set of 256 divination patterns. When one of the patterns is cast, the diviner recites the appropriate poems. The poems tell of real-life problems experienced by the gods and ancestors in the past. Without telling the diviner his problem, the client chooses the poem that best fits his situation. He then asks more questions of the diviner, who makes additional casts of his divination chain, until the client discovers all the potential dangers and benefits his destiny holds for him, together with the ritual means of ensuring the best possible outcome. Like all systems of divination, Ifa's predictions are general and open to interpretation. The value of divination lies not in the precision of prediction but in the decision-making processes that it offers to the client. Divination procedures require the client (and often his or her family) to examine problems fully, to consider alternative courses of action, and to obtain professional guidance. The result is a course of action that is objectively based, divinely sanctioned, and socially acceptable.

Diviners and mediums employ methods of treatment that usually involve a mixture of psychological, social, medical, and ritual means. Many illnesses are regarded as uniquely African in nature and hence as untreatable by Western methods. They include cases of infertility, stomach disorders, and a variety of ailments indicative of psychological stress and anxiety. The causes of such illnesses are generally attributed to social, spiritual, or physiological factors, either separately or in some combination. Typically, a person's problems will be attributed to his misdeeds or to the ill will of other people because of the belief in the social source of illness and misfortune. Equally fundamental is the notion that religion concerns the total person, his physical as well as his spiritual well-being.

To the extent that European Christianity relates only to spiritual matters, African societies have fashioned their own forms of Christianity whose rituals are aimed at both the physical and spiritual ills of society. These tend to be prophet-led, independent churches that utilize the power of Christian prayer and ritual to heal physiological and psychological maladies, much like the indigenous religions. Islam has been adapted along similar lines. Although Western medicine is recognized and sought after for the treatment of infectious diseases and physical injuries, ritual techniques continue to be used in both rural and urban areas because of African ideas about the social and spiritual foundation of personal health and well-being. Where the two systems are available, people often utilize both. Increased urbanization has tended to break down certain elements of traditional religions, for example, rites for ancestor spirits and nature gods, but urbanization has created its own social, psychological, and spiritual problems for which diviners and mediums have developed methods of treatment. . . .

RITUAL: SACRIFICE AND RITES OF PASSAGE

Ritual is the foundation of African religions. To become possessed by the gods, to speak ritual words, to perform offerings and sacrifices, or to make children into adults is to shape experience according to normative patterns of meaning and thereby to control and renew the world. The ritual sphere is the sphere in which the everyday world and the spiritual world communicate with each other and blend into one reality. Almost every African ritual is therefore an occasion in which human experience is morally and spiritually transformed. The two most important forms of African ritual are animal sacrifice and rites of passage. Both follow common patterns.

The sacrifice of animals and the offering of vegetable foods accomplish a two-way transaction between the realm of divinity and the realm of humanity. The vegetable offerings and animal victims are the mediating principles. They are given to the gods and spirits in return for their favors. Animal sacrifice is especially prominent because the life of the victim and its blood are potent spiritual forces. By killing the victim, its life is released and offered to the gods for their sustenance in exchange for their blessings, especially in the case of human life that is threatened. The act of sacrifice may also transfer the illness to the animal victim, which thus serves as a scapegoat. An animal may also be sacrificed so that its blood may act as a barrier against malevolent spiritual forces. Fowl, sheep, and goats are the most common sacrificial animals; cattle are frequently sacrificed among pastoralist peoples. Animal victims usually possess certain characteristics of color, size, shape, and behavior that make them symbolically appropriate for certain spiritual beings. Through invocations, prayers, and songs, human desires are made known, sins are confessed, and spiritual powers attracted to the sacrificial scene. Generally, the ritual word performs a dual function: it says what is desired and helps to bring about the desired through the power of ritual speech. . . .

Sacrifices are performed on a variety of occasions in seasonal, curative, life-crisis, divinatory, and other kinds of rituals, and always as isolable ritual sequences. Sacrifices that involve the sharing of the victim's flesh con-

firm the bond between the people and the spiritual power, to which a portion is given. Purifications may also be performed so that the participants may be cleansed of the potent sacred elements of the sacrifice. Major sacrificial rites usually have the following structure: consecration, invocation, immolation, communion, and purification. At the social level, sacrifices and offerings bring together individuals and groups and reinforce common moral bonds. Fundamentally, blood sacrifice is a reciprocal act, bringing gods and people together in a circuit of moral, spiritual, and social unity. In this way sacrifice restores moral and spiritual balance—the healthy equilibrium between person and person, group and group, human beings and spiritual powers—which permits the positive flow of life on earth. As a sacred gift of life to the gods, sacrifice atones for human misdeeds and overcomes the human impediments to the flow of life; thus it is one of the keystones of African religions.

Rites of passage possess a threefold pattern consisting of rites of separation, transition, and reincorporation. Their purpose is to create and maintain fixed and meaningful transformations in the life cycle (birth, naming, puberty, marriage, death, ancestorhood), in the ecological and temporal cycle (planting, harvest, seasonal change, lunar and solar cycles, new year), and in the accession of persons to high office. Without these rites there would be no significant pattern to traditional life and no enduring social institutions.

The important phase in these ceremonies is the middle, or liminal, period of transition. In this phase people are morally remade into "new" social beings. Newborn infants are made into human persons, children are made into adults, men and women are made into husbands and wives, adults are made into elders, princes are made into kings, deceased persons are made into ancestor spirits. Seasonal transitions are also marked and celebrated in this way. Thus the old year is made into the new and the season of drought is made into the season of rain.

This remaking of persons and time involves the symbolic destruction of the old and the creation of the new. It is a dual process of death and rebirth, involving symbols of reversal, bisexuality, disguise, nakedness, death, humility, dirt, intoxication, pain, and infantilism. These symbols of ritual liminality have both negative and positive connotations representing the paradoxical situation of the womb/tomb—the betwixt and between period when people are neither what they were nor what they will become. In the liminal stage, people are momentary anomalies, stripped of their former selves, ready to become something new. Similarly, the time between the seasons and the time between the years belongs neither to the old nor to the new but to both. The transition phase is a time out of time, when the usual order of things is reversed or suspended, ready to become reestablished and renewed. During the Apo New Year ceremony of the Ashanti, people openly express their resentments against their neighbors, chiefs, and king in order to "cool" themselves and rid society of its tensions, which may cause harm before order is restored and the new year begins.

The most fundamental rite of passage is that which initiates the young into adulthood. In this way a society not only moves its young into new social roles but also transforms them inwardly by molding their moral and mental disposition toward the world. A period of instruction may or may not be part of this process. A Nuer boy simply tells his father that he is ready to receive the marks of *gar*, six horizontal lines cut across the forehead. His socialization is already assumed. In many West African societies the rite is held in the confines of initiation groves where the initiates are given intensified moral and religious instruction. These rites may take place over a period of years and are organized into men's and women's initiation societies, such as the Poro society among the Senufo of the Ivory Coast, Mali, and Burkina Faso. By means of stories, proverbs, songs, dances, games, masks, and sacred objects, the children and youths are taught the mysteries of life and the values of the adult world. The rites define the position of the initiates in relation to God, to society, to themselves, and to the world. Some form of bodily marking is usually done, and circumcision and clitoridectomy are widely practiced. The significance of bodily marking varies. Among the Gbaya of Mali, the initiates are cut slightly on the stomach with a "mortal wound" to signify their "death" to childhood. Generally, the marks indicate that the transition to adulthood is permanent, personal, and often painful and that society has successfully imprinted itself upon the individual.

PERSONS, ANCESTORS, AND ETHICS

African concepts of the person, or self, share several characteristics. Generally, the self is regarded as composite and dynamic; it consists of several aspects, social, spiritual, and physical, and admits of degrees of vitality. The self is also open to possession by divinity, and its life history may be predestined before birth. After death, the self becomes a ghost, and in the course of several generations it becomes merged with the impersonal ancestors. Each of these aspects and potentialities of the person,

sometimes misleadingly described as multiple souls, is important in different contexts and receives special ritual attention.

In West African societies, the success or failure of a person's life is explained by reference to a personal destiny that is given to the individual by the creator god before birth. A person's destiny stems from a family ancestor (usually a grandparent) who is partly reborn in the person at birth and serves as a spiritual guardian throughout life. Although destinies are largely predetermined, they are also somewhat alterable for better or worse by the gods, witches, and guardian ancestors. To realize the full potential of one's destiny, frequent recourse to divination is required to discover what destiny has in store and to ensure the best outcome. Successes and failures in life are therefore attributed both to personal initiative and to inherited destiny. After death, this immortal aspect of the personality returns to the creator god, ready to be reborn in the same lineage group. In societies where the concept of destiny is absent, the most important life-determining principle is the person's inherited lineage component, and it is this that survives after death.

The human personality is also permeable by divinity. On ritual occasions the consciousness of an individual may become temporarily replaced by the presence of a spiritual being. Often the personality of the god resembles that of the individual, and professional mediums may have several gods or spirits at their command. These are said to mount "on the head" or "on the back" of the medium. Almost everyone is susceptible to spirit possession of some sort, and when controlled in a ritual manner it has therapeutic effect.

At death, new problems of social and spiritual identity arise. When a family loses one of its members, especially a senior male or female, a significant moral and social gap occurs. The family, together with other kinsmen, must close this gap through funerary procedures. At the same time the deceased must undergo spiritual adjustment if he or she is to find a secure place in the afterlife and remain in contact with the family left behind. This is accomplished by the construction of an ancestor shrine and sometimes also by the making of an ancestor mask and costume.

Almost every family and village has its ancestor shrines, and every town its heroes who founded and protected it. From the beginning, the ancestors helped to create the world; they gave birth to the people, led them to their present homeland, created agriculture, established social rules, founded kingdoms, and invented metalworking and the arts. Their deeds laid the foundations of African myth, history, and culture. Whether the ancestors lived in the remote past or in more recent times, they are regarded as immortal spirits who transcend historical time. Through spirit possession and mediumship rites, the ancestors continue to communicate with their living descendants, who seek their help in the affairs of everyday life.

The carved images of the ancestors are not intended to be representational or abstract but conceptual and evocative. By means of stylized form and symbolic details the image conveys the characteristics of the ancestor and also helps to make the spiritual reality of the ancestor present among the people. Thus the carved ancestral icon enables the world of the living and the world of the living dead to come together for the benefit of human life.

The relationship between the community of the living and the spirits of the dead, sometimes misleadingly called "ancestor worship," has powerful social and psychological dimensions and plays a vital role in almost every African society. This is especially true in small-scale stateless societies in which sociopolitical rules are almost entirely governed by a descent system. In such societies ancestors are the focus of ritual activity, not because of a special fear of the dead or because of a strong belief in the afterlife, but because of the importance of the descent system in defining social relationships. In larger polities the royal ancestors often become the gods of the state. Superior to living kings and elders, the ancestors define and regulate social and political relations. It is they who own the land and the livestock, and it is they who regulate the prosperity of the lineage groups, villages, and kingdoms. Typically, when misfortune strikes, the ancestors are consulted through divination to discover what misdeeds have aroused their anger. The ancestors are also regularly thanked at ceremonial feasts for their watchful care, upon which the welfare of the community depends.

Not everyone may become an ancestor. Only those who led families and communities in the past as founders, elders, chiefs, or kings may serve in the afterlife as the social and political guides of the future. By contrast, ordinary people become ghosts after death. Such spirits require ritual attention at their graves, but they are finally sent away to "rest in peace," while the more positive influence of the ancestors is invoked generation after generation. The more recent ancestors receive the most frequent attention, especially at family shrines. Such ancestors are not worshiped in either a devotional or idolatrous sense but are honored and prayed to as the senior leaders of the living community.

The sufferings and misfortunes brought by the gods and ancestors are punishments aimed at correcting human behavior. By contrast, the sufferings and misfortunes caused by witches and sorcerers are undeserved and socially destructive; they are unequivocally evil. The African concept of evil is that of perverse humanity: the human witch and sorcerer. The African image of the witch and sorcerer is of humanity turned against itself. Witches act only at night, they fly through the air, walk on their hands or heads, dance naked, feast on corpses, possess unsatiable and incestuous lusts (despite sexual impotence), murder their relatives, and live in the bush with wild animals. This symbolic imagery is consistent with the sociological characteristics of the witch: disagreeable, ambitious, lying, and envious.

Accusations of witchcraft and sorcery therefore function as a means of social control. In the past accused witches and sorcerers were forced to confess or were killed or expelled from society. Witchcraft accusations also enabled quarreling members of the same lineage to separate from each other and establish their own residences, thus restoring village order. For the most part witchcraft accusations in Africa flourished in contexts where social interaction was intense but loosely defined, as between members of the same extended family or lineage group. In such cases witchcraft was sometimes thought to be an inherited power of which the individual might be unaware until accused. In other instances it existed in the form of deliberately practiced sorcery procedures, so-called black magic, which was effective at long range and across lineage groups. Whether deliberate or not, the witch and the sorcerer were regarded as fundamentally antihuman and thus as principles of evil in a world governed by fundamentally moral and social forces. . . .

SHRINES, TEMPLES, AND RELIGIOUS ART

Shrines and temples serve as channels of communication with the spiritual world, and they may also serve as dwelling places of gods and spirits. Shrines may exist in purely natural forms, such as forest groves, large rocks, rivers, and trees, where gods and spirits dwell. Every African landscape has places of this kind that are the focus of ritual activity. Man-made shrines vary in form. A simple tree branch stuck into the ground is a shrine for a family ghost among the Nuer. A large rectangular building serves as the ancestor stool chapel among the Ashanti. Whatever its form, an African shrine acts as a symbolic crossroads, a place where paths of communication between the human and spiritual worlds intersect.

If the shrine serves as a temple, that is, as the dwelling place of a spiritual being, it is built in houselike fashion, like the "palaces" of the royal ancestors in Buganda. Such shrines usually have two parts: the front section, where the priest and the people gather, and the rear section, where the god or spirit dwells. An altar stands between the two and links them together.

Shrines and temples often contain carved images of gods, spirits, and ancestors; indeed, such images sometimes serve as shrines themselves. . . . Carved figures may function as altars for communication with spiritual beings and as physical embodiments of the spirits themselves. The Baule of the Ivory Coast carve figures to represent the spiritual spouse who everyone has in the otherworld before being born into this one. The human-shaped figure becomes a shrine through which the spirit may be propitiated. The Dan-speaking peoples of Liberia and the Ivory Coast carve wooden masks to represent and to embody forest spirits so that they may appear before the people of the villages.

More generally, African ritual art, including masks, headdresses, sacred staffs, and ceremonial implements, is fashioned according to definite stylistic forms in order to express religious ideas and major social values. The carved *chi wara* antelope headdress of the Bamana of Mali represents the mythic farming animal, called Chi Wara, that originally showed the people how to cultivate, and the antelope shape of the headdress expresses the qualities of the ideal farmer: strength, industriousness, and graceful form. Male and female headdresses are danced together, while women sing songs to encourage the young men's cultivation groups to compete with each other for high agricultural achievements. The Gẹlẹdẹ masks of the Yoruba honor the spiritual power of women, collectively known as "our mothers." This power is both creative (birth) and destructive (witchcraft). The Gẹlẹdẹ mask depicts the calm and serene face of a woman and expresses the feminine virtue of patience. The face is often surmounted by elaborately carved scenes of daily activity, for the spiritual power of "the mothers" is involved in every aspect of human life.

African traditional art is primarily concerned with the human figure because of the anthropocentric and anthropomorphic character of African religions. As we have seen, religion in Africa deals with the problems of human life, the causes of which are seen to be fundamentally human in nature. Thus social conflict produces illness, human misdeeds cause the gods and ancestors to bring misfortune, and the gods themselves are essentially human in character. African thought typically conceives of the unknown and invisible forces of life by analogy with human realities that are both knowable and controllable. Hence African sculpture represents the gods, spirits, and ancestors in a basically human form.

SOURCES

In the space available and given the diversity of African religions, I can provide you with only a sampling of the diverse ways of being religious that have developed among indigenous African peoples. We shall sample six themes: creation, god, first humans, death, sacrifice, and healing. There are a number of different variations on these themes, and most indigenous religions weave them into a complex tapestry.

4.2 CREATION

The African people have many different stories about how the world came to be. The following excerpt from a long and complex story was recorded in 1946 by Marcel Griaule (1898–1956), a French ethnologist. Griaule engaged in field studies in Africa for more than twenty-five years and came to be held in high regard by the Dogon, a West African people found today in the country of Mali. Ogotemmêli, an elder of the Dogon who lost his eyesight in a hunting accident, was authorized to tell Griaule secret teachings usually withheld from outsiders. Over time, Griaule was led through deeper and deeper layers of often conflicting stories about the origins of many things important to the Dogon people.

Stories regarded as sacred by some people about the origin of things are called **myths.** This is a technical term in religious studies, and it is not intended to connote that the stories are untrue (although other people who do not regard them as sacred might think them untrue). A sacred story or myth is considered authoritative by the people who accept it. Myths often explain how practices significant to a certain people originate and why they are of utmost importance to the continued life of the people.

RECORDED BY MARCEL GRIAULE

Conversations with Ogotemmêli

READING QUESTIONS

1. How does this creation story illustrate the claim that "myths deal with the origins of things"?
2. According to this version of the Dogon creation myth, what is the cause of disorder?
3. What is the significance of the **Nummo**?
4. What important function do circumcision and clitoridectomy (here referred to as an act of excision) play?

The God **Amma** took a lump of clay, squeezed it in his hand and flung it from him, as he had done with the stars. The clay spread and fell on the north, which is the top, and from there stretched out to the south, which is the bottom, of the world, although the whole movement was horizontal. The earth lies flat, but the north is at the top. It extends east and west with separate members like a foetus in the womb. It is a body, that is to say, a thing with members branching out from a central mass. This body, lying flat, face upwards, in a line from north to south, is feminine. Its sexual organ is an ant-hill, and its clitoris a termite hill. Amma, being lonely and desirous of intercourse with this creature, approached it. That was the occasion of the first breach of the order of the universe.

Ogotemmêli ceased speaking. His hands crossed above his head, he sought to distinguish the different sounds coming from the courtyards and roofs. He had reached the point of the origin of troubles and of the primordial blunder of God.

"If they overheard me, I should be fined an ox!"

At God's approach the termite hill rose up, barring the passage and displaying its masculinity. It was as strong as the organ of the stranger, and intercourse could not take place. But God is all-powerful. He cut down the termite hill, and had intercourse with the excised earth. But the original incident was destined to affect the course of things for ever; from this defective

union there was born, instead of the intended twins, a single being, the *Thos aureus* or jackal, symbol of the difficulties of God. Ogotemmêli's voice sank lower and lower. It was no longer a question of women's ears listening to what he was saying; other, non-material, eardrums might vibrate to his important discourse. The European and his African assistant, Sergeant Koguem, were leaning towards the old man as if hatching plots of the most alarming nature.

But, when he came to the beneficent acts of God, Ogotemmêli's voice again assumed its normal tone.

God had further intercourse with his earth-wife, and this time without mishaps of any kind, the excision of the offending member having removed the cause of the former disorder. Water, which is the divine seed, was thus able to enter the womb of the earth and the normal reproductive cycle resulted in the birth of twins. Two beings were thus formed. God created them like water. They were green in colour, half human beings and half serpents. From the head to the loins they were human: below that they were serpents. Their red eyes were wide open like human eyes, and their tongues were forked like the tongues of reptiles. Their arms were flexible and without joints. Their bodies were green and sleek all over, shining like the surface of water, and covered with short green hairs, a presage of vegetation and germination.

These spirits, called Nummo, were thus two homogeneous products of God, of divine essence like himself, conceived without untoward incidents and developed normally in the womb of the earth. Their destiny took them to Heaven, where they received the instructions of their father. Not that God had to teach them speech, that indispensable necessity of all beings, as it is of the world-system; the Pair were born perfect and complete; they had eight members, and their number was eight, which is the symbol of speech.

They were also of the essence of God, since they were made of his seed, which is at once the ground, the form, and the substance of the life-force of the world, from which derives the motion and the persistence of created being. This force is water, and the Pair are present in all water: they *are* water, the water of the seas, of coasts, of torrents, of storms, and of the spoonfuls we drink.

Ogotemmêli used the terms "Water" and "Nummo" indiscriminately. . . .

He returned to the subject of the Nummo spirits, or (as he more usually put it, in the singular) of Nummo, for this pair of twins, he explained, represented the perfect, the ideal unit.

The Nummo, looking down from Heaven, saw their mother, the earth, naked and speechless, as a conse-

From Marcel Griaule, *Conversations with Ogotemmêli: An Introduction to Dogon Religious Ideas*, pp. 17–23. Published for the International African Institute by Oxford University Press. © 1965 International African Institute. Reprinted by permission.

quence no doubt of the original incident in her relations with the God Amma. It was necessary to put an end to this state of disorder. The Nummo accordingly came down to earth, bringing with them fibres pulled from plants already created in the heavenly regions. They took ten bunches of these fibres, corresponding to the number of their ten fingers, and made two strands of them, one for the front and one for behind. To this day masked men still wear these appendages hanging down to their feet in thick tendrils.

But the purpose of this garment was not merely modesty. It manifested on earth the first act in the ordering of the universe and the revelation of the helicoid sign in the form of an undulating broken line.

For the fibres fell in coils, symbol of tornadoes, of the windings of torrents, of eddies and whirlwinds, of the undulating movement of reptiles. They recall also the eight-fold spirals of the sun, which sucks up moisture. They were themselves a channel of moisture, impregnated as they were with the freshness of the celestial plants. They were full of the essence of Nummo: they *were* Nummo in motion, as shown in the undulating line, which can be prolonged to infinity.

When Nummo speaks, what comes from his mouth is a warm vapour which conveys, and itself constitutes, speech. This vapour, like all water, has sound, dies away in a helicoid line. The coiled fringes of the skirt were therefore the chosen vehicle for the words which the Spirit desired to reveal to the earth. He endued his hands with magic power by raising them to his lips while he plaited the skirt, so that the moisture of his words was imparted to the damp plaits, and the spiritual revelation was embodied in the technical instruction.

In these fibres full of water and words, placed over his mother's genitalia, Nummo is thus always present.

Thus clothed, the earth had a language, the first language of this world and the most primitive of all time. Its syntax was elementary, its verbs few, and its vocabulary without elegance. The words were breathed sounds scarcely differentiated from one another, but nevertheless vehicles. Such as it was, this ill-defined speech sufficed for the great works of the beginning of all things. . . .

The conversation reverted to the subject of speech. Its function was organization, and therefore it was good; nevertheless from the start it let loose disorder.

This was because the jackal, the deluded and deceitful son of God, desired to possess speech, and laid hands on the fibres in which language was embodied, that is to say, on his mother's skirt. His mother, the earth, resisted this incestuous action. She buried herself in her own womb, that is to say, in the anthill, disguised as an ant. But the jackal followed her. There was, it should be ex-

plained, no other woman in the world whom he could desire. The hole which the earth made in the anthill was never deep enough, and in the end she had to admit defeat. This prefigured the even-handed struggles between men and women, which, however, always end in the victory of the male.

The incestuous act was of great consequence. In the first place it endowed the jackal with the gift of speech so that ever afterwards he was able to reveal to diviners the designs of God.

It was also the cause of the flow of menstrual blood which stained the fibres. The resulting defilement of the earth was incompatible with the reign of God. God rejected that spouse, and decided to create living beings directly. Modelling a womb in damp clay, he placed it on the earth and covered it with a pellet flung out into space from heaven. He made a male organ in the same way and having put it on the ground, he flung out a sphere which stuck to it.

The two lumps forthwith took organic shape; their life began to develop. Members separated from the central core, bodies appeared, and a human pair arose out of the lumps of earth.

At this point the Nummo Pair appeared on the scene for the purpose of further action. The Nummo foresaw that the original rule of twin births was bound to disappear, and that errors might result comparable to those of the jackal, whose birth was single. For it was because of his solitary state that the first son of God acted as he did.

"The jackal was alone from birth," said Ogotemmêli, "and because of this he did more things than can be told."

The Spirit drew two outlines on the ground, one on top of the other, one male and the other female. The man stretched himself out on these two shadows of himself, and took both of them for his own. The same thing was done for the woman. Thus it came about that each human being from the first was endowed with two souls of different sex, or rather with two principles corresponding to two distinct persons. In the man the female soul was located in the prepuce; in the woman the male soul was in the clitoris.

But the foreknowledge of the Nummo no doubt revealed to him the disadvantages of this makeshift. Man's life was not capable of supporting both beings: each person would have to merge himself in the sex for which he appeared to be best fitted.

The Nummo accordingly circumcised the man, thus removing from him all the femininity of his prepuce. The prepuce, however, changed itself into an animal which is "neither a serpent nor an insect, but is classed with serpents." This animal is called a *nay*. It is said to be a sort of lizard, black and white like the pall which covers the dead. Its name also means "four," the female number, and "Sun," which is a female being. The *nay* symbolized the pain of circumcision and the need for the man to suffer in his sex as the woman does.

The man then had intercourse with the woman, who later bore the first two children of a series of eight, who were to become the ancestors of the Dogon people. In the moment of birth the pain of parturition was concentrated in the woman's clitoris, which was excised by an invisible hand, detached itself and left her, and was changed into the form of a scorpion. The pouch and the sting symbolized the organ: the venom was the water and the blood of the pain. . . .

4.3 GOD THE ETERNAL

Christian missionaries faced with the task of selecting indigenous words for "God" paid particular attention to African notions of a **high god** who was often associated with the sky and sometimes with the creation of the world. They thought that African notions of this high god were vague and that the high god seemed remote from the day-to-day activities of life and ritual practice. For example, few sacrifices were offered directly to the high god. These "findings" suited the missionaries' purposes nicely since they could now proclaim the gospel as the good news that this vague and remote high god has been made known and present in Jesus the Christ.

Scholars of African religions built on this idea and thus proclaimed the primary god of the Africans to be a *deus incertus* and a *deus remotus* (an uncertain and remote deity). E. Bolaji Idowu, an African cultural nationalist, was eager to show that African religion was not as primitive as missionaries and others thought. He rejected the notion that the high god was uncertain and remote, contending that African conceptions of god were well developed and monotheistic. He introduced the term *diffused monotheism* to indicate the idea of a supreme being who was partially diffused through other gods.[1]

Kenyan scholar and theologian John S. Mbiti built on Idowu's ideas and, in an influential book (*African Religions and Philosophy*, 1970), tried to show that the indigenous African conception of the nature of the high god is very much like the Christian conception of god. In citing evidence for this claim, Mbiti quotes the following Pygmy hymn, which he found in T. C. Young's *African Ways and Wisdom* (London, 1937). Unfortunately, Young does not identify the precise Pygmy group from which he got this hymn. Mbiti believes this hymn clearly shows that indigenous African people believe the supreme god to be a spirit and eternal.

Pygmy Hymn on God

READING QUESTIONS

1. Do you think this hymn is intended to make theological claims about the nature of god (if so, what are they?), or is it intended to state how the Pygmies feel about god (if so, how do they feel?), or is it intended to do both?
2. What additional information would you need in order to properly interpret this hymn? How would this additional information help you understand the hymn better?

In the beginning was God,
  Today is God
  Tomorrow will be God.
Who can make an image of God?
He has no body.
He is as a word
  which comes out of your mouth.
That word! It is no more,
  It is past, and still it lives!
So is God.

4.4 THE FIRST MAN/KING AND DEATH

Uganda is an East African country with many different ethnic groups ranging in size from the Upale (several hundred) to the Rwanda (several million).

---

[1] For a brief discussion of this and other topics relating to the study of African religions along with references to Idowu's writings, see the important article by Rosalind Shaw, "The Invention of 'African Traditional Religion,'" *Religion* 20 (1990): 339–353.

Quoted on p. 44 of John S. Mbiti's *African Religions and Philosophy* (Garden City, N.Y.: Anchor Books, 1970).

Among the Ganda, stories are told about **Kintu** who, in some versions, appears to be the first human being and, in others, the first king of the Ganda. In some accounts he arrives from some other place on earth, and in others he comes from heaven.

The story of Kintu is often classified by mythologists as a hero tale. Like most heroes, Kintu must overcome tests and trials in order to gain a prize and must rely on strength, cunning, help from others, and even miraculous interventions. Some mythologists interpret the hero tale as the journey of "everyperson" through life since, for all of us, we must overcome obstacles to obtain our goals.

The story of Kintu also contains the story of the origin of death. There are various versions of how death came about, but its arrival marks the beginning of a sharper separation between the people of the earth and the beings of heaven. People die. The gods are immortal.

⧫⧫⧫

KINTU
A Story of the Ganda

READING QUESTIONS

1. Nambi is described as a "woman," that is, as a female, yet she comes from heaven and lives there with her father, the King of Heaven, and her brothers. Is she divine or human? Do you think that distinction would make much sense to the teller of this tale?
2. What are the tests Kintu must pass, and how does he pass them? What do you think is the significance of these specific tests? Would any kind of test suffice?
3. How do you interpret the story about how death came to be? Are there features of the story that strike you as odd in some way? If so, what are they? Why do they seem odd to you?

When Kintu first came to Uganda he found there was no food at all in the country; he brought with him one cow and had only the food which the animal supplied him with. In the course of time a woman named Nambi

From John Roscoe, *The Baganda: An Account of Their Native Customs and Beliefs* (London: Frank Cass and Co., 1911). Paragraph breaks added.

came with her brother to the earth and saw Kintu; the woman fell in love with him, and wishing to be married to him pointedly told him so. She, however, had to return with her brother to her people and father, Gulu, who was King of Heaven. Nambi's relations objected to the marriage because they said that the man did not know of any food except that which the cow yielded, and they despised him. Gulu, their father, however, said they had better test Kintu before he consented to the marriage, and he accordingly sent and robbed Kintu of his cow. For a time Kintu was at a loss what to eat, but managed to find different kinds of herbs and leaves which he cooked and ate. Nambi happened to see the cow and recognized it, and complaining that her brothers wished to kill the man she loved, she went to the earth and told Kintu where his cow was, and invited him to return with her to take it away. Kintu consented to go, and when he reached Heaven he was greatly surprised to see how many people there were with houses, [and] cows, goats, sheep and fowls running about.

When Nambi's brothers saw Kintu sitting with their sister at her house, they went and told their father, who ordered them to build a house for Kintu and said they were to give him a further testing to see whether he was worthy of their sister. An enormous meal was cooked, enough food for a hundred people, and brought to Kintu, who was told that unless he ate it all he would be killed as an impostor; failure to eat it, they said, would be proof that he was not the great Kintu. He was then shut up in a house and left. After he had eaten and drunk as much as he wished, he was at a loss to know what to do with the rest of the food; fortunately he discovered a deep hole in the floor of the house, so he turned all the food and beer into it and covered it over so that no one could detect the place. He then called the people outside to come and take away the baskets. The sons of Gulu came in, but would not believe he had eaten all the food; they therefore searched the house, but failed to find it. They went to their father and told him that Kintu had eaten all the food.

He was incredulous, and said Kintu must be further tested; a copper axe was sent by Gulu, who said: "Go and cut me firewood from the rock, because I do not use ordinary firewood." When Kintu went with the axe he said to himself: "What am I to do? If I strike the rock, the axe will only turn its edge or rebound." However, after he had examined the rock he found there were cracks in it, so he broke off pieces and returned with them to Gulu, who was surprised to get them; still he said Kintu must be further tried before they gave their consent to the marriage.

Kintu was next sent to fetch water and told he must bring dew only, because Gulu did not drink water from wells. Kintu took the waterpot and went off to a field where he put the pot down and began to ponder what he was to do to collect the dew. He was sorely puzzled, but upon returning to the pot he found it full of water, so he carried it back to Gulu. Gulu was most surprised and said, "This man is a wonderful being; he shall have his cow back and marry my daughter." Kintu was told he was to pick his cow from the herd and take it; this was a more difficult task than the others, because there were so many cows like his own he feared he would mistake it and take the wrong one. While he was thus perplexed a large bee came and said: "Take the one upon whose horns I shall alight; it is yours." The next morning he went to the appointed place and stood and watched the bee which was resting on a tree near him; a large herd of cows was brought before him, and he pretended to look for his cow, but in reality he watched the bee, which did not move. After a time Kintu said, "My cow is not there." A second herd was brought, and again he said, "My cow is not there." A third, much larger, herd was brought, and the bee flew at once and rested upon a cow which was a very large one, and Kintu said, "That is my cow." The bee then flew to another cow, and Kintu said, "That is one of the calves from my cow," and so on to a second and third which he claimed as the calves that had been born during the cow's stay with Gulu.

Gulu was delighted with Kintu and said: "You are truly Kintu, take your cows; no one can deceive or rob you, you are too clever for that." He called Nambi and said to Kintu, "Take my daughter who loves you, marry her and go back to your home." Gulu further said, "You must hurry away and go back before Death (Walumbe) comes, because he will want to go with you and you must not take him; he will only cause you trouble and unhappiness." Nambi agreed to what her father said and went to pack up her things. Kintu and Nambi then took leave of Gulu, who said, "Be sure if you have forgotten anything not to come back, because Death will want to go with you and you must go without him."

They started off home, taking with them, besides Nambi's things and the cows, a goat, a sheep, a fowl, and a plantain tree. On the way Nambi remembered that she had forgotten the grain for the fowl, and said to Kintu, "I must go back for the grain for the fowl, or it will die." Kintu tried to dissuade her, but in vain; she said, "I will hurry back and get it without anyone seeing me." He said, "Your brother Death will be on the watch and see you." She would not listen to her husband, but went back and said to her father, "I have forgotten the grain for the fowl, and I am come to take it from the doorway where I put it." He replied: "Did I not tell you that you were not to return if you forgot anything, because your brother Death would see you, and want to go with you?

Now he will accompany you." She tried to steal away without Death, but he followed her; when she rejoined Kintu, he was angry at seeing Death, and said: "Why have you brought your brother with you? Who can live with him?" Nambi was sorry, so Kintu said, "Let us go on and see what will happen."

When they reached the earth Nambi planted her garden, and the plantains grew rapidly, and she soon had a large plantain grove at Manyagalya. They lived happily for some time and had a number of children, until one day Death asked Kintu to send one of his children to be his cook. Kintu replied: "If Gulu comes and asks me for one of my children, what am I to say to him? Shall I tell him that I have given her to be your cook?" Death was silent and went away, but he again asked for a child to be his cook, and again Kintu refused to send one of his daughters, so Death said, "I will kill them." Kintu, who did not know what he meant, asked, "What is it you will do?" In a short time, however, one of the children fell ill and died, and from that time they began to die at intervals. Kintu returned to Gulu and told him about the deaths of the children, and accused Death of being the cause. Gulu replied: "Did I not tell you when you were going away to go at once with your wife and not to return if you had forgotten anything, but you allowed Nambi to return for the grain? Now you have Death living with you: had you obeyed me you would have been free from him and not lost any of your children."

After some further entreaty, Gulu sent Kaikuzi, the brother of Death, to assist Nambi, and to prevent Death from killing the children. Kaikuzi went to the earth with Kintu and was met by Nambi, who told him her pitiful story; he said he would call Death and try to dissuade him from killing the children. When Death came to greet his brother they had quite a warm and affectionate meeting, and Kaikuzi told him he had come to take him back, because their father wanted him. Death said, "Let us take our sister too," but Kaikuzi said he was not sent to take her, because she was married and had to stay with her husband. Death refused to go without his sister, and Kaikuzi was angry with him and ordered him to do as he was told. Death, however, escaped from Kaikuzi's grip and fled away into the earth.

For a long time there was enmity between the two brothers; Kaikuzi tried in every possible way to catch his brother Death, who always escaped. At last Kaikuzi told the people to remain in their houses for several days and not let any of the animals out, and he would have a final hunt for Death. He further told them that if they saw Death they must not call out nor raise the usual cry (ndulu) of fear. The instructions were followed for two or three days, and Kaikuzi got his brother to come out of the earth and was about to capture him, when some children took their goats to the pasture and saw Death and called out. Kaikuzi rushed to the spot and asked why they called, and was told they had seen Death; he was angry, because Death had again gone into the earth; so he went to Kintu and told him he was tired of hunting Death and wanted to return home; he also complained that the children had frightened Death into the earth again. Kintu thanked Kaikuzi for his help and said he feared nothing more could be done, and hoped Death would not kill all the people. From that time Death has lived upon the earth and killed people whenever he could, and then escaped into the earth at Tanda in Singo.

4.5 SACRIFICE

Sacrifice plays a central role in many African as well as other religions. There are many different kinds of sacrifice and almost as many different theories concerning its meaning. The word *sacrifice* derives from a Latin word meaning "to make sacred." Sacrifices may involve the spilling of blood (for example, the ritual slaying of an animal), or they may be bloodless when vegetable or cultural products are used.

Every sacrifice has at least four elements: (1) the people who perform the sacrifice, (2) what is sacrificed, (3) the mode of sacrifice, and (4) those (gods, spirits, ancestors, etc.) who receive the sacrifice. As the entry on sacrifice in the *HarperCollins Dictionary of Religion* (1995:948) indicates, there are numerous explanations, both native and academic, for sacrifice. As we discussed in chapter 3, to explain something involves interpreting it in light of some theory. Some theories of sacrifice postulate that sacrifices are gifts, or are attempts to establish reciprocity between humans and spirits or gods. Still other theories view them as a substitution, or an expiation, or a reenactment of primal events. Sacrifices are also explained as a means of communication between the gods and humans. Which of these explanations should be taken as basic (if any) cannot be decided on empirical grounds alone because sacrifices function in multiple ways.

The evidence for sacrificial rituals and their meanings among Africans consists primarily of observations made by outside observers (trained or untrained) and by reports of participants. The following report is by a distinguished anthropologist, E. E. Evans-Pritchard (1902–1973), who wrote a definitive work on Nuer religion. The Nuer are, like the Ganda, an East African group whose life centers on raising cattle.

According to Evans-Pritchard, sacrifices among the Nuer can be roughly divided into two main types: personal and collective. The first type involves sacrifices offered on behalf of individual persons, and the second involves sacrifices offered on behalf of social groups. Evans-Pritchard believes the intention behind the first type is piacular (expiatory) and the intention behind the second confirmatory. In other words, personal sacrifices are intended to get rid of some wrongdoing, illness, or danger and collective sacrifices are intended to make some social event (marriage, for example) holy or blessed.

Among the Nuer, the usual sacrifice is an ox, slain with a spear (although other methods are used). Youth and women cannot engage actively in the rites surrounding the sacrifice, but the sacrificer need not be a priest. Any adult male who has some status and interest in the affair may perform the sacrifice. Even though sacrifices are made to various spirits, Evans-Pritchard believes they are all directly or indirectly offered to what he calls "Spirit."

E. E. EVANS-PRITCHARD

Nuer Sacrifice

READING QUESTIONS

1. Describe each of the four acts of the sacrifice and their significance.
2. How does Evans-Pritchard's description of Nuer sacrifice involve his own interpretation? Be specific.
3. Do you think a Nuer would accept Evans-Pritchard's description of sacrifice as accurate? If she or he did not, what difference would it make to you?

Almost all sacrifices, whether personal or collective, have the same general features. A description of one is therefore, apart from details, a description of almost all. The

From E. E. Evans-Pritchard, *Nuer Religion* (Oxford: Clarendon Press, 1956), pp. 208–215. Reprinted by permission of Oxford University Press.

victim is brought to the place of sacrifice and there are performed in succession the four acts which compose the sacrificial drama: presentation, consecration, invocation, and immolation. Other features may be added, such as libations and aspersions and, mostly in sacrifices to spirits, hymn-singing, but these are supernumerary acts. The essential rites of the sacrifice proper are the four I have mentioned. They form what might be called the canon of sacrifice.

The first act is the *pwot*, the driving into the ground of a tethering-peg and the tethering of the animal to it. The officiant presents the victim to God. The man who stakes the victim is called *pwot yang*, the tetherer of the cow, and as in collective sacrifices this is generally done by the master of ceremonies of the family concerned he is commonly referred to in a sacrificial context by this title. Sometimes, after the victim has been staked, a libation, of milk, beer, or water, is poured over, or at the foot of, the peg.

Then takes place the *buk*, the rubbing (with ashes), the act of consecration. . . . The man who is about to speak the first invocation rubs ashes of cattle-dung lightly on the victim's back with his right hand. Each speaker does this in turn, and in some sacrifices all present place ash on the victim's back whether they make invocations or not. I discuss later . . . the meaning of rubbing ashes, when I shall try to show that it is not only a consecration of the beast to God but also an identification of man with ox.

Then takes place the *lam*, the invocation. . . . The officiant, holding his spear in his right hand, speaks to God over the consecrated victim. The invocation states the intention of the sacrifice and matters relevant to it. Occasionally, when a sacrifice is a very perfunctory affair, no words are spoken. When asked about the omission Nuer say that the sacrifice is the *lam*, by which they mean that the intention is implied in the sacrifice itself in the circumstances in which it is made. However, even in the most perfunctory rites, it is more usual for a few formal phrases to be spoken by the officiant as he consecrates the victim, either in a scarcely audible patter or even silently. He is addressing God and not the people present. This is what Nuer call a *lam me tot*, a short invocation. They say "*ca be lam e bec*," "they will not invoke (God) much." Normally, however, and always in a serious situation which also permits leisurely action, there is a *lam me dit*, a long invocation. The officiant walks up and down past the tethered beast, brandishing his spear, and uttering his words loud and clear he is then addressing the audience as well as God, and they may interrupt him with promptings, advice, and even argument. In a long address of this kind certain petitionary

formulae recur again and again but it has no set form or prescribed words. Each speaker may say what he likes so long as what he says is true and also in some way relevant to the intention of the sacrifice. These long rambling addresses, sometimes taking over an hour to deliver, contain, besides a statement of intention and petitions, all sorts of affirmations, exhortations, reflections about life, anecdotes, and opinions; and also complaints, for on very formal occasions the speaker must reveal any grievance he may have in his heart. As there may be several such invocations by different persons before the victim is slain, a sacrifice may be a very lengthy affair, and for a European rather tedious to assist at. He has to sit in the sun for several hours listening to addresses which are difficult for him to follow. Some of the sentences may be inaudible, the speaker speaking too low or having his back turned to the audience, who may also be talking among themselves; and the invocations are apt to require a more detailed knowledge of past events and relationships than a stranger is likely to have. . . .

The word *lam*, which has much the same range of meaning in other Nilotic languages, expresses a number of interconnected ideas, one or other of which is stressed according to the direction of interest. In reference to God it has to be translated "to invoke." In reference to a sacrificial victim it can be translated "to sacrifice." With reference to a man the ordinary meaning is "to curse," more rarely "to bless." It may also refer to a formal pronouncement in ordeals, and in animal stories to the ordeal itself. "Invocation" would seem best to cover all these special senses. For the verbal form I shall generally use the phrase "to make an invocation." Nuer usually employ it in what we call a passive or intransitive mood when speaking of sacrifices, saying "*ba lam*," "an invocation is made," or "*be lam ke lam*," "he will invoke with an invocation"; but since it is understood that it is God (though it may be in some refraction and sometimes coupled with ghosts) who is invoked it is legitimate also to use the phrase "to invoke God" even when this is not a word-for-word translation of what is said in Nuer. Even in curses and blessings it is God who is implicitly, if not explicitly, invoked, since the desired action can come only from him. A curse is therefore an imprecatory, and a blessing a benedictory, address to God. . . .

Now takes place the immolation, what Nuer generally call the *kam yang*, the giving, or offering, of the victim when speaking of personal sacrifices, and the *nak*, the killing, when speaking of collective sacrifices. By the use of one or the other word they indicate whether a sacrifice is for them more a religious or a festal event, whether its purpose is mainly piacular or social. Nuer do not, in so far as I have observed or heard, wait for the animal to urinate before killing it, as do some of the other Nilotic peoples. An ox is speared on the right side, and so expert are the Nuer that I have never known a second thrust to be necessary or the beast to move for more than a few seconds after the thrust has been made. Sheep and goats have their throats cut. . . . A bovine victim should fall well to make a perfect sacrifice. Falling well means falling cleanly on its side, preferably on its right side, and with its head in the desired direction, which in most sacrifices is towards the huts and the people who sit outside them. I have been told that should an ox fall badly, and there is another handy, they repeat the sacrifice. I have not, however, seen this done, and in my experience those present say that the animal has fallen well whichever way it falls. I have also been told that a lion will not eat an animal it has killed if it falls on its left side, but most Nuer ridiculed this statement.

We may, indeed, note here that Nuer are not a highly ritualistic people. We have already noted that they are not particular about the time and place of sacrifice or who performs the rite, that neither sacrificer nor officiant has to submit to any ceremonial interdictions, and that there is no prescribed content of their invocations, neglect of which would invalidate the rite. There is a certain air of casualness and lack of ceremony about the whole sacrificial procedure. So, although it is better if the ox falls well, it does not much matter if it does not. Nuer are more interested in purpose than in details of procedure. An oblation must be made to validate a social status or relationship or so that people may be free from evil and danger—small details of ceremony do not matter.

Sacrifice proper finishes with the *kam yang* or *nak*, the offering or killing of the victim, and since these expressions describe the culminating movement of the drama they can stand for the whole sacrifice and have the general sense of "to sacrifice." In this final moment, at which the invocation may be intensified . . ., the consecrated life has gone to God.

Nuer say that God takes the *yiegh*, the life, and I have heard them say also that he takes the *tie*, the soul. . . . They also say that what in sacrifice belongs to God are the *riem*, blood, which soaks into the ground, and the *wau*, chyme or perhaps a mixture of chyme and chyle. In what sense do Nuer speak of the blood and the chyme being what God receives? No doubt we have here to take into consideration the different levels at which Nuer conceive of Spirit. I have heard them say that after sacrifice to a spirit you can see the flesh of the speared beast twitching as the spirit pulls at it, and we have earlier noted in the hymn to the river-spirit *buk* the emphasis on red blood and also how the fetishes are said to "eat" the "soul" of offerings. But, as I have said before, the word *cam*, to eat, even in reference to fetishes is a metaphorical usage. I think that it may be accepted that there is no question of Nuer believing that in animal sacrifice Spirit, even as most materially conceived of, eats the blood and the chyme, not even in the sense of consuming their essence. Clearly, they are not materially consumed. Nuer do not say that Spirit feeds on (*mieth*) or eats (*cam*) or drinks (*madh, ruidh*) them. They do not use these words, but say that God, or a spirit, *kan*, takes, them. It is not a question of eating anything—what eating there is is done by the people—but of taking something, the life. This would seem to be a matter of great importance in an estimation of Nuer religious thought.

When, therefore, Nuer say that the blood and the chyme belong to God we are to understand, I would suggest, that this is a way of saying that the life belongs to him. It is true that we cannot say for the Nuer, as for the Hebrews, that the blood is the life. The word for life, *yiegh*, is also the word for breath, so that if we were to say that anything "is" the life we would have to say it of the breath; though even here the word "is" must not be taken to imply identity but a symbolic relationship. We must rather suppose that the blood and the chyme, and especially the blood, are also symbols of the life. . . .

God takes the *yiegh*, the life. Man takes the *ring*, the flesh, what is left over after the sacrifice. The carcass is cut up and skinned as soon as the animal falls. In most sacrifices the meat is consumed by members of the family and kin of the person on whose behalf it was made. In marriage and most other collective sacrifices it is divided among relatives, both paternal and maternal, in traditional portions; and the age-mates of the owner of the beast and representatives of lineages collateral to his may also have rights to shares. If the principal officiant is not a member of the family or of the close kin but a master of ceremonies of the family or a priest or a prophet, he also receives his share. This part of the proceedings is of general interest and not merely for those directly concerned in the rites. If it is at all a public occasion people, whether they are concerned in the matter or not, gather round to watch the meat being cut up and handed to those to whom it is due, and there is often much shouting and argument as the distribution is good-humouredly disputed and men tug at the carcass and snatch or beg pieces of meat. Even outsiders who get in the way and beg persistently enough are likely to receive pieces of it. According to the circumstances those who on such an occasion receive meat take it to their homes, maybe in different villages, for cooking and eating, or it is cooked by women of the homestead in which the sacrifice took place and eaten there by groups, according to sex, age, and kinship. The meat is cooked, served, and eaten as would be that of a wild beast slaughtered in hunting. It is boiled, though tit-bits may be roasted in the embers of a fire. I want to make it clear indeed that the cutting up of the victim, the preparation of its flesh, and the eating of it are not parts of the sacrifice. To regard the eating of the animal as part of the sacrificial rite would be like regarding a wedding feast as part of the marriage service in our own country. But if it does not form part of the rite and has no sacramental significance it forms part of the whole ceremony in the broader sense and has a social significance. We have always to remember that a sacrifice, even piacular sacrifice, furnishes a feast and that in the circumstances in which Nuer live and by convention this means that neighbours are likely in one way or another to share in it.

4.6 HEALING

African societies, like most other societies, are patriarchal to one degree or another. Men have more power, more control, and a greater range of options than women. Women are subordinate to men in a variety of ways and have less status and control over their lives. Unfortunately, religions often support such gender inequality by giving it divine sanction: It is the way the gods intended it to be.

Despite this inequality, women play important roles in both the religious and the secular realms in African societies. They are often, for example, skilled in traditional medicine and practice the arts of healing. Healing in Africa, as elsewhere, is sometimes associated with altered states of consciousness called trance states, which are thought to release healing power.

The following account is by Nisa, a woman !Kung healer ("!" indicates a clicking sound made by popping the tip of the tongue off the roof of the mouth). The !Kung are a hunting/gathering people who live in small village units in Botswana and Namibia. Among the !Kung there is a high level of gender equality (contemporary hunting/gathering societies are usually less patriarchal than agricultural and herding societies). Both women and men can be leaders, and women have considerable influence. There is a division of labor (women gather, men hunt) that is rather rigidly enforced (although some women also hunt), and even though the gathering activities of women account for more than sixty percent of the diet, meat hunted by the men is considered more valuable.

The gender inequality that does exist emerges most noticeably in religious matters. The main reli-

gious activities consist in ritual healing. The !Kung believe that most illness is caused by invisible arrows shot by the supreme god, lesser gods, or ancestors usually because they have been offended in some way. Humans (both men and women) can, via trance states, get the power to heal called *n/um* (the "/" indicates a sound similar to "tsk" in English). This power can be accessed in trance states brought about by ritual dancing. The healer, in trance, goes to the gods or ancestors responsible for the arrow of illness and intercedes on behalf of the victim. The healer lays hands on the ill people gathered at the dance and if the intercession is successful, they get well. If it is not, the illness persists or gets worse. About half the !Kung men and a third of the !Kung women have *n/um*, but men usually engage in the healing activities and the women sing and clap as the men dance.

In the past one hundred years, !Kung women have been developing a drum dance in which a male drummer beats out a rhythm and the females dance. However, while the women may enter trance, only a small number lay on hands and heal. Since healing, not the ability to enter trance, is the most prestigious spiritual activity of the !Kung, men tend to dominate in religious matters.

Nisa's description of trance and healing was recorded in Botswana in 1970 and 1971 and published by Marjorie Shostak. Dr. Shostak was part of a long-term anthropological study conducted by Harvard University.

❧

RECORDED BY MARJORIE SHOSTAK

Nisa—A Woman Healer

READING QUESTIONS

1. How does one, according to Nisa, get *n/um?*
2. According to Nisa, what is being in trance like?
3. Nisa explains that men do more healing than women because women are more afraid of pain

Reprinted by permission of the publisher from *Nisa: The Life and Words of a !Kung Woman* by Marjorie Shostak, pp. 299–303. Cambridge, Mass.: Harvard University Press. Copyright © 1981 by Marjorie Shostak.

than are men. Do you think there might be other explanations for gender inequality in healing? If so, what might they be?

N/um—the power to heal—is a very good thing. This is a medicine very much like your medicine because it is strong. As your medicine helps people, our n/um helps people. But to heal with n/um means knowing how to trance. Because, it is in trance that the healing power sitting inside the healer's body—the n/um—starts to work. Both men and women learn how to cure with it, but not everyone wants to. Trance-medicine really hurts! As you begin to trance, the n/um slowly heats inside you and pulls at you. It rises until it grabs your insides and takes your thoughts away. Your mind and your senses leave and you don't think clearly. Things become strange and start to change. You can't listen to people or understand what they say. You look at them and they suddenly become very tiny. You think, "What's happening? Is God doing this?" All that is inside you is the n/um; that is all you can feel.

You touch people, laying on hands, curing those you touch. When you finish, other people hold you and blow around your head and your face. Suddenly your senses go "Phah!" and come back to you. You think, "Eh hey, there are people here," and you see again as you usually do.

My father had the power to cure people with trance medicine, with gemsbok-song trance medicine. Certain animals—gemsbok, eland, and giraffe—have trance songs named after them, songs long ago given by God. These songs were given to us to sing and to work with. That work is very important and good work; it is part of how we live.

It is the same with everything—even the animals of the bush. If a hunter is walking in the bush and God wants to, God will tell him, "There's an animal lying dead over there for you to eat." The person is just walking, but soon sees an animal lying dead in the bush. He says, "What killed this? It must have been God wanting to give me a present." Then he skins it and eats it; that's the way he lives.

But if God hadn't wanted, even if the hunter had seen many animals, his arrows would never strike them. Because if God refuses to part with an animal, the man's arrows won't be able to kill it. Even if the animal is standing close beside him, his arrows will miss every time. Finally he gives up or the animal runs away. It is only when God's heart says that a person should kill something, be it a gemsbok or a giraffe, that he will have it to eat. He'll say "What a huge giraffe! I, a person, have just killed a small something that is God's." Or it may be a big eland that his arrows strike.

That is God's way; that is how God does things and how it is for us as we live. Because God controls everything.

God is the power that made people. He is like a person, with a person's body and covered with beautiful clothes. He has a horse on which he puts people who are just learning to trance and becoming healers. God will have the person in trance ride to where he is, so God can see the new healer and talk to him. There are two different ways of learning how to trance and of becoming a healer. Some people learn to trance and to heal only to drum-medicine songs. My mother knew how to trance to these, although she never learned to heal. There are other people who know how to trance and to heal to drum-medicine songs as well as to ceremony-dance songs. The n/um is the same in both. If a person is lying down, close to death, and someone beats out drum-medicine songs, a healer will enter a trance and cure the sick person until he is better. Both men and women have n/um, and their power is equal. Just as a man brings a sick person back to health, so does a woman bring a sick person back to health.

My father was a very powerful healer. He could trance to both kinds of songs, and he taught n/um to my older brother. He also taught it to my younger brother. But when my father died, he stole Kumsa's medicine from him. He left Dau with it, but not Kumsa. Today, even if someone is lying down sick, Kumsa doesn't try to cure him. Only Dau does that.

My present husband, Bo, doesn't have n/um. He was afraid. People wanted to teach him but he refused. He said it would hurt too much.

N/um is powerful, but it is also very tricky. Sometimes it helps and sometimes it doesn't, because God doesn't always want a sick person to get better. Sometimes he tells a healer in trance, "Today I want this sick person. Tomorrow, too. But the next day, if you try to cure her, then I will help you. I will let you have her for a while." God watches the sick person, and the healer trances for her. Finally, God says, "All right, I only made her slightly sick. Now, she can get up." When she feels better, she thinks, "Oh, if this healer hadn't been here, I would have surely died. He's given me my life back again."

That's n/um—a very helpful thing!

I was a young woman when my mother and her younger sister started to teach me about drum-medicine. There is a root that helps you learn to trance, which they dug for me. My mother put it in my little leather pouch and said, "Now you will start learning this, because you are a young woman already." She had me keep it in my pouch for a few days. Then one day, she took it and pounded it along with some bulbs and some beans and cooked them together. It had a horrible taste and made my mouth feel foul. I threw some of it up. If she hadn't pounded it with the other foods, my stomach would have been much more upset and I would have thrown it all up; then it wouldn't have done anything for me. I drank it a number of times and threw up again and again. Finally I started to tremble. People rubbed my body as I sat there, feeling the effect getting stronger and stronger. My body shook harder and I started to cry. I cried while people touched me and helped me with what was happening to me.

Eventually, I learned how to break out of myself and trance. When the drum-medicine songs sounded, that's when I would start. Others would string beads and copper rings into my hair. As I began to trance, the women would say, "She's started to trance, now, so watch her carefully. Don't let her fall." They would take care of me, touching me and helping. If another woman was also in trance, she laid on hands and helped me. They rubbed oil on my face and I stood there—a lovely young woman, trembling in trance—until I was finished.

I loved when my mother taught me, and after I had learned, I was very happy to know it. Whenever I heard people beating out drum-medicine songs, I felt happy. Sometimes I even dug the root for myself and, if I felt like it, cooked it and drank it. Others would ask for some, but if they hadn't learned how to trance, I'd say, "No, if I gave it to you, you might not handle it well." But once I really knew how to trance, I no longer drank the medicine; I only needed that in the beginning.

When my niece gets older, I'll dig some of the root for her, put it in her kaross for a few days, and then prepare it. She will learn how to drink it and to trance. I will stand beside her and teach her.

Unlike my mother, I know how to cure people to drum-medicine songs. An elderly uncle taught me a few years ago. He struck me with spiritual medicine arrows; that's how everyone starts. Now when the drum starts sounding, "dong . . . dong . . . dong . . . dong," my n/um grabs me. That's when I can cure people and make them better.

Lately, though, I haven't wanted to cure anyone, even when they've asked. I've refused because of the pain. I sometimes become afraid of the way it pulls at my insides, over and over, pulling deep within me. The pain scares me. That's why I refuse. Also, sometimes after I cure someone, I get sick for a while. That happened not long ago when I cured my older brother's wife. The next day, I was sick. I thought, "I won't do that again. I cured

her and now I'm sick!" Recently, Dau cured her again. I sat and sang the medicine songs for him. He asked me to help, but I said, "No, I was so sick the last time I almost died. Today, my medicine is not strong enough."

I am a master at trancing to drum-medicine songs. I lay hands on people and they usually get better. I know how to trick God from wanting to kill someone and how to have God give the person back to me. But I, myself, have never spoken directly to God nor have I seen or gone to where he lives. I am still very small when it comes to healing and I haven't made these trips. Others have, but young healers like myself haven't. Because I don't heal very often, only once in a while. I am a woman, and women don't do most of the healing. They fear the pain of the medicine inside them because it really hurts! I don't really know why women don't do more of it. Men just fear it less. It's really funny—women don't fear childbirth, but they fear medicine! . . .

CONTEMPORARY SCHOLARSHIP

Space permits only one example of a scholarly study of African religions. Many recent studies reflect a social scientific point of view (see chapter 3) because much of the study of African religions has been conducted by anthropologists. They are particularly interested in how religion relates to and is an expression of African culture. Many such studies focus on the function religion plays in constructing and maintaining a meaningful world, a world that makes sense given the African experience.

Increasingly, philosophers have been looking at the information gathered by anthropologists, historians, and ethnographers. They seek to engage this material with a critical and analytical eye, hoping to uncover the philosophical implications and assumptions behind religious practices and beliefs.

4.7 AFRICAN RELIGION AND PHILOSOPHY

Kwasi Wiredu, author of the next selection, studied philosophy at the Universities of Ghana and Oxford. Formerly the head of the philosophy department at the University of Ghana for a number of years, he now teaches at the University of South Florida, Tampa.

His article is a good illustration of philosophical inquiry. He carefully distinguishes different senses of the word *religion*, develops and argues a thesis, probes the relationship between religion and morality, and wonders whether concepts like natural and supernatural are appropriate in the African context. Wiredu recognizes that the concepts we use to interpret religion are inherently comparative. Meaning depends on contrasts, and so we must be careful about what is implied, but not stated explicitly, in terms that are inherently comparative.

Professor Wiredu's essay is not only a good example of the philosophical study of religion, it also underscores how central the issue of defining religion is to our interpretive endeavors (see chapter 2). Much of what Wiredu has to say about African religions hinges on how one defines religion.

~ষ্ঠX৯~

KWASI WIREDU

African Religions from a Philosophical Point of View

READING QUESTIONS

1. How does Wiredu distinguish between **religion and *a* religion**?
2. What is one of Wiredu's theses?
3. According to Wiredu, the notion of God's commands as the basis of morality does not apply widely to African religions. Why?
4. Why does Wiredu think it is misleading to characterize African religion by the categories "natural" and "supernatural"?
5. How do African attitudes toward God differ from attitudes toward spirits, ancestors, and lesser gods?
6. What are some of the negative consequences of calling beliefs and practices associated with lesser gods, spirits, and ancestors religion?
7. Based on what you know about African religions, do you think Wiredu is right in claiming the category "supernatural" does not apply to African cosmological views? Why or why not?

From Kwasi Wiredu, "African Religions from a Philosophical Point of View," in *A Companion to Philosophy of Religion*, edited by Philip L. Quinn and Charles Taliaferro (Cambridge: Blackwell Publishers, 1997), pp. 34–42. © 1997 Blackwell Publishers, Ltd. Reprinted by permission. References omitted.

If there is wisdom in starting with first things first, then a philosophical discussion of African religions should start with an inquiry into the applicability of the concept of religion to African life and thought. Not only is the word "religion" not an African word—this in itself is not necessarily a problem—but also, as Mbiti suggests, it is doubtful whether there is a single word or even periphrastic translation of the word in any African language. This does not mean, of course, that the phenomenon itself does not exist among Africans. One may have something without being given to talking about it. Mbiti himself, for example, maintains in his *African Religions and Philosophy* that Africans are pre-eminently religious, not even knowing how to live without religion. . . . Be that as it may, there is at this stage an assumption that we need to disavow, at least methodologically. We must not assume that having a religion is necessarily either a moral or an intellectual credit. Some of the early European visitors to Africa, going, it would seem, principally on a cheeky ignorance, freely opined that the African mind was in too rude a condition to be capable of a religious feeling or perception. By contrast, many African scholars have been keen to prove that Africans, by their own unsupplemented lights, were able to develop a belief in God and related matters before ever a European set foot in Africa. In either case there is the presupposition that having a religion is a kind of achievement. This assumption, unfortunately, is likely to handicap a dispassionate examination of the sense, if any, in which religion may be said to have a place in African culture.

Obviously, we need in this connection to be clear about what religion itself is. In this enterprise we need not be unduly intimidated by the well-known multiplicity of definitions of religion; for, when the willfully idiosyncratic ones are discounted, what this situation really presents is a legion of sufficient conditions. And if that is an embarrassment, it is only an embarrassment of riches. Moreover, there is a necessary distinction, not often enough drawn, which can gain us considerable simplification. It is the distinction between religion and *a* religion. Religion as such is, in essence, simply a metaphysic joined to a particular type of attitude. A religion, on the other hand, is, typically, all this plus an ethic, a system of ritual, and an officialdom (usually hierarchical) for exhorting, reinforcing or monitoring conformity to them. In the first sense, religion can be purely personal—one can be religious without having a religion; which, actually, is not at all uncommon. In the second, religion is both personal and institutional. One of the theses of the present discussion is going to be that, contrary to frequent suggestions, religion in Africa is predominantly of a personal rather than an institutional character. The claim, in other words, is that the concept of religion applies to African culture in most instances only in the minimal sense.

In this minimal sense to be religious is to entertain certain ontological and/or cosmological beliefs about the nature of the world and about human destiny and to have an attitude of trust, dependency, or unconditional reverence toward that which is taken to be the determiner of that destiny, whether it be an intelligent being or an aspect of reality. In terms of this characterization, it is not necessary for religion to include belief in a deity. In Africa, however, as in a great many areas of the world, that belief is the centerpiece of religion. But in Africa, unlike elsewhere, it also frequently more or less exhausts its scope. African world views usually, though not invariably, feature a supreme being who is regarded as responsible for the world order. Generally, that being is explicitly conceived to be omniscient, omnibenevolent and, subject to a rider to be entered in due course, omnipotent. . . . A sense of dependency, trust, and unconditional reverence is almost everywhere evident in African attitudes to the supreme being.

Strikingly, however, rituals of God-worship are often absent from African life. Mbiti . . . has observed that the word "worship" has no counterpart in many African languages. While this does not necessarily imply that the practice did not exist, it would explain it, if that were the case. In the particular case of the Akans, Abraham . . . has pointed out (correctly) not only that they "never had a word for worship" but also that "worship is a concept that had no place in Akan thought." Even when there is a simulacrum of worship among an African people, there is nothing comparable to the regular, rigorously organized and officer-led, group-praying and divine praise-singing characteristic of Christianity, for example. Nor is there an analogue to the weekly moral and metaphysical discourses from Christian pulpits. Many African peoples are, indeed, known to pray, and some to make offerings and sacrifices, to God. But these activities are often personal and informal or, when formal, as in some of the sacrifices, rather episodic; while some African groups, such as the Ankore and the Banyarwandas, are positive that an omnibenevolent being does not need or expect such things as sacrifices. . . . Indeed, it is difficult to see what use a perfect being could have for worship or how he could welcome it at all. But what, from a philosophical point of view, is of the utmost importance in all this is that Africans tend not to base their conceptions of the meaning of morality on their belief in God. And this must account largely for the non-institutional character of their religion. Given, however, the prevalence of the contrary impression in the literature, these claims require a lot of explaining.

Consider, then, the general idea of the dependency of morality on religion. If this relation is interpreted in a causal or genetic sense, there is an iota, though only an iota, of truth in it. Some people in Africa (and presumably outside Africa) are discouraged from mischief by the fear of divine retribution. But freedom from this kind of reason for action or inaction is, in fact, one of the marks of moral maturity recognized among the wise folks of well-known traditional African societies. But even if this were not the case, it still would not follow that *evil* is understood to mean *that which will bring divine retribution*; for, in that case, to warn that evil will bring those consequences will amount to announcing that what will bring divine retribution will bring divine retribution—a splendid truth, regrettably lacking in moral information. The suggestion is not necessarily that traditional sages are known to have formulated this particular consideration, though the philosophic ones among them are capable of even more incisive argumentation; it is rather that the communalist ethic typical of many traditional African societies is just such as to inhibit trafficking in such tautologies. From the communalist standpoint, morality is the adjustment of the interests of the individual to the interests of the community on the principle of sympathetic impartiality. On this view, morality derives, rationally, from the desiderata of social existence, not from any transcendent source. In the African example this is easily inferred from the corpus of moral maxims commonplace among the people. . . . Given some such conception of morality and an unqualified belief in the justice of God, there is no reason why a flagging virtue may not be bolstered up by thoughts of divine sanctions even if good and evil are conceived in a manner logically independent of the will of God. . . . Again, although it is true to say that most Africans believe that it is God who, as Idowu . . . puts it, implanted in human beings the sense of right and wrong, it does not follow that we should expect them to hold for this reason that "right," for example, means "approved by God"; just as it would not occur to anyone to suppose that if people believe that the sense of beauty and ugliness was implanted in us by God, then they will take "beautiful" to mean something like "appreciated by God."

One reason why morality has so often been thought to be closely connected with religion in Africa is because the scope of African religion has been routinely enlarged to include the beliefs and procedures relating to the great assortment of extra-human beings that is a component of various African worldviews. There is, indeed, no doubt that these worldviews usually postulate a hierarchy of beings. At the top is God; and, in the middle, various kinds of "spirits," some supposed to be resident in certain remarkable trees, mountains, and rivers, together with the departed ancestors. Below these are the human species, the lower animals, vegetation, and the realm of inanimate objects, in descending order. The "spirits" are credited with the ability to help or harm human beings in ways that surpass the causes and effects familiar in everyday life. For this reason people are careful to try to establish good relations with the more susceptible ones, and this often involves "rituals" replete with supplications sweetened with flattery. Among these extra-human beings the ancestors occupy a special position. They are not the most powerful, but they are, in the great majority of African societies, the best loved and respected. The world of the ancestors is conceived to be continuous and analogous to that of the living, and the interactions between the two realms are, by common reckoning, regular and on a day-to-day basis. In this setup the ancestors may be called the extra-mundane guardians of morality; their entire concern is to watch over the affairs of the living members of their families, rewarding right conduct and punishing its opposite, with unquestioned justice, while, at all times, working for their well-being. It is on this ground that the ancestors are so highly venerated. Notice that, on this showing, the orientation of the afterlife in the African "eschatology" is thoroughly this-worldly. . . . Not surprisingly, many African customs and institutions have some connection with the belief in the ancestors in particular and the world of spirits at large.

What, however, is the justification for calling the attitude to the ancestors and the other "spirits" religious? It is apparent that this is based on certain ways of ontologically compartmentalizing the worldview just adumbrated. The orders of existence above the human sphere are categorized as supernatural, spiritual, and, in some connections, transcendent, while the rest is designated as natural, material, and temporal. If to this is added the characterization of the activities dedicated to establishing useful relations with the extra-human powers and forces as worship, then the stage is set for attributing to Africans not only an intense religious sense but also a particularly pervasive institutional religion with unmistakable imprints on all major aspects of life. . . . In this perception of African religion it is not even necessary to bring God into the picture. It seems sufficient, under some available definition of religion, that Africans be seen to believe in, and worship, a great many "supernatural" and "spiritual" entities who are credited with power over the life and fate of human beings and in some cases invested with a moral authority. This, actually, is how Christian missionaries saw African religion, which they called paganism. Missionary semantics in Ghana offer an almost picturesque illustration of this fact. In ver-

nacular communication in the Akan area of Ghana the missionaries called the indigenous religion *Abosomsom* which means "stone-service" (*Abo* means "stones" and *som* means "service," which, in the evangelical translation, is a forced approximation to the concept of worship). Their own religion they called *Nyamesom*, meaning the service of God (*Nyame* means "God" and *som*, as we have seen, means "service"). Interestingly, what many Akan Christians, sincere in the faith and, at the same time, proud of the indigenous religion—conceptual incompatibilities notwithstanding—have done about this linguistic anomaly is merely to insist that the indigenous religion includes, in addition to the business about the "spirits," recognition of the existence of the Almighty God.

The incompatibilities, however, cut too deep to be so cheerfully skated over. Not only are there radical disparities between the Christian worldview and its African counterparts with respect to specific ontological issues, but also the categories of thought underpinning the concept of religion which has just been used have a questionable coherence in the relevant African contexts. A most fundamental pair of such categories is the natural/supernatural distinction. In describing the "spirits" in question as supernatural, it is assumed that this distinction is intelligible within the conceptual framework of the African peoples concerned. Yet one who consults any average text on African religion will be readily furnished with stories of spirits not only living in material circumstances but also indulging in physical ventures, gyrating upon the head not excluded. Moreover, spirits are not spoken of in any other terms. The conceptual implications of this have rarely been seriously explored *from the point of view of the African worldviews themselves*. Occasionally, though, a foreign researcher into African thought has come close to the beginnings of wisdom in this matter. Thus, Kenneth Little . . ., in a study of the Mende of Sierra Leone, notes that "the situation seems to be that they regard 'supernatural' phenomena in much the same kind of way and frame of mind as they regard the material circumstances of their environment and the motives and actions of human beings. . . . Such an attitude is [also], within the bounds of Mende knowledge, quite empirical." The quotes around the word "supernatural" do not betray any uneasiness regarding the intelligibility of the metaphysical dichotomy of the natural and the supernatural in the abstract; they are merely indicative of Little's suspicion that the Mende do not employ it in their thinking. His explanation is that "they have an essentially 'practical' attitude to life" which manifests itself as a "lack of interest in metaphysics." It is arguable, however, that they don't use that dichotomy because it is fundamentally incompatible with their metaphysic. At all events, in the conceptual framework of the African group to which the present writer belongs, namely, that of the Akans of Ghana, which, on the evidence of various studies . . ., is very similar to that of the Mende in many important respects, it makes scant sense to divide the world order into two, calling one nature and the other supernature.

Within the system of thought just alluded to, the world (*wiase*) is a unified order of created things (*abode*). (*Bo* means "to make" and (*a)de* means "thing(s)." But see the comment on creation in our final paragraph.) The so-called spirits are as creaturely as the humblest animal. The world order operates in every detail according to laws, some commonplace, others more recondite; but the latter do not contradict or abrogate the former, and interactions between the realms predominantly governed by these kinds of laws are perfectly regular in a cosmological sense. Accordingly, explanations of some puzzling phenomena in common experience in terms of the activities of "spirits," for example, do not generate the sense of "going out of this world" which the ascent, in another worldview, from the natural to the supernatural would seem to suggest. Certainly, "spirits" are regarded as being out of the ordinary, but they are not felt to be out of this world. Moreover—so the belief goes —they can actually be seen and communicated with by those who have medicinally reinforced eyes and appropriate resources of communication. And there is no lack of such "specialists" in many African societies. Significantly, when descriptions are given of what is thus seen, they are positively material in imagery. It is apparent, on these considerations, that calling the "spirits" supernatural represents a substantial misunderstanding. The same considerations must give pause to those who would speak of the "spirits" as spiritual. But there is a very much more fundamental objection. The word "spiritual" has a neo-Cartesian sense; it connotes non-spatiality. But —to turn to the African language that I know from the inside—in the Akan language the concept of existence, as Gyekye . . . rightly insists, is intrinsically spatial: to exist (*wo ho*) is to be somewhere. Consequently, in the Akan understanding, if "spirits" exist, they must be spatial and cannot be spiritual in a neo-Cartesian sense.[1] . . . They are not, on that account, fully material; for to be such it is necessary to be not just spatial but also subject to the causal laws of common experience. By all indications, however, the extra-human beings in question are supposed to be exempt, for example, from some of the

dynamical laws that constrain the motion and efficiency of ordinary objects. Thus they are thought to be capable of affecting human beings without, *normally*, being seen, and the action can be at a great distance. Such entities may, for convenience, be called quasi-material or quasi-physical. It is because they are quasi-material rather than spiritual that I have so far used the word "spirits" with quotational reservations. The aim has been to forestall the common fallacy of supposing that spirits must be necessarily spiritual. In fact, it is not only with respect to Akan discourse that this is not the case: Western spiritualist literature also is full of stories of quasi-material apparitions. The difference is that Western metaphysics additionally harbors schools of thought dedicated to the propagation of notions of spiritual entities in the Cartesian sense, and Akan traditional thought is devoid of such an inclination for the deep semantical reason already adduced. It is probably unnecessary at this stage to belabor the point that in being quasi-material, the spirits of the Akan worldview are quasi-empirical and therefore not transcendent in any useful sense. The decidedly empirical bent of discourse about spirits among various African peoples suggests that the Akan language is not unique in the present respect.

Revisiting now the question of the worship of the ancestors and certain other spirits, it emerges that if the attitude involved is that of worship, then it is not the worship of anything that may appropriately be called supernatural or spiritual or transcendent. But is it really worship, religious worship, that is? The following considerations do not encourage an affirmative answer. Leaving the ancestors out of account for a moment, it is a commonplace of African studies that the African attitude to the spirits, often hyperbolically called "lesser gods," is purely utilitarian. Ritualized praise is rendered unto them only because of expected benefits. As Busia . . . remarks: "the gods are treated with respect if they deliver the goods, and with contempt if they fail." Or worse: if devotees develop a confirmed impression of futility, attention is withdrawn, and the "god" concerned is left in fatal solitude. The reference to fatality is intended with all seriousness. In 1975 the African Nobel laureate Wole Soyinka startled an audience of African scholars at the University of Ghana when, in remarks enthusiastic of the Yoruba "gods," he pointed out quite serenely that the Yorubas create their own "gods" (such as the god of electricity) and can on occasion kill them. Yet the idea that an inefficient "god" can be denuded of all vital power through an enforced shortage of attention or other, more technical, means is widely received among traditional folks.

Allied to the last reflection is the consideration that the "gods," not unlike the Greek varieties of old, are not

---

[1] [Neo-Cartesian refers to philosophical ideas stemming from the French philosopher René Descartes that regard spirit as incorporeal (without a body) and hence nonspatial.—Ed.]

of a uniform moral standing: some are good, some bad, others nondescript; from which it is apparent that the devotee reserves the right of periodic review of their moral credentials. It follows, in turn, that the wishes of the "gods"—of even the moral elite among them—do not define moral goodness, notwithstanding the fact that the reactions of some of them may have a policing influence on conduct. The same is true of the ancestors, although, except in a few cases in Africa, such as among the Nuer and the Dinka, . . . they are held in higher and warmer esteem and are more irreversibly credited with immortality. . . . The ancestors are frequently so important in African life that something called ancestor worship is sometimes elevated into the veritable essence of African religion. But, in truth, the veneration of the ancestors is only an accentuated form of the respect given to the living elders of the group, and their moral authority is exerted only in the enforcement of morals established on pre-mortem criteria. These criteria of good conduct, as noted earlier, are founded on the quest for the impartial harmonization of human interests. It might be said, on this ground, by the way, that the ethic in question is a rational, humanistic one. . . . It should be noted, furthermore, that in most traditional African societies the average individual hopes eventually to gain a place in the community of the honored ancestors. If the ancestors were standardly worshiped and thought of as a species of gods, this would mean that a hankering after self-apotheosis is routine in those societies, suggesting a generalized megalomania quite frightening to contemplate. As it happens, the truth is less frightening. "Worship" is an elastic word, but it is stretching it rather far to call the attitude to the ancestors worship in any strict religious sense. And if this is so with respect to the ancestors, it is even more evident with respect to the assortment of spirits mentioned above.

If we now compare African attitudes to God with their attitudes to the spirits as just characterized, the contrast is tremendous. True, the will of God also does not define goodness, but, on the other hand, goodness (along with other qualities) does define God. And this is unique to God. Not even the ancestors are considered good by definition. In consequence, the reverence accorded to God is, as previously noted, unconditional, which is what the object of a genuinely religious attitude must evoke. The ancestors and "lesser gods" certainly fail to elicit this kind of respect. If, in spite of all this, one insists—as many do—on including the doctrines and doings regarding the spirits in the scope of African religions, this can only be by dint of a considerable extension of the concept of religion. Aside from the gratuitous assumption that, of religion, the more the better,

it is not clear what the point of it is. But it is clear what some of its negative consequences are. One such consequence is that skepticism, on the part of contemporary Africans, regarding the spirits and their capabilities tends to be perceived by them (and others as well) as disenchantment with the traditional religion. Adherence to a foreign religion, say Islam . . . or Christianity . . ., is then seen as a desirable substitution. If it had been realized that the beliefs and practices revolving round the spirits do not really constitute a part of the religion, conversion might still conceivably have taken place, but it might perhaps have been for weightier reasons. A reverse side of this phenomenon is that other Africans, wishing to demonstrate their indigenous authenticity in the matter of religion, are apt to engage in proud exhibitions of spirit-oriented rituals with calls on their compatriots to join in the preservation of our religious heritage. But the beliefs involved will probably not survive the advance of modern knowledge. One cannot, of course, be dogmatic in this, for in the West progress in scientific knowledge has not, by any stretch of the imagination, wiped out the belief in all kinds of spirits and related practices. Still, a properly discriminating understanding of the nature of African religions is likely to promote more pertinent programs for their preservation, if preserved they must be.

Philosophically speaking, whether a religion is worthy of preservation should depend on the validity of its metaphysic. In Africa, however, a judicious metaphysical evaluation is impeded by conceptual distortions resulting from the fact that the reigning traditions of scholarship in African religions, for reasons connected with colonialism, were established by foreign scholars who, naturally enough, articulated their accounts in terms of the intellectual categories of their own culture. Among the most basic of these are the dualisms of the natural and the supernatural, the material and the spiritual and the transcendent and the empirical. I have argued that these categorial distinctions are not coherent within typical African conceptual frameworks. Whether this incoherence is due to a defect in those schemes of thought or in the dualisms themselves is a cross-cultural issue, which, *pace* relativism, can be fruitfully investigated. In the present connection, however, it only needs to be noted that, on account, partly, of this contextual incoherence, the concept of religion itself applies to African thinking (in at least many cases) only in the most minimal sense. It should be clear from the above discussion that we can speak of religion in African life only because of the widespread belief and trust in a supreme being who is the author of the world order. Incidentally, although the belief is widespread in Africa, it is not universal. If p'Bitek . . . is right, the central Luo, for instance, do not even operate with the concept of a supreme being. Besides, individual traditional skeptics are not unknown even in the God-believing societies. In any case, because of the non-transcendental cast of much African thought, even when the belief is entertained its meaning is usually more radically different from Christian conceptions, for instance, than it has been orthodox to suppose. Thus the supreme being is conceived to be the author of the world in the sense of a cosmic designer or architect rather than a creator *ex nihilo* (from nothing) . . . , and his omnipotence is understood to mean that he can accomplish any well-defined project, not that he can do absolutely everything, including, for example, abrogating the world order or even aspects of it. Taken together with the independence of morality from this belief, both conceptually and institutionally, the frequent absence or marginality of the worship of God, and the this-worldliness of the afterlife, a distinctive picture of African religions emerges that will have to be deeply pondered in any study of the religions of the world.

KEY TERMS AND CONCEPTS

Amma Creator god of the Dogon.

divination Methods for discovering the human significance of present and future events.

high god A god associated with the sky or heavens who appears to be a *deus remotus* (remote deity) because sacrifices are usually not offered directly to him (high gods are usually spoken of as male) and a *deus incertus* (uncertain or vague deity) because his exact nature sometimes seems to be both incorporeal (without a body) and corporeal (embodied).

Kintu The first man/king of the Ganda people, who marries a being from the sky named Nambi, who is the daughter of the King of Heaven, Gulu.

myth From a Greek word for story and used technically in religious studies to refer to sacred stories about divine or semidivine beings and the origin of things, in particular the world.

n/um A term used by Nisa, a woman !Kung healer, for the power to heal.

nummo A Dogon word that refers to water as well as **Amma**'s seed and the half-human/half-serpent twins born of that seed. Nummo appears to refer to life force in general

religion and *a* religion A distinction employed by Kwasi Wiredu between a metaphysical view joined with a particular type of attitude (religion) and a metaphysical view joined with a particular attitude plus a system of ritual, a clergy or officialdom, and an ethic (*a* religion). Religion is personal while *a* religion is both personal and institutional.

rites of passage Rituals designed to mark and aid people through the major transitions of life (birth, adulthood, marriage, death). These rituals symbolically separate a person from the previous stage of life, place him or her in a liminal, or transitional, state between the old and the new, and finally reincorporate the person into society in the new stage or role.

sacrifice This word, derived from a Latin word meaning "to make sacred," refers to rituals involving the slaying of animals (blood sacrifice) or the offering of vegetables and culture products (bloodless sacrifice). Every sacrifice has at least four elements: the people who conduct the sacrifice, what is sacrificed, the mode of sacrifice, and those (gods, spirits, ancestors, etc.) who receive the sacrifice. Sacrifices may be personal (an offering to promote healing) or collective (an animal slain at a funeral). Some sacrifices have a fivefold structure—consecration, invocation, immolation, communion, purification—and others a fourfold structure—presentation, consecration, invocation, immolation.

traditional African religions A controversial designation usually intended to refer to African religious beliefs and practices dating from precolonial times found primarily among sub-Saharan groups.

trickster A figure (often represented by an animal) appearing in myths and folktales who expresses the ambiguities and uncertainties of life. The trickster character is both cunning and stupid, fooler and fooled, creator and created.

SUGGESTIONS FOR FURTHER READING

Evans-Pritchard, E. E. *Witchcraft, Oracles and Magic Among the Azande.* Oxford: Clarendon Press, 1937. A classic study still widely used. His theory of witchcraft as a means of explaining unfortunate events emphasizes its social functions.

Idowu, E. G. *Olodumare: God in Yoruba Belief.* London: Longman, 1962. Idowu argues for a diffused monotheism.

King, Noel Q. *African Cosmos: An Introduction to Re-*

ligion in Africa. Belmont, Calif.: Wadsworth, 1986. Intended for the beginning student. King organizes his material by ethnic groups such as the Yoruba, Akan, Bantu, and others.

Lienhardt, G. *Divinity and Experience: The Religion of the Dinka.* Oxford: Oxford University Press, 1961. Along with Evans-Pritchard's work, a classic in anthropological studies of African religions.

Mbiti, John S. *African Religions and Philosophy.* Garden City, N.Y.: Anchor Books, 1970. An influential book (most later studies cite it) filled with insight and information although criticized for its theological viewpoint.

Parrinder, E. G. *African Traditional Religion.* London: S.P.C.K., 1971. An important introduction with valuable information although criticized for decontextualizing African religion.

Parrinder, Geoffrey. *African Mythology.* Rev. ed. New York: Peter Bedrick Books, 1986. Parrinder summarizes many of the fascinating and provocative myths, legends, folktales, and fables from Africa. Includes excellent photographs.

RESEARCH PROJECTS

1. Collect from secondary sources three different myths of creation. Select them all from sub-Saharan groups, one from East Africa, one from West Africa, and one from Central or Southern Africa. Write a report that compares the three myths.

2. After doing some research, have a debate with other members of the class on the topic "African witchcraft is real." (Note: Careful definitions of both *witchcraft* and *real* will play a key part in this debate.)

3. Collect or make some slides of African art. Show them to the class, and describe their religious symbolism.

5

Ways of Being Religious
Among Native North Americans

INTRODUCTION

Our images of Native Americans, which come from movies and pictures, are "imagined." In fact, European Americans have been imagining Native Americans ever since the Europeans arrived on the American continent five hundred years ago. The Europeans were puzzled and wondered, "Who are these people, where did they come from, how do they live?" As they slowly destroyed many of the indigenous peoples through disease and war, stealing their lands, enslaving them, and forcing them to move further West, they kept imagining mostly wrong answers to their questions of who, where, and how.

In 1492, when Columbus landed on an island in the Caribbean, he believed he had landed in India. So he called the people he found living on the land "los Indios," and this wrong name has stuck. Columbus also found the people without religion and therefore thought they could be quickly Christianized. Wrong again!

Later explorers soon realized Columbus had not found India. Instead, they thought that he had discovered a New World. They got it wrong again. It was, in fact, a very old world that had been slowly discovered, explored, and settled by the indigenous peoples over thousands of years.

Images of these native peoples and their way of life soon began to polarize. Some Europeans thought the Native Americans were disgusting, repugnant, and barely human and described them as wild, heathen savages. Their religious practices were characterized as devil worship. Others found these "savages" noble, innocent, and the best examples of humanity before the corrupting influence of civilization.

The notions of religion, history, and civilization the Europeans brought with them largely determined their images. Using the Bible as their history book, some argued that the natives were the descendants of the ten lost tribes of Israel. Knowing only Christianity, Judaism, and Islam as examples of religion, they thought the natives either had no religion or were Jews. Some argued the natives had a religion but that it was a false religion, that is, idolatry. In the midst of the controversies about who the Native Americans were, where they came from, and what sort of religion, if any, they practiced, there was near universal agreement that they were in *need* of both civilization and Christianity.

The early missionaries carried a wide variety of these images with them as they preached the gospel to the natives. Some believed along with Roger Williams (1603?–1683), the Baptist founder of the Rhode Island Colony, that "by nature Europeans and Americans" were no different since God made all humans of "one blood" (Acts 17), but since by nature we are all "children of wrath" (Ephes. 2) missionary work was important. Others, like the Puritan Cotton Mather (1663–1728), believed that even though the "Indians were dispersed and rejected Israelites," they had become savages and must be "civilized ere they could be Christianized."[1]

The missionaries had to learn the languages and ways of the Native Americans before they could effectively "civilize" and Christianize them. They wrote down the stories and legends told to them and, in some cases, made detailed notes about ritual practices. These accounts, plus others of "archaic" and "primitive" peoples from around the globe, even-

---

[1] For a selection of sources on early European images of Native Americans, see *Native American Traditions: Sources and Interpretations*, by Sam D. Gill (Belmont, Calif.: Wadsworth, 1983), pp. 1–18.

tually led to the founding of the scholarly discipline of ethnography (a part of anthropology), which hoped to introduce scientific objectivity by breaking through all of these false images to the "reality" of Native American beliefs and practices. Thus, when the Smithsonian Institution was established in 1846, Henry R. Schoolcraft submitted a plan for the systematic investigation of American Indians.

It may be doubted that the scholarly study of Native American religions has broken through the false images and discovered the "reality." However, a new tradition of "imagining" the Native Americans did begin with ethnographic, anthropological, archaeological, and historical studies, which did break many of the old stereotypes. The stereotypes, of course, continue to persist, and the European conquest of and contact with "los Indios" has forever changed the traditional, pre-contact religions of the Native Americans. We must not overlook the fact that European religions and attitudes have also been changed by this contact—and the change is still going on. Although Native Americans were granted U.S. citizenship in 1924 by the descendants of those who stole much of their land, their religious freedom was not officially guaranteed until August 1978 with the passage of the American Indian Religious Freedom Act.

The images of Native American religions emerging today go beyond the older popular stereotypes and picture a rich religious tradition of great spiritual depth. This chapter provides glimpses that will, hopefully, enrich the images you have of Indians.

5.1 AN OVERVIEW

Åke Hultkrantz, a Swedish historian of religions, is concerned with American Indian religious beliefs and the ideology surrounding religious rites. This concern is intended to counterbalance the behavioral studies done by many American anthropologists. However, like anthropologists, he is concerned with the functions of religion. Many of his books have become classics in the field, and he has influenced several generations of scholars.

In the following selection, he introduces us to North American Indian religions by describing four prominent features: a similar worldview, a shared notion of cosmic harmony, emphasis on experiencing directly powers and visions, and a common view of the cycle of life and death. Some scholars would find Hultkrantz's attempt to isolate four common features too simplistic in that it obscures the great diversity one finds. Here the problem that plagues comparative religions (see chapter 3) comes to the fore once again: Comparison always involves finding similarities and differences. However, how do we decide what is more important, the similarities or the differences? Hultkrantz here opts for emphasizing similarities.

One can also see in the following reading the role that interpretive categories play in organizing and making sense of data. Hultkrantz uses the concept of a **worldview** (a comprehensive outlook on life) to interpret a wide range of data relating to Native North American religions.

ÅKE HULTKRANTZ

Native North American Religions

READING QUESTIONS

1. As you read, make a list of all the words and ideas you do not understand or are uncertain about. Discuss them with a classmate, look them up in a dictionary, or bring them up in class for discussion and clarification.
2. What are the four prominent features of North American Indian religions?
3. Explain in your own words what is meant by "cosmic harmony."
4. What is animalism?
5. Do you agree with Hultkrantz that the concepts of "supernatural" and "natural" apply to the Native American worldview given the differences between that worldview and the worldview of the "Judeo-Christian" tradition? Why or why not?
6. What is Pan-Indianism? Why do you think an outside observer like Hultkrantz finds it inaccurate and an insider like Jackson Beardy finds it attractive?
7. What is the vision quest, and why is it important?
8. What is a shaman?
9. What is the difference between a **linear** and a **cyclical** notion of time? What are the implications of the cyclical view for the possibility of life after death?

From Åke Hultkrantz, Native Religions of North America, HarperSanFrancisco, pp. 20–34. © 1987 by Åke Hultkrantz. Reprinted by permission of HarperCollins Publishers, Inc. Endnotes deleted.

10. If you read chapter 4 on African religions, state two similarities and two differences between ways of being religious in Africa and in North America that you believe are important. What makes them significant similarities and differences?

Four prominent features in North American Indian religions are a similar worldview, a shared notion of cosmic harmony, emphasis on experiencing directly powers and visions, and a common view of the cycle of life and death. These features will be treated separately, but it is useful to provide an initial identification of each. Worldview is the total understanding of life and the universe held by a particular people or culture. North American Indians have worldviews that in many respects are remarkably similar, particularly in the way they perceive the interrelationship of humans and animals. Many North American Indians also share a notion of cosmic harmony, in which humans, animals, plants, all of nature, and even supernatural figures cooperate to bring about a balanced and harmonious universe. North American Indian traditions emphasize a direct experience of spiritual power through dreams and visions; . . . the sacredness and prestige of these striking revelations often results in the modification or replacement of previous traditional elements. Native Americans have a common view of time as a recurring cycle; they are interested mainly in how this cycle affects people in this life and have only a vague notion of another existence after death.

WORLDVIEW

If we want to grasp the essential character of North American Indian religions, it is natural to start with their worldview. Worldview is a concept that may be interpreted in different ways. The American anthropologist Robert Redfield defines worldview as "the way a people characteristically look outward upon the universe," and it may be convenient to apply that definition here. In our context worldview then stands for a people's concept of existence and their view of the universe and its powers.

Most North American Indians consider that human existence was designed by the creator divinities at the time of the "first beginning." Mythological tales report that in those days all beings on earth were more or less human, but a change took place that turned many primeval beings into animals and birds. Only those who today are human beings retained their forms. Because of this genesis there is still today a close affinity between people and animals: they are brothers, and it is people's task to respect and be in harmony with the animals. It is interesting that domesticated animals such as dogs have not been included in this brotherhood, whereas domesticated horses have. Indeed, on the Plains there is even a cult of the horse. It is difficult to tell whether the fact that the horse is of foreign, European origin has contributed to its lofty position. In the main, however, it is the wild, independent animals to which Native Americans' religious attention has been paid. All over the Americas they have been thought to manifest the mysterious qualities of existence.

One consequence of the close kinship between humans and animals has been the tendency for Native Americans to imitate the animals in dress, actions, and projective thought. The feather-lined shirts, the feather ornaments for dancing, and the feather plumes in the hair of the American Indians are all measures to instill the capacities of birds (spirit birds) in the human being. Some feather arrangements in the hair seem to have obtained a secondary meaning—marking the number of enemies killed, success in scalping an enemy, or other deeds. The Mandan and their neighbors near the Upper Missouri developed the large war bonnets with a row of feathers in a headband, trailing down the back; these were more a symbol of dignity and intrepidity than of spiritual assistance—although the latter possibility cannot be excluded. These war bonnets were then later adopted by other Indians. The feather decorations of American Indians remind us of those of the Siberian **shaman,** which is a further testimony of the spiritual background of the "feather complex." Apparently feathers manifest spiritual essence, particularly of beings on high.

The bond between animals and humans is also expressed in ritual activities. Plains Indian dances in which the men imitate the movements of buffaloes or wear their horns and skins are supposed to bring forth this valuable game. They are not, as earlier research took for granted, magic rituals to multiply the animals. They are rather acts of supplication in which Indians, by imitating the wild, express their desires and expectations. Such a ritual tells us of the Indian's veneration for the active powers of the universe: it is a prayer.

The final consequence of Native Americans' close affinity to the animals is **animalism,** that is, the concept of spirits as animals. This is a characteristic feature in North American Indian religions. Of course, wherever hunting cultures are to be found, supernatural beings come dressed in animal attire. In North America, however, the vision complex, of which more will be said shortly, has strengthened and perpetuated the belief in animal spirits.

NATIVE AMERICAN TRIBES OF NORTH
AND CENTRAL AMERICA

Source: From Åke Hultkrantz, *Native Religions of North America*, Harper San Francisco. © 1987 by Åke Hultkrantz. Reprinted by permission of HarperCollins Publishers, Inc.

Here we may well ask whether we should speak about "animal spirits" or "spirit animals." The former term may indicate either the notion of spirits in animal form or the concept of the spirits—or souls—of animals. The latter term suggests that some animals may not be real animals, but spirits. In North American traditions both designations seem to apply, because the boundary between animals and spirits here is very vague. Therefore, both terms will be used in the following.

Indians think that animals are by nature mysterious since their behavior is both similar and different to that of humans. Such a tension between known and understood and unknown and not understood usually creates a sentiment of something uncanny, something not quite belonging to normal reality. The Ojibway of the Great Lakes think that, although most stones are not alive, some are. They can be seen rolling of their own accord, and a **medicine man** or a **medicine woman** can talk to them and receive their answers. Apparently, stones are divided according to their possession or lack of mysterious qualities. A similar rule holds for animals. All bears are mysterious in their various ways, but some bears are more mysterious than others, being able to talk or change forms (as experienced in dreams and visions). The former bears are in spite of everything ordinary bears, the latter are spirits. However, sometimes it is difficult to find out which category of bears Indian informants are referring to.

We are here reminded of the fact that to Native American religious thinking there is a dividing line between what belongs to the ordinary or natural world around us and what belongs to the supernatural or spiritual world. In some scholarly quarters it has been denied that any such categorization exists among the Indians, or it has been said that it only occurs among those Indians who have been touched by Christianity. However, a consideration of all the evidence makes it quite clear that in their spontaneous experience of religious miracles and in some cases in their thinking about such experiences and existence as such, Indians distinguish between an ordinary and a spiritual world. It is difficult for us to pinpoint which things belong to either category. As mentioned above, a bear may be an ordinary animal, or it may represent the shape of a supernatural being. To some tribes certain mountains are supernatural, to others they are not.

Indeed, some natural phenomena and cultural objects are so saturated with supernaturalness that they are set aside from all other things. They are sacred and therefore dangerous, **taboo.** For instance, the Indians surrounding Yellowstone Park feared its spouting geysers. Their eruptions were thought to spring from the operations of capricious spirits. Archaeological evidence seems to suggest that the Indians may have offered axes and other implements to the underground spirits. Otherwise, however, they avoided the dangerous spots. There are many other examples of the distinction between natural and supernatural. Plains Indians received in visions spirit instructions to leave alone certain tools or abstain from certain actions. The sacred Arapaho flatpipe cannot be touched except under proper ritual conditions. It is preserved in a special lodge and carefully wrapped up in blankets. One Shoshoni medicine man refused to dine with me at a restaurant because his spirit had forbidden him to eat with cutlery. Whoever transgresses such taboo rules runs the risk of becoming sick or paralyzed, or even dying. That person will bring misery and misfortune not only to himself, family, and kin, but to the whole community.

Some Indian pronouncements sound as if the whole universe, particularly the natural environment, is sacred. This is not so; if it were, Indians would not point out certain stones, mountains, and lakes as sacred. Conserva-

tionists have mistakenly assumed that Indians are ecologists because they supposedly care for all of nature. In fact, there are many proofs of the devastation of nature by Indians. However, Indians have paid more attention to nature than perhaps any other peoples, and Indian hunters have tended to protect nature, or parts of nature, as a manifestation of the supernatural. They care about the trees, because they give evidence of the supernatural; they care about the animals, because they may represent spirits; they care about the vast lands, because they may reveal God. Nature is potentially sacred, or rather, it turns into sacred matter when humans experience the supernatural in vision, meditation, or ritual.

There has been no remarkable speculation on the relations between the natural world and the spiritual world in the Indian worldview. Perhaps one could say that for the Indians the spiritual reveals the true nature of the ordinary world around us, but this inference should not be emphasized. The Western religious dichotomy between a world of spiritual plenitude and a world of material imperfection, a dualism pertaining to Christian and Gnostic doctrines, has no counterpart in American Indian thinking. Indians value highly life on earth, and their religion supports their existence in this world. The whole spirit of their religion is one of harmony, vitality, and appreciation of the world around them.

Perhaps the Western concept of "nature" is too narrow to use in this connection. Nature, the world, and the universe are concepts that flow into each other in Indian consciousness. What some scholars describe as "nature rituals" Indians view as affecting the whole of the universe. The Sun Dance is not just a ritual that promotes the vegetation and animal life during the new year that it introduces, it is a recapitulation of the creation; in fact, it is creation and its effects concern the whole evolution and sustenance of the universe.

The universe is usually divided into three levels—heaven, earth, and underworld, a division that is a heritage from ancient times and is also known in northern Eurasia. However, there are some variations in this world picture. The Bella Coola of British Columbia believe that there are five worlds on top of each other, of which ours is the middle one. Many Pueblo peoples of the Southwest believe in the existence of four underworlds and four upper worlds, and the Navajo have taken over their idea of the four subterranean realms, one over the other.

The various worlds are often united through the World Tree, which has its roots in the underworld, stretches through the world of humans and animals, and has its crown in the sky world. The World Tree is represented by such ritual structures as the Sun Dance post (which is an uprooted tree) or the Omaha sacred pole.

The three levels of the universe are marked on the Sun Dance post: the eagle at its top manifests the sky world, the buffalo skull on its trunk or at its base is the world of animals and humans, and the offerings of tobacco and water on the earth close to the base, destined for Mother Earth, symbolize the relations to the underworld. The myths of the tree or vine on which the ancestors climbed up from the underworld(s), according to Southwestern Indians, also remind us of the idea of the World Tree.

In myths and rituals the sacred areas of the supernatural powers are drawing close to people. They may become identical with the areas people occupy today. Thus, the mythic world of the Navajo supernatural beings is situated between the four sacred mountains that enclose the central country of the Navajo people: Big Sheep Peak in the north, Pelado Mountain in the east, Mount Taylor in the south, and the San Francisco Peaks in the west. To take another example, the Shoshonean myths portray a landscape in the Great Basin that still is the home of many Shoshoni groups today.

The supernatural powers that govern the universe are multifarious. There is usually a heavenly god who rules over the sky, a host of spirits who control the atmospheric powers, an innumerable crowd of spirits who influence human life on earth, and also some beings, including Mother Earth, who roam the nether world. Very often these spirits, or a large number of them, are conceived as a unity. This unity may consist of a collectivity of spirits or of a Supreme Being (usually identified with the sky god) supervising or taking in the functions of various spiritual powers. On the Plains, both these concepts may exist side by side. Thus **Wakan Tanka** of the Lakota Sioux is a term comprehending a set of spirits from different levels, functions, and areas—sixteen all together. (The number is the speculation of holy men.) However, it is also the name of a personal god, the quintessence of all powers. To one Lakota division, the Oglala Lakota, the concept of *Wakan Tanka* swings between the two poles of unity and collectivity.

Psychologically seen, the two cognitive elaborations represent two ways of looking at the supernatural. When people perceive the universe as a unit, whole and indivisible, the figure of the single godhead stands in focus. When human attention is drawn to the particular acts of the divine, such as thunder, food giving, and healing, particular powers appear that express the activities referred to. The Supreme Being fades into the background, unless he is especially bound up with one of these activities. There is thus a tension between universalism and particularism in the concepts of the supernatural and the universe.

The worldview of North American Indians reveals a concept of existence contrasting sharply with that of the Western world and the Judeo-Christian tradition. There is no sharp differentiation between divinity and humans, nor is there a clear distinction between humans and animals. Not only is there a different relationship between these beings, but also the beings themselves are viewed in a distinctive fashion calling for their own terms. The Western world focuses on one divinity as "God," but Native Americans, although they have the notion of a Supreme Being, emphasize an abundance of "powers" and "spirits." These powers are not far removed from humans but interact freely with humans, especially in dreams and visions. . . . Some animals are spirits, as some spirits are animals. In general, the Native American view of "nature" is much more alive and filled with spiritual activity than the Western view of nature. The Native American worldview can in some instances be characterized as emphasizing cosmic harmony.

COSMIC HARMONY

Today's Indians often emphasize the unitary, balanced system of the universe as made up of humans, animals, trees and plants, nature as a whole, and the supernaturals. For instance, Jackson Beardy, a modern Cree Indian artist, sees the world as a unit dominated by the sacred number four. He told me that the world has four basic elements: air, water, fire, and stone. The creation took place in four processes: the creation of the earth, the plants, the animals, and the human beings. There are four basic colors in the universe; and so on. Now, this is scarcely the original worldview of the artist's people, the Woodland Cree of Manitoba, because Canadian Woodland Indians are not known to have such concepts. It is rather a worldview that has striking resemblances with the cosmic speculations of Plains and Pueblo Indians. As a matter of fact, when questioned, Jackson Beardy admitted that he had absorbed ideas from the Plains Indians, the Northwest Coast Indians, and other Indians. He is convinced that there are no real differences between Indian religions, only different names.

The same position is taken today by most young Indians who believe in **Pan-Indianism**; that is, they consider that all Native American tribes basically share the same culture and the same religion and they want to revert to this culture and religion. They present a "North American religion" as an integrated system of beliefs and rituals with fixed symbolism, the same for all tribes. This is, however, a late idea, formed under the pressure of white domination. Still, its foundation, the concept of cosmic harmony, a harmony in which living beings also take part, is much older. It is an outgrowth of the speculations among priests in predominantly agrarian societies where religious ideas, natural phenomena, humans, and other beings have been drawn together as parallels, analogues, and symbols in a connected religiophilosophical pattern. Certainly, the very germs of this speculation may be retraced to the ancient hunting milieu. However, it is particularly in the horticultural milieu with its developed and intricate ritualism, its grandiose mythology, and speculating priest-thinkers that the idea of cosmic harmony is really at home.

To show the uniqueness of this ideology we may here contrast the thought systems of a hunting tribe like the Naskapi of Labrador and a horticultural group like the Tewa of New Mexico. The Naskapi, says an expert on their religion, Frank G. Speck, do not classify their religious ideas. "For a system is scarcely to be expected to appear on the surface as covering the aggregation of metaphysical ideas so rudimentary as those exhibited in Montagnais-Naskapi thought. . . . That any conception of categories is alien to the thought of the people must be apparent to anyone who has viewed their undisciplined life." On the other hand, there is an unconscious thought system that sometimes has a ring of Platonism, because earthly forms are seen as having their supernatural ideal forms. Each animal species has its master (lord, boss); this **master of the animals** is usually conceived as a mysterious animal spirit larger than ordinary animals of the same kind. Thus, the giant beaver who governs the beavers decides their allotment as game food to the hunters and their return to the world after death. The fish also have a master, but he is identified with the moose-fly, strangely enough. The principle remains, however: living beings have their supernatural guardians. In the case of humans, it is the Supreme Being who plays the superior role.

This simple system of the hunters contrasts with the rich symbolism of the agricultural Tewa, a Pueblo tribe in New Mexico described in detail in an excellent work by a Tewa (San Juan) Indian scholar, Alfonso Ortiz. The Tewa are organized in two **ceremonial moieties** or halves that are responsible in particular for the rituals of the calendar. These rituals regulate the seasons and serve the supernatural cosmic system. Whereas in the inchoate religion of the Naskapi the supernatural beings stand out as the powers who decide the course of events, in the Tewa worldview they are part of the ritual machinery, impersonated in the rituals by members of the moiety divisions. It is the cooperation between the two moieties that brings together the wholeness of Tewa existence. A symbol of this wholeness is the sacred center, the navel of the Earth Mother, a keyhole-shaped arrangement of stones on the southern plaza. Late in the winter seeds are placed in this navel to symbolize the

reawakening of nature. From this navel the world is oriented. The world has four quarters, and so has its ritual manifestation on earth, the pueblo.

The complementary powers of the universe are contained in the two moieties, which represent summer and winter and are protected by the Blue Corn Mother and the White Corn Mother, respectively. The summer moiety is particularly associated with the furthering of vegetation, the winter moiety with the furthering of hunting. Moreover, the moieties are combined with symbolic colors, the summer moiety with black (for clouds), green (for crops), and yellow (for sunshine), the winter moiety with white (for winter moisture) and red (for warfare and hunting). As a consequence of this division, the summer moiety stands for femaleness and the winter moiety for maleness. The summer moiety impersonates in its rituals the gods from the warm south, the winter moiety the gods from the cold north. In this way everything that exists is divided up between the ceremonial moieties.

There are also secret societies belonging to the moieties or balancing between them. In the annual cycle of rituals (called "works") these societies perform retreats and prayer sessions associated with the progression of the year and its economic activities. "The intent of each work is to harmonize man's relations with the spirits, and to insure that the desired cyclical changes will continue to come about in nature."

Why is there this difference in outlook between the Naskapi and the Tewa? One reason is certainly the wide differences in their conditions of existence. In their hard struggle in an Arctic environment the Naskapi, strewn over the country in small hunting camps, had few possibilities and few incentives to create bodies of speculative thought and little ritualism that made such speculation necessary. The agricultural, closely connected Tewa Indians, inhabiting a circumscribed pueblo and living in a more pleasant climate, had enough surplus time to consider their affinity with the universe. The picture of this universe was taken from their own cultural structure. Their dualistic cosmology may, as Ortiz suggests, have been stimulated by a dual subsistence system (hunting and horticulture). In a wider perspective their thought system is part of a Pueblo Indian philosophy that may go back to tendencies in archaic American Indian thinking.

POWERS AND VISIONS

The Jesuit missionaries of the 1630s who had arrived in the area of the Great Lakes to convert the Indians there were astonished to find religions so different in structure and expression from their own Catholic faith. "Their superstitions are infinite," wrote Father de Brébeuf on the Huron, an Iroquoian people, and Father Francois du Perron made the following statement: "All their actions are dictated to them directly by the devil, who speaks to them now in the form of a crow or some similar bird, now in the form of a flame or a ghost, and all this in dreams, to which they show great deference. They consider the dream as the master of their lives; it is the God of the country. It is this which dictates to them their feasts, their hunting, their fishing, their war, their trade with the French, their remedies, their dances, their games, their songs."

Behind these theological comments we have here the earliest Western descriptions of the role that dreams and visions have played in Native American religion. All over North America, with exception of the Southwest, spiritual power has come to people in their dreams or in visions they have received in isolated places in the wilderness. Indeed, it is possible to say that the **vision quest** is the most characteristic feature of North American religions outside the Pueblo area. For the lone hunter safety and success depended on the guardian spirit acquired through the vision quest. The guardian spirit was closer at hand than the high god or other spirits. The connection between a person and a protective spirit could become so intense that the person took part in the spirit's qualities and even in its life. In northern Mexico, this close bond is called **nagualism,** after the Indian term *nagual* (the guardian animal that is the individual's second ego). When the spirit died (and spirits could die), the person also succumbed.

The relationship to a guardian spirit through vision is evidence of the importance of spiritual contact in American Indian religion. Indians "believe" when they see or feel the supernatural being. A historical document from the seventeenth-century Southwest illustrates this point. The Spanish missionary Fray Alonso de Benavides tells us how he was visited by a Jicarilla Apache chieftain who much admired his altar and was informed that God was on that altar. However, the Apache was not satisfied, for God was not visible on the altar. When he left he was very disappointed, for he wished to have seen God. In Indian religion, the vision quest provided an opportunity for direct contact with the supernatural.

The basic vision quest in North America is connected with puberty or the years immediately preceding puberty. The young boy (girls do not usually participate in the vision quest) is required to seek the assistance of a guardian spirit to withstand the trials of existence and have luck in hunting, warfare, love, and so on. The parents or elders send him out, usually together with other boys, into the forest or mountains to fast and suffer from the cold and the attacks of dangerous wild animals. In

his weakened state he may have a vision of the spirit that henceforth becomes his guardian spirit. (There are many cases told of supplicants who were not blessed by spirits.) This quest, which we may call the "**puberty quest,**" was transformed into a quest for full-grown men on the Plains and in parts of adjacent territories. On the Plains the warriors repeatedly withdrew into the wilderness to seek spirits. A Plains Indian may therefore have a variety of guardian spirits, each of which is good for a different purpose.

Consequently, the boundary line between common visionaries and medicine men has been very slight among Plains Indians. . . . One can say that in comparison with ordinary Indians medicine men have more spirits, and their spirits are specialized to help cure the diseases of their clients. The medicine man receives his mission to cure from the spirits that come to him, and in his visions he receives instructions in the ways of doctoring.

The most common therapeutic method is to remove the agent of the disease, whether it be an object or a spirit. Sucking, blowing, and drawing it out (with a feather fan) are the most common techniques. In some areas, and particularly along the Northwest Coast, the medicine man falls into a trance or ecstasy to enable his soul to transcend the boundaries to the other world. In his trance he gathers information from the spirits of the dead, or even steals away the soul of a patient that has gone to the realm of the dead during the feverish coma of its owner. The medicine man then brings the soul back to the sick person, usually by pressing his hands against the latter's crown. Such a medicine man who falls recurrently into a deep trance to save a person's life is called a **shaman.**

Shamans, however, are not only doctors. They are able to divine the whereabouts of game, the location of a missing person, and the course of future events. Among the Athapascans of the Southwest (Apache and Navajo) the shaman goes into a trance to find out the nature of the disease before other medicine men start their doctoring.

Common visionaries, medicine men, and shamans all have their authority from spiritual revelations in visions. As said before, this direct contact with the supernatural world through visions means more to American Indians outside of the Pueblo area than the knowledge of supernatural powers through traditional lore. Sometimes spiritual revelation comes not through the sought vision, but in a spontaneous dream, particularly among the Iroquois in New York State and the Mohave in western Arizona and southern California. The Iroquois decide their actions from interpretations of dreams, and the Mohave even dream their myths, that is, construct their myths on the basis of dream contents. Medicine men and shamans west of the Rocky Mountains receive their powers not through the vision quest, but through spontaneous dreams and visions.

Since time immemorial Indian shamans have facilitated their contacts with the supernatural through potent psychotropic drugs, drugs that affect consciousness and behavior. Tobacco is a well-known and important ingredient in American Indian rituals. In the Eastern Woodlands and on the Plains, the smoking of a pipe introduces most ceremonies and most peace talks. There is reasonable evidence to suggest that in bygone times the pipe without the bowl functioned as a suction instrument through which the shaman could both remove a disease object from a patient and intoxicate himself with tobacco fumes.

Many psychotropic plants have been used for the attainment of trance states. Datura was used in California, the Southwest, and the Southeast. In recent times peyote, the small spineless cactus, plays a similar role. A whole religion has grown up around peyote, particularly on the Plains. . . .

THE CYCLE OF LIFE AND DEATH

In contrast to those in Western cultures, Native Americans conceive of time not in a linear, but in a cyclical form. Western time concepts include a beginning and an end; American Indians understand time as an eternally recurring cycle of events and years. Some Indian languages lack terms for the past and the future; everything is resting in the present. This explains to us how mythical events apparently thought to have happened long ago may repeat themselves in present ritual occurrences. The Lakota define the year as a circle around the border of the world. The circle is a symbol of both the earth (with its encircling horizons) and time. The changes of sunup and sundown around the horizon during the course of the year delineate the contours of time, time as a part of space. An illustration of this way of counting time is indicated in stone arrangements on mountaintops and plateaus in the Rocky Mountains: the stones are laid in a wide circle around a central hub, and the place of the summer solstice is marked. The **"medicine wheels,"** as these stone structures are called, served as some sort of calendars, among other things.

The cyclical time concept applies not only to the macrocosmos, the world and the year's rhythm, but also to the microcosmos, the human being. Each person makes a cycle of time from birth to death. Rituals mark the important changes of life: birth ceremonies, puberty rituals, initiation rites into tribal societies, and death rit-

uals. The cyclical concept demands that death is not an end, but a beginning of new life, either on this earth (**reincarnation** as another human or **transmigration** into some animal, most often an owl) or in a transcendent hereafter. Very often one individual might hold several ideas about the dead at the same time: the dead as residing in the other world, the dead as reincarnated in other persons, and the dead as haunting ghosts. This may appear to be a logical inconsistency in Indian thinking, but it should not be so considered. Different situations call for different interpretations of the fate of humans after death. (And in fact Western people themselves do not reconcile their apparent inconsistencies on the fate of individuals following death.)

Native Americans usually avoided the issue of death, thinking that nothing could be known with certainty about the state of the dead. The question of a person's survival after his or her demise has never been a prominent theme for American Indian speculation (although the Jesuit fathers thought so). As said before, religion in aboriginal America has always been in the service of life, not death. Beliefs about the dead are abstruse, vague, and of little consequence. The best descriptions there are emanate from shamans who have gone beyond life to liberate sick people's souls entrapped by the dead. These descriptions tell us much about the difficult roads to the other world and the obstacles to be met. With Paul Radin we may say that these tales are folkloristically reworked, rich in detail, but scarcely meaningful to the ordinary person who primarily trusts his or her own religious experiences. Conditions in the next life are not so well documented, although there are occasionally illuminating reports. These are usually modeled on the setting and conditions in this life and consequently vary with cultural background.

In popular contexts we often talk about the "happy hunting grounds." It has been said by some authorities that Indians never believed in them, but this is wrong. Hunting tribes usually think that there is a happy land after death, at least for those who have conformed to the norms of society. There is plenty of game in that land. Horticulturists tend to believe in a subterranean realm of the dead, the place of Mother Earth who produces the new life of vegetation. For obvious reasons this realm portrays a more gloomy picture of afterlife. However, often the horticulturists retain the old idea of a happy paradise, whatever its location, filled with the bounty of the earth. The question of whether there were different realms of the dead based on good and bad deeds in pre-Columbian Indian belief is difficult to answer. However, we know definitely that such ideas developed under the impact of Christianity, for cyclical thinking does not provide for a resuscitation of the dead in this life. As an

Indian told me, those who are gone are gone forever. Only in religious movements that have been inspired by Christian ideas, such as the **Ghost Dance** around 1890, is the return of the dead possible.

[This] overview of Native American religions . . . provides us with a general understanding of the worldview, cosmic harmony, powers and visions, and the cycle of life and death so important to this religious heritage. But because this overview has attempted to characterize Native American religion as a whole, especially in North America, it has necessarily been quite general. . . .

SOURCES

Space permits a representative sampling of traditional religious ways from only a few groups of North American Indians. Hopefully, the readings in this section will inspire you to find out about other groups as well. I shall emphasize the themes of creation, the divine, death, ritual dancing, visions, and shamans in a handful of nations.

5.2 CREATION

Stories about creation are often called creation myths by scholars of religion. As I mentioned in the previous chapter, myths are stories that are considered sacred and authoritative by the people who orient their lives around the ideas and values the stories convey. To many Native Americans, however, *myth* is a pejorative term that indicates misunderstanding of their sacred stories. Out of concern for native sensitivity, it is probably best to use *story* or *sacred story* instead of *myth* when examining the native literature about creation.

There are many different types of North American Indian creation stories. Most of them are about the beginning of the world the Native Americans live in, not the absolute beginning of everything. These stories tell of the origin of plants, animals, humans, the sun, moon, and stars as well as aspects of human life such as death and illness. One major type, usually called **earth diver,** tells about the origin of the earth. The earth comes about because some being (often an animal) dives to the bottom of primordial waters, gets a bit of soil or sand, and uses this to create solid ground. Another type, called **emergence,** tells of the ascent of human beings from an underground world

and their travel to the lands the people now inhabit. Still another type involves a **trickster** character who, acting as a **culture hero** (a being who creates religious and cultural institutions), steals some important necessity (fire, light, water, game) for the welfare of the people.

The first selection is from a long and complex story told by the Hopi about the emergence of the people from three worlds into the fourth world in which they now live. The excerpt relates some events from the first world, called Tokpela, and from the fourth and present world, called Túwaqachi. Taiowa is the supreme Creator, but he creates an assistant named Sótuknang to carry out his plans. Sótuknang in turn creates Kókyangwúti (**Spider Woman**) who in turn creates the primordial twins and human beings.

I have taken this story from a book by Frank Waters called *Book of the Hopi*. Waters, who is part Cheyenne, compiled these stories from translations of recorded interviews with Hopi elders. However, the Hopi have criticized his book because they believe it sensationalizes and distorts Hopi religion. In fact, the Hopi so resent outsiders writing about them, they are claiming an exclusive right to represent their own cultures. In Arizona, some tribal counsels demand the right to preapprove any scholarly writing pertaining to their traditions. This situation not only introduces political considerations into scholarly activities (have they been there all along?), but highlights the insider/outsider issue discussed in chapter 1 and the reductionism issue discussed in chapter 3. Should the conclusions of religious scholarship have to be acceptable to the insiders? If so, which insiders have the authority? Does this requirement destroy objectivity? Is objectivity even possible in the first place?

It is clear that Waters did not just transcribe what had been recorded. He, in effect, rewrote it. While he self-consciously places his interpretations in footnotes and at the end of sections, it is clear that his views intermingle with the "reports" throughout. The very organization of the material raises many questions in light of the fact that Waters hoped to produce a "Hopi Bible" complete with "Old Testament" and "New Testament." The Hopi criticism raises important points not only about issues of objectivity, but also about the reliability of our sources for understanding Native American religions. Everything, even so-called reports, must be carefully examined with a critical eye and cross-checked with other sources.

The Hopi are part of the Pueblo cultures of the southwestern United States. There are approximately 50,000 Pueblo peoples, many living in the same area the Spanish invaded in 1540. They practice agriculture (maize or corn is a central food, cultural object, and religious symbol), hunting (they have ceremonies for the bear and the deer), and foraging. The Hopi and Zuni (another Pueblo culture) practice elaborate ceremonialism and may be best known for their corn dances and the **kachina** dancers. Kachinas represent ancestral spirits and spirits of animals, humans, or superhuman beings whose arrivals and departures follow seasonal fluctuations. Their ceremonial houses, called **kivas,** represent the various underworlds connected by a central world axis (*Sipaapuni*). Their core narratives (such as the emergence story) are considered sacred, secret knowledge possessing great power and are often told in the form of liturgical dialogues between the priests and masked representatives of important deities.

Our second selection is a trickster story. It comes from the Tsimshian, who, along with the Tlingit, Haida, Kwakiutl, Chinook, and other groups, are part of a Northwest Coast cultural group extending 1,500 miles from Alaska to California. They are best known for their highly developed woodworking technology, especially the **totem pole,** a heraldic carved pole erected to commemorate important events. The Tsimshian first met Europeans in the late eighteenth century, but it was not until the nineteenth century that missionization, colonization, and governmental coercion began long-term processes ending in near extension of the culture. Successive epidemics (smallpox, measles, malaria) brought by the Europeans killed eighty percent of the population. Today there are about 100,000 people, speaking more than forty-five languages and experiencing a cultural, artistic, and religious renewal.

One of the basic ideas of these Northwest peoples is that humans exist in a complex web of relationships with the physical world, animals, spirits, and the dead. Hence, transformation stories and rituals abound, usually involving the elaborate use of masks and sometimes masks within masks. Among the Kwakiutl, it is said the masked gods came to earth and, when they removed their masks, they became human. Shamans wear transformation costumes and masks when they go into trance or perform cures.

In the story related here (of which there are many different versions), a figure called Giant transforms in and out of Raven's skin (a trickster and culture hero figure) and manages to steal light (mā) for the people. In a Haida version, the light is the sun kept secure inside a box that in turn is inside six other boxes.

✺

RECORDED BY FRANK WATERS

Spider Woman and Creation

READING QUESTIONS

1. What is the First World like?
2. What are the duties of the Twins?
3. What do you think is the significance of the claim that "all sound echoes the creator"?
4. What does this story tell you about the values of the Hopi?
5. Given what is said about Giant-Raven in the second story, why is Raven so often classified as both a culture hero and a trickster figure?
6. How would you describe the worldview that is expressed in this story?

Sótuknang went to the universe wherein was that to be Tokpela, the First World, and out of it he created her who was to remain on that earth and be his helper. Her name was Kókyangwúti, Spider Woman.

When she awoke to life and received her name, she asked, "Why am I here?"

"Look about you," answered Sótuknang. "Here is this earth we have created. It was shape and substance, direction and time, a beginning and an end. But there is no life upon it. We see no joyful movement. We hear no joyful sound. What is life without sound and movement? So you have been given the power to help us create this life. You have been given the knowledge, wisdom, and love to bless all the beings you create. That is why you are here."

Following his instructions, Spider Woman took some earth, mixed with it some *túchvala* (liquid from mouth: saliva), and molded it into two beings. Then she covered them with a cape made of white substance which was the creative wisdom itself, and sang the Creation Song over them. When she uncovered them the two beings, twins, sat up and asked, "Who are we? Why are we here?"

From *Book of the Hopi* by Frank Waters, pp. 4–7, 21. Copyright © 1963 by Frank Waters. Used by permission of Viking Penguin, a division of Penguin Putnam, Inc.

To the one on the right Spider Woman said, "You are Pöqánghoya and you are to help keep this world in order when life is put upon it. Go now around all the world and put your hands upon the earth so that it will become fully solidified. This is your duty."

Spider Woman then said to the twin on the left, "You are Palöngawhoya and you are to help keep this world in order when life is put upon it. This is your duty now: go about all the world and send out sound so that it may be heard throughout all the land. When this is heard you will also be known as 'Echo,' for all sound echoes the Creator."

Pöqánghoya, traveling throughout the earth, solidified the higher reaches into great mountains. The lower reaches he made firm but still pliable enough to be used by those beings to be placed upon it and who would call it their mother.

Palöngawhoya, traveling throughout the earth, sounded out his call as he was bidden. All the vibratory centers along the earth's axis from pole to pole resounded his call; the whole earth trembled; the universe quivered in tune. Thus he made the whole world an instrument of sound, and sound an instrument for carrying messages, resounding praise to the Creator of all.

"This is your voice, Uncle," Sótuknang said to Taiowa. "Everything is tuned to your sound."

"It is very good," said Taiowa.

When they had accomplished their duties, Pöqánghoya was sent to the north pole of the world axis and Palöngawhoya to the south pole, where they were jointly commanded to keep the world properly rotating. Pöqánghoya was also given the power to keep the earth in a stable form of solidness. Palöngawhoya was given the power to keep the air in gentle ordered movement, and instructed to send out his call for good or for warning through the vibratory centers of the earth.

"These will be your duties in time to come," said Spider Woman.

She then created from the earth trees, bushes, plants, flowers, all kinds of seed-bearers and nut-bearers to clothe the earth, giving to each a life and name. In the same manner she created all kinds of birds and animals —molding them out of earth, covering them with her white-substance cape, and singing over them. Some she placed to her right, some to her left, others before and behind her, indicating how they should spread to all four corners of the earth to live.

Sótuknang was happy, seeing how beautiful it all was—the land, the plants, the birds and animals, and the power working through them all. Joyfully he said to Taiowa, "Come see what our world looks like now!"

"It is very good," said Taiowa. "It is ready now for human life, the final touch to complete my plan."

CREATION OF MANKIND

So Spider Woman gathered earth, this time of four colors, yellow, red, white, and black; mixed with *túchvala*, the liquid of her mouth; molded them; and covered them with her white-substance cape which was the creative wisdom itself. As before, she sang over them the Creation Song, and when she uncovered them these forms were human beings in the image of Sótuknang. Then she created four other beings after her own form. They were *wúti*, female partners, for the first four male beings.

When Spider Woman uncovered them the forms came to life. This was at the time of the dark purple light, Qoyangnuptu, the first phase of the dawn of Creation, which first reveals the mystery of man's creation. . . .

THE NATURE OF MAN

With the pristine wisdom granted them, they understood that the earth was a living entity like themselves. She was their mother; they were made from her flesh; they suckled at her breast. For her milk was the grass upon which all animals grazed and the corn which had been created specially to supply food for mankind. But the corn plant was also a living entity with a body similar to man's in many respects, and the people built its flesh into their own. Hence corn was also their mother. Thus they knew their mother in two aspects which were often synonymous—as Mother Earth and the Corn Mother.

In their wisdom they also knew their father in two aspects.

TÚWAQACHI: THE FOURTH WORLD

"I have something more to say before I leave you," Sótuknang told the people as they stood at their Place of Emergence on the shore of the present Fourth World. This is what he said:

"The name of this Fourth World is Túwaqachi, World Complete. You will find out why. It is not all beautiful and easy like the previous ones. It has height and depth, heat and cold, beauty and barrenness; it has everything for you to choose from. What you choose will determine if this time you can carry out the plan of Creation on it or whether it must in time be destroyed too. Now you will separate and go different ways to claim all the earth for the Creator. Each group of you will follow your own star until it stops. There you will settle. Now I must go. But you will have help from the proper deities, from your good spirits. Just keep your own doors open and always remember what I have told you. This is what I say."

Then he disappeared.

TSIMSHIAN

Raven and the Light

Giant flew inland (toward the east). He went on for a long time, and finally he was very tired, so he dropped down on the sea the little round stone which his father had given to him. It became a large rock way out at sea. Giant rested on it and refreshed himself, and took off the raven skin.

At that time there was always darkness. There was no daylight then. Again Giant put on the raven skin and flew toward the east. Now, Giant reached the mainland and arrived at the mouth of Skeena River. There he stopped and scattered the salmon roe and trout roe. He said while he was scattering them, "Let every river and creek have all kinds of fish!" Then he took the dried sea-lion bladder and scattered the fruits all over the land, saying, "Let every mountain, hill, valley, plain, the whole land, be full of fruits!"

The whole world was still covered with darkness. When the sky was clear, the people would have a little light from the stars; and when clouds were in the sky, it was very dark all over the land. The people were distressed by this. Then Giant thought that it would be hard for him to obtain his food if it were always dark. He remembered that there was light in heaven, whence he had come. Then he made up his mind to bring down the light to our world. On the following day Giant put on his raven skin, which his father the chief had given to him, and flew upward. Finally he found the hole in the sky, and he flew through it. Giant reached the inside of the sky. He took off the raven skin and put it down near the hole of the sky. He went on, and came to a spring near the house of the chief of heaven. There he sat down and waited.

Then the chief's daughter came out, carrying a small bucket in which she was about to fetch water. She went down to the big spring in front of her father's house. When Giant saw her coming along, he transformed himself into the leaf of a cedar and floated on the water. The chief's daughter dipped it up in her bucket and drank it. Then she returned to her father's house and entered.

After a short time she was with child, and not long after she gave birth to a boy. Then the chief and the chieftainess were very glad. They washed the boy regularly. He began to grow up. Now he was beginning to creep about. They washed him often, and the chief smoothed and cleaned the floor of the house. Now the child was strong and crept about every day. He began to cry, "Hama, hama!" He was crying all the time, and the great chief was troubled, and called in some of his slaves to carry about the boy. The slaves did so, but he would not sleep for several nights. He kept on crying, "Hama, hama!" Therefore the chief invited all his wise men, and said to them that he did not know what the boy wanted and why he was crying. He wanted the box that was hanging in the chief's house.

This box, in which the daylight was kept, was hanging in one corner of the house. Its name was Mā. Giant had known it before he descended to our world. The child cried for it. The chief was annoyed, and the wise men listened to what the chief told them. When the wise men heard the child crying aloud, they did not know what he was saying. He was crying all the time, "Hama, hama, hama!"

One of the wise men, who understood him, said to the chief, "He is crying for the mā." Therefore the chief ordered it to be taken down. The man put it down. They put it down near the fire, and the boy sat down near it and ceased crying. He stopped crying, for he was glad. Then he rolled the mā about inside the house. He did so for four days. Sometimes he would carry it to the door. Now the great chief did not think of it. He had quite forgotten it. Then the boy really took up the mā, put it on his shoulders, and ran out with it. While he was running, some one said, "Giant is running away with the mā!" He ran away, and the hosts of heaven pursued him. They shouted that Giant was running away with the mā. He came to the hole of the sky, put on the skin of the raven, and flew down, carrying the mā. Then the hosts of heaven returned to their houses, and he flew down with it to our world.

At that time he world was still dark. He arrived farther up the river, and went down river. Giant had come down near the mouth of Nass River. He went to the mouth of Nass River. It was always dark, and he carried the mā about with him. He went on, and went up the river in the dark. A little farther up he heard the noise of the people, who were catching olachen in bag nets in their canoes. There was much noise out on the river, be-

From Frank Boas, *Tsimshian Mythology* (Washington, D.C.: Bureau of American Ethnology, Annual Report no. 31, 1916), p. 60. Notes omitted.

cause they were working hard. Giant, who was sitting on the shore, said, "Throw ashore one of the things that you are catching, my dear people!" After a while, Giant said again, "Throw ashore one of the things you are catching!" Then those on the water scolded him. "Where did you come from, great liar, whom they call Txä′msem?" [sounds like Chemsem] The (animal) people knew that it was Giant. Therefore they made fun of him. Then Giant said again, "Throw ashore one of the things that you are catching, or I shall break the mā!" and all those who were on the water answered, "Where did you get what you are talking about, you liar?" Giant said once more, "Throw ashore one of the things that you are catching, my dear people, or I shall break the mā for you!" One person replied, scolding him.

Giant had repeated his request four times, but those on the water refused what he had asked for. Therefore Giant broke the mā. It broke, and it was daylight. The north wind began to blow hard; and all the fishermen, the Frogs, were driven away by the north wind. All the Frogs who had made fun of Giant were driven away down river until they arrived at one of the large mountainous islands. Here the Frogs tried to climb up the rock; but they stuck to the rock, being frozen by the north wind, and became stone. They are still on the rock. The fishing frogs named him Txä′msem, and all the world had the daylight.

5.3 THE DIVINE

Just as Christian missionaries tried to find a counterpart to the monotheistic god of Christianity among the Africans (see chapter 4), so there has been a similar search for a high god among Native Americans. One problem that missionaries and scholars encountered is that the metaphysical and theological concept of monotheism did not appear to fit the religious situation the Europeans found in North America very well. They found creator gods, sky gods, chief spirits, and many other kinds of gods. Their search for a "primitive monotheism" finally led them to **Wakan Tanka** (Wakantanka), translated variously as God, Great Spirit, Great Sacred, and Great Mysteriousness.

The following brief selection was recorded by J. R. Walker. It was told to him by Sword, an Oglala of the Teton division of the Dakota Sioux. The term *Sioux* is a French corruption of an Algonquin pejorative term meaning "lesser, or small, adder or enemy." The Algonquins used this word to refer to the Teton, who left Minnesota and moved to the Great Plains in the early eighteenth century. The term the Sioux used for themselves was *Oceti Sakowin*, or "the Seven Fireplaces," which refers to the seven divisions of the Teton. However, the Algonquin term has stuck and the natives themselves now use Sioux. The Teton are the second most populous Native American group in the United States and are sometimes called Lakota after the dialect they speak.

The Teton were known as the scourge of the northern Plains. They were fierce warriors who, along with other groups, defeated Custer in 1876. They suffered a tragic massacre in 1890 at Wounded Knee, and their century of greatness ended on reservations, mostly in South Dakota. Because of their defeat of Custer, their skill as horsepeople and buffalo hunters, their talents and bravery as warriors, and their resistance to the ever-advancing whites, the Teton have lived on in the American imagination as the "fierce Indian warrior."

Anything has the potential to become *wakan* ("sacred"), from natural to cultural phenomena. Things that have become permanently wakan are collectively called Wakan Tanka or Great Wakan. Sword, in the following selection, refers to sixteen "different persons" that are Wakan Tanka. Many consider this a later interpretation referring to the eight powers who created the universe and the eight who came into existence when the earth was created. The first eight are Sun, Moon, Sky, Wind, Earth, Falling Star, Rock, and Thunder-being. The second eight are Buffalo, Bear-man, the Four Winds, the Shade, Breath, Whirlwind, Shadelike, and Potency.

Whether the reference to sixteen different persons is a later interpretation or not, it appears that translating Wakan Tanka as God is misleading. The word *God* has become so closely identified with a monotheistic notion of the divine, it simply does not work well as an analytic category. Perhaps words like *divine* or *deity* are not much better. Perhaps it is appropriate that Wakan Tanka, the Great Mysteriousness, should challenge if not completely escape our analytic and comparative categories.

SWORD (RECORDED BY J. R. WALKER)

Wakan Tanka

READING QUESTIONS

1. What is a wakan being like?
2. According to Sword, what does Wakan Tanka refer to?
3. What makes the Wakan Tanka "the same as one"?

Every object in the world has a spirit and that spirit is wakan. Thus the spirits of the tree or things of that kind, while not like the spirit of man, are also wakan. Wakan comes from the wakan beings. These wakan beings are greater than mankind in the same way that mankind is greater than animals. They are never born and never die. They can do many things that mankind cannot do. Mankind can pray to the wakan beings for help. There are many of these beings but all are of four kinds. The word Wakan Tanka means all of the wakan beings because they are all as if one. Wakan Tanka Kin signifies the chief or leading wakan being which is the Sun. However, the most powerful of the wakan beings is Nagk Tanka, the Great Spirit who is also Taku Skanskan. Taku Skanskan signifies the Blue, in other words, the Sky. . . . Mankind is permitted to pray to the wakan beings. If their prayer is directed to all the good wakan beings, they should pray to Wakan Tanka; but if the prayer is offered to only one of these beings, then the one addressed should be named. . . . Wakan Tanka is like sixteen different persons; but each person is kan. Therefore, they are only the same as one.

5.4 THE ORIGIN OF DEATH

Stories about **Coyote** are found among many Plains Indians including the Caddo, who moved from the Red River section of Louisiana to the southern Plains

From J. R. Walker, *The Sun Dance and Other Ceremonies of the Oglala Division of the Teton Dakota.* American Museum of Natural History, Anthropological Papers, vol. XVI, part II (1917), pp. 152–153.

area. They were a leading tribe in the Caddo Confederacy, which included the Kichai, Wischita, Tawakoni, and Waco. The Caddos were descended from the natives who once made up a rich and prosperous Mississippian culture with lush farmlands and major urban centers. The Spanish pillaged these urban centers in the sixteenth century, destroying much of the Caddoan culture.

The Caddo did not fair well in their contact with the descendants of other European cultures either. Between 1845 and 1861, Texas renegade soldiers and land-hungry settlers virtually eradicated the Caddo. Some Caddo stories have managed to survive, among them the following fine representative of a group of stories sometimes referred to as the trickster cycle. As mentioned earlier, trickster figures are culture heroes as well as creator figures. They usually perform lesser creative tasks, such as the founding of religious and cultural institutions, or make rather ambiguous contributions to the creation such as the introduction of death.

Coyote and the Origin of Death
A Story of the Caddo

READING QUESTIONS

1. How does death originate?
2. What kinds of lessons might Coyote's actions teach?

In the beginning of this world there was no such thing as death. Every one continued to live until there were so many people that there was not room for any more on the earth. The chiefs held a council to determine what to do. One man arose and said that he thought it would be a good plan to have the people die and be gone for a little while, and then to return. As soon as he sat down Coyote jumped up and said that he thought that people ought to die forever, for this little world was not large enough to hold all of the people, and if the people who

From George A. Dorsey, *Traditions of the Caddo* (Washington, D.C.: Publications of the Carnegie Institution of Washington, no. 41, 1905), pp. 15–16.

died came back to life there would not be food enough for all. All of the other men objected, saying that they did not want their friends and relatives to die and be gone forever, for then people would grieve and worry and there would not be any happiness in the world. All except Coyote decided to have the people die and be gone for a little while, and then to come back to life.

The medicine-men built a large grass house facing the east, and when they had completed it they called all of the men of the tribe together and told them that they had decided to have the people who died come to the medicine-house and there be restored to life. The chief medicine-man said that he would put a large white and black eagle feather on top of the grass house, and that when the feather became bloody and fell over, the people would know that someone had died. Then all of the medicine-men were to come to the grass house and sing. They would sing a song that would call the spirit of the dead to the grass house, and when the spirit came they would cause it to assume the form that it had while living, and then they would restore it to life again. All of the people were glad when the medicine-men announced these rules about death, for they were anxious for the dead to be restored to life and come again to live with them.

After a time they saw the eagle feather turn bloody and fall, and so they knew that someone had died. The medicine-men assembled in the grass house and sang, as they had promised that they would, for the spirit of the dead to come to them. In about ten days a whirlwind blew from the west, circled about the grass house, and finally entered through the entrance in the east. From the whirlwind appeared a handsome young man who had been murdered by another tribe. All of the people saw him and rejoiced except Coyote, who was displeased because his rules about dead were not carried out. In a short time the feather became bloody and fell again. Coyote saw it and at once went to the grass house. He took his seat near the door, and there sat with the singers for many days, and when at last he heard the whirlwind coming he slipped near the door, and as the whirlwind circled about the house and was about to enter, he closed the door. The spirit in the whirlwind, finding the door closed, whirled on by. Death forever was then introduced, and people from that time on grieved about the dead and were unhappy. Now whenever any one meets a whirlwind or hears the wind whistle he says: "There is some one wandering about." Ever since Coyote closed the door the spirits of the dead have wandered over the earth, trying to find some place to go, until at last they find the road to spirit land.

Coyote jumped up and ran away and never came back, for when he saw what he had done he was afraid. Ever after that he ran from one place to another, always looking back over first one shoulder and then over the other, to see if any one was pursuing him, and ever since then he has been starving, for no one will give him anything to eat.

5.5 RITUAL DANCING AND SINGING

It has been said that Native American religion is not so much a matter of believing as it is a matter of dancing. While Native Americans clearly have beliefs, it is in ritual dancing and singing that those beliefs come alive. The image of Native Americans dancing and chanting is still a very strong one, and most people have heard of the war dance, the rain dance, the corn dance, and the sun dance. Singing, drumming, and dancing are sources of power that unite individuals into a community through the coordination of sound and movement. Participants call on the powers of spirits to animate the dance, enter the body, and make sacred a space. One cannot go to a contemporary powwow (originally a Lenape [Delaware] word meaning "one who dreams") without sensing the importance of dancing, drumming, and singing to Native American life.

Sun Dance is a generic term used to refer to a rich complex of rituals, prayers, songs, dances, and ceremonies with specific variations relating to more than thirty distinct tribal groups. The name for the ritual varies considerably. The Shoshoni and Crow refer to it as the Thirst Lodge while the Cheyenne call it the Medicine Lodge.

Exactly where the Sun Dance started is unknown. It reflects shamanistic elements, and there are parallels to New Year rites among the Tunguzic people of Siberia. The U.S. government banned the Sun Dance in 1881 but relented in 1934. In modified forms, it has made a recent comeback as part of the Pan-Indian revitalization movement.

Among the Oglala Sioux (see Reading 5.3 for background), there is a sacred story that tells how, during a period of famine, **White Buffalo Calf Woman** appeared and gave them seven major rituals integrated around the symbolism of the pipe. These seven rituals are the sweat lodge (for purification), the vision quest, ghost-keeping (a vigil for departed relatives), a ritual to make strangers relatives (a sort of "blood-brother" rite), a girl's puberty rite, a religious ball game, and the Sun Dance.

The Sun Dance is the most well known of these rituals. It is called the "sun-gazing dance" by the Oglala and is the only calendrical ceremonial (usually celebrated once a year, in June) among the Oglala. It is filled with complex and detailed symbolism. At the heart of the traditional ceremony are four types of sacrifice: sun-gazing all day; piercing the breasts with skewers attached to the central pole that symbolizes the **World Tree,** a symbolic vertical axis of the universe connecting earth and sky; piercing the breasts and the back with skewers attached to rawhide ropes and hanging suspended from four posts (representing the four directions); and piercing the back with skewers attached to thongs connected to buffalo skulls that are dragged around the dance area. Those who select the latter three types of sacrifice dance until the flesh is torn through.

What follows is a remarkable description by Thomas Tyon, an Oglala Sioux. I have omitted some of the complex, detailed descriptions of selecting and cutting the wakan tree. This activity, however, is vital. If the wakan tree is not correctly selected, the power of the dance will be decreased. It is clear from Tyon's full account that careful attention to detail and doing things properly is of paramount importance.

⧯

THOMAS TYON

The Sun Dance

READING QUESTIONS

1. Select two or three symbols in the Sun Dance, and state what you think they mean. How would you find out what they really do mean?
2. What do you think the functions of the Sun Dance are? Support your answer with evidence from the description.

Reprinted from *Lakota Belief and Ritual*, by James R. Walker, edited by Raymond J. DeMallie and Elaine A. Jahner, pp. 176–180, by permission of the University of Nebraska Press. Copyright © 1980, 1991 by the University of Nebraska Press. Notes omitted.

If a man's child is very sick, or his wife, or if enemies shoot at him in a fight and he fears very much, yet he survives and is not killed, in such case he may vow the Sun Dance. Hence on account of such vows, they seek a good man, one without offense who knows the complete ceremony. The man who is to dance the Sun Dance bears a pipe, and at sunrise he goes and extends the pipe and prays for that which he desires. When he is finished, the man, from then on, proceeds very carefully. In the days to come, the one who is to dance the Sun Dance should always try to do what is proper. . . . The leader of the Sun Dancers, along with the people living about, fills a pipe and carries it in procession on foot. And they select a place for the camp circle so that all may come together properly in camp and do all things properly.

Now the leader of the Sun Dancers erects a tipi in the middle of the camp circle for them and inside the tipi he covers the floor well with sage. The man who will dance the Sun Dance now makes a sweat bath for himself in a formal way and cleanses himself. . . .

Well now, the people all camp in a big formal camp circle, and then the Sun Dancers will properly observe the rules made for them. No one laughs in the tipi and they regard everything within as *wakan* [sacred, powerful, spiritual]. Also, outside, around the tipi, they spread a blanket of tree leaves. They make a good place inside. They place a buffalo bull head inside. They place a pipe there also. The pipe belongs to the leader. Well, these men dress themselves as follows. They fold blue blankets around themselves and they also use scarlet blankets for skirts. Then the men repeatedly paint themselves red. They wear twisted sage around their head; they have buffalo hair tied on both wrists and on both ankles. They also have the same made of rabbit skin. Also they make a hoop covered with otter skin and they wear an otter skin cape.

Well, having finished these things properly, now during the nights, they feast. An old man cries out for those men who are skillful singers to assemble there; women also go. They sit in the tipi and they make no fire and sing. . . . Well now, they feast each night for four nights and [in this way] four days pass and then those who are to seek the *wakan* tree get busy with their work.

Now the men who are leaders decide how to divide up the work agreeably. And now the beloved children are gathered together; they assemble them, and they command them to go to seek the *wakan* tree. . . .

. . . Now the entire people go to bring the *wakan* tree. Now they go there together. When they arrive at the *wakan* tree, a holy man again stands there and talks. Then he sings. During this time all the people stand very quietly. Then the men who are leaders gather the beloved children together again. Again the holy man talks there, and again he sings. And then he stands and looks toward the four winds and now he stands by the *wakan* tree holding an ax and in that place he talks again, and he pretends to strike the *wakan* tree three times and the fourth time he strikes it. Then he stops striking with the ax. Therefore the leaders now meditate. . . .

They dance the White Owners dance (*Ska yuha wacipi*). At this time, those who choose to give to them make many presents to the children one by one in a line, and when they have finished there, then they choose a good woman and she alone cuts down the *wakan* tree and completely separates the branches from it. And when they have completely finished this, they pick some very good men who have never done anything bad. And those will bear the *wakan* tree as they go, returning to camp. . . .

Well now, the place where the sacred pole is has been made *wakan*; no one goes near that place. Now again the holy man goes there and commands them to bring the offerings. The *wakan* tree is forked. The top of the tree is towards where the sun goes down. First are the stems of chokecherry bushes that have no leaves and then the fat of a ruminant's heart and then red clay and then the fat of a buffalo loin, and a wooden rod, the stem of a chokecherry bush completely peeled, thrust into the buffalo loin. They mix the red clay in one of a pair of parfleches. They paint red the entire green bark of the forks. They mix Pawnee and common tobacco and put it on, and a feather decorated with red-dyed porcupine quills down the middle. Then they wrap the chokecherry stems in a bundle. And now they put them in the forks of the *wakan* tree.

Now all the people stand respectfully and quietly. They make an image of a man of rawhide and paint it entirely red. They place a plume on the head completely reddened. And they also make an image of a buffalo and paint it entirely black. They tie on the pole two small thongs so they will hang down from it. Now they carefully push upright the *wakan* tree, the forked tree. Now they place it erect and the people all shout together excitedly. Then all the women sing. At the top of the tree they tie a red blanket and then they paint the *wakan* tree on the sides of the four winds. Then the women raise the tremolo (*ongna kical*).

Well now, the entire people move about very excitedly and they set up the Sun Dance lodge. When they finish the lodge, a man again proclaims in a loud voice. Now all the young men paint themselves red. Now they will have the ground-smoothing dance. . . .

Well now, when they come to the place of the Sun Dance they run excitedly around the lodge. And now they go within the lodge. Within the lodge they dance around firing guns. They shoot both the image of the man and the image of the buffalo. There is the song for the dance. Then there is a song for the *wasicunpi* [guardian spirits]. Now they come outside altogether, moving quietly. Now those who will dance the Sun Dance separate and the Sun Dancers go together into the tipi.

Now they have finished the lodge for the Sun Dance so they come around the lodge praying. Now they stand at the entrance of the lodge. They go to the *catku* [place of honor]. The leader of the Sun Dance goes first, formally bearing the buffalo head. Bearing it to the *catku*, he stands there. He feigns four times to lay it down and then lays it down. And again they feign laying their hands on it three times and the fourth time they really lay their hands on it formally and then take them away. They all sit at the *catku*. These men will sing but they will not use a drum. A dried buffalo hide is used for the singers. They use quite a long wooden rod with a ruminant's tail tied on the end to beat the dried buffalo hide. And again they sing a song. And then they dance all around the lodge. They sing a song. Well, from now on they dance throughout the night. And thus the day passes.

So now the leader of all the Sun Dancers prepares the ground. At first he stands facing the west. He talks. Then the people stand looking toward him and say, "We wish you life." And with an ax he feigns three times to strike the ground and the fourth time he strikes it. And then in the same manner he strikes towards the east. And then he strikes the middle of the ground. Well now, he digs the ground and pulverizes it. Now he replaces all the earth and makes a star at the center of it. And there he sprinkles Pawnee tobacco and red clay. And then he erects on this pulverized earth a pipe and a rod of chokecherry stem completely painted blue. This pipe is formally filled with tobacco. And then he places the pipe on a dried buffalo chip.

Well now, the sun is at the meridian, so they will now mark the Sun Dancers. So they first take two braided thongs and approach the *wakan* tree and then tie them to the *wakan* tree so that they will hang suspended from it. And now when the sun is at the meridian the holy man again sings. Men, for the sake of the people, give names to the children. As long as they are Sun Dancing, they run to give away presents.

The men drink no water while they dance and they do not eat. They will compose and sing songs on this day. While dancing in the circle they sing.

Well now, the ceremony is completed and the people disperse widely. All go to whatever place they wish. All the Sun Dancers sound a large whistle while dancing and look at the sun as it moves (*hinapa*). And the words of the songs for the dance are such as are appropriate. If they wish for many buffalo, they will sing of them; if victory, sing of it; and if they wish to bring good weather, they will sing of it.

5.6 VISIONS

Visions play an important role in Native American religions. The **vision quest** was a widely practiced ritual, and the trance experiences of the **shamans** have always been particularly valued because of the benefits, often in the form of healing, to the community.

Most visions and trance states were induced by dancing, drumming, peyote use, fasting, isolation, and other means. These states often involved encounters with sacred beings and marvelous travel. Some visions occurred spontaneously and unexpectedly, but they were no less important.

The use of peyote, a small spineless psychotropic cactus from the Rio Grande area, has stirred considerable controversy. Peyote is a hallucinogen, and both state and federal governments have sought to ban its use even though it has been used in religious vision quests for centuries. In 1918 the Native American Church was incorporated in an effort to retain legal protection under the First Amendment to use peyote as a sacrament. This has not been entirely effective, however, and the religious right to use peyote is still hotly contested. This issue raises questions about the limits of tolerance discussed in chapter 1.

Not all visions involved the use of psychotropic plants. In 1873 a young man named **Black Elk** (1863–1950) of the Oglala Lakota Sioux had a great vision. During his youth the sacred myths, legends, and rituals of the Lakota were still very much alive, but by the time he reached adulthood, white civilization had destroyed that world. Like so many other Native Americans, Black Elk had to adjust to the white world. He converted to Roman Catholicism, assumed the name Nicholas, and put aside the "old ways." The old Lakota religion, however, lived on in him, and eventually he came to see that he had been given a sacred duty in his youth to transmit the "old ways" to a new generation.

John G. Neihardt interviewed Black Elk and immortalized his teachings in two important books: *Black Elk Speaks* (1932) and *When the Tree Flowered* (1951). In these books, Neihardt provides a literary interpretation of what Black Elk taught him. Both of these books, but especially the first, have had a major impact on the revival of traditional ways among contemporary Native Americans.

In 1984 Raymond J. DeMallie published the stenographic notes on which Neihardt's books were based. These notes provide a fuller and more accurate record of what Black Elk said to Neihardt. Central to this material is Black Elk's account of his great vision. DeMallie divides Black Elk's vision into eleven parts. Three of these eleven parts are included below.

❧✕❧

BLACK ELK

The Great Vision

READING QUESTIONS

1. What role does the bay horse play in the first part of the vision?
2. What is the significance of going to the center of the earth and receiving the daybreak star herb?
3. What do you think Black Elk's vision means?
4. What do you think is the most important part of the vision as recorded here? Why?

BLACK ELK FALLS ILL

When I was nine years old, many Pawnees got killed and the camp was now going toward the Rocky Mountains. I was now able to shoot a prairie chicken, a grouse, and other things quite well. I was also training in slinging the mud at this time.

Close to the Crow camp on the Little Big Horn I was riding along and I heard something calling me again. Just before we got to Greasy Grass Creek [the Little Big Horn], they camped again for the night. There was a man by the name of Man Hip who invited me for supper. While eating I heard a voice. I heard someone say,

Reprinted from *The Sixth Grandfather: Black Elk's Teachings Given to John G. Neihardt*, edited by Raymond J. DeMallie, pp. 111–115, 133–135, by permission of the University of Nebraska Press. Copyright © 1984 by University of Nebraska Press. Footnotes omitted.

"It is time, now they are calling you." I knew then that I was called upon by the spirits so I thought I'd just go where they wanted me to. As I came out of the tent both of my thighs hurt me.

The next morning [*they broke camp and*] I started out with some others on horseback. We stopped at a creek to get a drink. When I got off my horse I crumbled down, helpless, and I couldn't walk. The boys helped me up and when the camp camped again, I was very sick. They went on, taking me to the Sioux band camp and I was still pretty sick. Both my legs and arms were swollen badly and even my face. This all came suddenly.

THE TWO MEN TAKE BLACK ELK UP INTO THE CLOUDS

As I lay in the tipi I could see through the tipi the same two men whom I saw before and they were coming from the clouds. Then I recognized them as the same men I had seen before in my first vision. They came and stood off aways from me and stopped, saying: "Hurry up, your grandfather is calling you." When they started back I got up and started to follow them. Just as I got out of the tipi I could see the two men going back into the clouds and there was a small cloud coming down toward me at the same time, which stood before me. I got on top of the cloud and was raised up, following the two men, and when I looked back, I saw my father and mother looking at me. When I looked back I felt sorry that I was leaving them.

BLACK ELK IS SHOWN THE HORSES OF THE FOUR DIRECTIONS

I followed those men on up into the clouds and they showed me a vision of a bay horse standing there in the middle of the clouds. One of the men said: "Behold him, the horse who has four legs, you shall see." I stood there and looked at the horse and it began to speak. It said: "Behold me; my life history you shall see. Furthermore, behold them, those where the sun goes down, their lives' history you shall see."

I looked over there and saw twelve black horses toward the west, where the sun goes down. All the horses had on their necks necklaces of buffalo hoofs. [*I saw above the twelve head of horses birds.*] I was very scared of those twelve head of horses because I could see the light[ning] and thunder around them.

Then they showed me twelve white horses with necklaces of elks' teeth and said: "Behold them, those who are where the giant lives [the north]." Then I saw some white geese flying around over the horses.

Then I turned around toward the east, where the sun shines continually. The men said: "Behold them, those where the sun shines continually." I saw twelve head of horses, all sorrels [*and these sorrels had horns and there were some eagles flying above the sorrels*].

Then I turned to the place where you always face, the south, and saw twelve head of buckskin horses. They said: "Behold him, those where you always face." These horses had horns.

[*At the beginning of the vision they were all horses, only two* (sets) *had necklaces* (the blacks and the whites) *and two had horns* (the sorrels and the buckskins).]

When I had seen it all, the bay horse said to me: "Your grandfathers are having a council, these shall take you; so take courage." Then these horses went into formation of twelve abreast in four lines—blacks, whites, sorrels, buckskins. As they stood, the bay horse looked to the west and neighed. I looked over there and saw great clouds of horses in all colors and they all neighed back to this horse and it sounded like thunder. Then the horse neighed toward the north and the horses came through there and neighed back again. These horses were in all colors also. Then the bay looked toward the east and he neighed and some more horses neighed back. The bay looked southward and neighed and the horses neighed back to him from there.

The bay horse said to me: "Behold them, your horses come dancing." I looked around and saw millions of horses circling around me—a sky full of horses. Then the bay horse said: "Make haste." The horse began to go beside me and the forty-eight horses followed us. I looked around and all the horses that were running changed into buffalo, elk, and all kinds of animals and fowls and they all went back to the four quarters.

BLACK ELK IS TAKEN TO THE CENTER OF THE EARTH AND RECEIVES THE DAYBREAK STAR HERB

[The] western black spirit said: "Behold this day, for this day is yours." [*I will have the power to shed many happy days on people, they tell me.*] "Take courage, for we shall take you to the center of the earth." They [the spirits] said: "Behold the center of the earth for we are taking you there." As I looked I could see great mountains with rocks and forests on them. I could see all colors of light flashing out of the mountains toward the four quarters. Then they took me on top of a high mountain where I could see all over the earth. Then they told me to take courage for they were taking me to the center of the earth. All the sixteen riders of the four quarters were with me going to the center of the earth and also this man by the name of One Side.

We were facing the east and I noticed something queer and found out that it was two men coming from the east and they had wings. On each one's breast was a bright star. The two men came and stood right in front of us and the west black spirit said: "Behold them, for you shall depend upon them." Then as we stood there the daybreak star stood between the two men from the east. There was a little star beside the daybreak star also. They had an herb in their hands and they gave it to me, saying: "Behold this; with this on earth you shall undertake anything and accomplish it." As they presented the herb to me they told me to drop it on earth and when it hit the earth it took root and grew and flowered. You could see a ray of light coming up from the flower, reaching the heavens, and all the creatures of the universe saw this light. (Herbs used by Black Elk are in four colors —yellow, blue, red, white flowers all on one bush. The four-colored flowers represent the four quarters of the earth. This herb is called daybreak star herb.)

[The] western black spirit said: "Behold all over the universe." As I looked around I could see the country full of sickness and in need of help. This was the future and I was going to cure these people. On the east and north people were rejoicing, and on the south and west they were sick and there was a cloud over them. They said: "Behold them who need help. You shall make them over in the future." After a while I noticed the cloud over the people was a white one and it was probably the white people coming.

The western black spirit sang:

Here and there may you behold. (twice)
All may you behold.
Here and there may you behold. (twice)

They had taken me all over the world and showed me all the powers. They took me to the center of the earth and to the top of the peak they took me to review it all. This last song means that I have already seen it. I was to see the bad and the good. I was to see what is good for humans and what is not good for humans.

5.7 SHAMANS AND FEMININE POWER

The status of women among Native American groups varied a great deal. In some they were little more than slaves, belonging first to their father then, after marriage, to their husband. In other groups they enjoyed much higher status often controlling the line of inheritance and playing major roles in religious and other activities.

Women often play a decisive role in the sacred stories. We have already seen one example, the important role Spider Woman plays in the Hopi creation story, in an earlier reading. Another example comes from the Far North. It is a story of the origin of sea animals and the mistress of the deep, **Sedna,** who plays a major role in shamanic rites. When taboos are transgressed by anyone in the community, Sedna's hair becomes tangled and she withholds animals from hunters. The shaman's job is to enter into trance, descend to Sedna's home in the sea, and brush her hair so that she will free the animals again and the people will have food.

This story is told by the Central Inuit (Eskimos) whose life depends on hunting. Hunting is a dangerous activity that involves braving the sea, its storms, bitter cold, and the harm large mammals such as whales can do to the hunters. Shamans helped reduce the dangers of the hunt and ensured a food supply for the people. Thus, as in most Arctic hunting societies, shamanism plays a significant role in the life of the people. Both health and food depend on the shamans and their skills in communicating with the spirits (*inua*) that control so much of the Inuit environment.

The Inuit and their kinsmen the Aleut are excellent artists and artisans, taking great pride in decorating their hunting and fishing gear made of bone and walrus-tooth ivory. Their skin-covered kayaks are the most seaworthy boats of their kind.

Today most Inuit are Christian. However, the "old ways" have not entirely died out and, despite television and modern technology, the Inuit's special feeling of kinship with the animals lives on.

Franz Boas transcribed the story of Sedna, part of which appears on the following page, in the late nineteenth century. Sedna probably means "the one down there," and she is an important *master inua* because she controls the sea animals.

INUIT

Sedna

READING QUESTIONS

1. What do you think Sedna represents?
2. Is there anything of significance in the way the sea animals come into existence? If so, what?

Once upon a time there lived on a solitary shore an Inung with his daughter Sedna. His wife had been dead for some time and the two led a quiet life. Sedna grew up to be a handsome girl and the youths came from all around to sue for her hand, but none of them could touch her proud heart. Finally, at the breaking up of the ice in the spring a fulmar flew from over the ice and wooed Sedna with enticing song. "Come to me," it said; "come into the land of the birds, where there is never hunger, where my tent is made of the most beautiful skins. You shall rest on soft bearskins. My fellows, the fulmars, shall bring you all your heart may desire; their feathers shall clothe you; your lamp shall always be filled with oil, your pot with meat." Sedna could not long resist such wooing and they went together over the vast sea. When at last they reached the country of the fulmar, after a long and hard journey, Sedna discovered that her spouse had shamefully deceived her. Her new home was not built of beautiful pelts, but was covered with wretched fishskins, full of holes, that gave free entrance to wind and snow. Instead of soft reindeer skins her bed was made of hard walrus hides and she had to live on miserable fish, which the birds brought her. Too soon she discovered that she had thrown away her opportunities when in her foolish pride she had rejected the Inuit youth. In her woe she sang: "Aja. O father, if you knew how wretched I am you would come to me and we would hurry away in your boat over the waters. The birds look unkindly upon me the stranger; cold winds roar about my bed; they give me but miserable food. O come and take me back home. Aja."

When a year had passed and the sea was again stirred by warmer winds, the father left his country to visit Sedna. His daughter greeted him joyfully and besought

him to take her back home. The father, hearing of the outrages wrought upon his daughter, determined upon revenge. He killed the fulmar, took Sedna into his boat, and they quickly left the country which had brought so much sorrow to Sedna. When the other fulmars came home and found their companion dead and his wife gone, they all flew away in search of the fugitives. They were very sad over the death of their poor murdered comrade and continue to mourn and cry until this day.

Having flown a short distance they discerned the boat and stirred up a heavy storm. The sea rose in immense waves that threatened the pair with destruction. In this mortal peril the father determined to offer Sedna to the birds and flung her overboard. She clung to the edge of the boat with a death grip. The cruel father then took a knife and cut off the first joints of her fingers. Falling into the sea they were transformed into whales, the nails turning into whalebone. Sedna holding on to the boat more tightly, the second finger joints fell under the sharp knife and swam away as seals; when the father cut off the stumps of the fingers they became ground seals.

Meantime the storm subsided, for the fulmars thought Sedna was drowned. The father then allowed her to come into the boat. But from that time she cherished a deadly hatred against him and swore bitter revenge. After they got ashore, she called her dogs and let them gnaw off the feet and hands of her father while he was asleep. Upon this he cursed himself, his daughter, and the dogs which had maimed him; whereupon the earth opened and swallowed the hut, the father, the daughter, and the dogs. They have since lived in the land of Adlivun, of which Sedna is the mistress.

From Franz Boas, *The Central Eskimo* (Washington, D.C.: Bureau of American Ethnology, Annual Report no. 6, 1888), pp. 583–585.

CONTEMPORARY SCHOLARSHIP

The two examples of recent scholarship on Native American religions that follow use different methods. The first employs literary methods and focuses on the importance of language and storytelling in Native American culture and religion. The religion of Native Americans lives not only in singing and dancing but in stories as well. To understand such a religion, one must appreciate the power of words.

The second example uses the methods of ethnohistory to illuminate the spiritual values of Native American religion. As you read this scholarly sample, keep in mind the role that a definition of religion plays in scholarship. How we conceptualize religion (see chapter 2) profoundly affects the way we evaluate a religion.

Interestingly, both examples combine an insider's with an outsider's viewpoint (see chapter 1). One gets the impression from both essays that, in the final analysis, the insider's viewpoint is what matters most when it comes to understanding and appreciating Native American religions.

5.8 LAND ETHIC AND LANGUAGE

N. Scott Momaday is a celebrated Kiowa writer who approaches the study of Native American religions from a literary point of view. In an address to the First Convocation of American Indian Scholars in 1970, he spoke about how important Native American culture is for the development of a **land ethic** and why storytelling is so significant to the Native American. The following selection comes from this address.

N. SCOTT MOMADAY

The Man Made of Words

READING QUESTIONS

1. What does Momaday mean by a land ethic, and why is it so important?
2. Why do you think Momaday makes the "absolute assumption" that we "are what we imagine"?
3. Does Momaday's explication of the importance of storytelling help you appreciate the Native American stories you have just read? Why or why not?

I want to try to put several different ideas together this morning. And in the process, I hope to indicate something about the nature of the relationship between language and experience. It seems to me that in a certain sense we are all made of words; that our most essential being consists in language. It is the element in which we

From N. Scott Momaday, "The Man Made of Words," in *Indian Voices: The First Convocation of American Indian Scholars* (San Francisco: The Indian Historian Press, 1970), pp. 49–62. Reprinted by permission.

think and dream and act, in which we live our daily lives. There is no way in which we can exist apart from the morality of a verbal dimension.

In one of the discussions yesterday the question "What is an American Indian?" was raised.

The answer of course is that an Indian is an idea which a given man has of himself. And it is a moral idea, for it accounts for the way in which he reacts to other men and to the world in general. And that idea, in order to be realized completely, has to be expressed.

I want to say some things then about this moral and verbal dimension in which we live. I want to say something about such things as ecology and storytelling and the imagination. Let me tell you a story:

One night a strange thing happened. I had written the greater part of *The Way to Rainy Mountain*—all of it, in fact, except the epilogue. I had set down the last of the old Kiowa tales, and I had composed both the historical and the autobiographical commentaries for it. I had the sense of being out of breath, of having said what it was in me to say on that subject. The manuscript lay before me in the bright light, small, to be sure, but complete; or nearly so. I had written the second of the two poems in which that book is framed. I had uttered the last word, as it were. And yet a whole, penultimate piece was missing. I began once again to write.

During the first hours after midnight on the morning of November 13, 1833, it seemed that the world was coming to an end. Suddenly the stillness of the night was broken; there were brilliant flashes of light in the sky, light of such intensity that people were awakened by it. With the speed and density of a driving rain, stars were falling in the universe. Some were brighter than Venus; one was said to be as large as the moon. I went on to say that that event, the falling of the stars on North America, that explosion of meteors which occurred 137 years ago, is among the earliest entries in the Kiowa calendars. So deeply impressed upon the imagination of the Kiowas is that old phenomenon that it is remembered still; it has become a part of the racial memory.

"The living memory," I wrote, "and the verbal tradition which transcends it, were brought together for me once and for all in the person of Ko-sahn." It seemed eminently right for me to deal, after all, with that old woman. Ko-sahn is among the most venerable people I have ever known. She spoke and sang to me one summer afternoon in Oklahoma. It was like a dream. When I was born she was already old: she was a grown woman when my grandparents came into the world. She sat perfectly still, folded over on herself. It did not seem possible that so many years—a century of years—could be so compacted and distilled. Her voice shuddered, but it did not fail. Her songs were sad. An old whimsy, a delight in language and in remembrance, shone in her one good eye. She conjured up the past, imagining perfectly the long continuity of her being. She imagined the lovely young girl, wild and vital, she had been. She imagined the Sun Dance:

There was an old, old woman. She had something on her back. The boys went out to see. The old woman had a bag full of earth on her back. It was a certain kind of sandy earth. That is what they must have in the lodge. The dancers must dance upon the sandy earth. The old woman held a digging tool in her hand. She turned towards the south and pointed with her lips. It was like a kiss. . . .

Once in his life a man ought to concentrate his mind upon the remembered earth, I believe. He ought to give himself up to a particular landscape in his experience, to look at it from as many angles as he can, to wonder about it, to dwell upon it. He ought to imagine that he touches it with his hands at every season and listens to the sounds that are made upon it. He ought to imagine the creatures that are there and all the faintest motions in the wind. He ought to recollect the glare of noon and all the colors of the dawn and dusk.

The Wichita Mountains rise out of the Southern Plains in a long crooked line that runs from east to west. The mountains are made of red earth, and of rock that is neither red nor blue but some very rare admixture of the two like the feathers of certain birds. They are not so high and mighty as the mountains of the Far West, and they bear a different relationship to the land around them. One does not imagine that they are distinctive in themselves, or indeed that they exist apart from the plain in any sense. If you try to think of them in the abstract, they lose the look of mountains. They are preeminently an expression of the larger landscape, more perfectly organic than one can easily imagine. To behold these mountains from the plain is one thing; to see the plain from the mountains is something else. I have stood on the top of Mt. Scott and seen the earth below, bending out into the whole circle of the sky. The wind runs always close upon the slopes, and there are times when you can hear the rush of it like water in the ravines.

Here is the hub of an old commerce. A hundred years ago the Kiowas and Comanches journeyed outward from the Wichitas in every direction, seeking after mischief and medicine, horses and hostages. Sometimes they went away for years, but they always returned, for the land had got hold of them. It is a consecrated place, and even now there is something of the wilderness about it. There is a game preserve in the hills. Animals graze away in the open meadows or, closer by, keep to the shadows of the groves: antelope and deer, longhorn

and buffalo. It was here, the Kiowas say, that the first buffalo came into the world.

The yellow grassy knoll that is called Rainy Mountain lies a short distance to the north and west. There, on the west side, is the ruin of an old school where my grandmother went as a wild young girl in blanket and braids to learn of numbers and of names in English. And there she is buried.

Most is your name the name of this dark stone.
Deranged in death, the mind to be inheres
Forever in the nominal unknown,
Who listens here and now to hear your name.
The early sun, red as a hunter's moon,
Runs in the plain. The mountain burns and shines;
And silence is the long approach of noon
Upon the shadow that your name defines—
And death this cold, black density of stone.

I am interested in the way that a man looks at a given landscape and takes possession of it in his blood and brain. For this happens, I am certain, in the ordinary motion of life. None of us lives apart from the land entirely; such an isolation is unimaginable. We have sooner or later to come to terms with the world around us— and I mean especially the physical world, not only as it is revealed to us immediately through our senses, but also as it is perceived more truly in the long turn of seasons and of years. And we must come to moral terms. There is no alternative, I believe, if we are to realize and maintain our humanity; for our humanity must consist in part in the ethical as well as the practical ideal of preservation. And particularly here and now is that true. We Americans need now more than ever before—and indeed more than we know—to imagine who and what we are with respect to the earth and sky. I am talking about an act of the imagination essentially, and the concept of an American land ethic.

It is no doubt more difficult to imagine in 1970 the landscape of America as it was in, say, 1900. Our whole experience as a nation in this century has been a repudiation of the pastoral ideal which informs so much of the art and literature of the nineteenth century. One effect of the Technological Revolution has been to uproot us from the soil. We have become disoriented, I believe; we have suffered a kind of psychic dislocation of ourselves in time and space. We may be perfectly sure of where we are in relation to the supermarket and the next coffee break, but I doubt that any of us knows where he is in relation to the stars and to the solstices. Our sense of the natural order has become dull and unreliable. Like the wilderness itself, our sphere of instinct has diminished in proportion as we have failed to imagine truly what it is. And yet I believe that it is possible to formulate an ethical idea of the land—a notion of what it is and must be in our daily lives—and I believe moreover that it is absolutely necessary to do so.

It would seem on the surface of things that a land ethic is something that is alien to, or at least dormant in, most Americans. Most of us in general have developed an attitude of indifference toward the land. In terms of my own experience, it is difficult to see how such an attitude could ever have come about.

Ko-sahn could remember where my grandmother was born. "It was just there," she said, pointing to a tree, and the tree was like a hundred others that grew up in the broad depression of the Washita River. I could see nothing to indicate that anyone had ever been there, spoken so much as a word, or touched the tips of his fingers to the tree. But in her memory Ko-sahn could see the child. I think she must have remembered my grandmother's voice, for she seemed for a long moment to listen and to hear. There was a still, heavy heat upon that place; I had the sense that ghosts were gathering there.

And in the racial memory, Ko-sahn had seen the falling stars. For her there was no distinction between the individual and the racial experience, even as there was none between the mythical and the historical. Both were realized for her in the one memory, and that was of the land. This landscape, in which she had lived for a hundred years, was the common denominator of everything that she knew and would ever know—and her knowledge was profound. Her roots ran deep into the earth, and from those depths she drew strength enough to hold still against all the forces of chance and disorder. And she drew strength enough to hold still against all the forces of change and disorder. And she drew therefrom the sustenance of meaning and of mystery as well. The falling stars were not for Ko-sahn an isolated or accidental phenomenon. She had a great personal investment in that awful commotion of light in the night sky. For it remained to be imagined. She must at last deal with it in words; she must appropriate it to her understanding of the whole universe. And, again, when she spoke of the Sun Dance, it was an essential expression of her relationship to the life of the earth and to the sun and moon.

In Ko-sahn and in her people we have always had the example of a deep, ethical regard for the land. We had better learn from it: Surely that ethic is merely latent in ourselves. It must now be activated, I believe. We Americans must come again to a moral comprehension of the earth and air. We must live according to the principle of a land ethic. The alternative is that we shall not live at all.

Ecology is perhaps the most important subject of our time. I can't think of an issue in which the Indian has more authority or a greater stake. If there is one thing which truly distinguishes him, it is surely his regard of and for the natural world. . . .

If there is any absolute assumption in back of my thoughts tonight, it is this: We are what we imagine. Our very existence consists in our imagination of ourselves. Our best destiny is to imagine, at least, completely, who and what, and *that* we are. The greatest tragedy that can befall us is to go unimagined.

Writing is recorded speech. In order to consider seriously the meaning of language and of literature, we must consider first the meaning of the oral tradition.

By way of suggesting one or two definitions which may be useful to us, let me pose a few basic questions and tentative answers:

1. What is the oral tradition?

The **oral tradition** is that process by which the myths, legends, tales, and lore of a people are formulated, communicated, and preserved in language by word of mouth, as opposed to writing. Or, it is a *collection* of such things.

2. With reference to the matter of oral tradition, what is the relationship between art and reality?

In the context of these remarks, the matter of oral tradition suggests certain particularities of art and reality. Art, for example . . . involves an oral dimension which is based markedly upon such considerations as memorization, intonation, inflection, precision of statement, brevity, rhythm, pace, and dramatic effect. Moreover, myth, legend, and lore, according to our definitions of these terms, imply a separate and distinct order of reality. We are concerned here not so much with an accurate representation of actuality, but with the realization of the imaginative experience.

3. How are we to conceive of language? What are words?

For our purposes, words are audible sounds, invented by man to communicate his thoughts and feelings. Each word has a conceptual content, however slight; and each word communicates associations of feeling. Language is the means by which words proceed to the formulation of meaning and emotional effect.

4. What is the nature of storytelling? What are the purposes and possibilities of that act?

Storytelling is imaginative and creative in nature. It is an act by which man strives to realize his capacity for wonder, meaning and delight. It is also a process in which man invests and preserves himself in the context of ideas. Man tells stories in order to understand his experience, whatever it may be. The possibilities of storytelling are precisely those of understanding the human experience.

5. What is the relationship between what a man is and what he says—or between what he is, and what he thinks he is?

This relationship is both tenuous and complicated. Generally speaking, man has consummate being in language, and there only. The state of human *being* is an idea, an idea which man has of himself. Only when he is embodied in an idea, and the idea is realized in language, can man take possession of himself. In our particular frame of reference, this is to say that man achieves the fullest realization of his humanity in such an art and product of the imagination as literature—and here I use the term "literature" in its broadest sense. This is admittedly a moral view of the question, but literature is itself a moral view, and it is a view of morality.

Now let us return to the falling stars. And let me apply a new angle of vision to that event—let me proceed this time from a slightly different point of view:

In this winter of 1833 the Kiowas were camped on Elm Fork, a branch of the Red River west of the Wichita Mountains. In the preceding summer they had suffered a massacre at the hands of the Osages, and Tai-me, the sacred Sun Dance Doll and most powerful medicine of the tribe, had been stolen. At no time in the history of their migration from the north, and in the evolution of their plains culture, had the Kiowas been more vulnerable to despair. The loss of Tai-me was a deep psychological wound. In the early cold of November 13 there occurred over North America an explosion of meteors. The Kiowas were awakened by the sterile light of falling stars, and they ran out into the false day and were terrified.

The year the stars fell is, as I have said, among the earliest entries in the Kiowa calendars, and it is permanent in the Kiowa mind. There was symbolic meaning in that November sky. With the coming of natural dawn there began a new and darker age for the Kiowa people; the last culture to evolve on this continent began to decline. Within four years of the falling stars the Kiowas signed their first treaty with the government: within twenty, four major epidemics of smallpox and Asiatic cholera destroyed more than half their number; and within scarcely more than a generation their horses were taken from them and the herds of buffalo were slaughtered and left to waste upon the plains.

Do you see what happens when the imagination is superimposed upon the historical event? It becomes a story. The whole piece becomes more deeply invested with meaning. The terrified Kiowas, when they had regained possession of themselves, did indeed imagine that the falling stars were symbolic of their being and their destiny. They accounted for themselves with reference to that awful memory. They appropriated it, recreated it, fashioned it into an image of themselves—imagined it.

Only by means of that act could they bear what happened to them thereafter. No defeat, no humiliation, no suffering was beyond their power to endure, for none of it was meaningless. They could say to themselves, "Yes, it was all meant to be in its turn. The order of the world was broken, it was clear. Even the stars were shaken loose in the night sky." The imagination of meaning was not much, perhaps, but it was all they had, and it was enough to sustain them.

One of my very favorite writers, Isak Dinesen, said this: "All sorrows can be borne if you put them into a story or tell a story about them." . . .

5.9 SPIRITUAL VALUES

Joseph Epes Brown is a distinguished ethnohistorian of Native American religions who is now retired from teaching at the University of Montana. He is best known for his book *The Sacred Pipe: Black Elk's Account of the Seven Rites of the Oglala Sioux* (1953), which was the result of his having lived with Black Elk (Reading 5.6) for eight months.

JOSEPH EPES BROWN

Becoming Part of It

READING QUESTIONS

1. According to Brown, tribal cultures model what a religious tradition truly is. What does he mean by this, and what do you think about this claim?
2. What does Brown mean by interconnectedness and reciprocity? How is the latter concept related to the circle?

From Joseph Epes Brown, "Becoming Part of It," in *I Became Part of It*, edited by D. M. Dooling and Paul Jordan-Smith (New York: Parabola Books, 1989), pp. 10–20. Reprinted by permission of the author.

3. What is the distinctive Native American view of language and arts/crafts?
4. What is the spiritual value of the "guardian spirit quest" and the Sun Dance?
5. How does the sacred pipe represent the "three cumulative possibilities" of all spiritually effective rites?
6. What is **oneness of experience**?
7. Do you think Brown has overstepped the proper bounds of a historian with his evaluative comments about spiritual values of Native American religions? Why or why not?

Although greatly oversimplified and generalized, let me give at least a brief sampling of what I think are some of the core Native American values and perspectives, through which we can perhaps come to relearn a little bit about ourselves and about our own proper spiritual heritage, the hope being that what has been lost can still be rediscovered. Certainly the Native American people themselves, especially the younger ones today, are trying to regain and revitalize their own traditions which may have been lost, or taken from them through a variety of pressures and prejudices. We have, I suggest, in this struggle a model for our own proper quest. What are some of its contours?

Tribal cultures, it seems to me, present a model of what a religious tradition *is;* and this is a basic reality which we have lost sight of. That is, what really is a true religious tradition? What does it encompass, what are its dimensions? These cultures demonstrate how all components of a culture can be interconnected: how the presence of the sacred can permeate all lifeways to such a degree that what we call religion is here integrated into the totality of life and into all of life's activities. Religion here is so pervasive in life that there is probably no Native American language in which there is a term which could be translated as "religion" in the way we understand it. As Peter Nabokov tells us in his book, *Indian Running,* when you track down a seemingly isolated or minimal feature of Indian life, such as running, the whole system opens before your eyes; and this is true because of the interrelatedness of all the components of a genuine tradition. Obviously in such a system life cannot be fragmented, due to that binding and interconnecting thread of the presence of the sacred.

In terms of interconnections, a dominant theme in all Native American cultures is that of relationship, or a series of relationships that are always reaching further and further out; relationships within the immediate family reaching out to the extended family, to the band, outward again to the clan, to the tribal group; and relationships do not stop there but extend out to embrace and relate to the environment; to the land, to the animals, to the plants, and to the clouds, the elements, the heavens, the stars; and ultimately those relationships that people express and live, extend to embrace the entire universe.

In the Plains area, to give an example, one of the most profound rites is that of the smoking of the pipe. In this ritual smoking of the pipe, all who participate are joined in a communal ritual, and when it is finished, everybody who has shared in the smoking of the pipe recites the phrase, in Lakota in this case, "*mitakuye oya-sin*"—"we are all relatives." We *are* all related, because in this rite we have all become one within a mystery that is greater than any of its parts. I shall talk more about the general importance of rituals and ceremonies later.

Associated with relationship there should be mentioned the theme of reciprocity which permeates so many aspects of North American cultures. Put very simply, reciprocity here refers again to that process wherein if you receive or take away you must also give back. This is a living statement of the importance of the cycle permeating all of life. Everything in their world of experience is conceived in terms of such cycles or of the circle; everything comes back upon itself. Black Elk so often said that all the forces of the world work in cycles or circles; the birds build their nests in circular form, the foxes have their dens in circles, the wind in its greatest power moves in a circle, and life is as a circle. I recall once how this reality was beautifully expressed in a living manner, when I noticed how this dignified old man would relate to little children. He would get down on his hands and knees and pretend he was a horse, and the children would squeal with joy on the old man's back. Here there obviously was no generation gap; he was one with the child. I once asked him how it was that he could so relate to the child, and he replied: "I who am an old man am about to return *to* the Great Mysterious" (*Wakan Tanka*, Lakota) "and a young child is a being who has just come *from* the Great Mysterious; so it is that we are very close together." Because of such cyclical understanding, both are very nearly at the same point.

Such attitudes could be spelled out in terms of any number of cultural expressions, but the point I want to draw from this is that we have here an example which contrasts with our own dominant concept of process which is in terms of linearity—the straight line which moves from here to there and onward indefinitely. Indeed, this theme of linearity permeates all aspects of our life. The way we read, for instance, is in lines; we have sayings in our vocabulary that tell us to "Line up!" "Let's get this straight!" Or if we refer to somebody who is a little bit crazy, we make a circular motion alongside our head, by which we indicate the reason is going in circles. There is something here from which we can learn, something about ourselves and our concept of progress, with all the loaded meanings which this term bears.

One must mention also the special nature of Native American languages, which contrasts with our understanding of language and our use of words. In Native languages the understanding is that the meaning *is* in the sound, it *is* in the word; the word is not a symbol for a meaning which has been abstracted out, word and meaning are together in one experience. Thus, to name a being, for example an animal, is actually to conjure up the powers latent in that animal. Added to this is the fact that when we create words we use our breath, and for these people and these traditions breath is associated with the principle of life; breath is life itself. And so if a word is born from this sacred principle of breath, this lends an added sacred dimension to the spoken word. It is because of this special feeling about words that people avoid using sacred personal names, because they contain the power of the beings named, and if you use them too much the power becomes dissipated. So usually one has to refer to a person in a very circuitous manner, or use a term which expresses relationship.

In this context one must also emphasize the positive values that could be attached to non-literacy. I use that term rather than illiteracy, which connotes the *inability* to read and write, which is negative and derogatory. Too often we have branded people as being backward and uncivilized if they are *illiterate*, whereas one can make a strong case for the advantages of growing up and living in a society which is *non-literate*. For in such a society all the lore which is central and sacred to the culture is borne *within* the individual in a living manner; you do not have to go outside of yourself, for all that is essential to life is carried with you, is ever-present. It seems that where you have people who are non-literate in this positive sense, you tend to have a special quality of person, a quality of being that cannot be described—a very different quality from that of the literate person. It has been my experience when among primal peoples in many parts of the world that there is something here that is very special.

Paralleling this primal concept of language, and of the word not as "symbol" but as an immediate event, is the quality of experiencing the visual arts and crafts. I should stress first of all that for primal peoples generally there is no dichotomy between the arts and crafts, in the manner that our art historians insist on, where art is one kind of thing that can be placed on a mantelpiece or hung on the wall, and the craft item is inferior because it is made for utilitarian ends. This seems to me a most artificial distinction and I think it is time that we outgrew it; indeed there is today evidence that we *are* re-

evaluating such prejudiced dichotomies. For why cannot a utilitarian object also be beautiful? All necessary implements, utensils, and tools in Native American life-ways are of technical excellence and are also beautiful. They must be made in special sacred ways, and the materials of the tools and objects made have to be gathered with prayer and offerings. Beauty and truth are here one! When a Pomo basketmaker, for example, goes out to collect the grasses for her basket, she prays to the grasses, she enters into a relationship with them as she gathers, and makes offerings in return for having taken their life. When a woman weaves a basket she will pass the grass between her lips to moisten it, but also to breathe upon it, to give her life breath into the grass and thus give to the basket a special sacred quality that is always present in its use and tangible presence.

Through these few selected examples which have been given, I am suggesting that, where such traditions are still alive and spiritually viable, there tend to be present, within all of life's necessary activities, dimensions and expressions of the sacred. Actions of such quality could therefore be considered to manifest a ritual element in the sense that they tend to *order* life around and toward a Center. In this context, however, one must also speak of those special great rites and ceremonies, many often related to the seasonal cycles, which serve not just to support continuing orientations toward the sacred in everyday activities, but work for the *intensification* of such Presence and experience; such rites may also be the source and origin of new rites, ceremonies, and other sacred expressions through the visual arts, songs, or special dance forms.

One example of a ritual complex which is central to the lives of Plains people is the well-known "vision" or "guardian spirit quest." This ritualized retreat is for the benefit of the individual man and woman, and yet means are present for the eventual sharing of received vision powers or messages with the larger community. After rigorous preparations, which always include the rites of the purifying sweat lodge and instructions by a qualified elder, the candidate goes to a high and remote place with the resolve to fast and pray continually and to suffer through acts of sacrifice and exposure to the elements for a specified number of days. The ordeal is highly ritualized and may involve the establishing of an altar, or the setting out of poles at the center and to the four directions of space. The person may also be instructed to remain within this established space and not to move about casually but to walk only out from the center to each of the poles in turn, always returning to the center. Prayers may be addressed to the powers of the four directions, and one may also use repetitive prayers such as the one the Lakota Black Elk has given us: "Grandfather, Great Mysterious, have pity on me." One may also remain silent, for it has been said that "silence *is* the voice of *Wakan Tanka*, the *Great Mysterious.*" If tired, one may sleep, for dreams of power may come to the candidate in this manner; yet it is understood that the true vision is of greater power than the dream. Often the sacred experience comes in the mysterious appearance of an animal or a winged being, or perhaps in one of the powers of nature. A special message is often communicated to the seeker, and this will serve as a guide and reminder throughout the person's life. After three or four days one returns to camp where a sweat lodge has again been prepared; within this lodge the candidate will explain the vision or dream which will be interpreted by the guiding elder, who will then give instructions as to what should now be accomplished in order to insure the continuity of the participation of the spiritual throughout the person's life. From such experiences have come the "medicine bundles" with rich and complex rites specific to each bundle and their ceremonial opening on special occasions. They have also been the origin of sacred types of art forms, such as the painted shields, or special songs of power, or even the great ritual dances, such as the horse dance, involving four groups of eight horses not representing, but *being* the powers of the four directions of space. It is in this manner that something of the sacred experience which had come to a particular individual is shared by all members of the larger community.

What is remarkable about the rites of the vision quest among the Plains peoples is that it is accomplished not just by special people as is the case in the Arctic, but that every man or woman after the age of puberty is expected to participate either once or even repeatedly throughout his or her life.

What concerns us in this example is not just the detailed pattern of the ritual elements of the quest as such, which can encompass a multitude of very diverse possibilities, but that here we have one sample as a model of traditional ritual structures and acts which must involve initial purification, choice of appropriate site, the defining and delimiting of a special sacred place, and the fixing of a center. Further, ritualized *actions* are prescribed for the participant, which means that participation is not just with the mind, or a part of one's being, but with the totality of who one is. Also provided are means for continuity and development of the sacred experiences received, and the eventual responsibility for sharing something of them with the larger community.

As complement to the individually oriented "vision quest," one could mention the great communal "Sun Dance," referred to in different terms across the Plains groups. For this great complex of solemn rites, ceremonies, fasting, sacred song and dance fulfills not just the particular spiritual needs of the actively participating individuals, but also those of the entire tribal group gathered in circular camp for the occasion. The event is indeed for the welfare of the entire world. These are ceremonies, interspersed with special sacred rites, which celebrate world and life renewal at the time of spring. The ritualized dance forms again involve orientation around and towards a center which is either the sun itself or the cottonwood tree as axis of the world, standing at the center of a circular frame lodge carefully constructed in imitation of the cosmos. The ritual and ceremonial language of the total celebration speaks to and encompasses a plurality of spiritual possibilities at the levels of microcosm, macrocosm, and metacosm. It is believed by many that should the sacrificial rites of this "thirst lodge" be neglected or forgotten, the energy of the world will run out and the cycle in which we are living will close. It is an example to the world that these rites and ceremonies are far from being neglected, for today in ever increasing numbers the people are participating and are finding renewed strength and spiritual resolve.

All spiritually effective rites must accomplish three cumulative possibilities which may be termed purification, expansion—in wholeness or virtue—and identity. A ritual means which embodies these possibilities may be found in the sacred nature and use of the Plains Indian tobacco pipe, the smoking of which constitutes a communion. The shape of the pipe with its stem, bowl or "heart," and foot, is identified with the human person. In purifying the pipe before a ritual smoking there is an analogy to man's own purification; for in concentrating on the hollow of the straight stem leading to the bowl comes the understanding that one's mind should be this straight and pure. In filling the bowl of the pipe a prayer is said for each grain of tobacco in such a manner that everything in the world is mentioned. The filled bowl or the heart of man, in thus containing all possibilities, is then the universe. Finally, the fire which is put to the tobacco is the Presence of the ultimate all-inclusive Principle, *Wakan Tanka*, the "Great Mysterious." In smoking the pipe, through the aid of breath the totality of all creation is absorbed within this ultimate Principle. And since in the pipe there is a grain of tobacco identified with the one who smokes, there is here enacted a sacrificial communion of identity. With this understanding, the phrase "we are all related," recited by the individual or group after the smoking, takes on the deepest possible meaning.

I will sum up by simply saying that in all that I have tried to speak of in such brief fashion, we have expressions through different means of a special quality among traditional peoples that could be called oneness of experience: a lack of dichotomizing or fragmenting, a unity in the word and in visual image. In the painted image, for example, the understanding is that in the being that is represented, or even in a depicted part of that being—the paw of a bear, let us say—all the power of the animal is present. One can draw from all Native American cultures examples to reinforce such interpretation. One final example I will use is that of the Navajo dry painting or "sand painting" as it is sometimes called. These are made in a rich ceremonial context for the curing of individuals who have gotten out of balance with their world. They are long ceremonies which can go on for four or five or up to ten days, during which time sacred chants are used with all the meaning of the *word* as I have tried to explain it. At a certain moment during the ceremony the ill person is placed at the center of one of the dry paintings; the understanding is that the person thus becomes identified with the power that is in the image painted on the earth with colored sand and pollen. And the singer takes some of the painted image and presses it to the body of the ill person, again to emphasize this element of identity: the painting is not a symbol of some meaning or power, the power *is* there present in it, and as the person identifies with it the appropriate cure is accomplished.

I conclude with this portion of a Navajo chant:

The mountains, I become part of it . . .
The herbs, the fir tree, I become part of it.
The morning mists, the clouds, the gathering waters,
I become part of it.
The wilderness, the dew drops, the pollen . . .
I become part of it.

And in the context of other chants, there is always the conclusion that indeed, I *am* the universe. We are not separate, but are one.

KEY TERMS AND CONCEPTS

animalism The harmonious relationship found in hunting cultures between humans and animals.

Black Elk Medicine man of the Oglala Sioux whose teachings have kept alive some of the traditional religion practices.

ceremonial moieties In some tribes, the two halves into which the population is divided for the purpose of alternating at ritual performances; for example, one moiety may have the task of burying the dead of the other moiety.

coyote A **culture hero** and **trickster** figure found in a wide range of stories. In some stories, he is the one who introduces death into the world.

culture hero A creative power who introduces cultural and religious institutions.

earth diver The name for a widespread creation story attributing the origin of the earth to the result of some being (usually an animal) diving to the bottom of the primordial waters to get dirt for making the earth.

emergence A sacred story about the emergence of the primeval mankind from the underworld.

Ghost Dance A revivalistic movement (1870–1890) originating among the Paiute of Nevada and California. It spread to the Plains Indians where it caused clashes between Sioux Indians and the U.S. military. The dance is named for its round-dancing, which was supposed to contribute to the return of the dead and the good times prior to the coming of the whites.

Inua The word for spirit or soul in Inuit (Eskimo). All things have souls or spirits (trees, rocks, animals, people, etc.), but some *inua* are more important than others because of their special power.

Kachina (Katsina) The collective ancestral dead and rain deities artistically depicted as masked beings by Southwest indigenous peoples. Also the name for cult societies centering on the katsinas.

kivas Male lodge houses and ritual chambers representing the universe and the place of emergence from the underworld.

land ethic A moral concern for the environment and ecological balance often arising out of a sense of affinity, even oneness, with nature.

linear vs. cyclical views of time The concept that time has a beginning and an end and runs in a "straight" line from one to the other is called linear. The view that time is like a circle without beginning and end is called cyclical.

master of the animals The idea that every animal species of importance has its own master who protects the animals of that species and either offers them to hunters or withholds them from hunters.

medicine man/woman A person who has received the power to heal.

medicine wheel Arrangements of stones in circles around a central hub by which certain dates, such as the summer solstice, are indicated.

nagualism A Mexican Indian term denoting such an intimate connection between a human and the human's guardian spirit that they share the same qualities and life force.

oneness of experience A term used by Joseph Epes Brown to summarize what he takes to be the basic spiritual values of Native American religions.

oral tradition The passing on of the sacred stories and lore of a particular people from one generation to the next by word of mouth.

Pan-Indianism The (Native American) interpretation that Indian religious symbols have the same meaning in all tribes since all Indians are ethnically and culturally related. It can also refer to the movement that advocates this idea.

puberty quest A **vision quest** at the time of puberty.

reincarnation Rebirth as a human being.

Sedna According to an Inuit story, the goddess who created and controls the sea animals.

shaman A religious practitioner who, on behalf of society and with the aid of guardian spirit(s), enters into a trance to establish contact with the greater powers in some other world.

Spider Woman A being, according to the Hopis and others, that played a decisive role in the creation, especially the origin of the primordial twins and humans.

Sun Dance The annual cosmic rejuvenation ceremony of the Plains Indians.

taboo A term denoting what is forbidden, dangerous, and prohibited.

totem poles Heraldic poles among the Indians of the Northwest Coast raised to celebrate and commemorate important events or to preserve the remains of a dead person. The poles often portray guardian spirits, the pole's owner, or the owner's ancestors.

transmigration Rebirth as an animal, tree, or inanimate thing.

trickster A character in the mythologies of many Native American peoples, often identical with the **culture hero** in his cosmic aspects.

vision quest The ritual quest for a guardian spirit that is performed in early youth or (on the Plains) repeatedly on later occasions. The individual seeks the spirit by going out alone to remote places where it may appear to him or her in a vision.

wakan tanka The term for sacred powers of the Lakota (Dakota) Indians. Although it is often translated as God or Supreme Being, a better translation might be "Great Mysteriousness."

White Buffalo Calf Woman A spirit who revealed the sacred pipe and seven primary rites to the Sioux.

worldview Robert Redfield defines this term as "the way a people characteristically look outward upon the universe."

World Tree The cosmic tree that connects sky, earth, and underworld. It serves as a communication channel between the sky powers and humans.

SUGGESTIONS FOR FURTHER READING

Gill, Sam D. *Native American Religions: An Introduction.* Belmont, Calif.: Wadsworth, 1982. An introductory survey of Native American religious beliefs and practices.

Gill, Sam D. *Native American Traditions: Sources and Interpretations.* Belmont, Calif.: Wadsworth, 1983. A useful collection of sources.

Sullivan, Lawrence E., ed. *Native American Religions: North America.* New York: Macmillan, 1987, 1989. A valuable collection of articles from *The Encyclopedia of Religion.*

Thompson, Stith. *Tales of the North American Indians.* Bloomington: Indiana University Press, 1929, 1966, 1967. A collection of sources arranged according to themes.

RESEARCH PROJECTS

1. Write a one-page paper answering two questions: (1) What was the most important thing you learned from reading this chapter? and (2) What questions remain uppermost in your mind?

2. Find several different versions of one of the stories included in the "Sources" section (such as Raven stealing the light or the origin of death) and compare them. Focus on the differences and generate a hypothesis to explain them.

3. Collect or make some slides of Native American art, show them to the class, and describe their religious symbolism.

PART 3

WAYS OF BEING RELIGIOUS ORIGINATING IN ASIA

6

Hindu Ways of Being Religious

INTRODUCTION

There are many different ways of being religious in India. There are Jains, Sikhs, Muslims, Christians, Jews, Parses, Buddhists—to name only a few—who are practicing their own distinct religious ways. Here our focus will be on Hinduism. It should be noted, however, that Hinduism is found in other places besides India. While the majority of the estimated 700 to 800 million Hindus live in India, many live in such places as Bali, the Caribbean, South Africa, Europe, Canada, and the United States.

The word *Hinduism* is not an Indian word. It comes from an Arabic word originally used to refer to the people who lived in the Indus Valley. European scholars coined the word *Hinduism* as a collective term for the religious beliefs and practices of some of the people who live in India. The word is very misleading—so misleading that some scholars have argued we should abandon its use.

While it is doubtful whether we can or should abandon its use, we must be aware of why it is misleading. First, the word *Hinduism* implies that Hinduism is a separate and distinct religious tradition comparable to Christianity or Islam. However, Hinduism displays few of the characteristics generally associated with religion. There is no founder, no divinely revealed scriptures, no creed or dogmas, no ecclesiastical organization or "church," and, in many of its forms, the concept of a personal divinity is not of central importance. Given conventional understandings of the word *religion*, it is difficult to categorize all of Hinduism's forms as a "religion." Again the issue, discussed in chapter 2, of how best to define religion emerges as central to the problems involved in the academic study of Hinduism.

Second, Hinduism is extraordinarily diverse. On one end of the scale are small, local village cults focused on local gods and saints whose followers may

encompass no more than two or three villages. At the other end of the scale are large religious movements with millions of adherents throughout India and elsewhere. In between are numerous movements, sects, **audience cults** (groups that gather to hear some **guru** teach but are otherwise unorganized), and **client cults** (people who visit practitioners for therapy, meditation instruction, or help with personal problems) such as astrology. Each of these, from the smallest to the largest, has its own mythologies, theologies, rituals, and moral codes. It is possible to find groups referred to by the umbrella term *Hinduism* that have little in common.

The diversity and the unity of a religious tradition are often in the eye of the beholder. If we wish to focus on the diversity of Hinduism in the hope of painting a more accurate picture of its richness and variety, we risk ignoring the fact that many Hindus affirm that it is, despite the diversity, a single religious tradition. This affirmation is based on a sense of a shared heritage and historical continuity as well as family resemblances among various groups. In this chapter, we sample a few of the rich religious and spiritual foods offered to us by the complexity and diversity of Hinduism.

6.1 AN OVERVIEW

David R. Kinsley is professor of medieval Hinduism at McMaster University in Hamilton, Canada. He studied at the University of Chicago (Ph.D. 1970) and in the following selection offers an introduction to and historical overview of Hinduism. He notes the complexity and diversity of this "religious tradition" and the difficulty that poses for introducing it to someone who knows little about it. His perspective is cultural and historical, offering insights into the ideas, folk beliefs, practices, social organizations,

GENERAL MAP OF INDIA

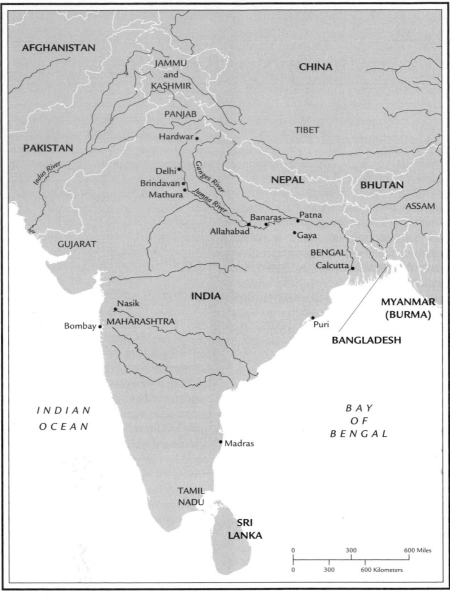

From *A Handbook of Living Religions*, edited by John R. Hinnells (London: Blackwell, 1997), p. 265, Fig. 5.1.

and historical dynamics that weave together to form the tapestry called Hinduism.

Like all complex religions, Hinduism teaches that human life has many different purposes because there are many different things that are good for humans and contribute to human flourishing. And, like all complex religions, Hinduism identifies those things that prevent humans from realizing the variety of goods that contribute to human flourishing. This means that Hinduism is not *exclusively* concerned with such "spiritual" values as salvation (to use a Western term). However, it is definitely concerned with what is the highest good and what, among all the hindrances to good, is the worst. Hinduism understands ignorance (*avidya*) as primarily responsible for keeping humans from realizing the highest good, and hence knowledge (*vidya* or *jnana*) plays an important role in realizing complete human flourishing or freedom (*moksha*) from the ignorance and unhappiness that plagues human lives. However, precisely what is ignorance, what is knowledge, and what is *moksha*, the highest human good? Hinduism, like all religions, provides a variety of provocative answers.

DAVID R. KINSLEY

Hinduism

READING QUESTIONS

1. As you read, make a list of all the words and ideas you do not understand or are uncertain about. Discuss them with a classmate, look them up in a dictionary, or bring them up in class for discussion and clarification.
2. The author offers several generalizations about Hinduism. What are they?
3. What is a "very common definition" of Hinduism?
4. What do you think are the most important differences among the Vedic, devotional, ascetic, and popular traditions?
5. What is the tension reflected in the epics, and what are the three "solutions" to this tension? In your opinion, do these solutions relieve the tension? Why or why not?
6. Make a list of the things from the various historical periods you would like to know more about. Discuss them in class.

Even before the sun has risen, the streets and alleyways of Varanasi[1] leading to the Ganges River swirl with devout pilgrims making their way to the broad steps that lead down into the river. By the time the sun is up the steps teem with pilgrims and devout residents taking ritual baths in Mother Ganges' sacred waters, which are believed to cleanse one of all sins. Small shops specializing in religious paraphernalia crowd the area around the

From *Hinduism: A Cultural Perspective*, by David R. Kinsley © 1993 Prentice-Hall, Inc. Reprinted by permission of Prentice-Hall, Inc. Upper Saddle River, N.J. pp. 2–25. Footnotes omitted.
[1] Also known as Banaras or Benares.

steps and do a thriving business. Hundreds of priests whose task it is to aid pilgrims are setting up their large umbrellas against the heat of the sun, and by midday the steps leading to the river look as if they are overgrown with immense mushrooms.

Dawn also signals the beginning of activity in the hundreds of temples and shrines throughout the city dedicated to the many gods and goddesses of the Hindu pantheon. In the impressive Vishvanath temple of the ascetic god Shiva, hereditary priests prepare to do puja (worship by personally waiting upon a deity), and devotees crowd the temple precincts to have a view of the image of the deity, a sight that is held to be auspicious, and to watch the colorful ceremony. Throughout the day devotees stream to the hundreds of temples scattered all over Varanasi to worship their favorite god or goddess. The variety of images from which they can choose reflects the extraordinary richness through which the divine has revealed itself in the Hindu tradition.

Enshrined in these temples is a veritable kaleidoscope of divinity: Vishnu, the great heavenly king who descends to the world from time to time in various forms to maintain cosmic stability; Shiva, the ascetic god who dwells in yogic meditation in the Himalayas, storing up his energy so that he can release it periodically into the world to refresh its vigor; Krishna, the adorable cowherd god who frolics with his women companions in the idyllic forests of Vrindavana; Hanuman, the monkey god, who embodies strength, courage, and loyalty to the Lord Rama; Ganesha, the elephant-headed god who destroys all obstacles for his devotees; Durga, the warrior goddess who periodically defeats the forces of evil in order to protect the world; Kali, the black goddess who dwells in cremation grounds and is served with blood; and many more.

Dawn is a busy time at the cremation grounds on the Ganges too. A steady stream of funeral processions wends its way to a particular set of steps where several funeral pyres burn constantly. At the funeral grounds the stretcher-borne corpses are set down to await their turn in the purifying fires. The constant activity at this particular burning ground reflects the belief of pious Hindus that death in or near the Ganges at Varanasi results in moksha, the final liberation from the endless cycles of birth and rebirth that is the ultimate spiritual goal of most Hindus. Thousands of devout Hindus, in their old age, come to die in Varanasi, and many funeral processions seem joyous, reflecting the auspicious circumstances of the person's death. As one watches the crackling fires consume the corpse, the rising tendrils of smoke suggest the soul's final and longed-for liberation.

Varanasi is the center of several religious orders, and the city's population includes a great number of ascetics who have chosen to live in the holy city permanently or who are simply wandering through. It is not unusual to see several of these holy men or women sitting in meditation around the steps. The burning ground itself is an auspicious site to perform meditation, as the funeral pyres remind the ascetics of the transcience of the worldly life they have renounced. The appearance of these renouncers is striking. Ascetics often wear saffron-colored robes, a minimum of clothes, or perhaps are even naked. Their bodies may be smeared with ashes, sometimes taken from the cremation grounds. Their hair is long and matted, indicating their utter neglect of bodily appearance, or their heads may be shaven. Their only possessions are a water pot and a staff. In the midst of a bustling city like Varanasi, which like all cities caters to the inexhaustible worldly desires of its populace with markets, cinemas, shops, and so on, the ascetics look like wayfarers from another world. They are a common sight in Varanasi, however, and remind one of the importance of world renunciation and asceticism in the Hindu tradition.

Before the day is over, a visitor to Varanasi will have witnessed many scenes common to the Hindu tradition: Brahmins performing ancient Vedic rituals; devotees from Bengal performing communal worship to Lord Krishna with much singing and dancing; students at Banares Hindu University consulting an astrologer to determine if the day on which their exams will be held will be auspicious; a low-caste pilgrim making an offering at the shrine of a beloved saint who is little known outside the pilgrim's own caste; a traditional pundit, or teacher, expounding the ethereal subtleties of Hindu philosophy to students; a priest or storyteller telling stories from Hindu scriptures to groups of devotees in the precincts of a temple; a woman pouring sacred Ganges water on an image of Shiva; a pious person ritually worshiping a cow; and a woman performing a ritual for the well-being of her household.

By the end of the day the visitor to Varanasi seeking to discern the essential outlines of the Hindu religious tradition probably will be very confused and tempted to conclude that Varanasi, with all its diversity, is not the best place to look for the essential ingredients of Hinduism. Indeed, Hinduism itself, like Varanasi, tends to defy neat analysis and description and leaves the impression that what happens in the name of Hinduism is chaotic. Hinduism, it seems, eludes and frustrates attempts to summarize it neatly because it offers exceptions or even contradictions to what at first might seem essential or generally true.

For example, many Hindus in Varanasi say that ahimsa (noninjury) is essential to the Hindu vision of reality, and they will be able to cite countless texts to support that view. They will mention Mahatma Gandhi as a recent example of the centrality of this theme in Hinduism, and possibly also the Hindu respect for cows and the emphasis on vegetarianism. You may be convinced that here, indeed, is an essential aspect of Hinduism. Thanking your informant, you will go on your way, only to come upon a temple of Kali or Durga, where worshipers are beheading a goat in sacrifice to the goddess. Or you might happen upon a copy of the *Artha Shastra* of Kautiliya, an ancient and authoritative text on Hindu political philosophy from around the fourth century C.E. You will look in vain for Gandhian political principles in this book, because the *Artha Shastra* is consistently ruthless and cunning in its approach to seizing and holding power.

You might, on the other hand, be told by an ascetic in Varanasi that Hinduism involves essentially the renunciation of society and all egotistical desires and the achievement of liberation from the lures of the world. But before long you would find a group of orthodox Brahmins performing ancient rituals from the *Vedas*, also affirmed to be the essence of Hinduism, the explicit aim of which is the stability and welfare of the world, what the Hindus call *loka-samgraha*, one of the central teachings of Hinduism's most famous scripture, the **Bhagavad Gita**.

Who is right? The orthodox Brahmin who performs daily rituals prescribed by the ancient *Vedas?* The ascetic who performs no such rituals, who may even show disdain for them, and who denies any obligation to society? The low-caste farmer who daily praises the Lord Rama and celebrates his heroic exploits? The untouchable who makes a pilgrimage to Varanasi to honor a saint beloved by his or her entire caste but virtually unknown to most high-caste Hindus? Or the pious businessman who consults his astrologer before closing a deal? One must believe them all, it seems, for they are all Hindus undertaking common and acceptable Hindu practices. And this leads to our first generalizations about the Hindu religious tradition.

One cannot find the equivalent of a Hindu pope or an authoritative Hindu council in Varanasi. Historically, Hinduism has never insisted on the necessity of a supreme figure in religious matters and has never agreed on certain articles of belief as essential for all Hindus. Throughout its long history, Hinduism has been highly decentralized.

Another feature of Hinduism follows from this one, a feature reflected in both the caste system and the different paths one may take in the religious quest. Hinduism affirms in a variety of ways that people are different from one another and that these differences are both crucial and distinctive. People have different *adhikaras*, different aptitudes, predilections, and abilities. What is natural to one person is unnatural to another. So it is that different ways are made available to different types. Some may have an aptitude for philosophy, and a path centering on knowledge is available for them. Others may be of a devotional aptitude, and so a path of devotion is appropriate for them. Over the centuries, then, Hinduism has accepted a variety of paths, spiritual techniques, and views of the spiritual quest that all succeed in helping humans fulfill their religious destiny.

On the social level the Hindu emphasis on differences manifests itself in the caste system. Human differences are systematically arranged in hierarchical order, and people are segregated into specialized cohesive groups called castes. Social contact with other castes is carefully circumscribed in such a way that the religious beliefs and practices of a particular Hindu often reflects his or her caste tradition and differs markedly from the religious practices of other castes. The philosophical ideas underlying the caste system are karma, the moral law of cause and effect according to which a person reaps what he or she sows, and samsara, rebirth according to the nature of a person's karma. The basic idea is that what one is now is the result of all that one has done in the past, and what one will become in the future is being determined by all one's actions in the present. In effect, a person's present caste identity is only a brief scene in an endless drama of lives that will end only with moksha, liberation from this endless round of birth, death, and rebirth.

Hinduism also affirms that during one's life a person changes, and different kinds of activities are appropriate to various stages of life. Traditionally four stages have been described, with different obligations for each one. The ideal was designed primarily for men, and only very rarely did a woman follow the pattern. Ideally, a high-caste male is to pass through these stages in the following order: student, householder, forest recluse, and wandering holy man. As a student, a male's duty is to study his tradition, particularly the *Vedas* if he is a Brahmin. As a householder he is to foster a family, undertake an occupation appropriate to his caste, and perform rituals, usually Vedic rituals, that help insure the stability of the world. As a forest hermit, he is supposed to leave his home, retire to the forest with his wife, continue Vedic rituals, and meditate on those realities that will bring about liberation from the world and rebirth. Finally, he is to abandon even his wife, give up Vedic rituals, wander continually, begging his food, and strive for the knowledge that emancipates him from the cycles of rebirth. Although this pattern is not always followed, it affirms the tradition's liberality in permitting a variety of approaches in one's spiritual sojourn: study; support of the

world through rituals, work, and family life; meditation away from society; and renunciation of the world through extreme asceticism.

The Hindu insistence on differences between people, then, leads to the very common definition of Hinduism in sacred texts as varna-ashrama-dharma, which may be loosely translated as performing the duty (dharma) of one's stage of life (ashrama) and caste or social station (varna).

Hindus also have acknowledged that differences exist among the regional areas of the Indian subcontinent, and the Hindu Law Books accept regional customs and peculiarities as authoritative. These regional dissimilarities help us understand another aspect of the diversity of belief and practice among Hindus in Varanasi. Hindus from Tamilnad in the South have a cultural history that differs greatly from, say, Hindus from Bengal. Each region has its own vernacular tradition, its favorite gods and goddesses, its own distinctive customs and rituals. In Varanasi, where pilgrims from all over India congregate, these differences further complicate any attempt to discern common themes, patterns, and beliefs. The history of Hinduism is, to a great extent, the record of what has gone on in the regions of India and is therefore marked by much diversity in belief and practice.

On the other hand, a strong, articulate, and authoritative tradition, called the Great, Sanskrit, or Aryan tradition, has counterbalanced this diversity by imposing on it certain myths, beliefs, customs, and patterns of social organization. Dominated by a literate Brahmin elite, Hinduism over the centuries always has manifested a certain coherence because of the prestige of this tradition throughout India. Thus, today Hinduism is, as it always has been, the dynamic interaction of various regional traditions with an all-India tradition in which the particular beliefs and rituals of any given Hindu are a combination. For orthodox Varanasi Brahmins, very little if any of the regional traditions may affect their brand of Hinduism. For low-caste Bengali peasants, on the other hand, very little of the Sanskrit tradition may be a part of their religion.

All this adds up to what one might call a liberal tendency in Hinduism that permits and even encourages men and women to undertake their religious sojourns in a variety of ways. Some things, to be sure, are encouraged for all Hindus: caste purity (intermarriage between castes is discouraged strongly), respect for Brahmins, and life-cycle rituals, for example. Certain ethical precepts also are encouraged for all, and certain underlying beliefs are accepted by most Hindus, such as karma, samsara, and moksha. In Varanasi, then, we find very general parameters defining Hinduism that for the most part are provided by the Sanskrit tradition and that permit a great diversity of belief and practice. What goes on within these parameters, finally, may be summed up as representing four accents within the Hindu tradition.

1. *The Vedic Tradition.* Historically, the Aryans, who composed the *Vedas*, were foreigners who succeeded in superimposing on the indigenous peoples of India their language, culture, and religion. This Vedic religion is still dominant in living Hinduism and is best represented by the orthodox Brahmins. One of the central aims of this religion is the stability and welfare of the world, which is achieved through a great variety of rituals. In Varanasi today this accent is represented by those Brahmins who study the traditional Law Books and sponsor elaborate Vedic rituals.

2. *The Devotional Tradition.* The Hinduism of the majority of people in Varanasi is devotional, and this accent within the tradition goes all the way back to at least the time of the *Bhagavad Gita* (around 200 B.C.E.). Devotion is of varying types and is directed to a great variety of gods and goddesses, but generally we can speak of three strands within this tradition: (1) devotion to Shiva or to one of his family; (2) devotion to Vishnu or to one of his avatars (incarnations), the two most popular of which in the Varanasi area are Krishna and Rama; and (3) devotion to one of the many manifestations of the Great Goddess, the Mahadevi. It is primarily against the background of the devotional tradition that Hindus identify themselves as Shaiva (devotees of Shiva), Vaishnava (devotees of Vishnu), or Shakta (devotees of the Goddess). Devotion to all three manifestations of the divine is concerned with eternal proximity to the deity in his or her heaven or with liberation from the cycle of endless births (Moksha).

3. *The Ascetic Tradition.* The several thousand ascetics in Varanasi are the living representatives of a tradition that is probably as ancient as the *Vedas* and that has been highly honored in Hinduism for over twenty-five hundred years. The underlying assumptions of this tradition are that (1) life in the world is a hindrance to realizing one's spiritual destiny; (2) renunciation of society, including family ties, is necessary to realize one's spiritual essence; (3) various kinds of austerities are the necessary means of purifying oneself of both ignorance and attachments; and (4) the ultimate goal of this arduous path is complete liberation from the wheel of rebirth. There are various types of ascetics, ascetic orders, and spiritual exercises undertaken by ascetics. Generally, though, they all share these ideas and emphasize the importance of the individual's emancipation rather than one's obligations to the social order and its maintenance. In this respect there has often been a tension

between the Vedic tradition and the ascetic tradition, a tension we shall return to later.

4. *The Popular Tradition.* This tradition refers to all those other rites and beliefs of Varanasi Hindus that do not fit neatly under the other three traditions. The sanctity of Varanasi itself, and of the River Ganges that flows through it, points to the central importance of sacred places and pilgrimage in the Hindu tradition. For Hindus the entire subcontinent bubbles with sacred places where immediate access to sacred and purifying power is obtainable. Most prominent geographical features, such as mountains and rivers, are sacred and are the focal points of pilgrimage. Most cities contain famous temples and are also sacred centers. In addition to geographical sites and cities, some plants are held to be sacred. To the worshipers of Vishnu, the *tulasi* plant is particularly sacred, whereas to many devotees of the Goddess, it is the *bilva* tree. Time is punctuated by auspicious and inauspicious moments that are determined by the movements of the stars, the planets, the sun, and the moon. Many Hindus are extremely sensitive to these rhythms and will undertake nothing of significance unless they have been assured by their astrologer that the time is auspicious. Most Hindus know precisely at what time they were born, because they, and their parents, need that information to determine the compatibility of marriage partners. We also include under the popular tradition the preoccupation many Hindus have with diet. Many Hindu scriptures give lists of pure and impure foods and characterize the different properties of foods according to the physical and spiritual effects they produce. The preoccupation of many Hindus and many Hindu scriptures with signs and omens is also part of the popular tradition, as are rituals that have to do with gaining control over enemies and members of the opposite sex. In short, the popular tradition refers to things that we might call magical or superstitious simply because we do not understand them fully; we are unable to do so because those who practice them cannot articulate in ways we can understand what these practices and beliefs mean to them or meant to their ancestors.

By way of concluding this introductory portrait of Hinduism, let me suggest an image that might be useful in thinking about its diversity. We all know someone who is a collector, who rarely throws anything away, whose possessions include the exquisite treasure, the tackiest bauble, the unidentifiable photograph, the neglected and dusty item, and the latest flashy gadget. The Hindu religious tradition has shown itself to be an incurable collector, and it contains in the nooks and crannies of its house many different things. Today this great collector may hold one or another thing in fashion and seem to be utterly fascinated by it. But very few things are ever discarded altogether, and this is probably one of the most interesting and distinctive features of Hinduism. Like a big family, with its diversity, quarrels, eccentricities, and stubborn loyalty to tradition, Hinduism is a religion that expresses the ongoing history of a subcontinent of people for over thirty-five hundred years. The family album is too immense to describe in a single book, but I hope that what follows succeeds in at least suggesting the extraordinary wisdom, richness, and beauty of that particular family of humanity we call Hinduism.

HISTORICAL OUTLINE

The Formative Period (2500–800 B.C.E.)

From the middle of the third millenniun B.C.E. to the second millennium B.C.E. there was a thriving city civilization in Northwest India, the Indus Valley civilization, which was centered in two cities, Harappa and Mohenjo-Daro. This civilization undertook extensive trade with the city civilizations of the ancient Near East, was based on an agricultural economy, and seems to have had a complex, hierarchical social structure. Writing was known, but it has not yet been deciphered by scholars.

It is difficult to say anything definite about the religion of the Indus Valley civilization. Many female figurines have been found, and it is probable that goddesses were worshiped in connection with the fertility of the crops. The bulls depicted on seals, the intriguing scenes depicted in the art, and a variety of stone objects are tantalizing in suggesting possible prototypes of later Indian religion, but until the script is deciphered most aspects of the religion of this ancient culture must remain unknown or at best vague.

The Indus Valley civilization came to an abrupt end around 1500 B.C.E. at about the time an energetic people known as the Indo-Aryans migrated into Northwest India. Although many aspects of later Hinduism may well have been inspired by the Indus Valley civilization or regional peasant cultures in India, it is the Indo-Aryans and their religion that Hinduism traditionally has looked to as its source and inspiration; the earliest scriptures of the Indo-Aryans, the *Vedas*, have been acknowledged for thousands of years to embody the primordial truths upon which Hinduism bases itself.

The *Vedas* represent a diversified and continuous tradition that extends from around 1200 B.C.E., the probable date of the *Rig Veda*, the earliest Vedic text, to around 400 B.C.E., the probable date of some of the late *Upanishads*. Generally, Vedic literature is of three types: (1) *Samhitas*, hymns in praise of various deities; (2) *Brahmanas*, sacrificial texts dealing with the meaning and technicalities of rituals; and (3) *Aranyakas* and *Upanishads*, philosophical and mystical texts dealing with the quest to realize ultimate reality.

The central figure of the *Samhita* texts is the rishi, a heroic visionary figure and poet who was able to experience directly the various gods and powers that pervaded the Vedic world. In the quest to commune with these sacred powers, the rishi does not seem to have employed ascetic techniques, as later Hindu visionaries were to do. The rishis did, however, employ a plant called *soma*, which was most likely a hallucinogenic mushroom. Drinking soma, the rishi was transported to the realm of the gods. Having experienced the gods, the rishis subsequently were inspired to compose hymns in their praise. The Vedic gods themselves are said to enjoy soma, and one of the most popular gods, Indra, a mighty warrior, is often described as drinking soma and experiencing its exhilarating effects. The centrality of the rishis' quest for an unmediated vision of the divine in the earliest Vedic literature has persisted in the Hindu tradition to this day, although the means of achieving this vision and the nature of the vision itself have changed over the centuries. In the later Hindu tradition, asceticism and devotion replaced the use of soma, and the polytheistic vision of the rishis has been replaced by visions emphasizing the underlying unity of reality.

Complementing the visionary dimension of the rishis in Vedic religion is a priestly, sacrificial cult centered on the great Vedic god Agni. Agni represents fire and heat. He is present at the sacrificial fire, at the domestic hearth, in the primordial fire of precreation, in the digestive fires of the stomach; he pervades all creatures as the fire of life. In addition, Agni is the intermediary between humans and gods because he transmits their offerings to the gods in the sacrificial fire. In general, nearly all Vedic sacrificial rituals aim at aiding, strengthening, or reinvigorating Agni so that the creative and vital powers of the world may remain fresh and strong.

At the daily and domestic level, the *agnihotra* ritual, performed by the head of most Vedic households three times each day, nourishes Agni in the form of the sun through simple offerings of clarified butter. At sunrise, midday, and twilight the householder makes offerings to Agni to help him in his perpetual and lifegiving round. On a much more elaborate scale, such as the ritual of building the fire altar, a similar aim is clear. The sacrificer, with the aid of Brahmin priests, builds an elaborate structure infused with elements and objects representing Agni in his many forms that have been collected over a year's period. The resulting fire altar in the form of a bird represents the rebuilt, distilled essence of Agni before he diffused himself throughout the created order. Agni is put back together again, as it were, so that he can regain the strength necessary to reinvigorate the world. This ritual, and others like it, then, is part of a cyclical pattern. Initially, Agni, representing the divine forces generally, diffused himself into the creation for the benefit of humans. Humans in turn sustain and reinvigorate Agni and the gods through rituals that enable Agni to redistribute himself periodically in the creation. In this ritual scheme the gods and humans are partners in maintaining the ongoing creative processes of the world.

The Speculative Period
(800–400 B.C.E.)

The sacrificial texts concern themselves to a great extent with the underlying potency of the rituals they describe and as such are metaphysical in nature. However, philosophical and metaphysical concerns only come to dominate Vedic literature in the *Upanishads*, in which we find a third dimension of Vedic religion. This dimension may be described as the quest for redemptive knowledge, or the search for the truth that will make people free. The *Upanishads* are primarily dialogues between a teacher and a student, they usually take place away from society, and from time to time they criticize the performance of rituals as superfluous to the religious quest. Some of the texts extol the renunciation of society and the performance of austerities that in later Hinduism become increasingly important techniques for liberation.

Although the *Upanishads* are somewhat diverse in their teachings, all agree that underlying reality is a spiritual essence called Brahman. Brahman is One, is usually said to be without delimiting attributes, is impersonal, and is essentially present in all people in the form of the Atman, a person's inmost self, or soul. The religious quest in the *Upanishads* involves realizing the fundamental identity of Brahman and Atman and realizing that one's essential self transcends individuality, limitation, decay, and death. The realization of this truth wins the adept liberation or release (moksha) from the shifting world of constant flux and the endless cycle of rebirth (samsara), which is perpetuated and determined by all one's actions (karma).

Unlike earlier Vedic texts, then, the *Upanishads* do not associate the religious quest with the vitality of the physical world but rather aim at a goal that transcends or overcomes the world. In later Hinduism moksha comes to represent the highest religious goal in nearly all texts,

and the *Upanishads* are therefore important in the history of Hinduism as the earliest scriptures to describe the religious quest for liberation from the world. The *Upanishads* are also important because they are the earliest texts to advocate withdrawal from society and the use of ascetic and meditational techniques in this quest. In the *Upanishads* it is clear that the Aryan-Vedic tradition has been influenced by one that was probably indigenous to India, the ascetic tradition.

The earliest systematic presentation of the ascetic tradition is found in the *Yoga Sutras.* Yoga is a technique of ascetic and meditational exercises that aims at isolating humans from the flux of the material world in order for them to recapture their original spiritual purity. Yoga seeks to disentangle the individual from involvement in prakriti (nature, matter, the phenomenal world generally) so that one may glimpse, and be liberated by, one's pure spiritual essence, purusha. Yoga represents an ancient Indian view of the world that emphasizes the transient nature of existence and seeks to overcome it by discovering and isolating one's eternal, unchanging, spiritual essence. Although this tendency is most clearly expressed in other Indian religions such as Jainism and Buddhism, it gains increasing importance in the Hindu tradition and remains central to that tradition to this day.

The Epic and Classical Periods
(400 B.C.E.–600 C.E.)

The period from around 400 B.C.E. to 400 C.E. in Hinduism is known as the epic period. During this time the Indo-Aryans ceased to be a nomadic people. They settled into towns and cities, especially in the Gangetic plains of North India, and began to infuse their religion with elements of the religion of the indigenous peoples they had come to dominate. It was during this period that the two great Hindu epics were written, the *Mahabharata* and the *Ramayana.* Both epics concern themselves with royal rivalries, perhaps reflecting political turmoil during this period, and exhibit, in their rambling ways, a tension between a religion aimed at supporting and upholding the world order and one aimed at isolating a person from society in order to achieve individual liberation.

As both epics are explicitly concerned with royal heroes, they have much to say about the world-supporting aspects of Hinduism. Vedic rituals, the ideal social system, and the preservation of order are essential concerns of the ideal king in Hinduism, and the heroes in both epics grapple with the subtleties and complexities of these concerns in their kingly roles. Rama, the hero of the *Ramayana*, for example, must come to terms with a dilemma that contrasts the written law (in this case, that the eldest son should inherit his father's kingdom) with the unwritten law of obeying one's father (for complicated reasons Rama's father commands him to exile himself to the forest for fourteen years so that Rama's half-brother may inherit the kingdom). Both epics emphasize that the king is a crucial figure in maintaining the harmonious realm of dharma (social and moral obligation) and rarely question the ultimate good involved in the preservation and refinement of the social order and those rituals and religious practices that insure it.

In the background of the epics, however, a host of characters call into question the ultimate good of the order of dharma. Called by a variety of names, these individuals have usually renounced the world, live in forests or small settlements, and are said to possess extraordinary powers. The epic heroes almost always treat these world renouncers with great respect and are often their students or beneficiaries.

The epics, like Hinduism itself, manage in various ways to hold together the tension between the aims of the royal heroes, which have to do with worldly order, and the aims of the world renouncers, which have to do primarily with individual liberation. On the narrative plane, first of all, both sets of epic heroes must wander for many years in the forest away from civilization and the realm of dharmic order among those who have renounced the world before gaining world sovereignty. In the disorder of the forest and from the teachings and examples of the world renouncers, the royal heroes acquire the knowledge and means to become rulers.

The epics offer a second solution to the tension between supporting or renouncing the world by defining the stages of life each person passes through. When Yudhishthira, the eldest of the five brothers who are the heroes of the *Mahabharata*, wishes to renounce the world because he is depressed at the slaughter that has taken place as a result of his desire to become king, his brothers and wife argue against him by saying that it is not proper to renounce the world until one has fulfilled one's social obligations. Increasingly this becomes the Hindu tradition's official position in seeking to wed the world-supporting and world-renouncing traditions. First one must fulfill one's obligation to society, and in performing this obligation the religion of the *Vedas*, with its emphasis on refreshing and sustaining the world, is appropriate. Second, there is one's ultimate obligation to achieve final liberation, and this may be pursued when it is timely, preferably after one's grey hairs have appeared and one has seen one's grandchildren. In performing this obligation, asceticism and renunciation of the world are appropriate.

A third solution to the tension between these two religious aims is found in the *Bhagavad Gita*, which forms a part of the *Mahabharata*. The *Gita*'s solution is philosophical, suggesting that true renunciation involves the renunciation of desires for the fruits of actions and that this renunciation may be undertaken in the world while fulfilling one's social duty. Selfless action without desire for reward, action as an end in itself, is true renunciation for the *Gita*, and as such no tension need exist between one's dual obligation to support the world and to seek individual liberation.

Roughly contemporary with the epics is a whole genre of literature concerned with the ideal nature of society, the Law Books. It is in this literature that the definition of the ideal society as varna-ashrama-dharma, the duty of acting according to one's stage of life (ashrama) and position in society (varna), is arrived at as most descriptive of Hindu society specifically and of Hinduism in general. The writers of these works have considerable respect for renouncing the world and seeking moksha in ascetic isolation, but they quite carefully relegate this aspect of the religious quest to old age. These works are concerned primarily with social stability, and underlying all the Law Books is the strong Hindu affirmation that an orderly, refined, stable society is to be cherished. Order, stability, and refinement have primarily and essentially to do with the proper functioning of the various castes and the proper observance of interaction among castes and among members of the same castes. Although the Law Books tolerate certain regional idiosyncrasies concerning social customs, all of them share a unified vision of society as hierarchically arranged according to caste. In the Law Books the social system has as its primary aim the support of Brahmins, who undertake Vedic rituals to maintain and renew the cosmic forces that periodically must be refreshed in order to keep the world bounteous and habitable. Beneath the Brahmins are the Kshatriyas (warriors) and Vaishyas (merchants). These three highest social groups (Brahmins, Kshatriyas, and Vaishyas) are called the twice-born classes, as they alone are permitted to perform the initiation ceremony of the sacred thread, which is believed to result in a second birth for the initiate. These groups alone, according to the Law Books, are qualified to study the *Vedas* and to undertake Vedic rituals. The serfs, or Shudras, are ranked below the twice-born classes, and their proper task is to support the higher castes by performing services for them. Beneath the Shudras, and barely even mentioned in the Law Books, are the untouchables, whose occupations are held to be highly polluting or who are so classed because they belong to tribal groups in India that are not yet acculturated.

Although the social ideal of the Law Books probably was never realized in the past, and although current Hindu society is quite different from this idealized model, the ideal society of the Law Books has had a great influence on Hindu thought and does succeed in capturing its underlying hierarchical assumptions and the preoccupation with ritual purity in Hindu religious practice and social intercourse.

The Medieval Period (600–1800 C.E.)

The medieval period in Hinduism is characterized by three developments: (1) the rise of devotional movements with a corresponding outburst in the construction of temples; (2) the systematization of Hindu philosophy into six schools dominated by the school of Advaita Vedanta (nondualistic Vedanta); and (3) the rise of Tantrism, a movement employing ritual techniques to achieve liberation.

Although devotion (called *bhakti* in Hinduism) enters the Hindu tradition as early as the *Bhagavad Gita* (around 200 B.C.E.), it was not until about the sixth century C.E. that devotion began to dominate the religious landscape of Hinduism. Beginning in the South with the Nayanars, devotional saints who praised Shiva, and the Alvars, devotional saints who worshiped Vishnu, an emotional, ecstatic kind of devotion became increasingly central to Hindu piety. By the seventeenth century, bhakti of this type had come to dominate the entire Hindu tradition. Devotion as described in the *Bhagavad Gita* was primarily a mental discipline aimed at controlling one's actions in the world in such a way that social obligations and religious fulfillment could be harmonized. In the later devotional movements, devotion is typically described as a love affair with God in which the devotee is willing to sacrifice anything in order to revel with the Lord in ecstatic bliss. The best example of this theme is the devotion to the cowherd Krishna, whose ideal devotees are married women who leave their husbands and homes to revel with Krishna in the woods. Unlike the *Bhagavad Gita*'s rather staid description of devotion, the later movements delight in describing the devotional experience as causing uncontrollable joy, fainting, frenzy, tears of anguish, madness, and sometimes social censure. Underlying most of these movements is the theological assumption that, although men and women may have differing inherited or ascribed duties and social positions, all creatures share the same inherent duty, which is to love and serve God. Although few devotional movements actually criticize the traditional social structure, it is sometimes the case that they are indifferent to traditional society, which they describe as confining when one undertakes the task of loving God. Two famous women devotees, Mahadeviyakka, a Virashaiva saint, and Mirabai, a Rajastani princess and devotee of Krishna, for example, both chafed

under traditional marriages and eventually left their husbands to devote themselves entirely to their respective gods.

Contemporary with the rise and spread of devotional movements, and perhaps reflecting their importance, was the rise of temples as important religious centers in Hinduism. Hindu temples, as the earthly dwelling places of the gods, are usually patterned on the model of a divine mountain or palace. They are centers of worship, centers for religious instruction, and often the homes of devotees who have renounced the world to pursue their service to God. Traditionally some temples dominated by the high castes have excluded low-caste devotees, but Hindus of all castes take part in temple worship, either at grand temples famous throughout India or at village temples that may consist of nothing more than a mud hut.

At these temples a great variety of deities are worshiped. Generally, however, the deity belongs to one of three strands within the Hindu pantheon: the Shaivite strand, which includes Shiva and members of his family; the Vaishnavite strand, which includes Vishnu and his avatars (incarnations); and the Shakta strand, which includes Hindu goddesses. The worship may be elaborate or simple but usually consists of some form of puja, a type of ritual service to the deity. This rite is normally performed by a priest, who is usually a Brahmin in temples frequented by high-caste Hindus but who may be a low-caste non-Brahmin in humbler temples used by the low castes.

The mythology of the deities worshiped, which is often portrayed in temple artwork, became systematized during the medieval period in a genre of works known as the *Puranas*, or "stories of old." As elsewhere in the Hindu tradition, the tension between *loka-samgraha*, supporting the world, and moksha, striving for release from the world, is reflected in these texts. Dominating the *Puranas* are two quite different manifestations of the divine: Shiva and Vishnu.

Shiva is the ascetic god, the great yogi who meditates in isolation on Kailasa Mountain in the Himalayas, who burns the god of love to ashes with the fury from his middle eye when the god tries to distract him. He is often portrayed as an outsider with matted hair, his body smeared with ashes and clothed in animal skins, with snakes and a garland of skulls as ornaments. Although a good deal of Shiva's mythology concerns his eventual marriage to the goddess Parvati and his most typical emblem is the lingam, the phallus, Shiva clearly embodies the world-renouncing tendencies of Hinduism and as such provides a model for this aspect of the tradition.

Vishnu, on the other hand, is usually described as a cosmic king who lives in the heavenly splendor of his palace in Vaikuntha. His primary role in the divine economy is to supervise universal order and prosperity. As the cosmic policeman he descends from time to time in various forms to defeat enemies of world stability, and as such he provides a model for supporting the world.

Turning to the second major development of the medieval period, the systematization of Hindu philosophical thought, we find a considerable diversity tolerated. The six schools that eventually came to be accepted as orthodox emphasize very differing points of view and reveal again the underlying tension between dharma, supporting the world, and moksha, release from the world. The tension is best seen in the rivalry between the Purva Mimamsa and Uttara Mimamsa schools. Although both schools emphasize the *Vedas* as their source of inspiration, the former preoccupies itself with the ritual aspects of the *Vedas* and affirms the centrality of Vedic rituals as the key to realizing both religious duty and personal salvation. For this school, Vedic rituals are the most potent of all actions and are crucial in maintaining the world. One's ultimate duty, according to Purva Mimamsa, is continually to support the world by performing those rituals that are revealed in the *Vedas*.

The Uttara Mimamsa school, more commonly known as Vedanta, occupies itself with the *Upanishads*, which as we have noted emphasize individual release from the world by realizing the essential unity of Brahman, the Absolute, and Atman, the essential self in each person. The most brilliant and systematic exponent of this school was the eighth-century South Indian, Shankara, whose particular school of Vedanta is known as Advaita Vedanta (the Vedanta of no difference, or nondualism). For Shankara, actions per se, whether good or bad, are of no ultimate significance in achieving liberation because they arise from a false sense of individuality. Knowledge alone, a transforming, experiential knowledge of one's identity with Brahman, is the goal of the religious quest and is not dependent upon social obligations. However, Shankara's own life is often taken as a model for adepts of this path, and as Shankara himself was a world renouncer, most followers of his philosophy extol renunciation as helpful, if not necessary, in achieving liberating knowledge. Although Shankara did not criticize traditional society and traditional religious practices that aim at supporting the world, he was clear that a person's ultimate spiritual goal is not achieved by or through them. Not surprisingly, Shankara is held by the Hindu tradition to have been an incarnation of the ascetic god Shiva.

The *Tantras*, the third major development of the medieval period, seem to have arisen outside the elite Brahmin tradition. The *Tantras*, of which there are hundreds, often criticize established religious practices and the upholders of those practices, the Brahmins. In many ways, however, the *Tantras* express central, traditional Hindu ideas and practices. Underlying Tantric practice, for example, is the assumption that an individual is a miniature or microcosm of the cosmos and that by learning the sacred geography of one's body one may, by means of various yogic techniques, bring about one's own spiritual fulfillment, which in most Tantric texts is the result of uniting various opposites within one's body/cosmos.

The *Tantras* claim to be appropriate to the present era, which is decadent and in which people are less spiritual and less inclined to perform the elaborate rituals prescribed in earlier ages. The *Tantras* claim to introduce techniques that lead directly to liberation without traditional practices and routines. Vedic study, Vedic rituals, pilgrimage, puja, and other traditional practices, although not always disregarded in the *Tantras*, are often held to be superfluous in the present age. The *Tantras*, then, offer a variety of rituals that employ mantras (sacred formulas), mandalas (schematic diagrams), and yogic techniques that are believed to achieve either complete liberation from the mundane world or extraordinary powers, such as omniscience and the ability to fly.

The *Tantras* themselves distinguish between a right-handed path and a left-handed path. The right-handed path is for all adepts and consists primarily in the use of mantras, mandalas, and ritual techniques based upon Tantric sacred bodily geography. The left-handed path, appropriate only for those of a special heroic temperament, centers on a particular ritual in which the adept partakes of five forbidden things, thereby transcending the tension between the sacred and the profane and gaining liberation. This left-handed aspect of Tantrism has been greatly criticized by the Brahmin establishment.

The Modern Period (1800 to the Present)

Increasing contact with the West, including the political and economic domination by England from the middle of the nineteenth century to the middle of the twentieth century, provides the background for three important developments in the modern period of the Hindu tradition: (1) the Hindu revival of the nineteenth century; (2) the independence movement of the nineteenth and twentieth centuries; and (3) the introduction of Hinduism in a variety of forms to the West, particularly to North America.

As early as the eighth century C.E. Muslims had entered India, and by the thirteenth century Islam had come to a position of political dominance in North India. Increasingly Hindus found themselves ruled by non-

Hindus, and British domination, beginning in the eighteenth century, represented to Hindus a continuation of foreign rule. Although many Indians were attracted by the teaching of the equality of all believers in Islam and converted to that religion, the majority remained at least nominal Hindus and in various ways continued the traditions of the past. With the arrival of Western powers in the eighteenth century, however, both Westerners and Hindus began to articulate an increasingly vocal criticism of the Hindu tradition. Many aspects of traditional Hinduism were castigated, and in the nineteenth century Hindu reform movements arose that sought to meet these criticisms by distilling what was most central to the Hindu tradition and doing away with the rest. Two movements in particular gained all-India fame: the Brahmo Samaj, founded by Ram Mohan Roy, and the Arya Samaj, founded by Swami Dayananda.

Ram Mohan Roy (1774–1833) was a prominent citizen of Bengal, and before he founded the Brahmo Samaj (the Society of Brahman) he had considerable contact with Christian missionaries. He was acquainted with Western humanistic traditions and made a journey to England, where he became even more familiar with Western ideas. In 1828 he founded the Brahmo Samaj, which represented his vision of a reformed Hinduism. For Ram Mohan the essence of Hinduism was found in the *Upanishads*. There, he said, was revealed the One Nameless Absolute God of all people, who was to be worshiped through meditation and a pious life. Such Hindu customs as image worship, pilgrimage, festivals, and the rules of caste, he held, were superfluous in the service of this God. The Brahmo Samaj, then, instituted worship services and a type of piety that were rationalistic, humanistic, and devoid of distinctive Hindu symbols and customs. Many Westerners applauded this movement, but it never gained popularity among Hindus.

The Arya Samaj was founded in 1875 by Swami Dayananda (1824–1883) as another attempt to restore Hinduism to its original purity. Like Ram Mohan Roy, Dayananda found the essence of Hinduism in the *Vedas*, which he said taught monotheism and morality. Dayananda was particularly keen on abolishing image worship and caste discrimination. His basis for criticizing the Hindu tradition as it existed in his own day was the *Vedas*. He was suspicious of Western ideas and insisted that a purified Hinduism must involve a return to the *Vedas*. Although the Arya Samaj had a wider appeal than the Brahmo Samaj, it did not succeed in gaining a very wide audience either. Both movements, however, were important in revitalizing Hindu pride and helped to lay the spiritual groundwork for the independence movement, with its championing of Indian traditions and criticisms of Western values and domination.

A third important religious phenomenon of this time was the Bengali saint, Ramakrishna. Ramakrishna (1836–1886) in most ways represented traditional Hindu beliefs and spiritual techniques. He was a temple priest of the goddess Kali, and though he found in this goddess his favorite object of devotion, he worshiped other deities as well in an attempt to discover the special blessing of each god. He also experimented with the different Hindu paths, such as Tantrism and the path of knowledge. His reaction to Western religions was simply to experiment with them in his own religious life. In these experiments he is said to have been successful, several times having visions of Muslim and Christian heroes. Ramakrishna sought, then, to incorporate Western ideas and religions into the expansive Hindu context and not to reform Hinduism by making it conform to Western ideas of monotheism or humanism. Unlike Ram Mohan Roy and Dayananda, Ramakrishna was widely considered a great saint by his fellow Hindus even before his death and probably represents the most typical Hindu response to foreign influence.

Ramakrishna's favorite disciple was Vivekananda (1863–1902), who is often considered the first successful Hindu missionary to the West. In 1893 he addressed the First World Parliament of Religions at Chicago and was enthusiastically received there and by many Americans in his subsequent travels throughout the United States. Returning to India a national hero, he instituted plans for fellow members of his movement to set up centers in the West to foster the teachings and practice of Hinduism. The Hinduism of Vivekananda was much less devotional than Ramakrishna's own piety and stressed the monistic teachings of the *Upanishads* and the Vedanta of Shankara. The Ramakrishna Mission was thus inaugurated in the West and became the first successful attempt to transplant Hinduism to that part of the world.

Both the persistence and modification of traditional Hindu themes are clear in the Indian independence movement, particularly in its two most famous leaders, Bal Gangadhar Tilak (1856–1920) and Mohandas Karamchand Gandhi (1869–1948). Both Tilak and Gandhi took the *Bhagavad Gita* and its teachings concerning *loka-samgraha*, supporting the world, as central to their positions, and both were considered karma-yogis, masters of disciplined action. However, the two differed considerably in their styles and provide a modern expression of the continuing tension between renunciation and support of the world.

Tilak's greatest work was his commentary on the *Bhagavad Gita*, the *Gita Rahasya*, in which he argued that the Hindu's primary responsibility is to work out his or her spiritual destiny while remaining in the world and acting without desire for the fruits of his or her actions.

He systematically refuted all earlier commentaries on the *Gita* and saw in this most famous of Hindu scriptures the theoretical foundation of political activism. Tilak, opposing all Hindus who argued for gradual reform and eventual independence, advocated no compromise with foreign rulers. For Tilak the *Gita* was a manual for action that, given its context, the battlefield, permitted the use of violence in a just cause. Renunciation of the world was unpatriotic and a sign of weakness. In his many speeches and writings Tilak never tired of calling his fellow Hindus to responsible action in and for the world.

Gandhi, too, interpreted the *Gita* as teaching involvement in the world, and it was the *Gita* that provided the theoretical background for his teaching and technique of satyagraha, holding to the truth. Satyagraha for Gandhi was the task of expressing the truth in every action, no matter what the result, the task of acting without regard for rewards. Gandhi, however, chose to read the *Gita* as a nonviolent text and refused to permit violence in his various political campaigns; he urged restraint, negotiation, and self-sacrifice instead. His style of life also differed from Tilak's and is reminiscent of the ascetic tradition in Hinduism. Although a householder, Gandhi early in his career practiced strict poverty, restricting his possessions to a few necessities, and later in life took a vow of celibacy. He wore little clothing and lived on a very restricted diet. Gandhi added to the role of the classic Hindu world renouncer, however, the element of community service. His asceticism was aimed at harnessing energy and vitality that would be used to support India's poor and oppressed. His spiritual mission, in addition to personal liberation, was the liberation of his fellow Hindus from ignorance, caste hatred, economic and political domination by foreigners, and material poverty. Gandhi's quest represented the inextricable combination of personal purification with the purification of the world.

In recent years varied expressions of Hinduism have found their way to the West, in a continuation of the precedent set by Vivekananda in 1893. Although Hinduism had moved beyond its own borders before the modern period, it was primarily a result of Indian emigration to other countries and the resulting establishment of Hindu culture in such places as Sri Lanka and Indonesia. In the modern period, however, beginning with Vivekananda, various Hindus have self-consciously sought to spread Hinduism outside of India. These figures have been many and diverse in their interpretations of the Hindu religion.

Two recent gurus (spiritual masters) who have gained a degree of popularity in the West are Maharishi Mahesh Yogi (ca. 1911), founder of the Spiritual Regeneration Movement, or Transcendental Meditation, and Swami

A. C. Bhaktivedanta (1896–1977), founder of the International Society for Krishna Consciousness. Although both movements have begun to take on certain pragmatic aspects suitable to the West, by emphasizing the scientific laws underlying their teachings and the practical or emotional benefits obtained from them, both movements, especially in their early phases, represent authentic Hindu traditions. Transcendental Meditation looks to Vedanta for its theoretical basis, emphasizing each person's inner divine essence and the liberating powers that may be harnessed when one's true identity is known. Maharishi is a typical modern exponent, then, of the ancient tradition in Hinduism that emphasizes the inward search for liberating knowledge. The International Society for Krishna Consciousness, on the other hand, emphasizes enthusiastic devotion to Lord Krishna and is a direct descendent of the Bengali devotionalism of Chaitanya (1485–1536). As such the movement expresses the kind of devotion to personal gods that has dominated Hinduism since the sixth century C.E.

SOURCES

I have organized the sources historically to provide an overview of some of the important religious literature of Hinduism. This organization departs from the topical organization used in chapters 4 and 5 in part because it is easier to date written material than oral traditions. However, the same topics will be covered—creation, gods and goddesses, ritual and moral practices, religious experiences, and the like—so that those who wish to do comparative studies by topics can do so. Nevertheless, we must not forget that comparison of topics is like comparing pictures of a similar scene. Pictures, however interesting, are extracted from a living, changing, dynamic process that is more like a moving picture than a scrapbook.

To facilitate readability, I have left out diacritical marks in my spelling of Sanskrit terms, but the translations I have used frequently include them. Diacritical marks indicate how sounds in a language other than English are to be made. See the Pronunciation Guide at the end of this chapter for more information.

6.2 THE VEDIC PERIOD

I am using the term *Vedic period* to designate the later part (ca. 1200–400 B.C.E.) of what Kinsley calls the formative and speculative periods. While there is much archaeological evidence surviving from pre-Vedic times (ca. 2500–1500 B.C.E.), the script has not yet been deciphered. As we learn more about this period, it is likely we will discover a greater influence on Vedic literature than presently imagined.

The **Vedas** are the earliest sacred writings of the Indo-Aryans who migrated into Northwest India from the North around 1500 B.C.E. The word *veda* means "knowledge" in Sanskrit (the language in which the *Vedas* are written) and in the *narrow* sense refers to the four *Vedas* (*Rig, Sama, Yajur,* and *Atharva*). In the *broad* sense, the *Vedas* also refer to a collection of three types of literature developed by the priestly specialists who produced the four *Vedas*. These three types are called the *Brahmanas* (ca. 1100–700 B.C.E.), the *Aranyakas* (ca. 800–600 B.C.E.), and the *Upanishads* (ca. 700–400 B.C.E.). This whole vast collection of literature is also called **shruti,** which literally means "that which is heard" and is sometimes translated as "revelation." Because these texts are religiously authoritative, they have been referred to as the Hindu scriptures. Both the words *revelation* and *scripture*, however, are misleading. There is no divine author of the *Vedas* (they are said to be "authorless"), and, while this collection constitutes sacred writing (scripture in the broad sense), it is not scripture in the narrow sense of a divinely inspired set of texts.

The claim that the *Vedas* are sacred yet without a divine author may strike you as odd if you have been raised in a Christian, Jewish, or Islamic tradition. However, according to later philosophical thought in India, one of the valid sources of knowledge is testimony. It is valid provided the person giving the testimony knows what she or he is talking about and testifies truthfully. If a testimony has no author, then its validity is difficult to doubt because there is no testifier to question. The doctrine that the *Vedas* are authorless is another way of saying that these writings have no human imperfection. Of course, there were "authors" in the conventional sense, some of whom were priests and poets called **rishis**—persons who have visions that they believe put them directly in touch with sacred powers and sources, including gods and goddesses. The *rishis*, it is said, *heard eternal truths*, and thus no stamp of these individual, historical "authors" is (presumably) found in the texts.

The gods of the Aryan religion referred to in the *Vedas* are, like the gods of the Greeks, in charge of various natural forces. Dyaüs Pitr (whose name means "shining father") is, like his Greek counterpart Zeus Pater, father of the gods. Indra, the god of storm and war, receives great attention in the *Vedas*, suggesting that the early Aryan invaders were predominately from a warrior class. Agni, whose name is related to the English word *ignite*, is the fire god who carries the sacrifices to the gods in the sky. Ushas or Dawn is one of the few goddesses mentioned in the *Vedas*. Rudra is in charge of the wind, Varuna oversees justice, Vishnu is responsible for order, and Surya is the major sun god. Yama is the god of the dead, and the god Soma was able to give a foretaste of immortality even in this mortal life.

Many of these Aryan gods are no longer worshiped, but elements of this ancient Aryan religion live on in modern Hinduism especially in the lore and ritual activity. Fire, for example, still plays a major role in Hindu ritual life, and many of the ancient chants are still used.

6.2.1 *Rig Veda*

The *Rig Veda*, the oldest of the *Vedas*, consists of more than a thousand hymns composed and collected over hundreds of years. I include only four here. The first stands quite appropriately at the beginning of the *Rig Veda*. It is a prayer to Agni, the god of fire. The heart of Vedic religion is the performance of sacrifices to the gods. Fire transforms the sacrificed into smoke that ascends to the heavens and feeds the gods. Without sacrifice, the gods would go hungry and disorder rather than order would consume the universe.

The *Rig Veda* recognizes that, within the natural order, everything can be divided into food and the eaters of food. A vast food chain stretches from the gods to water. The gods feed on humans, symbolically represented by sacrificial victims. Humans feed on animals, animals on plants, and plants on water, the sustainer of life. Agni and the sacrifices connect this vast hierarchical food chain. Fire makes the world go round.

However, Agni is not the only means facilitating the divine-human relationship. **Soma,** the divine, sacrificial drink and the liquid (water) counterpart of fire, provides visions of the gods, goddesses, and the heavens. Scholars do not agree about which plant was used to make *Soma*, but it may have been a hallucinogenic mushroom. In any case, those who ritually drank it felt free of the bounds of mortality, as our second selection testifies.

The third selection, called the *Purusha-Sukta,* or "The Hymn of Man," celebrates the creation of the universe from the parts of a primal person called

Purusha (here translated as "Man"). Note that creation results from the sacrifice of Purusha, thus establishing the importance of ritual sacrifice for the maintenance of the world order.

The final hymn, usually called the "Creation Hymn," raises a skeptical note about how mere mortals can know anything about the absolute beginning of everything. Creation is a puzzle, challenging humans to raise what seem to be unanswerable questions.

TRANSLATED BY WENDY DONIGER O'FLAHERTY

Hymns from the Rig Veda

READING QUESTIONS

1. What is being prayed for in "I Pray to *Agni*"?
2. What benefits can *Soma* bestow?
3. How does the traditional organization of Hindu society into four general classes (*varnas*, sometimes translated as "castes") receive a cosmic sanction in this hymn?
4. What do you think the "Creation Hymn" means?

1.1 I PRAY TO AGNI

1 I pray to Agni, the household priest who is the god of the sacrifice, the one who chants and invokes and brings most treasure.

2 Agni earned the prayers of the ancient sages, and of those of the present, too; he will bring the gods here.

3 Through Agni one may win wealth, and growth from day to day, glorious and most abounding in heroic sons.

4 Agni, the sacrificial ritual that you encompass on all sides—only that one goes to the gods.

5 Agni, the priest with the sharp sight of a poet, the true and most brilliant, the god will come with the gods.

6 Whatever good you wish to do for the one who worships you, Agni, through you, O Angiras,[1] that comes true.

From *The Rig Veda: An Anthology*, translated by Wendy Doniger O'Flaherty (London: Penguin Books, Ltd., 1981), selections 1.1 (p. 99), 8.48 (pp. 134–135), 10.90 (pp. 30–31), and 10.129 (pp. 25–26). Copyright © 1981 Wendy Doniger O'Flaherty. Reprinted by permission of Penguin Books, Ltd. Footnotes edited.
[1] The Angirases were an ancient family of priests, often identified with Vedic gods such as Agni and Indra.

7 To you, Agni, who shine upon darkness, we come day after day, bringing our thoughts and homage

8 to you, the king over sacrifices, the shining guardian of the Order, growing in your own house.

9 Be easy for us to reach, like a father to his son. Abide with us, Agni, for our happiness.

8.48 WE HAVE DRUNK THE SOMA

1 I have tasted the sweet drink of life, knowing that it inspires good thoughts and joyous expansiveness to the extreme, that all the gods and mortals seek it together, calling it honey.

2 When you penetrate inside, you will know no limits, and you will avert the wrath of the gods. Enjoying Indra's friendship, O drop of Soma, bring riches as a docile cow brings the yoke.

3 We have drunk the Soma; we have become immortal; we have gone to the light; we have found the gods. What can hatred and the malice of a mortal do to us now, O immortal one?

4 When we have drunk you, O drop of Soma, be good to our heart, kind as a father to his son, thoughtful as a friend to a friend. Far-famed Soma, stretch out our life-span so that we may live.

5 The glorious drops that I have drunk set me free in wide space. You have bound me together in my limbs as thongs bind a chariot. Let the drops protect me from the foot that stumbles and keep lameness away from me.

6 Inflame me like a fire kindled by friction; make us see far; make us richer, better. For when I am intoxicated with you, Soma, I think myself rich. Draw near and make us thrive.

7 We would enjoy you, pressed with a fervent heart, like riches from a father. King Soma, stretch out our life-spans as the sun stretches the spring days.

8 King Soma, have mercy on us for our well-being. Know that we are devoted to your laws. Passion and fury are stirred up. O drop of Soma, do not hand us over to the pleasure of the enemy.

9 For you, Soma, are the guardian of our body; watching over men, you have settled down in every limb. If we break your laws, O god, have mercy on us like a good friend, to make us better.

10 Let me join closely with my compassionate friend so that he will not injure me when I have drunk him. O lord of bay horses, for the Soma that is lodged in us I approach Indra to stretch out our life-span.

11 Weaknesses and diseases have gone; the forces of darkness have fled in terror. Soma has climbed up in us, expanding. We have come to the place where they stretch out life-spans.

12 The drop that we have drunk has entered our hearts, an immortal inside mortals. O fathers, let us serve that

Soma with the oblations and abide in his mercy and kindness.

13 Uniting in agreement with the fathers, O drop of Soma, you have extended yourself through sky and earth. Let us serve him with an oblation; let us be masters of riches.

14 You protecting gods, speak out for us. Do not let sleep or harmful speech seize us. Let us, always dear to Soma, speak as men of power in the sacrificial gathering.

15 Soma, you give us the force of life on every side. Enter into us, finding the sunlight, watching over men. O drop of Soma, summon your helpers and protect us before and after.

10.90 PURUṢA-SŪKTA, OR THE HYMN OF MAN

1 The Man has a thousand heads, a thousand eyes, a thousand feet. He pervaded the earth on all sides and extended beyond it as far as ten fingers.

2 It is the Man who is all this, whatever has been and whatever is to be. He is the ruler of immortality, when he grows beyond everything through food.

3 Such is his greatness, and the Man is yet more than this. All creatures are a quarter of him; three quarters are what is immortal in heaven.

4 With three quarters the Man rose upwards, and one quarter of him still remains here. From this he spread out in all directions, into that which eats and that which does not eat.

5 From him Virāj[1] was born, and from Virāj came the Man. When he was born, he ranged beyond the earth behind and before.

6 When the gods spread the sacrifice with the Man as the offering, spring was the clarified butter, summer the fuel, autumn the oblation.

7 They anointed the Man, the sacrifice born at the beginning, upon the sacred grass. With him the gods, Sādhyas, and sages sacrificed.

8 From that sacrifice in which everything was offered, the melted fat was collected, and he made it into those beasts who live in the air, in the forest, and in villages.

9 From that sacrifice in which everything was offered, the verses and chants were born, the metres were born from it, and from it the formulas were born.

10 Horses were born from it, and those other animals that have two rows of teeth; cows were born from it, and from it goats and sheep were born.

11 When they divided the Man, into how many parts did they apportion him? What do they call his mouth, his two arms and thighs and feet?

12 His mouth became the Brahmin; his arms were made into the Warrior, his thighs the People, and from his feet the Servants were born.

13 The moon was born from his mind; from his eye the sun was born. Indra and Agni came from his mouth, and from his vital breath the Wind was born.

14 From his navel the middle realm of space arose; from his head the sky evolved. From his two feet came the earth, and the quarters of the sky from his ear. Thus they set the worlds in order.

15 There were seven enclosing-sticks for him, and thrice seven fuel-sticks, when the gods, spreading the sacrifice, bound the Man as the sacrificial beast.

16 With the sacrifice the gods sacrificed to the sacrifice. These were the first ritual laws. These very powers reached the dome of the sky where dwell the Sādhyas, the ancient gods.

10.129 CREATION HYMN (NĀSADĪYA)

1 There was neither non-existence nor existence then; there was neither the realm of space nor the sky which is beyond. What stirred? Where? In whose protection? Was there water, bottomlessly deep?

2 There was neither death nor immortality then. There was no distinguishing sign of night nor of day. That one breathed, windless, by its own impulse. Other than that there was nothing beyond.

3 Darkness was hidden by darkness in the beginning; with no distinguishing sign, all this was water. The life force that was covered with emptiness, that one arose through the power of heat.

4 Desire came upon that one in the beginning; that was the first seed of mind. Poets seeking in their heart with wisdom found the bond of existence in non-existence.

5 Their cord was extended across. Was there below? Was there above? There were seed-placers; there were powers. There was impulse beneath; there was giving-forth above.

6 Who really knows? Who will here proclaim it? Whence was it produced? Whence is this creation? The gods came afterwards, with the creation of this universe. Who then knows whence it has arisen?

7 Whence this creation his arisen—perhaps it formed itself, or perhaps it did not—the one who looks down on it, in the highest heaven, only he knows—or perhaps he does not know.

---

[1] The active female creative principle, Virāj, is later replaced by Prakṛti, or material nature. . . .

6.2.2 Upanishads

The Upanishadic literature indicates that religious and philosophical reflection on the meaning and significance of sacrifice inspired many thinkers to explore questions about the nature of reality, the self, and life after death. Doubt arises about the effectiveness of ritual sacrifice since the law of *karma* represents a strict and universal cause-effect continuum. Any action (**karma**), including sacrifice, that is motivated by desire results in bondage to a universal round of reincarnations (**samsara**). The spiritual goal is to become liberated or released (*moksha* or *mukti*) from the cycle of *samsara*. It is ignorance about reality and the self that keeps us bound to *samsara*. Hence, genuine knowledge must replace ignorance if true freedom is to be achieved.

The ideas of *karma* and *samsara* are related. *Karma* is what determines one's rebirth in the samsaric cycle. Acting in any way at all produces *karma*, because *karma* is not only action but also the results of action. *Karma* is what you do and what happens to you. What happens to you in this life is a result of what you did in a previous life, and what will happen to you in the future is the result of what you do now. Your *jiva*, or individual soul, carries the imprints of your actions from one life to the next. Could one somehow leave the *jiva* behind and thereby break the samsaric cycle?

The idea of *moksha*, or release, indicates that it is possible to escape karmic results and gain liberation from the samsaric cycle. Just how best to do this became an intense religious debate in India, but that such release was possible is repeated many times in the *Upanishads*. The discipline (*yoga*) required to obtain *moksha* attracted much attention as religious ideas embedded deep in the *Upanishads* are explicated in later centuries.

Selections from two *Upanishads* follow. The *Brihadaranyaka Upanishad* is held in high esteem. Its first chapter revisits the theme of creation, and the second chapter reports a conversation about immortality between a sage named Yajnavalkya and his wife, Maitreyi. The *Chandogya Upanishad* contains a famous and influential conversation between a father and a son on the true nature of one's identity.

TRANSLATED BY PATRICK OLIVELLE

Brihadaranyaka and Chandogya Upanishads

READING QUESTIONS

1. How does the creative process start, and how are every male and female pair created?
2. What is *Brahman*'s super-creation?
3. Interpret verses 7 and 8 of chapter 1 of *Brihadaranyaka* in your own words. What do you think is the central message here? What evidence would you cite to support your views?
4. Why does Yajnavalkya say to Maitreyi, "by reflecting and concentrating on one's self, one gains the knowledge of this whole world"?
5. Yajnavalkya offers several analogies to illuminate his claim that "all that is nothing but this self." Explain how the analogies aid us in understanding this claim.
6. How does Yajnavalkya explain the meaning of his claim that "after death there is no awareness"?
7. What is the rule of substitution?
8. What do you think the phrase "that's how you are" means?

BRIHADARANYAKA

Chapter 1

4

In the beginning this world was just a single body (*ātman*) shaped like a man. He looked around and saw nothing but himself. The first thing he said was, "Here I am!" and from that the name "I" came into being. Therefore, even today when you call someone, he first says, "It's I," and then states whatever other name he may have. That first being received the name "man" (*puruṣa*), because ahead (*pūrva*) of all this he burnt up (*uṣ*) all evils.

From *Brihadaranyaka* 1.4.1–8, 2.4.1–14; *Chandogya* 6.1.1–7, 6.2.1–4, 6.10.1–3, 6.11.1–3; in *Upanishads*, translated by Patrick Olivelle (Oxford's World Classics, 1998), pp. 13–15, 28–30, 148–149, 153–154. Reprinted by permission of Oxford University Press.

When someone knows this, he burns up anyone who may try to get ahead of him.

²That first being became afraid; therefore, one becomes afraid when one is alone. Then he thought to himself: "Of what should I be afraid, when there is no one but me?" So his fear left him, for what was he going to be afraid of? One is, after all, afraid of another.

³He found no pleasure at all; so one finds no pleasure when one is alone. He wanted to have a companion. Now he was as large as a man and a woman in close embrace. So he split (*pat*) his body into two, giving rise to husband (*pati*) and wife (*patnī*). Surely this is why Yājñavalkya used to say: "The two of us are like two halves of a block." The space here, therefore, is completely filled by the woman.

He copulated with her, and from their union human beings were born.⁴ She then thought to herself: "After begetting me from his own body (*ātman*), how could he copulate with me? I know—I'll hide myself." So she became a cow. But he became a bull and copulated with her. From their union cattle were born. Then she became a mare, and he a stallion; she became a female donkey, and he, a male donkey. And again he copulated with her, and from their union one-hoofed animals were born. Then she became a female goat, and he, a male goat; she became a ewe, and he, a ram. And again he copulated with her, and from their union goats and sheep were born. In this way he created every male and female pair that exists, down to the very ants.

⁵It then occurred to him: "I alone am the creation, for I created all this." From this "creation" came into being. Anyone who knows this prospers in this creation of his.

⁶Then he churned like this and, using his hands, produced fire from his mouth as from a vagina. As a result the inner sides of both these—the hands and the mouth—are without hair, for the inside of the vagina is without hair. "Sacrifice to this god. Sacrifice to that god"—people do say these things, but in reality each of these gods is his own creation, for he himself is all these gods. From his semen, then, he created all that is moist here, which is really Soma. Food and eater—that is the extent of this whole world. Food is simply Soma, and the eater is fire.

This is *brahman*'s super-creation. It is a super-creation because he created the gods, who are superior to him, and, being a mortal himself, he created the immortals. Anyone who knows this stands within this super-creation of his.

⁷At that time this world was without real distinctions; it was distinguished simply in terms of name and visible appearance—"He is so and so by name and has this sort of an appearance." So even today this world is distin-

guished simply in terms of name and visible appearance, as when we say, "He is so and so by name and has this sort of an appearance."

Penetrating this body up to the very nailtips, he remains there like a razor within a case or a termite within a termite-hill. People do not see him, for he is incomplete as he comes to be called breath when he is breathing, speech when he is speaking, sight when he is seeing, hearing when he is hearing, and mind when he is thinking. These are only the names of his various activities. A man who considers him to be any one of these does not understand him, for he is incomplete within any one of these. One should consider them as simply his self (*ātman*), for in it all these become one. This same self (*ātman*) is the trail to this entire world, for by following it one comes to know this entire world, just as by following their tracks one finds [the cattle]. Whoever knows this finds fame and glory.

⁸This innermost thing, this self (*ātman*)—it is dearer than a son, it is dearer than wealth, it is dearer than everything else. If a man claims that something other than his self is dear to him, and someone were to tell him that he will lose what he holds dear, that is liable to happen. So a man should regard only his self as dear to him. When a man regards only his self as dear to him, what he holds dear will never perish.

Chapter 2

4

"Maitreyī!" Yājñavalkya once said. "Look—I am about to depart from this place. So come, let me make a settlement between you and Kātyāyanī."

²Maitreyī asked in reply: "If I were to possess the entire world filled with wealth, sir, would it make me immortal?" "No," said Yājñavalkya, "it will only permit you to live the life of a wealthy person. Through wealth one cannot expect immortality."

³"What is the point in getting something that will not make me immortal?" retorted Maitreyī. "Tell me instead, sir, all that you know."

⁴Yājñavalkya said in reply: "You have always been very dear to me, and now you speak something very dear to me! Come and sit down. I will explain it to you. But while I am explaining, try to concentrate." ⁵Then he spoke:

"One holds a husband dear, you see, not out of love for the husband; rather, it is out of love for oneself (*ātman*) that one holds a husband dear. One holds a wife dear not out of love for the wife; rather, it is out of love for oneself that one holds a wife dear. One holds children dear not out of love for the children; rather, it is out of love for oneself that one holds children dear. One holds wealth dear not out of love for wealth; rather, it is out of love for oneself that one holds wealth dear. One holds the priestly power dear not out of love for the priestly power; rather, it is out of love for oneself that one holds the priestly power dear. One holds the royal power dear not out of love for the royal power; rather, it is out of love for oneself that one holds the royal power dear. One holds the worlds dear not out of love for the worlds; rather, it is out of love for oneself that one holds the worlds dear. One holds the gods dear not out of love for the gods; rather, it is out of love for oneself that one holds the gods dear. One holds beings dear not out of love for beings; rather, it is out of love for oneself that one holds beings dear. One holds the Whole dear not out of love for the Whole; rather, it is out of love for oneself that one holds the Whole dear.

"You see, Maitreyī—it is one's self (*ātman*) which one should see and hear, and on which one should reflect and concentrate. For by seeing and hearing one's self, and by reflecting and concentrating on one's self, one gains the knowledge of this whole world.

⁶"May the priestly power forsake anyone who considers the priestly power to reside in something other than his self (*ātman*). May the royal power forsake anyone who considers the royal power to reside in something other than his self. May the gods forsake anyone who considers the gods to reside in something other than his self. May beings forsake anyone who considers beings to reside in something other than his self. May the Whole forsake anyone who considers the Whole to reside in something other than his self.

"All these—the priestly power, the royal power, worlds, gods, beings, the Whole—all that is nothing but this self.

⁷"It is like this. When a drum is being beaten, you cannot catch the external sounds; you catch them only by getting hold of the drum or the man beating that drum. ⁸Or when a conch is being blown, you cannot catch the external sounds; you catch them only by getting hold of the conch or the man blowing that conch. ⁹Or when a lute is being played, you cannot catch the external sounds; you catch them only by getting hold of the lute or the man playing that lute.

¹⁰"It is like this. As clouds of smoke billow from a fire lit with damp fuel, so indeed this Immense Being has exhaled all this: Ṛgveda, Yajurveda, Sāmaveda, the Atharva-Aṅgirasa, histories, ancient tales, sciences, hidden teachings (*upaniṣad*), verses, aphorisms, explanations, and glosses—it is that Immense Being who has exhaled all this.

¹¹"It is like this. As the ocean is the point of convergence of all the waters, so the skin is the point of convergence of all sensations of touch; the nostrils, of all odours; the tongue, of all tastes; sight, of all visible appearances; hearing, of all sounds; the mind, of all thoughts; the heart, of all sciences; the hands, of all activities; the sexual organ, of all pleasures; the anus, of all excretions; the feet, of all travels; and speech, of all the Vedas.

¹²"It is like this. When a chunk of salt is thrown in water, it dissolves into that very water, and it cannot be picked up in any way. Yet, from whichever place one may take a sip, the salt is there! In the same way this Immense Being has no limit or boundary and is a single mass of perception. It arises out of and together with these beings and disappears after them—so I say, after death there is no awareness."

After Yājñavalkya said this, ¹³Maitreyī exclaimed: "Now, sir, you have totally confused me by saying 'after death there is no awareness.'" He replied:

"Look, I haven't said anything confusing; this body, you see, has the capacity to perceive. ¹⁴For when there is a duality of some kind, then the one can smell the other, the one can see the other, the one can hear the other, the one can greet the other, the one can think of the other, and the one can perceive the other. When, however, the Whole has become one's very self (*ātman*), then who is there for one to smell and by what means? Who is there for one to see and by what means? Who is there for one to hear and by what means? Who is there for one to greet and by what means? Who is there for one to think of and by what means? Who is there for one to perceive and by what means?

"By what means can one perceive him by means of whom one perceives this whole world? Look—by what means can one perceive the perceiver?"

CHANDOGYA

Chapter 6

1

There was one Śvetaketu, the son of Āruṇi. One day his father told him: "Śvetaketu, take up the celibate life of a student, for there is no one in our family, my son, who has not studied and is the kind of Brahmin who is so only because of birth."

²So he went away to become a student at the age of 12 and, after learning all the Vedas, returned when he was 24, swell-headed, thinking himself to be learned, and arrogant. ³His father then said to him: Śvetaketu, here you are, my son, swell-headed, thinking yourself to be learned, and arrogant; so you must have surely asked

about that rule of substitution by which one hears what has not been heard of before, thinks of what has not been thought of before, and perceives what has not been perceived before?"

[4] "How indeed does that rule of substitution work, sir?"

"It is like this, son. By means of just one lump of clay one would perceive everything made of clay—the transformation is a verbal handle, a name—while the reality is just this: 'It's clay.'

[5] "It is like this, son. By means of just one copper trinket one would perceive everything made of copper—the transformation is a verbal handle, a name—while the reality is just this: 'It's copper.'

[6] "It is like this, son. By means of just one nail-cutter one would perceive everything made of iron—the transformation is a verbal handle, a name—while the reality is just this: 'It's iron.'

"That, son, is how this rule of substitution works."

[7] "Surely, those illustrious men did not know this, for had they known, how could they have not told it to me? So, why don't you, sir, tell me yourself?"

"All right, son," he replied.

2

"In the beginning, son, this world was simply what is existent—one only, without a second. Now, on this point some do say: In the beginning this world was simply what is non-existent—one only, without a second. And from what is non-existent was born what is existent.

[2] "But, son, how can that possibly be?" he continued. "How can what is existent be born from what is non-existent? On the contrary, son, in the beginning this world was simply what is existent—one only, without a second.

[3] "And it thought to itself: 'Let me become many. Let me propagate myself.' It emitted heat. The heat thought to itself: 'Let me become many. Let me propagate myself.' It emitted water. Whenever it is hot, therefore, a man surely perspires; and thus it is from heat that water is produced. [4] The water thought to itself: 'Let me become many. Let me propagate myself.' It emitted food. Whenever it rains, therefore, food becomes abundant; and thus it is from water that foodstuffs are produced. . . .

10

"Now, take these rivers, son. The easterly ones flow towards the east, and the westerly ones flow towards the west. From the ocean, they merge into the very ocean;

they become just the ocean. In that state they are not aware that: 'I am that river,' and 'I am this river.' [2] In exactly the same way, son, when all these creatures reach the existent, they are not aware that: 'We are reaching the existent.' No matter what they are in this world—whether it is a tiger, a lion, a wolf, a boar, a worm, a moth, a gnat, or a mosquito—they all merge into that.

[3] "The finest essence here—that constitutes the self of this whole world; that is the truth; that is the self (*ātman*). And that's how you are, Śvetaketu."

"Sir, teach me more."

"Very well, son.

11

"Now, take this huge tree here, son. If someone were to hack it at the bottom, its living sap would flow. Likewise, if someone were to hack it in the middle, its living sap would flow; and if someone were to hack it at the top, its living sap would flow. Pervaded by the living (*jīva*) essence (*ātman*), this tree stands here ceaselessly drinking water and flourishing. [2] When, however, life (*jīva*) leaves one of its branches, that branch withers away. When it leaves a second branch, that likewise withers away, and when it leaves a third branch, that also withers away. When it leaves the entire tree, the whole tree withers away.

[3] "In exactly the same way," he continued, "know that this, of course, dies when it is bereft of life (*jīva*); but life itself does not die.

"The finest essence here—that constitutes the self of this whole world; that is the truth; that is the self (*ātman*). And that's how you are, Śvetaketu." . . .

6.3 THE CLASSICAL PERIOD

The classical period (ca. 500 B.C.E.–500) is often identified as one of "synthesis." During this period many of the beliefs and practices associated with orthodox Hinduism became solidified. It is sometimes called the epic period because the great Hindu epics, especially the *Mahabharata*, were composed at this time. However, the development of Hindu religious literature went far beyond the epics.

During this period the important distinction between **shruti** ("what is heard") and **smriti** ("what is remembered" or "tradition") develops. *Smriti* refers to all the literature that falls outside *shruti*, and, unlike *shruti*, which designates the eternal and author-less *Vedas*, *smriti* is historical and does have authors (some human and some divine). *Smriti* texts of this period proclaim the authority of the *Vedas* and thus declare their orthodoxy (right teaching). Hence any religious or philosophical ideas that developed in India and did not recognize the authority of the *Vedas* are heterodox ("other teaching") from the point of view of those religious movements (later called Hinduism) that did recognize the authority of the *Vedas*.

The **orthodox/heterodox** distinction arose because this was a time of political, social, and religious turbulence. Foreign peoples (Greeks, Scythians, Parthians, and others) encountered the Hindus, and Buddhist and Jainist groups (who rejected the authority of the *Vedas*) were beginning to gain followers. The need of Hindus to establish a religious and cultural identity grew as pluralism developed.

We will sample four of the most important *smriti* texts from this period. The first (*Laws of Manu*) represents developments in moral and legal ideas and the second and third (*Ramayana* and *Bhagavad Gita*) provide a look at the epic literature. Finally, the *Yoga Sutra* introduces us to a spiritual practice that was gaining widespread attention.

6.3.1 Laws of Manu

Tradition says that Manu, the author of the *Laws*, is the name of a king who is the ancestor of the human race. He is sometimes called the "Indian Adam," and his name means "wise one." Although he is said to be a king and hence a member of the *kshatriya*, or warrior class, clearly the priestly class, or **brahmins,** are portrayed as the superior class. Hence it seems safe to conclude that these *Laws* were written by priests to instruct other priests on what sort of law and morality they should teach. It should also be noted that they were written by males who were concerned with controlling the conduct of females.

I have referred to the priests and kings as **classes** (*varnas*) rather than **castes,** because there were many castes (*jatis*, meaning "birth") assigned to the four *varnas* (priests, warriors, merchant-farmers, and ser-

vants). Besides the four classes, the *Laws of Manu* detail the *ashramas*, or **four stages of life:** student, householder, forest dweller, and wandering-ascetic or world renouncer. The task of the priestly authors was to detail the **dharma** (a term that can be translated as duty, law, religion, right, justice, practice, teaching, and principle) appropriate for each class at each stage of life.

The duties outlined in the *Laws of Manu* codified and idealized a way of life. They established and reinforced a hierarchical structuring of society that concentrated social power and wealth in the hands of males who occupied the top rungs of the social ladder. The *Laws of Manu* (and similar texts from other religions) have provided fertile evidence for sociological theories of religion (see chapter 3) that seek to uncover the role religion plays in distributing power and maintaining social control.

We must, however, always keep in mind that written texts do not always reflect what is going on in society. Women and men do not necessarily act in the idealized ways the priests described in the *Laws of Manu*. Clearly, not every person between the ages of 8 and 20 fulfills the priestly ideal of a celibate student life devoted to learning religious texts. Nor, during the householder stage of marriage, does every wife accept without question the authority of her husband and live a life of complete domestic service. While many husbands may have tried in ancient times and are trying even today to "guard" their wives, their efforts have not always been appreciated. Likewise, after the householder stage of marriage and family, not every Hindu is able, when the grandchildren arrive, to retire to the forest and once again become devoted to the study of religious matters.

The final stage of world renouncer (*sannyasin*) allows one the freedom to wander homeless outside of caste or settle in a religious community (*ashram*). The purpose of this sort of life is to devote all one's energy to attaining *moksha*, but most people do not have either the opportunity or the luxury of complete abandonment of all worldly ties and responsibilities. Although many in India may admire a life of spiritual freedom, few are able to practice it.

TRANSLATED BY WENDY DONIGER WITH BRIAN K. SMITH

Laws of Manu

READING QUESTIONS

1. Where does the power of a king come from, what are the duties of a king, and what happens if the king fails to inflict just punishment?
2. How do you think the difference in duties for husbands and wives arose, and how does this codification of duties make it harder to deviate from expected social roles?
3. What are the duties of commoners (merchant-farmer class) during the householder stage of life?
4. What is the supreme good of the servant class?
5. How is the promise of rebirth into a higher class used to reinforce social control and order?

CHAPTER 7

[1] I will explain the duties of kings, how a king should behave, how he came to exist, and how (he may have) complete success. [2] A ruler who has undergone his transformative Vedic ritual in accordance with the rules should protect this entire (realm) properly. [3] For when this world was without a king and people ran about in all directions out of fear, the Lord emitted a king in order to guard this entire (realm), [4] taking lasting elements from Indra, the Wind, Yama, the Sun, Fire, Varuṇa, the Moon, and (Kubera) the Lord of Wealth. [5] Because a king is made from particles of these lords of the gods, therefore he surpasses all living beings in brilliant energy, [6] and, like the Sun, he burns eyes and hearts, and no one on earth is able even to look at him. [7] Through his special power he becomes Fire and Wind; he is the Sun and the Moon, and he is (Yama) the King of Justice, he is Kubera and he is Varuṇa, and he is great Indra. [8] Even a boy king should not be treated with disrespect, with the thought, "He is just a human being"; for this is a great deity standing there in the form of a man.

From *The Laws of Manu*, translated by Wendy Doniger with Brian K. Smith (London: Penguin Books, 1991), 7.1–24, 87–98 (pp. 128–130, 137–138); 9.1–19, 326–335 (pp. 197–199, 232–233). Copyright © 1991 Wendy Doniger and Brian K. Smith. Reprinted by permission from Penguin Books. Footnotes omitted.

[9] Fire burns just one man who approaches it wrongly, but the fire of a king burns the whole family, with its livestock and its heap of possessions. [10] In order to make justice succeed, he takes all forms again and again, taking into consideration realistically what is to be done, (his) power, and the time and place. [11] The lotus goddess of Good Fortune resides in his favour, victory in his aggression, and death in his anger; for he is made of the brilliant energy of all (the gods). [12] The man who is so deluded as to hate him will certainly be destroyed, for the king quickly makes up his mind to destroy him. [13] Therefore no one should violate the justice that the king dispenses for those that please him nor the unpleasant justice (that he dispenses) differently for those that displease him. [14] For (the king's) sake the Lord in ancient times emitted the Rod of Punishment, his own son, (the incarnation of) Justice, to be the protector of all living beings, made of the brilliant energy of ultimate reality. [15] Through fear of him all living beings, stationary and moving, allow themselves to be used and do not swerve from their own duty. [16] Upon men who persist in behaving unjustly he should inflict the punishment they deserve, taking into consideration realistically (the offender's) power and learning and the time and place. [17] The Rod is the king and the man, he is the inflicter and he is the chastiser, traditionally regarded as the guarantor for the duty of the four stages of life. [18] The Rod alone chastises all the subjects, the Rod protects them, the Rod stays awake while they sleep; wise men know that justice is the Rod. [19] Properly wielded, with due consideration, it makes all the subjects happy; but inflicted without due consideration, it destroys everything.

[20] If the king did not tirelessly inflict punishment on those who should be punished, the stronger would roast the weaker like fish on a spit. [21] The crow would eat the sacrificial cake and the dog would lick the oblation; there would be no ownership in anyone, and (everything) would be upside down. [22] The whole world is mastered by punishment, for an unpolluted man is hard to find. Through fear of punishment everything that moves allows itself to be used. [23] The gods, the titans, the centaurs, the ogres, the birds and the snakes, even they allow themselves to be used, but only when under pressure from punishment. [24] All the classes would be corrupted, and all barriers broken, all people would erupt in fury as a result of a serious error in punishment. . . .

[87] When a king who protects his subjects is challenged by kings who are his equal or stronger or weaker, he should remember the duties of rulers and not turn away from battle. [88] Not turning away from battle,

protecting subjects, and obedience to priests are the ultimate source of what is best for kings. [89] Kings who try to kill one another in battle and fight to their utmost ability, never averting their faces, go to heaven. [90] Fighting in a battle, he should not kill his enemies with weapons that are concealed, barbed, or smeared with poison or whose points blaze with fire. [91] He should not kill anyone who has climbed on a mound, or an impotent man, or a man who folds his hands in supplication, or whose hair is unbound, or anyone who is seated or who says, "I am yours"; [92] nor anyone asleep, without armour, naked, without a weapon, not fighting, looking on, or engaged with someone else; [93] nor anyone whose weapons have been broken, or who is in pain, badly wounded, terrified, or fleeing—for he should remember the duties of good men. [94] But if a man flees from a battle in terror and is killed by others, he takes upon himself all the evil deeds of his master, whatever they may be; [95] and whatever (credit for) good deeds a man has earned for the hereafter, if he is killed while fleeing, his master takes all that upon himself. [96] Horses and chariots, elephants, parasols, money, grain, livestock, women, all sorts of things and non-precious metals belong to the man who wins them. [97] But the revealed Vedic canon says, "They must give the king a special portion of the booty." And the king must distribute to all the fighters whatever has not been won individually.

[98] The unembellished, eternal duty of warriors has thus been explained; a ruler who kills his enemies in battle should not slip from this duty. . . .

CHAPTER 9

[1] I will tell the eternal duties of a man and wife who stay on the path of duty both in union and in separation. [2] Men must make their women dependent day and night, and keep under their own control those who are attached to sensory objects. [3] Her father guards her in childhood, her husband guards her in youth, and her sons guard her in old age. A woman is not fit for independence. [4] A father who does not give her away at the proper time should be blamed, and a husband who does not have sex with her at the proper time should be blamed; and the son who does not guard his mother when her husband is dead should be blamed.

[5] Women should especially be guarded against addictions, even trifling ones, for unguarded (women) would bring sorrow upon both families. [6] Regarding this as the supreme duty of all the classes, husbands, even weak ones, try to guard their wives. [7] For by zealously guarding his wife he guards his own descendants, practices, family, and himself, as well as his own duty. [8] The husband enters the wife, becomes an embryo, and is born here on earth. That is why a wife is called a wife (*jāyā*), because he is born (*jāyate*) again in her. [9] The wife brings forth a son who is just like the man she makes love with; that is why he should guard his wife zealously, in order to keep his progeny clean.

[10] No man is able to guard women entirely by force, but they can be entirely guarded by using these means: [11] he should keep her busy amassing and spending money, engaging in purification, attending to her duty, cooking food, and looking after the furniture. [12] Women are not guarded when they are confined in a house by men who can be trusted to do their jobs well; but women who guard themselves by themselves are well guarded. [13] Drinking, associating with bad people, being separated from their husbands, wandering about, sleeping, and living in other people's houses are the six things that corrupt women. [14] Good looks do not matter to them, nor do they care about youth; "A man!" they say, and enjoy sex with him, whether he is good-looking or ugly. [15] By running after men like whores, by their fickle minds, and by their natural lack of affection these women are unfaithful to their husbands even when they are zealously guarded here. [16] Knowing that their very own nature is like this, as it was born at the creation by the Lord of Creatures, a man should make the utmost effort to guard them. [17] The bed and the seat, jewellery, lust, anger, crookedness, a malicious nature, and bad conduct are what Manu assigned to women. [18] There is no ritual with Vedic verses for women; this is a firmly established point of law. For women, who have no virile strength and no Vedic verses, are falsehood; this is well established.

[19] There are many revealed canonical texts to this effect that are sung even in treatises on the meaning of the Vedas, so that women's distinctive traits may be carefully inspected. . . .

[326] When a commoner has undergone the transformative rituals and has married a wife, he should constantly dedicate himself to making a living and tending livestock. [327] For when the Lord of Creatures emitted livestock he gave them over to the commoner, and he gave all creatures over to the priest and the king. [328] A commoner must never express the wish, "I would rather not tend livestock," nor should they ever be tended by anyone else when a commoner is willing. [329] He should know the high or low value of gems, pearls, coral, metals, woven cloth, perfumes, and spices. [330] He should know how to sow seeds, and recognize

the virtues and faults of a field, and he should know how to use all sorts of weights and measures; [331] and the worth or worthlessness of merchandise, the good and bad qualities of countries, the profit or loss from trades, and the way to raise livestock. [332] And he should know the wages of hired servants, the various languages of men, the way to preserve goods, and buying and selling. [333] He should make the utmost effort to increase his goods by means in keeping with his duty, and take pains to give food to all creatures.

[334] The servant's duty and supreme good is nothing but obedience to famous priestly householders who know the Veda. [335] If he is unpolluted, obedient to his superiors, gentle in his speech, without a sense of "I," and always dependent on the priests and the other (twice-born classes), he attains a superior birth (in the next life). . . .

6.3.2 Sita and Rama

During the classical, or epic, period, the *Ramayana* (ca. 400–200 B.C.E.) and the *Mahabharata* (ca. 500 B.C.E.– 400) were written. Like the *Laws of Manu*, these epics helped consolidate various strands of religious practices and ideas into a more integrated tradition. In particular, they gave renewed energy and recognition to the *bhakti*, or the devotional tradition.

The religious, moral, and intellectual activities celebrated in the *Vedas* and the law books like the *Laws of Manu* primarily express the religious concerns of the elite classes. The religious practices and concerns of the ordinary people were and are often very different from those of the elite. By focusing on texts written by the elite, we often overlook the unwritten beliefs and practices of the average villager. In many ways, the epics give written voice to the songs and stories told on the streets.

Devotion to various gods, goddesses, and saints is at the heart of the religious practices of the villagers. Incarnations (*avatara*) of the divine attract widespread devotion. The *Mahabharata* centers on **Krishna** and the *Ramayana* centers on **Rama,** both of whom are incarnations of the god Vishnu.

The *Vedas* refer to Vishnu, and, in later times, Vishnu is associated with the gods Brahma and Shiva. These three gods are the *trimurti,* or triple form of the divine. **Brahma** represents the creative power that makes the universe and is often depicted as a king with four faces that look in all four directions. **Vishnu** represents the power that preserves and sustains the created universe and is often depicted with four arms, which hold symbols of power. Ten major incarnations of Vishnu are commonly mentioned. Besides Rama and Krishna, Vishnu has incarnated as a fish, a boar, and a tortoise. Even the Buddha is an incarnation of Vishnu (an idea that helped reabsorb Indian Buddhism), and there is one incarnation yet to come, a savior figure on horseback who will judge the human race.

Shiva represents the power of destruction. The most familiar icon of Shiva is the Shiva Nataraja (ruler of the dance), which depicts Shiva with long yogi hair and dancing within a ring of fire, a drum in one hand symbolizing creation and fire in another hand symbolizing destruction. The universe, like everything else, is subject to cycles of rebirth. Before the creation of a new universe by Brahma, the old must be destroyed by Shiva. Destruction and death make way for new life. Death and life are parts of a single cycle. The fingers of a third arm point to Shiva's feet, inviting all of us to join the dance of life, and his fourth arm is extended in a blessing on all who do.

The *trimurti* (Brahma, Vishnu, and Shiva) is at the heart of much of the popular devotional, or *bhakti,* tradition of India. Temples, art, priests, and **puja** (the ritual offering of flowers, food, and incense to the images of these gods and their female consorts, the goddesses) sustain this tradition. It is also sustained by a rich storytelling tradition that celebrates the exploits of the divine incarnations. Sage-poets who went from village to village spreading the tales of gods and goddesses shaped and kept these traditions alive.

Valmiki was one of the most renowned sage-poets of ancient India and the author of the *Ramayana*. Book I of the epic opens with King Dasa-ratha of Ayodhya performing a sacrifice to get a son. At this time **Ravana,** a great and powerful demon, had conquered much of the world and the gods need a hero to fight and kill him. So Vishnu, the god who sustains the universe, becomes incarnate in the four sons—Rama, Bharat, Lakshmana, and Shatrughna—born to the three wives of King Dasa-ratha. He is most fully incarnate in Rama, who eventually wins the hand in marriage of **Sita,** the daughter of King Janaka in the neighboring kingdom of Videha. The wedding rite, included in the selection that follows, describes rites and vows that are still repeated in many Hindu weddings today.

Book II recounts how King Dasa-ratha intends to make Rama the heir to his kingdom, but he must relent and banish Rama from the kingdom for four-teen years in order to fulfill a vow made to his second queen, Kaikeyi. Kaikeyi wants her son, Bharat, to be king. Rama dutifully obeys his father and plans to leave without Sita but, as the account below indicates, she proves her devotion, love, and loyalty by ac-companying Rama into exile. When King Dasa-ratha dies, Bharat, the new heir and divine brother of Rama, thinks it only just that Rama be king and tries to per-suade him to return. However, as the following ex-cerpt indicates, Rama holds fast to what he believes is the duty of a son to a father.

Books III through VI recount how Sita is kid-napped by the demon Ravana, how Rama and his brother Lakshmana enlist the aid of King Sugriva, the leader of a monkey tribe, whose chief minister is **Hanuman,** and how Rama and the monkey ar-mies find Sita and rescue her after a series of pitched battles with the demons. Hanuman, the monkey gen-eral, becomes the foremost devotee and servant of Rama, and Ravana is finally slain by Rama, the hero of gods and humans. Because Rama questions Sita's virtue after having been a prisoner of Ravana, she must undergo an ordeal by fire in order to prove her faithfulness. Passing the test successfully, Sita and Rama return to Ayodhya to reign as king and queen.

Book VII, sometimes referred to as an epilogue, recounts how the people of Ayodhya spread rumors about Queen Sita's virtue and Rama banishes her to the forest. There she lives with the poet Valmiki and raises the two royal sons Kusha and Lava of whom Rama knows nothing. Finally discovering Sita and his sons, Rama asks for forgiveness and invites Sita to rule as his queen once more. She declines, as the last excerpt indicates, and returns to her mother earth, much to the sorrow of Rama. Rama eventually turns the kingdom over to his sons and ascends into heaven.

Throughout this story there are various subplots and exploits of one sort or another woven together in 48,000 lines of verse. Rama and Sita represent the ideal husband and wife. The geographic locations mentioned in the *Ramayana* have become holy pil-grimage sites. Legends and stories about Rama, Sita, and others are associated with brooks, hills, caverns, and glens in the region where the story is set. The wild fruits that grow there are "Sita-phal," being the reputed food of Rama and Sita in exile. It is said that one who recites the *Ramayana* in the morning, at noon, and at dusk, will never suffer adversity.

Ram Janmabhoomi, the reputed birthplace of Rama in Ayodhya, is today a focus of religious con-flict between Muslims and Hindus. It is the symbolic battleground for those who claim to defend the Hindu tradition against the Muslim threat. The *Ra-mayana* still casts a long shadow over Indian devotion, culture, and politics.

There are many different translations of the *Ra-mayana.* The one used here is by Romesh C. Dutt (1848–1909), a Bengali poet, scholar, and divisional administrator. Although the language is dated in many ways, it still gives, unlike prose translations, the English reader some feeling for the poetic and epic qualities of the original.

VALMIKI

Ramayana

READING QUESTIONS

1. How does the wedding rite compare to others you know about?
2. What are Sita's primary virtues?
3. Whose point of view do you think this picture of Sita represents? Why?
4. Why does Rama reject Bharat's request that he re-turn to Ayodhya and assume his rightful role as king?
5. What kind of ethical reasoning underlies Bharat's arguments and Rama's replies?
6. How do you interpret Sita's final departure?

BOOK I

VI THE WEDDING

Sage Vasishtha skilled in duty placed Videha's
  honoured king,
Viswa-mitra, Sata-nanda, all within the sacred ring,

And he raised the holy altar as the ancient writs ordain,
Decked and graced with scented garlands grateful unto
  gods and men,

And he set the golden ladles, vases pierced by artists
  skilled,

From *The Ramayana and The Mahabharata,* condensed into En-glish verse by Romesh C. Dutt (London: J. M. Dent & Sons, 1910), pp. 9–10, 34, 57–59, 150–152. Selections from Books 1, III, IV, and XI.

Holy censers fresh and fragrant, cups with sacred
　　honey filled,
Sanka bowls and shining salvers, *arghya* plates for
　　honoured guest,
Parchéd rice arranged in dishes, corn unhusked that
　　filled the rest,
And with careful hand Vasishtha grass around the altar
　　flung,
Offered gift to lighted AGNI and the sacred *mantra* sung!

Softly came the sweet-eyed Sita,—bridal blush upon
　　her brow,—
Rama in his manly beauty came to take the sacred vow,

Janak placed his beauteous daughter facing
　　Dasa-ratha's son,
Spake with father's fond emotion and the holy rite
　　was done:

"This is Sita child of Janak, dearer unto him than life,
Henceforth sharer of thy virtue, be she, prince, thy faithful
　　wife,

Of thy weal and woe partaker, be she thine in every land,
Cherish her in joy and sorrow, clasp her hand within thy
　　hand,

As the shadow to the substance, to her lord is faithful wife,
And my Sita best of women follows thee in death or life!"

Tears bedew his ancient bosom, gods and men his
　　wishes share,
And he sprinkles holy water on the blest and wedded
　　pair.

BOOK III [RAMA ADDRESSES
SITA ON PARTING]

"Bharat's will with deep devotion and with faultless
　　faith obey,
Truth and virtue on thy bosom ever hold their gentle
　　away,

And to please each dear relation, gentle Sita, be it
　　thine,
Part we love! for years of wand'ring in the pathless
　　woods is mine!"

Rama spake, and soft-eyed Sita, ever sweet in speech
　　and word,
Stirred by loving woman's passion boldly answered
　　thus her lord:

"Do I hear my husband rightly, are these words my
　　Rama spake,
And her banished lord and husband will the wedded
　　wife forsake?

Lightly I dismiss the counsel which my lord hath lightly
　　said,

For it ill beseems a warrior and my husband's princely
　　grade!

For the faithful woman follows where her wedded lord may
　　lead,
In the banishment of Rama, Sita's exile is decreed,

Sire nor son nor loving brother rules the wedded woman's
　　state,
With her lord she falls or rises, with her consort courts her
　　fate,

If the righteous son of Raghu wends to forests dark and drear,
Sita steps before her husband wild and thorny paths to clear!

Like the tasted refuse water cast thy timid thoughts
　　aside,
Take me to the pathless jungle, bid me by my lord abide,

Car and steed and gilded palace, vain are these to
　　woman's life,
Dearer is her husband's shadow to the loved and loving
　　wife!

For my mother often taught me and my father often
　　spake,
That her home the wedded woman doth beside her
　　husband make,

As the shadow to the substance, to her lord is faithful
　　wife,
And she parts not from her consort till she parts with
　　fleeting life!

Therefore bid me seek the jungle and in pathless
　　forests roam,
Where the wild deer freely ranges and the tiger makes
　　his home,

Happier than in father's mansions in the woods will
　　Sita rove,
Waste no thought on home or kindred, nestling in her
　　husband's love!

World-renowned is Rama's valour, fearless by her
　　Rama's side,
Sita will still live and wander with a faithful woman's
　　pride,

And the wild fruit she will gather from the fresh and
　　fragrant wood,
And the food by Rama tasted shall be Sita's cherished
　　food!

BOOK IV

II BHARAT'S ENTREATY
AND RAMA'S REPLY

"Speak, my true, my faithful Bharat," so the righteous
　　Rama cried,

"Wherefore to this jungle dwelling hast thou from
Ayodhya hied,

Speak, my fond and loving brother, if our father bade
thee come,

Leaving throne and spacious empire in this wilderness
to roam?

Heir and Regent of Kosala! Dost thou tend our father
well,

And obey the lofty mandate from his royal lips that
fell,

And the ancient Dasa-ratha, glorious still in regal
might,

Doth he pass his bright life's evening in each pure and
holy rite?

Doth my mother, Queen Kausalya, still for Rama wet
her eye,

And the gentle Queen Sumitra for her banished
Lakshman sigh,

Doth the peerless Queen Kaikeyi pass her days in
duties fair,

Guard her Bharat's mighty empire, tend him with a
mother's care?

Is each holy rite and homage to the Gods and Fathers
done,

Is the honour due to elders rendered by each duteous
son,

Do thy warriors guard thy kingdom as of yore with
matchless skill,

And with counsel deep and duteous do thy min'sters
serve thy will?

Rich thy fields in corn and produce fed by rivers broad
and deep,

Rich thy green unending pastures with the kine and
fattened sheep,

Tend the herdsman and his cattle, tend the tiller of
the soil,

Watch and help with all thy bounty workmen in their
peaceful toil,

For the monarch's highest duty is to serve his people's
weal

And the ruler's richest glory is to labour and to heal!

Guard thy forts with sleepless caution with the engines
of the war,

With the men who shoot the arrow and who drive the
flying car,

Guard Kosala's royal treasure, make thy gifts of wealth
and food,

Not to lords and proud retainers, but to worthy and
the good!

Render justice pure and spotless as befits thy royal line,
And to save the good and guiltless, Bharat, be it ever
thine,

For the tears of suffering virtue wither like the thunder
levin,

And they slay our men and cattle like the wrath of
righteous heaven,

Fruitful be thy lore of Veda, fruitful be each pious rite,
Be thy queen a fruitful mother, be thy empire full of
might!"

Weeping, weeping, Bharat answered Dasa-ratha's
eldest son,

"Dasa-ratha walks the bright sky, for his earthly task
is done!

For impelled by Queen Kaikeyi to the woods he bade
thee go,

And his spotless fame was clouded and his bosom sank
in woe,

And my mother, late repenting, weeps her deed of
deepest shame,

Weeps her wedded lord departed, and a woman's
tarnished fame!

Thou alone canst wipe this insult by a deed of kindness
done,—

Rule o'er Dasa-ratha's empire, Dasa-ratha's eldest son,

Weeping queens and loyal subjects supplicate thy
noble grace,—

Rule o'er Raghu's ancient empire, son of Raghu's
royal race!

For our ancient Law ordaineth and thy Duty makes
it plain,

Eldest-born succeeds his father as the king of earth
and main,

By the fair Earth loved and welcomed, Rama, be her
wedded lord,

As by planet-jewelled Midnight is the radiant Moon
adored!

And thy father's ancient min'sters and thy courtiers
faithful still,

Wait to do thy righteous mandate and to serve thy
royal will,

As a pupil, as a brother, as a slave, I seek thy grace,—
Come and rule thy father's empire, king of Raghu's
royal race!"

Weeping, on the feet of Rama, Bharat placed his lowly
head,

Weeping for his sire departed, tears of sorrow Rama
shed,

Then he raised his loving brother with an elder's
  deathless love,
Sorrow wakes our deepest kindness and our holiest
  feelings prove!

"But I may not," answered Rama, "seek Ayodhya's
  ancient throne,
For a righteous father's mandate duteous son may not
  disown,

And I may not, gentle brother, break the word of
  promise given,
To a king and to a father who is now a saint in heaven!

Not on thee, nor on thy mother, rests the censure or
  the blame,
Faithful to his father's wishes Rama to the forest came,

For the son and duteous consort serve the father and
  the lord,
Higher than an empire's glory is a father's spoken word!

All inviolate is his mandate,— on Ayodhya's jewelled
  throne,
Or in pathless woods and jungle Rama shall his duty own,

All inviolate is the blessing by a loving mother given,
For she blessed my life in exile like a pitying saint of
  heaven!

*Thou shall rule the kingdom, Bharat, guard our loving
  people well,*
Clad in wild bark and in deer-skin I shall in the forests dwell,

So spake saintly Dasa-ratha in Ayodhya's palace hall,
*And a righteous father's mandate duteous son may not
  recall!"*

BOOK XI

V SITA LOST

Morning dawned; and with Valmiki, Sita to the
  gathering came,
Banished wife and weeping mother, sorrow-stricken,
  suffering dame,

Pure in thought and deed, Valmiki gave his troth and
  plighted word,—
Faithful still the banished Sita in her bosom held
  her lord!

"Mighty Saint," so Rama answered as he bowed his
  humble head,
"Listening world will hear thy mandate and the word
  that thou hast said,

Never in his bosom Rama questioned Sita's faithful
  love,
And the God of Fire incarnate did her stainless virtue
  prove!

Pardon, if the voice of rumour drove me to a deed of
  shame,
Bowing to my people's wishes I disowned my sinless
  dame,

Pardon, if to please my subjects I have bade my Sita
  roam,
Tore her from my throne and empire, tore her from
  my heart and home!

In the dark and dreary forest was my Sita left to mourn,
In the lone and gloomy jungle were my royal children
  born,

Help me, Gods, to wipe this error and this deed of
  sinful pride,
May my Sita prove her virtue, be again my loving
  bride!"

Gods and Spirits, bright Immortals to that royal *Yajna*
  came,
Men of every race and nation, kings and chiefs of
  righteous fame,

Softly through the halls of splendour cool and scented
  breezes blew,
Fragrance of celestial blossoms o'er the royal chambers
  flew.

Sita saw the bright Celestials, monarchs gathered
  from afar,
Saw her royal lord and husband bright as heaven-
  ascending star,

Saw her sons as hermit-minstrels beaming with a
  radiance high,
Milk of love suffused her bosom, tear of sorrow filled
  her eye!

Rama's queen and Janak's daughter, will she stoop her
  cause to plead,
Witness of her truth and virtue can a loving woman
  need?

Oh! her woman's heart is bursting, and her day on
  earth is done,
And she pressed her heaving bosom, slow and sadly
  thus begun:

*"If unstained in thought and action I have lived from day
  of birth,*
*Spare a daughter's shame and anguish and receive her,
  Mother Earth!*

If in duty and devotion I have laboured undefiled,
*Mother Earth! who bore this woman, once again receive thy
  child!*

If in truth unto my husband I have proved a faithful wife,
Mother Earth! relieve thy Sita from the burden of this life!"

Then the earth was rent and parted, and a golden
  throne arose,
Held aloft by jewelled *Nagas* as the leaves enfold
  the rose,
And the Mother in embraces held her spotless sinless
  Child,
Saintly Janak's saintly daughter, pure and true and
  undefiled,
Gods and men proclaim her virtue! But fair Sita is
  no more,
Lone is Rama's loveless bosom and his days of bliss
  are o'er!

6.3.3 Bhagavad Gita

The *Bhagavad Gita*, or *Song of God*, is part of the *Mahabharata* and recounts how Krishna comes to the aid of the Pandava brothers in a civil war with their cousins. The "song" is a dialogue between Krishna (posing as a chariot driver) and the warrior Arjuna, one of the five Pandava brothers.

Arjuna is caught in a dilemma. If he fulfills his duty (*dharma*) as a warrior and fights, he will be fighting and killing members of his own family (his cousins). To kill family members is to fail in one's duty. Arjuna is damned if he does fight and damned if he does not fight. Either way he fails to do his duty and hence gets bad *karma* leading to rebirth.

Here the logic of the law of *karma* and rebirth reaches a startling and disturbing impasse. As mentioned earlier, the word *karma* means both action and the consequences of action. Taking the law of *karma* to its logical extreme, then everything one does, good or bad, leads to rebirth because every action has consequences. There appears no way out of *samsara* (the cycle of suffering and rebirth) because even the paths to liberation (sacrifice, the pursuit of knowledge, doing one's duty) amount to actions. *Moksha*, liberation from rebirth, appears either forever out of reach or possible only if one renounces everything and does absolutely nothing!

Krishna teaches Arjuna the way out of this impasse. He acknowledges and reinforces three paths, or *yogas*, to liberation: action (*karmayoga*), knowledge (*jnanayoga*), and devotion (*bhaktiyoga*). The discipline of *karma* teaches us how to act without attachment to the consequences of our action; the discipline of knowledge teaches us the immortal nature of the true self; and devotion to the divine Krishna teaches us the true nature of sacrifice (surrendering all to the divine). Genuine ritual actions and genuine knowledge are, Krishna teaches, incomplete without genuine devotion to the divine.

As the battle is about to start, Dhritarashtra, the blind brother of Arjuna's father, is granted a boon by the sage Vyasa (the traditional author of the *Mahabharata*). Sanjaya, Dhritarashtra's personal bard and charioteer, is granted a "divine eye" so that he can see and report all the events of the battle directly. Sanjaya thus becomes the narrator of the unfolding events knowing, by virtue of his "divine eye," even the thoughts and feelings of Arjuna.

The first book describes Arjuna's dilemma. The second book, included in the selection, states some key assumptions of Krishna's teaching about the nature of the self and one's duty. The other sixteen books, or teachings, elaborate on the themes found in the second book. The proper relationship between sacrifice and action is discussed in books three and four. The fifth and sixth books examine the tension between a life of renunciation and a life of action. The final six books recapitulate basic teachings and integrate them with the need for religious devotion.

In the eleventh teaching, Krishna gives Arjuna a "divine eye" by which he can see the grandeur and majesty of Krishna's cosmic order. Krishna reveals his deadly destructiveness in an explosion of countless mouths, weapons, eyes, ornaments, and fangs that leaves Arjuna filled with amazement, "his hair bristling on his flesh" as the "god of gods" reveals the cosmic dance of destruction and creation *ad infinitum;* worlds upon worlds upon worlds.

The twelfth book, included in the selection, describes the result of this theophany (revelation of the divine), and, in the thirteenth teaching, Krishna shows that the true battlefield is the human body—the place where we all struggle to know ourselves, discipline our lives, and figure out our duties. The last words of Arjuna to Krishna as the *Gita* closes in book eighteen are "I stand here, my doubt dispelled, ready to act on your words."

TRANSLATED BY BARBARA STOLER MILLER

Bhagavad Gita

READING QUESTIONS

1. Why does Krishna urge Arjuna to fight?
2. What type of spiritual discipline does Krishna recommend?
3. What is the person "deep in concentration" like?
4. What is the point of the twelfth teaching of the *Gita*?

THE SECOND TEACHING

Philosophy and Spiritual Discipline

Sanjaya
> Arjuna sat dejected,
> filled with pity,
> his sad eyes blurred by tears.
> Krishna gave him counsel.

Lord Krishna
> Why this cowardice
> in time of crisis, Arjuna?
> The coward is ignoble, shameful,
> foreign to the ways of heaven.

> Don't yield to impotence!
> it is unnatural in you!
> Banish this petty weakness from your heart.
> Rise to the fight, Arjuna!

Arjuna
> Krishna, how can I fight
> against Bhishma and Drona
> with arrows
> when they deserve my worship?

> It is better in this world
> to beg for scraps of food
> than to eat meals
> smeared with the blood

> of elders I killed
> at the height of their power
> while their goals
> were still desires.

> We don't know which weight
> is worse to bear—
> our conquering them
> or their conquering us.
> We will not want to live
> if we kill
> the sons of Dhritarashtra
> assembled before us.

> The flaw of pity
> blights my very being;
> conflicting sacred duties
> confound my reason.
> I ask you to tell me
> decisively—Which is better?
> I am your pupil.
> Teach me what I seek!

> I see nothing
> that could drive away
> the grief
> that withers my senses;
> even if I won kingdoms
> of unrivaled wealth
> on earth
> and sovereignty over gods.

Sanjaya
> Arjuna told this
> to Krishna—then saying,
> "I shall not fight,"
> he fell silent.

> Mocking him gently,
> Krishna gave this counsel
> as Arjuna sat dejected,
> between the two armies.

Lord Krishna
> You grieve for those beyond grief;
> and you speak words of insight;
> but learned men do not grieve
> for the dead or the living.

> Never have I not existed,
> nor you, nor these kings;
> and never in the future
> shall we cease to exist.

> Just as the embodied self
> enters childhood, youth, and old age,
> so does it enter another body;
> this does not confound a steadfast man.

Contacts with matter make us feel
heat and cold, pleasure and pain.
Arjuna, you must learn to endure
fleeting things—they come and go!

When these cannot torment a man,
when suffering and joy are equal
for him and he has courage,
he is fit for immortality.

Nothing of nonbeing comes to be,
nor does being cease to exist;
the boundary between these two
is seen by men who see reality.

Indestructible is the presence
that pervades all this;
no one can destroy
this unchanging reality.

Our bodies are known to end,
but the embodied self is enduring,
indestructible, and immeasurable;
therefore, Arjuna, fight the battle!

He who thinks this self a killer
and he who thinks it killed,
both fail to understand;
it does not kill, nor is it killed.

It is not born,
it does not die;
having been,
it will never not be;
unborn, enduring,
constant, and primordial,
it is not killed
when the body is killed.

Arjuna, when a man knows the self
to be indestructible, enduring, unborn,
unchanging, how does he kill
or cause anyone to kill?

As a man discards
worn-out clothes
to put on new
and different ones,
so the embodied self
discards
its worn-out bodies
to take on other new ones.

Weapons do not cut it,
fire does not burn it,
waters do not wet it,
wind does not wither it.

It cannot be cut or burned;
it cannot be wet or withered;

it is enduring, all-pervasive,
fixed, immovable, and timeless.

It is called unmanifest,
inconceivable, and immutable;
since you know that to be so,
you should not grieve!

If you think of its birth
and death as ever-recurring,
then too, Great Warrior,
you have no cause to grieve!

Death is certain for anyone born,
and birth is certain for the dead;
since the cycle is inevitable,
you have no cause to grieve!

Creatures are unmanifest in origin,
manifest in the midst of life,
and unmanifest again in the end.
Since this is so, why do you lament?

Rarely someone
sees it,
rarely another
speaks it,
rarely anyone
hears it—
even hearing it,
no one really knows it.

The self embodied in the body
of every being is indestructible;
you have no cause to grieve
for all these creatures, Arjuna!

Look to your own duty;
do not tremble before it;
nothing is better for a warrior
than a battle of sacred duty.

The doors of heaven open
for warriors who rejoice
to have a battle like this
thrust on them by chance.

If you fail to wage this war
of sacred duty,
you will abandon your own duty
and fame only to gain evil.

People will tell
of your undying shame,
and for a man of honor
shame is worse than death.

The great chariot warriors will think
you deserted in fear of battle;
you will be despised
by those who held you in esteem.

Your enemies will slander you,
scorning your skill
in so many unspeakable ways—
could any suffering be worse?

If you are killed, you win heaven;
if you triumph, you enjoy the earth;
therefore, Arjuna, stand up
and resolve to fight the battle!

Impartial to joy and suffering,
gain and loss, victory and defeat,
arm yourself for the battle,
lest you fall into evil.

Understanding is defined in terms of philosophy;
now hear it in spiritual discipline.
Armed with this understanding, Arjuna,
you will escape the bondage of action.

No effort in this world
is lost or wasted;
a fragment of sacred duty
saves you from great fear.

This understanding is unique
in its inner core of resolve;
diffuse and pointless are the ways
irresolute men understand.

Undiscerning men who delight
in the tenets of ritual lore
utter florid speech, proclaiming,
"There is nothing else!"

Driven by desire, they strive after heaven
and contrive to win powers and delights,
but their intricate ritual language
bears only the fruit of action in rebirth.

Obsessed with powers and delights,
their reason lost in words,
they do not find in contemplation
this understanding of inner resolve.

Arjuna, the realm of sacred lore
is nature—beyond its triad of qualities,
dualities, and mundane rewards,
be forever lucid, alive to your self.

For the discerning priest,
all of sacred lore
has no more value than a well
when water flows everywhere.

Be intent on action,
not on the fruits of action;
avoid attraction to the fruits
and attachment to inaction!

Perform actions, firm in discipline,
relinquishing attachment;

be impartial to failure and success—
this equanimity is called discipline.

Arjuna, action is far inferior
to the discipline of understanding,
so seek refuge in understanding—pitiful
are men drawn by fruits of action.

Disciplined by understanding,
one abandons both good and evil deeds;
so arm yourself for discipline—
discipline is skill in actions.

Wise men disciplined by understanding
relinquish the fruit born of action;
freed from these bonds of rebirth,
they reach a place beyond decay.

When your understanding passes beyond
the swamp of delusion,
you will be indifferent to all
that is heard in sacred lore.

When your understanding turns
from sacred lore to stand fixed,
immovable in contemplation,
then you will reach discipline.

Arjuna
Krishna, what defines a man
deep in contemplation whose insight
and thought are sure? How would he speak?
How would he sit? How would he move?

Lord Krishna
When he gives up desires in his mind,
is content with the self within himself,
then he is said to be a man
whose insight is sure, Arjuna.

When suffering does not disturb his mind,
when his craving for pleasures has vanished,
when attraction, fear, and anger are gone,
he is called a sage whose thought is sure.

When he shows no preference
in fortune or misfortune
and neither exults nor hates,
his insight is sure.

When, like a tortoise retracting
its limbs, he withdraws his senses
completely from sensuous objects,
his insight is sure.

Sensuous objects fade
when the embodied self abstains from food;
the taste lingers, but it too fades
in the vision of higher truth.

Even when a man of wisdom
tries to control them, Arjuna,

the bewildering senses
attack his mind with violence.

Controlling them all,
with discipline he should focus on me;
when his senses are under control,
his insight is sure.

Brooding about sensuous objects
makes attachment to them grow;
from attachment desire arises,
from desire anger is born.

From anger comes confusion;
from confusion memory lapses;
from broken memory understanding is lost;
from loss of understanding, he is ruined.

But a man of inner strength
whose senses experience objects
without attraction and hatred,
in self-control, finds serenity.

In serenity, all his sorrows
dissolve;
his reason becomes serene,
his understanding sure.

Without discipline,
he has no understanding or inner power
without inner power, he has no peace
and without peace where is joy?

If his mind submits to the play
of the senses,
they drive away insight,
as wind drives a ship on water.

So, Great Warrior, when withdrawal
of the senses
from sense objects is complete,
discernment is firm.

When it is night for all creatures,
a master of restraint is awake;
when they are awake, it is night
for the sage who sees reality.

As the mountainous depths
of the ocean
are unmoved when waters
rush into it,
so the man unmoved
when desires enter him
attains a peace that eludes
the man of many desires.

When he renounces all desires
and acts without craving,
possessiveness,
or individuality, he finds peace.

This is the place of the infinite spirit;
achieving it, one is freed from delusion;
abiding in it even at the time of death,
one finds the pure calm of infinity.

THE TWELFTH TEACHING

Devotion

Arjuna

Who best knows discipline:
men who worship you with devotion,
ever disciplined, or men who worship
the imperishable, unmanifest?

Lord Krishna

I deem most disciplined
men of enduring discipline
who worship me with true faith,
entrusting their minds to me.

Men reach me too who worship
what is imperishable, ineffable, unmanifest,
omnipresent, inconceivable,
immutable at the summit of existence.

Mastering their senses,
with equanimity toward everything,
they reach me, rejoining
in the welfare of all creatures.

It is more arduous when their reason
clings to my unmanifest nature;
for men constrained by bodies,
the unmanifest way is hard to attain.

But men intent on me
renounce all actions to me
and worship me, meditating
with singular discipline.

When they entrust reason to me,
Arjuna, I soon arise
to rescue them from the ocean
of death and rebirth.

Focus your mind on me,
let your understanding enter me;
then you will dwell
in me without doubt.

If you cannot concentrate
your thought firmly on me,
then seek to reach me, Arjuna,
by discipline in practice.

Even if you fail in practice,
dedicate yourself to action;

performing actions for my sake,
you will achieve success.

If you are powerless to do
even this, rely on my discipline,
be self-controlled,
and reject all fruit of action.

Knowledge is better than practice,
meditation better than knowledge,
rejecting fruits of action
is better still—it brings peace.

One who bears hate for no creature
is friendly, compassionate, unselfish,
free of individuality, patient,
the same in suffering and joy.

Content always, disciplined,
self-controlled, firm in his resolve,
his mind and understanding dedicated to me,
devoted to me, he is dear to me.

The world does not flee from him,
nor does he flee from the world;
free of delight, rage, fear,
and disgust, he is dear to me.

Disinterested, pure, skilled,
indifferent, untroubled,
relinquishing all involvements,
devoted to me, he is dear to me.

He does not rejoice or hate,
grieve or feel desire;
relinquishing fortune and misfortune,
the man of devotion is dear to me.

Impartial to foe and friend,
honor and contempt,
cold and heat, joy and suffering,
he is free from attachment.

Neutral to blame and praise,
silent, content with his fate,
unsheltered, firm in thought,
the man of devotion is dear to me.

Even more dear to me are devotees
who cherish this elixir of sacred duty
as I have taught it,
intent on me in their faith.

6.3.4 Yoga Sutra

The *Gita*, as we have seen, acknowledges that the way out of rebirth may be difficult because everything we do (*karma*) has the potential of keeping us bound to the cycle of *samsara*. Krishna suggests the practice of various *yogas* as the way to liberation. Arjuna is a war-

rior and must act, so when Krishna defines *yoga* as equanimity, Arjuna protests by saying that such a state of mind is impossible. Krishna answers by claiming that practice and dispassion can quiet the mind. Here, Krishna hints at a radical type of *yoga* aimed at liberation through controlling the mind.

This type of **yoga** is the subject of a book called the *Yoga Sutra*. Although practice of a mind-stilling *yoga* is much older than the *Yoga Sutra*, this text is the earliest known systematic statement on the subject. The dating of the text varies by centuries, some placing it as early as the third century B.C.E. and others around the third century C.E. According to legend, **Patanjali,** who is an incarnation of the serpent Ananta on whom the god Vishnu rests before the start of each new cycle of creation, is the author.

The *yoga* expounded by Patanjali is closely tied to a cosmological theory developed by the philosophical school known as *Sankhya*. According to *Sankhya*, reality is structured dualistically in terms of the two fundamental principles of **purusha** (spirit or pure consciousness) and **prakriti** (nature or matter). In an ideal state, reality is a balance between *purusha* and *prakriti* in which *purusha* is completely isolated from *prakriti*. *Purusha* is eternally inactive while *prakriti* is active. From within *prakriti*, the worlds of creation and destruction evolve.

In the course of evolution, thought (*citta*), mind (*manas*), intelligence (*buddhi*), and ego (*ahamkara*) develop. These are material in nature, but through ignorance humans often confuse them with spirit or consciousness (*purusha*). Physical forces are gross manifestations of these subtle mental forces, and the "turnings of thought" sustain them. If these constant turnings of thought can be stopped, it is possible to realize one's true identity as *purusha* and hence be liberated from a false identification with aspects of *prakriti*. For *Sankhya* and for Patanjali's *yoga*, the turnings of thought are fundamental to the confusion of *purusha* with material nature. It follows that the way to extricate oneself is to still the movements of thought, thereby becoming invulnerable to the chaotic change of both mental and physical stimuli. Patanjali presents *yoga* as the way to gain this release and hence as the way to stop rebirth.

Patanjali's *yoga* is a complex system involving the development of a virtuous life, mastering difficult postures and breathing exercises, and gaining gradual control of the senses and the mind. Hatha yoga (force yoga), a set of physical exercises involving stretching and balancing, has gained much attention, especially in the West, because of its health benefits. It originally developed to make long periods of meditation physically easier. It is, however, only one small (although important) part of Patanjali's "eight-limbed" system.

TRANSLATED AND COMMENTED ON BY BARBARA STOLER MILLER

Yoga Sutra

READING QUESTIONS

1. Describe the eight limbs of *yoga* and state what you think each means.
2. What kind of logic do you see at work in the eight limbs of *yoga*?

PART TWO

THE PRACTICE OF YOGA

The Purpose of Yoga

The active performance of yoga involves ascetic practice, study of sacred lore, and dedication to the Lord of Yoga. (1)
Its purpose is to cultivate pure contemplation and attenuate the forces of corruption. (2)
The forces of corruption are ignorance, egoism, passion, hatred, and the will to live. (3)

Definition of the Forces of Corruption

Ignorance is the field where the other forces of corruption develop, whether dormant, attenuated, intermittent, or active. (4)
Ignorance is misperceiving permanence in transience, purity in impurity, pleasure in suffering, an essential self where there is no self. (5)

Egoism is ascribing a unified self to the organs and powers of perception, such as the eye and the power to see. (6)
Passion follows from attachment to pleasure. (7)
Hatred follows from attachment to suffering. (8)
The will to live is instinctive and overwhelming, even for a learned sage. (9)

Removing the Forces of Corruption

The subtle forces of corruption can be escaped by reversing their course. (10)
One can escape the effect of their turnings through meditation. (11)
Subliminal intention formed in actions, rooted in the forces of corruption, is realized in present or potential births. (12)
As long as this root exists, actions ripen into birth, a term of life, and experience in the world. (13)
These actions bear joyful or sorrowful fruits according to the actor's virtue or vice. (14)
All life is suffering for a man of discrimination, because of the sufferings inherent in change and its corrupting subliminal impressions, and because of the way qualities of material nature turn against themselves. (15)
Suffering that has not yet come can be escaped. (16)

Patanjali now calls on Sankhya philosophy to explain how evolution is the transformation of primary, undifferentiated material nature (*prakṛti*) into the constituents of existence, such as egoism, mind, reason, the senses, and the subtle and gross elements. "Reversing the course" of the subtle forces of corruption is a kind of involution, the opposite of the evolutionary process. . . .

. . . In Patanjali's analysis, the aggregate of impressions expresses itself in thought (*citta*) and action (*karma*), which account for subconscious predispositions that condition the character and behavior of an individual throughout many reincarnations. Thought and action then become involved in an endless round of reciprocal causality. Actions create memory traces, which fuel the mental processes and are stored in memory that endures through many rebirths. The store of subliminal impressions is obliterated only when the chain of causal relations is broken.

When the fruits of action (*karma*) and the seeds of thought are eliminated by means of meditation, thought no longer sustains the world, and what has evolved collapses into itself, like a black hole. The turnings (*vṛtti*) of the subtle forces of corruption can be eliminated, not by physical means, but through meditative insight, which cleans out the stock of invisible seeds that would otherwise germinate into new thoughts and actions.

The discriminating person knows that suffering is inherent in change, in the anxiety over change, and in the subliminal impressions left by this anxiety. The past and present are intertwined, and even pleasant experiences are tinged with pain. Suffering that is yet to come can be avoided, however, by relinquishing attachment to any desired outcome in the future, since such outcomes are illusory. Thus one eliminates the potential for suffering stored in subliminal impressions.

This section on the forces of corruption exhibits similarities with Buddhist discussions of methods by which defilements (*kleśa*) can be removed to eliminate suffering. Even though psychological modeling is crucial in both the yogic and Buddhist analyses, the objective is not merely a psychological shift but the actual removal of concrete defilements. This is the purificatory dimension of both yogic and Buddhist practice.

The Observer and the Phenomenal World

The cause of suffering, which can be escaped, is the connection between the observer and the phenomenal world. (17)

The phenomenal world consists of material elements and sense organs characterized by their clarity, activity, or stillness; this world can serve the goals of sensual experience or spiritual liberation. (18)

The qualities of material things are structured as specific, nonspecific, marked, and unmarked. (19)

The observer is simply the subject of observing—although pure, it sees itself in terms of conceptual categories. (20)

In its essence the phenomenal world exists only in relation to an observer. (21)

Even if the phenomenal world ceases to be relevant for an observer who has realized freedom, it continues to exist because it is common to other observers. (22)

The connection between the observer and the phenomenal world causes a misperceived identity between active power and its master. (23)

The cause of this connection is ignorance. (24)

When there is no ignorance, there is no such connection —the freedom of the observer lies in its absence. (25)

The way to eliminate ignorance is through steady, focused discrimination between the observer and the world. (26)

Wisdom is the final stage of the sevenfold way of the observer. (27)

In these aphorisms, Patanjali analyzes the misunderstanding that binds the observing spirit (*puruṣa*, also called "the observer," *draṣṭṛ*), to the phenomenal world (*prakṛti*). Ignorance of the true nature of this relation

misleads us into egoistically believing in a unified self and falsely identifying spirit with matter. Since worldly existence occurs in an environment of corruptive forces, the unliberated spirit tends to be attracted by the phenomenal world, and misidentifies itself with it. This misidentification, together with the attachment to that misidentification, is the source of pain—but the connection can be severed by discrimination, which comes about through the practice of yoga. When ignorance is dispelled, the spirit becomes an observer to the world, detached from the world's painful transience.

In order to effect this detachment, the yogi must understand the multidimensional structure of the world, in which everything is composed of the three qualities of material nature (*guṇa*). These qualities—lucidity (*sattva*), passion (*rajas*), and dark inertia (*tamas*)—are like energy existing in potential form. Among them, Patanjali is mainly concerned with lucidity, which he contrasts with spirit. . . .

The qualities of material nature are structured into gross elements that can be particular or specific, subtle elements that can be universal or nonspecific, subtle matter that is differentiated or marked, and gross matter that is undifferentiated or unmarked. The misidentification of the power to act in the world (*śakti*) with its master, the spirit (*puruṣa*), is brought about by the false attribution of the qualities of material nature to the nature of the spirit itself.

The reference to a "sevenfold way" is somewhat obscure, since Patanjali does not elaborate on it. Commentators have proposed several versions of the sevenfold way and how its stages relate to the eight limbs of yogic practice described in the following sections.

The Limbs of Yogic Practice

When impurity is destroyed by practicing the limbs of yoga, the light of knowledge shines in focused discrimination. (28)

The eight limbs of yoga are moral principles, observances, posture, breath control, withdrawal of the senses, concentration, meditation, and pure contemplation. (29)

Patanjali's eight-limbed practice includes moral principles (*yama*), observances (*niyama*), posture (*āsana*), breath control (*prāṇāyāma*), withdrawal of the senses (*pratyāhāra*), concentration (*dhāraṇā*), meditation (*dhyāna*), and pure contemplation (*samādhi*). The eight limbs are essentially eight stages in the cumulative acquisition of yogic power. The first five will be elaborated in the remaining aphorisms of Part Two and the last three, which constitute the final stage of yoga, will be addressed in Part Three.

Patanjali's set of practices is parallel to the eight-limbed path of early Buddhism. In both yoga and Buddhism, this set of practices is crucial to the realization of spiritual freedom. The Buddhist eight-limbed path comprises right views, right speech, right conduct, right livelihood, right effort, right mindfulness, and right contemplation. Several of these are also central elements in Patanjali's practice: right conduct encompasses moral principles and observances, right mindfulness includes breath control and withdrawal of the senses, and right contemplation is equivalent to pure contemplation (*samādhi*).

The Moral Principles and Observances

The moral principles are nonviolence, truthfulness, abjuration of stealing, celibacy, and absence of greed. (30)

These universal moral principles, unrestricted by conditions of birth, place, time, or circumstance, are the great vow of yoga. (31)

The observances are bodily purification, contentment, ascetic practice, study of sacred lore, and dedication to the Lord of Yoga. (32)

When one is plagued by ideas that pervert the moral principles and observances, one can counter them by cultivating the opposite. (33)

Cultivating the opposite is realizing that perverse ideas, such as the idea of violence, result in endless suffering and ignorance—whether the ideas are acted out, instigated, or sanctioned, whether motivated by greed, anger, or delusion, whether mild, moderate, or extreme. (34)

A commitment to live according to the five universal moral principles (*yama*), without restrictions, constitutes the great vow (*mahāvrata*), which is the first step in undertaking yogic practice. In distinct contrast to the relativity of values that characterizes caste Hinduism, where moral obligations and relations are relative to one's birth, for Patanjali social status is irrelevant to moral behavior. . . .

The Moral Principles

When one perseveres in nonviolence, hostility vanishes in its presence. (35)

When one abides in truthfulness, activity and its fruition are grounded in the truth. (36)

When one abjures stealing, jewels shower down. (37)

When one observes celibacy, heroic energy accrues. (38)

When one is without greed, the riddle of rebirth is revealed. (39)

The Observances

Aversion to one's own body and avoidance of contact with others comes from bodily purification. (40)

Also purity of intelligence, mental satisfaction, psychic focus, victory over the sense organs, and a vision of one's inner being. (41)

Perfect happiness is attained through contentment. (42)

Perfection of the body and senses comes from ascetic practice, which destroys impurities. (43)

Communion with one's chosen deity comes from the study of sacred lore. (44)

The perfection of pure contemplation comes from dedication to the Lord of Yoga. (45)

Posture

The posture of yoga is steady and easy. (46)

It is realized by relaxing one's effort and resting like the cosmic serpent on the waters of infinity. (47)

Then one is unconstrained by opposing dualities. (48)

Breath Control

When the posture of yoga is steady, then breath is controlled by regulation of the course of exhalation and inhalation. (49)

The modification of breath in exhalation, inhalation, and retention is perceptible as deep and shallow breathing regulated by where the breath is held, for how long, and for how many cycles. (50)

A fourth type of breath control goes beyond the range of exhalation and inhalation. (51)

Then the cover over the light of truth dissolves. (52)

And the mind is fit for concentration. (53)

Withdrawal of the Senses

When each sense organ severs contact with its objects, withdrawal of the senses corresponds to the intrinsic form of thought. (54)

From this comes complete control of the senses. (55)

PART THREE

Perfect Discipline

Concentration is binding thought in one place. (1)

Meditation is focusing on a single conceptual flow. (2)

Pure contemplation is meditation that illumines the object alone, as if the subject were devoid of intrinsic form. (3)

Concentration, meditation, and pure contemplation
focused on a single object constitute perfect
discipline. (4)

The light of wisdom comes from mastery of perfect
discipline. (5)

The practice of perfect discipline is achieved in
stages. (6)

In contrast with the prior limbs of yoga, the final triad
is internal. (7)

Yet it is only an external limb of seedless
contemplation. (8)

This section defines the final three limbs of the eight-fold way, collectively the hyperconscious state known as "perfect discipline" (*saṃyama*). Concentration, meditation, and pure contemplation are the internal limbs of yoga, which concentrate the yogi's energy and free his thought of constraints, allowing it to experience limitless knowledge and powers, such as the ability to know past and future, enter into other bodies, and understand the languages of animals and birds.

Each of the three limbs of perfect discipline is a stage in the process of achieving spiritual freedom. Concentration (*dhāraṇā*) involves focusing attention on a particular spot, such as the navel, the heart, the tip of the nose, or an internally visualized image. Meditation (*dhyāna*) is unwavering attention to a single object—a continuous flow of attention that, like the flow of oil, is uninterrupted by any extraneous idea. Pure contemplation (*samādhi*) is achieved when the meditative subject is so absorbed in the object of meditation that the distinction between subject and object disappears. The observer, transcending all awareness of a separate personal identity, takes the form of the object contemplated, attains complete control over it, and is absorbed in it—obliterating the artificial, conceptual separation between the observer and object.

Patanjali closes his account of the limbs of perfect discipline by reminding us that even pure contemplation (*samādhi*) is not the deepest level in the process of spiritual transformation. Beyond it, at the culmination of yogic practice, is seedless contemplation (*nirbīja-samādhi*). . . .

6.4 MEDIEVAL PERIOD

Kinsley (Reading 6.1) speaks of three major developments during the medieval period (ca. 600–1800). The first is the spread and growing popularity of **bhakti,** or devotion to one of the incarnations of the divine such as Krishna. The second is the resur-gence of a philosophical school popularly known as Vedanta because of its concern with interpreting the *Upanishads.* The third is the development of a tradition known as **tantra** that criticized established religious rituals and the priests who supported such practices.

Advocates of these three traditions produced a vast amount of very important literature. What follows is a small sample.

6.4.1 Mirabai

We have seen in the *Laws of Manu* (Reading 6.3.1) that the duties and rights of women in Hindu society were very different from those of men. Many women suffered because their actions, rights, and choices were so much more restricted than men's. One consequence of this was the development of female *bhakti*-saints who became known for their ardent religious devotion and achieved significant influence as role models for those who would strive to be the perfect devotee.

Typically, these female saints leave unhappy marriages and male religious authorities reject them, but nonetheless they triumph by the example of their lives. Mirabai (ca. 1500–1550) was one of these saints. She was born in Rajasthan in northern India, but her reputation spread throughout India. Her arranged marriage was to a local prince, but she came to regard her true husband as Krishna. Running away from her marriage, she joined a group of Krishna devotees in Brindavan. At first the male leader of the group refused even to speak with her because he had made a vow never to speak to a woman. However, she made the point that there was really only one male at Brindavan, Hari (Lord) Krishna, because *all true devotees* are *females* in relation to him.

Mirabai is no dependent female guarded by men. She is not a passive agent, but actively takes charge of her life. However, she uses the traditional image of the passive and dependent female as a symbol for both male and female devotion to Krishna. Just as all females are to be devoted to their husbands (which she is not), all people (male and female) are to be totally devoted to Krishna (which she is). Indeed, it is Mirabai's devotion to Krishna that justifies her lack of devotion to her husband. Here is a good example of the complex functions religious symbols and ideas can play in social life. We should not too quickly conclude that religious ideals of female devotion necessarily reinforce traditional ideas of social control.

Here are three of Mirabai's songs to her Lord. They express a spiritual longing in erotic imagery focusing on Krishna's beautiful dark skin, handsome face, and great power.

MIRA

Songs

READING QUESTIONS

1. How does the first poem begin and end?
2. What images come to mind as you read aloud the second poem?
3. What value do you think might be found in complete and intense devotion to the divine?

Life without Hari is no life, friend,
And though my mother-in-law fights,
    my sister-in-law teases,
    the *rana* is angered,
A guard is stationed on a stool outside,
    and a lock is mounted on the door,
How can I abandon the love I have loved
    in life after life?
Mira's Lord is the clever Mountain Lifter:
    Why would I want anyone else?

[Caturvedi, no. 42]

I saw the dark clouds burst,
    dark Lord,
Saw the clouds and tumbling down
In black and yellow streams
    they thicken,
Rain and rain two hours long.
See—
    my eyes see only rain and water,
    watering the thirsty earth green.
Me—
    my love's in a distant land
    and wet, I stubbornly stand at the door,

For Hari is indelibly green,
    Mira's Lord,
And he has invited a standing,
    stubborn love.

[Caturvedi, no. 82]

I have talked to you, talked,
    dark Lifter of Mountains,
About this old love,
    from birth after birth.
Don't go, don't,
    Lifter of Mountains,
Let me offer a sacrifice—myself—
    beloved,
        to your beautiful face.
Come, here in the courtyard,
    dark Lord,
The women are singing auspicious wedding songs;
My eyes have fashioned
    an altar of pearl tears,
And here is my sacrifice:
    the body and mind
Of Mira,
    the servant who clings to your feet,
        through life after life,
            a virginal harvest for you to reap.

[Caturvedi, no. 51]

6.4.2 Birth of Kali

Goddess worship became increasingly popular from around the fourth century C.E. in India and continues into the present. As the goddess in her many forms gained increased popularity, an elaborate mythology developed around the goddess's exploits. One very well known story occurs in the *Markandeya Devi-Mahatmya Purana*. It tells about the goddess **Durga** slaying a buffalo demon. This demon threatens to upset the order of the cosmos, and the male gods, who fear it, call on Durga to save them. In some versions, the male gods create Durga specifically to fight the buffalo demon (Chanda). During the heat of battle, Durga gives birth to Kali, who battles the demons (*asuras*) who make up the Daitya (demon) army. Durga and Kali are often interchangeable in popular devotion.

In this account, Durga is called Ambika and the Kali she gives birth to is portrayed in her fierce warrior aspect. **Kali** is a being who dwells on the boundary of society, threatening to subvert the status quo. She is a bloodthirsty warrior goddess in revolt. We often see her wearing a necklace of human skulls, her fanged teeth dripping blood and her many arms full of fearsome weapons. These weapons destroy her enemies but protect her children. Kali, like Shiva, embodies what some consider an eternal truth: Destruction is necessary for new order to emerge. Creation and destruction are two sides of the same coin. Life and death belong together. Those who know Kali, know this truth.

❧❧❧

Devi-Mahatmya

READING QUESTIONS

1. Retell this story in your own words.
2. Why do you think this story is so popular?
3. Since the story of Kali's birth and battle with the demons ends by emphasizing the positive side of the goddess (a side more commonly emphasized in contemporary Hindu worship of Kali), why must Kali have a destructive side and appear so terrifying?

As they had been commanded, the Daityas, led by Caṇḍa and Muṇḍa, formed a four-fold army and sallied forth, their weapons raised aloft. They saw the goddess, smiling slightly, positioned on her lion atop the great golden peak of a mighty mountain. When they saw her, they made zealous efforts to seize her, while other demons from the battle approached her with bows and swords drawn. Then Ambikā became violently angry with her enemies, her face growing black as ink with rage. Suddenly there issued forth from between her eyebrows Kālī, with protruding fangs, carrying a sword and a noose, with a mottled, skull-topped staff, adorned with a necklace of human skulls, covered with a tiger-skin, gruesome with shriveled flesh. Her mouth gaping wide, her lolling tongue terrifying, her eyes red and sunken, she filled the whole of space with her howling. Attacking and killing the mighty demons, she devoured the armed force of the enemies of the gods. Seizing with

one hand the elephants with their back-riders, drivers, warriors and bells, she hurled them into her maw. In the same way she chewed up warriors with their horses, chariots and charioteers, grinding them up most horribly with her teeth. One she grabbed by the hair of the head, another by the nape of the neck, another she trod underfoot while another she crushed against her chest. The mighty striking and throwing weapons loosed by those demons she caught in her mouth and pulverised in fury. She ravaged the entire army of powerful evil-souled Asuras; some she devoured while others she trampled; some were slain by the sword, others bashed by her skull-topped club, while other demons went to perdition crushed by the sharp points of her teeth.

Seeing the sudden demise of the whole Daitya army, Caṇḍa rushed to attack that most horrendous goddess Kālī. The great demon covered the terrible-eyed goddess with a shower of arrows while Muṇḍa hurled discuses by the thousands. Caught in her mouth, those weapons shone like myriad orbs of the sun entering the belly of the clouds. Then howling horribly, Kālī laughed aloud malevolently, her maw gaping wide, her fangs glittering, awful to behold. Astride her huge lion, the goddess rushed against Caṇḍa; grabbing his head by the hair, she decapitated him with her sword. When he saw Caṇḍa dead, Muṇḍa attacked, but she threw him too to the ground, stabbing him with her sword in rage. Seeing both Caṇḍa and the mighty Muṇḍa felled, the remains of the army fled in all directions, overcome with fear.

Grabbing the heads of the two demons, Kālī approached Caṇḍikā and shrieked, cackling with fierce, demoniac laughter, "I offer you Caṇḍa and Muṇḍa as the grand victims in the sacrifice of battle. Now you yourself will kill Śumbha and Niśumbha!" Witnessing this presentation of the two great Asuras, the eminent Caṇḍikā spoke graciously to Kālī, "Since you have captured Caṇḍa and Muṇḍa and have brought them to me, O goddess, you will be known as Cāmuṇḍā!" . . .

So speaking, the honorable goddess Caṇḍikā of fierce mettle vanished on the spot before the eyes of the gods. And all the gods, their enemies felled, performed their tasks without harassment and enjoyed their shares of the sacrifices. When Śumbha, enemy of the gods, world-destroyer, of mighty power and valor, had been slain in battle and the most valiant Niśumbha had been crushed, the rest of the Daityas went to the netherworld.

In such a way, then, does the divine goddess, although eternal, take birth again and again to protect creation. This world is deluded by her; it is begotten by her; it is she who gives knowledge when prayed to and prosperity when pleased. By Mahākālī is this entire egg of Brahmā pervaded, lord of men. At the awful time of dissolution

From *Classical Hindu Mythology: A Reader in the Sanskrit Puranas*, edited and translated by Cornelia Dimmitt and J. A. B. van Buitenen, pp. 238–240. Reprinted by permission of Temple University Press. © 1978 by Temple University. All Rights Reserved.

she takes on the form of Mahāmārī, the great destructress of the world. She is also its unborn source; eternal, she sustains creatures in time. As Lakṣmī, or Good Fortune, she bestows wealth on men's homes in times of prosperity. In times of disaster she appears as Misfortune for their annihilation. When the goddess is praised and worshiped with flowers, incense, perfume and other gifts, she gives wealth, sons, a mind set upon Dharma, and happiness to all mankind.

6.4.3 Vedanta

Who are you? You might reasonably respond to that question by giving your name. What if I persisted and asked, "Who are you really?" Perhaps I challenge you a little: "Does your name designate who you really are? Could you have a different name and still be you?" Abandoning the use of a name, you might point to your body. You are your body. However, again I might ask, "Are you identical with your body? Could you be you even in a different body? What about the breath that keeps you alive? Are you that? Maybe you are your mind that thinks and receives sensations or the intellect that reasons?" It seems you are many things. However, is there any one thing you might be?

"I am none of these many things," you might say, "I am myself, me, my ego." Shankara (ca. 788–820), the great Hindu philosopher and teacher of **Advaita** (nondualistic) Vedanta, might say you were an "almost" good student if you said that. According to Shankara, we are all victims of *maya* (illusion), which causes us to missidentify our true selves. We are not the "five coverings" (body, vital energy, mind, intellect, ego) even though we often think we are. Indeed, you may have stopped with the ego, that sense of "I" we all have, because it is so natural to say "I am I." That is why Shankara would find you an "almost" good student. Shankara would demand that you go beyond even your sense of ego to the **Atman,** or true self. However, even when you got there, you would need to go further.

But how much further? In the following selection, Shankara, or one of his students (this text is attributed to Shankara, but there is some doubt he is its author), tells us. This text is a philosophical meditation on the Upanishadic claim "*Tat tvam asi*" ("that art thou") found in the *Chandogya Upanishad* (Reading 6.2.2). The "that" is not just the *Atman* understood as consciousness purified of all its erroneous

identifications, but it is also ***Brahman***, the essence of all that is real.

Just as we can imagine stripping away all the layers that we think of as our self until we come to consciousness itself (*Atman*), we can imagine stripping away all the layers of what we think of as an external world until we get to what is fundamentally real. The real itself, or *Brahman*, is that permanent, unchanging essence at the heart of all things. So, according to Shankara, the deeper awareness or higher knowledge of self and universe leads us to the realization that *Atman* (Pure Consciousness) is Brahman (Pure Being). That is what you truly are and what everything truly is. To realize this experientially is to experience bliss. Hence, ultimate reality may be characterized as Satchitananda; Being (*sat*), Consciousness (*chit*), and Bliss (*ananda*).

Other members of the Vedanta school of philosophy disagreed with Shankara's interpretation of the *Upanishads*. Ramanuja (eleventh century) was an exponent of devotionalism who rejected Shankara's nondualistic interpretation, in part, because it would make devotion absurd. If Shankara was right, both the worshiper and the worshiped would be *maya* (illusion). It makes no sense, Ramanuja thought, to worship oneself. Religious devotion, or *bhakti*, becomes, on Shankara's account, an activity caught in the realm of illusion and make-believe.

Therefore, instead of nondualism, Ramanuja offered a theory called **qualified nondualism**. *Brahman* has two aspects: selves and matter. While these aspects are dependent on *Brahman*, they are not reducible to *Brahman*. Your life is dependent on *Brahman*, but you are not the same as *Brahman*. Thus, genuine devotion is preserved along with the authority of the *Upanishadic* phrase "that art thou," which indicates, given Ramanuja's interpretation, that our life depends on the divine reality. This provides one more good reason why worship of and devotion to God is the right way to live.

For many religions that have written sacred texts, in time controversies erupt about the proper interpretation of those texts. Such controversies lead to different schools of thought and often different religious movements, yet they also energize religious traditions and restore their vitality. Here we listen in on one such controversy in Hinduism. Although Advaita Vedanta seems to have won the day among intellectuals in modern India, the devotionalism of Ramanuja is still very much alive.

SHANKARA

Crest-Jewel of Discrimination (Viveka-Chudamani)

READING QUESTIONS

1. What arguments and analogies does Shankara use to convince the reader that *Atman* is *Brahman?*
2. How does Shankara characterize *Brahman?*
3. How does Ramanuja analyze the meaning of "thou" and "that," and what arguments does he present to support his analysis?
4. Why, according to Ramanuja, can ignorance not be ended by the act of knowing *Brahman* as the Universal Self?

THAT ART THOU

The scriptures establish the absolute identity of Atman and Brahman by declaring repeatedly: "That art Thou." The terms "Brahman" and "Atman," in their true meaning, refer to "That" and "Thou" respectively.

In their literal, superficial meaning, "Brahman" and "Atman" have opposite attributes, like the sun and the glow-worm, the king and his servant, the ocean and the well, or Mount Meru and the atom. Their identity is established only when they are understood in their true significance, and not in a superficial sense.

"Brahman" may refer to God, the ruler of Maya and creator of the universe. The "Atman" may refer to the individual soul, associated with the five coverings which are effects of Maya. Thus regarded, they possess opposite attributes. But this apparent opposition is caused by Maya and her effects. It is not real, therefore, but superimposed.

These attributes caused by Maya and her effects are superimposed upon God and upon the individual soul. When they have been completely eliminated, neither soul nor God remains. If you take the kingdom from a king and the weapons from a soldier, there is neither soldier nor king.

The scriptures repudiate any idea of a duality in Brahman. Let a man seek illumination in the knowledge of Brahman, as the scriptures direct. Then those attributes, which our ignorance has superimposed upon Brahman, will disappear.

"Brahman is neither the gross nor the subtle universe. The apparent world is caused by our imagination, in its ignorance. It is not real. It is like seeing the snake in the rope. It is like a passing dream"—that is how a man should practice spiritual discrimination, and free himself from his consciousness of this objective world. Then let him meditate upon the identity of Brahman and Atman, and so realize the truth.

Through spiritual discrimination, let him understand the true inner meaning of the terms "Brahman" and "Atman," thus realizing their absolute identity. See the reality in both, and you will find that there is but one.

When we say: "This man is that same Devadatta whom I have previously met," we establish a person's identity by disregarding those attributes superimposed upon him by the circumstances of our former meeting. In just the same way, when we consider the scriptural teaching "That art Thou," we must disregard those attributes which have been superimposed upon "That" and "Thou."

The wise men of true discrimination understand that the essence of both Brahman and Atman is Pure Consciousness, and thus realize their absolute identity. The identity of Brahman and Atman is declared in hundreds of holy texts.

Give up the false notion that the Atman is this body, this phantom. Meditate upon the truth that the Atman is "neither gross nor subtle, neither short nor tall," that it is self-existent, free as the sky, beyond the grasp of thought. Purify the heart until you know that "I am Brahman." Realize your own Atman, the pure and infinite consciousness.

Just as a clay jar or vessel is understood to be nothing but clay, so this whole universe, born of Brahman, essentially Brahman, is Brahman only—for there is nothing else but Brahman, nothing beyond That. That is the reality. That is our Atman. Therefore, "That art Thou" —pure, blissful, supreme Brahman, the one without a second.

You may dream of place, time, objects, individuals, and so forth. But they are unreal. In your waking state, you experience this world, but that experience arises from your ignorance. It is a prolonged dream, and therefore unreal. Unreal also are this body, these organs, this life-breath, this sense of ego. Therefore, "That art Thou"—pure, blissful, supreme Brahman, the one without a second.

From *Shankara's Crest-Jewel of Discrimination: Viveka-Chudamani*, translated by Swami Prabhavananda and Christopher Isherwood (Hollywood, Calif.: Vedanta Press, 1947, 1975), pp. 72–76. Reprinted by permisson.

Because of delusion, you may mistake one thing for another. But, when you know its real nature, then that nature alone exists, there is nothing else but that. When the dream breaks, the dream-universe has vanished. Does it appear, when you wake, that you are other than yourself?

Caste, creed, family and lineage do not exist in Brahman. Brahman has neither name nor form; it transcends merit and demerit; it is beyond time, space and the objects of sense-experience. Such is Brahman, and "That art Thou." Meditate upon this truth.

It is supreme. It is beyond the expression of speech; but it is known by the eye of pure illumination. It is pure, absolute consciousness, the eternal reality. Such is Brahman, and "That art Thou." Meditate upon this truth.

It is untouched by those six waves—hunger, thirst, grief, delusion, decay and death—which sweep the ocean of worldliness. He who seeks union with it must meditate upon it within the shrine of the heart. It is beyond the grasp of the senses. The intellect cannot understand it. It is out of the reach of thought. Such is Brahman, and "That art Thou." Meditate upon this truth.

It is the ground upon which this manifold universe, the creation of ignorance, appears to rest. It is its own support. It is neither the gross nor the subtle universe. It is indivisible. It is beyond comparison. Such is Brahman, and "That art Thou." Meditate upon this truth.

It is free from birth, growth, change, decline, sickness and death. It is eternal. It is the cause of the evolution of the universe, its preservation and its dissolution. Such is Brahman, and "That art Thou." Meditate upon this truth.

It knows no differentiation or death. It is calm, like a vast, waveless expanse of water. It is eternally free and indivisible. Such is Brahman, and "That art Thou." Meditate upon this truth.

Though one, it is the cause of the many. It is the one and only cause, no other beside it. It has no cause but itself. It is independent, also, of the law of causation. It stands alone. Such is Brahman, and "That art Thou." Meditate upon this truth.

It is unchangeable, infinite, imperishable. It is beyond Maya and her effects. It is eternal, undying bliss. It is pure. Such is Brahman, and "That art Thou." Meditate upon this truth.

It is that one Reality which appears to our ignorance as a manifold universe of names and forms and changes. Like the gold of which many ornaments are made, it remains in itself unchanged. Such is Brahman, and "That art Thou." Meditate upon this truth.

There is nothing beyond it. It is greater than the greatest. It is the innermost self, the ceaseless joy within us. It is absolute existence, knowledge and bliss. It is endless, eternal. Such is Brahman, and "That art Thou." Meditate upon this truth.

Meditate upon this truth, following the arguments of the scriptures by the aid of reason and intellect. Thus you will be freed from doubt and confusion, and realize the truth of Brahman. This truth will become as plain to you as water held in the palm of your hand.

RAMANUJA

Vedanta Sutra Commentary (Shri-Bhashya)

Scripture does not teach that release is due to knowledge of a non-qualified Brahman

Nor can we admit the assertion that scripture teaches the cessation of ignorance to spring only from the cognition of a *Brahman* devoid of all difference. . . . For the reason that *Brahman* is characterised by difference all Vedic texts declare that final release results from the cognition of a qualified *Brahman*. And that even those texts which describe *Brahman* by means of negations really aim at setting forth a *Brahman* possessing attributes, we have already shown above.

In texts, again, such as "Thou art that," the co-ordination of the constituent parts is not meant to convey the idea of the absolute unity of a non-differenced substance; on the contrary, the words "that" and "thou" denote a *Brahman* distinguished by difference. The word "that" refers to *Brahman* omniscient, etc., which had been introduced as the general topic of consideration in previous passages of the same section, such as "It thought, may I be many"; the word "thou," which stands in co-ordination to "that," conveys the idea of *Brahman* in so far as having for its body the individual selves connected with non-intelligent matter. This is in accordance with the

---

From *The Vedanta Sutras with the Commentary of Ramanuja*, translated by George Thibaut, *Sacred Books of the East*, vol. XLVII (Oxford, England: Clarendon Press, 1904), pp. 129–132, 134.

general principle that co-ordination is meant to express one thing subsisting in a twofold form. If such doubleness of form (or character) were abandoned, there could be no difference of aspects giving rise to the application of different terms, and the entire principle of co-ordination would thus be given up. . . . If the text "Thou art that" were meant to express absolute oneness, it would, moreover, conflict with a previous statement in the same section, viz. "It thought, may I be many"; and, further, the promise (also made in the same section) that by the knowledge of one thing all things are to be known could not be considered as fulfilled. It, moreover, is not possible (while, however, it would result from the absolute oneness of "*tat*" and "*tvam*") that *Brahman*, whose essential nature is knowledge, which is free from all imperfections, omniscient, comprising within itself all auspicious qualities, there should belong ignorance; and that it should be the substrate of all those defects and afflictions which spring from ignorance. . . . If . . . the text is understood to refer to *Brahman* as having the individual selves for its body, both words ("that" and "thou") keep their primary denotation; and, the text thus making a declaration about one substance distinguished by two aspects, the fundamental principle of "co-ordination" is preserved. On this interpretation the text further intimates that *Brahman*—free from all imperfection and comprising within itself all auspicious qualities—is the internal ruler of the individual selves and possesses lordly power. It moreover satisfies the demand of agreement with the teaching of the previous part of the section, and it also fulfils the promise as to all things being known through one thing, viz. in so far as *Brahman* having for its body all intelligent and non-intelligent beings in their gross state is the effect of *Brahman* having for its body the same things in their subtle state. . . .

. . . From all this it follows that the entire aggregate of things, intelligent and non-intelligent, has its Self in *Brahman* in so far as it constitutes *Brahman*'s body. And as, thus, the whole world different from *Brahman* derives its substantial being only from constituting *Brahman*'s body, any term denoting the world or something in it conveys a meaning which has its proper consummation in *Brahman* only: in other words all terms whatsoever denote *Brahman* in so far as distinguished by the different things which we associate with those terms on the basis of ordinary use of speech and etymology.—The text "that art thou" we therefore understand merely as a special expression of the truth already propounded in the clause "in that all this has its Self."

Ignorance cannot be terminated by the simple act of cognising Brahman as the Universal Self

The doctrine, again, that ignorance is put an end to by the cognition of *Brahman* being the Self of all can in no way be upheld, for as bondage is something real it cannot be put an end to by knowledge. How, we ask, can any one assert that bondage—which consists in the experience of pleasure and pain caused by the connexion of selves with bodies of various kind, a connexion springing from good or evil actions—is something false, unreal? . . . the cessation of such bondage is to be obtained only through the grace of the highest Self pleased by the devout meditation of the worshipper, . . .

i.ii.12. And on account of distinctive qualities.

. . . Those, however, who understand the Vedānta, teach as follows: There is a highest *Brahman* which is the sole cause of the entire universe, which is antagonistic to all evil, whose essential nature is infinite knowledge and blessedness, which comprises within itself numberless auspicious qualities of supreme excellence, which is different in nature from all other beings, and which constitutes the inner Self of all. Of this *Brahman*, the individual selves—whose true nature is unlimited knowledge, and whose only essential attribute is the intuition of the supreme Self—are modes, in so far, namely, as they constitute its body. The true nature of these selves is, however, obscured by ignorance, i.e., the influence of the beginningless chain of works; and by release then we have to understand that intuition of the highest Self, which is the natural state of the individual selves, and which follows on the destruction of ignorance. . . .

6.4.4 Tantra of the Great Liberation

Tantric Hinduism developed in the fourth to sixth centuries C.E. in areas where Brahmanic influence was weakest. It sought to extend (*tantra* literally means "what extends") Vedic practices and the implications of *bhakti* Hinduism. Tantric beliefs and practices seek to balance and integrate the usually male-centered *bhakti* by emphasizing the goddess as **shakti** (power or energy). Tantric practice (sadhana) promotes the experience of the unity of *purusha* (understood as both soul and male deity) with *prakriti* (understood as both matter and goddess). The gendered material body itself becomes the vehicle for liberation.

Tantric Hinduism intentionally criticizes Brahmanic Hinduism, which is controlled by a male priesthood. Adepts come from all castes and use different types of yogic techniques, the most famous being *kundaliniyoga*, which is designed to awaken the dormant *shakti* power (imaged as a coiled serpent resting between the genitals and the anus). Once awake *shakti* transforms the various *chakras* (energy centers, usually six in number) by rising through the body's channels (**nadis**) to unite with Shiva in the "thousand petaled *chakra*" in the brain.

The practice of *kundaliniyoga* is common to the two main strands of Tantrism—the right-handed path and the left-handed path. However, the left-handed path goes further by engaging in the practice of the "five m's": eating fish (*matsya*), eating meat (*mamsa*), eating parched grain (*mudra*), drinking wine (*madya*), and engaging in ritualized sexual intercourse (*maithuna*). The uniting of male and female can be the means for uniting the energies of the universe and the divine into a harmonious whole. The spiritual goal of the unification of opposites becomes concretely symbolized and realized in tantric practice.

Excerpts from the *Mahanirvana Tantra* (*Tantra of the Great Liberation*) are presented in the selection. This translation was done by Arthur Avalon in 1913, and I have made some changes primarily to update the language and explain technical terminology. Arthur Avalon is a pseudonym for Sir John Woodroffe, an eminent jurist and professor at the University of Calcutta during colonial rule.

This *Tantra* is a series of conversations between the god *Shiva* and *shakti* (consort-energy) in which *Shiva* gives instructions for meditation exercises and rituals involving shaktic worship. In Indian devotional religion, female consorts accompany male deities and are so much a part of the male god that the god cannot be active without them. These female consorts are thus called *shaktis*, or energies, because they are essential for the power of the male gods.

The *Mahanirvana Tantra* presents itself as the teaching most appropriate for the *Kali* age. In classical devotional Hinduism, time is structured in three main rhythms. The longest is a *mahakalpa* (311,040 billion human years), which is made up of *kalpas*. Each *kalpa* is made up of a thousand *mahayugas* (4,320 million human years), which in turn is made up of four *yugas*. A full four-yuga cycle lasts 12,000 years, or one *mahayuga* (great yuga).

The *yugas* are not just time periods, but outline a progressive religious and moral decline from an age of perfection (*kritayuga*) to an imperfect and degenerate age (*kaliyuga*). Each age has teachings and teachers most appropriate to it. These teachings become more important and more urgent as degeneration sets in. We here sample part of a teaching meant to aid us in these terrible *kaliyuga* times.

Mahanirvana Tantra

READING QUESTIONS

1. What do you think is the significance of establishing that Shiva reveals a truth appropriate for each age?
2. What is the truth that Shiva reveals?
3. While tantric rituals and teachings refer to the complementary nature of the sexes and the need to unite female-male energy to achieve liberation, do you detect any elements in this account that might signal gender inequality? If so, what are they and why do you think they show gender inequality?

Shri Parvati [Shiva's spouse] said: "O God of the Gods, Lord of the World, Jewel of Mercy, my husband, you are my Lord on whom I am ever dependent and to whom I am ever obedient. Nor can I say ought without your word. If you have affection for me, I desire to lay before you that which passes in my mind. Who else but you, O Great Lord, in the three worlds is able to solve these doubts of mine. You who know all and all the scriptures."

Shri Sadashiva responded: "What is that you say, O You Great Wise One and Beloved of My Heart, I will tell you anything, be it ever so bound in mystery, even that which should not be spoken of before **Ganesha** [elephant-headed god and son of Shiva and Shakti] and Skanda [another son], Commander of the hosts of heaven. What is there in all the three worlds which should be concealed from you? For you, O Goddess, are my very self. There is no difference between me and you. You too are omnipresent. What is it then that you do not know and question like one who knows nothing?"

Shri Adaya [Primordial Shakti, another title for Shiva's wife] said: "O Lord of All and Greatest Among Those Versed in Dharma, you in former ages in your mercy did through Brahma [creator god] reveal the four Vedas which are the propagators of all dharmas and which ordain the rules of life for all the varying castes of humans and for the different stages of their lives. In the First Age, people by the practice of yoga . . . were virtuous and pleasing to gods and ancestors. By the study of the Vedas, meditation, asceticism, and the conquest of the senses, by acts of mercy and charity people were of

---

From *Tantra of The Great Liberation (Mahanirvana Tantra)*, translated by Arthur Avalon (London: Luzac & Company, 1913), pp. 4–9, 13–17, 103–104.

exceeding power and courage, strength and vigor, adherents of the true Dharma, wise and truthful and of firm resolve, and mortals though they were, they were yet like gods and went to the abode of gods. . . . After the Krita Age had passed, you in Treta Age, perceived the Dharma was in disorder and people were no longer able by Vedic rites to get what they desired . . . and you made known on earth the scripture in the form of Smriti which explains the meaning of the Vedas.

. . . Then in the Dvapara Age, when humans abandoned the good works prescribed in the Smritis, and were deprived of one half of Dharma and were afflicted by the ills of mind and body, they were yet again saved by you, through the instructions of the Sanghita and other religious lore. Now the sinful Kalic Age is upon them, when dharma is destroyed, an Age full of evil customs and deceit. People pursue evil ways. The *Vedas* have lost their power, the Smritis are forgotten, and many of the Puranas, which contain stories of the past, and show the many ways (which lead to liberation), will O Lord! be destroyed. People will become averse from religious rites, without restraint, maddened with pride, ever given over to sinful acts, lustful, gluttonous, cruel, heartless, harsh of speech, deceitful, short-lived, poverty-stricken, harassed by sickness and sorrow, ugly, feeble, low, stupid, mean and addicted to mean habits. . . . Say, O Lord of all the distressed in your mercy, how, without great pains, men may obtain longevity, health, and energy, increase of strength and courage, learning, intelligence, and happiness; and how they may become great in strength and valor, pure of heart, obedient to parents, not seeking the love of others' wives but devoted to their own, mindful of the good of their neighbors, reverent to the gods and to their gurus, cherishers of their children and kinsmen, possessing the knowledge of the Brahman, learned in the lore of and ever meditating on the Brahman. Say, O Lord for the good of the world, what people should and should not do according to their different castes and states of life. For who but you is their protector in all the three worlds?" . . .

[Shiva speaks]: "Truly, truly and yet again truly I say to you that in this Age there is no way to liberation but that proclaimed by the Tantra. I, O Blissful One, have already foretold in the *Vedas*, Smritis, and Puranas, that in this Age the wise shall worship after the doctrine of the Tantra. Truly, truly, and beyond all doubt, I say to you that there is no liberation for him who in this Age, heedless of such doctrine, follows another. There is no Lord but I in this world, and I alone am He who is spoken of in the *Vedas*, Puranas, and Smritis and Sanghitas. . . . In this Age the **mantras** [holy sounds] of the Tantras are efficacious, yield immediate fruit, and are auspicious for Japa (recitation), Yajna (sacrificial rites)

and all such practices and ceremonies. The Vedic rites and mantras which were efficacious in the First Age have ceased to be so in this."

[The rest of the text describes in detail various meditations, mantras, purifications, rituals, duties, and the like appropriate for the pious in this the Kali age. I include below the beginning of chapter VI, which describes the rites of the Pancha-tattvas, or five elements of worship—wine, meat, fish, parched food, and *maithuna* (ritualized sexual intercourse)—Ed.]

Shri Devi [goddess] said: "As you have kindness for me, pray tell me, O Lord, more particularly about the Pancha-tattvas and the other observances of which you have spoken."

Shri Sadashiva said: "There are three kinds of wine which are excellent, namely, that which is made from molasses, rice, or the Madhuka flower. . . . Howsoever it may have been produced, and by whomsoever it is brought, the wine, when purified, gives to the worshipper all siddhi (supernormal powers). There are no distinctions of caste in the taking of wine so sanctified. Meat, again, is of three kinds, that of animals of the waters, of the earth, and of the sky. From wheresoever it may be brought, and by whomsoever it may have been killed, it gives, without doubt, pleasure to the gods. Let the desire of the disciple determine what should be offered to the gods. Whatsoever he himself likes, the offering of that conduces to his well-being. Only male animals should be decapitated in sacrifice. It is the command of Shambhu that female animals should not be slain. There are three superior kinds of fish . . . there are also three kinds of parched food, superior, middle, and inferior. . . . O Great Goddess when the weakness of the Kali Age becomes great, one's own shakti or wife should alone be known as the fifth tattva [element]. This is devoid of all defect. . . ."

6.5 MODERN PERIOD

Since the eighteenth century, India and the Hindu tradition have undergone profound and far-reaching changes, first under the impact of British colonialism and then under the impact of independence. There are two intertwined directions of change: first, developments stemming from the revival and renewal within the Hindu tradition and, second, the emergence of a Neo-Hinduism. The first involves a restatement of the tradition referred to as *Sanatana Dharma* (roughly, "old-style religion"). Many local associations were created to protect the tradition and, in many cases, to re-create it in light of the colonial experience and the impact of modernization. The second strand (Neo-Hinduism) is a representation of the Hindu tradition created by English-speaking, educated elite Hindus.

6.5.1 Adherence to Truth

The leaders and the accomplishments of the Hindu revival are too numerous to recount here. We will look at one example, perhaps the most famous, the work of Mohandas Karamchand Gandhi (1869–1948). Gandhi combined what he considered the best in all religions including Hinduism into a social philosophy designed to win independence for India and, eventually, justice for all oppressed peoples. While he won fame as a political leader, he was first a religious leader.

In his teachings he combined three central ideas: adherence to the truth (*satyagraha*), nonviolence (*ahimsa*), and increasing the welfare of all or universal uplift (*sarvodaya*). In the selection from his autobiography that follows, Gandhi speaks of some of his deepest convictions—convictions that reveal the power of the Hindu tradition to inspire the human effort toward understanding and peace.

GANDHI

Experiments with Truth

READING QUESTION

1. What elements of traditional Hinduism do you find in Gandhi's experiments with truth?

This time has come to bring these chapters to a close.

My life from this point onward has been so public that there is hardly anything about it that people do not know. Moreover, since 1921 I have worked in such association with the Congress leaders that I can hardly describe any episode in my life since then without referring

From M. K. Gandhi, *An Autobiography or The Story of My Experiments with Truth* (London: Penguin, 1927), pp. 452–454. Reprinted by permission of the Navajivan trust.

to my relations with them. For though Shraddhanandji, the Deshabandhu, Hakim Saheb and Llalji are no more with us today, we have the good luck to have a host of other veteran Congress leaders still living and working in our midst. The history of the Congress, since the great changes in it that I have described above, is still in the making. And my principal experiments during the past seven years have all been made through the Congress. A reference to my relations with the leaders would therefore be unavoidable, if I set about describing my experiments further. And this I may do, at any rate for the present, if only from a sense of propriety. Lastly, my conclusions from my current experiments can hardly as yet be decisive. It therefore seems to me to be my plain duty to close this narrative here. In fact my pen instinctively refuses to proceed further.

It is not without a wrench that I have to take leave of the reader. I set high value on my experiments. I do not know whether I have been able to do justice to them. I can only say that I have spared no pains to give a faithful narrative. To describe truth, as it has appeared to me, and in the exact manner in which I have arrived at it, has been my ceaseless effort. The exercise has given me ineffable mental peace, because it has been my fond hope that it might bring faith in Truth and *Ahimsa* to waverers. My uniform experience has convinced me that there is no other God than Truth. And if every page of these chapters does not proclaim to the reader that the only means for the realization of Truth is *Ahimsa*, I shall deem all my labour in writing these chapters to have been in vain. And, even though my efforts in this behalf may prove fruitless, let the readers know that the vehicle, not the great principle, is at fault. After all, however sincere my strivings after *Ahimsa* may have been, they have still been imperfect and inadequate. The little fleeting glimpses, therefore, that I have been able to have of Truth can hardly convey an idea of the indescribable lustre of Truth, a million times more intense than that of the sun we daily see with our eyes. In fact what I have caught is only the faintest glimmer of that mighty effulgence. But this much I can say with assurance, as a result of all my experiments, that a perfect vision of Truth can only follow a complete realization of *Ahimsa*.

To see the universal and all-pervading Spirit Truth face to face one must be able to love the meanest of creation as oneself. And a man who aspires after that cannot afford to keep out of any field of life. That is why my devotion to Truth has drawn me into the field of politics; and I can say without the slightest hesitation, and yet in all humility, that those who say that religion has nothing to do with politics do not know what religion means.

Identification with everything that lives is impossible without self-purification; the observance of the law of *Ahimsa* must remain an empty dream; God can never be realized by one who is not pure of heart. Self-purification therefore must mean purification in all the walks of life. And purification being highly infectious, purification of oneself necessarily leads to the purification of one's surroundings.

But the path of self-purification is hard and steep. To attain to perfect purity one has to become absolutely passion-free in thought, speech and action; to rise above the opposing currents of love and hatred, attachment and repulsion. I know that I have not in me as yet that triple purity, in spite of constant ceaseless striving for it. That is why the world's praise fails to move me, indeed it very often stings me. To conquer the subtle passions seems to me to be harder far than the physical conquest of the world by the force of arms. Ever since my return to India I have had experiences of the dormant passions lying hidden within me. The knowledge of them has made me feel humiliated though not defeated. The experiences and experiments have sustained me and given me great joy. But I know that I have still before me a difficult path to traverse. I must reduce myself to zero. So long as a man does not of his own free will put himself last among his fellow creatures, there is no salvation for him. *Ahimsa* is the farthest limit of humility.

In bidding farewell to the reader, for the time being at any rate, I ask him to join with me in prayer to the God of Truth that He may grant me the boon of *Ahimsa* in mind, word and deed.

6.5.2 Religion and Politics

Hindu myths, legends, and moral literature often celebrate the subordination of women to men. Sita, the perfect wife of the *Ramayana*, is loyal to her husband, Rama, even when he mistreats her (Reading 6.3.2). The rights and responsibilities afforded women by Manu, the First Man, are not at all equal to men (Reading 6.3.1). The practices of seclusion and *sati* (or *suttee*, meaning "good wife" and referring to the self-immolation of widows on their husband's funeral pyre) promote negative stereotypes of the treatment of women in traditional India. Although *suttee* is now illegal, many suspect that the view of women it represents is far from dead.

However, the Hindu tradition also has its goddesses who destroy demons, women who actively fight for justice, and female saints whose devotion is often portrayed as greater than men's piety (Readings 6.4.1 and 6.4.2). In today's India these two views of women—one as passive and obedient, the other as active and independent—often clash and mix as modern Indian governments seek to accommodate the civil and domestic laws of different religious groups with the equality guaranteed by the constitution.

In the selection that follows, Katherine K. Young, who teaches Hinduism at McGill University and is an editor of the *Annual Review of Women in World Religions*, reports on an interview with Uma Bharati, who is not only an activist in promoting the cause of women in India but also a member of the Bharatiya Janata Party (BJP), which is often labeled "fundamentalist." The BJP supports more political power for Hindus and the promotion of traditional religious ideals and practices. There is a growing polarization between the secularists and the religiously conservative political parties like the BJP. Religious minorities prefer the present secular state because India is eighty-two percent Hindu, and they fear they would lose their religious freedom in a state based on Hindu tradition and law. Leaders of the movement for more rights for women also fear a religious state because of the traditional teachings about the role of women found in some Hindu literature.

Uma Bharati reveals that the situation in present-day India is more complex than this distinction between secularists and conservative Hindus indicates. Although a member of the BJP and a religious traditionalist, she nevertheless is a supporter of women's rights and is a political activist.

❧

KATHERINE K. YOUNG

The Case of Uma Bharati

READING QUESTIONS

1. How do you think Uma Bharati harmonizes her support of more rights for women and her traditional religious commitments?
2. How does Bharati use traditional religious language for political purposes?

Reprinted by permission of the State University of New York Press, from *Today's Women in World Religions*, by Arvind Sharma (Ed.) © 1994. State University of New York. Katherine K. Young, "Women in Hinduism," pp. 97–100. Notes omitted. All rights reserved.

A different style of activism on women's issues is represented by Ms. Uma Bharati. She has been a BJP member of Parliament from Khajuraho. When she was interviewed in December, 1989, for *Times of India News*, she described her life in the style of a sacred biography. She recalled, for instance, her early, extraordinary religious experiences:

> I began having unusual experiences. At the age of six, I found myself giving discourses on the scriptures to the villagers. As far back as I can remember I have had this feeling of two existences within me—dual voices—one of a philosopher-scholar, the other of a child. It was almost an organic phenomenon; I can't explain it. It was as natural as breathing, to orate on religious matters or on the need for a spiritual revolution.

The interviewer then asked how she was discovered as a religious prodigy. Bharati answered:

> Well, one day some professors from a Tikamgarh degree college came to the village as part of a *baraat* (marriage party). When they heard me, they were so amazed, they did not even wait for the *bidaai* (nuptials). They bundled me into a car and I was admitted to a school in the town. Then followed years of participation at religious *sammelans*. I travelled abroad, toured in private planes, was feted and banqueted, nearly drowned in flowers from admirers. When the initial glamour of the adulation wore off, I began to feel caged in the worship. I wanted to appear ordinary, not the image of a *devi* or *avatar*, or live up to a created image.

Bharati remarks that she was once engaged but broke off the relationship because of her "religious commitments." She thought of becoming a *brahmacāriṇī* until her mentor told her that being a *brahmacāriṇī* meant total renunciation—that is, complete withdrawal from the world. Because she wanted to serve the people and work for the welfare of the world (*lokasaṅgraha*), she decided against total renunciation (hence her sporadic wearing of the ochre robe). Working for the "welfare of the world" has meant working with outcastes and women in her native village and in Khajuraho. Of women, she said:

> Women are inherently superior as a created species. Men are not such noble beings that women should fight for equality. Instead they should fight to be treated with respect. . . .
>
> If Indian women combine the *madhurya* (sweetness), their femininity, with self-pride and political awareness, they can teach the whole world the path of liberation. . . .

> You cannot sacrifice either aspect—sword in the hand and child on the back. Our women have to combine the heroism of Draupadi, Gargi, Savitri, Jabala, and Kunti. It is self-respect that will free us, not legislation. I don't eat in houses where, as per the tradition, women eat after men and observe *purdah* . . . for crimes like rape, I feel there should be [the] death sentence.

When the interviewer asked her whether she has ever experienced sexual discrimination in political life, she replied, "No, because I am well known in my area. And in the BJP we give the woman a very exalted status." Then, with a twinkle in her eye, she told the reporter, "my religious image has helped women overcome their prejudices." Folding her ochre robes, she added "I have faith in myself. . . . And may God give me some of the reformist energy of my idols—Rani Laxmi Bai and Swami Vivekananda."

Uma Bharati sees no contradiction between working for the cause of women and being a member of the BJP Party, usually portrayed in the press as the Hindu fundamentalist or militant party, and stereotyped as a regressive force on women's issues. Bharati is a Hindu liberal, at least on women's issues. But like many other Hindus she is disturbed at the loss of Hindu values and perceives secularism under leaders such as Rajiv Gandhi negatively. When defending Indian voters, she remarks: "maybe they didn't like Rajiv's foreign wife . . . or his elite coterie of friends . . . or his mania for computerisation and breakneck modernisation in certain sectors when so many lakhs [100,000] were denied basic amenities."

Her remedy for conflict brought on by communalism and religious extremism is to make room for moderate religion in the public square:

> The fact is the Indians can only understand religion. We are an instinctively religious people. The police, law, science—these are external controls; even our communists are "astiks" (theists) in their heart of hearts. The best methods of controlling communalism is to get moderate religious leaders on public forums to address the masses, spiced with examples from the scriptures. Those who are inflamed by religion can only be calmed down by religion, not by a slick or rational explanation.

Bharati told the interviewer that all parties exploit religious sentiment: "But the BJP believe in Hindutva ("Hinduness") and are proud of it and just because of this we are branded communal." More recently, Bharati has become much more militant and vociferous against the Muslims. Prior to the projected showdown (regarding the rebuilding of a Hindu temple to Lord Rāma at the site of a mosque) at Ayodhya on October 30, 1990, she made speeches in Hindi that were later made into cassettes and sold. The message was virulent:

On October 30, by beginning the construction of the temple, our holy men will be laying the foundations of making Hindustan a Hindu [state]. Bharat Mata Ki jai . . . Glory to Mahadev [the Great Deity]. Destroy the tyrant in the same way that Ravana was vanquished. Do not display any love (nij preet). This is the order of Ram. Announce it boldly to the world that anyone who opposes Ram cannot be an Indian. Muslims, remember Rahim who longed for the dust of Lord Ram's feet. . . . Songs of Hindu Muslim brotherhood were sung by Mahatma Gandhi. We got ready to hear the Azaan along with the temple bells, but they can't do this, nor does their heritage permit them to do so. . . . The two cultures are polar opposites. But still we preached brotherhood. . . . We could not teach them with words, now let us teach them with kicks. . . . Let there be bloodshed once and for all. . . . Leftists and communists ask me if we desire to turn this land into a Hindu rashtra. I say it was declared one at the time of Partition in 1947— Hindustan, a nation of Hindus and Pakistan, a nation of the Muslims. Those Muslims who stayed behind could do so because of the tolerance and large-heartedness of the Hindus. . . . Declare without hesitation that this is a Hindu rashtra, a nation of Hindus.

Uma Bharati finally took saṁnyāsa (formal renunciation) in 1992. It was prompted, some say, to clear her reputation after she was accused by the opposition parties of having an affair. Be that as it may, she shaved her head, was renamed Uma Shri Bharati, and began to wear only ochre robes. As the opposition was quick to point out, she did not give up her status as a member of parliament. She also continued to support the cause of rebuilding the Rām Janmabhoomi temple. . . .

CONTEMPORARY SCHOLARSHIP

Reading about Hinduism has, perhaps, left you with more questions than it has answered. If so, that is good. The more we learn, the more questions we have, and the more questions we have the more likely we are to keep on learning. There is always more to discover and understand.

We turn here to two historians of religion who seek to deepen their own understanding and, by sharing their scholarship, our understanding as well about issues relating to gender complementarity in cosmogonic myths (stories about the origin of the universe) and the use of images in Hindu worship. The references to the roles of male and female divinities on the mythological level have sometimes been praised as a refreshing escape from the male-centeredness of Western religions and, at the same time, have been found incongruent with the treatment of females in India society. The use of images has often struck the Christian, Jew, and Muslim as little more than idol worship. Perhaps your reading of this material has raised similar issues in your own mind.

6.6 PURANIC ACCOUNTS OF CREATION

Purana, which means "belonging to ancient times," is the name of a class of Hindu writings containing stories about creation, gods, goddesses, demons, ancestors, rituals, and much more. These stories have had widespread appeal to the peoples of India and, in some cases, are the primary means by which they learn Hinduism, just as the stories in the Bible and Qur'an are the means by which Jews, Christians, and Muslims learn about their religions.

Creation stories are of particular importance because, by recounting how everything got started, they provide models of how everything should be. The meanings conveyed by stories, especially those thought to be sacred and telling us the way things were meant to be, can be enormously influential in shaping people's values, attitudes, and practices. Often such stories mask things such as gender inequality and thereby give it a divine sanction, even when official teachings tell us all humans are equal in the sight of the divine.

Tracy Pintchman is an assistant professor of Hindu studies at Loyola University in Chicago. Her Ph.D. is from the University of California, Santa Barbara. In the following selection she probes the hidden gender inequality embedded in Hindu stories that, on the surface, support gender complementarity.

TRACY PINTCHMAN

Gender Complementarity and Hierarchy

READING QUESTION

1. Summarize Pintchman's argument in your own words. Do you think she is right? Why or why not?

In his impressive study, *Classifying the Universe: The Ancient Indian Varṇa System and the Origins of Caste*, Brian K. Smith notes the role that cosmogonies recorded in Vedic texts play in supporting, legitimating, and perpetuating caste divisions in Hindu society. Vedic cosmogonies portray the *varṇas*, the broad classes comprising Indian society on which caste divisions are based, as being created, "in the beginning" in conjunction with the creation of all other things, beings, and worlds; hence the division of people into *varṇas* is "represented as aboriginal, as hard-wired into the essence of reality, as the 'way things are' because they were created that way." This is significant because as sources of legitimation, Smith notes, cosmogonic myths carry weight: "Cosmogony legitimizes the present insofar as it conforms to what things were like 'in the beginning.' Creation stories ensure that departures from a status quo appear as deviations from a god-given norm, as degenerations vis-à-vis a pristine time of original perfection. To pronounce on how things were at the dawn of time is to describe how things really are—or at least how they really should be. Religions have always depended on myths of origins to validate the dictates of particular human beings living in particular historical eras. Both Vedic and Hindu religions bestowed such cosmogonic legitimations on the social system they advocated and instituted in India. . . .

Smith further argues that the portrayal of the *varṇa* system in Vedic cosmogonies as primordial, "natural," and "the way things are" (instead of human in origin) serves well the interests of the Brahmin authors of the Vedic texts. By affirming the validity of *varṇa* divisions,

---

Excerpts from Tracy Pintchman, "Gender Complementarity and Gender Hierarchy in Puranic Accounts of Creation," *Journal of the American Academy of Religion* 66 (Summer 1998): 257–261, 274–275, 277–279. Reprinted by permission. References and notes omitted.

Vedic cosmogonies implicitly affirm the superiority of the Brahmins. The Vedas consistently portray the Brahmin class as the highest of the *varṇas*, the "hierarchically superior social entity" that is "invariably found in the top spot in any taxonomy; in the classification of society, the Brahmins are also and always given the highest position." . . . But the Brahmin authors of the Vedic texts conceal their own authorship and achieve the "illusion of objectivity necessary for authority" by portraying Vedic texts as authorless, eternal, and embodying absolute truth. . . .

Since Smith is concerned primarily with *varṇa* and caste (*jāti*), he does not engage questions regarding the role that Brahmanical cosmogonic myths might play in supporting the other powerful and pervasive hierarchy in Brahmanical Hinduism—that of gender. But the authors of Brahmanical scriptures, after all, were not just Brahmin, but also male, and it was in their interest to perpetuate an ideology of superiority that encompasses both of these dimensions of their identity. Vedic and post-Vedic Brahmanical texts do in fact tend to favor both Brahminhood and maleness, and caste and gender tend to function in similar ways in determining social hierarchy. In Brahmanical scriptures high-caste males are usually privileged over their subordinates, who comprise both low-caste individuals and all females. In the ancient Brahmanical law book, the Laws of Manu, for example, both women and Shudras (the lowest of the four *varṇas*) are often portrayed as inherently inferior beings and are excluded, at least theoretically, from studying the Veda, reciting the Veda, and performing sacrifices. . . .

There is, of course, an important distinction between caste and gender as markers of difference: there is no empirically verifiable biological basis for caste differentiation, whereas the biological realities of gender difference are obvious to all. But caste and gender tend to function socially in similar ways. Like caste, gender plays an important role in structuring social hierarchy in contemporary Indian culture, and both caste and gender have been invoked to legitimate inequitable distributions of wealth and power, differences in status, discrepancies in rights, divisions of labor, and hierarchical notions of inherent worth. Gender may in fact be even more fundamental than caste as a principle of hierarchy. In his study of Newars in Nepal, for example, Steven M. Parish notes that for some Newars, "not the opposition of pure and impure, or of Brahman and untouchable, but the opposition of male and female seems to be the most basic prototype of hierarchy. God, they say, originally made only two castes—male and female. All the rest came later—as surplus difference, the mere construction of kings, history, society. The original difference of male and female is the key to order; the caste hierarchy can go, but the gender hierarchy is natural and necessary." . . .

The most elaborate Brahmanical cosmogonies and the richest portrayals of gender and gender dynamics in cosmogonic processes are found in the Purāṇas, which are post-Vedic. Smith focuses his concerns with *varṇa* and caste on Vedism and the world of Vedic texts and hence does not venture into the world of post-Vedic Brahmanical scripture, but post-Vedic Brahmanical texts are equally part of the Brahmanical Hindu tradition, and cosmogonies found in these texts are equally "weighty." Furthermore, in matters concerning the ideology of gender Purāṇic cosmogonies are richer than their earlier Vedic counterparts and tend to be more consistent in their descriptions of gender dynamics in accounts of creation. During the Vedic period religious and social values and practices were probably less affected by gender difference than in later Hinduism; . . . the increased attention given to gender dynamics in Purāṇic cosmogonies and the way in which these dynamics are portrayed may reflect increased attention to gender and gender roles in the social realm.

One finds numerous accounts of creation scattered throughout different Brahmanical scriptures, and they represent a variety of divergent views regarding cosmogony. But there are predominant patterns and tendencies in these narratives. Purāṇic cosmogonies tend to portray male and female cosmogonic principles and actors as complementary, and processes associated with creation are driven by their mutual interaction. Many of the numerous creation narratives in the Mahā-Purāṇas maintain the need for balanced and fruitful interaction between female and male principles on different levels and at different stages of cosmogony in order for the process to succeed and for creation to be maintained.

What might the portrayal of gender and the complementary nature of gender roles in these narratives suggest about underlying gender ideologies? First, Purāṇic cosmogonies repeatedly acknowledge female contributions to the process of creation. In this regard they affirm the importance of the feminine principle in cosmogony. It is also important to note that an emphasis on gender complementarity reflects the biological realities of procreation, which, of course, requires both male and female participation. Beyond the basic biological facts, these descriptions of creation also have a good deal in common with Brahmanical ideologies regarding procreation, as we shall see. Finally, however, I believe there is another overriding agenda here that is rooted neither in the affirmation of female creativity nor in the biological facts of reproduction.

Many scholars have noted that assertions of gender complementarity frequently move beyond the biological and are invoked to support androcentric social biases. In her discussion of complementarity with respect to male-female roles in Jewish law, for example, Rebecca Alpert notes underlying gender prejudice, remarking, "Because of the essential androcentric bias of Jewish law, men are the central category. . . . All issues related to women are delineated in terms of their relationship to men." Gender biases are especially effective when they are concealed and give the impression of being natural or divine, not social, in origin. The account of the creation of Eve from Adam's rib in Genesis 2:18–25, for example, has often been invoked as evidence that women are inferior to men by nature and by divine decree. Gerda Lerner notes that the creation of woman from Adam's rib "has been interpreted in the most literal sense for thousands of years to denote the God-given inferiority of woman. Whether that interpretation has rested upon the rib as being one of Adam's 'lower' parts, and therefore denoting inferiority, or on the fact that Eve was created from Adam's flesh and bone, while he was created from earth, the passage has historically had profoundly patriarchal symbolic meaning." . . . I am reminded also of a passage from Dennis Covington's *Salvation on Sand Mountain*, a book about snake handling in Southern Appalachia. Covington describes a church service he attended led by Brother Carl, who launches into a diatribe about the need for women to stay in their place: " 'It's not godly for a woman to do a man's job!' he said. 'To wear a man's pants! Or cut her hair like a man does his! It doesn't please God to go on like that, acting like Adam was made out of Eve's rib instead of the other way around! . . . A woman's got to stay in her place!' Carl shouted. 'God made her for a helpmate to man! It wasn't intended for her to have a life of her own! If God had wanted to give her a life of her own, he'd have made her first instead of Adam, and then where would we be!' "

In the creation narratives of the Purāṇas models of gender complementarity tend to mask underlying androcentric biases even though they also acknowledge female contributions to cosmogony. Just as Vedic accounts of creation portray distinctions among the *varṇas* and the consequent inherent superiority of the Brahmins over everybody else as part of the natural order of things —the "way things are"—Purāṇic cosmogonies similarly communicate notions concerning the "inherent" attributes of maleness and femaleness that move beyond the biological to support Brahmanical notions concerning the "natural" dominance of maleness over femaleness. Throughout the Purāṇas at various stages of the cosmogonic process the dynamics between male and female suggest that male hegemony is built into "the way things are" from the very beginning and hence is "natural," although such evaluations are not made explicit in the accounts of creation themselves. . . .

GENDER COMPLEMENTARITY AS GENDER HIERARCHY? AN ASSESSMENT

In the patterns described above interaction between male and female elements provides the energy that drives and sustains the creative process. In these narratives cosmogony could not take place without the abiding presence of the feminine, and the roles that females play at different stages of creation are different from but no less essential than those played by males. This emphasis on the necessity of not only the male principle but also the female principle—especially at the "crisis point" in secondary creation when the female temporarily drops out and the process threatens to come to a standstill—might tempt one to see these myths as generally supportive of women in their stance toward gender. These narratives do, in fact, imply that creation is not a uniquely male activity and convey the importance of the female contribution to the cosmogonic process. In this regard the Purāṇic creation narratives detailed above stand in contradistinction to creation narratives like the biblical accounts of creation found in the first two chapters of Genesis, where the participation of a female agent in cosmogony is so remarkably absent.

Ultimately, however, these cosmogonies seem to reflect gender biases in Brahmanical Hinduism that favor the dominance of males over females. These biases have to do with the relative status ascribed to male and female principles and roles during the different stages of cosmogony. The male is consistently portrayed as an autonomous agent that takes charge and directs the process, whereas the female is portrayed as lacking autonomy and submissive to male command. In the descriptions of primary creation detailed above, for example, the ultimate source of creation, Brahman, may be best described as a formless androgyne. Brahman is understood to be *nirguṇa* on the highest level, so Brahman transcends both male and female dimensions. But since this formless Brahman is also understood to be the ultimate identity of an essentially male god—in the Mahā-Purāṇas Śiva, Viṣṇu, or one of the forms of Viṣṇu—how androgynous can Brahman really be? As [Wendy] O'Flaherty has observed, not all androgynes are equal; while there are true mythological androgynes, many are

either primarily male or primarily female. . . . This Purāṇic image of androgyny, which is really a male androgyny, is carried over from earlier Brahmanical scriptures. In her discussion of late Vedic texts, for example, O'Flaherty notes the presence of "the image of the pregnant male, the truly androgynous figure, though it is usually a *male* androgyne . . . Most ancient Indian androgynes are primarily male—men who can have babies as women do. . . . On the other hand, it does not happen that some woman or goddess suddenly finds herself endowed with a phallus or, to her surprise and ours, becomes able to produce children all by herself." . . . In the Mahā-Purāṇas Brahman tends to be this type of male androgyne. Femaleness is portrayed as a power (*śakti*) of the male with no autonomous ontological status. . . .

In telling the story of creation in the ways that they do, Purāṇic cosmogonies suggest notions about how at the time of creation male and female emerged and established patterns of relating to one another; "how things were at the dawn of time," as Smith puts it, and therefore "how they really should be" in the present —whatever that present may be—with respect to the proper dynamics between males and females. Males contain, females are contained; males are active creative agents, females are submissive ones; male seed is the source of new life, the female womb is merely an incubator; males are allied with spiritual processes, females are allied with material—especially sexual—processes. While there is a stress on complementarity of roles in these dynamics—both male and female have a part to play—the ways in which their mutual roles are constructed and the relative status of male and female principles at each stage of creation suggest the dominance of male over female and the primacy of the male contribution to creative processes. Brahmanical values would hold those activities associated in these cosmogonies with male creativity to be allied with "higher" human functions engaging the spiritual faculties, and therefore inherently better than those associated with femaleness, which tend to be allied with material and bodily functions.

Ideology underlying these portrayals of gender in Purāṇic cosmogonies is echoed in notions regarding the biology of conception and reproduction found both in Brahmanical teachings and in popular Hinduism. The Laws of Manu establishes the metaphor of the female as the "field" that acts as passive recipient of the male seed; while both contribute to the process of procreation, the seed is said to be superior (*utkṛṣṭa*), with the offspring of all beings marked with the characteristics of the seed. . . . The likening of a female to a vessel or field and a male to a seed or plower of the field is also fairly common in

Hindu culture, as in other cultures. . . . There is, of course, an ideological agenda here. In commenting upon how this metaphor operates among the Newars of Nepal, Parish notes that "there is a tacit rhetoric here, an implicit ideology that validates patriarchal patterns in the Newar family. The essential qualities of personhood—thought, knowledge, judgment—are constituted by the active male principle of 'seed.' Life and spirit reside in the seed." . . .

The gender ideology detailed above is also mirrored both in social teachings expounded in Brahmanical texts and in the realm of contemporary Hindu culture in notions concerning the complementary relationship of husband and wife. The Laws of Manu, for example, suggests that a woman who marries becomes a part of her husband and takes on his qualities, like a river that merges into an ocean. . . . The ocean, of course, does not mutually flow toward the river. Hence, the married couple, like the cosmogonic male androgyne, represents a complementary balance of male and female, but the female is the lesser of the two and must conform to her male counterpart. In her study of marriage in Bengal, Lina Fruzzetti notes that, when a woman becomes a wife, she becomes encompassed by the male lineage of her husband . . . just as *śakti* is encompassed; in many parts of India when a woman gets married, she loses her separate identity and becomes the "half-body" of her husband. . . . Vanaja Dhruvarajan notes in her study of women's lives in a village in south-central India that a wife refers to her husband as "my lord" or by using the formal third person "they," whereas a husband refers to his wife as "she who is mine" or "she who shares half of my being." . . . While it would be naive, of course, to draw a direct line from Purāṇic cosmogonies to Brahmanical ideology to related dimensions of contemporary Hindu social thought and practice, a similar ideology of gender appears to inform all three.

Such biases are not, of course, unique to the Hindu tradition, although different texts and traditions frame gender ideologies differently in accordance with their own particular emphases. The creation of Eve from Adam's rib in Genesis 2.21–22, for example, echoes the male-as-container, female-as-contained imagery that we find in the Purāṇas. As Rosemary Radford Ruether notes, in the story of Adam's rib the male gives "birth" to the female—the reverse of normal, everyday experience. . . . Lerner notes an emphasis on the male seed as the sole source of life, such as we find in the Hindu tradition, at work in Genesis 15–17, where God blesses Abraham's seed "as though it were self-generating." . . . Aristotle proclaimed a similar understanding of procreation, as Ruether points out, portraying the female womb as "merely the passive incubators of the male seed" that is the real source of life. . . . Ruether also observes that in much of Greek thought male gender is associated with human consciousness and the transcendent realm of spirit, whereas female gender is associated with the body and its passions or appetites. . . . Hence, gender associations at play in Purāṇic cosmogonies and more generally in Hindu culture are not unique but exemplify much more widespread biases.

There are, of course, other ways to tell the story of creation and other ways of portraying gender roles in cosmogony than what we find in the Purāṇas. William Sax has recorded a Garhwali song, for example, that portrays the primary creator as the goddess Ādiśakti, who produces offspring from blood that flows from her womb. . . . Similarly, Ann Gold has recorded a cosmogonic narrative in Rajasthan in which a goddess is accorded pride of place. . . . Accounts of creation narrated in some Tantric texts, such as the Lakṣmī Tantra, also ascribe more independence and active agency to female participants. But this is not the way the Mahā-Purāṇas tend to tell it. While they do not explicitly assert that females should be subordinate to males, Purāṇic cosmogonies like those above imply that in the "order of things" males are in charge. . . .

6.7 DARSAN

Darsan means "to see" and can refer to the act of seeing an image of the divine. However, what is "seen" (understood) when images are seen? Is the image simply an idol? What do the images *mean* to the devotee?

Diana L. Eck, a professor of comparative religion and Indian studies at Harvard University, explores, in the next selection, the meaning of what we might call "sacred seeing." She was first attracted to the study of Hinduism by seeing the arts, images, and landscapes of India. In the preface to the book from which this selection is taken, she indicates that she wrote this "for those who want to 'see' something of India, in the hope that what catches the eye may change our minds."

∾⧫∾

DIANA L. ECK

Seeing the Divine

READING QUESTIONS

1. Why, according to Eck, is the Hindu use of images not idolatry?
2. How does the ritual use of images help us to understand their meaning to the Hindu?

THE IMAGE OF GOD

The vivid variety of Hindu deities is visible everywhere in India. Rural India is filled with countless wayside shrines. In every town of some size there are many temples, and every major temple will contain its own panoply of shrines and images. One can see the silver mask of the goddess Durgā, or the stone shaft of the Śiva *linga*, or the four-armed form of the god Viṣṇu. Over the doorway of a temple or a home sits the plump, orange, elephant-headed Gaṇeśa or the benign and auspicious Lakṣmī. Moreover, it is not only in temples and homes that one sees the images of the deities. Small icons are mounted at the front of taxis and buses. They decorate the walls of tea stalls, sweet shops, tailors, and movie theatres. They are painted on public buildings and homes by local folk artists. They are carried through the streets in great festival processions.

It is visibly apparent to anyone who visits India or who sees something of India through the medium of film that this is a culture in which the mythic imagination has been very generative. The images and myths of the Hindu imagination constitute a basic cultural vocabulary and a common idiom of discourse. Since India has "written" prolifically in its images, learning to read its mythology and iconography is a primary task for the student of Hinduism. In learning about Hinduism, it might be argued that perhaps it makes more sense to begin with Gaṇeśa, the elephant-headed god who sits at the thresholds of space and time and who blesses all

beginnings, and then proceed through the deities of the Hindu pantheon, rather than to begin with the Indus Valley civilization and proceed through the ages of Hindu history. Certainly for a student who wishes to visit India, the development of a basic iconographic vocabulary is essential, for deities such as the monkey Hanumān or the fierce Kālī confront one at every turn.

When the first European traders and travelers visited India, they were astonished at the multitude of images of the various deities which they saw there. They called them "idols" and described them with combined fascination and repugnance. For example, Ralph Fitch, who traveled as a merchant through north India in the 1500s, writes of the images of deities in Vārāṇasī (Benares): "Their chiefe idols bee blacke and evill favoured, their mouths monstrous, their eares gilded and full of jewels, their teeth and eyes of gold, silver and glasse, some having one thing in their hands and some another."

Fitch had no interpretive categories, save those of a very general Western Christian background, with which to make sense of what he saw. Three hundred years did little to aid interpretation. When M.A. Sherring lived in Benares in the middle of the 1800s he could still write, after studying the city for a long time, of "the worship of uncouth idols, of monsters, of the linga and other indecent figures, and of a multitude of grotesque, ill-shapen, and hideous objects." When Mark Twain traveled through India in the last decade of the nineteenth century, he brought a certain imaginative humor to the array of "idols" in Benares, but he remained without what Arnheim would call "manageable models" for placing the visible data of India in a recognizable context. Of the "idols" he wrote, "And what a swarm of them there is! The town is a vast museum of idols—and all of them crude, misshapen, and ugly. They flock through one's dreams at night, a wild mob of nightmares."

Without some interpretation, some visual hermeneutic, icons and images can be alienating rather than enlightening. Instead of being keys to understanding, they can kindle xenophobia and pose barriers to understanding by appearing as a "wild mob of nightmares," utterly foreign to and unassimilable by our minds. To understand India, we need to raise our eyes from the book to the image, but we also need some means of interpreting and comprehending the images we see.

The bafflement of many who first behold the array of Hindu images springs from the deep-rooted Western antagonism to imaging the divine at all. The Hebraic hostility to "graven images" expressed in the Commandments is echoed repeatedly in the Hebrew Bible: "You shall not make for yourself a graven image, or any likeness of anything that is in heaven above, or that is in the earth beneath, or that is in the water under the earth."

The Hebraic resistance to imaging the divine has combined with a certain distrust of the senses in the world of the Greek tradition as well. While the Greeks were famous for their anthropomorphic images of the gods, the prevalent suspicion in the philosophies of classical Greece was that "what the eyes reported was not true." Like those of dim vision in Plato's cave, it was thought that people generally accept the mere shadows of reality as "true." Nevertheless, if dim vision described human perception of the ordinary world, the Greeks continued to use the notion of true vision to describe wisdom, that which is seen directly in the full light of day rather than obliquely in the shadowy light of the cave. Arnheim writes, "The Greeks learned to distrust the senses, but they never forgot that direct vision is the first and final source of wisdom. They refined the techniques of reasoning, but they also believed that, in the words of Aristotle, 'the soul never thinks without an image.'"

On the whole, it would be fair to say that the Western traditions, especially the religious traditions of the "Book"—Judaism, Christianity, and Islam—have trusted the Word more than the Image as a mediator of the divine truth. The Qur'ān and the Hebrew Bible are filled with injunctions to "proclaim" and to "hear" the word. The ears were somehow more trustworthy than the eyes. In the Christian tradition this suspicion of the eyes and the image has been a particularly Protestant position.

And yet the visible image has not been without some force in the religious thinking of the West. The verbal icon of God as "Father" or "King" has had considerable power in shaping the Judeo-Christian religious imagination. The Orthodox Christian traditions, after much debate in the eighth and ninth centuries, granted an important place to the honoring of icons as those "windows" through which one might look toward God. They were careful, however, to say that the icon should not be "realistic" and should be only two-dimensional. In the Catholic tradition as well, the art and iconography, especially of Mary and the saints, has had a long and rich history. And all three traditions of the "Book" have developed the art of embellishing the word into a virtual icon in the elaboration of calligraphic and decorative arts. Finally, it should be said that there is a great diversity within each of these traditions. The Mexican villager who comes on his knees to the Virgin of Guadalupe, leaves a bundle of beans, and lights a candle, would no doubt feel more at home in a Hindu temple than in a stark, white New England Protestant church. Similarly, the Moroccan Muslim woman who visits the shrines of Muslim saints, would find India less foreign than did the eleventh century Muslim scholar Alberuni, who wrote that "the Hindus entirely differ from us in every respect."

Worshiping as God those "things" which are not God has been despised in the Western traditions as "idolatry," a mere bowing down to "sticks and stones." The difficulty with such a view of idolatry, however, is that anyone who bows down to such things clearly does not understand them to be sticks and stones. No people would identify themselves as "idolators," by faith. Thus, idolatry can be only an outsider's term for the symbols and visual images of some other culture. Theodore Roszak, writing in *Where the Wasteland Ends*, locates the "sin of idolatry" precisely where it belongs: in the eye of the beholder.

In beginning to understand the consciousness of the Hindu worshiper who bows to "sticks and stones," an anecdote of the Indian novelist U. R. Anantha Murthy is provocative. He tells of an artist friend who was studying folk art in rural north India. Looking into one hut, he saw a stone daubed with red *kunkum* powder, and he asked the villager if he might bring the stone outside to photograph it. The villager agreed, and after the artist had photographed the stone he realized that he might have polluted this sacred object by moving it outside. Horrified, he apologized to the villager, who replied, "It doesn't matter. I will have to bring another stone and anoint *kunkum* on it." Anantha Murthy comments, "Any piece of stone on which he put *kunkum* became God for the peasant. What mattered was his faith, not the stone." We might add that, of course, the stone matters too. If it did not, the peasant would not bother with a stone at all.

Unlike the zealous Protestant missionaries of a century ago, we are not much given to the use of the term "idolatry" to condemn what "other people" do. Yet those who misunderstood have still left us with the task of understanding, and they have raised an important and subtle issue in the comparative study of religion: What is the nature of the divine image? Is it considered to be intrinsically sacred? Is it a symbol of the sacred? A mediator of the sacred? How are images made, consecrated, and used, and what does this tell us about the way they are understood? But still another question remains to be addressed before we take up these topics. That is the question of the multitude of images. Why are there so many gods?

THE RITUAL USES OF THE IMAGE

How is the divine image regarded by Hindus? And how is it used in a ritual context? Pursuing these questions is important to our understanding of the nature of the divine image which Hindus "see."

Two principal attitudes may be discerned in the treatment of images. The first is that the image is primarily a focus for concentration, and the second is that the image is the embodiment of the divine.

In the first view, the image is a kind of *yantra*, literally a "device" for harnessing the eye and the mind so that the one-pointedness of thought (*ekāgrata*) which is fundamental to meditation can be attained. The image is a support for meditation. As the *Viṣṇu Saṁhitā*, a ritual *āgama* text, puts it:

Without a form, how can God be mediated upon?
If (He is) without any form, where will the mind
fix itself? When there is nothing for the mind to
attach itself to, it will slip away from meditation
or will glide into a state of slumber. Therefore the
wise will meditate on some form, remembering,
however, that the form is a superimposition and
not a reality.

The Jābāla Upaniṣad goes even a step further, intimating that such an image, while it may be a support for the beginner, is of absolutely no use to the yogi. "Yogins see Śiva in the soul and not in images. Images are meant for the imagination of the ignorant."

It is the second attitude toward images that most concerns us in the context of this essay. That is, that the image is the real embodiment of the deity. It is not just a device for the focusing of human vision, but is charged with the presence of the god. This stance toward images emerged primarily from the devotional *bhakti* movement, which cherished the personal Lord "with qualities" (*saguṇa*) and which saw the image as one of the many ways in which the Lord becomes accessible to men and women, evoking their affections.

In the early theistic traditions of the Bhāgavatas or Pāñcarātras, who emphasized devotional worship (*pūjā*) rather than the Vedic sacrifice (*yajña*), the image was considered to be one of the five forms of the Lord. The five are the Supreme form (*para*), the emanations or powers of the Supreme (*vyūha*), the immanence of the Supreme in the heart of the individual and in the heart of the universe (*antaryāmin*), the incarnations of the Supreme (*vibhava*), and, finally, the presence of the Supreme Lord in a properly consecrated image (*arcā*). Later, the Śrī Vaiṣṇavas used the term *arcāvatāra* to refer to the "image-incarnation" of the Lord: the form Viṣṇu graciously takes so that he may be worshiped by his devotees. Indeed, the very theology of the Śrī Vaiṣṇava community, as articulated by Rāmānuja in the 11th century, is based on the faith that the Lord is characterized both by his utter Supremacy (*paratva*) and his gracious Accessibility (*saulabhya*).

God has become accessible not only in incarnations, but also in images. In the *Bhagavad Gītā* (4.11), Kṛṣṇa tells Arjuna, "In whatever way people approach me, in that way do I show them favor." The word *bhajāmi* translated here as "I show favor," is from the same root as *bhakti*. It could equally be translated "in that way do I love them," or "in that way do I share myself with them." Rāmānuja, in commenting on this passage, says that it means "in that way do I make myself visible (*darśayāmi*) to them." He goes on to comment, "God does not only rescue those, who resort to him in the shape of one of his *avatāras*, by descending into that shape alone, but He reveals himself to all who resort to him, whatever the shape in which they represent him."

Following Rāmānuja, another theologian of the Śrī Vaiṣṇava movement, Piḷḷai Lokācārya, writes of the grace by which the Lord enters and dwells in the image for the sake of the devotee:

This is the greatest grace of the Lord, that being
free He becomes bound, being independent He
becomes dependent for all His service on His
devotee. . . . In other forms the man belonged to
God but behold the supreme sacrifice of Isvara,
here the Almighty becomes the property of the
devotee. . . . He carries Him about, fans Him, feeds
Him, plays with Him—yea, the Infinite has become
finite, that the child soul may grasp, understand and
love Him."

The image, which may be seen, bathed, adorned, touched, and honored does not stand *between* the worshiper and the Lord, somehow receiving the honor properly due to the Supreme Lord. Rather, because the image is a form of the Supreme Lord, it is precisely the image that facilitates and enhances the close relationship of the worshiper and God and makes possible the deepest outpouring of emotions in worship.

In observing Hindu worship, in the home or in the temple, many Western students are baffled by the sense in which it appears to be an elaborate form of "playing house" with God. The image is wakened in the morning, honored with incense and song, dressed, and fed. Throughout the day, other such rites appropriate to the time of day are performed until, finally, the deity is put to bed in the evening.

How is one to honor God? What human acts and gestures most directly convey the devotion of *bhakti*? For Hindus and for people of many religious traditions, they are the gestures of humility, with which a servant approaches his master, or a host his guest—gestures such as bowing, kneeling, prostrating, and, in the Hindu world, touching the feet of a revered superior. In addition to such servant-master gestures, however, the Hindus utilize the entire range of intimate and ordinary domestic acts as an important part of ritual. These are common, affectionate activities, family activities, which are symbolically powerful because of their very simplicity and their domestic nature: cooking, eating, serving, washing, dressing, waking, and putting to sleep. These are precisely the acts which ordinary people have most carefully refined through daily practice with loved ones in the home. In summary, Hindu worship reveals not only an attitude of honor but also an attitude of affection in the range of ritual act and gesture utilized in the treatment of the image.

The general term for rites of worship and honor is *pūjā*. The simple lay rites of making offerings of flowers and water, and receiving both *darśan*, the "sight" of the deity, and *prasād*, the sanctified food offerings, may be called *pūjā*. More specifically, however, *pūjā* consists of elaborate forms of worship performed in the home by the householder and in the temple by special priests called *pūjārīs* who are designated for that purpose. These rites involved the presentation of a number of articles of worship, called *upacāras*, "honor offerings," to the deity. The number of *upacāras* presented may vary, but sixteen is considered a proper number for a complete *pūjā*. The *upacāras* include food, water, fresh leaves, sandalwood perfume, incense, betel nuts, and cloth. They are the type of hospitality offerings with which one would honor a guest, or a revered elder, or a king. In addition to such tangible offerings, the waving of the fan and the flywhisk are considered *upacāras*, since they are pleasing to the deity, and the rite of circumambulation is an *upacāra*, since it shows honor to the deity.

An important *upacāra* is the honoring of the deity with light. The priest or the householder slowly circles a five-wicked oil lamp or camphor lamp before the deity, often to the accompaniment of the ringing of handbells and the singing of hymns. This lamp-offering is called *āratī*, and the rite is so central to Hindu worship that *arati* has become the common general name for the daily rites of honoring the deity, often replacing the term *pūjā* completely. In a temple there will ordinarily be several *āratīs* during the day and into the evening. . . .

PRONUNCIATION GUIDE

Vowels

1. *e*, *ai*, *o*, and *au* are long and are pronounced as in *gray*, *aisle*, *open*, and *cow*.
2. *ā*, *ī*, *ū*, with lines over them (macrons) are long and are pronounced as in *father*, *machine*, and *rude*.
3. The same vowels without macrons are short as in *but*, *tin*, and *full*.
4. *ṛ* is sounded as in *rill* and is lightly trilled.

Consonants

5. *c* as in *church*, *j* as in *jungle*, *ṣ* as in *ship*, *ś* as in *sun*, and *jn* as in *gyana*.
6. Aspirated consonants should be pronounced distinctly: thus, *bh* as in *caB-House*, *dh* as in *maD-House*, *gh* as in *doG-House*, *jh* as in *fudGE-House*, *kh* as in *rocK-House*, *ph* as in *toP-Hat*, and *th* as in *goaT-Herd*.

Accent

7. Words of two syllables are accented on the first syllable: *VEda*.
8. Words of more than two syllables are accented on the penult (second syllable from end) when the penult is long or has a short vowel followed by two or more consonants: *veDANta*.
9. Words of more than two syllables are accented on the antepenult (third syllable from the end) in cases where the penult is short and *not* followed by two consonants: *UpaniSHAD*.

KEY TERMS AND CONCEPTS

Advaita Vedanta Nondualistic interpretation of the books at the end of the **Vedas** called the **Upanishads.** Shankara was a leading exponent of this philosophy/theology.

agni Primordial fire of creation. Also a god.

ahimsa Nonviolence or noninjury.

atman Usually translated as Self or Soul if referring to the universal S̲elf or as s̲elf (soul) if referring to the individual.

audience cults Religious groups consisting primarily of people who temporarily assemble to hear teachings.

avatara Incarnations or appearances of the divine in material forms.

avidya Ignorance.

Bhagavad Gita *The Song of God*, known in India as *Gita*. It is about Krishna's advice to Arjuna on how to avoid *karma*. Part of the epic poem *Mahabharata*.

bhakti Devotion to the divine.

Brahma The creator god.

Brahman Usually used to refer to absolute or ultimate reality.

brahmin A priest or priestly class.

caste (*jatis*) A grouping of people according to birth. Castes usually have no social mobility.

chakra Literally "wheel." In Tantric Buddhism, refers to centers of energy within the human body.

class In classical India, a grouping of people according to occupation. In India classes are called *varnas* and there are four main groups: **brahmins** (priests), **kshatriyas** (warriors or kings), **vaishyas** (merchants), and **shudras** (laborers). These classes are assigned specific duties, are arranged hierarchically, and within each are various castes (*jatis*).

client cults Groups of people who go to religious practitioners for various specific services such as therapy or spiritual advice.

dharma Can mean law, teaching, and duty. Sometimes translated as "religion."

Durga A warrior goddess.

four stages of life (*ashramas*) Student, householder, forest recluse or hermit, wandering ascetic. These four stages present an ideal picture of human spiritual development.

Ganesha The elephant-headed god.

guru A religious teacher often thought to be a representative if not a manifestation of the divine or, at least, a perfected soul.

Hanuman The monkey god.

jnana In general, means knowledge and is usually contrasted with ignorance (*avidya*). Hence it is one important key to liberation (*moksha*).

Kali Known as the Black Goddess and usually identified with **Durga**. She has both fierce and gentle aspects.

karma Means action or the law of action, viz., that every act produces a result. Usually tied to the idea of reincarnation or rebirth. The *karma* accumulated in this life determines one's birth in the next life.

Krishna Incarnation of the god **Vishnu**. See *Bhagavad Gita*. A devotee of Krishna is called a Vaishnava.

kundalini A latent power to be awakened in the practice of *kundaliniyoga*.

laws of Manu (Manu Dharma Shastra) A law book attributed to the ancestor of the human race, Manu, detailing the rules and duties for each *varna*, or class.

mantra Sacred sounds recited in worship and meditation. The most famous mantra is "OM."

moksha Release or liberation from suffering, ignorance, and the seemingly endless round of reincarnation, or *samsara*.

nadi A system of channels connecting the various *chakras* through which *kundalini* is to travel.

orthodox/heterodox Literally, "correct" or "right" teaching in contrast to "other than correct" teaching. In Hinduism, orthodoxy is determined by acknowledging the authority of the **Vedas.**

Patanjali Alleged author of the *Yoga Sutra*, which is a manual for yogic instruction.

puja Service or worship by personally attending the image of a god or goddess.

purusha/prakriti Usually translated as "consciousness" and "material nature," respectively. These concepts play a major role in *Sankhya* philosophy whose goal is to help people recognize the radical difference between spirit and matter.

qualified nondualism A rival of Shankara's interpretation of the **Upanishads** taught by Ramanuja. It claims that while individual souls and the material universe are attributes or qualities of the single substance **Brahman,** they are not identical to it.

Rama An incarnation of the divine whose exploits are recounted in the epic *Ramayana*.

Ravana The great demon of the *Ramayana* who kidnaps **Sita** and is killed by **Rama.**

rishi A visionary or seer who "saw" or "heard" the truths recorded in the *Vedas*.

samsara A word used for the world of change and rebirth.

sarvodaya A word used by Gandhi to refer to our obligation to increase the welfare of all people.

satyagraha Gandhi's principle of holding to the truth.

shakta Derived from *shakti* meaning creative energy or power and a general designation for the goddess.

Shaivas Devotees of the god *Shiva*.

Shiva The divine power of destruction that makes way for new life.

shruti Literally that which is heard. Sometimes translated as "revelation" and used to refer to *Vedas.*

Sita The wife of **Rama** who is presented as the ideal

wife in the *Ramayana* and must be rescued by **Rama** from the demon **Ravana.**

smriti Usually translated as "tradition" or "memory." It refers to all religiously authoritative writings that are not *shruti* such as **laws of Manu.**

soma A god and a drink (probably hallucinogenic) used in Vedic times.

Tantras A group of writings setting forth the ideas of Tantrism, a religious movement critical of the priestly dominated traditions.

trimurti The name for the three forms of the divine: **Brahma** the creator, **Vishnu** the preserver, and **Shiva** the destroyer/renewer.

Upanishads A collection of writings at the end of the *Vedas* recording philosophical ideas about the nature of the divine, human beings, and immortality.

Vedas A collection of writings considered **shruti,** consisting of hymns, sacrificial texts, and philosophical texts.

vidya Knowledge.

Vishnu A Hindu god who sustains the universe and appears as an *avatar* (incarnation) such as **Rama** and **Krishna** from time to time to save the world.

yoga Usually used to refer to a spiritual discipline leading to **moksha** such as *bhaktiyoga, jnanayoga, karmayoga,* and the like.

SUGGESTIONS FOR FURTHER READING

Basham, A. L. *The Wonder That Was India.* London: Sidgwick & Jackson, 1954, 3rd rev. ed. 1967; New York: Taplinger, 1968; London: Fontana, 1971. A classic study still widely cited as an authoritative historical study of Indian culture and civilization.

De Bary, W. T., et al., ed. *Sources of Indian Tradition.* New York: Columbia University Press, 1958, repr. 1969. An excellent collection of important and representative source material with introductions.

Flood, Gavin. *An Introduction to Hinduism.* New York: Cambridge University Press, 1996. An overview of Hinduism, utilizing the latest research, that is both clearly written and well organized.

Fuller, C. J. *The Camphor Flame: Popular Hinduism and Society in India.* Princeton: Princeton University Press, 1992. A very good introduction to Hinduism taking into account recent scholarship with a useful annotated bibliography.

Klostermaier, Klaus K. *A Survey of Hinduism.* 2nd ed. Albany: State University of New York Press, 1994. A topical approach that emphasizes the diversity of the Hindu tradition.

O'Flaherty, W. E. ed. *Hindu Myths: A Sourcebook: Translated from the Sanskrit.* Harmondsworth, England: Penguin, 1975. Mythological source materials arranged by topics in a very readable translation.

Shattuck, Cybelle. *Hinduism.* Upper Saddle River, N.J.: Prentice-Hall, 1999. This little book presents a clear and accurate historical survey including a list of holy days and festivals along with a peek at the possible future of Hinduism in the modern world.

RESEARCH PROJECTS

1. If there is a Hindu temple near you, visit it and speak with the priest about the temple and its activities. Write a report on your visit for the class.

2. View the video *Gandhi* and write down your observations on how religion influenced Gandhi's political career.

3. Collect or make some slides of Indian art and/or some recordings of Indian music. Present them to the class, and describe their religious symbolism. (Mira's songs are available by M. S. Subbalaxmi, *Meera Bhajans,* serial number EALP 1297 [Dum Dum: Gramophone Company of India, 1965]. Also, over ten films have been made about her life —see Kusum Gokarn, "Popularity of Devotional Films [Hindi]," *National Film Archive of India Research Project* 689/5/84.)

4. Many Indian "comic books" are about religious heroes, saints, and gods. See if you can locate some of these, analyze their religious message, and share them with the class.

5. Gather news accounts of the clashes between Hindus and Muslims at Rama's birthplace that resulted in the destruction of the Babri Masjid in 1992. Indicate, in a written report, the sequence of events and the role traditional religious symbolism played in the events. A brief summary can be found in Shattuck's *Hinduism,* pp. 97–101.

7

Buddhist Ways of Being Religious

INTRODUCTION

Are most people you know happy and content? Have you been emotionally upset or hurt in a deep way? Have you experienced the death of loved ones or seen people suffer from disease? What is suffering and what causes it? Why is there so much suffering in life? Would it not be good to live without suffering? Are we hopelessly trapped in a world of suffering?

If you have thought about these questions and wondered about the answers, you have been concerned about some of the same questions that pressed themselves on an Indian prince named Siddhartha **Gautama** 2,500 years ago. Siddhartha became so deeply concerned about the suffering that characterizes so much of life that he devoted his life to finding out the causes of suffering and how suffering might be overcome and helping others to find release from suffering. When he found the answers he became known as a **Buddha,** that is, as someone who has gained enlightenment. To this day, millions of people all over the world still listen to his teachings and follow the practices that he and his followers recommended in the hope that they too might learn how to live happy and contented lives.

For 2,500 years, there has existed a complex and bewildering variety of beliefs, practices, rituals, arts, philosophies, sects, cults, politics, gods, goddesses, demons, saints, buddhas, cultures, and more associated with Siddhartha, the Buddha of this age. When Westerners first began traveling to Asian countries like Sri Lanka, China, Korea, Thailand, Tibet, and Japan, they observed this wonderful variety and richness. At first it was just thought of as a kind of "Orientalism"—an idea invented by Europeans to refer rather vaguely to an Asian cultural mix of exotic creatures, romance, strange religions, and remarkable experiences. Eventually, about 300 years ago, Western

scholars settled on the term *Buddhism* in order to distinguish what they saw in some Asian countries from what they encountered in India.

What is it that is being named by the term *Buddhism?* Is it a religion? If religion must involve a belief in the divine, then some of what is called Buddhism might count and some might not because, for some Buddhists, divinities of one kind or another play an important role in their stories and practices and for other Buddhists the divine is essentially unimportant when it comes to understanding life, suffering, and the way to overcome suffering. Is Buddhism a culture? It certainly has inspired great cultural achievements in politics, language, art, literature, philosophy, and architecture. However, it clearly is not a single culture since it has equally inspired the lavish ornamentalism of the Tibetan tradition and the austere simplicity of Japanese Zen.

The recent academic study of Buddhism tends to treat it as a "total social phenomenon" to use the words of Stanley Tambiah, an anthropologist. Buddhism is a name for a religion (if it names religion at all) and much more. Space does not permit introducing Buddhism as a political, artistic, economic, cultural, and social phenomenon here. Since our concern is primarily with religious traditions, we will focus on the more typically religious aspects of Buddhism. However, we need to remind ourselves that Buddhism is much more than a religion. It is, in the fullest sense, a way of life.

7.1 AN OVERVIEW

It is uncertain precisely when Prince Siddhartha, the Sage of the Sakya Clan (**Sakyamuni**) lived. Western and Indian scholars suggest either 566–486 B.C.E. or 563–483 B.C.E., whereas Sri Lankan and Southeast

Asian Buddhists believe he lived earlier, around 624–544 B.C.E. Japanese scholars, using Chinese and Tibetan texts, put the dates at 448–368 B.C.E.

Although there is disagreement about precisely when the Buddha lived, there is little disagreement about where he lived. He lived in a region of the Ganges river basin in northeastern India. A great civilization had existed in this region starting around 2000 B.C.E. However, around 1500 B.C.E. it was replaced by nomadic peoples probably migrating from eastern Turkey, northern Iran, and southern Russia. Their religion centered on the myths, gods, and sacrifices described in the *Vedas* (see chapter 6).

Central to this Vedic religion was a Brahmin, or priestly, caste. Many Brahmins hoped to attain immortality by studying the *Vedas*, performing sacrifices, and living in accord with a priestly code of duties, or **dharmas.** During the seventh and sixth centuries B.C.E., the region where the Buddha lived underwent political, economic, and cultural transformation. Small kingdoms and clan-based communities were united into four large kingdoms, economy and trade flourished, a banking and money system was begun (perhaps the first in world history), populations grew and settled in large cities, and many in the priestly and warrior classes became very rich. While some Brahmins enjoyed the worldly fruits of these changes, others felt them to be spiritually corrupting.

Along with the prosperity came spiritual discontent. Religious camps were set up along the Ganges where spiritual teachers discussed religious and philosophical questions with interested students. *Samanas,* wandering priests and philosophers, dissatisfied with Vedic practices and ideas, expounded and debated a variety of views in such camps. Many came to believe that renouncing violence was the only way to attain lasting peace and happiness. Violence and the suffering associated with it were such a pronounced feature of everyday life that one could not even go to worship without seeing bloody sacrifices of animals. Surely violent sacrifice was not the way to alleviate suffering. All it did was to increase suffering.

One of the major *samana* groups was the Jains, led by Vardhamana the Mahavira, or Great Hero. Mahavira taught that all things are alive, each containing a *jiva,* or life principle. The goal of human life and hence the goal of Jainism, the religion he founded, is to liberate the *jiva* from the round of rebirths by destroying the results of previous **karma** (actions or deeds) through the practice of such austerities as fasting, going unwashed, pulling out one's hair, practic-

ing self-restraint, and vegetarianism. Most important of all is to live a life of complete nonviolence, or *ahimsa,* so that new, bad *karma* will not be created. Jainism today still teaches nonviolence, an idea that has profound political consequences in the hands of such leaders as Mohandas (Mahatma) Gandhi in India and Martin Luther King Jr. in the United States.

In origin, Buddhism is another one of these *samana* groups. While Prince Siddhartha found the Jain emphasis on nonviolence laudable, he opposed its asceticism as too extreme. He also did not think that there are individually distinct *jivas* or souls, that pass from one life to the next until released from the round of reincarnation (although he did believe in rebirth and karmic continuity). Nevertheless, he did come to believe, with many other *samanas* of his day, that a life of luxury, lavish consumption, meat eating, and bloody sacrifices to gods was spiritually corrupting.

In the following selection, Donald S. Lopez Jr., who is a professor of Buddhist and Tibetan studies at the University of Michigan, introduces us to the Buddha, the Buddha's teachings, and the community he founded. The foreign words will seem strange at first but, after a while, will seem less strange. You can refer to the Pronunciation Guide for Sanskrit in chapter 6 since many of these words are either Sanskrit or Pali (a language closely associated with Sanskrit). The Key Terms and Concepts at the end of this chapter will also provide a quick and convenient reference.

❧❦❧

DONALD S. LOPEZ JR.

Buddhism: An Overview

READING QUESTIONS

1. As you read, make a list of all the words and ideas you do not understand or are uncertain about. Discuss them with a classmate, look them up in a dictionary, or bring them up in class for discussion and clarification.
2. What is the point of the story about Siddhartha's early life before enlightenment?

3. What does the word *noble* signify in the phrase "the Four Noble Truths"?
4. Explain each of the Four Noble Truths in your own words.
5. What is one factor that accounts for the variety of practices described as "Buddhist"?
6. What is a **stupa**, and what role does it, along with icons, play in Buddhism?
7. What is the three-body doctrine, and why is it important?
8. What impact has the "absence" of the Buddha had on the development of Buddhist practice and teaching?
9. How did the goal of the religious life shift from the early tradition to the Mahayana, and how did this affect the length of time it took to become enlightened as well as the concept of the *bodhisattva?*
10. What are the two kinds of "tantric **sadhanas**"?
11. What is the meaning of *dharma?*
12. What were some of the objections of the Hinayana tradition to the Mahayana, and how did the doctrine of skillful means figure in this debate?
13. What role have texts played in the development of Buddhism?
14. What is the *sangha* and **vinaya?**
15. Why do you think there are different rules for monks and nuns?

THE BUDDHA

Scholars are increasingly reluctant to make unqualified claims about the historical facts of the Buddha's life and teachings. There is even a difference of opinion concerning the years of his birth and death. The long accepted dates of 563–483 B.C.E. have recently been called into question with the suggestion that the Buddha may have lived and died as much as a century later.

The traditional accounts of the Buddha's life are largely hagiographic and tend to include the following narrative. It tells of the miraculous birth of a prince of the warrior (*kṣatriya*) caste in a kingdom in what is today southern Nepal. Astrologers predict that the prince, named Siddhārtha ("He Who Achieves His Goal") will be either a great king or a great religious teacher. His father the king, apparently convinced that dissatisfaction with the world is what causes one's mind to turn to existential questions and the spiritual quest, is determined to protect his son from all that is unpleasant, and keeps him in a palace where he is surrounded by beauty and all forms of sport and delight. Only at the age of twenty-nine does the prince become sufficiently curious about the world beyond the palace walls to venture forth on four chariot rides. During the first he sees an old person for the first time in his life, and is informed by his charioteer that this is not the only old man in the world, but

that old age eventually befalls everyone. On the next tour he sees a sick person, on the next a corpse. It is only then that he learns of the existence of sickness and death. On his final chariot ride he sees a religious mendicant, who has renounced the world in search of freedom from birth and death. He decides to follow a similar path and, against his father's orders and leaving behind his wife and infant son, goes forth from the life of a householder in search of liberation from suffering.

Over a period of six years he engages in a number of the yogic disciplines current in India at the time, including severe asceticism, and concludes that mortification of the flesh is not conducive to progress toward his goal of freedom from birth, aging, sickness, and death. He eventually sits beneath a tree and meditates all night. After repulsing an attack by the evil deity Māra and his armies, at dawn he comes to a realization that makes him the Buddha ("Awakened One"), forever free from future rebirth. Exactly what it was that he understood on that full-moon night has remained a source of both inspiration and contention throughout the history of Buddhism. Some accounts say that the content of the enlightenment was so profound that the Buddha was initially reluctant to try to teach it to others, and decided otherwise only after being beseeched by the great god Brahmā, himself subject to rebirth and hence desirous of liberation. . . .

The Buddha was one of an infinite series of buddhas, all of whom reached their exalted state in the same manner, at exactly the same spot in India under one or another species of bodhi tree. When the Buddha gained enlightenment (*bodhi*), he did so all at once, in an instant, and his realization of the truth was perfect. He also made his momentous discovery by himself, without the aid of a teacher. It was this fact above all that distinguished the Buddha from his enlightened disciples, called *arhats*, in the early tradition. The disciples had to rely on his teachings to realize nirvāṇa, and typically did so only in stages. The Buddha was able to reach his enlightenment on his own and in a single night of meditation because he had previously devoted himself to the practice of virtues such as generosity, patience, and effort over countless previous lifetimes. In one of his previous lives, in the presence of a previous buddha, he had made the firm resolution to become a buddha himself at a future time when the path to liberation had been lost; he had dedicated his practice of virtue over the next eons of rebirth to that goal.

Seven weeks after his enlightenment, the Buddha is said to have walked to the city of Varanasi (Banaras) and to a deer park on its outskirts, where he encountered five renunciates with whom he had previously practiced asceticism. To them he gave his first teaching, usually referred to as the "four noble truths." However, it is not the truths that are noble. The term is perhaps less euphoniously but more accurately rendered as the "four truths for nobles." The term "noble" or "superior" in Sanskrit is *āryan*, the term with which the Indo-European invaders of India had described themselves and which Buddhism appropriated to mean one who is spiritually superior, that is, who has had a vision of a state beyond birth and death. The four things that the Buddha set forth to the five ascetics are known to be true by such people, not by others. Although some Mahāyāna texts dispute that this was the Buddha's very first teaching after his enlightenment, all agree that the teaching of the four truths was of great importance. Over the centuries it has received numerous renditions, the general contours of which follow.

The first truth is that life is inherently unsatisfactory, qualified as it inevitably is by birth, aging, sickness, and death. Various forms of suffering are delineated in Buddhist texts, including the fact that beings must separate from friends and meet with enemies, that they encounter what they do not want, and do not find what they want. The fundamental problem is presented as one of a lack of control over future events; a person wanders constantly from situation to situation, from rebirth to rebirth without companions, discarding one body to take on another, with no certainty or satisfaction, sometimes exalted and sometimes debased. Briefly stated, the problem is change or, as more commonly rendered, impermanence (*anitya*). Because suffering can occur at any moment without warning, even pleasure is in a sense a form of pain, because it will eventually be replaced by pain; there is no activity in which one can engage that will not, in the short or long term, become either physically or mentally painful.

The second truth is the cause of this suffering, identified as action (*karma*), specifically nonvirtuous action, and the negative mental states that motivate such action. As described above, the experience of pleasure and pain is the direct result of actions performed in the past. These actions are motivated by states of mind called *kleśas* (often translated as "afflictions" or "defilements"), the most important of which are desire, hatred, and ignorance. The exact content of this ignorance is again the subject of extensive discussion in Buddhist literature, but it is represented as an active misconception of the nature of reality, usually described as a belief in self (*ātman*). There is, in fact, no permanent and autonomous self in the mind or the body, and to believe otherwise is the root cause of all suffering. It is this imagined self that is inflamed by desire and defended by hatred. As long as one believes in the illusion of self, one will continue to engage in deeds and accumulate karma, and will remain in the cycle of rebirth. This belief in self, in short, is not merely a philosophical problem, but is the cause of the egotism and selfishness that harm others now and oneself in the future through the negative karma they create. . . .

The third truth is the truth of cessation, the postulation of a state beyond suffering. If suffering is caused by negative karma, and karma is caused by desire and hatred, and desire and hatred are caused by ignorance, it follows that if one could destroy ignorance then everything caused by ignorance, directly or indirectly, would also be destroyed. There would be a cessation of suffering. This state of cessation is called *nirvāṇa* ("passing away") and, again, a remarkable range of opinion has been expressed concerning the precise nature of this state beyond suffering—whether it is the cessation also of mind and body or whether the person persists in nirvāṇa.

The postulation of a state beyond suffering would be of little interest if there were not some means to achieve it. The fourth truth, then, is the path, the technique for putting an end to ignorance. Diverse renditions of this path are represented. . . . One useful way to approach the topic is through the traditional triad of ethics, meditation, and wisdom. Ethics refers to the conscious restraint of nonvirtuous deeds of body and speech, usually through observing some form of vows. Meditation (*dhyāna*), in this context, refers to developing a sufficient level of concentration (through a wide variety of techniques) to make the mind a suitable tool for breaking through the illusion of self to the vision of nirvāṇa. Wisdom is insight, at a deep level of concentration, into the fact that there is no self. Such wisdom is said not only to prevent the accumulation of future karma but eventually to destroy all past karma so that upon death one is not reborn but passes into nirvāṇa. A person who has achieved that state is called an *arhat* ("worthy one"). Two paths to becoming an arhat were set forth. The first was that of the *śrāvaka* ("listener"), who hears the Buddha's teachings and then puts them into practice The second was the *pratyekabuddha* ("privately awakened one") who becomes an arhat in solitude.

It is important to reiterate that although many Buddhists throughout history have known the teaching of the four truths in more or less detail, not very many have actively set out to destroy the ignorance of self and achieve nirvāṇa through the practice of meditation. Lay people tended to see this as the business of monks, and most monks tended to see it as the business of the relatively few among them who seriously practiced meditation. Even for such monks, the practice of meditation should be understood as a ritual act in a ritual setting. . . .

If the Buddha taught the four truths, he also must have taught many other things over the course of the four decades that followed his enlightenment. He is renowned for his ability to teach what was appropriate for a particular person, for adapting his message to the situation. Indeed, in the more spectacular descriptions of his pedagogical powers it was said that the Buddha could sit before an audience and simply utter the letter *a* and each person in the audience would hear a discourse designed specifically to meet his or her needs and capacities, in his or her native language. What he taught was represented as a truth that he had not invented but discovered, a truth that had been discovered by other buddhas in the past and would be discovered by buddhas in the future. Importantly, this truth, whatever it may be, was portrayed as something that could be taught, that could be passed on from one person to another, in a variety of languages. It is in this sense that we may speak of a Buddhist tradition. At the same time, the emphasis on the flexibility of the Buddha's teaching helps to account for the remarkable range of practices described as "Buddhist."

According to traditional accounts, at the age of eighty the Buddha died, or passed into nirvāṇa. He is said to have instructed his followers to cremate his body and distribute the relics that remained among various groups of his followers, who were to enshrine them in hemispherical reliquaries called stūpas. For all Buddhist schools, the stūpa became a reference point denoting the Buddha's presence in the landscape. Early texts and the archeological records link stūpa worship with the Buddha's life and especially the key sites in his career, such as the site of his birth, enlightenment, first teaching, and death. A standard list of eight shrines is recommended for pilgrimage and veneration. However, stūpas are also found at places that were sacred for other reasons, often associated with a local deity. Stūpas were constructed for past buddhas and for prominent disciples of the Buddha. Indeed, . . . stūpas dedicated to disciples of the Buddha may have been especially popular because the monastic rules stipulate that donations to such stūpas became the property of the monastery, whereas donations to stūpas of the Buddha remained the property of the Buddha, who continued to function as a legal resident of most monasteries in what was called "the perfumed chamber."

The Mahāyāna stūpa later became a symbol of buddhahood's omnipresence, a center of text revelation, a place guaranteeing rebirth in a pure land. By the seventh century, the practice of enshrining the physical relics of the Buddha ceases to appear in the archaeological record. Instead, one finds stūpas filled with small clay tablets that have been stamped or engraved with a four-line verse that was regarded as the essence of the Buddha's teaching: "The Tathāgata has explained the cause of all things that arise from a cause. The great renunciate has

also explained their cessation." Although this pithy statement is subject to wide interpretation, we can see here an intimation of the four truths: the Buddha has identified that suffering arises from the cause of ignorance and he has also identified nirvāṇa, the cessation of suffering. It is said that the wisest of the disciples, Śāriputra, decided to become the Buddha's follower upon simply hearing these words spoken by a monk, in the absence of the Buddha. But of perhaps greater importance in this context is the fact that this statement functions as a slogan, a mantra, and as a substitute for the relics of the Buddha to be enshrined in a stūpa. The teaching has become the teacher. . . .

Stūpas were pivotal in the social history of Buddhism: these monuments became magnets attracting monastery building and votive construction, as well as local ritual traditions and regional pilgrimage. The economics of Buddhist devotionalism at these centers generated income for local monasteries, artisans, and merchants, an alliance basic to Buddhism throughout its history. At these geographical centers arrayed around the symbolic monument, diverse devotional exertions, textual studies, and devotees' mercantile pursuits could all prosper. The great stūpa complexes—monasteries with endowed lands, a pilgrimage center, a market, and support from the state—represent central points in the Buddhist polities of Central, South, and Southeast Asia. . . .

The Buddha was also worshiped in paintings and statues. The production and worship of Buddhist icons —whether images of buddhas such as Śākyamuni and Amitābha, or bodhisattvas such as Avalokiteśvara and Maitreya—has been a central feature of Buddhist religious life throughout Asian history. . . . The worship of Buddhist icons was promoted by sūtras, and sponsoring the production of an icon was considered an act of great merit, as was bathing an image, a practice that continues in Southeast Asia, China, and Japan. A common goal of both devotional and ascetic Buddhist practice was to recollect the good qualities of the Buddha, which sometimes led to seeing the Buddha "face to face." Images of the Buddha seem to have been important aids in such practices, in part because, far from being a "symbol" of the departed master, images of the Buddha were ritually animated in consecration ceremonies intended to transform an inanimate image into a living deity. . . . Icons thus empowered were treated as spiritual beings possessed of magical powers, to be worshiped with regular offerings of incense, flowers, food, money, and other associated valuables. Buddhist literature from all over Asia is replete with tales of miraculous occurrences associated with such images.

The Buddha was thus the object of elaborate ritual devotions, often accompanied by recitations of his myriad virtues and powers. . . . These devotions were later incorporated into a larger liturgy that included the visualization of vast offerings and the confession of misdeeds. . . . But not all buddhas were so extraordinary. Indeed, the Japanese Zen master Dōgen went to some lengths to explain why the extraordinary telepathic powers that were supposedly a standard byproduct of enlightenment were not necessarily possessed by enlightened Zen masters in China. The true Zen master is utterly beyond all such categories of Buddhist doctrine. . . .

The question arose early as to the object of devotion in the universal practice of taking refuge in the three jewels: the Buddha, the dharma, and the saṅgha. In some formulations, the Buddha was regarded as having a physical body that was the result of past karma; it consisted of his contaminated aggregates (*skandha*), the final residue of the ignorance that had bound him in saṃsāra until his last lifetime. Because that body was the product of ignorance and subject to disintegration, it was not considered suitable as an object of veneration, as the Buddha-jewel. The Buddha was at the same time said to possess certain qualities (also called *dharma*) that are uncontaminated by ignorance, such as his pure ethics, his deep concentration, his wisdom, his knowledge that he has destroyed all afflictions, and his knowledge that the afflictions will not recur. The qualities were later categorized as the eighteen unshared qualities of a buddha's uncontaminated wisdom. . . . This "body of [uncontaminated] qualities" was deemed the true object of the practice of refuge. Thus, the term "body" came to shift its meaning from the physical form of the Buddha, corporeal extension in space and over time, to a collection of timeless abstract virtues. In addition, the early community had to account for those fantastic elements in the Buddha's hagiography such as his visit to his mother, who had died shortly after his birth and been reborn in the Heaven of the Thirty-Three. The Buddha is said to have made use of a "mind-made body" for his celestial journey. These notions were later systematized into a three-body theory encompassing the physical body (*rūpakāya*), the body of uncontaminated qualities (*dharmakāya*), and the mind-made or emanation body (*nirmāṇakāya*).

In Mahāyāna literature also there is a doctrine of the three bodies of the Buddha. There we find references to the dharmakāya as almost a cosmic principle, an ultimate reality in which all buddhas partake through their omniscient minds. After the dharmakāya comes the enjoyment body (*saṃbhogakāya*), a fantastic form of a buddha that resides only in the highest pure lands, adorned with thirty-two major and eighty minor physical marks, eternally teaching the Mahāyāna to highly advanced bodhisattvas; the enjoyment body does not appear to ordinary beings. The third body is the emanation body (*nirmāṇakāya*). It is this body that appears in the world to teach the dharma. Thus we can discern an important change in the development of the conception of the Buddha in India: whereas in the earlier tradition, the nirmāṇakāya had been that specialized body employed by the Buddha for the performance of occasional supernormal excursions, in the Mahāyāna there is no buddha that ever appears in the world other than the nirmāṇakāya. All of the deeds of the Buddha are permutations of the emanation body—they are all magical creations, the reflexive functions of the dharmakāya. These functions are by no means random. Indeed, the biography of the Buddha is transformed from the linear narration of a unique event into a paradigm, reduplicated precisely by all the buddhas of the past, present, and future in twelve deeds: descent from the Joyous Pure land, entry into his mother's womb, being born, becoming skilled in arts and sports as a youth, keeping a harem, taking four trips outside the city that cause him to renounce the world, practicing austerities for six years, sitting under the bodhi tree, defeating Māra and his hosts, attaining enlightenment, turning the wheel of doctrine, and passing into nirvāṇa.

The effects of this final deed have long been felt by Buddhist communities. Their sense of loss was not limited to the direct disciples of the Buddha but has been expressed by generations of future followers, often in the form of the lament that one's negative karma caused one to be reborn someplace other than northern India during the lifetime of the Buddha, that one's misdeeds prevented one from joining the audience of the Buddha's teaching. A standard part of Buddhist rituals became the request that other buddhas not pass into nirvāṇa but remain in the world for an eon, which they could do if they wished. . . .

The absence of the Buddha has remained a powerful motif in Buddhist history, and remedies have taken a wide variety of forms. In Burma, secret societies, with possible antecedents in tantric traditions, concentrate their energies on kinds of supernormal power that the mainstream tradition regards with some suspicion. Specifically, they engage in longevity practices to allow them to live until the coming of the next buddha, Maitreya. . . . In China and Japan, rituals constructed around the chanting of the name of the buddha Amitābha offer a means of being delivered at death into the presence of a buddha who is not present here but is present now, elsewhere, in the western paradise of Sukhāvatī. . . .

With the absence of the historical Buddha, a variety of substitutes were conceived to take his place. One such substitute was the icon, as we already noted. Another was the written text of his teaching, the sūtra, described below. In the absence of the Buddha, the transcendent principle of his enlightenment, sometimes called the buddha nature, became the subject of a wide range of doctrinal speculation, devotion, and practice. This impersonal principle, which made possible the transformation of Prince Siddhārtha from an ignorant and suffering human being into an omniscient and blissful buddha, was most commonly referred to as the *tathāgatagarbha*. *Tathāgata*, "One Who Has Thus Come [or Gone]" is one of the standard epithets of the Buddha. *Garbha* has a wide range of meanings, including "essence" and "womb," which were exploited in works like the *Tathāgatagarbha Sūtra* . . . , a popular and influential Mahāyāna work which declared that this seed or potential for buddhahood resides equally in all beings, and it needs only to be developed. A related work . . . states that everything in the universe contains in itself the entire universe, and that, therefore, the wisdom of a buddha is fully present in each and every being. Such an impersonal principle was not only an important point of doctrine but could also be the object of devotion and praise, prompting the Japanese monk Myōe to address an island as the Buddha. In so doing, Myōe, who had desired to go to India, was able to find the Buddha in Japan. . . .

There is a vacillation in the metaphors and similes employed in these texts as if between two models of the means of making manifest the buddha nature, of achieving enlightenment. One model regards the buddha nature as something pure that has been polluted. The process of the path, therefore, is a gradual process of purification, removing defilements through a variety of practices until the utter transformation from afflicted sentient being to perfect buddha has been effected. Other tropes in these texts, however, do not suggest a developmental model but employ instead a rhetoric of discovery: buddhahood is always already fully present in each being. It need only be recognized. It was this latter model that exercised particular influence in the Chan and Zen schools of China and Japan, which were at least rhetorically dismissive of standard doctrinal categories and traditional practices. . . .

One of the earliest substitutes for the Buddha was the wisdom by which he became enlightened and, by extension, the texts that contained that wisdom. This wisdom was called the "perfection of wisdom" (*prajñāpāramitā*). In part because it was this wisdom that metaphorically gave birth to the Buddha and, in part, because the word *prajñāpāramitā* is in the feminine gender in Sanskrit, this wisdom was anthropomorphized and worshiped as a goddess, referred to sometimes as Prajñāpāramitā, sometimes as "the Great Mother." But not all of the important female figures in Buddhism have been anthropomorphized principles. . . . The eighth-century queen of Tibet is identified as a female buddha, and the tantric

symbolism of her vagina as the source of enlightenment is set forth. . . . Gotamī, not the Buddha's metaphorical mother, but his aunt and foster-mother (his own mother died shortly after his birth), was instrumental in convincing the Buddha to establish the order of nuns, and her life story has served as a female parallel to the life of the Buddha. The account of her passage into nirvāṇa . . . clearly mimics the story of the Buddha's death.

Perhaps the most popular substitute for the absent Buddha, however, was the bodhisattva. The Buddha is said to have been able to remember all of his past lives, and he is said to have employed his prodigious memory to recount events from those lives. The Buddha's remarkable memory provided a scriptural justification for the appropriation of a diverse body of folklore into the canon. The **Jātakas** ("Birth Stories"), of which there are over five hundred, were transformed from an Indian version of Aesop's Fables into the word of the Buddha by a conclusion appended to each story, in which the Buddha represents the tale as the recollection of one of his former lives and inevitably identifies himself as the protagonist ("in that existence the otter was Ānanda, the jackal was Maudgalyāyana, the monkey was Śāriputra, and I was the wise hare"). In these tales, the Buddha is referred to as the *bodhisattva*, a term widely etymologized in later literature, but which generally means a person who is intent on the attainment of bodhi, enlightenment. If very few Buddhists felt that they could emulate the Buddha in his last life by leaving their families, living the life of an ascetic, and practicing meditation, the stories of the Buddha's previous lives provided a more accessible model. Stories of the Bodhisattva's deeds of generosity, morality, patience, and perseverance against great odds have remained among the most popular forms of Buddhist literature, both written and oral, and both in the Jātaka tales and in another genre called Avadāna. . . .

In the early Mahāyāna sūtras, the bodhisattva's deeds were represented not merely as an inspiration but as a model to be scrupulously emulated. Earlier in the tradition, the goal had been to follow the path set forth by the Buddha and become liberated from rebirth as an arhat. But in the Mahāyāna, the goal became to do not what the Buddha said but what he did: to follow a much, much longer path to become a buddha oneself. It seems that, at least in the time of the Buddha, it had been possible to become an arhat in one lifetime. Later Mahāyāna exegetes would calculate that, from the time that one made buddhahood one's goal until buddhahood was achieved, a minimum of 384×10^{58} years was required. This amount of time was needed to accumulate the vast stores of merit and wisdom that would result in the omniscience of a buddha, who was able to teach the path to liberation more effectively than any other because of his telepathic knowledge of the capacities and interests of his disciples. It was not the case, then, that bodhisattvas were postponing their enlightenment as buddhas; instead, they would forego the lesser enlightenment of the arhat, which offered freedom from suffering for oneself alone, in favor of the greater enlightenment of a buddha, whereby others could also be liberated.

Formal ceremonies were designed for taking the vow to become a bodhisattva and then follow the long bodhisattva path to buddhahood in order to liberate others from saṃsāra. This included the promise to follow a specific code of conduct. . . . At those ceremonies, the officiant, speaking as the Buddha, would declare that a particular disciple, at a point several eons in the future, would complete the long bodhisattva path and become a buddha of such and such a name, presiding over such and such a pure land. So, with the rise of the Mahāyāna we see the goal of enlightenment recede to a point beyond the horizon, but with the millions of intervening lives, beginning with this one, consecrated by the Buddha's prophecy that these present lives are a future buddha's former lives, part of a buddha's story and thus sacred history.

But the bodhisattva was not simply an object of emulation; the bodhisattva was also an object of devotion, for if the bodhisattva had vowed to liberate all beings in the universe from suffering, all beings were the object of the bodhisattva's compassionate deeds. The bodhisattvas mentioned in the Mahāyāna sūtras were worshiped for the varieties of mundane and supramundane succor they could bestow—bodhisattvas such as Mañjuśrī, the bodhisattva of wisdom; Kṣitigarbha, who as Jizō in Japan rescues children, both born and unborn; Maitreya, the bodhisattva who will become the next buddha; and most of all, Avalokiteśvara, the most widely worshiped bodhisattva, who takes a female form as Guanyin in China . . . and Kannon in Japan, and who in Tibet takes human form in the succession of Dalai Lamas. . . .

Yet another substitute for the absent Buddha is to be found in the Vajrayāna, in which rituals (called sādhana, literally, "means of achievement") are set forth in which the practitioner, through a practice of visualization, petitions a buddha or bodhisattva to come into the practitioner's presence. Much of the practice described in tantric sādhanas involves the enactment of a world—the fantastic jewel-encrusted world of the Mahāyāna sūtras or the horrific world of the charnel ground. In the sūtras, these worlds appear before the audience of the sūtra at the command of the Buddha, as in the Lotus Sūtra, or are described by him, as in the Pure Land sūtras. In the tantric sādhana, the practitioner manifests that world through visualization, through a process of invitation, descent, and identification, evoking the world that the sūtras declare to be immanent, yet only describe. The tantric sādhana is, in this sense, the making of the world of the Mahāyāna sūtras here and now. Tantric sādhanas usually take one of two forms. In the first, the buddha or bodhisattva is requested to appear before the meditator and is then worshiped in the hope of receiving blessings. . . . In the other type of tantric sādhana, the meditator imagines himself or herself to be a fully enlightened buddha or bodhisattva now, to have the exalted body, speech, and mind of an enlightened being. Those who become particularly skillful at this practice, it is said, gain the ability to appear in this form to others. . . .

DHARMA

Before the Buddha passed away, it is said that he was asked who would succeed him as leader of the community. He answered that his teaching should be the teacher. That teaching is most commonly referred to with the name dharma, a word derived from the root dhṛ, "to hold," a term with a wide range of meanings. Indeed, ten meanings of dharma, including "path," "virtue," "quality," "vow," and "nirvāṇa" were enumerated by a fifth-century scholar. Nineteenth-century translators often rendered dharma as "the law." But two meanings predominate. The first is the teaching of the Buddha, creatively etymologized from dhṛ to mean "that which holds one back from falling into suffering." The second meaning of dharma, appearing particularly in philosophical contexts, is often rendered in English as "phenomenon" or "thing," as in "all dharmas lack self."

The ambiguities encountered in translating the term are emblematic of a wide range of practices that have been regarded as the teaching of the Buddha. And because the Buddha adapted his teachings to the situation and because (at least according to the Mahāyāna), the Buddha did not actually disappear into nirvāṇa but remains forever present, works that represented themselves as his teaching (which begin with the standard formula, "Thus did I hear") have continued to be composed throughout the history of Buddhism. The term "Buddhist apocrypha" has generally been used to describe those texts composed outside of India (in China, for example) which represent themselves as being of Indian origin. Yet strictly speaking all Buddhist texts, even those composed in Indian languages, are apocryphal because none can be identified with complete certainty as a record of the teaching of the historical Buddha. This has, on the one hand, led to a certain tolerance for accepting diverse doctrines and practices as Buddhist. Sometimes new texts were written as ways of summarizing what was most important from an unwieldy and overwhelming canon. In some cases, these new texts represented themselves as the words of the historical Buddha . . . ; in other cases, essays were composed in poetry and prose with the purpose of explicating for a newly converted society the most essential teachings from a bewildering scriptural tradition. . . .

The absence of the Buddha did not merely occasion the creation of substitutes for him. Over the course of the history of Buddhism in Asia, it also portended crisis, notably in a variety of texts that responded to the notion of the decline of the dharma. Within a century or two after the Buddha's death, there were predictions of the eventual disappearance of the dharma from the world. Various reasons were given for its demise, ranging from a general deterioration in human virtue to the fact that the Buddha had agreed to admit women into the order. These texts, like most Buddhist sūtras, are set at the time of the Buddha, and the dire circumstances that signal the demise of the dharma are expressed in terms of prophecies by the Buddha of what will happen in the future. We can assume that the authors of the sūtras were in fact describing the events of their own day, usually including the corrupt and greedy behavior of monks, the persecution of Buddhism by the state, or the threat posed by foreign invaders. Some works of this genre not only prophesied decline of the dharma but offered prescriptions so that decline could be averted. . . .

When works such as these were composed to respond to a particular historical circumstance, it was sometimes necessary to account for the fact that there had been no previous record of such a text. It was explained that [some] texts . . . had been found locked inside an iron stūpa, having been placed there long ago to be discovered at the appropriate time. The fact that the version which eventually reached China seemed little more than an outline was the result of an unfortunate circumstance: the larger and more comprehensive version of the work had inadvertently been thrown overboard on the sea journey from India to China. Likewise, the Tibetan ritual text of the Great Bliss Queen . . . is an example of a Tibetan genre of texts known as *gter ma* (treasures). It is believed that the Indian tantric master who visited Tibet in the late eighth century, Padmasambhava, and his followers buried texts all over Tibet, knowing that they would be uncovered at an appropriate time in the future.

As one might imagine, there were those who found such claims fantastic, and the Mahāyāna was challenged by the foundational schools for fabricating new sūtras and distorting the Buddhist teaching. A sixth-century Mahāyāna author, Bhāvaviveka, summarizes the Hīnayāna argument that the Mahāyāna is not the word of the Buddha: the Mahāyāna sūtras were not included in ei-

ther the original or subsequent compilations of the word of the Buddha; by teaching that the Buddha is permanent, the Mahāyāna contradicts the dictum that all conditioned phenomena are impermanent; because the Mahāyāna teaches that the buddha nature is all-pervasive, it does not relinquish the belief in self; because the Mahāyāna teaches that the Buddha did not pass into nirvāṇa, it suggests that nirvāṇa is not the final state of peace; the Mahāyāna contains prophecies that the great early disciples will become buddhas; the Mahāyāna belittles the arhats, the Mahāyāna praises bodhisattvas above the Buddha; the Mahāyāna perverts the entire teaching by claiming that the historical Buddha was an emanation; the statement in the Mahāyāna sūtras that the Buddha was constantly in meditative absorption is unfeasible; by teaching that great sins can be completely absolved, the Mahāyāna teaches that actions have no effects, contradicting the law of karma. Therefore, the opponents of the Mahāyāna claim, the Buddha did not set forth the Mahāyāna; it was created by beings who were demonic in order to deceive the obtuse and those with evil minds.

Centuries earlier we find implied responses to these criticisms in the Mahāyāna sūtras themselves, side by side with the assertions that the Hīnayāna found so heretical. The most influential defense of new sūtras as authoritative teachings of the Buddha is found in the *Lotus Sūtra*, with its doctrine of skillful means (*upāya*). In that work the validity of the Mahāyāna and the Mahāyāna vision of buddhahood is defended by the use of parables. Because the *Lotus* is the most influential of Buddhist texts in all of East Asia, it is worthwhile to consider some of these.

The *Lotus Sūtra* must somehow account for the fact that the Mahāyāna has appeared late, after the Buddha had taught a path to nirvāṇa that had already been successfully followed to its terminus by his original disciples, the great arhats such as Śāriputra, Maudgalyāyana, and Kāśyapa. If the Mahāyāna is the superior teaching, why had it not been evident earlier? Several of the parables place the fault with the disciples themselves. Thus, in the parable of the hidden jewel, a man falls asleep drunk in the house of a friend who, unbeknownst to him, sews a jewel into the hem of his garment. The man awakes and goes on his way, only to suffer great poverty and hardship. He encounters his friend, who reveals the jewel, showing him that he had been endowed with great wealth all the while. In the same way, the disciples of the Buddha have constant access to the path to supreme enlightenment but are unaware of it; they are bodhisattvas unaware of their true identity. Again, the Buddha compares his teaching to the rainfall that descends without discrimination on the earth. That this rain causes some seeds to grow into flowers and some into great trees implies no differentiation in the rain but rather is due to the capacities of the seeds that it nurtures. Thus, the teaching of the Buddha is of a single flavor but benefits beings in a variety of ways according to their capacity. The Buddha knows the abilities and dispositions of his disciples and causes them to hear his dharma in a way most suitable to them.

Other parables employ a more radical strategy of authorization, suggesting that the Hīnayāna nirvāṇa is but a fiction. The oft-cited parable of the burning house tells of a father distraught as his children blithely play, unaware that the house is ablaze. Knowing of their respective predilections for playthings, he lures them from the inferno with the promise that he has a cart for each waiting outside, a deer-drawn cart for one, a goat-drawn cart for another, and so on. When they emerge from the conflagration, they find only one cart, a magnificent conveyance drawn by a great white ox, something that they had never even dreamed of. The burning house is saṃsāra, the children are ignorant sentient beings, unaware of the dangers of their abode, the father is the Buddha, who lures them out of saṃsāra with the teaching of a variety of vehicles—the vehicle of the śrāvaka, the vehicle of the pratyekabuddha, the vehicle of the bodhisattva—knowing that in fact there is but one vehicle, the buddha vehicle whereby all beings will be conveyed to unsurpassed enlightenment. And the Buddha tells the parable of the conjured city, in which a skillful guide leads a group of travelers on a long journey in search of a cache of jewels. Along the way, the travelers become exhausted and discouraged and decide to turn back. The guide magically conjures a great city in the near distance, where the travelers can rest before continuing toward their ultimate goal. The travelers enter the city where they regain their strength, at which point the guide dissolves the city and announces that the jewel cache is near. The travelers are those sentient beings who are weak and cowardly, intimidated by the thought of traversing the long Mahāyāna path to buddhahood. For their benefit, the Buddha creates the Hīnayāna nirvāṇa, more easily attained, which they mistakenly believe to be their final goal. He then announces to them that they have not reached their ultimate destination and exhorts them on to buddhahood, revealing that the nirvāṇa they had attained was but an illusion.

Thus, the claim to legitimacy of the earlier tradition is usurped by the Mahāyāna through the explanation that what the Buddha had taught before was in fact a lie, that there is no such thing as the path of the arhat, no such thing as nirvāṇa. There is only the Mahāyāna (also called the *ekayāna*, the "one vehicle"), which the Buddha intentionally misrepresents out of his compassionate understanding that there are many among his disciples who are incapable of assimilating so far-reaching a vision. But what of those disciples of the Buddha who are reported in the early sūtras to have become arhats, to have passed into nirvāṇa—what of their attainment? In an ingenious device (found also in other Mahāyāna sūtras) the great heroes of the Hīnayāna are drafted into the Mahāyāna by the Buddha's prophecies that even they will surpass the trifling goal of nirvāṇa and go on to follow the Mahāyāna path to eventual buddhahood. The first such prophecy is for the monk Śāriputra, renowned in the works of the foundational tradition as the wisest of the Buddha's disciples, who is transformed into a stock character in the Mahāyāna sūtras as one who is oblivious of the higher teaching. When his ignorance is revealed to him, he desires to learn more, coming to denounce as parochial the wisdom that he had once deemed supreme. The champion of the Hīnayāna is shown to reject it and embrace that which many adherents of the foundational tradition judged to be spurious. Thus the early history of the movement, already highly mythologized into a sacred history, was fictionalized further in the Mahāyāna sūtras, and another sacred history was eventually created. To legitimate these newly appearing texts, their authors claimed the principal figures of the earlier tradition, indeed its very codifiers, as converts to the Buddha's true teaching and central characters in its drama. The early story of Gautama Buddha and his disciples, preserved in the Pāli canon and already accepted as an historical account by the "pre-Mahāyāna" traditions, is radically rewritten in the *Lotus* in such a way as to glorify the *Lotus* itself as the record of what really happened. Such rewriting recurs throughout the history of the Buddhist traditions in the perpetual attempt to recount "what the Buddha taught."

And who is this Buddha that the *Lotus Sūtra* represents? In the fifteenth chapter, billions of bodhisattvas well up out of the earth and make offerings to the Buddha. The Buddha declares that all of these bodhisattvas who have been practicing the path for innumerable eons are in fact his own disciples, that he had set each of them on the long path to buddhahood. The bodhisattva Maitreya, who has witnessed this fantastic scene, asks the obvious question. He reckons that it had only been some forty years since the Buddha had achieved enlightenment under the tree at Bodhgayā. He finds it incredible that in that short period of time the Buddha could have trained so many bodhisattvas who had progressed so far on the path. "It is as if there were a man, his natural color fair and his hair black, twenty-five years of age, who pointed to men a hundred years of age and said, 'These are my sons!'" Maitreya, representing the self-doubt of the early Mahāyāna and reflecting the Hīnayāna critique, is deeply troubled by this inconsistency, fearing that people who hear of this after the Buddha's passing will doubt the truth of the Buddha's words and attack his teaching.

It is at this point that the Buddha reveals another lie. He explains that even though he is widely believed to have left the palace of his father in search of freedom from suffering and to have found that freedom six years later under a tree near Gayā, in fact, that is not the case. He achieved enlightenment innumerable billions of eons ago and has been preaching the dharma in this world and simultaneously in myriad other worlds ever since. Yet he recognizes the meager intelligence of many beings, and out of his wish to benefit them resorts to the use of skillful methods (upāya), recounting how he renounced his princely life and attained unsurpassed enlightenment. And, further recognizing that his continued presence in the world might cause those of little virtue to become complacent and not ardently seek to put his teaching into practice, he declares that he is soon to pass into nirvāṇa. But this also is a lie, because his lifespan will not be exhausted for many innumerable billions of eons.

Thus, the prince's deep anxiety at being confronted with the facts of sickness, aging, and death, his difficult decision to abandon his wife and child and go forth into the forest in search of a state beyond sorrow, his ardent practice of meditation and asceticism for six years, his triumphant attainment of the liberation and his imminent passage into the extinction of nirvāṇa—all are a pretense. He was enlightened all the time, yet feigned these deeds to inspire the world.

But we should not conclude that once the Lotus and other Mahāyāna sūtras declared the superiority of the bodhisattva path, the supremacy and authority of the Mahāyāna was finally and unequivocally established. Defenses of the Mahāyāna as the word of the Buddha remained the preoccupation of Mahāyāna scholastics throughout the history of Buddhism in India. . . . Nor should we assume that teachings were ranked only as Hīnayāna and Mahāyāna. Even sects that exalted the Lotus Sūtra above all others, for example, could disagree about whether there was more than one true practice, one true sūtra, one true buddha. In Japan, a dispute over the meaning of "original enlightenment" in what is called the Matsumoto Debate led to a bloody conflict in 1536 that involved thousands of troops on each side. . . . In China, the promotion and control of sacred scripture was the prerogative of the highest imperial offices. A sect that came into conflict with this authority, the "Teaching of the Three Stages," had its texts de-

clared heretical and banned from the official collection of Buddhist texts. . . .

. . . The significance of Buddhist texts does not lie simply in their doctrinal or philosophical content but in the uses to which they have been put. We find, for example, . . . that the Abhidharma (literally, "higher dharma," sometimes rendered as "phenomenology"), a class of Buddhist scriptures concerned with minute analyses of mental states, is chanted at Thai funerals. Contained in virtually every Mahāyāna sūtra was a proclamation of the marvelous benefits that would accrue to those who piously handled, recited, worshiped, copied, or circulated the text itself—again, the teaching had become the teacher. Ritual enshrinement and devotion to the sūtra as a vital embodiment of the dharma and, in a certain sense, as a substitute for the Buddha himself was instrumental to the rise of the disparate collections of cults of the book that came to be known as the Mahāyāna. In China, no text was more venerated than the Lotus, and tales were told of the miracles that attended its worship. . . .

The importance of texts in Buddhism derives in part from the fact that the tradition represents the Buddha as being eventually persuaded to teach others after his enlightenment. This suggests that the dharma is something that can be passed on, something that is transmittable, transferable. The Buddha is said to have spoken not in Sanskrit, the formal language of the priests of his day, but in the vernacular, and he is said to have forbidden monks from composing his teachings in formal verses for chanting. The implication was that the content was more important than the form. This led to the notion that the dharma could be translated from one language to another, and the act of translation (and the sponsorship of translation) has been regarded throughout Asia as one of the most pious and meritorious acts that could be performed. It was therefore common for Buddhist kings and emperors to sponsor the translation of texts from one language into another: from Sanskrit into Chinese, from Sanskrit into Tibetan, from Tibetan into Manchu, from Pāli into Burmese, and so on. Adding to this notion of translatability was the fact that the primary objects of Buddhist devotion—texts, relics, icons—were all portable; stories of the transportation and enshrinement of a particularly potent image of the Buddha figure in the histories of almost all Buddhist cultures. We should not conclude, however, as Buddhist sometimes do, that the dharma is something self-identical and transcendent, that showers over the cultures of Asia, transforming and pacifying them. . . . For example, Buddhism is portrayed [in one instance] as a Korean possession that can be offered in tribute to the Japanese court as a means of protecting the state. It is this universalism of the Buddhist dharma with its plastic pantheon into which any local deity could easily be enlisted, its doctrine of the Buddha's skillful methods for accommodating conflicting views, and its claims about the pervasive nature of reality that have made it a sometimes useful ideology for rulership and empire.

Buddhism has indeed transformed Asia, but it has been transformed in the process. We may consider even whether there ever was some entity called "Buddhism" to be transformed in the first place. What cannot be disputed is that if Buddhism exists, it is impossible to understand it outside the lives of Buddhists, outside the saṅgha.

Saṅgha

The last of the three jewels is the saṅgha, "the community." Technically taken to mean the assembly of enlightened disciples of the Buddha, the term more commonly connotes the community of Buddhist monks and nuns. In the rules governing the ordination ceremony, the saṅgha is said to be present when four fully ordained monks are in attendance. However, in its broadest sense the saṅgha is the whole body of Buddhist faithful. . . .

As mentioned earlier, Buddhist practice was traditionally subsumed under three headings: ethics (*śīla*), meditation (*dhyāna*), and wisdom (*prajñā*). Ethics, which in this context refers to refraining from nonvirtue through the conscious control of body and speech, was regarded as the essential prerequisite for progress in meditation and wisdom. It was the element of the triad most widely practiced both by lay people and monks and nuns, and this practice generally took the form of the observance of vows. Since in Buddhist ethical theory karma, both good and bad, depended not on the deed but on the intention, if one could make a promise not to kill humans, for example, and maintain that promise, the good karma accumulated by such restraint would be far greater than had one simply not had the occasion to commit murder. From the early days of the tradition, therefore, elaborate systems of rules for living one's life, called *vinaya*, were established, along with ceremonies for their conferral and maintenance. Laypeople could take vows not to kill humans, not to steal, not to commit sexual misconduct, not to lie about spiritual attainments (for example, not to claim to be telepathic when one actually was not), and not to use intoxicants. Novice monks and nuns took these five vows, plus vows not to eat after the noon meal (a rule widely transgressed in some Buddhist cultures through recourse to the evening "medicinal meal"), not to handle gold or silver, not to adorn their bodies, not to sleep in high beds, and not to attend musical performances. Fully ordained monks (*bhikṣu*) and nuns (*bhikṣuṇī*) took many more vows, which covered the entire range of personal and public decorum, and regulated physical movements, social intercourse, and property. Monks and nuns convened twice monthly to confess their transgressions of the rules in a ceremony and reaffirm their commitment to the code, with transgressions carrying punishments of various weights. The gravest misdeeds entailed expulsion from the order, whereas others could be expiated simply by confessing them aloud. In Buddhist traditions across Asia, ritual maintenance of these monastic codes has served as the mark of orthodoxy, much more than adherence to a particular belief or doctrine. Indeed, it is said that the teaching of the Buddha will endure only as long as the vinaya endures.

The Buddha and his followers were probably originally a group of wandering ascetics. However, they adopted the practice of other ascetic groups in India of remaining in one place during the rainy season. Wealthy patrons had shelters built for their use, and these shelters evolved into monasteries that were inhabited throughout the year. It seems that early in the tradition, the saṅgha became largely sedentary, although the tradition of the wandering monk continued. Still, the saṅgha was by no means a homogeneous community. The vinaya texts describe monks from a wide variety of social backgrounds. Mention is made of monks from all four of India's social castes. There were also a wide variety of monastic specialties. The vinaya texts describe monks who are skilled in speech, those who memorize and recite the sūtras, those who memorize and recite the vinaya, and those who memorize and recite lists of technical terms. There are monks who live in the forest, who wear robes of felt, who wear robes made from discarded rags, who live only on the alms they have begged for, who live at the foot of a tree, who live in a cemetery, who live in the open air, who sleep sitting up, and so on. There were also monks who specialized in meditation, monks who served as advisors to kings, and monks responsible for the administration of the monastery and its property. One of the tasks of this administrator was to insure that the wandering monks were not given mundane work, that meditating monks not be disturbed by noise, and that monks who begged for alms received good food. Whether they wandered without a fixed abode or lived in monasteries, monks and nuns that lived in a designated region, called a *sīmā*, were to gather twice a month to confess and affirm their vows communally, a ceremony that laypeople also attended.

Throughout the Buddhist world, monks and laypeople have lived in a symbiotic relationship: the laity provide material support for monks while monks provide a locus for the layperson's accumulation of merit (by supporting monks who maintained their vows). The rules and regulations in the vinaya texts were meant to govern the lives of Buddhist monks and to structure their relations with the laity. Monks in the vinaya literature are caught in a web of social and ritual obligations, are fully and elaborately housed and permanently settled, and are preoccupied not with nirvāṇa, but with bowls and robes, bathrooms and buckets, and proper behavior in public. . . . The saṅgha was also a community where disputes arose and had to be settled. Because it is said that the Buddha only prescribed a rule in response to a specific misdeed, the vinaya texts often provide the story of that first offense and the Buddha's pronouncement of a rule against such behavior in the future. . . .

There were also rules for nuns, although these receive much less attention in the vinaya literature. According to several traditions, the Buddha was approached early in his career by his aunt and step-mother, Mahāpajāpatī . . . , at the head of a delegation of women who wished him to institute a Buddhist order of nuns. The Buddha initially declined to institute such an order. But when the Buddha's cousin and personal attendant, Ānanda, asked him whether women were able to attain the fruits of the practice of the dharma, the Buddha unhesitatingly answered in the affirmative and agreed to establish an order for women. However, the same text states that if the Buddha had not agreed to establish an order for nuns, his teaching would not disappear from the world so quickly. The rules for nuns are both more numerous and stricter than those for monks, and placed nuns in a position of clear subordination to monks. For example, seniority in the order of monks and nuns is measured by the length of time one has been ordained, such that someone who has been a monk for five years must pay respect to a monk of six years, even if the first monk is chronologically older. However, the rules for nuns state that a woman who has been a nun for one hundred years must pay respect to a man who was ordained as a monk for one day. The difficulties entailed in maintaining the strict nuns' vows and a lack of institutional support led to the decline and eventual disappearance of the order of nuns in India, Sri Lanka, and Southeast Asia, and to an order of novices alone (rather than fully ordained nuns) in Tibet. The tradition of full ordination for women was maintained only in China.

Throughout the development of the Mahāyāna and the Vajrayāna, the rules for monks and nuns seems to have remained fairly uniform and the adherents of the new vehicles seem to have seen no contradiction between the monastic life and the practices of the Mahāyāna and the Vajrayāna. But if we understand the vinaya not as that which restricts individuals and their actions but as that which creates them, we will not be surprised that additional vows were formulated for the bodhisattva and the tantric practitioner, and that rituals which mimicked the monastic confession ceremony were designed for their administration. The vows of a bodhisattva included not only the vow to liberate all beings in the universe from suffering but also to act compassionately by always accepting an apology, not to praise oneself and belittle others, to give gifts and teachings upon request, and so on. Those who took the bodhisattva vows also promised never to claim that the Mahāyāna sūtras were not the word of the Buddha. . . .

Vajrayāna practice also entailed extensive sets of vows. . . . As mentioned above, it was common for Buddhist monks, especially in late Indian Buddhism and in Tibet, to hold bodhisattva and tantric vows in addition to their monk's vows. In the case of the more advanced tantric initiations, which involved sexual union with a consort, this presented problems, for monks were bound by the rule of celibacy. Whether or not monks were permitted to participate in such initiations became a question of some gravity when Buddhism was being established in Tibet. . . .

. . . Because of the portability of relics, texts, and icons, sacred sites were established across the Buddhist world and pilgrimages to those sites was a popular form of buddhist practice throughout Asia. Pilgrimage was sometimes to a stūpa associated with the life of the Buddha; Bodhgayā, the site of the Buddha's enlightenment, has drawn pilgrims from the outer reaches of the Buddhist world for centuries. Particularly powerful buddha images also attracted pilgrims; it was not uncommon for pilgrims from as far east as Manchuria and as far west as the Mongol regions of Russia to travel to Lhasa, the capital of Tibet, to visit the statue of the Buddha there. They would travel on foot or on horseback; the most pious would proceed by prostration—bowing and then stretching their bodies on the ground before rising, taking one step forward and prostrating again, along the entire route. In China, mountains believed to be the abodes of munificent bodhisattvas were (and are) popular destinations of communal pilgrimages. . . . But we should not assume that Buddhist travel was always directed from the periphery to the center. [There is a] story of a renowned Buddhist scholar who left one of the great monastic universities of India on a perilous sea voyage to Sumatra, where the preeminent teacher of the practice of compassion was said to reside. Nor was the travel always so concerned with what or who was to be found at the end of the journey; the Japanese monk Ippen saw travel itself as essential to his practice of devotion to Amitābha. . . .

WORLD DISTRIBUTION OF BUDDHISTS

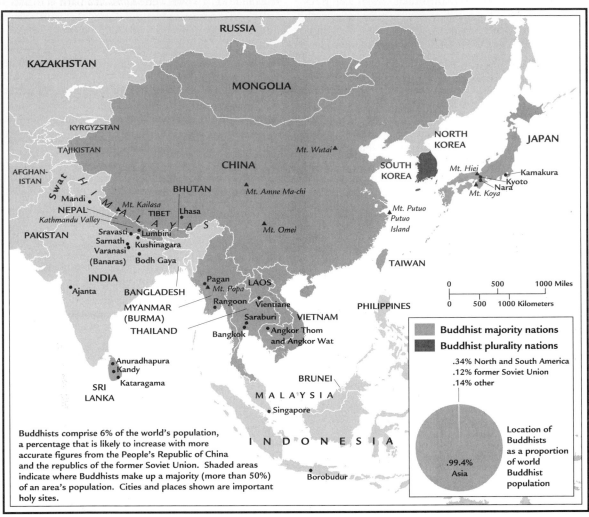

From *The HarperCollins Dictionary of Religion* by Jonathan Z. Smith. Copyright © 1995 by the American Academy of Religion. Reprinted by permission of HarperCollins Publishers, Inc.

SOURCES

I have organized the sources historically and by traditions (vehicles) in order to provide a developmental overview of some of the important religious literature of Buddhism. However, one should not assume that this structure indicates that one vehicle somehow stopped developing when our attention shifts to another vehicle. Neither does this sequence—Nikaya (Hinayana), Mahayana, and Vajrayana—imply a value judgment about which is the "original" form or which is the "best" tradition.

I have selected material that has been particularly important in the development of Buddhism. However, we must remember that this literature was created by a small religious elite, most of whom were monks or nuns as well as scholars and much of it was not well known or even read by the vast majority of Buddhist practitioners. I have included descriptions of practices, such as meditation and pilgrimage, that will give you an idea of what these practices are like. Buddhism, like many religions, lives, for most of its followers, more in what is done than in what is known about the fine points of doctrines or philosophical/theological arguments.

Nothing was written down for 400 to 500 years after the Buddha's *parinirvana* (final release from rebirth and suffering after death). Hence it is extremely difficult to recover the original teachings of the historical Buddha. Monks orally preserved material for centuries. During this time other material dating from after the time of the Buddha was added as problems arose in the monasteries, there were divisions among Buddhists into different groups, and questions needed to be clarified and answered. Add to this popular stories circulating among the laity and you have a vast mix of materials dealing with a wide variety of issues and topics. Only when the oral traditions were in danger of being lost did the task of recording them begin.

Over time, as Buddhism spread from one culture to another, new materials were added from local traditions. As encounters intensified with new indigenous traditions, new ideas, interpretations, and writings were added. For example, as Buddhism moved into China, it encountered the Confucian and Taoist traditions. It adapted, adopted, and disputed in reaction to this experience.

Buddhism has shown a remarkable flexibility. It both transforms and is transformed by the religions and cultures it comes into contact with. Hence the literature has, over the centuries, become both immense and complex. Thich Nhat Hanh, a Vietnamese Buddhist monk who has helped bring Buddhism to America, has expressed the situation well:

> Buddhism is not one. The teachings of Buddhism are many. When Buddhism enters a country, that country always acquires a new form of Buddhism. . . . The teaching of Buddhism in this country [America] will be different from other countries. Buddhism, in order to be Buddhism, must be suitable, appropriate to the psychology and the culture of the society that it serves. (*The Heart of Understanding*, Berkeley: Parallax Press, 1988, p. viii)

7.2 ENLIGHTENMENT

Enlightenment is that for which every Buddhist ultimately hopes although most will settle for rebirth in a better place than this world of suffering and pain. With enlightenment come wisdom, serenity, and release from suffering. Sakyamuni's own enlightenment is the model. Before enlightenment a person who has

taken the appropriate vows is called a **bodhisattva,** or *buddha to be.* To walk the *bodhisattva* path is to aim at enlightenment or buddhahood if not in this life, then in some future life.

We do not have a psychological description of Sakyamuni's enlightenment from his own mouth. What we do have is a pious reconstruction written sometime in the first and second centuries C.E. in a document, attributed to a poet named Ashvaghosha, called *The Deeds of the Buddha* (*Buddhacarita*). The author presents what he considers to be the basic moral and spiritual teachings of the Buddha. Even when writing about events such as the enlightenment experience, Ashvaghosha's primary concern is to instruct his readers rather than simply describe an event.

Ashvaghosha's text gained wide popularity not only among the Mahayana Buddhists in East Asia but also throughout India and South Asia. Enlightenment is a concern of Buddhists everywhere and of all schools of Buddhism. The story of the Buddha's enlightenment belongs to the whole of Buddhism.

✦

ASHVAGHOSHA

Enlightenment (Buddhacarita)

READING QUESTION

1. Write a brief commentary on two or three of the most important parts of this account. Why are these significant in your view? What do they mean? What spiritual insight do they show?

THE DEFEAT OF MARA

Because the great Sage, the scion of a line of royal seers, had made his vow to win emancipation, and had seated himself in the effort to carry it out, the whole world rejoiced—but Mara, the inveterate foe of the true Dharma, shook with fright. People address him gladly as the God of Love, the one who shoots with flower-arrows, and yet they dread this Mara as the one who

From *Buddhist Scriptures*, translated by Edward Conze (Middlesex, England: Penguin Books, Ltd., 1959), pp. 48–53. Copyright © 1959 Edward Conze. Reprinted by permission of Penguin Books, Ltd.

rules events connected with a life of passion, as the one who hates the very thought of freedom. He had with him his three sons—Flurry, Gaiety, and Sullen Pride—and his three daughters—Discontent, Delight, and Thirst. These asked him why he was so disconcerted in his mind. And he replied to them with these words: "Look over there at that sage, clad in the armour of determination, with truth and spiritual virtue as his weapons, the arrows of his intellect drawn ready to shoot! He has sat down with the firm intention of conquering my realm. No wonder that my mind is plunged in deep despondency! If he should succeed in overcoming me, and could proclaim to the world the way to final beatitude, then my realm would be empty today, like that of the king of Videha of whom we hear in the Epics that he lost his kingdom because he misconducted himself by carrying off a Brahmin's daughter. But so far he has not yet won the eye of full knowledge. He is still within my sphere of influence. While there is time I therefore will attempt to break his solemn purpose, and throw myself against him like the rush of a swollen river breaking against the embankment!"

But Mara could achieve nothing against the Bodhisattva, and he and his army were defeated, and fled in all directions—their elation gone, their toil rendered fruitless, their rocks, logs, and trees scattered everywhere. They behaved like a hostile army whose commander had been slain in battle. So Mara, defeated, ran away together with his followers. The great seer, free from the dust of passion, victorious over darkness' gloom, had vanquished him. And the moon, like a maiden's gentle smile, lit up the heavens, while a rain of sweet-scented flowers, filled with moisture, fell down on the earth from above.

THE ENLIGHTENMENT

Now that he had defeated Mara's violence by his firmness and calm, the Bodhisattva, possessed of great skill in Transic meditation, put himself into trance, intent on discerning both the ultimate reality of things and the final goal of existence. After he had gained complete mastery over all the degrees and kinds of trance:

1. In the first watch of the night he recollected the successive series of his former births. "There was I so and so; that was my name; deceased from there I came here"—in this way he remembered thousands of births, as though living them over again. When he had recalled his own births and deaths in all these various lives of his, the Sage, full of pity, turned his compassionate mind towards other living beings, and he thought to himself: "Again and again they must leave the people they regard as their own, and must go on elsewhere, and that without ever stopping. Surely this world is unprotected and helpless, and like a wheel it turns round and round." As he continued steadily to recollect the past thus, he came to the definite conviction that this world of Samsara is as unsubstantial as the pith of a plantain tree.

2. Second to none in valour, he then, in the second watch of the night, acquired the supreme heavenly eye, for he himself was the best of all those who have sight. Thereupon with the perfectly pure heavenly eye he looked upon the entire world, which appeared to him as though reflected in a spotless mirror. He saw that the decease and rebirth of beings depend on whether they have done superior or inferior deeds. And his compassionateness grew still further. It became clear to him that no security can be found in this flood of Samsaric existence, and that the threat of death is ever-present. Beset on all sides, creatures can find no resting place. In this way he surveyed the five places of rebirth with his heavenly eye. And he found nothing substantial in the world of becoming, just as no core of heartwood is found in a plantain tree when its layers are peeled off one by one.

3. Then, as the third watch of that night drew on, the supreme master of trance turned his meditation to the real and essential nature of this world: "Alas, living beings wear themselves out in vain! Over and over again they are born, they age, die, pass on to a new life, and are reborn! What is more, greed and dark delusion obscure their sight, and they are blind from birth. Greatly apprehensive, they yet do not know how to get out of this great mass of ill." He then surveyed the twelve links of conditioned co-production, and saw that, beginning with ignorance, they lead to old age and death, and, beginning with the cessation of ignorance, they lead to the cessation of birth, old age, death, and all kinds of ill.

When the great seer had comprehended that where there is no ignorance whatever, there also the karma-formations are stopped—then he had achieved a correct knowledge of all there is to be known, and he stood out in the world as a Buddha. He passed through the eight stages of Transic insight, and quickly reached their highest point. From the summit of the world downwards he could detect no self anywhere. Like the fire, when its fuel is burnt up, he became tranquil. He had reached perfection, and he thought to himself: "This is the authentic Way on which in the past so many great seers, who also knew all higher and all lower things, have travelled on to ultimate and real truth. And now I obtained it!"

4. At that moment, in the fourth watch of the night, when dawn broke and all the ghosts that move and those that move not went to rest, the great seer took up the position which knows no more alteration, and the leader of all reached the state of all-knowledge. When, through his Buddhahood, he had cognized this fact, the earth swayed like a woman drunken with wine, the sky shone bright with the Siddhas who appeared in crowds in all the directions, and the mighty drums of thunder resounded through the air. Pleasant breezes blew softly, rain fell from a cloudless sky, flowers and fruits dropped from the trees out of season—in an effort, as it were, to show reverence for him. Mandarava flowers and lotus blossoms, and also water lillies made of gold and beryl, fell from the sky on to the ground near the Shakya sage, so that it looked like a place in the world of the gods. At the moment no one anywhere was angry, ill, or sad; no one did evil, none was proud; the world became quite quiet, as though it had reached full perfection. Joy spread through the ranks of those gods who longed for salvation; joy also spread among those who lived in the regions below. Everywhere the virtuous were strengthened, the influence of Dharma increased, and the world rose from the dirt of the passions and the darkness of ignorance. Filled with joy and wonder at the Sage's work, the seers of the solar race who had been protectors of men, who had been royal seers, who had been great seers, stood in their mansions in the heavens and showed him their reverence. The great seers among the hosts of invisible beings could be heard widely proclaiming his fame. All living things rejoiced and sensed that things went well. Mara alone felt deep displeasure, as though subjected to a sudden fall.

For seven days He dwelt there—his body gave him no trouble, his eyes never closed, and he looked into his own mind. He thought: "Here I have found freedom," and he knew that the longings of his heart had at last come to fulfillment. Now that he had grasped the principle of causation, and finally convinced himself of the lack of self in all that is, he roused himself again from his deep trance, and in his great compassion he surveyed the world with his Buddha-eye, intent on giving it peace. When, however, he saw on the one side the world lost in low views and confused efforts, thickly covered with the dirt of the passions, and saw on the other side the exceeding subtlety of the Dharma of emancipation, he felt inclined to take no action. But when he weighed up the significance of the pledge to enlighten all things he had

taken in the past, he became again more favourable to the idea of proclaiming the path to Peace. Reflecting in his mind on this question, he also considered that, while some people have a great deal of passion, others have but little. As soon as Indra and Brahma, the two chiefs of those who dwell in the heavens, had grasped the Sugata's intention to proclaim the path to Peace, they shone brightly and came up to him, the weal of the world their concern. He remained there on his seat, free from all evil and successful in his aim. The most excellent Dharma which he had seen was his most excellent companion. His two visitors gently and reverently spoke to him these words, which were meant for the weal of the world: "Please do not condemn all those that live as unworthy of such treasure! Oh, please engender pity in your heart for beings in this world! So varied is their endowment, and while some have much passion, others have only very little. Now that you, O Sage, have yourself crossed the ocean of the world of becoming, please rescue also the other living beings who have sunk so deep into suffering! As a generous lord shares his wealth, so may also you bestow your own virtues on others! Most of those who know what for them is good in this world and the next, act only for their own advantage. In the world of men and in heaven it is hard to find anyone who is impelled by concern for the weal of the world's." Having made this request to the great seer, the two gods returned to their celestial abode by the way they had come. And the sage pondered over their words. In consequence he was confirmed in his decision to set the world free.

Then came the time for the alms-round, and the World-Guardians of the four quarters presented the seer with begging-bowls. Gautama accepted the four, but for the sake of his Dharma he turned them into one. At that time two merchants of a passing caravan came that way. Instigated by a friendly deity, they joyfully saluted the seer, and, elated in their hearts, gave him alms. They were the first to do so. After that the sage saw that Arada and Udraka Ramaputra were the two people best equipped to grasp the Dharma. But then he saw that both had gone to live among the gods in heaven. His mind thereupon turned to the five mendicants. In order to proclaim the path to Peace, thereby dispelling the darkness of ignorance, just as the rising sun conquers the darkness of night, Gautama betook himself to the blessed city of Kashi, to which Bhimaratha gave his love, and which is adorned with the Varanasi river and with many splendid forests. Then, before he carried out his wish to go into the region of Kashi, the Sage, whose eyes were like those of a bull, and whose gait like that of an elephant in rut, once more fixed his steady gaze on the root of the Bodhi tree, after he had turned his entire body like an elephant.

7.3 NIKAYA, OR HINAYANA, BUDDHISM

In the third century B.C.E., there were eighteen sects of Buddhism. These were given the pejorative name **Hinayana** ("Little Vehicle") by later Mahayana (Great Vehicle) Buddhists because the Mahayanists argued that the Hinayana tradition, concentrating as it did on the life of monks, carried fewer people to enlightenment. Of these eighteen sects only the **Theravada** (Way of the Elders) survives today, mostly in Sri Lanka and Southeast Asia. Hence, sometimes this whole tradition is called Theravada.

I have used the term **Nikaya** in order to avoid the pejorative term Hinayana and the misleading term Theravada, but Nikaya (often used to refer to a textual collection of discourses attributed to the Buddha or to an ordination lineage of the *sangha*) is not yet in widespread use in the textbooks. Nikaya Buddhism (Buddhism of the Schools) is not without its own problems, but it is sometimes used by Buddhists themselves and is increasingly being adopted by scholars.

We know little about the early history of the Theravada school in India, but we do know it was and is a conservative tradition and considers itself as preserving the original form of Buddhism. It refuses to deify the Buddha as some later traditions have and rejects any scriptures written after the formation of the **Tripitika** ("The Three Baskets," a term for the Buddhist canon). It tends to be individualistic in the sense that each individual is responsible for treading the path to enlightenment relying primarily on his or her own efforts. Of course, the Buddhist community (*sangha*) provides support in general, and those who can become monks and nuns live and practice in a community of like-minded individuals.

7.3.1 The Evolution of the World

There is no creation myth in early Buddhism because there is no creation or creator god. The universe or world is eternal. However, it does go through a cycle of beginning, evolving, and decaying and, then, repeats itself endlessly. The standard cosmology divides the universe into three realms, or worlds—the realm of desire, of form, and of the formless.

The realm of desire is inhabited by humans and organized into four islands surrounding a central mountain, **Mount Meru** (or Sumeru). On the lower elevation of Mount Meru live a class of beings called **asuras,** often translated as "demigods" or "titans." *Asuras* are often depicted as mean-spirited and causing harm to humans. At a higher elevation and above Mount Meru live six classes of gods. These gods, while living a long time, are not immortal and they too eventually die and are reborn. These gods are usually honored for the benefits they bestow. *Pretas*, or hungry ghosts, also inhabit the realm of desire. Monks and nuns have a special responsibility of feeding these ghosts, who have enormous stomachs and throats the size of the eye of a needle and hence are always hungry and thirsty.

Still in the realm of desire, but below the Southern Island on which humans live, are numerous hells, some burning hot and others freezing cold. It is desirable not to be reborn here, since beings here undergo a variety of tortures. These hells, however, are more like purgatories because it is possible to be reborn out of them.

The realm of form is situated above the realm of desire. Gods who experience the pleasures of sight, sound, and touch (but not taste and smell) live here. These gods have great powers of concentration that provide them with mental bliss.

Even more sublime than the realm of form is the formless realm. Here, gods exist in states of pure consciousness without bodies and sense organs of any kind. This is the most blissful of abodes and one of the most desirable places to be reborn.

The following story tells about the beginning of a new cycle of the universe and is referred to as the *Sutra on Knowing the Beginning* (*Agganna sutta*). At the start of a new cycle, humans live in a paradise, in which there is no need for food and their life span is immeasurable. But things change for the worse. Unfortunately, it seems, they always do.

Sutra on Knowing the Beginning (Agganna Sutta)

READING QUESTIONS

1. What are the beings like who fall from the Realm of the Radiant Gods, and why do they fall?
2. Why does one of these beings begin to eat the earth-essence and why do others follow suit? What effect does this activity have on the beings?
3. What is the sequence of events after the earth-essence disappears?
4. What is the point of this story?

O monks, eventually there comes a time when, after a long period, this world starts to wind down. And as the world is winding down, beings for the most part are reborn out of it, in the Realm of the Radiant Gods. Eventually, after another long period, it happens that this world that has ended begins to reevolve. And as it is reevolving, settling, and becoming established, certain beings, in order to work out their karma, fall from the Realm of the Radiant Gods and come to be once again in this world. These beings by nature are self-luminescent and move through the air. They are made of mind, feed on joy, dwell in bliss, and go where they will.

When at first they reappear, there is no knowledge in the world of the sun and the moon. And likewise there is no knowledge of the forms of the stars, of the paths of the constellations, of night and day, month and fortnight, seasons and years. . . .

Eventually, this Great Earth appears; it is like a pool of water. It is pretty and savory and tastes just like pure sweet honey, and in physical appearance it is like the scum on milk or ghee.

Now, monks, it happens that a certain being, fickle and greedy by nature, tastes some of this earth-essence with his finger. He enjoys its color, its smell, and its savor. Then other beings, seeing what he has done, imitate him. They also taste some of the earth-essence with their fingers, and they too take pleasure in its color, its smell, its savor.

Then, on another occasion, that being takes a morsel of earth-essence and eats it, and the other beings too,

seeing what he has done, imitate him. . . . And because they take morsels of earth-essence and eat them, in due course their bodies become heavy, solid, and hard, and their former qualities—of being self-luminescent, of moving through the air, being made of mind, feeding on joy, dwelling in bliss, and going where they will—disappear. And when this happens, the sun and the moon and likewise the forms of the stars, the paths of the constellations, night and day, month and fortnight, seasons and years come to be known in the world.

Now, monks, for a very long time these beings continue to consume this earth-essence. It is their food, what they eat, and it shapes them. Those who eat a lot of it take on an ugly appearance, whereas those who consume only a little of it become good looking. And the ones who are good looking become contemptuous of those who are ugly. "We are handsome," they declare, "and you look bad." While they go in this way, convinced of their own superior beauty, proud and arrogant, the earth-essence disappears. . . .

Now monks, when those beings eat the rice that is huskless, polished, and sweet smelling, bodily features of femininity appear in those who are women, and bodily features of masculinity appear in those who are men. Then, overflowing thoughts of passion for each other arise in their minds; they are pleased with each other, consumed by passion for each other, and have illicit sex together.

Then, other beings see them having illicit sex together and throw sticks and clods of dirt and dust at them. . . . Nowadays, when a girl is carried off to be married, people throw sticks and clods of dirt. In this way, they repeat an ancient primeval custom without realizing the meaning of it. In former times, it was thought to be immoral, profane, and undisciplined, but nowadays it is deemed moral, sacred, and disciplined. . . .

Then, it occurs to a certain being who has gone out to gather rice that he is needlessly wearying himself. "Why," he reflects, "should I go on tiring myself by getting rice for supper in the evening and rice for breakfast in the morning, when I could be gathering it for both evening and morning meals just once a day?" And that is what he begins to do.

Then, one evening, some other being says to him: "Come, my friend, let's go get some rice."

But the first being replies: "You go, friend. I already brought back rice for both evening and morning meals."

Then it occurs to that second being: "This is a wonderful way of doing things! Why, I could be gathering rice all at once for two or three days!" And that is what he begins to do.

Then, monks, it happens that a third being says to him: "Come, my friend, let's go get some rice."

And he replies: "You go, my friend. I already brought back rice for two or three days."

Then it occurs to that third being: "Now this is a wonderful way of doing things! Why, I could be gathering rice all at once for four or five days!" And that is what he begins to do.

But because these beings are now hoarding and consuming that rice that is huskless, polished, and sweet smelling, husks and reddish coatings begin to appear on it. And if it is reaped in the evening, by daybreak it has not sprouted, ripened, or grown back, and it is clear that it has been cut.

Then, those beings quickly assemble together and take counsel with one another. . . . "Now what if we were to divide the rice fields and draw boundaries between them?"

And that, monks, is what those beings do, declaring, "This field is yours, and this field is mine."

Then it occurs to one of those beings who has gone to gather rice: "How will I get my livelihood if my allotment of rice is destroyed? Why don't I now go and steal someone else's rice?"

And so that being, while guarding his own share of rice, goes and steals somebody else's portion. But another being happens to see him stealing that other person's portion, and he goes up to him and says, "Ho, my friend, you have taken someone else's rice!"

To which he replies: "Yes, my friend, but it will not happen again."

Nonetheless, it occurs a second time . . . and a third time. He goes and steals somebody else's portion, and another being sees him. But this time, that other being goes up to him and beats him with a stick, and says: "This is the third time, friend, that you have taken someone else's rice!"

Then that being holds up his arms, wails, and cries out: "Friends, immorality has appeared in the world! Irreligion has appeared in the world, for the taking up of sticks is now known!" But, the first being throws his stick on the ground, holds up his arms, wails, and cries out: "Friends, immorality and irreligion have appeared in the world, because stealing and lying are now known!"

In this way, monks, these three evil and demeritorious things first come to be known in the world: theft, lying, and violence. . . .

7.3.2 The Three Marks of Existence

If I asked you to name three things that characterize human existence, what would you name? You might say that while humans are happy and satisfied some of the time, they also suffer to one degree or another.

You also might notice a link between human suffering and change or impermanence. We have desires for things that please us and want to avoid pain and experience as much pleasure as is reasonably possible. When we find something that gives us pleasure, we become attached to it and do not want it to change. However, sooner or later it does change. We cannot avoid the passage of time, and inevitably the pleasures of childhood will give way to adulthood, old age, and eventually death. It makes us sad to lose the pleasures and innocence of childhood, and the thought of death often scares us.

Who is, however, being scared? Who is it that desires pleasure, becomes attached, experiences change, and then suffers? The answer seems obvious: I do. But who is this I? "Your self," you might reply. Quite so, but who is this self? Is it your soul? Probably many of us would answer yes, because the idea of a soul is so deeply rooted in Western culture and tradition. But what exactly is the soul? Is it a thing, a spiritual substance of some sort? How long does it live? Is it also impermanent?

In the Buddha's India, some Brahmins and others taught that the self (*atman* in Sanskrit) is an eternal, permanent substance (see previous chapter on Hinduism). The Buddha disagreed. Careful introspection showed there is no such self or soul (*anatman* in Sanskrit, **anatta** in Pali). The Buddha thought that this lack of a permanent self, along with suffering and impermanence, constitute the three main marks of existence. He also thought that if there is no such thing as a substantial soul or self, then the problem of attachment and suffering takes on a new light. It becomes possible to experience a freedom from suffering and attachment once one is free from a false view of the self. All this talk of suffering seems pointless if there is no self to suffer, no self to become attached, no self to cling to the momentary but passing existence of things.

Even if this idea of no self can help us see the problem of suffering and attachment in a new light, it seems to undercut both moral responsibility and the idea of rebirth. If there is no self, one would not be able to say that a particular individual had made merit or attained enlightenment. And what would pass from one life to the next? How could my *karma*, good or bad, get passed along?

This denial of a permanent self (the no-self doctrine) startled and puzzled many people in Buddha's day, and today many find it a rather strange idea. In fact, some Buddhists, called the Personalists, while admitting that there is no universal self or *atman* as the Hindus taught, argue that there is something they call the person (*pudgala* in Sanskrit, *puggala* in Pali). If there is a person, then moral responsibility and rebirth make sense. But other Buddhists disagree, arguing that the mark of impermanence applies to everything, including person.

Below are three brief selections dealing with the three marks of existence. The first, from the *Samyutta-Nikaya*, deals with suffering and co-dependent origination. The second, from the *Anityatasutra*, claims that impermanence extends to the Triple World of desire, form, and formlessness. In the final selection, also from the *Samyutta-Nikaya*, a Buddhist nun Vajira encounters **Mara,** the Evil One, who tempted the Buddha himself just before his enlightenment, and she sets him straight about "this Being" called "the self."

∽✕∾

Suffering, Co-Dependent Arising, Impermanence, and No-Self (Samyutta-Nikaya and Anityatasutra)

READING QUESTIONS

1. What is the "**Middle Way**" between eternalism and annihilationism, and how does it answer the question about what causes suffering?
2. What does impermanence mean?
3. What, according to Vajira, is the meaning of no-self?

SUFFERING

Thus have I heard. Once, when the Blessed One was dwelling in Rājagaha, . . . he got dressed early in the morning, took his bowl and his robe, and went into town

From *Experience of Buddhism*, 1st ed., by J. S. Strong, pp. 90, 94–95, 100–101. Copyright © 1995 Wadsworth Publishing. Reprinted by permission of Wadsworth Publishing, a division of International Thomson Publishing. Fax 800-730-2215.

for alms. Kassapa, the naked ascetic, saw his coming from a distance. He approached him, they exchanged greetings, and Kassapa, standing to one side, said: "If it is all right, good Gotama, I would like to ask you to explain something."

"Kassapa," the Buddha replied, "this is not a good time for questions; I am visiting houses. . . ."

But Kassapa repeated his request, and added: "I do not have many things to ask, good Gotama."

"Then go ahead and ask if you wish to, Kassapa."

"Good Gotama," Kassapa began, "is the suffering that one suffers caused by oneself?"

"No, it is not, Kassapa," replied the Blessed One.

"Then is the suffering that one suffers caused by someone else?"

"No, it is not Kassapa."

"Well, then, is it caused both by oneself and by someone else?"

"No, it is not, Kassapa."

"Well, then, . . . does it arise spontaneously?"

"No, it does not."

"Then suffering is nonexistent, good Gotama."

"No, Kassapa, it is not nonexistent; there *is* suffering."

"But you do not know it, nor do you see it?"

"Not so, Kassapa, I both know it and see it."

"Good Gotama, to all these questions that I have asked you . . . you have answered no. So please tell me, please teach me about suffering."

"Kassapa, if you say, 'The same individual who does a deed experiences its results'—what you called 'suffering caused by oneself'—then you fall into the view of eternalism. But if you say, 'One individual does a deed and another experiences its results'—what a sufferer would call 'suffering caused by another'—then you fall into the view of annihilationism. Kassapa, avoiding these two extremes, the Tathāgata teaches the Dharma in the manner of a Middle Way:

"Conditioned by ignorance are karmic constituents; conditioned by karmic constituents is consciousness; conditioned by consciousness is individuality (name and form); conditioned by individuality are the six senses; conditioned by the six senses is contact; conditioned by contact is feeling; conditioned by feeling is desire; conditioned by desire is clinging; conditioned by clinging is becoming; conditioned by becoming is rebirth; conditioned by rebirth are old age, death, sorrow, lamentation, suffering, depression, and dismay. In this way, this whole great heap of suffering originates.

"But from the complete cessation and dissipation of ignorance comes the cessation of karmic constituents; and from the complete cessation and dissipation of karmic constituents comes the cessation of consciousness;

and from the complete cessation and dissipation of consciousness comes the cessation of individuality; and from the complete cessation of individuality . . . [and so forth until]: from the complete cessation and dissipation of rebirth comes the cessation of old age, death, sorrow, lamentation, suffering, depression, and dismay. In this way, this whole great heap of suffering ceases."

IMPERMANENCE

Thus have I heard: Once the Blessed One was dwelling in Śrāvastī at the Jetavana monastery together with a great company of monks. And he said: "O monks, all karmically constituted things are impermanent; they are not fixed, not comforting, and are characterized by constant change. . . . For all beings, all creatures, all living things, life is limited by death; for them there is no termination of death and rebirth.

"And, monks, those who are householders from prominent families, brahmins, nobles, rich people . . .—their lives too are limited by death; for them there is no termination of death and rebirth.

"And, monks, nobles who have been annointed king, who have attained power and sovereignty over the people, and who have conquered the whole earth—their lives too are limited by death; for them there is no termination of death and rebirth.

"And, monks, brahmanical ascetics who dwell in the forest, who grasp for the fruit of liberation, who enjoy the fruit of liberation, who live by the fruit of liberation —their lives too are limited by death; for them there is no termination of death and rebirth.

"And, monks, those gods of the realm of desire, the four great guardian kings, the gods of the Trāyastriṃśa, Yama, Tuṣita, and other heavens—their lives too are limited by death; for them there is no termination of death and rebirth.

"And, monks, those gods of the realm of form— those who have attained the first, the second, the third, or the fourth trance levels—their lives too are limited by death; for them there is no termination of death and rebirth.

"And, monks, those gods of the formless realm, those who dwell in the contemplation of endless space, those who dwell in the contemplation of endless consciousness, those who dwell in the contemplation of nothingness, and those who dwell in the contemplation of neither perception nor nonperception—their lives too are limited by death; for them there is no termination of death and rebirth. Thus it is for the Triple World. . . .

NO-SELF

One morning, the nun Vajirā got dressed in her robes, and, taking her bowl, she entered the city of Sāvatthi for alms and went about the town on her begging round. On her way back, after her noonday meal, she entered into the Andhavana woods and seated herself at the foot of a tree to take her midday rest.

Then Māra, the Evil One, wishing to engender fear, shock, and dread in the nun Vajirā and hoping to disturb her meditation, approached her and spoke these verses:

Vajirā, who created this Being?
Where is Being's maker?
Where did Being come from?
Where will it disappear to?

But the nun Vajirā replied:

Māra, why do you keep coming back to Being?
You are resorting to false views.
There is no Being to be found here—
only a heap of karmic constituents.
Just as the word *chariot* is used,
when we come across a combination of parts,
so we speak conventionally of a Being
when the five skandhas are present.
But, truly, it is only suffering that arises,
suffering that persists and passes away,
nothing other than suffering that arises,
nothing else than suffering that ceases to be.

7.3.3 The Path to Enlightenment

The **Eightfold Path** or Way (the Fourth Noble Truth) is often divided into three parts: wisdom, moral conduct, and mental discipline or meditation. The Buddhist, seeking the middle way between extremes, must develop a right understanding of the **Four Noble Truths** and realize the truth of the three marks of existence. Right understanding or wisdom, however, cannot be developed in isolation from moral conduct and the practice of meditation.

The two selections that follow deal with moral conduct in relation to the life of a monk and the practice of meditation. Buddhist texts have much to say about meditation—how to do it, what to meditate on, what trance states to expect. They also contain practical advice for beginners, who inevitably will face difficulties. The second selection (from the *Saundarananda of Ashvaghosha*) recounts advice the Buddha reputedly gave to his half-brother, Nanda. Nanda was happily married and reluctant to join the *sangha* and leave his family. When he does leave, the Buddha instructs him in his meditation practice in order to help him concentrate on his new life on the path to *nirvana*.

⚜

Moral Conduct and Meditation

READING QUESTIONS

1. How do you respond to these moral ideals? In your view, what is positive about them and what is negative?
2. How do you think disciplining the mind by meditation practice helps one attain liberation?

MORAL CONDUCT

"Life in a household is confining and polluting; the monastic life is like open air. Living in a home, it is not easy to lead an utterly fulfilling, pure, chaste, and studious life, polished like mother of pearl. Why don't I, therefore, cut off my hair and beard, put on a yellow robe, leave home, and adopt the homeless life?"

Thus thinking, a householder or his son . . . abandons his accumulated wealth, whether great or small, and leaves behind the circle of his relations, whether many or few. And once he has wandered forth, he lives . . . endowed with good conduct, careful of the slightest transgressions, undertaking to observe the precepts, doing meritorious deeds of body, speech, and mind and leading a pure life, perfect in morality. . . .

In what ways . . . is a monk perfect in morality? Forsaking the taking of life, he abstains from killing. Having laid down his stick and his sword, he lives in modesty, showing kindness, compassion, and concern for the welfare of all living beings. Such is his moral conduct.

Forsaking the taking of what is not given, he abstains from theft. He lives, openly accepting and ex-

From *Experience of Buddhism*, 1st ed., by J. S. Strong, pp. 113–114, 122–123. Copyright © 1995 Wadsworth Publishing. Reprinted by permission of Wadsworth Publishing, a division of International Thomson Publishing. Fax 800-730-2215.

pecting gifts, keeping himself pure. Such is his moral conduct.

Forsaking unchastity, he leads a chaste life, aloof, abstaining from the vulgar practice of sex. Such is his moral conduct.

Forsaking uttering falsehoods, he abstains from lying. He . . . speaks the truth and is reliable, open, and trustworthy, not deceiving the world. Such is his moral conduct.

Forsaking malicious speech, he abstains from slander. What he hears here he does not repeat there so as to create factions; and what he hears there he does not repeat here for the same reason. In this way, he reconciles those who are at odds, he encourages those who are united, and he rejoices, delights, and takes pleasure in concord and promotes it when he speaks. Such is his moral conduct.

Forsaking harsh speech, he abstains from rudeness. Instead, he speaks words that are blameless, pleasing to the ear, kind, heart-warming, polite, delightful, and charming to many people. Such is his moral conduct.

Forsaking frivolous talk, he abstains from trivial conversations. His speech is timely, factual, and to the point, dealing with Dharma and the Vinaya. At the right time, he speaks words that are worth treasuring, that are reasonable, well defined, and purposeful. Such is his moral conduct.

He refrains from harvesting seeds or plants. He takes one meal a day and refrains from eating after noon or at night. He avoids watching shows that involve dancing, singing, and music. He abstains from bodily ornaments or jewelry and from wearing garlands, perfumes, or cosmetics. He does not use high or large beds. He refuses to accept gold or silver. . . .

MEDITATION

. . . Sit down cross-legged in some solitary place, hold your back straight, and direct your mindfulness in front of you, to the tip of your nose, your forehead, or the space between your eyebrows. Make your wandering mind focus entirely on one thing. Now if that mental affliction—a lustful imagination—should rear its head, do not abide it but brush it off as though it were dust on your clothes. For even if you have consciously rid yourself of desires, . . . there remains an innate proclivity toward them, like a fire hidden in the ashes. This, my friend, must be extinguished by meditation, like a fire put out by water. Otherwise, from that innate proclivity, desires will grow back again, as plants do from a seed. Only by its destruction will they cease to be, as plants whose roots are destroyed. . . .

Now if malice or thoughts of violence should unsettle your mind, you should use their antidotes to make it calm, the way a jewel settles muddied water. Know that their antidotes are love and compassion, for the opposition between them is eternal, like that between light and darkness. Those who have controlled wickedness but still harbor malicious thoughts throw dirt onto themselves, the way an elephant does after a bath. What noble, compassionate person could wish to impose further suffering on mortals who are already afflicted by sickness, death, old age, and so forth? . . . Therefore, abandon what is demeritorious, and meditate on what is meritorious, for that will cause you to attain your goals in this world, as well as the ultimate goal. . . .

Now if your thoughts should turn to the prosperity or lack thereof of your own family members, you should examine the inherent nature of the world of living beings in order to suppress them. Among beings who are being dragged along through saṃsāra by the force of karma, who is a stranger, who is a relative? It is due to delusion that one person seems attached to another. Your relative in a past life has become a stranger, and in a future life a stranger may become a relative. Just as birds assemble here and there in the evening to roost, so it is with the closeness of relatives and strangers from one birth to the next. . . . He who was your beloved relative in another existence—what is he to you now, or you to him? Therefore, you should not let your mind dwell on thoughts of your family; in saṃsāra there is no steady distinction between relatives and nonrelatives. . . .

Now if thoughts should arise in your mind that this country or that country is peaceful or fortunate or that alms are easy to get there, discard them, my friend, and do not dwell on them in any way whatsoever. For you know that the whole world everywhere is plagued by one problem or another. . . . Whether by cold, heat, disease, or danger, people are always being oppressed; nowhere in this world is there a refuge. There is no country where fear does not exist, where the people are not in terror of old age, sickness, and death. . . .

Now if you should have any thoughts that assume that there is no death, make efforts to ward them off, as though they were an illness you had come down with. Not even for a moment should you trust in the continuity of life. Like a tiger lying in wait, death can strike down the unsuspecting at any time. Do not think "I am strong, I am young." Death does not consider age but kills in all circumstances. Realizing the world to be in-substantial and ephemeral like a bubble, what sane person could ever fail to take death into consideration?

In summation then, my friend, in order to avoid having all of these thoughts, you should become a master of mindfulness. . . . In order to obtain gold, one must wash away the dirt—first the big clods and then, to cleanse it further, the smaller ones, until finally one retains pure particles of gold. Just so, in order to obtain liberation, one must discipline the mind and wash away from it first the big clods of one's faults and then, to purify it further, the smaller ones until finally one retains pure particles of Dharma.

7.3.4 The Goal

Nirvana (*nibbana* in Pali), or release from suffering, is the Buddhist equivalent of salvation. Buddhism usually distinguishes between two kinds of *nirvana*: *nirvana* with remaining *karma* and *nirvana* without remaining *karma* (*parinirvana*). The first is possible in this physical world and is what the Buddha experienced at enlightenment. The second is possible after death. To enter *parinirvana* is never to return again to this physical world of sorrow and rebirth (*samsara*).

What exactly is *nirvana?* Although it is, according to Buddhists, a bliss ultimately beyond the ability of human language to describe, much is said about it. The selections that follow deal with some aspects of it. The first selection, from the *Udana*, recounts what the Buddha presumably said about *nirvana* to his monks and discusses the sense in which *nirvana* is the end of suffering. The second selection, from the *Therigatha* (*Songs of Nuns*), was written by Patacara after she became an **arbati** (a female **arhat** or saint who has attained *nirvana* with remaining *karma*).

Patacara lived a tragic life. Her entire family is killed one by one, and she was almost driven mad with suffering. While in a state of despair, she meets the Buddha, who counsels her and allows her to become a nun. After years of meditative practice, she severs all attachments to worldly things.

The third selection, also from the *Therigatha*, was written by the mother of a monk who became an *arhat*. She left her unhappy home and became a nun. When she becomes an *arhati*, she celebrates her freedom.

Nirvana, The Cessation of Suffering (by Patacara), and The Joy of Release

READING QUESTIONS

1. What terms would you use to describe *nirvana*?
2. Would you like to experience *nirvana*? Why or why not?
3. What notion of freedom is found in these selections?

NIRVANA

Monks, there exists something in which there is neither earth nor water, fire nor air. It is not the sphere of infinite space, nor the sphere of infinite consciousness, nor the sphere of nothingness, nor the sphere of neither perception nor non-perception. It is neither this world nor another world, nor both, neither sun nor moon.

Monks, I do not state that it comes nor that it goes. It neither abides nor passes away. It is not caused, established, arisen, supported. It is the end of suffering. . . .

What I call the selfless is difficult to perceive, for it is not easy to perceive the truth. But one who knows it cuts through craving, and for one who knows it, there is nothing to hold onto. . . .

Monks, there exists something that is unborn, unmade, uncreated, unconditioned. Monks, if there were not an unborn, unmade, uncreated, unconditioned, then there would be no way to indicate how to escape from the born, made, created, and conditioned. However, monks, since there exists something that is unborn, unmade, uncreated, and unconditioned, it is known that there is an escape from that which is born, made, created, and conditioned. . . .

There is wandering for those who are attached, but there is no wandering for those who are unattached. There is serenity when there is no wandering, and when there is serenity, there is no desire. When there is no desire, there is neither coming nor going, and when there

is no coming nor going there is neither death nor rebirth. When there is neither death nor rebirth, there is neither this life nor the next life, nor anything in between. It is the end of suffering.

[*Udana*, ch. 8.1–4]

THE CESSATION OF SUFFERING

Ploughing their fields, sowing seeds in the ground,
Men care for their wives and children and prosper.
Why is it that I, endowed with morality and adhering to the teachings,
Do not attain nirvana? I am neither lazy nor conceited.
After washing my feet, I observed the water; watching the water flow downwards,
I focused my mind as one [trains] a noble thoroughbred horse.
Then I took a lamp and entered my cell. After observing the bed, I sat on the couch.
Holding a pin, I pulled out the wick.
The lamp goes out: nirvana. My mind is free!

[*Therigatha*, psalm 47]

THE JOY OF RELEASE

Free, I am free!
I am completely free from my kitchen pestle!
[I am free from] my worthless husband and even his sun umbrella!
And my pot that smells like a water snake!
I have eliminated all desire and hatred,
Going to the base of a tree, [I think,] "What happiness!"
And contemplate this happiness.

[*Therigatha*, psalm 22]

From *Scriptures of the World's Religions*, by James Fieser and John Powers (Boston: McGraw-Hill, 1998), pp. 86–87, 94–95. Translation by John Powers from the 1948 edition of *Udana*, edited by Paul Steinthal (London: Geoffrey Cumberlege), pp. 80–81, and the 1883 edition of *Therigatha*, edited by Hermann Oldenberg and Richard Pischel (London: Pali Text Society), pp. 134–135. Reprinted by permission of John Powers.

7.4 MAHAYANA BUDDHISM

Mahayana (Great Vehicle) Buddhism probably emerged in India five hundred years after the Buddha's death, although its proponents claim that its teachings go back to the Buddha himself. Mahayana lived side by side with Nikaya Buddhism for several centuries, but by the third or fourth century C.E. there were ordination lineages that distinguished themselves from earlier forms of Buddhism. As the Theravada sect of Nikaya moved south, Mahayana moved east and north, eventually becoming the dominant form of Buddhism in China, Vietnam, Korea, and Japan. However, elements of both can be found in southern as well as northern Asia.

Exactly what factors led to Mahayana formation we do not know. Possibly one or more of the eighteen sects of early Buddhism developed the ideas and practices that eventually became characteristic of Mahayana. Perhaps it arose out of a new movement in southern India and spread across several early Buddhist sects. One thing is clear, however: Mahayanists wanted to give a greater role to lay disciples. In early Buddhism, the monks were the full-time religious professionals and the laity gave them material support (food, clothing, land, buildings, and the like) in exchange for merit. However, if a layperson wanted to make serious spiritual progress toward enlightenment in this lifetime, he or she would have to "depart of the world" and become a monk or nun. Mahayanists, in contrast, gave the laity a greater religious role and held it was possible to make serious spiritual progress, even gain enlightenment, without becoming a monk or nun.

The greater role afforded the laity by Mahayanists slowly changed the *sangha* and Buddhism itself. For one thing, it increased the religious importance of the laity. It also led to greater emphasis on the Buddha's compassion and his role as a savior figure who could dispense grace to those whose faith and worship is sincere. Pilgrimages to stupas enshrining holy relics had been a part of early Buddhism, but now became more popular and widespread. Merit that could change one's karmic future could be made by participating in such pilgrimages and even transferred to others (such as dead relatives). Veneration of *bodhisattvas* who now, unlike the *arhat* ideal of Theravada, dedicated themselves primarily to the salvation of all living beings also became increasingly popular. And, as we shall shortly see, distinctive teachings arose claiming to convey a perfect wisdom.

7.4.1 Parable of the Lost Son

Do you think it is sometimes necessary to trick people for their own good? Does a good teacher tailor her or his message for the level the students can understand? Perhaps religious teachers say things that appear contradictory because they are tailoring their message for the abilities of their audience. Maybe they employ "skillful means" (**upaya**) in their words and deeds in order to bring people of different capacities to the truth.

The *Saddharma-Pundarika* (*The Lotus of the True Law*), better known as the *Lotus Sutra*, is a Mahayana text that treats many Buddhist teachings (particularly the Nikaya teachings) as provisionally expedient. They are steps toward the true teaching, the true law revealed in the *Lotus Sutra*. The situation is like a father who cannot get his children to come out of a burning house. Finally, he promises them toys if they will come out. It is a deceptive lure, but it leads to an expedient rescue. Is the father justified in deceiving his children? Is his lie a noble one? Is all well that ends well?

This story is a brief summary of the famous "Parable of the Burning House" found in the *Lotus Sutra*. However, it is not the only parable dealing with the issue of *upaya*, or skillful means. There is also the "Parable of the Lost Son." Although this story reminds many readers of the "Parable of the Prodigal Son" found in the Christian New Testament, there are important differences. For one thing, Mahayana Buddhism uses the story of the "Lost Son" along with the story of the "Burning House" to emphasize that teachings are like rafts. The purpose of the raft is to get you from one shore to another. Once you are successfully on the other side, do you need the raft anymore? So the Buddha's teachings are like rafts or vehicles intended to get you to enlightenment. Their value is in where they take you. They are not ends in themselves.

✥

The Lost Son

READING QUESTIONS

1. Why does the poor son run away when he sees the rich man?
2. How does the rich father get his poor son to come back and work for him?
3. What did the poor son think when his father revealed his identity and gave him his inheritance?
4. State what you take to be the point of the parable.
5. Read the "Parable of the Prodigal Son" in the New Testament (Luke 15:11–32), and compare the Bud-

---

From *Saddharma-Pundarika, or The Lotus of the True Law*, translated by Hendrik Kern. Volume XXI of *The Sacred Books of the East*, edited by F. Max Mueller (Oxford, England: Clarendon Press, 1884), pp. 99–108.

dhist story of the Lost Son with the story of the Prodigal Son. How are they alike and how are they different?

It is a case, O Lord, as if a certain man went away from his father and betook himself to some other place. He lives there in foreign parts for many years, twenty or thirty or forty or fifty. In course of time the one (the father) becomes a great man; the other (the son) is poor; in seeking a livelihood for the sake of food and clothing he roams in all directions and goes to some place, whereas his father removes to another country. . . .

In course of time, Lord, that poor man, in quest of food and clothing, roaming through villages, towns, boroughs, provinces, kingdoms, and royal capitals, reaches the place where his father, the owner of much wealth and gold, treasures and granaries, is residing. Now the poor man's father, Lord, the owner of much wealth and gold, treasures and granaries, who was residing in that town, had always and ever been thinking of the son he had lost fifty years ago, but he gave no utterance to his thoughts before others, and was only pining in himself and thinking: I am old, aged, advanced in years, and possess abundance of bullion, gold, money and corn, treasures and granaries, but have no son. It is to be feared lest death shall overtake me and all this perish unused. Repeatedly he was thinking of that son: O how happy should I be, were my son to enjoy this mass of wealth!

Meanwhile, Lord, the poor man in search of food and clothing was gradually approaching the house of the rich man, the owner of abundant bullion, gold, money and corn, treasures and granaries. And the father of the poor man happened to sit at the door of his house, surrounded and waited upon by a great crowd of Brâhmans, Kshatriyas, Vaiśyas, and Sûdras; he was sitting on a magnificent throne with a footstool decorated with gold and silver, while dealing with hundred thousands of koṭis of gold-pieces, and fanned with a chowrie, on a spot under an extended awning inlaid with pearls and flowers and adorned with hanging garlands of jewels; sitting (in short) in great pomp. The poor man, Lord, saw his own father in such pomp sitting at the door of the house, surrounded with a great crowd of people and doing a householder's business. The poor man frightened, terrified, alarmed, seized with a feeling of horripilation all over the body, and agitated in mind, reflects thus: Unexpectedly have I here fallen in with a king or grandee. People like me have nothing to do here; let me go; in the street of the poor I am likely to find food and clothing without much difficulty. Let me no longer tarry at this place, lest I be taken to do forced labour or incur some other injury.

Thereupon, Lord, the poor man quickly departs, runs off, does not tarry from fear of a series of supposed dangers. But the rich man, sitting on the throne at the door of his mansion, has recognised his son at first sight, in consequence whereof he is content, in high spirits, charmed, delighted, filled with joy and cheerfulness. He thinks: Wonderful! he who is to enjoy this plenty of bullion, gold, money and corn, treasures and granaries, has been found! He of whom I have been thinking again and again, is here now that I am old, aged, advanced in years.

At the same time, moment, and instant, Lord, he despatches couriers, to whom he says: Go, sirs, and quickly fetch me that man. The fellows thereon all run forth in full speed and overtake the poor man, who, frightened, terrified, alarmed, seized with a feeling of horripilation all over his body, agitated in mind, utters a lamentable cry of distress, screams, and exclaims: I have given you no offence. But the fellows drag the poor man, however lamenting, violently with them. He, frightened, terrified, alarmed, seized with a feeling of horripilation all over his body, and agitated in mind, thinks by himself: I fear lest I shall be punished with capital punishment; I am lost. He faints away, and falls on the earth. His father dismayed and near despondency says to those fellows: Do not carry the man in that manner. With these words he sprinkles him with cold water without addressing him any further. For that householder knows the poor man's humble disposition and his own elevated position; yet he feels that the man is his son.

The householder, Lord, skilfully conceals from every one that it is his son. He calls one of his servants and says to him: Go, sirrah, and tell that poor man: Go, sirrah, whither thou likest; thou art free. The servant obeys, approaches the poor man and tells him: Go, sirrah, whither thou likest; thou art free. The poor man is astonished and amazed at hearing these words; he leaves that spot and wanders to the street of the poor in search of food and clothing. In order to attract him the householder practises an able device. He employs for it two men ill-favoured and of little splendour. Go, says he, go to the man you saw in this place; hire him in your own name for a double daily fee, and order him to do work here in my house. And if he asks: What work shall I have to do? tell him: Help us in clearing the heap of dirt. The two fellows go and seek the poor man and engage him for such work as mentioned. . . .

Then the householder descends from his mansion, lays off his wreath and ornaments, parts with his soft, clean, and gorgeous attire, puts on dirty raiment, takes a basket in his right hand, smears his body with dust, and goes to his son, whom he greets from afar, and thus addresses: Please, take the baskets and without delay remove the dust. By this device he manages to speak to his son, to have a talk with him and say: Do, sirrah, remain here in my service; do not go again to another place; I will give thee extra pay, and whatever thou wantest thou mayst confidently ask me, be it the price of a pot, a smaller pot, a boiler or wood, or be it the price of salt, food, or clothing. . . . Be at ease, fellow; look upon me as if I were thy father, for I am older and thou art younger, and thou hast rendered me much service by clearing this heap of dirt, and as long as thou hast been in my service thou hast never shown nor art showing wickedness, crookedness, arrogance, or hypocrisy; I have discovered in thee no vice at all of such as are commonly seen in other man-servants. From henceforward thou art to me like my own son. . . .

After a while, Lord, the householder falls sick, and feels that the time of his death is near at hand. He says to the poor man: Come hither, man, I possess abundant bullion, gold, money and corn, treasures and granaries. I am very sick, and wish to have one upon whom to bestow (my wealth); by whom it is to be received, and with whom it is to be deposited. Accept it. For in the same manner as I am the owner of it, so art thou, but thou shalt not suffer anything of it to be wasted. . . .

After a while, Lord, the householder perceives that his son is able to save, mature and mentally developed; that in the consciousness of his nobility he feels abashed, ashamed, disgusted, when thinking of his former poverty. The time of his death approaching, he sends for the poor man, presents him to a gathering of his relations, and before the king or king's peer and in the presence of citizens and country-people makes the following speech: Hear, gentlemen! this is my own son, by me begotten. It is now fifty years that he disappeared from such and such a town. He is called so and so, and myself am called so and so. In searching after him I have from that town come hither. He is my son, I am his father. To him I leave all my revenues, and all my personal (or private) wealth shall he acknowledge (his own).

The poor man, Lord, hearing this speech was astonished and amazed; he thought by himself: Unexpectedly have I obtained this bullion, gold, money and corn, treasures and granaries.

Even so, O Lord, do we represent the sons of the Tathâgata, and the Tathâgata says to us: Ye are my sons, as the householder did. We were oppressed, O Lord, with three difficulties, viz. the difficulty of pain, the difficulty of conceptions, the difficulty of transition (or evolution); and in the worldly whirl we were disposed to what is low. Then have we been prompted by the Lord to ponder on the numerous inferior laws (or conditions, things) that are similar to a heap of dirt. Once directed to them we have been practising, making efforts, and seek-

ing for nothing but Nirvâna as our fee. We were content, O Lord, with the Nirvâna obtained, and thought to have gained much at the hands of the Tathâgata because of our having applied ourselves to these laws, practised, and made efforts. But the Lord takes no notice of us, does not mix with us, nor tell us that this treasure of the Tathâgata's knowledge shall belong to us, though the Lord skilfully appoints us as heirs to this treasure of the knowledge of the Tathâgata. And we, O Lord, are not (impatiently) longing to enjoy it, because we deem it a great gain already to receive from the Lord Nirvâna as our fee. We preach to the Bodhisattvas Mahâsattvas a sublime sermon about the knowledge of the Tathâgata; we explain, show, demonstrate the knowledge of the Tathâgata, O Lord, without longing. For the Tathâgata by his skilfulness knows our disposition, whereas we ourselves do not know, nor apprehend. It is for this very reason that the Lord just now tells us that we are to him as sons, and that he reminds us of being heirs to the Tathâgata. For the case stands thus: we are as sons to the Tathâgata, but low (or humble) of disposition; the Lord perceives the strength of our disposition and applies to us the denomination of Bodhisattvas; we are, however, charged with a double office in so far as in presence of Bodhisattvas we are called persons of low disposition and at the same time have to rouse them to Buddha-enlightenment. Knowing the strength of our disposition the Lord has thus spoken, and in this way, O Lord, do we say that we have obtained unexpectedly and without longing the jewel of omniscience, which we did not desire, nor seek, nor search after, nor expect, nor require; and that inasmuch as we are the sons of the Tathâgata. . . .

7.4.2 Perfection of Wisdom

A voluminous literature starts to appear around the beginning of the common era known as *Prajnaparamita*, usually translated as the "perfection of wisdom," but literally it means the "wisdom gone beyond." To enter the world created by this literature is something like accompanying Alice in her trip to wonderland in that it carries you beyond ordinary ways of thinking and speaking.

One of the best-known *Prajnaparamita* texts is the *Heart Sutra*. It is recited by monks and laity throughout East Asia, Tibet, and, most recently, Europe and the United States. The **sutra** is put in the mouth of **Avalokiteshvara,** one of the most important *bodhisattvas* of the Mahayana tradition. He instructs Sariputra, a disciple of the Buddha. There is a polemical intent in the text. Sariputra represents Nikaya Buddhism. Hence his instruction by a Mahayana *bodhisattva* in a wisdom that "goes beyond" clearly proclaims the superiority of Mahayana teachings.

At the heart of the text is the concept of emptiness. The **Abhidharma** (advanced doctrine) section of the Theravada scripture discusses the self-existence (*svabhava*), or essence, of *dharmas*. The *dharmas* here name elements of existence, and Avalokiteshvara, in the *Heart Sutra*, proclaims all such *dharmas* to be "empty of any inherent self-existence." This is a logical extension of the doctrines of impermanence and No-Self (see 7.3.2). However, calling the *dharmas* empty does not mean that they do not exist. It just means that their nature is not what the Abhidharmists said it was, namely, self-existence (*svabhava*). In other words, things have no abiding essence or substantial self-identity.

The *Heart Sutra* ends with a **mantra,** or formula, that not only sums up the *sutra* but also presumably is effective in saving people from suffering through its sincere repetition. As you say it, it carries you to a wisdom beyond conventional thought and into a wonderland of new insight into the insubstantial fluidity of reality providing you with an opportunity to awaken beyond this present dream. I recommend that you read this short *sutra* aloud and, at first, with enough speed to allow your mind to be disoriented by the negations that tumble over one another undermining any stable place to stand.

❧

Heart Sutra

READING QUESTIONS

1. How did reading this sutra make you feel, and what did it make you think?
2. Why is the *mantra* of the perfection of wisdom the *mantra* of great knowledge?

From *Scriptures of the World's Religions*, by James Fieser and John Powers (Boston: McGraw-Hill, 1998), pp. 98 101. Translation by John Powers from the 1960 edition of *Samyutta*, edited by Leon Feer (London: Pali Text Society), pp. 134–135. Reprinted by permission of John Powers.

Thus have I heard: At one time the Exalted One was dwelling on the Vulture Peak in Rajagriha together with a great assembly of monks and a great assembly of bodhisattvas. At that time, the Exalted One was immersed in a meditative absorption (*samadhi*) on the enumerations of phenomena called "perception of the profound." Also at that time, the bodhisattva, the great being, the superior Avalokiteshvara was considering the meaning of the profound perfection of wisdom, and he saw that the five aggregates (*skandha*) are empty of inherent existence. Then, due to the inspiration of the Buddha, the venerable Shariputra spoke thus to the bodhisattva, the great being, the superior Avalokiteshvara: "How should a son of good lineage train if he wants to practice the profound perfection of wisdom?"

The bodhisattva, the great being, the superior Avalokiteshvara spoke thus to the venerable Shariputra: "Shariputra, sons of good lineage or daughters of good lineage who want to practice the profound perfection of wisdom should perceive [reality] in this way: They should correctly perceive the five aggregates also as empty of inherent existence. Form is emptiness; emptiness is form. Emptiness is not other than form; form is not other than emptiness. In the same way, feelings, discriminations, compositional factors, and consciousness are empty. Shariputra, in that way, all phenomena are empty, without characteristics, unproduced, unceasing, undefiled, not undefiled, not decreasing, not increasing. Therefore, Shariputra, in emptiness there is no form, no feelings, no discriminations, no compositional factors, no consciousness, no eye, no ear, no nose, no tongue, no body, no mind, no form, no sound, no odor, no taste, no object of touch, no phenomenon. There is no eye constituent, no mental constituent, up to and including no mental consciousness constituent. There is no ignorance, no existence of ignorance, up to and including no aging and death and no extinction of aging and death. In the same way, there is no suffering, no source [of suffering], no cessation [of suffering], no path, no exalted wisdom, no attainment, and also no non-attainment.

"Therefore, Shariputra, because bodhisattvas have no attainment, they depend on and abide in the perfection of wisdom. Because their minds are unobstructed, they are without fear. Having completely passed beyond all error, they go to the fulfillment of nirvana. All the buddhas who live in the three times [past, present, and future] have been completely awakened into unsurpassable, complete, perfect awakening through relying on the perfection of wisdom.

"Therefore, the *mantra* of the perfection of wisdom is the *mantra* of great knowledge, the unsurpassable *mantra*, the *mantra* that is equal to the unequaled, the *mantra* that thoroughly pacifies all suffering. Because it is not false, it should be known to be true. The *mantra* of the perfection wisdom is as follows:

> *Om gate gate paragate parasamgate bodhir svaha* [*Om* gone, gone, gone beyond, gone completely beyond; praise to awakening.]

"Shariputra, bodhisattvas, great beings, should train in the profound perfection of wisdom in that way."

Then the Exalted One arose from that meditative absorption and said to the bodhisattva, the great being, the superior Avalokiteshvara: "Well done! Well done, well done, son of good lineage, it is just so. Son of good lineage, it is like that; the profound perfection of wisdom should be practiced just as you have indicated. Even the Tathagatas admire this." When the Exalted One had spoken thus, the venerable Shariputra, the bodhisattva, the great being, the superior Avalokiteshvara, and all those around them, and those of the world, the gods, humans, demigods, and *gandharvas* were filled with admiration and praised the words of the Exalted One.

7.4.3 Mahayana Philosophy

Most adherents of religious traditions probably know little about the theological and philosophical controversies that develop within their traditions. For most people, religion consists of devotional practices like prayer and worship, pilgrimages to sacred sites, participation in charitable activities, and listening to the stories told and teachings given by their priests, pastors, gurus, or other religious leaders.

However, any full appreciation of a religious tradition requires some familiarity with its theological and philosophical literature. Therefore, the student of religion cannot ignore the intellectual developments of religious traditions even though such developments are often difficult to comprehend and may appear far removed from the life of devotion that concerns most adherents.

Below we will sample the thoughts of two influential Buddhist philosophers: Nagarjuna (first or second century C.E.?), founder of the Madhyamika school of Mahayana Buddhism, and Vasubandhu (320–400), a representative of the Yogacara philosophical school of Mahayana Buddhism.

Nagarjuna detects an apparent inconsistency in the early philosophical interpretations of Nikaya Buddhism. According to Nikaya, the Buddha taught both the no-self (*anatman*) and *dharma* doctrines.

Dharma here refers to the notion that things are made up of basic indivisible elements or essences (*svabhava*). Some Hindu scholars taught that with respect to human beings the self (*atman*) is the essence. Nikaya Buddhism denied that *atman* is the essence (*anatman*), yet affirmed that there are essences. Nagarjuna argues that consistency requires the extension of the *anatman* doctrine to all things (*dharmas*).

This philosophical expansion of the no-self doctrine is equivalent, Nagarjuna believes, to applying the concept of emptiness or **shunyata** of the Perfection of Wisdom literature to all *dharmas* (see Reading 7.4.2, especially that section of the *Heart Sutra* which reads, "Form is emptiness; emptiness is form"). Things are empty of essences. *Shunyata* is, for Nagarjuna, simply the logical development of the Buddha's teaching about co-dependent origination. If things (*dharmas*) have an inherent nature (*svabhava*) that makes them separate and independent, then true interdependency is impossible. If change truly characterizes the nature of *all* existence, and everything is interdependent, then reality must be empty of those things that make for independence and separateness.

Is the claim that things are empty of essences the same as claiming that there are no essences? The answer, according to Nagarjuna, is no. Nagarjuna develops the tetralemma (1. X is; 2. X is not; 3. X is both X and not X; 4. X is neither X nor not X) in order to make his teaching about emptiness clear. The tetralemma confounds those who would make Nagarjuna's doctrine of emptiness into a metaphysical category that is equivalent to claiming there are no essences. Nagarjuna makes no claims at all. According to the tetralemma, Nagarjuna does not assert that (1) essences exist, and he does not assert that (2) essences do not exist. Further, he does not assert that (3) essences both exist and do not exist. However, do not be fooled. Even the fourth logical possibility, (4) essences neither exist nor do they not exist, is not asserted by Nagarjuna.

The tetralemma pulls the logical rug out from under our feet. Nagarjuna refuses to assert anything at all about essences. If Nagarjuna did assert anything about essences, his very assertion would be empty because it would be a form and "form is emptiness; emptiness is form" according to the "wisdom that goes beyond."

In our first selection, Nagarjuna applies the tetralemma to *nirvana* thereby confounding those who would make *nirvana* a kind of heaven or place where the faithful go after death. Emptiness, as used by Nagarjuna, means that all of our basic concepts such as self, essence, and nirvana cannot convey the true nature of reality. According to Nagarjuna, when it comes to dealing with the true nature of reality all human concepts are inadequate. This is one of the most profound and least understood philosophical implications of what the Buddha taught.

Nagarjuna's ideas about emptiness may strike you as a negative philosophical viewpoint. What are we to make of a philosophy that does not tell us about the nature of reality (shouldn't philosophies do that sort of thing?) but, rather, tells us that we cannot conceptually grasp the nature of reality? Some Mahayana philosophers thought more can be said than Nagarjuna allows. Vasubandhu, author of our second selection, is one of those philosophers.

Vasubandhu represents a Yogacara philosophical approach to the issue of reality. This philosophical school is often called "Mind-Only" or "Consciousness-Only" because of what appear to be its idealistic tendencies. Vasubandhu seeks to deny the conventional dualistic distinction between subject (my consciousness or awareness) and object (some object of my consciousness) that pervades so much of our ordinary thinking. Just as Nagarjuna and the Madhyamika school developed the idea of emptiness (*shunyata*) to counter the idea of essences (*svabhava*), so Vasubandhu develops the idea of consciousness-only to counter subject/object dualism.

According to Vasubandhu, the problem of the nature of things (*dharmas*) is really a problem about consciousness or awareness. There are eight different types of consciousness. The first five types result from the activities of the five senses: seeing, hearing, smelling, tasting, and touching. The "sixth sense" is associated with the brain and involves thinking. These six types were recognized and analyzed by Nikaya thinkers, but they missed two more types. The seventh is the mind (*manas*) which, through reflection, falsely attributes individuality to ourselves and other things. The eighth Vasubandhu calls the "granary consciousness" or "storehouse consciousness." In this storehouse, seeds for what become conscious moments or events are stored.

In this selection, Vasubandhu begins with the granary consciousness and moves on to the other types. All things (*dharmas*) can be seen as a part of or associated with a type of consciousness. Does this mean that the true nature of reality is perception? Does it mean that the objects of awareness are themselves made up of seeds of awareness? Vasubandhu

warns that if we think like this, then we have reestablished the subject/object dualism he has worked so hard to dispel. The notion that "all this is merely perception" should *not* be construed as some sort of external object of perception.

It is time to turn to the words of Nagarjuna and Vasubandhu themselves. Both philosophers express a viewpoint that goes beyond most of our conventional wisdom. Our conventional thought relies on the concept of essence and presupposes a subject/object dualism. Nagarjuna and Vasubandhu articulate a wisdom that goes beyond conventional modes of thinking and thereby challenge us to rethink some of our fundamental views about the nature of reality.

⟨⟨⟩⟩

NAGARJUNA AND VASUBANDHU

Nirvana and *Consciousness-Only*

READING QUESTIONS

1. Restate in your own words the argument Nagarjuna presents that supports the conclusion that *nirvana* is "not a thing and not a nothing."
2. Why, according to Nagarjuna, should we *not* assert that *nirvana* is "both a thing and a nonthing" and that *nirvana* is "neither a thing nor a nonthing"?
3. What do you think Nagarjuna means when he says, "There is no distinction whatsoever between *samsara* and *nirvana*"? Why does he say this? If there is no distinction, why follow the Buddhist path?
4. What is "consciousness-only," and what would it be like to experience such a state?
5. Do you think nondualistic consciousness is possible? Why or why not?

NIRVANA

An opponent argues:

1. If everything is empty, there can be no arising or passing away; therefore, by what abandonment, by what cessation can nirvāṇa be expected?

From *Experience of Buddhism*, 1st ed., by J. S. Strong, pp. 147–149, 152–154. Copyright © 1995 Wadsworth Publishing. Reprinted by permission of Wadsworth Publishing, a division of International Thomson Publishing. Fax 800-730-2215.

Nāgārjuna replies:

2. [It is only] if everything is *not* empty that there can be no arising or passing away [and that one can ask]: by what abandonment, by what cessation can nirvāṇa be expected?

3. This is said about nirvāṇa: no abandonment, no attainment, no annihilation, no eternality, no cessation, no arising.

4. Nirvāṇa is not a thing, for then it would follow that it would be characterized by old age and death, for no thing is free from old age and death.

5. And if nirvāṇa were a thing, it would be karmically constituted, for no thing anywhere has ever been found not to be karmically constituted.

6. And if nirvāṇa were a thing, how could it not be dependent on other things, for no independent thing has ever been found.

7. If nirvāṇa is not a thing, can it be that it is a "nonthing"? [No, because] wherever there is no thing, neither can there be a nonthing.

8. And if nirvāṇa were a nonthing, how could it not be dependent on other things, for no independent nonthing has ever been found.

9. The state of moving restlessly to and fro [in saṃsāra] is dependent and conditioned; independent and unconditioned, it is said to be nirvāṇa.

10. The Buddha said that both existence and freedom from existence are abandoned. Therefore it is fitting to say that nirvāṇa is not a thing and not a nonthing.

11. If nirvāṇa were *both* a thing and a nonthing, liberation would also be *both* a thing and a nonthing, but that does not make sense.

12. If nirvāṇa were *both* a thing and a nonthing, it would not be independent [of other things], for both [things and nonthings] are dependent.

13. And how could nirvāṇa be both a thing and a nonthing? Nirvāṇa is not karmically constituted, but things and nonthings are.

14. [And anyhow,] how could nirvāṇa be both a thing and a nonthing? Like light and darkness, these two are opposites and cannot both exist at the same place.

15. Only if things and nonthings are established can the proposition "Nirvāṇa is *neither* a thing nor a nonthing" be established.

16. But how could it be asserted that nirvāṇa was found to be "neither a thing nor a nonthing"?

17. It is not asserted that the Blessed One exists after his passing away; nor is it asserted that he

does not exist, that he both exists and does not exist, or that he neither exists nor does not exist.

18. Even while he is living, it is not asserted that the Blessed One exists; nor is it asserted that he does not exist, both exists and does not exist, or neither exists nor does not exist.

19. There is no distinction whatsoever between saṃsāra and nirvāṇa; and there is no distinction whatsoever between nirvāṇa and saṃsāra.

20. The limit of nirvāṇa and the limit of saṃsāra: one cannot find even the slightest difference between them.

21. Views about such things as the finitude or infinitude of the state coming after death, are related to the issue of nirvāṇa having beginning and ending limits.

22. Given that all elements of reality are empty, what is infinite? What is finite? What is both finite and infinite? What is neither finite nor infinite?

23. What is just this? What is that other? What is eternal? What is noneternal? What is both eternal and noneternal? What is neither eternal nor noneternal?

24. Ceasing to fancy everything and falsely to imagine it as real is good; nowhere did the Buddha ever teach any such element of reality.

CONSCIOUSNESS-ONLY

Vasubandhu

. . . The transformation of consciousness is of three kinds: coming to fruition, intellectualizing, and perceiving sense-objects.

The consciousness that is called "coming to fruition" is the granary consciousness (ālayna-vijñāna); it comprises all of the seeds (bīja). Its substratum, its disposition, its perceptions cannot be discerned, but it is always accompanied by the following factors: linkage to sense objects, attention, feeling, conceptualization, and volition. Its feelings are [neither pleasant nor unpleasant but] neutral, and it is undefiled and karmically indeterminate. . . . Its behavior is like the current of a stream. At arhatship, there occurs in it a fundamental revolution.

The intellectualizing consciousness is called "the mind" [manas]. As it develops, it is dependent on the granary consciousness and takes it as its object. It is karmically indeterminate but obstructed by four defilements to which it is always connected. These are called false view of the Self, delusion about the Self, pride of the Self, and love of the Self. Whenever the mind comes into being, it is accompanied by linkage to sense objects and by the other mental factors: attention, feeling, conceptualization, and volition. It ceases to exist at arhatship, or in the trance of cessation, or on the supramundane path. That is the second transformation of consciousness.

The third transformation concerns the consciousnesses dependent on the six senses: [the visual, auditory, olfactory, gustatory, tactile, and mental consciousnesses]. They are meritorious and/or demeritorious. They are accompanied by the three kinds of feeling [that is, pleasant, unpleasant, and neutral sensations] and they are connected to the following mental factors: the five mental factors that accompany them everywhere; the five special [mental factors which are not always present]; the meritorious mental states; the defilements, which are demeritorious; and the secondary defilements, which are also demeritorious.

First, the five mental factors that accompany the sense consciousnesses everywhere are: linkage to sense objects, attention, feeling, conceptualization, and volition.

The special mental factors are; zeal, resolve, mindfulness, concentration, and wisdom.

The meritorious mental states are: faith, modesty, fear of blame, lack of desire, lack of hatred, lack of delusion, striving, serenity, carefulness, and noninjury.

The defilements are: greed, hatred, confusion, pride, false views, and doubt.

The secondary defilements are: anger, enmity, disparaging others, irritation, envy, selfishness, deception, guile, assault, immodesty, nonfear of blame, sluggishness, excitability, lack of faith, sloth, carelessness, loss of mindfulness, distraction, and nondiscernment; there are also remorse and sleepiness, reflection and investigation, two pairs which are double factors [that can be either defiled or undefiled].

The first five sense consciousnesses [that is, the visual, auditory, olfactory, gustatory, and tactile consciousnesses] arise in the granary consciousness, either together or not, depending on conditions. They are like waves on the water. The sixth sense consciousness, the mental consciousness, always arises with them except in a situation where there is no recognition; in the two trance states where there is no mental consciousness; in dreamless sleep; in fainting; or in unconsciousness.

The whole transformation of consciousness is itself ultimately a false discrimination, and because it is a false discrimination, it does not exist. Therefore, all this is merely perception.

The granary consciousness contains all the seeds; its transformation takes place according to a process of give and take between it and the false discriminations to

which it gives rise [and which in turn affect it. This process leaves in the granary consciousness] residual impressions [vāsanā] of actions, which along with the residual impressions of dualistic grasping give rise to a new "coming to fruition" when the former "fruition" has died out. [. . .]

As long as consciousness is not content with being perception only, there will continue to be a tendency toward dualistic grasping. This is so even with the thought "All this is perception only." If you come to apprehend this and set it up in front of you, you are not being content with "this only." But when consciousness truly no longer apprehends any object of consciousness, it abides as consciousness only; for when what it grasps does not exist, there is no grasping. It is then free of thought, nondependent, transcendent knowledge. This is the fundamental revolution of all consciousness, the destruction of the double depravity. This element is also free from evil attachments, unimaginable, meritorious, constant, blissful. It is the liberation body, which is called the Dharma body of the Buddha.

7.4.4 The Bodhisattva Vow

As mentioned earlier, *bodhisattva* is a being headed for buddhahood. In Nikaya Buddhism the title is used primarily for Siddhartha prior to his enlightenment. In Mahayana Buddhism the idea is broadened to include, potentially, every being. We are all potentially headed for enlightenment, and the first step toward actualizing that is to take the *bodhisattva* vow.

In its simplest form, this vow is a solemn commitment to sincerely walk the path to enlightenment. Central to the vow is the idea of compassion. You should not tread the path for selfish reasons. If you do, you shall never reach the goal. Rather, you undertake this journey motivated by compassion. The true *bodhisattva*, even after enlightenment, postpones final *nirvana* (*nirvana* without remainder, or *parinirvana*) in order to help others.

Taking the *bodhisattva* vow can be a simple act of promising to pursue enlightenment and postpone one's own *parinirvana* to help others, or it can be a ritualized event beginning with the worship of Buddhas, reaffirming refuge, confessing sins, expressing thanksgiving for merit, asking the Buddhas for help, and making a declaration to lead an altruistic life.

The following selection is from the *Bodhicaryavatara* (*Entering the Path of Enlightenment*), written by the eighth-century poet Shantideva. Shantideva gives eloquent expression to the ideal *bodhisattva* mindset.

SHANTIDEVA

Entering the Path

READING QUESTIONS

1. How would you characterize the attitude expressed in the section "Worship and Devotion"?
2. What sorts of things are confessed?
3. What connection do you see between the sections on rejoicing at the merit of others and altruistic intent?
4. What sort of outlook on beings and reality motivates a *bodhisattva* to take such a vow?

WORSHIP AND DEVOTION

So as to obtain this gem of the mind set on enlightenment, I make devotional offerings to the Tathāgatas, to the immaculate jewel of the good Dharma, and to the Sangha, consisting of the sons of the Buddha, who are oceans of virtue.

However many flowers and fruits, medicinal plants, and previous gems there are in the world, as well as clear delightful waters;

and mountains made of jewels, and forest retreats where solitude is pleasant, where the creepers are resplendent with blossoms and the trees laden with fruit;

and sweet-smelling incenses from, among other places, the worlds of the gods; and wish-granting trees, and trees made of gems, and ponds bedecked with lotuses, made enchanting by the loud cries of wild geese;

and cultivated and uncultivated crops, and other things to honor those deserving devotional offerings; everything stretching as far as the limits of space, even those things that cannot be grasped—

All this I mentally give to the most eminent sages and their sons. . . .

From *Experience of Buddhism*, 1st ed., by J. S. Strong, pp. 161–163. Copyright © 1995 Wadsworth Publishing. Reprinted by permission of Wadsworth Publishing, a division of International Thomson Publishing. Fax 800-730-2215.

REFUGE AND CONFESSION

And I sing the praises of these oceans of virtue, with verses, with a flood of utterances. May the clouds of my hymns reach them without fail.

I go to the Buddha for refuge, taking enlightenment as my highest aim; and I go to the Dharma for refuge, as well as to the troop of bodhisattvas.

With folded hands, I make this confession to the Buddhas, spread out in all directions, as well as to the greatly compassionate bodhisattvas:

"Consumed by remorse, I hereby confess the evil deeds that I, no better than a beast, have committed or caused others to commit, either here in this life or throughout beginningless saṃsāra; and I confess the things that I deludedly took pleasure in and that led to self-destruction.

"And I confess all the wrongs that I have done with my body, speech, and mind, lacking respect for the Three Jewels, my parents, my teachers, and others; and the cruel evil deeds that I, guilty of many faults, have committed.

"Lords, how can I be rid of this burden? Help me quickly, lest death arrive soon while my pile of evil is still undiminished. . . .

"Lords, accept the sins I have committed. What was not good, I will not do again. . . ."

REJOICING AT THE MERIT OF OTHERS AND SUPPLICATING THE BUDDHAS

And I joyously applaud the good done by all beings that results in the cessation of the suffering of rebirth in the lower realms. May all those who suffer be happy!

And I applaud the liberation of embodied beings from the sufferings of saṃsāra, and I applaud the bodhisattvahood and Buddhahood of those so liberated.

And I applaud the Teachers, who are oceans of resolution, who bring happiness and welfare to all beings.

And with folded hands, I request the Buddhas in all directions to be a lamp of Dharma for those who have fallen into suffering because of their delusion.

With folded hands, I ask the Victorious Ones, who desire cessation, to stay in this world for endless aeons lest it remain blind.

ALTRUISTIC INTENT

May I too, through whatever good I have accomplished by doing all this, become one who works for the complete alleviation of the sufferings of all beings.

May I be medicine for the sick; may I also be their physician and attend to them until their disease no longer recurs.

With showers of food and water, may I eliminate the pain of hunger and thirst, and during the intermediate periods of great famine between aeons, may I *be* food and drink.

And may I be an inexhaustible storehouse for the poor, and may I always be first in being ready to serve them in various ways.

So that all beings may achieve their aims, may I sacrifice, without regret, the bodies, as well as the pleasures that I have had, and the merit of all the good that I have accomplished and will accomplish in the past, present, and future.

Nirvāṇa means to renounce everything. My mind is set on nirvāṇa, so because I am to renounce everything, it is best for me to give it to others.

I therefore dedicate this self of mine to the happiness of all beings. Let them smite me, constantly mock me, or throw dirt at me.

Let them make sport with my body, laugh, and make fun of me! I have given my body away to them: what could its misfortune mean to me?

Let them do to me whatever pleases them, but let no one suffer any mishap on my account.

Whether they direct toward me thoughts that are angry or kindly, may those very thoughts be a constant cause for their achieving all their aims.

Those who accuse me falsely, others who do me wrong, and still others who deride me—may they attain enlightenment!

May I be a protector of the unprotected, a guide for travelers on the way, a boat, a bridge, a means of crossing for those who seek the other shore.

For all creatures, may I be a light for those who need a light, a bed for those who need a bed, and a slave for those who need a slave.

For all creatures, may I be a wish-fulfilling gem, a vase of fortune, a spell that works, a true panacea, a wish-granting tree, a cow of plenty. . . .

Just as the Buddhas of the past grasped the mind set on enlightenment and went on to follow the bodhisattva-training,

so too will I give rise to the mind set on enlightenment for the well-being of the world, and so will I train in the stages of the bodhisattva discipline.

7.4.5 Savior *Bodhisattvas* and Buddhas

Mahayana Buddhism, unlike Theravada Buddhism, has given rise to devotional cults centered on the saving power of buddhas and *bodhisattvas* living in celestial realms. These savior figures are available not only to aid you along the path to enlightenment, but to help you out in other ways as well.

Avalokiteshvara, whose mercy and compassion was celebrated in the *Lotus Sutra*, became particularly popular in China and Japan where he took the female form of the Goddess of Mercy (Kuan-yin in Chinese and Kannon in Japanese). In Tibet his mantra *"Om Mani Padme Hum"* is used to call upon his compassion, and his devotional following became so great that Avalokiteshvara became the guardian deity of Tibet.

Also popular in Tibet and elsewhere is the Goddess **Tara,** who sometimes is paired with Avalokiteshvara. She is both compassionate, tirelessly providing aid to the oppressed, and ferocious in fiercely destroying the enemies of sentient beings.

Somewhere to "the West," where the sun sets and the dead travel, there is a **Pure Land,** a land of bliss, called *Sukhavati*. There lives the **Tathagata Amitabha,** a celestial buddha who long ago was the Bodhisattva Dharmakara. When Dharmakara took his *bodhisattva* vows, he guaranteed that when he became a buddha he would give entry into his Pure Land to anyone who repeats his name ten times with sincere faith.

The description of the Pure Land included below is from a Sanskrit text called *Smaller Description of the Land of Bliss*, and it gives you some idea of why entry into the Pure Land is so desirable to Buddhists. Although beginning in India, Pure Land Buddhism became particularly popular in China and Japan. In Japan, Amitabha is known as Amida, and chanting the phrase *"Namu Amida Butsu"* ("Praise to the Buddha Amitabha") with sincere faith can become your ticket into the Pure Land. Although some celestial buddhas in Pure Lands to the East would allow entry of women as women, *Sukhavati* was different because Dharmakara had vowed (vow #33) that those who entered his Pure Land to the West would be "freed from being women."

༄

Avalokiteshvara, Tara, and Amitabha

READING QUESTIONS

1. Why do you think beliefs in savior *bodhisattvas* and in Pure Land buddhas became important as Buddhism developed?
2. What possible tensions do you see among the concepts merit, grace, faith, and a life of true compassion? Explain.

AVALOKITESHVARA

Listen to the conduct of Avalokitesvara.

3. Hear from my indication how for numerous, inconceivable Æons he has accomplished his vows under many thousand kotis [millions] of Buddhas.

4. Hearing, seeing, regularly and constantly thinking will infallibly destroy all suffering, (mundane) existence, and grief of living beings here on earth.

5. If one be thrown into a pit of fire, by a wicked enemy with the object of killing him, he has but to think of Avalokitesvara, and the fire shall be quenched as if sprinkled with water.

Selection on Avalokiteshvara from *Saddharma-Pundarika, or the Lotus of the True Law*, translated by Hendrik Kern. Volume XXI of *The Sacred Books of the East*, edited by F. Max Mueller (Oxford, England: Clarendon Press, 1884), pp. 413–417. Selections on Tara and Amitabha from *Experience of Buddhism*, 1st ed., by J. S. Strong, pp. 184–185, 189–190. Copyright © 1995 Wadsworth Publishing. Reprinted by permission of Wadsworth Publishing, a division of International Thomson Publishing. Fax 800-730-2215.

6. If one happens to fall into the dreadful ocean, the abode of Nâgas, marine monsters, and demons, he has but to think of Avalokitesvara, and he shall never sink down in the king of waters.

7. If a man happens to be hurled down from the brink of the Meru, by some wicked person with the object of killing him, he has but to think of Avalokitesvara, and he shall, sunlike, stand firm in the sky.

8. If rocks of thunderstone and thunderbolts are thrown at a man's head to kill him, he has but to think of Avalokitesvara, and they shall not be able to hurt one hair of the body.

9. If a man be surrounded by a host of enemies armed with swords, who have the intention of killing him, he has but to think of Avalokitesvara, and they shall instantaneously become kind-hearted.

10. If a man, delivered to the power of the executioners, is already standing at the place of execution, he has but to think of Avalokitesvara, and their swords shall go to pieces.

11. If a person happens to be fettered in shackles of wood or iron, he has but to think of Avalokitesvara, and the bonds shall be speedily loosened.

12. Mighty spells, witchcraft, herbs, ghosts, and spectres, pernicious to life, revert thither whence they come, when one thinks of Avalokitesvara.

13. If a man is surrounded by goblins, Nâgas, demons, ghosts, or giants, who are in the habit of taking away bodily vigour, he has but to think of Avalokitesvara, and they shall not be able to hurt one hair of his body. . . .

[Then Akshayamati in the joy of his heart uttered the following stanzas:]

20. O thou whose eyes are clear, whose eyes are kind, distinguished by wisdom and knowledge, whose eyes are full of pity and benevolence; thou so lovely by thy beautiful face and beautiful eyes!

21. Pure one, whose shine is spotless bright, whose knowledge is free from darkness, thou shining as the sun, not to be beaten away, radiant as the blaze of fire, thou spreadest in thy flying course thy lustre in the world. . . .

25. Think, O think with tranquil mood of Avalokitesvara, that pure being; he is a protector, a refuge, a recourse in death, disaster, and calamity.

26. He who possesses the perfection of all virtues, and beholds all beings with compassion and benevolence, he, an ocean of virtues, Virtue itself, he, Avalokitesvara, is worthy of adoration.

27. He, so compassionate for the world, shall once become a Buddha, destroying all dangers and sorrows; I humbly bow to Avalokiteśvara.

28. This universal Lord, chief of kings, who is a [rich] mine of monastic virtues, he, universally worshipped, has reached pure, supreme enlightenment, after plying his course (of duty) during many hundreds of Æons. . . .

TARA

Oṃ! Praise to the Blessed Noble Tārā! [. . .]

Your compassion truly extends equally to all beings on the pathways of rebirth; therefore, I am surely among those whom it embraces.

Your unequaled capacity to save beings shines like the sun on the dark passions, the impurities of the whole world; and I too suffer and am tormented! Oh! The impure misdeeds that I have committed!

Woe! Woe! Ill-fated am I! I am blind, even in the light of the sun! I am thirsty even on the banks of a refreshing icy mountain stream! I am poor even with access to abundant jewels in the mines of the Isle of Gems! Being without refuge, I make you my protector, Blessed Lady, you who are the support of the whole world.

Even a mother gets tired of a baby who constantly cries for milk. Even a father gets angry at a son who daily asks for things he does not have. But you, like a great wish-granting tree, fulfill the desires of this Triple World. You never fail to grant the requests of all those who reverence you. [. . .]

When those who are injured—whose limbs are being fed on by vermin that have attached themselves to their oozing open wounds, smelling of flesh, flowing with blood, suppurating with stinking pus, filled with impurities due to their past evil deeds—devote themselves . . . to service at your feet, their physical bodies become beautiful like gold, and their eyes like lotuses.

Those in whose ear the gurus have not repeated the sacred texts (as though they were putting alms in a bowl) and those who, lacking a wealth of knowledge, become mute in the fellowship of the learned—they will become the Lord of Speech as a result of devotion to you. . . .

Those whose loins are covered with rags that are torn and dark with dirt from lying on the ground; who pick lice and seek food from others in a broken pot— they will gain universal sovereignty over the earth by propitiating you. . . .

Those who are tired of seeking ways in which to make a living by bartering, by carrying out a trade, or by being employed in the service of others and who fail to get money even though they have amassed merit in previous lives—by turning to you who surpass the gods, Mother of the destitute, they . . . will obtain a treasure of gold spewed forth from the earth. [. . .]

Some see you in your fierce form, striking out with bright weapons uplifted and swinging, breaking and pervading the sky, your arms entwined with bracelets that are hooded serpents. Taking on this frightful aspect, you scare enemies away, your laughter causes great tumult, like the rolling and striking of a great drum. . . .

But for others, in each of your hairs is visible the expanse of heaven and earth wherein dwell in bliss the gods Brahmā, Indra, and Rudra as well as humans, maruts, siddhas, gandharvas, and nāgas. And all directions are pervaded by hundreds of Buddhas without end, which you have magically fashioned. Worthy of worship by the Triple World, in your own being, you contain all creatures. . . .

Some see you red like the sun whose rays are redder than red lacquer or vermillion. Others see you blue like dust made of the pulverized fragments of a magnificent precious sapphire. And some see you white, more dazzling than the churned ocean of milk and brighter than gold. Your form, like a crystal, takes on various aspects, changing according to the different things that are placed near it.

AMITABHA

Then the Blessed One spoke to the Venerable Śāriputra: "Śāriputra, over a hundred thousand billion Buddha fields to the west of here, there is a Buddha field called the world of Sukhāvatī. And there dwells a Tathāgata, an altogether enlightened Buddha named Amitāyus [Amitābha]. . . . Now what do you think, Śāriputra, why do they call that world the land of bliss? Because, Śāriputra, in that world, Sukhāvatī, beings do not experience suffering [duḥkha], neither with their body nor with their mind, and the things causing happiness are innumerable. . . .

"Śāriputra, Sukhāvatī is adorned and enclosed by seven railings, seven rows of palm trees and strings of bells. And it is beautiful and embellished with four kinds of precious materials: gold, silver, lapis lazuli, and crystal. . . . And, Śāriputra, there are lotus pools there made of seven precious materials: gold, silver, lapis lazuli, crystal, red pearls, diamonds, and coral. They are filled with water endowed with eight good qualities . . . and they are strewn with sand of gold. And going down into those lotus pools, from all four sides, are four flights of steps, beautiful, and embellished with four precious materials, . . . and all around the lotus pools jewel-trees are growing, beautiful, and embellished with seven precious materials. . . . And in those lotus pools, lotuses are growing: various kinds of blue ones, and various kinds of yellow ones, and various kinds of red ones, and various kinds of white ones, beautiful, beautifully colored, beautifully resplendent, beautiful to look at, and as big around as the wheel of a cart. . . .

"Furthermore, Śāriputra, in that Buddha field, divine musical instruments are always playing, and the earth is pleasant and golden colored. And in that Buddha field, three times each night and three times each day, showers of blossoms fall, divine mandārava blossoms. And the beings there, during the time it takes to eat one morning meal, can pay homage to a hundred thousand billion Buddhas, by going to other universes. And after showering each Tathāgata with a hundred thousand billion flowers, they return to their own world in time for a nap. . . .

"Furthermore, Śāriputra, in that Buddha field, there are geese, snipe, and peacocks. Three times each night and three times each day, they come and sing together, each uttering its own cries. . . . And when the people there hear that sound, they become mindful of the Buddha, mindful of the Dharma, and mindful of the Sangha. Now, Śāriputra, [because of these birds] are you thinking that there are beings who have been reborn in that Buddha land as animals? That is not the way you should see it. Why? Because, in that Buddha field, Śāriputra, no one is born as a hell being, an animal, or a hungry ghost in the dominion of Yama the god of the dead. These birds were magically fashioned by the Tathāgata Amitāyus, and their cries are the sound of the Dharma. With such marvelous Buddha-field qualities, Śāriputra, is that Buddha field Sukhāvatī arrayed."

7.5 MAHAYANA BUDDHISM IN CHINA AND JAPAN

Mahayana Buddhism began to move into China sometime around the first century and reached Korea and Japan by the sixth century. Buddhist monks tell a more dramatic story than present-day historians do. According to a widely circulated story among Chinese Buddhists, the Emperor Ming (58–75) dreamed about a golden deity flying near his palace in Loyang,

the capital of China at that time. Emperor Ming's ministers of state informed him that the deity he dreamt about was named Buddha, who lived in India. Immediately the Emperor sent ambassadors to India, and they returned with monks and scriptures, which were translated into Chinese.

Chinese indigenous religions such as Taoism and Confucianism had their impact on Buddhism, and, as a result of this creative encounter, there were new Buddhist developments. However, at first, the various schools of Mahayana Buddhism in India made converts and established religious centers. Both the *Madhyamika* (*San-lun* in Chinese) and the *Yogacara* (*Fahsiang* in Chinese) schools made a significant impact along with Pure Land Buddhism.

For comments on translation and pronunciation of Chinese words, see the Pronunciation Guide at the end of chapter 8.

7.5.1 The Goddess

The Indian Buddhist stories of *bodhisattvas* and celestial buddhas made a strong impression on the Chinese. Particularly popular were stories of Vimalakirti, a kind of rogue Indian *bodhisattva* often portrayed as upsetting the disciples of the Buddha and his fellow *bodhisattvas* by his unorthodox teaching methods and life style. He was not a monk but a layperson, and this added to his popularity in China.

Stories about Vimalakirti are recounted in *The Holy Teaching of Vimalakirti*, probably written sometime in the first century B.C.E. The stories elaborate on the Perfect Wisdom (*Prajnaparamita*) tradition, often in a playful way. In one story, Vimalakirti invites Shariputra, a direct disciple of the Buddha, to his home. Shariputra represents the "old" Buddhism (perhaps the Theravadan perspective), having mastered only the "outer" (exoteric) teachings of the Buddha, not their "inner" (esoteric) meaning. At one point Shariputra encounters a goddess in Vimalakirti's home, and, believing in the inferiority of women and their need to be reborn as males in order to attain spiritual enlightenment, asks her why she does not use her supernatural powers to become a man. Her answer is surprising, especially to Shariputra.

The Goddess

READING QUESTION

1. What do you think the quotation "In all things, there is neither male nor female," attributed to the Buddha by the goddess, means?

Śāriputra:

Goddess, what prevents you from transforming yourself out of your female state?

Goddess:

Although I have sought my "female state" for these twelve years, I have not yet found it. Reverend Śāriputra, if a magician were to incarnate a woman by magic, would you ask her, "What prevents you from transforming yourself out of your female state?"

Śāriputra:

No! Such a woman would not really exist, so what would there be to transform?

Goddess:

Just so, reverend Śāriputra, all things do not really exist. Now, would you think, "What prevents one whose nature is that of a magical incarnation from transforming herself out of her female state?"

Thereupon, the goddess employed her magical power to cause the elder Śāriputra to appear in her form and to cause herself to appear in his form. Then the goddess, transformed into Śāriputra, said to Śāriputra, transformed into a goddess, "Reverend Śāriputra, what prevents you from transforming yourself out of your female state?"

And Śāriputra, transformed into the goddess, replied, "I no longer appear in the form of a male! My body has changed into the body of a woman! I do not know what to transform!"

The goddess continued, "If the elder could again change out of the female state, then all women could also change out of their female states. All women appear in the form of women in just the same way as the elder appears in the form of a woman. While they are not women in reality, they appear in the form of women. With this in mind, the Buddha said, 'In all things, there is neither male nor female.'"

Then, the goddess released her magical power and each returned to his ordinary form. She then said to him, "Reverend Śāriputra, what have you done with your female form?"

Śāriputra:

I neither made it nor did I change it.

Goddess:

Just so, all things are neither made nor changed, and that they are not made and not changed, that is the teaching of the Buddha.

Śāriputra:

Goddess, where will you be born when you transmigrate after death?

Goddess:

I will be born where all the magical incarnations of the Tathāgata are born.

Śāriputra:

But the emanated incarnations of the Tathāgata do not transmigrate nor are they born.

Goddess:

All things and living beings are just the same; they do not transmigrate nor are they born!

Śāriputra:

Goddess, how soon will you attain the perfect enlightenment of Buddhahood?

Goddess:

At such time as you, elder, become endowed once more with the qualities of an ordinary individual, then will I attain the perfect enlightenment of Buddhahood.

Śāriputra:

Goddess, it is impossible that I should become endowed once more with the qualities of an ordinary individual.

Goddess:

Just so, reverend Śāriputra, it is impossible that I should attain the perfect enlightenment of Buddhahood! Why? Because perfect enlightenment stands upon the impossible. Because it is impossible, no one attains the perfect enlightenment of Buddhahood.

Śāriputra:

But the Tathāgata has declared: "The Tathāgatas, who are as numerous as the sands of the Ganges, have attained perfect Buddhahood, are attaining

From Robert A. F. Thurman, *The Holy Teaching of Vimalakirti*, University Park, Pa.: The Pennsylvania State University Press, 1976. Copyright © 1976 by The Pennsylvania State University. Reproduced by permission of the publisher.

perfect Buddhahood, and will go on attaining perfect Buddhahood."

Goddess:

Reverend Śāriputra, the expression, "the Buddhas of the past, present and future," is a conventional expression made up of a certain number of syllables. The Buddhas are neither past, nor present, nor future. Their enlightenment transcends the three times! But tell me, elder, have you attained sainthood?

Śāriputra:

It is attained, because there is no attainment.

Goddess:

Just so, there is perfect enlightenment because there is no attainment of perfect enlightenment.

Then the Licchavi Vimalakīrti said to the venerable elder Śāriputra, "Reverend Śāriputra, this goddess has already served ninety-two million billion Buddhas. She plays with the superknowledges. She has truly succeeded in all her vows. She has gained the tolerance of the birthlessness of things. She has actually attained irreversibility. She can live wherever she wishes on the strength of her vow to develop living beings."

7.5.2 Buddha Nature

There is a common saying in Chinese Buddhism, "Hua-yen and T'ien-t'ai for doctrines and Ch'an and Pure Land for practice." We have already discussed Pure Land Buddhism in the Indian tradition, and in the next section we will discuss Ch'an Buddhism (Zen in Japanese). Here we will get a glimpse of teaching common to Hua-yen and T'ien-t'ai.

The T'ien-t'ai school is also called the Lotus School because it claims the *Lotus Sutra* (see Readings 7.4.1 and 7.4.5) represents the culmination of the Buddha's teaching. Chih-yi (538–597), its greatest systematic thinker, was concerned with reconciling what appeared to be very different teachings of the Buddha. His answer was to develop the notion of skillful means. The Buddha, employing skillful means, teaches different things at different times depending on the level of understanding of his audience.

The Hua-yen, or Flower Garland School, was also concerned with reconciling the different teachings of the Buddha. In addition, it sought to harmonize Buddhism with both Confucianism and Taoism. While the Hua-yen had Indian roots, no similar school existed in India, so its development is essentially Chinese.

Fa-tsang (643–712) is the founder of the Flower Garland School, and his *Treatise on the Golden Lion* is an influential work that uses a statue of a golden lion to teach that one thing is in all things and all things are in one thing. This teaching allowed the Hua-yen school to argue that the Buddha said essentially the same thing in different ways, to synthesize the teachings of various Buddhist schools with Confucianism and Taoism, and to argue that all things contain the Buddha Nature. However, it still claims that Buddhism, especially as understood by Hua-yen, is the most complete spiritual teaching.

The author of the following selection is Tsung-mi (780–841), the fifth patriarch of the Hua-yen school. This treatise is not a basic scripture nor particularly well known, but it applies the philosophical teachings about unity, characteristic of the Hua-yen, to the religious life.

≈≈≈

TSUNG-MI

An Inquiry on Man

READING QUESTIONS

1. What is meant by **Tathagatagarbha?**
2. What advice for living the religious life does Tsung-mi find in the teaching of the *Tathagatagarbha?*

DIRECTLY MANIFESTING THE TRUE SOURCE

The Doctrine of the Manifestation of Dharma-nature in the One Vehicle (of the T'ien-t'ai and Hua-yen Schools) preaches that all sentient beings possess the true mind of natural enlightenment, which from time immemorial has always been there, clear and pure, shining and not obscured, understanding and always know-

From *The Great Asian Religions: An Anthology*, edited by Wing-tsit Chan, Isma'il Ragi al Fārāgui, Joseph M. Kitagawa, and P. T. R. Raju (New York: Macmillan Publishing Co., Inc., 1969), p. 209. © Copyright 1969, Macmillan Publishing Co., Inc. Reprinted by permission. Endnotes omitted.

ing. It is also called Buddha-nature and Tathāgatagarbha (Store of the Thus-come). From the beginning of time, it has been obscured by erroneous ideas without knowing its own (Buddha-nature), but only recognizing its ordinary nature, loving it and being attached to it, accumulating action-influence, and suffering from the pain of life and death. The Buddha pitied these sentient beings. He preached to them that all things are empty. He also revealed to them that the true mind of spiritual enlightenment, being clear and pure, is completely identical with that of the Buddhas. Therefore the *Flower Splendor Scripture* says, "Among the Buddhas-sons (all sentient beings), none is without the wisdom of the Tathāgata complete in him. Only because of their erroneous ideas and clinging have they not realized it. If they are freed from erroneous ideas, the knowledge of all that exists, the knowledge naturally present from the beginning, and the knowledge without obstacle will immediately come to the fore." The scripture forthwith gives the analogy of one speck of dust containing a great scripture whose quantity is equivalent to the world system of 1,000 million worlds, equating the dust to the sentient beings and the great scripture to the Buddha-wisdom. Following this, it also says, "At that time the Tathāgata surveyed all sentient beings in the realm of dharmas and said these words: How strange! How strange! Why are the sentient beings deceived and deluded and do not see the wisdom of the Tathāgata complete in them? I must teach them the Holy Path to enable them to be free forever from erroneous thoughts and see the great and vast Tathāgata-wisdom in their own persons, making them the same as the Buddha."

Comment: For many aeons we have not encountered the True Doctrine. We have not learned how to reflect on our own bodies, but have merely clung to false characters and willingly admit that we are ordinary or inferior—perhaps we are animals or perhaps we are men. Only now that we make the inquiry in accordance with the perfect doctrine do we realize that we are originally Buddhas. Therefore our deeds must be in accordance with those of the Buddha, and our minds must be harmonious with the mind of the Buddha. We must revert to the foundation and return to the source, and cut off the habits of an ordinary man. "Decrease and further decrease until one reaches the point of taking no action." One will then naturally respond and function in as many ways as the number of sand grains in the Ganges River, and will be called a Buddha. We should know that both the deluded and the awakened share the same true mind. Great is this wonderful gate. This is the point to which our inquiry on man has come. (*Taishō daizōkyō* [Taishō edition of the Buddhist Canon], 45:710)

7.5.3 Ch'an Buddhism

"Point directly to the human mind." This is one of the mottos of Ch'an Buddhism (Son in Korea, Zen in Japan). Ch'an Buddhism began as a reformation movement in Buddhism. As the other schools of Chinese Buddhism translated Indian scriptures, argued over their interpretation, discussed which rituals brought the most merit, and asserted their own superiority over the other schools, Ch'an Buddhists started a "get back to basics" movement.

Why do we revere the Buddha? "Because he is enlightened," the Ch'an replied. And under what circumstances did his enlightenment happen? "While he was meditating under the Bodhi tree," the Ch'an replied. It is a very short step from these answers to the view that the heart of Buddhist practice should be meditation. Indeed, *Ch'an* is the way the Chinese say the Sanskrit word for meditation, *dhyana.* Ch'an Buddhism is meditation Buddhism.

Bodhidarma (460–534?) is the Indian monk credited with bringing meditation Buddhism to China. He is a semilegendary figure who arrived at the Shao-lin monastery where he sat in silent meditation in front of a wall for several years. Needless to say, this strange behavior attracted attention, and when he broke silence and began to teach, he had a ready following. The first Chinese patriarch of the school was one of his disciples. However, according to the Ch'an school, their teachings go back to the Buddha himself and constitute a "special transmission outside the scriptures."

In China, Ch'an eventually split between two major schools, the Northern School that stressed gradual enlightenment and the Southern School that stressed sudden enlightenment. Both schools agreed that *nirvana* is identical to the Buddha-mind and therefore is the Buddha-Nature in all sentient beings. However, the Northern School believed that you could realize your own Buddha-Nature only by gradually, through the practice of *samadhi* (concentration), removing the erroneous and impure thoughts that have obscured that nature. The practice of *samadhi* will eventually lead you to wisdom (*prajna*) buried within.

The Southern School, which eventually became the most dominant, insisted that all mental activities are functions of suchness. There are not two minds, a true original Buddha-mind and a false mind that obscures it. There is one mind, the Buddha-mind, and it is everywhere. Anything can be an occasion for its realization. It can happen at any moment and in any way. It can happen to a monk or a layperson, to someone early on in the transmigration cycle or someone who has lived millions of lives.

It follows from this that, although reading scriptures, debating fine philosophical points about the no-self, making offerings to the Buddha, reciting his name, joining monastic orders, and the like may be occasions for enlightenment, they are not necessary. Enlightenment could happen to a child at the sound of a bell.

Clearly these ideas are reforming, if not revolutionary, because the whole Buddhist organization is threatened by the claim that the heart of true Buddhism is to be concerned about truly getting in touch with your mind and that this can be done immediately and "in this very body." And so another Ch'an motto, "See one's nature and become a Buddha," struck Chinese Buddhism like a bomb.

Like many religious reformations, however, Ch'an Buddhism developed organizations, teachings, and rituals—the very things it maintained were not necessary for enlightenment! The most important teachings are found in the *Platform Sutra* (*Liu-tsu*), written by the sixth patriarch, Hui-neng (638–713). A selection follows.

⋘◈⋙

HUI-NENG

Platform Sutra

READING QUESTIONS

1. Why do you think the teachings contained in this selection of the *Platform Sutra* would become so popular? Be specific.
2. Can you think of any parallels to the movement of Ch'an Buddhism in other religions? If so, what are the parallels?

13. "Good and learned friends, calmness (*samādhi*) and wisdom (*prajñā*) are the foundations of my method.

From Chan, Wing-tsit, *A Source Book in Chinese Philosophy*, pp. 433–436. Copyright © 1963, renewed 1991 by Princeton University Press. Reprinted by permission of Princeton University Press. Footnotes and comments omitted.

First of all, do not be deceived into thinking that the two are different. They are one substance and not two. Calmness is the substance of wisdom and wisdom is the function of calmness. Whenever wisdom is at work, calmness is within it. Whenever calmness is at work, wisdom is within it. Good and learned friends, the meaning here is that [calmness and] wisdom are identified. Seekers of the Way, arouse your minds. Do not say that wisdom follows calmness or vice versa, or that the two are different. To hold such a view [would imply that] the dharmas (elements of existence) possess two different characters. In the case of those whose words are good but whose hearts are not good, wisdom and calmness are not identified. But in the case of those whose hearts and words are both good and in whom the internal and the external are one, calmness and wisdom are identified. Self-enlightenment and practice do not consist in argument. If one is concerned about which comes first, he is a [deluded] person. If he is not freed from the consideration of victory or defeat, he will produce the dharmas as real entities and cannot be free from the Four Characters [of coming into existence, remaining in the same state, change, and going out of existence]." . . .

16. "Good and learned friends, in method there is no distinction between sudden enlightenment and gradual enlightenment. Among men, however, some are intelligent and others are stupid. Those who are deluded understand gradually, while the enlightened achieve understanding suddenly. But when they know their own minds, then they see their own nature, and there is no difference in their enlightenment. Without enlightenment, they remain forever bound in transmigration."

17. "Good and learned friends, in this method of mine, from the very beginning, whether in the sudden-enlightenment or gradual-enlightenment tradition, absence-of-thought has been instituted as the main doctrine, absence-of-characters as the substance, and nonattachment as the foundation. What is meant by absence-of-characters? Absence-of-characters means to be free from characters while in the midst of them. Absence-of-thought means not to be carried away by thought in the process of thought. Nonattachment is man's original nature. Thought after thought goes on without remaining. Past, present, and future thoughts continue without termination. But if we cut off and terminate thought one instant, the dharma-body (Law-body or spiritual body) is freed from the physical body. At no time should a single instant of thought be attached to any dharma. If one single instant of thought is attached to anything, then every thought will be attached. That is bondage. But if in regard to dharmas no thought is attached to anything, that is freedom.

[This is] the meaning of having nonattachment as the foundation.

"Good and learned friends, to be free from all characters means the absence of characters. Only if we can be free from characters will the substance of our nature be pure. That is the meaning of taking the absence-of-character as the substance.

"Absence-of-thought means not to be defiled by external objects. It is to free our thoughts from external objects and not to have thoughts arise over dharmas. But do not stop thinking about everything and eliminate all thought. As soon as thought stops, one dies and is reborn elsewhere. Take heed of this, followers of the Way. If one does not think over the meaning of the Law and becomes mistaken himself, that is excusable. How much worse is it to encourage others to be [mistaken]! Deluded, he does not realize that he is so, and he even blasphemes the scripture and the Law! That is the reason why absence-of-thought is instituted as the doctrine. Because people who are deluded have thoughts about the spheres of objects, perverse views arise in them, and all sorts of afflictions resulting from passions and erroneous thoughts are produced. . . .

"However, this school has instituted absence-of-thought as the doctrine. When people of the world are free from erroneous views, no thoughts will arise. If there are no thoughts, there will not even be an 'absence-of-thought.' Absence means absence of what? Thought means thought of what? Absence-of-thought means freedom from the character of the duality (existence or nonexistence of characters) and from all afflictions resulting from passions. [Thought means thought of the true nature of True Thusness (True Reality).] True Thusness is the substance of thought and thought is the function of True Thusness. It is the self-nature that gives rise to thought. Therefore in spite of the functioning of seeing, hearing, sensing, and knowing, self-nature is not defiled by the many spheres of objects and always remains free and at ease. As the *Wei-mo-chieh [so-shuo] ching* (Scripture Spoken by Vimalakīrti) says, "Externally it skillfully differentiates the various dharma-characters while internally it abides immovably in the First Principle."

18. "Good and learned friends, according to this method sitting in meditation is at bottom neither looking at the mind nor looking at purity. Nor do we say that there should be imperturbability. Suppose we say to look at the mind. The mind is at bottom false. Since being false is the same as being illusory, there is nothing to look at. Suppose we say to look at purity. Man's nature is originally pure. It is by false thoughts that True Thusness is obscured. Our original nature is pure as long as it is free from false thoughts. If one does not realize that his own nature is originally pure and makes up his mind to look at purity, he is creating a false purity. Such purity has no objective existence. Hence we know that what is looked at is false. Purity has neither physical form nor character, but some people set up characters of purity and say that this is the object of our task. People who take this view hinder their own original nature and become bound by purity. If those who cultivate imperturbability would ignore people's mistakes and defeats, their nature would not be perturbed. Deluded people may not be perturbed physically themselves, but whenever they speak, they criticize others and thus violate the Way. Thus looking at the mind or at purity causes a hindrance to the Way."

19. "Now, this being the case, in this method, what is meant by sitting in meditation? In this method, to sit means to be free from all obstacles, and externally not to allow thoughts to rise from the mind over any sphere of objects. To meditate means to realize the imperturbability of one's original nature. What is meant by meditation and calmness? Meditation means to be free from all characters externally; calmness means to be unperturbed internally. If there are characters outside and the inner mind is not disturbed, one's original nature is naturally pure and calm. It is only because of the spheres of objects that there is contact, and contact leads to perturbation. There is calmness when one is free from characters and is not perturbed. There is meditation when one is externally free from characters, and there is calmness when one is internally undisturbed. Meditation and calmness mean that external meditation is attained and internal calmness is achieved. The *Wei-mo-chieh [so-shuo] ching* says, 'Immediately we become completely clear and recover our original mind.' The *P'u-sa chieh ching* (Scripture of Disciplines for Bodhisattvahood) says, 'We are originally pure in our self-nature.' Good and learned friends, realize that your self-nature is naturally pure. Cultivate and achieve for yourselves the Law-body of your self-nature. Follow the Way of the Buddha yourselves. Act and achieve Buddhahood for yourselves." . . .

7.5.4 Zen Buddhism

It took six hundred years for Mahayana Buddhism to spread across China, into Korea and then to Japan. According to legend, Prince Shotoku (574–622) welcomed Buddhist missionary monks and formulated the *Seventeen-Article Constitution*, which urged reverence for the Three Gems or Refuges: the Buddha, the *Dharma* (teachings), and the *sangha* (community). It also counseled harmony with the indigenous religion of Shinto. Today, Japan presents the broadest surviving range of the rich variety of Mahayana Buddhist schools and practices.

Among the various schools that came to Japan from China, *Ch'an* Buddhism, now known as **Zen,** left a deep and lasting impression on Japanese art, literature, architecture, military training, and general life style from the tea ceremony to bathing.

Both the Northern and Southern schools of Ch'an that had developed in China were established in Japan. The Rinzai school (*Lin-chi* in China) was introduced by Eisai (1141–1215) in 1191, and the Soto school (*Ts'ao-tung* in China) was established in 1227 by Dogen (1200–1253). Rinzai, with its emphasis on sudden enlightenment, emphasized the use of the *koan* (Chinese: *kung-an;* Korean: *kongan*) in meditation. *Koans* are enigmatic sayings or questions such as "What is the sound of one hand clapping?" that are given to students who are instructed to wrestle with them with all their strength until they reach a sudden insight called *satori*. The first *koan* often given to meditators is "Joshu's Mu." "Mu" means "no" and is said to have been the answer that the Chinese Ch'an master Chao Chou (Joshu in Japanese) gave to a monk who asked whether a dog had the Buddha-Nature.

Soto Zen placed more emphasis on gradual enlightenment, and thus monks were taught a more traditional type of meditation called **zazen,** or seated meditation. The following selection is a translation of three passages from the teachings of Dogen (*Shobogenzo Zuimonki,* or *Eye and Treasure of the True Law*) as recorded by his disciple Ejo. Note that in the first passage Dogen criticizes other Buddhist schools and in the last passage he answers a charge leveled against Buddhists, first by the Confucianists in China and then by those in Japan who believed that reverence and loyalty to one's parents and ancestors was of central importance to the moral life and the stability of society. Since Buddhism advocated the life of a monk or a nun, such a life appeared to lead to the abandonment of an important moral standard in both Chinese and Japanese society.

DOGEN

Eye and Treasure of the True Law

READING QUESTIONS

1. Why is *zazen* important?
2. How does Dogen answer the question about indebtedness to one's parents?
3. If you are a member of a religious tradition, and someone asked you what is the one thing in your tradition that everyone should practice, what would you say? How does your answer compare to Dogen's?

Once Dōgen taught, "One must remember how quickly the wind of transitoriness blows our life away, and how important are life and death. If one wishes to do and study something worthwhile during his short life, he ought to practice Buddhist disciplines and study the Law. It goes without saying that one should discard literary composition and writing poems inasmuch as they are of no value. One should not attempt to cover to many subjects even in his study and practice of Buddhism. Moreover, one should have nothing to do with those schools of Buddhism such as all the exoteric and esoteric sects, which unlike Zen build their doctrines based on scriptures and commentaries. Even the Buddha's own sayings should not be studied indiscriminately. Most people with limited abilities can hardly concentrate even on one thing. It is not desirable, therefore, for them to indulge in many things simultaneously, for in so doing their minds will lose control. . . .

Once, Ejō inquired, "What is the one thing in the Buddhist Law which we should practice?" The Master said, "What you should practice depends on your own abilities. However, the one practice which has been handed down in the tradition of Bodhidharma is *zazen* (meditation). This practice is suited for all people, regardless of differences of innate ability. When I learned this principle under the tutelage of the late master (Ju-ching,

From *The Great Asian Religions: An Anthology,* edited by Wing-tsit Chan et al. (New York: Macmillan Publishing Co., Inc., 1969), pp. 284–285. © Copyright 1969, Macmillan Publishing Co., Inc. Reprinted by permission. Endnotes omitted.

1163–1268) of the T'ien-t'ung Monastery [in China], I started practicing *zazen* day and night and continued it even when some other monks gave it up in the extremely hot and cold days. I then said to myself, 'I should practice *zazen* even if I should become ill or die on account of it. What good would it do if I, who am not sick, failed to do so! If I should die in following the practice of *zazen* before attaining enlightenment, I might at least create a cause to be born in future life as a follower of the Buddha. After all, it is useless simply to live long without undergoing Buddhist disciplines. Even if I take great care of my health, I might drown or encounter unexpected death, and then I will surely have cause to regret.' I, therefore, urge all of you to practice *zazen* most intensely. All of you without exception will find the true path. Such was the teaching of my late master [Ju-ching]." . . .

During one of the evening conversations Ejō asked, "What shall we do to repay our indebtedness to our parents?" Dōgen replied, "One should observe filial piety, of course. However, there is a difference between the filial piety of the monk and that of the layman. In the case of the layman, he should, as taught in the *Classic of Filial Piety*, serve his parents during their lifetime and engage in acts of repaying gratitude to them after their death. On the other hand, the monk who has entered the Buddhist life—which is characterized by inactivity, [by forsaking the indebtedness toward his parents]— should not try to repay gratitude only toward his physical parents. His sense of indebtedness toward all living beings must be considered as deep as his sense of indebtedness toward his parents of this lifetime, so that the latter should not be singled out as special objects of filial piety. This attitude is in keeping with the Buddhist principle of inactivity. To follow the path of the Buddha in one's daily disciplines and in one's study of the Law is the true filial piety. Holding a memorial service on the memorial days of the parents or doing charitable deeds for the repose of the parents during the forty-nine days following their death are examples of the way of the laity, [and not the way of the monks]. . . .

7.5.5 Nichiren Buddhism

Ch'an was only one of many forms of Mahayana Buddhism imported from China. T'ien-t'ai became Tendai in Japan. It was brought by the Japanese monk Saicho (766–822) and established on Mount Hiei, which became a Buddhist stronghold. Another Japanese monk, named Kukai (774–835), established

Shingon (True Word) in Japan after studying Chenyen Buddhism in China. Kukai, who became known as Kobo Daishi after his death, made Mount Koya (near Osaka) his home base and taught the mystery of the three rituals: body **mudras,** or hand gestures, speech (*mantras,* or mystical sounds), and mind (contemplation of celestial *buddhas* and *bodhisattvas*). However, one of the most popular schools was Pure Land Buddhism (*Jodo* in Japanese, *Ching-t'u* in Chinese), also called Amida Buddhism (from the Japanese name Amitabha).

Honen (1133–1212) taught Amida devotion, advocating that we need to rely on the grace of Amida for enlightenment. Devotion consisted of the recitation of Amida's name called the **nembutsu.** Honen's disciple, Shinran (1173–1262), contrasted "other power" (*tariki*) with self-power (*jiriki*). We live, Shinran thought, in a degenerate age called *mappo* in which the self-power taught by Zen is not sufficient for enlightenment. Only the "other power" of Amida can save us. Thus it might appear that the rallying cry of Martin Luther's Protestant Reformation in Germany—salvation by faith alone—had already been heard in Japan some three centuries earlier. However, the faith Luther advocated was faith in Jesus Christ's loving grace while the faith Honen and Shinran advocated was faith in the loving grace of Amida.

The path of faith became far more popular than Zen in Japan, in part because it did not require one to enter a monastery, practice *zazen*, and struggle with *koans*. A sincere recitation of *nembutsu* was enough to guarantee a place with Amida in the Pure Land to the West. However, even as Shinran preached, another Japanese Buddhist named Nichiren (1222–1282) proclaimed that these evil times of the *mappo*—the end of all decency, morality, and true teaching of the *Dharma*—required more drastic measures than silly chants. In order to save Japan and Buddhism, the people had to abandon their heretical beliefs in things like the *nembutsu*, repent of their sins, and turn in faith to the power of the *Lotus Sutra* (Japanese *Myhohorengekyo*, or, in its abbreviated form, *Hokekyo*). According to Nichiren, the *Lotus Sutra* is the only *sutra* containing the true teachings of the Buddha for these degenerate times. He did not hesitate to call the followers of Zen devils, to claim that the three Shingon rituals would destroy the land, and to declare that the Pure Land *nembutsu* chanters would go to hell. He called on the Japanese government to outlaw all Buddhist sects but his own.

As you might expect, this got him into a lot of trouble. He was attacked by a mob, arrested, exiled twice, and nearly executed, but, persecution only made his convictions and the convictions of his followers stronger. His movement grew strong and inspired intense patriotism to the ideal of a glorious Japan in which the power of the Buddha and the *kamis* (traditional gods and spirits of the indigenous Shinto religion) would save the nation from corruption and destruction. Today, new religious groups in Japan such as Reiyukai (1925), Soka Gakkai (1937), and Rossho Koseikai (1938) have been inspired by Nichiren's teachings.

The following is a summary translation of *The Establishment of Righteousness and the Security of the Nation* (*Rissho ankoku ron*), written in 1260.

NICHIREN

Righteousness and Security

READING QUESTIONS

1. List the main points of this summary. Do you notice any parallels between what is said here and other religious teachings that you have heard or heard about? If so, what are they?
2. Why do you think some religious groups are led to denounce other groups within their own religious traditions?

A visitor came and lamented, saying, "In recent years there have been strange phenomena in heaven, while famines and plagues have occurred all over the earth, so that it is not uncommon to find not only dead animals but also human corpses on the streets. I rather fancy that death has claimed over half of our population, and every family without exception has been in grief. In this situation, people have been prompted to seek various forms of superhuman help, such as uttering the holy name of the Buddha of the Western Pure Land [Amida], or offer-

From *The Great Asian Religions: An Anthology*, edited by Wing-tsit Chan et al. (New York: Macmillan Publishing Co., Inc., 1969), pp. 281–283. © Copyright 1969, Macmillan Publishing Co., Inc. Reprinted by permission. Endnotes omitted.

ing the incantations of esoteric Buddhism to avoid calamities, or practicing Zen meditation to attain liberation from worldly cares, or worshiping the Shintō kami of heaven and earth at various places to avoid pestilence. The rulers, too, are concerned with the plight of peasants and people, and they have remitted taxes. In spite of such kindness to the people, the famine and the plague are more oppressing, there are beggars everywhere, the dead can be seen everywhere, and more corpses are piled up each day. The sun, moon, and five stars follow their proper courses, Buddhism is respected, and the influence of the ruler is still great, and yet the life has gone out of the world, and religion too is losing its [spiritual] vitality. What is the cause of all this, I wonder?"

The Master of the house said, "I too have been anxious about these things and feel very indignant. Now that we share the same concerns, let us exchange our views on the subject. As far as I can ascertain, on the basis of my reflections and reading of the scriptures, all kinds of calamities have descended on us because the people have violated righteousness and turned to evil. That is why good kami have left the land, and sages have not returned, and thus demons and evil spirits have come."

The visitor said, "I have learned for the first time from you [that our troubles were caused by the departure of good kami and holy men and by the arrival of demons and evil spirits]. I would like to know the scriptural evidences for your view, though."

The Master replied, "Scriptural passages and their evidences are extensive. Among them, let me mention the *Scripture of the Golden Light* (*Konkōmyō kyō*), *Mahāsannipāta sūtra* (*Daishū kyō* or Scripture of great assembly), the *Scripture of the Divine Healer* (*Yakushi kyō*), and the *Scripture of the Benevolent Kings* (*Ninnō kyō*). The contents of these four scriptures are so clear that no one can question their meaning. However, those whose eyes have been blinded and those whose minds have been misguided would rather believe in the false teaching, not realizing the true doctrine. This accounts for the fact that people are discarding the Buddhas and scriptures instead of protecting them. And, since good kami and sages have left this country, evil spirits and heretical teachings are causing various kinds of troubles and calamities."

The visitor, who was now angered by the foregoing answer, stated, "Emperor Ming (r. 58–75) of the Eastern Han dynasty (25–220) was guided by a dream of a golden image and opened the door for the introduction of Buddhism to China. . . . [In our own country, since the time of the noble Prince Shōtoku, 573–621] . . . the sovereign as well as all his subjects have venerated Buddhist statues and scriptures. Our country is dotted with great temples, and scriptures are found in every corner of the land. Seeing all this, on what ground do you say that Buddhism is being neglected and discarded in our country?"

The Master explained to the guest, saying, "You are right in stating that there are many temples, many storehouses for scriptures, and many monks, and that Buddhism has for a long time been venerated and is still venerated. However, the monks are so degraded and lead people astray with flattery, whereas the sovereign as well as his subjects cannot tell good from evil because of their ignorance. . . . [Our present tragic situation is exactly like what was prophesied in the *Scripture of Benevolent Kings*, the *Nirvāṇa Scripture*, and the *Lotus Scripture*.] In this situation, righteousness cannot be restored unless we first remonstrate and correct the evil monks."

The guest, now angrier than ever, asked, "Isn't it the duty of the monarch to influence the nation according to the [great way of] heaven and earth, while the sages bring order by distinguishing right and wrong? Now, the monks of the world are highly respected by the people, [and that implies that these monks are not evil]. Otherwise, why does the wise monarch trust them? Why do you speak so disparagingly of the venerable clergy? Tell me, for instance, who is an evil monk?"

The Master replied, "I shall tell you. During the reign of Emperor Go-Toba (r. 1184–1198) there was a certain monk called Hōnen who wrote a book entitled "Collection of passages" [on the original vow of Amida in which the *nembutsu* is chosen above all ways of achieving rebirth]. In this "Collection," following the false interpretations by Donran (Tan-luan in Chinese, 476–542), Dōshaku (Tao-ch'o, d. 645), and Zendō (Shen-tao, d. 681), which divided Buddhism into the Gate of the Holy Path or the Path of Difficult Practice and the Gate of Pure Land or the Path of Easy Practice, [Hōnen classified all teachings except that of Pure Land into the former category.] Thus, he urged people to give up, close, discard, or destroy 637 scriptures, 2,883 sections in all, including those of the Lotus, the esoteric, and all the Mahāyāna teachings taught during the life of the Buddha, all other Buddhas and bodhisattvas and heavenly beings. . . . Hōnen's teaching is counter to the [original] vow of Amida, who pledged to save all beings except those who commit the Five Great Sins and those who falsely accuse the True Law, as clearly stated in the three Pure Land Scriptures from which Hōnen presumably derived his own views. However, in this period of Latter End of Law there is no holy man; rather, [many clergy] have forgotten the right path and lead others to distorted faith instead of helping them to see things clearly. [Under the influence of Hōnen's writing, people] venerate only Amida, the Buddha of the Western Pure Land, for-

getting even the supreme Buddha Śākyamuni. No wonder temples other than those of Amida are neglected, and offerings are given only to the priests of the *nembutsu* sect. Since the main traditions of Buddhism, such as the most comprehensive and central vehicle of the Lotus (the Tendai School), are neglected in favor of the Pure Land teaching, which lies at the border of historic Buddhism, it is understandable that the good kami are angry and evil spirits take advantage of the situation. Thus, the foremost task before us is not to offer various kinds of prayers to ward off famine and pestilence, but to forbid the very evil which is the cause of all these troubles."

The visitor, now looking a little more pleasant, said, "I now realize [Hōnen's mistakes in renouncing all other scriptures, and you have explained how Hōnen's writing has been the cause of all our troubles]. Now, everyone, from the sovereign to all his subjects, are concerned with the peace of the land. If the nation declines and the people vanish, who will be left to venerate Buddha and his Law? Thus, I feel that we must first pray for the security of the nation before thinking about Buddhism, and would like to know the means of eliminating the troubles which are now confronting the nation."

The Master replied, "Being stupid by nature, I cannot offer any clever solution of my own. However, based on the scriptures, I am convinced that the nation will attain peace and prosperity if those who slander the True Law are rejected and those who preach the true doctrine are given important positions. Concretely, if we want the security of the nation, we must first eliminate the false teaching [of Hōnen]. All the scriptures consider the act of slandering the Law a grave sin. Is it not foolish for one to be caught by the net of this grave sin and eventually descend into the flame of hell? Let me exhort you to be converted straightway to the true teaching of the Lotus, and when people follow the teaching of the Lotus, the Three Worlds and the ten regions will be transformed into the Buddha Land, and be it noted that the Buddha Land will never be destroyed by any calamity or trouble. When the nation thus attains security, we will all attain the safety of the body and peace of mind. You should believe and respect this statement." (*Nihon Bukkyō shisō shiryōshū* [Collection of source materials on the history of Japanese Buddhist thought], pp. 537–52)

7.6 VAJRAYANA OR TANTRIC BUDDHISM IN TIBET

Tantric Buddhism is based on a group of texts called **tantras** as distinguished from *sutras*. It began in India and is sometimes treated as an outgrowth of the Mahayana tradition. However, it is sufficiently distinct to be regarded as a "vehicle" in itself along with Nikaya (Hinayana) and Mahayana. As such it is often called the **Vajrayana,** or "Diamond Vehicle." Introduced to Tibet in the seventh century, it transformed Tibetan culture and political life. According to legend, the Tibetan king was converted to Buddhism by two princesses—one from China and one from Nepal—whom he married as the result of political treaties.

Tantric Buddhism took seriously the Madhyamika teaching of the identity of *nirvana* and *samsara* (see Reading 7.4.3). If *samsara* is truly *nirvana*, then at least two important things follow. First, polar opposites in thought are, in reality, unified; second, anything could become a means to enlightenment. Followers of "left-handed" tantrism engaged in meat-eating, wine-drinking, and ritualized sexual intercourse along with other behaviors forbidden to monks in order to symbolize the union of opposites and the freedom that enlightenment brings. Tantrism of the "right-handed" form took a less transgressive approach.

In general, Vajrayana urged people to identify with the Buddha in body, speech, and mind. If one could do so successfully, enlightenment was possible in this lifetime. One did not have to live for eons through thousands of reincarnations seeking *nirvana*. The Vajrayana commonly came to be known as the "shortcut" to enlightenment and developed elaborate visualization techniques that employ ***mandalas*** (elaborate structures symbolizing the unity of opposites) and figures of *buddhas* and *bodhisattvas*. During *mandala* meditation, one can merge with the sacred symbols and thereby realize one's Buddha-Nature.

7.6.1 The Tibetan Book of the Dead

In addition to the story of princesses from China and Nepal converting the king to Buddhism, there is the story that Vajrayana Buddhism was brought to Tibet by an Indian monk named Padmasambhava, now revered as the Guru Rimpoche ("precious teacher"). The indigenous religion of Tibet is known as Bon ("truth"), and one of its main ritual objectives was the safe conduct of the souls of the dead to an afterlife. Bon religion combined and interacted with Buddhism leaving its imprint in various ways. Among them are Buddhist shamanistic practices, including trance dances, oracular utterances, possession by gods and goddesses, and healing.

Another influence of the Bon concern with life after death is found in a special body of literature containing instructions to both the dead and the living about afterlife states. These instructions are the *Bardo Thodal (Liberation by Hearing on the After-Death Plane),* better known as the *Tibetan Book of the Dead.* These instructions are read aloud to the dying in order to help them achieve liberation during the three stages of the *bardo* state between death and rebirth.

During the first stage (*chikhai bardo*), after a period of unconsciousness, one sees a colorless bright light. If this light is recognized as the Dharma Body of the Buddha, one will experience *nirvana*. If not (and most of us do not because of our bad *karma*), one enters the *chonyid bardo* (second stage) where both kind and wrathful deities are met. Once again there is a chance for *nirvana*, but if it is missed, the *sidpa bardo* (third stage) is entered during which one experiences judgment according to one's *karma* followed by rebirth. ·

⟨✦⟩

Bardo Thodal

READING QUESTIONS

1. How should one conceive the spirit of enlightenment at death?
2. What is the clear light?
3. Why do you think there are different instructions about the clear light for a spiritual teacher?
4. What are the six kinds of "between"?
5. What causes one to miss the chances at liberation?
6. Why is it important to recognize the "sounds, lights, and rays" as one's own perceptions?

Hey, noble one! Now you have arrived at so-called "death," so you should conduct yourself according to your conception of the spirit of enlightenment. You should conceive your spirit of enlightenment thus: "Alas! I have arrived at the time of death. From now, relying on this death, I will develop my spirit only by contemplating the conception of the spirit of enlightenment of love and compassion. For the sake of the whole space-full of beings, I must attain perfect Buddhahood." And especially you should think, "Now for the sake of all beings, I will recognize the death clear light as the Body of Truth. Within its experience, I will attain the supreme accomplishment of the Great Seal, and I will accomplish the purposes of all beings. If I don't attain that, then in the time of the between, I will recognize it as the between. I will realize that between as the Great Seal Body of Integration, and I will accomplish the purposes of all the infinite space-full of beings by manifesting whatsoever is needed to tame whomsoever." Thus never losing the willpower of that spiritual conception, you should remember the experience of whatever instructions you have previously practiced.

This should be clearly enunciated with the lips near the ear. In this way, not allowing even an instant's distraction, you should pray for the deceased to accomplish this practice.

Then, when the outer breath has ceased, you should press the sleep channels (at the neck) forcefully and say the following; first, to a spiritual teacher or spiritual superior:

Venerable teacher! Right now the objective clear light dawns for you. Recognize it! Please incorporate it within your experience.

You should describe it to all others as follows:

Hey, noble one, you named So-and-so, listen here! Now the pure clear light of reality dawns for you. Recognize it! Hey, noble one, this, your present conscious natural clear void awareness, this presence in clear voidness without any objectivity of substance, sign, of color—just this is the reality, the Mother, Buddha All-around Goodness! And this, your conscious awareness natural voidness, not succumbing to a false annihilative voidness, just your own conscious awareness, unceasing, bright, distinct, and vibrant—just this awareness is the Father, Buddha All-around Goodness! Just this presence of the indivisibility of your awareness's natural insubstantial voidness and the vibrant bright presence of your conscious awareness—just this is the Buddha Body of Truth. Your awareness thus abides in this vast mass of light of clarity-void indivisible. You are free of birth or death—just this is the Buddha Changeless Light. It is enough just to recognize this. Recognizing this your own conscious awareness's purity nature as the Buddha, yourself beholding your own awareness—that is to dwell in the inner realization of all Buddhas. . . .

THE MILD DEITY
REALITY BETWEEN

. . . If the deceased is still not liberated, it is then called the "third between phase." The reality between dawns. This becomes the third between, in which the evolutionary hallucinations dawn. Therefore it is crucial to read this great orientation to the reality between at that time, with its very great power and benefits. At that time, her loved ones will weep and wail, her share of food is no longer served, her clothes are stripped off, her bed is broken. She can see them, but they cannot see her. She can hear them calling her, but they cannot hear when she calls them. So she must depart, her heart sinking in despair. Perceptions arise of sounds, lights, and rays, and she feels faint with fear, terror, and panic. Then you must use this great description of the reality between. You should call the deceased by name, and clearly and distinctly say as follows:

Hey, noble one! Listen unwavering with intense concentration! There are six kinds of between: the natural life between, the dream between, the contemplation between, the death-point between, the reality between, and the emergent existence between.

Hey, noble one, three betweens will dawn for you: the death-point between, the reality between, and the existence between will dawn. Until yesterday, in the death-point between, the reality clear light dawned. But you did not recognize it, so you had to wander here. Now the reality between and the existence between will dawn for you. As I describe them, you must recognize them without fail.

Hey, noble one! Now you have arrived at what is called "death." You are going from this world to the beyond. You are not alone; it happens to everyone. You must not indulge in attachment and insistence on this life. Though you are attached and you insist, you have no power to stay, you will not avoid wandering in the life cycle. Do not lust! Do not cling! Be mindful of the Three Jewels!

Hey, noble child! Whatever terrifying visions of the reality between may dawn upon you, you should not forget the following words. You must proceed remembering in your mind the meaning of these words. Therein lies the key of recognition.

Hey! Now when the reality between dawns upon me,
I will let go of the hallucinations of instinctive terror,
Enter the recognition of all objects as my mind's own
* visions,*
and understand this as the pattern of perception in the
* between;*

*Come to this moment, arrived at this most critical
  cessation,
I will not fear my own visions of deities mild and
  fierce!* . . .

You should proceed clearly saying this verse aloud and remembering its meaning. Do not forget this, as it is the key to recognizing whatever terrifying visions dawn as certainly being your own perceptions.

Hey, noble one! At this time when your mind and body are parting ways, pure reality manifests in subtle, dazzling visions, vividly experienced, naturally frightening and worrisome, shimmering like a mirage on the plains in autumn. Do not fear them. Do not be terrified! Do not panic! You have what is called an "instinctual mental body," not a material, flesh and blood body. Thus whatever sounds, lights, and rays may come at you, they cannot hurt you. You cannot die. It is enough just for you to recognize them as your own perceptions. Understand that this is the between.

Hey, noble one! If you don't recognize them as your own perceptions in this way—whatever other meditations and achievements you may have experienced in the human world, if you did not meet this particular instruction—the lights will frighten you, the sounds will panic you, the rays will terrify you. If you don't know the key of this instruction, you will not recognize the sounds, lights, and rays, and you will wander in the life cycle. . . .

7.6.2 Pilgrimage to Mount Kailasa

Going on pilgrimages to sacred sites is a common practice in many religions including Buddhism. From Sri Lanka to Japan, Buddhist sacred sites dot the landscape and attract pilgrims. Pilgrimage is widely regarded as a meritorious practice as well as an act of devotion that will contribute to one's spiritual development.

In Tibet, Mount Kailasa, a peak in the western Himalayas that some Tibetans believe is at the center of the world, is a sacred pilgrimage site second only to Lhasa, the holy city of Tibet. Mount Kailasa is called Gang Rimpoche and is associated with Milarepa, an eleventh-century saint. Pilgrims journey hundreds of miles, many on foot, to reach this mountain. Once there, the devotees go around Gang Rimpoche in a clockwise direction, called circumambulation, which is a common act of veneration. They also engage in prostration (placing one's body full length on the ground), and some use successive grand prostrations to travel all the way around Gang Rimpoche, body length by body length.

The following description is by a Japanese sociologist, Kazuhiko Tamamura, who visited Gang Rimpoche in 1985.

❧

KAZUHIKO TAMAMURA

Seizan Junrei

READING QUESTIONS

1. Make a list of as many different factors as you can think of that would motivate people to undertake this pilgrimage.
2. How might such pilgrimages contribute to the development of spiritual qualities?

What is known as the Gang Rimpoche [Mount Kailāsa] pilgrimage involves circumambulating the circumference of the sacred peak any number of times. . . . The pilgrims, coming from various directions, "appear" in Tarchen, the village near the base of the mountain [which serves as the takeoff point for the circumambulation path]. The word "appear" is entirely appropriate, for these people pay no attention to existing roads and simply take the shortest route. Some of them arrive, driving several dozen sheep on which they have loaded their baggage; some ride on horseback or in trucks or tractors; but the vast majority of them come on foot, their belongings on their back neatly packed in panniers made of willow branches. They carry staffs or tent poles in their hands in order to drive off ferocious dogs.

Except for those pilgrims travelling alone or in very small groups, most of the parties bring with them tents of white cotton cloth. As soon as they arrive in Tarchen, they set up these tents . . . and begin searching for fuel, yak dung, which they collect and carry in the folds of their aprons or shepherds' robes.

The fatigue of the long journey they have made to reach Tarchen is great [some have come on foot from Eastern Tibet as much as three thousand kilometers

From *Experience of Buddhism*, 1st ed., by J. S. Strong, pp. 267, 270. Copyright © 1995 Wadsworth. Reprinted by permission of Wadsworth Publishing, a division of International Thomson Publishing. Fax 800-730-2215. Translated from Kazuhiko Tamamura's *Seizan Junrei* (Tokyo: Yama to Keikoku Sha, 1987), pp. 41, 147.

away], but the very next day after their arrival, they set out on the Gang Rimpoche pilgrimage circuit with eager anticipation. Their fervent desire to make the circuit of the holy mountain as soon as possible prompts them to take to the road again. . . .

The pilgrimage route around Gang Rimpoche is 52 kilometers long. If you were to extend your arms in front of you to make a circle corresponding to the route, Tarchen would be where your head is, and Gang Rimpoche itself would tower majestically from a spot just inside of the place where the tips of your fingers meet. The pilgrimage route thus leaves from Tarchen, at an altitude of 4,700 meters, follows the La Chu River upstream (corresponding to your left arm), crosses the Dorma Pass at 5,600 meters [located roughly where your right hand would be], and returns to Tarchen along a course that follows the Son Chu River (your right arm).

Tibetans make this circumambulation in one fourteen-hour day. If they were to spend the night on the road, they would require a good deal of baggage including their tents, so they choose to go all out and make the circuit in a day. It is also considered to be more meritorious to make the trip in a single day. . . . They make the circumambulation with the same joy and high spirits that we associate with going on a picnic, and return to Tarchen in the evening. Then, after resting in Tarchen for a day or two, they once again make the circuit. In this way, they go around the sacred mountain many times [13 and 26 times are popular numbers], and so end up staying in Tarchen for quite a long while. . . .

A Note on Grand Prostrations

The special feature of the Tibetan Buddhists' grand prostration is the repetition with which it is performed. In front of a temple, around a temple, facing holy ground, around holy ground, and, at times, on the way to temples and holy areas, the grand prostration is repeated constantly time and again. I could not help feeling a sense of awe at the rigorous and strenuous nature of the practice of Tibetan Buddhists which involved completing the 52 kilometer circuit around Gang Rimpoche by making grand prostrations. . . .

In Tibetan, this type of practice is called "kyang chak." "Kyang" means "to extend the body," and "chak" means "to worship." First, one holds one's two hands together on top of one's head, and one prays: "May the sins that I have committed up until now with this body be cleansed." Then one lowers the hands cupping them in front of one's face, and one says: "May the sins that

I have committed up until now with this mouth be cleansed." Then one lowers one's hands further to chest level and says: "May the sins that I have committed up until now with this mind be cleansed." Then one falls to one's knees, forcefully extends the body forward, reaching the hands out as far as possible and bringing the palms together while flat on one's face. Then, getting up, one advances to the point to which one's hands extended, and one repeats the whole thing again. Each time, one can only move the distance one has measured out with one's body. Thus the ground that can be covered in a day is not very great. They say that it takes two weeks to cover the 52 kilometers around Gang Rimpoche by this method. . . . In the course of the circuit, any number of fords across rivers need to be made, but the pilgrims keep up their grand prostrations right across the stones in the stream. . . .

7.6.3 The White Lotus

Vajrayana Buddhism in Tibet is divided into four major groups: Karma-pa, Kagyu-pa, Sakya-pa, and Geluga-pa. The Karma-pa (the ancients) trace their line back to Padmasambhava and base their doctrines on tantric texts. There are strong Bon elements in this line, and other schools do not always accept them.

The Kagyu-pa began in the eleventh century with Marpa (1012–1096), who presumably learned from the Indian master Naropa (956–1040). The Kagyu-pa place emphasis on certain yogic practices such as *tum-mo* (generating inner body heat) and the quick path to enlightenment. Milarepa, one of the great saints of Tibet, is one of Marpa's disciples.

The Sakya-pa are most closely associated with the principality of Sakya and emphasize tantric practices that focus attention on the universal consciousness within.

Perhaps the best-known tradition, the Geluga-pa began as a reform movement started by the great scholar Tsongkha-pa (1357–1419), who emphasized learning, discipline, and celibacy (in contrast to the Karma-pa and Kagyu-pa, who allow monks to marry). In the seventeenth century, the head of the Geluga-pa, the fifth **Dalai Lama,** was able to consolidate political power and a succession of Dalai Lamas or their regents continued to rule Tibet until 1959.

Since the 1959 takeover of Tibet by the Chinese, the present Dalai Lama, who was born in 1935, has lived in exile. He has traveled the world teaching, supporting his people, and seeking freedom for Tibet. He was awarded the Nobel Peace Prize in 1989. He is, as he likes to say, "a simple Buddhist monk" whose love of peace and deep spirituality have impressed many. Among his many books is *Freedom in Exile*, from which the following selection is taken.

☙❧

THE DALAI LAMA

Freedom in Exile

READING QUESTIONS

1. According to the Dalai Lama, what is the fundamental precept of Buddhism, and how do the theories of consciousness and rebirth derive from this precept?
2. Who is this Dalai Lama, and how was he found?
3. How do you think the Dalai Lama's Buddhism influenced his impressions of the West?
4. While the Dalai Lama is traveling abroad, what approach does he take when addressing groups of people?
5. What is the Dalai Lama's attitude toward religions other than Buddhism?
6. How does the Dalai Lama answer the question "What is religion?"?
7. What impresses you most about the Dalai Lama's religious practice? Why?

Before going on to tell about my discovery as Dalai Lama, I must first say something about Buddhism and its history in Tibet. The founder of Buddhism was an historical figure, Siddhartha, who came to be recognized as the Buddha Shakyamuni. He was born more than 2,500 years ago. His teachings, now known as the *Dharma*, or Buddhism, were introduced to Tibet during the fourth century A.D. They took several centuries to supplant the native Bon religion and become fully established, but eventually the country was so thoroughly converted that Buddhist principles governed all society, at every level. And whilst Tibetans are by nature quite aggressive people and quite warlike, their increasing interest in religious practice was a major factor in bringing about the country's isolation. Before then, Tibet

Pages 9–12, 199–207 from *Freedom in Exile: The Autobiography of the Dalai Lama* by Tenzin Gyatso. Copyright © 1990 by Tenzin Gyatso, His Holiness, the Fourteenth Dalai Lama of Tibet. Reprinted by permission of HarperCollins Publishers, Inc.

possessed a vast empire, which dominated Central Asia with territories covering large parts of northern India, Nepal and Bhutan in the south. It also included much Chinese territory. In 763 A.D., Tibetan forces actually captured the Chinese capital, where they extracted promises of tribute and other concessions. However, as Tibetans' enthusiasm for Buddhism increased, so Tibet's relations with her neighbours became of a spiritual rather than a political nature. This was especially true of China, where a "priest-patron" relationship developed. The Manchu Emperors, who were Buddhists, referred to the Dalai Lama as "King of Expounding Buddhism."

The fundamental precept of Buddhism is Interdependence or the Law of Cause and Effect. This simply states that everything which an individual being experiences is derived through action from motivation. Motivation is thus the root of both action and experience. From this understanding are derived the Buddhist theories of consciousness and rebirth.

The first holds that, because cause gives rise to effect which in turn becomes the cause of further effect, consciousness must be continual. It flows on and on, gathering experiences and impressions from one moment to the next. At the point of physical death, it follows that a being's consciousness contains an imprint of all these past experiences and impressions, and the actions which preceded them. This is known as *karma*, which means "action." It is thus consciousness, with its attendant *karma*, which then becomes "reborn" in a new body— animal, human or divine.

So, to give a simple example, a person who has spent his or her life mistreating animals could quite easily be reborn in the next life as a dog belonging to someone who is unkind to animals. Similarly, meritorious conduct in this life will assist in a favourable rebirth in the next.

Buddhists further believe that because the basic nature of consciousness is neutral, it is possible to escape from the unending cycle of birth, suffering, death and rebirth that life inevitably entails, but only when all negative *karma* has been eliminated along with all worldly attachments. When this point is reached, the consciousness in question is believed to attain first liberation and then ultimately Buddhahood. However, according to Buddhism in the Tibetan tradition, a being that achieves Buddhahood, although freed from *Samsara*, the "wheel of suffering," as the phenomenon of existence is known, will continue to return to work for the benefit of all other sentient beings until such time as each one is similarly liberated.

Now in my own case, I am held to be the reincarnation of each of the previous thirteen Dalai Lamas of Tibet (the first having been born in 1351 A.D.), who are in turn considered to be manifestations of Avalokiteshvara, or Chenrezig, Bodhisattva of Compassion, holder of the White Lotus. Thus I am believed also to be a manifestation of Chenrezig, in fact the seventy-fourth in a lineage that can be traced back to a Brahmin boy who lived in the time of Buddha Shakyamuni. I am often asked whether I truly believe this. The answer is not simple to give. But as a fifty-six year old, when I consider my experiences during this present life, and given my Buddhist beliefs, I have no difficulty accepting that I am spiritually connected both to the thirteen previous Dalai Lamas, to Chenrezig and to the Buddha himself.

When I was not quite three years old, a search party that had been sent out by the Government to find the new incarnation of the Dalai Lama arrived at Kumbum monastery. It had been led there by a number of signs. One of these concerned the embalmed body of my predecessor, Thupten Gyatso, the Thirteenth Dalai Lama, who had died aged fifty-seven in 1933. During its period of sitting in state, the head was discovered to have turned from facing south to north-east. Shortly after that the Regent, himself a senior lama, had a vision. Looking into the waters of the sacred lake, Lhamoi Lhatso, in southern Tibet, he clearly saw the Tibetan letters *Ah*, *Ka* and *Ma* float into view. These were followed by the image of a three-storeyed monastery with a turquoise and gold roof and a path running from it to a hill. Finally, he saw a small house with strangely shaped guttering. He was sure that the letter *Ah* referred to Amdo, the north-eastern province, so it was there that the search party was sent.

By the time they reached Kumbum, the members of the search party felt that they were on the right track. It seemed likely that if the letter *Ah* referred to Amdo, then *Ka* must indicate the monastery at Kumbum—which was indeed three storeyed and turquoise roofed. They now only needed to locate a hill and a house with peculiar guttering. So they began to search the neighbouring villages. When they saw the gnarled branches of juniper wood on the roof of my parents' house, they were certain that the new Dalai Lama would not be far away. Nevertheless, rather than reveal the purpose of their visit, the group asked only to stay the night. The leader of the party, Kewtsang Rinpoché, then pretended to be a servant and spent much of the evening observing and playing with the youngest child in the house.

The child recognised him and called out "Sera Lama, Sera Lama." Sera was Kewtsang Rinpoché's monastery. Next day they left—only to return a few days later as a formal deputation. This time they brought with them a number of things that had belonged to my predecessor, together with several similar items that did not. In every case, the infant correctly identified those belonging to

the Thirteenth Dalai Lama saying, "It's mine. It's mine." This more or less convinced the search party that they had found the new incarnation. However, there was another candidate to be seen before a final decision could be reached. But it was not long before the boy from Taktser was acknowledged to be the new Dalai Lama. I was that child.

Needless to say, I do not remember very much of these events. I was too small. My only real recollection is of a man with piercing eyes. These turned out to belong to a man named Kenrap Tenzin, who became my Master of the Robes and later taught me to write.

As soon as the search party had concluded that the child from Taktser was the true incarnation of the Dalai Lama, word was sent back to Lhasa informing the Regent. It would be several months before official confirmation was received. Until then, I was to remain at home. In the meantime, Ma Pu-feng, the local Governor, began to make trouble. But eventually I was taken by my parents to Kumbum monastery, where I was installed in a ceremony that took place at dawn. I remember this fact particularly as I was surprised to be woken and dressed before the sun had risen. I also remember being seated on a throne. . . .

Overall I have found much that is impressive about western society. In particular, I admire its energy and creativity and hunger for knowledge. On the other hand, a number of things about the western way of life cause me concern. One thing I have noticed is an inclination for people to think in terms of "black and white" and "either, or," which ignores the fact of interdependence and relativity. They have a tendency to lose sight of the grey areas which inevitably exist between two points of view.

Another observation is that there are a lot of people in the West who live very comfortably in large cities, but virtually isolated from the broad mass of humanity. I find this very strange—that under the circumstance of such material well-being and with thousands of brothers and sisters for neighbours, so many people appear able to show their true feelings only to their cats and dogs. This indicates a lack of spiritual values, I feel. Part of the problem here is perhaps the intense competitiveness of life in these countries, which seems to breed fear and a deep sense of insecurity.

For me, this sense of alienation is symbolised by something I once saw at the home of a very rich man whose guest I was on one of my trips abroad. It was a very large private house, obviously designed expressly for convenience and comfort, and fitted with every kind of appliance. However, when I went into the bathroom, I could not help noticing two large bottles of pills on the shelf above the hand basin. One contained tranquillisers, the other sleeping pills. This was proof, too, that material prosperity alone cannot bring about lasting happiness.

As I have already said, I usually go abroad at the invitation of others. Very often, I am also asked to address groups of people. When this happens, my approach is threefold. Firstly, as a human being, I talk about what I have termed Universal Responsibility. By this I mean the responsibility that we all have for each other and for all sentient beings and also for all of Nature.

Secondly, as a Buddhist monk I try to contribute what I can towards better harmony and understanding between different religions. As I have said, it is my firm belief that all religions aim at making people better human beings and that, despite philosophical differences, some of them fundamental, they all aim at helping humanity to find happiness. This does not mean that I advocate any sort of world religion or "super religion." Rather, I look on religion as medicine. For different complaints, doctors will prescribe different remedies. Therefore, because not everyone's spiritual "illness" is the same, different spiritual medicines are required.

Finally, as a Tibetan, and furthermore as the Dalai Lama, I talk about my own country, people and culture whenever anyone shows interest in these matters. However, although I am greatly encouraged when people do show concern for my homeland and my suffering fellow countrymen and women in occupied Tibet, and although it gives fuel to my determination to continue the fight for justice, I do not consider those who support our cause to be "pro-Tibet." Instead, I consider them to be pro-Justice.

One of the things that I have noticed whilst travelling is the amount of interest shown by young people in the things that I talk about. This enthusiasm could, I suppose, be due to the fact that my insistence on absolute informality appeals to them. For my own part, I greatly value exchanges with younger audiences. They ask all sorts of questions concerning everything from the Buddhist theory of Emptiness, through my ideas about cosmology and modern physics, to sex and morality. Those questions which are unexpected and complicated are the ones I appreciate most. They can help me a great deal as I am compelled to take an interest in something that might not otherwise have occurred to me. It becomes a bit like debating.

Another observation is that many of the people I talk to, especially in the West, have a highly sceptical cast of mind. This can be very positive, I feel, but with the proviso that it is used as the basis for further enquiry. . . .

Whenever I go abroad, I try to contact as many other religious practitioners as possible, with a view to fostering inter-faith dialogue. On one of my foreign visits, I met some Christians with a similar desire. This led to a monastic exchange whereby for a few weeks some Tibetan monks went to a Christian monastery, while a similar number of Christian monks came out to India. It proved to be an extremely useful exercise for both parties. In particular, it enabled us to gain a deeper understanding of other people's way of thinking.

Amongst the many religious personalities that I have met, I will single out a few notable Christians (though I should add that I have been fortunate enough to meet wonderful people from a great variety of different religious backgrounds). The present Pope is a man I hold in high regard. To begin with, our somewhat similar backgrounds give us an immediate common ground. The first time we met, he struck me as a very practical sort of person, very broad-minded and open. I have no doubt that he is a great spiritual leader. Any man who can call out "Brother" to his would-be assassin, as Pope John Paul did, must be a highly evolved spiritual practitioner.

Mother Teresa, whom I met at Delhi airport on my way back from a conference at Oxford, England, during 1988 (which she had also attended), is someone for whom I have the deepest respect. I was at once struck by her demeanour of absolute humility. From the Buddhist point of view she could be considered to be a Bodhisattva.

Another person whom I think of as a highly evolved spiritual master is a Catholic monk I met at his hermitage near Monserrat in Spain. He had spent a great many years there, just like an eastern sage, surviving off nothing more than bread and water and a little tea. He spoke very little English—even less than me—but from his eyes I could see that I was in the presence of an extraordinary person, a true practitioner of religion. When I asked him what his meditations were about, he answered simply, "Love." Since then, I have always thought of him as a modern Milarepa, after the Tibetan master of that name who spent much of his life hidden away in a cave, meditating and composing spiritual verses.

One religious leader with whom I have had several good conversations is the outgoing Archbishop of Canterbury, Dr. Robert Runcie (whose courageous emissary, Terry Waite, I always remember in my prayers). We share the view that religion and politics do mix and both agree that it is the clear duty of religion to serve humanity, that it must not ignore reality. It is not sufficient for religious people to be involved with prayer. Rather, they are morally obliged to contribute all they can to solving the world's problems. . . .

Religion should never become a source of conflict, a further factor of division within the human community.

For my own part, I have even, on the basis of my deep respect for the contribution that other faiths can make towards human happiness, participated in the ceremonies of other religions. And, following the example of a great many Tibetan lamas both ancient and modern, I continue to take teachings from as many different traditions as possible. For whilst it is true that some schools of thought felt it desirable for a practitioner to stay within his or her own tradition, people have always been free to do as they think fit. Furthermore, Tibetan society has always been highly tolerant of other people's beliefs. Not only was there a flourishing Muslim community in Tibet, but also there were a number of Christian missions which were admitted without hindrance. I am therefore firmly in favour of a liberal approach. Sectarianism is poison. . . .

What is religion? As far as I am concerned, any deed done with good motivation is a religious act. On the other hand, a gathering of people in a temple or church who do not have good motivation are not performing a religious act when they pray together. . . .

As for my own religious practice, I try to live my life pursuing what I call the Bodhisattva ideal. According to Buddhist thought, a Bodhisattva is someone on the path to Buddhahood who dedicates themselves entirely to helping all other sentient beings towards release from suffering. The word Bodhisattva can best be understood by translating the *Bodhi* and *Sattva* separately: *Bodhi* means the understanding or wisdom of the ultimate nature of reality, and a *Sattva* is someone who is motivated by universal compassion. The Bodhisattva ideal is thus the aspiration to practise infinite compassion with infinite wisdom. As a means of helping myself in this quest, I choose to be a Buddhist monk. There are 253 rules of Tibetan monasticism (364 for nuns) and by observing them as closely as I can, I free myself from many of the distractions and worries of life. Some of these rules mainly deal with etiquette, such as the physical distance a monk should walk behind the abbot of his monastery; others are concerned with behaviour. The four root vows concern simple prohibitions: namely that a monk must not kill, steal, or lie about his spiritual attainment. He must also be celibate. If he breaks any one of these, he is no longer a monk.

I am sometimes asked whether this vow of celibacy is really desirable and indeed whether it is really possible. Suffice to say that its practice is not simply a matter of suppressing sexual desires. On the contrary, it is necessary fully to accept the existence of these desires and to transcend them by the power of reasoning. When suc-

cessful, the result on the mind can be very beneficial. The trouble with sexual desire is that it is a blind desire. To say "I want to have sex with this person" is to express a desire which is not intellectually directed in the way that "I want to eradicate poverty in the world" is an intellectually directed desire. Furthermore, the gratification of sexual desire can only ever give temporary satisfaction. Thus as Nagarjuna, the great Indian scholar, said:

When you have an itch, you scratch.
But not to itch at all
Is better than any amount of scratching.

Regarding my actual daily practice, I spend, at the very least, five and a half hours per day in prayer, meditation, and study. On top of this, I also pray whenever I can during odd moments of the day, for example over meals and whilst travelling. In this last case, I have three main reasons for doing so: firstly, it contributes towards fulfilment of my daily duty; secondly, it helps to pass the time productively; thirdly, it assuages fear! More seriously though, as a Buddhist, I see no distinction between religious practice and daily life. Religious practice is a twenty-four-hour occupation. In fact, there are prayers prescribed for every activity from waking to washing, eating and even sleeping. For Tantric practitioners, those exercises which are undertaken during deep sleep and in the dream state are the most important preparation for death.

However, for myself, early morning is the best time for practice. The mind is at its freshest and sharpest then. I therefore get up at around four o'clock. On waking, I begin the day with the recitation of *mantras*. I then drink hot water and take my medicine before making prostrations in salutation of the Buddhas for about half an hour. The purpose of this is twofold. Firstly, it increases one's own merit (assuming proper motivation) and secondly, it is good exercise. After my prostrations, I wash—saying prayers as I do so. Then I generally go outside for a walk, during which I make further recitations, until breakfast at around 5:15 A.M. I allow about half an hour for this meal (which is quite substantial) and whilst eating read scriptures.

From 5:45 A.M. until around 8:00 A.M., I meditate, pausing only to listen to the 6:30 news bulletin of the BBC World Service. Then, from 8:00 A.M. until noon, I study Buddhist philosophy. Between then and lunch at 12:30, I might read either official papers or newspapers, but during the meal itself I again read scripture. At 1:00 P.M., I go to my office, where I deal with government and other matters and give audiences until 5:00 P.M. This is followed by another short period of prayer and meditation as soon as I get back home. If there is any-thing worthwhile on television, I watch it now before having tea at 6:00 P.M. Finally, after tea, during which I read scripture once more, I say prayers until 8:30 or 9:00 P.M., when I go to bed. Then follows very sound sleep.

Of course, there are variations to this routine. Some-times during the morning I will participate in a *puja* or, in the afternoon, I will deliver a teaching. But, all the same, I very rarely have to modify my daily practice—that is my morning and evening prayers and meditation.

The rationale behind this practice is quite simple. During the first part of it when I make prostrations, I am "taking refuge" in the Buddha, the *Dharma*, and the *Sangha*. The next stage is to develop *Bodhichitta* or a Good Heart. This is done firstly by recognising the impermanence of all things and secondly by realising the true nature of being which is suffering. On the ba-sis of these two considerations, it is possible to generate altruism.

To engender altruism, or compassion, in myself, I practise certain mental exercises which promote love towards all sentient beings, including especially my so-called enemies. For example, I remind myself that it is the actions of human beings rather than human beings themselves that make them my enemy. Given a change of behaviour, that same person could easily become a good friend.

The remainder of my meditation is concerned with *Sunya* or Emptiness, during which I concentrate on the most subtle meaning of Interdependence. Part of this practice involves what is termed "deity yoga," *lhāi naljor*, during which I use different *mandalas* to visualise myself as a succession of different "deities." (This should not, however, be taken to imply belief in independent exter-nal beings.) In so doing, I focus my mind to the point where it is no longer preoccupied with the data produced by the senses. This is not a trance, as my mind remains fully alert; rather it is an exercise in pure consciousness. What exactly I mean by this is hard to explain: just as it is difficult for a scientist to explain in words what is meant by the term "space-time." Neither language nor every-day experience can really communicate the mean-ing experience of "pure mind." Suffice to say that it is not an easy practice. It takes many years to master.

One important aspect of my daily practice is its con-cern with the idea of death. To my mind, there are two things that, in life, you can do about death. Either you can choose to ignore it, in which case you may have some success in making the idea of it go away for a lim-ited period of time, or you can confront the prospect of your own death and try to analyse it and, in so doing, try

to minimise some of the inevitable suffering that it causes. Neither way can you actually overcome it. How-ever, as a Buddhist, I view death as a normal process of life, I accept it as a reality that will occur while I am in *Samsara*. Knowing that I cannot escape it, I see no point in worrying about it. I hold the view that death is rather like changing one's clothes when they are torn and old. It is not an end in itself. Yet death is unpredictable—you do not know when and how it will take place. So it is only sensible to take certain precautions before it actu-ally happens. . . .

CONTEMPORARY SCHOLARSHIP

The contemporary scholarship on Buddhism by Bud-dhists and non-Buddhists alike is immense. Scholar-ship by Buddhists has sometimes been questioned on the grounds that it reflects too much of a sympathetic bias. It compromises, some claim, that critical dis-tance that only an outsider can bring.

It is necessary to recognize that both the insider and the outsider bring perspectives (and in that sense biases) to their scholarship. Perspectives cannot be avoided, but they can be acknowledged and their dis-tinct advantages (and disadvantages) recognized. If one automatically questions the quality of all schol-arship done from an insider's viewpoint, then one should also automatically question the quality of all scholarship done from an outsider's viewpoint.

What follows are two selections written by schol-ars who are also followers of Buddhist traditions. Both combine the insider's understanding with the rigors of scholarly distance. The first selection is by D. T. Suzuki, a Japanese scholar and follower of Zen Buddhism, who helped make that type of Buddhism popular in the United States and Europe. The second selection is by Rita M. Gross, an American scholar of comparative religions, a feminist, and a follower of Vajrayana Buddhism.

7.7 SATORI

In 1927, Daisetz Teitaro Suzuki (1870–1966), author of the next selection, awakened the interest of Amer-icans and Europeans to the world of Zen Buddhism with his book *Essays in Zen Buddhism*. D. T. Suzuki was a professor of Buddhist philosophy at Otani University in Kyoto, Japan, and he took his training in Zen meditation at the Zen monastery in Kamakura. He was also a visiting professor at many universities, including Columbia University in New York where he became particularly interested in the comparative study of mystical experiences.

Suzuki believed that there are deep similarities between the Zen experience of *satori* (sudden awakening) and the experiences of other mystics, in particular, the German Roman Catholic Meister Eckhart (1260–1328). However, he also found that one of the major differences between Christian mystical experiences and Zen *satori* is the characterization of the experience as "union with God." While this characterization appears to be a central part of Christian mysticism, it is not found among Zen Buddhist characterizations of *satori*.

D. T. SUZUKI

The Essence of Zen

READING QUESTIONS

1. According to Suzuki, what is the essence of Zen Buddhism?
2. Suzuki defines *satori* as "an intuitive looking into the nature of things." What does he mean by this?
3. How is *satori* similar to and different from the "eureka!" experience sometimes involved in solving a mathematical or scientific problem?

The essence of Zen Buddhism consists in acquiring a new viewpoint on life and things generally. By this I mean that if we want to get into the inmost life of Zen, we must forgo all our ordinary habits of thinking which control our everyday life, we must try to see if there is any other way of judging things, or rather if our ordinary way is always sufficient to give us the ultimate satisfac-

Excerpts from D. T. Suzuki, "Satori or Enlightenment," in *Zen Buddhism: Selected Writings of D. T. Suzuki*, edited by William Barrett (New York: Doubleday & Company, 1956), pp. 83–85. Copyright © 1956 by William Barrett. Reprinted by permission of Susan Barrett. Footnotes omitted.

tion of our spiritual needs. If we feel dissatisfied somehow with this life, if there is something in our ordinary way of living that deprives us of freedom in its most sanctified sense, we must endeavour to find a way somewhere which gives us a sense of finality and contentment. Zen proposes to do this for us and assures us of the acquirement of a new point of view in which life assumes a fresher, deeper, and more satisfying aspect. This acquirement, however, is really and naturally the greatest mental cataclysm one can go through with in life. It is no easy task, it is a kind of fiery baptism, and one has to go through the story, the earthquake, the overthrowing of the mountains, and the breaking in pieces of the rocks.

This acquiring of a new point of view in our dealings with life and the world is popularly called by Japanese Zen students "satori" (*wu* in Chinese). It is really another name for Enlightenment (*anuttara-samyak-sambodhi*), which is the word used by the Buddha and his Indian followers ever since his realization under the Bodhi-tree by the River Nairanjana. There are several other phrases in Chinese designating this spiritual experience, each of which has a special connotation, showing tentatively how this phenomenon is interpreted. At all events there is no Zen without satori, which is indeed the Alpha and Omega of Zen Buddhism. Zen devoid of satori is like a sun without its light and heat. Zen may lose all its literature, all its monasteries, and all its paraphernalia; but as long as there is satori in it, it will survive to eternity. I want to emphasize this most fundamental fact concerning the very life of Zen; for there are some even among the students of Zen themselves who are blind to this central fact and are apt to think when Zen has been explained away logically or psychologically, or as one of the Buddhist philosophies which can be summed up by using highly technical and conceptual Buddhist phrases, Zen is exhausted, and there remains nothing in it that makes it what it is. But my contention is, the life of Zen begins with the opening of satori (*kai wu* in Chinese).

Satori may be defined as an intuitive looking into the nature of things in contradistinction to the analytical or logical understanding of it. Practically, it means the unfolding of a new world hitherto unperceived in the confusion of a dualistically-trained mind. Or we may say that with satori our entire surroundings are viewed from quite an unexpected angle of perception. Whatever this is, the world for those who have gained a satori is no more the old world as it used to be; even with all its flowing streams and burning fires, it is never the same one again. Logically stated, all its opposites and contradictions are united and harmonized into a consistent organic whole. This is a mystery and a miracle, but according to the Zen masters such is being performed every day. Satori can thus be had only through our once personally experiencing it.

Its semblance or analogy in a more or less feeble and fragmentary way is gained when a difficult mathematical problem is solved, or when a great discovery is made, or when a sudden means of escape is realized in the midst of most desperate complications; in short, when one exclaims "Eureka! Eureka!" But this refers only to the intellectual aspect of satori, which is therefore necessarily partial and incomplete and does not touch the very foundations of life considered one indivisible whole. Satori as the Zen experience must be concerned with the entirety of life. For what Zen proposes to do is the revolution, and the revaluation as well, of oneself as a spiritual unity. The solving of a mathematical problem ends with the solution, it does not affect one's whole life. So with all other particular questions, practical or scientific, they do not enter the basic life-tone of the individual concerned. But the opening of satori is the remaking of life itself. When it is genuine—for there are many simulacra of it—its effects on one's moral and spiritual life are revolutionary, and they are so enhancing, purifying, as well as exacting. When a master was asked what constituted Buddhahood, he answered, "The bottom of a pail is broken through." From this we can see what a complete revolution is produced by this spiritual experience. The birth of a new man is really cataclysmic.

In the psychology of religion this spiritual enhancement of one's whole life is called "conversion." But as the term is generally used by Christian converts, it cannot be applied in its strict sense to the Buddhist experience, especially to that of the Zen followers; the term has too affective or emotional a shade to take the place of satori, which is above all noetic. The general tendency of Buddhism is, as we know, more intellectual than emotional, and its doctrine of Enlightenment distinguishes it sharply from the Christian view of salvation; Zen as one of the Mahayana schools naturally shares a large amount of what we may call transcendental intellectualism, which does not issue in logical dualism. When poetically or figuratively expressed, satori is "the opening of the mind-flower," or "the removing of the bar," or "the brightening up of the mind-works." . . .

7.8 GENDER AND EMPTINESS

Rita M. Gross teaches comparative religions at the University of Wisconsin–Eau Claire. She is an author and editor of numerous articles, essays, and books. Dr. Gross studied the history of religions at the University of Chicago and the practice of Buddhism with teachers from the Vajrayana tradition. She characterizes herself as an "engaged historian of religions" because she is simultaneously engaged in what she calls the "practice of theology and of the history of religions."

Many scholars take an "either/or" stance with respect to theology and history of religions: *Either* one engages in a "constructive-theological-normative" study of religion from an insider's viewpoint *or* one engages in a historical-comparative study from an outsider's viewpoint. Dr. Gross rejects this dichotomy and, instead, practices a "method of inseparability" that combines both of these approaches. She believes that the student of religions must not only practice objectivity and empathy but also has an obligation to promote genuine religious pluralism and criticize dysfunctional traditional religious values.

❧

RITA M. GROSS

Feminist Comments on the Mahayana

READING QUESTIONS

1. According to Gross, what are two common misunderstandings of emptiness?
2. How can the "two levels of truth" teaching be applied to gender issues? When so applied, what does it show?
3. Why are concepts of sex neutrality never sufficient as a corrective to androcentrism?

The earliest, best-known, and most widespread Mahayana teachings are a philosophical concept—*shunyata*—and an ethical precept—the Bodhisattva path. Here we are considering them as teachings of the second turning, following the system that sees some of the later Mahayana concepts as yet another complete revolution of the wheel of *dharma*, a classification scheme not agreed

From Rita M. Gross, *Buddhism After Patriarchy: A Feminist History, Analysis, and Reconstruction of Buddhism* (Albany, N.Y.: State University of New York Press, 1993), pp. 173–178. Copyright © 1993 State University of New York. Reprinted by permission. All rights reserved. Notes omitted.

upon even by all Mahayanists. Mythically, the Buddha himself taught the doctrine of emptiness at Rajagriha on Vulture Peak Mountain to a congregation of both Bodhisattvas and *arahants*, as narrated in Prajnaparamita literature, especially the Heart Sutra, the most famous and widely used succinct summary of Mahayana teachings. In the "three turnings" organizational framework, the second-turning teachings are particularly associated with the Madyamika school of Mahayana philosophy, while the third-turning teachings are particularly associated with the school often called the Yogacara school. However, the concepts of emptiness and the Bodhisattva path are also centrally important to all Mahayanists.

The second-turning refers especially to a specific emphasis on and interpretation of emptiness. The interpretation of emptiness to be discussed in this chapter emphasizes "what *shunyata* is *not*." This interpretation is the foundation for understanding that "*shunyata is not nothing*" in subsequent sections of this feminist analysis of key Buddhist concepts. Furthermore, in the context of this chapter, the philosophical outlook and the ethical precept are interdependent with each other: because emptiness is, the bodhisattva path is possible.

Shunyata, Two Truths, and Gender: The Classic Buddhist Argument

Even more than the term "egolessness," the term *shunyata*, "emptiness," confuses both outsider and insider. Buddhist texts themselves warn of the ease with which the concept can be misunderstood and of the extremely serious consequences of such misunderstanding. Like many another Buddhist concept that posits what is not, rather than what is, non-Buddhists have persistently attributed to it a negativity that is foreign to the concept itself. The concept has proved interesting and elusive to Westerners, especially those who look to Buddhism as a possible source of philosophical and spiritual inspiration for dealing with certain difficult issues in Western thought. Perhaps no other Buddhist concept has attracted similar attention or proved more interesting to such seekers.

As we have seen, the concept of emptiness has already been directly and explicitly connected with the issue of gender by Buddhists. It is the only Buddhist concept to have been used in classical Buddhist texts to criticize Buddhist practices of gender discrimination. Buddhists long ago saw that, logically, the fact of emptiness makes gender discriminations, like all other discriminations, inappropriate.

Though arguments and analyses regarding *shunyata* can become incredibly complex and, therefore, confusing, if one keeps returning to the basics, much of the complexity and confusion can be defused. It is simplest to see that, from the Mahayana perspective, *shunyata* is the logical outcome of thoroughly understanding egolessness and interdependent co-arising. When things are said to be empty, the important question is "empty of what?" The answer is that they are empty of, or lack "own-being," inherent existence. They do not exist in and of themselves, but only relative to their matrix, dependent on causes and conditions. For Mahayana Buddhism, such emptiness is thoroughgoing and pervasive. Nothing escapes it to exist inherently, in its own right, independent of its matrix, not subject to causes and conditions. There is no exempted, privileged corner somewhere, whether a Supreme Being or an eternal Soul, or even Buddhist *nirvana*, that is not completely and thoroughly characterized by *shunyata*.

Mahayanists have always emphasized that emptiness is nothing but thoroughgoing egolessness. The early Buddhist analysis primarily focused on the first object of reification, the thing most likely to be taken as really existing, substantially, inherently, and eternally by those who absolutize conventional psychological reactions—the Self or Soul. That reified ego was examined, broken down into its component parts, and found to be lacking any metaphysical glue that held those parts together, which means that ego does not exist. Instead of focusing only on ego itself, Mahayana analysis also focuses on the constituents of ego, which in the Mahayana analysis, are comprised of just basic space, openness, all-pervasive egolessness, *shunyata*. Mahayanists claim that earlier Buddhist analysis stopped too soon; it understood clearly the egolessness of ego, but did not thoroughly comprehend the egolessness of the components of ego; instead it reified them. The Mahayanists claim that even at the subtle level of analysis involved in discerning the component parts of ego, we do not find "ultimate realities at all but only mental constructions." One finds no fixed reference points, but only empty, interdependent, relatively existing fluidity.

Mahayanists claim that fully understanding the doctrine of interdependent co-arising, which can be seen as the central doctrine of early Buddhism, compels one to the conclusion of all-pervading emptiness. "To be dependent means to be devoid of self-nature or own-being (*svabhava*). What is devoid of self-nature is said to be empty (*sunya*). Conditionality and emptiness are the same thing." Therefore, the most famous line of Nagarjuna's root text on the Madyamika: "*Pratityasamutpada* is *shunyata*." According to Mahayana analysis, *nothing*, including the unconditioned elements posited by earlier

Buddhist analysis, escapes this verdict. They exist only as mental constructs and only in relation to the conditioned elements; they do not exist as ultimate realities, since they are imaginable or thinkable only in relation to the conditioned elements. The unconditioned elements, including *nirvana*, are unthinkable by themselves; they are thinkable only in relation to, and therefore dependent upon, conditioned elements. Therefore, such asserted unconditioned elements cannot exist as genuinely unconditioned, but only as empty, conditioned interdependent, relative elements. This is the logic behind the assertions that so often baffle students of Buddhism and that so infuriated advocates of the earlier Buddhist systems—that *samsara* and *nirvana* can be equated, and that the Four Noble Truths are not absolutes.

Mahayanists see this analysis as the Middle Way, so important to all Buddhist endeavors, between eternalism and nihilism, between granting ultimacy either to assertions or to negations. But they also see this middle way as a razor's edge, from which it is easy to fall into either extreme. Falling into the extreme of nihilism was always considered to be the more dangerous pitfall. To emphasize this point, Mahanyanists warned of the "poison of *shunyata*," which they compare to a snake seized by the wrong end; it can easily wound a person fatally. Probably the most common version of the poison of *shunyata* is belief that, since, everything is relative rather than ultimate, nothing really matters and one can do anything one wants. To see emptiness, however, cuts only one's habitual tendency towards fixated attachment to things as if they were ultimate, not their existence in relative terms. Some things are still more or less helpful or satisfying than other things, even in a world devoid of ultimates.

The other way of retreating from the razor's edge is probably more abstract and less likely, though it is a way of understanding emptiness that often allures Westerners. It is often assumed that emptiness is what everything is made of, that it is a kind of negative substance underlying the appearance of things. Such assumptions sometimes underlie the equation of God and emptiness that is so popular in some comparisons of Buddhism and Christianity. But Mahayanists are careful to point out that emptiness should not itself be reified. *Everything* lacks own-being, including emptiness, which is a tool used to cut conceptual fixation, not an alternative concept out of which to build a worldview. It is important to realize not just emptiness, but the emptiness of emptiness.

Because this understanding of emptiness would undercut all assertions, Mahayanists also developed a tool, already known to early Indian Buddhism, for using and evaluating language more effectively. It was recognized

that there are two levels of language, or more accurately, two levels of truth—absolute truth and relative truth. It was always conceded by Buddhists that conventional ways of speaking about persons and things are convenient and useful, relatively speaking. That all things are empty of own-being does not obviate their relative existence and the need to operate in the world of relative things. To believe otherwise would be to fall into the poison of *shunyata*. It also must be conceded that within the realm of relative truth, some analyses are more cogent and some actions more appropriate than others. The temptation is to fixate and reify. The constant reminder that relative truth is only relative truth, not absolute or ultimate, cuts that temptation. The level of absolute truth transcends verbalization or conceptualization. To say anything at all about it is already to return to the level of relative truth, according to Buddhism, which does not mean that one should never speak of Absolute Reality, but only that one should regard one's words as nothing more than tools and pointers. The difficulty of speaking about Truth accurately does not, for Buddhists, undercut the expectation that it is possible to experience intuition into Things-As-They-Are (*tathata*).

Fortunately, some implications of these concepts to the problem of gender are found in classic Buddhist texts. . . .

The application is quite simple. "Male" and "female," like all other labels and designations, are empty and lack substantial reality. Therefore, they cannot be used in a rigid and fixed way to delimit people. In the classic Mahayana texts, this argument is used against those who hold to a belief that high levels of spiritual attainment and Buddhist understanding cannot be combined with a female body. As we have seen, girls and women demonstrate by their skill in presenting complex Buddhist concepts that women can attain high levels of accomplishment. They also demonstrate how fluid sexual identity can be, as they change their sex into the male sex, and sometimes back again. All this can happen because maleness and femaleness do not exist as fixed, inherently existing forms, but only as convenient designations and mere tokens. And finally, they argue decisively that gender traits cannot really be found; therefore, they cannot be used as a basis for discrimination or challenges to change one's body into a male body in order to prove that one's understanding is as deep as it appears to be.

The goddess of the *Vimalakirtinirdesa Sutra* says it best, in words that could be echoed by many a contemporary liberal or equal-rights feminist. After being taunted to change her sex, as genuine proof of the depth of her understanding of emptiness (as if having a penis helped one understand abstract concepts), she says: "I have been here for twelve years and have looked for the innate characteristics of the female sex and haven't been able to find them." Many a woman, held back from her life choices and unable to find comfort or relevance in the female gender role, has made similar statements about the lack of inherent, essential traits of femininity, supposedly possessed by all women, by virtue of their female anatomy. These traits simply cannot be found, even in the quantified research of contemporary psychology. Furthermore, the attempt to limit and classify people on the basis of sex, to say that women can't do something or that men should behave in a certain way, is to make absolute determinations and discriminations on the basis of a relative, empty trait. Or one could say that such judgments and limitations absolutize the relative. In either case, conventional social arrangements, including those common to Buddhist institutions contradict the essential Mahayana teaching of emptiness.

Though not explicitly citing the theory of the two truths, these texts also utilize that concept. After changing herself into a man and her interlocutor into a woman, the goddess says to him (who is now temporarily "her"), "Just as you are not really a woman but appear to be female in form, all women also only appear to be female in form but are not really women. Therefore, the Buddha said all are not really men or women." In terms of the two truths, the level of convention and appearance is the level of gender roles and stereotypes, but at the level of absolute truth, "all are not really men or women." Notice that, consonant with the unspeakability of absolute truth, the text does not try to say what people really are beyond maleness and femaleness, but it does state clearly that they are not *really*, but only apparently, men or women.

The conclusions to be drawn are obvious and were drawn in theory in the Buddhist texts, though the practical applications of those conclusions have never been integrated into Buddhist institutions and everyday life. You cannot predict, on the basis of gender, who is likely to be able to comprehend and practice "the dharma which is neither male nor female." The whole apparatus of preselecting people for roles on the basis of their gender, of forcing people to fit gender roles, and of limiting their options on the basis of gender would become inadmissible if the emptiness and relativity of maleness and femaleness were to be taken seriously.

Strong as these traditional arguments from emptiness, the assertions that the "*dharma* is neither male nor female" and that maleness and femaleness do not really exist, may be, they are not sufficient to undercut patriarchal conventions. These assertions are certainly useful and accurate. But they do not really break free of the androcentrism that so pervades Buddhist thought. The Buddhist statement that "the *dharma* is neither male

nor female" is strikingly similar to the Christian Pauline statement that "in Christ there is neither male nor female," a statement that, however often quoted, has not kept Christianity from developing male dominance, any more than its Buddhist parallel has been effective in ridding Buddhism of male dominance. It is important to ascertain why.

In both cases, the statement about the irrelevance of gender is made in an androcentric context. Given that context, those statements are only superficially gender neutral. In fact, they always mean, "You can make it, even if you are female." They never mean, "You can make it even if you are male." Often the sex-neutral language hides the fact that women become acceptable only by transcending their femaleness and becoming "manly." They are supposedly given the opportunity to match the human norm, but that human norm is collapsed into the male ideal. Men are rarely, if ever, expected to become "unmanly" to the extent that women are expected to become "unfeminine" in order to achieve the same level of spiritual attainment, though, to be fair, it must be admitted that men must transcend their culture's version of the macho male. The point is, however, that the ideal "spiritual person," for both Buddhism and Christianity, is not androgynous or neutral, and certainly is not feminine; it is male, and the qualities that make a person spiritual are conflated with the qualities that make a person male, while the qualities that make a person overtly female are shunned as spiritual ideals by both traditions. Therefore, concepts of sex-neutrality as a corrective to androcentrism are never sufficient because the neutral ideal is in fact much more male than female. As a result, both Buddhism and Christianity waver between a male-defined sex neutrality that a few women might be able to achieve and an outright favoring of biological males. Clearly, these two options are not sufficient. . . .

KEY TERMS AND CONCEPTS

Abhidharma (Pali: *Abhidhamma*) One of the principal divisions of the *Tripitika* containing elaboration on the teachings of the Buddha.

Amitabha (Japanese: **Amida**) Savior Buddha of the **Pure Land** in the West and the Buddha of central importance to the **Pure Land** movement. Also named Amitayus (Buddha of Infinite Life).

anatman (Pali: *anatta*) Denial of the existence of a permanent, unchanging self.

Anitya (Pali: **anicca**) Impermanence. Along with *anatman* and *duhkha* (suffering), one of the "Three Marks" of existence.

arhat (female: **arhati**) A term used in Theravada Buddhism for a saint or one who has attained enlightenment.

asura One of a class of extraordinary beings. Sometimes translated as "titans" and pictured as waging war with the gods (*devas*).

Avalokiteshvara (Chinese: **Kuan-yin;** Japanese: **Kannon;** Tibetan: **Chenrezik**) Compassionate savior *bodhisattva* and protector of Tibet.

bodhisattva (Pali: **bodhisatta**) Any person who has taken a vow to become a buddha and lives a life of compassion intent on the goal of his or her own enlightenment and the enlightenment of others.

Buddha The title for someone who is enlightened. When capitalized, it usually refers to the Buddha **Sakyamuni.**

Ch'an (Korean: **Son;** Japanese: **Zen**) A school of Buddhism that emphasizes meditation as the heart of Buddhist practice.

Dalai Lama Temporal and spiritual leader of Tibet thought to be one of a line of successive reincarnations of **Avalokiteshvara.**

dharma (Pali: **dhamma**) The word has many meanings most of which refer to what is true or real. Often used specifically to refer to the teachings of the Buddha **Sakyamuni** and philosophically to refer to basic elements of reality. Also translated as Truth, Doctrine, and Law.

dhyana (Pali: **Jhana;** Chinese: **Ch'an;** Korean: **Son;** Japanese: **Zen**) In general, it refers to meditation and specifically to one of the levels of trance.

Dukkha (Pali: **dukkha**) The first of the **Four Noble Truths** usually translated as suffering or unsatisfactoriness.

Eightfold Path The development of wisdom, moral purity, and mental discipline leading to *nirvana.* Usually listed as right view, right thought, right speech, right conduct, right livelihood, right effort, right mindfulness, and right meditation. Also known as the **Middle Way.**

Four Noble Truths These Aryan (Noble) truths are considered by many to be the heart of the Buddha's teaching. They are (1) suffering, (2) cause of suffering, (3) cessation of suffering, and (4) **Eightfold Path,** or **Middle Way.**

Gautama (Pali: **Gotama**) The family name of the historical **buddha** of this age, Buddha **Sakyamuni,** whose personal name is Siddhartha.

Hinayana *Yana* means "vehicle," and *hina* can be translated as "smaller, lesser, baser." A pejorative name given by Mahayana Buddhists to some of the other schools.

Jātaka Stories of the past lives of the Buddha **Sakyamuni** that are very popular and well known among many Buddhists.

karma In general it refers to action or deed, specifically, to any intentional deed (often ritualistic or moral) that will cause effects in this life or the next. Also refers to the Law of Karma, which is the principle of cause and effect in general and specifically the principle that good deeds bring good results and bad deeds bring bad results.

koan A riddle used for meditation in **Zen** Buddhism.

Mahayana Sanskrit term meaning Great Vehicle used by one of the three main branches of Buddhism.

Maitreya (Pali: **Metteyya**) The next **buddha** due to come at some point in the future.

mandala A Sanskrit word meaning circle and used to refer to structured space symbolically depicting various levels of the universe and different **buddhas** and **bodhisattvas.** Widely used in Tantric Buddhism for purposes of visualization meditations.

mantra A set of sounds that have spiritual potency. They are frequently chanted in worship and as a focus for meditation.

Mappo A Japanese word that refers to a time near the end of the *Dharma* when following the path to enlightenment becomes very difficult.

Mara The tempter of Buddha and others who is concerned with keeping people living in the realm of desire over which he rules.

Middle Way A term used broadly to refer to the Buddha's teachings as a whole as a moderate way to release from suffering that avoids the extremes of asceticism and indulgence. More narrowly it refers to the **Eightfold Path.**

Mount Meru The mythic mountain at the center of the Buddhist cosmos and the dwelling place of *asuras* and *devas.*

mudra Symbolic hand gestures widely used in *Vajrayana* ritual.

nembutsu Japanese term for calling on Amida Buddha involving the recitation of the **mantra** "*Namu Amida Butsu.*"

Nikaya A section of the Pali canon and sometimes used as a nonderogatory term for **Hinayana** Buddhism.

nirvana (Pali: **nibbana**) The third **Noble Truth** and the soteriological goal of Buddhism—release from desire, ignorance, hatred, and, in general, suffering. Sometimes used to refer to enlightenment and also used to refer to *parinirvana.*

parinirvana nirvana without remainder.

prajna (Pali: *panna*) Wisdom or a true understanding of the nature of reality.

Pure Land A paradise like heaven where devotees may be reborn after death. Often used specifically of the Western Pure Land of *Amitabha* and the Pure Land school centering on his worship.

sadhana A Vajrayana visualization meditation used to invoke and identify with a deity or **buddha.**

Sakyamuni Means the Sage of the Sakya Clan and is an honorific title frequently used for the Buddha, Siddhartha **Gautama.**

samadhi Meditative concentration and the trance state attained by yogic meditation.

sangha The Buddhist community in general (lay and monastic) and, more narrowly, the monastic community of monks and nuns.

satori Zen Buddhist term for a sudden awakening or insight.

shunyata Usually translated as "emptiness." It refers specifically to the lack of any inherent self-existence (*svabhava*) in things.

Skandha (Pali: *khandha*) Means "aggregate" and usually refers to the five aggregates of individual existence: form, feelings, perceptions, dispositions or karmic constituents, and consciousness.

stupa A moundlike structure usually containing a relic of the Buddha **Sakyamuni** and a place for pilgrimage and worship.

sutra (Pali: *sutta*) Any discourse attributed to the Buddha and one of the principal divisions of the Buddhist canon.

svabhava The substance of a thing understood as independently existing. Usually translated as "self-existent."

tantras A group of writings setting forth the ideas and practices of Tantric Buddhism, which some consider a shortcut to enlightenment. These practices often involve violating the traditional norms of society and traditional monastic vows (such as drinking and sexuality) in order to show that the truly enlightened are free from ordinary rules.

Tara (Tibetan: *Drolma*) Female savior *bodhisattva* often associated with **Avalokiteshvara** and popular in Tibet.

Tathagata Literally the "Thus-Come One" and a title used for the Buddha.

Tathagatagarbha Literally the "embryo or womb of the **Tathagata**" and refers to the potential for enlightenment within all beings.

Theravada A sect or school within **Nikaya** Buddhism meaning the "Teachings of the Elders."

Tripitika (Pali: *Tipitaka*) The Buddhist canon consisting of the *Vinaya, Sutra,* and *Abhidharma.*

Triple Gem The "Three Jewels" or "Three refuges": the Buddha, the *Dharma,* and the *Sangha.*

upaya The employment of "skillful means" in teaching.

Vajrayana Refers to the "Diamond (or Thunderbolt) Vehicle" that is one of the three main branches of Buddhism.

vinaya The code of conduct for monks and nuns as well as a name for one of the principal divisions of **Tripitika.**

zazen Seated meditation, a practice common in **Zen.**

Zen See *Ch'an.*

SUGGESTIONS FOR FURTHER READINGS

Buddhist Scriptures, selected and translated by Edward Conze. London: Penguin Books, 1959. A collection of sources arranged in three parts: The Teacher, Doctrines, and Other Worlds and Future Worlds.

Harvey, P. *An Introduction to Buddhism: Teaching, History and Practices.* Cambridge: Cambridge University Press, 1990. A clear and informative introduction to Buddhism.

Kitagawa, Joseph M., et al. eds. *Buddhism and Asian History.* New York: Macmillan, 1987, 1989. Articles on religion, history, and culture taken from *The Encyclopedia of Religion.*

Lopez Jr., Donald S. ed. *Buddhism in Practice.* Princeton: Princeton University Press, 1995. A good collection of difficult-to-locate source material with excellent introductions and interpretations.

Strong, John S. *The Experience of Buddhism: Sources and Interpretations.* Belmont, Calif.: Wadsworth, 1995. A good collection of sources with commentary.

RESEARCH PROJECTS

1. If you are interested in the possible influences of Buddhist stories on the Christian scriptures and the parallels between them, read Roy C.

Amore's *Two Masters, One Message* (Nashville, Tenn.: Abingdon, 1978) and write a critical review.

2. If you are interested in pursuing the topic of women and Buddhism, read Diana Y. Paul's *Women in Buddhism: Images of the Feminine in the Mahayana Tradition* (Berkeley: University of California Press, 1985) and write a critical review.

3. Locate and interview a local Buddhist about the things most important to her or him about Buddhism and why the person is a Buddhist. Analyze the results of your interview and write a report.

4. Do a Web search on some aspect of Buddhism, take notes on the information available, analyze it, and write a report that includes an annotated list of sources.

5. Get a copy of *The Teaching of Buddha* (Tokyo: Buddyo Dendo Kyokai, 1966), which, like the Gideon Bible, is a collection of Buddhist scripture placed in many hotel rooms and hospitals throughout Asia and Europe. Analyze how it presents information about Buddhism and the Buddha's teaching. You may order a copy from the Buddhist Promoting Foundation, c/o MTI Corporation, 18 Essex Road, Paramus, NJ 07652.

8

Confucian Ways of Being Religious

INTRODUCTION

When I was visiting the Temple of Heaven in Beijing, China, I got into a discussion with a Chinese guide about Chinese religion. Quoting a popular Chinese saying, he spoke of the "three teachings" and ended by saying that the three are fundamentally the same. These three teachings are what Western scholars call Confucianism, Taoism, and Buddhism.

Like all sayings, the claim that Chinese religion consists of "three teachings that are one" both reveals and conceals. There are indeed three relatively distinct teachings or religious traditions in China, but Chinese religion is more diverse and varied than the term "three teachings" reveals. While these three traditions have profoundly influenced one another and, over the centuries, blended somewhat, they have also been at odds and in conflict with one another.

Here our focus will be on Confucianism, but we must be aware that abstracting this teaching from the other two is misleading. In the previous chapter we discussed Chinese Buddhism, and in the next we shall look at Taoism, but this division is for convenience only. In reality the three are blended like threads in a tapestry.

This tapestry contains more than three threads. One of these other threads is called Chinese popular religion. The designation "popular religion" is usually used in two senses. In the first sense, it refers to the type of religion practiced by almost all Chinese people, regardless of explicit religious identification. These practices involve certain funeral rituals, consultation with fortune-tellers, health and medical routines, offerings to the ancestors, New Year's rites, seeking advice from spirit mediums, exorcism of ghosts, and the like. In another sense, the term "popular religion" is used to designate the religion of the masses or lower classes as distinguished from the religion of the elite. Although both groups may engage in the same or very similar religious practices, their understandings are very different. For the elite, such cults as those devoted to the veneration of ancestors are important for promoting morality, social order, and a venerable cultural tradition. The elite are more likely to be somewhat skeptical about the existence of ghosts and demons than the general populace.

Confucianism appears to have begun as a loose collection of moral, ritual, political, aesthetic, and historical teachings of the elite. Indeed, many have claimed that it is not really a religion, but, rather, a kind of humanistic philosophy largely attractive to scholars or the literati, as they are sometimes called. Others have claimed that there is no such thing as Confucianism, but that a number of different literary writings and figures have been lumped together into a school of thought labeled Confucian.

These issues will come up for further discussion below. For now it is sufficient to note two things. First, when we study any putative religious tradition, it is important to raise questions of social class. Who writes the literature and performs the rituals? What kind of people is their audience? Who participates? Second, although Confucianism is an elite movement, the Chinese family system and the Chinese form of bureaucracy have been deeply shaped by it, and hence Confucianism touches the lives of practically all Chinese regardless of social class.

Although I focus on China below, we need to be aware that Confucianism has spread outside of China to such places as Vietnam, Japan, and Korea. Immigration has brought it to the West, and, after a period of decline in China, aspects of it may now be entering a new phase of creativity sometimes referred to as New Confucianism.

8.1 AN OVERVIEW

Imagine that you are interested in the art of government, that you believe good government can improve the lives of people, that in the past there were great rulers who benefited the people they governed, and that, at the present time, when you live, social chaos reigns. Imagine that the present political leaders are corrupt, government officials take bribes, many are mean and some cruel, families are disintegrating, and injustice rather than justice is abroad in the land. What would you do? What would you say?

One thing you might do is seek some kind of governmental position of influence. One thing you might say is that there are important lessons to be learned from the great rulers of the past. You might start studying the past with a view to applying what you learn to the present. You might teach others what you are learning and try to get them to find positions of influence so that social conditions can be improved. You might try to restore "family values" and to figure out ways to get educated people of good moral character into office. You might, in short, do the sorts of things that Confucius (551–479 B.C.E.) seems to have done.

Julia Ching, Professor of Religious Studies at the University of Toronto and Fellow of the Royal Society of Canada, describes the origins and development of Confucianism in our first selection. She begins by asking the question "What do I mean by 'Confucianism'?" This is an important question because there is considerable doubt about our ability to neatly define what it is.

When Western scholars first encountered Confucianism, they wondered what they had found. Was it a religion, a form of Asian wisdom literature, a kind of philosophy, or a form of social ethics? Interestingly, the early Christian missionary-scholars called the most important Confucian texts "classics" rather than "scriptures." This indicates that they felt some uncertainty about how Confucian literature might be categorized in Western terms. "Classic literature" might be religious, ethical, political, philosophical, or all of these.

You will notice that Professor Ching gives two different spellings for Chinese terms. A word is first spelled according to the Wade-Giles system of rendering Chinese sounds. After the slash mark ("/"), the word is rendered according to the pinyin system. For more information on these spelling systems and pronunciation of Chinese terms, see the Pronunciation Guide at the end of this chapter.

As you read Professor Ching's overview, answer the reading questions. They will help you highlight key ideas.

JULIA CHING

Confucianism as Religious Humanism

READING QUESTIONS

1. As you read, make a list of all the words and ideas you do not understand or are uncertain about. Discuss them with a classmate, look them up in a dictionary, or bring them up in class for discussion and clarification.
2. Why are the Five Classics important?
3. What is the "negative Golden Rule"? What is the difference between the negative and positive formulation?
4. What are the Five Relationships, and why are they significant?
5. How is *jen* related to *li?*
6. Describe the cult of Heaven and the cult of ancestors.
7. What is the Mandate of Heaven, and when is the removal of the Mandate justified?
8. Why is the Han period important in the religious history of China?
9. What is Neo-Confucianism, and how is it related to the Four Books?
10. How are *T'ai-chi, li,* and *ch'i* related?

What do I mean by "Confucianism"? A Western designation of a Chinese tradition, the term itself is ambiguous, representing an ideology developed by a man of the name Confucius (552?–479 B.C.). The Chinese themselves have usually preferred *Ju-chia/Rujia* or *Ju-chiao/Rujiao,* the school or teachings of the scholars. Etymologically, it has been claimed that the word *ju/ru* is related to the word for "weaklings" or "cowards," and referred originally to those dispossessed aristocrats of an-

From Julia Ching, *Chinese Religions* (Maryknoll, N.Y.: Orbis Books, 1993), pp. 53–65, 72–75, 77–80, 153–160, 165–167. © 1993 Julia Ching. Reprinted by permission of the publisher. Footnotes omitted.

tiquity who were no longer warriors, but lived off their knowledge of rituals or history, music, numbers or archery. It is a case of a pejorative term becoming eventually a designation of honour, as also with the Christians. Eventually, the school of *Ju* came to refer to the ethical wisdom of the past that Confucius transmitted to later ages, as well as the entire development of the tradition after his time. . . .

THE HISTORICAL CONFUCIUS

In recent history, the *questioning* into Chinese tradition as such and Confucianism in particular involved also a *quest*—that for the historical Confucius, as distinct from the Confucius-image of popular veneration. The development in the 1920s and 1930s of a more scientifically critical historical method facilitated this task to a certain extent. It might be studied in terms parallel to the quest for the historical Jesus. But it is a much more difficult quest, since the oldest extant source, the *Analects*, was compiled at least a century after the Master's death, whereas the oldest document in the New Testament came from within a generation of Jesus' death.

First of all, *Confucius* is the Latin rendering by seventeenth-century Jesuit missionaries of K'ung Fu-tzu, or Master K'ung, whose name was K'ung Ch'iu, also styled K'ung Chung-ni. He was a native of the small state of Lu, whose birthplace is near modern Ch'ü-fu (Qufu, Shantung). As with the life of Jesus or even more, little can be established about his life, including the exact year of birth, and about his forebears and immediate family. However, legends (including very early ones) are abundant. He is sometimes said to be a direct descendant of the Shang royal house. However, at the time of his parents, the family's circumstances were far from comfortable. The highest public office he occupied at the age of fifty was as a kind of police commissioner in his home state, and only for about a year. In over ten years of travel, K'ung visited many feudal states, seeking, but never finding, a ruler who would use his advice. In old age, he devoted more time to teaching disciples, while also occupying himself with music and poetry, occasionally conversing with rulers or ministers.

Were we to judge him on the basis of his attainments in public office, we would not even give him a footnote in history. This is despite the praises sung about the good order he set up for the state of Lu, where the people allegedly could go to sleep without locking their house doors, and also despite the allegation from some sources that he had his deputy executed on dubious grounds— an allegation that fuelled the Anti-Confucius campaign

in 1973–74. Like many great personages, K'ung was to be remembered for reasons other than those goals to which he had oriented his life. Without doubt, he had a correct sense of his own mission to regenerate the culture of his time, without fully realising how that was to come about. Like Jesus, K'ung became historically influential only after his death, which was at around the age of seventy, from natural causes. Like Jesus, K'ung did not develop any systematic doctrinal structure in which manners, morals, law, philosophy and theology were clearly separated. In K'ung's case, the teachings were systematised only with Mencius (c. 371–289) and Hsün-tzu (c. 298–238).

The following passage gives us some insight into K'ung's own self-consciousness. His profound sense of reverence for the will of Heaven should help us appreciate the basically religious orientation of his life and character.

> At fifteen I set my heart on learning [to be a sage].
> At thirty I became firm.
> At forty I had no more doubts.
> At fifty I understood Heaven's Will.
> At sixty my ears were attuned [to this Will].
> At seventy I could follow my heart's desires, without overstepping the line.
>
> (*Analects* 2:4)

It is interesting to dwell on how his ears were attuned, presumably to Heaven's will. After all, the word *sage* was originally the graph for a large ear and a small mouth. But K'ung was a modest man who said, "How dare I rank myself with sages . . . ? I prefer to say of myself, that I strive without cease [for sageliness] and teach others without weariness." But then, what is sagehood, if not this constant striving—as his disciples recognised? They responded: "This is just what we, your disciples, have been unable to learn from you" (*Analects* 7:33).

It might also be inferred that K'ung was a believer in Heaven as personal deity, as higher power, order and law, displacing the many "gestalts" of the old gods. "He who sins against Heaven, has no one to whom he can pray" (*Analects* 3:13). K'ung lived in an age of turmoil, during which the ancient religious beliefs were questioned, and he contributed to the rationalist atmosphere of philosophical reflection. But why shouldn't he question them, knowing what we do of ancient religion, with its emphasis on divination and sacrifice, including human sacrifice? Understandably, K'ung distanced himself from this. Interestingly, he heralded in a new age of ethical wisdom, by appealing to the legacy of the ancients. Was he a conservative or a reformer, or perhaps a revolutionary? We may already have some clues to answering this question.

THE CONFUCIAN CLASSICS

While Confucius' teachings are best found in the *Analects*—the record of his conversations with his disciples—early Confucianism regards as its special texts the Five Classics. This group of books includes various genres. Let us take another look at this text and the others in proper focus:

- The *Book of Changes* or the *I-ching* probably existed at the time of Confucius, and was attributed to the sages of old. The manual centres upon short oracles arranged under sixty-four hexagrams, symbols made up of combinations of broken and unbroken lines in groups of six. Commentaries were later added to the oracles. The longest one is the *Hsi-tz'u* or Appended Remarks, which offer early cosmological and metaphysical speculation in a cryptic language. The text is reaching a wide audience in our own times, especially since the psychoanalyst Carl Jung introduced the notion of "synchronicity" to replace that of chance in evaluating the validity of divination.

- The *Book of History*, also called the *Book of Documents* (*Shang-shu*, literally, ancient documents), is allegedly a collection organised and introduced by Confucius. It is mainly an assortment of speeches from royalty and chief ministers, as well as certain narrative accounts of royal achievements and principles of government, arranged chronologically. While the materials describing early Chou times are more credible, some of the allegedly older chapters have been called forgeries.

- The *Book of Poetry*, also called the *Book of Songs*, or the *Odes* (*Shih-ching*) is basically a collection of three hundred and five songs. Probably compiled around 600 B.C., even if the materials could be much older, it includes four sections, with various genres, such as folk songs of love, courtship and desertion, as well as about hunts and dances. There are also banquet songs, or state hymns. Allegedly, Confucius compiled them from an ancient repertory of three thousand.

- The Classic of *Rites* is an entire corpus. This includes the *Ceremonials* (*I-li*), an early manual of etiquette for the nobility, detailing such occasions as marriages and funerals, sacrifices and archery contests. There is also the *Book of Rites* (*Li-chi*), with its forty-nine sections of ritual and government regulations, as well as treatises on education, the rites, music and philos-

ophy. Then there is the *Institutes of Chou* (*Chou-li*), apparently an idealised description of offices of government in early Chou times. It is believed that these texts were compiled in the early first century B.C., on the basis of somewhat earlier materials.

- The *Spring-Autumn Annals* (*Ch'un-ch'iu*) is basically a didactically and laconically written chronicle of the state of Lu, the Master's native state, which purports to explain the decline of the ancient political and moral code. The Annals cover the period dating from 722 to 481 B.C., and from this we have derived the "Spring-Autumn Period." It was attributed to Confucius as author, but this is no longer acceptable. It is usually associated with three commentaries, or rather appendages: the vividly narrative *Tso-chuan* or Tso Commentary, the catechetical (question-and-answer) Kung-yang Commentary and Ku-liang Commentary.

A sixth classic, the *Book of Music*, is no longer extant.

In the past, Confucius has been considered the author of the classics, or at least, as their editor. Contemporary scholarship no longer takes this seriously. True, the core of many of these classical texts goes back to Confucius, and even to the time preceding him, which shows the ancient lineage of the school of *Ju*. But each of them underwent a long period of evolution, receiving accretions postdating Confucius. . . .

THE MORALITY OF HUMAN RELATIONSHIPS

It has sometimes been said that Confucius' great merit is his discovery of the moral character of human relationships. He taught a doctrine of reciprocity and neighbourliness.

> To regard every one as a very important guest, to manage the people as one would assist at a sacrifice, *not to do to others what you would not have them do to you*. (*Analects* 15:23)

For its resemblance to Christian teachings, the last part of this quotation (my italics) has come to be called the *negative* Golden Rule.

Within Confucianism, the well-known "Five Relationships" include the ruler–minister, father–son, husband–wife, elder and younger brother, and friend and friend. Three of these are family relationships, while the other two are usually conceived in terms of the family models. For example, the ruler–minister relationship resembles the father–son, while friendship resembles brotherliness. For this reason, the Confucian society regards itself as a large family: "Within the four seas all men are brothers" (*Analects* 12:5).

The responsibilities ensuing from these relationships are mutual and reciprocal. A minister owes loyalty to his ruler, and a child filial respect to the parent. But the ruler must also care for his subjects, and the parent for the child. All the same, the Five Relationships emphasise the vertical sense of hierarchy. Even with the horizontal relationship between friends, seniority of age demands a certain respect; and if the conjugal relationship bears more natural resemblance to that between older and younger brothers, it is more usually compared to the ruler–minister relationship. Indeed, the duty of filial piety, the need for procuring progeny for the sake of assuring the continuance of the ancestral cult, has been for centuries the ethical justification for polygamy.

Confucius' main legacy is the teaching on *jen/ren*. Etymologically, it is written with the radical "human" and the word for "two," or, if one wishes, for a sign that might also be interpreted as "above." It is pronounced the same as the word for human being. Understandably, *jen* is always concerned with human relationship, with relating to others. It may also be explained as the virtue of the "superior man," the gentleman. It is associated with loyalty (*chung/zhong*)—referring basically to loyalty to one's own heart and conscience, rather than to a narrower political loyalty—and reciprocity (*shu*)—respect of, and consideration for others (*Analects* 4:15).

Jen is also related to *li* (propriety or ritual). But the latter refers more to social behavior, and the former, to the inner orientation of the person. *Jen* is translated variously as goodness, benevolence, humanity and human-heartedness. It was formerly a particular virtue, the kindness which distinguished the gentleman in his behaviour toward his inferiors. He transformed it into a universal virtue, that which *makes* the perfect human being, the sage. The later importance of his teachings gave this a social importance—that moral character and merit should replace birth as the criterion for a gentleman. . . .

If the natural feelings underlying kinship call for special consideration, the natural feelings aroused by the neighbour's—*any* neighbour's—need for help are also recognised. This is especially underlined by Mencius, who gives the example of a man witnessing a child falling into a well (Mencius 2A:6). The *natural* first impulse is to rescue the child, and this comes before any desire for praise or fear of blame. The following of this impulse is an act of commiseration, or love of neighbour. This example serves as a kind of Confucian parable of the Good Samaritan, illustrating the meaning of universal love. And natural feelings serve also as an experiential guide. For the follower of Confucius, parental love

for children can be extended to cover other people's children, just as filial respect for the aged can be extended to cover other people's parents and elders, so that the natural order serves as a starting point and an experiential guide in achieving universal love.

Familial relations provide a model for social behaviour. Respect your own elders, as well as others' elders; be kind to your own children and juniors, as well as those of others. These are the instructions of Mencius (1A:7), and have provided inspiration for generations of Confucians. They have been the reason for the strong sense of solidarity not only in the Chinese family, but also in Confucian social organisations even among overseas communities.

CONFUCIANISM AS RITUAL RELIGION

Rituals are an essential dimension of religious life, giving expression to communal beliefs. . . . The Chinese word for ritual (*li*) is related etymologically to the words "worship" and "sacrificial vessel" with a definite religious overtone. But, in fact, the term has a much broader range of meanings in the Chinese context, straddling the sacred and the profane spheres. Somewhat like the contemporary English term, it came to include social practices, partaking even of the nature of law, as a means of training in virtue and of avoiding evil. And going beyond the English term, it refers also to propriety, that is, proper behaviour.

Ritual is a very important part of Confucius' teachings, and has been understood as such by his disciples, who were also teachers of rituals. Thus, Confucianism also became known as the ritual religion *li-chiao/lijiao*, with its emphases upon the doctrinal as well as ritual prescriptions for "proper behaviour" in family and society. Confucian teachings helped to keep alive the older cult of veneration for ancestors, and the worship of Heaven, a formal cult practised by China's imperial rulers, who regarded themselves as the keepers of Heaven's Mandate of government, a kind of High Priest, a mediator figure between the human order and the divine order. With the official establishment of Confucianism, its classical texts were inscribed in stone, and collected a corpus of commentaries and sub-commentaries, establishing various traditions of textual exegesis. This took place during the period of time spanning the Han (B.C. 206–220 A.D.) and the T'ang (618–906 A.D.) dynasties. Among these texts, the *Spring-Autumn Annals* in particular gave rise to allegorical interpretations that drew in *yin-yang* metaphysics offering a new cosmological and historical vision, while the *Book of Rites*, with its elaborate instructions for correct deportment, especially regarding mourning and funerals, became the backbone of Chinese society.

Confucius also emphasised the need to have the right inner dispositions, without which ritual propriety becomes hypocrisy (*Analects* 15:17). He insisted that sacrifice is to be performed, with the consciousness of the presence of the spirits (3:12). Besides, "what can rites do for a person lacking in the virtue of humanity (*jen*)? What can music do for a person lacking in humanity?" (3:3). . . .

The Cult of Heaven

We made mention of the worship of Heaven. The phrase refers to the annual sacrifices offered by the emperor to heaven and earth. Today we may still visit the sites on which these rituals took place in Peking (Beijing). The Temple of Heaven, which goes back to the Ming dynasty (1368–1661), is situated in a wide park outside the former "forbidden city." There are several old structures there, including the well-known circular prayer hall for good harvests, with its blue tiles (blue being the colour of Heaven). What is even more impressive are the three circular open-air marble terraces, under the sky itself. Here is the altar for the cult of Heaven. The middle of the topmost terrace is the place where the emperor used to make sacrifices to the Lord-on-high at the time of the winter solstice.

To what religion does the Temple of Heaven belong? This is a question often posed by visitors. The correct answer is: to Chinese religion. But exactly what is Chinese religion? Tradition has transmitted a plurality including Confucianism and Taoism. We would have to say more specifically: that Chinese religion includes a dimension of nature worship which was transformed by Confucianism and Taoism and incorporated into each system in a different way. And, to the extent that the cult of Heaven has been approved by the Confucian tradition, one might even designate the Temple of Heaven as a *Confucian* temple. Indeed, the *Book of Rites* contains precise instructions for the performance of this cult to Heaven. This ritual surrounding the cult of Heaven developed very early, existing already at the time of Confucius, and remaining in many respects the main feature of Chinese religion until the twentieth century.

The cult to Heaven was a sacrifice of burnt offerings. . . . Attendance was strictly limited, as the population in general was not admitted, and individual citizens would be guilty of high treason should they attempt to perform it. Rather, the performance was the privilege as well as sacred duty of the Son of Heaven, the emperor.

This itself was not only proof that there was no separation between political and religious powers, between the *imperium* and the *sacerdotium*, but also that the office of the emperor was basically a continuation of the ancient office of the priest-shaman-king. . . .

In speaking of the cult to Heaven, one should not neglect the other cult, offered to Earth. The dual cults give an impression that Heaven and Earth are equals, each accepting a sacrifice. But the reality is not quite so. While the sacrifices of Heaven and Earth both belonged to the category of "great" sacrifices, performed by the emperor himself as Son of Heaven, Heaven takes on greater importance and is addressed as Lord-on-high. It would appear that these cults represented a mixture of beliefs, which came down with the interaction of Shang and Chou religions. Sacrifices were thus offered both to Heaven and Earth as cosmic forces, and to Heaven in particular as a supreme deity.

The Other State Cults

Starting from the time of the Han dynasty, an elaborate state cult was evolved, which has been, rightly or wrongly, attributed to Confucian teachings. They include expressions of very ancient beliefs, not just in a supreme deity, and in natural powers as deity symbols, as well as in the intercessory powers of deceased worthies or heroes. We mentioned the great rituals performed by the emperor himself, not only for the worship of Heaven but also for that of Earth, and of his imperial ancestors. There were also intermediate rituals, for the worship of the sun and the moon, and numerous spirits of earth and sky. There were the lesser sacrifices to minor gods, including those of mountains, lakes, and rivers as well as those well-known historical figures—in particular wise and incorrupt magistrates—honoured as "city gods." Besides, surrounded by his disciples, and also by later worthies, Confucius himself became the centre of an elaborate cult which possibly would have been most repugnant to him. While not deified, he received official sacrifices as the teacher *par excellence*, and was especially venerated by the scholarly class. The Confucian emphasis on rituals assured a continuity with the past, and offered also a ritual as well as a moral education for the would-be gentleman.

With the establishment of a republic in China (1912) the cult of Heaven, as well as the other state cults, came to an end. But their memory remains as witness to a theistic belief (be this monotheism or polytheism, depending on one's interpretations) present at the heart of traditional Chinese religion, and persisting throughout the ages, in spite of the changes in the philosophical interpretation of this belief.

The Cult of Ancestors

Any religion that focuses so much on ancestors presupposes some belief in the hereafter. The Confucian belief was that the human being is compounded of two "souls," an upper, or intellectual soul, called the *hun*, which becomes the spirit (*shen*), and ascends to the world above, and a lower, or animal soul, called the *p'o/po*, which becomes the ghost (*kuei*) and descends with the body into the grave. These ideas are especially found in the *Tso Commentary* (*Tso-chuan*), in a recording of a conversation dated 534 B.C., where these "souls" are also presumed to be possessed by everyone, not just nobility. Such ideas are confirmed by archaeological findings of tomb paintings of a heavenly realm, as in Ma-wang-tui, the Han site. They were also accepted by the Taoist religion, which greatly elaborated them. The Taoist cult of immortality, involving physical immortality or the ascent to Heaven as immortals, developed from these beliefs, especially regarding the *hun*.

The ancestral cult was a memorial service, held previously at ancestral temples, and after that at gravesides or at home. Wine and food libations were usually offered, with silent prostrations in front of the tablets. The ancestors were alleged to have tasted the food, before the whole family partook of the meal. Conversion to Christianity frequently represented a rupture with this tradition, since the converts were either forbidden, or no longer expected, to continue the cult.

Much better known than the cult of Heaven, the cult of ancestors goes back to the dawn of Chinese history, although originally it was the exclusive privilege of the nobility. It became associated with the state orthodoxy, while remaining very much a family practice—an expression of a community of both the living and the beloved deceased. While the ancestral cult may be regarded as a religion in itself, its persistence has also been considered as another indication of the religious character of Confucianism. Until today, in many Chinese houses in Hong Kong, Taiwan and Southeast Asia—as well as in Korea and Japan—the ancestral shrine is maintained. . . .

The Family Rituals

There are, of course, other rituals as well, recorded in the *Book of Rites* and practised during many centuries. I am referring especially to those ceremonies surrounding a person's growth and maturity, the affirmation of the family principle by marriage, and the mourning and funerary rites. These are the so-called Family Rituals, and they have been singled out for special attention by the great Neo-Confucian thinker Chu Hsi (1130–1200), who has helped to promote their influence not only in China itself, but also in traditional Korea and beyond. While many of these rituals are no longer observed, they offer useful evidence of the religious character of Confucianism.

The rituals include the male adolescent's "Capping," some time between the ages of fifteen and twenty, when he receives his formal hat and ceremonial gown, as well as his formal name. In addition, a wine libation is made and the young man is presented formally to his ancestors. . . . After that comes marriage, also a union of families, which begins with the announcement of the event to the ancestors in the temple, accompanied by a wine libation. . . .

The family rituals are obviously part and parcel of an ancestral cult. The invisible ancestors receive reports from the living members of the family regarding births and weddings, as well as during those occasions that mark the adolescent's entry into adult society. There are also other rituals dedicated more directly to the deceased, such as mourning and funerary rites, and the anniversaries attached to the memories of the deceased members of the family. These occupy much attention in the *Book of Rites;* one might say the entire classical text is preoccupied especially with these occasions and how such rituals should be enacted. . . .

HUMAN NATURE AND THE RITES: MENCIUS AND HSÜN-TZU

As we have described it, Confucianism was an ancient teaching, which Confucius himself preferred to attribute to the sages of old, even if we find in it facets that are new and distinct against the perspective of ancient religion. With time, the disciples of the school, called *Ju* or scholars, achieved greater social recognition. Etymologically, as we have mentioned, the word refers to a coward or weakling, and it became associated with these people probably because they preferred attention to ritual matters and the learning of the ancients rather than to the sword at a time when aristocrats were mostly fighting men. Eventually, the term would also achieve respectability, and the entire culture became tilted to scholarly rather than military virtues, even if conquests continued to be made by the sword.

The Confucian school was further developed by its later followers, including Mencius and Hsün-tzu. These differed not merely with Confucius himself on certain issues, but even more among themselves. Yet they share enough to contribute together to the building up of the Confucian tradition. On the other hand, Mo-tzu, who was once a follower of the Confucian school, moved away from it to begin a distinctive school of thought, and was much criticised, especially by Mencius, for ideas like universal love, as being subversive of family values.

The word Mencius, like the word Confucius, is the Latinised form for Master Meng (Meng-tzu), whose name was Meng Ko (372–289 B.C.), a native of a small state adjacent to Confucius' Lu. From the stories that have come down to us, Meng is described as having been an orphan boy, quite difficult when very young, and brought up by a wise and virtuous mother. Like Confucius, he travelled from one feudal state to another, looking for a ruler who would accept his advice. Unlike Confucius, his advise was often given bluntly, and of course, his time (the "Warring States") was in much greater turmoil than the earlier times (the "Spring and Autumn period"). It appears that the feuding lords regarded him as hopelessly impractical for preaching benevolence and righteousness when might was making right in the struggle for political survival. More than the *Analects*, the *Book of Mencius* possesses real eloquence, with passages of lofty idealism and even mysticism.

Hsün-tzu was no contemporary of Mencius. Master Hsün, called Hsün K'uang or Hsün Ch'ing (312?–238 B.C.), a native of the state of Chao, also in North China, from which came virtually all early Confucians and even Mohists. He was appointed magistrate of Lanling, in the powerful state of Ch'i, and served as such for a short period. He left behind a work of the same name (*Hsün-tzu*) with thirty-two sections. The extant version appears to include sections coming from his own hand as well as from his disciples. The work is organised around definite topics, such as the nature of Heaven, and the wickedness of human nature. The thinking is developed much more logically than in the other Confucian works.

Some of Hsün-tzu's teachings were diametrically opposed to those of Mencius. Besides, by career as well as by orientation of thinking, he has been associated with some Legalists. He is said to have had as disciples both Li Ssu, the chief minister of Ch'in who helped to propel the state to pre-eminence and became prime minister of the First Emperor of the Ch'in dynasty, and Han Fei, the aristocrat whose teachings on political power have come down in the work, *Han Fei Tzu*.

The Rites: Sacred or Secular?

In the *Book of Mencius*, we find a clear evolution in the meaning of the term Heaven. Where Confucius only makes infrequent mention of the personal deity, Mencius speaks much more of Heaven—but not always as personal deity. According to Mencius, Heaven is present within man's heart, so that he who knows his own heart and nature, knows Heaven (*Mencius* 7A:1). It represents,

therefore, a greater immanence. It also refers more and more to the source and principle of ethical laws and values. Nevertheless, Mencius continues to hold in esteem the practice of offering sacrifices to the Lord-on-high and to ancestors: "Though a man may be wicked, if he adjusts his thoughts, fasts and bathes, he may sacrifice to the Lord-on-high" (*Mencius* 4B:25).

Hsün-tzu sees a difference between a *gentleman* of education, who uses his rationality, and the common people, who believe in fortune and misfortune. Where we had earlier found divination in the royal ancestral temples of the Shang dynasty, and rain dances sponsored by the state, we find in *Hsün-tzu* the movement away from such religious practices, on the part of the higher classes, and the identification of such with the "superstitious" commoners. It is the beginning of the separation between Confucianism as an élite tradition, and so-called popular religion, at a grass-roots level. . . .

As an education, the rites are supported by music. In the *Book of Rites*, a text which manifests Hsün-tzu's influence, the chapter on music also extols it as a help in gaining inner equilibrium and tranquility—the equilibrium is the reflection of the harmony of elegant music. Together, music and the rites maintain or restore an inner harmony, which is or ought to be, a reflection of the harmony between Heaven and earth. This reflects the teachings of the Doctrine of the Mean, also a chapter from the same ritual text. The philosophical assumption here is the correlation between the microcosm and the macrocosm, between the inner workings of man's mind and heart and the creative processes of the universe. Here, we touch upon the heart of the Chinese meaning of harmony, with its obvious mystical dimension. . . .

Human Nature: Good or Evil?

The Chinese word for human nature is *hsing/xing*, a compound including the term for mind or heart, and life or offspring. Philological scholarship demonstrates the association between etymology and early religious worship. The human being is he or she who has received from Heaven the gift of life and all the innate endowments of human nature, especially the shared faculty of moral discernment. Thus the meaning of *hsin* as mind and heart is closer to the biblical Hebrew notion of *lev*, the seat of both reason and emotions, than it is to the somewhat more intellectual Greek *nous* or Latin *mens*, to which English "mind" is related. Mencius says that the sense of right and wrong is common to all (2A:6), distinguishing the human from the beast. From this flows another belief, that of the natural equality of all, which exists in spite of social hierarchy, or any distinction between the "civilised" and the "barbarian."

The Confucian tradition has sometimes been criticised for its inability to explain the place of evil in human existence. While the Shang dynasty's King T'ang publicly begged the Lord-on-high for forgiveness for his sins . . . , Confucian philosophy was not to develop a theory of sin as offence against God. Rather, it affirms the presence of evil, explaining this as either the product of contact between an originally good nature and its wicked environment, as Mencius tends to say, or as inherent in human nature itself, which is the position of Hsün-tzu. . . .

POLITICS: CONFUCIANISM AS "CIVIL RELIGION"

The term "civil religion" comes from the American sociologist Robert Bellah, who is also a Japan specialist. It refers to the religious or quasi-religious regard for civic values and traditions marked by feasts, rituals, dogmas and creeds. He applied the term especially to the American situation, with the coexistence of several faiths like Protestant and Roman Catholic Christianity and Judaism, sharing a common belief in one God and in a set of religious values, as well as in a religion of nationalism with its creed, catechism and dogma reflected in symbols of civil unity like the flag, and in documents like the Declaration of Independence and the Constitution. Certain addresses like Washington's Farewell and Lincoln's Second Inaugural took on religious overtones, while the Pledge of Allegiance became a standard rite for school children much as morning prayers had been.

We make use of the term here in the Chinese context, because we find certain parallels in the cases of a modern society like that of the United States and traditional Chinese society. Although not usually regarded as a high priest, the American President is expected to adhere to, and articulate, certain common tenets of the religious beliefs of the people, and does this in a near-ritual form on certain state occasions. In the Chinese case, state religion, which overlaps with Confucianism as the state ideology, actually embraces the tenets and practices of Taoism. Aside from the sacrifice to Heaven and the ancestral cult, which are not found in American civil religion, traditional China adhered to certain political principles with implicit religious sanctions. These bear similarity to some of the principles enshrined in the American Declaration of Independence, which offers the justification for the people's revolution against British rule. We refer here to the Chinese belief in Heaven's bestowing a mandate to govern to the rulers, who forfeit it if they become tyrants.

The Politics of Heaven's Mandate

Much more than Christianity, Confucian teachings are oriented to improving the political order, as a means of achieving human-heartedness. The teaching of *jen* is extended to the political order, where it is defined as benevolent government, a government of moral persuasion, in which the leader gives the example of personal integrity, and selfless devotion to the people. Confucian teaching prompted generations of scholars to strive for participation in government. For the human is never regarded as dualistic, as matter and mind, body and soul. It is always accepted as *one*, as existing in society, as striving as well for physical well-being, for social harmony, and for moral and spiritual perfection. The Confucian sage has been described as possessing the qualities of "sageliness within and kingliness without." In other words, he should have the heart of the sage, and the wisdom of the king. We have here what may be called "philosopher kings" as in Plato's *Republic*.

But while Confucian teachings were originally aimed at advising the rulers, they became increasingly applied to the training of those who would act as the rulers' advisors. The problem for the minister or would-be minister is: what should one do were the ruler not only less than sage, as most rulers turned out to be, but even despotic and tyrannical, as some of them definitely were? Confucius himself offers a doctrine of Rectification of Names, which has sometimes been misunderstood. In eight cryptic words, he says: "Ruler, ruler; minister, minister; father, father; son, son" (*Analects* 13:3). These have been misinterpreted as representing a caste system where the ruler is always ruler, the minister always minister. However, this is obviously a mistake, since every son is expected to become a father. The correct interpretation is that the ruler should be a *good* ruler, the minister a *good* minister, the father a *good* father, and the son a *good* son. Names should represent realities, but in Plato's sense of ideal forms. . . .

. . . And Mencius also offered a clear formulation of the doctrine of rebellion or revolution, known popularly as the "removal of the Mandate" (*ko-ming/geming*). It was Mencius who said that killing a tyrant was not regicide, since the tyrant no longer deserved to rule (1B:8); it was Mencius who declared: "The people come first; the altars of the earth and grain come afterwards; the ruler comes last" (7B:14). . . .

The Confucian tradition was to include political conservatives as well as moderate and radical reformers; there were those whose priority was to serve the state; there were also those who remained independent of the state, while seeking to change or transform it. Confucian scholars were usually activists, either serving the government, advising and admonishing the ruler or engaging in reforms, or even protesting against tyranny through passive or active resistance. . . .

COMPROMISES WITH OTHER SCHOOLS: HAN CONFUCIANISM

The Han period is important in religious history because during that time Confucianism became a state orthodoxy (some would say, the state religion), Taoism became an institutional religion, and Buddhism was introduced into the country. Han China represents an epoch when all under Heaven was unified under one emperor ruling by Heaven's mandate with the help of Confucian orthodoxy. . . .

Kingship: Real and Ideal

The Han scholar reputed to be the most influential in consolidating Confucian gains was the "political theologian" Tung Chung-shu (179–104 B.C.), who sought with metaphysical arguments to persuade the ruler to exercise benevolent government. Systematising traditional thought, he established Heaven, Earth and Man as a horizontal triad or trinity, with kingship as the vertical link between them:

> Those who in ancient times invented writing drew three lines and connected them through the middle, calling the character "king." The three lines are Heaven, earth and man, and that which passes through the middle joins the principles of all three. . . . Thus the king is but the executor of Heaven. He regulates its seasons and brings them to completion. . . .

Cosmology: Yin-Yang and the Five Agents

Tung Chung-shu and Han Confucians also incorporated ideas from the Yin-Yang and **Five Agents** schools. These were independent and ancient schools, but their ideas gradually fused with one another and were absorbed into both Taoism and Confucianism. We are here referring to cosmological ideas of two opposing yet complementary forces, *yin* and *yang*, as well as to a system of thinking focused on five primal elements that were also viewed as active cosmic agents always engaged in a process of mutual interaction and change. These five agents are water, fire, wood, metal and earth. Each has power over the other; that is, water is over fire, fire over earth, earth over metal, metal over wood, wood over water.

These five agents thus differ from the Greek or Hindu "Four Elements" of earth, air, fire and water. Not only does the Chinese group include an organic substance, wood, but it appears to exclude the very important and all-pervasive air. Actually, air or *ch'i* had always been regarded as fundamental and indeed, all-pervasive. The Five Agents, however, served another purpose. Together with *yin* and *yang*, they formed a system of correlation which integrated life and the universe.

Han Confucianism was tolerant of exaggerations and superstitions. Together with the reconstructed Five Classics, many apocryphal texts were also accepted; indeed, each classic had at least one apocryphal text associated with it. We hear of Confucius' alleged miraculous birth and many other legends. There were also widespread beliefs in omens and portents, supported by a wide array of prognostication and divination texts. Eventually, scholarly consensus would subordinate the nonrational and non-historical materials to stricter scrutiny. But the Chinese belief in omens and portents continued until our own times. During centuries of history, eclipses of the sun and moon were carefully predicted and studied for their values as portents or omens. Natural disasters, whether flood or droughts, were also regarded as signs from Heaven of displeasure of misrule. The earthquake in Tangshan, North China, that just preceded Mao Zedong's death in 1976, was widely seen as an omen, predicting drastic change.

NEO-CONFUCIANISM AS A RESPONSE TO BUDDHISM

As a term, "Neo-Confucianism" is also a Western coinage. The usual Chinese usage is to refer to the later development of Confucianism as the "Metaphysical Thought" (*Li-hsüeh*, literally "the learning of principle"). This was a *new* expression of Confucian thought, based on a smaller corpus of classical texts, reinterpreted in response to Buddhist challenges. In this respect, the Neo-Confucian movement parallels scholastic philosophy in the West, which sought to reinterpret Christian teachings with the assistance of Greek philosophical concepts. Ironically, since the rise of Neo-Confucianism signalled the decline of Buddhism, Buddhist influences on Chinese thought are best discerned afterwards in the structure of Neo-Confucian thinking.

During the Han dynasty and the later T'ang dynasty (when Buddhism became prominent), many commentaries and subcommentaries were written on the classical texts themselves, which also became the core of the examination curriculum. But all this was largely the work of philologists. The Neo-Confucian philosophers made a different kind of contribution, as they developed their new thinking in response to Taoist and Buddhist influences. These thinkers also turned away from Han philology and superstitions. They looked for the spiritual legacy of Confucianism itself—the "legacy of the mind and heart" that we may call spirituality. It was a new development, quite different from the direction of Han Confucianism, which oscillated between the rationalism of Hsün-tzu and the superstitions of signs and omens. It also marked all later Chinese thinking, drawing the wealth of spiritual doctrine into mainstream philosophy. While Western spirituality has its rightful place in ascetical and mystical theology, it remains the domain of the monks rather than the laity, and has never been part and parcel of Western philosophical heritage. In the Chinese context, the spirituality of Confucius and Mencius, and even of Lao-tzu and Chuang-tzu, became strengthened through the Buddhist experience and the Neo-Confucian response to this experience, which was primarily the response of lay teachers and thinkers on a quest for sageliness.

The Neo-Confucian movement also strengthened a new understanding of lineage, so central to Chinese religious as well as philosophical thought. According to Chu Hsi (1130–1200), the true understanding of Confucius' teachings was lost after Mencius, and only rediscovered by his own intellectual predecessors—the eleventh-century thinkers Chou Tun-yi, Chang Tsai and the Ch'eng brothers.

The Four Books as a New Canon

The Five Classics had stimulated philological exegesis, but had not promoted sufficient philosophical and religious commentaries. The Sung dynasty Neo-Confucian philosophers reformulated Confucian philosophy on the basis of a smaller corpus of texts, the **Four Books**. They contained the following texts:

- The *Analects* of Confucius (*Lun-yü*) includes twenty chapters, divided into nearly fifty sections, some of which are very brief. The earliest text with any historical information about Confucius, it goes back to about one century after the Master's death and gives the conversations between Confucius and his disciples. The chapters are not organised systematically, and the dialogues they offer are fragmentary.

- The *Book of Mencius*, a work in seven chapters, each subdivided into two parts, presents the conversations between Mencius and his disciples. Probably compiled after Mencius' death, although perhaps not that much later, it too is not systematically organised. But

the passages are longer and the contents livelier, and include many anecdotes.

- The *Great Learning* is a brief chapter taken from the *Book of Rites*. Its concern is less ritual, but rather moral and spiritual cultivation, considered the beginning of good rulership.

- The *Doctrine of the Mean* is a slightly longer text, also taken from the *Book of Rites*. Its spiritual and philosophical content focuses on the inner life of psychic equilibrium and harmony.

In giving these texts pre-eminence, Chu Hsi and the other Neo-Confucian philosophers oriented Confucian scholarship increasingly to metaphysical and spiritual questions, at a time when Buddhism had made great inroads. In fact, their own thinking shows signs of Buddhist and Taoist philosophical influence. The result is a new synthesis, a *Weltanschauung* that builds on the old moralist answers to questions about life and the world, with a clearer metaphysical framework and spiritual profundity. The basic Neo-Confucian quest, while it has its scholastic roots, is definitely oriented to self-transcendence in the achievement of sagehood, rather than to rising on the bureaucratic ladder simply by passing official examinations. The synthesis took shape especially during the Sung (960–1279) and Ming (1368–1661) dynasties.

Chu Hsi on the Absolute: T'ai-chi *and* Li

Chu Hsi's philosophy represents a conscious synthesis of previous philosophies, combining as it does the "naturalist" legacy of the Taoists and Buddhists, and the psychist and culturalist legacy of the Confucians themselves, modified also by an undercurrent of Buddhist influences. His theory of human nature draws from both sides. For Chu Hsi, as for the mainstream of Chinese philosophy, the human being and the cosmos are each paradigms, one of the other, so that evil loses its significance in the affirmation of human perfectibility, as expressed through the doctrine of sagehood.

A terse expression of the world regarded as an ontological paradigm is given in the philosophy of the Great Ultimate (*T'ai-chi*), which Chu Hsi took over from Chou Tun-yi. This is a symbolic expression of cosmology which emphasises the interrelatedness of the world and man in macrocosm/microcosm terms; it also hides within itself a secret Taoist formula for alchemy and yoga. And it points possibly to early Chinese beliefs in a supreme deity under symbols of astral bodies.

Chu Hsi interprets the *T'ai-chi* with the help of the concept of *li*, those "principles" which constitute all things, and which had been given prominence by the Ch'eng brothers, especially Ch'eng Yi. *Li* may be defined as forms of essences, as organising and normative principles, belonging to the realm "above shapes." It is prior—although not in a temporal sense—to its co-ordinate, *ch'i*, translated sometimes as "ether," or "matter-energy," which belongs to the realm "within shapes." All things are constituted of both *li* and *ch'i*, somewhat as with Aristotelian form and matter, with the difference that *li* is passive and *ch'i* is dynamic.

The Great Ultimate is the most perfect *li*, a kind of primal archetype. It is also the *totality* of all the principles (*li*) of the myriad things, as brought together into a single whole. It serves in Chinese philosophy the function of the Form of the Good in Platonism, and that of God in Aristotelianism.

In place of a personal deity, Chu Hsi was speaking about an absolute which he clearly identified with both Heaven and the Lord-on-high. He asserted that it is not correct to speak about "a man in Heaven" who is lord of the world, but that it is equally wrong to say that "there is no such Ruler." He was removing the anthropomorphic overtones of these terms while affirming the presence of a higher power, a metaphysical more than a personal Absolute.

> The Book of Poetry and the Book of History speak as though there is a human being there above, commanding things to come to pass, as in [passages] where they mention the Lord (***Ti***) as being filled with wrath, etc. But even here what they refer to is [the action of] *Li*. There is nothing more eminent under Heaven [i.e., in the universe] than *Li*. Hence it is called Ruler. "The august Lord-on-high has conferred even upon the inferior people a moral sense." [The word] "conferred" conveys the idea of a ruler. . . .

Chu Hsi was probably the greatest mind, and the most prolific author among the Neo-Confucian giants. Though he was not accepted as an orthodox thinker during his own life, his commentaries on the Four Books were eventually integrated into the curriculum of the civil service examinations (1313), making his philosophy the new state orthodoxy for six centuries to come. The history of Chinese philosophy after Chu Hsi may be described as a debate between those who, like him, wished to give more importance to *li*, and others who wished to give more emphasis to *ch'i*. The protagonists of *li* tended to presuppose a pre-established pattern of harmony in the universe and in human nature, to be recaptured and maintained by a proper balance of reason and the emotions. The protagonists of *ch'i*, on the other hand, were inclined to minimise the opposition between reason and

the emotions. In other words, the tendency was toward either idealism, in the first case, or materialism, in the second. It is interesting to note that Chinese Marxist scholars have consistently sought to discover in *ch'i* a materialist ancestry for Chinese Marxism. . . .

NEO-CONFUCIANISM IN MODERN TIMES

During most of the last thousand years, Neo-Confucianism has been the official philosophy for China. But the Jesuit missionaries, including especially Matteo Ricci, preferred classical Confucianism to the later development. They opposed the metaphysical dimensions of Neo-Confucian philosophy, which bore a pantheistic imprint of Buddhist influence. Actually, it has become impossible to separate Neo-Confucianism from earlier Confucianism, so that an onslaught on one meant the same on the other. In the late nineteenth century, Chinese intellectuals began a soul-searching questioning of the cultural heritage, particularly Confucianism. It was regarded by many of them as a weight and a burden —an intellectual shackle on the mind, preventing the country from modernisation. Its strongest critic was probably the early-twentieth-century writer Lu Hsün, whose short stories attacked the "cannibalistic" ritual religion that stifled human freedom and individual initiative in the name of passive, conformist virtues. These critiques satirised the dehumanising elements in a fossilised tradition until then inextricably bound up with the social-political establishment. They were also expressive of the newly awakened nationalism, desirous of asserting independence against the coming of the Western Powers and Japan. It was in the midst of these anti-traditionalist, anti-Confucian voices of the May Fourth Movement (1919) that the Chinese Communist Party was born (1921). What began as a search for intellectual freedom entailed finally a repudiation of the monopoly of tradition, with the Communist takeover of the mainland (1949).

Mainland scholars have sought as well to point out for the sake of attack the *religious* character of the Neo-Confucian movement, including Chu Hsi's teachings on meditation and spiritual cultivation and Wang Yangming's penchant for mysticism. However, Liu Shaoqi, former head of state in Communist China, had lauded both Confucian and Neo-Confucian ideas in his address, *How to Be a Good Communist*:

> The Chinese scholars of the Confucian school had a number of methods for the cultivation of their body and mind. Every religion has various

methods and forms of cultivation of its own. The "investigation of things, the extension of knowledge, sincerity of thought, the rectification of the heart, the cultivation of the person, the regulation of the family, the ordering well of the state and the making tranquil of the whole kingdom" as set forth in the Great Learning also means the same. All this shows that in achieving one's progress one must make serious and energetic efforts to carry on self-cultivation and study.

During the Cultural Revolution (1966–76), the Anti-Confucius movement entered a new phase, with diatribes in 1973–74 linking the fallen Defence chief Lin Piao with Confucius. This was the most vehement attack ever mounted. Long before that, Liu Shaoqi had become "enemy number one" to Chairman Mao. His writings were banned, and the Confucian and Neo-Confucian ideas he had praised also came under heavy attack.

While Marxist scholars were vigorously criticising the entire traditional legacy, a group of philosophers and scholars in Taiwan and Hong Kong expressed their concern for the survival of Chinese culture, which they identified especially with Neo-Confucianism. I refer here to the plea for a return to Neo-Confucian sources, in "A Manifesto for the Reappraisal of Sinology and Reconstruction of Chinese Culture," made public by a group of Chinese philosophers in Taipei in 1958. This statement speaks of the harmony of the "way of Heaven" (*t'ien-tao/tiandao*) and the "way of man" (*jen-tao/rendao*) as the central legacy of Confucianism. It also challenges Western Sinologists to give greater attention to Confucian spirituality as the core of Chinese culture, which it claims was not properly understood by the missionaries of the sixteenth and seventeenth centuries. In saying this, these scholars interestingly concurred with mainland scholars in the judgement that Neo-Confucianism in particular possesses an undeniably spiritual and religious character. . . .

SOURCES

I have organized the sources chronologically into six different periods in order to provide a developmental overview of the significant literature of Confucianism. A historical arrangement is particularly important in the case of Confucianism because so much of the later literature comments on and presupposes a knowledge of the earlier materials.

A wide variety of topics are discussed in this literature including rituals, the origin of the universe, the nature of morality, good government, how one should conduct one's life, and much more. Much of what you will find is instruction on how to become a sage, or wise person. This goal is of central importance in Confucianism and is as important to a Confucian as enlightenment is to a Buddhist.

8.2 THE CLASSICAL PERIOD (ca. 700–221 B.C.E.)

From the classical period stems the classical texts of Confucianism that have had a formative impact on the subsequent tradition. The texts attributed to the three most important Confucian thinkers, Confucius (551–479 B.C.E.), Mencius (371–289 B.C.E.), and Hsün Tzu (298–238 B.C.E.), come from this period. Also, the **Five Classics,** although containing material from a previous period, took shape during this period.

8.2.1 Book of Rites

The Confucian tradition does not begin with Confucius. Even though Confucius is respectfully called the First Teacher, he explicitly states that he is a transmitter of a tradition much older than he is. According to the Confucian tradition, he preserved, edited, transmitted, and commented on a wisdom he inherited from antiquity.

As do many religious traditions, Confucianism views innovation and newness suspiciously. Even when something radically new emerges, it is often claimed to be nothing more than a return to the classical teachings. Being faithful to the tradition is what counts. Religions, and Confucianism is no exception here, tend to view themselves as conserving a revered past. However, they also change, adapt, and give rise to innovative geniuses that keep the tradition alive and growing. Confucius was one of those innovative geniuses who both transmitted and changed a tradition.

The *Book of Rites* is part of the *Classic of Rites* (one of the Five Classics) Confucius supposedly edited and transmitted. It is a collection of discourses compiled during the Former or Western Han dynasty (206 B.C.E.–8 C.E.) from earlier materials. The Chinese word here translated as "rites" is *li. Li* encompasses all kinds of behavior, both public and private, ranging across such activities as seasonal festivals, table manners, rites of passage, and governmental functions.

According to some social scientists, ritual actions, like many actions, have both a manifest function and a latent function. The manifest function of some action is the conscious or intended function, and the latent, or hidden, function is unconscious or unintended. A function is what any belief or activity does to satisfy some social need. For example, beliefs and rituals surrounding death may manifestly (be intended to) reduce anxiety over death. However, these same beliefs may also unintentionally increase anxiety by reminding people of their own deaths (latent function).

In most activities, the manifest function is the same as the purpose of an action. So, for example, the manifest function of an economic activity like spending money is the same as its purpose, to gain something. However, in religious activities (only in religious activities?), the manifest function may not be the same as the purpose. A prayer for a safe fishing trip may manifestly reduce anxiety over traveling on the ocean, but its purpose may be to appease the anger of some storm deity or spirit thereby ensuring a safe trip. In order to discover the manifest functions of some activity, ask what *social needs* it may be intended to satisfy. Discovering the latent function is more difficult and requires a sensitivity to possible unintended consequences of human action.

The selections that follow come from three important chapters of the *Book of Rites:* "The Principles of Sacrifice," "The Mean," and "The Great Learning." A later Confucian scholar named Chu Hsi (1130–1200) excerpted both "The Mean" and "The Great Learning" and made them independent texts. These two books, along with the *Analects* and the *Mencius,* are known as the **Four Books,** and in the fourteenth century they became required reading for the civil service examination—a system of study and examination that lasted into the early twentieth century. Given their use, it seems appropriate that Chu Hsi rearranged the eight steps of "The Great Learning" to begin with "the investigation of things" rather than "making thoughts sincere," the latter being the original first step. Chu Hsi's arrangement has become standard and is followed in the translation below.

The Principles of Sacrifice, The Mean, and The Great Learning

READING QUESTIONS

1. What attitude is expressed through ritual, and what does "completion" (blessings) mean?
2. What is filial behavior?
3. What are the manifest and latent (hidden) functions of sacrifices in honor of the ancestors?
4. What does sacrifice teach?
5. What are centrality and harmony, and why are they important?
6. What does sincerity have to do with the trinity of heaven, earth, and humans?
7. What is the great learning, and what makes it "great"?

THE PRINCIPLES OF SACRIFICE

Of all the ways of governing human beings well, none is more compelling than ritual; of the five categories of rites, none is more important than sacrificial offerings. Sacrifice does not enter from without: it issues from within, in the mind. When the mind is in awe, it is expressed through ritual. Only worthies are able to plumb the meaning of sacrifice.

The sacrifices of worthy persons receive their blessings, but these are not what the world ordinarily calls blessings. The term "blessings" here means "completion," an expression that means complete accord. When everything is in accord, there is completion. This is to say that internally, there is full completion of the self; externally, there is complete accord with the Way. When loyal ministers serve their sovereigns and filial children serve their parents, they act from this same fundamental basis. When this happens, then on high there is complete accord with ghosts and spiritual beings; outside the family sphere, there is accord with sovereigns and seniors; inside the family sphere, there is filiality toward parents. This then is completion. Only worthy people can attain to this completion, and when they do they may then sacrifice. The sacrifices of worthy people may be described thus: the sacrificers perfect their sincerity and good faith with loyalty and reverence and then offer

From *Chinese Religion: An Anthology of Sources,* edited by Deborah Sommer, pp. 35–39. Copyright © 1995 by Oxford University Press. Used by permission of Oxford University Press, Inc.

their votive gifts following the way of ritual, accompanying the rites with music and performing them openly, without seeking anything. This then is the attitude of the filial child.

By sacrificing, one continues to care for one's parents and act with filiality. Filiality means "to care for," and caring means according with the Way and not transgressing proper conventions of behavior. Filial people serve their parents in three ways: in life, they care for them; in death, they mourn them; when mourning is over, they sacrifice to them. Caring for parents expresses accord; mourning expresses sorrow; sacrifice expresses reverence and timely attentiveness. Filial behavior lies in fulfilling these three criteria.

Upon fulfilling one's responsibilities within the family, one then seeks a helpmate from outside, and for this there are the rites of marriage. When a ruler seeks a wife, he says, "I ask from you this jadelike maiden to share with my humble self this poor state, to serve at the ancestral temple and at the altars of the land and grain." This is essentially how one seeks a helpmate. Husbands and wives must conduct sacrifices together, and each has his or her own respective duties, without and within. Only when these responsibilities are performed is there completion. Everything, of lesser and greater importance, must be prepared: minces and pickles made from the products of land and water, stands for the meats of the three sacrificial animals, condiments for the eight dishes, rare animals and plants—all the things of the yin and the yang forces. Everything, whether generated by heaven or grown upon the earth, is set forth. Outwardly, there is a complete profusion of things, and inwardly, there is a complete perfection of the will. This is the attitude appropriate to sacrificing.

Hence the Son of Heaven himself plows south of the city to provide grain for the sacrificial cauldrons, and the empress tends silkworms north of the city to supply ritual attire. The enfeoffed lords also plow east of the city to supply grain, and their wives likewise practice sericulture north of the city to supply caps and attire. It is not that the Son of Heaven and feudal lords have no one to do the plowing for them, or that the empress and the lords' wives have no one to do sericulture for them: it is just that they themselves want to express their sincerity and good faith. Such qualities are what is meant by perfection, and perfection means reverence; only when reverence is perfected can one serve the spiritual and the numinous. This is the way of sacrifice. . . .

Three aspects of sacrifice are especially important: of offerings, libations; of music, the high songs; and of dance performances, the "Night of the Battle of King Wu." These are the ways of the Chou, and they give outward expression to the will of the honorable person

and enhance it. One's will is expressed in the advancing and retreating motion of one's steps, lighter and heavier, proportionate to the sentiment behind them. Even a sage cannot be inwardly lighthearted and outwardly serious. Honorable people conduct sacrifices in person to clarify what is important, and they follow the way of ritual. Emphasizing the three important aspects of sacrificing, they present offerings to the august personator of the dead. This is the way of the sage.

After sacrificing there are foodstuffs left over, and even though these are the most peripheral aspects of rites, one must still know what to do with them. As the ancient saying goes, the ending must be as fine as the beginning, and leftovers must be considered in the same vein. As a gentleman of antiquity once said, "The personator of the dead eats what the ghosts and spirits leave behind." This is a kind practice that illustrates the workings of governance. When the personator arises after eating, the ruler and three great ministers eat, and when the ruler arises, the six great officers eat, consuming what the ruler has left over. The great officers get up, and then the eight officers eat, those of lower rank eating what their superiors have left. Then the officers get up, and taking what is left, go out, placing it in the hall below. Finally the lesser officials come in and take it away, and the subordinate officials eat what their superiors have left. At each change there are more people, illustrating the degrees of higher and lower rank. Everyone shares in this beneficent custom, and this is what happens to the contents of the four vessels of millet in the ancestral temple. The ancestral temple is itself symbolic of the whole land.

Sacrifice is a great benefaction. When superiors receive some benefit, they then bestow it on those below them. It is just that superiors receive the beneficence first and subordinates receive it later; it is not that superiors accumulate excess while subordinates suffer from cold and hunger. When people of higher rank receive some boon, those below wait for it to flow down to them, knowing that beneficence will reach them. One can see all this by considering the distribution of leftovers from sacrifice, and hence it is said that this practice illustrates the workings of governance.

Sacrifice is the greatest of things when all its preparations are complete. What do such preparations teach? Through them the ruler can teach respect for rulers and ministers in the sphere outside of the family, and within the family sphere he can teach people to be filial. So if the sovereign is enlightened, the ministers will follow him. When he discharges his duties in the ancestral temple and to the altars of the land and grain, then his sons and grandsons will be filial. His teaching is brought forth because he perfects this Way and perfects this kind of deportment. Honorable people should act this way themselves in serving the ruler. Misunderstandings that occur between higher-ranking people should not be taken out on their subordinates, and subordinates should not direct their own animosities toward their superiors. Criticizing the actions of others but then doing the same thing oneself goes contrary to this teaching. So these are the fundamentals of the instruction of the honorable person. Is this not truly the epitome of concord? Is this not truly what is meant by sacrificing? So it is said that sacrifice is the basis of instruction.

In sacrifice there are ten proper norms: the ways appropriate to serving ghosts and spirits, the proper comportment of rulers and ministers, the relationships between parent and child, the distinctions between those of higher and lower rank, the degrees of intimacy between close and distant relatives, the distributions of rank and emolument, the differences between husband and wife, fairness in the affairs of governance, the order of priorities between senior and junior, and the boundaries between higher and lower. These are the ten norms.

THE MEAN

What heaven has mandated is called the nature. According with this nature is called the Way (*Tao*). Cultivating the Way is called instruction.

This Way cannot be departed from for even an instant, and if it can be, then it is not really the Way. Hence the honorable person is cautious about things as yet unseen and apprehensive about things as yet unheard.

Nothing is more visible than what is darkly hidden, and nothing is more evident than what can be barely detected. So the honorable person is cautious even when alone.

The condition when pleasure, anger, sorrow, and joy have not yet arisen is called centrality; the condition when these do arise and all reach a measured expression is called harmony. Centrality is the fundamental basis of the world, and harmony is the attainment of the Way throughout the world.

When centrality and harmony are perfected, everything in heaven and earth finds its place and all things flourish.

[1.1–5]

Spirits

The master said, "The virtue of ghosts and spirits is truly marvelous. One looks for them but they cannot be seen; one listens for them but they cannot be heard. They are at the marrow of things but they cannot be

detected. They cause everyone in the world to observe vigils and purify themselves, dress in their richest attire, and present sacrificial offerings. Then the spirits seem to float just above the heads of the sacrifiers, all around them. As it is said in the *Book of Odes*, 'The approaches of spirits are unfathomable. How could one be unmoved by this?' So it is said that what can barely be detected becomes evident, and that sincerity cannot be kept concealed."

[16.1–5]

The Five Relationships

So that the Way may be attained throughout the land, people must consider five things, and for enacting the Way, one must consider three. The five are the relationships between ruler and minister, parent and child, husband and wife, elder and younger brother, and friend and friend. These five constitute the attainment of the Way throughout the land. Understanding, humanity, and fortitude are the three aspects of attaining to virtue throughout the land, and one enacts them with a single-minded oneness. Some people understand all this from birth, others understand it through study, and still others understand it only through painful experience; nevertheless, once they understand it, those people are all the same. Some are able to enact all this with ease; others, with some effort; still others, with strenuous effort. Nevertheless, once they succeed, they are all the same.

[20.8–9]

Sincerity

Sincerity is the Way of heaven, and the attainment of sincerity is the Way of human beings. A person who is possessed of sincerity, who achieves things effortlessly and apprehends things without excessive deliberation, who goes along with things and attains the Way, is a sage. Those possessed of sincerity embrace what is good and hold fast to it.

They study widely and inquire extensively, ponder things carefully and make clear deliberations; they act with earnestness.

They do not rest lest there be something they have not studied or studied but not yet grasped, or lest there be something they have not inquired about or have inquired about but do not yet understand. Nor do they rest lest there be something they have not yet pondered or have pondered but not yet apprehended, or lest there be something they have not yet deliberated, or have deliberated but have not yet clarified. They do not rest lest there be something they have not done or have done but without earnestness. If someone else accomplishes things after only one try, they will try a hundred times; if someone else accomplishes things after only ten attempts, they will try a thousand times.

If people are able to proceed in this way, then even if they are stupid they will become bright and intelligent, and even if they are weak they will become strong.

That this intelligence comes from sincerity is human nature itself. The fact that sincerity comes from intelligence is due to instruction. If there is sincerity there will be intelligence, and where there is intelligence there will be sincerity.

[20.18–20]

A Trinity with Heaven and Earth

In this world only those who have attained the epitome of sincerity can perfect their natures, and when they have perfected their own natures, they can then perfect the natures of other people. When they have perfected the natures of other people, they can then perfect the natures of things. When they have perfected the natures of things, they can then participate in the transforming and sustaining forces of heaven and earth and form a trinity with heaven and earth.

Next below these people are those who first develop themselves in small ways. When they are able to do that, they can attain to sincerity, and when they are sincere, they begin to take shape. Shape becomes lustrous and luster becomes brightness; brightness becomes vibrancy, vibrancy becomes change, and change becomes transformation. In this world when one attains sincerity, one can transform things.

Such is the Way of the perfection of sincerity that one can have foreknowledge of things before they happen. When a state is about to prosper, auspicious omens will appear, and when a state is about to perish, baneful prodigies become manifest. These can be seen in the milfoil stalks and the tortoiseshell, and they will vibrate within one's four limbs. When either misfortune or prosperity is about to happen, both the good and the bad will be foreknown. To perfect sincerity, then, is to become like a spirit.

[22–24]

Heaven and Earth

The ways of heaven and earth can be completely explained in one phrase: they are impartial to all things. How they generate things is unfathomable. The way of heaven and earth is expansive and generous, lofty and bright, far-reaching and enduring. Heaven seems to be but a glow of brightness, but if one gazes into its inexhaustible reaches, one will see the sun, moon, stars, and celestial bodies all suspended from it. It covers all things. The earth seems to be but a mass of soil, but if one looks farther into its breadth and depth, one will see that it effortlessly bears the weight of even the Hua peaks and carries the rivers and seas without their leaking away. It holds up all things. Mountains seem to be but lumps of rock, but looking at their breadth and height one sees plants and trees flourishing and birds and beasts thriving in their midst. Many treasures lie within them. Consider a spoonful of water, but then look at water's unfathomable depths where great turtles, sea tortoises, scaly creatures, dragons, fishes, and green turtles live. Precious things abound there.

[26.7–9]

THE GREAT LEARNING

The Way of the great learning lies in clarifying bright virtue, loving the people, and abiding in the highest good.

Only if one knows where to abide can one develop resolve, and only with resolve can one become tranquil. Only tranquility allows one to be restfully secure, and only with this security can one be reflective. Only by reflecting on things can one apprehend them.

Things have their roots and their branches, and affairs have their beginnings and their ends. If one knows what should be first and what should be last, then one can draw near the Way.

In antiquity, those who wanted to clarify their bright virtue throughout the entire realm first had to govern their states well. Those who wanted to govern their states well first had to manage their own families, and those who wanted to manage their families first had to develop their own selves. Those who wanted to develop themselves first rectified their own minds, and those who wanted to rectify their minds first made their thoughts sincere. Those who wanted to make their thoughts sincere first extended their knowledge. Those who wanted to extend their knowledge first had to investigate things.

Once things are investigated, knowledge can be extended. When knowledge is extended, thoughts can be made sincere; when thoughts are sincere, the mind can be rectified. When the mind is rectified, one can develop the self; once the self is developed, the family can be managed. When the family is managed, the state can be governed well; when the state is governed well, peace can prevail throughout the land.

From the Son of Heaven to the common people, everyone must consider developing the self to be the fundamental root of things. If the roots are confused, then the branches cannot be well governed. It should never happen that important things are trifled with, or that trifles are considered important.

8.2.2 Analects

The **Analects** (literally, "Sayings") are a collection of aphoristic sayings recorded and collected by Confucius's students. Some of his students are mentioned by name, and he is often referred to by the title "Master." It contains material that probably dates to Confucius himself mixed with other material.

Confucius claims that people who genuinely seek to cultivate their humanity in a social context of appropriate relationships can become a *chün-tzu,* a word sometimes translated as "honorable person," "superior man," "noble man," or "gentleman." Literally, *chün-tzu* means "scion of a ruling family." In Confucius's day, it was widely believed that one is a *chün-tzu* by birth, but Confucius lays the groundwork for a new and radical idea: A person can become noble and honorable by effort. In particular, one can achieve this status by cultivating such virtues as kindness (*jen*), mutual consideration (*shu*), loyalty (*chung*), and understanding (*chih*). The *tao,* or way to live properly, is not to retreat from society as some kind of recluse, but, rather, to engage society properly and live one's life as an example for others. This is particularly important for government officials and rulers: If peace, harmony, and good will are to arise in a state, the rulers must set good examples for the people to follow.

❧

CONFUCIUS

Selected Sayings

READING QUESTIONS

1. What is the honorable person like?
2. How are humanity, virtue, and consideration related?

From *Chinese Religion: An Anthology of Sources*, edited by Deborah Sommer, pp. 43–48. Copyright © 1995 by Oxford University Press. Used by permission of Oxford University Press, Inc.

3. What seems to be Confucius's attitude toward ritual, sacrifice, spirits, and praying?
4. What is the point of the two stories about "recluses"?

CONFUCIUS'S CHARACTER

The master said, "How delightful it is to study and to review from time to time what one has studied! How pleasant to have friends visit from afar!"

[1.1.1–2]

The master said, "One can still find happiness if one has only simple food to eat, water to drink, and a bent arm for a pillow. Wealth and high rank attained unrighteously are to me but floating clouds."

[7.15]

Tzu-kung said, "The master is congenial, pleasant, courteous, good tempered, and complaisant. Thus does he engage the world, and his way of engaging it is quite different from that of other people."

[1.10.2]

There were four things he was completely free of. He never showed a lack of forethought, he was not opinionated, he was not hidebound, and he was not egoistic.

[9.4]

The master offered instruction concerning four things: cultural refinement, proper conduct, loyalty, and good faith.

[7.24]

When the master was eating next to someone who was in mourning, he never ate to the full. He never sang on a day in which earlier he had been crying.

[7.9]

The master fished, but not with a net. When hunting he did not shoot at roosting birds.

[7.26]

HUMAN NATURE

Tzu-kung said, "One can apprehend the master's disquisitions on culture and refinement, but not his discussions of human nature or the way of heaven."

[5.12]

The master said, "In terms of human nature, people are much alike. But in terms of practice and effort, they are quite different."

[17.2]

Confucius said, "Those who are possessed of understanding from birth are the highest type of people. Those who understand things only after studying them are of the next lower type, and those who learn things from painful experience are yet the next. Those who have painful experiences but do not learn from them are the lowest type of people."

[16.9]

THE HONORABLE PERSON

The master said, "Isn't one truly an honorable person if one is not acknowledged by others yet still does not resent it!"

[1.1.3]

The master said, "Honorable people are modest in what they say but surpassing in what they do."

[14.29]

The master said, "There are three aspects to the way of the honorable person, but I am incapable of them: to be possessed of humanity and have no anxieties, to be wise and have no doubts, and to be strong and have no fears." Tzu-kung said, "Master, those are your ways."

[14.30]

The master said, "Honorable persons seek things within themselves. Small-minded people, on the other hand, seek things from others."

[15.20]

Confucius said, "There are three things of which the honorable person is in awe: the mandate of heaven, great people, and the words of the sages. Small-minded people do not understand the mandate of heaven and are not in awe of it; they are insolent toward great people and ridicule sages."

[16.8]

HUMANITY, VIRTUE, AND CONSIDERATION

The master rarely spoke of profit, of one's mandated fate, or of humanity.

[9.1]

The master said, "Persons possessed of humanity are like this: wanting to develop themselves, they also develop others; wanting to achieve things themselves, they also allow others to achieve what they want. This is the direction humanity takes: to use what is close to oneself as an analogy to be extended to others."

[6.28.2–3]

Chung-kung asked about humanity. The master said, "In your social affairs behave as if you are meeting with important guests, and treat people as if you were participating in a great sacrificial offering. Do not impose on other people anything you yourself dislike. Let there be no animosity either in the state or in the family." Chung-kung said, "Even though I am not gifted, I will try to practice what you have just said."

[12.2]

Fan Ch'ih asked about humanity. The master said, "Be solicitous of others." Fan Ch'ih asked about understanding. The master said, "Be understanding toward others."

[12.22]

The master said, "Only persons possessed of humanity can truly like other people or truly dislike them."

[4.3]

The master said, "Is humanity something far away? If I want to be humane, then humanity has already been attained."

[7.29]

Someone asked, "What of repaying animosity with virtue?" The master said, "How could one repay that with virtue? Repay animosity with directness, and repay virtue with virtue."

[14.36]

Tzu-kung asked, "Is there one word by which one may live one's entire life?" The master said, "Isn't that word 'consideration'? Do not impose on other people anything you yourself dislike."

[15.23]

THE WAY

The master said, "It is enough that someone who dies in the evening has heard of the Way only that morning."

[4.8]

The master said, "Tseng-tzu, my way has only one theme that holds it all together." Tseng-tzu replied, "That is so." When the master went out, the other disciples asked Tseng-tzu what Confucius had meant. Tseng-tzu replied, "The master's way is simply loyalty and consideration."

[4.15]

It is that human beings glorify the Way, not that the Way glorifies human beings.

[15.28]

GOVERNANCE

The master said, "Someone who governs with virtue is like the northern polar star, which stays in one place while all the other stars pay their respects to it."

[2.1]

Chi-k'ang Tzu asked Confucius about governance. Confucius replied, "To govern means to rectify. If you start by rectifying yourself, how would anyone else not do the same?"

[12.17]

The master said, "If you rectify your own self, then even if you give no orders they will still be carried out. If you don't rectify yourself, then even if you do give orders they will still not be followed."

[13.6]

The master said, "If one adopts administrative measures and implements punishments in a consistent fashion, the people will comply with them but will have no shame. But if one follows the Way of virtue and implements ritual consistently, the people will have a sense of shame and moreover will correct themselves."

[2.3]

Fan Ch'ih asked to study farming with him. The master said, "Better to ask an old farmer about it." He then asked to study gardening. "Better to ask an old gardener." When Fan Ch'ih left, the master said, "Fan Chih is such a small-minded person. If a superior loves ritual, then the people will be reverent. If a superior loves righteousness, the people will oblige him, and if he loves good faith, the people will respond to him. If he can be like this, then people from all directions will come to him, bearing their children on their backs. Why should he need to study farming?"

[13.4]

HEAVEN

The master said, "No one understands me." Tzu-kung said, "How can you say that no one understands you?" The master said, "I bear no animosity toward heaven and no ill-will toward human beings. My studies, while lowly, attain certain heights. It is heaven that understands me."

[14.37]

The master said, "I don't want to say anything." Tzu-kung said, "If you don't say anything, then what should we write down?" The master said, "Does heaven say anything? The four seasons proceed and all things are generated, but does heaven say anything?"

[17.19]

The master said, "Heaven has generated the virtue within me. What can Huan T'ui do to me?"

[7.22]

A great minister asked Tzu-kung, saying, "Can't your master be considered a sage? He is a man of many different abilities." Tzu-kung replied, "Heaven has granted that he has very nearly become a sage, and, moreover, he is a man of many skills." The master heard this, and said, "The great minister understands me. When I was young, I was of very humble background, and hence I am capable at many different but nevertheless common things. But does the honorable person need this diversity? No."

[9.6]

Ssu-ma Niu lamented, "All people have brothers, but only I do not." Tzu-hsia said, "I have heard it said that 'Death and life are mandated, and wealth and high honor lie with heaven.' If the honorable person is reverential and well mannered, is respectful of others and follows ritual, then within the four seas all people will be brothers. How could the honorable person be worried that he have no brothers?"

[12.5]

RITUAL

The master said, "People say 'ritual this' and 'ritual that.' But is ritual just jades and silks? They say 'music this' and 'music that.' But is music just bells and drums?"

[17.11]

When Fan Ch'ih was Confucius's charioteer, the master said, "Meng-sun asked me what filiality was and I said, 'Not being disobedient.'" Fan Ch'ih asked, "What did you mean by that?" The master replied, "I meant to serve one's parents with ritual when they are alive, to bury them with ritual when they die, and thereafter to sacrifice to them with ritual."

[2.5.2–3]

Tzu-kung wanted to eliminate the offering of the sacrificial sheep at the beginning of the lunar month. The master said, "Tzu-kung, you are concerned about the sheep, but I am concerned about the ritual."

[3.17]

The master said, "Honorable people, widely studied in cultural things and guided by ritual, will not overstep themselves."

[6.25]

The master said, "Respect without ritual becomes tiresome, circumspection without ritual becomes timidity, bold fortitude without ritual becomes unruly, and directness without ritual becomes twisted."

[8.2.1]

SACRIFICE

Someone asked about the meaning of the great Ti sacrifice. The master said, "I do not know. Someone who knew how to explain it would find the whole realm in the palm of his hand."

[3.11]

The master was very circumspect about observing the vigils before sacrificing, about warfare, and about illness.

[7.12]

When observing the vigils before sacrifice, Confucius wore immaculately clean clothing. He altered his diet, and he moved from the place where he commonly sat.

[10.7]

The food was spare, with only soup and vegetables, but when sacrificing that was how he observed the vigils.

[10.8.10]

SPIRITS

The master said, "To sacrifice to a spirit with which one has no proper association is merely to curry favor with it."

[2.24]

When he sacrificed to the ancestral spirits, he did so as if they were actually present; when he sacrificed to other spirits, he did so as if they were actually present. The master said, "If I do not really take part in the sacrifice, it is as if I did not sacrifice at all."

[3.12]

Fan Ch'ih asked about wisdom. The master said, "To perform the obligations properly due to the people; and to pay reverence to ghosts and spirits, while keeping a distance from them—this may be called wisdom."

[6.20]

The master did not talk about strange marvels, the use of force, chaos and disorder, or spirits.

[7.20]

PRAYER

When the master became very ill, Tzu-lu asked to be allowed to pray for him. The master asked, "Is this usually done?" and Tzu-lu replied, "It is. It is said in the eulogies that one prays to the spirits above and to the terrestrial divinities below." The master remarked, "Then I have been praying for a long time."

[7.34]

Wang-sun Chia asked, "What is meant by the expression 'Rather than supplicate the tutelary powers of the southwest corner of the house, supplicate those of the stove'?" The master replied, "That is not the case at all. Those who offend heaven have nothing to whom they might pray."

[3.13]

SHAMANISM, DIVINATION, AND EXORCISM

The master said, "The people of the south say that unless someone is a steady person, they cannot become either a shaman or a healer. That is an excellent saying! Unless one is of steady virtue, one will invite disgrace. This would come simply from not divining properly."

[13.22]

When the villagers were performing the Nuo exorcism, he donned court dress and stood on the eastern steps.

[10.10.2]

RECLUSES

Once when Ch'ang Chü and Chieh Ni were out plowing their fields together, Confucius passed by and had Tzu-lu ask them where the ford was. Ch'ang Chü asked, "Who is that there in the carriage?"

"Confucius."

"Confucius from Lu?"

"Yes," Tzu-lu replied.

"Well, if that's who it is," Ch'ang added, "then he knows where the ford is."

Tzu-lu then asked Chieh Ni, who said, "Who are you?"

"I am Tzu-lu."

"You're a disciple of Confucius from Lu?"

"That is so."

"The whole world is flooded," Chieh stated, without interrupting his raking, "and who can change it? It's better to be a follower of someone who withdraws from the whole world than of someone who withdraws only from certain people."

When Tzu-lu got back he told Confucius what they said. Surprised, the master said, "One cannot flock together with birds and beasts. If I do not associate with human beings, then with whom should I associate? If the Way prevailed within the world, then I would not try to change it."

[18.6]

Tzu-lu, following at some distance behind the master, encountered an elderly man carrying a bamboo basket slung over his shoulder on a pole. Tzu-lu asked, "Have you seen my master?" The old man replied, "You don't look too hard-working, and you probably can't even tell one kind of grain from another. Just who might your master be?" The man stuck his staff in the ground and started weeding, but Tzu-lu just stood there respectfully with his hands clasped in front of his chest. In the end the old man invited Tzu-lu to stay over; he killed a chicken and prepared some millet to feed him, and he introduced him to his two children. The next day, Tzu-lu went on his way, and when he caught

up with the master he told him what had happened. The master said, "He is a recluse." He had Tzu-lu go back so that he might meet him, but when they arrived, he had already gone out. Tzu-lu said, "Not to serve in office is not right. The proper customs between old and young cannot be set aside, but how much less can one set aside the righteousness between ruler and minister? By wanting to make himself pure, this man has thrown greater human relationships into disarray. When honorable persons serve in office, they enact this righteousness. When the Way is not enacted, they also know it of themselves."

[18.7]

8.2.3 Is Human Nature Good or Evil?

Do you think human beings are morally good or bad by nature? Do you think strong governments with strictly enforced laws and severe punishments are necessary for a good social order? Or do you think that the less government there is the better?

What role does education play in making people good? Can virtue be taught? Should our schools engage in moral education? Should education impart knowledge only, or should it also build character?

What exactly is the human potential? If people are uneducated and controlled by few laws, will they become more humane and civil or will they become more antisocial and uncivil? Can education and strict laws guarantee civility?

These questions and others like them arose as the Confucian tradition developed. Like many religions, Confucianism found society falling far short of its ideal. Societies were often riddled with crime, people did evil and cruel things, and rulers were corrupt. Why did evil and imperfection exist? If things were not wrong, there would be no need to set them right. However, why are they wrong in the first place? Could it be that humans are evil by nature?

Confucius had little to say directly about human nature, but he appears to have been optimistic about the human potential. According to Confucius, if people who are not honorable by birth can become so through the cultivation of virtue, then, given the proper education, most people, even those lowly born, should be able to become honorable and wise.

Mencius (371–289 B.C.E.), the author of the first selection, was taught, according to tradition, by the grandson of Confucius. Mencius believed that Confucius's teachings implied that humans are good by nature. However, if they are good by nature, whence comes evil? Mencius believed that evil comes from society: Bad societies corrupt humans who are *originally* good. Hence, he argued that education must center on recovering the innate knowledge of the good and the innate tendency to do the good thereby countering the effects of a corrupting culture.

Mencius's views represent the idealistic wing of Confucian philosophy. Hsün Tzu, the author of the second selection, was born sometime around 312 B.C.E., and his views represent the naturalistic wing. Whereas Mencius argued for the goodness of human nature, Hsün Tzu disputed Mencius's views and argued that humans are evil by nature.

Both Mencius and Hsün Tzu believed that heaven generates human nature. However, Mencius thought heaven is good and hence that humans have an inherent tendency to do good. Hsün Tzu thought heaven is neutral with respect to good and evil and that humans are generated by heaven to be what they are, creatures born with conflicting desires and an innate tendency to be selfish.

Although Hsün Tzu develops his views in opposition to Mencius, the difference between them is not as great as it might first appear. Both were strong supporters of education, but for different reasons. For Mencius proper education is essential to allowing our originally good nature to flourish, whereas for Hsün Tzu it can make "straight" an originally "crooked" nature.

Readers of this debate who are familiar with Christianity should not read Christian ideas into it. In Christian theology, the debate about human nature takes place in the context of the notion of an "original sin." According to Christianity, humans are created good by a good god, but they sin by rebelling against the divine. This sin of rebellion is prefigured by a cosmic rebellion led by Lucifer or Satan, who is an angel and who, in the form of a serpent, tempts the first humans to sin. Just as Satan is cast out of heaven because of his sin, so the first humans "fall" from an original goodness. This first sin has infected the whole human race. Such, according to Christianity, is the story of how evil came to be.

There is no "fall" for either Mencius or Hsün Tzu. Indeed, there is neither a personal creator god nor any Satan figure. For them the issue of good and evil centers on whether original human nature prior to social influences has an innate tendency to do good or whether it lacks the ability to control its many conflicting desires.

The selection from Mencius recounts part of a debate he had with Kao Tzu. Kao Tzu holds the view that there is neither good nor evil in human nature. Human nature, according to Kao Tzu, is morally neutral. The selection opens with a discussion of whether Kao Tzu's analogies are correct and moves on to Mencius's criticism of Kao Tzu's claim that "nature" means the same as "inborn." In the second selection, Hsün Tzu explains his view that humans are evil by nature and provides a refutation of Mencius's views.

Much argument in ancient Chinese philosophy took place by using analogies to support or refute ideas. This use of analogy will be illustrated in the selections that follow. One question to keep in mind as you read is, How strong and compelling are the analogies? Do they persuade you or not?

MENCIUS

Human Nature Is Good

READING QUESTIONS

1. According to Mencius, why is the native endowment of humans not the cause of evil?
2. What reason does Mencius give to support the claim that no human lacks a heart sensitive to the suffering of others? Do you think he is right about this? Why?
3. According to Hsün Tzu, why is Mencius wrong when he says, "Man learns because his nature is good"?
4. According to Hsün Tzu, from where do propriety and righteousness come?
5. How does Hsün Tzu define good and evil?
6. In your view, who is right about human nature, Mencius or Hsün Tzu, and why?

BOOK VI • PART A

1. Kao Tzu said, "Human nature is like the *ch'i* willow. Dutifulness is like cups and bowls. To make morality out of human nature is like making cups and bowls out of the willow."

From *Mencius*, translated by D. C. Lau, volume 2. Copyright © 1970 D. C. Lau. Reprinted by permission of Penguin Books, Ltd. Footnotes omitted.

"Can you," said Mencius, "make cups and bowls by following the nature of the willow? Or must you mutilate the willow before you can make it into cups and bowls? If you have to mutilate the willow to make it into cups and bowls, must you, then, also mutilate a man to make him moral? Surely it will be these words of yours men in the world will follow in bringing disaster upon morality."

2. Kao Tzu said, "Human nature is like whirling water. Give it an outlet in the east and it will flow east; give it an outlet in the west and it will flow west. Human nature does not show any preference for either good or bad just as water does not show any preference for either east or west."

"It certainly is the case," said Mencius, "that water does not show any preference for either east or west, but does it show the same indifference to high and low? Human nature is good just as water seeks low ground. There is no man who is not good; there is no water that does not flow downwards.

"Now in the case of water, by splashing it one can make it shoot up higher than one's forehead, and by forcing it one can make it stay on a hill. How can that be the nature of water? It is the circumstances being what they are. That man can be made bad shows that his nature is no different from that of water in this respect."

3. Kao Tzu said, "The inborn is what is meant by 'nature.'"

"Is that," said Mencius, "the same as 'white is what is meant by "white"'?"

"Yes."

"Is the whiteness of white feathers the same as the whiteness of white snow and the whiteness of white snow the same as the whiteness of white jade?"

"Yes."

"In that case, is the nature of a hound the same as the nature of an ox and the nature of an ox the same as the nature of a man?"

6. Kung-tu Tzu said, "Kao Tzu said, 'There is neither good nor bad in human nature,' but others say, 'Human nature can become good or it can become bad, and that is why with the rise of King Wen and King Wu, the people were given to goodness, while with the rise of King Yu and King Li, they were given to cruelty.' Then there are others who say, 'There are those who are good by nature, and there are those who are bad by nature.' For this reason, Hsiang could have Yao as prince, and Shun could have the Blind Man as father, and Ch'i, Viscount of Wei and Prince Pi Kan could have Chou as nephew as well as sovereign.' Now you say human nature is good. Does this mean that all the others are mistaken?"

"As far as what is genuinely in him is concerned, a man is capable of becoming good," said Mencius. "That is what I mean by good. As for his becoming bad, that is not the fault of his native endowment. The heart of compassion is possessed by all men alike; likewise the heart of shame, the heart of respect, and the heart of right and wrong. The heart of compassion pertains to benevolence, the heart of shame to dutifulness, the heart of respect to the observance of the rites, and the heart of right and wrong to wisdom. Benevolence, dutifulness, observance of the rites, and wisdom do not give me a lustre from the outside, they are in me originally. Only this has never dawned on me. That is why it is said, 'Seek and you will find it; let go and you will lose it.' There are cases where one man is twice, five times or countless times better than another man, but this is only because there are people who fail to make the best of their native endowment. The *Odes* say,

> Heaven produces the teeming masses,
> And where there is a thing there is a norm.
> If the people held on to their constant nature,
> They would be drawn to superior virtue.

Confucius commented, 'The author of this poem must have had knowledge of the Way.' Thus where there is a thing there is a norm, and because the people hold on to their constant nature they are drawn to superior virtue."

8. Mencius said, "There was a time when the trees were luxuriant on the Ox Mountain, but as it is on the outskirts of a great metropolis, the trees are constantly lopped by axes. Is it any wonder that they are no longer fine? With the respite they get in the day and in the night, and the moistening by the rain and dew, there is certainly no lack of new shoots coming out, but then the cattle and sheep come to graze upon the mountain. That is why it is as bald as it is. People, seeing only its baldness, tend to think that it never had any trees. But can this possibly be the nature of a mountain? Can what is in man be completely lacking in moral inclinations? A man's letting go of his true heart is like the case of the trees and the axes. When the trees are lopped day after day, is it any wonder that they are no longer fine? If, in spite of the respite a man gets in the day and in the night and of the effect of the morning air on him, scarcely any of his likes and dislikes resembles those of other men, it is because what he does in the course of the day once again dissipates what he has gained. If this dissipation happens repeatedly, then the influence of the air in the night will no longer able to preserve what was originally in him, and when that happens, the man is not far removed from an animal. Others, seeing his resemblance to an animal, will be led to think that he never had any

native endowment. But can that be what a man is genuinely like? Hence, given the right nourishment there is nothing that will not grow, while deprived of it there is nothing that will not wither away. Confucius said, 'Hold on to it and it will remain; let go of it and it will disappear. One never knows the time it comes or goes, neither does one know the direction.' It is perhaps to the heart this refers."

15. Kung-tu Tzu asked, "Though equally human, why are some men greater than others?"

"He who is guided by the interests of the parts of his person that are of greater importance is a great man; he who is guided by the interests of the parts of his person that are of smaller importance is a small man."

"Though equally human, why are some men guided one way and others guided another way?"

"The organs of hearing and sight are unable to think and can be misled by external things. When one thing acts on another, all it does is to attract it. The organ of the heart can think. But it will find the answer only if it does think; otherwise, it will not find the answer. This is what Heaven has given me. If one makes one's stand on what is of greater importance in the first instance, what is of smaller importance cannot displace it. In this way, one cannot but be a great man."

16. Mencius said, "No man is devoid of a heart sensitive to the suffering of others. Such a sensitive heart was possessed by the Former Kings and this manifested itself in compassionate government. With such a sensitive heart behind compassionate government, it was as easy to rule the Empire as rolling it on your palm.

"My reason for saying that no man is devoid of a heart sensitive to the suffering of others is this. Suppose a man were, all of a sudden, to see a young child on the verge of falling into a well. He would certainly be moved to compassion, not because he wanted to get in the good graces of the parents, nor because he wished to win the praise of his fellow villagers or friends, nor yet because he disliked the cry of the child. From this it can be seen that whoever is devoid of the heart of compassion is not human, whoever is devoid of the heart of shame is not human, whoever is devoid of the heart of courtesy and modesty is not human, and whoever is devoid of the heart of right and wrong is not human. The heart of compassion is the germ of benevolence; the heart of shame, of dutifulness; the heart of courtesy and modesty, of observance of the rites; the heart of right and wrong, of wisdom. Man has these four germs just as he has four limbs. For a man possessing these four germs to deny his own potentialities is for him to cripple himself; for him to deny the potentialities of his prince is for him to cripple his prince. If a man is able to develop all these four germs that he possesses, it will be like a fire starting up or a spring coming through. When these are fully developed, he can tend the whole realm within the Four Seas, but if he fails to develop them, he will not be able even to serve his parents."

✺

HSÜN TZU

Human Nature Is Evil

The nature of man is evil; his goodness is the result of his activity.[1] Now man's inborn nature is to seek for gain. If this tendency is followed, strife and rapacity result and deference and compliance disappear. By inborn nature one is envious and hates others. If these tendencies are followed, injury and destruction result and loyalty and faithfulness disappear. By inborn nature one possesses the desires of ear and eye and likes sound and beauty. If these tendencies are followed, lewdness and licentiousness result, and the pattern and order of propriety and righteousness disappear. Therefore to follow man's nature and his feelings will inevitably result in strife and rapacity, combine with rebellion and disorder, and end in violence. Therefore there must be the civilizing influence of teachers and laws and the guidance of propriety and righteousness, and then it will result in deference and compliance, combine with pattern and order, and end in discipline. From this point of view, it is clear that the nature of man is evil and that his goodness is the result of activity.

Crooked wood must be heated and bent before it becomes straight. Blunt metal must be ground and whetted before it becomes sharp. Now the nature of man is evil. It must depend on teachers and laws to become correct and achieve propriety and righteousness and then it becomes disciplined. Without teachers and laws, man is unbalanced, off the track, and incorrect. Without pro

From Chang, Wing-tsit, *A Source Book in Chinese Philosophy*, pp. 128–132. Copyright © 1963, renewed 1991 by Princeton University Press. Reprinted by permission of Princeton University Press. Footnotes edited.

[1]According to Yang Liang, *wei* (artificial) is "man's activity." It means what is created by man and not a result of natural conditions. This is accepted by most commentators, including Hao I-hsing, who has pointed out that in ancient times *wei* (ordinally meaning false or artificial) and *wei* (activity) were interchangeable.

priety and righteousness, there will be rebellion, disorder, and chaos. The sage-kings of antiquity, knowing that the nature of man is evil, and that it is unbalanced, off the track, incorrect, rebellious, disorderly, and undisciplined, created the rules of propriety and righteousness and instituted laws and systems in order to correct man's feelings, transform them, and direct them so that they all may become disciplined and conform with the Way (Tao). Now people who are influenced by teachers and laws, accumulate literature and knowledge, and follow propriety and righteousness are superior men, whereas those who give rein to their feelings, enjoy indulgence, and violate propriety and righteousness are inferior men. From this point of view, it is clear that the nature of man is evil and that his goodness is the result of his activity. . . .

Mencius said, "Man learns because his nature is good." This is not true. He did not know the nature of man and did not understand the distinction between man's nature and his effort. Man's nature is the product of Nature; it cannot be learned and cannot be worked for. Propriety and righteousness are produced by the sage. They can be learned by men and can be accomplished through work. What is in man but cannot be learned or worked for is his nature. What is in him and can be learned or accomplished through work is what can be achieved through activity. This is the difference between human nature and human activity. Now by nature man's eye can see and his ear can hear. But the clarity of vision is not outside his eye and the distinctness of hearing is not outside his ear. It is clear that clear vision and distinct hearing cannot be learned. Mencius said, "The nature of man is good; it [becomes evil] because man destroys his original nature." This is a mistake. By nature man departs from his primitive character and capacity as soon as he is born, and he is bound to destroy it. From this point of view, it is clear that man's nature is evil.

By the original goodness of human nature is meant [by Mencius] that man does not depart from his primitive character but makes it beautiful, and does not depart from his original capacity but utilizes it, so that beauty being [inherent] in his primitive character and goodness being [inherent] in his will are like clear vision being inherent in the eye and distinct hearing being inherent in the ear. Hence we say that the eye is clear and the ear is sharp. Now by nature man desires repletion when hungry, desires warmth when cold, and desires rest when tired. This is man's natural feeling. But now when a man is hungry and sees some elders before him, he does not eat ahead of them but yields to them. When he is tired, he dares not seek rest because he wants to take

over the work [of elders]. The son yielding to or taking over the work of his father, and the younger brother yielding to or taking over the work of his older brother —these two lines of action are contrary to original nature and violate natural feeling. Nevertheless, the way of filial piety is the pattern and order of propriety and righteousness. If one follows his natural feeling, he will have no deference or compliance. Deference and compliance are opposed to his natural feelings. From this point of view, it is clear that man's nature is evil and that his goodness is the result of his activity.

Someone may ask, "If man's nature is evil, whence come propriety and righteousness?" I answer that all propriety and righteousness are results of the activity of sages and not originally produced from man's nature. The potter pounds the clay and makes the vessel. This being the case, the vessel is the product of the artisan's activity and not the original product of man's nature. The artisan hews a piece of wood and makes a vessel. This being the case, the vessel is the product of the artisan's activity and not the original product of man's nature. The sages gathered together their ideas and thoughts and became familiar with activity, facts, and principles, and thus produced propriety and righteousness and instituted laws and systems. This being the case, propriety and righteousness, and laws and systems are the products of the activity of the sages and not the original products of man's nature.

As to the eye desiring color, the ear desiring sound, the mouth desiring flavor, the heart desiring gain, and the body desiring pleasure and ease—all these are products of man's original nature and feelings. They are natural reactions to stimuli and do not require any work to be produced. But if the reaction is not naturally produced by the stimulus but requires work before it can be produced, then it is the result of activity. Here lies the evidence of the difference between what is produced by man's nature and what is produced by his effort. Therefore the sages transformed man's nature and aroused him to activity. As activity was aroused, propriety and righteousness were produced, and as propriety and righteousness were produced, laws and systems were instituted. This being the case, propriety, righteousness, laws, and systems are all products of the sages. In his nature, the sage is common with and not different from ordinary people. It is in his effort that he is different from and superior to them.

It is the original nature and feelings of man to love profit and seek gain. Suppose some brothers are to divide their property. If they follow their natural feelings, they will love profit and seek gain, and thus will do violence to each other and grab the property. But if they are transformed by the civilizing influence of the pattern and order of propriety and righteousness, they will even yield to outsiders. Therefore, brothers will quarrel if they follow their original nature and feeling but, if they are transformed by righteousness and propriety, they will yield to outsiders.

People desire to be good because their nature is evil. If one has little, he wants abundance. If he is ugly, he wants good looks. If his circumstances are narrow, he wants them to be broad. If poor, he wants to be rich. And if he is in a low position, he wants a high position. If he does not have it himself, he will seek it outside. If he is rich, he does not desire more wealth, and if he is in a high position, he does not desire more power. If he has it himself, he will not seek it outside. From this point of view, [it is clear that] people desire to be good because their nature is evil. . . .

Mencius said, "The nature of man is good." I say that this is not true. By goodness at any time in any place is meant true principles and peaceful order, and by evil is meant imbalance, violence, and disorder. This is the distinction between good and evil. Now do we honestly regard man's nature as characterized by true principles and peaceful order? If so, why are sages necessary and why are propriety and righteousness necessary? What possible improvement can sages make on true principles and peaceful order?

Now this is not the case. Man's nature is evil. Therefore the sages of antiquity, knowing that man's nature is evil, that it is unbalanced and incorrect, and that it is violent, disorderly, and undisciplined, established the authority of rulers to govern the people, set forth clearly propriety and righteousness to transform them, instituted laws and governmental measures to rule them, and made punishment severe to restrain them, so that all will result in good order and be in accord with goodness. Such is the government of sage-kings and the transforming influence of propriety and righteousness.

But suppose we try to remove the authority of the ruler, do away with the transforming influence of propriety and righteousness, discard the rule of laws and governmental measure, do away with the restraint of punishment, and stand and see how people of the world deal with one another. In this situation, the strong would injure the weak and rob them, and the many would do violence to the few and shout them down. The whole world would be in violence and disorder and all would perish in an instant. From this point of view, it is clear that man's nature is evil and that his goodness is the result of his activity. . . .

8.3 HAN ORTHODOXY (206 B.C.E.–220 C.E.)

During the Han dynasty, scholars spent countless hours collecting, preserving, and editing the literature they had inherited from the past. One problem the Han scholars faced was that the transition from individual states to an empire had been destructive. Archives and written records, not to mention disfavored scholars, were burned by the first Ch'in emperor of a unified China. The demise of the Ch'in led to a protracted civil war before the Han were able to reestablish order and unity. In a society where books were hand-copied and rare, such political turmoil and destruction severely reduced the sources available for understanding and reconstructing the past.

An anti-Confucian school of political philosophy known as Legalism had gained power under the Ch'in. Advocating the use of strong and harsh laws to control the people, the Legalists helped the Ch'in replace the feudal domains with a system of provinces that still exists today. The Ch'in also standardized the Chinese written language, expanded military power, and finished the Great Wall. For the first hundred years of the Han dynasty, Taoism became more influential in government circles than Legalism. However, Confucians slowly came back into power and eventually their philosophy became the official ideology of the Han empire. Confucianism now became a state cult, and Confucius was elevated to a semidivine status. Temples were built in his honor, and sacrifices were offered to him as the supreme teacher of wisdom.

8.3.1 Correlative Thinking

Tung Chung-shu (176–104 B.C.E.), a Confucian scholar, was summoned, along with a hundred-odd scholars, to the Han court of Emperor Wu-ti (ruled 140–87 B.C.E.) in order to advise him. Tung Chung-shu told the emperor to practice the teachings of Confucius and to patronize only Confucianism. He advocated a Confucian system of education and government officials educated in the Six Classics. Emperor Wu was so impressed with Tung's ideas that he made Tung a chief minister and, in 125 B.C.E., founded a national academy based on the study of the Confucian classics. This school lasted until the twentieth century.

According to Tung's interpretation of the Confucian literature, there is a correspondence among

Heaven, Earth, and humans. Humans are a microcosm of the universe, and events in society are correlated with events in the natural order. The emperor ruled by Heaven's mandate and represented all humans before Heaven.

If there is, as Tung taught, an organic and dynamic correlation among Heaven, Earth, and humans, then a number of important inferences can be drawn. First, signs of Heaven's mandate can be gleaned from the study of natural events. Floods, eclipses, drought, and the like are omens and portents that must be carefully interpreted. Second, humans, especially the ruler, must act appropriately and cultivate virtue or risk disturbing the harmony of the universe. Third, there are "Three Bonds," the bonds between ruler and ruled, between father and son, and between husband and wife, which must be informed by righteousness and humaneness lest the natural order be upset and Heaven's mandate lost.

What follows are excerpts from Tung Chung-shu's book *Luxuriant Gems of the Spring and Autumn Annals (Ch'un-ch'iu fan-lu)*. As you read, you should be able to see how correlative thinking informs Tung's ideas. Joseph Needham, a scholar of Chinese science and thought, has described the correlative system as something like a huge Victorian roll-top desk with many small drawers inside: Order is created out of potential disorder by finding a place for everything *in relation* to everything else.

❧

TUNG CHUNG-SHU

Luxuriant Gems

READING QUESTIONS

1. In what sense are Heaven, Earth, and humans the basis of all creatures?
2. What are the threefold obligations of the ruler?
3. How do Tung's teachings on human nature compare to the teachings of Mencius and Hsün Tzu?

Republished with permission of Columbia University Press, 562 W. 113th St., New York, NY 10025. *Sources of the Chinese Tradition* (excerpt), compiled by Wm. Theodore De Bary, Wing-tsit Chan, and Burton Watson, 1960. Reproduced by permission of the publisher via Copyright Clearance Center, Inc. pp. 162–163, 166–167, 171–172. Footnotes edited.

4. What is the theory of portents, and how can this theory function as a justification of Heaven even though Heaven causes "evil" events like drought and famine?
5. Do you believe in omens and portents? Why or why not?

THE THREEFOLD OBLIGATIONS OF THE RULER

The ruler is the basis of the state. In administering the state, nothing is more effective for educating the people than reverence for the basis. If the basis is revered then the ruler may transform the people as though by supernatural power, but if the basis is not revered then the ruler will have nothing by which to lead his people. Then though he employ harsh penalties and severe punishments the people will not follow him. This is to drive the state to ruin, and there is no greater disaster. What do we mean by the basis? Heaven, earth, and man are the basis of all creatures. Heaven gives them birth, earth nourishes them, and man brings them to completion. Heaven provides them at birth with a sense of filial and brotherly love, earth nourishes them with clothing and food, and man completes them with rites and music. The three act together as hands and feet join to complete the body and none can be dispensed with. . . . If all three are lacking, then the people will become like deer, each person following his own desires, each family possessing its own ways. Fathers cannot employ their sons nor rulers their ministers, and though there be walls and battlements they will be called an "empty city." Then will the ruler lie down with a clod of earth for a pillow. No one menacing him, he will endanger himself; no one destroying him, he will destroy himself. This is called a spontaneous punishment, and when it descends, though he hide in halls of encircling stone or barricade himself behind steep defiles, he can never escape. But the enlightened and worthy ruler, being of good faith, is strictly attentive to the three bases. His sacrifices are conducted with utmost reverence; he makes offerings to and serves his ancestors; he advances brotherly affection and encourages filial conduct. In this way he serves the basis of Heaven. He personally grasps the plow handle and plows a furrow, plucks the mulberry himself and feeds the silkworms, breaks new ground to increase the grain supply and opens the way for a sufficiency of clothing and food. In this way he serves the basis of earth. He sets up schools for the nobles and in the towns and villages to teach filial piety and brotherly affection, reverence and humility. He enlightens the people with education and moves them with rites and music. Thus he serves the basis of man. If he rightly serves these three, then the people will be like sons and brothers, not daring to be unsubmissive. They will regard their country as a father or a mother, not waiting for favors to love it nor for coercion to serve it, and though they dwell in fields and camp beneath the sky they will count themselves more fortunate than if they lived in palaces. Then will the ruler go to rest on a secure pillow. Though none aid him he will grow mighty of himself, though none pacify his kingdom peace will come of its own. This is called a spontaneous reward, and when it comes, though he relinquish his throne, give up his kingdom and depart, the people will take up their children on their backs, follow him, and keep him as their lord, so that he can never leave them.

[From *Ch'un-ch'iu fan-lu*, Sec. 19, 6:7a–8a]

HUMAN NATURE AND EDUCATION

For discovering the truth about things there is no better way than to begin with names. Names show up truth and falsehood as a measuring-line shows up crooked and straight. If one inquires into the truth of a name and observes whether it is appropriate or not, then there will be no deception over the disposition of truth. Nowadays there is considerable ignorance on the question of human nature and theorists fail to agree. Why do they not try returning to the word "nature" itself? Does not the word "nature" (*hsing*) mean "birth" (*sheng*), that which one is born with?[1] The properties endowed spontaneously at birth are called the nature. The nature is the basic substance. Can the word "good," we inquire, be applied to the basic substance of the nature? No, it cannot. . . . Therefore the nature may be compared to growing rice, and goodness to refined rice. Refined rice is produced from raw rice, yet unrefined rice does not necessarily all become refined. Goodness comes from the nature of man, yet all natures do not necessarily become good. Goodness, like the refined rice, is the result of man's activities in continuing and completing Heaven's work; it is not actually existent in what Heaven itself has produced. Heaven acts to a certain degree and then ceases, and what has been created thus far is called the heavenly nature; beyond this point is called the work of man. This work lies outside of the nature, and yet by

it the nature is inevitably brought to the practice of virtue. The word "people" (*min*) is taken from the word "sleep" (*ming*). . . .

The nature may be compared to the eyes. In sleep the eyes are shut and there is darkness; they must await the wakening before they can see. At this time it may be said that they have the potential disposition to see, but it cannot be said that they see. Now the nature of all people has this potential disposition, but it is not yet awakened; it is as though it were asleep and awaiting the wakening. If it receives education, it may afterwards become good. In this condition of being not yet awakened, it can be said to have the potential disposition for goodness, but it cannot be said to be good. . . . Heaven begets the people; their nature is that of potential good, but has not yet become actual good. For this reason it sets up the king to make real their goodness. This is the will of Heaven. From Heaven the people receive their potentially good nature, and from the king the education which completes it. It is the duty and function of the king to submit to the will of Heaven, and thus to bring to completion the nature of the people.

[From *Ch'un-ch'iu fan-lu*, Sec. 35, 10:3a–5b]

THE THEORY OF PORTENTS

The creatures of Heaven and earth at times display unusual changes and these are called wonders. Lesser ones are called ominous portents. The portents always come first and are followed by wonders. Portents are Heaven's warnings, wonders are Heaven's threats. Heaven first sends warnings, and if men do not understand, then it sends wonders to awe them. This is what the *Book of Odes* means when it says: "We tremble at the awe and fearfulness of Heaven!" The genesis of all such portents and wonders is a direct result of errors in the state. When the first indications of error begin to appear in the state, Heaven sends forth ominous portents and calamities to warn men and announce the fact. If, in spite of these warnings and announcements, men still do not realize how they have gone wrong, then Heaven sends prodigies and wonders to terrify them. If, after these terrors, men still know no awe or fear, then calamity and misfortune will visit them. From this we may see that the will of Heaven is benevolent, for its has no desire to trap or betray mankind.

If we examine these wonders and portents carefully, we may discern the will of Heaven. The will of Heaven desires us to do certain things, and not to do others. As to those things which Heaven wishes and does not wish, if a man searches within himself, he will surely find

---

[1]Tung is using a favorite Chinese type of argument, that based upon the supposed affinities between characters of similar pronunciation. Such "puns," as we should call them, are intended to be taken in all seriousness.

warnings of them in his own heart, and if he looks about him at daily affairs, he will find verification of these warnings in the state. Thus we can discern the will of Heaven in these portents and wonders. We should not hate such signs, but stand in awe of them, considering that Heaven wishes to repair our faults and save us from our errors. Therefore it takes this way to warn us.

According to the principles used in writing the *Spring and Autumn Annals*, if when the ruler changed the ancient ways or departed from what was right Heaven responded and sent portents, then the country was called fortunate. . . . Because Heaven sent no portents and earth brought forth no calamities in his kingdom, King Chuang of Ch'u prayed to the mountains and streams, saying: "Will Heaven destroy me? It does not announce my faults nor show me my sins." Thus we can see how the portents of Heaven come about as a response to errors, and how wonders make these faults clear and fill us with awe. This is because of Heaven's desire to save us. Only those who receive such portents are called fortunate in the *Spring and Autumn Annals*. This is the reason why King Chuang prayed and beseeched Heaven. Now if a sage ruler or a wise lord delights in receiving remonstrances from his faithful ministers, how much more should he delight in receiving the warnings of Heaven!

[From *Ch'un-ch'iu fan-lu*, Sec. 30, 8:13b–14b]

8.3.2 The Perfect Confucian Woman

The principle of correlation, so highly valued by Han Confucianists like Tung Chung-shu, had important implications for women. One of the Three Bonds is the bond between husband and wife. Just as there are cosmological correlations between the ruler and the ruled, so too there are cosmological correspondences between husband and wife. The husband must be strong, firm, and dominant like Heaven, and the wife must be weak, pliant, and subservient like Earth. The husband's duty is to support and protect his wife, and the wife's duty is to serve her husband.

Traditional Chinese marriage practices require a daughter to leave her birth family and household upon marriage and live in her husband's house. Her husband's father and mother become her new parents, and her filial duty transfers from her birth parents to her parents-in-law. This practice places considerable stress on the new wife. It requires of women the practice of selfless virtue well beyond any demands placed on males. It is clear that women need some preparation for the demanding role of wife, es-

pecially because Confucians believe that the family is the foundation of the social order.

Pan Chao (ca. 48–ca. 112) provided that preparation in a short work called "Lessons for Women." From a prominent scholarly family, she was well educated and widely recognized for her scholarship and intellect. She became one of the foremost historians of the Han period. According to a fifth-century biography, Pan Chao worked at one of the imperial libraries editing treatises on astronomy and chronological tables of nobility. She served as court tutor for the women in the imperial family, but she wrote this particular text for the unmarried women of her own family, her daughters and nieces.

Pan Chao's "Lessons for Women" exerted considerable influence on the lives of Chinese women. This work became the model for all subsequent instructional texts for preparing women to accept the responsibilities of wives. It is something of an irony that a woman educated in the same way as a man and holding a position normally given to men should write an instructional manual admonishing women to fulfill traditional roles.

PAN CHAO

Lessons for Women

READING QUESTIONS

1. What does Pan Chao mean by "humility"?
2. What is the proper relationship between husband and wife? What makes it proper?
3. What is the main point of the chapter titled "Respect and Caution"?
4. What are the "womanly qualifications"?
5. What must a wife do to gain the love of her husband?
6. What role do the concepts of *yin* and *yang* play in Pan Chao's advice?
7. Does the advice of Pan Chao reinforce the moral, religious, and social conventions of her age, or does it subvert them? If you think it does some of both, what is subversive about her advice?

From Nancy Lee Swann, *Pan Chao: Foremost Woman Scholar of China* (New York: Russell & Russell, 1932), pp. 82–90. Copyright © 1968 by Russell & Russell. Reprinted by permission. Footnotes omitted.

INTRODUCTION

I, the unworthy writer, am unsophisticated, unenlightened, and by nature unintelligent, but I am fortunate both to have received not a little favor from my scholarly father, and to have had a (cultured) mother and instructresses upon whom to rely for a literary education as well as for training in good manners. More than forty years have passed since at the age of fourteen I took up the dustpan and the broom in the Ts'ao family. During this time with trembling heart I feared constantly that I might disgrace my parents, and that I might multiply difficulties for both the women and the men (of my husband's family). Day and night I was distressed in heart, (but) I labored without confessing weariness. Now and hereafter, however, I know how to escape (from such fears).

Being careless, and by nature stupid, I taught and trained (my children) without system. Consequently I fear that my son Ku may bring disgrace upon the Imperial Dynasty by whose Holy Grace he has unprecedentedly received the extraordinary privilege of wearing the Gold and the Purple, a privilege for the attainment of which (by my son, I) a humble subject never even hoped. Nevertheless, now that he is a man and able to plan his own life, I need not again have concern for him. But I do grieve that you, my daughters, just now at the age for marriage, have not at this time had gradual training and advice; that you still have not learned the proper customs for married women. I fear that by failure in good manners in other families you will humiliate both your ancestors and your clan. I am now seriously ill, life is uncertain. As I have thought of you all in so untrained a state, I have been uneasy many a time for you. At hours of leisure I have composed in seven chapters these instructions under the title, "Lessons for Women." In order that you have something wherewith to benefit your persons, I wish every one of you, my daughters, each to write out a copy for yourself.

From this time on every one of you strive to practise these (lessons).

CHAPTER I HUMILITY

On the third day after the birth of a girl the ancients observed three customs: (first) to place the baby below the bed; (second) to give her a potsherd with which to play; and (third) to announce her birth to her ancestors by an offering. Now to lay the baby below the bed plainly indicated that she is lowly and weak, and should regard it as her primary duty to humble herself before others. To

give her potsherds with which to play indubitably signified that she should practise labor and consider it her primary duty to be industrious. To announce her birth before her ancestors clearly meant that she ought to esteem as her primary duty the continuation of the observance of worship in the home.

These three ancient customs epitomize a woman's ordinary way of life and the teachings of the traditional ceremonial rites and regulations. Let a woman modestly yield to others; let her respect others; let her put others first, herself last. Should she do something good, let her not mention it; should she do something bad, let her not deny it. Let her bear disgrace; let her even endure when others speak or do evil to her. Always let her seem to tremble and to fear. (When a woman follows such maxims as these,) then she may be said to humble herself before others.

Let a woman retire late to bed, but rise early to duties; let her not dread tasks by day or by night. Let her not refuse to perform domestic duties whether easy or difficult. That which must be done, let her finish completely, tidily, and systematically. (When a woman follows such rules as these,) then she may be said to be industrious.

Let a woman be correct in manner and upright in character in order to serve her husband. Let her live in purity and quietness (of spirit), and attend to her own affairs. Let her love not gossip and silly laughter. Let her cleanse and purify and arrange in order the wine and the food for the offerings to the ancestors. (When a woman observes such principles as these,) then she may be said to continue ancestral worship.

No woman who observes these three (fundamentals of life) has ever had a bad reputation or fallen into disgrace. If a woman fail to observe them, how can her name be honored; how can she but bring disgrace upon herself?

CHAPTER II HUSBAND AND WIFE

The Way of husband and wife is intimately connected with *Yin* and *Yang*, and relates the individual to gods and ancestors. Truly it is the great principle of Heaven and Earth, and the great basis of human relationships. Therefore the "Rites" honor union of man and woman; and in the "Book of Poetry" the "First Ode" manifests the principle of marriage. For these reasons the relationship cannot but be an important one.

If a husband be unworthy, then he possesses nothing by which to control his wife. If a wife be unworthy, then she possesses nothing with which to serve her husband. If a husband does not control his wife, then the rules of conduct manifesting his authority are abandoned and broken. If a wife does not serve her husband, then the proper relationship (between men and women) and the natural order of things are neglected and destroyed. As a matter of fact the purpose of these two (the controlling of women by men, and the serving of men by women) is the same.

Now examine the gentlemen of the present age. They only know that wives must be controlled, and that the husband's rules of conduct manifesting his authority must be established. They therefore teach their boys to read books and (study) histories. But they do not in the least understand that husbands and masters must (also) be served, and that the proper relationship and the rites should be maintained.

Yet only to teach men and not to teach women,—is that not ignoring the essential relation between them? According to the "Rites," it is the rule to begin to teach children to read at the age of eight years, and by the age of fifteen years they ought then to be ready for cultural training. Only why should it not be (that girls' education as well as boys' be) according to this principle?

CHAPTER III RESPECT AND CAUTION

As *Yin* and *Yang* are not of the same nature, so man and woman have different characteristics. The distinctive quality of the *Yang* is rigidity; the function of the *Yin* is yielding. Man is honored for strength; a woman is beautiful on account of her gentleness. Hence there arose the common saying: "A man though born like a wolf may, it is feared, become a weak monstrosity; a woman though born like a mouse may, it is feared, become a tiger."

Now for self-culture nothing equals respect for others. To counteract firmness nothing equals compliance. Consequently it can be said that the Way of respect and acquiescence is woman's most important principle of conduct. So respect may be defined as nothing other than holding on to that which is permanent; and acquiescence nothing other than being liberal and generous. Those who are steadfast in devotion know that they should stay in their proper places; those who are liberal and generous esteem others, and honor and serve (them).

If husband and wife have the habit of staying together, never leaving one another, and following each other around within the limited space of their own rooms, then they will lust after and take liberties with one another. From such action improper language will arise between the two. This kind of discussion may lead

to licentiousness. Out of licentiousness will be born a heart of disrespect to the husband. Such a result comes from not knowing that one should stay in one's proper place.

Furthermore, affairs may be either crooked or straight; words may be either right or wrong. Straightforwardness cannot but lead to quarreling; crookedness cannot but lead to accusation. If there are really accusations and quarrels, then undoubtedly there will be angry affairs. Such a result comes from not esteeming others, and not honoring and serving (them).

(If wives) suppress not contempt for husbands, then it follows (that such wives) rebuke and scold (their husbands). (If husbands) stop not short of anger, then they are certain to beat (their wives). The correct relationship between husband and wife is based upon harmony and intimacy, and (conjugal) love is grounded in proper union. Should actual blows be dealt, how could matrimonial relationship be preserved? Should sharp words be spoken, how could (conjugal) love exist? If love and proper relationship both be destroyed, then husband and wife are divided.

CHAPTER IV WOMANLY QUALIFICATIONS

A woman (ought to) have four qualifications: (1) womanly virtue; (2) womanly words; (3) womanly bearing; and (4) womanly work. Now what is called womanly virtue need not be brilliant ability, exceptionally different from others. Womanly words need be neither clever in debate nor keen in conversation. Womanly appearance requires neither a pretty nor a perfect face and form. Womanly work need not be work done more skillfully than that of others.

To guard carefully her chastity; to control circumspectly her behavior; in every motion to exhibit modesty; and to model each act on the best usage, this is womanly virtue.

To choose her words with care; to avoid vulgar language; to speak at appropriate times; and not to weary others (with much conversation), may be called the characteristics of womanly words.

To wash and scrub filth away; to keep clothes and ornaments fresh and clean; to wash the head and bathe the body regularly, and to keep the person free from disgraceful filth, may be called the characteristics of womanly bearing.

With whole-hearted devotion to sew and to weave; to love not gossip and silly laughter; in cleanliness and order (to prepare) the wine and food for serving guests, may be called the characteristics of womanly work.

These four qualifications characterize the greatest virtue of a woman. No woman can afford to be without them. In fact they are very easy to possess if a woman only treasure them in her heart. The ancients had a saying: "Is Love afar off? If I desire love, then love is at hand!" So can it be said of these qualifications.

CHAPTER V
WHOLE-HEARTED DEVOTION

Now in the "Rites" is written the principle that a husband may marry again, but there is no Canon that authorizes a woman to be married the second time. Therefore it is said of husbands as of Heaven, that as certainly as people cannot run away from Heaven, so surely a wife cannot leave (a husband's home).

If people in action or character disobey the spirits of Heaven and of Earth, then Heaven punishes them. Likewise if a woman errs in the rites and in the proper mode of conduct, then her husband esteems her lightly. The ancient book, "A Pattern for Women" (*Nü Hsien*), says: "To obtain the love of one man is the crown of a woman's life; to lose the love of one man is to miss the aim in woman's life." For these reasons a woman cannot but seek to win her husband's heart. Nevertheless, the beseeching wife need not use flattery, coaxing words, and cheap methods to gain intimacy.

Decidedly nothing is better (to gain the heart of a husband) than whole-hearted devotion and correct manners. In accordance with the rites and the proper mode of conduct, (let a woman) live a pure life. Let her have ears that hear not licentiousness; and eyes that see not depravity. When she goes outside her own home, let her not be conspicuous in dress and manners. When at home let her not neglect her dress. Women should not assemble in groups, nor gather together, (for gossip and silly laughter). They should not stand watching in the gateways. (If a woman follows) these rules, she may be said to have whole-hearted devotion and correct manners.

If, in all her actions, she is frivolous, she sees and hears (only) that which pleases herself. At home her hair is dishevelled, and her dress is slovenly. Outside the home she emphasizes her femininity to attract attention; she says what ought not to be said; and she looks at what ought not to be seen. (If a woman does such as) these, (she may be) said to be without whole-hearted devotion and correct manners.

CHAPTER VI IMPLICIT OBEDIENCE

Now "to win the love of one man is the crown of a woman's life; to lose the love of one man is her eternal disgrace." This saying advises a fixed will and a whole-hearted devotion for a woman. Ought she then to lose the hearts of her father- and mother-in-law?

There are times when love may lead to differences of opinion (between individuals); there are times when duty may lead to disagreement. Even should the husband say that he loves something, when the parents-in-law say "no," this is called a case of duty leading to disagreement. This being so, then what about the hearts of the parents-in-law? Nothing is better than an obedience which sacrifices personal opinion.

Whenever the mother-in-law says, "Do not do that," and if what she says is right, unquestionably the daughter-in-law obeys. Whenever the mother-in-law says, "Do that," even if what she says is wrong, still the daughter-in-law submits unfailingly to the command.

Let a woman not act contrary to the wishes and the opinions of parents-in-law about right and wrong; let her not dispute with them what is straight and what is crooked. Such (docility) may be called obedience which sacrifices personal opinion. Therefore the ancient book, "A Pattern for Women," says: "If a daughter-in-law (who follows the wishes of her parents-in-law) is like an echo and a shadow, how could she not be praised?"

CHAPTER VII HARMONY
WITH YOUNGER BROTHERS-
AND SISTERS-IN-LAW

In order for a wife to gain the love of her husband, she must win for herself the love of her parents-in-law. To win for herself the love of her parents-in-law, she must secure for herself the good will of younger brothers- and sisters-in-law. For these reasons the right and the wrong, the praise and the blame of a woman alike depend upon younger brothers- and sisters-in-law. Consequently it will not do for a woman to lose their affection.

They are stupid both who know not that they must not lose (the hearts of) younger brothers- and sisters-in-law, and who cannot be in harmony with them in order to be intimate with them. Excepting only the Holy Men, few are able to be faultless. Now Yen Tzû's greatest virtue was that he was able to reform. Confucius praised him (for not committing a misdeed) the second time. (In comparison with him) a woman is the more likely (to make mistakes).

Although a woman possesses a worthy woman's qualifications, and is wise and discerning by nature, is she able to be perfect? Yet if a woman live in harmony with her immediate family, unfavorable criticism will be silenced (within the home. But) if a man and woman disagree, then this evil will be noised abroad. Such consequences are inevitable. The "Book of Changes" says:

Should two hearts harmonize,
The united strength can cut gold,
Words from hearts which agree,
Give forth fragrance like the orchid.

This saying may be applied to (harmony in the home).

Though a daughter-in-law and her younger sisters-in-law are equal in rank, nevertheless (they should) respect (each other); though love (between them may be) sparse, their proper relationship should be intimate. Only the virtuous, the beautiful, the modest, and the respectful (young women) can accordingly rely upon the sense of duty to make their affection sincere, and magnify love to bind their relationships firmly.

Then the excellence and the beauty of such a daughter-in-law becomes generally known. Moreover, any flaws and mistakes are hidden and unrevealed. Parents-in-law boast of her good deeds; her husband is satisfied with her. Praise of her radiates, making her illustrious in district and in neighborhood; and her brightness reaches to her own father and mother.

But a stupid and foolish person as an elder sister-in-law uses her rank to exalt herself; as a younger sister-in-law, because of parents' favor, she becomes filled with arrogance. If arrogant, how can a woman live in harmony with others? If love and proper relationships be perverted, how can praise be secured? In such instances the wife's good is hidden, and her faults are declared. The mother-in-law will be angry, and the husband will be indignant. Blame will reverberate and spread in and outside the home. Disgrace will gather upon the daughter-in-law's person, on the one hand to add humiliation to her own father and mother, and on the other to increase the difficulties of her husband.

Such then is the basis for both honor and disgrace; the foundation for reputation or for ill-repute. Can a woman be too cautious? Consequently to seek the hearts of young brothers- and sisters-in-law decidedly nothing can be esteemed better than modesty and Acquiescence.

Modesty is virtue's handle; acquiescence is the wife's (most refined) characteristic. All who possess these two have sufficient for harmony with others. In the "Book of Poetry" it is written that "here is no evil; there is no dart." So it may be said of (these two, modesty and acquiescence).

8.4 THE DEFENSE OF THE CONFUCIAN WAY (220–907)

From the fall of the Han dynasty in 220 to the end of the T'ang dynasty in 907, state-sponsored Confucianism lost some of its previous influence. This is the golden era of Chinese Buddhism, and, along with Taoism, it attracted imperial favor, the attention of the intellectual elite, and a widespread following among the masses.

When Confucianism became the officially recognized state cult under the Han, it enjoyed considerable imperial patronage. Temples, libraries, and a university were built. Artworks were commissioned, scholars were employed, Confucian music and dance flourished, and there were elaborate public rites, sacrifices, and seasonal rituals. However, there is always a price to pay for state favors. That price is independence.

Confucianism had become dependent on the state, and when imperial favoritism waned, so did the fortunes of Confucianism. The conquest of Northern China by people from Central Asia introduced Buddhism into China. At first Buddhism was considered a relative of Taoism, but in time it spread and broadened its appeal, thereby establishing its autonomy with respect to both Confucianism and Taoism. During this Confucian winter, Confucians found themselves in fierce competition with Buddhism and Taoism for the emperor's patronage, the intellectuals' minds, and the loyalty of the masses.

8.4.1 The True Way

Han Yü (768–829) was one Confucian among others who championed the Confucian cause. In his famous *An Inquiry on Human Nature* (*Yüan-hsing*), he revived the debate about human nature and offered his theory of the "Three Grades." According to this theory, human nature has three grades: superior, medium, and inferior. The superior grade is the only good grade because at this level the Five Virtues of humanity (*jen*), righteousness (*i*), propriety (*li*), wisdom (*chih*), and loyalty (*chung*) are practiced in their purity. At the other end of the scale, the inferior grade, a person rebels against at least one of these virtues and is out of harmony with the others. The medium grade, in between the superior and the inferior, tends toward one or the other end of the scale depending on how many of the Five Virtues are sincerely practiced.

Beyond reviving Confucian interest in the debate over human nature, Han Yü waged a campaign against both Buddhism and Taoism. He asserted the superiority of Confucianism and advised the emperor to favor Confucianism alone.

Confucianists had never been happy with the reclusive tendencies of Taoism and Buddhism. Buddhism, in particular, counseled sons and daughters to leave home and become monks or nuns. They should forsake the world, not marry, and thus not produce children. This violated the norms of Confucianism at its deepest level because if monastic lifestyles should prevail, the sacred ancestral line would stop. This would undermine the family and, eventually, according to Confucian thought, undermine humanity.

Below are two selections from Yan Yü, in which he attacks Buddhism and argues that Confucianism represents the true way. Han Yü did not find many adherents in his own day because the view of Taoism and Buddhism as complementary to Confucianism had become well entrenched. However, Han Yü was rediscovered later by one of the first leaders of the Confucian revival. He became a virtual patron saint of Neo-Confucianism.

HAN YÜ

Memorial on the Bone of Buddha and What Is the True Way?

READING QUESTIONS

1. What are Han Yü's objections to Buddhism in general and to the emperor's participation in a ceremony honoring a relic of the Buddha in particular?
2. How do you think Han Yü reconciled his commitment to the Confucian principle of benevolence (*jen*) and his attack on Taoism and Buddhism?

Republished with permission of Columbia University Press, 562 W. 113th St., New York, NY 10025. *Sources of the Chinese Tradition*, compiled by Wm. Theodore De Bary, Wing-tsit Chan, and Burton Watson, 1960. Reproduced by permission of the publisher via Copyright Clearance Center, Inc. pp. 372–374, 376–379. Footnotes edited.

3. Some advocates of different religious today also preach both love of humanity and hatred toward those seen as religiously different. Why do you think this is the case?

MEMORIAL ON THE BONE OF BUDDHA

Your servant begs leave to say that Buddhism is no more than a cult of the barbarian peoples which spread to China in the time of the Latter Han. It did not exist here in ancient times. . . . When Emperor Kao-tsu [founder of the T'ang] received the throne from the House of Sui, he deliberated upon the suppression of Buddhism. But at that time the various officials, being of small worth and knowledge, were unable fully to comprehend the ways of the ancient kings and the exigencies of past and present, and so could not implement the wisdom of the emperor and rescue the age from corruption. Thus the matter came to nought, to your servant's constant regret.

Now Your Majesty, wise in the arts of peace and war, unparalleled in divine glory from countless ages past, upon your accession prohibited men and women from taking Buddhist orders and forbade the erection of temples and monasteries, and your servant believed that at Your Majesty's hand the will of Kao-tsu would be carried out. Even if the suppression of Buddhism should be as yet impossible, your servant hardly thought that Your Majesty would encourage it and on the contrary cause it to spread. Yet now your servant hears that Your Majesty has ordered the community of monks to go to Feng-hsiang to greet the bone of Buddha, that Your Majesty will ascend a tower to watch as it is brought into the palace, and that the various temples have been commanded to welcome and worship it in turn. Though your servant is abundantly ignorant, he understands that Your Majesty is not so misled by Buddhism as to honor it thus in hopes of receiving some blessing or reward, but only that, the year being one of plenty and the people joyful, Your Majesty would accord with the hearts of the multitude in setting forth for the officials and citizens of the capital some curious show and toy for their amusement. How could it be, indeed, that with such sagely wisdom Your Majesty should in truth give credence to these affairs? But the common people are ignorant and dull, easily misled and hard to enlighten, and should they see their emperor do these things, they might say that Your Majesty was serving Buddhism with a true heart. "The Son of Heaven is a Great Sage," they would cry, "and yet he reverences and believes with all his heart! How should we, the common people, then begrudge our bodies and our lives?" Then would they set about singeing their heads and scorching their fingers,[1] binding together in groups of ten and a hundred, doffing their common clothes and scattering their money, from morning to evening urging each other on lest one be slow, till old and young alike had abandoned their occupations to follow [Buddhism]. If this is not checked and the bone is carried from one temple to another, there will be those who will cut off their arms and mutilate their flesh in offering [to the Buddha]. Then will our old ways be corrupted, our customs violated, and the tale will spread to make us the mockery of the world. This is no trifling matter!

Now Buddha was a man of the barbarians who did not speak the language of China and wore clothes of a different fashion. His sayings did not concern the ways of our ancient kings, nor did his manner of dress conform to their laws. He understood neither the duties that bind sovereign and subject, nor the affections of father and son. If he were still alive today and came to our court by order of his ruler, Your Majesty might condescend to receive him, but it would amount to no more than one audience in the Hsüan-cheng Hall, a banquet by the Office for Receiving Guests, the presentation of a suit of clothes, and he would then be escorted to the borders of the nation, dismissed, and not allowed to delude the masses. How then, when he has long been dead, could his rotten bones, the foul and unlucky remains of his body, be rightly admitted to the palace? Confucius said: "Respect ghosts and spirits, but keep them at a distance!" So when the princes of ancient times went to pay their condolences at a funeral within the state, they sent exorcists in advance with peach wands to drive out evil, and only then would they advance. Now without reason Your Majesty has caused this loathsome thing to be brought in and would personally go to view it. No exorcists have been sent ahead, no peach wands employed. The host of officials have not spoken out against this wrong, and the censors have failed to note its impropriety. Your servant is deeply shamed and begs that this bone be given to the proper authorities to be cast into fire and water, that this evil may be rooted out, the world freed from its error, and later generations spared this delusion. Then may all men know how the acts of their wise sovereign transcend the commonplace a thousandfold. Would this not be glorious? Would it not be joyful?

Should the Buddha indeed have supernatural power to send down curses and calamities, may they fall only upon the person of your servant, who calls upon High Heaven to witness that he does not regret his words.

With all gratitude and sincerity your servant presents this memorial for consideration, being filled with respect and awe.

[From *Ch'ang-li hsien-sheng wen-chi*, SPTK ed., 39:2b–4b]

WHAT IS THE TRUE WAY? (YÜAN TAO)

. . . To love universally is called humanity (*jen*); to apply this in a proper manner is called righteousness (*i*). The operation of these is the Way (*Tao*), and its inner power (*te*) is that it is self-sufficient, requiring nothing from outside itself. Humanity and righteousness are fixed principles, but the Way and its inner power are speculative concepts. Thus we have the way of the gentleman and the way of the small man, and both good and evil power. Lao Tzu made light of humanity and righteousness, but he did not thereby abolish them. His view was narrow like that of a man who sits at the bottom of a well and looks up at the sky, saying, "The sky is small." This does not mean that the sky is really small. Lao Tzu understood humanity and righteousness in only a very limited sense, and therefore it is natural that he belittled them. What he called the Way was only the Way as he saw it, and not what I call the Way; what he called inner power was only power as he saw it, and not what I call inner power. What I call the Way and power are a combination of humanity and righteousness and this is the definition accepted by the world at large. But what Lao Tzu called the Way and power are stripped of humanity and righteousness, and represent only the private view of one individual.

After the decline of the Chou and the death of Confucius, in the time of Ch'in's book burnings, the Taoism of the Han, and the Buddhism of the Wei, the Chin, the Liang, and the Sui, when men spoke of the Way and power, of humanity and righteousness, they were approaching them either as followers of Yang Chu or of Mo Tzu, of Lao Tzu or of Buddha. Being followers of these doctrines, they naturally rejected Confucianism. Acknowledging these men as their masters, they made of Confucius an outcast, adhering to new teachings and vilifying the old. Alas, though men of later ages long to know of humanity and righteousness, the Way and inner power, from whom may they hear of them? . . .

In ancient times there were only four classes of people, but now there are six.[2] There was only one teach-

---

[1] Acts symbolic of a person's renunciation of the world upon entering Buddhist orders.

[2] The four classes of traditional Chinese society—official, farmer, artisan, and merchant—to which were added the Taoist and the Buddhist clergy.

ing, where now there are three.[3] For each family growing grain, there are now six consuming it; for each family producing utensils, there are six using them; for one family engaged in trade, six others take their profits. Is it surprising then that the people are reduced to poverty and driven to theft?

In ancient times men faced many perils, but sages arose who taught them how to protect and nourish their lives, acting as their rulers and teachers. They drove away the harmful insects and reptiles, birds and beasts, and led men to settle in the center of the earth. The people were cold and they made them clothes, hungry and they gave them food. Because men had dwelt in danger in the tops of trees or grown sick sleeping on the ground, they built them halls and dwellings. They taught them handicrafts that they might have utensils to use, trades so that they could supply their wants, medicine to save them from early death, proper burial and sacrifices to enhance their sense of love and gratitude, rites to order the rules of precedence, music to express their repressed feelings, government to lead the indolent, and punishments to suppress the overbearing. Because men cheated each other, they made tallies and seals, measures and scales to insure confidence; because men plundered they made walls and fortifications, armor and weapons to protect them. Thus they taught men how to prepare against danger and prevent injury to their lives.

Now the Taoists tell us that "until the sages die off, robbers will never disappear," or that "if we destroy our measures and break our scales then the people will cease their contention." Alas, how thoughtless are such sayings! If there had been no sages in ancient times, then mankind would have perished, for men have no feathers or fur, no scales or shells to protect them from cold and heat, no claws and teeth to contend for food. Therefore those who are rulers give commands which are carried out by their officials and made known to the people, and the people produce grain, rice, hemp, and silk, make utensils and exchange commodities for the support of the superiors. If the ruler fails to issue commands, then he ceases to be a ruler, while if his subordinates do not carry them out and extend them to the people, and if the people do not produce goods for the support of their superiors, they must be punished. Yet the Way [of the Taoists and Buddhists] teaches men to reject the ideas of ruler and subject and of father and son, to cease from activities which sustain life and seek for some so-called purity and Nirvāna. Alas, it is fortunate for such doctrines that they appeared only after the time of the Three Reigns and thus escaped suppression at the hands of Yü

and T'ang, kings Wen and Wu, the Duke of Chou and Confucius, but unfortunate for us what they did not appear before the Three Reigns so that they could have been rectified by those sages. . . .

The *Book of Rites* says: "The ancients who wished to illustrate illustrious virtue throughout the kingdom first ordered well their own states. Wishing to order well their states, they first regulated their families. Wishing to regulate their families, they first cultivated their persons. Wishing to cultivate their persons, they first rectified their hearts. Wishing to rectify their hearts, they first sought to be sincere in their thoughts" [*Great Learning*, I]. Thus when the ancients spoke of rectifying the heart and being sincere in their thoughts, they had this purpose in mind. But now [the Taoists and Buddhists] seek to govern their hearts by escaping from the world, the state and the family. They violate the natural law, so that the son does not regard his father as a father, the subject does not look upon his ruler as a ruler, and the people do not serve those whom they must serve.

When Confucius wrote in the *Spring and Autumn Annals*, he treated as barbarians those feudal lords who observed barbarian customs, and as Chinese those who had advanced to the use of Chinese ways. The *Analects* [III, 5] says: "The barbarians with rulers are not the equal of the Chinese without rulers." The *Book of Odes* [Odes of Lu, 4] says: "Fight against the barbarians of the west and north, punish those of Ching and Shu." Yet now [the Buddhists] come with their barbarian ways and put them ahead of the teachings of our ancient kings. Are they not become practically barbarians themselves?

What were these teachings of our ancient kings? To love universally, which is called humanity; to apply this in the proper manner, which is called righteousness; to proceed from these to the Way and to be self-sufficient without seeking anything outside, which is called [inner] power. The *Odes* and the *History*, the *Changes* and the *Spring and Autumn Annals*, are their writings; rites and music, punishments and government, their methods. Their people were the four classes of officials, farmers, artisans, and merchants; their relationships were those of sovereign and subject, father and son, teacher and friend, guest and host, elder and younger brother, and husband and wife. Their clothing was hemp and silk; their dwelling halls and houses; their food grain and rice, fruit and vegetables, fish and meat. Their ways were easy to understand; their teachings simple to follow. Applied to oneself, they brought harmony and blessing; applied to others, love and fairness. To the mind they gave peace; to the state and the family all that was just and fitting. Thus in life men were able to satisfy their emotions, and at death the obligations due them were fulfilled. Men sacrificed to Heaven and the gods were

---

[3] Confucianism, to which was added Taoism and Buddhism.

pleased; to the spirits of their ancestors and the ancestors received their offerings. What Way is this? It is what *I* call the Way, and not what the Taoists and Buddhists call the Way. Yao taught it to Shun, Shun to Yü, Yü to T'ang, and T'ang to kings Wen and Wu and the Duke of Chou. These men taught it to Confucius and Confucius to Mencius, but when Mencius died it was no longer handed down. Hsün Tzu and Yang Hsiung understood elements of it, but their understanding lacked depth; they spoke of it but incompletely. In the days before the Duke of Chou, the sages were rulers and so they could put the Way into practice, but after the time of the Duke of Chou they were only officials and so they wrote at length about the Way.

What should be done now? I say that unless [Taoism and Buddhism] are suppressed, the Way will not prevail; unless these men are stopped, the Way will not be practiced. Let their priests be turned into ordinary men again, let their books be burned and their temples converted into homes. Let the Way of our former kings be made clear to lead them, and let the widower and the widow, the orphan and the lonely, the crippled and the sick be nourished. Then all will be well.

[From *Ch'ang-li hsien-sheng wen-chi*, SPTK ed., 11:1a–3b]

8.5 NEO-CONFUCIANISM (960–1644)

Some of the Chinese literati who had embraced Buddhism begin, in the eleventh century, to question it for a variety of reasons. Among them was the growing belief that Buddhism was a foreign religion, fit for "barbarians" who taught doctrines destructive of Chinese family traditions. These intellectuals began to embrace Confucianism once more and revived the tradition among the elite after the long Confucian winter that had begun with the fall of the Han dynasty in 220 and the state-supported cult of Confucius. This revival is known in China as the "Study of Nature and Propriety" and in the West as Neo-Confucianism.

Buddhist philosophical speculation on the nature of ultimate reality and the intellectual rigor of Buddhist metaphysical debates had appealed to the Chinese literati. In light of this, it is not surprising to find the renewal of Confucianism concerning itself with cosmological and ontological questions.

8.5.1 The Great Ultimate

One of the philosophers responsible for the Confucian revival is Chou Tun-i (1017–1073), who is sometimes referred to as the pioneer of Neo-Confucianism. He discussed what were to become some of its principal themes in two short treatises: *An Explanation of the Diagram of the Great Ultimate* (*T'ai-chi-t'u shuo*) and *Penetrating the Book of Changes* (*T'ung-shu*).

The *Book of Changes* (*I-Ching*) is one of the *Five Classics* and had long been used for purposes of divination as well as a source for understanding how nature operates. The book shows sixty-four abstract symbols made of solid (*yang*) and broken (*yin*) lines. **Yang** lines represent all strong, active, creative, dominate, male, bright, high, and other associated forces in the universe, whereas **yin** lines represent all the weak, passive, receptive, submissive, female, dark, low, and other associated forces. For example, the first hexagram (an image of six lines) is called the Creative Principle and the second is called the Receptive, or Passive, Principle.

The Creative	The Receptive
————	—— ——
————	—— ——
————	—— ——
————	—— ——
————	—— ——
————	—— ——

Each hexagram is made up of three trigrams (units of three lines). The remaining sixty-two hexagrams are made up of different combinations of *yang* and *yin* lines. If you faced a problem and wished advice, you could ask a question and throw some coins or sticks that yield a *yang/yin* pattern leading you to one of the hexagrams. That hexagram, rightly interpreted, is thought to contain the answer to your question. Over the centuries, various commentaries were written on the hexagrams in the belief that the secret workings of nature as a dynamic interaction of *yang/yin* forces were inscribed in the *Book of Changes*.

Chou Tun-i's comments on the *I-Ching* brought the book into the forefront of Confucian thought and thus made metaphysical speculation more prominent in Confucianism than it had been before. Likewise, his writing on the Great Ultimate, or **T'ai-chi,** reinforced the newfound interest in metaphysics and thereby made Confucianism more intellectually competitive with both Taoism and Buddhism. It is possible to see both Taoist and Buddhist metaphysical speculation in Chou Tun-i's claim that *T'ai-chi* is equal to the "Ultimate of Non-being" (*wu-chi*). The movement of *T'ai-chi* generates *yang* forces, and its rest generates *yin* forces. As these two forces interact, the "five elements" that make up the world as it appears to us are generated.

YIN/YANG

Yin-Yang

CHOU TUN-I

An Explanation of the Diagram of the Great Ultimate and Penetrating the Book of Changes

READING QUESTIONS

1. Some scholars have characterized the cosmology presupposed by Chou Tun-i's explanation of the diagram of the Great Ultimate as one of "organic harmony." Do you agree? Why or why not?
2. What do you think is meant by the claim that fundamentally the Great Ultimate is the Non-ultimate? (See "Comment" by the translator, Wing-tsit Chan.)
3. How does this cosmological explanation of the universe differ from creation stories you have read?

From Chan, Wing-tsit, *A Source Book in Chinese Philosophy*, pp. 463–467, 473–474, Copyright © 1963, renewed 1991 by Princeton University Press. Reprinted by permission of Princeton University Press. Footnotes edited.

4. What is sincerity, and how does it relate to "sagehood"?
5. How can sincerity be said to give rise to both "good and evil"? What exactly is "evil" in this context?
6. What are the marks of a sage, and how does one become a sage?

AN EXPLANATION OF THE DIAGRAM OF THE GREAT ULTIMATE

The Ultimate of Non-being and also the Great Ultimate (*T'ai-chi*)! The Great Ultimate through movement generates yang. When its activity reaches its limit, it becomes tranquil. Through tranquility the Great Ultimate generates yin. When tranquility reaches its limit, activity begins again. So movement and tranquility alternate and become the root of each other, giving rise to the distinction of yin and yang, and the two modes are thus established.

By the transformation of yang and its union with yin, the Five Agents of Water, Fire, Wood, Metal, and Earth arise. When these five material forces (*ch'i*) are distributed in harmonious order, the four seasons run their course.

The Five Agents constitute one system of yin and yang, and yin and yang constitute one Great Ultimate. The Great Ultimate is fundamentally the Non-ultimate. The Five Agents arise, each with its specific nature.

When the reality of the Ultimate of Non-being and the essence of yin, yang, and the Five Agents come into mysterious union, integration ensues. Ch'ien (Heaven) constitutes the male element, and k'un (Earth) constitutes the female element. The interaction of these two material forces engenders and transforms the myriad things. The myriad things produce and reproduce, resulting in an unending transformation.

It is man alone who receives (the Five Agents) in their highest excellence, and therefore he is most intelligent. His physical form appears, and his spirit develops consciousness. The five moral principles of his nature (humanity or *jen*, righteousness, propriety, wisdom, and faithfulness) are aroused by, and react to, the external world and engage in activity; good and evil are distinguished; and human affairs take place.

The sage settles these affairs by the principles of the Mean, correctness, humanity, and righteousness (for the way of the sage is none other than these four), regarding tranquility as fundamental. (Having no desire, there will therefore be tranquility.) Thus he establishes himself as the ultimate standard for man. Hence the character of the sage is "identical with that of Heaven and Earth; his brilliancy is identical with that of the sun and moon; his order is identical with that of the four seasons; and his good and evil fortunes are identical with those of spiritual beings." The superior man cultivates these moral qualities and enjoys good fortune, whereas the inferior man violates them and suffers evil fortune.

Therefore it is said that "yin and yang are established as the way of Heaven, the weak and the strong as the way of Earth, and humanity and righteousness as the way of man." It is also said that "if we investigate the cycle of things, we shall understand the concepts of life and death." Great is the *Book of Changes*! Herein lies its excellence! (*Chou Tzu ch'üan-shu*, chs. 1–2, pp. 4–32)

Comment. This *Explanation* has provided the essential outline of Neo-Confucian metaphysics and cosmology in the last eight hundred years. Few short Chinese treatises like this have exerted so much influence. Although the whole concept owes much to the *Book of Changes*, it is to be noted that it rejected the idea of the Eight Trigrams of the *Book of Changes* and used the Five Agents instead, thus showing that the system was the product of Chou Tun-i's own speculation.

A great amount of literature has grown up on the history of the diagram and on the concept of the Great Ultimate. So far as philosophy is concerned, most Neo-Confucianists have followed Chou although they have differed in many details. However, two of Chou's ideas have aroused considerable criticism. One is the idea of the Non-ultimate. One of the famous debates between Chu Hsi and Lu Hsiang-shan (Lu Chiu-yüan, 1139–1193) was over this idea. The word *erh* in the opening sentence means "and also" or "in turn." But it can be interpreted in the sense of "and then," in which case, the Non-ultimate and the Great Ultimate would be two separate entities. This was precisely what Lu Hsiang-shan was objecting to, as he saw in Chou Tun-i a bifurcation of reality as two. On the other hand, Chu Hsi claimed that Chou never meant that there is a Non-ultimate outside of the Great Ultimate, that the Non-ultimate is the state of reality before the appearance of forms whereas the Great Ultimate is the state after the appearance of forms, and that the two form a unity. This interpretation has been accepted by most Neo-Confucianists. . . .

PENETRATING THE BOOK OF CHANGES

Ch. 1. Sincerity, Pt. 1

Sincerity (*ch'eng*)[1] is the foundation of the sage. "Great is the *ch'ien*, the originator! All things, obtain their beginning from it." It is the source of sincerity. "The way of *ch'ien* is to change and transform so that everything will obtain its correct nature and destiny." In this way sincerity is established. It is pure and perfectly good. Therefore "the successive movement of yin and yang constitutes the Way (Tao). What issues from the Way is good, and that which realizes it is the individual nature." Origination and flourish characterize the penetration of sincerity, and advantage and firmness are its completion (or recovery). Great is the Change, the source of nature and destiny!

Ch. 2. Sincerity, Pt. 2

Sagehood is nothing but sincerity. It is the foundation of the Five Constant Virtues (humanity, righteousness, propriety, wisdom, and faithfulness) and the source of all activities. When tranquil, it is in the state of non-being, and when active, it is in the state of being. It is perfectly correct and clearly penetrating. Without sincerity, the Five Constant Virtues and all activities will be wrong. They will be depraved and obstructed. Therefore with sincerity very little effort is needed [to achieve the Mean]. [In itself] it is perfectly easy but it is difficult to put into practice. But with determination and firmness, there will be no difficulty. Therefore it is said, "If a man can for one day master himself and return to propriety, all under heaven will return to humanity."

Ch. 3. Sincerity Is the Subtle, Incipient, Activating Force (Chi) of Virtue

Sincerity [in its original substance] engages in no activity, but is the subtle, incipient, activating force giving rise to good and evil. The virtue of loving is called humanity, that of doing what is proper is called righteousness, that of putting things in order is called propriety, that of penetration is called wisdom, and that of abiding by one's commitments is called faithfulness. One who is in accord with his nature and acts with ease is a sage. One who returns to his nature and adheres to it is a wor-

---

[1]This word means not only sincerity in the narrow sense, but also honesty, absence of fault, seriousness, being true to one's true self, being true to the nature of being, actuality, realness.

thy. And one whose subtle emanation cannot be seen and whose [goodness] is abundant and all-pervasive without limit is a man of the spirit.

Comment. The first sentence of this chapter occasioned a great deal of discussion among Neo-Confucianists. Chou seems to contradict himself, for sincerity, being the original state of man's moral nature, is perfectly good and yet it gives rise to both good and evil. Actually the problem of evil had bothered Confucianists right along and there was no solution until Chang Tsai (Chang Heng-ch'ü, 1020–1077). Chou adheres to the traditional Confucian position that human nature is inherently good but as one's nature comes into contact with external things, good and evil appear. Whereas both Taoism and Buddhism maintain that this external influence corrupts. Confucianism puts the responsibility on man himself by holding that evil appears when man fails to adhere to the Mean. Thus the good moral nature is substance, and good and evil appear only in its function. This doctrine was upheld throughout the history of Neo-Confucianism. As Sun Ch'i-feng (1584–1675) has observed in commenting on this chapter, Chou teaches that good results from one's being correct and evil from one's being one-sided, a theory quite different from that of Hu Hung (Hu Wu-feng, 1100–1155), who said that both good and evil proceed from nature. Chou Tzu's important contribution in this connection is his idea of subtle, incipient activation. It is also found in chapters four and nine and, according to Chu Hsi, is implicit in chapter twenty-seven.

The word *chi* means an originating power, an inward spring of activity, an emergence not yet visible, a critical point at which one's direction toward good or evil is set. It is here and now that one must be absolutely sincere and true to his moral nature so he will not deviate from it either in going too far or not going far enough. Thus Chou turns a quietistic state into a dynamic one.

Ch. 4. Sagehood

"The state of absolute quiet and inactivity" is sincerity. The spirit is that which, "when acted on, immediately penetrates all things." And the state of subtle incipient activation is the undifferentiated state between existence and nonexistence when activity has started but has not manifested itself in physical form. Sincerity is infinitely

pure and hence evident. The spirit is responsive and hence works wonders. And incipient activation is subtle and hence abstruse. The sage is the one who is in the state of sincerity, spirit, and subtle incipient activation.

Ch. 20. Learning to Be a Sage

"Can one become a sage through learning?"
"Yes."
"Is there any essential way?"
"Yes."
"Please explain it to me."
"The essential way is to [concentrate on] one thing. By [concentrating on] one thing is meant having no desire. Having no desire, one is vacuous (*hsü*, being absolutely pure and peaceful) while tranquil, and straightforward while in action. Being vacuous while tranquil, one becomes intelligent and hence penetrating. Being straightforward while active, one becomes impartial and hence all-embracing. Being intelligent, penetrating, impartial, and all-embracing, one is almost a sage."

Comment. Confucianists had never advocated having no desire. Mencius merely advocated having few desires. The Taoist influence here is obvious. Hitherto, it was only a Taoist and Buddhist method of moral cultivation, but from now on, it became a Confucian method too. But as Chu Hsi said, Chou went too far, and as the prerequisite for concentrating on one thing, Ch'eng had to substitute seriousness (*ching*) for desirelessness, evidently in order to eliminate this Taoist influence.

8.5.2 Spiritual Beings

In Reading 8.1, Julia Ching provided an overview of Chu Hsi's ideas about the Great Ultimate, principle (*li*), and material energy (*ch'i*) as well as his important place in the development of Confucianism. Here I present a brief selection on spiritual beings from the *Complete Works of Chu Hsi (Chu Tzu ch'üan-shu)*.

It is helpful to remember that, according to some Confucians, human beings have two souls: an upper soul (***hun***) and a lower soul (***p'o***). At death the upper soul becomes a spirit (***shen***) and the lower soul a ghost (***kuei***). Because of the cult of the ancestors and the widespread belief in ghosts, considerable debate arose about the existence of spirits and ghosts. Sometimes the question of whether the dead are conscious and know what is happening was treated as a theme for wit. For example, a Queen who commanded that her lover be buried alive with her when she died was presumably dissuaded, as the following dialogue indicates.

"Do you think the dead have knowledge?"

"They do not," said the Queen.

"If Your Majesty's divine intelligence plainly knows that the dead lack knowledge, why uselessly bury the man you loved in life beside an unknowing corpse? But if the dead do have knowledge, his late Majesty's wrath has been mounting for a long time."

Wang Ch'ung (ca. 27–100) wrote a treatise on death in which he argued that people become neither ghosts nor spiritual beings at death. It was quite natural then that Chu Hsi should be asked about spiritual beings. His reply follows.

CHU HSI

Spiritual Beings and Forces

READING QUESTIONS

1. Make a list of all the ideas you do not understand and discuss them in class. First, state what you think they mean. Second, formulate as precise a question as you can about what you do not understand.
2. How does Chu Hsi relate his views on principle (*li*) and material energy (*ch'i*) to the issue of spiritual beings?
3. What is Chu Hsi's objection to Buddhist ideas of rebirth? Do you agree with this objection? Why or why not?

Someone asked whether there are spiritual beings (*kuei-shen*)?

Answer: How can this matter be quickly explained? Even if it could, would you believe it? You must look into all principles of things and gradually understand, and then this puzzling problem will be solved by itself. When Fan Ch'ih asked about wisdom, Confucius said, "Devote oneself earnestly to the duties due to men, and

From Chan, Wing-tsit, *A Source Book in Chinese Philosophy*, pp. 643–646. Copyright © 1963, renewed 1991 by Princeton University Press. Reprinted by permission of Princeton University Press. Footnotes edited.

respect spiritual beings but keep them at a distance. This may be called wisdom." Let us attend to those things that should be attended to. Those that cannot be attended to, let us set aside. By the time we have attended thoroughly to ordinary daily matters, the principles governing spiritual beings will naturally be understood. This is the way to wisdom. [When Confucius said], "If we are not yet able to serve man, how can we serve spiritual beings?" he expresses the same idea. (51:2a)

Is expansion positive spiritual force (*shen*) and contraction negative spiritual force (*kuei*)?

The Teacher drew a circle on the desk with his hand and pointed to its center and said: Principle is like a circle. Within it there is differentiation like this. All cases of material force which is coming forth belong to yang and are positive spiritual force. All cases of material force which is returning to its origin belong to yin and are the negative spiritual force. In the day, forenoon is the positive spiritual force, afternoon is the negative spiritual force. In the month, from the third day onward is the positive spiritual force; after the sixteenth day, it is the negative spiritual force.

T'ung Po-yü *asked:* Is it correct when speaking of the sun and moon as opposites, to say that the sun is the positive spiritual force and the moon is the negative spiritual force?

Answer: Yes, it is. Plants growing are the positive spiritual force, plants declining are the negative spiritual force. A person from childhood to maturity is the positive spiritual force, while a man in his declining years and old age is the negative spiritual force. In breathing, breath going out is the positive spiritual force, breath coming in is the negative spiritual force. (51:6b)

The positive and negative spiritual forces are so-called with respect to function. Spirit is so-called with respect to the wonderful functioning. In the cases of positive and negative spiritual forces, like yin and yang, contraction and expansion, going and coming, and diminution and augmentation, there are rough traces that can be seen. In the case of spirit which is so-called because of the mysterious functioning, it happens all of a sudden and is unfathomable. It suddenly comes, suddenly goes; it is suddenly here, suddenly there. (51:7b)

Question about the principles of life and death and spiritual beings. (*Question:* Although we know that spiritual beings and life and death are governed by one and the same principle, we do not understand the exact point. *Answer:* "Essence and material force are combined to be things. The wandering away of the spirit becomes change." This is the principle of life and death. The questioner did not understand. *Further remark:* Essence and material force consolidate to become man, and as they disintegrate, they become a spiritual being.

Further question: When essence and material force consolidate, is this principle attached to material force?)

Answer: As the Way of Heaven operates, the myriad things develop and grow. There is (logically) principle first and then material force. Although they coexist at the same time, in the final analysis principle is basic. Man receives it and thus possesses life. (But material force may be clear or turbid.) The clear part of material force becomes his vital force (*ch'i*), while the turbid part becomes his physical nature. (The clear part belongs to yang while the turbid part belongs to yin.) Consciousness and movement are due to yang, while physical form and body (bones and flesh, skin and hair) are due to yin. The vital force belongs to the heavenly aspect of the soul (*hun*) and the body is governed by the earthly aspect of the soul (*p'o*). In his commentary on the *Huai-nan Tzu,* Kao Yu . . . said, "*Hun* is the spirit of yang and *p'o* is the spirit of yin." By spirit is meant the master of the body and the vital force. Man is born as a result of integration of essence and material force. He possesses this material force only in a certain amount, which in time necessarily becomes exhausted. (This is what is meant by physicians when they say that yin or yang no longer rises or falls.) When exhaustion takes place, the heavenly aspect of the soul and the vital force return to Heaven, and the earthly aspect of the soul and the body return to the Earth, and the man dies. When a man is about to die, the warm material force leaves him and rises. This is called the *hun* rising. The lower part of his body gradually becomes cold. This is called the *p'o* falling. Thus as there is life, there is necessarily death, and as there is beginning, there must be an end. What integrates and disintegrates is material force. As to principle, it merely attaches itself to material force, but from the beginning it does not consolidate into a separate thing by itself. However, whatever in one's functioning that is correct is principle. It need not be spoken of in terms of integration and disintegration. When a man dies, his material force necessarily disintegrates. However, it does not disintegrate completely at once. Therefore in religious sacrifices we have the principle of spiritual influence and response. Whether the material force (or vital force) of ancestors of many generations ago is still there or not cannot be known. Nevertheless, since those who perform the sacrificial rites are their descendants, the material force between them is after all the same. Hence there is the principle by which they can penetrate and respond. But the material force that has disintegrated cannot again be integrated. And yet the Buddhists say that man after death becomes a spiritual being and the spiritual being again becomes a man. If so, then in the universe there would always be the same number of people coming and going, with no need of the creative process of production and reproduction. This is decidedly absurd. (51:18b–19b)

8.5.3 Why Does Great Learning Manifest Clear Character?

Wang Yang-ming (1472–1529) is the main representative of the idealistic wing of Neo-Confucianism. He argued against the rationalism of Chu Hsi that placed "the investigation of things" prior to "making thoughts sincere" in "The Great Learning," (Reading 8.2.1). According to Wang Yang-ming, the study of mind, not things, should be primary. Understanding the truth comes from within and not from externals.

WANG YANG-MING

Inquiry on the Great Learning

READING QUESTIONS

1. What does Master Wang mean by "one body"?
2. What are the differences between the "great man" and the "small man"?
3. Why does the learning of the "great man" consist in loving the people?
4. What is "clear character," and how is it related to "abiding in the highest good"?

Question: The *Great Learning* was considered by a former scholar [Chu Hsi] as the learning of the great man. I venture to ask why the learning of the great man should consist in "manifesting the clear character"?

Master Wang said: The great man regards Heaven and Earth and the myriad things as one body. He regards the world as one family and the country as one person. As to those who make a cleavage between objects and distinguish between the self and others, they are small men. That the great man can regard Heaven, Earth, and the myriad things as one body is not because he deliberately wants to do so, but because it is natural to the hu-

---

mane nature of his mind that he do so. Forming one body with Heaven, Earth, and the myriad things is not only true of the great man. Even the mind of the small man is no different. Only he himself makes it small. Therefore when he sees a child about to fall into a well, he cannot help a feeling of alarm and commiseration. This shows that his humanity (*jen*) forms one body with the child. It may be objected that the child belongs to the same species. Again, when he observes the pitiful cries and frightened appearance of birds and animals about to be slaughtered, he cannot help feeling an "inability to bear" their suffering. This shows that his humanity forms one body with birds and animals. It may be objected that birds and animals are sentient beings as he is. But when he sees plants broken and destroyed, he cannot help a feeling of pity. This shows that his humanity forms one body with plants. It may be said that plants are living things as he is. Yet even when he sees tiles and stones shattered and crushed, he cannot help a feeling of regret. This shows that his humanity forms one body with tiles and stones. This means that even the mind of the small man necessarily has the humanity that forms one body with all. Such a mind is rooted in his Heaven-endowed nature, and is naturally intelligent, clear, and not beclouded. For this reason it is called the "clear character." Although the mind of the small man is divided and narrow, yet his humanity that forms one body can remain free from darkness to this degree. This is due to the fact that his mind has not yet been aroused by desires and obscured by selfishness. When it is aroused by desires and obscured by selfishness, compelled by greed for gain and fear of harm, and stirred by anger, he will destroy things, kill members of his own species, and will do everything. In extreme cases he will even slaughter his own brothers, and the humanity that forms one body will disappear completely. Hence, if it is not obscured by selfish desires, even the mind of the small man has the humanity that forms one body with all as does the mind of the great man. As soon as it is obscured by selfish desires, even the mind of the great man will be divided and narrow like that of the small man. Thus the learning of the great man consists entirely in getting rid of the obscuration of selfish desires in order by his own efforts to make manifest his clear character, so as to restore the condition of forming one body with Heaven, Earth, and the myriad things, a condition that is originally so, that is all. It is not that outside of the original substance something can be added.

Question: Why, then, does the learning of the great man consist in loving the people?

Answer: To manifest the clear character is to bring about the substance of the state of forming one body with Heaven, Earth, and the myriad things, whereas loving the people is to put into universal operation the function of the state of forming one body. Hence manifesting the clear character consists in loving the people, and loving the people is the way to manifest the clear character. Therefore, only when I love my father, the fathers of others, and the fathers of all men can my humanity really form one body with my father, the fathers of others, and the fathers of all men. When it truly forms one body with them, then the clear character of filial piety will be manifested. Only when I love my brother, the brothers of others, and the brothers of all men can my humanity really form one body with my brother, the brothers of others, and the brothers of all men. When it truly forms one body with them, then the clear character of brotherly respect will be manifested. Everything from ruler, minister, husband, wife, and friends to mountains, rivers, spiritual beings, birds, animals, and plants should be truly loved in order to realize my humanity that forms one body with them, and then my clear character will be completely manifested, and I will really form one body with Heaven, Earth, and the myriad things. This is what is meant by "manifesting the clear character throughout the empire." This is what is meant by "regulation of the family," "ordering the state," and "bringing peace to the world." This is what is meant by "full development of one's nature."

Question: Then why does the learning of the great man consist in "abiding in the highest good"?

Answer: The highest good is the ultimate principle of manifesting character and loving people. The nature endowed in us by Heaven is pure and perfect. The fact that it is intelligent, clear, and not beclouded is evidence of the emanation and revelation of the highest good. It is the original substance of the clear character which is called innate knowledge of the good. As the highest good emanates and reveals itself, we will consider right as right and wrong as wrong. Things of greater or less importance and situations of grave or light character will be responded to as they act upon us. In all our changes and movements, we will stick to no particular point, but possess in ourselves the Mean that is perfectly natural. This is the ultimate of the normal nature of man and the principle of things. There can be no consideration of adding to or subtracting from it. If there is any, it means selfish ideas and shallow cunning, and cannot be said to be the highest good. Naturally, how can anyone who does not watch over himself carefully when alone, and who has no refinement and singleness of mind, attain to such a state of perfection? Later generations fail to realize that the highest good is inherent in their own minds, but exercise their selfish ideas and cunning and grope for it outside their minds, believing that every event and every object has its own peculiar definite principle. For this reason the law of right and wrong is obscured; the mind becomes concerned with fragmentary and isolated details and broken pieces; the selfish desires of man become rampant and the Principle of Nature is at an end. And thus the learning of manifesting character and loving people is everywhere thrown into confusion. In the past there have, of course, been people who wanted to manifest their clear character. But simply because they did not know how to abide in the highest good, but instead drove their own minds toward something too lofty, they thereby lost them in illusions, emptiness, and quietness, having nothing to do with the work of the family, the state, and the world. Such are the followers of Buddhism and Taoism. There have, of course, been those who wanted to love their people. Yet simply because they did not know how to abide in the highest good, but instead sank their own minds in base and trifling things, they thereby lost them in scheming strategy and cunning techniques, having neither the sincerity of humanity nor that of commiseration. Such are the followers of the Five Despots and the pursuers of success and profit. All of these defects are due to a failure to know how to abide in the highest good. Therefore abiding in the highest good is to manifesting character and loving people as the carpenter's square and compass are to the square and the circle, or rule and measure to length, or balances and scales to weight. If the square and the circle do not abide by the compass and the carpenter's square, their standard will be wrong; if length does not abide by the rule and measure, its adjustment will be lost; if weight does not abide by the balances, its exactness will be gone; and if manifesting clear character and loving people do not abide by the highest good, their foundation will disappear. Therefore, abiding in the highest good so as to love people and manifest the clear character is what is meant by the learning of the great man.

Question: "Only after knowing what to abide in can one be calm. Only after having been calm can one be tranquil. Only after having achieved tranquility can one have peaceful repose. Only after having peaceful repose can one begin to deliberate. Only after deliberation can the end be attained." How do you explain this?

Answer: People fail to realize that the highest good is in their minds and seek it outside. As they believe that everything or every event has its own definite principle, they search for the highest good in individual things. Consequently, the mind becomes fragmentary, isolated, broken into pieces; mixed and confused, it has no definite direction. Once it is realized that the highest good is in the mind and does not depend on any search outside,

then the mind will have definite direction and there will be no danger of its becoming fragmentary, isolated, broken into pieces, mixed, or confused. When there is no such danger, the mind will not be erroneously perturbed but will be tranquil. Not being erroneously perturbed but being tranquil, it will be leisurely and at ease in its daily functioning and will attain peaceful repose. Being in peaceful repose, whenever a thought arises or an event acts upon it, the mind with its innate knowledge will thoroughly sift and carefully examine whether or not the thought or event is in accord with the highest good, and thus the mind can deliberate. With deliberation, every decision will be excellent and every act will be proper, and in this way the highest good will be attained.

Question: "Things have their roots and their branches." A former scholar [Chu Hsi] considered manifesting the clear character as the root (or fundamental) and renovating the people as the branch (or secondary), and that they are two things opposing each other as internal and external. "Affairs have their beginnings and their ends." The former scholar considered knowing what to abide in as the beginning and the attainment of the highest good as the end, both being one thing in harmonious continuity. According to you, "renovating the people" (*hsin-min*) should be read as "loving the people" (*ch'in-min*). If so, isn't the theory of root and branches in some respect incorrect?

Answer: The theory of beginnings and ends is in general right. Even if we read "renovating the people" as "loving the people" and say that manifesting the character is the root and loving the people is the branches, it is not incorrect. The main thing is that root and branches should not be distinguished as two different things. The trunk of the tree is called the root (or essential part), and the twigs are called the branches. It is precisely because the tree is one that its parts can be called roots and branches. If they are said to be two different things, then since they are two distinct objects, how can we speak of them as root and branches of the same thing? Since the idea of renovating the people is different from that of loving the people, obviously the task of manifesting the character and that of loving the people are two different things. If it is realized that manifesting the clear character is to love the people and loving the people is to manifest the clear character, how can they be split in two? What the former scholar said is due to his failure to realize that manifesting the character and loving the people are basically one thing. Instead, he believed them to be two different things and consequently, although he knew that root and branches should be one, yet he could not help splitting them in two. . . .

8.6 CH'ING CONFUCIANISM (1644–1911)

During the Ch'ing dynasty, a critical reaction to the Neo-Confucian metaphysical emphasis on transcendence developed in the School of Evidential Research. The School of Evidential Research wanted to return to a more solid, concrete, and practical emphasis than was found in Neo-Confucianism. Although the work of Chu Hsi continued to be the basis for the civil service examinations, many Confucians believed his emphasis on nonphysical principle (*li*) and material energy (*ch'i*) moved dangerously close to dualism, thereby introducing an element of disharmony.

We shall look at one example below of how the potential bifurcation and disharmony of Chu Hsi's distinction between *li* and *ch'i* might be overcome.

8.6.1 The Harmony of Nature

Passions and desires are powerful sorts of things that drive us to eat, drink, sleep, and have sex. They move our bodies in ways that are natural, yet in ways that seem to take the control of our bodies away from us.

Many religious thinkers have had problems with passions and desires. They want to turn our minds toward heaven, not earth. They want us to contemplate the spiritual, not the bodily. Some Confucianists want us to restrain and always control our bodies, and Buddhists find human desires the cause of suffering. Indeed, both morality and salvation appear to depend, for many deeply religious people, on the suppression, if not the rejection, of the body and its desires.

If we learn that an antagonistic relationship exists between the bodily and the spiritual, then we may experience tension between what seems natural to us as humans and what seems appropriate for our spiritual development. Disharmony rather than harmony characterizes our lives as we strive to transcend the desires of our earthly bodies and focus on our heavenly homes. Maybe there is a better way to live.

Wang Fu-chih (1619–1692) did not like the dualistic tendency of Chu Hsi's rationalism. However, he also found Wang Yang-ming's idealistic emphasis on mind too subjective. Wang Fu-chih sought to reconstruct Confucianism in ways that avoided the twin pitfalls of dualism and subjectivism.

Wang Fu-chih believed that Chang Tsai (1020–1077), author of the *Western Inscription*, provided a fruitful starting point for recovering both the emphasis on harmony and the emphasis on moral practice. The opening lines of the *Western Inscription* read:

> Heaven is my father and Earth is my mother, and even such a small creature as I finds an intimate place in their midst. Therefore that which fills the universe I regard as my body and that which directs the universe I consider as my nature. All people are my brothers and sisters, and all things are my companions.

Wang Fu-chih thought the emphasis on a reality that transcends the world of space and time that is found among metaphysical Confucianists as well as Taoists and Buddhists takes our attention away from the world in which we live. In our world, both material and immaterial elements are aspects of a creative process of change. Wang Fu-chih wanted to emphasize a synthesis of principle (*li*) and material energy (*ch'i*) without positing something beyond the universe in which we live. Thus he finds a positive place for the passions (in opposition to much Buddhist and some Confucianist thinking) as natural human forces with which we need to learn how to live by developing a harmony between passion and proper restraint. He argues that the rules of ritual are themselves natural expressions, which must be embodied in human desires. There can, Wang claims, never be a "Heaven distinct from man."

❧

WANG FU-CHIH

The Principle of Nature and Human Desires

READING QUESTIONS

1. Create your own set of reading questions for this selection and answer them. Focus on what you think are the most important ideas.

From Chan, Wing-tsit, *A Source Book in Chinese Philosophy*, pp. 700–701. Copyright © 1963, renewed 1991 by Princeton University Press. Reprinted by permission of Princeton University Press. Footnotes edited.

2. According to Wang Fu-chih, what is wrong with Taoism and Buddhism?

Although rules of propriety are purely detailed expressions of the Principle of Nature, they must be embodied in human desires to be seen. Principle is a latent principle for activities, but its function will become prominent if it varies and conforms to them. It is precisely for this reason that there can never be a Heaven distinct from man or a principle distinct from desires. It is only with the Buddhists that principle and desires can be separated. . . . Take fondness for wealth and for sex. Heaven, working unseen, has provided all creatures with it, and with it man puts the great virtue of Heaven and Earth into operation. They all regard wealth and sex as preserved resources. Therefore the *Book of Changes* says, "The great characteristic of Heaven and Earth is to produce. The most precious thing for the sage is [the highest] position. To keep his position depends on humanity. How to collect a large population depends on wealth." Thus in sound, color, flavor, and fragrance we can broadly see the open desires of all creatures, and at the same time they also constitute the impartial principle for all of them. Let us be broad and greatly impartial, respond to things as they come, look at them, and listen to them, and follow this way in words and action without seeking anything outside. And let us be unlike Lao Tzu, who said that the five colors blind one's eyes and the five tones deafen one's ears, or the Buddha, who despised them as dust and hated them as robbers. . . . If we do not understand the Principle of Nature from human desires that go with it, then although there may be a principle that can be a basis, nevertheless, it will not have anything to do with the correct activities of our seeing, hearing, speech, and action. They thereupon cut off the universal operation of human life, and wipe it out completely. Aside from one meal a day, they would have nothing to do with material wealth and aside from one sleep under a tree, they would have nothing to do with sex. They exterminate the great character of Heaven and Earth and ruin the great treasure of the sage. They destroy institutions and eliminate culture. Their selfishness is ablaze while principles of humanity are destroyed. It is like the fire of thunder or a dragon. The more one tries to overcome it, the more it goes on. Mencius continued the teaching of Confucius which is that wherever human desires are found, the Principle of Nature is found. (*Tu Ssu shu ta-ch'üan shuo*, 8:10b–11a)

8.7 NEW CONFUCIANISM (1911–PRESENT)

Confucianism suffered many setbacks as Asia in general and China in particular went through the turmoil that greeted the dawn of the twentieth century. Two world wars, the spread of communism, and the rise of secularization stressed traditional Confucianism almost to the breaking point. Many predicted that the tradition was dying and soon would be dead.

However, the creativity of Confucianism proved more durable than the pundits had imagined. Slowly a new Confucianism took shape among scholars dedicated to the reform and renewal of the tradition from a critical perspective. They have tried to identify the themes that a genuine Confucianism must be concerned with from *jen* (humaneness) and *li* (ritual action/civility) to *ch'i* (energy). At the same time, they tried to reform the elitist tendencies of the tradition, its subservience to government authority, and its patriarchal denigration and oppression of women, and they tried to demonstrate its spiritual resources.

8.7.1 Does Confucianism Have a Religious Element?

When Christian missionaries entered China in the seventeenth century, they brought with them the concept of religion and tried to identify a Chinese religion. They asked, "Is Confucianism a religion?" The Chinese did not have a Western conception of religion, so this question had not bothered them. It was only during the nineteenth century, when the Western idea of a religion had become a part of Chinese thinking, that Chinese scholars began to debate whether or not Confucianism is a religion.

The Christian missionaries observed, when they came to China, both popular and elite traditions. Most classified the popular veneration of ancestors, the worship of various spirits and deities, and the ritual activities associated with temples as "mere superstition" and hence not genuine religion. The elite tradition they regarded as a kind of secular humanism and political theory designed to support imperial rule. The Neo-Confucianism they encountered was not organized or institutionalized in any way that resembled a "church." There were no clergy preaching to any laity, no revealed scriptures, and no liturgical worship. In short, there was nothing that looked like religion as the missionaries had come to define the term under the influence of Christianity.

If there is no Confucian church, how can there be a Confucian religion? The answer rests, in part, on how one thinks of religion. If religion equals an institutionalized form like Christian churches, then there is no Confucian religion. But if religion is a quest for transforming humans so that they live more in accord with the "way of Heaven," then there is a deep and profound religious aspect to Confucianism.

Once again the theoretical issue of how one defines religion (see chapter 2) takes center stage. This illustrates not only the way in which theory and definition influence interpretations of facts but also the way in which our thinking can be so strongly influenced by one tradition that neutral cross-cultural comparison becomes very difficult to achieve. However, these problems do not deter Tu Wei-ming from explicating the religious dimension of Confucianism as he understands it.

Tu Wei-ming is a professor of Chinese history and philosophy at Harvard University and one of the exponents of New Confucianism. In the following selection, he addresses the question of whether or not Confucianism is a religion. Earlier in the chapter from which this selection is taken, he defined the Confucian way of being religious as "ultimate self-transformation as a communal act and as a faithful dialogical response to the transcendent."

One of the profound Confucian insights into the human situation is that the process by which we become fully human is a process that must be carried out, according to Tu Wei-ming, in "a constant dialogical relationship with Heaven." But what does this mean? What is Heaven? Is Heaven something like God and, if so, does it exist independently of the world? Read and see how Tu Wei-ming answers these questions.

TU WEI-MING

On Confucian Religiousness

READING QUESTIONS

1. What does "ultimate self-transformation" imply?
2. What is the difference between the "great body" and the "small body," and why is this difference important?
3. What is *hsin*, and what does it have to do with religiousness?

In our examination of Confucian religiosity, we need to address the intriguing issue of transcendence. We must ask ourselves whether or not the idea of the theistic God, which features so prominently in Judaism, Christianity and Islam, is at all relevant to the Confucian mode of being religious. Such a line of questioning does not grow out of the Confucian tradition itself, but if we raise the issue here we can sharpen the contours of Confucian religiosity by defining the kind of transcendence that is most appropriate to Confucian self-understanding. Certainly the idea of theistic God, not to mention the "wholly other," is totally absent from the symbolic resources of the Confucian tradition. In exploring the issue of transcendence in Confucian religiosity, we must be careful not to impose an alien explanatory model or to introduce problems that are only peripheral to its central concerns.

Confucian religiousness begins with the phrase "ultimate self-transformation," which implies a critical moment in a person's life as well as a continuous process of spiritual cultivation. For us to be actively involved in ultimate self-transformation, we must make a conscious decision to do so. Since being religious is tantamount to learning to be fully human, we are not religious by default but by choice. This does not necessarily contradict the idea of *homo religiosus*, which is an ontological assertion about human nature. We are by nature religious, but we must make an existential decision to initiate our ultimate self-transformation.

Reprinted by permission of the State University of New York Press, from *Centrality and Commonality: An Essay on Confucian Religiousness* by Tu Wei-ming, pp. 116–121. © 1989 State University of New York. Footnotes omitted. All rights reserved.

Actually, the conscious choice or the existential decision can be understood in terms of the "either-or" dichotomy of Kierkegaard. Specifically, two kinds of "either-or" decisions are necessary. First, one must decide that learning to be human, which is a conventional Confucian way of denoting the process of ultimate self-transformation, is either "for the sake of others" (*wei-jen*) or "for the sake of the self" (*wei-chi*). Theoretically, learning to be human can be both "for the sake of others" and "for the sake of the self." Indeed, this preference for the inclusive "both-and" rather than the exclusive "either-or" solution to conflicts between self and society is a distinctive feature of Confucian ethics. Yet, in practice, the difference between learning for the sake of the self and learning for the sake of others is fundamental and crucial.

Learning for the sake of others may appear to be altruistic, but Confucius criticized it as inauthentic since it is often motivated by considerations other than a genuine desire to improve oneself. Strictly speaking, even though the demands of society and the urgings of parents are important for prompting us to become aware of our duty, they are secondary reasons for learning to become fully human. The primary reason is simply that learning is for our own good. A decision to turn our attention inward to come to terms with our inner self, the true self, is the precondition for embarking on the spiritual journey of ultimate self-transformation. Learning for the sake of the self is the authentic way of learning to be fully human.

However, inward reflection involves not only the choice of the self over others as the primary focus for learning but also a critical sense of developing the true self rather than the private ego. Another "either-or" decision is required: either the realization of the true self, which creatively establishes and enlarges itself as an open system by entering into fruitful communication with an ever-expanding network of human-relatedness; or the dominance of the private ego, which is encapsulated in its own "opinionatedness, dogmatism, inflexibility, and egoism." This inner decision to realize the true self does not lead to self-centeredness (nor does it lead to individualism), for it is never meant to be an isolated quest for spirituality devoid of social relevance. Yet we must also bear in mind that, despite its social relevance, it does not function primarily as a mechanism in social ethics and cannot be reduced to a choice in social relations.

In Mencian terms, the purpose of the inner decision to know our true self is to "recognize the great body" in us. The "great body" (*ta-t'i*) is contrasted with the "small body" (*hsiao-t'i*); it refers to the true self that can form a unity with Heaven, Earth, and the myriad things.

Mencius singled out sympathy-and-empathy ("the heart that cannot bear the suffering of others") as the unique and defining characteristic of our nature. Although he also accepted instinctive demands for food and sex as legitimately human (the "small body"), he noted that they are common to other animals as well. He acknowledged that since instinctive demands constitute much of what we naturally are, the difference between us and the birds and the beasts is not at all pronounced and studying birds and beasts can be immensely helpful in understanding humans on the biological level. However, Mencius was primarily interested in that difference that, in his view, makes humans unique. The slight difference between humans beings and the other animals, therefore, became the focus of his attention. For Mencius, the "great body" is both the basis for and the natural result of cultivating that which makes us uniquely human. This subtle point is vitally important for understanding how the Mencian project works.

The characterization of the "slight difference" between human beings and other animals as the "great body" implies that the uniqueness of being human is not a static quality but a dynamic process. Since sympathetic and empathic feeling is the source of our humanity, so it is also the basis of our ultimate self-transformation. By increasing our supply of sympathetic and empathic feeling, we can enrich our humanity; in this way we can become fully human. To employ the metaphor of the stream again, unless the supply from the source is sufficient, our humanity will not flow very far.

The Mencian idea of "recognizing the great body" is synonymous with the more common Confucian expression "establishing the will" (*li-chih*). As Mencius noted, when we acknowledge the slight difference that makes human beings unique, we recognize the great body inherent in our nature, take self-cultivation seriously, and aspire to become profound persons. A profound person preserves and increases what is common to us all. Yet we are not merely acknowledging and recognizing the principle that each of us is capable of sympathetic and empathic feelings. We are also asserting that we will be guided by these feelings in our conduct. "Establishing the will" can thus be interpreted as making the decision to act in accordance with the "great body," specifically with the sympathetic and empathic feelings that characterize the nature of the "great body."

Because the "great body" is not a static structure but a dynamic unfolding of human care, the decision to act in accord with it cannot be made once for all. Nor can the will be established by one momentous act. It can only be established by an infinite process of firm and continuous resolve. The decision so conceived is not a "function" of something else; it does not assume a finite form. It is a "substance" signifying the ontological reality of the "great body."

This decision can be seen as a self-illumination of the "great body"; it is, therefore, always enlightening as an autonomous center of creativity. Neither the loving care of our parents nor the inspiring guidance of our teachers can establish our will; we must self-consciously transcend the limitations of learning for the sake of others in order to learn for ourselves. Yet as soon as we are *willing* to learn ourselves, we have an inexhaustible supply of inner resources for self-transformation.

This decision is the necessary and sufficient condition for establishing the will. Here and only here can we be absolutely certain that willing entails having. Confucius assured us that if we desire humanity, it will automatically come. Mencius reiterated the confidence that only in this unique case, seeking implies getting. If we get it ourselves, we are truly "self-possessed" (*tzu-te*). This sense of being "self-possessed" is what Mencius recommended as the authentic way of learning to be human:

> The profound person steeps himself in the Way because he wishes to "get it" himself. When he gets it himself, he will be at ease with it. When he is at ease with it he can trust it deeply, and when he can trust it deeply, he can find its source wherever he turns. This is why the profound person wishes to take it himself.

The Way that the profound person wishes to get himself is not somewhere else, to be appropriated by departing from where we are here and now. On the contrary, it is right here, near at hand and inseparable from the existential conditions that underlie our daily lives. Paradoxically, once we get the Way by assuming full responsibility for our self-education, we can benefit from virtually every human encounter, including the loving care of our parents and the inspiring guidance of our teachers. In nurturing our human way, we can benefit from nature and the world beyond.

Our decision to establish the will signifies, then, the presence of the heart-and-mind (*hsin*), not only as an empirical entity but also, in the ontological sense, as an absolute, transcendental reality. This reading of the Confucian project may give the impression that it is yet another version of the "God talk" that has generated much controversy in theological circles recently. If the reference to an absolute, transcendental reality carries a particular theological flavor, it is not the result of a conscious design to think theologically about Confucian religiousness but the natural outcome of an attempt to understand Confucian humanism religiously.

The *hsin* (heart-and-mind) that enables us to make our inner decision to cultivate our sensitivity (humanity) is what Mencius referred to as the "great body." It is also the ultimate ground for "establishing the will." Yet it is not an objective reality separable from and independent of our lived concreteness. The temptation to reify *hsin* is mitigated by a strong preference for understanding it as an infinite being and as continuous creativity. *Hsin* manifests itself through a ceaseless process of internal illumination. It constantly transcends itself by fundamentally transforming the particular forms that crystallize its existence. No finite form, no matter how spectacular, can fully realize its inexhaustible possibilities. The multiplicity of forms that the heart-and-mind assumes demonstrates that its creativity cannot be incarnated fully in any given moment, place or person, even though it only manifests itself through the concrete in given moments, places, and persons.

Hsin can never maintain a pure objectivity as the absolute transcendental Mind by according itself the status of the wholly other. For its own realization, it must work through the subjectivity of a person in time and space. *Hsin* is omnipresent but not omnipotent. It cannot detach itself from the arena in which its creativity resides. Its true nature lies not in radical transcendence but in immanence with a transcendent dimension. In the last analysis, Confucian transcendence is an integral part of its inclusive humanism.

CONTEMPORARY SCHOLARSHIP

Contemporary scholarship on Chinese religions in general and Confucianism in particular is undergoing a renaissance. More students are learning Chinese, traveling to China, and discovering beneath the surface of older scholarship new and exciting information. We will sample only a small part of this renewed scholarship here, but I trust it will whet your appetite for more.

8.8 THE SECULAR AS SACRED

Many scholars, especially modern philosophers, find Confucius a parochial moralizer whose ideas are largely irrelevant to modern society and the larger world. From the modern philosophical view, Confucius barely qualifies as a philosopher and his level of ethical thinking seems archaic.

In 1972 an American philosopher, Herbert Fingarette, wrote a penetrating study of Confucius that transformed the conventional thinking about Confucius. Fingarette, a professor of philosophy at the University of California in Santa Barbara, found insights in Confucius's *Analects* that convinced him (and many others) that Confucius can be a "teacher to us today." In many ways, Fingarette, who is the author of the next selection, found Confucius "ahead of our times," especially with respect to his understanding of ritual.

⁕

HERBERT FINGARETTE

Human Community as Holy Rite

READING QUESTIONS

1. What does Fingarette mean by magic?
2. What, according to Fingarette, is Confucius's creative insight, and how does it relate to *li*?
3. In what sense is *li* characteristic of "human relationships at their most human" level?
4. What has Fingarette's interpretation of Confucius taught you about Confucius and about being human?

The remarks which follow are aimed at revealing the magic power which Confucius saw, quite correctly, as the very essence of human virtue. It is finally by way of the magical that we can also arrive at the best vantage point for seeing the holiness in human existence which Confucius saw as central. In the twentieth century this central role of the holy in Confucius's teaching has been largely ignored because we have failed to grasp the existential point of that teaching.

Specifically, what is needed (and is here proposed) is a reinterpretation which makes use of contemporary philosophical understanding. In fact such a reinterpretation casts, by reflection as it were, illumination into dimensions of our own philosophical thought, which have remained in shadow.

The distinctive philosophical insight in the *Analects*, or at least in its more authentic "core," was quickly obscured as the ideas of rival schools infected Confucius's teaching. It is not surprising that this insight, requiring as it does a certain emphasis on the magical and religious dimensions of the *Analects*, is absent from the usual Western-influenced interpretations of modern times. Today the *Analects* is read, in its main drift, either as an empirical, humanist, this-worldly teaching or as a parallel to Platonist-rationalist doctrines. Indeed, the teaching of the *Analects* is often viewed as a major step toward the explicit rejection of superstition or heavy reliance on "supernatural forces."

There is no doubt that the world of the *Analects* is profoundly different in its quality from that of Moses, Aeschylus, Jesus, Gautama Buddha, Lao-tzu or the Upanishadic teachers. In certain obvious respects the *Analects* does indeed represent the world of a humanist and a traditionalist, one who is, however, sufficiently traditional to render a kind of pragmatic homage, when necessary, to the spirits.

"Devote yourself to man's duties," says the Master; "respect spiritual beings but keep distance." (6:20) He suited the deed to the precept and himself, "never talked of prodigies, feats of strength, disorders, or spirits." (7:20) In response to direct questions about the transcendental and supernatural he said: "Until you are able to serve men, how can you serve spiritual being? Until you know about life, how can you know about death?" (11:11)

If we examine the substance of the *Analects* text, it is quickly evident that the topics and the chief concepts pertain primarily to our human nature, comportment and relationships. Merely to list some of the constantly recurring themes suffices for our present purposes: Rite (*li*), Humaneness (*jen*), Reciprocity (*shu*), Loyalty (*chung*), Learning (*hsueh*), Music (*yüeh*), and the concepts by which are defined the familial-social relationships and obligations (prince, father, etc.).

The this-worldly, practical humanism of the *Analects* is further deepened by the teaching that the moral and spiritual achievements of man do not depend on tricks or luck or on esoteric spells or on any purely external agency. One's spiritual condition depends on the "stuff" one has to begin with, on the amount and quality of study and good hard work one puts into "shaping" it. Spiritual

nobility calls for persistence and effort. "First the difficult. . . ." (6:20) "His burden is heavy and his course is
long. He has taken *jen* as his burden—is that not heavy?"
(8:7) What disquieted Confucius was "leaving virtue un-
tended and learning unperfected, hearing about what is
right but not managing either to turn toward it or to reform what is evil." (7:3) The disciple of Confucius was
surely all too aware that his task was one calling not for
amazement and miracle but for constant "cutting, filing,
carving, polishing" (1:15) in order to become a fully and
truly human being, a worthy participant in society. All
this seems the very essence of the antimagical in outlook.
Nor does it have the aura of the Divine.

Yet, in spite of this dedicated and apparently secular
prosaic moralism, we also find occasional comments in
the *Analects* which seem to reveal a belief in magical
powers of profound importance. By "magic" I mean the
power of a specific person to accomplish his will directly
and effortlessly through ritual, gesture and incantation.
The user of magic does not work by strategies and devices as a means toward an end; he does not use coercion
or physical forces. There are no pragmatically developed
and tested strategies or tactics. He simply wills the end
in the proper ritual setting and with the proper ritual gesture and word; without further effort on his part,
the deed is accomplished. Confucius's words at times
strongly suggest some fundamental magical power as
central to this way. (In the following citations, the Chinese terms all are central to Confucius's thought, and
they designate powers, states and forms of action of fundamental value. Insofar as necessary, they will be discussed later.)

"Is *jen* far away? As soon as I want it, it is here." (7:29)

"Self-disciplined and ever turning to *li*—everyone in
the world will respond to his *jen*." (12:1)

Shun, the great sage-ruler, "merely placed himself
gravely and reverently with his face due South (the
ruler's ritual posture); that was all" (i.e., and the affairs
of his reign proceeded without flaw). (15:4)

The magical element always involves great effects
produced effortlessly, marvelously, with an irresistible
power that is itself intangible, invisible, unmanifest.
"With correct comportment, no commands are necessary, yet affairs proceed." (13:6) "The character of a
noble man is like wind, that of ordinary men like grass;
when the wind blows the grass must bend." (12:19) "To
govern by *te* is to be like the North Polar Star; it remains
in place while all the other stars revolve in homage
about it." (2:1)

Such comments can be taken in various ways. One
may simply note that, as Duyvendak remarks, the "original magical meaning" of 2:1 is "unmistakable," or that

the ritual posture of Shun in 15:4 is "a state of the highest magical potency." In short, one may admit that these
are genuine residues of "superstition" in the *Analects*.

However, many modern interpreters of the *Analects*
have wished to read Confucius more "sympathetically,"
that is, as one whose philosophic claims would have max-
imum validity for us in our own familiar and accepted
terms. To do this, these commentators have generally
tried to minimize to the irreducible the magical claims
in the *Analects*. For it is accepted as an axiom in our
times that the goal of direct action by incantation and
ritual gesture cannot be taken as a serious possibility.
(The important exception to this general acceptance of
the axiom . . . is contemporary "linguistic analysis." But
the import of this work has as yet hardly extended beyond the world of professional philosophy.)

The suggestion of magic and marvel so uncongenial
to the contemporary taste may be dissipated in various
ways: only one of the sayings I have quoted comes from
the portion of the *Analects*—Books 3 to 8—that has been
most widely of all accepted as "authentic" in the main.
The other sayings might be among the many interpo-
lations, often alien in spirit to Confucius, which are
known to be in the received text. Or one might hold that
the magical element is quite restricted in scope, applying
only to the ruler or even the perfect ruler alone. Still another possible method of "interpreting away" the "magical" statements is to suppose that Confucius was merely
emphasizing and dramatizing the otherwise familiar
power of setting a good example. In short, on this view
we must take the "magical" sayings as being poetic statements of a prosaic truth. Finally, one might simply argue
that Confucius was not consistent on the issue—perhaps
that he was mainly and characteristically antimagic, but,
as might well be expected, he had not entirely freed himself of deep-rooted traditional beliefs.

All of these interpretations take the teaching of a
magical dimension to human virtue as an obstacle to
acceptance by the sophisticated citizen of the twentieth
century. The magic must be interpreted away or else
treated as a historically understandable failure on Confucius's part. I prefer to think we can still learn from
Confucius on this issue if we do not begin by supposing
the obvious meaning of his words as unacceptable.

Rather than engage in polemics regarding these
other interpretations, I shall devote the remainder of my
remarks to a positive exposition of what I take to be the
genuine and sound magical view of man in Confucius's
teaching. I do not hold that my interpretation is correct
to the exclusion of all others. There is no reason to suppose that an innovator such as Confucius distinguishes
all possible meanings of what he says and consciously in-

tends only one of these meanings to the exclusion of all others. One should assume the contrary. Of the various meanings of the Confucian magical teaching, I believe the one to be elaborated in the following remarks is authentic, central and still unappreciated.

Confucius saw, and tried to call to our attention, that the truly, distinctively human powers have, characteristically, a magical quality. His task, therefore, required, in effect, that he reveal what is already so familiar and universal as to be unnoticed. What is necessary in such cases is that one come upon this "obvious" dimension of our existence in a new way, in the right way. Where can one find such a new path to this familiar area, one which provides a new and revealing perspective? Confucius found the path: we go by way of the notion of *li*.

One has to labor long and hard to learn *li*. The word in its root meaning is close to "holy ritual," "sacred ceremony." Characteristic of Confucius's teaching is the use of the language and imagery of *li* as a medium within which to talk about the entire body of the *mores*, or more precisely, of the authentic tradition and reasonable conventions of society. Confucius taught that the ability to act according to *li* and the will to submit to *li* are essential to that perfect and peculiarly human virtue or power which can be man's. Confucius thus does two things here: he calls our attention to the entire body of tradition and convention, and he calls upon us to see all this by means of a metaphor, through the imagery of sacred ceremony, holy rite.

The (spiritually) noble man is one who has labored at the alchemy of fusing social forms (*li*) and raw personal existence in such a way that they transmitted into a way of being which realizes *te*, the distinctively human virtue of power.

Te is realized in concrete acts of human intercourse, the acts being of a pattern. These patterns have certain general features, features common to all such patterns of *li*: they are all expressive of "man-to-man-ness," of reciprocal loyalty and respect. But the patterns are also specific: they differentiate and they define in detail the ritual performance-repertoires which constitute civilized, i.e., truly human patterns of mourning, marrying and fighting, of being a prince, a father, a son and so on. However, men are by no means conceived as being mere standardized units mechanically carrying out prescribed routines in the service of some cosmic or social law. Nor are they self-sufficient, individual souls who happen to consent to a social contract. Men become truly human as their raw impulse is shaped by *li*. And *li* is the fulfillment of human impulse, the civilized expression of it —not a formalistic dehumanization. *Li* is the specifi-

cally humanizing form of the dynamic relation of man-to-man.

The novel and creative insight of Confucius was to see this aspect of human existence, its form as learned tradition and convention, in terms of a particular revelatory image: *li*, i.e., "holy rite," "sacred ceremony," in the usual meaning of the term prior to Confucius.

In well-learned ceremony, each person does what he is supposed to do according to a pattern. My gestures are coordinated harmoniously with yours—though neither of us has to force, push, demand, compel or otherwise "make" this happen. Our gestures are in turn smoothly followed by those of the other participants, all effortlessly. If all are "self-disciplined, ever turning to *li*," then all that is needed—quite literally—is an initial ritual gesture in the proper ceremonial context; from there onward everything "happens." What action did Shun (the Sage-ruler) take? "He merely placed himself gravely and reverently with his face due south; that was all." (15:4) Let us consider in at least a little detail the distinctive features of action emphasized by this revelatory image of Holy Rite.

It is important that we do not think of this effortlessness as "mechanical" or "automatic." If it is so, then, as Confucius repeatedly indicates, the ceremony is dead, sterile, empty: there is no *spirit* in it. The truly ceremonial "takes place"; there is a kind of spontaneity. It happens "of itself." There is life in it because the individuals involved do it with seriousness and sincerity. For ceremony to be authentic one must "participate in the sacrifice"; otherwise it is as if one "did not sacrifice at all." (3:12) To put it another way, there are two contrasting kinds of failure in carrying out *li*: the ceremony may be awkwardly performed for lack of learning and skill; or the ceremony may have a surface slickness but yet be dull, mechanical for lack of serious purpose and commitment. Beautiful and effective ceremony requires the personal "presence" to be fused with learned ceremonial skill. This ideal fusion is true *li* as sacred rite.

Confucius characteristically and sharply contrasts the ruler who uses *li* with the ruler who seeks to attain his ends by means of commands, threats, regulations, punishments and force. (2:3) The force of coercion is manifest and tangible, whereas the vast (and sacred) forces at work in *li* are invisible and intangible. *Li* works through spontaneous coordination rooted in reverent dignity. The perfection in Holy Rite is esthetic as well as spiritual.

Having considered holy ceremony in itself, we are now prepared to turn to more everyday aspects of life. This is in effect what Confucius invites us to do; it is the foundation for his perspective on man.

I see you on the street; I smile, walk toward you, put out my hand to shake yours. And behold—without any command, stratagem, force, special tricks or tools, without any effort on my part to make you do so, you spontaneously turn toward me, return my smile, raise your hand toward mine. We shake hands—not by my pulling your hand up and down on your pulling mine but by spontaneous and perfect cooperative action. Normally we do not notice the subtlety and amazing complexity of this coordinated "ritual" act. This subtlety and complexity become very evident, however, if one has had to learn the ceremony only from a book of instructions, or if one is a foreigner from a nonhandshaking culture.

Nor normally do we notice that the "ritual" has "life" in it, that we are "present" to each other, at least to some minimal extent. As Confucius said, there are always the general and fundamental requirements of reciprocal good faith and respect. This mutual respect is not the same as a conscious feeling of mutual respect; when I am *aware* of a respect for you, I am much more likely to be piously fatuous or perhaps self-consciously embarrassed; and no doubt our little "ceremony" will reveal this in certain awkwardnesses. (I put out my hand too soon and am left with it hanging in midair.) No, the authenticity of the mutual respect does not require that I consciously feel respect or focus my attention on my respect for you; it is fully expressed in the correct "live" and spontaneous performance of the *act*. Just as an aerial acrobat must, at least for the purpose at hand, possess (but not think about his) complete trust in his partner if the trick is to come off, so we who shake hands, though the stakes are less, must have (but not think about) respect and trust. Otherwise we find ourselves fumbling awkwardly or performing in a lifeless fashion, which easily conveys its meaninglessness to the other.

Clearly it is not necessary that our reciprocal respect and good faith go very far in order for us to accomplish a reasonably successful handshake and greeting. Yet even here, the sensitive person can often plumb the depths of another's attitude from a handshake. This depth of human relationship expressible in a "ceremonial" gesture is in good part possible because of the remarkable specificity of the ceremony. For example, if I am your former teacher, you will spontaneously be rather obvious in walking toward me rather than waiting for me to walk toward you. You will allow a certain subtle reserve in your handshake, even though it will be warm. You will not slap me on the back, though conceivably I might grasp you by the shoulder with my free hand. There are indescribably many subtleties in the distinctions, nuances and minute but meaningful variations in gesture. If we do try to describe these subtle variations and their rules, we immediately sound like Book 10 of the *Ana-*

lects, whose ceremonial recipes initially seem to the modern American reader to be the quintessence of quaint and extreme traditionalism. It is in just such ways that social activity is coordinated in civilized society, without effort or planning, but simply by spontaneously initiating the appropriate ritual gesture in an appropriate setting. This power of *li*, Confucius says, depends upon prior learning. It is not inborn.

The effortless power of *li* can also be used to accomplish physical ends, though we usually do not think of it this way. Let us suppose I wish to bring a book from my office to my classroom. If I have no magic powers, I must literally take steps—walk to my office, push the door open, lift the book with my own muscles, physically carry it back. But there is also magic—the proper ritual expression of my wish which will accomplish my wish with no such effort on my part. I turn politely, i.e., ceremonially, to one of my students in class and merely express in an appropriate and polite (ritual) formula my wish that he bring me the book. This proper ceremonial expression of my wish is all; I do not need to force him, threaten him, trick him. I do not need to do anything more myself. In almost no time the book is in my hands, as I wished! This is a uniquely human way of getting things done.

The examples of handshaking and of making a request are humble; the moral is profound. These complex but familiar gestures are characteristic of human relationships at their most human: we are least like anything else in the world when we do not treat each other as physical objects, as animals or even as subhuman creatures to be driven, threatened, forced, maneuvered. Looking at these "ceremonies" through the image of *li*, we realize that explicitly sacred rite can be seen as an emphatic, intensified and sharply elaborated extension of everyday *civilized* intercourse. . . .

In general, what Confucius brings out in connection with the workings of ceremony is not only its distinctively human character, its linguistic and magical character, but also its moral and religious character. Here, finally, we must recall and place at the focus of our analysis the fact that for Confucius it is the imagery of Holy Ceremony that unifies and infuses all these dimensions of human existence. Perhaps a modern Westerner would be tempted to speak of the "intelligent practice of learned conventions and language." This has a fashionably value-free, "scientific" ring. Indeed the contemporary analytical philosophers tend to speak this way and to be suitably common-sensical and restrained in their style. But this quite fails to accomplish what Confucius's central image did.

The image of Holy Rite as a metaphor of human existence brings foremost to our attention the dimension of the holy in man's existence. There are several dimensions of Holy Rite which culminate in its holiness. Rite brings out forcefully not only the harmony and beauty of social forms, the inherent and ultimate dignity of human intercourse; it brings out also the moral perfection implicit in achieving one's ends by dealing with others as beings of equal dignity, as free coparticipants in *li*. Furthermore, to act by ceremony is to be completely open to the other; for ceremony is public, shared, transparent; to act otherwise is to be secret, obscure and devious, or merely tyrannically coercive. It is in this beautiful and dignified, shared and open participation with others who are ultimately like oneself (12:2) that man realizes himself. Thus perfect community of men—the Confucian analogue to Christian brotherhood—becomes an inextricable part, the chief aspect, of Divine worship—again an analogy with the central Law taught by Jesus.

Confucius wanted to teach us, as a corollary, that sacred ceremony in its narrower, root meaning is not a totally mysterious appeasement of spirits external to human and earthly life. Spirit is no longer an external being influenced by the ceremony; it is that that is expressed and comes most alive *in* the ceremony. Instead of being diversion of attention from the human realm to another transcendent realm, the overtly holy ceremony is to be seen as the central symbol, both expressive of and participating in the holy as a dimension of all truly human existence. Explicitly Holy Rite is thus a luminous point of concentration in the greater and ideally all-inclusive ceremonial harmony of the perfectly humane civilization of the *Tao*, or ideal Way. Human life in its entirety finally appears as one vast, spontaneous and holy Rite: the community of man. This, for Confucius, was indeed an "ultimate concern"; it was, he said, again and again, the only thing that mattered, more than the individual's life itself. (3:17; 4:5, 6, 8)

8.9 CONFUCIAN WOMEN

We included as one of our sources (Reading 8.3.2) Pan Chao's *Lessons for Women*, which, even though written by a renowned female Confucian scholar, presented lessons reflecting a deeply entrenched patriarchal value system. The New Confucians, as we noted earlier, recognize the need to reform Confucianism with respect to the views of women. There is a long history and well-established Confucian literature stemming from Pan Chao that addresses the problems and needs of women. The instructional literature is an important source for contemporary historians interested in gender issues and religion.

In our final selection, Theresa Kelleher, a professor of religion and Asian studies at Manhattanville College, shares some of her research into traditional Chinese instructional literature for women. She shows how the position of women in traditional Confucian thought was reinforced by relating that position to the supposed cosmic order. Confucianism is not alone among religions in seeking sanctions for the *way things are* by showing that they are the *way things are supposed to be*.

THERESA KELLEHER

Confucianism

READING QUESTIONS

1. What three aspects of the cosmic order especially impressed Confucians, and what "lessons" for conducting one's life did these aspects of the cosmic order teach?
2. According to classical Confucianism, what were the implications of the cosmic order and its lessons for the life of women?
3. In what ways did Confucianism during the Han dynasty attempt to bring women "into the mainstream of the tradition"?
4. What sorts of stories about "good" girls and boys in contrast to "bad" girls and boys were you taught by your religious tradition (if you have one) or by your society? How do they compare to some of the stories told in the Confucian tradition?
5. What is the "new element" with respect to both women and men that Neo-Confucianism introduces?
6. Do you agree with Kelleher that there is a "positive legacy" for women in the Confucian tradition? Why or why not?
7. If you read the selection on ritual by Fingarette (Reading 8.8), compare his approach to Confucianism with Kelleher's approach. Fingarette is a philosopher, and Kelleher is a historian interested in feminist issues and theories. Focus specifically on how their approaches differ.

Reprinted by permission of the State University of New York Press, from *Women in World Religions*, by Arvind Sharma (Ed.). © 1987 State University of New York. "Confucianism," by Theresa Kelleher, pp. 135–144, 150–156, 158–159. Notes omitted. All rights reserved.

This chapter will examine the position of women in Confucianism, focusing primarily on the classical period and to a lesser extent on its later phase, Neo-Confucianism. As I shall show, women played a central role in Confucianism by virtue of their place in both the cosmic order and in the family. Nevertheless, since Confucianism was a patriarchal religious tradition, its estimation of women's nature was by and large a low one. Richard Guisso has summed up the negative attitudes toward women which appear in the canonical texts of early Confucianism, the Five Classics, as follows: "The female was inferior by nature, she was dark as the moon and changeable as water, jealous, narrow-minded, and insinuating. She was indiscreet, unintelligent, and dominated by emotion. Her beauty was a snare for the unwary male, the ruination of states."

I have chosen not to dwell so much on these negative attitudes as on the actual religious path set forth for women in the tradition. I will give particular attention to the types of attitudes and behavior considered desirable for a good Confucian woman and the models put forth for women to emulate. To do so, I will draw on various instructions for women found in the classical ritual texts and in pieces written by women for women, as well as biographies of exemplary women.

There are, of course, limitations in the use of these sources. They were all in support of the dominant male teachers and were addressed to an elite group in society. Social historians have pointed out the cruel use to which some of these teachings were put at different periods of Chinese history to make the lot of women difficult. Although there were surely discrepancies between the ideals articulated in the texts and the realities of women's lives in Chinese history, we have evidence that many women did take these teachings seriously, fervently believed in them, and were even willing to die to honor them. For this reason, though other readings of the texts are possible (and even necessary) to fully understand the position of women in Confucianism, I will keep to a fairly straightforward description of the texts and their teachings, supplying occasional critical commentary.

Since the basic religious orientation of Confucianism may not be well understood by many and since such an understanding is necessary if one is to appreciate the part women played in the tradition, I will begin with a brief overview of basic Confucian teachings. I will do so in terms of the cosmic order of Heaven and earth, the human order, which parallels the cosmic order with its roots in the family and its fullest expression in the state, and lastly, the proper response of humans to these two orders.

The cosmic order in its fullest sense is seen as comprised of the triad of Heaven, earth, and the human.

Humans are intimately linked to Heaven and earth, but not in the same way as they are related to the divine in the West. The call of the human community is not to worship Heaven and earth, but to learn from them, imitate their behavior, and thus form a human order modeled upon the cosmic order. Three aspects of the cosmic order especially impressed the Confucians as lessons worth learning in the human order.

First, Heaven and earth were seen as fundamentally life-giving; they continually bring new life into being, nurture and sustain it, and bring it to its completion. The fundamental optimism of Confucianism that life is good—indeed, that life is the most precious gift of all—comes from this sense of the universe as being fundamentally oriented toward the production and promotion of life.

The second aspect of the cosmic order valued by the Confucians was that everything in life is relational. Nothing comes into being in isolation, and nothing survives in isolation. Both the creative and the nurturing process depend on the coming together of two different elements in a relationship. Now the relationship between Heaven and earth is the most primal and most creative one in the universe. But these bodies do not function as equals; rather, they observe a hierarchy, with Heaven as the superior, creative element, positioned high above, and earth as the inferior, receptive element, positioned down below. What mattered was the overall effectiveness of the relationship rather than which was superior or inferior.

The third aspect of the cosmic order which impressed the Confucians was the orderly fashion in which it worked, with harmony rather than conflict prevailing among its parts. Each part seemed patterned to work for the good of the whole and yet at the same time to realize its own nature. It appeared to the Confucians that the parts observed a type of deference, or "polite form," with each other. For example, the sun dominates the day but yields its place to the moon at night with an absence of strife. Each of the four seasons gets its turn to dominate part of the year, but then gives way, or defers, to the season that follows.

In sum, the cosmic order was seen as life-giving, relational, and harmonious in the interaction of its parts. All these concepts formed the cornerstone of the Confucian ordering of human society.

The capacity of humans to be life-giving, for human life to be passed down from generation to generation in an unbroken chain, was an awesome thing for Confucians. The most direct and profound experience of this for any human was the gift of life at birth from one's parents. Birth brought one into this continuum of life, which was much larger than any one individual life. One felt oneself caught up in a flow of life which connected one to countless generations before and many more to come. A worshipful attitude was thus directed toward the progenitors of life: in the most concrete sense, one's own parents, but also their parents and their parents' parents. This reverence and gratitude for life formed the basis of ancestor worship.

The family, as the nexus of this life-giving activity and the custodian of the chain of life, thus came to be enshrined as a sacred community and was reverenced in a way that few religious traditions of the world have reverenced it. All other social groupings, including the state, had their basis in the family, and indeed, were often seen in terms of the family metaphor. Since Confucianism had no priesthood or special houses of worship, the roles of husband and wife took on a sacerdotal character. Marriage was a vocation to which all were called. Just as one received life at birth, one was to pass on that life to the next generation. Not to do so was a serious offense. As the philosopher Mencius said, "There are three things which are unfilial, and to have no posterity is the greatest of them" (Mencius 4A:26). As we shall see, this sense of the primacy of marriage and the sacredness of the family had an immense impact on the lives of women in Confucianism.

The second lesson that Confucians learned from the cosmic order was the relational aspect of things. All humans exist in relationships; there are no solitary individuals. These relationships are not just any relationships, but five very specific ones, known as the "Five Cardinal Relationships." The family generates three of them, and society generates the other two. Man and woman come together as husband and wife. They produce children, thus establishing the parent-child relationship as well as the older-younger sibling relationship. These bonds form the basis of the political relationship of ruler and subject and the social one of friend and friend.

For the Confucians, these relationships were not just biological or social; more importantly, they were moral. Since humans are not like plants and animals, they need more than food and shelter to sustain themselves—they need the empathetic response and support of other humans. Confucians had a profound awareness of the capacity of humans to nurture (be life-giving) or tear down (be life-destroying) in their interactions with others. Confucius thus made as the focus of his teachings in the Analects the virtue of *jen*, variously translated as "benevolence," "humaneness," "humanity," "love," or even just "virtue." The Chinese character for jen is composed of two elements: a human being on the left and the word for "two" on the right. The implication is that humans are structured to be in relationship, that our fundamental being is wrapped up in the existence of others. We

are called upon to be as responsible and as empathetic as possible, both for the sake of the other and for our own good. One of the descriptions of jen given by Confucius explains it thus:

> Now the man of perfect virtue, wishing to be established himself, seeks also to establish others; wishing to be enlarged himself, he seeks also to enlarge others. To be able to judge of others by what is nigh in ourselves: this may be called the art of virtue. (Analects 6:28)

Thus the Confucians were puzzled and disturbed when Buddhism made its way to China with its monastic system, which called for males to leave home and lead a celibate existence away from any family or social context.

The actual practice of jen in the Five Cardinal Relationships varied because of the hierarchical nature of these relationships. The same sense of hierarchy that exists in the cosmic order was seen as existing in the human order. Except for the friend-friend relation, all the others were conceived of as hierarchical in nature, with one party in the superior position and the other in the inferior position. This hierarchy was seen as necessary if the relationships were to work. Those who occupied the superior positions were parents, rulers, husbands, and older siblings; those in the inferior positions were children, subjects, wives, and younger siblings. Children were exhorted to be filial to their parents, subjects loyal to their rulers, wives submissive to their husbands, and younger siblings respectful to their older siblings. While most moral teachings in Confucianism were directed to those in the inferior positions, persons in the superior positions were obliged to use their superior status for the well-being of the other.

The third aspect of the cosmic order which impressed Confucians was the order and harmony which prevailed among the various elements, the correct positioning of each part in relation to the whole. Desirous of establishing the same order and harmony in the human community, from the family up to the state, Confucians attempted to choreograph the gestures, speech, and behavior of human beings with ritual. Here ritual included not just the more overtly religious ceremonials associated with coming-of-age ceremonies, weddings, funerals, and ancestral sacrifices (the four major rituals in Confucianism), but also what Westerners would put in the category of comportment and good manners. The classical ritual texts (notably, the Book of Rites, the Book of Etiquette and Ceremonial, the Rites of Chou) are filled with directives on the correct and proper behavior for every conceivable human interaction. The range extends from details for children to follow in serving their parents on a day-to-day basis in the household to the correct protocol for officials at court. While Confucius was all too aware of the dangers of formalism to which such a heavy emphasis on ritual could lead, nevertheless, he feared leaving the carrying out of virtue to chance. How as a child to be filial? Did he have to figure that duty out anew each day? Though one's understanding of filial piety should deepen over one's lifetime, one must begin with patterns to follow, both to ensure the smooth running of the household and also to initiate a person into a sense of what filial piety consists. Similar directions could be applied to the other relationships, including that of husband and wife.

From this brief presentation of the basic teachings of Confucianism, we see that the cosmic order is the primary source of divine revelation and the model for the human order, that the family is perceived as the nexus of the sacred community, and that all humans, both male and female, operate in a highly contextual, hierarchical, and choreographed setting. Relationships and the behavior considered appropriate to them are spelled out in quite specific terms. The religious pursuit for a Confucian is not to leave the world, but to realize the fullness of his or her humanity by a total immersion in human life, beginning with the family and extending outward to society through public service. By so doing, one achieves a mystic identification with the cosmic order, and one is "able to assist in the transforming and nourishing powers of Heaven and earth" (Doctrine of the Mean, ch. 22).

This, then, is the context in terms of which I will base my discussion of the role of women in Confucianism. I will show how that role was said to mirror the cosmic order, how women were identified in terms of their roles in the network of human relationships rather than as individuals, and how their behavior was informed by the elaborate ritual code.

In the cosmic order of things, the feminine as yin constitutes one of the two primary modes of being. This feminine force is identified with the earth, with all things lowly and inferior. It is characterized as yielding, receptive, and devoted, and it furthers itself through its sense of perseverence (Book of Changes, *k'un* hexagram). Though inferior to the masculine yang principle, the yin principle is nevertheless crucial and indispensable to the proper workings of the universe. From this cosmic pattern it was deduced that the position of women in the human order should be lowly and inferior like the earth, and that the proper behavior for a woman was to be yielding and weak, passive and still like the earth. It was left for men to be active and strong, to be initiators like Heaven. Though men were considered superior, they could not do without women as their complementary opposites.

In the human order, women were seen only in the context of the family, while men were seen in the wider social-political order. And within the family, a woman was subject to the "three obediences": as a daughter she was subject to her father; as a wife, to her husband; and when older, to her son. If the Confucian calling for men was "the way of the sages" (*sheng-tao*), for women it was "the wifely way" (*fu-tao*). The Chinese word for "wife" shows a woman with a broom, signifying the domestic sphere as her proper place. Marriage was indeed the focal point of a woman's life, and she was identified in terms of her role as wife, along with her two related roles as daughter-in-law and mother. In theory, females as step-daughters did not have much status within their natal families because, destined as they were to join the ranks of another family at marriage, they would never be official members of their natural families (no tablet would ever stand for them on the family's ancestral altar).

All childhood education for females was solely to prepare them for their future roles as wives and mothers. In contrast to boys, who went out of the house at age 10 for their education in history and the classics, girls remained at home, sequestered in the female quarters and under the guidance of a governess. They learned good manners and domestic skills like sewing and weaving.

> A girl at the age of ten ceased to go out [from the women's apartments]. Her governess taught her [the arts of] pleasing speech and manners, to be docile and obedient, to handle the hemper fibres, to learn [all] woman's work, how to furnish garments, to watch the sacrifices, to supply the liquors and sauces, to fill the various stands and dishes with pickles and brine, and to assist in setting forth the appurtenances for the ceremonies. (Book of Rites, ch. 12)

At age 15, according to this chronology, a girl would receive the hair pin in a coming-of-age ceremony. At 20 she was to marry. Three months before her marriage, a young woman was to be instructed in the four aspects of womanly character: virtue, speech, comportment, and work.

Both for the woman and the families, marriage and the wedding ceremony were extremely important events. As mentioned earlier, marriage marked the formation of a new link in the family chain of life, the sacred passing on of one generation to the next. The emphasis was on this sense of linkage or continuity rather than on any sense that marriage was the start of something new; that is why the Book of Rites says that no one congratulates anyone at the time of marriage. In addition, the Book of Rites comments on marriage as follows:

The ceremony of marriage was intended to be a bond of love between two [families of different] surnames, with a view, in its retrospective character, to secure the services in the ancestral temple, and in its prospective character, to secure the continuance of the family line. Therefore, the superior men (the ancient rulers), set a great value upon it. (Book of Rites, ch. 44)

Because the event had repercussions not just in the existing human order but also in the cosmic order and with the ancestors, the ceremony had to be done with careful attention to detail so that it would have its proper effect. Below are several of the most important details.

When the groom is about to set forth to fetch his bride, he receives the following command from his father: "Go meet your helpmeet, and so enable me to fulfill my duties in the ancestral temple. Be diligent in taking the lead as husband, but with respectful consideration, for she is the successor of your mother. Thus will the duties of the women in our family show no signs of decay" (I-li, or Book of Etiquette and Ceremonial, 4B). The groom then sets forth to the home of his bride. It is important that he take the initiative in this matter to remind all the parties that as husband, he is to be the active agent like Heaven, while the wife is to be the passive agent like earth.

Faithfulness is requisite in all service of others, and faithfulness is specially the virtue of a wife. Once mated with her husband, all her life she will not change her feeling of duty to him, and hence, when the husband dies, she will not marry again. (Book of Rites, ch. 11)

A good deal of the reason for this was that a woman's bond in marriage was not just with her husband, but also with his family. Thus, even with his death, she had duties to his living relations and his ancestors. Though women were encouraged not to remarry, the social sanctions against those who did, in classical and medieval Chinese history, were not nearly as heavy as they were to become in later Chinese history under the influence of Neo-Confucianism.

Such was the wifely way as outlined in the ritual texts of classical Confucianism. During the Han dynasty (206 B.C.E.–220 C.E.) when Confucianism was first made a state orthodoxy, there was a more conscious attempt to bring women into the mainstream of the tradition and to give them more specialized instructional writings and biographies of women to emulate. Specifically, we have in the Han dynasty two pieces, Instructions for Women

(Nü-chieh) by Pan Chao, and Biographies of Exemplary Women (Lieh-nü chuan) by Liu Hsiang. . . .

As Pan Chao's Instructions became the prototype of later instructional texts for women, so did the Biographies of Exemplary Women kept by the scholar-official Liu Hsiang (77–6 B.C.E.) with respect to collections of female biographies. This collection, which drew upon a variety of sources from the legendary past to his own day, presents biographies of over a hundred women, grouped according to seven types. The first six types are of good, moral women (exemplary mothers, worthy and astute women, benevolent and wise women, women of propriety, women of sexual integrity, and intellectual women), and the seventh group is of bad, wicked women.

This text is fairly remarkable. Even though it groups women into types, and even though most of the women are celebrated for some contribution they make to men, still, it is no mean thing that such a large number of lively women who show themselves skillful in the arts of moral persuasion, have a keen moral sense, and are ready to act on their beliefs are honored in the sociopolitical realm.

To appreciate the distinctiveness of this text, I wish to provide the reader with a sampling of the biographies, beginning with two of the model mothers from the first chapter. These two models give us a sense of how Confucians regarded the duties of a mother. The first is T'ai-jen, the mother of one of the classical sage-kings, who was honored for her ability in "prenatal instruction." Believing that the moral character of the child was formed during pregnancy, an expectant mother was urged to pay special attention to her attitudes and behavior during that period.

A woman with child did not lie on her side as she slept; neither would she sit sidewise nor stand on one foot. . . . She did not let her eyes gaze on lewd sights nor let her ears listen to depraved sounds. At night she ordered the blind musicians to chant poetry. (Lieh-nü chuan 1:4a)

Because T'ai-jen excelled in doing these things, her son "King Wen grew up and became an illustrious sage."

The next model mother is the most celebrated mother in Chinese history, the widowed mother of the great philosopher Mencius. Aware of the influence the environment had on the moral formation of children, she moved their residence three times before coming on one suitable for her son's upbringing. In their first two places of residence, one near a graveyard and one near a market place, Mencius had spent his time playing undertaker and businessman, two professions a good Confucian mother would hardly want for her son. Finally, she moved near a school, where Mencius engaged in play more along the Confucian lines of teacher and ritualist.

Several other incidents are given to show her vigilance in the care of her son, but the one which most endears her to women is one which takes place after Mencius was married. One day he entered his wife's room and found her not fully dressed as propriety would dictate, and he left immediately in disgust. Aware that in his stubbornness he would never return to her on his own, the wife appealed to Mencius's mother. Mencius's mother, with her down-to-earth, balanced moral sense, took her son aside and pointed out to him that while his wife might have transgressed the dictates of propriety, so had he by not giving her fair warning that he was approaching. "Mencius apologized and kept his wife. The superior person commented that Mencius's mother understood propriety and excelled in the way of the mother-in-law" (1:11a).

Elsewhere, in chapters 2, 3, and 6, we are presented with women, mostly wives, who excel in dispensing valuable moral advice to men, often in attempts to reform their conduct in the domestic or political sphere. These women are skillful in the art of persuasion, show that they are fully conversants with Confucian moral teachings, and even display a type of savvy in terms of the hard political realities of their day (which, for most of these biographies, is the chaotic and violent Warring States period, roughly 500–220 B.C.E.). Among these women, we find wives of rulers who criticize their husbands for failing in their role as father to the people, or for being inept in selecting good, capable advisors, or for short-sightedness in planning military campaigns. A daughter proves herself more astute about marriage politics than her father.

Many of these women are astute enough to realize that they must be indirect in their approach if their advice is to be taken seriously by the men in their lives. One wife, disturbed that her husband finds her so attractive that he neglects his duties at court to be with her, tried to reform him by making a public display of her guilt. In the palace tribunal, she tears off her hair ornaments and earrings, and has her governess deliver a statement of her guilt to her husband. "The stupidity and licentious heart of your wife have manifested themselves. It has come to such a pass that she causes the King to fail in propriety and to come late to court, so that it is seen that the King enjoys the beauty of women and has forgotten virtue" (2:1a). In so taking responsibility on herself, she awakens the king to his own responsibility in the matter. He refuses to accept her accusation and immediately reforms his ways, thereby becoming a more effective ruler.

In contrast to those wives who excel at advising and reforming their husbands, chapters 4 and 5 are filled with women dealing with their own sense of personal honor. These chapters have a great dramatic sense, with women often taking their own lives to protect their honor. While both chapter headings have a word meaning "chastity" (*chen* in chapter 4 and *chieh* in chapter 5), the interpretation of "chastity" has a broader sense than the narrow one of sexual continence, embracing a more general sense of integrity or honor.

Some of these women illustrate a strict adherence to proper ritual behavior as in the case of the widow who, when her room catches fire one night, will not leave the room because, according to ritual procedures, a woman does not go out at night unless accompanied by a matron and governess. Declaring herself willing to risk death rather than go against right principle, she perishes in the fire. She is praised as one who has perfectly realized the "wifely way" (4:1b–2a) Another example is that of the wife of the Duke of Ch'u. While he is away from home, a terrible flood threatens his home so he sends a messenger with others to relocate his wife. But because the messenger has forgotten the proper credentials, the wife refuses to go with him. She does so even though she is aware that her refusal almost certainly means death by drowning. She does indeed die in the flood, but is celebrated by her husband and others for preserving her chastity (4:6a–b).

Other biographies deal more explicitly with the matter of faithfulness to husbands, dead or alive. There is the woman of Wei who learns only when she has reached the gates of the town that her prospective husband has just died. Though she is advised to return home to her parents, she asserts her prerogative as his wife to enter his household, carry out the mourning rites for him, and to remain on as a member of the household. Her dead husband's younger brother proposes marriage to her, but she staunchly refuses, even when her own brothers pressure her to do so. "My heart is not a stone, it cannot be rolled. My heart is not a mat, it cannot be folded away" (4:2a–b).

There is also the case of the wife who refuses to obey her mother's order to return home when she learns that her husband has contracted leprosy. "If my husband is unfortunate, then his misfortune is mine. Why should I leave him? The way of the bride is that after one marriage cup of wine with the groom, she does not change in a lifetime. If unfortunately she meets with one having an incurable disease, she does not change her resolve" (4:2b–3a).

The suicides and killings continue in chapter 5, but here women are caught in divided loyalties to the various men in their lives. In one example, a wife's brother comes and murders her husband, takes over his kingdom, and then tries to take his sister back to his own kingdom. For her, the dilemma is that if she ignores what happened to her husband and excuses her brother, she will be going against righteousness; and yet, if on account of the loss of her husband she became angry with her brother, she will go against sibling love. What should she do so that she can be true to both men? With tears to Heaven, the woman goes out and kills herself (5:5b–6a). A second example is that of the "chaste woman of the capital." Her husband's enemy sees a way of getting revenge by exploiting the virtuous nature of the wife. He captures her father and threatens to kill him if she doesn't help him get to her husband. Her dilemma is that if she doesn't obey her father, she will be unfilial and he will be killed; if she obeys him, she will be unrighteous and her husband will be killed. Either way she will lose. She pretends to cooperate, advising the enemy where her husband will be sleeping on a certain night. She has her husband sleep elsewhere that night and arranges that it is she who is murdered, not her husband. Thus able to be faithful to both men, the woman earns the reputation of being humane and filial (5:11a–b).

From this sample of biographies from the first six chapters of this text, we have seen a variety of strong, moral women. In the domestic scene, they have shown themselves to be wise and able teachers of their sons and husbands; in the political sphere, they have proven themselves to be skillful and astute advisers. Often they have appeared more faithful in carrying out their Confucian duty than have the men, some even going so far as to give their lives on behalf of some Confucian principle. These are women with moral consciences who have the courage of their convictions. Thus does Liu Hsiang honor women as custodians of family and state morality.

But if he gives most of his attention to exemplary women (trying to exercise the power of positive thinking?), he does not completely leave out evil, selfish, wicked women. The last chapter of the text is given over to examples of "dangerous" women, women whose beauty distracts from their official duties and occasions the downfall of kingdoms. Among the example given are the concubines of the bad last rules of the Hsia and Shang dynasties (second millenium B.C.E.), Mo-hsi, the concubine of King Chieh, and Tan-chi, the concubine of King Chou. Not only do these two women ensnare the men in a life of sensual pleasure, but they also encourage sadistic treatment of servants and ministers. When the minister Pi-kan remonstrates with King Chou about his orgies, Tan-chi goads King Chou to have Pi-kan cut open to see if it is true that a sage has seven orifices (7:1a–2a). . . .

These women in the last chapter are the antithesis of the others, caring nothing for the betterment of the men in their lives, wrapped up instead in their own insatiable desires for sensual pleasure. They threaten the moral fabric of society, and rather than being the custodians of family and state morality, are its destroyers.

The texts that this paper has discussed so far can all be seen as attempts to bring women into the mainstream of male-dominated Confucianism. Though the modern reader might well have doubts as to whether they truly gave women much dignity in their own rights, still, when compared with the later position of women in Neo-Confucianism, they reflect a broad and generous approach to women. We turn now to take a brief look at women and Neo-Confucianism.

With the fall of the Han dynasty in 220 C.E., Confucianism was eclipsed by Buddhism and Taoism in the area of religion. It was not to play a significant role in that area until its reemergence in the form of Neo-Confucianism in the Sung dynasty (960–1279 C.E.). When it did reemerge in this form, a great shift had occurred which was to have a profound effect on the lives of women.

The early Neo-Confucians zealously worked to revitalize Confucianism to reclaim the territory it had earlier lost to the Buddhists. Their challenge was to reestablish the family and the state as the locus of religious duty. They attacked the Buddhists for selfishly trying to escape from the world rather than direct their energies to building up the human order. Nevertheless, they were quite impressed with the depths of Buddhist spirituality. How could they blend the best of the two? The Neo-Confucianism that resulted was a more overtly religious tradition than earlier Confucianism and was concerned more with metaphysical matters, human interiority, and religious practices such as meditation. There was a new sense of the profound depths of the human self, but with it a great awareness of the dangers and obstructions which hinder the full development of the self. They saw these dangers in terms of human desires and passions. As a result, in Neo-Confucianism there is a greater preoccupation with self-discipline and with controlling one's desires.

This great wariness about human desires and passions was directed to the area of human relationships, the cornerstone of Confucian religiosity. Ch'eng I (1033–1107), one of the leading Sung Neo-Confucians, reflects this wariness in the following statement which appears in the most famous anthology of Neo-Confucian writings, Reflections on Things at Hand (Chin-ssu lu):

In family relationships, parents and children usually overcome correct principles with affection and supplant righteousness with kindness. Only strong and resolute people can avoid sacrificing correct principles for the sake of personal affection. (Chin-ssu lu 6:1b)

Here we see a new element. In classical Confucianism, one fulfilled oneself by immersing oneself in the network of human relationships. Now there is more ambivalence about these relationships, a sense that they may be a source of obstruction rather than a contribution to one's pursuit of sagehood.

Women could not but be influenced by this change, especially because one of the most intimate ties of a Confucian male was with his wife. Women came to be seen as activators of desires both sensual and affective. There was a felt need to ensure that they controlled their desires and not upset men's progress toward sagehood. Thus the moral code for women, while in many ways a continuation of the earlier, classical one, focused to an almost obsessive degree on chastity. And within this, the chastity of widows was singled out for special emphasis.

To be sure, chastity had been an important virtue for women in the classical period, as we have seen in the Biographies of Exemplary Women, and widows were exhorted to remain faithful to their husbands by not remarrying. But nothing in the classical period can match the degree of preoccupation with chastity that Neo-Confucianism exhibited. The most chilling statement in this regard was made by Ch'eng I concerning the remarriage of widows. He is asked whether a widow can remarry in the extenuating circumstance that she is poor, all alone, and about to starve to death. Ch'eng I responds: "This theory has come about only because people of later generations are afraid of starving to death. But to starve to death is a very small matter. To lose one's integrity, however, is a very serious matter" (Chin-ssu lu 6:3a).

The models of women presented in an influential primer for young men, the Elementary Learning (Hsiao-hsüeh), compiled by the most famous Sung dynasty Neo-Confucian Chu Hsi (1130–1200), staunchly promote this moral code. In one case, we have a woman who progressively mutilates her body with each new exertion of pressure by her parents to remarry. First she cuts off her hair, then her ears, and finally her nose, all the while defiantly asserting her determination to remain faithful to her dead husband. Another example is of two unmarried sisters who are abducted by bandits. They both resist rape, the first by hurling herself off a high cliff and the second by dashing herself on the rocks (there is plenty of blood and gore in these tales) (Hsiao-

hsüeh 6:11a–12a). Since the bond of marriage is not just with the husband but with his parents as well, we are also presented with model widows who further prove their faithfulness by giving unstinting care to their mother-in-laws, even in the worst of conditions. One woman's husband dies in war while she is still young, leaving her childless. Rather than succumb to her parent's pressure to remarry, she cares for her mother-in-law even though it entails a life of poverty for her. What little she has at the time of her mother-in-law's death she sells to give the mother-in-law a proper funeral (6:10a–b). Another woman is praised for trying to ward off ten strong bandits when they attack her mother-in-law. She is able to succeed in saving the mother even though she herself is almost beaten to death (6:11b–12a).

What is noticeably absent among these models are mature, astute women of the kind who dispense good advice, who are skillful in the arts of persuasion, and who involve themselves in the political realm. There are no wise, discerning mothers. There are only nun-like martyrs in their young adulthood. This more dramatic and ascetical tone, I must add, also pervades the models set up for men to emulate. . . .

The legacy of Confucianism in the modern period is a complicated one. By the late nineteenth and early twentieth century, China was in a state of decline, overwhelmed by problems of poverty, overpopulation, corruption, and loss of morale in the government, and imperialism by Western powers. Radicals and reformers turned on Confucianism as one of the prime sources of their problems. Since the position of women was also seen as at an all-time low, as evidenced in the widespread practices of footbinding, female infanticide, and the buying and selling of women, women also turned against the tradition. Probably no other socioreligious tradition has been attacked in such a large-scale, systematic way. Mao Tse-tung was astute enough to see the potential in women as a revolutionary group and achieved much of his success from the support of women. The People's Republic of China has made sweeping reforms to improve the status of women in society, and has included large numbers of them in the work force and in political office. However, as several recent books have shown, much remains to be done to give women full equality. The recent one-child policy has brought to the surface the traditional bias in favor of male heirs.

But the larger question for us is the future of Confucianism. Does it indeed have a future? Can it exist in a scientific and technological world that does not reflect its cosmic orientation? Can it exist apart from the traditional Chinese political and family system? Despite all the repudiation of Confucianism in modern China, do many of its teachings persist, albeit in Communist form?

If there is no future for Confucianism, then there is no use asking what future role women might play in it. Indeed, there are few Chinese women today who want to identify themselves with Confucianism, linked as it is with the oppression of women. But will there come a time when the atmosphere is not so highly charged and when Chinese women will want to evaluate the positive legacy of their tradition as well? From the outsider's point of view, there is such a positive legacy. Though Confucianism contributed to the victimization of women, it also gave them a sense of self-discipline, esteem for education, and respect for public service that has enabled them to enter into today's political and social realm in the number and with the effectiveness that they have.

The Confucian tradition, with its appreciation for the gift of life, with its profound humanistic spirit, its sense of religious practice as building the human community, and its sense of the relational quality of things, has much to contribute to our global religious heritage. The challenge of giving women a more equitable place within that tradition remains. It seems obvious that unless that challenge is met, the appeal of many aspects of Confucianism will be greatly diminished.

PRONUNCIATION GUIDE

There are two methods in wide use today for romanticizing (translating into a Latin-based alphabetical system) Chinese words. One is called Wade-Giles and the other pinyin. I have used Wade-Giles spelling even though it is older than pinyin and is slowly being replaced by pinyin because most of my sources use it. Thus it minimizes confusion. However, Wade-Giles does require a pronunciation guide because some of the sounds indicated by the letters do not, to an English speaker, correspond to the sound in Chinese.

a as in father
e as in end
i as in the initial e in eve
o as in go
u as in rude
ü as in menu
ai as in ice
ao as in out
ou as in obey
ch pronunced as j
k pronunced as g
p pronunced as b

t pronounced as d
ts or tz pronounced as tz or dz
hs pronounced like sh
j pronounced like r
ch', k', p', ts', tz' pronounced as in English

KEY TERMS AND CONCEPTS

Analects (*Lun-yü*) The name for a collection of Confucius's sayings and one of the **Four Books**.

ch'eng The virtue of sincerity, or truthfulness.

ch'i A primary energy or force that may be thought of as both material and spiritual in Western terms.

chiao Usually translated as "teaching" or sometimes as "religion."

chih The Confucian virtue of understanding.

chung The Confucian virtue of loyalty.

chün-tzu A "noble person." Sometimes translated as "honorable person," "superior person," or "gentleman."

Five Agents (Five Elements) The elemental forces of the universe: water, earth, metal, fire, and wood.

Five Classics The classical literature derived from a time preceding Confucius consisting of the *Book of Changes, Book of History, Book of Poetry* or *Odes, Classic Rites* (includes *Ceremonials, Book of Rites,* and *Institutes of Chou*), and the *Spring-Autumn Annals.*

Four Books A widely influential collection of Confucian writings: *The Great Learning, Doctrine of the Mean, Analects,* and *Mencius.*

hun The upper soul or heavenly soul expressed in intelligence and as a vital force in the power to breathe, in contrast to *p'o.*

jen A primary Confucian concept that can be translated as humanity, human-heartedness, love, benevolence, altruism, and, in general, virtue. It is the general virtue out of which various moral virtues come.

kuei See *kuei-shen.*

kuei-shen Literally means ghosts and deities but is used in a variety of ways to indicate spiritual beings in general. In ancient times, *shen* usually referred to heavenly beings and *kuei* to spirits of deceased humans. In popular religion, *kuei* means something like demons and *shen* refers to good deities. In Confucianism, *kuei* often refers to positive spiritual forces and *shen* to negative ones. Some hold that at death the **hun** becomes *kuei* and the *p'o* becomes *shen.*

li Can be used to mean principle of conduct, rule of conduct, rules of propriety, good manners, civility, ceremonies, rituals, and rites. Philosophically, when it is used in contrast to *ch'i*, it means principle, reason, law, order, or pattern.

p'o The lower or earthly soul expressed in bodily movements. See *hun* and *kuei-shen*.

shen See *kuei-shen*.

shu The virtue of reciprocity.

T'ai-chi Often translated as the Great Ultimate.

tao Literally means the path along which one walks. As an abstract concept, it came to designate the right way. It can be used to refer to the right moral path or the right way to live as well as the way of nature or of heaven.

Ti Can mean emperor and often translated as Lord.

yang Can refer to the sun or the sunny side of a slope. As an abstract principle, it came to designate anything positive, active, strong, male, and creative. It is the complement of *yin.*

yin Can refer to the moon or the shady side of a slope. As an abstract principle, it came to designate anything negative, passive, weak, female, and receptive. It is the complement of *yang.*

SUGGESTIONS FOR FURTHER READING

Berthrong, John H. *Transformations of the Confucian Way.* Boulder, Colo.: Westview Press, 1998. A study of the historical development of Confucian thought.

Chang, Wing-tsit. "Confucian Thought." In *The Encyclopedia of Religion*, edited by Mircea Eliade, vol. 4, pp. 15–24. New York: Macmillan, 1987. An insightful treatment of the classical period.

Hall, David L., and Roger T. Ames. *Thinking Through Confucius.* Albany: State University of New York Press, 1987. A critical interpretation of the conceptual structure behind Confucius's thinking.

Taylor, Rodney Leon. *The Religious Dimensions of Confucianism.* Albany: State University of New York Press, 1990. Taylor focuses on the religious aspects of the Confucian tradition.

Thompson, Laurence G. *Chinese Religion: An Introduction.* 3rd ed. Belmont, Calif.: Wadsworth, 1996. A good introduction to Chinese religion in general with informative chapters on Confucianism or what Thompson calls the literati tradition.

Tu, Wei-ming. *Humanity and Self-Cultivation: Essays in Confucian Thought.* Berkeley, Calif.: Asian Humanities Press, 1978. Collected essays on various aspects of Confucianism as it relates to the process of fulfilling the human potential for humaneness.

RESEARCH PROJECTS

1. Select any one of the authors of the source material included in this chapter and do further research on his or her life, times, influence, and views. Write a report summarizing what you have found out. For example, you may wish to read Nancy Lee Swann's *Pan Chao: Foremost Woman Scholar of China* (New York: Russell & Russell, 1968), which provides information on Pan Chao's ancestry, life, and writings, then write your report on this interesting and influential Confucian woman.

2. Imagine growing up in a Confucian family and town. Write an account of what you think your life would be like.

3. View the video *A Confucian Life in America: Tu Wei-ming* available from Films for the Humanities and Sciences, 1994 (Princeton, N.J.) and write a report on what you learn.

9

Taoist Ways of Being Religious

INTRODUCTION

In the center of a home in Taiwan there is a room with an altar. On that altar are statues of ancient-looking men with long robes and beards. Into the room come two men. One listens as the other tells him about an illness that medicines have not been able to cure. After the illness has been described, and some questions asked and answered, one of the men, called a master, dips a brush in red ink and quickly draws a sign on a little piece of yellow paper. This sign is called a *fu* and is a talismanic symbol for a particular energy drawn from the body of the master. The paper is burned and the ashes dissolved in water, which is drunk by the sick man. Both men are confident that health will return because the *fu* is a specially selected energy distilled from the vital energy of the master and given to the sick man in order to restore his health. There is no charge for this service, even though the master has given from his own life force in order to restore the life force of another.

This description is based on a common ritual described in Kristofer Schipper's *The Taoist Body*. Curing rituals are the stock and trade of many religious practitioners the world over. Some might classify this particular one as a folk religious curing-ritual, others as part of Chinese popular religion. However, the master is a Taoist priest and Schipper refers to it as a Taoist ritual.

What exactly is Taoism? Some claim it is a sophisticated philosophy, and others that it is a degenerate form of a sophisticated philosophy. Some claim it is a form of popular or folk religion, and others that it is a political movement developed and supported by the imperial court for its own purposes. While some say it is primarily a misguided medical and alchemical attempt to attain health, longevity, and even immortality, others argue it is a messianic movement offering salvation for the masses. Some think it is an

unsystematic mass of beliefs, rituals, and other practices that has grown up more or less by chance, changing radically from century to century. The *Harper-Collins Dictionary of Religion* defines Taoism as "a traditional component of Chinese culture embracing a broad array of moral, social, philosophical, and religious values and activities," which is broad enough to include just about everything mentioned above.

It used to be common among scholars to distinguish between philosophical Taoism and religious Taoism, but the most recent scholarship recognizes that the difference between the two is not as clear as once thought. In the past ten years, the scholarship on Taoism by Western scholars has increased dramatically, and it is changing our understanding and appreciation of a unified tradition of thought, experience, and practice that has creatively reinvented itself to meet the demands of changing times and places.

9.1 AN OVERVIEW

In 142 a man named Chang Tao-ling claimed that a deity he called the Highest Venerable Lord appeared to him. This deity, Tao-ling maintained, was a manifestation of the Tao, or Way of Reality, about whom the ancient sage Lao Tzu wrote. In fact, Lao Tzu himself was an incarnation of the Tao. Tao-ling went on to establish one of the first organized Taoist schools or sects called Orthodox Unity, or **Celestial Masters.** It still exists today.

The Highest Venerable Lord may have appeared "out of the blue" to Chang Tao-ling, but that does not mean that there were no precursors to organized Taoism. The ancient philosophers Lao Tzu and Chuang Tzu, whose major works date from the fourth and third centuries B.C.E., laid the foundations on which Tao-ling described the world as created and sustained by the Tao, which literally means way, road, or path.

In the Former Han dynasty (206–8 B.C.E.), wandering healers and ascetics called *fang-shih* became famous for their abilities in a variety of arts including astrology, dream interpretation, acupuncture, pharmacology, dietetics, exorcisms, and the like. They sought longevity of the body and open channels to the world of gods and spirits. They too left an indelible mark on Taoism.

Then, around the beginning of the common era, a number of messianic movements emerged promising that the increasingly political and economic stresses of the time would soon end in a utopian Great Peace. Thousands of people took to the dusty roads of China, visionaries received numerous revelations, sacred talismans for protection and good luck were circulated, and rebellions against the prevailing authorities erupted. The insurrection of the Yellow Turbans, or Tao of Great Peace, in 184 is probably the most famous rebellion. It was cruelly smashed, as were many others. The Celestial Masters was one of these messianic movements, although less politically inclined than some of them. It somehow managed to survive as the others died.

Laurence G. Thompson, Professor Emeritus, University of Southern California, presents an overview of religious Taoism in the following selection. He quotes liberally from the sources thereby giving us a rich taste of the many fascinating Taoist ways of being religious.

✥

LAURENCE G. THOMPSON

The Taoist Tradition

READING QUESTIONS

1. As you read, make a list of all the words and ideas you do not understand or are uncertain about. Discuss them with a classmate, look them up in a dictionary, or bring them up in class for discussion and clarification.

2. According to Thompson, what is the goal of Taoism?
3. What is *wai-tan*, and how does it differ from *nei-tan?*
4. According to Thompson, why are the alchemical practices of Taoism more than protoscience?
5. What is the theory behind "Taoist yoga"?
6. What are the two main functions of the Taoist professional or clergy?
7. What is the difference between *fa-shih* and *tao-shih?*
8. Describe both the esoteric and exoteric meaning of *chiao.*

It is essential to understand that Taoism is not the same as "popular religion." The pervasive influence of various Taoistic principles in the popular culture should not obscure the special features that set Taoism apart as an organized, specialized religion. Such special features include a nearly two thousand-year-old tradition of ordained priesthood; the accumulation of an enormous "Bible" of esoteric texts comprehensible only to those with special competence; a grand liturgical tradition based on the ritual texts; a well-defined eremitic tradition; and many distinctive techniques conducive to the ultimate goal of transformation to transcendent immortality. We shall attempt, in what follows, to delineate the features of Taoism as a Way to ultimate transformation and then to depict the nature of its interactions with religious life in the communities.

The premise of religious Taoism is that life is good and to be enjoyed. The individual self is not set apart from the rest of nature but is, like all things, a product of *yin* and *yang* as the creative processes of *tao*. Neither the ego nor the rest of the phenomenal world is illusory —both are completely real. *The religious quest is for liberation of the spiritual element of the ego from physical limitations, so that it may enjoy immortality or at least longevity.* In other words, the goal is the triumph of the *yang* over *yin*. When one has attained this liberation, this triumph, one may choose either to remain in the physical body to enjoy mundane pleasures or to wander freely in the realm of space, to visit or dwell in one of the fabled abodes of the immortals.

It may seem difficult to reconcile this religious Taoism with the whole purport of the classic Taoist texts *The Old Master (Lao Tzû)*, i.e., the *Scripture of the Tao and Its Individuating Power (Tao Tê Ching)*, and *Master Chuang (Chuang Tzû)*. And yet, although the authors of these profoundly philosophical works would certainly have been bemused by many of the theories and practices of the religion that later claimed them as founders, it is, in fact, easy to find in their writings numerous passages that lend themselves to mystical and even esoteric interpretations. A literal, as opposed to a symbolic or poetic,

From *Chinese Religion*, 5th edition, by L. G. Thompson, pp. 81–94. © 1996 by Wadsworth Publishing. Reprinted with permission of Wadsworth Publishing, a division of International Thomson Publishing. Fax 800 730-2215. Footnotes omitted.

reading could find both the goal of immortality and some techniques for attaining it in such passages as the following:

One who does not lose his [proper] place endures for long; One who [apparently] dies but does not perish is long-lived. (*The Old Master* 33)

. . .

I have heard that one who is good at taking care of his life will not encounter wild bulls or tigers when traveling by land, and will not [be wounded] by weapons when in the army. [In his case] wild bulls will find no place in which to thrust their horns, tigers no place in which to put their claws, and weapons no place in which to insert their points. And why? Because in him there is no place (literally, no ground) of death. (*The Old Master* 50)

. . .

Attain utmost emptiness and preserve earnest stillness. (*The Old Master* 16)

. . .

Block the road, shut your gate, subdue your ardor, do away with your inner divisions, dim your light, and become one with the dusty world. (*The Old Master* 56)

. . .

[Controlled] exhaling and inhaling; disgorging old [breath] and taking in new; bearlike lurchings and birdlike stretchings are performed solely for the sake of longevity. These are what specialists in guiding [the vital breath] and men who nourish the form [in hope of attaining] the longevity of Ancestor P'êng like to do. (*Master Chuang*, scroll 15, "The Will Constrained"; *Chuang Tzû, K'ô Yi*)

. . .

Master Lieh traveled by charioteering on the wind with light and wonderful skill. (*Master Chuang*, scroll 1, "Taking It Easy"; *Chuang Tzû, Hsiao Yao Yu*)

. . .

In the mountains of Miao-ku-shê (supposedly in the Northern Sea—i.e., an island of the immortal transcendents) there live spiritlike men with flesh and skin like ice and snow, gentle and weak as unmarried maidens. They do not eat the five grains but inhale the wind and drink the dew. They ride on the breaths of the clouds and chariot on flying dragons, traveling beyond the Four Seas. (*Master Chuang*, scroll 1)

. . .

My Master, Master Lieh, asked the Guardian of the Pass, saying, The Perfect Man (i.e., the Taoist adept) walks under water without hindrance, treads on fire without being burned, and moves about on the heights without fear. May I ask how he has attained to this? The Guardian of the Pass replied, It is by the safeguarding of his pure vital breath. (*Master Chuang*, scroll 19, "The Fulfillment of Life"; *Chuang Tzû, Ta Shêng*)

. . .

The True Man (another term for the Taoist adept) breathes from his heels, while the masses of men breathe from their throats. (*Master Chuang*, scroll 6, "The Great Master"; *Chuang Tzû, Ta Tsung Shih*)

. . .

When he succeeded in transcending his own being, apprehension [of the true condition of things] dawned on him, and when that apprehension had dawned, he was able to perceive the One. When he succeeded in perceiving the One he was able [to understand] the nonexistence of "past" and "present." Understanding the nonexistence of past and present he was able to enter into the awareness of no death or birth. (*Master Chuang*, scroll 6)

The historical relationship between this sort of thinking as found in the first Taoist philosophers and the formulation of specific techniques for achieving the goals at which it hinted is obscure. The goal itself must, of course, be as old as humankind, but the kinds of practices characteristic of the religious Taoist system in China were perhaps developed no earlier than three to four centuries B.C.E. These practices have been divided into two inclusive categories: The first was called "outer elixir" (*wai-tan*); this involved the concoction of a drug of immortality. The second was called "inner elixir" (*nei-tan*), which was the refining by various means of the spiritual essence within the body in order to liberate this spiritual essence from its physical shackles.

WAI-TAN

The search for the elixir of immortality, closely related to, or identical with, "the philosopher's stone," apparently began in China and eventually spread to the West. The alchemical elixir, when ingested, would prolong life indefinitely; the alchemical philosopher's stone would be able to transmute base metals into gold. Gold was the common denominator. In the case of the elixir, the symbolism of gold was that of indestructible, incorruptible life. The hope of making cheaper ingredients into the most valuable needs no symbolism.

The earliest literary reference to the elixir is found in the first great history of China, written by Ssû-ma Ch'ien in the mid-second century B.C.E.:

At this time [133 B.C.] Li Shao-jün was also received in audience by Emperor [Wu], because, by worshipping the Stove and by a method of [not eating] grain [products], he said he knew how to avoid old age. . . .

[Li] Shao-jün spoke to the Emperor, saying You should worship the Stove and then you can make [spiritual] beings present themselves; when [spiritual] beings have presented themselves, cinnabar powder can be metamorphosed into gold . . . ; when this gold has been made, it can be used for vessels for drinking and eating, and will increase the length of your life; when the length of your life has been increased, the immortals of Peng-lai in the midst of the ocean can thereupon be given audience; when they have been given audience, by [making the sacrifices] *fêng* and *shan* you will never die. The Yellow Lord did this. Your subject has traveled on the ocean and had an audience with Master An-chi. Master An-chi fed your servant jujubes as large as melons. Master An-chi is an immortal who is in conununication with those on [the isle of] Peng-lai. When it suits him, he appears to people, and when it does not suit him, he remains hidden. . . .

Whereupon the Son of Heaven [Emperor Wu], for the first time worshipped the Stove in person, sent gentlemen [possessors] of recipes . . . out into the ocean to seek for Master An-chi and similar [beings from the isle of] Peng-lai, and paid attention to metamorphosing powdered cinnabar and potions of various drugs into gold.

The activities of the alchemists were of direct concern to the State, which was anxious to prevent counterfeiting of gold money. For this reason such activities were proscribed on penalty of public execution. The alchemists, therefore, to avoid prosecution and to protect an esoteric lore, kept their operations secretive, relaying their formulas orally or writing them down in a language so occult and obscure that none but initiates could find them intelligible. One rare text, dating from the midsecond century C.E., contains the following explanation of the elixir theory:

Tan-sha (Red Sand, cinnabar, mercury sulfide) is of wood and will combine with gold (metal). Gold (metal) and water live together; wood and fire keep one another company. [In the beginning] these four were in a confused state. They came to be classified as Tigers and Dragons. The numbers for the Dragons, which are *yang* (positive, male), are odd, and those for the Tigers, which are *yin* (negative, female), are even.

The blue liver is the father and the white lungs are the mother. The red heart is the daughter, the yellow spleen is the grandfather, and the black kidneys are the son. The son is the beginning of the *wu-hsing* (the Five Elements). The *three* things are of the same family and they all are of the ordinal numbers *Wu* and *Chi*.

Another passage from the same work pictures the alchemist at work, his ingredients in the cauldron, and explains the efficacy of the elixir:

Circumference three-five, diameter one tenth of an inch, mouth four-eight, two inches, length one and two-tenths feet, and thickness equal throughout. With its belly properly set, it is to be warmed up gradually. *Yin* (negativeness) is above and *yang* (positiveness) runs below. The ends are strongly heated and the middle mildly warmed. Start with seventy, and with thirty, and two hundred and sixty. There should be thorough mixing.

The *yin* . . . fire is white and produces the *huang-ya* (Yellow Sprout) from the lead. Two-seven gathers to bring forth the man. When the brain [head] is properly tended for the required length of time, one will certainly attain the miracle. The offspring, living securely in the center, plies back and forth without coming out of doors. By degrees he grows up and is endowed with a pure nature. He goes back to the one to return to his origin. . . .

Respectful care should be accorded, as by a subject to his ruler. To keep up the work for a year is indeed a strenuous task. There should be strict protection, so as not to get lost. The Way is long and obscurely mystical, at the end of which the *Ch'ien* (positiveness, male) and the *K'un* (negativeness, female) come together. The taking of so small a quantity of it as would cover the edge of a knife or spatula will be enough to confer tranquility on the *hun-p'o* (man's animal spirit), give him immortality, and enable him to live in the village of the immortals.

. . . Careful reflection is in order, but no discussion with others should take place. The secret should be carefully guarded and no writing should be done for its conveyance. . . .

When the aspirant is accomplished, he will ride on the white crane and the scaled dragon to pay respects to the Immortal Ruler in the Supreme Void. There he will be given the decorated diploma which entitles him to the name of a *Chên-jen* (True Man).

Had alchemy been no more than a technique for producing the elixir, it could be considered as simply protoscience and not as religion; but, in fact, the adepts of this technique were never simply experimenters with material substances. The major treatise of the alchemical school, written by one Kô Hung (253–333?) under the pen name Pao P'u Tzû, or The Master Who Holds in His Arms the Uncarved Block, contains many specifications such as the following:

> The rules of immortality demand an earnest desire for quietness, loneliness, nonactivity and forgetfulness of one's own body.
> The rules of immortality require that one extend his love to the creeping worm and do no harm to beings with the life-fluid. . . .
> The rules of immortality require that one entirely abstain from flesh, give up cereals and purify one's interior.
> The rules of immortality demand universal love for the whole world, that one regard one's neighbor as one's own self.

As in all religions, there is a moral imperative in this search for immortality through alchemy:

> He who aspires after immortality should, above all, regard as his main duties: loyalty, filial piety, friendship, obedience, goodness, fidelity (all good "Confucian" virtues). If one does not lead a virtuous life but exercises himself only in magical tricks, he can by no means attain long life. If one does evil, should this be of a grave nature, the god of the fate would take off one chi (300 days, according to translator's note), and for a small sin he would take off a suan (three days) of one's life. . . .
> If the number of good actions is not yet completed, he will have no profit from them, although he takes the elixir of immortality.

The life to be led by the aspirant is described by the same authority:

> This Way is of utmost importance. You must teach it only to those who are wise and virtuous. . . . Whoever receives this instruction, must as a pledge throw a golden effigy of a man and of a fish into a river which flows eastwards. He must smear on his mouth the blood of a victim to pledge allegiance to the cause. . . . One must compound the cinnabar in a famous mountain, uninhabited by human beings, in the company of not more than three persons. First, one must fast for a hundred days, washing and bathing in water mixed with five odoriferous substances and thus effect absolute purity. Avoid strictly proximity to filthy things and observe isolation from the vulgar crowd. Furthermore,

disbelievers of the Way should not be given any information, for these would slander and spoil the elixir, and thus the Medicine will fail.

NEI-TAN

The quest for the elixir continued on for centuries, becoming increasingly conceived more in spiritual than in physical terms. This development is summed up by Waley, who calls *nei-tan* "esoteric alchemy":

> *Exoteric alchemy* [i.e., *wai-tan*] . . . uses as its ingredients the tangible substances mercury, lead, cinnabar and so on . . . [whereas] *esoteric alchemy* . . . uses only the "souls" of these substances. . . . Presently a fresh step is made. These transcendental metals are identified with various parts of the human body, and alchemy comes to mean in China . . . a system of mental and physical re-education. This process is complete in the *Treatise on the Dragon and Tiger* (lead and mercury) of Su Tung-p'o, written c. 1100: "The dragon is mercury. He is the semen and the blood. He issues from the kidneys and is stored in the liver. His sign is the trigram *k'an*. The tiger is lead. He is breath and bodily strength. He issues from the mind and the lungs bear him. His sign is the trigram *li*. When the mind is moved, then the breath and strength act with it. When the kidneys are flushed then semen and blood flow with them."
> In the thirteenth century alchemy (if it may still so be called) no less than Confucianism is permeated by the teachings of the Buddhist Meditation Sect [i.e., Ch'an]. The chief exponent of the Buddhicized Taoism is Ko Ch'ang-kêng, also known as Po Yü-chuan. In his treatise . . . he describes three methods of esoteric alchemy: (1) the body supplies the element lead; the heart, the element mercury. Concentration supplies the necessary liquid; the sparks of intelligence, the necessary fire. "By this means a gestation usually demanding ten months may be brought to ripeness in the twinkling of an eye." . . . (2) The second method is: The breath supplies the element lead, the soul [*shên*] supplies the element mercury. The cyclic sign [*wu*] "horse" supplies fire; the cyclic sign [*tzu*] "rat" supplies water. (3) The semen supplies the element lead. The blood supplies mercury; the kidneys supply water; the mind supplies fire.
> "To the above it may be objected," continues Ko Ch'ang-kêng, "that this is practically the same

as the method of the Zen Buddhist. To this I reply that under Heaven there are no two Ways, and that the Wise are ever of the same heart."

Although *wai-tan*, an alchemy of substances, thus becomes more and more a technique for cultivating the "inner chemistry" of the body, it must not be assumed that this latter was historically an outgrowth of the former. On the contrary, . . . inner cultivation was already a feature of ancient Taoist philosophy. From these hints, the later adepts of religious Taoism developed a variety of yoga, based on a theory that may be called "spiritual physiology." This in turn formed the foundation for the protoscience of traditional Chinese medicine. The objective of Taoist yoga was, as we have said, liberation of the *yang* soul (that is, the *shên*) from the hindrances of the *yin*, or gross physical body, and thus it was, in fact, a development of the ancient concepts. That is, it had always been presumed that such a liberation was accomplished by death, but the religious Taoists believed it could be accomplished in this very life.

In the spiritual physiology of religious Taoism, the life-force was identified with such obviously vital components as breath, blood, and semen. To preserve life these components must be conserved, and the obstructions to their continuing nourishment of the *shên* must be reduced and finally eliminated. The peculiarity about the religious Taoist notion of breath was that it was not merely inhalation and exhalation of an exterior substance but that it was a progressive "using up" of the allotment of life-spirit with which one was born. Taoist yoga therefore endeavored to conserve the breath. In the same way exhaustion of the semen was equivalent to exhaustion of the life-spirit; therefore, adepts used a technique to retain it instead of ejaculating it during the sexual act. Not only did this prevent exhaustion of the life-spirit, but the method of retention was positively beneficial as well. It was believed that pressure on the urethra at the moment of ejaculation forced the semen back up through the spinal passage to the brain, where it nourished the **"Field of Cinnabar"** supposed to be located there. Through this circulation of the semen (as of the breath) throughout the various passages and organs predicated by Taoist physiological and anatomical theory, the practitioner was continually rejuvenated.

The same purpose lay behind the various gymnastic routines of Taoist devotees, some of which have been widely adopted in East Asia. The so-called Chinese boxing (*t'ai-chi ch'üan*), a slow-motion ballet performed by countless men and women every morning in China, is like the setting-up exercises used in the West. Its rationale, however, is that just described. Such Taoist gymnastics, when combined with the injunctions of the Old

Master to be nonassertive, "weak, like water," and so forth, further led to techniques of bodily combat that have recently become popular among some Westerners, particularly that called the "yielding way" (*rou-tao* in Chinese, or *jūdō* in Japanese).

The Taoist adept attempted to reduce his intake of food as far as possible, because the consumption of food merely contributed to maintenance of the physical body and produced excreta that clogged the various interior passages, which were to be kept open wide for circulation of the life-forces. Even cereals were to be avoided because the body was inhabited by maleficent spirits (*kuei*), who were nourished by cereals.

The notion of the body being inhabited by both beneficent and malevolent spirits was further extended to the conception of the body as a microcosm corresponding to the macrocosm of the universe. Such an imaginative conception might have had its origin, at least in part, in certain passages of *Master Chuang*, where the relativity of things is most powerfully delineated:

> There is nothing in the world larger than the tip of an autumn down; but Mt T'ai is small. There is no life so long as that which is cut off in youth. Ancestor P'êng (the Chinese Methuselah) may be considered to have died prematurely. Heaven-and-Earth were created together with me. The myriad things-and-beings and I are one. (*Master Chuang*, scroll 2, "An Essay on the Relativity of Things"; *Chuang Tzû, Ch'i Wu Lun*)

However, the same sort of thinking was stimulated by the paradoxes beloved of the philosophers of the sophist type who flourished in the fourth and third centuries B.C.E. And even in the more socially oriented thought of Master Mêng, one finds this curious passage: "The ten thousand things (i.e., all things) are complete within us."

At the highest level, among Taoists of superior intellectual and spiritual attainments, the religious quest led not only to the goal of immortality but to a mystical absorption in *tao* itself. Although the meditational techniques of Taoism were strongly influenced by Buddhism in later times, ultimately resulting in the Buddho-Taoist techniques of Ch'an, it seems certain that some form of meditation was already practiced in China long before the arrival of the Indian religion. What is hinted at in *The Old Master* seems to become explicit in *Master Chuang*:

> [Yen] Hui said, May I venture to ask about "fasting the mind"? Chung-ni (i.e., Master K'ung) replied, Concentrate the will. Do not listen with the ears but listen with the mind. Do not listen with the mind but listen with the vital breath. Hearing stops at the ears, the mind stops at tallying [with a stimulus],

but the vital breath is empty and awaits something. It is just the *Tao* that gathers in this emptiness, and this emptiness is the "fasting of the mind." (*Master Chuang*, scroll 4, "Society and the Times"; *Chuang Tzû, Rên Chien Shih*)

. . .

Sloughing off limbs and trunk, driving out intellectual apprehension, abandoning form and rejecting knowledge, identifying with the Great Pervader: this is what is meant by sitting in forgetfulness. (*Master Chuang*, scroll 6)

. . .

Light is produced in the empty room and felicity stops and abides there. If for a time it does not, this is called galloping about while sitting. When the eyes and ears are directed inward and the "knowledge" of the mind is cast out, the very spirits will come to lodge. (*Master Chuang*, scroll 4)

INSTITUTIONALIZATION OF TAOISM

The quest for transcending the limitations of the flesh that has been described thus far was based on esoteric interpretations of certain ancient texts and carried on by means of various techniques that Western scholars have called alchemy. These interpretations and practices constituted the essence of Taoism as a religious Way and required no professional ordination. Indeed, lay devotees of the arts of longevity or immortality must always have been far more numerous than the professional religious. By itself this sort of effort—corresponding in general intent to the search in the West for the "philosopher's stone" or the "fountain of youth"—would not have produced an institutionalized religion. That Taoism did become institutionalized may be ascribed to two major historical developments. On the one hand, the solitary retreats of recluses evolved into whole communities of aspirants living under the guidance of renowned masters, and as one result of this situation, the teachings of the latter were written down to become gospel texts of a Taoist Canon. On the other hand, a new type of religious specialist emerged in the "theocratic" regimes that arose during the time of troubles of the Later Han dynasty, in the second century of the common era.

By far the most important of these regimes for the history of Taoism was that established in the far western province of Ssuch'uan by one Chang Ling or Chang Tao-ling. It is Chang Tao-ling who must be identified, if any one figure can be, as the founder of Taoist religion in the institutionalized form. He stands conveniently for this purpose at the borders of history and legend, and in

the latter area he has been deified as one of popular Taoism's most puissant spiritual powers. Historically, it seems that he did gain political control over a considerable territory, which he administered through a bureaucracy whose officials were more religious than secular in authority. These officials, although deriving organizationally from the practices of the Han imperium, are said to have acted most importantly in the capacity of parish priests. They, like Chang Tao-ling, were evangelists of a new religion of faith healing and ritual adapted to the needs of the masses. Apparently this addition to the age-old popular religion was eagerly embraced by the multitudes, perhaps because it was the first time that their rulers had concerned themselves with the common people. Now, the services of common mediums, shaman-exorcists, and sorcerers were in a sense brought under the aegis of respectable, literate priest-officials, who could bring an unprecedented spiritual power to bear in popular religion. It was this literacy, or mastery of texts, that distinguished the Taoists (we shall use this term hereafter to designate the professional religious and not "believers" in general) from lower-level religious practitioners. At the same time, it was the involvement of the Taoists in the communities that made their services an integral part of the popular religion.

The original chief of these community priests, Chang Tao-ling, assumed a title that was to endure as the most prestigious both within and outside the Taoist institution: **T'ien Shih.** This title, obviously derived by analogy with the imperial title of T'ien Tzû (Son of Heaven), meant the Master Designated by the [Three] Heavens. It remained the hereditary property of the Chang lineage, was given official recognition by many imperial regimes throughout history, especially since the Sung dynasty, and is still acknowledged to have unique authority.

The great majority of Taoists remain in society to act as ritualists for the communities in which they live. They are identified as receiving a number of different ritual traditions, but that purporting to trace back to Chang Tao-ling, called the T'ien-Shih Chêng-yi Tao, or Way of the Orthodox One of the Master Designated by the Heavens, holds pride of place. Most important, it has been the T'ien Shih who has been the recognized source of orthodox ordination, which he would confer on aspirants in accordance with their mastery of specific texts from the whole range of sectarian traditions. On the other hand, Taoists who chose to leave the world and live secluded in monasteries in order to pursue the alchemical techniques that would gain them personal immortality might be said more closely to resemble Buddhist monks. The major tradition of this style of Taoist career was the Ch'üan-chên Chiao, or Sect of Total Perfection.

THE TAOIST AS EXORCIST AND RITUALIST

The two main functions of the Taoist are exorcism and protection of the well-being and security of the mortal world against the attacks of *kuei*, and performance of rituals on behalf of clients and community. Although both of these functions are also carried on by lower-level religious specialists, the Taoist is recognized to have more effective power under his control for exorcism and protection, and only he knows the complicated rubrics of the major liturgies. He is, to put it in brief, a better-educated specialist than those others, especially by virtue of his book learning. This was, of course, an outstanding qualification in those days when the mere ability to read and write made a person exceptional and constituted the very basis for qualifying one to enter elite status in the society. It should be stressed that the profession of Taoist is very much more demanding in its preparation than those of medium, shaman, or the like. While these latter may have literally no preparatory training but simply be "possessed" by their familiar deity—or even substitute only a convincing assertion of their occult powers for such possession—the Taoist has to undergo a long period of textual studies, supplemented by the oral instructions of his mentor. The latter is customarily his own father as, in common with most professions involving specialized technical knowledge in traditional China, the professional secrets were kept within the family. Following this long apprenticeship, the aspirant would seek service under an eminent master, in order to become his successor. His ordination was an impressive ceremony, preceded by many days of isolation and fasting and publicly performed during a sacrificial "mass" called *chiao*, which lasted a minimum of three days.

    . . . The basis for the Taoist's control over *kuei* and *shên* was a form of "name magic," an interesting survival, in a sophisticated religion, of a very ancient, even primitive, notion. He could summon and dismiss the deities of **macrocosm** (the universe) and **microcosm** (his own body) by virtue of his knowledge of their names, true descriptions, and functions. He further controlled them by means of cabalistic writing, the talismans or charms called *fu*. These *fu* were, in effect, orders or commands issued by the Taoist by virtue of his authority in the spiritual realm, and thereby they kept away *kuei* and invoked the beneficence of *shên*. . . .

It should be noted that there is generally understood to be a distinction between those Taoists (commonly called "Red-heads" in Taiwan) who are found practicing exorcism and other popular rites in the busy temples on an everyday basis and the supposedly higher-class Taoists (called "Black-heads" in Taiwan) who alone are competent to perform the extended liturgies of the *chiao*. The former will wear a red scarf tied about the head (or waist) and carry a buffalo horn, which they blow in loud blasts, while the latter are seen attired in their formal sacerdotal vestments complete with black "mandarin cap" with gold-colored knob. The essential distinction between the two types is that the former (called *fa-shih*, or occult specialists), knowing only the more rudimentary texts, are ordained in low rank and cannot perform the greater liturgies, while the latter have mastered the texts qualifying them to perform those greatly more complex and religiously profound rituals. However, the superior ranked *tao-shih* (Taoist masters) are, of course, able to carry out the popular rites that are the specialty of their inferiors and often do not disdain to do so in consideration of the pecuniary rewards.

The greater rituals whose liturgies are set forth in the advanced texts are known as *chiao* and **chai**. There apparently was not much difference between these two forms historically. A contemporary Chinese scholar, Liu Chih-wan, has suggested the following distinction: "Taking the broadest view, the difference in the results sought by the two [forms of ritual] is simply that their emphases are not the same: The *chai* places its emphasis upon the prayers of the individual for blessings and the salvation of the dead; whereas the emphasis of the *chiao* is upon the prayers of the public (i.e., the community) for averting calamities and ensuring tranquillity. [Thus] each has its special emphasis." According to the American authority Michael Saso, himself an ordained *tao-shih*, although the two sets of rituals are both performed during the several-day festivals in the communities in Taiwan, the *chiao* has as its purpose "to win blessing from heaven and union with the transcendent Tao," whereas the *chai* is intended "to free the souls from hell." A special feature of the latter is that it concludes with a great feast for the souls of those in purgatory, called by the Buddhist term **p'u-tu**.

The *chiao* has both esoteric and exoteric levels of meaning. For the Taoist himself, it is a procedure whereby he personally attains mystical union with Tao, or in other words, a form of *nei-tan*. To the public it is an impressive ceremonial and magical performance whereby the supreme powers of the universe are called down into the temple for a State visit and petitioned to give their spiritual support to the community. At the same time, while these highly formalized, canonically prescribed events are being enacted within a temple—which, incidentally, is only for this occasion made off-limits to the public—the people are themselves participating in the rituals according to traditional lay roles, and the joint efforts of priests and people comprise a total community "happening," a great festival both sacred and profane.

In Taiwan today such *chiao* are the most exciting and colorful affairs carried on in the communities. Like medieval European fairs, they combine the religious, the aesthetic, and the purely sensual, and they last for at least three days and nights. Large structures called *t'an*, or altars, are erected in vacant lots or fields, dedicated to major deities, and at night brightly illuminated. They are facades or skeletons of bamboo covered with cloth and paper, colorfully decorated with all sorts of ingenuous folk art. Every so often the Taoist retinue emerges from the temple to perform some public section of the liturgies, much to the enjoyment of the people. Huge crowds arrive, many from distant places, to share in the excitement. Everywhere the local people have set out their household offerings on tables at the roadside, of which pride of place goes to monstrous pigs that have been fattened for just this occasion and that are spread-eagled in hairless nudity on special stands. There are noisy theatricals, fortune-telling booths, hawkers of every kind, and carnival amusements. Day and night this animated scene astonishes by its vitality and the prodigality with which these people of so little material substance spend for their festival. The persistent theme of the festival as a whole is the dominance of the dead. Not only are canonical texts of merit and repentance for salvation of souls constantly being read by the Taoists during the entire *chiao*, but all of that mountain of food and drink set out by the households of the entire community is for the souls of the dead. The ancestors are of course expected to enjoy this feast, but there are many souls who must be appeased for fear of their vengeance—the spirits of those who have been deprived of their due sacrifices and the spirits of those who must suffer punishment in purgatory. Dominating the scene before the temple stands the figure of Ta Shih, the metamorphosed Kuan Shih Yin as King of these Ghosts, charged with keeping them in order when they flock to the feast prepared for them by the community. To that feast they have been invited by signal lamps and pennants hung on tall posts and by paper boats sent burning out on the waters. Not until these dangerous spirits have been respectfully banqueted on the essences of the sacrifices can the community feel secure and the hoped-for benefits of the *chiao* be assured.

We may seem here to have left the topic of the religious vocation and to have returned to religion in the community. But it will be seen that it is in fact the roles of exorcist and ritualist for the community that have constituted the profession, the raison d'etre, of the Taoist and ensured the continuing vitality of his public vocation through the centuries.

SOURCES

The source material for Taoism is massive. The official collection or canon of Taoist literature (*Tao-tsang*), published in 1445, is composed of 1,120 volumes and 1,476 titles. It is divided into three primary parts called the "Three Caverns" in which one will find moral codes, revelations from gods and goddesses, textual commentaries, ritual instructions, alchemical recipes, meditation instruction, philosophical musing, and much more.

Over the years there have been many supplements to the *Tao-tsang* and there is much literature pertaining to Taoism that is not part of the canon. The material I have selected is organized historically and covers a variety of themes. It includes both influential and representative material touching on some of the main themes of Taoism such as the Tao, discipline, meditation, physical practices, rituals, longevity, and immortality.

The promise of Taoism is freedom and immortality. The serious Taoist seeks to be free from conventional modes of thought and ways of living, hoping one day to live among the glorious immortals. The path to freedom and immortality is long and complex. Along the way the serious adept must discipline both body and mind, transforming not only her or his life in this world, but also securing a place in the world to come.

9.2 THE EARLY FOUNDATIONS

Although, as we noted earlier, the revelation on which the Taoist movement called Celestial Masters is based did not take place until 142, that revelation is intimately tied to earlier ideas. Among them are ideas attributed to two brilliant sages, Lao Tzu and Chuang Tzu. We must start with this foundation because its authority has been vital to Taoism for more than 2,000 years.

Even before Chang Tao-ling had his vision of Lao Tzu in 142, people had been inspired by the writings of Lao Tzu and Chuang Tzu. We have records of vivid visionary journeys inspired by the imagery of these two great sages. One, called "Far-Off Journey," relates a trip into a soundless, invisible Great Beginning.

9.2.1 The Way and Its Power

Imagine that you are instructed to describe the source of all things. You might begin by thinking about the things you know about like rocks, trees, cats, books, chairs, people, and the like. Could any one of these things be the source of all things? It seems unlikely because all of these things are limited by time, space, and matter. Is the source of all things limited too? If it is, how could it be the source of everything? Perhaps it is best to say that the source of all things is unlimited. Does that mean it is spaceless, timeless, and immaterial? If it is, how can we describe it except by saying what it is not?

Lao Tzu, the legendary author of the ***Tao Te Ching,*** faced this problem of describing the source of all. He gave it a name—the Tao, or Way—and he talked about its power (Te), but in the final analysis he knew that it is really the Nameless.

According to Taoist tradition, Lao Tzu, was an older contemporary of Confucius living in sixth century B.C.E. China. Supposedly he worked as an archivist for most of his life, and, when he became disturbed by the degeneration of his society, he decided to leave China by the "Western Gate." Before the gatekeeper would let him pass, the gatekeeper persuaded him to write down his wisdom concerning the Tao and its power. Later generations reported numerous sightings of the departed Lao Tzu, and soon a wealth of legends began to circulate about him, including one in which he instructed Confucius in the proper understanding of the Tao. After Lao Tzu purportedly went through the Western Gate, he traveled to India and there became known as the Buddha. Eventually he became an immortal deity, or, rather, he returned to his original state since it was rumored that he was really a deity incarnate all the while people had thought him mortal. However, he still appears in visions to people at crucial times to instruct them in the Way.

The Taoist tradition claims that the *Tao Te Ching* is the oldest text in the Taoist canon, dating from around 250 B.C.E. It is sometimes called the *Lao-tzu,* after its alleged author, and is popularly known as "The Five Thousand Character Classic" because it contains around five thousand characters. It is the foundational text of Taoism.

The *Tao Te Ching* has been translated numerous times and interpreted in a variety of ways. The text as we have it now is divided into two parts. The first deals with the Tao (Way) and the second with its Te (power or virtue). The selections that follow focus on the notion of the Tao, since this "nameless name" has played such a central role in Taoism.

❧

LAO TZU

Tao Te Ching

READING QUESTIONS

1. Why is the Tao that can be told not the eternal Tao?
2. What does it mean to manage affairs without action?
3. What kinds of metaphors are used to characterize Tao?
4. If we model our life after Tao, what sort of life would it be?
5. What is the order of production of the ten thousand things?

1

The Tao that can be told of is not the eternal Tao;
The name that can be named is not the eternal name.
The Nameless is the origin of Heaven and Earth;
The Named is the mother of all things.

Therefore let there always be non-being, so we may
  see their subtlety,
And let there always be being, so we may see their
  outcome.
The two are the same,
But after they are produced, they have different names.
They both may be called deep and profound.
Deeper and more profound,
The door of all subtleties!

From Chan, Wing-tsit, *A Source Book of Chinese Philosophy*. Copyright © 1963 by Princeton University Press; renewed 1991. Reprinted by permission of Princeton University Press. Footnotes and commentary omitted.

2

When the people of the world all know beauty as
  beauty,
There arises the recognition of ugliness.
When they all know the good as good,
There arises the recognition of evil.
Therefore:
  Being and non-being produce each other;
  Difficult and easy complete each other;
  Long and short contrast each other;
  High and low distinguish each other;
  Sound and voice harmonize each other;
  Front and behind accompany each other.
  Therefore the sage manages affairs without action
  And spreads doctrines without words.
  All things arise, and he does not turn away from
    them.
  He produces them but does not take possession of
    them.
  He acts but does not rely on his own ability.
  He accomplishes his task but does not claim credit
    for it.
  It is precisely because he does not claim credit that
    his accomplishment remains with him. . . .

4

Tao is empty (like a bowl).
  It may be used but its capacity is never exhausted.
  It is bottomless, perhaps the ancestor of all things.
  It blunts its sharpness,
  It unties its tangles.
  It softens its light.
  It becomes one with the dusty world.
  Deep and still, it appears to exist forever.
  I do not know whose son it is.
  It seems to have existed before the Lord. . . .

6

The spirit of the valley never dies.
  It is called the subtle and profound female.
The gate of the subtle and profound female
  Is the root of Heaven and Earth.
It is continuous, and seems to be always existing.
Use it and you will never wear it out. . . .

8

The best (man) is like water.
  Water is good; it benefits all things and does not
    compete with them.
It dwells in (lowly) places that all disdain.
This is why it is so near to Tao.

(The best man) in his dwelling loves the earth.
In his heart, he loves what is profound.
In his associations, he loves humanity.
In his words, he loves faithfulness.
In government, he loves order.
In handling affairs, he loves competence.
In his activities, he loves timeliness.
It is because he does not compete that he is without
  reproach. . . .

11

Thirty spokes are united around the hub to make a
  wheel,
  But it is on its non-being that the utility of the
    carriage depends.
Clay is molded to form a utensil,
  But it is on its non-being that the utility of the
    utensil depends.
Doors and windows are cut out to make a room,
  But it is on its non-being that the utility of the room
    depends.
Therefore turn being into advantage, and turn non-
  being into utility. . . .

14

We look at it and do not see it;
  Its name is The Invisible.
We listen to it and do not hear it;
  Its name is The Inaudible.
We touch it and do not find it;
  Its name is The Subtle (formless).

These three cannot be further inquired into,
And hence merge into one.
Going up high, it is not bright, and coming down low,
  it is not dark.
Infinite and boundless, it cannot be given any name;
It reverts to nothingness.

This is called shape without shape,
Form without objects.
It is The Vague and Elusive.
Meet it and you will not see its head.
Follow it and you will not see its back.
Hold on to the Tao of old in order to master the
  things of the present.
From this one may know the primeval beginning
  (of the universe).
This is called the bond of Tao. . . .

16

Attain complete vacuity.
Maintain steadfast quietude.

All things come into being,
And I see thereby their return.
All things flourish,
But each one returns to its root.
This return to its root means tranquillity.
It is called returning to its destiny.
To return to destiny is called the eternal (Tao).
To know the eternal is called enlightenment.
Not to know the eternal is to act blindly to result in
  disaster.
He who knows the eternal is all-embracing.
Being all-embracing, he is impartial.
Being impartial, he is kingly (universal).
Being kingly, he is one with Nature.
Being one with Nature, he is in accord with Tao.
Being in accord with Tao, he is everlasting
And is free from danger throughout his lifetime. . . .

22

To yield is to be preserved whole.
To be bent is to become straight.
To be empty is to be full.
To be worn out is to be renewed.
To have little is to possess.
To have plenty is to be perplexed.
Therefore the sage embraces the One
And becomes the model of the world.
He does not show himself; therefore he is luminous.
He does not justify himself; therefore he becomes
  prominent.

He does not boast of himself; therefore he is given
  credit.
He does not brag; therefore he can endure for long.

It is precisely because he does not compete that the
  world cannot compete with him.
Is the ancient saying, "To yield is to be preserved
  whole," empty words?
Truly he will be preserved and (prominence and credit)
  will come to him. . . .

25

There was something undifferentiated and yet
  complete,
Which existed before heaven and earth.
Soundless and formless, it depends on nothing and
  does not change.
It operates everywhere and is free from danger.
It may be considered the mother of the universe.
I do not know its name; I call it Tao.
If forced to give it a name, I shall call it Great.
Now being great means functioning everywhere.
Functioning everywhere means far-reaching.
Being far-reaching means returning to the original
  point.

Therefore Tao is great.
Heaven is great.
Earth is great.
And the king is also great.
There are four great things in the universe, and the
  king is one of them.
Man models himself after Earth.
Earth models itself after Heaven.
Heaven models itself after Tao.
And Tao models itself after Nature. . . .

34

The Great Tao flows everywhere.
It may go left or right.
All things depend on it for life, and it does not turn
  away from them.
It accomplishes its task, but does not claim credit for it.
It clothes and feeds all things but does not claim to be
  master over them.
Always without desires, it may be called The Small.

All things come to it and it does not master them; it may be called The Great.
Therefore (the sage) never strives himself for the great, and thereby the great is achieved. . . .

37

Tao invariably takes no action, and yet there is nothing left undone.
If kings and barons can keep it, all things will transform spontaneously.
If, after transformation, they should desire to be active, I would restrain them with simplicity, which has no name.
Simplicity, which has no name, is free of desires.
Being free of desires, it is tranquil.
And the world will be at peace of its own accord. . . .

42

Tao produced the One.
The One produced the two.
The two produced the three.
And the three produced the ten thousand things.
The ten thousand things carry the yin and embrace the yang, and through the blending of the material force they achieve harmony. . . .

9.2.2 Mystical Tales

After the *Tao Te Ching*, the *Chuang Tzu* is the second most important foundational text of Taoism. It is attributed to the philosopher **Chuang Tzu** after whom it is named. It is unlikely that Chuang Tzu, who lived in the fourth century B.C.E., is responsible for all of the thirty-three chapters in the book, but most scholars agree that the so-called "inner chapters" (chapters 1–7) may well be from his mouth, if not his brush.

The *Chuang Tzu* is a remarkable book. It is full of funny stories, brilliant philosophical asides, wry observations, illustrative anecdotes, tips on living, contradictory riddles, and questions upon questions upon questions. It is skeptical and mystical, brilliant and dark, stable and fluid, ancient and postmodern. It is constantly undermining itself while undermining

its undermining. It is very much like the Tao itself. Then again, it is not.

As you might imagine, the interpretations of the *Chuang Tzu* vary greatly. Some read the text as deeply mystical, teaching us to see the unity of all opposites. Others read the text as deeply skeptical, teaching us to doubt all conceptions of truth and reality. Still others think the *Chuang Tzu* teaches a radical value relativism that undermines all philosophical and religious claims to reveal absolute values. Burton Watson, whose translation I use, says in his introduction that the *Chuang Tzu* seeks to point the way to freedom from the baggage of conventional values. As you read, apply these various interpretations and see if they make sense of the text.

❧

CHUANG TZU

Chuang Tzu

READING QUESTION

1. Write a brief commentary on these passages from chapter 2, stating what you think they mean.

Now I am going to make a statement here. I don't know whether it fits into the category of other people's statements or not. But whether it fits into their category or whether it doesn't, it obviously fits into some category. So in that respect it is no different from their statements. However, let me try making my statement.

There is a beginning. There is a not yet beginning to be a beginning. There is a not yet beginning to be a not yet beginning to be a beginning. There is being. There is nonbeing. There is a not yet beginning to be nonbeing. There is a not yet beginning to be a not yet beginning to be nonbeing. Suddenly there is being and nonbeing. But between this being and nonbeing, I don't really know which is being and which is nonbeing. Now I have just said something. But I don't know whether

Republished with permission of Columbia University Press, 562 W. 113th St., New York, NY 10025. *Chuang Tzu: Basic Writings,* translated by Burton Watson, 1964/1996. Reproduced by permission of the publisher via Copyright Clearance Center, Inc. Pp. 38–45. Footnotes edited.

what I have said has really said something or whether it hasn't said something.

There is nothing in the world bigger than the tip of an autumn hair, and Mount T'ai is little. No one has lived longer than a dead child, and P'eng-tsu died young.[1] Heaven and earth were born at the same time I was, and the ten thousand things are one with me.

We have already become one, so how can I say anything? But I have just *said* that we are one, so how can I not be saying something? The one and what I said about it make two, and two and the original one make three. If we go on this way, then even the cleverest mathematician can't tell where we'll end, much less an ordinary man. If by moving from nonbeing to being we get to three, how far will we get if we move from being to being? Better not to move, but to let things be!

The Way has never known boundaries; speech has no contstancy. But because of [the recognition of a] "this," there came to be boundaries. Let me tell you what the boundaries are. There is left, there is right, there are theories, there are debates, there are divisions, there are discriminations, there are emulations, and there are contentions. These are called the Eight Virtues. As to what is beyond the Six Realms,[2] the sage admits it exists but does not theorize. As to what is within the Six Realms, he theorizes but does not debate. In the case of the *Spring and Autumn*, the record of the former kings of past ages, the sage debates but does not discriminate. So [I say,] those who divide fail to divide; those who discriminate fail to discriminate. What does this mean, you ask? The sage embraces things. Ordinary men discriminate among them and parade their discriminations before others. So I say, those who discriminate fail to see.

The Great Way is not named; Great Discriminations are not spoken; Great Benevolence is not benevolent; Great Modesty is not humble; Great Daring does not attack. If the Way is made clear, it is not the Way. If discriminations are put into words, they do not suffice. If benevolence has a constant object, it cannot be universal. If modesty is fastidious, it cannot be trusted. If daring attacks, it cannot be complete. These five are all round, but they tend toward the square.[3]

Therefore understanding that rests in what it does not understand is the finest. Who can understand discriminations that are not spoken, the Way that is not a

way? If he can understand this, he may be called the Reservoir of Heaven. Pour into it and it is never full, dip from it and it never runs dry, and yet it does not know where the supply comes from. This is called the Shaded Light.

So it is that long ago Yao said to Shun, "I want to attack the rulers of Tsung, K'uai, and Hsü-ao. Even as I sit on my throne, this thought nags at me. Why is this?"

Shun replied, "These three rulers are only little dwellers in the weeds and brush. Why this nagging desire? Long ago, ten suns came out all at once and the ten thousand things were all lighted up. And how much greater is virtue than these suns!"

Nieh Ch'üeh asked Wang Ni, "Do you know what all things agree in calling right?"

"How would I know that?" said Wang Ni.

"Do you know that you don't know it?"

"How would I know that?"

"Then do things know nothing?"

"How would I know that? However, suppose I try saying something. What way do I have of knowing that if I say I know something I don't really not know it? Or what way do I have of knowing that if I say I don't know something I don't really in fact know it? Now let me ask *you* some questions. If a man sleeps in a damp place, his back aches and he ends up half paralyzed, but is this true of a loach? If he lives in a tree, he is terrified and shakes with fright, but is this true of a monkey? Of these three creatures, then, which one knows the proper place to live? Men eat the flesh of grass-fed and grain-fed animals, deer eat grass, centipedes find snakes tasty, and hawks and falcons relish mice. Of these four, which knows how food ought to taste? Monkeys pair with monkeys, deer go out with deer, and fish play around with fish. Men claim that Mao-ch'iang and Lady Li were beautiful, but if fish saw them they would dive to the bottom of the stream, if birds saw them they would fly away, and if deer saw them they would break into a run. Of these four, which knows how to fix the standard of beauty for the world? The way I see it, the rules of benevolence and righteousness and the paths of right and wrong are all hopelessly snarled and jumbled. How could I know anything about such discriminations?"

Nieh Ch'üeh said, "If you don't know what is profitable or harmful, then does the Perfect Man likewise know nothing of such things?"

Wang Ni replied, "The Perfect Man is godlike. Though the great swamps blaze, they cannot burn him; though the great rivers freeze, they cannot chill him; though swift lightning splits the hills and howling gales shake the sea, they cannot frighten him. A man like this rides the clouds and mist, straddles the sun and moon, and wanders beyond the four seas. Even life and death

---

[1] The strands of animal fur were believed to grow particularly fine in autumn: hence "the tip of an autumn hair" is a cliché for something extremely tiny. P'eng-tsu [is] the Chinese Methuselah. . . .

[2] Heaven, earth, and the four directions, i.e., the universe.

[3] All are originally perfect, but may become "squared," i.e., impaired, by the misuses mentioned.

have no effect on him, much less the rules of profit and loss!"

Chü Ch'üeh-tzu said to Chang Wu-tzu, "I have heard Confucius say that the sage does not work at anything, does not pursue profit, does not dodge harm, does not enjoy being sought after, does not follow the Way, says nothing yet says something, says something yet says nothing, and wanders beyond the dust and grime. Confucius himself regarded these as wild and flippant words, though I believe they describe the working of the mysterious Way. What do you think of them?"

Chang Wu-tzu said, "Even the Yellow Emperor would be confused if he heard such words, so how could you expect Confucius to understand them? What's more, you're too hasty in your own appraisal. You see an egg and demand a crowing cock, see a crossbow pellet and demand a roast dove. I'm going to try speaking some reckless words and I want you to listen to them recklessly. How will that be? The sage leans on the sun and moon, tucks the universe under his arm, merges himself with things, leaves the confusion and muddle as it is, and looks on slaves as exalted. Ordinary men strain and struggle; the sage is stupid and blockish. He takes part in ten thousand ages and achieves simplicity in oneness. For him, all the ten thousand things are what they are, and thus they enfold each other.

"How do I know that loving life is not a delusion? How do I know that in hating death I am not like a man who, having left home in his youth, has forgotten the way back?

"Lady Li was the daughter of the border guard of Ai.[4] When she was first taken captive and brought to the state of Chin, she wept until her tears drenched the collar of her robe. But later, when she went to live in the palace of the ruler, shared his couch with him, and ate the delicious meats of his table, she wondered why she had ever wept. How do I know that the dead do not wonder why they ever longed for life?

"He who dreams of drinking wine may weep when morning comes; he who dreams of weeping may in the morning go off to hunt. While he is dreaming he does not know it is a dream, and in his dream he may even try to interpret a dream. Only after he wakes does he know it was a dream. And someday there will be a great awakening when we know that this is all a great dream. Yet the stupid believe they are awake, busily and brightly assuming they understand things, calling this man ruler, that one herdsman—how dense! Confucius and you are

both dreaming! And when I say you are dreaming, I am dreaming, too. Words like these will be labeled the Supreme Swindle. Yet, after ten thousand generations, a great sage may appear who will know their meaning, and it will still be as though he appeared with astonishing speed.

"Suppose you and I have had an argument. If you have beaten me instead of my beating you, then are you necessarily right and am I necessarily wrong? If I have beaten you instead of your beating me, then am I necessarily right and are you necessarily wrong? Is one of us right and the other wrong? Are both of us right or are both of us wrong? If you and I don't know the answer, then other people are bound to be even more in the dark. Whom shall we get to decide what is right? Shall we get someone who agrees with you to decide? But if he already agrees with you, how can he decide fairly? Shall we get someone who agrees with me? But if he already agrees with me, how can he decide? Shall we get someone who disagrees with both of us? But if he already disagrees with both of us, how can he decide? Shall we get someone who agrees with both of us? But if he already agrees with both of us, how can he decide? Obviously, then, neither you nor I nor anyone else can know the answer. Shall we wait for still another person?

"But waiting for one shifting voice [to pass judgment on] another is the same as waiting for none of them. Harmonize them all with the Heavenly Equality, leave them to their endless changes, and so live out your years. What do I mean by harmonizing them with the Heavenly Equality? Right is not right; so is not so. If right were really right, it would differ so clearly from not right that there would be no need for argument. If so were really so, it would differ so clearly from not so that there would be no need for argument. Forget the years; forget distinctions. Leap into the boundless and make it your home!"

Penumbra said to Shadow, "A little while ago you were walking and now you're standing still; a little while ago you were sitting and now you're standing up. Why this lack of independent action?"

Shadow said, "Do I have to wait for something before I can be like this? Does what I wait for also have to wait for something before it can be like this? Am I waiting for the scales of a snake or the wings of a cicada? How do I know why it is so? How do I know why it isn't so?"

Once Chuang Chou dreamt he was a butterfly, a butterfly flitting and fluttering around, happy with himself and doing as he pleased. He didn't know he was Chuang Chou. Suddenly he woke up and there he was, solid and unmistakable Chuang Chou. But he didn't know if he was Chuang Chou who had dreamt he was a butterfly,

---

[4] She was taken captive by Duke Hsien of Chin in 671 B.C., and later became his consort.

or a butterfly dreaming he was Chuang Chou. Between Chuang Chou and a butterfly there must be *some* distinction! This is called the Transformation of Things.

9.2.3 Ecstatic Travel

Taoists practice three different kinds of meditation: concentrative meditation, insight meditation, and **ecstatic journeys.** The first type is called "guarding the One" and involves learning how to fix one's mind on a single point. It is similar to Hindu and Buddhist *samadhi* practices. The second type, which appears to be borrowed from Buddhism, involves developing insight into the "true nature of things" by learning how to observe or witness self and others from the viewpoint of Taoism. Ecstatic travel involves spiritual journeys into the otherworld. The adept has an "out of body experience" in which he or she travels to the heavens and moves among the gods.

Ecstatic spirit travel probably derives from ancient shamanistic practices. Shamans developed various techniques for traveling to spirit worlds in order to find answers to various questions or bring back power for healing. Later, these journeys were linked with the physical journeys taken by emperors through their realm. Such journeys established the power and control of the emperors by making their presence known in the far reaches of their kingdoms.

A classical account of ecstatic travel ("Far-Off Journey") is found in a collection of ritual songs titled *Songs of the Chu* (also called *Songs of the South*), which date from the third century B.C.E. and later. They were compiled by a poet from South China named Ch'ü Yüan. A story recounts how Ch'ü Yüan drowned himself in despair over the corruptness of the world, having been unfairly slandered and banished from court. His death is associated with the Dragon Boat festival held in midsummer. During the festival, boat races reenact fishermen's attempts to save Ch'ü Yüan.

We do not know the author of "Far-Off Journey," but he or she draws on the imagery found in both the *Tao Te Ching* and the *Chuang Tzu.* One important concept found in all three writings is **wu-wei,** or nonaction (sometimes translated as "actionless action"). The Tao acts without acting, which means acting freely and without force. It is to allow or permit natural action to occur rather than to control and shape a situation by force. Both rulers and the ruled should model their own action after the Tao.

The journey you are about to undertake leads you not only to the realm of nonaction but also beyond. It not only takes you to the realm of the gods but transcends that realm as well. You come in contact with accomplished adepts and learn how to command the deities. Racing across the cosmos, traveling in all directions, surveying many marvels, you finally enter the silence of the Great Beginning.

༺ঔৢ৶ঌ༻

Far-Off Journey

READING QUESTIONS

1. Outline the structure of this poem. How does it start? How does it end? What happens in the middle?
2. What part of the poem do you find most gripping? Why?
3. How might experiences of ecstatic travel and their accounts function in religion?

Wrought with afflictions of the wonts of this age
I long to rise softly and journey afar,
But my meager powers are of trifling avail.
On what might I ride to soar upwards?
Confronting sunken depravity, a morass of corruption,
Alone and depressed, in whom might I confide?
Through the night I am wakeful and sleepless,
And my soul is restive until dawn;
I ponder the unfathomable reaches of heaven and earth,
Mourn the endless travails of human existence,
Lament those people already departed, whom I had
    never met,
And those yet to come, whom I would never know.
Pacing about, my thoughts adrift,
Nervously anxious and oddly pensive,
My thoughts run wild and unsettled,
And my heart is sadly despondent.
My spirit flashes forth and does not return,
And my physical frame withers and is left behind.
Reflecting inwardly I remain steadfast,
Searching for the source of the true vital force.
In silent vacuity and tranquillity I find quiet joy;

With still nonaction I accomplish things naturally. . . .
I am in awe of the regularity of heaven's seasons,
Of that shining ethereal brightness, in its westward
  journey;
But a light frost is settling, sinking downward,
And I worry lest my fragrant flowers fall early.
Would that I could drift and roam,
Forever passing the years with no particular design.
But with whom might I enjoy my few remaining
  fragrances?
At dawn, I unloose my feelings into the prevailing
  winds. . . .
I dine on the six vital forces and drink mists and vapors,
Rinse my mouth with the principal yang forces and
  imbibe the morning haze.
I safeguard the halcyon clarity of the spiritual and
  numinous,
And refined vital forces enter and coarser dregs are
  expelled.
Flowing with the gentle breezes, I roam about with
  them;
Arriving at the Southern Aerie, I stop at once,
And seeing Master Wang, I stay the night.
I ask him how the one vital force can be harmonized
  with virtue,
And he says, "The way can be received, but it cannot
  be transmitted to others.
It is so small that it has no inner space, so large that it
  has no outer limits.
When the soul is without artifice, one can deal with
  things naturally;
When the unitary vital force permeates the spirit,
  sustain it throughout the night.
Abide in vacuity prior to nonaction,
And everything will come to completion.
This is the gate of virtue."
I hear this and treasure it; I continue on,
Quickly preparing to set out.
I soon see the Feathered People of the Cinnabar Hills
And linger in that ancient deathless land.
I wash my hair in Boiling Valley,
And at night dry my bodily self at Nine Yang Forces;
I inhale the subtle secretions of the Flying Springs,
And embrace the shining emblems of the jade regalia.
The jade's colors radiate, casting a luster on my face;
My subtle essences, purified, start to strengthen;
My material self melts and dissolves, frothing away,
And my spirit floats about, loose and free.
I admire the warm, radiant virtues of the southern land,
And the winter blossoming of the beautiful cassia tree.
There desolate mountains are uninhabited by beasts,
And silent wildernesses harbor no human beings.

Bearing my corporeal soul, I ascend the mists of dawn,
And spread upon a floating cloud, I journey upward.
I order the porter of the gates of heaven to open his
  doors,
Swing back the gates, and keep a lookout for me.
I summon Feng Lung and place him in my vanguard
And ask him where Great Subtlety lies.
Collecting my redoubled yang forces, I enter the
  palace of the Lord;
I visit Temporal Origins and purview the City of
  Clarity.
Setting out at dawn, I stop at the Court of Grand
  Ceremony,
And by evening draw nigh to the Gate of Subtlety.
Marshalling a company of ten thousand chariots,
Rolling forward en masse at an even gallop,
I drive eight dragons, beautiful and sleek,
In a chariot strung with waving serpentine cloud banners
And mounted with bold rainbows of multicolored
  streamers,
Their five colors arrayed in dazzling brightness.
My inside steeds arch proudly, lowering and tossing;
The outside team writhes spiritedly, prancing.
Charging off, we ride tightly bunched and then fan out
  in a fray,
And the colorful stampede takes off.
Taking up the reins and unleashing the whip,
I set off to see Kou Mang.
Passing Grand Luminosity, I wheel to the right,
Sending Fei Lien ahead to clear the way.
As the light brightens just before sunrise,
I traverse the diameter of heaven and earth;
The Earl of the Wind courses ahead as my vanguard,
Sweeping away the dusts and ushering in clear coolness;
Soaring phoenixes bear my banners aloft,
And I encounter Ju Shou at the Western August
  Heavens.
Grasping a broom-star as my standard
And wielding aloft the Dipper's handle as my ensign,
In a glittering coruscation wending high and low,
I roam onward, scattering the flowing waves of mist.
Daylight clouds into darkness
As I summon Hsüan Wu to race in my retinue,
Charge Wen Ch'ang to direct the maneuvers at the
  rear guard,
And appoint a host of spirits to flank me on both sides.
The road spans far into the distance,
And I check the pace as I veer sharply upward.
At my right the Master of Rains serves as my scout,
And on the left, the Duke of Thunder is my escort.
Wanting to traverse the entire world, I forget to return
  home;

My thoughts are carefree and unconstrained,
And inwardly I rejoice and am at peace with myself,
Delighting in my own contentment.
But pacing the azure clouds, drifting and roaming,
I suddenly catch a glimpse of my old homeland;
My charioteers and grooms long for it, and my own
    heart grows sad.
Even the outside horses, turning back to look, do not
    go on.
Thinking of my old home, I envision it in my thoughts,
Drawing a deep breath as I hide my tears.
With a troubled countenance, I still advance upward,
Restraining my will and regaining composure.
Aiming for the Flaming Spirit, I gallop straight for it,
Heading toward the Southern Mountains.
I survey the barren reaches beyond space,
The floating mirages that drift of their own accord,
But Chu Jung warns me to turn back.
So I remount, bidding the simurgh to invite Fu Fei;
Strumming "In Many Ponds" and playing "Uplifting
    the Clouds,"
Two maidens present the Nine Shao Songs.
I bid the spirits of the Hsiang River to play the drum
    and zither,
And order the God of the Sea to dance with P'ing-i.
Lines of black dragons and sea-serpents weave in
    and out,
Their bodies wriggling and swaying in serpentines.
Lady Rainbow brightens ever more beautifully
As the simurgh soars and flies above
And the music rises in limitless crescendos.
I roam again, sporting to and fro,
Rolling onward at an even pace, galloping excitedly.
Striding ahead to the boundary limits at the Gate of
    Coldness;
Rushing forth swiftly with the wind at Clear Springs,
I follow Chuan Hsü over tiers of ice.
Crossing the land of Hsüan Ming, I diverge from
    my path;
Mounting the latitudes, I turn to look back,
Summoning Ch'ien Lei to manifest himself
To go before me and level the road.
I have traversed the Four Vastnesses,
Made a circuit of the Six Deserts,
Ascended to the lightning's cracks,
And descended into the Great Ravine.
Peaks rise high below, but there is no earth;
Empty vastness soars above, but there is no heaven.
Glancing this way and that, I see nothing;
Listening anxiously, I hear nothing.
Going beyond nonaction, I attain clarity,
And dwell in the Great Beginning.

9.3 TAOISM EXPANDS

As we have seen, Chang Tao-ling's revelation in 142 was the beginning of the Celestial Masters school of Taoism. In 364 a medium named Yang Hsi began to receive revelations from the Heaven of Highest Clarity, and, with those revelations, the second major Taoist school began. It was called, appropriately enough, the Highest Clarity (*Shang Ch'ing*) school. **Highest Clarity** practice aimed at transferring humans into the realms of the immortals by the use of visualizations, ecstatic journeys, and even by the ingestion of highly poisonous alchemical elixirs.

A few decades after Yang Hsi's revelations, yet another Taoist school formed around the revelations of Ge Chao-fu. Known as the Numinous Treasure (*Ling-bao*) school, it integrated Highest Clarity scriptures with some Buddhist ideas. Its practice was much simpler than that of Highest Clarity, requiring the recitation of its scriptures and participation in its rites, rather than arduous meditation exercises and alchemical elixirs, in order for humans to be perfected.

With the *Ling-bao* movement, Taoism emerged for the first time as an organized religion of *all* China. Copying from popular Buddhist movements, its leaders built monasteries, compiled scriptures, created representations of Taoist gods, and established order among its membership during the fifth and sixth centuries.

9.3.1 Commenting on the Tao

Commentaries are acts of interpretation and are vital for keeping a religion that is based on scriptures alive. As times change, the foundational scriptures must be reinterpreted to fit the changed circumstances. In a very real sense, commentaries constitute acts of rewriting scriptures because, wittingly or unwittingly, commentators rewrite the meaning of a text to reflect their own concerns.

The Celestial Masters remained an isolated and localized community for many years after Chang Tao-ling's encounter with a returned Lao Tzu. Eventually they were forced, by political and military circumstances, to spread out into a larger geographic area. As the community broke up and spread, it carried its ideas and practices with it, and soon new converts were entering the ranks. These new members needed to know about the values, beliefs, and practices of their newfound faith, and so instruction manuals were required.

The next selection (*Hsiang-erh*) is the earliest known Taoist commentary on the foundational scripture (*Tao Te Ching*) of the Celestial Masters school. It is less a commentary than a treatise in its own right that uses the *Tao Te Ching* as a point of departure in order to instruct new converts. Some attribute the authorship to either Chang Tao-ling or his grandson Chang Lu. The manuscript dates to the late fifth or early sixth century, but we do know versions were in existence prior to 255.

The graphs *hsiang* and *erh* can mean "thinking of or contemplating you" and may refer to the adepts' need to contemplate the celestial deities or may reassure the adepts that the celestial deities are thinking of them. Perhaps both.

Before you read the selection, here is a note about the translation. You will encounter the word *pneuma*, which the translator has used to translate the Chinese word *ch'i*. *Pneuma* means breath or spirit in Greek, and *ch'i* can mean a variety of things in Chinese, including material energy, spiritual energy, or the vital force or power that gives life. *Ch'i* appears in all things, but one of its most immediate manifestations in animals is the breath. Hence, learning how to control the breath meant learning how to control *ch'i*, and learning how to control *ch'i* meant, for the Taoists, the possibility of creating a longer and healthier life.

One further note. The translator has used pinyin spelling. Thus, Tao is spelled Dao.

❧

CELESTIAL MASTER

Hsiang-erh Commentary

READING QUESTIONS

1. The commentary is on various lines of the *Tao Te Ching*. Compare the comments to the lines in two or three instances and describe how the author has gone beyond the surface meaning of the line. For example, the author comments on the line "Then all is regulated" by interpreting it as a political comment equivalent to "the kingdom will be regulated."

From *Early Daoist Scripture*, by Stephen R. Bokenkamp (Berkeley: University of California Press, 1997), pp. 78–83. © 1997 by The Regents of the University of California. Reprinted by permission of the publisher. Footnotes edited.

2. What purpose do you think the author had in mind when writing this commentary?

Not seeing that which is desirable will make your heart unruffled.

. . . Not desiring to see something is like not seeing it at all. Do not allow your heart to be moved. If it is moved, restrain it. [If you do so,] though the Dao departs, it will return again. But if you follow the wild promptings of your heart, the Dao will leave for good.

The Sage regulates through emptying his heart and filling his belly,

The heart is a regulator. It may hold fortune or misfortune, good or evil. The belly is a sack for the Dao; its pneumas constantly wish to fill it. When the heart produces ill-omened and evil conduct, the Dao departs, leaving the sack empty. Once it is empty, deviance enters, killing the person. If one drives off the misfortune and evil in the heart, the Dao will return to it and the belly will be filled.

through weakening his will and strengthening his bones.

The will follows the heart in possessing both good and evil. The bones follow the belly in accommodating pneuma. When a strong will produces evil, the pneumas depart and the bones are desiccated. If one weakens the evil will, the pneumas return and marrow fills the bones.

He constantly causes the people to be without knowledge, without desire;

When the Dao is cut off and does not circulate, deviant writings flourish and bribery arises. Then the people contend in their avarice and in their desire to study these writings. Consequently, their bodies are placed into grave danger. Such things should be prohibited. The people should not know of deviant writings; nor should they covet precious goods. Once this is accomplished, the kingdom will be easy to rule. The transformative influence of those above over those below will be like a wind through the slender grasses. If you wish this, the essential thing is that you should know to keep faith with the Dao.

and causes the knowledgeable not to dare inaction.

If his highness tirelessly keeps faith with the Dao, the knowledgeable, even though their hearts have been perverted, will still outwardly mark right and wrong. Seeing his highness acting reverently, they will dare not act otherwise.

Then all is regulated.

In this manner, the kingdom will be regulated.

Employ the Dao as it rushes in. Further, do not allow it to overflow.

The Dao values the centrally harmonious. You should practice it in inner harmony. Your will should not flood over, for this is a transgression of the precepts of the Dao.

Be deep, resembling the primogenitor of the myriad things.

This refers to the Dao. When one practices the Dao and does not transgress the precepts, one is deep like the Dao.

Blunt its sharp edges; release its vexations.

The "sharp edge" refers to the heart as it is plotting evil. "Vexations" means anger. Both of these are things in which the Dao takes no delight. When your heart wishes to do evil, blunt and divert it; when anger is about to emerge, forgive and release it. Do not allow your five viscera to harbor anger and vexation. Strictly control yourself by means of the precepts of the Dao; urge yourself on with the [hope of] long life. By these means you will reach the desired state. The stirring of vexations is like the rapid vibrations of lute strings; this is why it leads to excess. You should strive to be slow to anger, for death and injury result from these violent urges. If the five viscera are injured by anger, the Dao is not able to govern. This is why the Dao has issued such heavy injunctions against anger and why the Dao teaches about it so diligently.

The five viscera are injured when the five pneumas [which fill them]—those of metal, wood, water, fire, and earth—are rendered inharmonious. When these are harmonious, they give birth to one another; when they clash, they attack one another. When you give vent to anger or follow your emotions, one of these pneumas will always issue forth. It issues from one of the viscera and then attacks the others. The victorious pneuma will then form an illness and kill you. If you are strong in yang, a declining pneuma will emerge to attack an ascendant pneuma and there will be no injury from the anger. Even so, in this way you are only a hair's breadth from death. If you are weak, an ascendant pneuma will emerge to attack a declining pneuma and disaster will result.

Harmonize your radiances; unify your dust.

When one's emotions are unmoved and one's joy and anger do not issue forth, the five viscera harmonize and are mutually productive. This is to be of one radiance and of one dust with the Dao.

Be deep and still and so perpetually present.

One who is still in this fashion endures perpetually without perishing.

Do you not yet know whose child I am? My image preceded the Thearchs.

"I" refers to the Dao, as does the phrase "preceded the Thearchs." The ten thousand things all alike originated in it, the nameless. It is not yet known which children from which families will be able to practice this Dao. Those who are able to practice it will pattern themselves on the Dao and will be as if they existed before the Thearchs.[1]

Heaven and earth are inhumane; they treat the myriad things as straw dogs.

Heaven and earth are patterned on the Dao. They are humane to all those who are good, inhumane to all those who do evil. Thus, when they destroy the myriad things, it is the evil whom they hate and whom they view as if they were grass or domestic dogs.

The Sage is inhumane; he treats the common people as if they were straw dogs.

The Sage models himself on heaven and earth. He is humane to good people, inhumane toward evil people. When kingly governance turns to destruction and evil, [the Sage] also views the king as a straw dog. Thus people should accumulate meritorious actions so that their essences and [internal] spirits communicate with heaven. In this way, when there are those who wish to attack and injure them, heaven will come to their aid. The common run of people are all straw dogs; their essences and spirits are unable to communicate with heaven. The reason for this is that, as robbers and thieves with evil intentions dare not be seen by government officials, their essences and spirits are not in touch with heaven, so that when they meet with dire extremities, heaven is unaware of it.

The Yellow Thearch was a humane sage and knew the inclinations of later generations, so he plaited straw to make a dog and hung it above the gate, desiring

---

[1] The "Thearchs" (*Di*) were, as early as the Shang period, regarded as the ascended ancestors of the king. From 221 B.C.E. on, living emperors adopted the title. In Daoism, *Di* are the god-kings of the heavens. In this text, the Yellow Thearch occupies a special place. . . . Although these lines are commonly taken to refer to the Dao, our commentator in effect reads them in two ways simultaneously; once as a description of the Dao, and the second time as a description of those who are able to successfully emulate the Dao. This is a reading strategy used throughout the commentary.

thereby to indicate that within these gates in later generations, all would be straw dogs. But people did not understand what the Yellow Thearch meant to imply. They merely copied this practice without reforming their evil hearts.[2] This is certainly a great evil.

The space between heaven and earth, is it not like a bellows?

The pneumas of the Dao reside in this space—clear, subtle, and invisible. All blood-bearing beings receive them in reverence. Only the ignorant do not believe this. As a result the space is here compared to a bellows. When the smelter works the bellows, air moves through the tube—that is, the hollow bamboo pipe—with a sound. [Although there is something there,] it cannot be seen. This is why it is here taken as a metaphor, meant to explain the matter for the ignorant.

Void, it cannot be exhausted. The more movement there is, the more it emits.

The clear pneumas are invisible, as if they were void. Yet their breathing never is exhausted. The more they move, the more it is that emerges.

Those with great learning are again and again depleted; best maintain the middle.

Those possessing great knowledge are superficial and ornate. They do not know how to hold to the Dao or to perfect the body. Once they live out their span of years, they will invariably be "depleted" [i.e., die]. "Again and again" means [that this has happened] more than once. It is better to study life, to maintain the centrally harmonious Dao.

Desiring that one's spirits do not die—this is called the mysterious feminine.

Gu [valley] means desire. Essence congeals to form [internal] spirits. If you desire to keep these spirits from perishing, you should congeal your essences and maintain them. The "feminine" is earth. The inborn nature of its body is stable. Women are patterned on it; therefore [their sexual organs] do not become rigid. If a man wishes to congeal his essence he should mentally pattern himself on earth and be like a woman. He should not work to give himself priority.

The gate of the mysterious feminine is the root of heaven and earth—

The "feminine" refers to the earth. Women are patterned after it. The vagina is the "gate," the comptroller of life and death. It is the very crux [of existence] and thus is called "the root." The penis is also called "the root." . . .

9.3.2 Immortality, Alchemy, and Merit

Taoist claims about people who could live ten thousand years and secret elixirs of immortality were bound to raise a few eyebrows. Both Buddhists and Confucianists scoffed at what they saw as superstition and the sad neglect of morality. The teachings of Taoism were, they believed, inferior not only to their own teachings but to the teachings of many other philosophical and religious schools as well.

Ko Hung (253–333?) took up these skeptical challenges in his *Pao-p'u Tzu (The Philosopher Who Embraces Simplicity)*. He offers a defense of the possibility of immortality, a justification of both external and internal alchemy, a detailed essay on the importance of morality, and comments on the relation of Taoism to other schools. His work paved the way for further elaboration of the Taoist religion and reinforced the notion that philosophy and religion are not as far apart as some might suppose.

❧

KO HUNG

The Philosopher Who Embraces Simplicity

READING QUESTIONS

1. How does Pao-p'u Tzu answer the question about the possibility of immortality?
2. What do you think is the main point of the essay on alchemy?

---

[2] According to standard commentaries, "straw dogs" were dogs made of plaited grass used in a scapegoat ritual. . . . The commentary, in tracing this popular practice back to a misunderstood warning from the Yellow Thearch, indicates at the same time that all who continue this practice are marking themselves as "disciples of the straw dog" and outside of the Dao.

Republished with permission of Columbia University Press, 562 W. 113th St., New York, NY 10025. *Sources of the Chinese Tradition*, compiled by Wm. Theodore De Bary, Wing-tsit Chan, and Burton Watson. Volume 1, 1960. Reproduced by permission of the publisher via Copyright Clearance Center, Inc. Pp. 258–265. Footnotes omitted.

3. How would you characterize Ko Hung's views on morality and merit?
4. How does Pao-p'u Tzu answer the question about the relationship of Taoism and Confucianism?

THE BELIEF IN IMMORTALS

Someone asked: Is it really possible that spiritual beings and immortals (*hsien*) do not die?

Pao-p'u Tzu said: Even if we had the greatest power of vision, we could not see all the things that have corporeal form. Even if we were endowed with the sharpest sense of hearing, we could not hear all the sounds there are. Even if we had the feet of Ta-chang and Hsu-hai [expert runners], what we had already trod upon would not be so much as what we have not. And even if we had the knowledge of [the sages] Yü, I, and Ch'i-hsieh, what we know would not be so much as what we do not know. The myriad things flourish. What is there that could not exist? Why not the immortals, whose accounts fill the historical records? Why should there not be a way to immortality?

Thereupon the questioner laughed heartily and said: Whatever has a beginning necessarily has an end, and whatever lives must eventually die. . . . I have only heard that some plants dry up and wither before frost, fade in color during the summer, bud but do not flower, or wither and are stripped of leaves before bearing fruit. But I have never heard of anyone who enjoys a life span of ten thousand years and an everlasting existence without end. Therefore people of antiquity did not aspire to be immortals in their pursuit of knowledge, and did not talk of strange things in their conversation. They cast aside perverse doctrines and adhered to what is natural. They set aside the tortoise and the crane [symbols of immortality] as creatures of a different species, and looked upon life and death as morning and evening. . . .

Pao-p'u Tzu answered: . . . Life and death, beginning and end, are indeed the great laws of the universe. Yet the similarities and differences of things are not uniform. Some are this way and some are that. Tens of thousands of varieties are in constant change and transformation, strange and without any definite pattern. Whether things are this way or that, and whether they are regular or irregular in their essential and subsidiary aspects, cannot be reduced to uniformity. There are many who say that whatever has a beginning must have an end. But it is not in accord with the principle [of existence] to muddle things together and try to make them all the same. People say that things are bound to grow in the summer, and yet the shepherd's-purse and the water

chestnut wilt. People say that plants are bound to wither in the winter, and yet the bamboo and the cypress flourish. People say whatever has a beginning will have an end, and yet Heaven and earth are unending. People say whatever is born will die, and yet the tortoise and the crane live forever. When the yang is at its height, it should be hot, and yet the summer is not without cool days. When the yin reaches its limit, it should be cold, and yet even a severe winter is not without brief warm periods. . . .

Among creatures none surpasses man in intelligence. As creatures of such superior nature, men should be equal and uniform. And yet they differ in being virtuous or stupid, in being perverse or upright, in being fair or ugly, tall or short, pure or impure, chaste or lewd, patient or impatient, slow or quick. What they pursue or avoid in their interests and what their eyes and ears desire are as different as Heaven and earth, and as incompatible as ice and coals. Why should you only wonder at the fact that immortals are different and do not die like ordinary people? . . . But people with superficial knowledge are bound by what is ordinary and adhere to what is common. They all say that immortals are not seen in the world, and therefore they say forthwith that there cannot be immortals. [2:1a–4a]

Among men some are wise and some are stupid, but they all know that in their bodies they have a heavenly component (*hun*) and an earthly component (*p'o*) of the soul. If these are partly gone, man becomes sick. If they are completely gone, man dies. If they are partially separated from the body, the occult expert has means to retain and restrict them. If they are entirely separated, there are principles in the established rites to recall them. These components of the soul as entities are extremely close to us. And yet although we are born with them and live with them throughout life, we never see or hear them. Should one say that they do not exist simply because we have not seen or heard them? [2:12a]

[From *Pao-p'u Tzu*, 2:1a–4a; 12a]

ALCHEMY

The immortals nourish their bodies with drugs and prolong their lives with the application of occult science, so that internal illness shall not arise and external ailment shall not enter. Although they enjoy everlasting existence and do not die, their old bodies do not change. If one knows the way to immortality, it is not to be considered so difficult. [2:3b–4a]

Among the creatures of nature, man is the most intelligent. Therefore those who understand [creation] slightly can employ the myriad things, and those who get to its depth can enjoy [what is called in the *Lao Tzu*] "long life and everlasting existence" [ch. 59]. As we know that the best medicine can prolong life, let us take it to obtain immortality, and as we know that the tortoise and the crane have longevity, let us imitate their activities to increase our span of life. . . . Those who have obtained Tao are able to lift themselves into the clouds and the heavens above and to dive and swim in the rivers and seas below. [3:1a, 5a]

Pao-p'u Tzu said: I have investigated and read books on the nourishment of human nature and collected formulas for everlasting existence. Those I have perused number thousands of volumes. They all consider reconverted cinnabar [after it has been turned into mercury] and gold fluid to be the most important. Thus these two things represent the acme of the way to immortality. . . . The transformations of the two substances are the more wonderful the more they are heated. Yellow gold does not disintegrate even after having been smelted a hundred times in fire, and does not rot even if buried in the ground until the end of the world. If these two medicines are eaten, they will strengthen our bodies and therefore enable us not to grow old nor to die. This is of course seeking assistance from external substances to strengthen ourselves. It is like feeding fat to the lamp so it will not die out. If we smear copperas on our feet, they will not deteriorate even if they remain in water. This is to borrow the strength of the copper to protect our flesh. Gold fluid and reconverted cinnabar, however, upon entering our body, permeate our whole system of blood and energy and are not like copperas which helps only on the outside. [4:1a–3a]

It is hoped that those who nourish life will learn extensively and comprehend the essential, gather whatever there is to see and choose the best. It is not sufficient to depend on cultivating only one thing. It is also dangerous for people who love life to rely on their own specialty. Those who know the techniques of the *Classic of the Mysterious Lady* and the *Classic of the Plain Lady* [books on sexual regimen no longer extant] will say that only the "art of the chamber" will lead to salvation. Those who understand the method of breathing exercises will say that only the permeation of the vital power can prolong life. Those who know the method of stretching and bending will say that only physical exercise can prevent old age. And those who know the formulas of herbs will say that only medicine will make life unending. They fail in their pursuit of Tao because they are so onesided. People of superficial knowledge think they have enough when they happen to know of only one way and do not realize that the true seeker will search unceasingly even after he has acquired some good formulas. [6:4a]

[From *Pao-p'u Tzu*, 2:3b–4a; 3:1a, 5a; 4:1a–3a; 6:4a]

THE MERIT SYSTEM

Furthermore, as Heaven and earth are the greatest of things, it is natural, from the point of view of universal principles, that they have spiritual power. Having spiritual power it is proper that they reward good and punish evil. Nevertheless their expanse is great and their net is wide-meshed. There is not necessarily an immediate response [result] as soon as this net is set in operation. As we glance over the Taoist books of discipline, however, all are unanimous in saying that those who seek immortality must set their minds to the accumulation of merits and the accomplishment of good work. Their hearts must be kind to all things. They must treat others as they treat themselves, and extend their humaneness (*jen*) even to insects. They must rejoice in the fortune of men and pity their suffering, relieve the destitute and save the poor. Their hands must never injure life, and their mouths must never encourage evil. They must consider the success and failure of others as their own. They must not regard themselves highly, nor praise themselves. They must not envy those superior to them, nor flatter dangerous and evil-minded people. In this way they may become virtuous and blessed by Heaven; they may be successful in whatever they do, and may hope to become immortal.

If, on the other hand, they hate good and love evil; if their words do not agree with their thoughts; if they say one thing in people's presence and the opposite behind their backs; if they twist the truth; if they are cruel to subordinates or deceive their superiors; if they betray their task and are ungrateful for kindness received; if they manipulate the law and accept bribes; if they tolerate injustice but suppress justice; if they destroy the public good for their selfish ends; if they punish the innocent, wreck people's homes, pocket their treasures, injure their bodies, or seize their positions; if they overthrow virtuous rulers or massacre those who have surrendered to them; if they slander saints and sages or hurt Taoist priests; if they shoot birds in flight or kill the unborn in womb or egg; if in spring or summer hunts they burn the forests or drive out the game; if they curse spiritual beings; if they teach others to do evil or conceal their good deeds or endanger others for their own security; if they claim the work of others as their own; if they spoil people's happy affairs or take away what others love; if they cause division in people's families or disgrace others in order to win; if they overcharge or underpay; if they set fire or inundate; if they injure people with trickery or coerce the weak; if they repay good with evil; if they take things by force or accumulate wealth through robbery and plunder; if they are unfair or unjust, licentious, indulgent, or perverted; if they oppress orphans or mistreat widows; if they squander inheritance and accept charity; if they cheat or deceive; if they love to gossip about people's private affairs or criticize them for their defects; if they drag Heaven and earth into their affairs and rail at people in order to seek vindication; if they fail to repay debts or play fair in the exchange of goods; if they seek to gratify their desires without end; if they hate and resist the faithful and sincere; if they disobey orders from above or do not respect their teachers; if they ridicule others for doing good; if they destroy people's crops or harm their tools so as to nullify their utility, and do not feed people with clean food; if they cheat in weights or measures; if they mix spurious articles with genuine; if they take dishonorable advantage; if they tempt others to steal; if they meddle in the affairs of others or go beyond their position in life; if they leap over wells or hearths [which provide water and fire for food]; if they sing in the last day of the month [when the end should be sent off with sorrow] or cry in the first day of the month [when the beginning should be welcomed with joy]; if they commit any of these evil deeds; it is a sin.

The Arbiter of Human Destiny will reduce their terms of life by units of three days or three hundred days in proportion to the gravity of the evil. When all days are deducted they will die. Those who have the intention to do evil but have not carried it out will have three-day units taken just as if they had acted with injury to others. If they die before all their evil deeds are punished, their posterity will suffer for them. [6:5b–7a]

Someone asked: Is it true that he who cultivates the way [to become an immortal] should first accomplish good deeds?

Pao-p'u Tzu answered: Yes, it is true. The middle section of the *Yu-ch'ien ching* says: "The most important thing is to accomplish good works. The next is the removal of faults. For him who cultivates the way, the highest accomplishment of good work is to save people from danger so they may escape from calamity, and to preserve people from sickness so that they may not die unjustly. Those who aspire to be immortals should regard loyalty, filial piety, harmony, obedience, love, and good faith as their essential principles of conduct. If they do not cultivate moral conduct but merely devote themselves to occult science, they will never attain everlasting life. If they do evil, the Arbiter of Human Destiny will take off units of three hundred days from their allotted life if the evil is great, or units of three days if the evil is small. Since [the punishment] depends on the degree of evil, the reduction in the span of life is in some cases great and in others small. When a man is endowed with life and given a life span, he has his own definite number of days. If his number is large, the units of three hundred days and of three days are not easily exhausted and therefore he dies later. On the other hand, if one's allotted number is small and offences are many, then the units are soon exhausted and he dies early."

The book also says: "Those who aspire to be terrestrial immortals should accomplish three hundred good deeds and those who aspire to be celestial immortals should accomplish 1,200. If the 1,199th good deed is followed by an evil one, they will lose all their accumulation and have to start all over. It does not matter whether the good deeds are great or the evil deed is small. Even if they do no evil but talk about their good deeds and demand reward for their charities, they will nullify the goodness of these deeds although the other good deeds are not affected." The book further says: "If good deeds are not sufficiently accumulated, taking the elixir of immortality will be of no help." [3:7b–8a, 10a–b]

[From *Pao-p'u Tzu*, 3:7b–10b; 6:5b–7a]

TAOISM IN RELATION TO OTHER SCHOOLS

Someone said: If it were certain that one could become an immortal, the sages would have trained themselves to be such. But neither Duke Chou nor Confucius did so. It is clear that there is no such possibility.

Pao-p'u Tzu answered: A sage need not be an immortal and an immortal need not be a sage. The sage receives a mandate [from Heaven], not to attend to the way of everlasting life, but to remove tyrants and eliminate robbers, to turn danger into security and violence into peace, to institute ceremonies and create musical systems, to propagate laws and give education, to correct improper manners and reform degenerate customs, to assist rulers who are in danger of downfall and to support those states that are about to collapse. . . . What the ordinary people call sages are all sages who regulate the world but not sages who attain Tao. The Yellow Emperor and Lao Tzu were sages who attained Tao, while

Duke Chou and Confucius were sages who regulated the world. [12:1a–b]

Someone asked: Which is first and which is last, Confucianism or Taoism?

Pao-p'u Tzu answered: Taoism is the essence of Confucianism and Confucianism is an appendage to Taoism. First of all, there was the "teaching of the yin-yang school which had many taboos that made people constrained and afraid." "The Confucianists had extensive learning but little that was essential; they worked hard but achieved little." "Mo-ism emphasized thrift but was difficult to follow," and could not be practiced exclusively. "The Legalists were severe and showed little kindness"; they destroyed humanity and righteousness. "The teachings of the Taoist school alone enable men's spirits to be concentrated and united and their action to be in harmony with the formless. . . . Taoism embraces the good points of both Confucianism and Mo-ism and combines the essentials the Legalists and Logicians. It changes with the times and responds to transformations of things. . . . Its precepts are simple and easy to understand; its works are few but its achievements many." It is devoted to the simplicity that preserves the Great Heritage and adheres to the true and correct source. [10:1a–b]

[From *Pao-p'u Tzu*, 10:1a–b; 12:1a–b]

9.3.3 Immortal Ladies

Fully accomplished Taoist adepts become immortal. When their allotted time on earth is over or when a summons suddenly arrives from the celestial court, the **immortals** ascend from this world to become heavenly hosts and serve in the celestial administration of the universe.

However, as long as these immortals are here and must live among ordinary mortals, they exhibit some very unusual characteristics. They have powers far above the ordinary. They are, in short, supermen and superwomen.

Biographies of these immortals became popular literature among the Chinese and the stories circulated far and wide, much like the stories of saints in the Middle Ages and superheroes in our own time. The story that follows is from an early collection called *Biographies of Spirit Immortals*. Originally compiled in the fourth century, it was lost and reassembled in the sixth century. One of the more interesting and entertaining stories is about "The Lady of Great Mystery." Although women were second-class citizens in ancient China, within Taoism they could attain ranks of great importance, as we shall soon see.

❧

The Lady of Great Mystery

READING QUESTION

1. What religious purpose do you think stories like this served, and what might be their social functions?

The Lady of Great Mystery had the family name Zhuan and was personally called He. When she was a little girl she lost first her father and after a little while also her mother.

Understanding that living beings often did not fulfill their destined lifespans, she felt sympathy and sadness. She used to say: "Once people have lost their existence in this world, they cannot recover it. Whatever has died cannot come back to life. Life is so limited! It is over so fast! Without cultivating the Tao, how can one extend one's life?"

She duly left to find enlightened teachers, wishing to purify her mind and pursue the Tao. She obtained the arts of the Jade Master and practiced them diligently for several years.

As a result she was able to enter the water and not get wet. Even in the severest cold of winter she would walk over frozen rivers wearing only a single garment. All the time her expression would not change, and her body would remain comfortably warm for a succession of days.

The Lady of Great Mystery could also move government offices, temples, cities, and lodges. They would appear in other places quite without moving from their original location. Whatever she pointed at would vanish into thin air. Doors, windows, boxes, or caskets that were securely locked needed only a short flexing of her finger to break wide open. Mountains would tumble, trees would fall at the pointing of her hand. Another short gesture would resurrect them to their former state.

One day she went into the mountains with her disciples. At sunset she took a staff and struck a stone. The stone at once opened wide, leading into a grotto-world

---

fully equipped with beds and benches, screens and curtains. It also had a kitchen and larder, full with wine and food. All was just like it would be in the world of everyday life.

The Lady of Great Mystery could travel ten thousand miles, yet at the same time continue to stay nearby. She could transform small things to be suddenly big, and big things to be small. She could spit fire so big it would rise up wildly into heaven, and yet in one breath she could extinguish it again.

She was also able to sit in the middle of a blazing fire, while her clothes would never be even touched by the flames. She could change her appearance at will: one moment she was an old man, the next a small child. She could also conjure up a cart and horse to ride back and forth in if she did not want to walk.

The Lady of Great Mystery perfectly mastered all thirty-six arts of the immortals. She could resurrect the dead and bring them back to life. She saved innumerable people, but nobody knew what she used for her dresses or her food, nor did anybody ever learn her arts from her. Her complexion was always that of a young girl; her hair stayed always black as a raven. Later she ascended into heaven in broad daylight. She was never seen again. (7.27a)

9.4 TAOISM FLOURISHES

Imperial favor reached its height during the T'ang dynasty (618–907) and Taoism flourished. The founder of the dynasty was named Li, the supposed surname of Lao Tzu, and so he was honored as a descendant of the immortal and divine Lao Tzu himself. He called himself the Most High Emperor of Mystic Origin and ranked himself above Confucius and Buddha. Princes, dukes, and other nobles were required to study the *Tao Te Ching*, and Taoist temples were built throughout the empire. In 742 Lao Tzu's illustrious followers were canonized as saints and immortals, and this included Chuang Tzu (who, one imagines, would have found all of this quite amusing).

9.4.1 The Path

In the mid T'ang dynasty, Ssu-ma Cheng Chen, a famous patriarch of the Highest Clarity school, published an essay recommending the practices outlined by someone called the Master of Heavenly Seclusion. Although we do not know (and neither did Ssu-ma Cheng Chen) who this person is, his or her essay is the first well-organized and clear summary of the

Taoist path. It has remained both popular and influential ever since and its guidelines are followed by practitioners today.

The Master of Heavenly Seclusion

READING QUESTIONS

1. What is spirit immortality?
2. What is the path of simplicity?
3. What do fasting and abstention mean?
4. What is meant by seclusion?
5. How is "sitting in oblivion" related to visualization and imagination?
6. Why do you think Taoists believe that the goal of spirit liberation can be attained by these practices?

1. SPIRIT IMMORTALITY

All people from birth are endowed with the energy of emptiness. Originally their essence and enlightenment are of penetrating awareness, learning has no obstructions, and the "spirit" is pure. Settle this spirit within and let it shine without! You will naturally become different from ordinary people. You will be a spirit immortal! Yet even as a spirit immortal, you are still human.

To accomplish spirit immortality you must cultivate the energy of emptiness. Never let the common world defile it. Find spirit immortality in spontaneously following your nature. Never let false views obstruct your path.

Joy, anger, sadness, happiness, love, hate, and desires are the seven perversions of the emotions. Wind, damp, cold, heat, hunger, satiation, labor, and idleness are the eight perversions of energy. Rid yourself of them! Establish immortality!

2. SIMPLICITY

The *Book of Changes* says: "The way of heaven and earth is simple." What does this mean?

The Master of Heavenly Seclusion says: "Heaven and earth are above my head and beneath my feet. When I

From Livia Kohn, "The Teaching of T'ien-yin-tzu," *Journal of Chinese Religions* (1987) 15:1–28. Reprinted by permission.

open my eyes I can see them. I can speak of them without complex devices. Thus I say: Consummate simplicity is the virtue of immortality."

What path should be used to seek this? He says: "Without seeking you cannot know; without a path you cannot attain the goal. All students of spirit immortality must first realize simplicity. Teachings that are marvelous, artful, and attractive only lead people astray. They do not lead to the root. They could never be my teaching."

3. GRADUAL PROGRESS TOWARD THE GATE OF THE TAO

In the *Book of Changes*, there is the hexagram called "Progressive Advance." Lao Tzu speaks of the "Marvelous Gate." Human beings should cultivate inner perfection and realize their original natures. They should not expect sudden enlightenment. Rather, they progress gradually and practice the techniques in peace. The following five are the progressive gateways to the Tao.

The first is fasting and abstention.
The second is seclusion.
The third is visualization and imagination.
The fourth is sitting in oblivion.
The fifth is spirit liberation.

What does fasting and abstention mean? It means cleansing the body and emptying the mind.
What does seclusion mean? It means withdrawing deep into the meditation chamber.
What does visualization and imagination mean? It means taming the mind and recovering original nature.
What does sitting in oblivion mean? It means letting go of the personal body and completely forgetting oneself.
What does spirit liberation mean? It means spirit pervasion of all existence.

Practice according to these five and perfect step one, then only proceed to step two. Perfect step two, then gradually move on to step three. Perfect step three, then approach step four. Perfect step four, then finally pass on to step five. Thus you attain spirit immortality!

4. FASTING AND ABSTENTION

Fasting and abstention not only mean to live on vegetables and mushrooms. Cleansing the body is not just bathing to remove the dirt. Rather, the method is to regulate the food so that it is perfectly balanced, to massage the body so that it glows in health.

All people are endowed with the energy of the five agents. They live on things that consist of the five agents. From the time they enter the womb people breathe in and out; blood and essence circulate in their bodies. How could one stop eating and yet attain long life?

Ordinary people do not realize that to abstain from food and nourish on pure energy are only temporary measures of the Taoists. These things do not mean that we completely abstain from all grain. We speak of fasting and abstention from food, yes. But we refer to the purification of nourishment and the moderation of intake. If one is hungry one eats—but never to satiation. Thus we establish a balanced diet.

Don't eat anything not well cooked! Don't eat strongly flavored dishes! Don't eat anything rotten or conserved! These are our basic abstentions. Massage your skin with your hands so that it becomes moist and hot! This drives out the cold energy and makes the body radiate with a glow.

Refrain from long sitting, long standing, long exhaustive labor! All these are basic abstentions. They serve to balance and regulate the body. If the body is strong, energy is whole. Thus, fasting and abstention are the first gateway to the Tao.

5. SECLUSION

What is meant by seclusion? It has nothing to do with living in ornate halls, in cavernous buildings, on double matting and thick carpeting. It means sitting with one's face to the south, sleeping with one's head to the east, complying in everything with the harmonious rhythm of yin and yang.

Light and darkness should be in balance. The room should not be too high. If it is too high, yang is predominant and there will be too much light. The room should not be too low. If it is too low, yin is predominant and there will be too much darkness. The reason for this precaution is that, when there is too much light, the material souls will be harmed. When there is too much darkness, the spirit souls will suffer. People's three spirit souls are yang, their seven material souls are yin. Harm them with light and darkness, and they will get sick.

When things are arranged in the proper balanced way, we have a chamber of seclusion. Still, don't forget how various the energies of heaven and earth can be. There may be, for example, a violent yang that attacks the flesh. Or there may be a lascivious yin that overpowers the body. Be wary and guard against these!

During the progressive advance of cultivation and nourishment there is no proper seclusion unless these instructions are carried out. Thus the Master of Heavenly Seclusion says:

"The room I live in has windows on all four sides. When wind arises I close them; as soon as the wind has died down I open them again. In front of my meditation seat a curtain is suspended; behind it a screen has been placed. When it is too light I draw the curtain to adjust the brightness inside. When it gets too dark I roll the curtain up again to let light in from outside.

"On the inside I calm my mind, on the outside I calm my eyes. Mind and eyes must be both completely at peace. If either light or darkness prevails, there are too many thoughts, too many desires. How could I ever calm myself inside and out?" Thus, in studying the Tao, seclusion marks the second step.

6. Visualization and Imagination

Visualization is to produce a vision of one's spirit. Imagination means to create an image of one's body. How to do this? Close your eyes and you can see your own eyes. Collect the mind and you can realize your own mind. Mind and eyes should never be separate from the body; they must not harm the spirit: this is what visualization and imagination are for.

Ordinary people, to the end of their days, direct their eyes only toward others. Thus their minds wander outside. When the mind is concerned only with outer affairs, it also causes the eyes to continue looking at things outside. Brightly sparkling, their light floats around and never reflects back on themselves. How can people not become sick from this and end up dying prematurely?

Therefore, "return to the root means tranquility, and tranquility means to recover life." To recover life and perfect one's inner nature is called "the gate of all subtleties." Thus, with the step of visualization and imagination the task of learning the Tao is half completed.

7. Sitting in Oblivion

Sitting in oblivion is the perfection of visualization and imagination. It is also the utter oblivion of visualization and imagination.

To put the Tao into action but not oneself act—isn't that the meaning of sitting? To see something and not act on it—isn't that the meaning of oblivion?

Why do we speak of not acting? Because the mind remains free from agitation. Why do we speak of not seeing? Because the body is completely obliterated.

Someone asks: "If the mind is unmoving, does it have the Tao then?" The Master of Heavenly Seclusion remains silent and does not answer.

Another asks: "If the body is obliterated, does it have the Tao then?" The Master of Heavenly Seclusion closes his eyes and does not look.

Then someone awakens to the Tao and, in withdrawing, says: "The Tao is really in me. What person is this 'me'? What person actually is this Master of Heavenly Seclusion?"

Thus, self and other are both forgotten. Nothing is left to shine forth.

8. Spirit Liberation

Step one, fasting and abstention, is called liberation through faith. Without faith, the mind cannot be liberated.

Step two, seclusion, is called liberation through tranquility. Without tranquility, the mind cannot be liberated.

Step three, visualization and imagination, is called liberation through insight. Without insight, the mind cannot be liberated.

Step four, sitting in oblivion, is called liberation through absorption. Without absorption, the mind cannot be liberated.

When the four gates of faith, tranquility, insight, and absorption have been pervaded by the spirit, then we speak of spirit liberation. By "spirit" we mean that which arrives without moving and is swift without hurrying. It pervades the rhythm of yin and yang and is as old as heaven and earth.

When the three forces, heaven, earth, and humanity, are combined, changes occur. When the myriad beings are equalized, then the Tao and the Virtue are active. When the one original nature of all is realized, there is pure suchness. Enter into suchness and return to non-action.

The Master of Heavenly Seclusion says: "I am born with the changes; I will die with the changes. In accordance with the myriad beings I move; going along with the myriad beings I rest. Pervasion comes from the one original nature; perfection comes from the one original nature. Through spirit I am liberated from all: life and death, movement and rest, pervasion and perfection."

Among human beings the liberated are spirit immortals: in heaven they are heavenly immortals; on earth they are earth immortals; in water they are water immortals. Only when they pervade all are they spirit immortals.

The path to spirit immortality consists of these five progressive gateways. They all lead to one goal only.

9.4.2 Gods and Goddesses

The gods and goddesses of Taoism are personifications of *yin* and *yang* energy. Although there are many deities of different ranks, two deities—the Lord King of the East and the Queen Mother of the West—embody the *yang* and *yin* forces all the deities represent.

The **Queen Mother,** in different forms, was known as a powerful deity from very ancient times, but she was not paired with her male counterpart (Lord King) until the Han dynasty (206 B.C.E.–220 C.E.). The following biography of the Queen Mother comes from the late T'ang dynasty. It is found in the *Records of the Assembled Immortals of the Heavenly Walled City,* written by Tu Kuangtin (850–933), an important Taoist liturgist and chronicler of the late T'ang.

As you read this selection, you may get visions of the imperial palaces of ancient China. This is not surprising because ideas of Heaven are modeled after human society. So, if you want to imagine heaven, what better place to look than the imperial palaces.

~※~

TU KUANGTIN

The Queen Mother of the West

READING QUESTIONS

1. Why do you think many religions, including Taoism, describe their heavens in such luxurious terms?
2. What is the Queen Mother's life like?
3. What message is contained in the story about the help the Queen Mother gives to the Yellow Emperor?

From Suzanne Cahill, "Practice Makes Perfect: Paths to Transcendence for Women in Medieval China," *Taoist Resources* (1990) 2.2:23–42. Reprinted by permission.

The goddess Mother of Metal is the Ninefold Numinous and Greatly Wondrous Mother of Metal of Tortoise Mountain. Sometimes she is also called the Greatly Numinous and Ninefold Radiant Mother of Metal of Tortoise Terrace. Another common name of hers is Queen Mother of the West. She is, in fact, the incarnate wondrousness of the innermost power of the west, the ultimate venerable of all-pervading yin-energy.

In old times, the energy of the Tao congealed in quietude and deepened into an organized structure. Resting in non-action, it desired to unfold and guide the mysterious accomplishments of creation, to bring forth and raise the myriad beings.

First it took the perfected true energy of the innermost power of the east and transformed it into the Lord of Wood. The Lord of Wood was born on the shore of the Bluegreen Sea, in the void of fresh-green spiritual power. Born from the energy of highest yang harmony, he rules in the east. Because of this, he is also called the Lord King of the East.

Then the Tao took the perfected wondrous energy of the innermost power of the west and transformed it into the Mother of Metal. The Mother of Metal was born on the shore of Yonder River on the Divine Continent. Jue is her surname, and Kou the clan to which she belongs. As soon as she was born, she soared up in flight. Born from the energy of highest yin spiritual power, she rules in the west. Because of this she is also called the Queen Mother of the West.

In the beginning, she derived her substance from great nonbeing. She floated along in spirit and was mysteriously hidden in the midst of the west's confused chaos of primordial energy. Then she divided the pure essential energy of the great Tao, to connect it back together again and form herself a body.

She and the Lord King of Wood and the East rule the two primal energies [yin and yang], nourish and raise heaven and earth, mold and develop the myriad beings.

The Queen Mother embodies the deepest foundation of the weak and yielding; she represents the origin of the ultimate yin. Therefore she rules over the direction of the west. She mothers and nourishes all kinds of beings, whether in heaven above or on the earth below, whether in any of the three worlds or in any of the ten directions. Especially all women who ascend to immortality and attain the Tao are her dependents.

The palaces and towers she resides in are located on Pestle Mountain in the Tortoise Mountain Range, in the splendid parks of Mount Kunlun with its hanging gardens and lofty atmosphere. Here there is a golden city a thousand levels high, with twelve-storied jade buildings and towers of jasper essence. There are halls of radiant lucid jade, nine-storied mysterious terraces, and purple kingfisher cinnabar chambers.

On the left, the palace compound is surrounded by the Fairy Pond; on the right, it is ringed by the Kingfisher River. Beneath the mountain, the weakwater stream rushes along in nine layers, its waves and swells a hundred thousand feet high. Without a whirlwind carriage on feathered wheels, no one can ever reach here.

The jade towers rise up all the way into the heavens; the luscious terraces reach into the empyrean. The buildings' eaves are of green gems; the chambers inside of vermilion-purple stone. Joined gems make colorful curtains, while a steady bright moon irradiates them on all four sides.

The Queen Mother wears a flowered *sheng* headdress and has marvelous ornaments suspended from her belt. Her attendants on the left are immortal maidens; her attendants on the right are feathered lads. Gem-studded canopies glimmer with their mutual reflections; feathered banners shade the courtyard.

Beneath the balustrades and staircases of the palaces, the grounds are planted with white bracelet trees and a cinnabar diamond forest. There are a myriad stalks of emptiness-pure greenery, a thousand stems of turquoise-jade trees. Even when there is no wind, the divine reeds spontaneously harmonize sounds, clinking like jade belt-pendants. They naturally produce the spheric timbres of the eight harmonies.

The Divine Continent where the Queen Mother was born is southeast of Mount Kunlun. Thus the *Erya Dictionary* claims: "The land of the Queen Mother of the West is directly beneath the sun. This place and the subsolar land are the same." It also says: "The Queen Mother has disheveled hair and wears a *sheng* headdress. She has tiger's teeth and is good at whistling." Now, this describes really the Queen Mother's envoy, the white tiger spirit of the direction of metal. Such are not in fact the Queen Mother's true looks!

To ensure her power, the Heavenly King of Primordial Beginning bestowed upon her the primordial lineage record of the myriad heavens and the Tortoise Mountain registers of ninefold radiance. He empowered her to control and summon the myriad spirit forces of the universe, to assemble and gather the perfected and the sages of the world, to oversee all covenants and examine the people's quality of faith.

Moreover, she presides over all formal observances in the various heavens as well as at all audiences and banquets held by the celestial worthies and supreme sages. In addition, it is her duty to supervise the correcting and editing of the sacred scriptures in heaven, to reflect due divine light on the proceedings. Her responsibility covers all the treasured scriptures of Highest Clarity, the jade writs of the Three Caverns, as well as the sacred texts that are bestowed at ordination.

Formerly the Yellow Emperor punished the Wormy Rebel when he rose and usurped power. Before he was subdued, the Wormy Rebel brought forth many magical transformations. He raised the wind, summoned the rain, puffed forth smoke, and spat mist, so that the generals and soldiers of the Yellow Emperor's army were greatly confused. Thereupon the emperor returned home and rested in a valley of Mount Tai. Bewildered, he lay down in deep distress.

Seeing his plight, the Queen Mother sent out an envoy wearing a dark fox cloak to give him a talisman. It said:

Great Unity just ahead!
Heavenly Unity just behind!
Obtain it and excel!
Attack and overcome!

The talisman was three inches wide and one foot long. It shone like jade with a greenish lustre. Cinnabar drops like blood formed a glistening pattern on it. The Yellow Emperor hung it at his waist.

When he had done this, the Queen Mother commanded a woman with a human head and the body of a bird to go to him. She introduced herself as the Mysterious Lady of the Nine Heavens and gave the emperor the plan of cosmic yin and yang. This included information also on the five basic human intentions and the three palaces within. In addition, she bestowed upon him various arts: how to calculate the times of attack and withdrawal with the help of Great Unity and how to control all space and time through pacing the Northern Dipper in the sky. Beyond that, she taught him the way to use a number of talismans of concealment, the five divine talismans of the Numinous Treasure, and the divine writ ensuring the five kinds of victory.

Thus equipped, the Yellow Emperor easily subdued the Wormy Rebel in Middleland. He then destroyed the descendents of the Divine Farmer and executed the Fiery Emperor's great-grandson at Blockspring. Thereafter all under heaven was greatly at peace.

The Yellow Emperor then built his capital at Dripping Deer in the Upper Valley. After he had thus been settled peacefully for a number of years, he received another envoy from the Queen Mother. This time the white tiger spirit came to him. Riding a white tiger, he descended to the emperor's courtyard. He bestowed upon him the cosmic maps of the unified empire.

Toward the end of his years, the Queen Mother moreover gave him the perfect true Tao of purity, tranquility, and non-action. Its instructions were:

Do not stop drinking and gobbling up food—and your body will never be light.

Do not stop fretting and worrying—and your spirit
will never be pure.

Do not stop craving for sounds and sights—and
your heart will never be calm.

No calm in your heart—and your spirit will never be
numinous.

No numen in your spirit—and the Tao cannot work
its wonders.

Success is not in homage to the stars or worship of
the Dipper.

That rather makes you suffer and exhausts your body.

Success is in deepening the spirit powers of your
heart.

There is no effort needed—the Tao of immortality
is there!

Now you can live long!

9.4.3 Ascension

Before you can join the Heavenly Immortals, you
must ascend. Stories of ascensions abound in Taoism and fascinated many because of their miraculous
qualities and for their confirmation of Taoist teachings and techniques. One finds eyewitness accounts
of sudden and unexpected ascensions, and stories of
Taoist masters publicly announcing and planning
their ascension with great drama.

The story that follows (recorded by Tu Kuangtin
in his *Records of the Assembled Immortals of the Heavenly
Walled City*), about the ascension of a Taoist priestess,
is particularly dramatic. Unlike other ascension accounts that indicate the physical body is left behind,
the "Flower Maiden" takes her corpse with her, astonishing all who watch.

TU KUANGTIN

The Flower Maiden

READING QUESTIONS

1. What impresses you most about this story?
2. Many different religions have ascension stories.
   What role do you think such stories play?

From Suzanne Cahill, "Practice Makes Perfect: Paths to Transcendence for Women in Medieval China," *Taoist Resources*
(1990) 2.2:23–42. Reprinted by permission.

In the ninth year of Kaiyuan [721], Huang Lingwei,
known as the Flower Maiden, wished to ascend through
transformation. So she said to her disciples: "My journey to immortality is coming close. I cannot stay here
much longer. After my body has been transformed, do
not nail my coffin shut, but just cover it with crimson
netted gauze."

The next day she came to an end without even being
sick. Her flesh and muscles were fragrant and clear; her
body and energy were still warm and genial. A strange
fragrance filled the courtyard and halls.

Her disciples followed her orders and did not nail the
coffin shut. Instead, they simply covered it with crimson
netted gauze.

Suddenly they all heard a massive clap of thunder.
When they looked at the coffin, there was a hole about
as big as a hen's egg in the gauze, and in the coffin itself
only her shroud and some slips of wood were left. In the
ceiling of the room, there was a hole big enough for a
person to pass through.

They duly presented an offering of a gourd at the
place of her ascension. After several days it sprouted
creepers and grew two fruits that looked like peaches.

Each time the anniversary of her death came around,
wind and clouds swelled up and suddenly entered the
room.

9.5 TAOISM ABIDES

After the heyday of the T'ang dynasty, the fortunes
of Chinese religions and culture faced troubled times
due to a rebellion in 755. By 960 the Song dynasty
reestablished political stability and, realizing the need
for a strong social order, the rulers of the Song emphasized "harmonizing the three teachings."

Many new sects of Taoism sprung up, especially in
South China. Among them was the Complete Perfection or **Perfect Truth** (*Ch'üan-chen*) monastic school,
which emphasized the practice of inner alchemy and
the integration of the three teachings. It obtained a
position of great influence, especially under the Mongol rulers. It still exists today along with the Celestial
Masters as one of the two surviving forms of organized Taoism.

While the fortunes of Taoism have waxed and
waned over the centuries and reached their lowest
point after the establishment of the People's Republic in this century, Taoism has not, contrary to many
predictions, died. In fact, it is making a comeback

as many of its ancient practices have become popular once more as both medical and spiritual techniques.

In a recent visit to the White Cloud Temple in Beijing, home of the Chinese Daoist Association and chief temple of the Perfect Truth sect, I observed many young monks attending the various shrines. There was a steady stream of laypeople offering incense and praying. The temple gift shop sold religious items such as tapes of chanting, statues of goddesses and gods, incense holders, books, good-luck charms, meditation beads, and even a Christian crucifix to hang around your neck.

9.5.1 Floating with the Tao

Ponder the statement "The bird is controlled by the air." Close your eyes and imagine a bird carried aloft by the wind, soaring on the currents. Does it look like fun? Do you feel the freedom? Without flying, the bird flies. Can we live like that?

Wang Ch'ung-yang (1112–1170), founder of Perfect Truth Taoism, thinks we can. Wang studied both Confucianism and Buddhism before becoming a Taoist adept. He recommends to his monastic followers that they read Taoist literature as well as Buddhist and Confucian texts. The influence of all of these viewpoints can be seen in the "Fifteen Teachings," which follows. In it, Wang teaches others how to float like the bird held aloft by the wind.

WANG CH'UNG-YANG

Fifteen Teachings

READING QUESTIONS

1. What are the differences between the two kinds of wandering?
2. What are the ecological implications of Wang's advice about residences and coverings?
3. How does Wang blend the ideas of Taoism, Confucianism, and Buddhism?
4. Do you think this would be a good way to live? Why or why not?

ON THE CLOISTERED LIFE

All those who choose to leave their families and homes should join a Taoist monastery, for it is a place where the body may find rest. Where the body rests, the mind also will gradually find peace; the spirit and the vital energy will be harmonized, and entry into the Way (*Tao*) will be attained.

In all action there should be no overexertion, for when there is overexertion, the vital energy is damaged. On the other hand, when there is total inaction, the blood and vital energy become sluggish. Thus a mean should be sought between activity and passivity, for only in this way can one cherish what is permanent and be at ease with one's lot. This is the way to the correct cloistered life.

ON CLOUD-LIKE WANDERING

There are two kinds of wandering. One involves observing the wonders of mountains and waters; lingering over the colors of flowers and trees; admiring the splendor of cities and the architecture of temples; or simply enjoying a visit with relatives and friends. However, in this type of wandering the mind is constantly possessed by things, so this is merely an empty, outward wandering. In fact, one can travel the world over and see the myriad sights, walk millions of miles and exhaust one's body, only in the end to confuse one's mind and weaken one's vital energy without having gained a thing.

In contrast, the other type of wandering, cloud-like wandering, is like a pilgrimage into one's own nature and destiny in search of their darkest, innermost mysteries. To do this one may have to climb fearsome mountain heights to seek instruction from some knowledgeable teacher or cross tumultuous rivers to inquire tirelessly after the Way. Yet if one can find that solitary word which can trigger enlightenment, one will have awakened in oneself perfect illumination; then the great matters of life and death will become magnificent, and one will become a master of the Perfect Truth. This is true cloud-like wandering. . . .

ON RESIDENCE AND COVERING

Sleeping in the open air would violate the sun and the moon, therefore some simple thatched covering is necessary. However, it is not the habit of the superior man to live in great halls and lavish palaces, because to cut down the trees that would be necessary for the building of such grand residences would be like cutting the arteries of the earth or cutting the veins of a man. Such deeds would only add to one's superficial external merits while actually damaging one's inner credits. It would be like drawing a picture of a cake to ward off hunger or piling up snow for a meal—much ado and nothing gained. Thus the Perfect Truth Taoist will daily seek out the palace hall within his own body and avoid the mundane mind which seeks to build lavish external residences. The man of wisdom will scrutinize and comprehend this principle.

ON COMPANIONSHIP

A Taoist should find true friends who can help each other in times of illness and take care of each other's burials at death. However he must observe the character of a person before making friends with him. Do not commit oneself to friendship and then investigate the person's character. Love makes the heart cling to things and should therefore be avoided. On the other hand, if there is no love, human feelings will be strained. To love and yet not to become attached to love—this is the middle path one should follow.

There are three dimensions of compatibility and three of incompatibility. The three dimensions of compatibility are an understanding mind, the possession of wisdom, and an intensity of aspiration. Inability to understand the external world, lack of wisdom accompanied by foolish acts, and lack of high aspiration accompanied by a quarrelsome nature are the three dimensions of incompatibility. The principle of establishing oneself lies in the grand monastic community. The choice of a companion should be motivated by an appreciation of the loftiness of a person's mind and not by mere feelings or external appearance.

ON SITTING IN MEDITATION

Sitting in meditation which consists only of the act of closing the eyes and seating oneself in an upright position is only a pretense. The true way of sitting in meditation is to have the mind as immovable as Mount T'ai all the hours of the day, whether walking, resting, sitting, or reclining. The four doors of the eyes, ears, mouth, and nose should be so pacified that no external sight can be let in to intrude upon the inner self. If ever an impure or wandering thought arises, it will no longer be true quiet sitting. For the person who is an accomplished meditator, even though his body may still reside within this

dusty world, his name will already be registered in the ranks of the immortals or free spirits (*hsien*) and there will be no need for him to travel to far-off places to seek them out; within his body the nature of the sage and the virtuous man will already be present. Through years of practice, a person by his own efforts can liberate his spirit from the shell of his body and send it soaring to the heights. A single session of meditation, when completed, will allow a person to rove through all the corners of the universe.

ON PACIFICATION OF THE MIND

There are two minds. One is quiet and unmoving, dark and silent, not reflecting on any of the myriad things. It is deep and subtle, makes no distinction between inner and outer, and contains not a single wandering thought. The other mind is that mind which, because it is in contact with external forms, will be dragged into all kinds of thoughts, pushed into seeking out beginnings and ends—a totally restless and confused mind. This confused mind must be eliminated. If one allows it to rule, then the Way and its power will be damaged, and one's Nature and Destiny will come to harm. Hearing, seeing, and conscious thoughts should be eliminated from all activities, from walking, resting, sitting, or reclining.

ON NURTURING ONE'S NATURE

The art of cultivating one's Nature is like that of playing on the strings of a musical instrument: too great a force can break the string, while too weak a pull will not produce any sound; one must find the perfect mean to produce the perfect note. The art of nurturing one's Nature is also like forging a sword: too much steel will make the sword too brittle while too much tin will make it too malleable. In training one's Nature, this principle must be recognized. When it is properly implemented, one can master one's Nature at will.

ON ALIGNING THE FIVE
PRIMAL ENERGIES

The Five Primal Energies are found in the Middle Hall. The Three Primal Energies are located at the top of the head. If the two are harmonized, then, beginning with the Green Dragon and the White Tiger [the supreme Yin-Yang pair], the ten thousand gods in the body will be arranged in perfect harmony. When this is accomplished, then the energy in the hundred veins will flow smoothly. Cinnabar [symbol for Nature] and mercury [symbol for Destiny] will coalesce into a unity. The body of the adept may still be within the realm of men, but the spirit is already roving in the universe.

ON THE UNION OF NATURE AND DESTINY

Nature is spirit. Destiny is material energy. When Nature is supported by Destiny it is like a bird buoyed up and carried along by the wind—flying freely with little effort. Whatever one wills to be, one can be. This is the meaning in the line from the *Classic of the Shadowy Talismans:* "The bird is controlled by the air." The Perfect Truth Taoist must treasure this line and not reveal its message casually to the uninitiated. The gods themselves will chide the person who disobeys this instruction. The search for the hidden meaning of Nature and mind is the basic motif of the art of self-cultivation. This must be remembered at all times.

ON THE PATH OF THE SAGE

In order to enter the path of the sage, one must accumulate patiently, over the course of many years, merit-actions and true practices. Men of high understanding, men of virtue, and men who have attained insight may all become sages. In attaining sagehood, the body of the person may still be in one room, but his nature will already be encompassing the world. The various sages in the various Heavens will protect him, and the free spirits and immortals in the highest realm of the Non-Ultimate will be around him. His name will be registered in the Hall of the Immortals, and he will be ranked among the free spirits. Although his bodily form is in the world of dust, his mind will have transcended all corporal things.

ON TRANSCENDING THE THREE REALMS

The Three Realms refer to the realms of desire, form, and formlessness. The mind that has freed itself from all impure or random thoughts will have transcended the first realm of desire. The mind that is no longer tied to the perception of objects in the object-realm will have transcended the realm of form. The mind that no longer

is fixed upon emptiness will further transcend the realm of formlessness. The spirit of the man who transcends all three of these realms will be in the realm of the immortals. His Nature will abide forever in the realm of Jade-like Purity.

ON CULTIVATING THE BODY OF THE LAW

The Body of the Law is formless form. It is neither empty nor full. It has neither front nor back and is neither high nor low, long nor short. When it is functioning, there is nothing it does not penetrate. When it is withdrawn into itself, it is obscure and leaves no trace; it must be cultivated in order to attain the true Way. If the cultivation is great, the merit will be great; if the cultivation is small, the merit will be small. One should not wish to return to it, nor should one be attached to this world of things. One must allow Nature to follow its own course.

ON LEAVING THE MUNDANE WORLD

Leaving the mundane world is not leaving the body; it is leaving behind the mundane mind. Consider the analogy of the lotus; although rooted in the mud, it blossoms pure and white into the clear air. The man who attains the Way, although corporally abiding in the world, may flourish through his mind in the realm of sages. Those people who presently seek after non-death or escape from the world do not know this true principle and commit the greatest folly.

The words of these fifteen precepts are for our disciples of aspiration. Examine them carefully!

9.5.2 The Great Tao Has No Form

The societies in which we live all have a certain amount of hierarchical structure to them. Some are more egalitarian than others, but all have some sort of structure, formal and informal, from the lowest to the highest levels. Chinese society, for a good portion of its history, exhibits a well-defined hierarchical structure stretching from the poor peasant to the emperor.

When Taoists speak of transcendence, they usually imagine moving up in a way analogous to someone bettering their lot in the social order. The pious

Taoist, however, is bettering his or her lot for all eternity, and the goal is to obtain earthly, then heavenly immortality. However, even in Heaven there is a hierarchy, and there the heavenly immortal Taoist has to repeat the earthly process by diligent work. Is there an end to advancement? Is there a place where the quest for transcendence stops? Is there something so transcendent that one cannot imagine going beyond it? Does one attain it by effort or by effortless action (*wu-wei*)? Perhaps the best way to get "ahead" is to be content with where one is.

The following text is a Taoist liturgical text that has been memorized and chanted in Taoist monasteries since the Song dynasty (960–1260). It is particularly popular in the Perfect Truth monastic school, and, because it extols the virtues of purity and tranquility, is titled *Scripture of Purity and Tranquility*. This text teaches the monks or nuns who chant it what sort of life they should live while in this world by making an analogy to the ultimate transcendent, the Great Tao.

Scripture of Purity and Tranquility (Ching-ching Ching)

READING QUESTIONS

1. What are the exhortations and warnings found in this liturgy?
2. Can you find Buddhist ideas in this text? What are they?
3. This liturgy reveals a quest for transcendence. How would you characterize that transcendence?

The Great Tao has no form;
It brings forth and raises heaven and earth.
The Great Tao has no feelings;
It regulates the course of the sun and the moon.

The Great Tao has no name;
It raises and nourishes the myriad beings.

I do not know its name—
So I call it Tao.

The Tao can be pure or turbid, moving or tranquil.
Heaven is pure, earth is turbid;
Heaven is moving, earth is tranquil.
The male is moving, the female is tranquil.

Descending from the origin,
Flowing toward the end,
The myriad beings are being born.

Purity—the source of turbidity,
Movement—the root of tranquility.

Always be pure and tranquil;
Heaven and earth
Return to the primordial.

The human spirit is fond of purity,
But the mind disturbs it.
The human mind is fond of tranquility,
But desires meddle with it.

Get rid of desires for good,
And the mind will be calm.
Cleanse your mind,
And the spirit will be pure.

Naturally the six desires won't arise,
The three poisons are destroyed.
Whoever cannot do this
Has not yet cleansed his mind,
His desires are not yet driven out.

Those who have abandoned their desires:
Observe your mind by introspection—
And see there is no mind.

Then observe the body,
Look at yourself from without—
And see there is no body.

Then observe others by glancing out afar—
And see there are no beings.

Once you have realized these three,
You observe emptiness!

Use emptiness to observe emptiness,
And see there is no emptiness.
When even emptiness is no more,
There is no more nonbeing either.

Without even the existence of nonbeing
There is only serenity,
Profound and everlasting.

When serenity dissolves in nothingness—
How could there be desires?

When no desires arise
You have found true tranquility.

In true tranquility, go along with beings;
In true permanence, realize inner nature.
Forever going along, forever tranquil—
This is permanent purity, lasting tranquility.

In purity and tranquility,
Gradually enter the true Tao.
When the true Tao is entered,
It is realized.

Though we speak of "realized,"
Actually there is nothing to attain.
Rather, we speak of realization
When someone begins to transform the myriad beings.

Only who has properly understood this
Is worthy to transmit the sages' Tao.

The highest gentleman does not fight;
The lesser gentleman loves to fight.
Highest Virtue is free from Virtue;
Lesser Virtue clings to Virtue.

All clinging and attachments
Have nothing to do with the Tao or the Virtue.

People fail to realize the Tao
Because they have deviant minds.
Deviance in the mind
Means the spirit is alarmed.

Spirit alarmed,
There is clinging to things.
Clinging to things,
There is searching and coveting.

Searching and coveting,
There are passions and afflictions.
Passions, afflictions, deviance, and imaginings
Trouble and pester body and mind.

Then one falls into turbidity and shame,
Ups and downs, life and death.
Forever immersed in the sea of misery,
One is in eternity lost to the true Tao.

The Tao of true permanence
Will naturally come to those who understand.
Those who understand the realization of the Tao
Will rest forever in the pure and tranquil.

9.5.3 Taoist Breathing Techniques

As the twenty-first century opens, Taoist practices remain important as both spiritual and medical techniques. Many exercises aimed at developing and fo-

cusing the body's vital energy (*ch'i*) abound. One of the most popular is called **Ch'i-kung**. Mental control, relaxed postures, and, above all, regulated breathing are paramount features of *Ch'i-kung*. Practitioners believe that by focusing the *ch'i* on weakened or ill parts of the body, health can be restored.

Ch'i-kung's popularity stems, in part, from the experience and writings of Jiang Weiqiao, known as Master Yinshi. He was a sickly child whose health worsened as he grew older. After reading an ancient text on inner alchemy, he decided to practice the exercises, adapting them to his own situation. His health improved, and he stopped the practices. His health got worse again and, at age twenty-two, he caught tuberculosis, a disease that had already killed his brother. He started his exercises again in earnest and was cured.

Master Yinshi first published his guide to these exercises in 1914 under the title *Quiet Sitting with Master Yinshi*. It has been made a part of the supplement to the Taoist canon and provides a particularly clear account of those parts of the exercises involving breathing. The techniques he describes have been modified and applied in a wide variety of settings to help people deal with everything from stopping smoking to battling cancer.

JIANG WEIQIAO

Quiet Sitting with Master Yinshi

READING QUESTIONS

1. Create your own set of reading questions for this selection and answer them.
2. Why do you think these breathing exercises might be beneficial?

Breathing is one of the most essential necessities of human life, even more so than food and drink. Ordinary people are quite familiar with the idea that food and

Reprinted by permission of the State University of New York Press, from *The Taoist Experience: An Anthology* by Livia Kohn (Ed.), pp. 136–141. © 1993 State University of New York. Notes omitted. All rights reserved.

drink are important to maintain life, that they will starve if left without it for a while. But they hardly ever turn around to think about the importance of breathing and that air is even more essential to life than anything else.

This has to do with the fact that in order to obtain food and drink people have to go to work and earn money, so they come to value these things as important commodities. Breathing, on the other hand, is done by taking in the air of the atmosphere of which there is no limit and which cannot be exhausted. There is no need to labor and pay for the air we breathe; thus people tend to overlook the importance of this function.

Yet if you stop eating and drinking, you may still survive for a couple of days, even as long as a whole week. However, if you stop up your nostrils and mouth you will be dead within minutes. This fact alone shows that breathing is far more important than food.

In discussing methods of breathing, two main types can be distinguished: natural breathing and regulated breathing.

NATURAL BREATHING

One exhalation and one inhalation are called one breath. The respiratory organs in the body are the nose on the outside and the lungs on the inside. The two wings of the lungs are positioned within the upper torso so that through the motion of the respiration the entire area expands and contracts. Such is the law of nature. However, in ordinary people, the respiration never expands or contracts the lungs to their full capacity. They only use the upper section of the lungs while their lower section hardly ever is employed at all. Because of this they cannot gain the full advantage of deep breathing, their blood and body fluids are not refreshed, and the various diseases gain easy entry. Any of this has as yet nothing to do with natural breathing.

Natural breathing is also called abdominal breathing. Every single inhalation, every single exhalation must always go deep down into the stomach area. During inhalation, when the air enters the lungs, they are filled to capacity and as a result their lower section expands. This in turn presses against the diaphragm and pushes it downward. Therefore, during inhalation, the chest area is completely relaxed while the stomach area is curved toward the outside.

Again, during exhalation the stomach area contracts, the diaphragm is pushed upward against the lungs and thereby causes the old and turbid breath to be expelled from their depth. Once it is all dispersed outside, no used air remains within. Therefore in this kind of breath-

ing, although it makes use mostly of the lungs, it is the area of the stomach and the diaphragm which expands and contracts. This is the great method of breathing naturally by which the blood and the body fluids are kept fresh and active.

Not only during and prior to meditation should this method be employed, but always: whether walking, staying, sitting, or lying down, one can breathe deeply and naturally in any given circumstance.

Breathing Instructions

1. Contract the lower abdomen when breathing out. Thereby the diaphragm is pushed upward, the chest area is tensed, and all used breath, even from the lower part of the lungs, is expelled entirely.

2. Breathe in fresh air through the nostrils. Let it fill the lungs to capacity so that the diaphragm is pushed down and the stomach area expands.

3. Gradually lengthen and deepen your inhalations and exhalations. The stomach will get stronger and more stable. Some people say that one should hold the breath for a short moment at the end of an inhalation. This is called stopping respiration. According to my own experience, this is not good for beginners.

4. As you go along, let the respiration gradually grow subtler and finer until the entering and leaving of the breath is very soft. With prolonged practice you will cease to be consciously aware of the respiration and feel as if you weren't breathing at all.

5. Once the state of non-respiration is reached, you can truly be without inhalations and exhalations. Even though you have special organs for breathing, you won't feel any longer that you are using them. At the same time the breath will by and by come to enter and leave through all the body. This is the perfection of harmonious breathing. However, as a beginner you should never try to attain this intentionally. Always obey nature and go along with what you can do.

REGULATED BREATHING

Regulated breathing is also known as "reversed breathing." It resembles natural breathing in that it is very deep and soft and should always reach as far as the stomach area. On the other hand, it reverses the movements of the stomach. The upward and downward movement of the diaphragm is accordingly different from its activity during natural breathing. It is called "reversed" precisely because it reverses the pattern proper to natural breathing.

Practical Instructions

1. Exhale slow and far, let the stomach area expand freely, and make sure that the stomach is strong and full.

2. Let the lower abdomen be full of breath, the chest area slack, and the diaphragm completely relaxed.

3. Inhale slowly and deeply into the diaphragm. Let the fresh air fill the lungs so that they expand naturally. At the same time contract the abdomen.

4. As the lungs are filled with breath they will press down, while the stomach, contracted, will push up. The diaphragm is therefore pressed in from above and below; its movement is thereby getting subtler and subtler.

5. When the chest area is fully expanded, the stomach region may be contracted, yet it should not be entirely empty. Independent of whether you inhale or exhale, the center of gravity must always be solidly established beneath the navel. Thus the stomach area remains strong and full.

6. All respiration should be subtle and quiet. Especially during the practice of quiet sitting it should be so fine that you don't hear the sound of your own breathing. In the old days some people claimed that inhalations should be slightly longer than exhalations. Nowadays some say that exhalations should be slightly longer than inhalations. As far as I can tell, it is best to keep their length equal.

To summarize: Independent of whether you practice natural breathing or regulated breathing, the aim is always to activate the diaphragm. In the case of regulated breathing, the diaphragm is worked by means of human power. It reverses natural breathing and thus causes the diaphragm to stretch even farther, to move even more smoothly. For this reason I never enter my meditation practice without first practicing regulated breathing for a little while.

This is also the reason why I have recommended its use in my book. Since its publication many students have begun the practice. Some found the prescribed breathing exercises useful, others didn't. For this reason, always remain aware that even though regulated breathing is controlled by the human mind, it cannot be learned by human means alone. It is not a mere distortion of natural breathing, but its development, and should be learned in accordance with nature.

BREATHING EXERCISES

Both natural and regulated breathing have the following eight instructions in common:

1. Sit cross-legged and erect; take the same posture as in quiet sitting.

2. First breathe short breaths, then gradually lengthen them.

3. All breaths should be slow and subtle, quiet and long. Gradually they enter deeper into the abdomen.

4. Always inhale through the nose. Do not inhale through the mouth. The nose is the specific organ of respiration. There are tiny hairs on the inside of the nostrils which are easily blocked and obstructed. The mouth, on the other hand, is not made primarily for respiration, and if you use it for breathing it will usurp the proper function of the nose. This in turn will lead to the gradual obstruction of the nose. More than that, by breathing through the mouth any number of bacteria and dirt particles will enter the body, and diseases are easily conceived. Therefore always keep the mouth closed, not only during breathing and meditation practice.

5. Once your breathing gets purer and warmer with prolonged practice, lengthen the individual breaths. The limit of lengthening is reached when it takes you a whole minute to breathe in and out one single breath. However, never forget that this cannot be forced.

6. The practice of slow and subtle breathing can be continued any time, any place.

7. During quiet sitting there should be no thoughts and no worries. If you have to pay constant attention to your respiration, the mind cannot be truly calm. Therefore it is best to practice breathing before and after every sitting.

8. Before and after quiet sitting, practice respiration. Pick a place that has good fresh air. Take about five to ten minutes for the exercise.

BREATHING AND THE LOWERING OF THE PIT OF THE STOMACH

In my discussion of posture above [in a separate section], I already spoke about the reason why the pit of the stomach should be lowered. Nevertheless, since this lowering is also of central importance in breathing, I come back to it now. Generally, if the pit of the stomach is not lowered, the respiration cannot be harmonized. Then the effectiveness of quiet sitting will not come to bear.

Repeating thus what I said before, students should pay attention to the following points:

1. During the breathing exercise, beginners should be aware of the pit of the stomach being firm and solid. It thus interferes with the breath, which cannot be harmonized properly. This is because the diaphragm is not yet able to move up and down freely. A beginner should overcome this difficulty with determination and not falter before it.

2. Should you become aware that your breathing is obstructed in this way, never try to force it open. Rather, let it take its natural course by gently focusing your attention on the lower abdomen.

3. Relax your chest so that the blood circulation does not press upon the heart. The pit of the stomach will then be lowered naturally.

4. Practice this over a long period. Gradually the chest and the diaphragm will feel open and relaxed. The breathing will be calm and subtle, deep and continuous. Every inhalation and exhalation will reach all the way to the center of gravity below the navel. This, then, is proof that the pit of the stomach has been effectively lowered.

CONTEMPORARY SCHOLARSHIP

Contemporary scholarship on Taoism is growing by leaps and bounds. More texts are being translated, more detailed histories compiled, more careful philological studies undertaken than ever before. The Western bias favoring the more philosophical aspects of Taoism is slowly giving way to a closer examination of Taoist liturgical traditions. Along with this explosion of knowledge about Taoism, an increased interest in Chinese popular religion has developed.

Increased interest in gender studies along with the new scholarship on Taoism naturally leads to exploring the topic of women and Taoism. In the *Tao Te Ching*, the Tao is often described in feminine imagery and symbolism, and, as we have seen, there have been impressive female Taoist masters. We shall look at one example of scholarship on Taoism and women.

One continuing problem in the study of Chinese religions involves determining the precise relationship between Taoism and Chinese popular religion. Laurence Thompson (Reading 9.1) says they are not to be confused. However, Kristofer Schipper, who is both an ordained Taoist priest and a scholar of Taoism, writes, "Taoism . . . can be seen as the most elevated expression of Chinese popular religion" (*The Taoist Body*, p. 2). The second selection that follows, while not directly treating the problem of how Taoism relates to popular religion, does give us an overview of key elements in Chinese popular religion. As you read it, look for connections with Taoism.

9.6 WOMEN AND TAOISM

Chinese literature tells many tales of women who have learned the secrets of the Tao. The Tao itself is called "Mother," and female divinities generously populate Taoist literature. Powerful dragon goddesses save the world, and Hsi Wang Mu, the Queen Mother of the West, rules over the Taoist immortals. Clearly there is much in the Taoist tradition to interest scholars who are particularly concerned with issues of gender.

Barbara E. Reed, who is a professor of religion at St. Olaf College and author of the next selection, is just such a scholar. She did graduate work at the University of Iowa and at the National Taiwan Normal University. She is particularly interested in symbolism, especially as it relates to women, found in the Chinese Taoist and Buddhist traditions.

BARBARA E. REED

Women in Taoism

READING QUESTIONS

1. What are the views of women found in Taoist philosophical literature?
2. How does the way we think of the relationships between *yin* and *yang* relate to the relationships between men and women?

Reprinted by permission of the State University of New York Press, from *Women in World Religions* by Arvind Sharma (Ed.). © 1987 State University of New York. Barbara E. Reed, "Taoism," pp. 161–166, 172–180. Notes omitted. All rights reserved.

3. How can sexuality be used for religious ends?
4. What role do female deities play in Taoism?
5. Why do you think that there seems to be a more positive view of women in Taoism than in Confucianism?

The Valley Spirit never dies.
It is named the Mysterious Female.
And the Doorway of the Mysterious Female
Is the base from which Heaven and Earth sprang.
It is there within us all the while;
Draw upon it as you will, it never runs dry.

(Tao te ching VI)

Any religious or philosophical tradition that symbolizes cosmic and personal creativity as the "Mysterious Female" has great potential for attracting women's participation. Taoism not only uses female images for creative powers, but also advocates the harmony and equality of all opposites, including male and female. Women's historical fate in Taoism is especially interesting because it developed within the extremely patriarchal culture of Confucian China.

Taoism is the native religious tradition of China. It has shaped Chinese culture along with the native philosophical tradition of Confucianism and the imported Buddhist religion. According to tradition, Taoism was founded by the legendary Lao tzu in the sixth century B.C.E. But its roots are traceable to ancient shamanistic practices, deities, and myths which were incorporated into a rich tradition of philosophy, ritual, and magic. The Taoist tradition has several interacting strands: the mystical and philosophical texts, such as the Tao te ching (compiled ca. third century B.C.E.) and the Chuang tzu (fourth century B.C.E.), the Taoist religious sects dating from the second century C.E., and various techniques of exorcising malevolent spirits and attaining immortality.

WOMEN IN TAOIST PHILOSOPHICAL LITERATURE

The two great classics of Taoist philosophy, the Tao te ching and Chuang tzu, extol the way of nature as the path to happiness. The mysterious way of nature is called Tao. One can know Tao by yielding to and following nature. One should act spontaneously, naturally, without purpose. These two Taoist texts describe similar paths to simplicity and happiness, but they address themselves to different audiences and use radically different styles.

The Tao te ching uses feminine imagery and traditional views of female roles to counter destructive male behavior. Chuang tzu illustrates the Tao by describing anecdotes in the lives of individuals who manifest the Tao.

The Tao te ching is a short, cryptic text addressed to the ruler. One who has the responsibility of rule could, it suggests, create a simple and happy society by allowing the Tao to govern. The mysterious Tao can transform all things spontaneously if the ruler does not intervene with obstructive behavior. The Sage Ruler says: "So long as I love quietude, the people will of themselves go straight. So long as I act only by inactivity the people will of themselves become prosperous" (Tao te ching LVII). To communicate the Tao, the path of quietude and inactivity, the Tao te ching relies heavily on female imagery. Ultimately, the Tao is ineffable: "The Way that can be told of is not an Unvarying Way." But the Tao manifests itself in creativity and in spontaneous, nonaggressive human behavior. The Tao te ching symbolizes this behavior in concrete images from nature: water, the uncarved block, the child, the female, the mother, the valley, the dark, the bellows, the door, the empty vessel, the mare, and the hen. Most of these symbols are explicitly female, and all of them point to the potentiality associated with female reproduction or the unqualified nature of motherly love. Ellen Chen has shown that in many ways the Tao represents the Great Mother, the creative power of the female.

Creation in the Tao te ching is the production of all things from the womb of the Mother. The Tao is named the "Mother," the "dark," and the "mysterious." She is the "doorway" through which things enter the visible world. All things were created by her and continue to rely on her for their sustenance. The creativity of the Tao depends on the womb of creation, on its emptiness, its potentiality. The Tao is nonbeing in the Taoist understanding of nonbeing as the potential for new being —not in the usual Western sense of the negation of being. The Tao as empty has unlimited potentiality.

The Way is like an empty vessel
That yet may be drawn from
Without ever needing to be filled.
It is bottomless; the very progenitor of all things in
  the world.

(Tao te ching IV)

Tao as nonbeing is the beginning of all things and should also be that to which all things return. Unless one realizes that nonbeing is the sacred quality of female creative power, the return to the darkness of nonbeing appears to be a morbid search for annihilation. The return to original nonbeing is truly the return to authentic existence. Perhaps the goal of returning to the Tao is rooted in an earlier worship of the mother goddess. Because the cycle of return is grounded in the creative power of the Tao, it has none of the terror or meaninglessness associated with Hindu conceptions of life in continuing cycles. As [Mircea] Eliade has suggested, the terror of cyclical views of time occurs only when the sacred nature of the cosmos has been forgotten. The Tao te ching does not envision a primordial beginning with specific gods and goddesses. The creative powers of the beginning are instead symbolized by the abstract Mother, the Tao. She provides the comfort and meaning for the return to the beginning.

Nonbeing and being are both described with female imagery. Tao as the nameless (nonbeing) is beyond categories, but in attempting to describe it the text uses images of the dark and mysterious female. Tao as the named (being) is the source of all things. In Ellen Chen's view, the creativity of the nameless Tao as Mother is based on her emptiness, and the creativity of the named Tao (being) is based on its potentiality. The Mother is nonbeing, and her child of unlimited potential is being.

The spirit and creativity of the Mother is also found within all her creatures.

> The Valley Spirit never dies.
> It is named the Mysterious Female.
> And the Doorway of the Mysterious Female
> Is the base from which Heaven and Earth sprang.
> It is there within us all the while;
> Draw upon it as you will, it never runs dry.
>
> (Tao te ching VI)

The Taoist follows the Tao by acting as a child and clinging to the Mother's breast. The way to act in the world is to follow the role traditionally assigned to women in society—to be weak, flexible, and lowly. Creative power comes from these positions, not from positions of strength, hardness, or superiority. "He who knows the male, yet cleaves to what is female/Becomes like a ravine, receiving all things under heaven." The lowly position is identified with women but is advocated for all—particularly for the ruler, to whom the entire text is addressed. If the ruler acts passively, all things spontaneously follow the creative principle within them.

The Tao te ching takes a negative view toward the achievements of traditionally male-dominant Chinese civilization—its books, laws, and travel. And it views the traditional love of the mother as the model for the relationship of the Tao to all creation. The Tao, like the love of a mother, makes no distinctions; it embraces both the "good" and the "bad." One who follows Tao also refrains from judgments and accepts all things that come

from the mother. Traditional sex roles and biological differences are recognized but denied determinative status. All people (male or female) should take the role of the infant clinging to the Mother or of the female animal beneath the male in order to live in harmony in the world and to return to the Tao.

The Tao te ching uses both female biological characteristics and traditional socially defined characteristics to symbolize the Taoist path. The biological imagery of the womb and breast dominates images of the Tao; the social role of passivity dominates the images of the person who follows the Tao.

Chuang tzu does not use female imagery to communicate the Tao. Whereas the Tao te ching uses universal female images abstracted from nature to counter the normal way of perceiving and acting, Chuang tzu teaches in concrete anecdotes. The text illustrates Tao by describing people who have lived in harmony with it. Although women are mentioned, most of the characters are men. But all those who follow Tao act in the yielding and spontaneous way suggested by the Tao te ching. Chuang tzu expands the meaning of returning to the Tao by expressing a joyful acceptance of the mysterious transformation called "death." One should yield to all things brought about by the Tao, even death.

There are two items in Chuang tzu that are particularly interesting for this investigation of women in Taoism. First, Chuang tzu mentions a myth of a utopian matrilinear society in which people "knew their mothers, but not their fathers." Second, Chuang tzu sees no sex restrictions for the immortal beings who are an important part of later popular legends and religious Taoism. Hsi Wang Mu, the Queen Mother of the West, appears as one who found Tao and became immortal. And there is also an old woman with the complexion of a child who knew Tao and tried to teach it to a sage.

The Tao te ching and Chuang tzu both reject the aggressive, highly structured societies of their times in favor of lives of simplicity close to nature. With no value placed on social hierarchy, there is no place for the denigration of women. In fact, in the Tao te ching women serve as models.

YIN AND YANG

The complementary principles of yin and yang are important in most of Chinese thought and religion. They are not unique to Taoism, but in Taoism they are fundamental. Yin is the dark side, the cold, the damp, the female. Yang is the sunny side, the hot, the dry, the male.

In Taoist thinking, yin and yang are the complementary principles of the cosmos. The ideal is balance, not the victory of one over the other. In the Tao te ching the balance is grounded in the yin, which has the lower position. In Chuang tzu the alternation of the two, such as life and death, is accepted as the transformation of the Tao. Neither is superior—the yin state of death is as acceptable as the yang state of life. One cannot exist without the other; they are both part of the wondrous Tao.

The yin-yang duality of balance is strikingly different from Western conceptions of conflict dualism. In Western dualism, the victory of good over evil is based on a conflict that separates everything and everyone into two opposing sides that cannot exist in peace. Violence, whether physical or mental, may be necessary for the victory of one side over the other. There is no room for compromise with the other side—"You are either for us or against us," as the saying goes. This conflict dualism gives great hope to those on the side of "good" because there is the assurance that good is stronger than evil. Good, usually represented as God, will win in the end. The closer the end, the more hope for the forces of good.

Taoist harmony is a radically different goal than the victory of good over evil. It is based on a complementary dualism rather than a conflict dualism. There are two sides, but they depend on each other for their existence. The goal is the balancing of the two sides, the mutual interaction of the two forces. This complementary dualism has been the core of much east Asian religion and philosophy. It is the yin-yang model that originated in ancient China. One attains harmony in society and nature through the balancing of the positive forces of yang and the negative forces of yin. The cooperative actions of male and female, summer and winter, the sun and rain are examples of this complementary dualism, in which neither side is better than nor independent of the other. Yin and yang are viewed as female and male principles or forces, but women and men contain both principles and need the harmony of the two for physical and mental health.

The idea of the balance and relativity of yin and yang is difficult to maintain. In later Confucian thought and in some religious Taoism, yang is evaluated as the superior. In the Taoist quest for immortality, the relativity of individual life and death is superseded by the development of techniques for holding off death by the accumulation of yang. Breathing exercises, special diets, laboratory alchemy, and sexual practices were all developed in the context of yin-yang theory to prolong life and to attain individual immortality.

Even though the desire for the yang principle of life dominates, however, the importance of the yin principle never dies. Taoist techniques for attaining immortality are based on the cooperation of yin and yang and maternal creativity. The union of yin and yang in sexual intercourse is one technique to produce an immortal body and serves as the paradigm for others. In laboratory alchemy, the crucible functions as the womb, the elements of cinnabar and lead as female and male sexual fluids, and the alchemic firing process as the sexual technique. The equal importance of yin and yang is central to most Taoist paths to immortality. Both yin and yang could be absorbed through the skin to further the Taoist's progress toward immortality. The Classic of the Five Sacred Talismans (Ling-pao wu fu ching) of the third or fourth century suggests that the adept "breathe" in yang from the light of the sun and yin from the light of the moon at midnight. . . .

VIEWS OF THE BODY

Religions often associate women more closely than men with the physical body. Whenever body is contrasted with spirit, this association means lower status for women. Fear and guilt about the body is then transferred to the female sex. Taoism does not have a body-spirit dualism. The complementary duality of yin and yang is within nature. The physical world is highly valued, and the physical human body in its most purified form is the Taoist's goal.

The natural universe is the transformation of yin and yang. It is the body of the Tao. The individual human body is a microcosm of the universe, and it undergoes the same transformations, is controlled by the same forces, and is of highest value. The goal of immortality in religious Taoism is not the immortality of a disembodied spirit; it is the prolongation of life in a purified physical body. Just as gold is the incorruptible and highest form of metal, the bodies of the highest Celestial Immortals are of the purest, most incorruptible substance.

The division of male and female in the body of the universe is most clearly the division of Heaven and Earth. Heaven and Earth are the father and mother of the macrocosm and are equally important. In the earliest Taoist scripture, the T'ai-p'ing ching, the Master says, "Father and mother are equally human beings, and Heaven and Earth are both 'celestial.'" The respect for Mother Earth is as important as that for Heaven, which traditionally had been associated with moral law and natural order. In this scripture, followers are prohibited from digging wells because it would be equivalent to wounding one's own mother. People must be content with the natural springs which serve as the nipples of Mother Earth. This Taoist vision of the world is clearly wholistic. Each being is part of the larger body of the universe, and to harm any part of the universe is to harm oneself, one's siblings, or one's own parents.

Taoism views even women's bodies and sexuality positively. Women's menstrual blood is powerful, not impure as in many religions. Menstrual blood is the essence (*ching*) of the woman, which she can use to increase her life span if she can nurture it; semen serves the same function for men. The bodily fluids of men and women are equally valuable as the sources of natural life and immortal life. Both menstrual blood and semen provide the raw material for creating an embryo for an immortal body. Human sexuality is valued as the obvious means of creation and is given religious and philosophical meaning. Sexual intercourse is the primary form of the interaction of yin and yang and thus represents the mysterious Tao.

The female body as symbol for creativity in the Tao te ching is not lost in the religious movement of Taoism. The Tao as the dark womb of creation is often given more mythological form. In a fifth century Taoist text (San-t'ien nei-chieh ching), creation proceeds from nonbeing, which produces the Three Breaths, which in turn produce the Jade Mother of Divine Mystery. The Jade Mother then gives birth to the legendary Lao tzu, who creates the world. In this type of myth, the creativity of the Tao manifests itself as a specific woman—the mother of Lao tzu. Early birth legends of Lao tzu do not mention a father but only his mother, from whom he took the surname Li. Elsewhere Lao tzu himself is Mother Li and gives birth to himself.

If the female body represents the creative power of the Tao, then it could be the model for all Taoists. In some instances, men apparently tried to imitate the physical characteristics of women. This imitation goes beyond the use of women's traditionally passive social role as a model. The Hsiang-erh commentary on the Tao te ching says that men should cultivate a female character, and modern lore tells of Taoist practices leading to the atrophy of male genitals or to old Taoist men urinating in a female position. In Chuang tzu, when the Taoist character Lieh tzu reaches the highest level of understanding he takes the place of his wife in the kitchen, but even more extreme is the case in the *Lü-chu chih* in which the man Lü T'ung-pin actually claims he is pregnant. Pregnancy is a basic Taoist model for attaining immortality. A Taoist, male or female, creates and nurtures an immortal embryo within the corruptible physical body. According to this model, males must become females, at least metaphorically, to achieve their goal of deathlessness.

Sometimes sexual transformation did go the other way in Taoism. A text from about the eighteenth century proposes Hsi Wang Mu's ethical and physiological path to immortality specifically to women Taoists, but the end of the path is the rejuvenated form of a young boy rather than a young girl.

FEMALE ADEPTS

Women such as Hsi Wang Mu attained the secret of Tao and thus immortality in legendary times. Chinese literature is full of women who have learned the secrets of Tao in historical times, either accidentally or through the study of alchemy or meditation. One source for these stories is Pao p'u-tzu, written by Ko Hung in the fourth century. He was a scholar who defended the claims of esoteric Taoism, especially the belief that normal human beings can attain the status of Immortals through Taoist arts. He argues that just because some people have not seen Immortals is no proof that they do not exist; they do exist, because people have reported their existence. Some of the stories he offers as proof describe female adepts who have learned the secrets of immortality.

Ko Hung reports a second-hand story of a 4-year-old girl who learned the secret of prolonging life. Her father, Chan Kuang-ting, had to flee from disaster, but his young daughter was unable to make the difficult trip. He abandoned her in a tomb with a few months' supply of food and drink and then fled. After three years the father returned and went to the tomb to collect his daughter's bones for burial. At the tomb he found his daughter alive and well. She explained that at first she was hungry but that then she imitated a large tortoise in the corner of the tomb that stretched its neck and swallowed its own breath. This story is used to prove that tortoises, known for their longevity in China, possess specific techniques leading to long life. It also demonstrates that gender is not relevant to the ability to master the Taoist arts leading to extreme longevity.

Another story tells of an amazing 200-year-old woman captured by hunters during the Han dynasty (202 B.C.E.–220 C.E.). She was naked and covered with thick black hair. When questioned, she told her unusual story.

> I was originally a Ch'in concubine. Learning that with the arrival of bandits from the East the King of Ch'in would surrender and the palace would be burned, I became frightened and ran away to the mountains where I famished for lack of food. I was on the point of dying when an old man taught me how to eat the leaves and fruits of pines. At first it

was bitter and unpleasant, but I gradually grew used to it until it produced lack of hunger and thirst. In the winter I suffered no cold, and in the summer I felt no heat.

Unfortunately this woman, who proved to be nearing immortality, was taken back to the court and fed a normal diet, whereupon she lost her hair and died. Ko Hung tells us that if left alone she would have become an Immortal.

The last story of a woman using Taoist arts in Pao p'u-tzu is that of a girl from a family who possessed the esoteric knowledge of Taoist alchemy. A Han courtier, Ch'eng Wei, married her but failed to convince her to give him the secrets. She believed her own efforts in the laboratory were successful because she was fated to master the Tao, but she did not believe that he was so fated. He harassed her to give him the secrets until she went crazy, fled, and later died.

A tale from the I-yüan gives further evidence of female adepts. The tale tells of a shrine to a certain Lady Mei-ku in the third century B.C.E. Mei-ku was an accomplished Taoist master who could walk on water. She once broke the law of the Tao, and her husband killed her in rage and threw her body in a lake. A shaman placed her corpse in a lakeside shrine, and thereafter she would appear twice a month standing on the water. Fishing and hunting were then prohibited in this area because the shaman said that Lady Mei-ku hated to see animals suffer and die as she had.

These four stories have one thing in common: all the women have experienced crises within a family relationship. The crisis that motivates or ends the practice of Taoist arts is caused by a male member of her family—father, husband, or patron/lover. These stories linking the practice of Taoist arts with family crises and the need for survival are similar to the stories of modern shamanesses who seek communication with the spirits only after family crises and financial necessity.

Not all women experienced crises in their search for the secrets of the Tao. The Taoist canon contains several texts that describe meditation techniques for any woman to follow. Women are important in these meditation texts as both practitioners and as representations of visualized deities.

The meditation techniques of religious Taoism demonstrate that the spiritual powers are not identified with one sex. The spirits that rule the internal world of the body and the external world of the universe are both male and female. Neither immortality nor spiritual powers are gender specific. The female spirits include various jade maidens, fairies, goddesses, and powerful spirit-generals who aid women and men in their meditation. These female spiritual beings are as diverse as the male spirits. Many are beautiful and even erotic maidens. Some are terrifying and ugly female spirits. An example of the diversity is found in Michael Saso's description of a ritual to counter black magic used by a contemporary Taoist priest. Of the six spirit-generals called on to fight the battle against evil, two are women. General Hsiao-lieh is a beautiful woman: "She is eight feet tall, and her face is white and clear complexioned, with pretty features and delicate eyes." General Kang-Hsien is hideous: "She is ten feet tall, with the face of an ugly woman, yellow hair, and large protruding white teeth." However, although differing in beauty, both women are courageous and strong. Here beauty is not associated with weakness.

Some meditation texts have separate spirits for women and men. The goals and techniques of the meditation are the same; only the register of spirits to be visualized differs. In the T'ai-p'ing ching women and men may both meditate on the Primordial one, or women may visualize the internal spirits that control the body as female and the men may visualize them as male. Another example of separate but equal participation in meditation requires marriage for the highest level of participation. When first initiated into the sect, young children receive a register of 1 or more spirit generals for meditation. At the second childhood initiation, they receive a register of 10 generals. At adolescence, sex distinctions begin, and women receive a register of 75 Superior Powers while the men receive 75 Superior Immortals. The highest station is not for the individual but for the married couple whose combined register amounts to 150 spirit generals. This practice follows the model of the complementarity of male and female, yang and yin, in which both are equal and necessary.

Sexual techniques were also used to prolong life and sometimes even to form an incorruptible embryo for a new existence. The state of Taoist texts and current research make it difficult to fully understand women's participation in the sexual techniques or their understanding of them. Much literature focuses on male techniques of preventing ejaculation and using the yang semen and the yin essence absorbed from the female during intercourse. All people have an essence within them, and when it is exhausted, they die. The essence for the man is his semen; the essence for the woman is her menstrual blood. Sexual intercourse is important for the nourishing of the essence, but only if it is done right. The Immortal P'eng-tsu recommends to men that they choose young women who do not know the techniques themselves because women who know the technique will seek to prolong their own lives and not give up their essence. The physical techniques for women are not as clear as the suggested male techniques for preventing ejaculation. But women were obviously using these techniques for their own benefit, as they used other Taoist meditative disciplines. Lest these Taoists seem to be involved in continual sexual orgies, we must add that the texts contain many restrictions limiting when these practices could be performed. The restricted days, based on regular monthly and yearly prohibitions, number over two hundred a year. In addition, there are restrictions based on weather and personal circumstances that reduce the possible days to only a few per year.

Taoist women found communal living most conducive to following these methods leading to immortality. Life in convents appealed even to high-ranking women during the T'ang dynasty (618–907 C.E.). Daughters of T'ang emperors T'ai Tsung and Jui Tsung chose to become Taoist priestesses. A new convent was built for Jui Tsung's daughters, who took the Taoist titles "Jade Realized Princess" and "Golden Transcendent Princess." Many T'ang Taoist priestesses were known for their beauty and dressed in the same rich costumes worn by the immortal goddesses whom they sought to imitate. T'ang poetry depicts them in their crowns and splendid cloaks as they seek their true love—immortality:

> To go off in search of transcendence—
> Halcyon filigrees and golden comb are discarded:
> She enters among the steep tors;
> Fog rolls up—as her yellow net-gauze cloak;
> Clouds sculptured—as her white jade crown.

Sexual intercourse was one form of inner alchemy practiced in Taoist convents that created, not surprisingly, suspicion and hostility in outsiders. This form was later superceded by an inner alchemy for combining the yin and yang within a woman's own body without intercourse. A text written around 1798 by Liu I-ming explains that a woman's menstrual blood alone was enough to create an immortal body. By this time, Confucian and Buddhist influences had permeated Taoist communal life. A list of rules for Taoist nuns from the late eighteenth century requires them to abstain from wine and meat, remain celibate, and preserve their hymens if possible.

Even with the increased restrictions, some Chinese continued to see Taoist nuns as models of transcendence. Liu T'ieh-yün (1857–1909) in the last chapters of his novel *The Travels of Lao Ts'an* (translated as "A nun of Taishan" by Lin Yutang, 1950), depicted a young Taoist nun as the embodiment of the freedom, self-determination, and compassion that he sought in a new China.

FEMALE DEITIES

Taoist texts, Chinese mythology, and popular literature are filled with female divinities. Most have been related to Taoism at either the popular level or in the rituals. Ancient China was filled with powerful dragon women, river goddesses, and rain goddesses who lived on the cloudy peaks of mountains. Edward Schafer has shown how the state cult of medieval China turned these goddesses into abstract and asexual deities and how T'ang prose and poetry depicted them as man-destroying evil creatures often disguised as beautiful women.

One example of a transformed creature is Nü-kua, a dragon goddess who, according to ancient Chinese mythology, created humanity and repaired the world. Huainan-tzu, the eclectic Taoist work of the second century B.C.E, contains the legend of her saving the world.

> In very ancient times, the four pillars [at the compass points] were broken down, the nine provinces [of the habitable world] were split apart, Heaven did not wholly cover [Earth] and Earth did not completely support [Heaven]. Fires flamed without being extinguished, waters inundated without being stopped, fierce beasts ate people, and birds of prey seized the old and weak in their claws. Thereupon Nü-kua fused together stones of the five colors with which she patched together azure Heaven. She cut off the feet of a turtle with which she set up the four pillars. She slaughtered the Black Dragon in order to save the province of Chi [the present Hopei and Shansi provinces in North China]. She collected the ashes of reeds with which to check the wild waters.

Nü-kua not only saved the world; in another myth, she also created humanity out of yellow mud. The fate of this powerful and benevolent dragon was unkind. She was preserved primarily as one of the three emperors of the golden age—covered with robes and deprived of her serpentine and female characteristics.

Some early goddesses survived better. Hsi Wang Mu (Queen Mother of the West) was first mentioned in Chuang tzu, and a full mythology and cult devoted to her developed by about 100 C.E. Chinese artists depicted her with a royal headdress and seated on a half-dragon and half-tiger creature. As symbols of yin and yang, the tiger and dragon represent the cosmic transformations over which Hsi Wang Mu reigns. Chinese worshippers believed her to be the source of immortality: she could provide the desired potion to eliminate death. Her gift of immortality was first mentioned in the third century B.C.E. text Mu t'ien tzu chuan, which describes the meeting between the divine Queen of the West and the earthly King Mu of Chou. King Mu offered precious gifts, and she responded with the promise of immortality and marriage. Hsi Wang Mu's meetings with King Mu are part of a larger cycle of Chinese myths of seasonal meetings between rulers and goddesses or between stellar gods and goddesses. These myths also reflect the ancient Chinese fertility rites, during which young men and women celebrated the beginning of the new season with poetry contests and sexual intercourse. The seasonal interaction of yin and yang brings both agricultural and human fertility.

The attraction and mythology of Hsi Wang Mu continued, and she became the Fairy Queen of all the Taoist Immortals. A biography of her from the fourth or fifth century describes her life and paradise in detail. Her paradise in the K'un-lun mountains is filled with magical beauty: jade towers, silk tents, charming music, and the youthful men and women who serve as attendants for the benevolent Queen. Hsi Wang Mu was also known for her concern for women's problems: she was invoked in Taoist rituals to dispel the White Tiger deity who causes miscarriages in women. Hsi Wang Mu's cult did not survive, but she continues to exist in Chinese literature and art as the Queen of all Immortals who cultivates the peaches of immortality. She is one of the characters in the popular novel *Journey to the West*.

Nature goddesses have also survived—the Mother of Lightning, the Old Woman Who Sweeps Heaven Clear, the Woman in the Moon, and the Mother of the Pole Star. Stellar deities are central to Taoist rituals, and the Mother of the Pole Star, Toumu, is one of the most important. As patroness of the contemporary Taoist Master Chuang, she appears on his altar as an eight-armed, four-headed goddess—a deity of awesome power.

Chinese domestic rituals often involve goddesses, usually paired with a male god to reflect yin-yang duality. The kitchen god and his wife keep records of the deeds of the household to ensure that justice is done—his wife is responsible for the records of the women of the family. Another couple, the Lord and Lady of the Bed, are worshipped for fertility and marital happiness. A solitary goddess, the goddess of the latrine, is sometimes worshipped by girls seeking a good husband. Although Taoism has encouraged such domestic rituals, there is nothing in them unique to Taoism.

Two goddesses enshrined in Taoist temples continue to be important in providing protection for the individual. The Empress of Heaven (T'ien-hou) protects sailors, aided by a deity who can see for one thousand *li* (Chinese mile) and one who can hear for one thousand li. Her cult has been popular since the eleventh century.

The Sacred Mother (Sheng-mu) or Lady Mother (Nai-nai niang-niang) protects women and children and is assisted by the popular goddess who brings children to women who worship her. These two Taoist goddesses avert disaster and send children just like the Buddhist *bodhisattva* Kuan-yin, who is given female form in China. . . .

9.7 RELIGION ON THE GROUND

A woman lights three sticks of incense and intones a prayer while clasping her hands above her head. She closes her eyes, joins her fingers, with the exception of the thumbs, at the fingertips, and enters a trance. Two women, who are sisters, wait expectantly. They have asked this woman, who is a medium, to contact their dead mother about some family problems, in particular, why a third sister, who lives elsewhere, has not answered their letters. The medium announces that their mother is occupied elsewhere but that their grandfather wishes to speak with them. Next, the medium recounts a brief history of the family in order to ensure the right spirit has been contacted, and the seance proceeds once all present are assured it is the correct spirit.

This brief description of a seance that occurred in Hong Kong in the 1940s is described by V. R. Burkhardt in *Chinese Creeds and Customs*. There is nothing remarkable about it, and seances like this occur every day throughout the world in many different religious settings. In this case, the religious setting is Chinese, but should this event be characterized as Buddhist, Confucian, or Taoist? Many Western scholars would argue that it is not a part of any organized religious tradition but is a part of Chinese popular religion.

As we noted earlier, some scholars draw a sharp distinction between Chinese Taoism and Chinese popular religion, but other scholars view them as closely related. Whatever their exact relationship may be, there undoubtedly has been mutual influence. The actual religious practices of most of the Chinese people are a blending of Confucian, Buddhist, Taoist, and popular practices.

We have learned something about Buddhism, Confucianism, and Taoism in China. However, we have not focused directly on popular religion. This final essay, by Daniel L. Overmyer, provides a brief description of popular religion.

DANIEL L. OVERMYER

Popular Religion

READING QUESTIONS

1. Where are the activities associated with Chinese popular religion carried out?
2. Who are the gods of popular religion, and what do they symbolize?
3. Who are the demons, and what function do they perform?
4. What is sectarian popular religion like?
5. What role does the Great Mother goddess play in sectarian popular religion?

Nevertheless, even if some intellectuals did not place much emphasis on religion, various kinds of rituals and beliefs continued to be important for the vast majority of the population. As far back as the records go, we read of a variety of religious activities practiced by all except a few of the more strict scholars, priests, monks, including ancestor worship, sacrifices to spirits of sacred objects and places, belief in ghosts and demons, **exorcism,** divination, and the use of spirit-mediums. By the eleventh century (Song period) these practices had been blended together with Buddhist ideas of karma and rebirth and Daoist teachings about many levels of gods to form the popular religious system common from then on. Chinese popular religion is carried out in the midst of ordinary social life, in family, village, and city neighborhoods. It has no full-time specialists but is led by people who have other jobs, such as a farmer who may serve on a temple managerial committee, or a mechanic who works as a spirit-medium at night. There are popular religious temples where the gods are believed to live, but they usually have no resident clergy, just a caretaker or two. They are run and paid for by local people, who hire Daoist priests or Buddhist monks to perform special rituals. Worship in these temples is by individuals or families in the area who bring food offerings and incense to pray for blessings whenever they feel the need, though most come on the first or fifteenth of the

Pages 51–54 from *Religions of China: The World as a Living System* by Daniel L. Overmyer. Copyright © 1986 by Daniel L. Overmyer. Reprinted by permission of HarperCollins Publishers, Inc.

lunar month or on festival days. In such temples there are no congregations or group worship, and usually no reciting of scriptures. In any event, most popular rituals are done at home before the family altar or at the shrine of the locality god who is responsible just for one field or neighborhood.

The gods of popular religion are almost all the spirits of former human beings who have been deified, unlike the star gods of Daoism or the natural powers worshiped in the state religion. Since these gods were once human, they understand the needs of their worshipers, and furthermore they need their offerings and recognition if they are to keep their position as gods. Under Daoist influence popular gods were organized into a system like offices in a bureaucracy, each responsible for a specific function, such as healing smallpox, bringing children, or protecting fishermen. This system is ruled by the **Jade Emperor** in heaven, parallel to the emperor on earth. The Jade Emperor appoints the spirits of virtuous people to divine offices, which they hold temporarily until they are promoted for doing well or demoted for not being effective. In fact, if people feel their prayers are not being answered, they can abandon a god, or even a temple, and look for aid somewhere else. The offices remain much the same, but gods to fill them appear and disappear.

These gods are symbols of order, and many of them are believed to be equipped with weapons and celestial troops, as are some Daoist deities as well. Such force is necessary because beneath the gods is a vast array of demons, hostile influences that bring disease, suffering, and death—in a word, disorder. Ultimately the gods are more powerful, but these demons are violent and unruly and can be subdued only through repeated commands and dramatic rituals of exorcism. Most demons, or *gui,* are the spirits of the restless dead who died unjustly or whose bodies are not properly cared for; they cause disruption in order to draw attention to their problems. Other demons represent natural forces that can be dangerous, such as mountains and wild animals. Since these harmful spirits are believed to cause most illnesses, fires, and destructive weather, much effort is devoted to keeping them under control. A common method for driving them away is for a spirit-medium or Daoist priest to write out a charm in the name of a powerful god, a charm that is really a command such as might be issued by an emperor. Such a charm says something like, "I, the Jade Emperor, hereby order the evil and crooked forces causing this illness to leave immediately. This order has the power to smash and drive away all demons." The priest reads the charm aloud, then burns it so that its message is communicated to the sky through the

smoke. There is a dramatic split in popular religion between the forces of good and evil. Most people in China
had to struggle just to survive every day, so they easily
felt threatened and did all they could to fight back, from
working hard in their fields and protesting against unfair landlords to hiring a spirit-medium to heal a daughter's fever. This spirit of struggle has a lot to do with the
success of Chinese people today.

There is another kind of Chinese popular religion,
organized as sects or denominations similar to Protestant Christian groups in North America and Europe that
are led and supported by ordinary people. These sects,
still active in Taiwan, have their own books of scripture,
which they chant or sing from in group worship. People
join these associations as individuals looking for their
own religious satisfaction, whereas in general popular
religion there are no members, just families who worship
in a village temple because they happen to live there.
The sects go back in Chinese history to groups like the
Yellow Turbans at the end of the Han dynasty, but they
took their present shape in the thirteenth century under
Buddhist influence. Some evangelistic monks started organizing groups of followers outside the monasteries,
teaching them Buddhist beliefs in simple form, mostly
about Amitabha's paradise. These groups grew so rapidly
that more conservative monks became jealous and reported them to the government, which outlawed them
because it was uneasy about any organized associations
among the people. Once the sects were declared illegal,
it was difficult for orthodox monks to work with them,
so they were left on their own, They picked up a lot of
ideas from Daoism and popular religion and tried to
protect themselves by forming communes to raise their
own food. When they were attacked by police or troops,
some of them resisted with weapons, and even raided
towns themselves; the government considered them just
bandits or rebels. Perhaps because of this pressure, some
sects started emphasizing Maitreya, the future Buddha, whom they said was coming soon to bring in a new
world where they would be safe and happy. In the fourteenth century a few sects rebelled against the Mongols
in the name of Maitreya, which confirmed their bad
reputation with the government.

However, for the most part, the sects were peaceful
and provided a way for some people to be more religious
if they wanted to be and go directly to paradise at death,
without going through purgatory first. By the sixteenth
century the beliefs of most of these groups were centered
on a great mother goddess who created the world and
humankind and loves everybody as her own children.
Unfortunately her children have forgotten the Mother,
their real parent, and where they came from, and so they
lead sinful lives and get into trouble because of sex,
drinking, dishonesty, and stealing. Sectarian scriptures
were regarded as having been revealed by the Mother or
her messengers to remind people of who they are, how
they should live, and how they can be saved. Those who
believe the message should join the sect and share the
good news with others. These scriptures were passed on
from one sect leader to the next and used as the basis of
preaching, ritual, and discussion. Sect members were
supposed to be more pious and good than their neighbors; their perception of themselves was very different
from that of the government.

KEY TERMS AND CONCEPTS

Note: See the Key Terms and Concepts and the Pronunciation Guide at the end of chapter 8 for more
information on Chinese words and meanings.

Celestial Masters A Taoist school still in existence
whose leaders trace their lineage to Chang Tao-
ling, who first claimed **Lao Tzu** appeared to him
in 142.

chai Rituals and prayers offered for individuals
and intended to secure good fortune and other
blessings.

chiao A major Taoist ritual in which the priest renews a community's beneficial relationship or covenant with the Three Pure Ones who are supreme
Taoist deities and a source of blessings.

Ch'i-kung Breathing techniques designed to promote a healthy and peaceful life.

Chuang Tzu The name of an early Chinese philosopher and the title of a book attributed to him.

ecstatic journey An elaborate visualization practice
involving out-of-body experiences and marvelous
travels. It probably relates to ancient shamanistic
practices.

exorcism The ritual expulsion of evil spirits or demons from a person or place.

fa-shih Taoist specialists in the occult or hidden sciences who cannot perform the greater liturgies
such as the *chiao.*

Field of Cinnabar The head, chest, and abdomen
are important power areas in inner alchemy and
associated with the cinnabar (mercuric sulfide) of
outer alchemy.

fu Written talismans or charms used in Taoist
rituals.

Highest Clarity One of the more important Taoist sects (*Shang Ch'ing*) that no longer exists, but
whose writings and practices are still part of the
Taoist canon.

immortals Humans who have become deified. They may live on earth and/or in the celestial realms. Some function as patrons of various professions and crafts.

Jade Emperor The ruler of the gods and supreme deity of popular Chinese religion.

Lao Tzu Legendary Chinese philosopher who supposedly authored the *Tao Te Ching*, a basic text in Taoism.

macrocosm The universe viewed as a whole. In other words, the cosmic large scale structure or order.

microcosm Some part of the universe thought to mirror in structure the whole of the universe. For example, some think that human beings or society reflect the cosmic structure.

nei-tan The practice of inner or spiritual alchemy whose purpose is to transform a mortal into an immortal.

Perfect Truth A monastic school of Taoism dating from the thirteenth century and still in existence.

p'u-tu A Buddhist term used by Taoists to refer to the great feast for the dead offered at the close of a *chai* ritual.

Queen Mother of the West The designation for an important Taoist goddess.

t'ai-chi ch'üan A Chinese form of exercise consisting of slow-motion ballet movements and coordinated breathing. Sometimes called "Chinese boxing."

Tao Te Ching (*The Way and Its Power*) One of the classics of Taoism. Authorship is unknown, but it is attributed to **Lao Tzu.** Sometimes titled *Lao Tzu.*

T'ien Shih Means "Master Designated by the Heavens" and is usually shortened to Heavenly or Celestial Masters. It is a title that Chang Tao-ling, founder of the Celestial Masters school, assumed and has been passed on to his successors.

wai-tan Outer alchemical practices.

wu-wei Literally means "no action" and is used by Taoists to describe how the Tao "acts" and how the ideal human should learn to act. Primarily refers to acting without force or artificial constraint.

SUGGESTIONS FOR FURTHER READING

Baldrian, Farzeen. "Taoism." In *The Encyclopedia of Religion*, edited by Mircea Eliade, vol. 14, pp. 288– 306. New York: Macmillan, 1987. Articles include an overview of major ideas and the history of Taoist development and literature.

Ching, Julia. *Chinese Religions.* Maryknoll, N.Y.: Orbis Books, 1993. Chapters 5 and 6 provide a good overview of Taoism.

Cleary, Thomas, ed. *Immortal Sisters: Secrets of Taoist Women.* Boston: Shambhala, 1989. Translations of texts by and about Taoist women.

Kohn, Livia. *Early Chinese Mysticism: Philosophy and Soteriology in the Taoist Tradition.* Princeton, N.J.: Princeton University Press, 1992. A good but advanced study of Taoist mysticism and theories of salvation (soteriology) by a leading scholar.

Robinet, Isabelle. *Taoism: Growth of a Religion.* Translated by Phyllis Brooks. Stanford, Calif.: Stanford University Press, 1997. Although advanced this is one of the best studies available on the history of Taoism. Robinet has been called one of the foremost contemporary scholars of Taoism.

Saso, Michael R. *Blue Dragon, White Tiger: Taoist Rites of Passage.* Washington, D.C.: Taoist Center, 1990. A study of Taoist ceremonies by a scholar and a Taoist.

Schipper, Kristofer. *The Taoist Body.* Translated by Karen C. Duval. Berkeley: University of California Press, 1993. First published in French in 1982, this important study combines the insights of a scholar with the views of an ordained Taoist priest.

RESEARCH PROJECTS

1. Do a comparative study of Taoist and Christian mysticism.
2. Do a Web search for information about Taoism, and write a report describing and evaluating some of the resources you find.
3. View the video *The Dragon Boat Festival*, which is about the life and death of Ch'ü Yüan, who is credited with the *Songs of Chu* (*Songs of the South*). Write a report on what you learn. (The video is available from the University of Washington Press, P.O. Box 50096, Seattle, WA, 98145.)

PART 4

WAYS OF BEING RELIGIOUS
ORIGINATING IN THE NEAR EAST

10

Jewish Ways of Being Religious

INTRODUCTION

"Hear, O Israel: The Lord our God, the Lord is One."

The most important teaching of Judaism is that there is one God. This belief is stated in the Shema ("Hear") quoted above. The **Shema,** however, is more than just this sentence. It refers to a group of prayers recited morning and evening that declare God is the creator of heaven and earth, the revealer of the Torah, and the redeemer of Israel. The prayers address God, but in the prayers God also addresses the people of God, Israel. To pray is to speak, but it is also to listen.

Judaism proclaims that God's voice is heard in history. It is in the events that constitute the lives of people—in particular, the lives of the Jewish people —that God speaks. Therefore, we must pay careful attention to the history of Judaism, because in a very real sense, that history defines the shape and the life of Judaic religion.

I have been speaking as if there is one Judaism when, in fact, there are a variety of Judaisms (just as there are varieties of Christianity, Buddhism, Hinduism, and other religions) and a variety of Jewish histories. These histories are complex and vary widely from place to place and time to time. In this chapter, we will tell some of the most important parts of these stories.

If the varieties of Judaism complicate our study, so too does the fact that not all people who belong to an ethnic group identified as Jews practice the religion of Judaism. In other words, not all Jews are Judaists —people who practice one or another form of the Judaic religion. While people continue to use the word *Jew* for those who practice Judaism and for those who do not, we must be alert to the ambiguity of the word. We must also be alert to the fact that there are Judaists who are not Jews.

Another factor complicating the academic study of Judaism is that Judaism has long played a role in Christian myth and thought. Since many who engage in the academic study of religion in general and Judaism in particular are Christians or come from a Christian background, they come with preconceived ideas about Judaism and Jews.

Christianity began as a sectarian movement within Judaism. As it moved toward becoming a distinct religion, it struggled to define itself in contrast to its parent religion and, in so doing, painted a negative portrait of its parental home. The "Jews" (confusing both the ethnic group and the Judaists among that group) became the "killers of Christ," the divine Messiah Jesus (a Jew and a Judaist!) whom Christians worship.

The continued existence of the Jews and their continued loyalty to their own religion became for Christianity a sign of stubbornness. The "Jews" were and are for many Christians worse than the "heathen." Many of the heathen do not know about Jesus, but the Jews do and still they remain faithful to their own religion. What Jews see as faithfulness in face of great adversity, some Christians see as unbelief. So, for much of its history, Christianity has been both anti-Judaic (against the religion) and anti-Semitic (against the ethnic group). This is one reason why the Christian German guards at the concentration camps and death factories of the Nazis could gather at Christmas in the midst of murder and sing "Silent Night."

The negative views about Judaism taught by Christian theology, combined with the varieties of Judaism and the ambiguity of the word *Jew*, complicate our study. They do not, however, make it impossible. Balanced analysis, fair and informed interpretations, accurate descriptions, and appreciation of the courageous faith of the Jews are not only possible but also imperative.

MAIN CENTERS OF JEWISH POPULATION, 1991

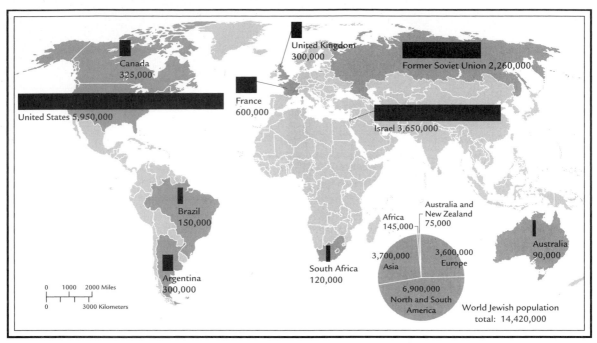

From *A New Handbook of Living World Religions,* edited by John R. Hinnells (Oxford, England: Blackwell Press, 1997), p. 17. Reprinted by permission.

10.1 AN OVERVIEW

A story is told of the creation of the world and human beings who disobey God. A story is told of Abraham who is called by God to migrate from his home in Mesopotamia to become a sojourner in the land of Canaan (the present-day land of Israel). Abraham is promised the land and great blessings and is assured that he will become the father (patriarch) of a great people. The story goes on to tell of Abraham's descendant Jacob (also called Israel) who must travel to Egypt during a famine. There his descendants multiply and eventually become enslaved by the Egyptians. God sends Moses to deliver them from their Egyptian exile and return them to the land promised by God. Eventually, God anoints (*messiah* means "anointed one") a great king, King David, who rules the promised land and the people on God's behalf. Soon disas-

ter strikes and the land is conquered, the great temple built by King Solomon, David's son, is destroyed, and the people are taken into exile once more. They yearn to return to the land God promised Abraham and eventually they do.

So goes the biblical story—the story of exile and return. It is a story adopted by the people as their story. And it is a story adopted personally, by individuals, as a story of their own spiritual struggles and journeys.

Jacob Neusner, professor of religion at Bard College and the University of South Florida, Tampa, continues this story of exile and return in the following selection. He shows how historical events have shaped and still shape the life and faith of the Jewish people.

JACOB NEUSNER

The Four Periods in the History of Judaism

READING QUESTIONS

1. As you read, make a list of all the words and ideas you do not understand or are uncertain about. Discuss them with a classmate, look them up in a dictionary, or bring them up in class for discussion and clarification.
2. What are the "five facts of political history" that are crucial for understanding the history of Judaism? Why are they crucial?
3. What is the "dual Torah"?
4. What are Mishnah and Talmud?
5. How did Judaism respond to the first destruction of the temple in 586 B.C.E.?
6. How did Judaism respond to the destruction of the second temple in 70 C.E.?
7. What is *Tanakh?*
8. In what sense does rabbinic Judaism remain "cogent" for nineteen centuries?
9. What caused the breakdown of rabbinic Judaism in "the second age of diversity"?

I must list the five facts of political history that mark off everything else. These facts derive from the histories of various groups of Jews, in diverse times and places, and govern the history of the Jews and also Judaism from the beginning to the present.

THE DESTRUCTION OF THE FIRST TEMPLE IN JERUSALEM BY THE BABYLONIANS IN 586 B.C.E.

The ancient Israelites, living in what they called the Land of Israel, produced Scriptures that reached their present form in the aftermath of the destruction of their capital city and Temple. Whatever happened before that time was reworked in the light of that event and the meaning imputed to it by authors who lived afterward. All Juda-

From *The Way of the Torah: An Introduction to Judaism*, 6th ed., by Jacob Neusner, pp. 22–34. © 1997. Reprinted with permission of Wadsworth Publishing, a division of International Thomson Publishing. Fax 800 730-2215.

isms, from 586 forward, appeal to the writings produced in the aftermath of the destruction of the first Temple. These writings encompass the Pentateuch—Genesis, Exodus, Leviticus, Numbers, and Deuteronomy—and also important prophetic works. Therefore, we must regard the destruction of that Temple as the date that marks the beginning of the formation of Judaism(s).

THE DESTRUCTION OF THE SECOND TEMPLE IN JERUSALEM BY THE ROMANS IN 70 C.E.

The Jews' leaders—the political classes and priesthood—after 586 were taken to Babylonia, the homeland of their conquerers, where they settled down. A generation later, Babylonia fell under the rule of the Persians, who permitted Jews to return to their ancient homeland. A small number did so, where they rebuilt the Temple and produced the Hebrew Scriptures. The second Temple of Jerusalem lasted from about 500 B.C.E. to 70 C.E., when the Romans—by that time ruling the entire Middle East, including the Land of Israel, mainly through their own friends and allies—put down a Jewish rebellion and, in the war, destroyed Jerusalem again. The second destruction proved final and marked the beginning of the Jews' history as a political entity defined in social and religious terms, but not in territorial ones. That is, the Jews formed a distinct religious-social group, but all of them did not live in any one place, and some of them lived nearly everywhere in the West, within the lands of Christendom and Islam alike.

THE CONQUEST OF THE NEAR AND MIDDLE EAST AND NORTH AFRICA BY THE MUSLIMS IN 640 C.E.

The definition of the world in which the Jews would live was completed when the main outlines of Western civilization had been worked out. These encompassed Christendom, in Western and Eastern Europe, inclusive of the world west of the Urals in Russia; and Islam, in command of North Africa and the Near and Middle East, later destined to conquer India and much of the Far East, Malaysia, and Indonesia in particular, as well as sub-Saharan Africa. During this long period, the Jews in Christendom and Islam alike ordinarily enjoyed the status of a tolerated but subordinated minority, and they were free to practice their religion and sustain their separate group existence. Of still greater importance, both Christianity and Islam affirmed the divine origin of the Jews' holy book, the Torah, and acknowledged the special status, among the nations, of Israel, the Jewish people.

THE AMERICAN CONSTITUTION (1789) AND THE FRENCH REVOLUTION (1787)

The American Constitution in the United States and the French Revolution in Western Europe marked the beginning of an age in which political change reshaped the world in which the West, including Western Jewries, lived. Politics became essentially secular, and political institutions no longer acknowledged supernatural claims of special status accorded to either a church or a religious community. The individual person, rather than the social group, formed the focus of politics. In the case of the Jews, the turning meant that the Jews would be received as individuals and given rights equal to those of all others, at the same time that "Israel" as a holy people and community no longer would enjoy special status and recognition.

THE DESTRUCTION OF THE JEWS IN EUROPE ("THE HOLOCAUST") AND THE CREATION OF THE STATE OF ISRAEL, 1933–1948

In 1933 Germany chose the National Socialist Party to govern. A principal doctrine of that party was that various groups among humanity, called races, possess traits that are inherent in the genes and passed on through time: racial characteristics. Some races have good traits, others, bad; and the worst of all of these "races" are the Jews. To save humanity from this dreadful "curse," all of the Jews of the world have to be murdered, which will constitute "the final solution of the Jewish problem." This racist doctrine, broadly held in Europe and elsewhere during World War II, from 1939 to 1945, led to the Germans' murder of nearly six million European Jews. In the aftermath of World War II, seeking a home for the remnants who had survived, the United Nations voted in 1947 to create a Jewish and an Arab state in what was then Palestine. The Jewish state came into being on May 15, 1948, as the State of Israel.

These events defined an entirely new ecology for Judaism. On the one hand, the problem of evil was restated with great intensity. On the other hand, the social and political life of the Jews was entirely redefined. The issue of "exile and return," paramount at the outset, was framed with fresh urgency, but with a new resolution. The formation of the State of Israel in the aftermath of the Holocaust opened a new chapter in the history of Judaism, but that chapter's story is not yet clear. . . .

How shall we organize the histories of various Judaisms, each with its beginning, middle, and (in some cases) end, into a single history of Judaism? The answer is to survey the long history of Judaisms and find the traits of the periods into which that history breaks down. One paramount fact imposes structure on the history of Judaism: for a long time, a single Judaism, rabbinic Judaism, predominated. Its success in defining the normative faith for nearly the whole Jewish world is marked in two ways. First, that Judaism absorbed into its own system new modes of thought and piety—philosophy and mysticism being the main ones. Second, that same Judaism defined the terms by which its competition—"heresies"—defined themselves. That is, the competition adopted doctrines antithetical to those of rabbinic Judaism, rather than building fresh and free-standing systems of its own. To define the issues of debate means to dominate, and rabbinic Judaism dominated, specifically, from ancient times to nearly our own day, for nearly 1,800 years. When we speak of Judaisms, in both ancient and modern times, we must not lose sight of the fact that, through most of the history of Judaism into contemporary times, rabbinic Judaism defined the norm.

In fact, the history of Judaism is the story of how diverse Judaisms before 70 C.E. gave way to that single Judaism that predominated from 70 onward and of how, in the modern age, rabbinic Judaism broke up into derivative Judaisms and lost its commanding position as the single, defining force in the life of the Jews as a social group. Here we consider the history of Judaism as a whole. . . . Seen whole, the history of Judaism the religion divides into the following four principal periods. (Note that in place of B.C., "before Christ," and A.D., "in the year of the Lord," we use the secular terms B.C.E., "before the Common Era," and C.E., "in the Common Era." They mean the same.)

The first age of diversity	About 586 B.C.E.–70 C.E.
The age of definition	About 70–640 C.E.
The age of cogency	About 640–1800 C.E.
The second age of diversity	About 1800–present

The first age of diversity begins with the writing down, in more or less their present form, of the Scriptures of ancient Israel, beginning with the Five Books of Moses. Drawing upon writings and oral traditions of the period before the destruction of the first Temple of Jerusalem in 586, the authors of the surviving leadership of that Temple and court, the priests, produced most of the books we now know as the Hebrew Bible (the "Old Testament" or "Tanakh")—specifically, the Pentateuch or Five Books of Moses; the prophetic writings from Joshua and Judges through Samuel and Kings and Isaiah, Jeremiah, and Ezekiel; the twelve smaller books of prophetic writings; and some of the other Scriptures as well. During this same period, several diverse groups of Jews, living in the Land of Israel and Babylonia, to the east, and in Alexandria, Egypt, to the west, took over these writings and interpreted them in various ways. Hence, during the period from the formation of the Torah to the destruction of the second Temple, there were many Judaisms.

The age of definition, beginning with the destruction of the second Temple in 70, saw the diverse Judaisms of the preceding period give way, over a long period of time, to a single Judaism. That was the system worked out by the sages who, after 70, developed a system of Judaism linked to Scripture but enriched by an autonomous corpus of holy writings in addition. This Judaism is marked by its doctrine of the dual media by which the Torah was formulated and transmitted, in writing on the one side, in formulation and transmission by memory, hence, orally, on the other. The doctrine of the dual Torah, written and oral, then defined the canon of Judaism. The written Torah encompassed pretty much the same books that Christians know as the Old Testament. The oral Torah added the writings of the sages, beginning with the Mishnah—a philosophical law code produced in approximately 200 C.E.—and two massive commentaries on the Mishnah—the two Talmuds, one produced in the Land of Israel and called the Yerushalmi, or Jerusalem Talmud, circa 400 C.E., the other in Babylonia and called the Bavli, or Talmud of Babylonia, circa 600 C.E. In that same age, alongside Mishnah commentary, systematic work on Scripture yielded works organized around particular books of the written Torah, parallel to works organized around particular tractates of the Mishnah: Sifra, to the book of Leviticus; Sifré, to Numbers; and another Sifré, to Deuteronomy. Also written during this time were works containing statements attributed to the same authorities who stand behind the Mishnah, to be dated sometime between 200 and 400; Genesis Rabbah and Leviticus Rabbah, discursive works on themes in Genesis and Leviticus, edited between 400 and 450; Pesiqta deRav Kahana, a profoundly eschatological treatment of topics in pentateuchal writings, of about 450; and similar works. These writings all together—organized around, first, the Mishnah, and, then, Scripture—comprised the first works of the oral Torah. That is, the teachings of the sages, originally formulated and transmitted in memory, were the written contents of the oral Torah that God had revealed (so the system maintained) to Moses at Sinai. During the age of definition, that Judaism of the dual Torah reached its literary statement and authoritative expression.

The age of cogency is characterized by the predominance, from the far West in Morocco, to Iran and India, and from Egypt to England, of the Judaism of the dual Torah. During this long period, the principal question facing Jews was how to explain the success of Christianity and Islam, which claimed to replace the Judaism of Sinai with a new testament, on the one side, or a final and perfect prophecy, on the other. Both religions affirmed but then claimed to succeed Judaism, and the Judaism of the dual Torah enjoyed success, among Jews, in making sense of the then-subordinated status of the enduring people and faith of Sinai. While heresies took shape during this long period, the beliefs of the new systems responded to the structure of the established one.

The second age of diversity is marked not by the breaking apart of the received system but by the development of competing systems of Judaism. In this period, new Judaisms came into being that entirely ignored the categories and doctrines of the received system, responding not to its concerns but to other issues altogether. Now the principal question addressed by new systems concerned matters other than those found urgent by the received Judaism of the dual Torah, with its powerful explanation of the Jews' status in the divine economy. The particular points of stress, the self-evident answers to urgent questions, came at the interstices of individual life. Specifically, Jews needed to explain to themselves how as individuals, able to make free choices on their own, they found a place also, within the commanded realm of the holy way of life and worldview of the Torah of Judaism. The issue again was political, but it concerned not the group but the individual. Judaisms produced in modern times answered the urgent question of individual citizenship, just as the Judaism of the long period of Christian and Muslim hegemony in Europe, Africa, and western Asia had taken up the (then equally pressing) question of a subordinated, but in its own view holy, society's standing and status as Israel in Islam or Christendom.

THE FIRST AGE OF DIVERSITY (CIRCA 586 B.C.E.–70 C.E.)

The destruction of Jerusalem in 586 B.C.E. produced a crisis of faith, because ordinary folk supposed that the god of the conquerors had conquered the God of Israel.

Israelite prophets saw matters otherwise. Israel had been punished for its sins, and it was God who had carried out the punishment. God was not conquered but vindicated. The pagans were merely his instruments. God could, moreover, be served anywhere, not only in the holy and promised Land of Israel. Israel in Babylonian exile continued the cult of the Lord through worship, psalms, and festivals; the synagogue, a place where God was worshipped without sacrifice, took shape. The Sabbath became Israel's sanctuary, the seventh day of rest and sanctification for God. When, for political reasons, the Persians chose to restore Jewry to Palestine and many returned (about 500 B.C.E.), the Jews were not surprised, for they had been led by prophecy to expect that with the expiation of sin through suffering and atonement, God would once more show mercy and bring them homeward. The prophets' message was authenticated by historical events.

In the early years of the Second Temple (about 450 B.C.E.), Ezra, the priest-scribe, came from Babylonia to Palestine and brought with him the Torah, the collection of ancient scrolls of law, prophecy, and narrative. Jews resolved to make the Torah the basis of national life. The Torah was publicly read on New Year's Day in 444 B.C.E., and those assembled pledged to keep it. Along with the canonical Scriptures, oral traditions, explanations, instructions on how to keep the law, and exegeses of Scripture were needed to apply the law to changing conditions of everyday life. A period of creative interpretation of the written Torah began, one that has yet to end in the history of Judaism. For that time forward, the history of Judaism became the history of the interpretation of Torah and its message for each successive age.

THE AGE OF DEFINITION (CIRCA 70–640 C.E.)

The next great event in Jews' history was the destruction of the Second Temple in 70 C.E. A political and military event, its religious consequences were drawn by Yohanan ben Zakkai and other great rabbis of the age. These rabbis, heirs of the tradition of oral interpretation and instruction in Torah and the continuators of the prophets of old, taught that the God of Israel could still be served by the Jewish people, who had not been abandoned by God but once more chastised. The rabbis in the following Talmudic story—told not after 70 but after a deep disappointment three hundred years later— taught that by obedience to Torah, Israel would again be restored to its land:

When a disciple of Yohanan ben Zakkai wept at seeing the Temple mount in ruins, Yohanan asked him, "Why do you weep, my son?"

"This place where the sins of Israel were atoned is in ruins, and should I not weep?" the disciple replied.

"Let it not be grievous to your eyes, my son," Yohanan replied, "for we have another means of atonement, as effective as Temple sacrifice. It is deeds of loving-kindness, as it is said [Hosea 6:6], *For I desire mercy and not sacrifice.*"

In our own century, we have seen how historical events—the destruction of European Jewry, the creation of the State of Israel—defined the issues that Judaic religious systems would have to address. So we cannot find it surprising that once again a historical event produced a major religious revolution in the life of Judaism. That revolution is embodied in the pages of the Palestinian and Babylonian Talmuds, compendia of Judaic law, lore, and theology produced by the rabbis of Palestine and Babylonia on the basis of the ancient oral tradition and finally edited in the fifth and sixth centuries C.E. Once and for all, the rabbis defined "being Jewish" in terms of laws universally applicable, laws that might be kept by Jews living in every civilization. Wherever Jews might go, they could serve God through prayer, study of Torah, practice of the commandments, and acts of loving-kindness. All Jews were able to study. No clerical class was required—only learned men. So rabbis took the priests' place as teachers of the people.

The Jews thus formed a commonwealth within an empire, a religious nation within other nations, living in conformity with the laws of alien governments, but in addition carrying out their own Torah. It was a commonwealth founded on religious belief, a holy community whose membership was defined by obedience to laws believed to have been given at Sinai and interpreted and applied by rabbinical sages to each circumstance of daily life.

We see, therefore, that the first age of diversity, the age from the formation of the Pentateuch in about 500, to before the first century C.E., was a period in which religious experiences and beliefs of various kinds, among diverse groups, took shape among the Jewish people, the people of ancient (and modern) Israel. One principal development in that long period was the Hebrew Scriptures, called by Christians the Old Testament and by Jews *Tanakh* (for the letters beginning the Hebrew words for the three parts of the document: *Torah* or Pentateuch, *Nebi'im* or Prophets, and *Ketubim* or Writings—hence *T–N–K*). As we must realize, the Hebrew

Scriptures are a mosaic of different kinds of books, about different sorts of religious experiences and teachings, all addressed to a single group of people, ancient Israel, and all brought together and united solely by their common audience.

The formative generations of rabbinic Judaism, the next period, drew upon more than the ancient Hebrew Scriptures. The formative generations flowed out of particular groups in the world of Judaism that read these Scriptures in a particular way and that had a distinctive approach to the religious life of the community of Israel. Three main components of Jews' religious life in the last two centuries B.C.E. and the first century C.E. deserve our attention. These components, not mutually exclusive, are (1) the priests, with their commitment to the Temple of Jerusalem and its sacred offerings and to governance of the people of Israel in accord with the orderly world created by and flowing out of the Temple; (2) the scribes, with their commitment to the ancient Scriptures and their capacity to interpret and apply these Scriptures to the diverse conditions of the life of the people (later on, the heirs of the scribes would gain the honorific title of "rabbi," which was not distinctive to their group of Jews or even to the Jews); and (3) the messianic Zealots, who believed that God would rule the Jews when foreign rulers had been driven out of the Holy Land. Obviously, these three components were talking about different things to different people.

Of these three groups, one predominated in the shaping of events in the first century C.E., and the other two fused thereafter. Until the destruction of the Temple of Jerusalem in 70 C.E., the messianic Zealots were the most powerful force in the history of the Jews. For they precipitated the single most important event of the time: the war fought against Rome from 66 to 73 C.E., climaxed by the fall of Jerusalem in 70 C.E. And the messianic Zealots must have remained paramount for another three generations, because the next major event in the Jews' history was yet a second, and still more disastrous, holy and messianic war against Rome fought under the leadership of Ben Kosiba (also called *Bar Kokhba*, the Star's Son) from 132 to 135 C.E. That war surely was a mass uprising, which tells us that a large part of the population was attracted to the Zealot way of thinking.

The other two groups—the priests and the scribes —with their interest in continuity, order, and regularity lost out both times. The priests of the Temple saw the destruction of their sanctuary in 70 C.E. and realized after 135 C.E. that it would not be rebuilt for a long time. The scribes who taught Scriptures and administered their law witnessed the upheavals of society and the destruction of the social order that war inevitably brings in

its aftermath. Although both groups doubtless shared in the messianic hopes, they most certainly could not have sympathized with the policies and disastrous programs of the messianic Zealots.

THE AGE OF COGENCY (CIRCA 640–1800 C.E.)

The age of cogency ran on into the nineteenth century, which does not mean no other Judaic systems existed. It means that the Judaism of the dual Torah set the standard. A heresy selected its "false doctrine" by defining in a way different from the Judaism of the dual Torah a category emerging in that Judaism of the dual Torah. Such a group was the Karaites, who believed that the Torah of Sinai encompassed only the written part and rejected the authority of the books that rabbinic Judaism called "the Oral Torah." Shifts and changes of all sorts occurred. But the Judaism of the dual Torah absorbed into itself and its structure powerful movements, such as philosophy, on the one side, and mysticism (called Qabbalah), on the other, and found strength in both of them. The philosopher defended the way of life and worldview of the Judaism of the dual Torah. The mystic observed the faith defined by that same way of life as the vehicle for gaining his or her mystical experience. So when we see the Judaism of the dual Torah as cogent for nineteen centuries, it is not because the system remained intact and unchanged but because it was forever able to take within itself, treat as part of its system of values and beliefs, a wide variety of new concepts and customs. This span is an amazingly long time for something so volatile as a religion to have remained essentially stable and to have endured without profound shifts in symbolic structure, ritual life, or modes of social organization for the religious community.

The Judaism that predominated during that long period and that has continued to flourish in the nineteenth and twentieth centuries bears a number of names: *rabbinic* because of the nature of its principal authorities, who are rabbis; *Talmudic* because of the name of its chief authoritative document after the Hebrew Scriptures, which is the Talmud; *classical* because of its basic quality of endurance and prominence; or, simply, *Judaism* because no other important alternative was explored by Jews.

What proved the stability and essential cogency of rabbinic Judaism during the long period of its predominance was the capacity of rabbinic Judaism—its modes of thought, its definitions of faith, worship, and the right way to live life—to take into itself and to turn into a support for its own system a wide variety of separate and distinct modes of belief and thought. Of importance were, first, the philosophical movement and, second, the mystical one. Both put forward modes of thought quite distinct from those of rabbinic Judaism.

Philosophers of Judaism raised a range of questions and dealt with those questions in ways essentially separate from the established and accepted rabbinic ways of thinking about religious issues. But all of the philosophers of Judaism not only lived in accord with the rabbinic way of life; all of them were entirely literate in the Talmud and related literature, and many of the greatest philosophers were also great Talmudists. The same can be said of the mystics. Their ideas about the inner character of God, their quest for a fully realized experience of union with the presence of God in the world, their particular doctrines, with no basis in the Talmudic literature produced by the early rabbis, and their intense spirituality were all thoroughly "rabbinized"—that is, brought into conformity with the lessons and way of life taught by the Talmud. In the end, rabbinic Judaism received extraordinary reinforcement from the spiritual resources generated by the mystic quest. Both philosophy and mysticism found their way into the center of rabbinic Judaism. Both of them were shaped by minds that, to begin with, were infused with the content and spirit of rabbinic Judaism.

THE SECOND AGE OF DIVERSITY (CIRCA 1800–THE PRESENT)

Only in modern times have other religious consequences been drawn from cataclysmic historical events. Because Judaism had developed prophecy and rabbinic leadership, it was able to overcome the disasters of 586 B.C.E. and 70 C.E. The challenge of modern times comes not only from the outside but also from within: the nurture of new religious leadership for Jews facing a world of new values and ideals. Religion provides a particularly subtle problem for students of the process of modernization. In other areas such as politics and economics, that which is "modern" may meaningfully be set apart and against that which is "traditional," but in religion the complexities of the process of social change become most evident, the certainties less sure.

What happened in modern times is that new questions arose that rabbinic Judaism did not address. In the nineteenth century, continuator-Judaisms, referring to the same authoritative books as rabbinic Judaism but finding in them answers to questions not previously addressed, came to the fore. They did not replace rabbinic

Judaism in its historical forms; they simply took shape as other Judaisms, alongside that Judaism and related to it in fundamental ways. The new Judaisms of the nineteenth century all wanted to know how people could be both "Israel"—God's holy people—and also other things, citizens of the nation-state in which they lived, for example. All of them differentiated a religious from a secular part of everyday life, making space in that secular corner for Jews' other commitments and concerns besides religion. Reform, integrationist-Orthodox, and Conservative Judaisms all responded to the critical issues Jews in Western countries wished to address.

In the twentieth century, essentially secular systems responded to yet another set of questions. These questions derived not from the challenges of other religions but rather from the political crisis represented by the rise of racist anti-Semitism, which identified the Jews as the source of all evil and denied them the right to live at all. Zionism in the first half of the twentieth century and the Judaism of Holocaust and Redemption in the second half responded to that crisis by explaining the conditions under which Jews could endure. From the last third of the nineteenth century onward, many Jews began to understand that the promises of Enlightenment and emancipation would never be kept; indeed, they were false to begin with. Western civilization had no place for the Jews, who had to build their own state as a refuge from the storms that were coming upon them. These Jews rejected that fundamental teleological optimism, rationalism, yielding patience, and quietism with which classical Judaism had viewed the world. They did not believe that the world was so orderly and reliable as Judaism had supposed. They regarded Judaism as a misleading and politically unwise view of the Jewish people and their worldly context. What was needed was not prayer, study of Torah, and a life of compassion and good deeds.

What the hour demanded was renewed action, a reentry into politics, and the repoliticization of the Jewish people. Zionism was the movement that redefined the Jewish people into a nation and revived the Jews' ancient political status. So far as Zionism saw the world as essentially irrational and unreliable, unable to proceed in the orderly, calm, reasonable fashion in which Judaism assumed the world would always do its business, Zionism marked an end to Judaism as it had been known. The fact that Zionism would in time take up the old messianic language and symbolism of Judaism and make over these ancient vessels into utensils bearing new meaning is not to be ignored. But at its beginning, Zionism marked a break from Judaism, not because of Zionism's messianic fervor but because of its rejection of the quiet confidence, rationalism, and optimism of rabbinic Judaism.

Thus, these two things—the promise of emancipation and the advent of racist and political anti-Semitism—fell so far outside the worldview of rabbinic Judaism that they could not be satisfactorily interpreted and explained within the established system. The result was the breakdown of the Judaic system for many, many Jews. The system of Judaism was not overturned; for these people, it simply had become implausible. It had lost the trait of self-evidence. To state matters very simply: rabbinic Judaism was and is a system of balance between cosmic, teleological optimism and short-term skepticism—a system of moderation and restraint, of rationalism and moderated feeling. Just as it came into being in response to the collapse of unrestrained Messianism, feelings unleashed and hopes unbounded by doubt, so it came to an end, where and when it did come to an end, in a renewed clash with those very emotions and aspirations that, in the beginning, it had overcome: passionate hope and unrestrained, total despair. A system of optimistic skepticism and skeptical optimism, a world grasped with open arms and loved with a breaking heart, could never survive those reaches toward the extremes, those violations of the rules and frontiers of moderate and balanced being, that characterize modern times.

THE HISTORY OF JUDAISM AND THE HISTORY OF THE JEWS

The Jews have written a diverse history that exhibits no single, continuous narrative. In each area of the world where Jews have lived, what happened to them in that place and time is to be examined in its own terms. Thus, at the same time that, in one part of the world, one group of Jews lived in peace and security, another, elsewhere, did not. In 1492, for example, with the Christian reunification of Spain, the Jews and Moors (Muslims) were expelled from the country, and in 1497, Portugal did the same. Jews had lived in Spain and Portugal from Roman times, so the end of nearly fifteen centuries of continuous history marks a considerable calamity. At the same time, however, Jews found a safe home in the Turkish Empire, which extended throughout the Middle East and into the Balkans. A history of the Jews in that part of the world would tell a very different story. That is why a single, unitary, harmonious, and linear history of the Jews, treating the history of diverse groups in various places as one story, is misleading.

The various Judaisms too have had their own histories, though, as we have seen, one of those Judaisms, the rabbinic, has enjoyed the longest continuous history and the greatest influence. A uniform and continuous history of a single Judaism would require us to treat as coherent and whole a vast variety of conflicting convictions and practices. In addition, we would then miss what made these convictions and practices important in their own distinctive settings. To understand a given Judaism, we need not tell everything that was happening to the Jews in all parts of the world of the age of that Judaism, let alone everything that came before or afterward. The history of rabbinic Judaism cannot be told by an account of the facts of the life of the Jews in Poland, Germany, Spain, or North Africa. As a matter of fact, no unitary, single history of the Jewish people, from the beginning to now, has ever succeeded in holding together in a sound, proportionate manner the remarkably diverse and distinctive histories of the Jews in Poland, Germany, Spain, or North Africa, let alone North America and Hispanic America. If the Jews have written no single, linear history, a number of Judaisms have; among them, the critical one, rabbinic Judaism, does cohere from its origins in ancient times to today.

At the same time, what has happened to the Jews—their diverse histories in various times and places—has shaped the histories of Judaisms in all times and places, because Jews bring to the Torah the concerns and challenges that everyday life presents. During prosperity, the issue of the purpose of the good life will predominate. In a society that accords Jews equality and welcomes them as part of society, the issue of why Jews should remain separate and distinct takes priority. The Holocaust made urgent the problem of evil—how could an all-powerful, loving God permit such things to happen? Every Judaism found itself required to frame an answer to that question. Hence, although we recognize the difference between the ethnic and the secular, and the religious and the sacred, we also must keep in mind how the Jews' experience as an ethnic group formulates for any Judaism a set of urgent questions, emerging from everyday life, that all Judaisms of that time and place must address. . . .

SOURCES

I have organized the sources historically following the pattern suggested by Jacob Neusner (see Reading 10.1). Within each period I have selected literature that represents some of the principal beliefs and practices of Judaism. The sampling of texts that follows will, hopefully, help you understand better the faith called Judaism.

10.2 THE FIRST AGE OF DIVERSITY (ca. 586 B.C.E.–70 C.E.)

The destruction of Solomon's temple (586 B.C.E.) and the exile to Babylon of many Jewish leaders produced not only a crisis of faith but also a need to record in writing the oral traditions of the people. Material was gathered, edited, combined, and recorded on scrolls. Those who engaged in this activity retold these old stories in ways that expressed their particular outlook. For example, priests naturally had interest in ritual matters and how certain practices such as the keeping of the Sabbath arose. They sought justifications for these rituals in the stories told of events from a previous era.

The eventual result of the interweaving of various strands of traditional stories, sayings, prayers, and hymns is one of the most influential books of Western culture—the *Tanakh*, or Hebrew Bible. Although this book is not exactly the same as the Christian Old Testament, there is considerable overlap. Many people who live in and are influenced by Western culture have come to believe that the stories contained in this book tell us not only how the world we live in came to be but also the purpose of human existence.

Scholars sometimes refer to the religion of the Jews prior to 586 B.C.E. as "ancient Israelite religion." Literary and archaeological evidence suggests that the practice of sacrifice was at the heart of ancient Israelite religion. Religions that center on sacrifice require priests to perform the sacrifices at temples and altars on special feast days or holy days. These sacrificial cults are usually localized and hence tied to a particular geographic location.

The "Babylonian captivity," as it came to be known, changed ancient Israelite religion into Judaism. The temple was destroyed, the place of sacrifice profaned, and the sacred land lost. The Babylonian exile required that ancient Israelite religion be made mobile. That is what happened and, when it did, Judaism was born.

Although the exiled Jews returned to Israel, the temple was rebuilt, the priests resumed sacrifices, and a tradition of prayer and study of sacred writings that had developed during the exile continued. This laid the foundations for the religious beliefs and practices that finally came to dominate Judaism after the destruction of the second temple in 70 C.E.

10.2.1 Torah

The word *Torah* means "teaching," "instruction," or "law." It is a word with many meanings used in a wide variety of ways in Judaism. In its broadest sense, it refers to God's teachings and in a more narrow sense to the first five books (also called the Pentateuch) of *Tanakh*.

According to traditional Jewish belief, Moses wrote these books. Biblical scholarship, however, finds in them a variety of different sources woven together. This theory of composition (called the Documentary Hypothesis) was articulated by Julius Wellhausen (1844–1918). According to Wellhausen and other scholars, the sources woven together in the Torah can be identified as J, E, P, and D. The J source acquired its name because of its continued use of **YHWH,** pronounced "Yahweh" (often mispronounced "Jehovah"), as the name of God even before the revelation of this name to Moses. This name is so sacred that it is not pronounced by pious Jews, who say *Adonai* or Lord in its place. The E source is so named because instead of YHWH it uses *Elohim* for God. The D source refers to Deuteronomy, and the P stands for a priestly source that reflects priestly concerns with ritual celebrations and practices.

Both the J and E source were written sometime between 922 and 722 B.C.E. They were redacted (spliced together) around 700 B.C.E., and the P source was created as an alternative to the JE story. About one hundred years later the D source was written, and all of them (JE, P, and D) were redacted (perhaps by the priest Ezra) into the Five Books of Moses, or the Torah, during or shortly after the Babylonian exile.

What follows is a sampling from three of the five Torah books. Genesis opens with two creation stories. The P source, with which it opens, emphasizes the cosmic structure of the created world and three mandates given by God. The J source, which follows (beginning in 2:4b), concentrates on the creation of the first humans, their disobedience, and the LORD God's (YHWH) punishment.

From the creation we move to the covenant with Abraham. The first covenant, or contract, God makes is with Noah. God, after destroying the earth with a great flood because of human wickedness, covenants with Noah. God promises that he will not again destroy the earth by water and permits humans to eat animal flesh. God makes a second contract with Abraham. God selects Abraham to be the father of a great nation and to inherit the land of Canaan. In the P account, which I have included, the seal of this contract is the institution of the practice of circumcision.

Some of Abraham's descendants go to Egypt during a famine in Canaan and eventually end up being enslaved. God calls Moses to lead the people out of slavery and back to Canaan. The pharaoh does not want to release the Jews, so God visits a series of plagues on the Egyptians that culminates in the killing of all the first-born humans and cattle in Egypt. One of the most important festivals in Judaism, **Passover,** celebrates the fact that God's angel of death passed over the homes of the Jews and celebrates the freedom from slavery that resulted.

God makes the third great covenant reported in the Torah with Moses at Mt. Sinai. It is the law (Torah) of God by which the people will become holy people, chosen to do God's will. The best-known part of the Mosaic Law is the Ten Commandments, but the presentation of the Law continues throughout the books of Exodus, Leviticus, Numbers, and Deuteronomy.

The Mosaic Law also contains a number of codes such as the Covenant Code (Exodus 21–23), the Purity Code (Leviticus 11–16), the Holiness Code (Leviticus 17–27), and the Law Code (Deuteronomy 12–26). I include the Holiness Code from Leviticus as one example.

The legal style of these codes is often compared to the Code of Hammurabi, King of Ur (Abraham's hometown) and one of the oldest known law codes. At a very early point in the development of Western civilization, people recognized the need to regulate both human relations and human-divine relations by laws.

From Genesis

READING QUESTIONS

1. What surprising or unusual things do you notice about the creation accounts?
2. What three mandates or commands does God give to humans?
3. How do you interpret the story of how death came to be?
4. What is the covenant El Shaddai makes with Abram?
5. What do you think is important, from a religious point of view, about the story of the Passover and Exodus?
6. Why do you think the people are not allowed, upon penalty of death, on the mountain with Moses?
7. What sorts of things do the commandments given in Exodus and Leviticus regulate?
8. Select two commands from the Holiness Code in Leviticus and analyze them in terms of the historical and social situation they presuppose.
9. Why do you think the refrain "I am the Lord" is so frequently repeated?

CREATION (GENESIS 1–3)

1

When God began to create heaven and earth—²the earth being unformed and void, with darkness over the surface of the deep and a wind from God sweeping over the water—³God said, "Let there be light"; and there was light. ⁴God saw that the light was good, and God separated the light from the darkness. ⁵God called the light Day, and the darkness He called Night. And there was evening and there was morning, a first day.

⁶God said, "Let there be an expanse in the midst of the water, that it may separate water from water." ⁷God made the expanse, and it separated the water which was below the expanse from the water which was above the expanse. And it was so. ⁸God called the expanse Sky. And there was evening and there was morning, a second day.

Genesis 1–3 and the following selections (Genesis 17; Exodus 12:29–42, 14, 19, 20; Leviticus 19) are from *Tanakh, the Holy Scriptures: The New JPS Translation According to the Traditional Hebrew Text* (Philadelphia: Jewish Publication Society, 5748, 1988). Copyright © 1985 by the Jewish Publication Society. Reprinted by permission. Footnotes omitted.

⁹God said, "Let the water below the sky be gathered into one area, that the dry land may appear." And it was so. ¹⁰God called the dry land Earth, and the gathering of waters He called Seas. And God saw that this was good. ¹¹And God said, "Let the earth sprout vegetation: seed-bearing plants, fruit trees of every kind on earth that bear fruit with the seed in it." And it was so. ¹²The earth brought forth vegetation: seed-bearing plants of every kind, and trees of every kind bearing fruit with the seed in it. And God saw that this was good. ¹³And there was evening and there was morning, a third day.

¹⁴God said, "Let there be lights in the expanse of the sky to separate day from night; they shall serve as signs for the set times—the days and the years; ¹⁵and they shall serve as lights in the expanse of the sky to shine upon the earth." And it was so. ¹⁶God made the two great lights, the greater light to dominate the day and the lesser light to dominate the night, and the stars. ¹⁷And God set them in the expanse of the sky to shine upon the earth, ¹⁸to dominate the day and the night, and to separate light from darkness. And God saw that this was good. ¹⁹And there was evening and there was morning, a fourth day.

²⁰God said, "Let the waters bring forth swarms of living creatures, and birds that fly above the earth across the expanse of the sky." ²¹God created the great sea monsters, and all the living creatures of every kind that creep, which the waters brought forth in swarms, and all the winged birds of every kind. And God saw that this was good. ²²God blessed them, saying, "Be fertile and increase, fill the waters in the seas, and let the birds increase on the earth." ²³And there was evening and there was morning, a fifth day.

²⁴God said, "Let the earth bring forth every kind of living creature: cattle, creeping things, and wild beasts of every kind." And it was so. ²⁵God made wild beasts of every kind and cattle of every kind, and all kinds of creeping things of the earth. And God saw that this was good. ²⁶And God said, "Let us make man in our image, after our likeness. They shall rule the fish of the sea, the birds of the sky, the cattle, the whole earth, and all the creeping things that creep on earth." ²⁷And God created man in His image, in the image of God He created him; male and female He created them. ²⁸God blessed them and God said to them, "Be fertile and increase, fill the earth and master it; and rule the fish of the sea, the birds of the sky, and all the living things that creep on earth."

²⁹God said, "See, I give you every seed-bearing plant that is upon all the earth, and every tree that has seed-bearing fruit; they shall be yours for food. ³⁰And to all the animals on land, to all the birds of the sky, and to everything that creeps on earth, in which there is the breath of life, [I give] all the green plants for food." And it was so. ³¹And God saw all that He had made, and found it very good. And there was evening and there was morning, the sixth day.

2

The heaven and the earth were finished, and all their array. ²On the seventh day God finished the work that He had been doing, and He ceased on the seventh day from all the work that He had done. ³And God blessed the seventh day and declared it holy, because on it God ceased from all the work of creation that He had done. ⁴Such is the story of heaven and earth when they were created.

When the Lord God made earth and heaven—⁵when no shrub of the field was yet on earth and no grasses of the field had yet sprouted, because the Lord God had not sent rain upon the earth and there was no man to till the soil, ⁶but a flow would well up from the ground and water the whole surface of the earth—⁷the Lord God formed man from the dust of the earth. He blew into his nostrils the breath of life, and man became a living being.

⁸The Lord God planted a garden in Eden, in the east, and placed there the man He had formed. ⁹And from the ground the Lord God caused to grow every tree that was pleasing to the sight and good for food, with the tree of life in the middle of the garden, and the tree of knowledge of good and bad.

¹⁰A river issues from Eden to water the garden, and it then divides and becomes four branches. ¹¹The name of the first is Pishon, the one that winds through the whole land of Havilah, where the gold is. (¹²The gold of that land is good; bdellium is there, and lapis lazuli.) ¹³The name of the second river is Gihon, the one that winds through the whole land of Cush. ¹⁴The name of the third river is Tigris, the one that flows east of Asshur. And the fourth river is the Euphrates.

¹⁵The Lord God took the man and placed him in the garden of Eden, to till it and tend it. ¹⁶And the Lord God commanded the man, saying, "Of every tree of the garden you are free to eat; ¹⁷but as for the tree of knowledge of good and bad, you must not eat of it; for as soon as you eat of it, you shall die."

¹⁸The Lord God said, "It is not good for man to be alone; I will make a fitting helper for him." ¹⁹And the Lord God formed out of the earth all the wild beasts and all the birds of the sky, and brought them to the

man to see what he would call them; and whatever the man called each living creature, that would be its name. ²⁰ And the man gave names to all the cattle and to the birds of the sky and to all the wild beasts; but for Adam no fitting helper was found. ²¹ So the LORD God cast a deep sleep upon the man; and, while he slept, He took one of his ribs and closed up the flesh at that spot. ²² And the LORD God fashioned the rib that He had taken from the man into a woman; and He brought her to the man. ²³ Then the man said,

> "This one at last
> Is bone of my bones
> And flesh of my flesh.
> This one shall be called Woman,
> For from man was she taken."

²⁴ Hence a man leaves his father and mother and clings to his wife, so that they become one flesh.

²⁵ The two of them were naked, the man and his wife, yet they felt no shame.

3

¹ Now the serpent was the shrewdest of all the wild beasts that the LORD God had made. He said to the woman, "Did God really say: You shall not eat of any tree of the garden?" ² The woman replied to the serpent, "We may eat of the fruit of the other trees of the garden. ³ It is only about fruit of the tree in the middle of the garden that God said: 'You shall not eat of it or touch it, lest you die.'" ⁴ And the serpent said to the woman, "You are not going to die, ⁵ but God knows that as soon as you eat of it your eyes will be opened and you will be like divine beings who know good and bad." ⁶ When the woman saw that the tree was good for eating and a delight to the eyes, and that the tree was desirable as a source of wisdom, she took of its fruit and ate. She also gave some to her husband, and he ate. ⁷ Then the eyes of both of them were opened and they perceived that they were naked; and they sewed together fig leaves and made themselves loincloths.

⁸ They heard the sound of the LORD God moving about in the garden at the breezy time of day; and the man and his wife hid from the LORD God among the trees of the garden. ⁹ The LORD God called out to the man and said to him, "Where are you?" ¹⁰ He replied, "I heard the sound of You in the garden, and I was afraid because I was naked, so I hid." ¹¹ Then He asked, "Who told you that you were naked? Did you eat of the tree from which I had forbidden you to eat?" ¹² The man said,

"The woman You put at my side—she gave me of the tree, and I ate." ¹³ And the LORD God said to the woman, "What is this you have done!" The woman replied, "The serpent duped me, and I ate." ¹⁴ Then the LORD God said to the serpent,

> "Because you did this,
> More cursed shall you be
> Than all cattle
> And all the wild beasts:
> On your belly shall you crawl
> And dirt shall you eat
> All the days of your life.
> ¹⁵ I will put enmity
> Between you and the woman,
> And between your offspring and hers;
> They shall strike at your head,
> And you shall strike at their heel."

¹⁶ And to the woman He said,

> "I will make most severe
> Your pangs in childbearing;
> In pain shall you bear children.
> Yet your urge shall be for your husband,
> And he shall rule over you."

¹⁷ To Adam He said, "Because you did as your wife said and ate of the tree about which I commanded you, 'You shall not eat of it,'

> Cursed be the ground because of you;
> By toil shall you eat of it
> All the days of your life:
> ¹⁸ Thorns and thistles shall it sprout for you.
> But your food shall be the grasses of the field;
> ¹⁹ By the sweat of your brow
> Shall you get bread to eat,
> Until you return to the ground—
> For from it you were taken.
> For dust you are,
> And to dust you shall return."

²⁰ The man named his wife Eve, because she was the mother of all the living. ²¹ And the LORD God made garments of skins for Adam and his wife, and clothed them.

²² And the LORD God said, "Now that the man has become like one of us, knowing good and bad, what if he should stretch out his hand and take also from the tree of life and eat, and live forever!" ²³ So the LORD God banished him from the garden of Eden, to till the soil from which he was taken. ²⁴ He drove the man out, and stationed east of the garden of Eden the cherubim and the fiery ever-turning sword, to guard the way to the tree of life.

COVENANT WITH ABRAHAM (GENESIS 17)

17

When Abram was ninety-nine years old, the LORD appeared to Abram and said to him, "I am El Shaddai. Walk in My ways and be blameless. [2] I will establish My covenant between Me and you, and I will make you exceedingly numerous."

[3] Abram threw himself on his face; and God spoke to him further, [4] "As for Me, this is My covenant with you: You shall be the father of a multitude of nations. [5] And you shall no longer be called Abram, but your name shall be Abraham, for I make you the father of a multitude of nations. [6] I will make you exceedingly fertile, and make nations of you; and kings shall come forth from you. [7] I will maintain My covenant between Me and you, and your offspring to come, as an everlasting covenant throughout the ages, to be God to you and to your offspring to come. [8] I assign the land you sojourn in to you and your offspring to come, all the land of Canaan, as an everlasting holding. I will be their God."

[9] God further said to Abraham, "As for you, you and your offspring to come throughout the ages shall keep My covenant. [10] Such shall be the covenant between Me and you and your offspring to follow which you shall keep: every male among you shall be circumcised. [11] You shall circumcise the flesh of your foreskin, and that shall be the sign of the covenant between Me and you. [12] And throughout the generations, every male among you shall be circumcised at the age of eight days. As for the homeborn slave and the one bought from an outsider who is not of your offspring, [13] they must be circumcised, homeborn and purchased alike. Thus shall My covenant be marked in your flesh as an everlasting pact. [14] And if any male who is uncircumcised fails to circumcise the flesh of his foreskin, that person shall be cut off from his kin; he has broken My covenant."

[15] And God said to Abraham, "As for your wife Sarai, you shall not call her Sarai, but her name shall be Sarah. [16] I will bless her; indeed, I will give you a son by her. I will bless her so that she shall give rise to nations; rulers of peoples shall issue from her." [17] Abraham threw himself on his face and laughed, as he said to himself, "Can a child be born to a man a hundred years old, or can Sarah bear a child at ninety?" [18] And Abraham said to God, "O that Ishmael might live by Your favor!" [19] God said, "Nevertheless, Sarah your wife shall bear you a son, and you shall name him Isaac; and I will maintain My covenant with him as an everlasting covenant for his offspring to come. [20] As for Ishmael, I have heeded you. I hereby bless him. I will make him fertile and exceedingly numerous. He shall be the father of twelve chieftains, and I will make of him a great nation. [21] But My covenant I will maintain with Isaac, whom Sarah shall bear to you at this season next year." [22] And when He was done speaking with him, God was gone from Abraham.

[23] Then Abraham took his son Ishmael, and all his homeborn slaves and all those he had bought, every male in Abraham's household, and he circumcised the flesh of their foreskins on that very day, as God had spoken to him. [24] Abraham was ninety-nine years old when he circumcised the flesh of his foreskin, [25] and his son Ishmael was thirteen years old when he was circumcised in the flesh of his foreskin. [26] Thus Abraham and his son Ishmael were circumcised on that very day; [27] and all his household, his homeborn slaves and those that had been bought from outsiders, were circumcised with him.

From Exodus

PASSOVER AND EXODUS (EXODUS 12:29–42, 14)

12

. . . [29] In the middle of the night the LORD struck down all the first-born in the land of Egypt, from the first-born of Pharaoh who sat on the throne to the first-born of the captive who was in the dungeon, and all the first-born of the cattle. [30] And Pharaoh arose in the night, with all his courtiers and all the Egyptians—because there was a loud cry in Egypt; for there was no house where there was not someone dead. [31] He summoned Moses and Aaron in the night and said, "Up, depart from among my people, you and the Israelites with you! Go, worship the LORD as you said! [32] Take also your flocks and your herds, as you said, and begone! And may you bring a blessing upon me also!"

[33] The Egyptians urged the people on, impatient to have them leave the country, for they said, "We shall all be dead." [34] So the people took their dough before it was leavened, their kneading bowls wrapped in their cloaks upon their shoulders. [35] The Israelites had done Moses' bidding and borrowed from the Egyptians objects of silver and gold, and clothing. [36] And the LORD had dis-

posed the Egyptians favorably toward the people, and they let them have their request; thus they stripped the Egyptians.

³⁷ The Israelites journeyed from Rameses to Succoth, about six hundred thousand men on foot, aside from children. ³⁸ Moreover, a mixed multitude went up with them, and very much livestock, both flocks and herds. ³⁹ And they baked unleavened cakes of the dough that they had taken out of Egypt, for it was not leavened, since they had been driven out of Egypt and could not delay; nor had they prepared any provisions for themselves.

⁴⁰ The length of time that the Israelites lived in Egypt was four hundred and thirty years; ⁴¹ at the end of the four hundred and thirtieth year, to the very day, all the ranks of the LORD departed from the land of Epypt. ⁴² That was for the LORD a night of vigil to bring them out of the land of Egypt; that same night is the LORD's, one of vigil for all the children of Israel throughout the ages. . . .

14

The LORD said to Moses: ² Tell the Israelites to turn back and encamp before Pi-hahiroth, between Migdol and the sea, before Baal-zephon; you shall encamp facing it, by the sea. ³ Pharaoh will say of the Israelites, "They are astray in the land; the wilderness has closed in on them." ⁴ Then I will stiffen Pharaoh's heart and he will pursue them, that I may gain glory through Pharaoh and all his host; and the Egyptians shall know that I am the LORD.

And they did so.

⁵ When the king of Egypt was told that the people had fled, Pharaoh and his courtiers had a change of heart about the people and said, "What is this we have done, releasing Israel from our service?" ⁶ He ordered his chariot and took his men with him; ⁷ he took six hundred of his picked chariots, and the rest of the chariots of Egypt, with officers in all of them. ⁸ The LORD stiffened the heart of Pharaoh king of Egypt, and he gave chase to the Israelites. As the Israelites were departing defiantly, ⁹ the Egyptians gave chase to them, and all the chariot horses of Pharoah, his horsemen, and his warriors overtook them encamped by the sea, near Pi-hahiroth, before Baal-zephon.

¹⁰ As Pharaoh drew near, the Israelites caught sight of the Egyptians advancing upon them. Greatly frightened, the Israelites cried out to the LORD. ¹¹ And they said to Moses, "Was it for want of graves in Egypt that you brought us to die in the wilderness? What have you done to us, taking us out of Egypt? ¹² Is this not the very thing we told you in Egypt, saying, 'Let us be, and we will serve the Egyptians, for it is better for us to serve the Egyptians than to die in the wilderness'?" ¹³ But Moses said to the people, "Have no fear! Stand by, and witness the deliverance which the LORD will work for you today; for the Egyptians whom you see today you will never see again. ¹⁴ The LORD will battle for you; you hold your peace!"

¹⁵ Then the LORD said to Moses, "Why do you cry out to Me? Tell the Israelites to go forward. ¹⁶ And you lift up your rod and hold out your arm over the sea and split it, so that the Israelites may march into the sea on dry ground. ¹⁷ And I will stiffen the hearts of the Egyptians so that they go in after them; and I will gain glory through Pharaoh and all his warriors, his chariots and his horsemen. ¹⁸ Let the Egyptians know that I am LORD, when I gain glory through Pharaoh, his chariots, and his horsemen."

¹⁹ The angel of God, who had been going ahead of the Israelite army, now moved and followed behind them; and the pillar of cloud shifted from in front of them and took up a place behind them, ²⁰ and it came between the army of the Egyptians and the army of Israel. Thus there was the cloud with the darkness, and it cast a spell upon the night, so that the one could not come near the other all through the night.

²¹ Then Moses held out his arm over the sea and the LORD drove back the sea with a strong east wind all that night, and turned the sea into dry ground. The waters were split, ²² and the Israelites went into the sea on dry ground, the waters forming a wall for them on their right and on their left. ²³ The Egyptians came in pursuit after them into the sea, all of Pharaoh's horses, chariots, and horsemen. ²⁴ At the morning watch, the LORD looked down upon the Egyptian army from a pillar of fire and cloud, and threw the Egyptian army into panic. ²⁵ He locked the wheels of their chariots so that they moved forward with difficulty. And the Egyptians said, "Let us flee from the Israelites, for the LORD is fighting for them against Egypt."

²⁶ Then the LORD said to Moses, "Hold out your arm over the sea, that the waters may come back upon the Egyptians and upon their chariots and upon their horsemen." ²⁷ Moses held out his arm over the sea, and at daybreak the sea returned to its normal state, and the Egyptians fled at its approach. But the LORD hurled the Egyptians into the sea. ²⁸ The waters turned back and covered the chariots and the horsemen—Pharaoh's entire army that followed them into the sea; not one of them remained. ²⁹ But the Israelites had marched through the sea on dry ground, the waters forming a wall for them on their right and on their left.

[30] Thus the Lord delivered Israel that day from the Egyptians. Israel saw the Egyptians dead on the shore of the sea. [31] And when Israel saw the wondrous power which the Lord had wielded against the Egyptians, the people feared the Lord; they had faith in the Lord and His servant Moses.

Mosaic Covenant (Exodus 19, 20)

19

On the third new moon after the Israelites had gone forth from the land of Egypt, on that very day, they entered the wilderness of Sinai. [2] Having journeyed from Rephidim, they entered the wilderness of Sinai and encamped in the wilderness. Israel encamped there in front of the mountain, [3] and Moses went up to God. The Lord called to him from the mountain, saying, "Thus shall you say to the house of Jacob and declare to the children of Israel: [4] 'You have seen what I did to the Egyptians, how I bore you on eagles' wings and brought you to Me. [5] Now then, if you will obey Me faithfully and keep My covenant, you shall be My treasured possession among all the peoples. Indeed, all the earth is Mine, [6] but you shall be to Me a kingdom of priests and a holy nation.' These are the words that you shall speak to the children of Israel.

[7] Moses came and summoned the elders of the people and put before them all that the Lord had commanded him. [8] All the people answered as one, saying, "All that the Lord has spoken we will do!" And Moses brought back the people's words to the Lord. [9] And the Lord said to Moses, "I will come to you in a thick cloud, in order that the people may hear when I speak with you and so trust you ever after." Then Moses reported the people's words to the Lord, [10] and the Lord said to Moses, "Go to the people and warn them to stay pure today and tomorrow. Let them wash their clothes. [11] Let them be ready for the third day; for on the third day the Lord will come down, in the sight of all the people, on Mount Sinai. [12] You shall set bounds for the people round about, saying, 'Beware of going up the mountain or touching the border of it. Whoever touches the mountain shall be put to death: [13] no hand shall touch him, but he shall be either stoned or shot; beast or man, he shall not live.' When the ram's horn sounds a long blast, they may go up on the mountain."

[14] Moses came down from the mountain to the people and warned the people to stay pure, and they washed their clothes. [15] And he said to the people, "Be ready for the third day: do not go near a woman."

[16] On the third day, as morning dawned, there was thunder, and lightning, and a dense cloud upon the mountain, and a very loud blast of the horn; and all the people who were in the camp trembled. [17] Moses led the people out of the camp toward God, and they took their places at the foot of the mountain.

[18] Now Mount Sinai was all in smoke, for the Lord had come down upon it in fire; the smoke rose like the smoke of a kiln, and the whole mountain trembled violently. [19] The blare of the horn grew louder and louder. As Moses spoke, God answered him in thunder. [20] The Lord came down upon Mount Sinai, on the top of the mountain, and the Lord called Moses to the top of the mountain and Moses went up. [21] The Lord said to Moses, "Go down, warn the people not to break through to the Lord to gaze, lest many of them perish. [22] The priests also, who come near the Lord, must stay pure, lest the Lord break out against them." [23] But Moses said to the Lord, "The people cannot come up to Mount Sinai, for You warned us saying, 'Set bounds about the mountain and sanctify it.'" [24] So the Lord said to him, "Go down, and come back together with Aaron; but let not the priests or the people break through to come up to the Lord, lest He break out against them." [25] And Moses went down to the people and spoke to them.

20

God spoke all these words, saying:

[2] I the Lord am your God who brought you out of the land of Egypt, the house of bondage: [3] You shall have no other gods besides Me.

[4] You shall not make for yourself a sculptured image, or any likeness of what is in the heavens above, or on the earth below, or in the waters under the earth. [5] You shall not bow down to them or serve them. For I the Lord your God am an impassioned God, visiting the guilt of the parents upon the children, upon the third and upon the fourth generations of those who reject Me, [6] but showing kindness to the thousandth generation of those who love Me and keep My commandments.

[7] You shall not swear falsely by the name of the Lord your God; for the Lord will not clear one who swears falsely by His name.

[8] Remember the sabbath day and keep it holy. [9] Six days you shall labor and do all your work, [10] but the seventh day is a sabbath of the Lord your God: you shall not do any work—you, your son or daughter, your male or female slave, or your cattle, or the stranger who is within your settlements. [11] For in six days the Lord made heaven and earth and sea, and all that is in them, and He rested on the seventh day; therefore the Lord blessed the sabbath day and hallowed it.

¹²Honor your father and your mother, that you may long endure on the land that the Lord your God is assigning to you.

¹³You shall not murder.

You shall not commit adultery.

You shall not steal.

You shall not bear false witness against your neighbor.

¹⁴You shall not covet your neighbor's house: you shall not covet your neighbor's wife, or his male or female slave, or his ox or his ass, or anything that is your neighbor's.

¹⁵All the people witnessed the thunder and lightning, the blare of the horn and the mountain smoking; and when the people saw it, they fell back and stood at a distance. ¹⁶"You speak to us," they said to Moses, "and we will obey; but let not God speak to us, lest we die." ¹⁷Moses answered the people, "Be not afraid; for God has come only in order to test you, and in order that the fear of Him may be ever with you, so that you do not go astray." ¹⁸So the people remained at a distance, while Moses approached the thick cloud where God was.

¹⁹The Lord said to Moses:

Thus shall you say to the Israelites: You yourselves saw that I spoke to you from the very heavens: ²⁰With Me, therefore, you shall not make any gods of silver, nor shall you make for yourselves any gods of gold. ²¹Make for Me an altar of earth and sacrifice on it your burnt offerings and your sacrifices of well-being, your sheep and your oxen; in every place where I cause My name to be mentioned I will come to you and bless you. ²²And if you make for Me an altar of stones, do not build it of hewn stones; for by wielding your tool upon them you have profaned them. ²³Do not ascend My altar by steps, that your nakedness may not be exposed upon it.

From Leviticus

Holiness Code (Leviticus 19)

19

The Lord spoke to Moses, saying: ²Speak to the whole Israelite community and say to them:

You shall be holy, for I, the Lord your God, am holy.

³You shall each revere his mother and his father, and keep My sabbaths: I the Lord am your God.

⁴Do not turn to idols or make molten gods for yourselves: I the Lord am your God.

⁵When you sacrifice an offering of well-being to the Lord, sacrifice it so that it may be accepted on your behalf. ⁶It shall be eaten on the day you sacrifice it, or on the day following; but what is left by the third day must be consumed in fire. ⁷If it should be eaten on the third day, it is an offensive thing, it will not be acceptable. ⁸And he who eats of it shall bear his guilt, for he has profaned what is sacred to the Lord; that person shall be cut off from his kin.

⁹When you reap the harvest of your land, you shall not reap all the way to the edges of your field, or gather the gleanings of your harvest. ¹⁰You shall not pick your vineyard bare, or gather the fallen fruit of your vineyard; you shall leave them for the poor and the stranger: I the Lord am your God.

¹¹You shall not steal; you shall not deal deceitfully or falsely with one another. ¹²You shall not swear falsely by My name, profaning the name of your God: I am the Lord.

¹³You shall not defraud your fellow. You shall not commit robbery. The wages of a laborer shall not remain with you until morning.

¹⁴You shall not insult the deaf, or place a stumbling block before the blind. You shall fear your God: I am the Lord.

¹⁵You shall not render an unfair decision: do not favor the poor or show deference to the rich; judge your kinsman fairly. ¹⁶Do not deal basely with your countrymen. Do not profit by the blood of your fellow: I am the Lord.

¹⁷You shall not hate your kinsfolk in your heart. Reprove your kinsman but incur no guilt because of him. ¹⁸You shall not take vengeance or bear a grudge against your countrymen. Love your fellow as yourself: I am the Lord.

¹⁹You shall observe My laws.

You shall not let your cattle mate with a different kind; you shall not sow your field with two kinds of seed; you shall not put on cloth from a mixture of two kinds of material.

²⁰If a man has carnal relations with a woman who is a slave and has been designated for another man, but has not been redeemed or given her freedom, there shall be an indemnity; they shall not, however, be put to death, since she has not been freed. ²¹But he must bring to the entrance of the Tent of Meeting, as his guilt offering to the Lord, a ram of guilt offering. ²²With the ram of guilt offering the priest shall make expiation for him before the Lord for the sin that he committed; and the sin that he committed will be forgiven him.

[23] When you enter the land and plant any tree for food, you shall regard its fruit as forbidden. Three years it shall be forbidden for you, not to be eaten. [24] In the fourth year all its fruit shall be set aside for jubilation before the LORD; [25] and only in the fifth year may you use its fruit—that its yield to you may be increased: I the LORD am your God.

[26] You shall not eat anything with its blood. You shall not practice divination or soothsaying. [27] You shall not round off the side-growth on your head, or destroy the side-growth of your beard. [28] You shall not make gashes in your flesh for the dead, or incise any marks on yourselves: I am the LORD.

[29] Do not degrade your daughter and make her a harlot, lest the land fall into harlotry and the land be filled with depravity. [30] You shall keep My sabbaths and venerate My sanctuary: I am the LORD.

[31] Do not turn to ghosts and do not inquire of familiar spirits, to be defiled by them: I the LORD am your God.

[32] You shall rise before the aged and show deference to the old; you shall fear your God: I am the LORD.

[33] When a stranger resides with you in your land, you shall not wrong him. [34] The stranger who resides with you shall be to you as one of your citizens; you shall love him as yourself, for you were strangers in the land of Egypt: I the LORD am your God.

[35] You shall not falsify measures of length, weight, or capacity. [36] You shall have an honest balance, honest weights, an honest *ephah*, and an honest *hin*.

I the LORD am your God who freed you from the land of Egypt. [37] You shall faithfully observe all My laws and all My rules: I am the LORD.

10.2.2 Nevi'im (Prophets)

Prophets were spokespersons for God. They spoke out or forth the will of God as they understood it. They believed, as did many of the kings and people of Israel, that God called them to serve a special purpose. Their pronouncements on God's behalf were considered so important that many were recorded and included, along with the Torah books, in the *Tanakh*.

One of the greatest of the many prophetic books included in the *Tanakh* is the Book of Isaiah. In 722 B.C.E. the northern Kingdom of Israel fell to the Assyrians. Although the southern Kingdom of Judah survived until 586 B.C.E., the Assyrians threatened its existence. The prophet Isaiah was an advisor to King Ahaz and his successor, Hezekiah, both kings of Judah. His advice to both kings was to trust God for deliverance.

The Book of Isaiah consists of sixty-six chapters and is an anthology of prophetic writings from Isaiah's time through the Babylonian exile. Isaiah's own words can be found in chapters 1–11 and 28–32. Included below is chapter 1:1–28, in which Isaiah indicts the people of Judah, and chapter 6, which records Isaiah's call to be a prophet.

⁂

From Isaiah

READING QUESTIONS

1. In whose name does Isaiah speak?
2. What messages do you find in Isaiah's prophecies?
3. What kind of social and religious function do you think prophesies such as these served?
4. What are the main elements of Isaiah's call to be a prophet?
5. How do you interpret the message given in verses 9 and 10?

1

The prophecies of Isaiah son of Amoz, who prophesied concerning Judah and Jerusalem in the reigns of Uzziah, Jotham, Ahaz, and Hezekiah, kings of Judah.

[2] Hear, O heavens, and give ear, O earth,
For the LORD has spoken:
"I reared children and brought them up—
And they have rebelled against Me!
[3] An ox knows its owner,
An ass its master's crib:
Israel does not know,
My people takes no thought."

[4] Ah, sinful nation!
People laden with iniquity!
Brood of evildoers!
Depraved children!

Isaiah 1:1–28 and 6 from *Tanakh, the Holy Scriptures: The New JPS Translation According to the Traditional Hebrew Text* (Philadelphia: Jewish Publication Society, 5748, 1988). Copyright © 1985 by the Jewish Publication Society. Reprinted by permission. Footnotes omitted.

They have forsaken the LORD,
Spurned the Holy One of Israel,
Turned their backs [on Him].

⁵ Why do you seek further beatings,
That you continue to offend?
Every head is ailing,
And every heart is sick.
⁶ From head to foot
No spot is sound:
All bruises, and welts,
And festering sores—
Not pressed out, not bound up,
Not softened with oil.
⁷ Your land is a waste,
Your cities burnt down;
Before your eyes, the yield of your soil
Is consumed by strangers—
A wasteland as overthrown by strangers!
⁸ Fair Zion is left
Like a booth in a vineyard,
Like a hut in a cucumber field,
Like a city beleaguered.
⁹ Had not the LORD of Hosts
Left us some survivors,
We should be like Sodom,
Another Gomorrah.

¹⁰ Hear the word of the LORD,
You chieftains of Sodom;
Give ear to our God's instruction,
You folk of Gomorrah!
¹¹ "What need have I of all your sacrifices?"
Says the LORD.
"I am sated with burnt offerings of rams,
And suet of fatlings,
and blood of bulls;
And I have no delight
In lambs and he-goats.
¹² That you come to appear before Me—
Who asked that of you?
Trample My courts
¹³   no more;
Bringing oblations is futile,
Incense is offensive to Me.
New moon and sabbath,
Proclaiming of solemnities,
Assemblies with iniquity,
I cannot abide.
¹⁴ Your new moons and fixed seasons
Fill Me with loathing;
They are become a burden to Me,
I cannot endure them.

¹⁵ And when you lift up your hands,
I will turn My eyes away from you;
Though you pray at length,
I will not listen.
Your hands are stained with crime—
¹⁶ Wash yourselves clean;
Put your evil doings
Away from My sight.
Cease to do evil;
¹⁷ Learn to do good.
Devote yourselves to justice;
Aid the wronged.
Uphold the rights of the orphan;
Defend the cause of the widow.

¹⁸ "Come, let us reach an understanding,
                                        —says the LORD.

Be your sins like crimson,
They can turn snow-white;
Be they red as dyed wool,
They can become like fleece."
¹⁹ If, then, you agree and give heed,
You will eat the good things of the earth;
²⁰ But if you refuse and disobey,
You will be devoured [by] the sword—
For it was the LORD who spoke.

²¹ Alas, she has become a harlot,
The faithful city
That was filled with justice,
Where righteousness dwelt—
But now murderers.
²² Your silver has turned to dross;
Your wine is cut with water.
²³ Your rulers are rogues
And cronies of thieves,
Every one avid for presents
And greedy for gifts;
They do not judge the case of the orphan,
And the widow's cause never reaches them.

²⁴ Assuredly, this is the declaration
Of the Sovereign, the LORD of Hosts,
The Mighty One of Israel:
"Ah, I will get satisfaction from My foes;
I will wreak vengeance on My enemies!
²⁵ I will turn My hand against you,
And smelt out your dross as with lye,
And remove all your slag:
²⁶ I will restore your magistrates as of old,
And your counselors as of yore.
After that you shall be called
City of Righteousness, Faithful City."

²⁷Zion shall be saved in the judgment;
Her repentant ones, in the retribution.
²⁸But rebels and sinners shall all be crushed,
And those who forsake the Lord shall perish. . . .

6

In the year that King Uzziah died, I beheld my Lord seated on a high and lofty throne; and the skirts of His robe filled the Temple. ²Seraphs stood in attendance on Him. Each of them had six wings: with two he covered his face, with two he covered his legs, and with two he would fly.

³And one would call to the other,
"Holy, holy, holy!
The Lord of Hosts!
His presence fills all the earth!"

⁴The doorposts would shake at the sound of the one who called, and the House kept filling with smoke. ⁵I cried,

"Woe is me; I am lost!
For I am a man of unclean lips
And I live among a people
of unclean lips;
Yet my own eyes have beheld
The King Lord of Hosts."

⁶Then one of the seraphs flew over to me with a live coal, which he had taken from the altar with a pair of tongs. ⁷He touched it to my lips and declared,

"Now that this has touched your lips,
Your guilt shall depart
And your sin be purged away."

⁸Then I heard the voice of my Lord saying, "Whom shall I send? Who will go for us?" And I said, "Here am I; send me." ⁹And He said, "Go, say to that people:

'Hear, indeed, but do not understand;
See, indeed, but do not grasp.'
¹⁰Dull that people's mind,
Stop its ears,
And seal its eyes—
Lest, seeing with its eyes
And hearing with its ears,
It also grasp with its mind,
And repent and save itself."

¹¹I asked, "How long, my Lord?" And He replied:

"Till towns lie waste without inhabitants
And houses without people,
And the ground lies waste and desolate—
¹²For the Lord will banish the population—

And deserted sites are many
In the midst of the land.

¹³"But while a tenth part yet remains in it, it shall repent. It shall be ravaged like the terebinth and the oak, of which stumps are left even when they are felled: its stump shall be a holy seed."

10.2.3 Ketuvim (Writings)

Included among the books of the *Tanakh* are a collection called "Writings." One of the more interesting parts of this collection is a hymn book, or Psalter, called the Psalms. It includes some 150 songs and prayers written over a 600-year period, many during the Babylonian exile. Although we cannot be sure of the authorship of these songs, 73 are ascribed to King David.

Because it took so long for the Book of Psalms to reach its final form, it is very difficult for a modern scholar to decipher the origins, history, and use of the many different hymns. Scholars do know the whole Psalter in its final form is intended to be a manual of devotion and meditation encompassing, among other themes, confession (Psalm 51), lament (Psalm 3), adoration (Psalm 8), and praise (Psalm 150). It is also likely that many of the Psalms were composed for ceremonial use in the Jerusalem Temple.

Until the time of Josiah (640–609 B.C.E.), the ordinary people probably did not use the Jerusalem Temple for worship. It was a royal chapel, used by the monarchs and their households. Exactly which hymns and prayers were used in the royal ceremonies conducted at the temple is impossible to determine with certainty. Psalm 2 may have been David's inaugural hymn, and Psalms 24, 47, and 68 may have been composed for the occasion of bringing the Ark to Jerusalem (2 Samuel 6). Psalm 44 could be used by a king prior to a battle, and Psalms 93 and 96–99 might have been used on the anniversary of the king's coronation or as part of a New Year's festival.

At one point the collection was framed by Psalm 1, which stresses the importance of delighting in the law (Torah), and Psalm 119, which is an elaborate meditation on the law in all of its aspects. This indicates one shift in the interpretation of the Psalter from an emphasis on the words of worshipers addressed to God to the word of God (Torah) addressed to worshipers. Although Psalm 119 may have once ended the Psalter, it now ends with a block of David hymns (138–145), followed by five *hallelujah* psalms. This shifts the interpretation once again from an emphasis on God's law to the life of King David, God's covenant with David, and David's life as the model of genuine piety.

Along with the Psalms, a book named Esther is included in the **Ketuvim.** It is one of two books in the *Tanakh* that focuses on the life of a Jewish heroine (Ruth is the other). Esther, we learn, is the queen of a Persian king named Ahasuerus (Xerxes I), one of the successors of King Cyrus who had allowed the Jews to return to Judah. King Ahasuerus does not know Esther is a Jew, so when Mordecai, her cousin, refuses to bow to Haman, a high official of his court, the king permits Haman to develop a plan to execute Mordecai and the Jews. Esther speaks to the king on behalf of the Jews, and they are spared. Poetic justice draws part of the story to a close as Haman is impaled on the stake he had prepared for Mordecai and the Jews are given the right to defend themselves.

The story of Esther is the basis for the Jewish feast Purim.

From Psalms

READING QUESTIONS

1. Assuming there was a cultic or ritual setting for Psalm 8, what do you think it might be?
2. How would you characterize the message of Psalm 23?
3. What message for the pious does Psalm 51 convey?
4. What do you think is the historical setting of Psalm 137?
5. Why do you think the story of Esther was preserved?

8

For the leader; on the *gittith*. A psalm of David.

[2] O Lord, our Lord,
   How majestic is Your name throughout the earth,
   You who have covered the heavens with Your splendor!

Psalms 8, 23, 51, 137 and Esther 3–5:5a, 7) from *Tanakh, the Holy Scriptures: The New JPS Translation According to the Traditional Hebrew Text* (Philadelphia: Jewish Publication Society, 5748, 1988). Copyright © 1985 by the Jewish Publication Society. Reprinted by permission. Footnotes omitted.

[3] From the mouths of infants and sucklings
   You have founded strength on account of Your foes,
   to put an end to enemy and avenger.
[4] When I behold Your heavens, the work of Your fingers,
   the moon and stars that You set in place,
[5] what is man that You have been mindful of him,
   mortal man that You have taken note of him,
[6] that You have made him little less than divine,
   and adorned him with glory and majesty;
[7] You have made him master over Your handiwork,
   laying the world at his feet,
[8] sheep and oxen, all of them,
   and wild beasts, too;
[9] the birds of the heavens, the fish of the sea,
   whatever travels the paths of the seas.
[10] O Lord, our Lord, how majestic is Your name
   throughout the earth!

23

A psalm of David.

The Lord is my shepherd;
   I lack nothing.
[2] He makes me lie down in green pastures;
   He leads me to water in places of repose;
[3] He renews my life;
   He guides me in right paths
   as befits His name.
[4] Though I walk through a valley of deepest darkness,
   I fear no harm, for You are with me;
   Your rod and Your staff—they comfort me.

[5] You spread a table for me in full view of my enemies;
   You anoint my head with oil;
   my drink is abundant.
[6] Only goodness and steadfast love shall pursue me
   all the days of my life,
   and I shall dwell in the house of the Lord
   for many long years.

51

For the leader. A psalm of David, [2] when Nathan the prophet came to him after he had come to Bathsheba.

[3] Have mercy upon me, O God,
   as befits Your faithfulness;
   in keeping with Your abundant compassion,
   blot out my transgressions.
[4] Wash me thoroughly of my iniquity,
   and purify me of my sin;
[5] for I recognize my transgressions,
   and am ever conscious of my sin.

⁶Against You alone have I sinned,
  and done what is evil in Your sight;
  so You are just in Your sentence,
  and right in Your judgment.
⁷Indeed I was born with iniquity;
  with sin my mother conceived me.
⁸Indeed You desire truth about that which is hidden;
  teach me wisdom about secret things.

⁹Purge me with hyssop till I am pure;
  wash me till I am whiter than snow.
¹⁰Let me hear tidings of joy and gladness;
  let the bones You have crushed exult.
¹¹Hide Your face from my sins;
  blot out all my iniquities.
¹²Fashion a pure heart for me, O God;
  create in me a steadfast spirit.
¹³Do not cast me out of Your presence,
  or take Your holy spirit away from me.
¹⁴Let me again rejoice in Your help;
  let a vigorous spirit sustain me.
¹⁵I will teach transgressors Your ways,
  that sinners may return to You.

¹⁶Save me from bloodguilt,
  O God, God, my deliverer,
  that I may sing forth Your beneficence.
¹⁷O Lord, open my lips,
  and let my mouth declare Your praise.
¹⁸You do not want me to bring sacrifices;
  You do not desire burnt offerings;
¹⁹True sacrifice to God is a contrite spirit;
  God, You will not despise
  a contrite and crushed heart.

²⁰May it please You to make Zion prosper;
  rebuild the walls of Jerusalem.
²¹Then You will want sacrifices offered in righteousness,
  burnt and whole offerings;
  then bulls will be offered on Your altar.

137

By the rivers of Babylon,
  there we sat,
  sat and wept,
  as we thought of Zion.
²There on the poplars
  we hung up our lyres,
  ³for our captors asked us there for songs,
  our tormentors, for amusement,
  "Sing us one of the songs of Zion."

⁴How can we sing a song of the Lord
  on alien soil?
⁵If I forget you, O Jerusalem,
  let my right hand wither;
  ⁶let my tongue stick to my palate
  if I cease to think of you,
  if I do not keep Jerusalem in memory
  even at my happiest hour.

⁷Remember, O Lord, against the Edomites
  the day of Jerusalem's fall;
  how they cried, "Strip her, strip her
  to her very foundations!"
⁸Fair Babylon, you predator,
  a blessing on him who repays you in kind
  what you have inflicted on us;
  ⁹a blessing on him who seizes your babies
  and dashes them against the rocks!

❧

From Esther

3

Some time afterward, King Ahasuerus promoted Haman son of Hammedatha the Agagite; he advanced him and seated him higher than any of his fellow officials. ²All the king's courtiers in the palace gate knelt and bowed low to Haman, for such was the king's order concerning him; but Mordecai would not kneel or bow low. ³Then the king's courtiers who were in the palace gate said to Mordecai, "Why do you disobey the king's order?" ⁴When they spoke to him day after day and he would not listen to them, they told Haman, in order to see whether Mordecai's resolve would prevail; for he had explained to them that he was a Jew. ⁵When Haman saw that Mordecai would not kneel or bow low to him, Haman was filled with rage. ⁶But he disdained to lay hands on Mordecai alone; having been told who Mordecai's people were, Haman plotted to do away with all the Jews, Mordecai's people, throughout the kingdom of Ahasuerus.

⁷In the first month, that is, the month of Nisan, in the twelfth year of King Ahasuerus, *pur*—which means "the lot"—was cast before Haman concerning every day and every month, [until it fell on] the twelfth month, that is, the month of Adar. ⁸Haman then said to King Ahasuerus, "There is a certain people, scattered and dis-

persed among the other peoples in all the provinces of your realm, whose laws are different from those of any other people and who do not obey the king's laws; and it is not in Your Majesty's interest to tolerate them. ⁹ If it please Your Majesty, let an edict be drawn for their destruction, and I will pay ten thousand talents of silver to the stewards for deposit in the royal treasury." ¹⁰ Thereupon the king removed his signet ring from his hand and gave it to Haman son of Hammedatha the Agagite, the foe of the Jews. ¹¹ And the king said, "The money and the people are yours to do with as you see fit."

¹² On the thirteenth day of the first month, the king's scribes were summoned and a decree was issued, as Haman directed, to the king's satraps, to the governors of every province, and to the officials of every people, to every province in its own script and to every people in its own language. The orders were issued in the name of King Ahasuerus and sealed with the king's signet. ¹³ Accordingly, written instructions were dispatched by couriers to all the king's provinces to destroy, massacre, and exterminate all the Jews, young and old, children and women, on a single day, on the thirteenth day of the twelfth month—that is, the month of Adar—and to plunder their possessions. ¹⁴ The text of the document was to the effect that a law should be proclaimed in every single province; it was to be publicly displayed to all the peoples, so that they might be ready for that day.

¹⁵ The couriers went out posthaste on the royal mission, and the decree was proclaimed in the fortress Shushan. The king and Haman sat down to feast, but the city of Shushan was dumfounded.

4

When Mordecai learned all that had happened, Mordecai tore his clothes and put on sackcloth and ashes. He went through the city, crying out loudly and bitterly, ² until he came in front of the palace gate; for one could not enter the palace gate wearing sackcloth.—³ Also, in every province that the king's command and decree reached, there was great mourning among the Jews, with fasting, weeping, and wailing, and everybody lay in sackcloth and ashes.—⁴ When Esther's maidens and eunuchs came and informed her, the queen was greatly agitated. She sent clothing for Mordecai to wear, so that he might take off his sackcloth; but he refused. ⁵ Thereupon Esther summoned Hathach, one of the eunuchs whom the king had appointed to serve her, and sent him to Mordecai to learn the why and wherefore of it all. ⁶ Hathach went out to Mordecai in the city square in front of the palace gate; ⁷ and Mordecai told him all

that had happened to him, and all about the money that Haman had offered to pay into the royal treasury for the destruction of the Jews. ⁸ He also gave him the written text of the law that had been proclaimed in Shushan for their destruction. [He bade him] show it to Esther and inform her, and charge her to go to the king and to appeal to him and to plead with him for her people. ⁹ When Hathach came and delivered Mordecai's message to Esther, ¹⁰ Esther told Hathach to take back to Mordecai the following reply: ¹¹ "All the king's courtiers and the people of the king's provinces know that if any person, man or woman, enters the king's presence in the inner court without having been summoned, there is but one law for him—that he be put to death. Only if the king extends the golden scepter to him may he live. Now I have not been summoned to visit the king for the last thirty days."

¹² When Mordecai was told what Esther had said, ¹³ Mordecai had this message delivered to Esther: "Do not imagine that you, of all the Jews, will escape with your life by being in the king's palace. ¹⁴ On the contrary, if you keep silent in this crisis, relief and deliverance will come to the Jews from another quarter, while you and your father's house will perish. And who knows, perhaps you have attained to royal position for just such a crisis." ¹⁵ Then Esther sent back this answer to Mordecai: ¹⁶ "Go, assemble all the Jews who live in Shushan, and fast in my behalf; do not eat or drink for three days, night or day. I and my maidens will observe the same fast. Then I shall go to the king, though it is contrary to the law; and if I am to perish, I shall perish!" ¹⁷ So Mordecai went about [the city] and did just as Esther had commanded him.

5

On the third day, Esther put on royal apparel and stood in the inner court of the king's palace, facing the king's palace, while the king was sitting on his royal throne in the throne room facing the entrance of the palace. ² As soon as the king saw Queen Esther standing in the court, she won his favor. The king extended to Esther the golden scepter which he had in his hand, and Esther approached and touched the tip of the scepter. ³ "What troubles you, Queen Esther?" the king asked her. "And what is your request? Even to half the kingdom, it shall be granted you." ⁴ "If it please Your Majesty," Esther replied, "let Your Majesty and Haman come today to the feast that I have prepared for him." ⁵ The king commanded, "Tell Haman to hurry and do Esther's bidding." . . .

7

So the king and Haman came to feast with Queen Esther. ²On the second day, the king again asked Esther at the wine feast, "What is your wish, Queen Esther? It shall be granted you. And what is your request? Even to half the kingdom, it shall be fulfilled." ³Queen Esther replied: "If Your Majesty will do me the favor, and if it pleases Your Majesty, let my life be granted me as my wish, and my people as my request. ⁴For we have been sold, my people and I, to be destroyed, massacred, and exterminated. Had we only been sold as bondmen and bondwomen, I would have kept silent; for the adversary is not worthy of the king's trouble."

⁵Thereupon King Ahasuerus demanded of Queen Esther, "Who is he and where is he who dared to do this?" ⁶"The adversary and enemy," replied Esther, "is this evil Haman!" And Haman cringed in terror before the king and the queen. ⁷The king, in his fury, left the wine feast for the palace garden, while Haman remained to plead with Queen Esther for his life; for he saw that the king had resolved to destroy him. ⁸When the king returned from the palace garden to the banquet room, Haman was lying prostrate on the couch on which Esther reclined. "Does he mean," cried the king, "to ravish the queen in my own palace?" No sooner did these words leave the king's lips than Haman's face was covered. ⁹Then Harbonah, one of the eunuchs in attendance on the king, said, "What is more, a stake is standing at Haman's house, fifty cubits high, which Haman made for Mordecai—the man whose words saved the king." "Impale him on it!" the king ordered. ¹⁰So they impaled Haman on the stake which he had put up for Mordecai, and the king's fury abated.

10.3 THE AGE OF DEFINITION (ca. 70–640 C.E.)

The first date of this formative period in the development of Judaism marks the destruction of the second temple by the Romans. The second date, 640, refers to the Arab conquest of the Near and Middle East and the establishment of Islam as the dominant religion.

During this period, Jewish faith faced serious problems. First, the second temple was lost and once again the Jews faced exile from Zion. Then Christianity, an offshoot of their own faith, became the official religion of the Roman Empire. The Jews now had to live in the world of Christendom. Then the Arab conquest pushed the Christians farther north

(along with many Jews) and established yet another religion, Islam, in lands the Jews held sacred. How could God let all of this happen to his chosen people? How could it be explained? How can the faith survive without the land God promised?

Not only did it survive, adversity brought one of the greatest creative surges in Jewish history. This creative response started before 70, but its energy flowed into later times. The destruction of the temple in 70 only served to give it further urgency. Jewish thinkers studied Greek and Roman philosophy, applying what they learned to the interpretation of Jewish Scriptures. These scriptures had been translated into Greek around 250 B.C.E. and named the Septuagint. Religious communities such as the Therapeutae and the Essenes sprung up, awaiting what they took to be the last days of judgment when God would establish his people once and for all by destroying their enemies. Jewish groups called Pharisees and Sadducees debated such issues as the resurrection of the dead. And great bodies of written materials—the Mishnah and the Talmud—reported the wisdom of Jewish sages, or rabbis.

10.3.1 Creation of the Intelligible World

When the first temple was destroyed in 586 B.C.E., a large number of Jews fled to Egypt. After Alexander the Great conquered Egypt and established the city of Alexandria, it became a center of learning and commerce in the Mediterranean world. Philo of Alexandria (ca. 20 B.C.E.–50 C.E.) was a Hellenized Jew who drank deeply at the well of Greek philosophy and science as well as Jewish lore and wisdom.

Philo believed that the truth of the Torah of Moses must coincide with the truth the Greek philosophers and scientists discovered. He developed the allegorical method of interpretation in order to show that buried in the Torah was an orderly and scientific account of the world and human life.

The Greek philosopher Plato (428–347 B.C.E.) had discovered that the visible world contained an order or pattern that the human mind, using logical and mathematical reasoning, could comprehend. It is as if the world in all of its ever-changing and seemingly chaotic splendor followed a hidden blueprint—a form or pattern that was unchanging and invariant. This intelligible pattern or, better, patterns, Plato called Forms. He believed they were discernible in human language and by human reason. Hence they constituted a *logos*, a Greek word meaning both "word" and "reason."

When the Torah was translated into Greek, the word *logos* was used to translate the creative word of God spoken about in Genesis. Thus, when Philo read his Torah through Greek and Platonic glasses, he found revealed there the intelligible world of Platonic Forms. The visible world is made according to this intelligible pattern, and thus the myth (Greek *mythos* means "story") of creation revealed to Moses contains, when allegorically interpreted, a true scientific account of how the world came to be. Indeed, it even improves on Plato's account because Plato had no place to locate the intelligible Forms, but Moses did. They eternally abide in the Divine Mind. God thinks the world before he creates it.

The passage included below tells how Philo went about showing that the wisdom of the Jewish Moses is no less than the wisdom of the best minds of the Greek world. According to Philo, the Jews' stories and writings represent a divinely revealed truth because they contain the best teachings about the origin of the world the science of the day had to offer.

⊱✖⊰

PHILO OF ALEXANDRIA

On the Intelligible World

READING QUESTIONS

1. What is the intelligible world, and what role does it play in creation?
2. How does Philo deduce the doctrine of the Incorporeal Ideas from Genesis?
3. What is the "Logos," and what role does it play in creation?
4. Why do you think Philo uses the sexual metaphor of the Creator having intercourse with his knowledge?

From *Philo of Alexandria: The Contemplative Life, the Giants, and Selections*, translated by David Winston (New York: Paulist Press, 1981), pp. 99–102. Copyright © 1981 by David Winston. Reprinted by permission. Notes omitted.

The Intelligible World within the Divine Mind Compared to a Blueprint within the Architect's Mind

For God, being God, judged in advance that a beautiful copy would never be produced except from a beautiful pattern and that no sense object would be irreproachable that was not modeled after an archetypal and intelligible idea. So when he willed to create this visible world, he first formed the intelligible world, so that he might employ a pattern completely Godlike and incorporeal for the production of the corporeal world, a more recent image of one that was older, which was to comprise as many sensible kinds as there were intelligible ones in the other.

To say or to suppose that that world composed of the ideas is in some place is improper; but how it was put together we shall know if we closely attend to some similitude taken from our own world. When a city is being founded to satisfy the great ambition of some king or ruler who pretends to absolute power, and magnificent in his pride further embellishes his good fortune, there comes forward now and then some trained architect who, after observing the mild climate and convenient location of the site, first maps out in his own mind virtually all the parts of the city that is to be brought to completion, temples, gymnasia, town halls, marketplaces, harbors, docks, lanes, wall constructions, the erection of houses as well as public buildings. Accordingly, after having received in his soul, as in wax, the impressions of each of these objects, he carries in his mind the image of an intelligible city. Then, after awakening these images through his innate power of memory, and imprinting their stamp even further, like a good craftsman keeping his eye on the model, he begins to build the city of stones and timber, adapting the corporeal objects to each of the incorporeal ideas.

Similarly must we think about God. When he was minded to found the Great City, he first conceived the forms of its parts, out of which he put together the intelligible world, and, using that as a model, he also brought to completion the sensible world. As, then, the city prefigured in the architect's mind held no place externally but was stamped in the soul of the artisan, so too the intelligible world could have no other location than the Divine Logos, which established the world order. For what other place could there be for his powers sufficient to receive and contain, I say not all, but any of them whatever unmixed. (*Op.* 16–20)

The Intelligible World Is the Divine Logos in the Act of Creation

If one should wish to express it more baldly, he would say that the Intelligible World is nothing else than the

Divine Logos already in the act of building the cosmos, for the intelligible city is nothing else than the reasoning of the architect already intent on founding the city. This is Moses' teaching, not mine; for in his description of man's creation in the sequel he explicitly acknowledges that he was molded after the image of God (Gen. 1:27). Now if the part is an image of an image, and the whole form, this entire sensible world since it is greater than the human image, is a copy of the divine image, it is clear that the archetypal seal, which we declare to be the intelligible world, would be the very Logos of God. (*Op.* 24–25)

Creation of the Intelligible World

First, then, the Creator made an incorporeal heaven and an invisible earth and the Form of air and void. The one he named "darkness," since air is by nature black; the other, "abyss," for the void is very deep and immense. Next came the incorporeal essence of water and pneuma (breath), and topping them all in the seventh place, that of light, which, in its turn incorporeal, was an intelligible pattern of the sun and all the luminous stars that were to take shape across the heavens. (*Op.* 29)

Creation of Incorporeal Ideas Deduced from Genesis 2:4–5

Concluding the creation narrative he says by way of summary:

> This is the book of the genesis of heaven and earth, when they came into being, on the day on which God made the heaven and the earth and every green shrub of the field before it appeared upon the earth, and all grass of the field before it sprang up. (Gen. 2:4–5)

Is he not manifestly setting before us the incorporeal and intelligible ideas that are the seals of the sensible objects of creation? For before the earth greened, young verdure itself existed in the nature of things, and before grass sprang up in the field, an invisible grass existed. We must suppose that prior also to each of all the other objects judged by the senses, there existed the more ancient forms and measures through which all things that come into being are shaped and measured, for even if he has not gone through all things severally but only collectively, taking thought as much as any for brevity, the few things said constitute nonetheless patterns for the whole of nature, which without an incorporeal model accomplishes nothing in the world of sense. (*Op.* 129–130)

The Logos Used as an Instrument in Creating the World

Bezalel means, then, "in the shadow of God"; but God's shadow is his Logos, which he used as an instrument and thus created the world. This shadow and representation, as it were, is in turn the archetype of other

things. For just as God is the Pattern of the Image, which was just named Shadow, so does the Image become the pattern of others, as Moses made clear at the beginning of the Law Code by saying, "And God made man after the Image of God" (Gen. 1:27); thus the Image had been modeled after God, but man after the Image, which had acquired the force of a pattern. (*LA* 3.96)

God Had Intercourse with His Knowledge and Begat Created Being

We should at once rightly say that the Craftsman who made this universe was at the same time the father of what was begotten, while the mother was the knowledge of its creator. With his knowledge God had intercourse, not in human fashion, and begat created being. Knowledge received the divine seed and with birththroes bearing perfect fruit bore the only beloved and sense-perceptible Son, this world. Thus wisdom is represented by one of the divine chorus as speaking of herself in this manner: "God obtained me first of all his world and founded me before the ages" (Prov. 8:22). For all that has come to birth must inevitably be younger than the mother and nurse of the All. (*Ebr.* 30–31) . . .

10.3.2 Dead Sea Scrolls

A few miles south of Jericho, on the western shore of the Dead Sea, lies some ruins known as Khirbet Qumran. These ruins were the center of an ancient Jewish religious community. One day, some two thousand years ago, members of this community hastily climbed the nearby cliffs in order to hide their precious scrolls in eleven caves. No one came back to get them, and they remained undisturbed until 1947 when a Bedouin shepherd boy accidentally discovered them. The information contained in the scrolls has led scholars to revise much of their thinking about religion, politics, Judaism, and the beginnings of Christianity at the start of a new millennium that saw Philo busy at work in Alexandria, Jews rebelling against Roman rule of Judah, and messianic Zealots roaming the streets of Jerusalem prophesying the coming of the **Messiah**—the "anointed one" of Israel.

Although the Qumran community has been identified by some scholars with a Jewish group known as the **Essenes,** this name is not used in the manuscripts, now called the **Dead Sea Scrolls.** The members of this religious community believed they were preparing for the final battle between the forces of good and evil. Apparently gripped by "eschatological fever" (**eschatology** refers to the end times, or last days, when God will establish his kingdom), they anticipated a decisive battle between the sons of light and the sons of darkness.

This theme of conflict between the forces of good and evil is as old as the human imagination and as recent as the latest Hollywood movie. This battle has a moral dimension that is fought over and over again whenever humans seek to do good but are tempted by evil. However, the members of the Qumran community thought it would be fought for the final time and that it would be a cosmic battle between truth and falsehood and a religious battle between purity and pollution.

The selection that follows, called "The Community Rule 1QS," was discovered in Cave 1. It is probably one of the oldest documents of the Qumran sect, originally written about 100 B.C.E. Apparently it was intended for the teachers or Masters of the community and contains statutes concerned with initiation into the sect and its common life and discipline, extracts from liturgical ceremonies, and a tract on the spirits of truth and falsehood. Below are parts III–IV dealing with entry into the covenant along with instruction about the two spirits.

Community Rule

READING QUESTIONS

1. How are the two spirits different?
2. What will happen "at the time of visitation"?
3. How do you think this sect might reconcile the strong emphasis on God's control and predestination with human freedom and responsibility?

The Master shall instruct all the sons of light and shall teach them the nature of all the children of men according to the kind of spirit which they possess, the signs identifying their works during their lifetime, their visitation for chastisement, and the time of their reward.

From the God of Knowledge comes all that is and shall be. Before ever they existed He established their whole design, and when, as ordained for them, they

From *The Complete Dead Sea Scrolls in English* by Geza Vermes, pp. 101–103. Published by Penguin Books. Reprinted by permission.

come into being, it is in accord with His glorious design that they accomplish their task without change. The laws of all things are in His hand and He provides them with all their needs.

He has created man to govern the world, and has appointed for him two spirits in which to walk until the time of His visitation: the spirits of truth and injustice. Those born of truth spring from a fountain of light, but those born of injustice spring from a source of darkness. All the children of righteousness are ruled by the Prince of Light and walk in the ways of light, but all the children of injustice are ruled by the Angel of Darkness and walk in the ways of darkness.

The Angel of Darkness leads all the children of righteousness astray, and until his end, all their sin, iniquities, wickedness, and all their unlawful deeds are caused by his dominion in accordance with the mysteries of God. Every one of their chastisements, and every one of the seasons of their distress, shall be brought about by the rule of his persecution; for all his allotted spirits seek the overthrow of the sons of light.

But the God of Israel and His Angel of Truth will succour all the sons of light. For it is He who created the spirits of Light and Darkness and founded every action upon them and established every deed [upon] their [ways]. And He loves the one everlastingly and delights in its works for ever; but the counsel of the other He loathes and for ever hates its ways.

These are their ways in the world for the enlightenment of the heart of man, and that all the paths of true righteousness may be made straight before him, and that the fear of the laws of God may be instilled in his heart: a spirit of humility, patience, abundant charity, unending goodness, understanding, and intelligence; (a spirit of) mighty wisdom which trusts in all the deeds of God and leans on His great loving-kindness; a spirit of discernment in every purpose, of zeal for just laws, of holy intent with steadfastness of heart, of great charity towards all the sons of truth, of admirable purity which detests all unclean idols, of humble conduct sprung from an understanding of all things, and of faithful concealment of the mysteries of truth. These are the counsels of the spirit to the sons of truth in this world.

And as for the visitation of all who walk in this spirit, it shall be healing, great peace in a long life, and fruitfulness, together with every everlasting blessing and eternal joy in life without end, a crown of glory and a garment of majesty in unending light.

But the ways of the spirit of falsehood are these: greed, and slackness in the search for righteousness, wickedness and lies, haughtiness and pride, falseness and deceit, cruelty and abundant evil, ill-temper and much folly and brazen insolence, abominable deeds (committed) in a spirit of lust, and ways of lewdness in the service of uncleanness, a blaspheming tongue, blindness of eye and dullness of ear, stiffness of neck and heaviness of heart, so that man walks in all the ways of darkness and guile.

And the visitation of all who walk in this spirit shall be a multitude of plagues by the hand of all the destroying angels, everlasting damnation by the avenging wrath of the fury of God, eternal torment and endless disgrace together with shameful extinction in the fire of the dark regions. The times of all their generations shall be spent in sorrowful mourning and in bitter misery and in calamities of darkness until they are destroyed without remnant or survivor.

The nature of all the children of men is ruled by these (two spirits), and during their life all the hosts of men have a portion of their divisions and walk in (both) their ways. And the whole reward for their deeds shall be, for everlasting ages, according to whether each man's portion in their two divisions is great or small. For God has established the spirits in equal measure until the final age, and has set everlasting hatred between their divisions. Truth abhors the works of injustice, and injustice hates all the ways of truth. And their struggle is fierce in all their arguments for they do not walk together.

But in the mysteries of His understanding, and in His glorious wisdom, God has ordained an end for injustice, and at the time of the visitation He will destroy it for ever. Then truth, which has wallowed in the ways of wickedness during the dominion of injustice until the appointed time of judgement, shall arise in the world for ever. God will then purify every deed of man with His truth; He will refine for Himself the human frame by rooting out all spirit of injustice from the bounds of his flesh. He will cleanse him of all wicked deeds with the spirit of holiness; like purifying waters He will shed upon him the spirit of truth (to cleanse him) of all abomination and injustice. And he shall be plunged into the spirit of purification that he may instruct the upright in the knowledge of the Most High and teach the wisdom of the sons of heaven to the perfect of way. [sic] For God has chosen them for an everlasting Covenant and all the glory of Adam shall be theirs. There shall be no more lies and all the works of injustice shall be put to shame.

Until now the spirits of truth and injustice struggle in the hearts of men and they walk in both wisdom and folly. According to his portion of truth so does a man hate injustice, and according to his inheritance in the realm of injustice so is he wicked and so hates truth. For God has established the two spirits in equal measure until the determined end, and until the Renewal, and

He knows the reward of their deeds from all eternity. He has allotted them to the children of men that they may know good [and evil, and] that the destiny of all the living may be according to the spirit within [them at the time] of the visitation. . . .

10.3.3 Wisdom of the Fathers

The **Mishnah** is largely a collection of legal discussions about what kinds of law apply to what sorts of situations. It was produced around 200 C.E. and over the next 400 years the rabbis created two massive commentaries on the Mishnah, both called **Talmud**. (See Neusner's discussion of the Jerusalem and Babylonian Talmuds in Reading 10.1.)

Below you will find one of the best-known sections of the Mishnah called *Abot* (literally, "fathers"). This section is so important that medieval copies of the Talmud have *Abot* at the end of each of the six key divisions. The typical style of the Mishnah is dialogical debate and argument, but the *Abot* is different. It is a collection of proverbs that were not debated. Another title for *Abot* is "The Ethics of the Fathers." As early as the ninth century, Jews formally studied this ethics manual on Saturday afternoons during summer months. Eventually it was added to the Prayer Book.

Although Judaism traces its oral Torah back to Moses (as the transmission recital that opens the *Abot* indicates), the Mishnah and the Talmudic commentary on it are obviously the collected sayings of the rabbis. How could these collected opinions of sages count as divine law? Surely, Moses did not receive from God and orally transmit laws that have to do with situations that did not even exist in his day? Besides, it is obvious from reading the text that these laws emerged from often heated discussion, debate, and disagreements among the **rabbis**.

The selection from the *Baba Mezia*, one of the most famous sections of the Talmud, explains that the majority position held by those sages who carry the oral law becomes the law. This notion of majority rule allowed the debate and exploration to continue while ensuring closure at some point. What is remarkable about this discussion is the authority invested in majority rule. Neither miracles nor voices from heaven have greater authority than consensus among those who transmit the oral Torah.

The Talmudic rabbis discussed many religious and civil matters. Among these matters were, quite naturally, laws relating to marriage and family. The *Trac-*

tate Yebamot, from which our third selection comes, deals specifically with levirate marriage—the obligation of a man to marry his deceased brother's wife if he died childless. The discussion of levirate marriage takes place in the more general context of the obligation to have children, which stems from the biblical command to be "fruitful and multiply" (Gn 1:28). Interestingly, the Mishnah exempts women from this duty of procreation.

Women did not have equal status with men under Talmudic law. For example, only a husband could initiate a divorce. Women were expected to engage primarily in domestic activities and were not encouraged to study the Torah, although some did. No law forbids women from studying the Torah, but only men are commanded to do so. Nevertheless, at least one second-century woman, believed to have been married to the famous Rabbi Meir, became a renowned Torah scholar. Her name is Beruriah and documents containing her story go back to the third century. It is said that her scholarship was so great that she learned three hundred traditions from three hundred masters in a single day. However, in the eleventh century a story was introduced into the Beruriah tradition that recounts how she mocked the rabbinic attitude toward women, committed adultery with one of her husband's students, then killed herself causing her husband to flee in disgrace.

Mishnah and Talmud

READING QUESTIONS

1. What do you think is meant by the command to make a fence around the Torah? Why does the Torah need a fence?
2. Why do you think the *Abot* is regarded as so important?
3. In your opinion, why would the sages of Israel regard miracles as less important as sources of authority than the majority opinion of the rabbis?
4. What strikes you as most important about the Talmudic discussion of levirate marriage?

From *The Talmud: Selected Writings*, translated by Ben Zion Bokser (New York: Paulist Press, 1989), pp. 219–221, 184–185, 131–132. Copyright © 1989 by Baruch M. Bokser. Reprinted by permission.

1. Moses received the Torah at Sinai. He conveyed it to Joshua; Joshua to the elders; the elders to the prophets; and the prophets transmitted it to the men of the Great Assembly. The latter emphasized three principles: Be deliberate in judgment; raise up many disciples; and make a fence to safeguard the Torah.

2. Simeon the Just was of the last survivors of the Great Assembly. He used to say: The world rests on three foundations: the Torah; the divine service; and the practices of lovingkindness between man and man.

3. Antigonus of Soho received the tradition from him. He was accustomed to say: Be not like servants who serve their master because of the expected reward, but be like those who serve a master without expecting a reward; and let the fear of God be upon you.

4. Yose ben Yoezer of Zeredah and Yose ben Yohanan of Jerusalem received the tradition from them. Yose ben Yoezer of Zeredah said: Let your house be a gathering place for wise men; sit attentively at their feet, and drink of their words of wisdom with eagerness.

5. Yose ben Yohanan of Jerusalem said: Let your home be a place of hospitality to strangers; and make the poor welcome in your household; and do not indulge in gossip with women. This applies even with one's own wife, and surely so with another man's wife. The sages generalized from this: He who engages in profuse gossiping with women causes evil for himself and neglects the study of the Torah, and he will bring upon himself retributions in the hereafter.

6. Joshua ben Perahya and Nittai the Arbelite received the tradition from them. Joshua ben Perahya said: Get yourself a teacher; and acquire for yourself a companion; and judge all people favorably.

7. Nittai the Arbelite said: Avoid an evil neighbor; do not associate with the wicked; and do not surrender your faith in divine retribution.

8. Judah ben Tabbai and Simeon ben Shatah received the traditions from them. Judah ben Tabbai said: Let not the judge play the part of the counselor; when they leave after submitting to the court's decree, regard them both as guiltless.

9. Simeon ben Shatah said: Search the witnesses thoroughly and be cautious with your own words lest you give them an opening to false testimony.

10. Shemaya and Abtalyon received the traditions from them. Shemaya said: love work; hate domineering over others; and do not seek the intimacy of public officials.

11. Abtalyon said: Sages, be precise in your teachings. You may suffer exile to a place where heresy is ram-

pant, and your inexact language may lead your disciples astray, and they will lose their faith, thus leading to a desecration of the divine name.

12. Hillel and Shammai received the tradition from them. Hillel said: Be of the disciples of Aaron. Love peace and pursue peace; love your fellow creatures and bring them near to the Torah.

13. He also said: He who strives to exalt his name will in the end destroy his name; he who does not increase his knowledge decreases it; he who does not study has undermined his right to life; and he who makes unworthy use of the crown of the Torah will perish.

14. He also said: If I am not for myself who will be? But if I am for myself only, what am I? And if not now, when?

15. Shammai said: Set a fixed time for the study of the Torah; say little and do much; and greet every person with a cheerful countenance.

16. Rabban Gamaliel said: Provide yourself with a teacher, and extricate yourself from doubt; and do not habitually contribute your tithes by rough estimates.

17. Simeon his son said: All my life I was raised among scholars and I found that no virtue becomes a man more than silence; what is more essential is not study but practice; and in the wake of many words is sin.

18. Rabban Simeon ben Gamaliel said: The world rests on three foundations: truth, justice, and peace. As it is written (Zech 8:16): "You shall administer truth, justice and peace within your gates."

[MISHNAH, *Abot*, ch. 1]

THE TALMUD ON RABBINIC AUTHORITY

We studied in the Mishnah (Eduyot 7:7) that if a pottery stove was cut into tiles, and cemented over with sand placed between the tiles, R. Eliezer declared it unsusceptible to ritual uncleanliness, while the other Sages declared it susceptible. This was the Akhnai Stove.

Why was it called Akhnai? Said R. Judah in the name of Samuel. They surrounded it with arguments as a snake winds its body around an object, and declared it unclean. It has been taught: On that day R. Eliezer marshaled every conceivable argument, but they did not accept them. Then he said: If the law is according to my views, let this carob tree prove it. There, upon the carob tree was thrust to a distance of a hundred cubits from its place, and some say four

hundred. They replied to him: We adduce no evidence from a carob tree. Again he said to them: If the law is in accordance with my views, let the stream of water prove it, and at once the stream of water flowed in the opposite direction. But they said: We adduce no evidence from a stream of water. Again he said to them: If the law agrees with my views, let the walls of the academy prove it, and the walls of the academy began to bend and were about to fall. R. Joshua rebuked them, saying: If scholars argue on a point of law, what business is it of yours? The walls did not fall out of respect for R. Joshua, but they did not become straight again out of respect for R. Eliezer.

Thereupon he said: If the law is in accordance with my views, let them prove it from heaven. A heavenly voice came forth, saying: What have you against R. Eliezer? The law is as he propounds it in all instances. R. Joshua then stood up and quoted: "It is not in the heavens" (Dt 30:12). What did he mean by quoting: "It is not in the heavens?" Said R. Jeremiah: That the Torah has already been given at Sinai, and we pay no attention to heavenly voices, for You have written at Sinai in the Torah: "Incline after the majority" (Ex 23:2).

R. Nathan met the prophet Elijah and he asked him: What did the Holy One, praised be He, do at that time? He replied: He laughed, and He said: My children have won over me, my chlordane have won over me!

[Talmud, *Baba Mezia* 59a–59b]

THE TALMUD ON LEVIRATE MARRIAGE

A person should not abstain from carrying out the obligation to "be fruitful and multiply" (Gn 1:28) unless he already has two chlordane. The Beit Shammai ruled: This means two sons, and the Beit Hillel ruled: A son and a daughter, because it is written: "Male and female He created them" (Gn 5:2). The duty of procreation applies to a man, but not to a woman. R. Yohanan b. Beroka said: Concerning both it is written: "And God blessed them and said to them: Be fruitful and multiply" (Gn 1:28). Mishnah 6:6

This means that if he has children he may abstain from the duty of procreation but he may not abstain from the duty of living with a wife. This supports the view of R. Nahman who reported a ruling in the name of Samuel, that even though a person has many children, he may not remain without a wife, as it is written: "It is not good for a man to be alone" (Gn 2:18). Others held the view that if he had children, he may abstain from the duty of procreation and he may also abstain from the duty of living with a wife. Shall we say that this contradicts what was reported by R. Nahman in the name of Samuel? No. If he has no children, he is to marry a woman capable of having a child, but if he already has children, he may marry a woman who is incapable of having children.

Elsewhere it was taught: R. Nathan said: According to the Beit Shammai, a person satisfies the obligation to "be fruitful and multiply" if he has a son and a daughter, and according to the Beit Hillel if he has a son or a daughter. Said Rava: what is the reason for the view of the Beit Hillel? It is written: "He created it not to be a waste, He formed it to be inhabited" (Is 45:18), and [by having a son or a daughter] he has already contributed to making it a place of habitation.

It was stated: If a person had children while he was an idolater, and was later converted [to Judaism], R. Yohanan said that he has already fulfilled the duty of procreation but Resh Lakish said that he has not fulfilled it, because when a person is converted he is like a born-again child.

The Mishnah does not agree with the view of R. Joshua, for it was taught that R. Joshua stated: if a person married in his youth he is also to marry in his old age; if he had children in his youth, he is also to have children in his old age, for it is written: "Sow your seed in the morning and do not withdraw your hand in the evening, for you do not know which will prosper, this or that, or whether both alike will be good" (Eccl 11:6).

Said R. Tanhum in the name of R. Hanilai: A person who is without a wife is without joy, without blessing, without good. Without joy—as it is written: "You shall rejoice, you and your household" (Dt 14:26); without blessing—as it is written: "That a blessing may rest on your house" (Ez 44:30) ["house" in such a context has generally been interpreted to mean one's wife]; without good—as it is written: "It is not good for a man to be alone" (Gn 2:18). In Palestine they said: He is without Torah, and without protection [from the ravages of life]. Without Torah—as it is written: "In truth, I have no one to help me [a wife], and sound wisdom [Torah] is driven from me" (Jb 6:13); without protection—as it is written: "A woman protects a man" (Jer 31:22). R. b. Ila said: He is without peace—as it is written: "And you shall know that your tent [when presided over by one's wife] is at peace, and you will visit your habitation and you will not sin" (Jb 5:24).

Said R. Joshua b. Levi: A person who knows his wife to be a God-fearing woman and he does not have marital relations with her is a sinner, as it is written: "And you shall visit your habitation [a euphemism for having relations with one's wife] and you will not sin."

The Rabbis taught: When one loves his wife as himself, and honors her more than himself, and trains his sons and daughters in the right path and arranges for their marriage at a young age—concerning such a person does the verse say: "And you shall know that your tent is at peace."

Said R. Eleazar: A man without a wife is not a complete man, as it is written: "Male and female created He them, and he called their name *adam*, 'man'" (Gn 5:2).

Turn away your eyes from the charms of another man's wife, lest you be trapped in her net. Do not join in fellowship with her husband, to drink with him wine and strong drink, for through the appearance of a beautiful woman have many been destroyed, and a mighty host are all her slain.

[Talmud, *Yebamot* 61b–64a]

10.4 THE AGE OF COGENCY (ca. 640–1800)

As Islam and Christianity tightened their temporal and spiritual power over large segments of the European, North African, Near Eastern, and Far Eastern world, Judaism survived in small pockets keeping the faith in the midst of persecutions and legal restrictions. The tradition of the dual Torah sustained the communities and set the norms for daily life. This is not to say that there were no dissenters—there were. The **Karaites,** for example, rejected the rabbinic conception of the dual Torah. Anan ben David (ca. 800), the founder of the Karaites, denied there was any oral Torah given by God to Moses at Sinai. According to him, there is only the written Torah and it is that by which the Jews should live. The so-called oral Torah of the rabbis amounts to human opinion, not divine law.

Rabbinic Judaism declared Karaites heretics and banned marriage to them. But they flourished among Middle Eastern Jews and in the Crimean area of Russia well into the twentieth century. During the invasion of the USSR from 1941 to 1944, the Germans classified Karaites as Gentiles and did not send them to the death camps.

Another challenge rabbinic Judaism faced came in 1648 when Sabbatai Zvi, a Jew from Smyrna, declared himself the Messiah. Great excitement arose in worldwide Jewry. Throughout 1665 Nathan of Gaza, a follower of Sabbatai Zvi, spread the news of his identity as the Messiah. Nathan's letters received an enthusiastic response throughout the Jewish world.

Sabbatai eventually traveled to Turkey to convert the sultan and the whole of Islam, but ended up converting to Islam. This shocked the Jewish world, dashed the hopes of many, and caused rabbinic Judaism to declare **Sabbateanism** a heresy and Sabbatai Zvi a "false Messiah," yet many persisted in believing in him as the Messiah promised by God.

Karaitism and Sabbateanism so threatened the authority of rabbinic Judaism that they had to be resisted. However, the rabbis accommodated other movements by incorporating them into the dual Torah tradition. Among these were both philosophical and mystical movements.

10.4.1 Principles of Faith

The best-known and most important Jewish philosopher during this classical period of rabbinic cogency is Moses ben Maimon (1135–1204), better known as Maimonides. He was born in Cordoba, Spain, and his importance is signaled by the saying "from Moses to Moses there is none like Moses."

Maimonides' fame rests on his many accomplishments as a physician, a rabbinic leader, an expert in Jewish law, and a philosopher. A book he published in 1190 titled *Guide for the Perplexed* is a philosophical classic. In it he harmonized traditional Jewish belief with the philosophical and scientific thinking of his day. His "Thirteen Principles of Faith," which follow, almost constitute a Jewish orthodox creed.

⇜⚜⇝

MOSES BEN MAIMON

The Thirteen Principles

READING QUESTIONS

1. What, according to these principles, are the main characteristics of the Creator?
2. What does Maimonides confess with respect to Moses and the Law (Torah)?

From *Authorized Daily Prayer Book*, translated by S. Singer, 9th American ed. (New York: Hebrew Publishing Company, 1912), pp. 89–90.

3. Why do you think so little is said about the Messiah?
4. Most of these "principles" are devoted to the Creator, and only a few deal with other matters. What does this tell you about Maimonides' understanding of Judaism?

1. I believe with perfect faith that the Creator, blessed be his name, is the Author and Guide of everything that has been created, and that he alone has made, does make, and will make all things.

2. I believe with perfect faith that the Creator, blessed be his name, is a Unity, and that there is no unity in any manner like unto his, and that he alone is our God, who was, and is, and will be.

3. I believe with perfect faith that the Creator, blessed be his name, is not a body, and that he is free from all the accidents of matter, and that he has not any form whatsoever.

4. I believe with perfect faith that the Creator, blessed be his name, is the first and the last.

5. I believe with perfect faith that to the Creator, blessed be his name, and to him alone it is right to pray, and that it is not right to pray to any being besides him.

6. I believe with perfect faith that all the words of the prophets are true.

7. I believe with perfect faith that the prophecy of Moses our teacher, peace be unto him, was true, and that he was the chief of the prophets, both of those that preceded and of those that followed him.

8. I believe with perfect faith that the whole Law, now in our possession, is the same that was given to Moses our teacher, peace be unto him.

9. I believe with perfect faith that this Law will not be changed, and that there will never be any other law from the Creator, blessed be his name.

10. I believe with perfect faith that the Creator, blessed be his name, knows every deed of the children of men, and all their thoughts, as it is said, It is he that fashioneth the hearts of them all, that giveth heed to all their deeds.

11. I believe with perfect faith that the Creator, blessed be his name, rewards those that keep his commandments, and punishes those that transgress them.

12. I believe with perfect faith in the coming of the Messiah, and, though he tarry, I will wait daily for his coming.

13. I believe with perfect faith that there will be a resurrection of the dead at the time when it shall please

the Creator, blessed be his name, and exalted be the remembrance of him for ever and ever.

10.4.2 Mystical Visions

There have been many different schools of Jewish mysticism, but since the twelfth century the **Kabbalah** has been the most dominant. The classical statements of early Kabbalah can be found in two thirteenth-century texts, the *Sefer ha-Bahir*, or *Book of Brightness*, and the *Sefer ha-Zohar*, or *Book of Splendor*. The **Zohar** became so influential that within a few centuries it became a sacred text. Moses de Leon, a Spanish Jew from Guadalajara, wrote it between 1280 and 1286. The central character in the book is Rabbi Shim'on, a second-century sage, who presents a verse-by-verse **midrash** (commentary) on several books of the *Tanakh*. Moses de Leon claimed that he discovered this ancient text and that Rabbi Shim'on had written it himself. For nearly six hundred years, Kabbalists believed Moses de Leon.

The key teaching of the *Zohar* centers on the ten emanations of God called the **Sefirot**. These ten divine attributes (Crown, Wisdom, Understanding, Love, Judgment, Beauty, Endurance, Majesty, Foundation, Presence) are the key to the structure of the created order and the key to the return of human beings to their divine source, the *Ein Sof*, or *Infinite*.

According to Genesis 1:27, God creates humans in his image. The *Sefirot* are the image of that image and hence are often (though not always) arranged visually to resemble a human body with the Crown (*Keter*) as the head and the other attributes arranged in left and right columns to form arms and legs. Beauty (*Tif'eret*) is in the center as a balancing power between God's Love and God's Judgment. Foundation (*Yesod*) is the phallus, and Presence (*Shekhinah*) is at the bottom. God's **Shekhinah** is the divine immanence that pervades and sustains all the universe. It is the *Keneset Yisra'el*, the mystical soul of the community of Israel.

The origin of evil lies deeply buried in this mystical body. If Judgment (the left arm) is not balanced by Love (the right arm), an imbalance can result. Both Judgment, which constitutes limitation, and Love, which constitutes grace and freedom, are necessary for the creation of the world. However, too much Judgment (limitation, restriction) and not enough Love (grace and freedom) lead to evil.

The human soul is the result of the union of God's Beauty (*Tif'eret*) and God's Presence (*Shekhinah*). This union gives birth to the human soul, and the mystical journey of the return of the soul to its source begins with the awareness of this mystical origin. Study, prayer, and meditation open the gate of the *Shekhinah*, and the mystic can begin the homeward journey through each of these *Sefirah* to God.

There is much more to this rich symbolism and mythology than I can convey here. These mystical insights fascinated the faithful Jew and the Gentile. The *Sefirot* were put to magical uses, and even fortune-telling *Tarot* cards embodied their symbols.

It is now time to read some of the *Zohar* for yourself and be ushered into a world of mystical wonder and splendor.

MOSES DE LEON

The Zohar

READING QUESTIONS

1. How should we look at the Torah?
2. What is the secret?
3. Who is Adam?

HOW TO LOOK AT TORAH

Rabbi Shim'on said
"Woe to the human being who says
that Torah presents mere stories and ordinary words!
If so, we could compose a Torah right now with ordinary words
and better than all of them!
To present matters of the world?
Even rulers of the world possess words more sublime.
If so, let us follow them and make a Torah out of them!

From *Zohar*, translation and introduction by Daniel Chanan Matt. © 1983 by Daniel Chanan Matt. Reprinted by permission of Paulist Press, Inc. Pp. 43–45, 49–50, 55–56, 153–157.

THE TEN SEFIROT

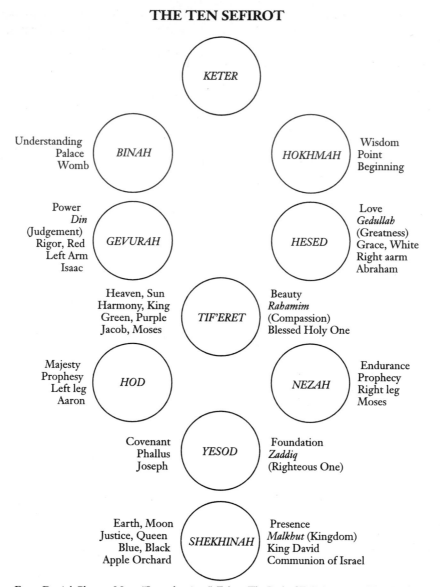

KETER

Understanding
Palace
Womb — BINAH

HOKHMAH — Wisdom
Point
Beginning

Power
Din
(Judgement)
Rigor, Red
Left Arm
Isaac — GEVURAH

HESED — Love
Gedullah
(Greatness)
Grace, White
Right aarm
Abraham

Heaven, Sun
Harmony, King
Green, Purple
Jacob, Moses — TIF'ERET — Beauty
Rahamim
(Compassion)
Blessed Holy One

Majesty
Prophesy
Left leg
Aaron — HOD

NEZAH — Endurance
Prophecy
Right leg
Moses

Covenant
Phallus
Joseph — YESOD — Foundation
Zaddiq
(Righteous One)

Earth, Moon
Justice, Queen
Blue, Black
Apple Orchard — SHEKHINAH — Presence
Malkhut (Kingdom)
King David
Communion of Israel

From Daniel Chanan Matt, "Introduction," *Zohar: The Book of Enlightenment* (New York: Paulist Press, 1983), p. 35. © 1983 Daniel Chanan Matt. Reprinted by permission.

Ah, but all the words of Torah are sublime words, sublime secrets!

Come and see:
The world above and the world below are perfectly balanced:
Israel below, the angels above.
Of the angels it is written:
'He makes His angels spirits'

(Psalms 104:4).
But when they descend, they put on the garment of this world.
If they did not put on a garment befitting this world they could not endure in this world
and the world could not endure them.

If this is so with the angels, how much more so with Torah

who created them and all the worlds
and for whose sake they all exist!
In descending to this world,
if she did not put on the garments of this world
the world could not endure.

So this story of Torah is the garment of Torah.
Whoever thinks that the garment is the real Torah
and not something else—
may his spirit deflate!
He will have no portion in the world that is coming.

That is why David said:
'Open my eyes
so I can see wonders out of Your Torah!'
(Psalms 119:18),
what is under the garment of Torah!

Come and see:
There is a garment visible to all.
When those fools see someone in a good-looking
  garment
they look no further.
But the essence of the garment is the body;
the essence of the body is the soul!

So it is with Torah.
She has a body:
the commandments of Torah,
called 'the embodiment of Torah.'

This body is clothed in garments:
the stories of this world.
Fools of the world look only at that garment, the story
  of Torah;
they know nothing more.
They do not look at what is under that garment.
Those who know more do not look at the garment
but rather at the body under that garment.
The wise ones, servants of the King on high,
those who stood at Mt. Sinai,
look only at the soul, root of all, real Torah!
In the time to come
they are destined to look at the soul of the soul of
  Torah!

Come and see:
So it is above.
There is garment and body and soul and soul of soul.
The heavens and their host are the garment.
The Communion of Israel is the body
who receives the soul, the Beauty of Israel.
So She is the body of the soul.
The soul we have mentioned is the Beauty of Israel
who is real Torah.

The soul of the soul is the Holy Ancient One.
All is connected, this one to that one.

Woe to the wicked
who say that Torah is merely a story!
They look at this garment and no further.
Happy are the righteous
who look at Torah properly!

As wine must sit in a jar,
so Torah must sit in this garment.
So look only at what is under the garment!
So all those words and all those stories—
they are garments!"

THE CREATION OF *ELOHIM*

In the Beginning

When the King conceived ordaining
He engraved engravings in the luster on high.
A blinding spark flashed
within the Concealed of the Concealed
from the mystery of the Infinite,
a cluster of vapor in formlessness,
set in a ring,
not white, not black, not red, not green,
no color at all.
When a band spanned, it yielded radiant colors.
Deep within the spark gushed a flow
imbuing colors below,
concealed within the concealed of the mystery of the
  Infinite.
The flow broke through and did not break through
  its aura.
It was not known at all
until, under the impact of breaking through,
one high and hidden point shone.
Beyond that point, nothing is known.
So it is called Beginning,
the first command of all.
"The enlightened will shine like the *zohar* of the sky,
and those who make the masses righteous
will shine like the stars forever and ever"
(Daniel 12:3).

Zohar, Concealed of the Concealed, struck its aura.
The aura touched and did not touch this point.
Then this Beginning emanated
and made itself a palace for its glory and its praise.
There it sowed the seed of holiness . . .

MALE AND FEMALE

This is the book of the generations of Adam.
On the day that God created Adam,
in the likeness of God He created him;
male and female He created them.
He blessed them and called their name Adam
on the day they were created.

(Genesis 5:1–2)

Rabbi Shim'on said
"High mysteries are revealed in these two verses.
'Male and female He created them'
to make known the Glory on high,
the mystery of faith.
Out of this mystery, Adam was created.

Come and see:
With the mystery by which heaven and earth were
   created
Adam was created.
Of them it is written:
'These are the generations of heaven and earth'
(Genesis 2:4).
Of Adam it is written:
'This is the book of the generations of Adam.'
Of them it is written:
'when they were created.'
Of Adam it is written:
'on the day they were created.'

'Male and female He created them.'
From here we learn:
Any image that does not embrace male and female
is not a high and true image.
We have established this in the mystery of our
   Mishnah.

Come and see:
The Blessed Holy One does not place His abode
in any place where male and female are not found
   together.
Blessings are found only in a place where male and
   female are found,
as it is written:
'He blessed them and called their name Adam
on the day they were created.'
It is not written:
'He blessed him and called his name Adam.'
A human being is only called Adam
when male and female are as one."

10.4.3 Spiritual Tales

Isaac Luria (1534–1572) developed the mysticism of the Kabbalah. Unlike Moses de Leon (see Reading 10.4.2), he did not understand creation in terms of the emanation of God's attributes but, rather, in terms of God's withdrawal. God withdraws into himself in order to make room for the created world. This withdrawal causes God's *Shekhinah*, or Presence, to become trapped in the world. It is not just the Jews who live in exile. Even God's Presence lives in exile!

The mystical return to God now becomes the return of God's *Shekhinah* to its rightful home. When harmony and unity are fully restored to the divine life, the redemption of all life will occur. When all aspects of God are restored to their original, unalienated condition, the universe will be similarly restored. When God's Presence is freed from captivity, the Jews will be freed from their oppressors.

In 1648 there was a widespread massacre of Jews after a Ukrainian uprising against Poland. Eighteen short years later came the elation and then the bitter disappointment caused by the messianic claims, then apostasy of Sabbatai Zvi (see 10.4). Rabbinic Judaism with its dual Torah was hard-pressed to preserve the morale of the Jews of eastern Europe.

Some rabbis and other Jewish leaders began to form various kinds of spiritual and pietistic movements drawing on the Talmud as well as the Kabbalistic mysticism of the *Zohar* and Isaac Luria's ideas about the exiled *Shekhinah*. Messianic expectations entered the picture as well. In the 1730s the **Baal Shem Tov** (1700–1760) began to attract a circle of Talmudic scholars, mystics, preachers, healers, rabbis, and others. This spiritually charged mix gave birth to the Hasidic movement.

There are a variety of Hasidic circles each centering on a **zadik**, or holy and pious leader who embodies an ideal of wisdom. Some scholars distinguish between the "Hasidut of Mysticism" and the "Hasidism of Faith." The former emphasizes God as an impersonal power or force who dwells in all existence. The latter emphasizes God as personal and transcendent, yet deeply involved in the major phases of history: creation, revelation, and redemption.

Nahman of Bratslav (1772–1810), a Ukrainian, was a Hasidic leader who, while deeply mystical, is more representative of the Hasidism of Faith. He developed a type of teaching device—the spiritual tale—that became typical of the Hasidic movement. Below we sample one of his tales.

⟨⟩

NAHMAN OF BRATSLAV

The Loss of the Princess

READING QUESTIONS

1. Write a commentary on this tale explaining what you think its religious meaning is. [*Hint:* The Princess is the *Shekhinah*.]
2. How might this story give comfort to Jews suffering persecution?

Rav Nahman answered and said: On the way, I told a tale (of such power) that whoever heard it had thoughts of repentance. This is it.

Once there was a king. The king had six sons and one daughter. The daughter was extremely important to him and he cherished her and enjoyed her company very much. Once, on a certain day when he was with her, he became enraged at her and from his mouth slipped the sentence: "May The Not-Good take you away." That night she went to her room, and in the morning no one knew where she was. Her father, the king, grieved deeply and he sent here and there searching for her.

Then the viceroy, seeing that the king was deeply grieved, rose and requested that a servant, a horse, and money (for expenses) be given to him. And he set out to search for her. And he searched for her for a very long time until he found her.

(Now Rav Nahman tells how he searched for her until he found her.)

He traveled for a long time, here and there, in deserts and fields and forests. And he searched for her for a very long time. While traveling in the desert, he saw a path off to the side and reflected: "Since I have been traveling such a long time in the desert and cannot find her, I shall follow this path—maybe I will come to a settled place." And he traveled for a long time. At last he saw a castle with many soldiers posted around it. The

castle was very beautiful and the soldiers were standing around it in perfect order. And he feared that the soldiers would not let him in, but he reflected: "I shall attempt it."

He left his horse and walked to the castle. They let him pass and did not hinder him at all. He walked from room to room without hindrance and came to a hall where he saw a king sitting with his crown, many soldiers standing guard, and many musicians playing instruments in his presence. And it was lovely and beautiful there. Neither the king nor any other person asked him anything. He saw delicacies and fine foods there, and he stopped to eat and went to lie down in a corner to observe what was going on there. He observed that the king ordered that they bring the queen and they went to bring her. When they brought in the queen, there was a great tumult and great joy and the musicians played and sang mightily. They placed a throne for her next to the king. And she was the lost princess! And the viceroy recognized her. After a time, the queen glanced about and saw someone lying in the corner and recognized the viceroy. She rose from the throne and went there and touched him.

She asked him: "Do you recognize me?"

He answered: "Yes. I recognize you. You are the princess who has been lost." And he asked: "How did you get here?"

She answered: "Because that sentence slipped from my father's mouth. And this place is *The Not-Good*."

He told her that her father was deeply grieved and that he had searched for her for many years. And he asked her: "How can I free you from here?"

She told him: "You cannot free me unless you choose a place and stay there for one whole year. During this entire year you must yearn for me, to free me from here. You will constantly yearn and search and hope to free me. And you will fast. On the last day of the year, you shall fast and not sleep from sunset to sunset."

And he went and did so. At the end of the year, on the last day, he fasted and did not sleep. He set out to go to the princess to free her. As he went, he saw a tree, and on it grew very fine apples. He craved them very much, and he went to eat from them. As soon as he ate from the apple, he fell over and sleep seized him. And he slept for a very long time. His servant shook him, but he did not wake up. After some time, he stirred from his sleep and asked the servant: "Where am I in the world?"

The servant told the viceroy the entire story: "You have been sleeping a very long time, several years, and I, in the meanwhile, have lived off the fruit." The viceroy grieved deeply and went to the castle and found the princess. And she wailed bitterly to him: "If you had only come on that day you would have freed me from here. Because of that one day, you have lost everything. It is true that not eating is very difficult, especially on the last day when the evil impulse waxes strong. And so, choose another place and stay there, too, for a whole year. On the last day you will be allowed to eat. Only do not sleep and do not drink wine so that you will not fall asleep, because the main thing is sleep."

He went and did so. On the last day he was walking back there and he saw a spring gushing forth and it looked red and smelled of wine. He asked the servant: "Do you see this spring? There should be water in it, but it looks reddish and smells of wine." And he went and tasted a bit from the spring. Immediately, he fell over and slept some seventy years. During this period many soldiers passed by with their baggage trains traveling behind them. And the servant hid from the soldiers. Afterwards, there passed a carriage and the princess was sitting in it. She stopped next to the viceroy and alighted and sat next to him and recognized him. She shook him vigorously, but he could not wake up. She began to wail about him, that all the labors performed and travails endured for so many years in order to free her were lost because of that one day when he could have freed her. She wept much about it: "It's a great pity both for him and for me, because I have been here such a long time and cannot get out." Afterwards she took the kerchief off her head and wrote on it with her tears and left it next to him. She rose and sat in her carriage and rode off.

Later, he woke up and asked the servant: "Where am I in the world?" The servant told him the whole story, that many soldiers had passed by and that the carriage had been there and the princess had wept and cried out: "It's a great pity for you and for me!" In the meanwhile, the viceroy glanced about and saw that the kerchief was lying next to him. And he asked: "Where did this come from?" And the servant answered that the princess had left it after having written on it with her tears. The viceroy took it and raised it to the sun. He began to see the letters and read what was written there, all her lament and cry, that she was no longer in the former castle, but that he should search for a golden mountain and pearly castle. "There you shall find me!"

He left the servant behind and went on alone to search for her. And he traveled for several years searching for her. He reasoned that surely there is no golden mountain and pearly castle in a settled place because he was expert in the map of the world. And so (he concluded): "I shall go to the deserts." He went to search for her in the deserts for many and many a year. At last he saw a man so huge that his size was not human and he was carrying a tree so huge that no such tree is found in any settled place.

That giant asked him: "Who are you?"

The viceroy answered: "I am a human being."

The giant wondered and said: "I have been in the desert for a long time, but I have never seen a human being here."

The viceroy told him the whole story, and that he was searching for a golden mountain and a pearly castle. The giant said to him: "Surely it does not exist at all." He rebuffed him and told him that they had deluded his mind with nonsense, that it surely did not exist at all. And the viceroy began to weep bitterly and said: "It surely, definitely exists somewhere." The wild man rebuffed him again saying that they surely had deluded him with nonsense. And the viceroy said that it surely exists.

The wild man said to the viceroy: "In my opinion, this is nonsense. But since you insist, I, who am in charge of all the animals, will do you a favor and summon them all. Since they roam throughout the entire world, one of them might know about that mountain and castle." And he summoned them all, from the smallest to the biggest, all kinds of animals. He asked them, but they answered that they had not seen anything of the sort. So he said to the viceroy: "See! They have deluded you with nonsense. If you listen to me, you will go back, because you will surely not find it since it does not exist anywhere in the world."

But the viceroy insisted vigorously and said that it surely, definitely exists. The wild man said to the viceroy: "Here, in the desert, I have a brother who is in charge of all the fowl. Perhaps they know since they fly high in the air. Perhaps they have seen that mountain and castle. Go to him and tell him that I have sent you." And the viceroy went on for many and many a year in search of him. Finally he again found a man as huge as the former one and he, too, carried a huge tree. And this giant asked the viceroy the same question. The viceroy told him the whole story adding that his brother had sent him. And he, too, rebuffed him saying that it surely does not exist. The viceroy insisted that it does. The giant said to the viceroy: "I am in charge of all the birds. I shall summon them—perhaps they know." He summoned all the birds and asked them all, from the smallest to the biggest, and they answered that they knew nothing about that mountain and castle. The man said to him: "You see that it surely does not exist anywhere in the world. If you listen to me, go back." But the viceroy insisted and said that it surely does exist somewhere in the world. The giant said: "Further in the desert you will find my brother who is in charge of all the winds. They roam throughout the whole world—perhaps they know."

The viceroy traveled and searched for many and many a year, and finally found a man as huge as the former one and he, too, carried a huge tree. This giant asked the viceroy the same question, and the viceroy told him the whole story. This giant, too, rebuffed him, but the viceroy insisted again. Finally, the third giant said to the viceroy that he would do him a favor and summon all the winds to come and he would ask them. He summoned them, and all the winds came and he asked them all. None of them knew anything about that mountain and castle. The giant said to the viceroy: "Don't you see that they have told you nonsense?" And the viceroy began to weep loudly and said: "I know that it surely must exist."

At that moment he saw that another wind had arrived. And the giant in charge of the winds was very angry with it: "Why are you late? Didn't I order all the winds to come? Why didn't you come with them?"

The wind answered him: "I was detained because I had to transport a princess to a golden mountain and a pearly castle."

And the viceroy was overjoyed to hear this.

The giant in charge asked the wind: "What is expensive there?"

The wind said: "Everything is very expensive there."

So the giant in charge of the winds told the viceroy: "Since you have been searching for her for such a long time and have performed so many labors, and money might now be an obstacle, I am giving you a purse, and whenever you put your hand in it you will draw money from it." And he ordered a wind to take him there. The storm wind came and carried him there and brought him up to the gate. The soldiers standing guard there would not let him enter the city, but he put his hand into the purse and took out the money and bribed them and entered the city. And it was a beautiful city. He went to a rich man and arranged for his board, knowing that he had to spend time there, because he had to employ intelligence and wisdom to free her.

(And how he freed her, Rav Nahman did not tell.)

And finally he did free her.

10.5 THE SECOND AGE OF DIVERSITY (ca. 1800– THE PRESENT)

The advent of the modern world brought many changes and challenges to Judaism. The Jews of western Europe, who had been largely restricted to ghetto life in closed communities, now were "emancipated" and given the same rights as all citizens. The emancipation was, however, a double-edged sword.

Along with emancipation came nationalism. Nationalism divides people into competing national groups sharing a common history, language, land, and political future. While it brought with it Jewish emancipation, it also threatened the existence of traditional Jewish communities. The nation-state demanded of the emancipated Jews, as it demanded of all citizens, allegiance. Prior to this, the ultimate allegiance of Jews was to their religious communities. Now, allegiance was threatened and pressures to assimilate threatened Jewish identity. Intermarriage with non-Jews, service to the state, becoming coworkers and fellow citizens with Gentile neighbors —all of this made undreamed of choices and opportunities possible, but the danger was the loss of a tradition that defined Judaism.

Modernity ushered in a new view of science called scientific naturalism. According to scientific naturalism, science is a process of discovering the objective and natural laws that govern the workings of the universe. The appeal to the supernatural as an explanatory power faded into the background, and the creation stories of Genesis began to appear as delightful, but quaint, old-fashioned myths.

In addition to the rise of nationalism and scientific naturalism in the modern period, scholars began to accept a new way of doing history called historicism. The past is best known, the historicist argued, by a critical and careful sifting of evidence. Knowledge of the past is established not by traditional stories but, rather, by careful assessment of historical facts. Historicism casts doubt on the historical reliability of the writings in the *Tanakh*. Valued stories became legends and folktales, and authoritative authors disappeared into the mists of time. Moses, the modern historians concluded, did not write the Torah.

Jewish reactions in Europe and North America to emancipation, nationalism, scientific naturalism, and historicism spawned a new creative force resulting in more variety and diversity in Judaism. One reaction is modernism. In general the modernistic reaction seeks to retain parts of the tradition, but update it so that it is compatible with the modern world. Precisely how to do that led to the creation of Reform, Conservative (Positive-Historical), Reconstructionist, and Orthodox Judaism.

Another reaction is secularism. Secularism turns the traditional religious ideology of the Jews into a political one. History replaces God as the source of moral norms, the notion of an oppressed people replaces the religious view of a chosen people, and the messianic age is reinterpreted as the people's liberation from oppression and persecution. Various socialists and Zionist Jewish movements preached this new torah.

Traditionalism constitutes a third reaction to modernity. Traditionalists retain the old ways complete with supernaturalistic and premodern understandings of God, Torah, Israel, and the Messiah. The Hasidic movements of the twentieth century exemplify this approach.

10.5.1 Reform and Conservative Judaism

In response to emancipation and the new knowledge created by the Enlightenment, some Jewish leaders in Germany began a reform movement. They attempted to adjust Judaism to the modern world by redefining what they took to be most important in the tradition. Although many people were involved in a number of stages of reform, the founding of **Reform Judaism** is usually associated with Abraham Geiger (1810–1874) and Samuel Holdheim (1806–1860).

Abraham Geiger understood both the written and oral Torah as a progressive, ever-changing body of tradition shaped by meaningful responses to historical events. If historical conditions have changed for the Jew, Geiger reasoned, then the law must be reformulated to make it more relevant to the present circumstances. Geiger also argued that the essence of Judaism is an "ethical monotheism." Judaism, at its heart, is a religion that emphasizes the importance of the highest moral standards. Ritual law is much less important than moral law.

Reform Judaism changed Judaism from a culture-religion based on ethnic identification to a voluntary association. Judaism became a religion in the modern sense of an organization that one can join (or not join) and that holds certain beliefs, recommends a particular way to live, and provides a set of rituals to practice.

Immigrants transferred German Reform Judaism to the United States as early as 1848 with the founding of the first successful Reform synagogue, Mt. Sinai, in Baltimore, Maryland. In 1885 the Pittsburgh Platform (see the selection) was written under the direction of Isaac Meyer Wise (1819–1900) and Kaufmann Kohler (1843–1926). They formulated the key ideas of American Reform Judaism.

Orthodox Judaism represents a negative reaction to the reform movement. **Orthodoxy** affirms that the written and oral Torah are revealed by God and should not be changed by humans. All of the law is binding, and the Jew is under an absolute and unchanging divine mandate to fulfill it. "The Thirteen Principles of Maimonides" (see Reading 10.4.1) constitute an unofficial creed for most Orthodox.

There is no simple uniformity in Orthodox Judaism today. The "modern/centrist" Orthodox affirm the Torah and its divine origin as do the "rightist/ultra" Orthodox. However, the ultra-Orthodox deny any intellectual or spiritual validity to the non-Jewish world and non-Orthodox forms of Judaism. This view leads to a deliberate policy of withdrawal and separatism in all matters. The ultra-Orthodox elevate even dress, hairstyles, and language to the level of religious commands.

Conservative Judaism began as an attempt to find a middle way between the extremes of Reform and Orthodox Judaism. Conservative Jews think that genuine Judaism embraces both tradition *and* change. In their view, the Orthodox are not responsive enough to changing historical circumstances and the Reform reject far too much of the rich tradition that has sustained the Jews over the centuries. What is needed, Conservative Jews reason, is a better balance between the old and the new.

The rabbinic scholar Solomon Schechter (1847–1915) is the chief architect of Conservative Judaism in America. During his presidency (1902–1915) of the Jewish Theological Seminary in New York, he created the model for the Conservative synagogue. His presidential address, in the second selection, provides an informative contrast to the Pittsburgh Platform of Reform Judaism.

❧❧❧

The Pittsburgh Platform

READING QUESTION

1. What differences do you notice between the Pittsburgh Platform and Schechter's address that, in your opinion, distinguishes Reform from Conservative Judaism?

From *The Jewish Encyclopedia*, edited by I. Singer (New York: Funk and Wagnalls Company, 1907), p. 215.

1. We recognize in every religion an attempt to grasp the Infinite, and in every mode, source, or book of revelation held sacred in any religious system the consciousness of the indwelling of God in man. We hold that Judaism presents the highest conception of the God-idea as taught in our Holy Scriptures and developed and spiritualized by the Jewish teachers, in accordance with the moral and philosophical progress of their respective ages. We maintain that Judaism preserved and defended, midst continual struggles and trials and under enforced isolation, this God-idea as the central religious truth for the human race.

2. We recognize in the Bible the record of the consecration of the Jewish people to its mission as the priest of the one God, and value it as the most potent instrument of religious and moral instruction. We hold that the modern discoveries of scientific researches in the domain of nature and history are not antagonistic to the doctrines of Judaism, the Bible reflecting the primitive ideas of its own age, and at times clothing its conception of divine Providence and Justice dealing with man in miraculous narrative.

3. We recognize in the Mosaic legislation a system of training the Jewish people for its mission during its national life in Palestine, and today we accept as binding only its moral laws, and maintain only such ceremonies as elevate and sanctify our lives, but reject all such as are not adapted to the views and habits of modern civilization.

4. We hold that all such Mosaic and rabbinical laws as regulate diet, priestly purity, and dress originated in ages and under the influence of ideas entirely foreign to our present mental and spiritual state. They fail to impress the modern Jew with a spirit of priestly holiness; their observance in our days is apt rather to obstruct than to further modern spiritual elevation.

5. We recognize, in the modern era of universal culture of heart and intellect, the approaching of the realization of Israel's great Messianic hope for the establishment of the kingdom of truth, justice, and peace among all men. We consider ourselves no longer a nation, but a religious community, and therefore expect neither a return to Palestine, nor a sacrificial worship under the sons of Aaron, nor the restoration of any of the laws concerning the Jewish State.

6. We recognize in Judaism a progressive religion, ever striving to be in accord with the postulates of reason. We are convinced of the utmost necessity of preserving the historical identity with our great past. Christianity and Islam being daughter religions of Judaism, we appreciate their providential mission to aid in the spreading of monotheistic and moral truth. We acknowledge that the spirit of broad humanity of our age is our ally in the fulfillment of our mission, and therefore we extend the hand of fellowship to all who operate with us in the establishment of the reign of truth and righteousness among men.

7. We reassert the doctrine of Judaism that the soul is immortal, grounding this belief on the divine nature of the human spirit, which forever finds bliss in righteousness and misery in wickedness. We reject as ideas not rooted in Judaism, the beliefs both in bodily resurrection and in Gehenna and Eden (Hell and Paradise) as abodes for everlasting punishment and reward.

8. In full accordance with the spirit of Mosaic legislation, which strives to regulate the relation between rich and poor, we deem it our duty to participate in the great task of modern times, to solve, on the basis of justice and righteousness, the problems presented by the contrasts and evils of the present organization of society.

SOLOMON SCHECHTER

The Charter of the Seminary

Let me say a few words about the general religious tendency this Seminary will follow. I am not unaware that this is a very delicate point, and prudence would dictate silence or evasion. But life would hardly be worth living without occasional blundering, "the only relief from dull correctness." Besides, if there be in American history one fact more clearly proved than any other it is that "know-nothing-ism" was an absolute and miserable failure. I must not fall into the same error. And thus, sincerely asking forgiveness of all my dearest friends and dearest enemies with whom it may be my misfortune to differ, I declare, in all humility, but most emphatically, that I do know something. And this is that the religion

From Solomon Schechter, "The Charter of the Seminary," in *Tradition and Change: The Development of Conservative Judaism*, edited by Mordecai Waxman (New York: Burning Bush Press, 1958), pp. 102–104. Reprinted with permission.

in which the Jewish ministry should be trained must be specifically and purely Jewish, without any alloy or adulteration. Judaism must stand or fall by that which distinguishes it from other religions as well as by that which it has in common with them. Judaism is not a religion which does not oppose itself to anything in particular. Judaism is opposed to any number of things, and says distinctly "thou shalt not." It permeates the whole of your life. It demands control over all your actions, and interferes even with your menu. It sanctifies the seasons, and regulates your history, both in the past and in the future. Above all, it teaches that disobedience is the strength of sin. It insists upon the observance both of the spirit and of the letter; spirit without letter belongs to the species known to the mystics as "nude souls" wandering about in the universe without balance and without consistency, the play of all possible currents and changes in the atmosphere. In a word Judaism is absolutely incompatible with the abandonment of the Torah. Nay, the very prophet or seer must bring his imprimatur from the Torah. The assertion that the destruction of the Law is its fulfillment is a mere paradox, and recalls strongly the doctrines of Sir Boyle Roche, "the inimitable maker of Irish bulls." He declared emphatically that he "would give up a part, and, if necessary, the whole of the constitution, to preserve the remainder!"

President Abraham Lincoln, the wisest and greatest of rulers, addressed Congress on some occasion of great emergency with the words: "Fellow citizens, we cannot escape history." Nor can we, my friends. The past, with its long chain of events, with its woes and joy, with its tragedies and romances; with its customs and usages, and above all; with its bequest of the Torah, the great entail of the children of Israel, has become an integral and inalienable part of ourselves, bone of our bone and flesh of our flesh. We must make an end to these constant amputations if we do not wish to see the body of "Israel" bleed to death before our very eyes. We must leave off talking about Occidentalizing our religion— as if the occident has ever shown the least genius for religion—or freeing the conscience by abolishing various laws. These, and similar platitudes and stock phrases borrowed from Christian apologetics, must be abandoned entirely, if we do not want to drift slowly but surely into Paulinism, which entered the world as the deadliest enemy of Judaism, pursued it through all its course and is still finding its abettors among us, working for their own destruction. Lord, forgive them, for they know nothing. Those who are entrusted with carrying out the purpose of this institution, which, as you have seen, aims at the perpetuation of the tenets of the Jewish religion, both pupils and masters, must faithfully and manfully maintain their loyalty to the Torah. There is no other Jewish religion but that taught by the Torah and confirmed by history and tradition, and sunk into the conscience of Catholic Israel.

I have just hinted at the desirability of masters and pupils working for one common end. You must not think that our intention is to convert this school of learning into a drill ground where young men will be forced into a certain groove of thinking, or, rather, not thinking; and after being equipped with a few devotional texts, and supplied with certain catchwords, will be let loose upon an unsuspecting public to proclaim their own virtues and the infallibility of their masters. Nothing is further from our thoughts. I once heard a friend of mine exclaim angrily to a pupil: "Sir, how dare you always agree with me?" I do not even profess to agree with myself always, and I would consider my work, to which, with the help of God, I am going to devote the rest of my life, a complete failure if this institution would not in the future produce such extremes as on the one side a raving mystic who would denounce me as a sober Philistine; on the other side, an advanced critic, who would rail at me as a narrow-minded fanatic, while a third devotee of strict orthodoxy would raise protest against any critical views I may entertain. "We take," says Montaigne, "other men's knowledge on trust, which is idle and superficial learning. We must make it our own." The Rabbis express the same thought with allusion to Ps. 1:2 which they explain to mean that what is first at the initiation of man into the Law—God's Torah, becomes, after a sufficient study man's own Torah. Nay, God even deigns to descend to man's own level so as not to interfere with his individuality and powers of conception. I reproduce in paraphrase a passage from a Midrash: "Behold now how the voice of Sinai goes forth to all in Israel attuned to the capacity of each; appealing to the sages according to their wisdom: to the virile according to their strength; to the young according to their aspiring youthfulness, and the children and babes according to their innocence; aye, even to the women according to their motherhood." All that I plead for is that the voice should come from Sinai, not from Golgotha; that it should be the voice of Jacob, not of Esau. The Torah gave spiritual accommodation for thousands of years to all sorts and conditions of men, sages, philosophers, scholars, mystics, casuists, schoolmen and skeptics; and it should also prove broad enough to harbor the different minds of the present century. Any attempt to place the centre of gravity outside of the Torah must end in disaster. We must not flatter ourselves that we shall be allowed to land somewhere midway, say in some Omar Khayyam cult or in some Positivists' society or in some other agnostic makeshift. No, my friends, there are laws of gravitation in the spiritual as there are in the physical world; we cannot create halting places at will. We must either remain faithful to history or go the way of all flesh, and join the great majority. The teaching in the Seminary will be in keeping with this spirit, and thus largely confined to the exposition and elucidation of historical Judaism in its various manifestations.

10.5.2 Zionism

Before the nineteenth century, anti-Jewish feelings were largely based on Christian religious prejudices. The Jews were the "unbelievers" who had crucified the Christ. This religious anti-Semitism led to sporadic persecutions and expulsions along with severe economic and personal restrictions. After emancipation, anti-Semitism became racially motivated as demagogues and reactionary governments blamed the Jews for political and economic problems. Pseudoscientific theories of "Aryan" superiority and spurious documents like the "Protocols of the Wise Men of Zion" purporting to outline a Jewish plan for world domination fed a growing willingness on the part of many people to blame their troubles on the Jews.

As wave after wave of anti-Semitism washed across Europe, people began to talk about and debate "the Jewish question": What should be done with the Jews? Fueled by Christian prejudices, resentment, and greed, the gentile world posed an ever greater threat to the Jews. Many Jews became alarmed. Perhaps emancipation and **assimilation** would not protect them from the hate and danger.

Theodor Herzl (1860–1904) was a secularized Jew. He trained as a lawyer and eventually became a correspondent for a Vienna newspaper. Alarmed by the growing incidents of anti-Semitism, he decided that only a Jewish state, a land where Jews could live together and govern each other, provided a safe haven. If such a land could be found and if Jews would immigrate there, they would be free from the dangers of a growing European anti-Semitism.

In 1896 Herzl wrote *Der Judenstaat (The Jewish State)*, which has become the classic expression of the Zionist cause. That cause stirred great controversy among Jews and non-Jews alike. Some religious Jews opposed **Zionism** because the state Herzl had in mind would be a secular state and, if located in Palestine, heresy to the Orthodox who believed the Jews should return to their beloved land of Zion only when the Messiah came. Many secular Jews were uncertain about leaving countries and cultures with which they identified.

THEODOR HERZL

The Jewish State

READING QUESTIONS

1. Why is Herzl proposing a Jewish state?
2. Why does he think assimilation will not solve "the Jewish question"?
3. Why does Herzl argue that the new Jewish state should not be a theocracy?

PREFACE

The idea which I have developed in this pamphlet is a very old one: it is the restoration of the Jewish State.

The world resounds with outcries against the Jews, and these outcries have awakened the slumbering idea. . . .

The present scheme . . . includes the employment of an existent propelling force. In consideration of my own inadequacy, I shall content myself with indicating the cogs and wheels of the machine to be constructed, and I shall rely on more skilled mechanicians than myself to put them together.

Everything depends on our propelling force. And what is that force? The misery of the Jews. . . .

The Jewish question still exists. It would be foolish to deny it. It is a remnant of the Middle Ages, which civilized nations do not even yet seem able to shake off, try as they will. They certainly showed a generous desire to do so when they emancipated us. The Jewish question exists wherever Jews live in perceptible numbers. Where it does not exist, it is carried by Jews in the course of their migrations. We naturally move to those places where we are not persecuted, and there our presence produces persecution. This is the case in every country, and will remain so, even in those highly civilized—for instance, France—until the Jewish question finds a solution on a political basis. The unfortunate Jews are now carrying the seeds of Anti-Semitism into England; they have already introduced it into America.

I believe that I understand Anti-Semitism, which is really a highly complex movement. I consider it from a

From Theodor Herzl, *The Jewish State: An Attempt at a Modern Solution of the Jewish Question* (New York: American Zionist Council, 1946), pp. 69, 70, 75–78, 82–83, 92–95, 146–147, 153, 156–157.

Jewish standpoint, yet without fear or hatred. I believe that I can see what elements there are in it of vulgar sport, of common trade jealousy, of inherited prejudice, of religious intolerance and also of pretended self-defence. I think the Jewish question is no more a social than a religious one, notwithstanding that it sometimes takes these and other forms. It is a national question, which can only be solved by making it a political world-question to be discussed and settled by the civilized nations of the world in council.

We are a people—one people.

We have honestly endeavored everywhere to merge ourselves in the social life of surrounding communities and to preserve the faith of our fathers. We are not permitted to do so. In vain are we loyal patriots, our loyalty in some places running to extremes; in vain do we make the same sacrifices of life and property as our fellow citizens; in vain do we strive to increase the fame of our native land in science and art, or our wealth by trade and commerce. In countries where we have lived for centuries we are still cried down as strangers, and often by those whose ancestors were not yet domiciled in the land where Jews had already had experience of suffering. . . .

Oppression and persecution cannot exterminate us. No nation on earth has survived such struggles and sufferings as we have gone through. Jew-baiting has merely stripped off our weaklings; the strong among us were invariably true to their race when persecution broke out against them. . . .

Assimilation, by which I understand not only external conformity in dress, habits, custom, and language but also identity of feeling and manner—assimilation of Jews could be effected only by intermarriage. But the need for mixed marriages would have to be felt by the majority; their mere recognition by law would certainly not suffice. . . .

Those who really wished to see the Jews disappear through intermixture with other nations, can only hope to see it come about in one way. The Jews must previously acquire economic power sufficiently great to overcome the old social prejudice against them. The aristocracy may serve as an example of this, for in its ranks occur the proportionately largest numbers of mixed marriages. The Jewish families which regild the old nobility with their money become gradually absorbed. But what form would this phenomenon assume in the middle classes, where (the Jews being a bourgeois people) the Jewish question is mainly concentrated? A previous acquisition of power could be synonymous with that economic supremacy which they are already erroneously declared to possess. And if the power they now possess creates rage and indignation among the Anti-Semites, what outbreaks would such an increase of power create?

Hence the first step towards absorption will never be taken, because this step would involve the subjection of the majority to a hitherto scorned minority, possessing neither military nor administrative power of its own. I think, therefore, that the absorption of Jews by means of their prosperity is unlikely to occur. . . .

No human being is wealthy or powerful enough to transplant a nation from one habitation to another. An idea alone can achieve that: and this idea of a State may have the requisite power to do so. The Jews have dreamt this kingly dream all through the long nights of their history. "Next year in Jerusalem" is our old phrase. It is now a question of showing that the dream can be converted into a living reality.

For this, many old, outgrown, confused and limited notions must first be entirely erased from the minds of men. Dull brains might, for instance, imagine that this exodus would be from civilized regions into the desert. That is not the case. It will be carried out in the midst of civilization. We shall not revert to a lower stage, we shall rise to a higher one. We shall not dwell in mud huts; we shall build new more beautiful and more modern houses, and possess them in safety. We shall not lose our acquired possessions; we shall realize them. We shall surrender our well earned rights only for better ones. We shall not sacrifice our beloved customs; we shall find them again. We shall not leave our old home before the new one is prepared for us. Those only will depart who are sure thereby to improve their position; those who are now desperate will go first, after them the poor; next the prosperous, and, last of all, the wealthy. Those who go in advance will raise themselves to a higher grade, equal to that whose representatives will shortly follow. Thus the exodus will be at the same time an ascent of the class.

The departure of the Jews will involve no economic disturbances, no crises, no persecutions; in fact, the countries they abandon will revive to a new period of prosperity. There will be an inner migration of Christian citizens into the positions evacuated by Jews. The outgoing current will be gradual, without any disturbance, and its initial movement will put an end to Anti-Semitism. The Jews will leave as honored friends, and if some of them return, they will receive the same favorable welcome and treatment at the hands of civilized nations as is accorded to all foreign visitors. Their exodus will have no resemblance to a flight, for it will be a well-regulated movement under control of public opinion. The movement will not only be inaugurated with absolute conformity to law, but it cannot even be carried out without the friendly cooperation of interested Governments, who would derive considerable benefits from it.

Security for the integrity of the idea and the vigor of its execution will be found in the creation of a body corporate, or corporation. This corporation will be called "The Society of Jews." In addition to it there will be a Jewish company, an economically productive body.

An individual who attempted even to undertake this huge task alone, would be either an impostor or a madman. The personal character of the members of the corporation will guarantee its integrity, and the adequate capital of the Company will prove its stability. . . .

THE PLAN

The whole plan is in its essence perfectly simple, as it must necessarily be if it is to come within the comprehension of all.

Let the sovereignty be granted us over a portion of the globe large enough to satisfy the rightful requirements of a nation; the rest we shall manage for ourselves. . . .

The plan, simple in design, but complicated in execution, will be carried out by two agencies: The Society of Jews and the Jewish Company.

The Society of Jews will do the preparatory work in the domains of science and politics, which the Jewish Company will afterwards apply practically.

The Jewish Company will be the liquidating agent of the business interests of departing Jews, and will organize commerce and trade in the new country. . . .

Those Jews who agree with our idea of a State will attach themselves to the Society, which will thereby be authorized to confer and treat with Governments in the name of our people. The Society will thus be acknowledged in its relations with Governments as a State-creating power. This acknowledgment will practically create the State. . . .

PALESTINE OR ARGENTINE?

Shall we choose Palestine or Argentine? We shall take what is given us, and what is selected by Jewish public opinion. The Society will determine both these points. . . .

THEOCRACY

Shall we end by having a theocracy? No, indeed. Faith unites us, knowledge gives us freedom. We shall therefore prevent any theocratic tendencies from coming to the fore on the part of our priesthood. We shall keep our priests within the confines of their temples in the same way as we shall keep our professional army within the confines of their barracks. Army and priesthood shall receive honors high as their valuable functions deserve. But they must not interfere in the administration of the State which confers distinction upon them, else they will conjure up difficulties without and within.

Every man will be as free and undisturbed in his faith or his disbelief as he is in his nationality. And if it should occur that men of other creeds and different nationalities come to live amongst us, we should accord them honorable protection and equality before the law. We have learnt toleration in Europe. This is not sarcastically said; for the Anti-Semitism of today could only in a very few places be taken for old religious intolerance. It is for the most part a movement among civilized nations by which they try to chase away the spectres of their own past.

CONCLUSION

How much has been left unexplained, how many defects, how many harmful superficialities, and how many useless repetitions in this pamphlet, which I have thought over so long and so often revised!

But a fair-minded reader, who has sufficient understanding to grasp the spirit of my words, will not be repelled by these defects. He will rather be roused thereby to cooperate with his intelligence and energy in a work which is not one man's task alone, and to improve it. . . .

Here it is, fellow Jews! Neither fable nor deception! Every man may test its reality for himself, for every man will carry over with him a portion of the Promised Land—one in his head, another in his arms, another in his acquired possessions. . . .

But we must first bring enlightenment to men's minds. The idea must make its way into the most distant, miserable holes where our people dwell. They will awaken from gloomy brooding, for into their lives will come a new significance. Every man need think only of himself, and the movement will assume vast proportions.

And what glory awaits those who fight unselfishly for the cause!

Therefore I believe that a wondrous generation of Jews will spring into existence. The Maccabeans will rise again.

Let me repeat once more my opening words: The Jews who wish for a State will have it.

We shall live at last as free men on our own soil, and die peacefully in our own home.

The world will be freed by our liberty, enriched by our wealth, magnified by our greatness.

And whatever we attempt there to accomplish for our own welfare, will react powerfully and beneficially for the good of humanity.

10.5.3 Judaism As a Life of Dialogue

Martin Buber (1878–1965) was a Jewish educator and philosopher whose book *Ich und Du* (*I and Thou*, 1923) combined in creative ways the spiritual depth of Hasidism with existential philosophy. Buber argued that open, nonmanipulative, personal, and mutually affirming dialogue not only improves relationships but also reveals God, the "Eternal Thou." These "I-Thou" relationships Buber contrasted with "I-It" relationships that treat others as objects, create alienation, depersonalize the world and people, and conceal rather than reveal the sacred quality of living.

Buber's philosophy stems, in part, from a deep appreciation of Judaism and its history as a dialogue between humans and God. When arguments about the dual Torah rage, when mystics dance in ecstasy, when people try to make sense of exile, suffering, and grief, when they seek reform, and when they seek to restore a lost tradition in all of its purity—these kinds of things are part of a dialogue between heaven and earth.

In 1938 Buber left Germany and immigrated to Palestine where he advocated Jewish-Arab rapprochement. It was a dialogue that has started and stopped over and over again in the midst of war and the threats of war.

<hr>

MARTIN BUBER

The Dialogue Between Heaven and Earth

READING QUESTIONS

1. What are the first and the second biblical axioms?
2. How, according to Buber, can humans be free in the face of God's foresight and predetermination?

3. How does Buber respond to the question "How is a Jewish life still possible after Auschwitz?"

<hr>

I

The most important of all that the biblical view of existence has opened up for all times is clearly recognized by a comparison of Israel's Holy Writ with those holy books of the nations that originated independently of it. None of those books is, like it, full of a dialogue between heaven and earth. It tells us how again and again God addresses man and is addressed by him. God announces to man what plan He has for the world; as the earliest of the "literary" prophets puts it (Amos 4:13), God lets him know "his soliloquy." He discloses to him His will and calls upon him to take part in its realization. But man is no blind tool; he was created as a free being—free also vis-à-vis God, free to surrender to Him or to refuse himself to Him. To God's sovereign address, man gives his autonomous answer; if he remains silent, his silence, too, is an answer. Very often we hear God's voice alone, as in much of the books of the prophets, where only in isolated cases—in certain accounts of visions, or in the diary-like records of Jeremiah—does the prophet's reply become articulate, and sometimes these records actually assume a dialogic form. But even in all those passages where God alone speaks, we are made to feel that the person addressed by Him answers with his wordless soul, that is to say, that he stands in the dialogic situation. And again, very often we hear the voice of man alone, as generally in the Psalms, where only in isolated cases the worshipper indicates the divine reply; but here, too, the dialogic situation is apparent: it is apparent to us that man, lamenting, suppliant, thanks-giving, praise-singing man, experiences himself as heard and understood, accepted and confirmed, by Him to whom he addresses himself. The basic teaching that fills the Hebrew Bible is that our life is a dialogue between the above and the below.

But does this still apply to our present-day life? Believers and unbelievers deny it. A view common among believers is that though everything contained in Scripture is literally true, though God did certainly speak to the men chosen by Him, yet, since then, the holy spirit has been taken from us; heaven is silent to us, and only through the books of the written and oral tradition is God's will made known to us as to what we shall do or not do. Certainly, even today, the worshipper stands immediately before his Creator, but how could he dare, like the Psalmist, to report to the world words of personal reply, of personal granting, as spoken immediately to him? And as for the unbelievers, it goes without saying that the atheists need not be mentioned at all, but only the adherents of a more or less philosophic God-concept, with which they cannot reconcile the idea of God's addressing and being addressed by man; to them, the entire dialogics of Scripture is nothing but a mythical figment, instructive from the point of view of the history of the human mind, but inapplicable to our life.

As against either opinion, a faithful and unbiased reader of Scripture must endorse the view he has learned from it: what happened once happens now and always, and the fact of its happening to us is a guarantee of its having happened. The Bible has, in the form of a glorified remembrance, given vivid, decisive expression to an ever recurrent happening. In the infinite language of events and situations, eternally changing, but plain to the truly attentive, transcendence speaks to our hearts at the essential moments of personal life. And there is a language in which we can answer it; it is the language of our actions and attitudes, our reactions and our abstentions. The totality of these responses is what we may call our responsibility in the proper sense of the word. This fundamental interpretation of our existence we owe to the Hebrew Bible; and whenever we truly read it, our self-understanding is renewed and deepened.

II

But in Scripture, not only the individual but the community too is addressed from above, in such a manner as is found in no other of the holy books of mankind.

Here the people, as a people, confronts God and receives, as a people, His never ceasing instruction. It, too, like the individual, is called upon to participate in the realization of the divine will on earth. Just as the individual is to hallow himself in his personal life, the people is to hallow itself in its communal life; it is to become a "holy people." Like the individual, it is free in its answer to the divine call, free to say yes or no to God by its doing and its not doing. The people is not a sum of individuals addressed by God; it is something existing beyond that, something essential and irreplaceable, meant by God as such, claimed by Him as such, and answerable to Him as such. God leads it and requires it to follow His sole leadership. He has created not only man as an individual, men as individuals, but also the human peoples; and He uses them, like the former, for His purpose, for the completion of His world-creation. He takes care of them in their history; not only Israel but all peoples are, as the prophet proclaims, led by Him to

freedom when enslaved by other peoples, and in freedom they shall serve Him, as peoples, each in its own way and according to its own character. Though He reprimands Israel with especial severity because, contrary to its mandate, it has not fulfilled divine justice in the life of the community, yet He reprimands the other peoples as well, because they, who are also His children, do not act toward each other as brothers should. Some day, however, so the prophecy runs, the representatives of all of them will crowd around Mount Moriah and there, as Israel once did, alone, at Mount Sinai, receive that divine instruction on the great peace between the peoples (Isaiah 2). "The noble ones of the peoples are gathered together," so the Psalmist says, "as the people of the God of Abraham" (Psalm 47:10)—of Abraham, who is called "the father of a multitude of nations" (Genesis 17:5), a description meaning more than genealogy. Since world history is the advance of the peoples toward this goal, it is, essentially, sacred history.

This is also why in Scripture the divine voice addresses man not as an isolated individual but always as an individual member of the people. Even before there is a people of Israel, its father-to-be, Abraham, is addressed as such: he is to become "a blessing" in his seed. And in the legislation, both in the Decalogue and in the injunctions supplementing it, God again and again addresses Himself to a "thou" that is certainly the "thou" of each individual in each generation of the people, but as he is conceived in his connection with the people, at whose communal life that legislation is aimed, so that everyone, when a commandment conveys to him the will of God with regard to his own life, conceives himself as the individual condensation of the people. This basic view unfolds itself up to the highest level of human existence: "Thou art My servant, the Israel in whom I will be glorified," says God (Isaiah 49:3) to His elect; the man who fulfills the mandate given to the people embodies the truth of the people's existence.

From this vantage point, modern life, both of peoples and of persons, is judged and sentence passed. This life is split in two: what is thought reprehensible in the relations between persons is thought commendable in the relations between peoples. This is contrary to the prophetic demand: the prophet accuses a people of sinning against another people because it "remembered not the brotherly convenant" (Amos 1:9). But that split naturally continues into the life of modern man as an individual: his existence is divided into a private and a public one, which are governed by very different laws. What he disapproves, in his fellow man and in himself, in the former sphere, he approves, in his fellow man and in himself, in the latter: lying degrades the private person, but it well befits the political partisan, provided that it is practiced skillfully and successfully. This duality of moral values is intolerable from the point of view of biblical faith: here, deceit is under all circumstances regarded as disgraceful (also, e.g., in the case of the patriarchs, as we see from the prophetical criticism of Jacob and from some other indications), even if it is prompted by a desire to promote the cause of justice; in fact, in the latter case, it is the more pernicious, since it poisons and disintegrates the good that it is supposed to serve.

If the first biblical axiom is: "Man is addressed by God in his life," the second is: "The life of man is meant by God as a unit."

III

As we have seen, in the biblical conception of existence God addresses the human person and the human people with a view to what shall be, what shall be realized through this person, through this people. This means that man is placed in freedom and that every hour in which he, in his current situation, feels himself to be addressed is an hour of genuine decision. In the first instance, of course, he decides only upon his own behavior, but by doing so he participates, in a measure that he is neither able nor authorized to determine, in the decision upon what the next hour will be like, and through this upon what the future generally will be like.

It is from here that the great biblical phenomenon of prophecy must be understood. The essential task of the prophets of Israel was not to foretell an already determined future, but to confront man and people in Israel, at each given moment, with the alternative that corresponded to the situation. It was announced not what would happen under any circumstances, but what would happen if the hearers of the message realized God's will, and what would happen if they refused themselves to its realization. The divine voice chose the prophet, as it were, for its "mouth," in order to bring home to man again and again, in the most immediate fashion, his freedom and its consequences. Even when the prophet did not speak in alternative form, but announced unconditionally that after such and such a time the catastrophe would happen, this announcement—as we learn from the paradigmatic Book of Jonah—nevertheless contained a hidden alternative: the people is driven into despair, but in precisely this state kindles the spark of "turning": the people turns to God—and is saved [sic]. By an extreme threat to existence, man is stirred to the depths of his soul and brought to a radical decision for

God, but his decision is at the same time a fateful decision in the strictest sense.

Post-biblical thinkers have pondered how the freedom of the human will and the resultant indetermination of the future can be reconciled with divine foresight and predetermination. Outstanding among all that has been said in the effort to overcome this contradiction is the well-known saying of Akiba's, "All is foreseen, yet the power is given," whose meaning is that to God, who sees them together, the times do not appear in succession but in progressless eternity, while in the progression of times in which man lives freedom reigns, at any given time, in the concrete moment of decision; beyond that, human wisdom has not attained. In the Bible itself there is no pondering; it does not deal with the essence of God but with His manifestation to mankind. The reality of which it treats is that of the human world, and in it the immutable truth of decision applies.

For guilty man this means the decision to turn from his wrong way to the way of God. We see most clearly what this means in the biblical view that our responsibility is essentially our answering to a divine address. The two great examples are Cain and David. Both have murdered (for so the Bible understands also David's deed, since it has God's messenger say to him that he "slew Uriah the Hittite with the sword") and both are called to account by God. Cain attempts evasion: "Am I my brother's keeper?" He is the man who shuns the dialogue with God. Not so David. He answers: "I have sinned against the Lord." This is the true answer: whomever one becomes guilty against, in truth one becomes guilty against God. David is the man who acknowledges the relations between God and himself, from which his responsibility arises, and realizes that he has betrayed it.

The Hebrew Bible is concerned with the terrible and at the same time merciful fact of the *immediacy* between God and ourselves. Even in the dark hour after he has become guilty against his brother, man is not abandoned to the forces of chaos. God Himself seeks him out, and even when He comes to call him to account, His coming is salvation.

IV

But there is, in the biblical view, a third, widest sphere of divine utterance. God speaks not only to the individual and to the community, within the limits and under the conditions of a particular biographical or historical situation. Everything, being and becoming, nature and history, is essentially a divine pronouncement (*Aussprache*), an infinite context of signs meant to be perceived and understood by perceiving and understanding creatures.

But here a fundamental difference exists between nature and human history. Nature, as a whole and in all its elements, enunciates something that may be regarded as a self-communication of God to all those ready to receive it. This is what the psalm means that has heaven and earth "declare," wordlessly, the glory of God. Not so human history—not only because mankind, being placed in freedom, cooperates incessantly in shaping its course, but quite especially because, in nature, it is God the Creator who speaks, and His creative act is never interrupted; in history, on the other hand, it is the revealing God who speaks, and revelation is essentially not a continuous process, but breaks in again and again upon the course of events and irradiates it. Nature is full of God's utterance, if one but hears it, but what is said here is always that one, though all-inclusive, something, that which the psalm calls the glory of God; in history, however, times of great utterance, when the mark of divine direction is recognizable in the conjunction of events, alternate with, as it were, mute times, when everything that occurs in the human world and pretends to historical significance appears to us as empty of God, with nowhere a beckoning of His finger, nowhere a sign that He is present and acts upon this our historical hour. In such times it is difficult for the individual, and more so for the people, to understand oneself to be addressed by God; the experience of concrete responsibility recedes more and more, because, in the seemingly God-forsaken space of history, man unlearns taking the relationship between God and himself seriously in the dialogic sense.

In an hour when the exiles in Babylon perceived God's passage through world history, in the hour when Cyrus was about to release them and send them home, the anonymous Prophet of the Exile, who like none before him felt called upon to interpret the history of peoples, in one of his pamphlets made God say to Israel: "From the beginning I have not spoken in secret" (Isaiah 48:16). God's utterance in history is unconcealed, for it is intended to be heard by the peoples. But Isaiah, to whose book the pronouncements of the anonymous prophet have been attached, not only speaks of a time when God "hideth His face from the house of Jacob" (8:17), but he also knows (28:21) that there are times when we are unable to recognize and acknowledge God's own deeds in history as His deeds, so uncanny and "barbarous" do they seem to us. And the same chapter of the Prophet of the Exile, in which God says, "Ask Me of the things to come" (45:11), states that in the hour of

the liberation of peoples the masses whom Egypt put to forced labor and Ethiopia sold as slaves will immediately, with the chains of serfdom still on their bodies, as it were, turn to God, throw themselves down, and pray: "Verily Thou art a God that hideth Himself, O God of Israel, Savior!" (45:15). During the long periods of enslavement it seemed to them as though there were nothing divine any more and the world were irretrievably abandoned to the forces of tyranny; only now do they recognize that there is a Savior, and that He is one—the Lord of History. And now they know and profess. He is a God that hides himself, or more exactly, the God that hides Himself and reveals Himself.

The Bible knows of God's hiding His face, of times when the contact between heaven and earth seems to be interrupted. God seems to withdraw Himself utterly from the earth and no longer to participate in its existence. The space of history is then full of noise, but empty of the divine breath. For one who believes in the living God, who knows about Him, and is fated to spend his life in a time of His hiddenness, it is very difficult to live.

There is a psalm, the 82nd, in which life in a time of God's hiddenness is described in a picture of startling cruelty. It is assumed that God has entrusted the government of mankind to a host of angels and commanded them to realize justice on earth and to protect the weak, the poor, and the helpless from the encroachments of the wrongdoers. But they "judge unjustly" and "respect the persons of the wicked." Now the Psalmist envisions how God draws the unfaithful angels before His seat, judges them, and passes sentence upon them: they are to become mortal. But the Psalmist awakes from his vision and looks about him: iniquity still reigns on earth with unlimited power. And he cries to God: "Arise, O God, judge the earth!"

This cry is to be understood as a late, but even more powerful, echo of that bold speech of the patriarch arguing with God: "The judge of all the earth, will He not do justice?!" It reinforces and augments that speech; its implication is: Will He allow injustice to reign further? And so the cry transmitted to us by Scripture becomes our own cry, which bursts from our hearts and rises to our lips in a time of God's hiddenness. For this is what the biblical word does to us: it confronts us with the human address as one that in spite of everything is heard and in spite of everything may expect an answer.

In this our own time, one asks again and again: how is a Jewish life still possible after Auschwitz? I would like to frame this question more correctly: how is a life with God still possible in a time in which there is an Auschwitz? The estrangement has become too cruel, the hiddenness too deep. One can still "believe" in the God who allowed those things to happen, but can one still speak to Him? Can one still hear His word? Can one still, as an individual and as a people, enter at all into a dialogic relationship with Him? Can one still call to Him? Dare we recommend to the survivors of Auschwitz, the Job of the gas chambers: "Give thanks unto the Lord, for He is good; for His mercy endureth forever"?

But how about Job himself? He not only laments, but he charges that the "cruel" God (30:21) has "removed his right" from him (27:2) and thus that the judge of all the earth acts against justice. And he receives an answer from God. But what God says to him does not answer the charge; it does not even touch upon it. The true answer that Job receives is God's appearance only, only this that distance turns into nearness, that "his eye sees Him" (42:5), that he knows Him again. Nothing is explained, nothing adjusted; wrong has not become right, nor cruelty kindness. Nothing has happened but that man again hears God's address.

The mystery has remained unsolved, but it has become his, it has become man's.

And we?

We—by that is meant all those who have not got over what happened and will not get over it. How is it with us? Do we stand overcome before the hidden face of God like the tragic hero of the Greeks before faceless fate? No, rather even now we contend, we too, with God, even with Him, the Lord of Being, whom we once, we here, chose for our Lord. We do not put up with earthly being; we struggle for its redemption, and struggling we appeal to the help of our Lord, who is again and still a hiding one. In such a state we await His voice, whether it comes out of the storm or out of a stillness that follows it. Though His coming appearance resemble no earlier one, we shall recognize again our cruel and merciful Lord.

CONTEMPORARY SCHOLARSHIP

I have not selected the typical historical or sociological scholarly studies of Judaism for this section. The essays I have selected are written by scholars, but they are not intended to be scholarly in the traditional sense. Rather, they are personal statements informed not only by scholarship but also by personal experience as Jews. The first, by a prominent literary figure, struggles with the question of what it means to be a Jew after the **Holocaust**. The second, by a professor of religious studies who is also a feminist theologian, examines the question of feminism and Judaism. These essays teach us that scholarship need not be impersonal to be informative and that it need not be disinterested to be illuminating.

10.6 AFTER AUSCHWITZ

The Nazi death camps before and during the Second World War devoured six million Jews. Over one million Jewish children were exterminated. The cruelty, barbarism, and suffering stagger the human mind. The skins of Jews were turned into lamp shades by their Nazi murderers. Old men and young men, small children and teenagers, old women and young women—all went to their deaths for no other reason than the fact that they happened to be born Jewish.

Europe had experienced anti-Semitism before, but nothing like this. Hitler set in motion a systematic program to exterminate a whole people from the face of the earth. It was his "final solution" to "the Jewish question." Judaism and the peoples of the world have not been the same since.

Many Jewish writers and thinkers have tried, in their own ways, to come to grips with the unbelievable horror of the Holocaust. How could a Messiah who is *able* to come to redeem his people fail to do so under these extreme circumstances? How could "good Christians" not only stand by and watch but actively participate as well? The Holocaust was not another Jewish exile. It was the end of a way of life. Can it also be the beginning of a new Judaism, a new return?

Elie Wiesel (1928–) is a survivor of the death camps and was a witness to the brutality. He is also a sensitive and gifted writer who explores in his many books and stories what it means to be a Jew after the Holocaust.

ELIE WIESEL

To Be a Jew

READING QUESTIONS

1. What did it mean, according to Wiesel, to be a Jew before the Holocaust?
2. According to Wiesel, what does it mean to be a Jew after the Holocaust?

Once upon a time, in a distant town surrounded by mountains, there lived a small Jewish boy who believed himself capable of seeing good in evil, of discovering dawn within dusk and, in general, of deciphering the symbols, both visible and invisible, lavished upon him by destiny.

To him, all things seemed simple and miraculous: life and death, love and hatred. On one side were the righteous, on the other the wicked. The just were always handsome and generous, the miscreants always ugly and cruel. And God in His heaven kept the accounts in a book only He could consult. In that book each people had its own page, and the Jewish people had the most beautiful page of all.

Naturally, this little boy felt at ease only among his own people, in his own setting. Everything alien frightened me. And alien meant not Moslem or Hindu, but Christian. The priest dressed in black, the woodcutter and his ax, the teacher and his ruler, old peasant women crossing themselves as their husbands uttered oath upon oath, constables looking gruff or merely preoccupied— all of them exuded a hostility I understood and considered normal, and therefore without remedy.

I *understood* that all these people, young and old, rich and poor, powerful and oppressed, exploiters and exploited, should want my undoing, even my death. True, we inhabited the same landscape, but that was yet another reason for them to hate me. Such is man's nature: he hates what disturbs him, what eludes him. We depended on the more or less unselfish tolerance of the "others," yet our life followed its own course independently of theirs, a fact they clearly resented. Our deter-

mination to maintain and enrich our separate history, our separate society, confused them as much as did that history itself. A living Jew, a believing Jew, proud of his faith, was for them a contradiction, a denial, an aberration. According to their calculations, this chosen and accursed people should long ago have ceased to haunt a mankind whose salvation was linked to the bloodstained symbol of the cross. They could not accept the idea of a Jew celebrating his Holy Days with song, just as they celebrated their own. That was inadmissible, illogical, even unjust. And the less they understood us, the more I understood them.

I felt no animosity. I did not even hate them at Christmas or Easter time when they imposed a climate of terror upon our frightened community. I told myself: They envy us, they persecute us because they envy us, and rightly so; surely *they* were the ones to be pitied. Their tormenting us was but an admission of weakness, of inner insecurity. If God's truth subsists on earth in the hearts of mortals, it is our doing. It is through us that God has chosen to manifest His will and outline His designs, and it is through us that He has chosen to sanctify His name. Were I in their place I, too, would feel rejected. How could they not be envious? In an odd way, the more they hunted me, the more I rationalized their behavior. Today I recognize my feelings for what they were: a mixture of pride, distrust and pity.

Yet I felt no curiosity. Not of any kind, or at any moment. We seemed to intrigue them, but they left me indifferent. I knew nothing of their catechism, and cared less. I made no attempt to comprehend the rites and canons of their faith. Their rituals held no interest for me; quite the contrary, I turned away from them. Whenever I met a priest I would avert my gaze and think of something else. Rather than walk in front of a church with its pointed and threatening belfry, I would cross the street. To see was as frightening as to be seen; I worried that a visual, physical link might somehow be created between us. So ignorant was I of their world that I had no idea that Judaism and Christianity claimed the same roots. Nor did I know that Christians who believe in the eternity and in the divinity of Christ also believe in those of God, *our* God. Though our universes existed side by side, I avoided penetrating theirs, whereas they sought to dominate ours by force. I had heard enough tales about the Crusades and the pogroms, and I had repeated enough litanies dedicated to their victims, to know where I stood. I had read and reread descriptions of what inquisitors, grand and small, had inflicted on Jews in Catholic kingdoms; how they had preached God's love to them even as they were leading them to the stake. All I knew of Christianity was its hate for my people. Christians were more present in my imagination than in my life. What did a Christian do when he was alone? What were his dreams made of? How did he use his time when he was not engaged in plotting against us? But none of this really troubled me. Beyond our immediate contact, our public and hereditary confrontations, he simply did not exist.

My knowledge of the Jew, on the other hand, sprang from an inexhaustible source: the more I learned, the more I wanted to know. There was inside me a thirst for knowledge that was all-enveloping, all-pervasive, a veritable obsession.

I knew what it meant to be a Jew in day-to-day life as well as in the absolute. What we required was to obey the Law; thus one needed first to learn it, then to remember it. What was required was to love God and that which in His creation bears His seal. And His will would be done.

Abraham's covenant, Isaac's suspended sacrifice, Jacob's fiery dreams, the revelation at Sinai, the long march through the desert, Moses' blessings, the conquest of Canaan, the pilgrimages to the Temple in Jerusalem, Isaiah's and Habakkuk's beautiful but harsh words, Jeremiah's lamentations, the Talmudic legends: my head was abuzz with ancient memories and debates, with tales teeming with kings and prophets, tragedies and miracles. Every story contained victims, always victims, and survivors, always survivors. To be a Jew meant to live with memory.

Nothing could have been easier. One needed only to follow tradition, to reproduce the gestures and sounds transmitted through generations whose end product I was. On the morning of Shavuoth there I was with Moses receiving the Law. On the eve of Tishah b'Av, seated on the floor, my head covered with ashes, I wept, together with Rabbi Yohanan Ben-Zakkai, over the destruction of the city that had been thought indestructible. During the week of Hanukkah, I rushed to the aid of the Maccabees; and on Purim, I laughed, how I laughed, with Mordecai, celebrating his victory over Haman. And week after week, as we blessed the wine during Shabbat meals, I accompanied the Jews out of Egypt—yes, I was forever leaving Egypt, freeing myself from bondage. To be a Jew meant creating links, a network of continuity.

With the years I learned a more "sophisticated," more modern vocabulary. I was told that to be a Jew means to place the accent simultaneously and equally on verb and noun, on the secular and the eternal, to prevent the one from excluding the other or succeeding at the expense of the other. That it means to serve God by espousing man's cause, to plead for man while recognizing his need of God. And to opt for the Creator *and* His creation, refusing to pit one against the other.

Of course, man must interrogate God, as did Abraham; articulate his anger, as did Moses; and shout his sorrow, as did Job. But only the Jew opts for Abraham—who questions—*and* for God—who is questioned. He claims every role and assumes every destiny: he is both sum and synthesis.

I shall long, perhaps forever, remember my Master, the one with the yellowish beard, telling me, "Only the Jew knows that he may oppose God as long as he does so in defense of His creation." Another time he told me, "God gave the Law, but it is up to man to interpret it —and his interpretation is binding on God and commits Him."

Surely this is an idealized concept of the Jew. And of man. And yet it is one that is tested every day, at every moment, in every circumstance.

At school I read in the Talmud: Why did God create only one man? The answer: All men have the same ancestor. So that no man, later, could claim superiority over another.

And also: A criminal who sets fire to the Temple, the most sacred, the most revered edifice in the world, is punishable with only thirty-nine lashes of the whip; let a fanatic kill him and *his* punishment would be death. For all the temples and all the sanctuaries are not worth the life of a single human being, be he arsonist, profanator, enemy of God and shame of God.

Painful irony: We were chased from country to country, our Houses of Study were burned, our sages assassinated, our school-children massacred, and still we went on tirelessly, fiercely, praising the inviolate sanctity of life and proclaiming faith in man, any man.

An extraordinary contradiction? Perhaps. But to be a Jew is precisely to reveal oneself within one's contradictions by accepting them. It means safeguarding one's past at a time when mankind aspires only to conquer the future; it means observing Shabbat when the official day of rest is Sunday or Friday; it means fervently exploring the Talmud, with its seemingly antiquated laws and discussions, while outside, not two steps away from the heder or the yeshiva, one's friends and parents are rounded up or beaten in a pogrom; it means asserting the right of spirituality in a world that denies spirituality; it means singing and singing again, louder and louder, when all around everything heralds the end of the world, the end of man.

All this was really so. The small Jewish boy is telling only what he heard and saw, what he lived himself, long ago. He vouches for its truth.

Yes, long ago in distant places it all seemed so simple to me, so real, so throbbing with truth. Like God, I looked at the world and found it good, fertile, full of meaning. Even in exile, every creature was in its place and every encounter was charged with promise. And with the advent of Shabbat, the town changed into a kingdom whose madmen and beggars became the princes of Shabbat.

I shall never forget Shabbat in my town. When I shall have forgotten everything else, my memory will still retain the atmosphere of holiday, of serenity pervading even the poorest houses: the white tablecloth, the candles, the meticulously combed little girls, the men on their way to synagogue. When my town shall fade into the abyss of time, I will continue to remember the light and the warmth it radiated on Shabbat. The exalting prayers, the wordless songs of the Hasidim, the fire and radiance of their Masters.

On that day of days, past and future suffering and anguish faded into the distance. Appeased man called on the divine presence to express his gratitude.

The jealousies and grudges, the petty rancors between neighbors could wait. As could the debts and worries, the dangers. Everything could wait. As it enveloped the universe, the Shabbat conferred on it a dimension of peace, an aura of love.

Those who were hungry came and ate; and those who felt abandoned seized the outstretched hand; and those who were alone, and those who were sad, the strangers, the refugees, the wanderers, as they left the synagogue were invited to share the meal in any home; and the grieving were urged to contain their tears and come draw on the collective joy of Shabbat.

The difference between us and the others? The others, how I pitied them. They did not even know what they were missing; they were unmoved by the beauty, the eternal splendor of Shabbat.

And then came the Holocaust, which shook history and by its dimensions and goals marked the end of a civilization. Concentration-camp man discovered the anti-savior.

We became witnesses to a huge simplification. On the one side there were the executioners and on the other the victims. What about the onlookers, those who remained neutral, those who served the executioner simply by not interfering? To be a Jew then meant to fight both the complacency of the neutral and the hate of the killers. And to resist—in any way, with any means. And not only with weapons. The Jew who refused death, who refused to believe in death, who chose to marry in the ghetto, to circumcise his son, to teach him the sacred language, to bind him to the threatened and weakened

lineage of Israel—that Jew was resisting. The professor or shopkeeper who disregarded facts and warnings and clung to illusion, refusing to admit that people could so succumb to degradation—he, too, was resisting. There was no essential difference between the Warsaw ghetto fighters and the old men getting off the train in Treblinka: because they were Jewish, they were all doomed to hate, and death.

In those days, more than ever, to be Jewish signified *refusal*. Above all, it was a refusal to see reality and life through the enemy's eyes—a refusal to resemble him, to grant him that victory, too.

Yet his victory seemed solid and, in the beginning, definitive. All those uprooted communities, ravaged and dissolved in smoke; all those trains that crisscrossed the nocturnal Polish landscapes; all those men, all those women, stripped of their language, their names, their faces, compelled to live and die according to the laws of the enemy, in anonymity and darkness. All those kingdoms of barbed wire where everyone looked alike and all words carried the same weight. Day followed day and hour followed hour, while thoughts, numb and bleak, groped their way among the corpses, through the mire and the blood.

And the adolescent in me, yearning for faith, questioned: Where was God in all this? Was this another test, one more? Or a punishment? And if so, for what sins? What crimes were being punished? Was there a misdeed that deserved so many mass graves? Would it ever again be possible to speak of justice, of truth, of divine charity, after the murder of one million Jewish children?

I did not understand, I was afraid to understand. Was this the end of the Jewish people, or the end perhaps of the human adventure? Surely it was the end of an era, the end of a world. That I knew, that was all I knew.

As for the rest, I accumulated uncertainties. The faith of some, the lack of faith of others added to my perplexity. How could one believe, how could one not believe, in God as one faced those mountains of ashes? Who would symbolize the concentration-camp experience—the killer or the victim? Their confrontation was so striking, so gigantic that it had to include a metaphysical, ontological aspect: would we ever penetrate its mystery?

Questions, doubts. I moved through the fog like a sleepwalker. Why did the God of Israel manifest such hostility toward the descendants of Israel? I did not know. Why did free men, liberals and humanists, remain untouched by Jewish suffering? I did not know.

I remember the midnight arrival at Birkenau. Shouts. Dogs barking. Families together for the last time, families about to be torn asunder. A young Jewish boy walks at his father's side in the convoy of men; they walk and they walk and night walks with them toward a place spewing monstrous flames, flames devouring the sky. Suddenly an inmate crosses the ranks and explains to the men what they are seeing; the truth of the night: the future, the absence of future; the key to the secret, the power of evil. As he speaks, the young boy touches his father's arm as though to reassure him, and whispers, "This is impossible, isn't it? Don't listen to what he is telling us, he only wants to frighten us. What he says is impossible, unthinkable, it is all part of another age, the Middle Ages, not the twentieth century, not modern history. The world, Father, the civilized world would not allow such things to happen."

And yet the civilized world did know, and remained silent. Where was man in all this? And culture, how did it reach this nadir? All those spiritual leaders, those thinkers, those philosophers enamored of truth, those moralists drunk with justice—how was one to reconcile their teachings with Josef Mengele, the great master of selections in Auschwitz? I told myself that a grave, a horrible error had been committed somewhere—only, I knew neither its nature nor its author. When and where had history taken so bad a turn?

I remember the words of a young Talmudist whose face was that of an old man. He and I had worked as a team, carrying boulders weighing more than the two of us.

"Let us suppose," he whispered, "let us suppose that our people had not transmitted the Law to other nations. Let us forget Abraham and his example, Moses and his justice, the prophets and their message. Let us suppose that our contributions to philosophy, to science, to literature are negligible or even nonexistent. Maimonides, Nahmanides, Rashi: nothing. Spinoza, Bergson, Einstein, Freud: nothing. Let us suppose that we have in no way added to progress, to the well-being of mankind. One thing cannot be contested: the great killers, history's great assassins—Pharaoh, Nero, Chmelnitzky, Hitler—not one was formed in our midst."

Which brings us back to where we started: to the relations between Jews and Christians, which, of course, we had been forced to revise. For we had been struck by a harsh truth: in Auschwitz all the Jews were victims, all the killers were Christian.

I mention this here neither to score points nor to embarrass anyone. I believe that no religion, people or nation is inferior or superior to another; I dislike facile triumphalism, for us and for others. I dislike self-righteousness. And I feel closer to certain Christians—as long as they do not try to convert me to their faith—than to certain Jews. I felt closer to John XXIII and to

François Mauriac than to self-hating Jews. I have more in common with an authentic and tolerant Christian than with a Jew who is neither authentic nor tolerant. I stress this because what I am about to say will surely hurt my Christian friends. Yet I have no right to hold back.

How is one to explain that neither Hitler nor Himmler was ever excommunicated by the church? That Pius XII never thought it necessary, not to say indispensable, to condemn Auschwitz and Treblinka? That among the S.S. a large proportion were believers who remained faithful to their Christian ties to the end? That there were killers who went to confession between massacres? And that they all came from Christian families and had received a Christian education?

In Poland, a stronghold of Christianity, it often happened that Jews who had escaped from the ghettos returned inside their walls, so hostile did they find the outside world; they feared the Poles as much as the Germans. This was also true in Lithuania, in the Ukraine, in White Russia and in Hungary. How is one to explain the passivity of the population as it watched the persecution of its Jews? How explain the cruelty of the killers? How explain that the Christian in them did not make their arms tremble as they shot at children or their conscience bridle as they shoved their naked, beaten victims into the factories of death? Of course, here and there, brave Christians came to the aid of Jews, but they were few: several dozen bishops and priests, a few hundred men and women in all of Europe.

It is a painful statement to make, but we cannot ignore it: as surely as the victims are a problem for the Jews, the killers are a problem for the Christians.

Yes, the victims remain a serious and troubling problem for us. No use covering it up. What was there about the Jew that he could be reduced so quickly, so easily to the status of victim? I have read all the answers, all the explanations. They are all inadequate. It is difficult to imagine the silent processions marching toward the pits. And the crowds that let themselves be duped. And the condemned who, inside the sealed wagons and sometimes on the very ramp at Birkenau, continued not to see. I do not understand. I understand neither the killers nor the victims.

To be a Jew during the Holocaust may have meant not to understand. Having rejected murder as a means of survival and death as a solution, men and women agreed to live and die without understanding.

For the survivor, the question presented itself differently: to remain or not to remain a Jew. I remember our tumultuous, anguished debates in France after the liberation. Should one leave for Palestine and fight in the name of Jewish nationalism, or should one, on the contrary, join the Communist movement and promulgate the ideal of internationalism? Should one delve deeper into tradition, or turn one's back on it? The options were extreme: total commitment or total alienation, unconditional loyalty or repudiation. There was no returning to the earlier ways and principles. The Jew could say: I have suffered, I have been made to suffer, all I can do is draw closer to my own people. And that was understandable. Or else: I have suffered too much, I have no strength left, I withdraw, I do not wish my children to inherit this suffering. And that, too, was understandable.

And yet, as in the past, the ordeal brought not a decline but a renascence of Jewish consciousness and a flourishing of Jewish history. Rather than break his ties, the Jew strengthened them. Auschwitz made him stronger. Even he among us who espouses so-called universal causes outside his community is motivated by the Jew in him trying to reform man even as he despairs of mankind. Though he may be in a position to become something else, the Jew remains a Jew.

Throughout a world in flux, young Jews, speaking every tongue, products of every social class, join in the adventure that Judaism represents for them, a phenomenon that reached its apex in Israel and Soviet Russia. Following different roads, these pilgrims take part in the same project and express the same defiance: "They want us to founder, but we will let our joy explode; they want to make us hard, closed to solidarity and love, well, we will be obstinate but filled with compassion." This is the challenge that justifies the hopes the Jew places in Judaism and explains the singular marks he leaves on his destiny.

Thus there would seem to be more than one way for the Jew to assume his condition. There is a time to question oneself and a time to act; there is a time to tell stories and a time to pray; there is a time to build and a time to rebuild. Whatever he chooses to do, the Jew becomes a spokesman for all Jews, dead and yet to be born, for all the beings who live through him and inside him.

His mission was never to make the world Jewish but, rather, to make it more human.

10.7 DILEMMAS OF A JEWISH FEMINIST

Judaism is, like many religions, patriarchal. Men have held positions of power, written the scriptures, made the decisions, led the worship, offered the sacrifices, and otherwise have run the show. Of course, women had a role—but a role largely determined by men.

When the Reform movement in 1844 tried to revise the Jewish liturgy to allow women full participation in the service, it failed—there was too much opposition. Judaism was not yet ready to admit women into full religious fellowship with men.

Things have changed since 1844. There are now female rabbis in both Reform and Conservative Judaism. However, Orthodox Judaism still does not allow women to hold rabbinical positions and Hasidism is still largely male dominated.

A woman who is Jewish and finds the tradition spiritually nourishing and enriching, but also believes in equality of women, faces a dilemma. Judith Plaskow, a professor of religion at Manhattan College and author of *Standing Again at Sinai*, a landmark book in feminist Jewish thought, tackles this question in the next selection.

JUDITH PLASKOW

The Wife/Sister Stories

READING QUESTIONS

1. What are the wife/sister stories?
2. Why do these stories and the situation they typify pose a dilemma for a Jewish feminist? What is that dilemma?
3. Why cannot the "invisibility of women" be remedied within the legal structure of Judaism?
4. What is Plaskow's solution to the dilemma?

Speaking as a *Jew* from the *Jewish* feminist perspective, I want to explore the complex situation in which the Jewish feminist finds herself, and the particular dilemma of one who seeks to forge a Jewish identity for herself in the midst of a culture that cannot imagine why she would bother.

My jumping off point is a Biblical passage or, actually, a series of passages which, to my mind, are paradigms of the Jewish woman's situation. Three times in the Bib-

From *Speaking of Faith: Global Perspectives on Women, Religion and Social Change*, edited by Diana L. Eck and Devaki Jain (Philadelphia: New Society Publishers, 1987) pp. 122–129. Copyright © 1987 Judith Plaskow Committee on Women, Religion and Social Change. Reprinted by permission. Notes omitted.

lical book of Genesis, twice with reference to Abraham and once with reference to Isaac, we are told that one of the patriarchs, spurred by famine in the land of Canaan, journeyed to a strange land with his wife in search of food. Afraid that the people of the land would kill him in order to be able to marry his beautiful wife, the patriarch asked her to say she was his sister in order that he might be treated well on her account. In the narratives concerning Abraham, the king then takes Sarah into his house on the assumption she is Abraham's sister, only to be punished or threatened with punishment by God for taking another man's wife. The king, realizing what has happened, indignantly confronts Abraham with his deception.

Three years ago, I was teaching a course in feminist theology at a Jewish conference at which there was also a course on the Jew as a stranger. A few days into the conference, one woman defected from the stranger course to mine. The teacher of this course had begun by using his wife/sister stories to illustrate the relation of the Jew to Gentile culture. Abraham, the first Jew, afraid of rejection by what he perceived as a hostile society, set up a situation in which he was bound to be rejected. "That's very interesting and useful," my woman friend said, "but what about what Abraham does to Sarah?" "Oh," the class groaned, "not the women's issue again; that's not what we're talking about here."

My class, of course, was more than happy to talk about the issue, and ever since, these stories have fascinated me. They seem to me to capture perfectly the position of the Jewish woman as the "other's other." In these stories, the male Jew, perceiving himself—however rightly or wrongly—as "other" in a Gentile culture uses the woman as a buffer between himself and that culture, doubling her otherness. Thus Abraham recapitulates in relation to Sarah his own relation to the wider culture. The male Jew as other in turn defines as other the woman who shares his otherness with him. And Sarah's capacity, the Jewish woman's capacity, to demur from this situation is hampered by the fact that there may be real danger out there. Perhaps the Egyptians or Abimelech *would* have killed Abraham, and thus how could Sarah refuse to go along with his ruse?

This is one way of looking at the Jewish feminist dilemma. In addition to illustrating women's situation as other, it helps us understand part of the reason why Jewish feminists have been less radical in our criticism of tradition than our Christian sisters: we are afraid of being without allies. But I don't want to focus on the precariousness of the Jewish woman's situation, because in fact Jewish feminists *are* refusing our otherness both in the tradition and in the wider culture. Like other women, we are taking upon ourselves the right to define ourselves rather than having our place and our being defined for us. Judaism, like all other traditions, is a patriarchal tradition we are trying to transform.

It has become clear, however, that while we may share a common commitment to change, the specific content and texture of our situations is very different. What does it mean to be "other" in the Jewish tradition, and what does it mean to move beyond that otherness? The central category of Jewish religious life from the first century to the end of the 18th century was *halachah*, or law. Deprived of the Temple and its sacrificial cult by the Roman destruction of Jerusalem, the Jews developed a portable religiosity based on prayer and the study and elaboration of Biblical texts. While this textual elaboration, or *midrash* as it is called, was partly narrative and theological, legal *midrash*, the application of legal texts to everyday situations, has had a certain priority in Jewish life. Women's situation has been defined, then, not so much by a set of ideas or concepts but by a legal system which seeks to realize the reality of God in every detail of human existence. Statements or opinions about women help us to understand the context of the law, but women are defined, first of all, by what they can and cannot and must *do*.

This does not mean, however, that we can generate from the law a comprehensive statement of women's position. The many laws pertaining to women in Jewish sources do not add up and are not intended to add up to an overarching statement of her position and status, and the search for such a statement leads to contradiction. Analysis of patterns of women's "exclusion and participation" as they appear in Jewish law makes clear that there are areas of obligation men and women share, areas from which women are excluded, and areas in which the law provides female oriented rituals. Thus feminists can focus on aspects of Jewish texts which assume women's subordination, and apologists on those aspects which seem to support "equality in difference," but only because both are imposing a foreign category on the literature.

These considerations, however, while cautionary, do not prevent us from making certain generalizations. First, whatever the legal sources have to say about women, good or bad, there is a sense in which women's real concerns are not represented. As Jacob Neusner has pointed out, women become important or are taken notice of in the law precisely when they ruffle the smooth ordering of things. When a woman is about to leave a marriage or leave her father's house to enter into one, or when she has taken a vow or is suspected of having committed adultery, the law then becomes interested in her. When her sexuality rears its head in a potentially threatening way, or she is about to be at the center of an important property transfer, the law must step in to regularize her irregularity and ensure her return to the normal state of daughter/wife/motherhood. But if we want to know how women functioned daily as mothers, wives and workers—let alone what they themselves felt about these roles—the texts tell us next to nothing. In fact, Neusner says he cannot think of a single sentence in the *Mishnah*, an important code of law, dealing with women as mothers.

Second, insofar as women's concerns are not represented by the legal texts, we do not really get from them a picture of women as moral agents. The question has been raised of how moral roles and models for women in Judaism are different from those for men. Insofar as the legal sources address only specific male concerns about regularizing women, the texts give us women not as actors but as persons acted upon. Here, I think the wife/sister stories, although narrative texts, are again instructive because they indicate that once women are defined relationally, we get to see their decision making only as circumscribed by particular sets of relations. Sarah can, in a variety of ways, make the best of a bad situation, but we do not get to see her formulating her moral choices from her own perspective.

Third—and for me, this is the most important point—the invisibility of women cannot be remedied within the legal structure. In fact, the Jewish feminist movement of the last ten years has focused largely on *halachah* and the rectification of certain problems it raises for women. For example, according to Jewish law, women are not required to put on a prayer shawl or phylacteries or say the *she'ma* three times daily. But since in Jewish law one who is not obligated to perform a commandment has a lower status in its performance than one who is obligated, women cannot form part of the minyon, or quorum for prayer, made up of those obligated to pray. Divorce is another important feminist issue. According to Jewish law, only a man can write and deliver the *get*, or divorce decree, which ends a Jewish marriage. This means that in a case in which a man cannot or will not give his wife a *get*, she is forever prevented from remarrying.

These concerns can and have been addressed within a halachic framework, and adjustments have been made. In fact, the tradition has been trying for hundreds of years to remedy the inequity of the divorce laws by finding ways to get a recalcitrant husband to give his wife a *get*. But these only partially successful efforts reveal very clearly that the desire to render justice to women is secondary to the preservation of the halachic system. For really the only way to solve the problem of divorce is to give women equal agency, to allow them to write a *get*. But this is precisely what has not been and cannot be done within the traditional framework, because it would

entail a recognition of women's situation as women, which goes beyond the system. It is to just such a recognition, however, that we as feminists are committed. Once we begin to see women as a class, and gender as a central category for the analysis of any culture or tradition, we are bound to break out of a system which renders women's status invisible. At this stage, in any case, a feminist Judaism must insist upon the importance of women's experience and, thus, on shaking up the categories and processes of Jewish life and thought.

I must add that, although I have been speaking about traditional Judaism, these last comments apply equally to liberalism. Over the past 150 years, the various forms of liberal Judaism—Reform, Conservative, Reconstructionist—have to different degrees rejected the binding authority of the law and with it the place assigned to women. Gradually, women have gained access to Jewish education, to the right to participate in synagogue ritual and—in the last ten years—even to the rabbinate. Women are now ordained as Reform and Reconstructionist rabbis and will soon be admitted to the Conservative seminary. While I do not want to underestimate the importance of these changes and the possibilities they have opened to women, since they are what enable me to question the tradition today, it remains the case that these changes have come out of a liberal commitment to equality which entirely fails to recognize that *real* equality of women is not the same as integrating women into male institutions and systems. Reform Judaism in particular, which is the oldest of these movements, assumed that if it abolished women's traditional legal status, women would simply become equal without there being any need to attend to the nature of or barriers to their equality. Thus, Reform has had no vocabulary for understanding why it took 140 years for the first woman to be ordained or what these ordinations yet portend. In other words, a thoroughgoing feminist analysis is as important to liberal Judaism as it is to Orthodox Judaism, although liberalism provides more space in which this analysis can be performed.

Let me reiterate, however, that insistence on feminist criticism is made more difficult by Jewish feminist awareness that feminist criticism of Judaism provides fuel for anti-Semites. According to the new feminist form of anti-Semitism, Christianity can perhaps be redeemed from sexism, but for some strange reason Judaism cannot. Actually, I think this is a problem Jews share with Muslim women: sexism becomes an excuse for dismissing a tradition which may be oppressive differently, but is really no more or less oppressive than the tradition of those doing the dismissing.

Let me also address the other side of the Jewish feminist situation: the theological and material resources for change which the Jewish tradition provides. Sometimes the situation of the Jewish woman feels to me like Wittgenstein's duck/rabbit: a simple figure that from one perspective appears to be a duck, from another a rabbit, but one that is hard to see as both at the same time. I use this image to express my sense of the duality of the Jewish woman's situation. Sometimes I perceive the Jewish tradition as the oppressor of women, systematically negating and excluding our experience, making us the "other's other." Obviously this is the perspective from which I have spoken thus far. But at other times, I look at the strength of Jewish women and see this perception as absurd. I know that we as Jewish women have not necessarily experienced ourselves as oppressed, and that the experience of non-oppression is not simply a matter of false consciousness—although I do not deny the reality of false consciousness—but comes out of a real history of integrity and power.

First, we American feminists for the last fifteen years have been trying to create womanspaces in which we could come together out of our fathers' and husbands' houses and share our experiences and visions as women. But in traditional Judaism, with its sharp sex-role division, women have always had and still have that womanspace. Whether it was in the market or the ritual bath, or whether it was in the form-creating idle chatter of the women's side of the synagogue, women shared a common life that we deeply desire and yet lost when liberal Judaism gave us the precious right sometimes to act as men. What women did with this common life is now our task to discover. For example, what have the rituals surrounding menstruation meant to women? Anthropological evidence suggests that blood taboos which appear very oppressive to women can and have been used by women to their own ends. Was this true in the Jewish tradition, and how? Or Rosh Hodesh, the celebration of the new moon, which was traditionally a women's holiday and which contemporary Jewish feminists are recovering and developing—what did it mean to women and how did it affect their lives? What can it mean to us?

Second, the Jewish male ideal is the scholar spending his time in uninterrupted study. This fact, combined with the precariousness of the Jewish economic situation in many times and places, gave women an important and sometimes crucial role in economic life. In the middle ages, for example, Jewish women were involved in a variety of occupations, some of which involved travel away from their families for extended periods of time. While the economic importance of women necessitated certain changes in Jewish civil law—so that women would be responsible for their own debts, for instance—it is unclear whether it had any impact on their religious status.

Bernadette Brooten has demonstrated, through examination of inscriptional evidence, that in a very early period of Jewish history women seem to have played some leadership role in the synagogue. Whether this correlated with some particular economic role in the community or whether there were other periods of female religious leadership is still being explored. But even if we find no correlation between significant economic roles for women and improvement of their religious status, we cannot ignore the impact of economic role on women's sense of self. Thus, if the duck is exclusion of women from public religious life, the rabbit is a role acknowledged by the whole community as vital and one which must have provided women with a sense of energy and worth.

I do not mean to suggest for one minute that either of these points obviates the need for change. It is clear that womanspaces, like halachic tinkering, can help preserve an unjust system by rendering it bearable and providing shared self-validation which does not threaten the status quo. The challenge is to use those spaces in a way which is transforming, knowing that we have not invented them, that we have a heritage of power to draw on.

Being the "other's other," we can use this power to articulate our claim to justice in a tradition which already partially knows our situation. I began by suggesting that Sarah shares with Abraham a sense of strangerhood which is recapitulated in her own relation to him. "Our ancestors were strangers in the land of Egypt"— this is where the Jewish story begins. As one Jewish feminist has pointed out, however, this shared experience can provide the basis for a new *halachah* and a new ethic which demands of the Jewish male the same decency he demands of the community at large. A decent Gentile should not join a golf club which excludes Jews; a decent Jew should not join a synagogue which excludes women. A decent Gentile should not attend a medical school which does not admit Jews; a decent Jew should not study at a Yeshivah which closes Talmud study to women. These are the injunctions to which liberal Judaism has already responded, but they are not enough.

We are not stopping here. We are also using our power to reclaim our heritage in an ongoing *midrash* which places Sarah at the center. I mentioned earlier that Jewish religiosity is based on the elaboration of Biblical texts. The wife/sister motif is no exception: the tradition plays with it in a variety of ways. Abraham committed a great sin in risking Sarah's honor, says one commentator. He failed to trust in God, says another, for God would have delivered him from famine in Canaan. The second time Abraham passed off Sarah as his sister, the *midrash* tell us, he did not ask her permission, for he knew she would refuse. The commentators know there's a problem. They circle round; they circle round. They're still concerned with Sarah's beauty, the immorality of the Egyptians, Sarah's honor defined in terms of her availability to only one man. But the process does not stop there. It is also in our hands. Judaism is open. We think we know something of what Sarah felt, and much more will we uncover and come to know. We are telling and retelling our own stories. We are speaking as Jewish feminists, taking self-definition into our own hands.

KEY TERMS AND CONCEPTS

assimilation Taking on the cultural traits and life-style of a culture different from the one in which a person is born.

Baal Shem Tov (1700–1760) The title for the founder of Hasidism, meaning "Master of the Good Name."

Conservative Judaism A religious movement reacting against the liberalism of **Reform Judaism.** It attempts to balance tradition with change.

Dead Sea Scrolls Ancient scrolls found near Qumran hidden by a Jewish **eschatological** sect.

El, *Elohim* God or divinity.

eschatology Theory of the last days or end of time that is usually associated with God's judgment, the messianic era, the resurrection of the dead, and the world or kingdom of God to come.

Essenes A Jewish sect usually associated with the **Dead Sea Scrolls.**

Holocaust An effort to destroy all Jews by mass murder. More than six million Jews were killed from 1933 to 1945 by the Nazis (German National Socialist Workers Party).

Kabbalah Literally means "tradition" but has come to designate a type of Jewish mysticism.

Karaites An eighth- to twelfth-century Jewish sect that rejected the oral **Torah** and lived by the written **Torah** alone.

Ketuvim Literally means "writings" and refers to one of the three main parts of the **Tanakh.**

Messiah Literally means "anointed one" and refers to the **eschatological** king who will rule in the end times.

midrash An interpretation of scripture or a collection of such interpretations.

Mishnah A code of law promulgated by Judah the Patriarch around 200 C.E.

Nevi'im Translated as "Prophets" and refers to a collection of writings in the **Tanakh.**

Orthodoxy Literally, "right opinion." Refers to a division of modern Judaism that stresses traditional values and beliefs with little accommodation to the modern world.

Passover A festival commemorating the Exodus from Egypt.

Purim A festival celebrating the deliverance of Persian Jews brought about by Queen Esther.

rabbi Means "my master" and is a title for a teacher of **Torah.**

Reform Judaism A Jewish religious movement advocating updating tradition to conform to the conditions of modern life.

Sabbateanism A movement centering on the messiahship of Sabbatai Zvi (1626–1676), who converted to Islam (probably under threat of death) and became known as the "false messiah." Some of his followers viewed his conversion as part of the divine plan.

Sefirot The divine emanations of God central to **kabbalistic** mysticism.

Shekhinah God's presence in the world.

Shema The proclamation of God's unity.

Talmud The **Mishnah** plus commentary on the **Mishnah** produced in rabbinic academies from about 200 to 500. Two Talmuds were written, one in Palestine and one in Babylon. From about 500 on, the Babylonian Talmud has been the primary source for Judaic theology and law.

Tanakh Name for the Hebrew Bible.

Torah At first this referred to the Five Books of Moses, then to Scriptures as a whole, then to the whole body of revelation both written and oral. In its broadest sense, it refers to teachings, instructions, and law based on divine revelation.

YHWH The divine name revealed to Moses in the burning bush. Pronounced "Yahweh," not "Jehovah," Jews do not pronounce this holy name but say *Adonai* or Lord instead.

zadik Means "a righteous person" and is a title used in Hasidism for a wise master and leader of a Hasidic circle.

Zionism A movement, founded in 1897 by Theodor Herzl, to secure a Jewish state.

Zohar A medieval **kabbalistic** book written in thirteenth-century Spain.

SUGGESTIONS FOR FURTHER READING

Cohn-Sherbok, Dan. *Judaism*. Upper Saddle River, N.J.: Prentice-Hall, 1999. A brief but valuable introduction to Jewish life, history, beliefs, and practices.

Friedman, Richard Elliot. *Who Wrote the Bible?* London: Cape, 1988. A clear and engrossing summary of the findings of modern biblical scholarship.

Heschel, Susannah. *On Being a Jewish Feminist: A Reader*. New York: Schocken Books, 1983. A collection of essays dealing with the role and place of women in Judaism.

Jacobs, Louis. *The Jewish Religion: A Companion*. Oxford, England: Oxford University Press, 1995. A comprehensive and excellent introduction to Judaism.

Rosenthal, Gilbert S. *Contemporary Judaism: Patterns of Survival*. New York: Human Sciences, 1986. A good introduction to the history and ideas of Orthodox, Conservative, Reform, and Reconstruction Judaism.

Weiner, Herbert. *9½ Mystics: The Kabbala Today*. New York: Holt, Rinehart & Winston, 1969. A fascinating account of a modern rabbi's visits to centers of Jewish mysticism.

Wigoder, Geoffrey. *The New Stanard Jewish Encyclopaedia*. Rev. ed. New York and Oxford, England: Facts on File, 1992. A concise source of basic information about Jewish civilization and religion.

RESEARCH PROJECTS

1. If there is a Jewish temple or synagogue near you, visit it and speak with the rabbi about his or her work and role in the community. Get permission to attend a worship service. Make a list of items ahead of time to guide your observations. Write a report on your interview and visit for the class.

2. View the video *The Chosen*. Write a paper analyzing the plot and comparing and contrasting the two lead characters, Danny Saunders and Reuven Maeter.

3. Read Elie Wiesel's *The Gates of the Forest* and write a paper on how the hero of this story deals with the Holocaust.

11

Christian Ways of Being Religious

INTRODUCTION

The designation "Christian" was first used, as far as we know, in Antioch in Syria around 35–40 to name an emerging religious movement made up of Jews and Gentiles who worshiped "*Christos.*" *Christos* (**Christ** in English) is the Greek translation of the Hebrew title "Messiah." The title was used for a Jewish teacher named Jesus of Nazareth whom the Romans executed as a political criminal in Judea.

This designation stuck as a number of different messianic groups confessing Jesus as the Christ spread from Judea and Syria into all parts of the Roman Empire and beyond to eventually become the most widely followed religion in the world. Today, as in the beginning, there is no single entity or group to which the term refers. Instead, there are Christiani*ties* with widely variant organizational and ritual structures, not to mention beliefs and histories.

This variety not only complicates the study of Christianity, it also makes it impossible even to sample all aspects of this religion in a book like this. While the study of worldwide Christianity has been distorted by the assumption that it is primarily a Western religion, I will focus primarily on its Western expression here because that is, in all likelihood, the most influential form for those who will read and use this book.

However, I do want to emphasize that there is much more to Christianity than its Western expression. Given present demographics and membership statistics, Christianity is growing most rapidly in places like Africa. It is more than likely that the distinctive history, experience, and culture of Africa will shape decisively the development of Christianity in the new millennium just as Europe and the United States shaped its development in the previous millennium.

11.1 AN OVERVIEW

Professor Lawrence S. Cunningham, Chair of Theology at the University of Notre Dame, undertakes, in the selection that follows, to do the nearly impossible—provide a succinct overview of the history of Christianity. He also speaks of its spiritual character and its problems and prospects as it enters the third millennium.

Western culture as we know it is unthinkable without Christianity. For good or for ill it has shaped the ideas, values, politics, and economies of the West. It has influenced art, music, architecture, holidays, education, charities, medicine, and more. Try to imagine Western culture and history without Christianity.

Although it may be difficult to imagine Western culture without Christianity, we need to remember that Christianity and Western culture are not the same. Christians are people who give their ultimate allegiance to Jesus Christ, and that can be done whether one lives in Ireland or Bolivia or China.

LAWRENCE S. CUNNINGHAM

Christianity

READING QUESTIONS

1. As you read, make a list of all the words and ideas you do not understand or are uncertain about. Discuss them with a classmate, look them up in a dic-

From pages 240–253 of *The HarperCollins Dictionary of Religion* by Jonathan Z. Smith. Copyright © 1995 by The American Academy of Religion. Reprinted by permission of HarperCollins Publishers, Inc.

WORLD DISTRIBUTION OF CHRISTIANS

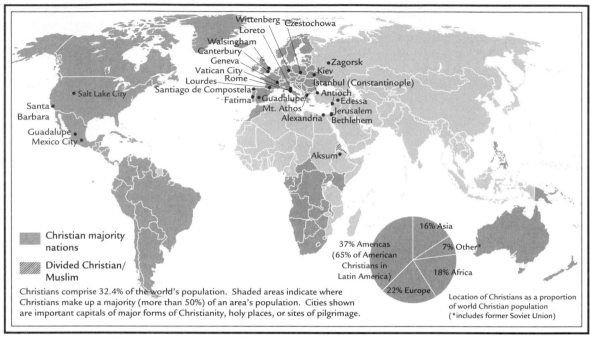

Wittenberg Czestochowa
Loreto
Walsingham
Canterbury
Geneva
Vatican City   Zagorsk
Lourdes   Rome   Kiev
Santiago de Compostela   Istanbul (Constantinople)
Fatima   Guadalupe   Antioch
Mt. Athos   Edessa
Alexandria   Jerusalem
Bethlehem

Salt Lake City

Santa
Barbara

Guadalupe
Mexico City

Aksum

Christian majority
nations

Divided Christian/
Muslim

16% Asia

37% Americas
(65% of American
Christians in
Latin America)

7% Other*

18% Africa

22% Europe

Location of Christians as a proportion
of world Christian population
(*includes former Soviet Union)

Christians comprise 32.4% of the world's population. Shaded areas indicate where
Christians make up a majority (more than 50%) of an area's population. Cities shown
are important capitals of major forms of Christianity, holy places, or sites of pilgrimage.

From *The HarperCollins Dictionary of Religion*, edited by Jonathan Z. Smith (San Francisco: Harper San Francisco © 1995 by the American Academy of Religion.), p. 241. Reprinted by permission of HarperCollins Publishers, Inc.

tionary, or bring them up in class for discussion and clarification.

2. How did Christianity start?
3. What are some of the reasons for Christianity's growth in the first four centuries?
4. What impact did official Roman recognition of Christianity have on its development?
5. What was the net result of the **ecumenical** councils?
6. What impact did the development of monasticism have on Christianity?
7. What sort of changes did the Protestant Reformation bring about?
8. What is secularization, and what impact did it have on Christian development?
9. What is a linear view of history?
10. As Christianity enters the twenty-first century, what challenges does it face?

Christianity is the religion that honors Jesus Christ as its founder and as the object of its worship. Its foundational document is the Bible, which is divided into the Old Testament and the New Testament.

Christianity is the largest of the world's organized religions, with particular strengths in Europe, the Americas, and Africa, but it is represented in most parts of the world. It represents just under a third of the world's population with roughly 1.5 billion adherents.

The three largest branches of Christianity, in order of their numerical strength, are traditionally given as Roman Catholic, Protestant, and Eastern Orthodox, although within those broad categories there are numerous denominations.

HISTORY

Christianity traces its origins to small assemblies of believers, largely (but not exclusively) Jewish in makeup, which arose in Roman Palestine and around the Mediterranean in the second quarter of the first century. These groups preached belief in Jesus Christ (the Greek word *Christ* translates the Hebrew *Messiah*, which means the "Anointed One"), who had been executed in Jerusalem but who, according to this belief, rose from the dead to be exalted in heaven. These early Christians saw Jesus as the fulfillment of the Messianic promises contained in the Hebrew Bible. Christianity, then, has intimate ties with Judaism, the religion from which it springs.

Although it is difficult to reconstruct exactly the character of these early congregations, there are hints in the sources (especially the Letters of Paul) that can help understand their broad shape and polity. Their initiation rite, called baptism, represented a symbolic death and rebirth by which the old person was put away in favor of a new state of being. The death and rebirth motif was also reflected in their language, which both described their peculiar inclusive character (e.g., the "saints" or the "elect"), as opposed to those who were not part of the community (the "unrighteous" or the "nonbelievers"). The celebration of a symbolic meal (called the Eucharist, "Thanksgiving") memorialized the risen Christ and his sacrificial death.

Early Christianity slowly separated from its roots in Judaism, but its increasing appeal to the gentile population of the Roman Empire did not exclude it from official suspicion. Indeed, the first four centuries of Christian growth were punctuated by outbreaks of persecution, although contrary to popular estimation there was no empire-wide or systematic persecution of Christians until 250 under the emperor Decius.

However sporadic these persecutions may have been, they exercised an enormous force on the Christian imagination. Christian martyrs' shrines were places of pilgrimage even before the fourth century. Their death anniversaries were memorialized (thus giving rise, in time, to a complex liturgical calendar that noted both events connected to Jesus Christ and to the sufferings of the martyrs) and churches were built over their tombs. Their courage seemed to have had a positive impact on the growth of the church; the North African theologian Tertullian (d. ca. 220) is famous for his observation that "the blood of the martyrs is the seed of the church."

The reasons for the widespread growth of Christianity in the Roman Empire have been the subject of much speculation. How a religion honoring an executed provincial criminal who came from a religion (Judaism) that was itself marginal in Roman eyes could become so entrenched that by the end of the fourth century it became the official state religion of the empire is hard to explain. Part of the explanation is external and cultural: the Roman Empire was at peace; it had a common commercial language (common Greek), a safe system of roads, and a tolerance for religious ideas despite its reflexive acts of persecution. All of those factors made it easy for a religion to spread to a willing population. To that must be added a yearning for monotheism among certain classes, the availability of entrance to the religion by all classes and both sexes, the mechanisms for excising remorse or guilt, and a moral and social code that stressed mutual aid and a strong sense of personal ethics.

From the evidence of early Christian history, it seems clear that the religion grew largely through the growth of small communities that then split off to found others. For the first four centuries Christianity's greatest growth occurred in the cities in the Roman Empire and in those places with which Rome had trade or colonial outposts. Indeed, the word *pagan* originally meant a noncity dweller, which, in context, meant one who was not Christianized.

Christians were granted toleration by the emperor Constantine by the Edict of Milan in 311, and Christianity became the official religion of the state by proclamation of the emperor Theodosius in 381. This official recognition had profound implications for Christianity.

Leaving its status as an illegal sect, it now enjoyed the patronage of the state. Inevitably, it absorbed both the sociolegal structures of the larger culture and many of its ideas. Christian communities became designated by geographical areas (parishes and dioceses) overseen by bishops and priests who were aided by deacons and deaconesses who ministered to the social needs of congregations. Large-scale building programs developed and the imperial court took an increasing interest in the social and doctrinal affairs of the church. The social development of Christianity brought with it an inevitable growth in differentiated social roles. By the fourth century there was a clear distinction between laity and clergy, with the latter enjoying an ever-increasing prestige and power.

By the fourth century Christianity was represented in urban settlements as far north as Roman Britain and south as Roman Africa; west to the Iberian Peninsula and east to Byzantium (Constantinople) and Roman Syria. In fact, the Syriac Church made incursions, over the centuries, as far east as India as well as possessing a toehold in China. With Constantine's edict of toleration in 311, Christianity absorbed large doses of Roman culture under official patronage. Ecclesiastical districts followed Roman administrative divisions; the legal code of the church reflected Roman jurisprudence; and the state involved itself more in church matters. The simple worship service of the Christians grew increasingly more complex and formal even though its bare outline of the celebration of the Word (i.e., the reading of scripture and preaching about it) and the Sacrament (the celebration of the sacred meal of bread and wine representing the body and blood of Christ) was still discernible.

A further development involved the church's efforts to state its belief in a manner that was coherent and faithful to the original intentions of its founder and his first disciples. This effort involved judgments about what was appropriate and inappropriate (with the inevitable distinction between orthodox and heretical teaching) as well as official statements of the former and condemnations of the latter. These controversies raged in the first five centuries of the church's life and were settled by various councils of bishops (some convened by the emperor) that were considered ecumenical (i.e., universal). The first eight of these ecumenical councils still stand as a source of special authority in the churches of the East and the West. The net result of these controversies was a series of fundamental doctrinal positions that characterize historic Christianity to the twentieth century: a belief in a trinity of Persons (Father, Son, and **Holy Spirit**) in one God; a belief that Jesus was born fully human and fully divine but was only one person; a canon of authentic books that make up the New Testament portion of the Bible; the place of bishops as the authentic teachers and pastors of the church.

Christianity's emergence as the religion of the Roman Empire coincided with the slow decline of that empire. Barbarian invasions from the North battered the western empire (the city of Rome was sacked in the early fifth century), and the Eastern empire with its center at Constantinople became increasingly separated from the West and developed its own theology and liturgical practice. Those divisions, centuries in the making, would end in a schism between the two churches in the eleventh century creating a division that has existed to the twentieth century between the Orthodox Church in the East and the Roman Catholic Church in the West.

One form of resistance to Roman culture, discernible from the late third century, was the exodus of religious seekers who fled urban areas for the deserts in order to live a more perfectly religious life. These desert dwellers were the seedbed from which monasticism evolved as they regularized their lives by specific rules and by rigid codes of moral conduct. Monasticism exerted an enormous influence on the shape of Christianity, especially in Syria, Roman Palestine, North Africa, and the Byzantine world. The monastic ideal of a celibate life, of a regular daily round of prayer, of self-denial and asceticism, and of an intense yearning for salvation would leave its mark on later Christianity. Many of the disciplinary practices of the Roman Catholic clergy (e.g., celibacy) have roots in the monastic and ascetical practices of early Christianity.

In the West, when urban life went into decline after the fifth century, the monastic life provided missionaries both to the Germanic countries and to Ireland. In the East, monasteries were centers of religious life in places such as Constantinople and the source for bishops of the church, since bishops were by law celibate. That is still the practice of the Orthodox world in the late twentieth century.

Monasticism (and other, more informal forms of ascetic life) was not the singular domain of men. From the earliest days, there were women ascetics. Organized monasteries of women grew in both the East and the West. In Anglo-Saxon England, for example, these establishments wielded enormous influence on church affairs in the seventh century. Religious orders of women have played an enormous role in the Christian world, especially in Roman Catholic circles, where they have provided not only the personnel for many of the church's social programs but also many of its greatest mystics and spiritual mistresses.

The whole concept of a religious rule of life (Lat. *vita regularis*), characteristic of monasticism, would take on different colorings in the history of Christianity with the rise of religious orders of men and women. Such orders flourished in the West in both the Middle Ages and after the Reformation, where in both eras they were often agents of renewal and reform in the church.

The rise of Islam in the seventh century radically changed the geographical face of Christianity. The traditional Christian strongholds of greater Palestine, Egypt, and North Africa fell to Islam with further Islamic incursions into the Iberian Peninsula in the West and Anatolia in the East. While, in later centuries, there would be pockets of toleration between Islam and Christianity and a fair amount of mutual cultural influence, the response of Christianity was, by and large, hostile. The medieval Crusades were a series of attempts, with varying degrees of success, to wrest the Christian holy places in Jerusalem from the "infidel" intruders. Armed struggles between Islamic cultures and Christian Europe persisted well into modern times, as the nineteenth-century Greek revolt against the Ottoman Turks attests.

By the early Middle Ages (roughly after the year 1000) Christianity had spread northward in Europe, balancing the loss of the Islamic South and East. Russia was evangelized from Constantinople at the end of the tenth century, giving it an Eastern form of worship and polity. In time, the Russian Church would see itself as an autonomous "Third Rome," standing as an equal with the patriarchs of ancient Rome and Constantinople. Missionaries from the West evangelized the Scandinavian countries and the rest of Eastern Europe, which was not under the direct influence of Russia or Constantinople.

With the reemergence of urban life in the Middle Ages, cities took on a more important part in the development of religious life. The rurally oriented monastic centers gave way to the preeminence of episcopal life centered around cathedrals. Schools and, eventually, universities were founded in cities. New religious orders such as the mendicant orders of Franciscans, Dominicans, Augustinians, and Carmelites ministered to urban populations. The papacy became increasingly bureaucratic and took to itself more centralized powers of administration and jurisdiction. Forms of devotional life (the cult of the Virgin, pilgrimage, popular devotions, etc.) multiplied, and religious ideals had an enormous impact on the emerging vernacular literatures (e.g., Dante and Geoffrey Chaucer). Intellectual life was robust, partially because of the rediscovery of Greek learning, which came to the West from Islamic sources, influencing both Christian and Jewish thinkers of the period. The fecund blend of Greek philosophy and Christian theology gave rise to a new synthesis of Christian learning called Scholasticism, a theology of the schools (i.e., of the medieval universities) that supplanted the older monastic theology of the late patristic and early medieval periods.

The eminence of Christian ideas and institutions in the Western medieval world was also its greatest weakness. Repeated attempts to reform the corruption in institutions or to disengage secular control of church life (and wealth) either by official church action (e.g., reforming councils) or charismatic leaders foundered on the embedded self-interest of those who flourished by a lack of reform.

The fifteenth and early sixteenth centuries were times of convulsive religious change. In 1453, Constantinople fell to the Ottoman Turks. The city that had been the center of Byzantine Christianity now became an Islamic stronghold, and its premier church of Holy Wisdom (Hagia Sophia) was turned into a mosque. In time, the Turks would control many of the traditional Byzantine strongholds, including Greece itself, and would maintain that control until the collapse of that empire's power beginning in the nineteenth century.

The flight of Greek scholars to the West at this time abetted the humanist learning of the Renaissance both in Italy and in the North. Many humanist scholars (preeminently in the North) saw the rise of this "new learning" as one possible vehicle for the reform of Christianity. Although that vision was not to be realized, these humanists did give the Christian world many of the intellectual tools (Bible translations, critical editions of the patristic period, etc.) that would aid the Reformation, both Protestant and Catholic. The humanist emphasis on interior piety and ethical conversion was a direct reaction against the more externalized religion of the medieval world.

The sixteenth-century Protestant Reformation, triggered by the efforts of Martin Luther, a German Augustinian friar, fractured the religious unity of Western Europe. Luther was excommunicated by papal edict in 1521. By the middle of the century, the religious map of Europe was totally changed. Reformers such as John Calvin, Martin Bucer, and Huldrych Zwingli brought the Reformed movement to Switzerland. England broke from Rome under the monarchy of Henry VIII. Scotland and Scandinavian countries participated in the Reformation, as did large segments of Northern Germany and parts of what in the 1990s was Czechoslovakia. Besides the classical reformers such as Luther and Calvin, more radical reform movements emerged as diverse sectarian movements that attempted to reconstitute a primitive form of Christianity based on literal readings of the Bible and an adamantine resistance to secular power and privilege.

The Protestant Reformation brought in its wake many cultural changes. It shifted religious sensibility away from the old Catholic sense of the iconic and sacramental toward a renewed interest in the Word of God enshrined in the scriptures. With that shift, vernacular translations of the Bible became crucial as did the concomitant need for greater literacy. The reformers also put great emphasis on music as a vehicle for worship, so that the tradition of vernacular hymnody as well as other musical forms (e.g., the chorale) flourished.

The Catholic response to the Reformation (the Counter-Reformation) took many forms. New religious orders such as the Jesuits attempted to reform the religious life of the Catholic Church. Authoritarian measures such as the Roman Inquisition, the censorship of books, and strong clerical discipline attempted to stem the spread of Reformed ideas in traditional Catholic countries. The Council of Trent, meeting sporadically from 1545 to 1563, defined its doctrine and practice in strong reaction to Reformation theology and practice. The increased centralization of Catholic polity at this time would distinguish modern Catholicism even until the watershed events following the Second Vatican Council in the 1960s.

Catholic missionary ventures were launched both to the New World of the Americas and, less successfully, to India and the Orient in the aftermath of the great period of Renaissance exploration. Similarly, Protestant churches expanded into the New World as a result of the colonizing impulses of England and Holland in the seventeenth century. Both Catholicism and Protestantism made further incursions into countries both in Asia and Africa as a result of colonial expansion that lasted into the early twentieth century.

The rise of the empirical sciences as well as the sociopolitical revolutions attendant on the European Enlightenment lessened the hold of traditional religion, whether Protestant or Catholic, on the minds of eighteenth- and nineteenth-century Europeans. Political revolutions in the United States (1776) and France (1789) triggered new understandings of the relationship of the church to the state. The rise of scientific historical studies and the sharpening of philosophy as an autonomous discipline eroded the eminence of theology both as an academic discipline and as an overarching framework for human understanding. This process (called **secularization**) brought about both new attempts on the part of the churches to invigorate themselves and a more noticeable shift of religion away from public power to the private sphere.

Looking back on the twentieth century, it is easy to see a series of shifts in the fortunes of Christianity. After long periods of persecution, Christianity seems to be undergoing a resurgence in Eastern Europe in its offer of an alternative meaning system to a discredited Marxism. Western Europe still reflects the secularizing tendencies of its inherited past with the continual erosion of church attendance. Christianity is still vigorous in the United States, a country that the English writer G. K. Chesterton (1874–1936) once characterized as a "nation with the soul of a church." The traditional Catholicism of Central and Latin America is being invigorated by liberation theology, but significant numbers of Catholics are also joining Protestant churches, especially those with a strong charismatic and evangelical tone. In the non-Western world, Christianity shows exceptional strength in places such as black Africa (where it competes with Islam), parts of India that have a historic Christian presence (e.g., Kerala), and newly independent countries such as Indonesia. Christianity's growth in these areas of the world is inevitably reshaping how Christianity looks as it acculturates itself in places less touched by European cultural modes of thought and action.

SPIRITUAL CHARACTER

As a total phenomenon, Christianity seems so complex in its history and practice one can forget that, at its core, Christianity is based on a simple premise. Christianity asserts that human beings exist in a state of alienation; that alienation (from each other, from God) has been healed through the life and saving deeds of a single person, Jesus of Nazareth. Christianity, then, has at its heart not an idea but a person. Since Christianity further asserts that this person is both fully human and fully divine, it is clear that this person, Jesus Christ, stands as the paradigmatic figure against which all human effort must be measured. Thus, Jesus does something for humanity and is something for humanity.

There are two traditional modes of assertion of these convictions in Christianity. First, there is the preaching of the Word both as an evangelizing technique and as a practice within worship. Second, there is the memorializing of these truths through symbolic actions or rites (e.g., sacraments, ordinances). It is broadly true that Reformed Christianity puts a stronger emphasis on the first mode (with its insistence on the scriptures, preaching, evangelizing, singing, etc.) and Orthodox and Roman Catholic Christianity assert the latter more strongly, as its more conspicuously sacramental, iconic, and liturgical character shows. Some church bodies (e.g., Anglicans, Lutherans) that have strong roots in both traditions often attempt a middle course between the two emphases.

Because of Christianity's insistent claim that Jesus was truly human there is an inevitable element of imitatability in Christianity; i.e., Jesus, as known through the New Testament, is offered to the believer as a model to imitate. Many scholars have insisted that each Christian generation has found a model of Jesus congenial to, or appropriate for, its own cultural era. Indeed, histories of Christianity tracing the changing models of Christ have been frequent in modern times. In times of persecution, churches would emphasize that Jesus suffered persecution and death, just as Byzantine emperors or medieval kings would find the triumphant Christ who "holds all things in his hands" (the Pantocrater of Byzantine mosaics) a congenial model to worship. In the late twentieth century the image of Jesus as lover and liberator of the poor has had an enormous impact on Christian preaching among the civilly deprived (South African blacks and, in the recent past, African Americans) and the socially marginalized (the *campesinos* of Central and Latin America).

This powerful notion of the imitation of Christ (Gk. ***christomimesis***) not only derives from the desire to imagine who Christ is and how he might relate to human life, but also forms the foundation of how people should live; i.e., there is a correlation between christomimesis and Christian ethics. Christianity not only inherits the moral formulations of the Hebrew scriptures (e.g., the Ten Commandments) and the ethical ideals of the ancient Greco-Roman philosophical world (e.g., Stoicism), but also attempts to construct an ethics based on the life and teachings of Jesus. While this ethics is often more honored in theory than in practice, Christianity did (and does) attempt to live out an ethic based on selfless love, care for the poor and the dispossessed, forgiveness of sin, and nonviolence, which Jesus preached as part of his own understanding of those teachings that came from the great classical prophets of ancient Israel.

The complex historical evolution of Christian care-giving institutions (orphanages, hospitals, leprosaria, schools for the poor, etc.) must be seen as attempts to provide instrumentalities for the execution of the command of Jesus to care for "the least of the brethren." Similarly, both historic movements and persons who served the poor and/or attempted betterment of their condition root themselves in this same impulse. Indeed, some commentators have insisted that the early successes of Christianity in the Roman Empire are partially explicable because of the strong commitment of the early Christian communities to provide such aids at a time when social services were rudimentary or nonexistent.

Because Christianity grew largely through the multiplication of communities, it was inevitable that the relationship would arise of these communities to the larger culture in general and the state in particular. Christianity went through three great macrodevelopments: from persecution, to establishment (i.e., enjoyment of full state support), to separation from the state and an autonomous existence in most parts of the world. That large picture, however, does not do full justice to the complexity of the issue.

Christianity holds a linear view of history: the world comes from God; history unfolds; and, finally, history will come to an end with the Second Coming of Christ. Inevitably, there is both a yearning for the "not yet" and a concomitant sense of the impermanence of earthly realities.

Historically, Christians of differing times and persuasions have given different emphases to this large worldview. There is a Christian strain of sectarianism that is profoundly ambivalent about "this world," shunning it as temporary and evanescent (e.g., in Catholic monasticism, in sectarian Protestantism) and placing a strong emphasis on the age to come. Another strain sees the coming kingdom as already present, and insists on human work in this world as the establishment of the kingdom in the here and now and as part of God's ultimate plan for the world and humanity.

Many contemporary debates in Christianity (about the role of Christians in the sociopolitical order, for example) ultimately root themselves in the emphasis one chooses to make about the nature of this world in relationship to the end of history. Everything from Third World liberation theology and the aftermath of the Second Vatican Council (1962–65) in Catholicism to the world-affirming Social Gospel or the strong apocalyptic character of some forms of Protestant fundamentalism may be seen as attempts to come to grips with what Augustine (d. 430) called the "two cities" of the world and God.

PROBLEMS AND PROSPECTS

As Christianity begins its third millennium, it is faced with serious challenges both in terms of its own self-understanding and in relation to those who do not share its beliefs.

One demographic fact seems inescapable: the greatest growth in Christianity occurs today outside of Western Europe, which has been the historic intellectual center of both Catholic and Reformed Christianity. With that demographic shift comes new expressions of Christianity that are acculturated into new patterns and symbols. The implications of this shift are profound, since these newer centers of Christianity will inevitably provide a new vocabulary and sensibility to Christian self-understanding. The great task of the future will be to hold in balance the essential Christian proclamation while doing justice to the new insights that derive from cultures other than European ones. As the theologian Karl Rahner (d. 1984) has noted, the day when Christianity can be viewed as an "export item" from the West seems largely over. Only the future will tell what shape African or Asian or Oceanic Christianity will look like.

From its beginnings, Christianity has had divisions and schisms within its own body. Only the most utopian of twentieth-century thinkers hopes for a totally undivided Christianity; more realistic commentators hope, and work for, a lessening of tensions and an increase of cooperation between diverse bodies who commonly profess faith in the person of Jesus Christ. Such internal ecumenism could palliate antagonisms between warring Christian bodies (e.g., Protestants and Catholics in Northern Ireland; Catholics and Orthodox in the Ukraine) as well as lessen the competition between Christian bodies where cooperation (e.g., in social work) would benefit all. This is the task of both the organized ecumenical movement in Christianity and the myriad attempts of Christian groups to grow in mutual trust and to work on common projects. Such trust and cooperation is of paramount importance, since many episodes in Christian history bear witness to how lethal a combination religious zealotry and national identity can be.

Although the foundational Christian documents proclaim the equality of all persons as a root belief springing from the doctrine of the Incarnation, it is only through long meditation, and many false starts, that Christianity has overcome its toleration of slavery, its acceptance of class distinctions, and its passivity in the form of racism. Too often in the past the Christian church was one more vehicle for colonial expansion as, for example, the modern history of Christianity in both Latin America and Africa attest. Current debates about the place of the emarginated and the emergence of Christian feminism indicate how slowly organized Christianity comes to grips with inequalities within its own ranks.

The relationship of Christianity with other faiths has not always been pacific, as, for example, the long history of Christian anti-Semitism demonstrates. With a rising sense of the complex diversity of religious sentiments in the world (brought to the fore by the globalization of information technologies), dialogue with the world's religions is an urgent task calling both for a greater appreciation of those religions and a lessening of the triumphalism endemic to certain forms of Christian proclamation.

Those same information technologies illustrate the vast inequalities in standards of living and the destitution of immense populations either through natural forces or indifferent political forces. Increasingly, Christian bodies have concerned themselves with the struggle for civil rights and for the amelioration of degraded living conditions. Nothing in current history indicates that such struggles are over.

That Christianity has not matched its own rhetoric with perfect performance should surprise no one, least of all Christians. Its founder asserted that the "wheat and the weeds" would coexist until the end of history. Authentic Christianity is not a perfectionist religion but one living in the ambiguities and disappointments of history. This fact does not absolve it from the need to realize the kingdom envisioned by Jesus of Nazareth, but it does mean that, for the Christian believer, the perfection of what Jesus was and what he preached will only come to full realization in the consummation of history. That point was made by Augustine of Hippo in his monumental work *City of God* (413–426): "For the City of the saints is up above, although it produces citizens here below, and in their persons the City is on pilgrimage until the time of its kingdom comes."

SOURCES

I have organized the sources, for the most part, chronologically to give you some sense of the development of Christianity in at least one part of the world. Space limitations prevent the inclusion of texts representing all the many varieties of Christianity. However, I have included some texts that have been important and influential in Christian history.

11.2 EARLY CHRISTIAN WRITINGS

There is a vast amount of early Christian writings covering a wide range of styles and types. There are letters, gospels, histories, theological defenses (**apologetics**), creeds, hymns, liturgies, martyrdom tales, and much more. This literature spans a time period from about 50 to 500. I will focus mostly on New Testament texts because of their decisive influence on the people who have become Christians. However, we will also sample some other texts of importance.

11.2.1 New Testament Letters

The **Old Testament** and the **New Testament** make up the two main parts of Christian scriptures. In chapter 10 we looked at some of the literature from the Jewish *Tanakh* that is also included in the Christian Old Testament. Here I will focus on some of the writings that were accepted into the New Testament **canon** (an authoritative collection of literature).

The story of the formation of the New Testament canon is a long, complex, and fascinating story. We cannot tell it here, but we must be aware that there existed a vast amount of literature that Christians had to sort through and argue about before any of it became part of what we call the New Testament (a name that was in common use by the fourth century). For example, there were numerous **gospel** writings (writings that tell about the Good News revealed by God in Jesus the Redeemer) of which only four now appear in the New Testament.

The New Testament is only one collection of some of these writings and, in fact, is not the earliest. Early converts circulated various collections of Paul's letters, and different congregations used individual gospels. A Christian teacher named Marcion, who lived in the middle of the second century, formulated a list of writings that did not include the Old Testament, but did include ten Pauline letters and an abridged Gospel of Luke.

Marcionism attracted large numbers of converts and continued well in the fifth century. Many Marcionite Christians became martyrs, giving up their life for their faith. However, these churches were opposed by some other groups of early Christians who claimed that their views about Christianity—not Marcion's views—were orthodox (correct). The orthodox group condemned Marcion and, in response to Marcion's canon, proposed a canon of its own. This new canon included the Septuagint (the Greek translation of the books in the Jewish *Tanakh* as well as additional literature) and, eventually, the twenty-seven books that are now part of the New Testament. The earliest list of the books that are part of the New Testament as we know it dates from 367, over three hundred years after the death of Jesus. Even after 367, different churches used differing canons.

The earliest writings in the New Testament are the writings of the apostle Paul, a Jewish convert to Christianity, who was primarily responsible for carrying the gospel of Christ to the Gentiles. He was well educated in Jewish literature and a devout Jew. It seems he was also familiar with Greek and Roman philosophy, especially the ethical thinking of the Stoics. When he heard that some Jews were claiming Jesus was the Messiah, he set about persecuting them. However, after a dramatic conversion experience involving a vision of the risen Christ, he became a leading advocate of the messianic movement centering on Jesus.

After his conversion, Paul established dozens of churches and corresponded with many of them. Our first sample of his correspondence comes from a letter to the church in Galatia (ca. 55), written after Jewish Christians attempted to persuade the new Gentile converts in Galatia that they had to adhere to Jewish law in order to be followers of Jesus. This letter is the earliest written account of first-century church politics.

In the same year, Paul also wrote to the church he founded in Corinth (see the second selection). The topic is not politics, but life after death. Two Jewish sects in Paul's day, the Pharisees and the Sadducees, had been arguing about the resurrection of the body. The Sadducees rejected the idea on the grounds that it was not mentioned in Hebrew scripture, but the Pharisees accepted the idea. Paul had been a member of the Pharisaic sect before converting to the messianic Jesus movement. The ideas he learned from the Pharisees provided a framework for interpreting the meaning of Jesus' death and resurrection.

Our final selection comes from Paul's famous and influential letter to the Romans (ca. 56–58). It appears Paul wrote this letter in Corinth while on his way to Jerusalem carrying contributions to the Jerusalem church from the Christians in Greece and Asia Minor. Paul planned a missionary trip to Spain after his work in Jerusalem was complete, and he was writing to Christians in Rome (where others had already established a church) to tell them he planned to visit on his way to Spain.

After a salutation and thanksgiving, Paul explains his understanding of the gospel. He wishes to clarify the relationship between the Jewish law and the good news about the Messiah (Christ) with respect to the issues of justification and salvation. He says, as you will shortly see, some very dramatic and radical things about the way of law and the way of faith.

From Paul's Letter to the Galatians (1–2)

READING QUESTIONS

1. Why do you think Paul is so insistent about Gentiles not having to follow the Jewish law?
2. How important is the doctrine of the resurrection of the dead?
3. How does Paul answer the questions about how the dead will be raised and what sort of bodies they will have?
4. If the law cannot save, what is its purpose?
5. How is salvation realized?

ON FAITH AND FREEDOM

1

From Paul, an apostle, not by human appointment or human commission, but by commission from Jesus Christ and from God the Father who raised him from the dead. [2] I and the group of friends now with me send greetings to the Christian congregations of Galatia.

[3] Grace and peace to you from God the Father and our Lord Jesus Christ, [4] who sacrificed himself for our sins, to rescue us out of this present age of wickedness, as our God and Father willed; [5] to whom be glory for ever and ever. Amen.

⁶I am astonished to find you turning so quickly away from him who called you by grace, and following a different gospel. ⁷Not that it is in fact another gospel; only there are persons who unsettle your minds by trying to distort the gospel of Christ. ⁸But if anyone, if we ourselves or an angel from heaven, should preach a gospel at variance with the gospel we preached to you, he shall be held outcast. ⁹I now repeat what I have said before: if anyone preaches a gospel at variance with the gospel which you received, let him be outcast!

¹⁰Does my language now sound as if I were canvassing for men's support? Whose support do I want but God's alone? Do you think I am currying favour with men? If I still sought men's favour, I should be no servant of Christ.

¹¹I must make it clear to you, my friends, that the gospel you heard me preach is no human invention. ¹²I did not take it over from any man; no man taught it me; I received it through a revelation of Jesus Christ.

¹³You have heard what my manner of life was when I was still a practising Jew: how savagely I persecuted the church of God, and tried to destroy it; ¹⁴and how in the practice of our national religion I was outstripping many of my Jewish contemporaries in my boundless devotion to the traditions of my ancestors. ¹⁵But then in his good pleasure God, who had set me apart from birth and called me through his grace, chose to ¹⁶reveal his Son to me and through me, in order that I might proclaim him among the Gentiles. When that happened, without consulting any human being, ¹⁷without going up to Jerusalem to see those who were apostles before me, I went off at once to Arabia, and afterwards returned to Damascus.

¹⁸Three years later I did go up to Jerusalem to get to know Cephas. I stayed with him for a fortnight, ¹⁹without seeing any other of the apostles, except James the Lord's brother. ²⁰What I write is plain truth; before God I am not lying.

²¹Next I went to the regions of Syria and Cilicia, ²²and remained unknown by sight to Christ's congregations in Judaea. ²³They only heard it said, "Our former persecutor is preaching the good news of the faith which once he tried to destroy"; ²⁴and they praised God for me.

2

Next, fourteen years later, I went again to Jerusalem with Barnabas, taking Titus with us. ²I went up because it had been revealed by God that I should do so. I laid before them—but at a private interview with the men of repute—the gospel which I am accustomed to preach to the Gentiles, to make sure that the race I had run, and was running, should not be run in vain. ³Yet even my companion Titus, Greek though he is, was not compelled to be circumcised. ⁴That course was urged only as a concession to certain sham-Christians, interlopers who had stolen in to spy upon the liberty we enjoy in the fellowship of Christ Jesus. These men wanted to bring us into bondage, ⁵but not for one moment did I yield to their dictation; I was determined that the full truth of the Gospel should be maintained for you.

⁶But as for the men of high reputation (not that their importance matters to me: God does not recognize these personal distinctions)—these men of repute, I say, did not prolong the consultation, ⁷but on the contrary acknowledged that I had been entrusted with the Gospel for Gentiles as surely as Peter had been entrusted with the Gospel for Jews. ⁸For God whose action made Peter an apostle to the Jews, also made me an apostle to the Gentiles.

⁹Recognizing, then, the favour thus bestowed upon me, those reputed pillars of our society, James, Cephas, and John, accepted Barnabas and myself as partners, and shook hands upon it, agreeing that we should go to the Gentiles while they went to the Jews. ¹⁰All they asked was that we should keep their poor in mind, which was the very thing I made it my business to do.

¹¹But when Cephas came to Antioch, I opposed him to his face, because he was clearly in the wrong. ¹²For until certain persons came from James he was taking his meals with gentile Christians; but when they came he drew back and began to hold aloof, because he was afraid of the advocates of circumcision. ¹³The other Jewish Christians showed the same lack of principle; even Barnabas was carried away and played false like the rest. ¹⁴But when I saw that their conduct did not square with the truth of the Gospel, I said to Cephas, before the whole congregation, "If you, a Jew born and bred, live like a Gentile, and not like a Jew, how can you insist that Gentiles must live like Jews?"

¹⁵We ourselves are Jews by birth, not Gentiles and sinners. ¹⁶But we know that no man is ever justified by doing what the law demands, but only through faith in Christ Jesus; so we too have put our faith in Jesus Christ, in order that we might be justified through this faith, and not through deeds dictated by law; for by such deeds, Scripture says, no mortal man shall be justified.

¹⁷If now, in seeking to be justified in Christ, we ourselves no less than the Gentiles turn out to be sinners against the law, does that mean that Christ is an abettor of sin? No, never! ¹⁸No, if I start building up again a system which I have pulled down, then it is that I show myself up as a transgressor of the law. ¹⁹For through the

law I died to law—to live for God. I have been crucified with Christ: [20] the life I now live is not my life, but the life which Christ lives in me; and my present bodily life is lived by faith in the Son of God, who loved me and gave himself up for me. [21] I will not nullify the grace of God; if righteousness comes by law, then Christ died for nothing.

From Paul's Letter to the First Corinthians (15: 12–28, 35–57)

ON LIFE AFTER DEATH

15

... [12] Now if this is what we proclaim, that Christ was raised from the dead, how can some of you say there is no resurrection of the dead? [13] If there be no resurrection, then Christ was not raised; [14] and if Christ was not raised, then our gospel is null and void, and so is your faith; [15] and we turn out to be lying witnesses for God, because we bore witness that he raised Christ to life, whereas, if the dead are not raised, he did not raise him. [16] For if the dead are not raised, it follows that Christ was not raised; [17] and if Christ was not raised, your faith has nothing in it and you are still in your old state of sin. [18] It follows also that those who have died within Christ's fellowship are utterly lost. [19] If it is for this life only that Christ has given us hope, we of all men are most to be pitied.

[20] But the truth is, Christ was raised to life—the firstfruits of the harvest of the dead. [21] For since it was a man who brought death into the world, a man also brought resurrection of the dead. [22] As in Adam all men die, so in Christ all will be brought to life; [23] but each in his own proper place: Christ the firstfruits, and afterwards, at his coming, those who belong to Christ. [24] Then comes the end, when he delivers up the kingdom to God the Father, after abolishing every kind of domination, authority, and power. [25] For he is destined to reign until God has put all enemies under his feet; [26] and the last enemy to be abolished is death. [27] Scripture says, "He has put all things in subjection under his feet." But in saying "all things," it clearly means to exclude God who subordinates them; [28] and when all things are thus subject to him, then the Son himself will also be made subordinate to God who made all things subject to him, and thus God will be all in all. ...

[35] But, you may ask, how are the dead raised? In what kind of body? [36] How foolish! The seed you sow does not come to life unless it has first died; [37] and what you sow is not the body that shall be, but a naked grain, perhaps of wheat, or of some other kind; [38] and God clothes it with the body of his choice, each seed with its own particular body. [39] All flesh is not the same flesh: there is flesh of men, flesh of beasts, of birds, and of fishes—all different. [40] There are heavenly bodies and earthly bodies; and the splendour of the heavenly bodies is one thing, the splendour of the earthly, another. [41] The sun has a splendour of its own, the moon another splendour, and the stars another, for star differs from star in brightness. [42] So it is with the resurrection of the dead. What is sown in the earth as a perishable thing is raised imperishable. [43] Sown in humiliation, it is raised in glory; sown in weakness, it is raised in power; [44] sown as an animal body, it is raised as a spiritual body.

If there is such a thing as an animal body, there is also a spiritual body. [45] It is in this sense that Scripture says, "The first man, Adam, became an animate being," whereas the last Adam has become a life-giving spirit. [46] Observe, the spiritual does not come first; the animal body comes first, and then the spiritual. [47] The first man was made "of the dust of the earth": the second man is from heaven. [48] The man made of dust is the pattern of all men of dust, and the heavenly man is the pattern of all the heavenly. [49] As we have worn the likeness of the man made of dust, so we shall wear the likeness of the heavenly man.

[50] What I mean, my brothers, is this: flesh and blood can never possess the kingdom of God, and the perishable cannot possess immortality. [51] Listen! I will unfold a mystery: we shall not all die, but we shall all be changed in a flash, [52] in the twinkling of an eye, at the last trumpet-call. For the trumpet will sound, and the dead will rise immortal, and we shall be changed. [53] This perishable being must be clothed with the imperishable, and what is mortal must be clothed with immortality. [54] And when our mortality has been clothed with immortality, then the saying of Scripture will come true: "Death is swallowed up; victory is won!" [55] "O Death, where is your victory? O Death, where is your sting?" [56] The sting of death is sin, and sin gains its power from the law; [57] but, God be praised, he gives us the victory through our Lord Jesus Christ.

∾⚭∾

From Paul's Letter to the Romans (3:9–28)

ON JUSTIFICATION BY FAITH (ROMANS 3)

3

. . . [9] What then? Are we Jews any better off? No, not at all! For we have already drawn up the accusation that Jews and Greeks alike are all under the power of sin. [10] This has scriptural warrant:

> "There is no just man, not one;
> [11] no one who understands, no one who seeks God.
> [12] All have swerved aside, all alike have become debased;
> there is no one to show kindness; no, not one.
>
> [13] Their throat is an open grave,
> they use their tongues for treachery,
> adders' venom is on their lips,
> [14] and their mouth is full of bitter curses.
>
> [15] Their feet hasten to shed blood,
> [16] ruin and misery lie along their paths,
> [17] they are strangers to the high-road of peace,
> [18] and reverence for God does not enter their thoughts."

[19] Now all the words of the law are addressed, as we know, to those who are within the pale of the law, so that no one may have anything to say in self-defence, but the whole world may be exposed to the judgement of God. [20] For (again from Scripture) "no human being can be justified in the sight of God" for having kept the law: law brings only the consciousness of sin.

[21] But now, quite independently of law, God's justice has been brought to light. The Law and the prophets both bear witness to it: [22] it is God's way of righting wrong, effective through faith in Christ for all who have such faith —all, without distinction. [23] For all alike have sinned, and are deprived of the divine splendour, [24] and all are justified by God's free grace alone, [25] through his act of liberation in the person of Christ Jesus. For God designed him to be the means of expiating sin by his sacrificial death, effective through faith. God meant by this to demonstrate his justice, because in his forbearance he had overlooked the sins of the past—[26] to demonstrate his justice now in the present, showing that he is himself just and also justifies any man who puts his faith in Jesus.

[27] What room then is left for human pride? It is excluded. And on what principle? The keeping of the law would not exclude it, but faith does. [28] For our argument is that a man is justified by faith quite apart from success in keeping the law.

11.2.2 Synoptic Gospels

The first three books (Matthew, Mark, and Luke) of the New Testament are called the **synoptic Gospels** because they contain similar, though not identical, accounts of Jesus' life and ministry. Matthew and Luke use material from Mark and from a collection of Jesus' sayings now lost. The collection of Jesus' sayings is called **Q** for the German word *Quelle* meaning "source." Some biblical scholars reject the notion that Q ever existed.

The Gospel of Mark appeared around 70 and Matthew and Luke around 85. All three Gospels, along with the Fourth Gospel (John), at first circulated among Christian communities anonymously and were not attributed to the **apostles** until around 150.

The authors of these Gospels present different interpretations of Jesus' life, and their writings were intended for different audiences. The Gospel of Matthew is a manual of Christian teaching designed to show that Jesus is the fulfillment of Jewish prophecy and is the Messiah anticipated by some Jews. The audience appears to be Jewish or at least people well versed in Jewish literature. According to some (but not all) ancient manuscripts, Mark opens his Gospel by giving to Jesus the title "Son of God," and that theme is reinforced in subsequent verses (1:11, 5:7, 9:7, 14:61–62, 15:39). Mark records far fewer sayings of Jesus than either Matthew or Luke. According to a very old tradition, Mark (also known as John) composed his Gospel at Rome as a summary of Peter's preaching. However, many scholars now believe that Mark's Gospel originated in Palestine or Syria. The Gospel of Luke is the first volume of a two-volume work (the second volume is the Book of Acts) in which the author describes the works and words of Jesus in terms of a divine-human savior figure whose mission is, among other things, to extend compassion to all who are needy. A special section, unique to Luke (9:51–18:14), contains many of the most famous parables including the Prodigal Son.

In the selections that follow are parallel accounts of the birth of Jesus, his sermons and parables, the

Passover meal Jesus shared with his disciples, and Jesus' death and resurrection so that you can compare both the similarities and differences in the synoptic Gospel accounts. Careful comparison will reveal how the different Gospel writers make different points with their versions of the same events.

The Birth of Jesus

READING QUESTIONS

1. How do the two birth stories differ? What do you think accounts for the differences?
2. Compare the "Beatitudes" in Matthew's account of the Sermon on the Mount (5:3–12) with those found in Luke's account of the Sermon on the Plain (6:17, 20–23). How are they the same and different? Do the differences change the meaning?
3. Why do you think Matthew portrays Jesus as being concerned with Jewish law and establishing a "higher righteousness," but Luke does not?
4. Why do you think Luke includes the "Alas" sayings (verses 24–26) and Matthew does not?
5. Assuming these teachings represent the teachings of the historical Jesus, what impression of Jesus do they leave you with?
6. How do you interpret the Parable of the Prodigal Son? Compare it to the Parable of the Lost Son found in the *Lotus Sutra* (Reading 7.4.1).
7. What differences and similarities do you notice in the three accounts of the Last Supper? How would you explain them?
8. Make a list of the differences and similarities you notice in the three accounts of the crucifixion and resurrection of Jesus. How would you explain them?
9. What religious significance do you find in these stories of death and resurrection?

MATTHEW 1:18–25, 2:1–15

1

. . . [18] This is the story of the birth of the Messiah. Mary his mother was betrothed to Joseph; before their marriage she found that she was with child by the Holy Spirit. [19] Being a man of principle, and at the same time wanting to save her from exposure, Joseph desired to have the marriage contract set aside quietly. [20] He had resolved on this, when an angel of the Lord appeared to him in a dream. "Joseph son of David," said the angel, "do not be afraid to take Mary home with you as your wife. It is by the Holy Spirit that she has conceived this child. [21] She will bear a son; and you shall give him the name Jesus (Saviour), for he will save his people from their sins." [22] All this happened in order to fulfil what the Lord declared through the prophet: [23] "The virgin will conceive and bear a son, and he shall be called Emmanuel," a name which means "God is with us." [24] Rising from sleep Joseph did as the angel had directed him; he took Mary home to be his wife, [25] but had no intercourse with her until her son was born. And he named the child Jesus.

2

Jesus was born at Bethlehem in Judaea during the reign of Herod. After his birth astrologers from the east arrived in Jerusalem, [2] asking, "Where is the child who is born to be king of the Jews? We observed the rising of his star, and we have come to pay him homage." [3] King Herod was greatly perturbed when he heard this; and so was the whole of Jerusalem. [4] He called a meeting of the chief priests and lawyers of the Jewish people, and put before them the question: "Where is it that the Messiah is to be born?" "At Bethlehem in Judaea," [5] they replied; and they referred him to the prophecy which reads: [6] "Bethlehem in the land of Judah, you are far from least in the eyes of the rulers of Judah; for out of you shall come a leader to be the shepherd of my people Israel."

[7] Herod next called the astrologers to meet him in private, and ascertained from them the time when the star had appeared. [8] He then sent them on to Bethlehem, and said, "Go and make a careful inquiry for the child. When you have found him, report to me, so that I may go myself and pay him homage."

[9] They set out at the king's bidding; and the star which they had seen at its rising went ahead of them until it stopped above the place where the child lay. [10] At the sight of the star they were overjoyed. [11] Entering the house, they saw the child with Mary his mother, and bowed to the ground in homage to him; then they opened their treasures and offered him gifts: gold, frankincense, and myrrh. [12] And being warned in a dream not to go back to Herod, they returned home another way.

[13] After they had gone, an angel of the Lord appeared to Joseph in a dream, and said to him, "Rise up, take the child and his mother and escape with them to Egypt, and stay there until I tell you; for Herod is going to search for the child to do away with him." [14] So Joseph rose from sleep, and taking mother and child by night he went away with them to Egypt, [15] and there he stayed till Herod's death. This was to fulfil what the Lord had declared through the prophet: "I called my son out of Egypt."

LUKE 2:1–21

2

In those days a decree was issued by the Emperor Augustus for a registration to be made throughout the Roman world. ²This was the first registration of its kind; it took place when Quirinius was governor of Syria. ³For this purpose everyone made his way to his own town; ⁴and so Joseph went up to Judaea from the town of Nazareth in Galilee, to register at the city of David, called Bethlehem, because he was of the house of David by descent; ⁵and with him went Mary who was betrothed to him. She was expecting a child, ⁶and while they were there the time came for her baby to be born, ⁷and she gave birth to a son, her first-born. She wrapped him in his swaddling clothes, and laid him in a manger, because there was no room for them to lodge in the house.

⁸Now in this same district there were shepherds out in the fields, keeping watch through the night over their flock, ⁹when suddenly there stood before them an angel of the Lord, and the splendour of the Lord shone round them. They were terror-stricken, ¹⁰but the angel said, "Do not be afraid; I have good news for you: there is great joy coming to the whole people. ¹¹Today in the city of David a deliverer has been born to you—the Messiah, the Lord. ¹²And this is your sign: you will find a baby lying wrapped in his swaddling clothes, in a manger." ¹³All at once there was with the angel a great company of the heavenly host, singing the praises of God:

¹⁴"Glory to God in highest heaven,
  and on earth his peace for men on whom his favour
    rests."

¹⁵After the angels had left them and gone into heaven the shepherds said to one another, "Come, we must go straight to Bethlehem and see this thing that has happened, which the Lord has made known to us." ¹⁶So they went with all speed and found their way to Mary and Joseph; and the baby was lying in the manger. ¹⁷When they saw him, they recounted what they had been told about this child; ¹⁸and all who heard were astonished at what the shepherds said. ¹⁹But Mary treasured up all these things and pondered over them. ²⁰Meanwhile the shepherds returned glorifying and praising God for what they had heard and seen; it had all happened as they had been told.

²¹Eight days later the time came to circumcise him, and he was given the name Jesus, the name given by the angel before he was conceived.

Sermons on the Mount

MATTHEW 5–7

5

When he saw the crowds he went up the hill. ²There he took his seat, and when his disciples had gathered round him he began to address them. And this is the teaching he gave:

³"How blest are those who know their need of
    God; the kingdom of Heaven is theirs.
⁴How blest are the sorrowful;
    they shall find consolation.
⁵How blest are those of a gentle spirit;
    they shall have the earth for their possession.
⁶How blest are those who hunger and thirst to see
    right prevail;
  they shall be satisfied.
⁷How blest are those who show mercy;
    mercy shall be shown to them.
⁸How blest are those whose hearts are pure;
    they shall see God.
⁹How blest are the peacemakers;
    God shall call them his sons.
¹⁰How blest are those who have suffered persecution
    for the cause of right;
  the kingdom of Heaven is theirs.

¹¹"How blest you are, when you suffer insults and persecution and every kind of calumny for my sake. ¹²Accept it with gladness and exultation, for you have a rich reward in heaven; in the same way they persecuted the prophets before you.

¹³"You are salt to the world. And if salt becomes tasteless, how is its saltness to be restored? It is now good for nothing but to be thrown away and trodden underfoot.

¹⁴"You are light for all the world. A town that stands on a hill cannot be hidden. ¹⁵When a lamp is lit, it is not put under the meal-tub, but on the lamp-stand, where it gives light to everyone in the house. ¹⁶And you, like the lamp, must shed light among your fellows, so that, when they see the good you do, they may give praise to your Father in heaven.

¹⁷"Do not suppose that I have come to abolish the Law and the prophets; I did not come to abolish, but to complete. ¹⁸I tell you this: so long as heaven and earth endure, not a letter, not a stroke, will disappear from the Law until all that must happen has happened. ¹⁹If any

man therefore sets aside even the least of the Law's demands, and teaches others to do the same, he will have the lowest place in the kingdom of Heaven, whereas anyone who keeps the Law, and teaches others so, will stand high in the kingdom of Heaven. [20] I tell you, unless you show yourselves far better men than the Pharisees and the doctors of the law, you can never enter the kingdom of Heaven.

[21] "You have learned that our forefathers were told, 'Do not commit murder; anyone who commits murder must be brought to judgement.' [22] But what I tell you is this: Anyone who nurses anger against his brother must be brought to judgement. If he abuses his brother he must answer for it to the court; if he sneers at him he will have to answer for it in the fires of hell.

[23] "If, when you are bringing your gift to the altar, you suddenly remember that your brother has a grievance against you, [24] leave your gift where it is before the altar. First go and make your peace with your brother, and only then come back and offer your gift.

[25] "If someone sues you, come to terms with him promptly while you are both on your way to court; otherwise he may hand you over to the judge, and the judge to the constable, and you will be put in jail. [26] I tell you, once you are there you will not be let out till you have paid the last farthing.

[27] "You have learned that they were told, 'Do not commit adultery.' [28] But what I tell you is this: If a man looks on a woman with a lustful eye, he has already committed adultery with her in his heart.

[29] "If your right eye is your undoing, tear it out and fling it away; it is better for you to lose one part of your body than for the whole of it to be thrown into hell. [30] And if your right hand is your undoing, cut it off and fling it away; it is better for you to lose one part of your body than for the whole of it to go to hell.

[31] "They were told, 'A man who divorces his wife must give her a note of dismissal.' [32] But what I tell you is this: If a man divorces his wife for any cause other than unchastity he involves her in adultery; and anyone who marries a divorced woman commits adultery.

[33] "Again, you have learned that our forefathers were told, 'Do not break your oath,' and, 'Oaths sworn to the Lord must be kept.' [34] But what I tell you is this: You are not to swear at all—not by heaven, for it is God's throne, [35] nor by earth, for it is his footstool, nor by Jerusalem, for it is the city of the great King, [36] nor by your own head, because you cannot turn one hair of it white or black. [37] Plain 'Yes' or 'No' is all you need to say; anything beyond that comes from the devil.

[38] "You have learned that they were told, 'Eye for eye, tooth for tooth.' [39] But what I tell you is this: Do not set yourself against the man who wrongs you. If someone slaps you on the right cheek, turn and offer him your left. [40] If a man wants to sue you for your shirt, let him have your coat as well. [41] If a man in authority makes you go one mile, go with him two. [42] Give when you are asked to give; and do not turn your back on a man who wants to borrow.

[43] "You have learned that they were told, 'Love your neighbour, hate your enemy.' [44] But what I tell you is this: Love your enemies and pray for your persecutors; [45] only so can you be children of your heavenly Father, who makes his sun rise on good and bad alike, and sends the rain on the honest and the dishonest. [46] If you love only those who love you, what reward can you expect? Surely the tax-gatherers do as much as that. [47] And if you greet only your brothers, what is there extraordinary about that? Even the heathen do as much. [48] There must be no limit to your goodness, as your heavenly Father's goodness knows no bounds.

6

"Be careful not to make a show of your religion before men; if you do, no reward awaits you in your Father's house in heaven.

[2] "Thus, when you do some act of charity, do not announce it with a flourish of trumpets, as the hypocrites do in synagogue and in the streets to win admiration from men. I tell you this: they have their reward already. [3] No; when you do some act of charity, do not let your left hand know what your right is doing; [4] your good deed must be secret, and your Father who sees what is done in secret will reward you.

[5] "Again, when you pray, do not be like the hypocrites; they love to say their prayers standing up in synagogue and at the street-corners, for everyone to see them. I tell you this: they have their reward already. [6] But when you pray, go into a room by yourself, shut the door, and pray to your Father who is there in the secret place; and your Father who sees what is secret will reward you.

[7] "In your prayers do not go babbling on like the heathen, who imagine that the more they say the more likely they are to be heard. [8] Do not imitate them. Your Father knows what your needs are before you ask him.

[9] "This is how you should pray:

'Our Father in heaven,
thy name be hallowed;
[10] thy kingdom come,
thy will be done,
on earth as in heaven.
[11] Give us today our daily bread.
[12] Forgive us the wrong we have done,

as we have forgiven those who have wronged us. [13] And do not bring us to the test, but save us from the evil one.'

[14] For if you forgive others the wrongs they have done, your heavenly Father will also forgive you; [15] but if you do not forgive others, then the wrongs you have done will not be forgiven by your Father.

[16] "So too when you fast, do not look gloomy like the hypocrites: they make their faces unsightly so that other people may see that they are fasting. I tell you this: they have their reward already. [17] But when you fast, anoint your head and wash your face, so that men may not see that you are fasting, [18] but only your Father who is in the secret place; and your Father who sees what is secret will give you your reward.

[19] "Do not store up for yourselves treasure on earth, where it grows rusty and moth-eaten, and thieves break in to steal it. [20] Store up treasure in heaven, where there is no moth and no rust to spoil it, no thieves to break in and steal. [21] For where your treasure is, there will your heart be also.

[22] "The lamp of the body is the eye. [23] If your eyes are sound, you will have light for your whole body; if the eyes are bad, your whole body will be in darkness. If then the only light you have is darkness, the darkness is doubly dark.

[24] "No servant can be the slave of two masters; for either he will hate the first and love the second, or he will be devoted to the first and think nothing of the second. You cannot serve God and Money.

[25] "Therefore I bid you put away anxious thoughts about food and drink to keep you alive, and clothes to cover your body. Surely life is more than food, the body more than clothes. [26] Look at the birds of the air; they do not sow and reap and store in barns, yet your heavenly Father feeds them. You are worth more than the birds! [27] Is there a man of you who by anxious thought can add a foot to his height? [28] And why be anxious about clothes? Consider how the lilies grow in the fields; they do not work, they do not spin; [29] and yet, I tell you, even Solomon in all his splendour was not attired like one of these. [30] But if that is how God clothes the grass in the fields, which is there today, and tomorrow is thrown on the stove, will he not all the more clothe you? How little faith you have! [31] No, do not ask anxiously, 'What are we to eat? What are we to drink? What shall we wear?' [32] All these are things for the heathen to run after, not for you, because your heavenly Father knows that you need them all. [33] Set your mind on God's kingdom and his justice before everything else, and all the rest will come to you

as well. [34] So do not be anxious about tomorrow; tomorrow will look after itself. Each day has troubles enough of its own.

7

[1] "Pass no judgement, and you will not be judged. [2] For as you judge others, so you will yourselves be judged, and whatever measure you deal out to others will be dealt back to you. [3] Why do you look at the speck of sawdust in your brother's eye, with never a thought for the great plank in your own? [4] Or how can you say to your brother, 'Let me take the speck out of your eye,' when all the time there is that plank in your own? [5] You hypocrite! First take the plank out of your own eye, and then you will see clearly to take the speck out of your brother's.

[6] "Do not give dogs what is holy; do not throw your pearls to the pigs: they will only trample on them, and turn and tear you to pieces.

[7] "Ask, and you will receive; seek, and you will find; knock, and the door will be opened. [8] For everyone who asks receives, he who seeks finds, and to him who knocks, the door will be opened.

[9] "Is there a man among you who will offer his son a stone when he asks for bread, [10] or a snake when he asks for fish? [11] If you, then, bad as you are, know how to give your children what is good for them, how much more will your heavenly Father give good things to those who ask him!

[12] "Always treat others as you would like them to treat you: that is the Law and the prophets.

[13] "Enter by the narrow gate. The gate is wide that leads to perdition, there is plenty of room on the road, and many go that way; [14] but the gate that leads to life is small and the road is narrow, and those who find it are few.

[15] "Beware of false prophets, men who come to you dressed up as sheep while underneath they are savage wolves. [16] You will recognize them by the fruits they bear. Can grapes be picked from briars, or figs from thistles? [17] In the same way, a good tree always yields good fruit, and a poor tree bad fruit. [18] A good tree cannot bear bad fruit, or a poor tree good fruit. [19] And when a tree does not yield good fruit it is cut down and burnt. [20] That is why I say you will recognize them by their fruits.

[21] "Not everyone who calls me 'Lord, Lord' will enter the kingdom of Heaven, but only those who do the will of my heavenly Father. [22] When that day comes, many will say to me, 'Lord, Lord, did we not prophesy

in your name, cast out devils in your name, and in your name perform many miracles?' ²³ Then I will tell them to their face, 'I never knew you; out of my sight, you and your wicked ways!'

²⁴ What then of the man who hears these words of mine and acts upon them? He is like a man who had the sense to build his house on rock. ²⁵ The rain came down, the floods rose, the wind blew, and beat upon that house; but it did not fall, because its foundations were on rock. ²⁶ But what of the man who hears these words of mine and does not act upon them? He is like a man who was foolish enough to build his house on sand. ²⁷ The rain came down, the floods rose, the wind blew, and beat upon that house; down it fell with a great crash."

²⁸ When Jesus had finished this discourse the people were astounded at his teaching; ²⁹ unlike their own teachers he taught with a note of authority.

Luke 6:17–49

6

. . . ¹⁷ He came down the hill with them and took his stand on level ground. There was a large concourse of his disciples and great numbers of people from Jerusalem and Judaea and from the seaboard of Tyre and Sidon, who had come to listen to him, and to be cured of their diseases. ¹⁸ Those who were troubled with unclean spirits were cured; ¹⁹ and everyone in the crowd was trying to touch him, because power went out from him and cured them all.

²⁰ Then turning to his disciples he began to speak:

"How blest are you who are in need; the kingdom of God is yours.

²¹ "How blest are you who now go hungry; your hunger shall be satisfied.

"How blest are you who weep now; you shall laugh.

²² "How blest you are when men hate you, when they outlaw you and insult you, and ban your very name as infamous, because of the Son of Man. ²³ On that day be glad and dance for joy; for assuredly you have a rich reward in heaven; in just the same way did their fathers treat the prophets.

²⁴ "But alas for you who are rich; you had your time of happiness.

²⁵ "Alas for you who are well-fed now; you shall go hungry.

"Alas for you who laugh now; you shall mourn and weep.

²⁶ "Alas for you when all speak well of you; just so did their fathers treat the false prophets.

²⁷ "But to you who hear me I say:

"Love your enemies; do good to those who hate you; ²⁸ bless those who curse you; pray for those who treat you spitefully. ²⁹ When a man hits you on the cheek, offer him the other cheek too; when a man takes your coat, let him have your shirt as well. ³⁰ Give to everyone who asks you; when a man takes what is yours, do not demand it back. ³¹ Treat others as you would like them to treat you.

³² "If you love only those who love you, what credit is that to you? Even sinners love those who love them. ³³ Again, if you do good only to those who do good to you, what credit is that to you? Even sinners do as much. ³⁴ And if you lend only where you expect to be repaid, what credit is that to you? Even sinners lend to each other to be repaid in full. ³⁵ But you must love your enemies and do good; and lend without expecting any return; and you will have a rich reward: you will be sons of the Most High, because he himself is kind to the ungrateful and wicked. ³⁶ Be compassionate as your Father is compassionate.

³⁷ "Pass no judgement, and you will not be judged; do not condemn, and you will not be condemned; acquit, and you will be acquitted; ³⁸ give, and gifts will be given you. Good measure, pressed down, shaken together, and running over, will be poured into your lap; for whatever measure you deal out to others will be dealt to you in return."

³⁹ He also offered them a parable: "Can one blind man be guide to another? Will they not both fall into the ditch? ⁴⁰ A pupil is not superior to his teacher; but everyone, when his training is complete, will reach his teacher's level.

⁴¹ "Why do you look at the speck of sawdust in your brother's eye, with never a thought for the great plank in your own? ⁴² How can you say to your brother, 'My dear brother, let me take the speck out of your eye,' when you are blind to the plank in your own? You hypocrite! First take the plank out of your own eye, and then you will see clearly to take the speck out of your brother's.

⁴³ "There is no such thing as a good tree producing worthless fruit, nor yet a worthless tree producing good fruit. ⁴⁴ For each tree is known by its own fruit: you do not gather figs from thistles, and you do not pick grapes from brambles. ⁴⁵ A good man produces good from the store of good within himself; and an evil man from evil within produces evil. For the words that the mouth utters come from the overflowing of the heart.

⁴⁶ "Why do you keep calling me 'Lord, Lord'—and never do what I tell you? ⁴⁷ Everyone who comes to me

and hears what I say, and acts upon it—I will show you what he is like. ⁴⁸He is like a man who, in building his house, dug deep and laid the foundations on rock. When the flood came, the river burst upon that house, but could not shift it, because it had been soundly built. ⁴⁹But he who hears and does not act is like a man who built his house on the soil without foundations. As soon as the river burst upon it, the house collapsed, and fell with a great crash."

The Prodigal Son

LUKE 15:11–32

15

. . . ¹¹Again he said: "There was once a man who had two sons; ¹²and the younger said to his father, 'Father, give me my share of the property.' So he divided his estate between them. ¹³A few days later the younger son turned the whole of his share into cash and left home for a distant country, where he squandered it in reckless living. ¹⁴He had spent it all, when a severe famine fell upon that country and he began to feel the pinch. ¹⁵So he went and attached himself to one of the local landowners, who sent him on to his farm to mind the pigs. ¹⁶He would have been glad to fill his belly with the pods that the pigs were eating; and no one gave him anything. ¹⁷Then he came to his senses and said, 'How many of my father's paid servants have more food than they can eat, and here am I, starving to death! ¹⁸I will set off and go to my father, and say to him, "Father, I have sinned, against God and against you; ¹⁹I am no longer fit to be called your son; treat me as one of your paid servants."' ²⁰So he set out for his father's house. But while he was still a long way off his father saw him, and his heart went out to him. He ran to meet him, flung his arms round him, and kissed him. ²¹The son said, 'Father, I have sinned, against God and against you; I am no longer fit to be called your son.' ²²But the father said to his servants, 'Quick! fetch a robe, my best one, and put it on him; put a ring on his finger and shoes on his feet. ²³Bring the fatted calf and kill it, and let us have a feast to celebrate the day. ²⁴For this son of mine was dead and has come back to life; he was lost and is found.' And the festivities began.

²⁵"Now the elder son was out on the farm; and on his way back, as he approached the house, he heard music and dancing. ²⁶He called one of the servants and asked what it meant. ²⁷The servant told him, 'Your brother has come home, and your father has killed the fatted calf because he has him back safe and sound.' ²⁸But he was angry and refused to go in. His father came out and pleaded with him; ²⁹but he retorted. 'You know how I have slaved for you all these years; I never once disobeyed your orders; and you never gave me so much as a kid, for a feast with my friends. ³⁰But now that this son of yours turns up, after running through your money with his women, you kill the fatted calf for him.' ³¹'My boy,' said the father, 'you are always with me, and everything I have is yours. ³²How could we help celebrating this happy day? Your brother here was dead and has come back to life, was lost and is found.'"

The Last Supper

MARK 14:1–25

14

Now the festival of Passover and Unleavened Bread was only two days off; and the chief priests and the doctors of the law were trying to devise some cunning plan to seize him and put him to death. ²"It must not be during the festival," they said, "or we should have rioting among the people."

³Jesus was at Bethany, in the house of Simon the leper. As he sat at table, a woman came in carrying a small bottle of very costly perfume, pure oil of nard. She broke it open and poured the oil over his head. ⁴Some of those present said to one another angrily, "Why this waste? ⁵The perfume might have been sold for thirty pounds and the money given to the poor"; and they turned upon her with fury. ⁶But Jesus said, "Let her alone. Why must you make trouble for her? It is a fine thing she has done for me. ⁷You have the poor among you always, and you can help them whenever you like; but you will not always have me. ⁸She has done what lay in her power; she is beforehand with anointing my body for burial. ⁹I tell you this: wherever in all the world the Gospel is proclaimed, what she has done will be told as her memorial."

[10]Then Judas Iscariot, one of the Twelve, went to the chief priests to betray him to them. [11]When they heard what he had come for, they were greatly pleased, and promised him money; and he began to look for a good opportunity to betray him.

[12]Now on the first day of Unleavened Bread, when the Passover lambs were being slaughtered, his disciples said to him, "Where would you like us to go and prepare for your Passover supper?" [13]So he sent out two of his disciples with these instructions: "Go into the city, and a man will meet you carrying a jar of water. Follow him, [14]and when he enters a house give this message to the householder: 'The Master says, "Where is the room reserved for me to eat the Passover with my disciples?"' [15]He will show you a large room upstairs, set out in readiness. Make the preparations for us there." [16]Then the disciples went off, and when they came into the city they found everything just as he had told them. So they prepared for Passover.

[17]In the evening he came to the house with the Twelve. [18]As they sat at supper Jesus said, "I tell you this: one of you will betray me—one who is eating with me." [19]At this they were dismayed; and one by one they said to him, "Not I, surely?" [20]"It is one of the Twelve," he said, "who is dipping into the same bowl with me. [21]The Son of Man is going the way appointed for him in the scriptures; but alas for that man by whom the Son of Man is betrayed! It would be better for that man if he had never been born."

[22]During supper he took bread, and having said the blessing he broke it and gave it to them, with the words: "Take this; this is my body." [23]Then he took a cup, and having offered thanks to God he gave it to them; and they all drank from it. [24]And he said, "This is my blood, the blood of the covenant, shed for many. [25]I tell you this: never again shall I drink from the fruit of the vine until that day when I drink it new in the kingdom of God."

MATTHEW 26:20–29

26

. . . [20]In the evening he sat down with the twelve disciples; [21]and during supper he said, "I tell you this: one of you will betray me." [22]In great distress they exclaimed one after the other, "Can you mean me, Lord?" [23]He answered, "One who has dipped his hand into this bowl with me will betray me. [24]The Son of Man is going the

way appointed for him in the scriptures; but alas for that man by whom the Son of Man is betrayed! It would be better for that man if he had never been born." [25]Then Judas spoke, the one who was to betray him: "Rabbi, can you mean me?" Jesus replied, "The words are yours."

[26]During supper Jesus took bread, and having said the blessing he broke it and gave it to the disciples with the words: "Take this and eat; this is my body." [27]Then he took a cup, and having offered thanks to God he gave it to them with the words: "Drink from it, all of you. [28]For this is my blood, the blood of the covenant, shed for many for the forgiveness of sins. [29]I tell you, never again shall I drink from the fruit of the vine until that day when I drink it new with you in the kingdom of my Father."

LUKE 22:7–38

22

. . . [7]Then came the day of Unleavened Bread, on which the Passover victim had to be slaughtered, [8]and Jesus sent Peter and John with these instructions: "Go and prepare for our Passover supper." [9]"Where would you like us to make the preparations?" they asked. [10]He replied, "As soon as you set foot in the city a man will meet you carrying a jar of water. Follow him into the house that he enters and give this message to the householder: [11]'The Master says, "Where is the room in which I may eat the Passover with my disciples?"' [12]He will show you a large room upstairs all set out: make the preparations there." [13]They went and found everything as he had said. So they prepared for Passover.

[14]When the time came he took his place at table, and the apostles with him; [15]and he said to them, "How I have longed to eat this Passover with you before my death! [16]For I tell you, never again shall I eat it until the time when it finds its fulfilment in the kingdom of God." [17]Then he took a cup, and after giving thanks he said, "Take this and share it among yourselves; [18]for I tell you, from this moment I shall drink from the fruit of the vine no more until the time when the kingdom of God comes." [19]And he took bread, gave thanks, and broke it; and he gave it to them, with the words: "This is my body."

[21]"But mark this—my betrayer is here, his hand with mine on the table. [22]For the Son of Man is going his appointed way; but alas for that man by whom he is betrayed!" [23]At this they began to ask among themselves

which of them it could possibly be who was to do this thing.

²⁴ Then a jealous dispute broke out: who among them should rank highest? ²⁵ But he said, "In the world, kings lord it over their subjects; and those in authority are called their country's 'Benefactors.' ²⁶ Not so with you: on the contrary, the highest among you must bear himself like the youngest, the chief of you like a servant. ²⁷ For who is greater—the one who sits at table or the servant who waits on him? Surely the one who sits at table. Yet here am I among you like a servant.

²⁸ "You are the men who have stood firmly by me in my times of trial; ²⁹ and now I vest in you the kingship which my Father vested in me; ³⁰ you shall eat and drink at my table in my kingdom and sit on thrones as judges of the twelve tribes of Israel.

³¹ "Simon, Simon, take heed: Satan has been given leave to sift all of you like wheat; ³² but for you I have prayed that your faith may not fail; and when you have come to yourself, you must lend strength to your brothers." ³³ "Lord," he replied, "I am ready to go with you to prison and death." ³⁴ Jesus said, "I tell you, Peter, the cock will not crow tonight until you have three times over denied that you know me."

³⁵ He said to them, "When I sent you out barefoot without purse or pack, were you ever short of anything?" "No," they answered. ³⁶ "It is different now," he said; "whoever has a purse had better take it with him, and his pack too; and if he has no sword, let him sell his cloak to buy one. ³⁷ For Scripture says, 'And he was counted among the outlaws,' and these words, I tell you, must find fulfilment in me; indeed, all that is written of me is being fulfilled." ³⁸ "Look, Lord," they said, "we have two swords here." "Enough, enough!" he replied.

Crucifixion and Resurrection

MARK 15:21–16:8

15

. . . ²¹ Then they took him out to crucify him. A man called Simon, from Cyrene, the father of Alexander and

---

You may wish to compare these accounts with John 19:17–20:18.

Rufus, was passing by on his way in from the country, and they pressed him into service to carry his cross.

²² They brought him to the place called Golgotha, which means "Place of a skull." ²³ He was offered drugged wine, but he would not take it. ²⁴ Then they fastened him to the cross. They divided his clothes among them, casting lots to decide what each should have.

²⁵ The hour of the crucifixion was nine in the morning, ²⁶ and the inscription giving the charge against him read, "The king of the Jews." ²⁷ Two bandits were crucified with him, one on his right and the other on his left.

²⁹ The passers-by hurled abuse at him: "Aha!" they cried, wagging their heads, "you would pull the temple down, would you, and build it in three days? ³⁰ Come down from the cross and save yourself!" ³¹ So too the chief priests and lawyers jested with one another: "He saved others," they said, "but he cannot save himself. ³² Let the Messiah, the king of Israel, come down now from the cross. If we see that, we shall believe." Even those who were crucified with him taunted him.

³³ At midday a darkness fell over the whole land, which lasted till three in the afternoon; ³⁴ and at three Jesus cried aloud, "*Eli, Eli, lema sabachthani?*," which means, "My God, my God, why hast thou forsaken me?" ³⁵ Some of the bystanders, on hearing this, said, "Hark, he is calling Elijah." ³⁶ A man ran and soaked a sponge in sour wine and held it to his lips on the end of a cane. "Let us see," he said, "if Elijah will come to take him down." ³⁷ Then Jesus gave a loud cry and died. ³⁸ And the curtain of the temple was torn in two from top to bottom. ³⁹ And when the centurion who was standing opposite him saw how he died, he said, "Truly this man was a son of God."

⁴⁰ A number of women were also present, watching from a distance. Among them were Mary of Magdala, Mary the mother of James the younger and of Joseph, and Salome, ⁴¹ who had all followed him and waited on him when he was in Galilee, and there were several others who had come up to Jerusalem with him.

⁴² By this time evening had come; and as it was Preparation-day (that is, the day before the Sabbath), ⁴³ Joseph of Arimathaea, a respected member of the Council, a man who looked forward to the kingdom of God, bravely went in to Pilate and asked for the body of Jesus. ⁴⁴ Pilate was surprised to hear that he was already dead; so he sent for the centurion and asked him whether it was long since he died. ⁴⁵ And when he heard the centurion's report, he gave Joseph leave to take the dead body. ⁴⁶ So Joseph bought a linen sheet, took him down from the cross, and wrapped him in the sheet. Then he laid him in a tomb cut out of the rock, and rolled a stone against the entrance. ⁴⁷ And Mary of Mag-

dala and Mary the mother of Joseph were watching and saw where he was laid.

16

When the Sabbath was over, Mary of Magdala, Mary the mother of James, and Salome bought aromatic oils intending to go and anoint him; [2] and very early on the Sunday morning, just after sunrise, they came to the tomb. [3] They were wondering among themselves who would roll away the stone for them from the entrance to the tomb, [4] when they looked up and saw that the stone, huge as it was, had been rolled back already. [5] They went into the tomb, where they saw a youth sitting on the right-hand side, wearing a white robe; and they were dumbfounded. [6] But he said to them, "Fear nothing; you are looking for Jesus of Nazareth, who was crucified. He has been raised again; he is not here; look, there is the place where they laid him. [7] But go and give this message to his disciples and Peter: 'He is going on before you into Galilee; there you will see him, as he told you.'" [8] Then they went out and ran away from the tomb, beside themselves with terror. They said nothing to anybody, for they were afraid.

And they delivered all these instructions briefly to Peter and his companions. Afterwards Jesus himself sent out by them from east to west the sacred and imperishable message of eternal salvation.

MATTHEW 27:32–28:20

27

. . . [32] Then they led him away to be crucified. On their way out they met a man from Cyrene, Simon by name, and pressed him into service to carry his cross.

[33] So they came to a place called Golgotha (which means "Place of a skull") [34] and there he was offered a draught of wine mixed with gall; but when he had tasted it he would not drink.

[35] After fastening him to the cross they divided his clothes among them by casting lots, [36] and then sat down there to keep watch. [37] Over his head was placed the inscription giving the charge: "This is Jesus the king of the Jews."

[38] Two bandits were crucified with him, one on his right and the other on his left.

[39] The passers-by hurled abuse at him: [40] they wagged their heads and cried, "You would pull the temple down, would you, and build it in three days? Come down from the cross and save yourself, if you are indeed the Son of God." [41] So too the chief priests with the lawyers and elders mocked at him: [42] "He saved others," they said, "but he cannot save himself. King of Israel, indeed! Let him come down now from the cross, and then we will believe him. [43] Did he trust in God? Let God rescue him, if he wants him—for he said he was God's Son." [44] Even the bandits who were crucified with him taunted him in the same way.

[45] From midday a darkness fell over the whole land, which lasted until three in the afternoon; [46] and about three Jesus cried aloud, *"Eli, Eli, lema sabachthani?,"* which means, "My God, my God, why hast thou forsaken me?" [47] Some of the bystanders, on hearing this, said, "He is calling Elijah." [48] One of them ran at once and fetched a sponge, which he soaked in sour wine, and held it to his lips on the end of a cane. [49] But the others said, "Let us see if Elijah will come to save him."

[50] Jesus again gave a loud cry, and breathed his last. [51] At that moment the curtain of the temple was torn in two from top to bottom. There was an earthquake, the rocks split [52] and the graves opened, and many of God's saints were raised from sleep; [53] and coming out of their graves after his resurrection they entered the Holy City, where many saw them. [54] And when the centurion and his men who were keeping watch over Jesus saw the earthquake and all that was happening, they were filled with awe, and they said, "Truly this man was a son of God."

[55] A number of women were also present, watching from a distance; they had followed Jesus from Galilee and waited on him. [56] Among them were Mary of Magdala, Mary the mother of James and Joseph, and the mother of the sons of Zebedee.

[57] When evening fell, there came a man of Arimathaea, Joseph by name, who was a man of means, and had himself become a disciple of Jesus. [58] He approached Pilate, and asked for the body of Jesus; and Pilate gave orders that he should have it. [59] Joseph took the body, wrapped it in a clean linen sheet, [60] and laid it in his own unused tomb, which he had cut out of the rock; he then rolled a large stone against the entrance, and went away. [61] Mary of Magdala was there, and the other Mary, sitting opposite the grave.

[62] Next day, the morning after that Friday, the chief priests and the Pharisees came in a body to Pilate. [63] "Your Excellency," they said, "we recall how that impostor said while he was still alive, 'I am to be raised again after three days.' [64] So will you give orders for the grave to be made secure until the third day? Otherwise his disciples may come, steal the body, and then tell the people that he has been raised from the dead; and the final de-

ception will be worse than the first." [65] You may have your guard," said Pilate; "go and make it secure as best you can." [66] So they went and made the grave secure; they sealed the stone, and left the guard in charge.

28

The Sabbath was over, and it was about daybreak on Sunday, when Mary of Magdala and the other Mary came to look at the grave. [2] Suddenly there was a violent earthquake; an angel of the Lord descended from heaven; he came to the stone and rolled it away, and sat himself down on it. [3] His face shone like lightning; his garments were white as snow. [4] At the sight of him the guards shook with fear and lay like the dead.

[5] The angel then addressed the women: "You," he said, "have nothing to fear. I know you are looking for Jesus who was crucified. [6] He is not here; he has been raised again, as he said he would be. Come and see the place where he was laid, [7] and then go quickly and tell his disciples: 'He has been raised from the dead and is going on before you into Galilee; there you will see him.' That is what I had to tell you."

[8] They hurried away from the tomb in awe and great joy, and ran to tell the disciples. [9] Suddenly Jesus was there in their path. He gave them his greeting, and they came up and clasped his feet, falling prostrate before him. [10] Then Jesus said to them, "Do not be afraid. Go and take word to my brothers that they are to leave for Galilee. They will see me there."

[11] The women had started on their way when some of the guards went into the city and reported to the chief priests everything that had happened. [12] After meeting with the elders and conferring together, the chief priests offered the soldiers a substantial bribe and [13] told them to say, "His disciples came by night and stole the body while we were asleep." They added, [14] "If this should reach the Governor's ears, we will put matters right with him and see that you do not suffer." [15] So they took the money and did as they were told. This story became widely known, and is current in Jewish circles to this day.

[16] The eleven disciples made their way to Galilee, to the mountain where Jesus had told them to meet him. [17] When they saw him, they fell prostrate before him, though some were doubtful. [18] Jesus then came up and spoke to them. He said, "Full authority in heaven and on earth has been committed to me. [19] Go forth therefore and make all nations my disciples; baptize men everywhere in the name of the Father and the Son and the Holy Spirit, [20] and teach them to observe all that I have commanded you. And be assured, I am with you always, to the end of time."

LUKE 23:26–24:11

23

. . . [26] As they led him away to execution they seized upon a man called Simon, from Cyrene, on his way in from the country, put the cross on his back, and made him walk behind Jesus carrying it.

[27] Great numbers of people followed, many women among them, who mourned and lamented over him. [28] Jesus turned to them and said, "Daughters of Jerusalem, do not weep for me; no, weep for yourselves and your children. [29] For the days are surely coming when they will say, 'Happy are the barren, the wombs that never bore a child, the breasts that never fed one.' [30] Then they will start saying to the mountains, 'Fall on us,' and to the hills, 'Cover us.' [31] For if these things are done when the wood is green, what will happen when it is dry?"

[32] There were two others with him, criminals who were being led away to execution; [33] and when they reached the place called The Skull, they crucified him there, and the criminals with him, one on his right and the other on his left. [34] Jesus said, "Father, forgive them; they do not know what they are doing."

[35] They divided his clothes among them by casting lots. The people stood looking on, and their rulers jeered at him: "He saved others: now let him save himself, if this is God's Messiah, his Chosen." [36] The soldiers joined in the mockery and came forward offering him their sour wine. [37] "If you are the king of the Jews," they said, "save yourself." [38] There was an inscription above his head which ran: "This is the king of the Jews."

[39] One of the criminals who hung there with him taunted him: "Are not you the Messiah? Save yourself, and us." [40] But the other rebuked him: "Have you no fear of God? You are under the same sentence as he. [41] For us it is plain justice; we are paying the price for our misdeeds; but this man has done nothing wrong." [42] And he said, "Jesus, remember me when you come to your throne." [43] He answered, "I tell you this: today you shall be with me in Paradise."

[44] By now it was about midday and a darkness fell over the whole land, which lasted until three in the afternoon; [45] the sun's light failed. And the curtain of the temple was torn in two. [46] Then Jesus gave a loud cry and said, "Father, into thy hands I commit my spirit"; and with these words he died. [47] The centurion saw it all, and gave praise to God. "Beyond all doubt," he said, "this man was innocent."

[48] The crowd who had assembled for the spectacle, when they saw what had happened, went home beating their breasts.

⁴⁹His friends had all been standing at a distance; the women who had accompanied him from Galilee stood with them and watched it all.

⁵⁰Now there was a man called Joseph, a member of the Council, a good, upright man, ⁵¹who had dissented from their policy and the action they had taken. He came from the Judaean town of Arimathaea, and he was one who looked forward to the kingdom of God. ⁵²This man now approached Pilate and asked for the body of Jesus. ⁵³Taking it down from the cross, he wrapped it in a linen sheet, and laid it in a tomb cut out of the rock, in which no one had been laid before. ⁵⁴It was Friday, and the Sabbath was about to begin.

⁵⁵The women who had accompanied him from Galilee followed; they took note of the tomb and observed how his body was laid. ⁵⁶Then they went home and prepared spices and perfumes; and on the Sabbath they rested in obedience to the commandment.

24

²But on the Sunday morning very early they came to the tomb bringing the spices they had prepared. Finding that the stone had been rolled away from the tomb, ³they went inside; but the body was not to be found. ⁴While they stood utterly at a loss, all of a sudden two men in dazzling garments were at their side. ⁵They were terrified, and stood with eyes cast down, but the men said, "Why search among the dead for one who lives? ⁶Remember what he told you while he was still in Galilee, ⁷about the Son of Man: how he must be given up into the power of sinful men and be crucified, and must rise again on the third day." ⁸Then they recalled his words ⁹and, returning from the tomb, they reported all this to the Eleven and all the others.

¹⁰The women were Mary of Magdala, Joanna, and Mary the mother of James, and they, with the other women, told the apostles. ¹¹But the story appeared to them to be nonsense, and they would not believe them.

11.2.3 The Gospel of John

The fourth Gospel, known as the Gospel of John, was written around 90. Tradition ascribes it to the apostle John, but we do not know who the author is. It is quite different in style, tone, purpose, and content from the synoptic Gospels. Ninety percent of the material in John does not appear in the synoptic Gospels, including the prologue and the miracle of the resurrection of Lazarus, which we will sample below.

John begins his Gospel not with a birth narrative, but with a philosophical statement about the relationships among God, the Word, or *Logos*, of God, and Jesus. The concept of **logos** already had a long philosophical history before John used it. A Greek philosopher named Heraclitus had used it to designate the rational order of the ever-changing universe. Stoic philosophers of John's day used it to designate not only a divine reason but also the power of reason humans possess that allows them to make sense of their experiences. Philo of Alexandria (see Reading 10.3.1), who died only forty years before this Gospel was written, had already used it to designate the creative Word of God referred to in Genesis. Now John uses it to interpret Jesus.

John's use of *logos* in this prologue is the foundation for one of the most influential **Christologies** (theories of Christ) found in Christianity. It is called, appropriately enough, the Logos Christology, and it lays the foundation for later struggles over the doctrine of the **Trinity** as we shall shortly see.

The Word Made Flesh
(John 1:1–18)

READING QUESTIONS

1. How does John characterize Jesus?
2. What message do you think John intends to send by paralleling his opening prologue with the opening verse of Genesis?
3. Do you think the story of the resurrection of Lazarus is intended to prefigure Jesus' own resurrection? Why or why not?

1

When all things began, the Word already was. The Word dwelt with God, and what God was, the Word was. ²The Word, then, was with God at the beginning, ³and through him all things came to be; no single thing was created without him. All that came to be was alive with his life, ⁴and that life was the light of men. ⁵The light shines on in the dark, and the darkness has never mastered it.

⁶There appeared a man named John, sent from God; ⁷he came as a witness to testify to the light, that all might become believers through him. ⁸He was not himself the light; he came to bear witness to the light. ⁹The real light which enlightens every man was even then coming into the world.

[10]He was in the world; but the world, though it owed its being to him, did not recognize him. [11]He entered his own realm, and his own would not receive him. [12]But to all who did receive him, to those who have yielded him their allegiance, he gave the right to become children of God, [13]not born of any human stock, or by the fleshly desire of a human father, but the offspring of God himself. [14]So the Word became flesh; he came to dwell among us, and we saw his glory, such glory as befits the Father's only Son, full of grace and truth.

[15]Here is John's testimony to him: he cried aloud, "This is the man I meant when I said, 'He comes after me, but takes rank before me'; for before I was born, he already was."

[16]Out of his full store we have all received grace upon grace; [17]for while the Law was given through Moses, grace and truth came through Jesus Christ. [18]No one has ever seen God; but God's only Son, he who is nearest to the Father's heart, he has made him known.

The Resurrection of Lazarus (John 11:17–44)

11

. . . [17]On his arrival Jesus found that Lazarus had already been four days in the tomb. [18]Bethany was just under two miles from Jerusalem, [19]and many of the people had come from the city to Martha and Mary to condole with them on their brother's death. [20]As soon as she heard that Jesus was on his way, Martha went to meet him, while Mary stayed at home.

[21]Martha said to Jesus, "If you had been here, sir, my brother would not have died. [22]Even now I know that whatever you ask of God, God will grant you." [23]Jesus said, "Your brother will rise again." [24]"I know that he will rise again," said Martha, "at the resurrection on the last day." [25]Jesus said, "I am the resurrection and I am life. If a man has faith in me, even though he die, he shall come to life; [26]and no one who is alive and has faith shall ever die. Do you believe this?" [27]"Lord, I do," she answered; "I now believe that you are the Messiah, the Son of God who was to come into the world."

[28]With these words she went to call her sister Mary, and taking her aside, she said, "The Master is here; he is asking for you." [29]When Mary heard this she rose up quickly and went to him. [30]Jesus had not yet reached the village, but was still at the place where Martha had met

him. [31]The Jews who were in the house condoling with Mary, when they saw her start up and leave the house, went after her, for they supposed that she was going to the tomb to weep there.

[32]So Mary came to the place where Jesus was. As soon as she caught sight of him she fell at his feet and said, "O sir, if you had only been here my brother would not have died." [33]When Jesus saw her weeping and the Jews her companions weeping, he sighed heavily and was deeply moved. [34]"Where have you laid him?" he asked. They replied, "Come and see, sir." [35]Jesus wept. [36]The Jews said, "How dearly he must have loved him!" [37]But some of them said, "Could not this man, who opened the blind man's eyes, have done something to keep Lazarus from dying?"

[38]Jesus again sighed deeply; then he went over to the tomb. It was a cave, with a stone placed against it. [39]Jesus said, "Take away the stone." Martha, the dead man's sister, said to him, "Sir, by now there will be a stench; he has been there four days." [40]Jesus said, "Did I not tell you that if you have faith you will see the glory of God?" [41]So they removed the stone.

Then Jesus looked upwards and said, "Father, I thank thee; thou hast heard me. [42]I knew already that thou always hearest me, but I spoke for the sake of the people standing round, that they might believe that thou didst send me."

[43]Then he raised his voice in a great cry: "Lazarus, come forth." [44]The dead man came out, his hands and feet swathed in linen bands, his face wrapped in a cloth. Jesus said, "Loose him; let him go."

11.2.4 The Gospel of Mary (Magdalene)

Imagine the excitement when, in 1945 in Nag Hammadi, Egypt, forty-five Coptic translations of Greek manuscripts dating from the fourth to the fifth century were found. The originals of these manuscripts, which go back even earlier, have revolutionized our understanding of early Christianity. They indicate that early Christianity was far more diverse than had previously been thought. One of these manuscripts, *The Gospel of Thomas*, contains 114 sayings attributed to Jesus that predate the sayings contained in the New Testament Gospels.

Scholars believe these texts belonged to a Christian movement named **Gnosticism** (*gnosis* means "knowledge"). The Gnostics claimed that Jesus had passed on a secret, oral tradition of teachings that stressed knowledge as the key to salvation. According to some of these teachings, the human soul is derived from the divine. Hence, to know the soul is to know its divine origin and destiny.

Although there are many different beliefs associated with Gnosticism, many Gnostic Christians apparently emphasized a sharp dualism between spirit and matter. Some believed that God is the primal, divine Mother and Father of all reality. Others believed God radiates divine qualities, one of which is the female spirit of Wisdom that is the womb of everything. Some Gnostic texts mention a divine trinity of father, mother, and son. These texts also defend the role of women as teachers of divine knowledge, although it is difficult to determine the exact role and status of women among Gnostic Christians. By 200, feminine imagery associated with God was disappearing among the Christian groups that eventually defeated Gnosticism's bid for acceptance as the true gospel. The emerging Orthodox Church was becoming more firmly dominated by male authority.

Below is what remains of a Gnostic text called the Gospel of Mary, named for an early female disciple of Jesus called Mary Magdalene. In the text we find Mary instructing Peter, who challenges her teaching, but Levi comes to her defense.

While hundreds of manuscript copies of the canonical Gospels survived into the modern period, only three fragmentary manuscripts of the Gospel of Mary survived; two third-century Greek fragments published in 1938 and 1983 and a longer, fifth-century Coptic translation. Roughly half the Gospel appears to be lost. We do not know who wrote it. Neither do we know when or where it was written, but the best scholarly evidence points to either Syria or Egypt in the late first or early second century.

꧁✕꧂

Mary Magdalene Teaches Peter

READING QUESTIONS

1. Why do you think Jesus, in this Gospel, says the disciples should lay down no new rules?
2. Why do you think the author has Peter question Mary's account and Levi come to her defense?

From *The Complete Gospels: Annotated Scholars Version*, edited by Robert J. Miller (San Francisco: HarperSanFrancisco, 1994), pp. 361–366. Copyright © 1992, 1994 by Polebridge Press. Reprinted by permission.

1. [Six manuscript pages are missing.]

2. ". . . Will matter then be utterly destroyed or not?"
The Savior replied, "Every nature, every modeled form, every creature, exists in and with each other. They will dissolve again into their own proper root. For the nature of matter is dissolved into what belongs to its nature. Anyone with two ears capable of hearing should listen!"

3. Then Peter said to him, "You have been expounding every topic to us; tell us one further thing. What is the sin of the world?"
The Savior replied, "There is no such thing as sin; rather, you yourselves are what produces sin when you act according to the nature of adultery, which is called 'sin.' For this reason, the Good came among you approaching what belongs to every nature. It will set it within its root."
Then he continued. He said, "This is why you get sick and die, for [you love] what de[c]ei[ve]s you. Anyone with a mind should use it to think!
[Ma]tter gav[e bi]rth to a passion which has no [true] image because it derives from what is contrary to nature. Then a disturbing confusion occurred in the whole body. This is why I told you. 'Be content of heart.' And do not conform [to the body], but form yourselves in the presence of that other image of nature. Anyone with two ears capable of hearing should listen!"

4. When the Blessed One had said this, he greeted them all. "Peace be with you!" he said. Acquire my peace within yourselves!
Be on your guard so that no one deceives you by saying, 'Look over here!' or 'Look over there!' For the seed of true humanity exists within you. Follow it! Those who search for it will find it.
Go then, preach the good news of the domain. Do not lay down any rule beyond what I ordained for you, nor promulgate law like the lawgiver, or else it will dominate you."
After he said these things, he left them.

5. But they were distressed and wept greatly. How are we going to go out to the rest of the world to preach the good news, about the domain of the seed of true humanity?" they said. "If they didn't spare him, how will they spare us?"
Then Mary stood up. She greeted them all and addressed her brothers: "Do not weep and be distressed nor let your hearts be irresolute. For his grace will be with you all and will shelter you. Rather we should praise his greatness, for he has joined us together and made us true human beings."
When Mary said these things, she turned their minds [to]ward the Good, and they began to [as]k about the wor[d]s of the Savi[or].

6. Peter said to Mary, "Sister, we know that the Savior loved you more than any other woman. Tell us the words of the Savior that you know, but which we haven't heard."

Mary responded, "I will rep[ort to you as much as] I remember that you don't know." And she began to speak these words to them.

7. She said, "I saw the Lord in a vision and I said to him, 'Lord, I saw you today in a vision.'

"He said to me, 'Congratulations to you for not wavering at seeing me. For where the mind is, there is the treasure.'

"I said to him, 'Lord, how does a person who sees a vision see it—[with] the soul [or] with the spirit?'

"The Savior answered, 'The [visionary] does not see with the soul or with the spirit, but with the mind which exists between these two—that is [what] sees the vision and that is w[hat . . .]'

8. [Four manuscript pages are missing.]

9. . . . "And Desire said, 'I did not see you go down, yet now I see you go up. So why do you lie since you belong to me?'

"The soul answered, 'I saw you. You did not see me nor did you know me. You [mis]took the garment [I wore] for my [true] self. And you did not recognize me.'

"After it had said these things, [the soul] left rejoicing greatly.

Again, it came to the third Power, which is called 'Ignorance.' [It] examined the soul closely, saying, 'Where are you going? You are bound by fornication. Indeed you are bound! Do not pass judgment!'

"And the soul said, 'Why do you judge me, since I have not passed judgment? I am bound, but I have not bound. They did not recognize me, but I have recognized that the universe is to be dissolved, both the things of earth and those of heaven.'

"When the soul had overcome the third Power, it went upward and it saw the fourth Power. It had seven forms. The first form is Darkness; the second, Desire; the third, Ignorance; the fourth Zeal of Death; the fifth, the Domain of the Flesh; the sixth, the Foolish Wisdom of the Flesh, and seventh is the Wisdom of the Wrathful Person. These are seven Powers of Wrath.

"They interrogated the soul, 'Where are you coming from, human-killer, and where are you going, space-conqueror?'

"The soul replied, 'What binds me has been slain, and what surrounds me has been destroyed, and my desire has been brought to an end, and my ignorance has died. In a world, I was set loose from a world and in a type, from a type which is above, and [from] the chain of forgetfulness that exists in time. For now on, for the rest of the course of the [due] measure of the time of the age, I will rest i[n] silence.'"

When Mary said these things, she fell silent, since it was up to this point that the Savior had spoken to her.

10. Andrew sai[d, "B]rothers, what is your opinion of what was just said? I for one don't believe that the S[a]vior said these things, be[cause] these opinions seem to be so different from h[is th]ought."

After reflecting on these ma[tt]ers, [Peter said], "Has the Sa[vior] spoken secretly to a wo[m]an and [not] openly so that [we] would all hear? [Surely] he did [not wish to indicate] that [she] is more worthy than we are?"

Then Mary wept and said to Peter, "Peter, my brother, what are you imagining about this? Do you think that I've made all this up secretly by myself or that I am telling lies about the Savior?"

Levi said to Peter, "Peter, you have a constant inclination to anger and you are always ready to give way to it. And even now you are doing exactly that by questioning the woman as if you're her adversary. If the Savior considered her to be worthy, who are you to disregard her? For he knew her completely [and] loved her devotedly.

"Instead, we should be ashamed and, once we clothe ourselves with perfect humanity, we should do what we were commanded. We should announce the good news as the Savior ordered, and not be laying down any rules or making laws."

After he said these things, Levi left [and] began to announce the good news.

11.2.5 The Martyrdom of Perpetua

It has been said that the blood of the martyrs is the seed of the church. No doubt those who were willing to die for their faith provided good examples to not only the faithful but also those non-Christians who witnessed or heard about their bravery.

It is difficult to know how many Christian martyrs there were prior to the end of the Roman persecutions. Recent evidence indicates that the Roman persecutions and killing of Christians was not as widespread as people once believed. However, it did happen, and what follows is a rare early first-person account. It is even more rare because it was written by a woman, named Perpetua, who died in Carthage on March 7 in 203.

Soon after Perpetua's death her story spread rapidly among Christians and a cult devoted to her developed. She was held up as a prime example of faithfulness in the face of death and as an inspiration to other Christians to remain faithful even unto death.

⁂

PERPETUA

Perpetua's Vision

READING QUESTION

1. Why do you think Perpetua interprets her vision as she does?

A few days later we were imprisoned. I was terrified because never before had I experienced such darkness. What a terrible day! Because of crowded conditions and rough treatment by the soldiers the heat was unbearable. My condition was aggravated by my anxiety for my baby. Then Tertius and Pomponius, those kind deacons who were taking care of our needs, paid for us to be moved for a few hours to a better part of the prison where we might refresh ourselves. Leaving the dungeon we all went about our own business. I nursed my child, who was already weak from hunger. In my anxiety for the infant I spoke to my mother about him, tried to console my brother, and asked that they care for my son. I suffered intensely because I sensed their agony on my account. These were the trials I had to endure for many days. Then I was granted the privilege of having my son remain with me in prison. Being relieved of my anxiety and concern for the infant, I immediately regained my strength. Suddenly the prison became my palace, and I loved being there rather than any other place.

Then my brother said to me, "Dear sister, you already have such a great reputation that you could ask for a vision indicating whether you will be condemned or freed." Since I knew that I could speak with the Lord, whose great favors I had already experienced, I confidently promised to do so. I said I would tell my brother about it the next day. Then I made my request and this is what I saw.

From Patricia Wilson-Kastner et al., *A Lost Tradition: Women Writers of the Early Church* (Lanham, Md.: University Press of America, 1981), pp. 20–22. Copyright © 1981 Patricia Kastner.

There was a bronze ladder of extraordinary height reaching up to heaven, but it was so narrow that only one person could ascend at a time. Every conceivable kind of iron weapon was attached to the sides of the ladder: swords, lances, hooks, and daggers. If anyone climbed up carelessly or without looking upwards, he/she would be mangled as the flesh adhered to the weapons. Crouching directly beneath the ladder was a monstrous dragon who threatened those climbing up and tried to frighten them from ascent.

Saturus went up first. Because of his concern for us he had given himself up voluntarily after we had been arrested. He had been our source of strength but was not with us at the time of the arrest. When he reached the top of the ladder he turned to me and said, "Perpetua, I'm waiting for you, but be careful not to be bitten by the dragon." I told him that in the name of Jesus Christ the dragon could not harm me. At this the dragon slowly lowered its head as though afraid of me. Using its head as the first step, I began my ascent.

At the summit I saw an immense garden, in the center of which sat a tall, grey-haired man dressed like a shepherd, milking sheep. Standing around him were several thousand white-robed people. As he raised his head he noticed me and said, "Welcome, my child." Then he beckoned me to approach and gave me a small morsel of the cheese he was making. I accepted it with cupped hands and ate it. When all those surrounding us said "Amen," I awoke, still tasting the sweet cheese. I immediately told my brother about the vision, and we both realized that we were to experience the sufferings of martyrdom. From then on we gave up having any hope in this world.

A few days later there was a rumor that our case was to be heard. My father, completely exhausted from his anxiety, came from the city to see me, with the intention of weakening my faith. "Daughter," he said, "have pity on my grey head. Have pity on your father if I have the honor to be called father by you, if with these hands I have brought you to the prime of your life, and if I have always favored you above your brothers, do not abandon me to the reproach of men. Consider your brothers; consider your mother and your aunt; consider your son who cannot live without you. Give up your stubbornness before you destroy all of us. None of us will be able to speak freely if anything happens to you."

These were the things my father said out of love, kissing my hands and throwing himself at my feet. With tears he called me not daughter, but woman. I was very upset because of my father's condition. He was the only member of my family who would find no reason for joy in my suffering. I tried to comfort him saying, "Whatever God wants at this tribunal will happen, for remember that our power comes not from ourselves but from God." But utterly dejected, my father left me.

One day as we were eating we were suddenly rushed off for a hearing. We arrived at the forum and the news spread quickly throughout the area near the forum, and a huge crowd gathered. We went up to the prisoners' platform. All the others confessed when they were questioned. When my turn came my father appeared with my son. Dragging me from the step, he begged: "Have pity on your son!"

Hilarion, the governor, who assumed power after the death of the proconsul Minucius Timinianus, said, "Have pity on your father's grey head; have pity on your infant son; offer sacrifice for the emperors' welfare." But I answered, "I will not." Hilarion asked, "Are you a Christian?" And I answered, "I am a Christian." And when my father persisted in his attempts to dissuade me, Hilarion ordered him thrown out, and he was beaten with a rod. My father's injury hurt me as much as if I myself had been beaten, and I grieved because of his pathetic old age. Then the sentence was passed; all of us were condemned to the beasts. We were overjoyed as we went back to the prison cell. Since I was still nursing my child who was ordinarily in the cell with me, I quickly sent the deacon Pomponius to my father's house to ask for the baby, but my father refused to give him up. Then God saw to it that my child no longer needed my nursing, nor were my breasts inflamed. After that I was no longer tortured by anxiety about my child or by pain in my breasts.

11.2.6 The Council of Nicaea

When the Roman emperor Constantine converted to Christianity, it not only meant the immediate end of any official persecutions of Christians, but also meant that being a Christian now became fashionable. This laid the foundations for what we call Christendom, the political and religious domination of Christianity.

Constantine needed a united Christianity in order to support a united empire that was increasingly feeling the strains between Latin culture in the West and Greek culture in the East. Christians, however, were not united. There were a number of different Christian churches with differing interpretations of the Christian message. Constantine asked the bishops of various sections of the empire to meet in Nicaea in 325 to hammer out differences.

One of the many issues the bishops had to face was the issue of how the three main divine powers (Father, Son, and Holy Spirit) in which Christians believed were related. Some Christians, following a teacher named Sabellius, developed a theory called **modalistic monarchianism.** According to this theory, there is one God who has different modes or ways of relating to humans. Sometimes God relates to us as Father the Creator, at other times as Son the Redeemer, or as Holy Spirit, the Teacher of Truth. Another group of Christians followed a teacher named Arius (250–336) who argued that the Father, Son, and Holy Spirit were not equally divine. The Father is the eternal God, and the Son and Spirit proceeded from the Father before the creation of the world.

Arius was an elder in the church at Alexandria. Another Alexandrian named Athanasius (296–373) opposed Arius's views. He thought they amounted to little more than tritheism (believing in three gods). An effort at compromise was made by suggesting that the Son and Spirit were of similar substance (*homoiousia* in Greek) as the eternal Father. The followers of Athanasius would not accept this wording—it was too weak. Nothing less than same substance (*homoousia* in Greek) would do.

So the debate came down to a single "iota," and people wondered what the bishops at Nicaea would do. What they did, with Constantine presiding, was take an already existing confession of faith, or **creed,** and insert *homoousia* into it so that it now read that the Son was of "one substance" with the Father.

This did not end the debate and Arian Christians, although condemned as heretical by the Council of Nicaea, did not cease to believe their own version. The Nicene Creed, as it came to be called, was further modified by the Council of Constantinople in 381 and, according to some scholars, was reformulated again at the Council of Chalcedon in 451.

In the interesting history of the creed, another debate over wording arose. At a local council in Toledo in 589, the Latin word *filioque* (meaning "and the son") was inserted so that the creed now read "I believe that the Holy Spirit . . . who proceeds from the Father *and the Son*." This change was unacceptable to the Eastern churches in part because it had been made by a local council of bishops in the West rather than an ecumenical council (a council of bishops of the whole church). There were already considerable tensions between East and West over such issues as the authority of the bishop of Rome, which the West acknowledged as pope and the East did not, and differences over modes of worship. The addition of the *filioque* clause was the straw that broke the camel's back, and in 1054 the **Great Schism** split the Eastern and Western Churches. Now there were two main branches of Christianity: the Roman Catholic and the Eastern Orthodox. The Nicene Creed is used by both branches to this day, but in the East the *filioque* clause is omitted (the version below includes it).

Many scholars have argued that these fights over correct belief ended up dividing Christians even more deeply and, by placing so much emphasis on belief, turned Christianity into more of an orthodoxy-type religion than an orthopraxy-type such as Judaism. Correct belief (*ortho-doxa*) became more important than correct practice (*ortho-praxis*).

While this is true to a certain extent, we must not forget some of the more important theological reasons for these debates. Even though these were debates over how to word doctrines, behind the debates was a deep religious concern with issues of worship and salvation. Many felt that nothing but a fully divine and eternal Son of God (Jesus) could firmly secure human salvation and be worthy of human worship.

∼✦∼

Nicene Creed

READING QUESTIONS

1. What qualities does the Nicene Creed attribute to Father, Son, and Holy Ghost (Spirit)?
2. Why do you think more is said about the Son than about the Father and the Holy Ghost?
3. What do you think the phrase "being of one substance with the father" means?

I believe in one God the father almighty, maker of heaven and earth, and of all things visible and invisible. And in one lord Jesus Christ, the only begotten son of God, begotten of his father before all worlds, God of God, light of light, true God of true God, begotten, not made, being of one substance with the father, by whom all things were made. Who for us men, and for our salvation came down from heaven, and was incarnate by the Holy Ghost of the Virgin Mary, and was made man, and was crucified also for us under Pontius Pilate. He suffered and was buried, and the third day he rose again

according to the scriptures, and ascended into heaven, and sits on the right hand of the father. And he shall come again with glory to judge both the quick and the dead: whose kingdom shall have no end. And I believe in the Holy Ghost, the lord and giver of life, who proceeds from the father and the son, who with the father and the son together is worshipped and glorified, who spoke by the prophets. And I believe in one catholic and apostolic church. I acknowledge one baptism for the remission of sins, and I look for the resurrection of the dead, and the life of the world to come. Amen.

11.3 CHRISTIANITY IN THE MIDDLE AGES

It is difficult to decide exactly what time period is named by the Middle Ages. Generally it refers to that time between the end of antiquity and the beginning of the Renaissance. The term is also culture bound since it refers primarily to a period in the development of Western European culture. However, it is generally agreed that during this time period Christianity spread throughout the European continent, both East and West, moving steadily North as Islam captured more and more territory formerly held by Christian rulers in the South and the East.

As the fortunes of the Roman Empire declined in the West, so did the quality of city life and civil order. However, the bishop of the church in Rome became increasingly powerful, and, as the quality of city life began an upward curve, the pope in Rome became the peer of emperors and the bishops of the church were at the side of princes. The Latin Christian church with headquarters in Rome became the largest landowner in Europe and a power no one could afford to ignore.

The Middle Ages saw the building of the great cathedrals of Europe and a flowering in art, architecture, and religious culture never before seen in western Europe. Crusades were launched to liberate land from the Islamic control, and the great universities of Europe were founded. Monastic life flourished, and more countries were steadily converted.

11.3.1 A Tale of Two Cities

Aurelius Augustinus (354–430), North African bishop of Hippo, is the most influential Christian theologian of late antiquity. He lived during the decline and fall of the Roman Empire and before the

From *The Book of Common Prayer* (London, 1855).

beginning of the Middle Ages. However, it is appropriate to open our discussion of Christianity during the Middle Ages with a selection of his writings because his way of thinking about Christianity, called Augustinianism, became a major influence in Christianity, especially in the West, throughout the Middle Ages and beyond. It has been said that every major renewal of the Christian church has begun with the rediscovery of Augustine's ideas.

In 410 Alaric, a barbarian from the North, sacked Rome, the eternal city of power and glory. Only some thirty years before, the Roman emperor had made the worship of the many gods of the Romans a crime. If you were a faithful Roman of the day and had been forbidden to worship your gods and if the city that symbolized the power and glory of your culture was then invaded and burned by barbarians, what might you think? You would probably think what many non-Christian citizens of the Roman Empire thought, namely, that the abandonment of the traditional gods had caused the sacking of the sacred city of Rome. Resentment against Christianity quite naturally developed, and some Romans laid the blame for this horrible calamity at the Christian doorstep.

Augustine wrote *The City of God* in response to this situation. In this book he provides a Christian interpretation of the whole of history. After arguing against the polytheistic interpretation of historical events, he describes the Christian version of the origin of humans and the division of humans into two cities or societies (heavenly and earthly). Wicked and evil people belong to the City of Man, the earthly society ruled by the devil, whereas good, faithful Christian people belong to the City of God, the heavenly society ruled by God. Augustine writes, "Two loves have built two cities, self-love in contempt of God has built the earthly city; love of God in contempt of oneself has built the heavenly city."

According to Augustine, the struggle between these two cities is the heart and soul of history and human experience. The struggle takes place on a social level among nations and on an individual level since these two cities are also in each of us as the tension between selfishness (wrongly ordered love) and unselfish love of God (rightly ordered love).

No one knows for sure who belongs to which city until the end of the world. Then, at the Last Judgment, God will separate the two societies. The citizens of the City of Man will go to hell for eternal punishment, and the citizens of the City of God will go to heaven where they will enjoy eternal happiness.

Ironically, the sharp distinction Augustine draws between the divine and human cities, while intended to refute the pagan claims that Christianity is to blame for the fall of Rome, is heavily dependent on pagan philosophy. The Greek philosopher Plato (427–347 B.C.E.) wrote a book called the *Republic*, in which he too characterizes the ideally just society. Although Plato's and Augustine's views are different in many respects, Augustine borrows from Plato a distinction between an eternal, unchanging reality and the fleeting material world of change.

Augustine's story of human history and destiny became so influential and so deeply embedded in Western minds that most of you probably have heard it, even if you have never heard of Augustine of Hippo. So, as you read the selection that follows, the ideas may have a familiar ring.

AUGUSTINE OF HIPPO

The City of God (Book 14)

READING QUESTIONS

1. What are the supreme good and evil, and how is the supreme good to be obtained?
2. Why are belief and faith necessary?
3. Why are the natural goods of body and mind and even the learned goods of virtue inadequate?
4. What is the "peace of Babylon," and in what sense are the people of God strangers on this earth?
5. What is justice in this life, and how does the peace of the life hereafter contrast with the life of those who experience supreme evil?
6. How does Augustine's postulation of the two cities refute his opponents' claim that Rome's disintegration results from the people's abandonment of the traditional gods?

CHAPTER FOUR

If, therefore, we are asked what the City of God replies when asked about these various points and, first, its opinion about the final good and evil, it will reply that

---

From *Augustine of Hippo: Selected Writings*, translation and introduction by Mary T. Clark. © 1984 by Mary T. Clark. Used by permission of Paulist Press, Inc. Pp. 440–443, 475–478. Notes omitted.

the supreme good is eternal life and that the supreme evil is eternal death and to obtain the one and escape the other we must live rightly. Thus it is written: "The just man lives by faith" (Hb 2:4). Since we do not yet see our good so it is appropriate for us to seek it by believing; neither have we in ourselves power to live rightly unless He who has given us faith to believe that we must ask help from him shall help us when we believe and pray. But those who have thought that the final good and final evil are to be had in the present life, whether placing the supreme good in the body or in the soul or in both, or, more explicitly, either in pleasure or in virtue or in both, in repose or in virtue or in both, in primary natural goods or in virtue or in both, all these have sought with a marvelous vanity to be happy in this life and to achieve happiness by their own efforts. Truth ridiculed these people through the words of the Prophet: "The Lord knows the thoughts of men" (Ps 94:11) or as the Apostle Paul testified: "The Lord knows the thoughts of the wise, that they are vain" (1 Cor 3:9).

For what torrent of eloquence suffices to explain the miseries of this life? Cicero lamented them as best he could in the *Consolation* on the death of his daughter, but how inadequate was his best! For when, where, how in this life can the so-called primary natural goods be so possessed as not to be threatened by unforeseen accidents? Why, what pain is there, the contrary of pleasure, what disquiet is there, the contrary of repose, that cannot befall the body of the wise man? Certainly amputation or weakening destroys its integrity; deformity destroys its beauty; weakness, its health; lassitude, its vigor; sleepiness or sluggishness, its activity—and which of these may not attack the flesh of the wise man? Comely fitting positions and movements of the body are also numbered among the primary natural goods; but suppose some disease makes the limbs quake and tremble? Suppose a man's spine is so curved that his hands reach the ground, making of him a quadruped, so to speak? Will this not ruin all beauty and grace of bodily stance or of movement?

What of the so-called primary natural goods of the mind itself, the sense and intellect, the first of the two for perception and the other for the comprehension of truth? But what kind of perception remains where a man becomes deaf and blind, to say nothing of other defects? And where do reason and intelligence withdraw, where do they sleep when a man is crazed by some disease? When the insane say or do many absurd things that are mostly alien to their own aims and characters— and are even contrary to their good aims and characters, when we consider or see the actions and words of these insane people we can scarcely refrain from tears, or perhaps we cannot. What shall I say of those afflicted by de-

monic possession? Where is their own intelligence hidden or buried while the evil spirit is using their souls and bodies according to his own will? And who can be confident that this evil will not befall the wise man in this life? Then as to the perception of truth, what kind can we hope for in this flesh and how much when, as we read in the truthful book of wisdom: "The corruptible body weighs down the soul, and the earthly frame lies heavy on a mind that ponders many things" (Wis 9:15)? And eagerness or an impulse to act, if either is the correct meaning for what the Greeks called *hormē*, is also considered to be among the primary natural goods. Yet, is not impulse itself accountable for those miserable movements and actions of the insane which horrify us, when sensation is deceived and reason deranged?

Finally, as to virtue itself, which is not among the primary natural goods, since it is added later through instruction, although it claims the highest place among human goods, what does it do here but make perpetual war with vices, not external but internal, not alien but plainly our own, a war waged especially by the virtue called *sōphrosynē* in Greek and temperance in Latin which checks the lusts of the flesh lest they win the mind's consent and drag it into every kind of crime?

For we must not suppose that there is no vice in us when, as the Apostle says, "The flesh lusts against the spirit" (Gal 5:17); for there is a virtue contrary to this vice, when, as the same Apostle says: "The spirit lusts against the flesh. For these two," he says, "are opposed one to the other, so that you do not what you would" (Gal 5:17). But what do we will to do when we wish to be made perfect by the Supreme Good unless that the flesh should not lust against the spirit, and that there should be in us no vice for the spirit to lust against? And since we cannot achieve this in the present life, no matter how much we desire it, let us with God's help achieve at least this, to restrain the soul from succumbing and yielding to the flesh lusting against it and to deny our consent to the commitment of sin. Far be it from us, therefore, to believe that as long as we are engaged in this internal war that we have already attained the happiness which we seek to reach by victory. And who is there so wise that he has no battle at all to wage against his vices?

What is to be said of that virtue called prudence? Is it not totally vigilant in discerning good from evil, so that in seeking the one and avoiding the other no error or mistake may occur about good and evil? Thus it is itself a witness to the existence of evil and of evils in us. For prudence itself teaches that it is evil to consent to sin and good to refuse this consent. Yet that evil to which prudence teaches us not to consent and temperance enables us not to consent is neither by prudence nor by temperance removed from this life. What is to be said of justice, whose task is to assign to each man his due, whence there exists in man a certain just order of nature so that the soul is subject to God, and flesh to the soul, and consequently both soul and flesh to God? Does justice not thereby demonstrate that she is still laboring at her task rather than reposing at the end of her labors? For the soul is so much the less subjected to God the less it keeps mindful of God; and flesh is so much the less subjected to the spirit as it lusts more strongly against the spirit. Hence as long as we are beset by this weakness, this plague, this sickness, how shall we dare to say that we are saved, and if not saved, how dare we say that we are already blessed with final happiness? Then truly that virtue called fortitude, though present with however great wisdom, testifies very clearly to human evils which it is compelled to endure with patience. . . .

CHAPTER TWENTY-FIVE

For however laudable may seem to be the rule of the soul over the body and the reason over the vices, if the soul and the reason do not serve God as God has commanded that He should be served, then in no way do they rightly rule the body and vices. For what kind of mistress over the body and the vices can that mind be which is ignorant of the true God, and which instead of being subject to his authority is prostituted to the corrupting power of the most vicious demons? Hence the very virtues which it thinks it possesses, through which it rules the body and vices in order to obtain or keep what it desires, if it does not subordinate them to God, are themselves vices rather than virtues. For although some suppose that virtues are true and honorable when they are referred to themselves and not sought on account of something else, even then they are puffed up and proud and so must be judged as vices, not virtues. For just as it is not that which comes from the flesh but that which is above the flesh which makes the flesh live, so it is not that which comes from man but that which is above man that makes him live a blessed life; and this is true not only of man but of every heavenly domination and power.

CHAPTER TWENTY-SIX

Therefore, as the life of the flesh is the soul, so the blessed life of man is God, of whom the sacred Scriptures of the Hebrews declare: "Blessed is the people

whose God is the Lord" (Ps 144:15). Wretched, therefore, is the people that is alienated from that God. Yet even this people has a peace of its own not to be rejected; but in the end it will not possess it because it does not make good use of it before the end. But it is to our interest that it enjoy this peace meanwhile in this life; for as long as the two cities are commingled, we also enjoy the peace of Babylon; and the people of God is by faith so freed from it as to live as a stranger in the midst of it. On this account the Apostle also admonished the Church to pray for its kings and other nobility, adding these words: "That we may live a quiet and tranquil life with all piety and love" (1 Tm 2:2). And the Prophet Jeremiah, in predicting the captivity to befall the ancient people of God, and in commanding them by divine inspiration to go obediently to Babylon, serving God by their very patience, admonished them to pray for Babylon, saying: "Because in her peace is your peace" (Jer 29:7), that is, of course, the temporal peace of the present which is common to good and wicked alike.

CHAPTER TWENTY-SEVEN

But the peace that is ours we already have with God by faith, and we shall forever have it with Him by sight. But peace in this life, whether common to all or our special possession, is such that it should be called a solace of our misery rather than an enjoyment of blessedness. Also, our very justice, although it is true in relation to the true final good to which it is subordinated, is nevertheless in this life only of such a kind as to consist rather in the remission of sins than in the perfecting of virtues. Witness the prayer of the entire City of God that is exiled on earth. Through all its members it cries out to God: "Forgive us our debts as we forgive our debtors" (Mt 6:12). Nor is this prayer efficacious for those whose faith is dead without works (Jas 2:17), but only for those whose faith brings forth works through love (Gal 5:6). For because the reason, though subjected to God, in this mortal condition and in the corruptible body, which weighs down the soul (Wis 9:15), does not perfectly rule the vices, such a prayer is necessary for just men. For although the reason exercises command over the vices, certainly this is not without struggle. And even if we fight the good fight and rule as master, after such foes have been defeated and subdued, still in this realm of weakness something creeps in so that sin is found if not in some swift action, certainly in some momentary utterance or some fleeting thought. And therefore there is no complete peace as long as the vices are being ruled, because the battle against resisting vices is precarious while those conquered do not allow for a triumph of carefree ease but one held down under a command that is full of anxiety. Among all these temptations, therefore, of which it has been briefly asserted in the divine oracles: "Is man's life on earth anything but temptation?" (Jb 7:1), who will assume that his life is such that he need not say to God: "Forgive us our debts," unless it be a proud man, not truly great, but puffed up and bloated, who is justly resisted by Him who gives grace abundantly to the humble? On this account it is written: "God resists the proud, but gives grace to the humble" (Jas 4:6; 1 Pt 5:5). And so in this life, accordingly, justice for the individual means that God rules and man obeys, the soul rules over the body and reason rules over the vices even when rebellious, whether by subduing or withstanding them, and that from God Himself we seek grace to do our duty and forgiveness for our sins, and that we offer our service of thanksgiving for the blessings received. But in that final peace to which this justice should be subordinated and for the sake of having it this justice should be maintained, since our nature will be healed of its sickness by immortality and incorruption and will have no vices and since nothing either in ourselves or in another will be at war with any one of us, the reason will not need to rule the vices, since they will no longer exist; but God will rule man, and soul the body, and in obeying we shall find a pleasure and ease as great as the felicity of our living and reigning. And there, for all and for everyone, this state will be everlasting, and its everlastingness will be certain; and therefore the peace of this blessedness or the blessedness of this peace will be the highest good.

CHAPTER TWENTY-EIGHT

But, on the other hand, those who do not belong to that City of God will receive everlasting misery, which is called also the second death (Rv 2:11), because neither the soul that is alienated from God's life can be said to live there, nor the body which will be subjected to everlasting torments; and this second death will be all the harder to bear in that it cannot be ended in death. But since just as misery is the opposite of blessedness, and death of life, so war is the opposite of peace, the question is properly raised: What or what kind of war can be understood to take place in the final state of the

wicked to correspond to the peace that is predicted and lauded in the final state of the righteous? But let the questioner attend to what is harmful or destructive in warfare, and he will see that it is nothing but the mutual opposition and conflict of things. Therefore, what war can he imagine more grievous and bitter than one in which the will is so opposed to passion and passion to will that their hostilities can be ended by the victory of neither, and in which the power of pain so struggles with the very nature of the body that neither yields to the other? For in this life, when such a conflict arises, either pain conquers, and death takes away feeling, or nature conquers, and health removes the pain. But in the life beyond, pain remains to torment and nature stays to feel it; neither ceases to be lest the punishment should also cease.

However, since these are the extremes of good and evil of which we should seek to gain the former and escape the latter, and since through judgment good men pass to the former, bad men to the latter, I will, so far as God may grant, discuss this judgment in the following book.

11.3.2 Spiritual Stillness

As early as the sixth century, one of the most influential forms of contemplation, called the Jesus Prayer, had developed. The Jesus Prayer involves continuously repeating "Lord Jesus Christ, Son of God, have mercy upon me." This practice became widespread among Eastern Christian monks and was called **hesychasm** (stillness). By the thirteenth century, this prayer was supplemented with breathing techniques and postures involving resting one's chin on one's chest with eyes fixed on the heart region. The purpose of this contemplation was to clear one's mind of all distractions and directly encounter God within one's heart.

Hesychists were criticized by other Eastern Orthodox Christians in the fourteenth century (by now the split between East and West had occurred) on the grounds that a direct experience of God is impossible for humans in this life. However, despite the controversy, hesychistic practices persisted.

The following selection is one of the earliest discussions of the Jesus Prayer. It is from *On Watchfulness and Holiness* by Hesychios of Sinai, and eighth-century abbot.

HESYCHIOS OF SINAI

The Jesus Prayer

READING QUESTIONS

1. What are the benefits of the Jesus Prayer?
2. Do you notice any similarities with other forms of prayer or meditation you know about?

102. Forgetfulness can extinguish our guard over our intellect as water extinguishes fire; but the continuous repetition of the Jesus Prayer combined with strict watchfulness uproots it from our heart. The Jesus Prayer requires watchfulness as a lantern requires a candle.

103. We should strive to preserve the previous gifts which preserve us from all evil, whether on the plane of the senses or on that of the intellect. These gifts are the guarding of the intellect with the invocation of Jesus Christ, continuous insight into the heart's depths, stillness of mind unbroken even by thoughts which appear to be good, and the capacity to be empty of all thought. In this way the demons will not steal in undetected; and if we suffer pain through remaining centered in the heart, consolation is at hand.

104. The heart which is constantly guarded, and is not allowed to receive the forms, images and fantasies of the dark and evil spirits, is conditioned by nature to give birth from within itself to thoughts filled with light. For just as coal engenders a flame, or a flame lights a candle, so will God, who from our baptism dwells in our heart, kindle our mind to contemplation when He finds it free from the winds of evil and protected by the guarding of the intellect.

105. The name of Jesus should be repeated over and over in the heart as flashes of lightning are repeated over and over in the sky before rain. Those who have experience of the intellect and of inner warfare know this very

well. We should wage this spiritual warfare with a precise sequence: first, with attentiveness; then, when we perceive the hostile thought attacking, we should strike at it angrily in the heart, cursing it as we do so; thirdly, we should direct our prayer against it, concentrating the heart through the invocation of Jesus Christ, so that the demonic fantasy may be dispersed at once, the intellect no longer pursuing it like a child deceived by some conjurer.

106. Let us exert ourselves like David, crying out "Lord Jesus Christ" until our throats are sore; and let our spiritual eyes never cease to give us hope in the Lord our God (cf. Ps. 69:3).

107. If we constantly bear in mind the parable of the unjust judge, which the Lord related in order to show us that we ought always to pray and not to lose heart, we shall both profit and be vindicated (cf. Luke 18:1–8).

108. Just as he who looks at the sun cannot but fill his eyes with light, so he who always gazes intently into his heart cannot fail to be illumined. . . .

174. The single-phrased Jesus Prayer destroys and consumes the deceits of the demons. For when we invoke Jesus, God and Son of God, constantly and tirelessly, He does not allow them to project in the mind's mirror even the first hint of their infiltration—that is to say, their provocation—or any form, nor does He allow them to have any converse with the heart. If no demonic form enters the heart, it will be empty of evil thoughts, as we have said; for it is the demons' habit to converse with the soul by means of evil thoughts and so deceitfully to pervert it.

175. It is through unceasing prayer that the mind is cleansed of the dark clouds, the tempests of the demons. And when it is cleansed, the divine light of Jesus cannot but shine in it, unless we are puffed up with self-esteem and delusion and a love of ostentation, and elevate ourselves towards the unattainable, and so are deprived of Jesus' help. For Christ, the paradigm of humility, loathes all such self-inflation.

176. Let us hold fast, therefore, to prayer and humility, for together with watchfulness they act like a burning sword against the demons. If we do this, we shall daily and hourly be able to celebrate a secret festival of joy within our hearts. . . .

188. Noxious foods give trouble when taken into the body; but as soon as he feels the pain, the person who has eaten them can quickly take some emetic and so be unharmed. Similarly, once the intellect that has imbibed evil thoughts senses their bitterness, it can easily expel them and get rid of them completely by means of the

Excerpts from "On Watchfulness and Holiness" from *The Philokalia: The Complete Text*, Volume I compiled by St. Nikodimos of the Holy Mountain and St. Makarios of Corinth, translated by G. E. H. Palmer, Philip Sherrard, and Kallistos Ware. Translation copyright © 1979 by The Eling Trust, 1979. Reprinted by permission of Faber and Faber, Inc. Pages 179–180, 193, 196.

Jesus Prayer uttered from the depths of the heart. This lesson, and the experience corresponding to it, have by God's grace conveyed understanding to those who practice watchfulness.

189. With your breathing combine watchfulness and the name of Jesus, or humility and the unremitting study of death. Both may confer great blessing.

11.3.3 Nature, Grace, and the Sacraments

The two most important Christian rituals, dating back to the New Testament, are **baptism** and the **Eucharist** (a ritual meal of thanksgiving and fellowship based on the last supper Jesus had with his disciples—see Reading 11.2.2). These rituals came to be regarded as **sacraments** because they employed natural objects (water, bread, and wine) as sacred objects. Eventually, other sacraments developed (such as Penance, Marriage, and Ordination), and debates about the nature of sacraments developed with them.

Many Christians agreed that the sacraments were a means by which God bestows **grace.** The incarnation of God in Jesus is itself the ultimate sacramental act insofar as God makes the human flesh of Jesus a vehicle for bestowing the gift (grace) of eternal life. However, was grace really needed? Is not eternal life based on doing good and obeying God's laws? Granted, not all humans do that, but surely humans are capable of doing it? Why would God give commandments to humans if they were unable to follow them? Are means of grace, like the sacraments, really necessary?

Very early in the history of Christianity, many thought the sacraments were necessary. "There is no salvation outside the Church," proclaimed Cyprian (d. 258), bishop of Carthage and martyr for the faith. Why? Because the church dispenses the sacraments, the means by which humans receive saving grace. However, are not faith and good works necessary for salvation? Surely, grace is not automatically bestowed to anyone and everyone who participates in sacraments?

Thomas Aquinas (1225–1274), the greatest Christian thinker of the Middle Ages, tackled these questions and others in his remarkable *Summa Theologica* (*Summary of Theology*). Thomas was a Dominican monk who taught at the Universities of Paris, Rome, and Naples. Although his ideas were controversial in his day, eventually the Roman Catholic Church made him a doctor of the church.

Many of the writings on natural philosophy by the Greek philosopher Aristotle (384–322 B.C.E.) had been lost to Western culture for several centuries. They were reintroduced by Islamic and Jewish philosophers and theologians, which caused considerable controversy. Augustine (Reading 11.3.1) had based his theology on a Platonic view of reality as a duality of eternity and temporality. Aristotle, a pupil of Plato, had rejected Platonic dualism. Many Christian theologians perceived this rejection of Platonic dualism as a threat to the division between nature and supernature that lay, as Augustine had taught them, at the foundation of Christianity and the teachings of Jesus. Thomas showed how Aristotle's ideas (to whom he simply referred to as The Philosopher) could be reconciled with Christianity.

He is famous for expounding five proofs for God's existence (the arguments from motion, from efficient causation, from possibility and necessity, from degrees of value, and from the order or design of things), at least two of which (from motion and from efficient causation) are directly dependent on Aristotle. If a nondualistic pagan philosopher like Aristotle could help us prove the existence of God, his ideas might also help us prove many other doctrines of the Christian faith.

In the selections from the *Summa*, Thomas argues that God's grace is an "infused quality," that God is the sole cause of grace but the sacraments are his means, and that humans cannot merit eternal life without grace.

Thomas's style may take a little getting used to. He writes in what is called the "**scholastic** style" because it had become the standard format among the "school men" or scholars who taught at the universities in the Middle Ages. Each section or article deals with a particular issue. Arguments pro and con are summarized by Thomas, then Thomas offers his own answer along with supporting arguments. He ends by refuting the initial objections.

THOMAS AQUINAS

Summa Theologica

READING QUESTIONS

1. Why, according to Thomas, should we think of grace as an infused quality?
2. What does Thomas mean when he says that grace is caused "instrumentally by the sacraments themselves"?
3. How does Thomas answer the question whether one can merit eternal life without grace?

QUESTION 110: THE ESSENCE OF GOD'S GRACE

. . .

Article Two: Whether Grace Is a Quality of the Soul

We proceed to the second article thus:

1. It seems that grace is not a quality of the soul. No quality acts on the subject to which it belongs. If it did, the subject would have to act on itself, since there is no action of a quality without the action of its subject. But grace acts on the soul, in justifying it. It follows that grace is not a quality.

2. Again, a substance is nobler than its quality. But grace is nobler than the soul's nature, since we can do many things by grace which we cannot do by nature, as was said in Q. 109, Arts. 1, 2, and 3. It follows that grace is not a quality.

3. Again, no quality persists after it ceases to be in its subject. But grace persists, since it is not corrupted. If grace were corrupted it would be reduced to nothing, since it is created out of nothing—wherefore it is called a "new creature" in Galatians. It follows that grace is not a quality.

On the other hand: the gloss by Augustine on Ps. 104:15, "Oil to make his face to shine," says that "grace is a beauty of the soul, which wins the divine love."

Reproduced from *Aquinas on Nature and Grace*, edited by A. M. Fairweather *(Library of Christian Classics)*, pp. 159–160, 174–175, 205–206. Used by permission of Westminster John Knox Press.

Beauty of soul is a quality, just as comeliness of body is a quality. It follows that grace is a quality.

I answer: as we maintained in the preceding article, to say that a man has the grace of God is to say that there is within him an effect of God's gracious will. Now God's gracious will helps a man in two ways, as we said in Q. 109, Art. 1. In the first place, a man's mind is helped by God to know, to will, or to act. Such an effect of grace is not a quality, but a movement of the soul, since "in the moved, the act of the mover is a movement," as is said in 3 *Physics*, text 18. Secondly, God infuses a habitual gift into the soul, for the reason that it would not be fitting that God should give less to those whom he loves in order that they may attain supernatural good, than he gives to creatures whom he loves in order that they may attain only natural good. Now God provides for natural creatures not only by moving them to their natural actions, but by endowing them with forms and powers which are the principles of actions, so that they may incline to such movements of their own accord. In this way the movements to which God moves them become natural to creatures, and easy for them, in accordance with Wisdom 8:1: ". . . and disposes all things sweetly." Much more, then, does God infuse certain forms or supernatural qualities into those whom he moves to seek after supernatural and eternal good, that they may be thus moved by him to seek it sweetly and readily. The gift of grace, therefore, is a certain quality.

On the first point: as a quality, grace is said to act on the soul not as an efficient cause, but as a formal cause, as whiteness makes things white, or as justice makes things just.

On the second point: any substance is either the nature of that of which it is the substance, or a part of its nature. In this sense, matter and form are both called "substance." But grace is higher than human nature. It cannot then be its substance, nor yet the form of its substance. Grace is a form accidental to the soul. What exists as substance in God occurs as accident in the soul which shares in divine good, as is obvious in the case of knowledge. But since the soul shares in divine good imperfectly, this participation itself, which is grace, exists in the soul in a less perfect mode than that in which the soul exists in itself. Such grace is nevertheless nobler than the soul's nature, in so far as it is an expression or sharing of the divine goodness, even though it is not nobler than the soul in respect of its mode of being.

On the third point: as Boethius says (*Isagogue Porphyri*): "the being of an accident is to inhere." Thus an accident is said to "be," not as if it existed by itself, but because some subject "is" through possessing it. It is thus affirmed of an existence, rather than affirmed to be an existence, as is said in 7 *Metaph.*, text 2. Now since coming to be and passing away are affirmed of what exists, properly speaking no accident comes to be or passes away. But an accident is said to come to be or to pass away when its subject begins or ceases to be actualized through possession of it. In this sense, grace is said to be created when it is men who are created in grace, i.e., when they are created anew out of nothing, and not on account of merit, according to Eph. 2:10: "created in Christ Jesus unto good works."

Question 112: The Cause of Grace

We must now consider the cause of grace, concerning which there are five questions. 1. Whether God is the sole efficient cause of grace. 2. Whether any disposition for grace is required on the part of the recipient, by an act of free will. 3. Whether such a disposition can ensure grace. 4. Whether grace is equal in everyone. 5. Whether any man can know that he has grace.

Article One: Whether God Is the Sole Cause of Grace

We proceed to the first article thus:

1. It seems that God is not the sole cause of grace. For it is said in John 1:17 that "grace and truth came by Jesus Christ," and the name Jesus Christ means the creaturely nature assumed as well as the divine nature which assumed it. It follows that what is creaturely can be the cause of grace.

2. Again, the sacraments of the new law are said to differ from those of the old in this respect, namely that the sacraments of the new law are causes of the grace which those of the old law only signify. Now the sacraments of the new law are visible elements. It follows that God is not the sole cause of grace.

3. Again, according to Dionysius (Coel. Hier. 3, 4): "angels purge, enlighten, and perfect both lesser angels and men." But rational creatures are purged, enlightened, and perfected through grace. It follows that God is not the sole cause of grace.

On the other hand: it is said in Ps. 84:11: "the Lord will give grace and glory."

I answer: nothing can act upon what is above its own species, since a cause must always be greater than its effect. Now the gift of grace exceeds every capacity of nature, since it is none other than a participation of

the divine nature, which exceeds every other nature. It is therefore impossible for any creature to be a cause of grace. Hence it is just as inevitable that God alone should deify, by communicating a sharing of the divine nature through a participation of likeness, as it is impossible that anything save fire alone should ignite.

On the first point: the humanity of Christ is "an organ of his divinity," as the Damascene says (3 De Fid. Orth. 15). Now an instrument carries out the action of a principal agent by the power of the principal agent, not by its own power. Thus the humanity of Christ does not cause grace by its own power, but by the power of the divinity conjoined with it, through which the actions of the humanity of Christ are redemptive.

On the second point: just as in the person of Christ humanity is the cause of our salvation through the divine power which operates as the principal agent, so it is with the sacraments of the new law. Grace is caused instrumentally by the sacraments themselves, yet principally by the power of the Holy Spirit operating in the sacraments.

On the third point: an angel purges, enlightens, and perfects an angel or a man by instruction, not by justification through grace. Wherefore Dionysius says (Coel. Hier. 7): "this kind of purging, enlightening, and perfecting is nothing other than the acquisition of divine knowledge."

Question 114: Concerning Merit, Which Is the Effect of Cooperative Grace

. . .

Article Two: Whether One Can Merit Eternal Life Without Grace

We proceed to the second article thus:

1. It seems that one can merit eternal life without grace. It was said in the preceding article that a man merits from God that to which he is divinely ordained. Now it is of the very nature of man that he is ordained to blessedness as his end, which is indeed the reason why he naturally seeks to be blessed. A man can therefore merit blessedness, which is eternal life, by his own natural powers and without grace.

2. Again, a work is the more meritorious the less it is incumbent upon one, and a good work is the less incumbent if it is done by him who has received the fewer benefits. Now a man who has only his own natural good has received less from God than one who has received

gifts of grace in addition. His work is therefore the more meritorious in God's sight. Hence if one who has grace can in any wise merit eternal life, much more can one who is without grace.

3. Again, the mercy and liberality of God are infinitely greater than the mercy and liberality of man. Now one man can merit something from another, even though he has never had his grace. Much more, then, does it seem that a man without grace can merit eternal life from God.

On the other hand: the apostle says (Rom. 6:23): "the gift of God is eternal life."

I answer: there are two states of man without grace, as we said in Q. 109, Art. 2. One is the state of pure nature, such as was in Adam before his sin. The other is the state of corrupt nature, such as is in ourselves before restoration through grace. If we are speaking of man in the first of these states, there is one reason why he cannot merit eternal life by his natural powers alone, and that is that his merit depends on a divine preordination. No action of anything whatsoever is divinely ordained to that which exceeds what is commensurate with the power which is its principle of action. It is indeed an ordinance of divine providence that nothing shall act beyond its own power. Now eternal life is a good which exceeds what is commensurate with created nature, since it transcends both natural knowledge and natural desire, according to I Cor. 2:9: "Eye hath not seen, nor ear heard, neither have entered into the heart of man. . . ." No created nature, therefore, can suffice as the principle of an action which merits eternal life, unless there is added to it a supernatural gift, which we call grace. But if we are speaking of man as he exists in sin, there is a second reason why this is so, namely, the impediment of sin. Sin is an offence against God which excludes us from eternal life, as we said in Q. 71, Art. 6, and Q. 113, Art. 2. Hence no one who lives in sin can merit eternal life unless he is first reconciled to God by the remission of sin. Now sin is remitted by grace, since the sinner merits not life but death, according to Rom. 6:23: "The wages of sin is death."

On the first point: God has ordained that human nature shall attain the end of eternal life by the help of grace, not by its own power. Its own action can merit eternal life by the help of grace.

On the second point: a man without grace cannot have it in him to perform a work equal to that which proceeds from grace, since action is the more perfect the more perfect is its principle. This reasoning would be valid, however, if such works were equal in each case.

On the third point: the first reason to which we have referred relates to God and to man in dissimilar ways.

For it is from God, and not from man, that a man has every power of well-doing which he possesses. He cannot therefore merit anything from God except by means of God's gift. The apostle expresses this pointedly when he says: "who hath first given to him, and it shall be recompensed unto him again?" (Rom. 11:35). The second reason, on the other hand, which is concerned with the impediment of sin, relates to man and to God in a similar way, since one man cannot merit anything even from another man whom he has offended, unless he first makes retribution, and is reconciled to him.

11.4 REFORMING CHRISTIANITY

As with many religions, so too with Christianity—from time to time reform movements develop hoping to purge a religious community of perceived corruption. Throughout the Middle Ages there were various reform movements, but in the sixteenth century a reform attempt was launched by a German Roman Catholic Augustinian monk named Martin Luther (1483–1546) that was to have far-reaching consequences. Although it failed in its goal of reforming the Roman Catholic Church, it did create the third main branch of Christianity called Protestantism. After the sixteenth century, it became customary to speak of three main types of Christianity: **Eastern Orthodox, Roman Catholic,** and **Protestant.**

While we still speak this way, it is, like many categorical systems, oversimplified. There are numerous subdivisions of the Protestant branch, different types of Orthodoxy and Roman Catholicism, and many Christian groups that do not fall into any of these three categories such as the Coptic Christian churches and the Church of Jesus Christ of Latter-day Saints.

Luther's reform movement, known as the Protestant Reformation, was not the only reform attempt. In Spain, Teresa of Avila (1515–1582), a Roman Catholic Carmelite nun, launched, against much opposition, a reform of monastic life. She was eventually successful in establishing a reformed Carmelite order, and in 1568 John of the Cross and several other men founded a reformed house for men at her urging.

Perhaps Teresa's success was due to her limited goals and her refusal to side with Luther's movement in Germany. Perhaps it was due to the obvious spiritual and mystical qualities of her life and the purity of her intentions. Whatever the reasons, Teresa of Avila emerged as a leading figure in the reform of the Carmelite order in Spain.

11.4.1 Attacking the Roman Defense

Like many reform efforts, Luther's began modestly. He started preaching in his local church against the practice of selling indulgences. Indulgences were pieces of paper people could buy from a representative of the pope guaranteeing so many years off purgatory, an intermediate state between hell and heaven where Christians suffered and did penance for their sins. Indulgences were selling quite well (you could buy them for dead relatives) and filling the treasury in Rome with the much needed money to build the magnificent St. Peter's Cathedral.

There was, however, a lot of resentment in northern Europe about money being drained off to head south to the Italian states. Luther tapped into that resentment when he asked his parishioners not to waste their precious money on pieces of worthless paper. But he did more than that: He indirectly attacked the sacramental system of the Roman Catholic Church.

The Roman Catholic Church claimed that it, as God's representative on earth, had the right to dispense grace. In other words, it controlled the keys that unlocked heaven's gates. Luther, by attacking the church's right to sell indulgences, began to chip away at this sacramental system. Eventually he attacked it outright, denying that grace was an infused quality as Thomas had taught (see Reading 11.3.3), emphasizing justification by faith not meritorious works (see Paul's Letter to the Romans, Reading 11.2.1), and proclaiming such radical ideas as the "priesthood of all believers."

According to Roman Catholic teachings, only a properly ordained priest could validly perform certain rituals such as the sacrament of the Lord's Supper (the Mass). The laity or nonordained could not do this, and hence an official priesthood was needed if God's grace was to flow to the people. Ordination itself had, by this time, become a sacrament, and those ordained were thought to have a special grace the laity did not have. In denying this important distinction between priest and laity, Luther was indirectly attacking the structural power and authority of the Roman Catholic Church. However, it should be noted that Luther did not intend to abolish different offices or functions among Christians. He meant only to deny the notion that priests held some special status or dignity that elevated them above ordinary Christians.

Luther and the other reformers also emphasized the absolute authority of scripture (Scripture alone). Disagreements in matters of faith were to be settled, the reformers argued, not by appeals to priestly officials like the pope but, rather, by appeals to the "plain words of scripture." Of course, as the continuous splintering of Protestantism into various sects since the Reformation testifies, the "plain words" often did not seem so "plain."

Luther also believed that the Roman Catholic Church wrongly emphasized "works" or good deeds as the means to salvation. We, Luther argued, are not justified by what we do, but by what God does for us. Therefore, we are justified by faith in the work of Christ, not by our own good deeds. Hence, a rallying cry of the Reformation was "scripture alone and faith alone" (*sola scriptura et sola fide*).

In the following selection from *An Appeal to the Ruling Class of German Nationality as to the Amelioration of the State of Christendom* (1520), Luther calls on the secular ruling classes (princes and nobles) to aid in the reform of the church since the papacy will not do it. Historically, councils of bishops met to settle controversial issues. However, the papacy had, by Luther's time, asserted its authority over councils. One can hear, in Luther's plea, a note of desperation. Although he did receive the protection of the German nobility, he did not succeed in his reform efforts within the Roman Catholic Church and Christian Protestantism as a separate Christian movement was born.

⚜

MARTIN LUTHER

The Three Walls

READING QUESTIONS

1. What are the three walls, and what arguments does Luther use to "demolish" them?
2. How does Luther use the Bible in developing his argument?
3. Why do you think Luther's attempt to reform the Roman Catholic Church failed and resulted in another schism in Christianity?

From *The Reformation Writings of Martin Luther*, Volume I: *The Basis of the Protestant Reformation*, translated and edited by Bertram Lee Woolf (London: Lutterworth Press, 1953). Reprinted by permission.

i

The Romanists have very cleverly surrounded themselves with three walls, which have protected them till now in such a way that no one could reform them. As a result, the whole of Christendom has suffered woeful corruption. In the first place, when under the threat of secular force, they have stood firm and declared that secular force had no jurisdiction over them; rather the opposite was the case, and the spiritual was superior to the secular. In the second place, when the Holy Scriptures have been used to reprove them, they have responded that no one except the pope was competent to expound Scripture. In the third place, when threatened with a council, they have pretended that no one but the pope could summon a council. In this way, they have adroitly nullified these three means of correction, and avoided punishment. Thus they still remain in secure possession of these three walls, and practise all the villainy and wickedness we see to-day. When they have been compelled to hold a council, they have made it nugatory by compelling the princes to swear in advance that the present position shall remain undisturbed. In addition they have given the pope full authority over all the decisions of a council, till it is a matter of indifference whether there be many councils or none, for they only deceive us with make-believes and sham-fights. So terribly fearful are they for their skins, if a truly free council were held. Further, the Romanists have overawed kings and princes till the latter believe it would be impious not to obey them in spite of all the deceitful and cunning dodges of theirs.

May God now help us, and give us one of those trumpets with which the walls of Jericho were overthrown; that we may blow away these walls of paper and straw, and set free the Christian, corrective measures to punish sin, and to bring the devil's deceits and wiles to the light of day. In this way, may we be reformed through suffering and again receive God's blessing.

Let us begin by attacking the first wall. To call popes, bishops, priests, monks, and nuns, the religious class, but princes, lords, artisans, and farmworkers the secular class, is a specious device invented by certain timeservers; but no one ought to be frightened by it, and for good reason. For all Christians whatsoever really and truly belong to the religious class, and there is no difference among them except in so far as they do different work. That is St. Paul's meaning in I Corinthians 12:12f., when he says: "We are all one body, yet each member hath his own work for serving others." This applies to us all, because we have one baptism, one gospel, one faith, and are all equally Christian. For baptism, gospel, and faith alone make men religious and create a Christian people. When a pope or bishop anoints, grants tonsures, ordains, consecrates, dresses differently from laymen, he may make a hypocrite of a man, or an anointed image, but never a Christian or a spiritually-minded man. The fact is that our baptism consecrates us all without exception, and makes us all priests. As St. Peter says, I Pet. 2 [:9], "You are a royal priesthood and a realm of priests," and Revelation, "Thou hast made us priests and kings by Thy blood" [Rev. 5:9 f.]. If we ourselves as Christians did not receive a higher consecration than that given by pope or bishop, then no one would be made priest even by consecration at the hands of pope or bishop; nor would anyone be authorized to celebrate Eucharist, or preach, or pronounce absolution. ◆

When a bishop consecrates, he simply acts on behalf of the entire congregation, all of whom have the same authority. They may select one of their number and command him to exercise this authority on behalf of the others. It would be similar if ten brothers, king's sons and equal heirs, were to choose one of themselves to rule the kingdom for them. All would be kings and of equal authority, although one was appointed to rule. To put it more plainly, suppose a small group of earnest Christian laymen were taken prisoner and settled in the middle of a desert without any episcopally ordained priest among them; and they then agreed to choose one of themselves, whether married or not, and endow him with the office of baptizing, administering the sacrament, pronouncing absolution, and preaching; that man would be as truly a priest as if he had been ordained by all the bishops and the popes. It follows that, if needs be, anyone may baptize or pronounce absolution, an impossible situation if we were not all priests. The fact that baptism, and the Christian status which it confers, possess such great grace and authority, is what the Romanists have overridden by their canon law, and kept us in ignorance thereof. But, in former days, Christians used to choose their bishops and priests from their own members, and these were afterwards confirmed by other bishops without any of the pomp of present custom. St. Augustine, Ambrose, and Cyprian each became bishops in this way.

Those who exercise secular authority have been baptized like the rest of us, and have the same faith and the same gospel; therefore we must admit that they are priests and bishops. They discharge their office as an office of the Christian community, and for the benefit of that community. Every one who has been baptized may claim that he has already been consecrated priest, bishop, or pope, even though it is not seemly for any particular person arbitrarily to exercise the office. Just because we are all priests of equal standing, no one must push himself forward and, without the consent and choice of the rest, presume to do that for which we all have equal authority. Only by the consent and command of the community should any individual person claim for himself what belongs equally to all. If it should happen that anyone abuses an office for which he has been chosen, and is dismissed for that reason, he would resume his former status. It follows that the status of a priest among Christians is merely that of an office-bearer; while he holds the office he exercises it; if he be deposed he resumes his status in the community and becomes like the rest. Certainly a priest is no longer a priest after being unfrocked. Yet the Romanists have devised the claim to *characteres indelebiles*, and assert that a priest, even if deposed, is different from a mere layman. They even hold the illusion that a priest can never be anything else than a priest, and therefore never a layman again. All these are human inventions and regulations.

Hence we deduce that there is, at bottom, really no other difference between laymen, priests, princes, bishops, or, in Romanist terminology, between religious and secular, than that of office or occupation, and not that of Christian status. All have spiritual status, and all are truly priests, bishops, and popes. But Christians do not all follow the same occupation. Similarly, priests and monks do not all work at the same task. . . .

Therefore those now called "the religious," i.e., priests, bishops, and popes, possess no further or greater dignity than other Christians, except that their duty is to expound the word of God and administer the sacraments—that being their office. In the same way, the secular authorities "hold the sword and the rod," their function being to punish evil-doers and protect the law-abiding. A shoemaker, a smith, a farmer, each has his manual occupation and work; and yet, at the same time, all are eligible to act as priests and bishops. Every one of them in his occupation or handicraft ought to be useful to his fellows, and serve them in such a way that the various trades are all directed to the best advantage of the community, and promote the well-being of body and soul, just as all the organs of the body serve each other. . . .

ii

The second wall is more loosely built and less indefensible. The Romanists profess to be the only interpreters of Scripture, even though they never learn anything contained in it their lives long. They claim authority for themselves alone, juggle with words shamelessly before

our eyes, saying that the pope cannot err as to the faith, whether he be bad or good; although they cannot quote a single letter of Scripture to support their claim. Thus it comes about that so many heretical, unchristian, and even unnatural laws are contained in the canon law—matters of which there is no need for discussion at the present juncture. Just because the Romanists profess to believe that the Holy Spirit has not abandoned them, no matter if they are as ignorant and bad as they could be, they presume to assert whatever they please. In such a case, what is the need or the value of Holy Scripture? Let it be burned, and let us be content with the ignorant gentlemen at Rome who "possess the Holy Spirit within," who, however, in fact, dwells in pious souls only. Had I not read it, I should have thought it incredible that the devil should have produced such ineptitudes at Rome, and have gained adherents to them. But lest we fight them with mere words, let us adduce Scripture. St. Paul says, I Corinthians 14 [:30], "If something superior be revealed to any one sitting there and listening to another speaking God's word, the first speaker must be silent and give place." What would be the virtue of this commandment if only the speaker, or the person in the highest position, were to be believed? Christ Himself says, John 6 [:45], "that all Christians shall be taught by God." Then if the pope and his adherents were bad men, and not true Christians, i.e., not taught by God to have a true understanding; and if, on the other hand, a humble person should have the true understanding, why ever should we not follow him? Has not the pope made many errors? Who could enlighten Christian people if the pope erred, unless someone else, who had the support of Scripture, were more to be believed than he? . . .

iii

The third wall falls without more ado when the first two are demolished; for, even if the pope acts contrary to Scripture, we ourselves are bound to abide by Scripture. We must punish him and constrain him, according to the passage, "If thy brother sin against thee, go and tell it him between thee and him alone; but if he hear thee not, take with thee one or two more; and if he hear them not, tell it to the church; and if he hear not the church, let him be unto thee as a Gentile" [Matt. 18:15–17]. This passage commands each member to exercise concern for his fellow; much more is it our duty when the wrong-doer is one who rules over us all alike, and who causes much harm and offence to the rest by his conduct. And if I am to lay a charge against him before the church, then I must call it together.

Romanists have no Scriptural basis for their contention that the pope alone has the right to summon or sanction a council. This is their own ruling, and only valid as long as it is not harmful to Christian well-being or contrary to God's laws. If, however, the pope is in the wrong, this ruling becomes invalid, because it is harmful to Christian well-being not to punish him through a council. . . .

It is empty talk when the Romanists boast of possessing an authority such as cannot properly be contested. No one in Christendom has authority to do evil, or to forbid evil from being resisted. The church has no authority except to promote the greater good. Hence, if the pope should exercise his authority to prevent a free council, and so hinder the reform of the church, we ought to pay no regard to him and his authority. If he should excommunicate and fulminate, that ought to be despised as the proceedings of a foolish man. Trusting in God's protection, we ought to excommunicate him in return, and manage as best we can; for this authority of his would be presumptuous and empty. He does not possess it, and he would fall an easy victim to a passage of Scripture; for Paul says to the Corinthians, "For God gave us authority, not to cast down Christendom, but to build it up" [II Cor. 10:8]. Who would pretend to ignore this text? Only the power of the devil and the Antichrist attempting to arrest whatever serves the reform of Christendom. Wherefore, we must resist that power with life and limb, and might and main.

Even if some supernatural sign should be given, and appear to support the pope against the secular authority; e.g., if a plague were to strike someone down, as they boast has happened sometimes, we ought only to regard it as caused by the devil on account of our lack of faith in God. It is what Christ proclaimed, "False Christs and false prophets will come in my name, and will do signs and wonders, so as to lead astray, if possible, even the elect" [Matt. 24:24]. St. Paul says to the Thessalonians [II Thess. 2:9] that the Antichrist shall, through Satan, be mighty in false, miraculous signs.

Therefore, let us firmly maintain that no Christian authority is valid when exercised contrary to Christ. St. Paul says, "We can do nothing against Christ, but only for Christ" [II Cor. 13:8]. But if an authority does anything against Christ, it is due to the power of the Antichrist and of the devil, even if that authority makes it rain and hail miracles and plagues. Miracles and plagues prove nothing, especially in these latter days of evil, for specious miracles of this kind are foretold everywhere in Scripture. Therefore, we must hold to God's Word with firm faith. The devil will soon abandon his miracles.

And now, I hope that I have laid these false and deceptive terrors, though the Romanists have long used them to make us diffident and of a fearful conscience. It is obvious to all that they like us, are subject to the authority of the state, that they have no warrant to expound Scripture arbitrarily and without special knowledge. They are not empowered to prohibit a council or, according to their pleasure, to determine its decisions in advance, to bind it and to rob it of freedom. But if they do so, I hope I have shown that of a truth they belong to the community of Antichrist and the devil, and have nothing in common with Christ except the name.

11.4.2 Spiritual Marriage

Teresa of Avila entered a Carmelite convent at the age of nineteen. In 1538 she became seriously ill, lapsed into a three-day coma, and was taken for dead. She managed to revive, but she was left so paralyzed that it took her three years before she could walk.

Teresa was intensely devout and began to have visions and "raptures" (being carried away by ecstatic love or joy). She founded a strict order of Carmelites called the Discalced (sandaless) Carmelites. In one memorable vision, an angel pierced her heart with a flaming arrow, which left her with a burning love for God. Her spiritual directors were, however, suspicious of her many visions and raptures, fearing she might be either mentally unbalanced or, worse yet, seduced by Satan. After a terrifying vision of hell, she vowed to reform the Carmelite order.

News of the conflicts tearing Christians apart in northern Europe, the corrupt lifestyles of many priests in Rome, the many souls yet to be saved in the New Indies, made her heart burn even more intensely with a devotion to serve God perfectly. Teresa thought that if Christ has so few friends, these few must serve "His Majesty" (Teresa's way of referring to Jesus Christ) more deeply.

A brief selection from her book, *The Interior Castle* (1577) follows. In this book Teresa uses the metaphor of seven series of mansions or rooms to represent various stages of spiritual development. The castle is the soul, which the Christian enters through prayer. In the fifth mansion, the soul is possessed by God through the Prayer of Union. Progressing through the sixth and seventh mansions, the soul experiences a spiritual betrothal and finally a spiritual marriage—the most intimate of unions with the divine.

⧉

TERESA OF AVILA

The Interior Castle (7.2)

READING QUESTIONS

1. How does the spiritual marriage begin?
2. What is the difference between spiritual betrothal and spiritual marriage?
3. In describing the spiritual marriage, do you think Teresa is saying that God and the human soul become identical? Why or why not?

Now then let us deal with the divine and spiritual marriage, although this great favor does not come to its perfect fullness as long as we live; for if we were to withdraw from God, this remarkable blessing would be lost.

The first time the favor is granted, His Majesty desires to show Himself to the soul through an imaginative vision of His most sacred humanity so that the soul will understand and not be ignorant of receiving this sovereign gift; with other persons the favor will be received in another form. With regard to the one of whom we are speaking, the Lord represented Himself to her, just after she had received Communion, in the form of shining splendor, beauty, and majesty, as He was after His resurrection, and told her that now it was time that she consider as her own what belonged to Him and that He would take care of what was hers, and He spoke other words destined more to be heard than to be mentioned.

It may seem that this experience was nothing new since at other times the Lord had represented Himself to the soul in such a way. The experience was so different that it left her indeed stupefied and frightened: first, because this vision came with great force; second, because of the words the Lord spoke to her and also because in the interior of her soul, where He represented Himself to her, she had not seen other visions except the former one. You must understand that there is the

From *Teresa of Avila: The Interior Castle*, translation by Kieran Kavanaugh, O.C.D., and Otilio Rodriguez, O.C.D. © 1979 by the Washington Province of Discalced Carmelites, Inc. Used by permission of Paulist Press. Pp. 177–182. Endnotes omitted.

greatest difference between all the previous visions and those of this dwelling place. Between the spiritual betrothal and the spiritual marriage the difference is as great as that which exists between two who are betrothed and between two who can no longer be separated.

I have already said that even though these comparisons are used, because there are no others better suited to our purpose, it should be understood that in this state there is no more thought of the body than if the soul were not in it, but one's thought is only of the spirit. In the spiritual marriage, there is still much less remembrance of the body because this secret union takes place in the very interior center of the soul, which must be where God Himself is, and in my opinion there is no need of any door for Him to enter. I say there is no need of any door because everything that has been said up until now seems to take place by means of the senses and faculties, and this appearance of the humanity of the Lord must also. But that which comes to pass in the union of the spiritual marriage is very different. The Lord appears in this center of the soul, not in an imaginative vision but in an intellectual one, although more delicate than those mentioned, as He appeared to the apostles without entering through the door when He said to them *pax vobis*. What God communicates here to the soul in an instant is a secret so great and a favor so sublime—and the delight the soul experiences so extreme—that I don't know what to compare it to. I can say only that the Lord wishes to reveal for that moment, in a more sublime manner than through any spiritual vision or taste, the glory of heaven. One can say no more—insofar as can be understood—than that the soul, I mean the spirit, is made one with God. For since His Majesty is also spirit, He has wished to show His love for us by giving some persons understanding of the point to which this love reaches so that we might praise His grandeur. For He has desired to be so joined with the creature that, just as those who are married cannot be separated, He doesn't want to be separated from the soul.

The spiritual betrothal is different, for the two often separate. And the union is also different because, even though it is the joining of two things into one, in the end the two can be separated and each remains by itself. We observe this ordinarily, for the favor of union with the Lord passes quickly, and afterward the soul remains without that company; I mean, without awareness of it. In this other favor from the Lord, no. The soul always remains with its God in that center. Let us say that the union is like the joining of two wax candles to such an extent that the flame coming from them is but one, or that the wick, the flame, and the wax are all one. But afterward one candle can be easily separated from the other and there are two candles; the same holds for the wick. In the spiritual marriage the union is like what we have when rain falls from the sky into a river or fount; all is water, for the rain that fell from heaven cannot be divided or separated from the water of the river. Or it is like what we have when a little stream enters the sea, there is no means of separating the two. Or, like the bright light entering a room through two different windows; although the streams of light are separate when entering the room, they become one.

Perhaps this is what Saint Paul means in saying *He that is joined or united to the Lord becomes one spirit with him*, and is referring to this sovereign marriage, presupposing that His Majesty has brought the soul to it through union. And he also says: *For me to live is Christ, and to die is gain*. The soul as well, I think, can say these words now because this state is the place where the little butterfly we mentioned dies, and with the greatest joy because its life is now Christ.

And that its life is Christ is understood better, with the passing of time, by the effects this life has. Through some secret aspirations the soul understands clearly that it is God who gives life to our soul. These aspirations come very, very often in such a living way that they can in no way be doubted. The soul feels them very clearly even though they are indescribable. But the feeling is so powerful that sometimes the soul cannot avoid the loving expressions they cause, such as: O Life of my life! Sustenance that sustains me! and things of this sort. For from those divine breasts where it seems God is always sustaining the soul there flow streams of milk bringing comfort to all the people of the castle. It seems the Lord desires that in some manner these others in the castle may enjoy the great deal the soul is enjoying and that from that full-flowing river, where this tiny fount is swallowed up, a spurt of that water will sometimes be directed toward the sustenance of those who in corporeal things must serve these two who are wed. Just as a distracted person would feel this water if he were suddenly bathed in it, and would be unable to avoid feeling it, so are these operations recognized, and even with greater certitude. For just as a great gush of water could not reach us if it didn't have a source, as I have said, so it is understood clearly that there is Someone in the interior depths who shoots these arrows and gives life to this life, and that there is a Sun in the interior of the soul from which a brilliant light proceeds and is sent to the faculties. The soul, as I have said, does not move from that center nor is its peace lost; for the very One who gave peace to the apostles when they were together can give it to the soul.

It has occurred to me that this greeting of the Lord must have amounted to much more than is apparent from its sound, as well as our Lord's words to the glorious Magdalene that she go in peace. Since the Lord's words are effected in us as deeds, they must have worked in those souls already disposed in such a manner that everything corporeal in them was taken away and they were left in pure spirit. Thus the soul could be joined in this heavenly union with the uncreated spirit. For it is very certain that in emptying ourselves of all that is creature and detaching ourselves from it for the love of God, the same Lord will fill us with Himself. And thus, while Jesus our Lord was once praying for His apostles —I don't remember where—He said that they were one with the Father and with Him, just as Jesus Christ our Lord is in the Father and the Father is in Him. I don't know what greater love there can be than this. And all of us are included here, for His Majesty said: *I ask not only for them but for all those who also will believe in me*; and He says: *I am in them*.

O God help me, how true these words are! And how well they are understood by the soul who is in this prayer and sees for itself. How well we would all understand them if it were not for our own fault, since the words of Jesus Christ, our King and Lord, cannot fail. But since we fail by not disposing ourselves and turning away from all that can hinder this light, we do not see ourselves in this mirror that we contemplate, where our image is engraved.

Well, to return to what we were saying. The Lord puts the soul in this dwelling of His, which is the center of the soul itself. They say that the empyreal heaven where the Lord is does not move as do the other heavens; similarly, it seems, in the soul that enters here there are none of those movements that usually take place in the faculties and the imagination and do harm to the soul, nor do these stirrings take away its peace.

It seems I'm saying that when the soul reaches this state in which God grants it this favor, it is sure of its salvation and safe from falling apart. I do not say such a thing, and wherever I so speak that it seems the soul is secure, this should be taken to mean as long as the divine Majesty keeps it in His hand and it does not offend Him. At least I know certainly that the soul doesn't consider itself safe even though it sees itself in this state and the state has lasted for some years. But it goes about with much greater fear than before, guarding itself from any small offense against God and with the strongest desire to serve Him, as will be said further on, and with habitual pain and confusion at seeing the little it can do and the great deal to which it is obliged. This pain is no small cross but a very great penance. For when this soul does penance, the delight will be greater in the measure that the penance is greater. The true penance comes when God takes away the soul's health and strength for doing penance. Even though I have mentioned elsewhere the great pain this lack causes, the pain is much more intense here. All these things must come to the soul from its roots, from where it is planted. The tree that is beside the running water is fresher and gives more fruit. What is there, then, to marvel at in the desires this soul has since its true spirit has become one with the heavenly water we mentioned?

Now then, to return to what I was saying, it should not be thought that the faculties, senses, and passions are always in this peace; the soul is, yes. But in those other dwelling places, times of war, trial, and fatigue are never lacking; however, they are such that they do not take the soul from its place and its peace; that is, as a rule.

This center of our soul, or this spirit, is something so difficult to explain, and even believe in, that I think, Sisters, I'll not give you the temptation to disbelieve what I say, for I do not know how to explain this center. That there are trials and sufferings and that at the same time the soul is in peace is a difficult thing to explain. I want to make one or more comparisons for you. Please God, I may be saying something through them; but if not, I know that I'm speaking the truth in what I say.

The King is in His palace and there are many wars in his kingdom and many painful things going on, but not on that account does he fail to be at his post. So here, even though in those other dwelling places there is much tumult and there are many poisonous creatures and the noise is heard, no one enters that center dwelling place and makes the soul leave. Nor do the things the soul hears make it leave; even though they cause it some pain, the suffering is not such as to disturb it and take away its peace. The passions are now conquered and have a fear of entering the center because they would go away from there more subdued.

Our entire body may ache; but if the head is sound, the head will not ache just because the body aches.

I am laughing to myself over these comparisons for they do not satisfy me, but I don't know any others. You may think what you want; what I have said is true.

11.5 SOME CHRISTIAN CURRENTS IN NINETEENTH- AND TWENTIETH-CENTURY AMERICA

The spread of Christianity from Europe to North and South America created conditions conducive to new religious movements. Two of the more successful of these movements will be sampled here, the

Church of Jesus Christ of Latter-day Saints (LDS), better known as the Mormons, and the Church of Christ, Scientist.

As modern biblical scholarship spread from Europe to America, conservative Christians responded by countering papal claims to infallibility with the claim that the Bible is infallible. This became a hallmark of American fundamentalism—so called because of its insistence that there are certain fundamentals Christians must believe in order to be saved. Among them is some form of the idea that scripture is infallible, free from all error, and should be interpreted literally.

The Roman Catholic Church, after a battle with modernism, went through its own reformation when Pope John XXIII called for a Second Vatican Council in 1959. This council opened the Roman Catholic Church to renewal and new currents of thought. A renewal of the contemplative mystical tradition was one of many results.

11.5.1 New Revelations

After the accession of Elizabeth I in 1558, some Christians in England began a movement to "purify" the Church of England of the remnants of Roman Catholicism. The "Puritans," as they came to be called, drank deeply from the theological cup of French Protestant reformer John Calvin (1509–1551). For Calvin, God is absolutely sovereign. Two consequences flow from this: first, the utter and complete sinfulness of humans and, second, the absolute power of God to predestine some humans to salvation and allow others to go to hell (double predestination).

When the Puritans began to migrate to New England in the 1630s, where they established Congregational churches in Massachusetts and Connecticut, they brought with them the Calvinistic doctrines of the total human depravity, or sinfulness, and double predestination. They also brought with them a zeal to purify sinners and revive the intense and serious piety of early Christianity. These ideas profoundly influenced the development of Christianity in the New World. In particular, the idea of purifying Christianity through the revival of a sincere and earnest piety—a piety based on the confession of human sin and complete reliance on the power of God for salvation—took deep root in the new soil of America.

Two centuries later, in an attempt to reach the unchurched of a young United States, Protestant Christianity would draw on this heritage to develop the technique known as the revival. Preachers would travel to the small farming regions of a largely agrarian America and hold revival meetings featuring singing, praying, and fervent preaching. Preachers asked people to accept Jesus as their Savior and Lord. Many did.

Upstate New York became known as "burned over" because so many different revival preachers had passed through the area seeking and making converts. Some people became upset and confused by all the different sects and all the different claims to absolute truth. Where, in all this variety, can one find the true Christian church?

In 1820, when he was fourteen, Joseph Smith Jr., who lived on his family's farm near Paltry, New York, was visited by what he took to be two divine personages. They told him not to join any existing sect. Smith interpreted this to mean that a "sect to end all sects" would soon be revealed. In 1823, according to Mormon tradition, Smith's eagerly awaited revelation occurred when the angel Moroni appeared to Smith and told him about records written on gold plates detailing what happened to the lost tribes of Israel.

Four years later Smith found these hidden plates, translated them from "reformed Egyptian" into English, and published his translation as *The Book of Mormon* in 1830. The story in that book purports to bridge the gap between the true church of the apostolic age—before apostasy—and its restoration in the "latter days" in America. It tells how ancient Israelites sailed to America in 600 B.C.E. long before the Puritans arrived on these shores, how they built a great civilization, how the resurrected Christ visited them and preached the gospel, and how the Lamanites (ancestors of Native Americans) fought and destroyed the Nephites. The angel Moroni, who was the last of the Nephite prophets, recorded this history on golden plates. He buried them and now, resurrected as an angel, visited Smith and told him about their existence. Smith recovered them after fourteen centuries of being buried and translated them, and Moroni bore them away.

The story of the progress of the Mormon Church based on this book is a story of persecution, westward movement seeking a new Zion, division into sects, and triumph. Today there are more than 7 million Mormons worldwide with, at any given time, 35,000 missionaries spreading what they understand to be the true gospel of the restored church of Jesus the Christ. This story, in effect, tells Americans that they do not have to rely on a gospel brought here from Europe. Instead, they can rely on a gospel brought here by Christ himself.

Below is a brief selection from one of the books in *The Book of Mormon* featuring a sermon by the prophet Moroni to the unbelievers in his own day. One can hear the fiery tone of the revival preacher in Moroni's words and an argument why we should believe that the age of miracles still exists.

⚜

The Book of Mormon ("Mormon," Chapter 9)

READING QUESTIONS

1. Do you detect in this sermon a criticism of the established churches of Smith's day? If so, what is it?
2. Outline this sermon. What is its structure like?
3. What argument does Moroni make to support his claim that, for those who believe, the age of miracles has not ended?

Moroni calls upon those who do not believe in Christ to repent—He proclaims a God of miracles, who gives revelations and pours out gifts and signs upon the faithful—Miracles cease because of unbelief—Signs follow those who believe—Men are exhorted to be wise and keep the commandments.

And now, I speak also concerning those who do not believe in Christ.

² Behold, will ye believe in the day of your visitation—behold, when the Lord shall come, yea, even that "great day when the earth shall be rolled together as a scroll, and the elements shall melt with fervent heat, yea, in that great day when ye shall be brought to stand before the Lamb of God—then will ye say that there is no God?

³ Then will ye longer deny the Christ, or can ye behold the Lamb of God? Do ye suppose that ye shall dwell with him under a consciousness of your guilt? Do ye suppose that ye could be happy to dwell with that holy Being, when your souls are racked with a consciousness of guilt that ye have ever abused his laws?

From *The Book of Mormon* (Salt Lake City, Utah: The Church of Jesus Christ of the Latter-day Saints, 1981), pp. 484–487. Reprinted by permission.

⁴Behold, I say unto you that ye would be more miserable to dwell with a holy and just God, under a consciousness of your filthiness before him, than ye would to dwell with the damned souls in hell.

⁵For behold, when ye shall be brought to see your nakedness before God, and also the glory of God, and the holiness of Jesus Christ, it will kindle a flame of unquenchable fire upon you.

⁶O then ye unbelieving, turn ye unto the Lord; cry mightily unto the Father in the name of Jesus, that perhaps ye may be found spotless, pure, fair, and white, having been cleansed by the blood of the Lamb, at that great and last day.

⁷And again I speak unto you who deny the revelations of God, and say that they are done away, that there are no revelations, nor prophecies, nor gifts, nor healing, nor speaking with tongues, and the interpretation of tongues;

⁸Behold I say unto you, he that denieth these things knoweth not the gospel of Christ; yea, he has not read the scriptures; if so, he does not understand them.

⁹For do we not read that God is the same yesterday, today, and forever, and in him there is no variableness neither shadow of changing?

¹⁰And now, if ye have imagined up unto yourselves a god who doth vary, and in whom there is shadow of changing, then have ye imagined up unto yourselves a god who is not a God of miracles.

¹¹But behold, I will show unto you a God of miracles, even the God of Abraham, and the God of Isaac, and the God of Jacob; and it is that same God who created the heavens and the earth, and all things that in them are.

¹²Behold, he created Adam, and by Adam came the fall of man. And because of the fall of man came Jesus Christ, even the Father and the Son; and because of Jesus Christ came the redemption of man.

¹³And because of the redemption of man, which came by Jesus Christ, they are brought back into the presence of the Lord; yea, this is wherein all men are redeemed, because the death of Christ bringeth to pass the resurrection, which bringeth to pass a redemption from an endless sleep, from which sleep all men shall be awakened by the power of God when the trump shall sound; and they shall come forth, both small and great, and all shall stand before his bar, being redeemed and loosed from this eternal band of death, which death is a temporal death.

¹⁴And then cometh the judgment of the Holy One upon them; and then cometh the time that he that is filthy shall be filthy still; and he that is righteous shall be righteous still; he that is happy shall be happy still; and he that is unhappy shall be unhappy still.

¹⁵And now, O all ye that have imagined up unto yourselves a god who can do no miracles, I would ask of you, have all these things passed, of which I have spoken? Has the end come yet? Behold I say unto you, Nay; and God has not ceased to be a God of miracles.

¹⁶Behold, are not the things that God hath wrought marvelous in our eyes? Yea, and who can comprehend the marvelous works of God?

¹⁷Who shall say that it was not a miracle that by his word the heaven and the earth should be; and by the power of his word man was created by the dust of the earth; and by the power of his word have miracles been wrought?

¹⁸And who shall say that Jesus Christ did not do many mighty miracles? And there were many mighty miracles wrought by the hands of the apostles.

¹⁹And if there were miracles wrought then, why has God ceased to be a God of miracles and yet be an unchangeable Being? And behold, I say unto you he changeth not; if so he would cease to be God; and he ceaseth not to be God, and is a God of miracles.

²⁰And the reason why he ceaseth to do miracles among the children of men is because that they dwindle in unbelief, and depart from the right way, and know not the God in whom they should trust.

²¹Behold, I say unto you that whoso believeth in Christ, doubting nothing, whatsoever he shall ask the Father in the name of Christ it shall be granted him; and this promise is unto all, even unto the ends of the earth.

²²For behold, thus said Jesus Christ, the Son of God, unto his disciples who should tarry, yea, and also to all his disciples, in the hearing of the multitude: Go ye into all the world, and preach the gospel to every creature;

²³And he that believeth and is baptized shall be saved, but he that believeth not shall be damned;

²⁴And these signs shall follow them that believe—in my name shall they cast out devils; they shall speak with new tongues; they shall take up serpents; and if they drink any deadly thing it shall not hurt them; they shall lay hands on the sick and they shall recover;

²⁵And whosoever shall believe in my name, doubting nothing, unto him will I confirm all my words, even unto the ends of the earth.

²⁶And now, behold, who can stand against the works of the Lord? Who can deny his sayings? Who will rise up against the almighty power of the Lord? Who will despise the works of the Lord? Who will despise the children of Christ? Behold, all ye who are despisers of the works of the Lord, for ye shall wonder and perish.

²⁷O then despise not, and wonder not, but hearken unto the words of the Lord, and ask the Father in the name of Jesus for what things soever ye shall stand in

need. Doubt not, but be believing, and begin as in times of old, and come unto the Lord with all your heart, and work out your own salvation with fear and trembling before him.

[28] Be wise in the days of your probation; strip yourselves of all uncleanness; ask not, that ye may consume it on your lusts, but ask with a firmness unshaken, that ye will yield to no temptation, but that ye will serve the true and living God.

[29] See that ye are not baptized unworthily; see that ye partake not of the sacrament of Christ unworthily; but see that ye do all things in worthiness, and do it in the name of Jesus Christ, the Son of the living God; and if ye do this, and endure to the end, ye will in nowise be cast out.

[30] Behold, I speak unto you as though I spake from the dead; for I know that ye shall have my words.

[31] Condemn me not because of mine imperfection, neither my father, because of his imperfection, neither them who have written before him; but rather give thanks unto God that he hath made manifest unto you our imperfections, that ye may learn to be more wise than we have been.

[32] And now, behold, we have written this record according to our knowledge, in the characters which are called among us the reformed Egyptian, being handed down and altered by us, according to our manner of speech.

[33] And if our plates had been sufficiently large we should have written in Hebrew; but the Hebrew hath been altered by us also; and if we could have written in Hebrew, behold, ye would have had no imperfection in our record.

[34] But the Lord knoweth the things which we have written, and also that none other people knoweth our language; and because that none other people knoweth our language, therefore he hath prepared means for the interpretation thereof.

[35] And these things are written that we may rid our garments of the blood of our brethren, who have dwindled in unbelief.

[36] And behold, these things which we have desired concerning our brethren, yea, even their restoration to the knowledge of Christ, are according to the prayers of all the saints who have dwelt in the land.

[37] And may the Lord Jesus Christ grant that their prayers may be answered according to their faith; and may God the Father remember the covenant which he hath made with the house of Israel; and may he bless them forever, through faith on the name of Jesus Christ. Amen.

11.5.2 Christian Science

In 1866 a woman named Mary Baker Eddy (1821–1910) had a healing experience that affected her deeply. She translated her experience into a theological and philosophical system known as Christian Science. Her experience convinced her that God has the power to heal illness and that the healing ministry of Jesus has been neglected by Christianity.

God is Mind, according to Mrs. Eddy, and the universe and humans are reflections of this one divine Mind. Mind or Spirit is the only real substance. Matter appears to be real, but it is not. Hence illness, disease, and even death, all of which afflict the material body, only seem to be real as a dream seems to be real.

Before her cure in 1866, Mrs. Eddy had been a semi-invalid and sought help from the leading therapies of the day. None proved satisfactory, although she worked with Phineas P. Quimby, a noted healer, for four years. Shortly after Quimby's death in 1866, Mrs. Eddy's cure took place. She devoted herself to nine years of study and healing practice in order to demonstrate the principles she believed were central to a "Christian science" of healing. This work eventually led, in 1875, to the publication of *Science and Health with Key to the Scriptures*.

In 1879 she founded the Church of Christ, Scientist, in Massachusetts. Its stated purpose is "to commemorate the word and works of our Master, which should reinstate primitive Christianity and its lost element of healing." She became the pastor of the Boston church, which became known as the Mother Church. Mrs. Eddy wrote the *Manual of the Mother Church*, which still governs what is today a worldwide movement.

Mary Baker Eddy was a strong leader and maintained strict organizational control of Church of Christ, Scientist. When disagreements developed and former adherents went off to found other movements (generally referred to as New Thought), Mrs. Eddy insisted on retaining an explicitly Christian identification. "Many imagine," she wrote in the Preface to *Science and Health*, "that the phenomena of physical healing in Christian Science present only a phase of the action of the human mind . . . [but] the physical healing of Christian Science results now, as in Jesus' time, from the operation of divine Principle, before which sin and disease lose their reality in human consciousness and disappear as naturally and as necessarily as darkness gives place to light and sin to reformation" (p. xi).

What follows is a selection from a section called "Recapitulation" from *Science and Health with Key to the Scriptures*. In it Mary Baker Eddy strongly affirms her belief in the power of the divine Mind to heal. One of the things that makes this religious movement interesting to students of religion is that it is one of the few churches founded and shaped by a woman. Its emphasis on healing, health, and science gives it a distinctive character.

MARY BAKER EDDY

Science and Health with Key to the Scriptures

READING QUESTIONS

1. What are the demands of the "Science of Soul," and what is "the scientific statement of being"?
2. By what reasoning does Mary Baker Eddy reach the conclusion that "evil is unreal"?
3. What is sickness, and how can it be healed?

CHAPTER XIV: RECAPITULATION

For precept must be upon precept, precept upon precept; line upon line, line upon line; here a little, and there a little.

—Isaiah

This chapter is from the first edition of the author's class-book, copyrighted in 1870. After much labor and increased spiritual understanding, she revised that treatise for this volume in 1875. Absolute Christian Science pervades its statements, to elucidate scientific metaphysics.

Questions and Answers

Question.—What is God?
Answer.—God is incorporeal, divine, supreme, infinite Mind, Spirit, Soul, Principle, Life, Truth, Love.

From *Science and Health with Key to the Scriptures*, by Mary Baker Eddy, Pp. 465–471, 493–495. © 1994 The Christian Science Board of Directors. ISBN 0-087952-038-8. Reprinted by permission of The Christian Science Board of Directors.

Question.—Are these terms synonymous?
Answer.—They are. They refer to one absolute God. They are also intended to express the nature, essence, and wholeness of Deity. The attributes of God are justice, mercy, wisdom, goodness, and so on.

Question.—Is there more than one God or Principle?
Answer.—There is not. Principle and its idea is one, and this one is God, omnipotent, omniscient, and omnipresent Being, and His reflection is man and the universe. *Omni* is adopted from the Latin adjective signifying *all*. Hence God combines all-power or potency, all-science or true knowledge, all-presence. The varied manifestations of Christian Science indicate Mind, never matter, and have one Principle.

Question.—What are spirits and souls?
Answer.—To human belief, they are personalities constituted of mind and matter, life and death, truth and error, good and evil; but these contrasting pairs of terms represent contraries, as Christian Science reveals, which neither dwell together nor assimilate. Truth is immortal; error is mortal. Truth is limitless; error is limited. Truth is intelligent; error is non-intelligent. Moreover, Truth is real, and error is unreal. This last statement contains the point you will most reluctantly admit, although first and last it is the most important to understand.

The term *souls* or *spirits* is as improper as the term *gods*. Soul or Spirit signifies Deity and nothing else. There is no finite soul nor spirit. Soul or Spirit means only one Mind, and cannot be rendered in the plural. Heathen mythology and Jewish theology have perpetuated the fallacy that intelligence, soul, and life can be in matter; and idolatry and ritualism are the outcome of all man-made beliefs. The Science of Christianity comes with fan in hand to separate the chaff from the wheat. Science will declare God aright, and Christianity will demonstrate this declaration and its divine Principle, making mankind better physically, morally, and spiritually.

Question.—What are the demands of the Science of Soul?
Answer.—The first demand of this Science is, "Thou shalt have no other gods before me." This *me* is Spirit. Therefore the command means this: Thou shalt have no intelligence, no life, no substance, no truth, no love, but that which is spiritual. The second is like unto it, "Thou shalt love thy neighbor as thyself." It should be thoroughly understood that all men have one Mind, one God and Father, one Life, Truth, and Love. Mankind will become perfect in proportion as this fact becomes apparent, war will cease and the true brotherhood of

man will be established. Having no other gods, turning to no other but the one perfect Mind to guide him, man is the likeness of God, pure and eternal, having that Mind which was also in Christ.

Science reveals Spirit, Soul, as not in the body, and God as not in man but as reflected by man. The greater cannot be in the lesser. The belief that the greater can be in the lesser is an error that works ill. This is a leading point in the Science of Soul, that Principle is not in its idea. Spirit, Soul, is not confined in man, and is never in matter. We reason imperfectly from effect to cause, when we conclude that matter is the effect of Spirit; but *a priori* reasoning shows material existence to be enigmatical. Spirit gives the true mental idea. We cannot interpret Spirit, Mind, through matter. Matter neither sees, hears, nor feels.

Reasoning from cause to effect in the Science of Mind, we begin with Mind, which must be understood through the idea which expresses it and cannot be learned from its opposite, matter. Thus we arrive at Truth, or intelligence, which evolves its own unerring idea and never can be coordinate with human illusions. If Soul sinned, it would be mortal, for sin is mortality's self, because it kills itself. If Truth is immortal, error must be mortal, because error is unlike Truth. Because Soul is immortal, Soul cannot sin, for sin is not the eternal verity of being.

Question.—What is the scientific statement of being?
Answer.—There is no life, truth, intelligence, nor substance in matter. All is infinite Mind and its infinite manifestation, for God is All-in-all. Spirit is immortal Truth; matter is mortal error. Spirit is the real and eternal; matter is the unreal and temporal. Spirit is God, and man is His image and likeness. Therefore man is not material; he is spiritual.

Question.—What is substance?
Answer.—Substance is that which is eternal and incapable of discord and decay. Truth, Life, and Love are substance, as the Scriptures use this word in Hebrews: "The substance of things hoped for, the evidence of things not seen." Spirit, the synonym of Mind, Soul, or God, is the only real substance. The spiritual universe, including individual man, is a compound idea, reflecting the divine substance of Spirit.

Question.—What is Life?
Answer.—Life is divine Principle, Mind, Soul, Spirit. Life is without beginning and without end. Eternity, not time, expresses the thought of Life, and time is no part of eternity. One ceases in proportion as the other is recognized. Time is finite; eternity is forever infinite. Life

is neither in nor of matter. What is termed matter is unknown to Spirit, which includes in itself all substance and is Life eternal. Matter is a human concept. Life is divine Mind. Life is not limited. Death and finiteness are unknown to Life. If Life ever had a beginning, it would also have an ending.

Question.—What is intelligence?
Answer.—Intelligence is omniscience, omnipresence, and omnipotence. It is the primal and eternal quality of infinite Mind, of the triune Principle,—Life, Truth, and Love,—named God.

Question.—What is Mind?
Answer.—Mind is God. The exterminator of error is the great truth that God, good, is the *only* Mind, and that the supposititious opposite of infinite Mind—called *devil* or evil—is not Mind, is not Truth, but error, without intelligence or reality. There can be but one Mind, because there is but one God; and if mortals claimed no other Mind and accepted no other, sin would be unknown. We can have but one Mind, if that one is infinite. We bury the sense of infinitude, when we admit that, although God is infinite, evil has a place in this infinity, for evil can have no place, where all space is filled with God.

We lose the high signification of omnipotence, when after admitting that God, or good, is omnipresent and has all-power, we still believe there is another power, named *evil*. This belief that there is more than one mind is as pernicious to divine theology as are ancient mythology and pagan idolatry. With one Father, even God, the whole family of man would be brethren; and with one Mind and that God, or good, the brotherhood of man would consist of Love and Truth, and have unity of Principle and spiritual power which constitute divine Science. The supposed existence of more than one mind was the basic error of idolatry. This error assumed the loss of spiritual power, the loss of the spiritual presence of Life as infinite Truth without an unlikeness, and the loss of Love as ever present and universal.

Divine Science explains the abstract statement that there is one Mind by the following self-evident proposition: If God, or good, is real, then evil, the unlikeness of God, is unreal. And evil can only seem to be real by giving reality to the unreal. The children of God have but one Mind. How can good lapse into evil, when God, the Mind of man, never sins? The standard of perfection was originally God and man. Has God taken down His own standard, and has man fallen?

God is the creator of man, and, the divine Principle of man remaining perfect, the divine idea or reflection, man, remains perfect. Man is the expression of God's being. If there ever was a moment when man did not express the divine perfection, then there was a moment when man did not express God, and consequently a time when Deity was unexpressed—that is, without entity. If man has lost perfection, then he has lost his perfect Principle, the divine Mind. If man ever existed without this perfect Principle or Mind, then man's existence was a myth.

The relations of God and man, divine Principle and idea, are indestructible in Science; and Science knows no lapse from nor return to harmony, but holds the divine order or spiritual law, in which God and all that He creates are perfect and eternal, to have remained unchanged in its eternal history.

The unlikeness of Truth,—named *error*,—the opposite of Science, and the evidence before the five corporeal senses, afford no indication of the grand facts of being; even as these so-called senses receive no intimation of the earth's motions or of the science of astronomy, but yield assent to astronomical propositions on the authority of natural science.

The facts of divine Science should be admitted,—although the evidence as to these facts is not supported by evil, by matter, or by material sense,—because the evidence that God and man coexist is fully sustained by spiritual sense. Man is, and forever has been, God's reflection. God is infinite, therefore ever present, and there is no other power nor presence. Hence the spirituality of the universe is the only fact of creation. "Let God be true, but every [material] man a liar." . . .

Question.—Will you explain sickness and show how it is to be healed?

Answer.—The method of Christian Science Mind-healing is touched upon in a previous chapter entitled Christian Science Practice. A full answer to the above question involves teaching, which enables the healer to demonstrate and prove for himself the principle and rule of Christian Science or metaphysical healing.

Mind must be found superior to all the beliefs of the five corporeal senses, and able to destroy all ills. Sickness is a belief, which must be annihilated by the divine Mind. Disease is an experience of so-called mortal mind. It is fear made manifest on the body. Christian Science takes away this physical sense of discord, just as it removes any other sense of moral or mental inharmony. That man is material, and that matter suffers,—these propositions can only seem real and natural in illusion. Any sense of soul in matter is not the reality of being.

If Jesus awakened Lazarus from the dream, illusion, of death, this proved that the Christ could improve on a false sense. Who dares to doubt this consummate test of the power and willingness of divine Mind to hold man forever intact in his perfect state, and to govern man's entire action? Jesus said: "Destroy this temple [body], and in three days I [Mind] will raise it up"; and he did this for tired humanity's reassurance.

Is it not a species of infidelity to believe that so great a work as the Messiah's was done for himself or for God, who needed no help from Jesus' example to preserve the eternal harmony? But mortals did need this help, and Jesus pointed the way for them. Divine Love always has met and always will meet every human need. It is not well to imagine that Jesus demonstrated the divine power to heal only for a select number or for a limited period of time, since to all mankind and in every hour, divine Love supplies all good.

The miracle of grace is no miracle to Love. Jesus demonstrated the inability of corporeality, as well as the infinite ability of Spirit, thus helping erring human sense to flee from its own convictions and seek safety in divine Science. Reason, rightly directed, serves to correct the errors of corporeal sense; but sin, sickness, and death, will seem real (even as the experiences of the sleeping dream seem real) until the Science of man's eternal harmony breaks their illusion with the unbroken reality of scientific being.

Which of these two theories concerning man are you ready to accept? One is the mortal testimony, changing, dying, unreal. The other is the eternal and real evidence, bearing Truth's signet, its lap piled high with immortal fruits.

Our Master cast out devils (evils) and healed the sick. It should be said of his followers also, that they cast fear and all evil out of themselves and others and heal the sick. God will heal the sick through man, whenever man is governed by God. Truth casts out error now as surely as it did nineteen centuries ago. All of Truth is not understood; hence its healing power is not fully demonstrated.

If sickness is true or the idea of Truth, you cannot destroy sickness, and it would be absurd to try. Then classify sickness and error as our Master did, when he spoke of the sick, "whom Satan hath bound," and find a sovereign antidote for error in the life-giving power of Truth acting on human belief, a power which opens the prison doors to such as are bound, and sets the captive free physically and morally.

When the illusion of sickness or sin tempts you, cling steadfastly to God and His idea. Allow nothing but His likeness to abide in your thought. Let neither fear nor doubt overshadow your clear sense and calm trust, that the recognition of life harmonious—as Life eternally is—can destroy any painful sense of, or belief in, that which Life is not. Let Christian Science, instead of corporeal sense, support your understanding of being, and this understanding will supplant error with Truth, replace mortality with immortality, and silence discord with harmony. . . .

11.5.3 Battles Over the Bible

Among European Protestant scholars, the so-called "higher criticism" of biblical literature began making headway in the nineteenth century. This scholarship called into question many traditional views about dating, authorship, and composition of biblical writings. Liberal Protestants in Europe and America accepted this scholarship because of their conviction that the true Word of God is Jesus and the Bible is only indirectly God's word insofar as it witnesses to the true Word. The Bible is not infallible, only God is infallible.

Higher criticism was part of the general movement known as modernism. Growing out of the Enlightenment in the eighteenth century, the spirit of modernism convinced many that human reason could be applied to the study of anything, including religion and religious scriptures, and that humans had a duty to "follow reason wherever it may lead."

Many reacted negatively to the application of Enlightenment reason to the Bible. It seemed, for many Christians, to undermine the authority of revelation. Conservatives among Roman Catholics reacted by claiming that the pope, when speaking *ex cathedra* (in his official capacity as the Vicar of Christ on earth), is infallible. Conservative Protestants reacted by claiming the written words of the Bible are infallible.

Princeton Theological Seminary became the home of a number of Protestant Presbyterian theologians in the nineteenth century who opposed the "higher criticism" and defended the infallibility of scripture. Although not fundamentalist in the strict sense, but conservative evangelicals, they nevertheless helped formulate what became an important part of the credo of American fundamentalism, the belief that the Christian scripture is literally God's word and the original autographs (no longer extant) are without error.

Benjamin B. Warfield (1851–1921) was a professor of theology at Princeton for many years. His many publications in the field of biblical studies are scholarly and influential. We find in one of his writings, in the selection that follows, one of the clearest statements of the belief that the Bible is infallible.

BENJAMIN B. WARFIELD

The Inspiration of Scripture

READING QUESTIONS

1. What is inspiration, and what is its result?
2. How can the words of the Scriptures be both human and divine?
3. Liberals have often accused Warfield's position of being a kind of "bibliolatry" or Bible worship. Given what you have read, do you think that charge is fair?

Inspiration is that extraordinary, supernatural influence (or, passively, the result of it,) exerted by the Holy Ghost on the writers of our Sacred Books, by which their words were rendered also the words of God, and, therefore, perfectly infallible. In this definition, it is to be noted: 1st. That this influence is a supernatural one—something different from the inspiration of the poet or man of genius. Luke's accuracy is not left by it with only the safeguards which "the diligent and accurate Suetonius" had. 2d. That it is an extraordinary influence— something different from the ordinary action of the Spirit in the conversion and sanctifying guidance of believers. Paul had some more prevalent safeguard against false-teaching than Luther or even the saintly Rutherford. 3d. That it is such an influence as makes the words written under its guidance, the words of God; by which is meant to be affirmed an absolute infallibility (as alone fitted to divine words), admitting no degrees whatever—extending to the very word, and to all the words. So that every part of Holy Writ is thus held alike infallibly true in all its statements, of whatever kind.

Fencing around and explaining this definition, it is to be remarked further:

1st. That it purposely declares nothing as to the mode of inspiration. The Reformed Churches admit that this is inscrutable. They content themselves with defining carefully and holding fast the effects of the divine influence, leaving the mode of divine action by which it is brought about draped in mystery.

2d. It is purposely so framed as to distinguish it from revelation;—seeing that it has to do with the communication of truth not its acquirement.

From Benjamin B. Warfield, *The Inspiration and Authority of the Bible* (Philadelphia, Pa.: Presbyterian and Reformed Publishing Company, 1948), pp. 420–422. Reprinted by permission.

3d. It is by no means to be imagined that it is meant to proclaim a mechanical theory of inspiration. The Reformed Churches have never held such a theory: though dishonest, careless, ignorant or over eager controverters of its doctrine have often brought the charge. Even those special theologians in whose teeth such an accusation has been oftenest thrown (e.g., Gaussen) are explicit in teaching that the human element is never absent. The Reformed Churches hold, indeed, that every word of the Scriptures, without exception, is the word of God; but, alongside of that they hold equally explicitly that every word is the word of man. And, therefore, though strong and uncompromising in resisting the attribution to the Scriptures of any failure in absolute truth and infallibility, they are before all others in seeking, and finding, and gazing on in loving rapture, the marks of the fervid impetuosity of a Paul—the tender saintliness of a John—the practical genius of a James, in the writings which through them the Holy Ghost has given for our guidance. Though strong and uncompromising in resisting all effort to separate the human and divine, they distance all competitors in giving honor alike to both by proclaiming in one breath that all is divine and all is human. As Gaussen so well expresses it, "We all hold that every verse, without exception, is from men, and every verse, without exception, is from God"; "every word of the Bible is as really from man as it is from God."

4th. Nor is this a mysterious doctrine—except, indeed, in the sense in which everything supernatural is mysterious. We are not dealing in puzzles, but in the plainest facts of spiritual experience. How close, indeed, is the analogy here with all that we know of the Spirit's action in other spheres! Just as the first act of loving faith by which the regenerated soul flows out of itself to its Saviour, is at once the consciously-chosen act of that soul and the direct work of the Holy Ghost; so, every word indited under the analogous influence of inspiration was at one and the same time the consciously self-chosen word of the writer and the divine-inspired word of the Spirit. I cannot help thinking that it is through failure to note and assimilate this fact, that the doctrine of verbal inspiration is so summarily set aside and so unthinkingly inveighed against by divines otherwise cautious and reverent. Once grasp this idea, and how impossible is it to separate in any measure the human and divine. It is all human—every word, and all divine. The human characteristics are to be noted and exhibited; the divine perfection and infallibility, no less.

This, then, is what we understand by the church doctrine:—a doctrine which claims that by a special, supernatural, extraordinary influence of the Holy Ghost, the sacred writers have been guided in their writing in such a way, as while their humanity was not superseded, it was yet so dominated that their words became at the same time the words of God, and thus, in every case and all alike, absolutely infallible.

11.5.4 Contemplation

Thomas Merton (1919–1968) died tragically. He was electrocuted by a faultily wired fan in his room in Bangkok while visiting Buddhist monks. He was on a trip to learn more about spirituality and mysticism in Buddhism. Christians, Merton believed, could learn much from the spirituality found in other religions.

Merton had converted to Roman Catholicism in 1939 and, at twenty-six, became a Trappist monk. His best-selling autobiography, *The Seven Story Mountain*, published in 1948, helped to renew interest in Catholic spiritualism and mysticism.

Merton did not fear encountering religions other than Christianity and was open to the valuable lessons they could teach. One of his finest works is *Mystics and Zen Masters*. His love of God, and his life devoted to contemplation, spiritual dialogue, and writing, reveal a deep sensitivity to spiritual matters. The Dalai Lama (see Reading 7.6.3) remarked after meeting with Merton just weeks before his death, "This was the first time that I had been struck by such a feeling of spirituality in anyone who professed Christianity. Since then I have come across others with similar qualities, but it was Merton who introduced me to the real meaning of the word "Christian.""

Read a little Merton for yourself and see if you experience in his writings what the Dalai Lama experienced when he met Merton.

THOMAS MERTON

New Seeds of Contemplation

READING QUESTIONS

1. What is contemplation, and what are its seeds?
2. How does Merton answer the question, "How can I know God's will?"

3. What sort of spirituality do you find in Merton's words and ideas? Is it distinctively Christian or more universal? Explain your answer.

Contemplation is the highest expression of man's intellectual and spiritual life. It is that life itself, fully awake, fully active, fully aware that it is alive. It is spiritual wonder. It is spontaneous awe at the sacredness of life, of being. It is gratitude for life, for awareness and for being. It is a vivid realization of the fact that life and being in us proceed from an invisible, transcendent, and infinitely abundant Source. Contemplation is, above all, awareness of the reality of that Source. It *knows* the Source, obscurely, inexplicably, but with a certitude that goes both beyond reason and beyond simple faith. For contemplation is a kind of spiritual vision to which both reason and faith aspire, by their very nature, because without it they must always remain incomplete. Yet contemplation is not vision because it sees "without seeing" and knows "without knowing." It is a more profound depth of faith, a knowledge too deep to be grasped in images, in words or even in clear concepts. It can be suggested by words, by symbols, but in the very moment of trying to indicate what it knows the contemplative mind takes back what it has said, and denies what it has affirmed. For in contemplation we know by "unknowing." Or, better, we know *beyond* all knowing or "unknowing."

Poetry, music, and art have something in common with the contemplative experience. But contemplation is beyond aesthetic intuition, beyond art, beyond poetry. Indeed, it is also beyond philosophy, beyond speculative theology. It resumes, transcends, and fulfills them all, and yet at the same time it seems, in a certain way, to supersede and to deny them all. Contemplation is always beyond our own knowledge, beyond our own light, beyond systems, beyond explanations, beyond discourse, beyond dialogue, beyond ourself. To enter into the realm of contemplation one must in a certain sense die: but this death is in fact the entrance into a higher life. It is a death for the sake of life, which leaves behind all that we can know or treasure as life, as thought, as experience, as joy, as being.

And so contemplation seems to supersede and to discard every other form of intuition and experience—whether in art, in philosophy, in theology, in liturgy, or in ordinary levels of love and of belief. This rejection is of course only apparent. Contemplation is and must be compatible with all these things, for it is their highest fulfillment. But in the actual experience of contemplation all other experiences are momentarily lost. They "die" to be born again on a higher level of life.

In other words, then, contemplation reaches out to the knowledge and even to the experience of the transcendent and inexpressible God. It knows God by seeming to touch Him. Or rather it knows Him as if it had been invisibly touched by Him. . . . Touched by Him Who has no hands, but Who is pure Reality and the source of all that is real! Hence contemplation is a sudden gift of awareness, an awakening to the Real within all that is real. A vivid awareness of infinite Being at the roots of our own limited being. An awareness of our contingent reality as received, as a present from God, as a free gift of love. This is the existential contact of which we speak when we use the metaphor of being "touched by God."

Contemplation is also the response to a call: a call from Him Who has no voice, and yet Who speaks in everything that is, and Who, most of all, speaks in the depths of our own being: for we ourselves are words of His. But we are words that are meant to respond to Him, to answer to Him, to echo Him, and even in some way to contain Him and signify Him. Contemplation is this echo. It is a deep resonance in the inmost center of our spirit in which our very life loses its separate voice and resounds with the majesty and the mercy of the Hidden and Living One. He answers Himself in us and this answer is divine life, divine creativity, making all things new. We ourselves become His echo and His answer. It is as if in creating us God asked a question, and in awakening us to contemplation He answered the question, so that the contemplative is at the same time, question and answer.

The life of contemplation implies two levels of awareness: first, awareness of the question, and second, awareness of the answer. Though these are two distinct and enormously different levels, yet they are in fact an awareness of the same thing. The question is, itself, the answer. And we ourselves are both. But we cannot know this until we have moved into the second kind of awareness. We awaken, not to find an answer absolutely distinct from the question, but to realize that the question is its own answer. And all is summed up in one awareness—not a proposition, but an experience: "I Am."

The contemplation of which I speak here is not philosophical. It is not the static awareness of metaphysical essences apprehended as spiritual objects, unchanging and eternal. It is not the contemplation of abstract ideas. It is the religious apprehension of God, through my life in God, or through "sonship" as the New Testament says. "For whoever are led by the Spirit of God, they are the sons of God. . . . The Spirit Himself gives testimony to our own spirit that we are the sons of God." "To as many as received Him He gave the power to become the sons of God. . . ." And so the contemplation of which I speak is a religious and transcendent gift. It is not something to which we can attain alone, by intellectual effort, by perfecting our natural powers. It is not a kind of self-hypnosis, resulting from concentration on our own inner spiritual being. It is not the fruit of our own efforts. It is the gift of God Who, in His mercy, completes the hidden and mysterious work of creation in us by enlightening our minds and hearts, by awakening in us the awareness that we are words spoken in His One Word, and that Creating Spirit (*Creator Spiritus*) dwells in us, and we in Him. That we are "in Christ" and that Christ lives in us. That the natural life in us has been completed, elevated, transformed and fulfilled in Christ by the Holy Spirit. Contemplation is the awareness and realization, even in some sense *experience*, of what each Christian obscurely believes: "It is now no longer I that live but Christ lives in me."

Hence contemplation is more than a consideration of abstract truths about God, more even than affective meditation on the things we believe. It is awakening, enlightenment, and the amazing intuitive grasp by which love gains certitude of God's creative and dynamic intervention in our daily life. Hence contemplation does not simply "find" a clear idea of God and confine Him within the limits of that idea, and hold Him there as a prisoner to Whom it can always return. On the contrary, contemplation is carried away by Him into His own realm, His own mystery, and His own freedom. It is a pure and a virginal knowledge, poor in concepts, poorer still in reasoning, but able, by its very poverty and purity, to follow the Word "wherever He may go."

SEEDS

Every moment and every event of every man's life on earth plants something in his soul. For just as the wind carries thousands of winged seeds, so each moment brings with it germs of spiritual vitality that come to rest imperceptibly in the minds and and wills of men. Most of these unnumbered seeds perish and are lost, because men are not prepared to receive them: for such seeds as these cannot spring up anywhere except in the good soil of freedom, spontaneity, and love.

This is no new idea. Christ in the parable of the sower long ago told us that "The seed is the word of God." We often think this applies only to the word of the Gospel as formally preached in churches on Sundays (if indeed it is preached in churches any more!). But every expression of the will of God is in some sense a "word" of God and therefore a "seed" of new life. The ever-changing reality in the midst of which we live should awaken us to the possibility of an uninterrupted dialogue with God. By this I do not mean continuous "talk," or a frivolously conversational form of affective prayer which is sometimes cultivated in convents, but a dialogue of love and of choice. A dialogue of deep wills.

In all the situations of life the "will of God" comes to us not merely as an external dictate of impersonal law but above all as an interior invitation of personal love. Too often the conventional conception of "God's will" as a sphinx-like and arbitrary force bearing down upon us with implacable hostility, leads men to lose faith in a God they cannot find it possible to love. Such a view of the divine will drives human weakness to despair and one wonders if it is not, itself, often the expression of a despair too intolerable to be admitted to conscious consideration. These arbitrary "dictates" of a domineering and insensible Father are more often seeds of hatred than of love. If that is our concept of the will of God, we cannot possibly seek the obscure and intimate mystery of the encounter that takes place in contemplation. We will desire only to fly as far as possible from Him and hide from His Face forever. So much depends on our idea of God! Yet no idea of Him, however pure and perfect, is adequate to express Him as He really is. Our idea of God tells us more about ourselves than about Him.

We must learn to realize that the love of God seeks us in every situation, and seeks our good. His inscrutable love seeks our awakening. True, since this awakening implies a kind of death to our exterior self, we will dread His coming in proportion as we are identified with this exterior self and attached to it. But when we understand the dialectic of life and death we will learn to take the risks implied by faith, to make the choices that deliver us from our routine self and open to us the door of a new being, a new reality.

The mind that is the prisoner of conventional ideas, and the will that is the captive of its own desire cannot accept the seeds of an unfamiliar truth and a supernatural desire. For how can I receive the seeds of freedom if I am in love with slavery and how can I cherish the desire of God if I am filled with another and an opposite desire? God cannot plant His liberty in me because I am a prisoner and I do not even desire to be free. I love my captivity and I imprison myself in the desire for the things that I hate, and I have hardened my heart against true love. I must learn therefore to let go of the familiar and the usual and consent to what is new and unknown to me. I must learn to "leave myself" in order to find myself by yielding to the love of God. If I were looking for God, every event and every moment would sow, in my will, grains of His life that would spring up one day in a tremendous harvest.

For it is God's love that warms me in the sun and God's love that sends the cold rain. It is God's love that feeds me in the bread I eat and God that feeds me also by hunger and fasting. It is the love of God that sends the winter days when I am cold and sick, and the hot summer when I labor and my clothes are full of sweat: but it is God Who breathes on me with light winds off the river and in the breezes out of the wood. His love spreads the shade of the sycamore over my head and sends the water-boy along the edge of the wheat field with a bucket from the spring, while the laborers are resting and the mules stand under the tree.

It is God's love that speaks to me in the birds and streams; but also behind the clamor of the city God speaks to me in His judgments, and all these things are seeds sent to me from His will.

If these seeds would take root in my liberty, and if His will would grow from my freedom, I would become the love that He is, and my harvest would be His glory and my own joy.

And I would grow together with thousands and millions of other freedoms into the gold of one huge field praising God, loaded with increase, loaded with wheat. If in all things I consider only the heat and the cold, the food or the hunger, the sickness or labor, the beauty or pleasure, the success and failure, or the material good or evil my works have won for my own will, I will find only emptiness and not happiness. I shall not be fed, I shall not be full. For my food is the will of Him Who made me and Who made all things in order to give Himself to me through them.

My chief care should not be to find pleasure or success, health or life or money or rest or even things like virtue and wisdom—still less their opposites, pain, failure, sickness, death. But in all that happens, my one desire and my one joy should be to know: "Here is the thing that God has willed for me. In this His love is found, and in accepting this I can give back His love to Him and give myself with it to Him. For in giving myself I shall find Him and He is life everlasting."

By consenting to His will with joy and doing it with gladness I have His love in my heart, because my will is now the same as His love and I am on the way to becoming what He is, Who is Love. And by accepting all things from Him I receive His joy into my soul, not because things are what they are but because God is Who He is, and His love has willed my joy in them all.

How am I to know the will of God? Even where there is no other more explicit claim on my obedience, such as a legitimate command, the very nature of each situation usually bears written into itself some indication of God's will. For whatever is demanded by truth, by justice, by mercy, or by love must surely be taken to be willed by God. To consent to His will is, then, to consent to be true, or to speak truth, or at least to seek it. To obey Him is to respond to His will expressed in the need of another person, or at least to respect the rights of others. For the right of another man is the expression of God's love and God's will. In demanding that I respect the rights of another God is not merely asking me to conform to some abstract, arbitrary law: He is enabling me to share, as His son, in His own care for my brother. No man who ignores the rights and needs of others can hope to walk in the light of contemplation, because his way has turned aside from truth, from compassion, and therefore from God.

The requirements of a work to be done can be understood as the will of God. If I am supposed to hoe a garden or make a table, then I will be obeying God if I am true to the task I am performing. To do the work carefully and well, with love and respect for the nature of my task and with due attention to its purpose, is to unite myself to God's will in my work. In this way I become His instrument. He works through me. When I act as His instrument my labor cannot become an obstacle to contemplation, even though it may temporarily so occupy my mind that I cannot engage in it while I am actually doing my job. Yet my work itself will purify and pacify my mind and dispose me for contemplation.

Unnatural, frantic, anxious work, work done under pressure of greed or fear or any other inordinate passion, cannot properly speaking be dedicated to God, because God never wills such work directly. He may permit that through no fault we may have to work madly and distractedly, due to our sins, and to the sins of the society in which we live. In that case we must tolerate it and make the best of what we cannot avoid. But let us not be blind to the distinction between sound, healthy work and unnatural toil.

In any case, we should always seek to conform to the *logos* or truth of the duty before us, the work to be done, or our own God-given nature. Contemplative obedience and abandonment to the will of God can never mean a cultivated indifference to the natural values implanted by Him in human life and work. Insensitivity must not be confused with detachment. The contemplative must certainly be detached, but he can never allow himself to become insensible to true human values, whether in society, in other men, or in himself. If he does so, then his contemplation stands condemned as vitiated in its very root.

CONTEMPORARY SCHOLARSHIP

My selections for this section represent both historical and theological approaches. Historical studies, as indicated in chapter 3, describe and explain the development of religious traditions. Some historians also seek to evaluate traditions, although evaluation always runs the risk of compromising objectivity. Theological studies stand on the boundary between the academic study of religions as found in secular universities and the insiders' study of their own religious traditions. They combine the commitment of an insider with the careful, critical scholarship of an outsider.

The following selections rely heavily on careful historical scholarship. However, they also engage in theological assessment. Both provide interesting examples of the interplay of historical and theological concerns.

11.6 THE ORTHODOX CHURCH

We have had occasion to mention the Eastern Orthodox Church and to look at some of its sources. Here we take a closer look through the eyes of Ernst Benz (1907–1978), a German professor of church history who, after the Second World War, founded the Ecumenical Seminar at the University of Marburg to encourage mutual study and dialogue between the Eastern and Western branches of Christianity.

The Byzantine Empire, or eastern Roman Empire, lasted for more than a thousand years after Constantine. Characteristic of Byzantine Christianity and other Eastern Orthodox traditions is a close association between the affairs of the church and the ruling regime. Scholars refer to this involvement of emperors (caesars) in the affairs of the church as "caesaropapism." Also characteristic of the Orthodox tradition is a deep and abiding commitment to the liturgical life of the church. The liturgies of the Orthodox traditions are among the most beautiful and inspiring rituals of worship found in any religious tradition.

Currently, there are fifteen self-governing churches in the Orthodox fold, including the four ancient patriarchates of Constantinople, Alexandria, Antioch, and Jerusalem. The Patriarch of Constantinople is called the Ecumenical Patriarch and is given primacy of honor within the Orthodox Church. However, he has no authority comparable to the Roman pope. Patriarchs also lead the Orthodox churches of Russia, Serbia, Georgia, Romania, and Bulgaria. Archbishops or metropolitans head the Orthodox churches of Greece, Cyprus, Albania, Poland, the former Czechoslovakia, and the United States.

In the selection below, Benz is particularly concerned to assess the strengths and weaknesses of Orthodoxy. He believes that Western Christians have misunderstood and underestimated Orthodoxy's spiritual resources. He is not unaware of problems, however, and he attempts to provide a balanced assessment.

ERNST BENZ

The Greatness and Weakness of Orthodoxy

READING QUESTIONS

1. What, according to Benz, are the strengths of the Orthodox Church?
2. What, according to Benz, are the weaknesses of the Orthodox Church?
3. How do you interpret Benz's claim that the Orthodox Church is itself the "Burning Bush"?

1. THE STRENGTH OF ORTHODOXY

Within contemporary Christendom, Orthodoxy shines with a light all its own. Especially impressive is the fact that it has preserved faithfully the catholicity of the primitive Church. This is true for all its vital functions.

Its liturgy is a wonderful repository of all the early Church's interpretations and practices of worship. Whatever the early Church and the Byzantine Church created in the way of liturgical drama, meditation and contemplation, in beauty of prayers and hymns, has

From Ernst Benz, *The Eastern Orthodox Church: Its Thought and Life*, translated from the German by Richard and Clara Winston (Garden City, N.Y.: Doubleday & Company, 1963), pp. 206–217. Reprinted by permission.

been integrated and retained in the Orthodox liturgy. Similarly the content of Scripture has been kept ever present in the form of generous readings from both the Old and the New Testaments at various prescribed times through the liturgical year. The entire historical tradition of the Church is constantly communicated to the members in readings from the lives of the great saints and mystics. The sermon has its fixed place in the sacramental service; originally it came immediately after the reading of the Gospel text in the service for cate-chumens, but nowadays it frequently comes elsewhere —for example, after Communion. Verbal service and sacramental service are meaningfully interlocked so that total separation of them, such as has occurred in West-ern Reformed churches, can never occur. The full doc-trine of the early Church, as it was defined by the seven ecumenical councils, is immediate and vital in the liturgy, and also in the hymn of worship that elaborates the fun-damental ideas of both Orthodox and lay prayer. Here there is no divorce between liturgy and theology, wor-ship and dogma.

This Church has clung to the original consciousness of universality and catholicity. Its sense of itself as the one holy, ecumenical and apostolic Church is based not upon a judicial idea, but upon the consciousness of rep-resenting the Mystical Body of Christ. According to the Orthodox outlook, the celestial and the earthly Church, and the Church of the dead, belong indissolubly to-gether. In taking part in the liturgy the earthly Church is reminded that it belongs to the higher Church. In the liturgy the earthly congregation experiences the pres-ence of the angels, patriarchs, prophets, apostles, mar-tyrs, saints and all the redeemed; in the sacrament of the Eucharist it experiences the Presence of its Lord. Within the Mystical Body there takes place a unique communication and correlation: within that communion the gifts of the Holy Spirit—the power to forgive sins, to transmit salvation, to suffer by proxy for one another, and the power of intercession—become effective. And these powers extend down to the domain of the dead, for God is "a Lord of the living, not the dead."

In this way the Church has preserved the early Chris-tian combination of genuine personalism, of apprecia-tion for the uniqueness and singularity of the individual, along with the early Christian sense of communion. But the catholicity of the Orthodox Church is not in any way synonymous with uniformity. Thanks to its principle of letting every people possess the gospel, liturgy and doc-trine in its own language, Orthodoxy has been able to adapt to the natural national differences within mankind. The broad framework of Orthodoxy has been able to accommodate a wealth of ecclesiastical traditions. The result has been that the Orthodox Church has shown itself as an extraordinarily creative force. It has exerted great religious, social and ethical influence upon the cultures of Orthodox nations and taken a leading part in the intellectual and political development of those na-tions. This function of the Orthodox Church has been especially significant during the periods in which the political existence of Orthodox nations was threatened or destroyed.

Orthodoxy's unity within variety has been sustained by a unified canon of the New and Old Testaments, by a unified episcopal organization based on apostolic suc-cession, by a unified liturgy that is the same in all lan-guages, and by unity of doctrine and dogmatic tradition.

The durability of the Orthodox Church is all the more remarkable in that it has been exposed to enor-mous historical disasters, to persecutions of all kinds, es-pecially from Islam; in great stretches of its former do-minions, Orthodoxy has been completely exterminated. Nevertheless it has adhered with the greatest loyalty, down to the present day, to the early Church's liturgical and dogmatic heritage.

This heritage is not at all a museum piece as has of-ten been asserted. On the contrary, it is a living force capable of development. In a certain sense the great-ness of Orthodoxy rests on the very fact that the doc-trine is not so carefully defined down to details, is not so strictly regulated by canons. Orthodoxy's system is by no means closed; it is still full of potential. The char-ismatic life of Orthodoxy has not been confined within sets of legal and institutional forms. There is a signifi-cant degree of intellectual mobility, even in theology; thus, teachers of theology are frequently laymen rather than ordained priests. Alongside the offices of deacon, priest and bishop, the Church has from the beginning left room for the charismatic office of the teacher— *didaskalos.*

A further essential trait of the Orthodox Church is Christian universalism. This manifests itself in Ortho-doxy's view of the cosmos as well as its view of history. Western Christianity has more or less underplayed the question of a Christian natural philosophy. The Eastern Church, on the other hand, has endeavored to frame its Christian interpretation of creation in an unending se-ries of sketches for a Christian cosmology and natural philosophy. It views the process of redemption not only as an event that has taken place for the benefit of man, within the framework of human history, but also as a cosmic event in which the evolution of the entire uni-verse is included. Anthropology, cosmology and the doc-trine of salvation are indissolubly interconnected. Ac-cording to the Orthodox theory, the fall of man carried along the entire universe into rebellion against God, exposing everything to the powers of sin and death. Similarly, the incarnation of God in Jesus Christ and his resurrection likewise had cosmic effects. The "whole of creation" participated in the salvation brought by Christ, and all creatures yearn for the day of redemption along with man. Thus, at the end of time, when salvation is fulfilled, the old earth and the old heaven will be transformed along with man into a new earth and a new heaven. The reshaping of creation will involve the entire universe.

This universalism is also magnificently present in the Church's interpretation of redemption. It does not restrict the effects of divine redemption to the narrow confines traditionally promised by the Old Testament. According to the Orthodox Church, it is not only the Chosen People, but all the peoples of the globe who are involved in the story of man's redemption. The universalism of Orthodox thought is based upon the doctrine of the Logos. Orthodox theologians grant that the divine Logos spoke chiefly through the voices of the Old Testament prophets before the Incarnation, but there are evidences of his presence among other peoples. Both Clement of Alexandria and Origen pointed out that traces of the divine Logos could also be found in Greek, Indian, Egyptian and Persian philosophy. Thus all of mankind has been from the beginning included in the history of redemption, a history whose culmination and fulfillment is to be found in Jesus Christ.

Another element making for the greatness of Orthodoxy is its unwavering emphasis on the idea of God's beauty. Its prayers and hymns have never ceased to praise the beauty of God. This picture of God does not accord with the picture of a wrathful God of justice and predestination as has been painted by Occidental theology. It can only be tenable if paired with a universalism that sees Christ as the perfector of the cosmos and of salvation, as the conqueror not only of sin but also of physical annihilation, as the victor over death and the demonic powers of the entire cosmos.

In consequence, Orthodoxy has preserved the original mood of the Christian fellowships, the *chara*—rejoicing and jubilation—which the New Testament mentions as the characteristic spirit of the first Christian fellowship. This rejoicing has remained the fundamental mood of divine service in the Orthodox Church, especially of the Eucharistic service: joy in union with the living Lord; jubilation that the powers of sin and death have been overcome, the demons defeated, and that the reign of Satan has already been shattered. Its basic assumption is that at bottom evil is already overcome, that to the reborn the new eon of life in God, of glory in

God and the beauty of God, the life of new creatures in a new cosmos, has already dawned.

2. THE WEAKNESSES OF ORTHODOXY

The validity of the Orthodox Church has always depended on its maintaining an equilibrium among the various vital spheres on which it touches. Whenever that equilibrium has been upset the Orthodox Church has, historically, been exposed to four dangers.

Establishment

The first danger is inherent in the nature of the Church as an "established" church. Because of this, any displacement of the equilibrium between state and Church in favor of the state will have unfortunate results. True, Orthodox doctrine upholds the ideal of "harmony" or "symphony" between state and Church. But in the history of Orthodoxy the balance has shifted, time and time again, to the point at which the state outweighs the Church. In Orthodox countries the Church is constantly in danger of losing its internal freedom to the state. This has indeed happened repeatedly, especially in Russia. Even today the tradition of the Russian established Church continues to operate. Although the Russian Church today lives in an atheistic state, whose constitution proclaims the complete separation of Church and state, the old tradition of the establishment comes to the fore again and again, and the hierarchy permits itself to be used as an instrument of the Soviet Union's internal and foreign policy.

On the whole Orthodoxy's relation to the state has had unfortunate consequences; the Church has suffered from the union. The state has been led to influence excessively the inner life and organization of the Church, employing for this purpose methods inappropriate to the nature of the Church. It has adapted Christianity to the aims and advantages of the state. The Church has been seduced into using the political and police powers of the state when it should have employed the means peculiar to its own nature as a spiritual institution. All this gave rise to the suspicion, which having once struck root was hard to dislodge, that the Church's basic aim was something other than giving man, through the gospel, faith and the freedom of the children of God. The most pernicious effect, however, was this: the existence of an established Church made the gospel a law for those who did not believe in it. This was alienating Christianity from its true nature, which is to be a law only for those who are reborn in God.

Nationalism (Phyletism)

The second danger lay in a displacement of the equilibrium between the ecumenical and the nationalistic spirit of the Orthodox Church in favor of nationalism. This danger of nationalism was already implicit in the peculiar structure of Orthodoxy which permitted each nation its own language, constitution and ecclesiastical autonomy. Thus the development of the Church was intimately connected with the development of state and nation in the history of Russia, and above all in the history of the Balkan peoples.

We have already seen that the attempt by the Bulgarian Church to free itself from the ecumenical patriarchate of Constantinople and to set up its own autocephalous national church, was branded as a heresy —"phyletism"—by the Greek patriarch. In point of fact phyletism is a latent heresy that has constantly threatened the entire Orthodox world. Modern Orthodox efforts to achieve closer ties among the member churches have only revealed that national egoism is stronger than the consciousness of membership in a universal church. Even among the emigrant churches with their ecumenically minded world organizations, such as Syndesmos, a league of Orthodox youth organizations, national tensions are forever asserting themselves. Grave difficulties crop up in any collaboration among Greeks, Arabs and Slavs. And in Syria, Palestine and Egypt, joint work between the Greek and Arab or Coptic portions of the Church has been impeded by rivalries for spiritual and practical leadership within the Church. Too frequently Orthodoxy failed to prove itself a bond of spiritual unity sufficiently strong to overcome the nationalistic quarrels among the Balkan peoples. The Orthodox Church has never been able to prevent these conflicts from precipitating terrible carnage. The emigrant churchs, too, are rent by nationalistic disputes. To the outsider they present a painful picture of nationalistic and political dissensions that make a mockery of the ecumenical claims of Orthodoxy.

Independence in the Liturgy

The third peril lies in a displacement of the equilibrium between sacrament and social work accompanied by propagation of the faith, in favor of sacrament. This might be termed the danger of liturgical isolationism. When the liturgical and sacramental elements become preponderant, the liturgy can easily become a shell into which the Church withdraws like a turtle, losing all contact with living reality. This danger of liturgical isolationism is inherent in the very nature of Orthodoxy.

Political conditions, however, have intensified this tendency. The holders of political power have always been only too pleased when the Church confined itself to its liturgical, sacramental functions and withdrew from its other obligation, such as propagating the faith by active preaching, or seeking the realization of Christian ethics within the body politic. The Orthodox tsars, emperors and kings, as well as their present atheistic successors, have as a rule encouraged the liturgical self-isolation of the Church. In this way they hoped to render the Church innocuous and to divert it from its further purpose of shaping the world along Christian lines.

This bent has been furthered by the fact that most Orthodox churches were for centuries forced to lead at best a tolerated life under rulers and governments of alien faiths. Under the dominion of Mongols, Arabs and Turks the various Orthodox churches of Russia and the Near and Middle East, have in fact crawled back into their liturgical shell and have necessarily renounced outward activity. It is therefore not surprising that the Orthodox Church in Russia today, with its history of centuries of such self-isolation under non-Christian governments, under Bolshevism has once again taken refuge in an attitude of liturgical isolationism. This position has one great virtue: it protects Orthodoxy in a remarkable manner against the intrusion of non-Christian influences into its innermost realm of liturgy. But on the other hand this long-standing attitude of self-isolation can easily become a condition of permanent paralysis.

Renunciation of the "World"

In saying this we have already forecast the fourth danger: the displacement of equilibrium between transcendentalism and Christianity's task of renewing the world, in favor of transcendentalism. In divine worship the Orthodox Christian experiences an encounter with the celestial Church, with the kingdom of heaven. Out of this encounter grace, forgiveness, hope and salvation pour down upon him. Under the pressure of political events the Orthodox believer manifests a tendency to excessive otherworldliness that keeps him from engaging in the Christian's specific task of being a "co-worker of God" who, as the Apostle Paul says, will shape the world in the spirit of Christ. Here again the tendency to renounce both social activity and the cultural fulfillment of the Church is reinforced. Significantly enough, the kind of Christian mysticism Eastern Orthodoxy has produced tends to make the world and even fellowmen vanish from the gaze of the believer. There is no neighbor left to love; there remains only the inner meeting between the self and the transcendental, in which ultimately even the self is submerged and disappears. Thus Orthodoxy has often all too readily excused itself from the task of shaping the world in a Christian sense and has consoled itself with the thought that in any case this world will remain "of evil" until Judgment Day. Most of the social movements in Russian politics have come not from Orthodox believers, but from opponents of the Church and religion —in contrast to the Anglo-Saxon countries, where conscious Christians—especially those belonging to free churches—have for the most part been in the forefront of all the movements for social betterment.

3. CAN THESE WEAKNESSES BE OVERCOME?

These weaknesses, however, can be overcome. Orthodoxy contains within itself the spiritual strength to correct these disequilibriums. But that is not entirely a matter of free choice. The restoration of the equilibrium between state and Church in most cases—and certainly in the Soviet Union—depends almost exclusively upon the attitude of the state, that is, upon its readiness to permit the Church a fair degree of activity in public life. The history of Orthodoxy shows that a responsible leadership of the Church can go far in reinvigorating the social dynamism of the Church even after long paralysis —provided such a leadership keeps the end in view, namely, a Christian reshaping of the world.

The evils of nationalism can likewise be overcome. Here, too, the history of the Orthodox Church shows that the ecumenical idea can form the basis for genuine collaboration among national churches extremely different in habits and languages. The modern ecumenical movement whose outlines we have traced has certainly brought about a reawakening of the feeling of identity among various national Orthodox churches. It has brought about a return of the original ecumenical consciousness of Orthodoxy, a rediscovery of Orthodoxy's "internal universalism."

The danger of liturgical isolationism, too, can be conquered. The liturgy does not necessarily have to drive the Church into self-isolation. On the contrary, it can serve the Church as the source of a fresh access of spirit and vitality. The liturgy contains within itself forces that could revive the theology and the mysticism of the Church and could lead to the sanctification and Christian shaping of all of life. It can also spur a revival of preaching. For it is significant that wherever in the world violent repression has receded and Orthodox revival movements have arisen, these movements have

taken their inspiration from the liturgy and have looked to it for the source of their vitality.

We all know the biblical story of Moses in the wilderness and how he saw a bush that "was burning, yet it was not consumed" (Ex. 3:2). And "the angel of the Lord appeared to him in a flame of fire out of the midst of a bush." When he went up to it "God called to him out of the bush. . . . 'Do not come near; put off your shoes from your feet, for the place on which you are standing is holy ground.'"

Orthodoxy has incorporated into its liturgy the various typological interpretations that the great ascetics have given to this scene. Orthodoxy sees in it three mysteries:

The mystery of the Holy Trinity:

"As Thou hast appeared to Moses in the thornbush in the form of fire, Thou wast called angel, Word of the Father, who revealedst Thy coming to us, whereby Thou plainly proclaimedst to all men the tripersonal power of the one Deity."

The mystery of the Incarnation:

"As the Mysteries tell us, Moses foresaw in holy vision Thine image: the thornbush not burning in the fire, O Virgin, O sublime one beyond all reproach. For the Maker, dwelling in Thee, did not burn Thee who art elevated above all things made, Bride of God."

The mystery of the Mother of God:

"Thou wert imaged long ago by the thornbush on Sinai, which did not burn, O Virgin, in the touch of the fire. For as a Virgin thou didst bear. And exceeding all sense thou, Mother-Virgin, hast remained Virgin."

But in the deepest sense the Orthodox Church itself —sprung from the mystery of the Incarnation and preserving that mystery in itself, sprouting in the wilderness as the Church of ascetics, ravaged by the sandstorms of persecution, harassed by enemies of the faith and hostile fellows of the same faith, parched by immeasurable suffering and by inner and outer temptations, but yet unconsumed; burning with the fire of the Holy Spirit, aglow with the love of God, irradiated by the nuptial joy of the heavenly feast, illumined by the all-transfiguring power of the resurrected Lord—the Orthodox Church itself is

THE BURNING BUSH.

11.7 AFRICAN AMERICAN WOMEN AND CHRISTIAN REDEMPTION

Christianity has always been concerned with liberation and freedom. The ring of freedom sounds throughout the Bible from the exodus of the Jews from slavery in Egypt to the freedom from suffering Jesus offered the poor and others in need.

In the twentieth century, the Christian message of freedom has been reformulated in terms of various types of liberation theologics. These theologies began in South America as Roman Catholic theologians, appalled by the misery of the poor and the role the institutional church had played in helping the rich keep the poor oppressed, called for a new Christian commitment to liberating not just souls from sin but the whole person, body and soul, from the bondage of poverty and oppression.

The ideas of Karl Marx (1818–1883) also played an important role in the development of Latin American liberation theology. At first it may seem strange to discover a positive connection between atheistic Marxism and theistic Christianity. However, Marxism provided Christian thinkers with important analytic tools for uncovering the power structures that encourage and support economic exploitation. The Marxist concerns for social justice and social activism meshed nicely with the same concerns liberation theologians found in the message of the prophets and of Jesus.

This message of liberation echoed throughout the world, and oppressed peoples heeded its call. In North America, various kinds of Christian liberation movements have had a deep impact on the culture. Martin Luther King Jr. used the Christian message of hope and freedom along with Gandhi's message of nonviolence (see Reading 6.5.1) in his fight to end racial segregation. Although Marxist thought plays less of a role in the liberation theologies of North America than in those of Latin America, Christian churches are heavily involved in the fight against poverty and the fight for economic justice among the poor. Also, Christian churches have played and continue to play a role in women's liberation movements, working for equal opportunity for women both in and outside the church.

Delores S. Williams, author of our last selection, is a professor of theology and culture at Union Theological Seminary in New York. She argues that the experiences of black women require a rethinking of Christian views of redemption. Notice how her argument employs both historical and theological analyses. She reminds us that people can and have used Christianity to foster both liberation and oppression.

❧

DELORES S. WILLIAMS

Black Women's Surrogacy Experience

READING QUESTIONS

1. What are the two faces of surrogacy?
2. What are the ransom, satisfaction, substitution, and moral theories of atonement?
3. How does Williams interpret atonement?
4. What do you think about Williams's argument?

Often, African-American women in church and society have characterized their oppression as unique. Some black female scholars define this uniqueness on the basis of the interfacing of racial, class, and gender oppression in the experience of black women. However, this interfacing of oppressions is not unique to black women's experience. Jewish, Hispanic, Asian, and other women of color in America can also experience this reality. My exploration of black women's sources has revealed a heretofore undetected structure of domination that has been operative in African-American women's lives since slavery. This structure of domination is surrogacy, and it gives black women's oppression its unique character—and raises challenging questions about the way redemption is imaged in a Christian context.

TWO FACES OF SURROGACY

On the basis of African-American women's sources it is possible to identify two kinds of surrogacy that have given rise to the unique character of black women's oppression. They are *coerced surrogacy* and *voluntary sur-*

From Delores S. Williams, "Black Women's Surrogacy Experience and the Christian Notion of Redemption," in *After Patriarchy: Feminist Transformations of the World Religions*, edited by Paula M Cooey et al. (Maryknoll, N.Y.: Orbis Books, 1991), pp. 1–13. Reprinted by permission. Works Cited omitted.

rogacy. Coerced surrogacy, belonging to the pre–Civil War period, was a forced condition in which people and systems more powerful than black women and black people forced black women to function in roles that ordinarily would have been filled by someone else. For example, black female slaves were forced to substitute for the slave owner's wife in nurturing roles involving white children. Black women were forced to take the place of men in work roles that, according to the larger society's understanding of male and female roles, belonged to men. Frederick Law Olmstead, a Northern architect writing in the nineteenth century, said he "stood for a long time watching slave women repair a road on a South Carolina Plantation." During the antebellum period this coerced surrogacy was legally supported in the ownership rights by which slave masters controlled their property, for example, black women. Slave women could not exercise the choice of refusing the surrogacy role.

After emancipation the coercion associated with antebellum surrogacy was replaced by social pressures that influenced black women to continue to fill some surrogacy roles. But surrogacy in the antebellum period differed from surrogacy in the postbellum period. The difference was that black women, after emancipation, could exercise the choice of refusing the surrogate role. Because of this element of choice, postbellum surrogacy can be referred to as voluntary surrogacy, even though social pressures influenced the choices black women made as they adjusted to life in a "free" world.

A closer look at these two modes of surrogacy in the two different periods (antebellum and postbellum) provides an in-depth view of the differences between the two modes.

COERCED SURROGACY AND ANTEBELLUM REALITIES

In the period before the Civil War coerced surrogacy roles involving black women were in the areas of nurturance, field labor, and sexuality.

The mammy role was the direct result of the demands slavocracy made upon black women's nurturing capacities. Standing in the place of the slave owner's wife, mammy nurtured the entire white family. A long and respected tradition among many southern whites, mammy was an empowered (but not autonomous) house slave who was given considerable authority by her owners. According to the existing scattered reports of mammies and how the tradition operated, we know many southerners thought "mammy could do anything, and do it better than anyone else. Because of her expertise in all domestic matters, she was the premier house ser-

vant and all others were her subordinates." . . . According to [Deborah] White, Eliza Riply, a southern white woman who received nurture from a mammy, remembers her as

> a "supernumerary" who, after the children grew up . . . managed the whole big and mixed household. In her [Eliza Riply's] father's house, everyone was made to understand that . . . all applications were to go through Mammy Charlotte. Nobody thought to go to the judge or his wife for anything.

The testimony of ex-slaves themselves also attests to the value and power of mammies in the slaveholders' household. Drucella Martin remembers "that her mother was in full charge of the house and all marse children." Katherine Epps of Alabama said that her mother "worked in the Big House, 'aspinnin and 'anussin de white chillun." Epps also claimed that the slave owner's wife was so fond of her mother "that when she learned . . . the overseer had whipped the woman whom everyone called 'Mammy,' she dismissed him and gave him until sundown to remove himself and his family from the plantation."

Mammy was not always so well-treated, however. Frederick Douglass tells of his grandmother, who was mammy to a white family. When she became too old and frail to work, "they took her to the woods, built her a little hut with a mud chimney, and left her there to support and care for herself." As Douglass put it, "they turned her out to die." And there is the awful fate of one mammy told by ex-slave Jacob Stroyer. This mammy was named Aunt Betty. "She nursed her master through infancy, lived to see him become a drunk, and then became his victim when, during one of his drunken rampages, he took his shotgun and killed her." Nevertheless, the mammy role was probably the most powerful and authoritative one slave women could fill. Though slave women in their coerced roles as mammies were often abused, they were also empowered.[1]

This was not the case for slave women laboring beyond the "big house," that is, the slave owner's dwelling. In the area of field labor, black women were forced into work usually associated with male roles.[2] Feminist scholar Bell Hooks claims that on large plantations "Women plowed, planted . . . harvested crops. On some plantations black women worked longer hours in the fields than black men." What this amounted to, in terms of coerced surrogacy, was black female energy substituting for male energy. This resulted in what Hooks refers to as the masculinization of the black female.

In their autobiographies some ex-slave women describe the masculine work roles black women were forced to fill. Bethany Veney tells of helping her cruel slave owner haul logs, drive out hogs, and set posts into the ground for fences. Louisa Picquet told of slave women who drove ox wagons, tended mills, and plowed just like men. Another ex-slave Mary Prince tells of a slave woman who drove cattle, tended sheep and did general farming work in the fields.

Unlike the mammy role of the female house slave, the masculinized roles of the female field slave did not empower black women in the slave structure to the extent that mammies were empowered. In the fields the greatest amount of power a slave could hold was in the position of slave driver or overseer. Usually, only males could ascend to these roles. Thus the driver was a male slave. Though a few black males served as overseers, this role was usually filled by white men of lower social class than the slave owner. Females who filled the masculinized roles in the fields were less respected than mammies and drivers. Field women were not often given recognition for their service, seldom realized the endearment of the white folks as did some of the mammies, got worse food and clothing, and often received more brutal punishment. These masculinized female field slaves were thought to be of a lower class than the female house slaves, who usually did "women's work" consisting of cleaning, spinning, cooking, sewing, and tending to the children.

More than in the areas of nurturance and field labor, coerced surrogacy in the area of sexuality was threatening to slave women's sense of self-worth. This is the area in which slave women were forced to stand in the place of white women to provide sexual pleasure for white male slave owners. The Victorian ideal of true womanhood (for Anglo-American women) supported a consciousness which, in the area of sexual relations, imagined sex between free white men and their wives to be for the purpose of procreation rather than for pleasure. Many white males turned to slave women for sexual pleasure and forced these women to fulfill needs which, according to racist ideology concerning male-female relations, should have been fulfilled by white women.

In her narrative *Incidents in the Life of a Slave Girl*, Linda Brent presents a vivid description of her slave owner Dr. Flint, who tried to force her into one of these illicit female slave/slave master sexual liaisons. Brent escaped his advances by fleeing from his house and hiding for seven years in a crawl space in the roof of her grandmother's home. The octoroon slave woman Louisa Picquet was not as fortunate as Linda Brent. Louisa was purchased by a Mr. Williams when she was about fourteen years old. He forced her into sexual relations with him. From these relations four children issued. Another slave woman, Cynthia, was purchased by a slave trader who told her she would either accompany him home and become his "housekeeper" or he would sell her as a field worker to one of the worst plantations on the Mississippi River. Cynthia thus became the slave trader's mistress and housekeeper.

There was in the antebellum South a kind of institutionalizing of female slave/slave master sexual liaisons that was maintained through the "fancy trade." This was a special kind of slave trading involving the sale of what were thought to be beautiful black women for the exclusive purpose of becoming mistresses of wealthy slave owners. Though New Orleans seems to have been the center of this trade, it also flourished in Charleston and Columbia, South Carolina; St. Louis, Missouri; and Lexington and Richmond, Virginia. The famous octoroon balls that occurred in New Orleans allowed rich white men to meet and purchase these black women who became their mistresses and often bore children by these slave owners.

Beyond this special kind of arrangement, slave owners also frequented the slave quarters and established sexual relations with any female slave they chose. The slave woman in either kind of arrangement had no power to refuse this coerced surrogacy in which she stood in the place of the white woman. Sometimes these slave women hoped for (and were promised) their freedom through sexual liaisons with the slave master. But more often than not their expectations were futile, and they were "sold off to plantations where . . . [they] shared the misery of all slaves."

All three forms of coerced surrogacy illustrate a unique kind of oppression only black women experienced in the slavocracy. Only black women were mammies. Only black women were permanently assigned to field labor. Only black women permanently lost control of their bodies to the lust of white men. During slavery, black women were bound to a system that had respect for neither their bodies, their dignity, their labor, nor their motherhood except as it was put to the service of securing the well-being of ruling class white families. In North America fierce and violent struggle had to afflict the entire nation before southern slave women could experience a measure of relief from coerced surrogacy roles.

VOLUNTARY SURROGACY AND POSTBELLUM REALITIES

When the American Civil War ended and the master-slave relation was officially terminated in the South, black people tried to determine for whom or what black women *would not* stand in place. They were especially anxious to relieve black women those coerced surrogacy roles related to field work and to black women's sexuality involving black female/white male sexual liaisons. [According to Paula Giddings,] ex-slave women themselves are reported to have said "they never mean to do any outdoor work, that white men support their wives and the [black women] mean that their husbands shall support them." Black men were just as anxious for black women to quit the fields. According to historians Carter G. Woodson and Lorenzo Greene, "The Negro male when he worked for wages . . . tended to imitate the whites by keeping his wife and daughters at home."

Of even greater concern to black males and females were their efforts to terminate the forced sexual relations between black women and white men that existed during slavery. Inasmuch as marriage between African-American women and men became legal after freedom and droves of black women and men came to official locations to be married, sexual liaisons between white men and black women could be curtailed, although white men (without regard for black marriage) still took advantage of some black women. Bell Hooks points out that after black reconstruction (1867–77) "black women were often . . . [pressured] into sexual liaisons with white employers who would threaten to fire them unless they capitulated to sexual demands."

Nevertheless, there was not nearly as much sexual activity between black women and white men after slavery because black women themselves could refuse to substitute for white women in providing sexual pleasure for white males. Nancy White, a contemporary black female domestic worker, testified about refusing this role of playmate to white male employers:

I've had to ask some [white male employers] to keep their hands off me and I've had to just give up some jobs if they got too hot behind me. . . . I have lost some money that way, but that's all right. When you lose control of your body, you have just about lost all you have in this world.

Nancy White makes it clear that some white female employers approved of black women standing in their places to provide sexual favors for their husbands. White says:

One day that woman [her white female employer] told me that she wouldn't be mad if I let her husband treat me the same way he treated her. I told her I would be mad . . . if he tried to treat me like I was as married to him as she was.

Nancy White goes on to describe her method of declining this surrogate role her female and male employers wanted to assign her. Says White: "I had to threaten that devil [the white male employer] with a pot of hot grease to get him to keep his hands to hisself."

While black women and men did realize a small measure of success in determining the surrogate roles black women would not fill after emancipation, certain social and economic realities limited black women's power to choose full exemption from all surrogacy roles. Poverty and the nature of the work available, especially to southern black families, demanded black women's participation in some of the most strenuous areas of the work force. There was also the attempt among newly freed black families to adopt some of the values of the people they took to be "quality white folk" during slavery.[3] This meant that efforts were made to influence black women to choose to continue in two of the surrogate roles they had filled during slavery: substituting female power and energy for male power and energy, and acting in mammy capacities.

After emancipation black women chose to substitute their energy and power for male energy and power in the area of farm labor. Greene and Woodson tell of urban Negro male laborers in 1901 who saved money and invested in farms. "It was not uncommon . . . to see Negro mechanics owning well-kept farms, which were cared for chiefly by wives and families." The United States Census of 1910 reported that 967,837 black women were farm laborer's and 79,309 were farmers. Also in 1910 Addie W. Hunton reported that

More than half of the 2,000,000 wage earning women of the [black] race are engaged in agriculture from its roughest and rudest form to its highest and most attractive form. . . . The 15,792,579 acres owned and cultivated by Negroes, which with buildings and equipment and rented farm lands reach a valuation approaching a billion dollars, represent not only the hardihood and perseverance of the Negro man but the power for physical and mental endurance of the woman working by his side. Many of the farms owned by colored men are managed entirely by the women of the family while these men give themselves to other employment.

It was, however, the surrogate role of mammy that some black males and white people consciously tried to perpetuate into the future beyond slavery and reconstruction. In Athens, Georgia, in the early twentieth century, Samuel Harris, the black principal of Athens Colored High School, dreamed up the idea of starting the Black Mammy Memorial Institute in that city. With the help of prominent white citizens this institute was chartered on September 19, 1910, and was authorized to operate for twenty years. According to a brochure published by the Black Mammy Memorial Association, the institute was to be

> a memorial where men and women learn . . . how to work and to love their work; where the mantle of the "Old Black Mammy" may fall on those who go forth to serve; where the story of these women will be told to the generations that come and go; where better mothers for homes will be trained; a building from which those who go forth in life may speak louder in their works than their words. . . . The MONUMENTAL INDUSTRIAL INSTITUTE to the OLD BLACK MAMMY of the South will be devoted to the industrial and moral training of young Negro men and women. The work that is to receive special emphasis is the training of young women in Domestic Art.

Obviously the prominent white citizens wanted to perpetuate the mammy roles so that the comfort of the white family could be assured by a type of black female servant who (after slavery) was properly trained in the skills of nurturing, supporting, and caring about the well-being of white children. Not so obvious, but probable, is the suggestion that to the black man Mr. Harris, black women trained in the mammy skills could learn to organize and manage the black households in the same way that the slave owners' households were organized and managed. This meant that the black family had to become more patriarchal in its structure and values in order to resemble the slave owners' households.

Mammy had a variety of skills that could accommodate this process. She was skillful at exerting authority in the household while being careful not to offend or usurp the power of the patriarchal authority figures: the slave master and his wife. Mammy was skilled in about every form of what was thought of as women's work: sewing, spinning, cooking, cleaning, tending to children, and so on. Hence she could train female children in this work. According to Deborah Gray White, mammy was often the advisor of the slave master in business matters. With regard to the quality of relationships in the master's family, she knew how to be a diplomat and a peacemaker who often healed relations that had gone awry. The mammy skills could promote and support black males as they became the patriarchal heads of the black household after slavery. And the black family could therefore resemble the patriarchal model of family sanctioned in mainline American society.

One could also suggest that the institution of Mothers of the Church, which developed in some black churches after emancipation, has kinship with the mammy tradition. Like the antebellum mammy, a mother of the church exerts considerable authority in the church family. But more often than not she uses her power in such a way that it does not challenge the power and authority of the patriarchal head of the church, usually a male preacher. She is sometimes called upon to be a healer of relationships within the congregation. She is well-versed in and knows how to pass along the church's highest values for living the Christian life. Her power and influence often extend beyond the church into her community because she has been empowered by one of the central authority agents of the community (the black church) to provide care and nurture for the children of God.

Black women's history of filling surrogacy roles has fed into negative stereotypes of black women that exist until this day. From the mammy tradition has emerged the image of black women as perpetual mother figures, religious, fat, asexual, loving children better than themselves, self-sacrificing, giving up self-concern for group advancement. The antebellum tradition of masculinizing black women through their work has given rise to the image of black women as unfeminine, physically strong, and having the capacity to bear considerably more pain than white women. These kinds of ideas helped create the notion of black women as superwomen. The sexual liaisons between white men and slave women created the image of the black woman as Jezebel, as one "governed almost entirely by her libido . . . the counterimage of the mid-nineteenth-century ideal of the Victorian lady" [according to White]. Hence the surrogacy roles black women have filled during slavery and beyond are exploitative. They rob African-American women of self-consciousness, self-care, and self-esteem, and put them in the service of other people's desires, tasks, and goals. This has serious implications for Christian theologians attempting to use black women's history as a source for constructive theology.

FROM BLACK WOMAN SURROGATE TO SURROGATE-JESUS

One of the results of focusing upon African-American women's historic experience with surrogacy is that it raises significant questions about the way many Christians, including black women, have been taught to image redemption. More often than not the theology in mainline Christian churches, including black ones, teaches believers that sinful humankind has been redeemed because Jesus died on the cross in the place of humans, thereby taking human sin upon himself. In this sense Jesus represents the ultimate surrogate figure standing in the place of someone else: sinful humankind. Surrogacy, attached to this divine personage, thus takes on an aura of the sacred. It is therefore altogether fitting and proper for black women to ask whether the image of a surrogate-God has salvific power for black women, or whether this image of redemption supports and reinforces the exploitation that has accompanied their experience with surrogacy. If black women accept this image of redemption, can they not also passively accept the exploitation surrogacy brings?

This essay recognizes that reflection upon these questions causes many complex theological issues to surface. For instance, there is the issue of the part God the Father played in determining the redemptive, surrogate role filled by Jesus, the Son. For black women there is also the question of whether Jesus on the cross represents coerced surrogacy (willed by the father) or voluntary surrogacy (chosen by the son) or both. At any rate, a major theological problem here is the place of the cross in any theology significantly informed by African-American women's experience with surrogacy. Even if one buys into Moltmann's notion of the cross as the meeting place of the will of God to give up the Son (coerced surrogacy?) and the will of the Son to give up himself (voluntary surrogacy?) so that "the spirit of abandonment and self-giving love" proceed from the cross "to raise up abandoned men," African-American women are still left with this question: Can there be salvific power in Christian images of oppression (for example, Jesus on the cross) meant to teach something about redemption?

Theologians since the time of Origen have been trying to make the Christian principle of atonement believable by shaping theories about it in the language and thought that people of a particular time understood and were grounded in. Thus most theories of atonement, classical and contemporary, are time-bound (as well as ideologically bound with patriarchy) and do not respond meaningfully to the questions of people living beyond the particular time period. For instance, Origen (183–253 C.E.), capitalizing on people's belief in devils and spirits, provided what Alan Richardson speaks of as a ransom theory, claiming that the death of Jesus on the cross was a ransom paid by God to the devil for the sins of humankind. This view of atonement declined when another age dawned. Thus Anselm emerged in the eleventh century and spoke of atonement using the chivalric language and sociopolitical thought of his time. He shaped a theory describing sin as the human way of dishonoring God. People owed honor to God just as peasants and squires owed honor and loyalty to the feudal overlord. However, men had no power to render satisfaction to God for their massive disloyalty to God through sin. According to the codes of chivalry in An-

selm's time, one atoned for a crime either by receiving punishment or by providing satisfaction to the injured person. Since God did not want to punish humans forever (which the sin deserved) and since humans had no means to render satisfaction to God's injured honor, the deity, Godself, made restitution for humanity. God satisfied God's own violated honor by sending the Son to earth in human form ultimately to die on the cross.

There were also the theories of atonement associated with Abelard (1079–1142). Since the church in Abelard's time put great stress upon the penitential life of believers, it was reasonable for Abelard to see Calvary as "the school of penitence of the human race, for there men of all ages and races have learned the depth and power of the love of God" [according to Richardson]. Often referred to as the moral theories of atonement, these emphasized God's love in the work of atonement and claimed that, when humans look upon the death of Jesus, they see the love of God manifested. The cross brings repentance to humankind and shows simultaneously God the Father's love and the suffering inflicted upon that love by human sin. The moral theories of atonement taught that the cross was "the most powerful moral influence in history, bringing to men that repentance which renders them able to be forgiven."

As the Renaissance approached and the medieval worldview collapsed, the Anselmian and Abelardian ways of understanding the atonement began to fade. The Renaissance was a time of great interest in the revival of ancient law. So it was reasonable to expect the reformers to work out their theories of atonement in legal terms grounded in the new political and legal thought of the sixteenth century. Thus Calvin and others spoke of the justice of God the judge, of the divine law of punishment that could not be ignored, and of the infinite character of human sin that deserved infinite harsh punishment. But, according to the Reformers, God is both just and merciful. Therefore, in infinite mercy God provided a substitute who would bear the punishment for human sin. Jesus Christ came to offer himself as a substitute for humans. He took their punishment upon himself. Thus the Reformers provided a substitution theory of atonement.

While these ransom, satisfaction, substitution, and moral theories of atonement may not be serviceable for providing an acceptable response to African-American women's questions about redemption and surrogacy, they do illustrate a serviceable practice for female theologians attempting today to respond to this question. That practice (as shown by the theologians above) was to use the language and sociopolitical thought of the time to render Christian principles understandable. This fits well the task of the black female theologian. For that task is to use the language and sociopolitical thought of black women's world to show them that their salvation does not depend upon any form of surrogacy made sacred by human understandings of God. This means using the language and thought of liberation to liberate redemption from the cross and to liberate the cross from the "sacred aura" put around it by existing patriarchal responses to the question of what Jesus' death represents. To find resources to accomplish this task, the black female theologian is led to the scriptures.

The synoptic gospels (more than Paul's letters) provide resources for constructing a Christian understanding of redemption that speaks meaningfully to black women, given their historic experience with surrogacy. Jesus' own words in Luke 4 and his ministry of healing the human body, mind, and spirit (described in Matthew, Mark, and Luke) suggest that Jesus did not come to redeem humans by showing them God's love "manifested" in the death of God's innocent child on a cross erected by cruel, imperialistic, patriarchal power. Rather, the spirit of God in Jesus came to show humans *life*—to show redemption through a perfect *ministerial* vision of righting relationships. A female-male inclusive vision, Jesus' ministry of righting relationships involved raising the dead (for example, those appearing to be lost from life), casting out demons (for example, ridding the mind of destructive forces prohibiting the flourishing of positive, peaceful life), and proclaiming the word of life that demanded the transformation of tradition so that life could be lived more abundantly. Jesus was quick to remind his disciples that humans were not made for the Sabbath; rather, the Sabbath was made for humans. God's gift to humans, through Jesus, was to invite them to participate in this ministerial vision ("whosoever will, let them come") of righting relations. The response to this invitation by human principalities and powers was the horrible deed that the cross represents—the evil of humankind trying to kill the ministerial vision of life in relation that Jesus brought to humanity. The resurrection does not depend upon the cross for life, for the cross only represents historical evil trying to defeat good. The resurrection of Jesus and the flourishing of God's spirit in the world as the result of resurrection, represents the life of the ministerial vision gaining victory over the evil attempt to kill it. Thus, to respond meaningfully to black women's historic experience of surrogacy-oppression, the theologian must show that redemption of humans can have nothing to do with any kind of surrogate role Jesus was reputed to have played in a bloody act that supposedly gained victory over sin and/or evil. Black women are intelligent people living in a technological world where nuclear bombs, defilement of the earth, racism, sexism, and economic injustices attest to the presence and power of evil in the world. Perhaps not many people today can believe that evil and sin were overcome by Jesus' death on the cross, that is, that Jesus took human sin upon himself and therefore saved humankind. Rather, it seems more intelligent to understand that redemption had to do with God, through Jesus, giving humankind new vision to see resources for positive, abundant relational life—a vision humankind did not have before. Hence, the kingdom of God theme in the ministerial vision of Jesus does not point to death; that is, it is not something one has to die to get to. Rather, the kingdom of God is a metaphor of hope God gives those attempting to right the relations between self and self, between self and others, between self and God as prescribed in the sermon on the mount and the golden rule.

Though space limitations here prohibit more extensive reconstruction of this Christian understanding of redemption (given black women's surrogacy experience), there are a few things that can be said about sin in this kind of reconstruction. The image of Jesus on the cross is the image of human sin in its most desecrated form. This execution destroyed the body but not before it mocked and defiled Jesus by publicly exposing his nakedness and private parts, by mocking the ministerial vision as they labeled him king of the Jews, by placing a crown of thorns upon his head mocking his dignity and the integrity of his divine mission. The cross thus becomes an image of defilement, a gross manifestation of collective human sin. Jesus, then, does not conquer sin through death on the cross. Rather, Jesus conquers the sin of temptation in the wilderness (Mt 4:1–11) by resistance—by resisting the temptation to value the material over the spiritual ("Man shall not live by bread alone"); by resisting death (not attempting suicide; "if you are the son of God, throw yourself down"); by resisting the greedy urge of monopolistic ownership ("He showed him all the kingdoms of the world and the glory of them; and he said to him, 'All these I will give you, if you will fall down and worship me'"). Jesus therefore conquered sin in life, not in death. In the wilderness he refused to allow evil forces to defile the balanced relation between the material and the spiritual, between life and death, between power and the exertion of it.

What this allows the black female theologian to show black women is that God did not intend the surrogacy roles they have been forced to perform. God did not intend the defilement of their bodies as white patriarchal power put them in the place of white women to provide sexual pleasure for white men during the slavocracy. This was rape. Rape is defilement, and defilement means wanton desecration. Worse, deeper and more wounding than alienation, the sin of defilement is the one of which today's technological world is most guilty. Nature—the land, the seas, the animals in the sea—are every day defiled by humans. Cultures such as Native American and African have been defiled by the onslaught of Western, patriarchal imperialism. The oceans are defiled by oil spills and human waste, destroying marine life. The rain forest is being defiled. The cross is a reminder of how humans have tried throughout history to destroy visions of righting relationships that involve transformation of tradition and transformation of social relations and arrangements sanctioned by the status quo. The resurrection of Jesus and the kingdom of God theme in Jesus' ministerial vision provide black women with the knowledge that God has, through Jesus, shown humankind how to live peacefully, productively, and abundantly in relationship. Humankind is therefore redeemed through Jesus' life and not through Jesus' death. There is nothing of God in the blood of the cross. God does not intend black women's surrogacy experience. Neither can Christian faith affirm such an idea. Jesus did not come to be a surrogate. Jesus came for life, to show humans a perfect vision of ministerial relation that humans had forgotten long ago. However, as Christians, black women cannot forget the cross. But neither can they glorify it. To do so is to make their exploitation sacred. To do so is to glorify sin.

NOTES

1. This is not to suggest that such empowerment led to autonomy for slave women. Quite to the contrary. Slave women, like slave men, were always subject to the control of the slave owners. And as historian Deborah Gray White's description of mammy reveals, the empowerment of mammy was also directly related to the attempt of pro-slavery advocates to provide an image of black women which proved that the institution of slavery was vital for molding some black women in accord with the maternal ideals of the Victorian understanding of true womanhood.

2. Some scholars estimate that about eighty percent of slave women worked in the fields. Twenty percent worked as house servants. See Robert Fogel and Stanley Engerman, *Time on the Cross* (Boston: Little, Brown and Co., 1974), pp. 38–58.

3. Historian Joel Williamson discusses this in relation to a process of acculturation he says existed among slaves and continued into and beyond the reconstruc-

tion. Williamson refers to the slaves as trying to "become more white."

KEY TERMS AND CONCEPTS

apologetics A type of theology that seeks to defend the truth of Christianity and provide arguments that might persuade nonbelievers to convert.

apostles Early followers of Jesus who took leadership roles in the church after his death. Defined in Acts 1 more narrowly as those who had followed Jesus and witnessed his resurrection.

baptism A Christian **sacrament** involving the use of water to symbolize the washing away of sin and the birth of a new person in Christ.

canonization Derived from the Greek word for rule or measure, it can refer to (1) the process by which certain writings become authoritative scripture or (2) the process that declares a person holy and makes him or her eligible to become a saint.

Christ Greek word used to translate the Hebrew word *Messiah* and applied to Jesus of Nazareth by early Christians.

Christology Theories about the nature of Christ.

christomimesis Means "imitation of Christ." This has become a spiritual goal for many Christians.

creed Derives from the Latin *credo* ("I believe") and refers to official teachings of the Christian Church approved by **ecumenical** councils of the church. The Nicene Creed is one example.

Eastern Orthodox One of the three main branches of Christianity that developed in the eastern Roman Empire.

ecumenical A movement to create greater unity and cooperation among various Christian groups. It derives from a Greek word for universal, and theologians use it to characterize the early councils of the church.

Ecumenical creeds Creeds, such as the Nicene Creed, adopted by the ecumenical councils of the early church, that is, councils with representatives from different Christian groups. Although these councils claimed to be universal in their representation, not all the different varieties of Christianity were represented.

eschatology Denotes the study of the end time (*eschaton*). The end time is usually associated with God's judgment, the messianic era, the resurrection of the dead, and the world or kingdom of God to come. Christians associate the *eschaton* with the Second Coming of Christ.

Eucharist Means "thanksgiving" in Greek and refers to the **sacrament** of the Lord's Supper or Holy Communion.

filioque Means "and the son" and was inserted into the Nicene Creed by the Latin Church but rejected by the Eastern Orthodox Church.

Gnosticism An early group of Christians holding diverse beliefs. Gnosticism is often sharply dualistic with respect to such notions as spirit and matter. Orthodox groups branded it heretical.

gospel Means "Good News" and is often applied to the first four books of the New Testament (the **synoptics** plus John).

grace Gifts given by God including salvation.

Great Schism Division of Christianity between the Roman Catholic Church and the Eastern Orthodox Church in 1054.

hesychasm A method of contemplation developed among Eastern Orthodox monks involving controlled breathing, special body postures, and the repetition of the Jesus Prayer: "Lord Jesus Christ, Son of God, have mercy upon me."

Holy Spirit (Ghost) one of the persons of the **Trinity** (along with Father and Son) who operates as a teacher and guide.

homoiousia **and** *homoousia* The first word mans "similar substance" and the second means "same substance." Arius favored the first wording to describe the relationship of the Son and God and Athanasius favored the second, which was eventually accepted by the Council of Nicaea.

logos Greek word meaning "word" and "reason." The Gospel of John uses it to represent Jesus' prehuman existence and the Johannine view of the incarnation.

Marcionism A second-century Christian movement led by Marcion that rejected the Old Testament, formulated one of the earliest canons, and distinguished between a god of hate and a god of love. it was eventually declared heretical.

modalist monarchianism A theory of the **Trinity** ascribed to Sabellius that claims there is one God manifested in three modes (Father, Son, and Holy Spirit). This view was rejected as heretical.

New Testament A collection of twenty-seven documents Christians recognize as scripture and which they added to a Greek edition of the Hebrew Bible.

Old Testament A collection of writings Christians recognize as scripture. It is nearly identical to the Jewish *Tanakh*.

Protestant Derives from "protest" and was used to name reformers like Martin Luther who protested the abuses they saw in Roman Catholicism. Now often used to name the third main branch of Christianity (along with Roman Catholicism and Eastern Orthodoxy).

Q (for *Quelle*) The name for a document (now lost) that some scholars believe was a very early collection of Jesus' sayings used by the **Gospel** writers.

Roman Catholic Means "universal" or "worldwide" and was adopted by the Latin, or Western, Church centered in Rome, hence the term Roman Catholic.

sacraments Defined in Christian theology as a "means of Grace." Among Protestants there are two: Baptism and Communion (Eucharist or Lord's Supper). Among Roman Catholics there are seven: Baptism, Penance, Confirmation, Eucharist (Mass), Marriage, Ordination, and Last Rites.

scholasticism The name for a kind of theology developed by Christian scholars at medieval universities that stressed careful critical analysis of theological and philosophical ideas.

secularization A social process that deemphasizes the importance of religion and spirituality. It claims that society should be free from ecclesiastical (church) control.

synoptic Gospels The Gospels called Matthew, Mark, and Luke, which are similar in content.

Trinity (tri-unity) The teaching approved at the Council of Nicea that states God is one substance in three persons (Father, Son, and Holy Spirit). This means that all three persons are totally and completely divine in substance, but distinct with respect to personhood. The Son and Holy Spirit are no less divine than the Father, but they are not the same persons as the Father.

SUGGESTIONS FOR FURTHER READING

Helm, Thomas E. *The Christian Religion: An Introduction.* Englewood Cliffs, N.J.: Prentice-Hall, 1991. Clearly explains Christian history and some of its key movements and ideas.

Tucker, Ruth A., and Walter L. Liefeld. *Daughters of the Church: Women and Ministry From New Testament Times to the Present.* Grand Rapids, Mich.: Academie Books, 1987. A history of the role women have played in the development of Christianity that challenges a number of popularly held assumptions.

Wiggins, James, and Robert S. Ellwood. *Christianity: A Cultural Perspective.* Englewood Cliffs, N.J.: Prentice-Hall, 1988. A clear exposition of the history of Christianity and the structure of Christian life.

Wilson, Brian. *Christianity.* Upper Saddle River, N.J.: Prentice-Hall, 1999. A brief overview of the history of Christianity with a helpful list of holy days and festivals along with an excellent beginning bibliography.

RESEARCH PROJECTS

1. Visit two different Christian worship services. If you belong to a Christian church, select two that are different from your own. Make a list of items ahead of time to guide your observations. Write a report comparing and contrasting the two worship services.

2. View the video series *From Jesus to Christ: The First Christians* (available from PBS) and write a critical review.

3. Research and write a paper comparing and contrasting Roman Catholic Christianity with Mormon Christianity. Deal particularly with their histories, main beliefs, and positions on contemporary social issues.

4. Research and write a paper on liberation theology. Explain what it is, how it developed, and its significance, as you see it, in the development of Christianity.

12

Islamic Ways of Being Religious

INTRODUCTION

One night in 610 a forty-year-old Arab was in a cave on Mount Hira near a city called Mecca in the western part of Arabia. He was holding a night vigil and thinking about his life, the ills of his society, and the turbulent times in which he lived, when he heard a voice, a voice like reverberating bells. The voice said, "Recite!" Startled and frightened, the man, whose name was Muhammad ibn Abdullah, stammered that he did not know what to say. Again the voice commanded him to recite, and again Muhammad replied that he did not know what to say. Finally the words came to him, "Recite in the name of your Lord who has created, Created man out of a germ-cell. Recite for your Lord is the Most Generous One Who has taught by the pen, Taught humans what they did not know" (Qur'an 96:1–5).

Muhammad ibn Abdullah, whose nickname was al-Amin (the trusted one), did not know what to make of this experience. Where did the voice come from? What did it mean? Was this an evil spirit speaking? Could it be a *jinn*? Perhaps he was going mad.

Islamic tradition tells us that Muhammad consulted with his wife, **Khadija,** who assured him he was not mad. She suggested they consult her cousin Waraqa ibn Qusayy, who was a Christian and, she thought, might know about such things since Christians had prophets. Waraqa told Muhammad that the voice had been "sent down" by God through an angel (identified as Gabriel) and that Muhammad had been called to be a prophet to his people.

This night, called by later Islamic tradition "The Night of Power and Excellence," was the beginning of a series of revelations to Muhammad lasting from 610 to 632 and later collected in a book titled, appropriately enough, "The Recitation" or, in Arabic, the Qur'an (sometimes spelled Koran). **Muhammad**

was eventually accepted as a prophet by his fellow Arabs and many other people. He became known as the "Messenger (**Rasul**) of God," and the religion that stems from his revelations (**Islam**) is, some 1400 years later, the second largest world missionary religion.

Muhammad was born about 570 in Mecca. We do not know many details of the religion of the tribe into which he was born, the Quraysh. We do know that Arabic religious practices at that time centered around a variety of gods and goddesses, superhuman agents called *jinn* (from which we get the word *genie*), and demons. Hubal, god of the moon, was the principal deity of Meccans along with three chief goddesses, Al-Lat, Al-Manat, and Al-Uzza. **Allah** (the Arabic word for God) was the deity responsible for creation.

In Mecca, the **Kaaba,** housing statues of various gods and a sacred Black Stone which, it was said, had dropped from heaven, was a major pilgrimage site. When Muhammad, having been convinced by his revelations that "there is no god, but Allah," returned to Mecca after some years in Medina, he cleansed the Kaaba of these "idols" and converted it to a pilgrimage site for Muslims.

In addition to the indigenous Arabic religions, there were Christians and Jews living in Arabia at the time Muhammad was born. It is clear he knew some of the stories from the Jewish Torah, especially the stories about Abraham and other prophets as well as stories about Jesus. He came to believe that he was the last of the great Semitic prophets extending back through Jesus to Adam and that God (Allah) had visited him in order to restore the true divine message that these prophets had delivered, but which was now corrupted by false teachings such as the Christian doctrine of the Trinity and the divinity of Jesus (see chapter 11).

So Muhammad, setting his doubts aside, came to make sense of that voice in the cave on Mount Hira

WORLD DISTRIBUTION OF MUSLIMS

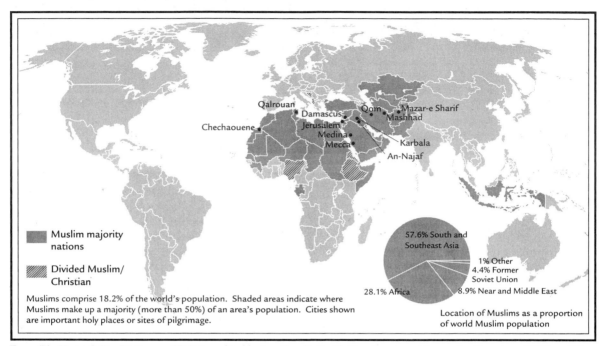

From *The HarperCollins Dictionary of Religion*, edited by Jonathan Z. Smith (San Francisco: Harper San Francisco, 1995), p. 499. Copyright © 1995 by the American Academy of Religion. Reprinted by permission of HarperCollins Publishers, Inc.

by understanding it as nothing less than a call by Allah to restore the truth about God and God's relationship to humans. It seems quite fitting, then, that the first of the Five Pillars of Islam should be "Witness that there is no god, but Allah and Muhammad is the Messenger of God."

12.1 AN OVERVIEW

Richard C. Martin, a professor of religion at Emory University and a specialist in Islamic studies, introduces us (see the following section) to Islam by providing a historical overview, some general observations, and a discussion of some of the difficulties associated with the study of Islam. He is well aware of how difficult it is for people in Europe and the

United States to study Islam fairly and present a balanced account of its beliefs, practices, and histories.

One reason for this difficulty is the immense diversity of Islam. It is a world religion embracing different sects, different languages, different ethnic groups, and different histories. Another reason stems from the history of conflict between Islam and Christianity. Within a few short years of Muhammad's death (632), his followers were conquering territory controlled by Christian rulers and would have captured most of Europe if Muslim armies were not stopped in France in 732. Later, Christians launched crusades to recapture the "Holy Land" from the "infidel." Armed conflict continues to this day along with considerable political tensions. At the same time, Islam is the fastest growing religion in North America and many Muslim families are establishing their homes and their **mosques** (places of worship) in Canada and the United States.

RICHARD C. MARTIN

Islam

READING QUESTIONS

1. As you read, make a list of all the words and ideas you do not understand or are uncertain about. Discuss them with a classmate, look them up in a dictionary, or bring them up in class for discussion and clarification.
2. What do the words *Islam* and *Muslim* mean, and what are the two main divisions of Islam?
3. Why is the popular image of Muslims as Bedouin nomads wrong?
4. What did the Bedouin Arabs contribute to Islam?
5. What is important about the dates 1500, 1300, and 1200?
6. What are the four roots of the law, and on what four sources do they draw?
7. Who are the *ulama*, and what is their role?
8. What is Sufism?
9. What was the religious message contained in the early revelations to Muhammad, and how did the message change after the *hijra*?
10. What is the difference between *shirk* and *tawhid*?
11. What is the result of the confusion between normative statements and descriptions of actual situations in thinking about any religion, including Islam?

Islam is an Arabic term meaning "submission" to the will of the one God, Allah. The Arabic root "s-l-m" (like its Hebrew cognate "sh-l-m") means "peace," the peace and human social accord gained by submission to the will of God. Closely associated with this act of submission is acceptance of the seventh-century prophet Muhammad (ca. 570–632) as the last and final Messenger of God, the "seal of the prophets." Those who submit—who "fear God and obey His messengers," which scripture, the Qur'an, frequently admonishes humans to do—are known as Muslims.

Islam is a global religion. The vast majority of Muslims around the world (about 85 percent) identify themselves as "Sunni," and follow one of the four accepted schools of legal interpretation: Malikite (Africa); Hanafite (Egypt, Turkey, Central Asia); Hanbalite (Arabia, Gulf Arab states); and Shafiite (Middle East, Southeast Asia). A significant minority identify themselves as "Shii" or "Shiites," living primarily in Iran, Syria, and Lebanon. Although both Sunni and Shii Muslims practice their religion in nearly identical ways, their worldviews differ somewhat owing to conflicts that occurred during the first generation after Muhammad's death and about which there are significant differences of interpretation.

Until the latter half of the twentieth century, most North Americans knew little about Islamic religion. Much of the non-Muslim world's sudden interest in Islam has arisen in part as a result of tragic conflict in the Middle East and elsewhere in the Muslim world. That conflict has had many causes, but European colonialism in the nineteenth and twentieth centuries produced many of the conditions and motivations that led to it. News reports and political analysis of more recent disputes involving Muslim populations, such as the Arab/Israeli conflict (1948), the Iranian Revolution resulting in the taking of American hostages (1979), and the U.S.-led Allied war against Iraq ("Desert Storm," 1991), have contributed to a climate of negative information and disinformation about Arabs and Muslim peoples more generally.

In the 1980s, representations of Islamic religion and cultures began to appear more frequently in the media, in public-school history and social studies textbooks, and in university general studies and elective curricular offerings. Yet the common assessment of Muslims and specialists on Islam is that much of the information about Islam that gets published is less than accurate and often misleading. On the other side, exponents of such movements as multiculturalism have sought to remedy the problem by encouraging public schools and the media to provide unbiased information about Islamic peoples and their cultures. However, raw information about Islamic societies and cultural symbolism without proper analysis of social and cultural systems can also be misleading. An example is the tendency, when conflict has erupted in the Muslim world, to invite specialists to speak in the media or in the schools on the Five Pillars of Islam, as though analysis of the traditional beliefs and practices of a religious community can explain everything that takes place in that society.

There is a need for more nuanced understanding of the increasing amount of information, much of it still inaccurate, about Islam. Speaking and writing responsibly about Islam is a task facing students and teachers, reporters in the print and broadcast media, government officials, international businesses, as well as domestic businesses that operate in markets that include rapidly growing Muslim communities in North America. First, however, some general information and observations about Islamic civilization will be useful.

General Observations

Islam is the youngest of the major world religions, dating from the seventh century. Historians of religion classify Islam as a universal missionary religion, the second largest tradition belonging to this category. The other two are Christianity (the largest) and Buddhism. A global ethnographic survey of Muslim peoples in 1984 estimated the world population of Muslims at 837 million; in 1992 the Encyclopedia Britannica Book of the Year estimated 950 million Muslims worldwide (as compared to 1.7 billion Christians, 17 million Jews, and 884 million nonreligious peoples). Muslims form the majority in some fifty-six nations and close to 50 percent in four other countries. Most of these countries lie in a belt of economically poorer, less well-industrialized nations across Africa and Asia, the so-called Third World.

A notable exception to this pattern with respect to personal income levels (among the highest in the world in the late twentieth century) is the Persian (or Arabian) Gulf region. Gulf Muslim societies nonetheless exhibit a socioreligious ethos that is among the most conservative, exclusive, and tightly controlled in the Muslim world. Gulf Arab expressions of social and theological conservatism stem from one of the four schools of law to which Sunni Muslims adhere, the Hanbali school, named after the popular legal and religious scholar, Ahmad Ibn Hanbal (d. 855); reformist and "puritanical" expressions of Islam, including the Wahhabi (named after Muhammad Ibn Abd al-Wahhab, 1703–92) movement in Arabia, have frequently come from Muslims who have subscribed to Hanbali interpretations of Islamic law.

A popular image of Muslims in the West is that of camel-driving Arab nomads, the Bedouin. This view is inaccurate in two ways. First, only a small minority of Muslims are Arabs (and not all Arabs are Muslim). In 1984 the world population of Arab Muslims was estimated to be under 137 million, some 16 percent of the world Muslim population. After Arabs come Bengalis (93 million), Punjabis (57 million), and Javanese (53 million). Persians rank as the eighth largest ethnic group of Muslims at 23.5 million, Kurds as the seventeenth largest, at 10.4 million, Somalis as the twenty-first at 7.6 million, and Bosnians (in the former Yugoslavia) as the fiftieth at 2.2 million. Second, the representation of

Muslims by Hollywood and the media as camel drivers bears little relation to cultural realities. Only a small minority even of Arab Muslims are nomads. Throughout the diverse ethnic/linguistic and geographic world of Islam, the vast majority—nearly 70 percent—are peasants living in rural areas in an agrarian economy. By contrast, about 30 percent of the world Muslim population lives in urban areas. Only about 2 percent of the Muslims in the world today are pastoral peoples living nomadic lifestyles.

In North America, Islam is estimated by some demographers to become the second largest religious community (after Christianity but ahead of Judaism) sometime early in the twenty-first century. Thus, Islam is not only one of the largest and fastest growing religions in Africa and Asia; it is quickly becoming a major confessional community in North America. Consequently, large Muslim communities thrive in some of the biggest media markets across the United States. Smaller inland cities, such as Cedar Rapids, Iowa, have well-established Muslim communities with mosques, religious schools, and community centers. Muslim children are enrolling in increasing numbers in public schools; Muslim parents are joining parent-teacher organizations and running, often successfully, for local school boards and for political office.

Despite the smaller percentage of Muslims living in urban areas, the city has always been an essential social environment for Islamic practice. The Muslim place of worship, the mosque (from the Arabic term *masjid*, "place of prostration"), has played an important role in urban centers, where it often serves also as a place for advanced study of the religious sciences. Indeed, the major mosque and gathering place in any predominantly Muslim city is called the *iami* ("congregating"), which in many locales is a work of architectural majesty. Hospitals and schools are often associated with major mosques in Islamic cities. The Friday noon gathering for the most important weekly prayer in Islam is particularly important in cities, where Muslim rulers and distinguished personages often lead the prayer or give the sermon. Among the major cities in the Muslim world today are Cairo, Baghdad, Damascus, Tehran, Lahore, and Yogjakarta.

If Bedouin nomads comprise only a small portion of the world Muslim population, nonetheless the contribution of these Arab pastoral societies and their relation to the urban growth and social ethos in some parts of the Islamic world should not be overlooked. The Muslim philosopher of history and social theorist Ibn Khaldun (1332–1406) argued that the tough self-reliance of nomadic lifestyles, when combined with tribal loyalties, produces an important factor called "group solidarity," or *asabiyya*, in the formation of civilization. In time, asa-biyya gives way to the social and cultural patterns of higher urban cultures that are less hardy and self-reliant, and thus a civilization will fall back into social conditions for which tribal lifestyles provide more effective means of survival. Ibn Khaldun's theory of the vicissitudes of Islamic history has earned him the title "father of the social sciences." His three-volume *Muqaddimah* (Introduction to History) has been translated into English and has been the subject of several studies of modern scholars.

What the Arab Bedouin did contribute to Islamic religion and society, of significance far beyond the demographic limits of the Arab component in Islamic civilization, was their language, Arabic. Although Persian, Turkish, Indian, Malay, and other ethnic Muslim communities are often critical of the exaggerated role the Arabs have claimed for themselves in the unfolding of Islamic history, all Muslims cherish the Arabic language and try to learn at least some quranic and other religious phrases in Arabic. Today, as in classical times, the religious sciences of Islam (including quranic recitation and commentary, prophetic traditions [*hadith*], law, and theology) are studied and taught in Arabic by Muslims around the world. Indeed, at the beginning of the twentieth century, a revival of Arabic language and literature occurred in Arab lands, leading to the development of a modern standard form of Arabic for the classroom, public speaking, and the media. At the end of the twentieth century, the revival of Arabic applies to non-Arab Muslims as well. One of the marks of the modern reassertion of Islamic identity in virtually all parts of the world where significant Muslim communities live has been the study of the Arabic language.

The importance of Arabic as a significant factor in Islamic identity is as much theological as linguistic, and this has been the case throughout Islamic history. It is important to Muslims that Arabic was the language in which the Qur'an was revealed, in stylistic perfection so remarkable that Islam has seen the Qur'an itself as God's miracle through the Prophet Muhammad. By the ninth century, Muslim theologians argued that just as God had given to Moses, as a sign of his prophethood, the power to change rods into serpents and divide the Red Sea; and just as God had given to Jesus, as a sign of his prophethood, the power to heal the sick and raise the dead; so God gave to Muhammad the ability to recite his word in language so beautiful that even the most gifted Arab poets and orators could not imitate it when challenged by Muhammad to do so. Even non-Arab Muslims, most of whom must approach the Qur'an in translation in order to grasp its intellectual content, join Arab Muslims in asserting the ultimate untranslatability of the Qur'an.

HISTORICAL OVERVIEW

Looking at the long expanse of Muslim civilization from the seventh century to the present, Islamic history can be divided into two parts. The question is where to locate the divide. Many contemporary Western historians have seen 1500 as the rough dividing line between traditional Islamic civilization and the rise of modern Islamic societies. In the late fifteenth and early sixteenth centuries, three Islamic empires arose, in Anatolia (Ottoman), Iran (Safavid), and the Indian subcontinent (Mughul). These empires lasted until the beginning of the modern period, when growing European influence and eventually colonialism, among other factors, hastened their collapse. Others have seen 1300 as the major divide between classical and modern Islam, for in 1258 the Mongols destroyed the imperial office of the caliphate in Baghdad, thus bringing to an end the practical hope of a universal Sunni Islam under one Muslim ruler.

By 1200, however, the Islamic religious tradition achieved its present religious institutional forms. The last of the twelve descendants of Muhammad's family through his paternal cousin and son-in-law, Ali son of Abu Talib, to be recognized as *imam* (spiritual leader of the Shiite communities) had disappeared. The twelfth imam, according to the majority of the Shia, was believed to have gone into occultation in the latter part of the ninth century. By the mid-tenth century, the main body of the Shia of Ali declared the Greater Occultation of the Twelfth Alid Imam. For the next three generations, until the mid-eleventh century, Shiite theologians established the main texts and practices of Shiite Islam. The devotees of the seventh imam, Ismail, whom they believed had gone into occultation, became a significant heterodox (and sometimes subversive) sect in medieval Islam. Still another alternative sect of the Shia, the followers of the fifth imam were named *Zaydis* after him. Until 1200, the Zaydis represented a theological posture that was strongly critical of the Sunni caliphate, but that nonetheless accepted more of Sunni doctrine than the other Shia groups.

The four schools of Sunni jurisprudence (Shafite, Hanafite, Hanbalite, and Malikite), along with the main Shiite tradition in jurisprudence (Jafarite), became entrenched in Islamic society by the end of the twelfth century. Moreover, by this time, Islamic religious thought had become completely identified in method and worldview with jurisprudence, and less so with theological speculation and reflection. Matters of faith and practice were decided, case by case, in written opinions (*fatwas*) according to how the legal scholars interpreted and applied the four roots of law: the Qur'an, *Sunna*, the consensus of the community, and reasoning by analogy from known divine commandments or prophetic practice to newer situations. The primary authority of these four roots had been established by al-Shafii (767–820), one of the founders of the four law schools. These roots of the law combined four sources—divine word, prophetic example, communal precedent, and individual reasoning—with much room for difference of opinion and debate on virtually every issue.

The process of public and disciplined disputation on virtually every point of interpretation in faith and practice is known in Arabic as *khilaf*. Religious and legal disputation became a chief cultural expression, not only among Islamic schools of jurisprudence, but also between Muslim and non-Muslim theological virtuosos and among heterodox sectarians, philosophers, and other factions within Islamic society in the early Middle Ages (until 1100, at least). What united the Islamic world was (and is) far less a single polity (the caliphate was in receivership to local warlords by 950) or a supreme spiritual leader (there was none in Islam) than a set of sources and methods of interpreting those sources (namely, Qur'an and Sunna).

Those charged with carrying on this tradition of education in the religious sciences and interpreting them continually as differences arise are known as *ulama* ("knowers," "learned ones"). Unlike Christian clergy, who are ordained and who bear sacramental authority, the ulama are men recognized by their communities for their learning in the religious sciences of Islam. The ulama seldom command political power as such. Rather, they are teachers, jurisconsults, and religious intellectuals, situated between the rulers and the ruled in Islamic societies. Historians often note that the major difference between Shiite and Sunni ulama is that the former have tended to take a stance of opposition to Muslim political regimes, while the latter have usually been more accommodating to the wishes of rulers.

Still another social institution of traditional Islamic religion that was well established by 1200 was Sufism, the Islamic form of mysticism. The Sufi worldview was based on the same sources as other Muslims, the Qur'an and Sunna. But the early mystics (and ascetics) stressed spiritual discipline and the inner meaning of the religious duties required by Islamic law. Above all, they pursued methods of attaining union with God. Virtuoso mystics in the early centuries of Islam drew disciples. In time, Sufi brotherhoods, known as *tariqas*, became powerful alternative modes of living the Islamic religion. Today, Sufi brotherhoods are still active in the Nile Valley and elsewhere in the Muslim world.

If the major Islamic institutions were established by the year 1200, the symbols and forms they took had been established in the beginning generation of Is-lam, the time of the Prophet Muhammad and the four Rightly Guided Caliphs, who ruled Islam for the next thirty years.

ISLAMIC BEGINNINGS

The story of its beginnings has been for Islam, as for most religions, an important framework in all ages for self-understanding. A chief concern is for what constitutes the Muslim community, or *umma*. Islam traces its rise to the historical appearance of Muhammad, who later sources say was born ca. 570 in the Arabian trading and pilgrimage shrine town of Mecca. Arabia was dominated by tribal social and cultural patterns, including alliances and conflicts with other tribes. The Quraysh tribe, into which Muhammad was born, had dominated Mecca and its shrine, the Kaaba, and commercial markets (mostly caravanserai) for several generations. In Islamic cosmology, the appearance of the Prophet Muhammad among his own Arab people brought an end to a global period of crude human ignorance, or *jahiliyya*. The other "Peoples of the Book" (primarily Jews, Christians, and Zoroastrians), who had preceded the Muslim community, had perverted the scriptures brought to them from God by their prophets. The notion that jahiliyya symbolizes the need for the renewal of true religion had been an important theme for Muslim reformers, especially in modern times.

According to Muslim biographical and historical works in Arabic dating from the ninth century, Muhammad's call to prophethood began when he was forty years old (ca. 610). In a dramatic moment during a night of vigil in a cave in the mountains near Mecca, Muhammad was ordered by the angel Gabriel to "recite in the name of the Lord . . . who teaches man by the pen what he knows not" (Qur'an 96:1–4 passim). Though Muhammad was reported to have been sore afraid and unsure of himself in the first instance, those recitations of God's word in miraculously beautiful Arabic were to continue to come to him throughout his life, until his death in 632. In Mecca during the first years of Muhammad's prophethood, the revelations of the divine word that were "sent down" took the form of strong warnings to Meccan society to repent of social immorality and to give up pagan polytheism. The message was met with derision and scorn on the part of most Meccans.

The entire collection of recitations, forming a book about the length of the Christian New Testament, is known in Arabic as the Qur'an (lit., "recitals"). The cardinal importance of the Qur'an in Muslim life—in educational foundations, legal formulations, moral expectations, social behavior, liturgical practice, artistic performance (chanting and calligraphy), and in everyday speech—is a hallmark of Islam that is at once theological and aesthetic. Islamic societies are infused with the message, as well as the aesthetic appeal, of the Qur'an at many conscious and subconscious levels.

From the beginning, the message of the Qur'an and the moral and spiritual precedents established by the living example of the Prophet claimed authority over all of life, including religious duties, as well as matters pertaining to family, the market, and the state. The revelation of the Qur'an, however, was incomplete when, in 622 (year one in Muslim chronology), after several years of harassment by the elders of the Meccan Quraysh tribe, the followers of Muhammad decided to leave Mecca for an agricultural oasis town called Yathrib, later named Medina (city [of the Prophet]), an event celebrated as the Hijra.

In Medina, Muhammad was recognized as Prophet not only by the Meccan followers who had emigrated with him, known as Muhajirun, but also by the citizens of Medina known as the Ansar ("helpers"), who had invited Muhammad to preside over their tribally divided community in the traditional manner of the Middle Eastern judicious tribal leader. The revelations that were "sent down" to Muhammad in Medina now pertained to his growing community of followers, containing prescriptions for social behavior and ritual performance.

Moreover, what Muhammad said, when asked questions in Medina about religion, or *din*, and what he did in the practice of it became known as *sunna* ("path," "practice"). The Sunna of the Prophet Muhammad became the second major source of scriptural authority after the Qur'an. The Prophet's Sunna, that is, his words and deeds and matters on which he otherwise indicated approval or disapproval, were remembered by his Companions and transmitted by them to subsequent generations. These verbal traditions about the Prophet's Sunna are known as *hadith*. The most authoritative generations of transmitters were the first three, known respectively as the Companions, the Followers, and the Followers of the Followers.

By the ninth century the hadiths numbered in the tens of thousands. Several collections were made and written down, organized either according to the Companions and Followers, etc., who transmitted them, or according to the topics of their content. Six collections, each in several volumes, became known as "The Sound" collections. Of these, the most famous and oft-quoted is that of al-Bukhari (d. 870), which has been printed in many Arabic editions and translated into English.

Bukhari's collection begins with a brief section on the inspiration of the Qur'an. The following sections are on faith, religious knowledge, and purity, including ritual lustrations (baths) after polluting activities, and lesser ablutions performed before the prayer. Among the most polluting substances are semen and blood. Many hadiths in these sections pertain to the need for lustrations following sexual intercourse, as well as for women experiencing postpartum or menstrual bleeding. Many of the hadiths in this section are traced back to Ayisha, the Prophet's youngest and, reputedly, his favorite wife.

Several sections in Bukhari's collection contain prophetic sayings on the religious duties of Islam (prayer, alms, fasting, and pilgrimage). The last few volumes contain hadiths on such topics as *jihad* ("struggle," "effort"), the virtues and merits of Muhammad and other prophets, wills and testaments, inheritance, marriage, good manners, taking and keeping oaths, the divinely set punishments (for stealing, murder, etc.), and the interpretation of dreams. Significantly, the last section of Bukhari's collection is on *tawhid* ("divine unity"), the doctrine that lies at the basis of the Islamic concept of monotheism.

Ten years after the Hijra to Medina, Muhammad died in his own home of natural causes. The Islamic rejection of the doctrine of Jesus' divinity is based on the quranic conviction that Muhammad, like all prophets before him, including Jesus, was a mortal human being. Yet Muslims believe, as Christians do, in the virgin birth of Jesus and in the perfect moral nature of all prophets. Hence, to say that Muhammad and all the preceding prophets from Adam to Jesus were mortal and not divine is not to say that they were merely "ordinary" human beings, in the Islamic worldview. If the central problem of Christology for the church fathers was to resist the attraction of Arianism, which emphasized the humanity of Jesus the Christ to the exclusion of his divinity, the problem surrounding Muhammad's prophethood has been the temptation for Muslims to exalt his extraordinary nature. A ritual and festal occasion for celebrating and remembering the Prophet Muhammad is the *Mawlid* ("birthday") ceremony, which is popular in North Africa, Southeast Asia, and in many other parts of the Islamic world. However, in Arabia, among those Muslims who follow the Hanbali Sunni interpretation of law, celebrating the birthday of the Prophet is forbidden and regarded as *bida* ("[unlawful] innovation").

Muhammad experienced many struggles and conflicts with opponents and enemies during his lifetime. These experiences and the terms for them, along with the struggles for power among various factions after Muhammad's death, became paradigmatic for later Islamic history. The Muslim community's sense of self-identity in relation to non-Muslim communities, as well as its sense of what separates Muslims from non-Muslim peoples, is derived largely from events in the lifetime of the Prophet and of his companions who survived in the seventh century. For example, the message of submission to the one God Allah was sharply critical of Arab pagan polytheism. Islam viewed polytheism from the vantage point of strict monotheism, declaring that the worst form of false belief was to "associate" (*shirk*) other deities with Allah. Shirk is the opposite of the aforementioned *tawhid*. Long after the polytheism of Arabia, and other lands to which Islam spread, was no longer a challenge to Islamic belief, the concept of shirk has remained potent nonetheless. Leaders who do not rule Muslim nations according to Islamic precepts, for example, are often accused of shirk, that is, of not being good Muslim theists; their accusers claim they do not rule according to divine legislation, or *Sharia*. In modern times, those rulers who have sought Western support, and who (in the eyes of their Muslim subjects) have abandoned rule according to the Sharia, are often accused of shirk.

Speaking About Islam . . .

A significant problem for those who read, speak, or write about Islamic topics is the cultural stereotypes that many Muslims find offensive. This is not a trivial problem. Those writing for broadcast and print news media, as well as for features and school curricula, now find that what they say about Islam circulates widely in the Muslim world, thanks to modern technology and telecommunications.

For example, despite the above-mentioned statistics about the extent of the world Muslim population, and the fact that Americans have more information about Islam and Muslims than ever before, ignorance and misinformation still exist. According to a survey conducted by a North American professional association of scholars in Middle Eastern studies, in the 1990s, social studies textbooks on the Middle East and other regions that include Islamic societies often still represent Muslims as camel-driving nomads. In fact, as mentioned already, only about 2 percent of Muslims are pastoral nomads.

A related problem for the growing number (and percentage) of writers, teachers, and speakers who deal with Islamic topics is the inevitable ethnocentrism of persons culturally situated in North America. It would not be surprising for a Southern Baptist and an agnostic secular humanist to have quite different conceptions of the significance of religion in American public life. Often, however, little thought seems to be given to the fact that neither the Baptist nor the agnostic will understand religion in public life the way it would be understood by a Sunni Muslim in Egypt or a Shiite Muslim in Iran.

In Western textbooks, the historical encounter with Muslim peoples often has been portrayed primarily in terms of armed conflict motivated by religion—from the defeat by Charles Martel (the Hammer) of the advancing Arab Muslim armies at Poitiers in the eighth century (blocking Arabs from further entry into Europe through Gaul); to the Crusades beginning in the eleventh century (recapturing the Holy Land from Muslim "infidels"); to the Reconquista in Spain in the late fifteenth century (repulsing Muslims from southern Europe altogether); to the struggles between Turks and Europeans in the Balkans (stopping the "Saracen hordes" at the gates of Vienna); down to late-twentieth-century counterterrorism (protecting North American tourists, business, and military interests endangered by a putative global Islamic threat).

Some measure of understanding the converse experience, the Islamic experience of the West during the past two centuries, is important for those who may seek to understand why many Muslims represent modern Islam in anti-Western dialectical terms. Historically speaking, Muslim encounters with Christian European civilization around the Mediterranean did not much affect the vast majority of Muslim societies in Africa and Asia (including the Middle East, Central Asia, and the Indian subcontinent) until the colonial period. The Islamic response to the concept of "the West" (Euro-American civilization; Judeo-Christianity; capitalist-driven colonial subjugation of Muslim societies) did not develop until the nineteenth century. At first, the common image of the West among the Muslim intelligentsia (at least, those writing for and read by Western scholars) was of a society that educationally, economically, and militarily was vastly superior to Islamic civilization; Islam was seen as having fallen into relative impotence since the great achievements of the ages of the Prophet Muhammad, the conquests under the Rightly Guided Caliphs, and the Golden Age of the Abbasid Empire.

Less visible in Europe and America were indigenous eighteenth- and nineteenth-century Islamic movements to "renew" traditional religion and social systems. These movements are now seen by most historians as a response to the decline of the premodern regimes that once bound much of the Islamic world together in regional empires: the Ottomans in the eastern and southern Mediterranean, the Safavids in Iran and parts of Central Asia, and the Moghuls in South Asia. In the twentieth century, the mood began to shift from admiration of Western achievements to resentment of Western colonialism and imperialism. Muslim discourses against the West—specifically against secularism, capitalism, and communism as failed systems—intensified during the twentieth century.

Those who read and write about Islam today do so not only in the wake of Western colonial (economic and military) control of much of the Muslim world, but also within a Western-constructed discourse about Islam—a discourse that has come to be known as orientalism. Since 1979, when Edward Said published a book titled *Orientalism*, offering a scathing indictment of European studies of Arabs and Muslims, much of earlier Western scholarship on Islam has come under increasing criticism by both Muslim and non-Muslim scholars. Nonetheless, in the ongoing study of Islam in Western scholarship, contemporary historians, religionists, and social scientists are heavily indebted to the pioneering contribution of previous generations of Arabists and Islamicists.

North American as well as Muslim writers often confuse normative descriptions of religious beliefs and practices with historical expression and social behavior. Under the impact of acceptable argument in the social sciences, some North American writers represent Islam in terms of what they perceive Muslims actually to be doing—in the mosque and home, and in society more generally, in gender relationships, and in the treatment of Muslim sects and non-Muslim minorities. In this view, the adjective "Islamic" qualifies virtually all social behavior observed in Muslim societies. The popular confusion of normative religion with the things religious people actually do, or seem to be doing, can lead to pernicious, self-serving comparisons: "My religion teaches 'thou shalt not kill,' but the people of religion *X* seem to kill each other all the time." Creedal demand and actual behavior can be two quite different things.

Many Muslim scholars, on the other side, mean by "Islam" a system of beliefs and practices revealed by God in scripture (the Qur'an) and perfectly exemplified in the life of the Prophet (the Sunna). In this latter view, some of what outsiders observe ordinary Muslims believing and doing is regarded as un-Islamic, heretical, or even blasphemous. Thus, Western writers may come under criticism for characterizing observed phenomena within the full range of Muslim social and religious practices in ways that orthodox Sunni or Shii Islam does not recognize as essentially Islamic. One way to avoid potential misunderstanding when writing about Islam (or any religious tradition) is to be clear in the beginning as to whether one is speaking about a normative system of beliefs, ritual performances, and social practices, or whether one is dealing with observed social behavior and the manifestation of culture in actual circumstances.

In comparative religious studies generally, more information and analysis is needed on how Muslims negotiate the disparity between what the Qur'an and Sunna require of them and what they may do in apparent conflict with those ideals. This is a central problem in religious studies more generally. One of the best sources for seeing how Muslims experience and cope with this disparity, found in all religions (and indeed in human existence universally), can be found in the poetry and novels of Muslim writers, such as the 1988 Nobel Laureate, Naguib Mahfouz of Egypt.

SOURCES

I have organized the sources in three broad historical periods to provide some sense of the development of Islam. There is so much Islamic literature and so many different varieties of Islam that I have had to exclude much that is important. However, what I have managed to include will hopefully introduce some of the more important literature and, through that literature, provide some insights into the power of the Muslim faith.

12.2 THE FORMATIVE PERIOD

The writings from the earliest period in Islamic history that have been most influential on the development of the tradition are the Qur'an and the various collections of *hadith*. The Qur'an is the most significant because Muslims believe it contains the actual words of God. The ***hadith*** are sayings attributed to Muhammad and his earlier companions along with stories about the Messenger's deeds. Although these are not considered revelation in the strict sense, their influence in the development of Islam has been almost as important as the Qur'an.

12.2.1 Qur'an

The **Qur'an,** the collection of the revelations received by Muhammad, is the primary sacred text for all Islamic sects. It is divided into 114 sections called ***surahs.*** The traditional arrangement is from the longest *surah* to the shortest (with the exception of *surah* 1). The titles are derived from a recurring word such as Abraham, Mary, Angels, Muhammad.

After each of Muhammad's revelations, specially assigned reciters or recorders either memorized them or wrote them down. When Muhammad died, there was no complete written record and, a year later, many of the reciters who had memorized a large number of the revelations were killed in battle. **Abu Bakr,** the first **caliph** (successor of Muhammad), fearing that the revelations might be lost, ordered a compilation of the first complete text. The third caliph, Uthman, ordered Zayd ibn Thabit, an aide to Muhammad, to supervise the creation of a definitive edition in 650 because by then there were different versions of some parts circulating among Muslims and causing dissension. Once the definitive version was created, Uthman ordered all other versions destroyed. Although variant editions appeared later, the definitive text is the one Zayd edited.

For Muslims, the Qur'an contains the eternal words of Allah. Many believe there is an original engraved tablet of the Qur'an in heaven written in Arabic. Hence, authentic copies can only be in Arabic, and the true Qur'an can never be translated.

Tradition says that Muhammad was illiterate. Hence, the literary quality of the Qur'an is considered proof of its authenticity. That an illiterate man could produce such a great work is, for Muslims, nothing less than a divine miracle.

The selections that follow come from various surahs. The first is "The Opening" (*Al-Fatiha, surah* 1), which contains the most commonly repeated prayer in Islam. *Surah* 15 (*Al-Hijr*) deals with several themes from the validity of the revelation to creation and paradise, while the selection from *surah* 2 ("The Cow") focuses on the "fall" from paradise. It should be noted that there is no "original sin" in Islam in the same sense as there is in Christianity. The sin of Adam and Eve is theirs alone. Brief selections from *surah* 2 and *surah* 112 deal with the nature of Allah and the importance of belief in Allah, the one and only God.

The next selection, *surah* 10, is from the late Meccan period before the *hijra* to Medina. It deals with the fate of those who deny Qur'anic authority and persist in idol worship. Although the Qur'an condemns idolaters, it acknowledges that certain people received revelations prior to the Qur'an. These people (Jews, Christians, Zoroastrians, and Sabians) were called People of the Book. These people were allowed to practice their own religion within Islamic-held territories if they did not wish to convert to Islam. However, as *surah* 5 ("The Table") indicates, many of these people, according to Allah, had strayed from the revelations given them and thus needed to be admonished by Muhammad to return to a pure monotheism. Muhammad had hoped that Jews, Christians, Zoroastrians, and others would recognize him as a prophet and accept the Qur'an as divine revelation. His intention was to reform and purify the monotheism already revealed, but, as with so many other reform movements, a different religion was the final result.

The selection from *surah* 17 is sometimes referred to as the Decalogue because of its similarity to the Ten Commandments. It provides moral advice to the faithful Muslim. It is followed by selections from *surah* 4 dealing with marriage. By contemporary Western standards, the treatment of women in Islam is unfair. However, in Muhammad's day in Arabia where women had few if any rights, the Qur'anic sayings on women's rights must have seemed quite radical. Parts of *surah* 4, written in 624, set forth laws pertaining to women that improve their status considerably since prior to this women were regarded as property.

Many of you have probably heard of the Five Pillars of Islam. They are (1) sincerely witnessing and confessing that there is no god but Allah and that Muhammad is his messenger (**shahada**), (2) praying five times during the day while facing Mecca (**salat**), (3) giving alms to those in need (**zakat**), (4) fasting from sunup to sundown during the holy month of **Ramadan** (**sawn**), and (5) making a pilgrimage to Mecca, if possible, once in one's life (**hajj**). To these five some add a sixth, **jihad,** which is often translated as "holy war" but literally means "exertion" in the cause of Allah. The explicit obligation of *jihad* appears in the *Hadith*, but its roots are in the Qur'an. It refers to both the inner struggle between belief and unbelief and between good and evil (the "greater" *jihad*) and the outer struggle against unbelievers (the "lesser" *jihad*).

The last day of judgment and the resurrection of the dead are predominant themes in the Qur'an. *Surah* 75 is called "The Resurrection," and we end our selections from the Qur'an with it.

The Opening (Surah 1)

1. What do you think is meant by "the straight path"?
2. How does the story of the creation and fall differ from the story in Genesis?
3. What is Allah like?
4. What is wrong with idolatry?
5. What does *surah* 5 reveal about early Islamic attitudes toward Judaism and Christianity?
6. What do you find more interesting about the moral commandments given in *surah* 17?
7. To whom are the laws about women addressed? Why?
8. In your opinion, how do the Pillars of Islam promote spirituality?
9. Why is *jihad* an obligation?
10. How does the *surah* on the resurrection try to convince doubters?

1.1
IN THE NAME OF ALLAH
THE COMPASSIONATE
THE MERCIFUL

Praise be to Allah, Lord of the Creation,
The Compassionate, the Merciful,
King of Judgement-day!
You alone we worship, and to You alone
we pray for help.
Guide us to the straight path
1:7 The path of those whom You have favoured,
Not of those who have incurred Your wrath,
Nor of those who have gone astray.

Creation (Surahs 15:1–48, 2:28–39)

In the Name of Allah, the Compassionate, the Merciful

15:1 Alif *lam ra*. These are the versus of the Book, the Glorious Koran:

All of the selections from the Qur'an are from *The Koran*, translated by N. J. Dawood (London: Penguin Books, 1990). Copyright © 1956, 1959, 1966, 1968, 1974, 1990 N. J. Dawood. Reprinted by permission. Footnotes edited.

The day will surely come when the unbelievers will wish that they were Muslims. Let them feast and make merry; and let their hopes beguile them. They shall know the truth.

Never have We destroyed a nation whose term of life was not ordained beforehand. Men cannot forestall their doom, nor can they retard it.

They say: "You to whom the warning was revealed, you are surely possessed. Bring down the angels, if what you say be true."

We shall send down the angels only when Our judgement has been passed. Then they shall never be reprieved.

It was We that revealed the Koran, and shall Ourself *15:9* preserve it. We have sent forth apostles before you to the older nations: but they scoffed at each apostle We sent them. Thus We will put doubt in the hearts of the guilty: they will deny their apostle despite the example of the ancients.

If We opened for the unbelievers a gate in heaven and they ascended through it higher and higher, still they would say: "Our eyes were dazzled: truly, we must have been bewitched."

We have decked the heavens with constellations and guarded them from all accursed devils. Eavesdroppers are pursued by fiery comets.

We have spread out the earth and set upon it immovable mountains. We have planted it with every seasonable fruit, thus providing sustenance for man and *15:20* beast. We hold the store of every blessing and send it down in appropriate measure. We let loose the fertiliz- *15:21* ing winds and bring down water from the sky for you to drink; its stores are beyond your reach.

We ordain life and death. We are the Heir of all things.

We know those who have gone before you, and those who will come hereafter. Your Lord will gather them all before Him. He is wise and all-knowing.

We created man from dry clay, from black moulded loam, and before him Satan from smokeless fire. Your Lord said to the angels: "I am creating man from dry clay, from black moulded loam. When I have fashioned him and breathed of My spirit into him, kneel down and prostrate yourselves before him."

All the angels prostrated themselves, except Satan. He refused to prostrate himself.

"Satan," said Allah, "why do you not prostrate *15:32* yourself?"

He replied: "I will not bow to a mortal created of dry clay, of black moulded loam."

"Begone," said Allah, "you are accursed. My curse shall be on you till Judgement-day."

"Lord," said Satan, "reprieve me till the Day of Resurrection."

He answered: "You are reprieved till the Appointed Day."

"Lord," said Satan, "since you have led me astray, I will seduce mankind on earth: I will seduce them all, except those that faithfully serve you."

He replied: "This is the right course for Me. You shall have no power over My servants, except the sinners who follow you. They are all destined for Hell. It has seven gates, and through these they shall come in separate bands. But the righteous shall dwell amongst gardens and fountains; in peace and safety they shall enter them. We shall remove all hatred from their hearts, and they shall recline on couches face to face, a band of brothers. Toil shall not weary them, nor shall they ever leave their Paradise." . . .

15:48

2:28 How can you deny Allah? Did He not give life when you were dead, and will He not cause you to die and then re-
2:29 store you to life? Will you not return to Him at last? He created for you all that the earth contains; then, ascending to the sky, fashioned it into seven heavens. He has knowledge of all things.

When your Lord said to the angels: "I am placing on the earth one that shall rule as My deputy," they replied: "Will You put there one that will do evil and shed blood, when we have for so long sung Your praises and sanctified Your name?"

He said: "I know what you do not know."

He taught Adam the names of all things and then set them before the angels, saying: "Tell Me the names of these, if what you say be true."

2:32 "Glory to You," they replied, "we have no knowledge except that which You have given us. You alone are wise and all-knowing."

Then said He to Adam: "Tell them their names." And when Adam had named them, He said: "Did I not tell you that I know the secrets of heaven and earth, and all that you hide and all that you reveal?"

And when We said to the angels: "Prostrate yourselves before Adam," they all prostrated themselves except Satan, who in his pride refused and became an unbeliever.

To Adam We said: "Dwell with your wife in Paradise and eat of its fruits to your hearts' content wherever you will. But never approach this tree or you shall both become transgressors."

But Satan made them fall from Paradise and brought about their banishment. "Go hence," We said, "and may your offspring be enemies to each other. The earth will for a while provide your sustenance and dwelling-place."

Then Adam received commandments from his Lord, 2:37 and his Lord relented towards him. He is the Forgiving One, the Merciful.

"Go down hence, all," We said. "When Our guidance is revealed those that accept it shall have nothing to fear or to regret; but those that deny and reject Our revela- 2:39 tions shall be the heirs of Hell, and there they shall abide for ever." . . .

Allah Reveals Himself
(Surahs 2:255–257, 112:1–4)

Allah: there is no god but Him, the Living, the Eternal 2:255 One. Neither slumber nor sleep overtakes Him. His is what the heavens and the earth contain. Who can intercede with Him except by His permission? He knows what is before and behind men. They can grasp only that part of His knowledge which He wills. His throne is as vast as the heavens and the earth, and the preservation of both does not weary Him. He is the Exalted, the Immense One.

There shall be no compulsion in religion. True guid- 2:256 ance is now distinct from error. He that renounces idol-worship and puts his faith in Allah shall grasp a firm handle that will never break. Allah hears all and knows all.

Allah is the Patron of the faithful. He leads them from darkness to the light. As for the unbelievers, their patrons are false gods, who lead them from light to darkness. They are the heirs of Hell and shall abide in it for ever. . . .

UNITY

In the Name of Allah, the Compassionate, the Merciful

Say: "Allah is One, the Eternal God. He begot none, 112:1 nor was He begotten. None is equal to Him." 112:4

Evils of Idolatry
(Surah 10:26–38)

Allah invites you to the Home of Peace. He guides whom He will to a straight path. Those that do good works shall be rewarded with abundant blessings. Neither blackness nor misery shall cover their faces. They are the heirs of Paradise: in it they shall abide for ever.

10:27 As for those that have earned evil, evil shall be rewarded with like evil. Misery will cover them (they shall have none to defend them from Allah), as though their faces were veiled with the night's black darkness. They are the heirs of Hell: in it they shall abide for ever.

10:28 On the day when We assemble them all together, We shall say to the idolaters: "Keep to your places, you and your idols!" We will separate them one from another, and then their idols will say to them: "It was not us that you worshipped. Allah is our all-sufficient witness: we were unaware of your worship."

Thereupon each soul will know what it has done. They shall be sent back to Allah, their true Lord, and the idols they invented will forsake them.

Say: "Who provides for you from heaven and earth? Who has endowed you with sight and hearing? Who brings forth the living from the dead, and the dead from the living? Who ordains all things?"

They will reply: "Allah."

Say: "Will you not take heed, then? Such is Allah, your true Lord. That which is not true must needs be false. How then can you turn away from him?"

Thus the word of your Lord is made good. The evil-doers have no faith.

10:34 Say: "Can any of your idols conceive Creation, then renew it? Allah conceives Creation, then renews it. How is it that you are so misled?"

Say: "Can any of your idols guide you to the truth? Allah can guide you to the truth. Who is more worthy to be followed: He that can guide to the truth or he that cannot and is himself in need of guidance? What has come over you that you cannot judge?"

Most of them follow nothing but mere conjecture. But conjecture is no substitute for Truth. Allah is cognizant of all their actions.

This Koran could not have been composed by any but Allah. It confirms what was revealed before it and fully explains the Scriptures. It is beyond doubt from the Lord of the Creation.

If they say: "It is your own invention," say: "Compose one chapter like it. Call on your false gods to help you, if what you say be true!" . . .

People of the Book
(Surah 5:44–51, 65–78)

There is guidance, and there is light, in the Torah which *5:44* We have revealed. By it the prophets who surrendered themselves to Allah judged the Jews, and so did the rabbis and the divines; they gave judgement according to Allah's scriptures which had been committed to their keeping and to which they themselves were witnesses.

Have no fear of man; fear Me, and do not sell My revelations for a paltry end. Unbelievers are those who do not judge in accordance with Allah's revelations.

In the Torah We decreed for them a life for a life, an *5:45* eye for an eye, a nose for a nose, an ear for an ear, a tooth for a tooth, and a wound for a wound. But if a man charitably forbears from retaliation, his remission shall atone for him. Transgressors are those that do not judge in accordance with Allah's revelations.

After those prophets We sent forth Jesus, the son of Mary, confirming the Torah already revealed, and gave him the Gospel, in which there is guidance and light, corroborating that which was revealed before it in the Torah, a guide and an admonition to the righteous. Therefore let the followers of the Gospel judge in accordance with what Allah has revealed therein. Evil-doers are those that do not base their judgements on Allah's revelations.

And to you We have revealed the Book with the truth. *5:48* It confirms the Scriptures which came before it and stands as a guardian over them. Therefore give judgement among men in accordance with Allah's revelations and do not yield to their fancies or swerve from the truth that has been made known to you.

We have ordained a law and assigned a path for each of you. Had Allah pleased, He could have made you one nation: but it is His wish to prove you by that which He has bestowed upon you. Vie with each other in good works, for to Allah you shall all return and He will declare to you what you have disagreed about.

Pronounce judgement among them in accordance *5:49* with Allah's revelations and do not be led by their desires. Take heed lest they should turn you away from a part of that which Allah has revealed to you. If they reject your judgement, know that it is Allah's wish to scourge them for their sins. Many of them are wrongdoers.

Is it pagan laws that they wish to be judged by? Who is a better judge than Allah for men whose faith is firm?

Believers, take neither Jews nor Christians for your friends. They are friends with one another. Whoever of you seeks their friendship shall become one of their number. Allah does not guide the wrongdoers. . . .

If the People of the Book accept the true faith and keep from evil, We will pardon them their sins and ad-5:66 mit them to the gardens of delight. If they observe the Torah and the Gospel and what is revealed to them from Allah, they shall be given abundance from above and from beneath.

Some of them are righteous men; but many of them do nothing but evil.

5:67 Apostle, proclaim what is revealed to you from your Lord; if you do not, you will surely fail to convey His message. Allah will protect you from all men. He does not guide the unbelievers.

Say: "People of the Book, you shall not be guided until you observe the Torah and the Gospel and that which is revealed to you from your Lord."

That which is revealed to you from your Lord will surely increase the wickedness and unbelief of many of them. But do not grieve for the unbelievers.

Believers, Jews, Sabaeans, or Christians—whoever believes in Allah and the Last Day and does what is right —shall have nothing to fear or to regret.

5:70 We made a covenant with the Israelites and sent forth apostles among them. But whenever an apostle came to them with a message that did not suit their fancies they either rejected him or slew him. They thought no harm would come to them: they were blind and deaf. Allah turned to them in mercy, but many of them again became blind and deaf. Allah is ever watching over their actions.

Unbelievers are those that say: "Allah is the Messiah, the son of Mary." For the Messiah himself said: "Children of Israel, serve Allah, my Lord and your Lord." He that worships other gods besides Allah shall be forbidden Paradise and shall be cast into the fire of Hell. None shall help the evil-doers.

Unbelievers are those that say: "Allah is one of three." There is but one God. If they do not desist from so saying, those of them that disbelieve shall be sternly punished.

Will they not turn to Allah in repentance and seek forgiveness of Him? He is forgiving and merciful.

The Messiah, the son of Mary, was no more than 5:75 an apostle: other apostles passed away before him. His mother was a saintly woman. They both ate earthly food.

See how We make plain to them Our revelations. See how they ignore the truth. . . .

❧❧❧

Ethics (Surah 17:21–37)

Serve no other gods besides Allah, lest you incur disgrace and ruin. Your Lord has enjoined you to worship none but Him, and to show kindness to your parents. If either or both of them attain old age in your dwelling, show them no sign of impatience, nor rebuke them; but speak to them kind words. Treat them with humility and tenderness and say: "Lord, be merciful to them. They nursed me when I was an infant."

Your Lord best knows what is in your hearts; He knows if you are good. He will forgive those that turn to Him.

Give to the near of kin their due, and also to the destitute and to the wayfarers. Do not squander your substance wastefully, for the wasteful are Satan's brothers; and Satan is ever ungrateful to his Lord. But if, while waiting for your Lord's bounty, you lack the means to assist them, then at least speak to them kindly.

Be neither miserly nor prodigal, for then you should either be reproached or be reduced to penury.

Your Lord gives abundantly to whom He will and sparingly to whom He pleases. He knows and observes His servants.

You shall not kill your children for fear of want.[1] 17:31 We will provide for them and for you. To kill them is a great sin.

You shall not commit adultery, for it is foul and 17:32 indecent.

You shall not kill any man whom Allah has forbidden you to kill, except for a just cause. If a man is slain unjustly, his heir is entitled to satisfaction. But let him not carry his vengeance too far, for his victim will in turn be assisted and avenged.

Do not interfere with the property of orphans except with the best of motives, until they reach maturity.

---

[1] In allusion to the pre-Islamic custom of burying alive unwanted newborn girls.

Keep your promises; you are accountable for all that you promise.

Give full measure, when you measure, and weigh with even scales. That is fair, and better in the end.

Do not follow what you do not know. Man's eyes, ears, and heart—each of his senses shall be closely questioned.

17:37 Do not walk proudly on the earth. You cannot cleave the earth, nor can you rival the mountains in stature.

All this is evil; odious in the sight of your Lord.

These injunctions are but a part of the wisdom with which your Lord has inspired you. Serve no other god besides Allah, lest you should be cast into Hell, despised and helpless. . . .

Laws on Marriage
(Surah 4:13–25, 34–35, 128–135)

4:13 Such are the bounds set by Allah. He that obeys Allah and His apostle shall dwell for ever in gardens watered by running streams. That is the supreme triumph. But he that defies Allah and His apostle and transgresses His bounds, shall be cast into Hell-fire and shall abide in it for ever. A shameful punishment awaits him.

If any of your women commit fornication, call in four witnesses from among yourselves against them; if they testify to their guilt confine them to their houses till death overtakes them or till Allah finds another way for them.

If two men among you commit indecency punish them both. If they repent and mend their ways, let them be. Allah is forgiving and merciful.

4:17 Allah forgives those who commit evil in ignorance and then quickly turn to Him in repentance. He will pardon them. Allah is wise and all-knowing. But Allah will not forgive those who do evil all their lives and, when death comes to them, say: "Now we repent!" Nor will He forgive those who die unbelievers. For these We have prepared a woeful scourge.

Believers, it is unlawful for you to inherit the women of your deceased kinsmen against their will, or to bar them from re-remarrying, in order that you may force them to give up a part of what you have given them, unless they be guilty of a proven crime. Treat them with kindness; for even if you do not love them, it may well

be that you may dislike a thing which Allah has meant for your own good.

If you wish to divorce a woman in order to wed another, do not take from her the dowry you have given her even if it be a talent of gold. That would be improper and grossly unjust; for how can you take it back when you have lain with each other and entered into a firm contract?

Henceforth you shall not marry the women who were married to your fathers. That was an evil practice, indecent and abominable.

4:23 You are forbidden to take in marriage your mothers, your daughters, your sisters, and your paternal and maternal aunts, the daughters of your brothers and sisters, your foster-mothers, your foster sisters, the mothers of your wives, your step-daughters who are in your charge, born of the wives with whom you have lain (it is no offence for you to marry your step-daughters if you have not consummated your marriage with their mothers), and the wives of your own begotten sons. Henceforth you are also forbidden to take in marriage two sisters at one and the same time. Allah is forgiving and merciful.

4:24 You are also forbidden to take in marriage married women, except captives whom you own as slaves. Such is the decree of Allah. All women other than these are lawful to you, provided you seek them with your wealth in modest conduct, not in fornication. Give them their dowry for the enjoyment you have had of them as a duty; but it shall be no offence for you to make any other agreement among yourselves after you have fulfilled your duty. Allah is wise and all-knowing.

4:25 If any one of you cannot afford to marry a free believing woman, let him marry a slave-girl who is a believer (Allah best knows your faith: you are born one of another). Marry them with the permission of their masters and give them their dowry in all justice, provided they are honourable and chaste and have not entertained other men. If after marriage they commit adultery, they shall suffer half the penalty inflicted upon free adulteresses. Such is the law for those of you who fear to commit sin: but if you abstain, it will be better for you. Allah is forgiving and merciful. . . .

4:34 Men have authority over women because Allah has made the one superior to the others, and because they spend their wealth to maintain them. Good women are obedient. They guard their unseen parts because Allah has guarded them. As for those from whom you fear disobedience, admonish them and send them to beds apart and beat them. Then if they obey you, take no further action against them. Allah is high, supreme.

4:35 If you fear a breach between a man and his wife, appoint an arbiter from his people and another from hers.

If they wish to be reconciled Allah will bring them together again. Allah is wise and all-knowing. . . .

4:128   If a woman fear ill-treatment or desertion on the part of her husband, it shall be no offence for them to seek a mutual agreement, for agreement is best. Man is prone to avarice. But if you do what is right and guard yourselves against evil, know then that Allah is cognizant of all your actions.

4:129   Try as you may, you cannot treat all your wives impartially. Do not set yourself altogether against any of them, leaving her, as it were, in suspense. If you do what is right and guard yourselves against evil, you will find Allah forgiving and merciful. If you separate, Allah will compensate you both out of His own abundance: He is munificent and wise.

4:131   To Allah belongs all that the heavens and the earth contain. We exhort you, as We have exhorted those to whom the Book was given before you, to fear Allah. If you deny Him, know that to Allah belongs all that the heavens and the earth contain. He is self-sufficient and worthy of praise.

To Allah belongs all that is in heaven and earth. Allah is your all-sufficient guardian. If He pleased, He could destroy you all and replace you by other men. This He has power to do.

Let the man who seeks the reward of this life know that Allah holds the rewards of this life and of the next. He hears all and sees all.

4:135   Believers, conduct yourselves with justice and bear true witness before Allah, even though it be against yourselves, your parents, or your kinsfolk. Whether the man concerned be rich or poor, know that Allah is nearer to him than you are. Do not be led by passion, lest you should swerve from the truth. If you distort your testimony or decline to give it, know that Allah is cognizant of all your actions.

Believers, have faith in Allah and His apostle, in the Book He has revealed to His apostle, and in the Scriptures He formerly revealed. He that denies Allah, His angels, His Scriptures, His apostles, and the Last Day, has strayed far from the truth. . . .

Pillars of Islam and Jihad
(Surah 2:144–150,
183–200, 216–218)

Many a time We have seen you turn your face towards   *2:144*
heaven. We will make you turn towards a *qiblah* that will please you. Turn towards the Holy Mosque; wherever you be face towards it.

Those to whom the Scriptures were given know this to be the truth from their Lord. Allah is watching over all their actions. But even if you gave them every proof they would not accept your *qiblah*, nor would you accept theirs; nor would any of their sects accept the *qiblah* of the other. If after all the knowledge you have been given you yield to their desires, then you will surely become an evil-doer.

Those to whom We gave the Scriptures know Our apostle as they know their own sons. But some of them deliberately conceal the truth. This is the truth from your Lord: therefore never doubt it.

Each one has a goal towards which he turns. But wherever you be, emulate one another in good works. Allah will bring you all before Him. He has power over all things.

Whichever way you depart, face towards the Holy Mosque. This is surely the truth from your Lord. Allah is never heedless of what you do.

Whichever way you depart, face towards the Holy Mosque: and wherever you face, face towards it, so that   *2:150*
men will have no cause to reproach you, except the evil-doers among them. Have no fear of them; fear Me, so that I may perfect My favour to you and that you may be rightly guided. . . .

Believers, fasting is decreed for you as it was decreed   *2:183*
for those before you; perchance you will guard yourselves against evil. Fast a certain number of days, but if   *2:184*
any one of you is ill or on a journey let him fast a similar number of days later on; and for those that can afford it there is a ransom: the feeding of a poor man. He that does good of his own account shall be well rewarded; but to fast is better for you, if you but knew it.

In the month of Ramadhan the Koran was revealed, a book of guidance with proofs of guidance distinguishing right from wrong. Therefore whoever of you is present in that month let him fast. But he who is ill or on a journey shall fast a similar number of days later on.

Allah desires your well-being, not your discomfort. He desires you to fast the whole month so that you may magnify Him and render to Him for giving you His guidance.

2:186   When My servants question you about Me, tell them that I am near. I answer the prayer of the suppliant when he calls to Me; therefore let them answer My call and put their trust in Me, that they may be rightly guided.

It is now lawful for you to lie with your wives on the night of the fast; they are a comfort to you as you are to them. Allah knew that you were deceiving yourselves. He has relented towards you and pardoned you. Therefore you may now lie with them and seek what Allah has ordained for you. Eat and drink until you can tell a white thread from a black one in the light of the coming dawn. Then resume the fast till nightfall and do not approach them, but stay at your prayers in the mosques.

These are the bounds set by Allah; do not come near them. Thus He makes known His revelations to mankind that they may guard themselves against evil.

Do not usurp one another's property by unjust means, nor bribe with it the judges in order that you may knowingly and wrongfully deprive others of their possessions.

2:189   They question you about the phases of the moon. Say: "They are seasons fixed for mankind and for the pilgrimage."

Righteousness does not consist in entering your dwellings from the back.[1] The righteous man is he that fears Allah. Enter your dwellings by their doors and fear Allah, so that you may prosper.

2:190   Fight for the sake of Allah those that fight against you, but do not attack them first. Allah does not love the aggressors.

Kill them wherever you find them. Drive them out of the places from which they drove you. Idolatry is worse than carnage. But do not fight them within the precincts of the Holy Mosque unless they attack you there; if they attack you put them to the sword. Thus shall the unbelievers be rewarded: but if they mend their ways, know that Allah is forgiving and merciful.

Fight against them until idolatry is no more and Allah's religion reigns supreme. But if they mend their ways, fight none except the evil-doers.

2:194   A sacred month for a sacred month: sacred things too are subject to retaliation. If any one attacks you, attack him as he attacked you. Have fear of Allah, and know that Allah is with the righteous.

Give generously for the cause of Allah and do not with your own hands cast yourselves into destruction. Be charitable; Allah loves the charitable.

Make the pilgrimage and visit the Sacred House for   2:196
His sake. If you cannot, send such offerings as you can afford and do not shave your heads until the offerings have reached their destination. But if any of you is ill or suffers from an ailment of the head, he must pay a ransom either by fasting or by alms-giving or by offering a sacrifice.

If in peacetime anyone of you combines the visit with the pilgrimage, he must offer such gifts as he can afford; but if he lacks the means let him fast three days during the pilgrimage and seven when he has returned; that is, ten days in all. That is incumbent on him whose family are not present at the Holy Mosque. Have fear of Allah: know that He is stern in retribution.

Make the pilgrimage in the appointed months. He   2:197
that intends to perform it in those months must abstain from sexual intercourse, obscene language, and acrimonious disputes while on pilgrimage. Allah is aware of whatever good you do. Provide yourselves well: the best provision is piety. Fear Me, then, you that are endowed with understanding.

It shall be no offence for you to seek the bounty of your Lord by trading. When you come running from Arafat remember Allah as you approach the sacred monument. Remember Him that gave you guidance when you were in error. Then go out from the place whence the pilgrims will go out and implore the forgiveness of Allah. He is forgiving and merciful. And when you have fulfilled your sacred duties, remember Allah as you remember your forefathers or with deeper reverence. . . .

Fighting is obligatory for you, much as you dislike it.   2:216
But you may hate a thing although it is good for you, and love a thing although it is bad for you. Allah knows, but you do not.

They ask you about the sacred months. Say: "To   2:217
fight in this month is a grave offence; but to debar others from the path of Allah, to deny Him, and to expel His worshippers from the Holy Mosque, is far more grave in His sight. Idolatry is worse than carnage."

They will not cease to fight against you until they force you to renounce your faith—if they are able. But whoever of you recants and dies an unbeliever, his works shall come to nothing in this world and in the world to come. Such men shall be the tenants of Hell, and there they shall abide for ever.

Those that have embraced the faith and those that have fled their land and fought for the cause of Allah, may hope for Allah's mercy. Allah is forgiving and merciful. . . .

---

[1] It was the custom of pagan Arabs, on returning from pilgrimage, to enter their homes from the back.

The Resurrection (Surah 75)

In the Name of Allah, the Compassionate, the Merciful

75:1 I swear by the Day of Resurrection, and by the self-reproaching soul!

Does man think We shall never put his bones together again? Indeed, We can remould his very fingers!

Yet man would ever deny what is to come. "When will this be," he asks, "this day of Resurrection?"

But when the sight of mortals is confounded and the moon eclipsed; when sun and moon are brought together—on that day man will ask: "Whither shall I flee?"

No, there shall be no escape. For on that day all shall return to your Lord.

On that day man shall be informed of all that he has done and all that he has failed to do. He shall become his own witness; his pleas shall go unheeded.

75:16 (You need not move your tongue too fast to learn this revelation. We Ourself shall see to its collection and recital. When We read it, follow its words attentively; We shall Ourself explain its meaning.)

Yet you love this fleeting life and are heedless of the life to come.

On that day there shall be joyous faces, looking towards their Lord. On that day there shall be mournful faces, dreading some great affliction.

But when a man's soul is about to leave him and those around him cry: Will no one save him? When he knows it is the final parting and the pangs of death assail him—on that day to your Lord he shall be driven. For in this life he neither believed nor prayed; he denied the truth and, turning his back, went to his kinsfolk elated with pride.

75:34 Well have you deserved this doom; well have you de-
75:35 served it. Well have you deserved this doom: too well have you deserved it!

Does man think that he lives in vain? Was he not a drop of ejected semen? He became a clot of blood; then Allah formed and moulded him and gave him male and
75:40 female parts. Is He then not able to raise the dead to life?

12.2.2 Hadith

Hadith means "report," and it refers to a collection of narratives reporting the sayings and actions of Muhammad. Next to the Qur'an, it is the second most authoritative collection of texts in Islam.

During the first two hundred years after Muhammad's death, booklets of *hadith* began to appear on a variety of topics. The number of *hadith* grew substantially and, when systematically compiled in the ninth and tenth centuries, filled 12 multivolume collections.

The **Sunnis,** the majority sect of Islam, recognize nine different collections, but the most widely accepted are the *Two Sahih* (authentic): *Sahih al-Bukhari* and *Sahih Muslim*. The first was carefully compiled and authenticated by al-Bukhari (810–870), a noted Islamic scholar. The second was compiled by a student of al-Bukhari named Muslim ibn al-Hajjaj (d. 875).

There are three Shi'a collections (called *akhbar* rather than *hadith*). According to tradition, they originated with **Ali** and the first **imams** (leaders).

Hadith sayings typically have two parts. The first is the story itself, and the second is a list of names constituting the chain of sources that establish its authenticity. Some stories are considered especially sacred because they contain divine revelations, and others, the noble *hadith* or *hadith sharif*, relate to Muhammad's personal life. *Hadith* were used to answer questions of law, to serve political needs, and to support one or another religious faction. Thousands were rejected as inauthentic, and critical scholarship still debates the authenticity of those that have been accepted.

Below we sample four selections from the *Sahih al-Bukhari*. The first is called "The Night Journey," and it expands on a verse in the Qur'an that reads, "Glory be to him who made his servant go by night from the sacred temple [of Mecca] to the farther temple [of Jerusalem] whose surroundings we have blessed, that we might show him some of our signs" (*surah* 17:1). Some Muslims interpret the night journey as a vision, but others take it literally. In commemoration of this event, Muslims built the famous shrine "The Dome of the Rock" on the former site of the Jewish temple.

Memorization and recitation of the Qur'an is a pious act. Muhammad ritually recited its passages and praised his companions who did the same. Special reciters memorized the Qur'an in its entirety and recited it daily in prescribed tonal songlike vocalizations. However, as the second selection indicates, variations of vocalization were permitted.

Muhammad died in the house of his favorite wife, **A'isha.** His death, described in the third selection, prompted concerns about a new leader of the Muslim community and fear that Muhammad might become an object of worship. While Muslims have argued and divided over Muhammad's legitimate successor, the following *hadith*, attributed to A'isha herself, claims he appointed no successor.

The last selection from the *Hadith* tells the story of how the third caliph, Uthman, ordered the compilation of the definitive edition of the Qur'an.

༄

The Night Journey (Sahih al-Bukhari, 5:227)

READING QUESTIONS

1. What do you think is the religious significance for Muslims of "The Night Journey"?
2. Why do you think reciting the Qur'an became a religious act?
3. Explain why you think the concern to recite the Qur'an correctly became so religiously significant.
4. Why do you think there was so much concern about both a successor to Muhammad and the possibility of people worshiping him?
5. What advantages can you see in having one written version of the Qur'an?

Narrated Anas ibn Malik from Malik ibn Sa'sa'a that Allah's Apostle described to them his Night Journey saying, While I was lying in Al-Hatim or Al-Hijr, suddenly someone came to me and cut my body open from here to here [across the chest]. He then took out my heart. Then a gold tray full of Belief was brought to me and my heart was washed and was filled (with Belief) and then returned to its original place. Then a white animal which was smaller than a mule and bigger than a donkey was brought to me. . . . The animal's step (was so wide that it) reached the nearest heaven. When he asked for the gate to be opened it was asked, "Who is it?" Gabriel answered, "Gabriel." It was asked, "Who was accompanying you?" Gabriel replied, "Muhammad." It was asked, "Has Muhammad been called?" Gabriel replied

This and the following *hadith* selections are from *The Translation of the Meanings of Sahih al-Bukhari*, translated by Muhammad Muhsin Khan, 9 volumes (Chicago: Kazi Publications), 1979. Copyright © Kazi Publications, Inc. Reprinted by permission.

in the affirmative. Then it was said, "He is welcomed. What an excellent visit his is!" The gate was opened, and when I went over the first heaven, I saw Adam there. Gabriel said (to me), "This is your father, Adam; pay him your greetings." So I greeted him and he returned the greeting to me and said, "You are welcomed, o pious son and pious Prophet." Then Gabriel ascended with me till we reached the second heaven. . . . There I saw Yahya (i.e., John) and 'Isa (i.e., Jesus) who were cousins of each other. . . . Then Gabriel ascended with me to the third heaven and . . . there I saw Joseph. . . . Then Gabriel ascended with me to the fourth heaven and . . . there I saw Idris. . . .

Then Gabriel ascended with me to the fifth heaven and . . . there I saw Harun (i.e., Aaron). Then Gabriel ascended with me to the sixth heaven and . . . there I saw Moses. . . . When I left him (i.e., Moses) he wept. Someone asked him, "What makes you weep?" Moses said, "I weep because after me there has been sent (as Prophet) a young man whose followers will enter Paradise in greater numbers than my followers." Then Gabriel ascended with me to the seventh heaven and . . . there I saw Abraham. . . . Then I was made to ascend to Sidratul-Muntaha (i.e., the Lote Tree of the farthest limit). Behold! Its fruits were like the jars of Har (i.e., a place near Medina) and its leaves were as big as the ears of elephants. Gabriel said, "This is the Lote Tree of the farthest limit." Behold! There ran four rivers, two were hidden and two were visible. I asked, "What are these two kinds of rivers, O Gabriel?" He replied, "As for the hidden rivers, they are two rivers in Paradise, and the visible rivers are the Nile and the Euphrates." Then Al-Bait-ul-Ma'mur (i.e., the Sacred House) was shown to me and a container full of wine and another full of milk and a third full of honey were brought to me. I took the milk. Gabriel remarked, "This is the Islamic religion which you and your followers are following." Then the prayers were enjoined on me: They were fifty prayers a day.

When I returned, I passed by Moses who asked (me), "What have you been ordered to do?" I replied, "I have been ordered to offer fifty prayers a day." Moses said, "Your followers cannot bear fifty prayers a day, and by Allah, I have tested people before you, and I have tried my level best with Bani Israil (in vain). Go back to your Lord and ask for reducing your followers' burden." So I went back, and Allah reduced ten prayers for me. Then again I went back to Allah and he reduced ten more prayers. When I came back to Moses he said the same, I went back to Allah and he ordered me to observe ten prayers a day. When I came back to Moses, he repeated the same advice, so I went back to Allah and was ordered to observe five prayers a day. When I came back to

Moses, he said . . . go back to your Lord and ask for reducing your followers' burden." I said, "I have requested so much of my Lord that I feel ashamed, but I am satisfied now and surrender to Allah's Order." When I left, I heard a voice saying, "I have passed My Order and have reduced the burden of My Worshippers."

⚜

Reciting the Qur'an
(Sahih al-Bukhari, 6:514)

Narrated Umar ibn Al-Khattab: I heard Hisham ibn Hakim reciting *surah* Al-Furqan during the lifetime of Allah's Apostle and I listened to his recitation and noticed that he recited in several different ways which Allah's Apostle had not taught me. I was about to jump over him during his prayer, but I controlled my temper, and when he had completed his prayer, I put his upper garment around his neck and seized him by it and said, "Who taught you this Surah which I heard you reciting?" He replied, "Allah's Apostle taught it to me." I said, "You have told a lie, for Allah's Apostle has taught it to me in a different way from yours." So I dragged him to Allah's Apostle and said (to Allah's Apostle), "I heard this person reciting Surah Al-Furqan in a way which you haven't taught me!" On that Allah's Apostle said, "Release him (O 'Umar)! Recite, O Hisham!" Then he recited in the same way as I heard him reciting. Then Allah's Apostle said, "It was revealed in this way," and added "Recite, O 'Umar!" I recited it as he had taught me. Allah's Apostle then said, "It was revealed in this way. This Koran has been revealed to be recited in seven different ways, so recite of it whichever is easier for you."

⚜

The Death of Muhammad
(Sahih al-Bukhari,
5:727, 730, 736)

A'isha, the wife of the Prophet said, When the ailment of Allah's Apostle became aggravated, he requested his wives to permit him to be treated in my house, and they gave him permission. He came out (to my house), walking between two men with his feet dragging on the ground. . . . When Allah's Apostle entered my house and his disease became aggravated, he said, "Pour on me the water of seven waterskins, the mouths of which have not been untied, so that I may give advice to the people." So we let him sit in a big basin . . . and then started to pour water on him from these waterskins till he started pointing to us with his hands intending to say "You have done your job." . . . Then he went out to the people and led them in prayer and preached to them. . . .

When Allah's Apostle became ill seriously, he started covering his face with his woolen sheet, and when he felt short of breath, he removed it from his face and said, "That is so! Allah's curse be on the Jews and the Christians, as they took the graves of their prophets as (places of worship)," intending to warn (the Muslims) of what they had done. . . . I argued with Allah's Apostle repeatedly about the matter (i.e., his order that Abu Bakr should lead the people in prayer in his place when he was ill), and what made me argue so much was that it never occurred to my mind that after the Prophet, the people would ever love a man who had taken his place, and I felt that anybody standing in his place would be a bad omen to the people, so I wanted Allah's Apostle to give up the idea of choosing Abu Bakr (to lead his people in prayer).

Narrated A'isha: It was one of favors towards me that Allah's Apostle expired in my house on the day of my turn while leaning against my chest and Allah made my saliva mix with his saliva at his death. 'Abdur-Rahman entered upon me with a Siwak in his hand and I was supporting (the back of) Allah's Apostle (against my chest). I saw the Prophet looking at the Siwak and I knew that he loved the Siwak, so I said (to him), "Shall I take it for you?" He nodded in agreement. So I took it and it was too stiff for him to use, so I said, "Shall I soften it for you?" He nodded his approval. So I softened it and he cleaned his teeth with it. In front to him there was a jug or a tin containing water. He started dipping his hand in the water and rubbing his face with it. He said, "None has the right to be worshipped except Allah. Death has its agonies." He then lifted his hands (towards the sky) and started saying, "With the highest companion," till he expired and his hand dropped down.

Narrated Al-Aswad: It was mentioned in the presence of A'isha that the Prophet had appointed Ali as successor by will. Thereupon she said, "Who said so? I saw the Prophet while I was supporting him against my chest. He asked for a tray, and then fell on one side and expired, and I did not feel it. So how (do the people say) he appointed Ali as his successor?

The Definitive Qur'an
(Sahih al-Bukhari, 6:510)

Narrated Anas ibn Malik: Hudhaifa ibn Al-Yaman came to 'Uthman at the time when the people of Sha'm and the people of Iraq were waging war to conquer Arminya and Adharbijan. Hudhaifa was afraid of their (the people of Sha'm and Iraq) differences in the recitation of the Koran, so he said to 'Uthman, "O the chief of the Believers! Save this nation before they differ about the Book (Koran) as Jews and the Christians did before." So 'Uthman sent a message to Hafsa saying, "Send us the manuscripts of the Koran so that we may compile the Koranic materials in perfect copies and return the manuscripts to you." Hafsa sent it to 'Uthman. 'Uthman then ordered Zayd ibn Thabit, 'Abdullah ibn Az-Zubair, Sa'id ibn Al-As and 'Abdur-Rahman ibn Harith ibn Hisham to rewrite the manuscripts in perfect copies. 'Uthman said to the three Quaishi men, "In case you disagree with Zayd ibn Thabit on any point in the Koran, then write it in the dialect of Quraish as the Koran was revealed in their tongue." They did so, and when they had written many copies, 'Uthman returned the original manuscripts to Hafsa. 'Uthman sent to every Muslim province one copy of what they had copied, and ordered that all the other Qur'anic materials, whether written in fragmentary manuscripts or whole copies, be burnt. Zayd ibn Thabit added, "A verse from Surah Ahzab was missed by me when we copied the Koran, and I used to hear Allah's Apostle reciting it. So we searched for it and found it with Khuzaima ibn Thabit Al-Ansari. (That verse was): "Among the believers are men who have been true in their covenant with Allah" (22:23).

12.3 MEDIEVAL DEVELOPMENTS

Under the **Abbasid** caliphs (750–1258), the dynasty that succeeded the **Umayyad** caliphs (661–750), the Islamic world experienced a time of unprecedented prosperity accompanied by a flowering of literature, art, architecture, law, theology, medicine, mathematics, and philosophy. The mythic glory immortalized in *The Arabian Nights (The One Thousand and One Nights)* reflects the high culture that developed under the Abbasids and lingered after their rule.

In this section we will sample a small part of some of the developments in law, theology, and mystical literature. I must remind you, however, that intricate details of legal, theological, and philosophical debate had little immediate or direct impact on most Muslims who lived during this time. Islam has always been more of an orthopraxy (correct action) than an orthodoxy (correct belief). Most people went about their daily business and daily prayers often unaware of the debates that preoccupied the intellectual elites. However, in time theological and philosophical ideas did influence Islamic practice and, most importantly, legal decisions, when backed by the judicial and police powers of the state, had a direct impact on how people lived.

12.3.1 Law (*Shari'a*)

Islamic religious law, or **shari'a**, is a dynamic system that has been changing and evolving since the earliest days. Large numbers of Muslims take it very seriously not only because they consider it one of the most impressive aspects of their religion but also because it makes Islam a comprehensive religion, that is, one that integrates all aspects of one's life from diet and dress to business and prayer.

Islamic jurisprudence is called **fiqh**, and its four basic principles are called **Usul al-fiqh**. These principles allow the law to be extended to new situations, situations not discussed in the Qur'an or by the Prophet. The *Usul al-fiqh* (Principles of Jurisprudence) are the Qur'an, sunna, qiyas, and ijma. Laws explicitly and clearly stated in the Qur'an are beyond debate because they represent the will of Allah. The **sunna** (traditions) refer to stories about how Muhammad lived his life. These are found in the "living *sunna*" and the "recorded *sunna*." The living *sunna* are the practices of virtuous Islamic communities, and the recorded *sunna* are found in the *Hadith* or authentic stories about the Prophet's life. Both provide examples of how one is to live. **Qiyas** refers to reasoning by analogy and **ijma** to the consensus of the community.

Reasoning by analogy (*qiyas*) and consensus (*ijma*) constitutes a system of legal reasoning called **ijtihad,** and someone who is qualified to do it is called a *mujtahid*. Not all situations are covered by the laws of the Qur'an and *sunna*, and it is not always clear how to apply the laws that are found there. In such situations, *ijtihad* comes into play and a *mujtahid* can, through the use of analogy and consensus, create new laws or apply and extend old ones.

Scholars of Islamic law are called **faqaha.** They engage in theoretical and historical studies, but do not create new laws or rule on new applications. People with legal questions go to a **mufti** for advice about the law and what to do. The *mufti* issues an opinion known as a **fatwa**. In theory the views of the *mufti* are binding, but in practice many people ignore their views if they dislike the advice. There is no institution to enforce the *mufti's* views so there is no punishment (outside of social sanctions) for ignoring his advice. Judges and other government officials administer the laws of the state. Depending on the country, the state legal administration may or may not recognize the *shari'a*, or religious law, as part of its responsibility to enforce.

While all the law schools of Islam recognize the four principles of jurisprudence (*Usul al-fiqh*), they differ on specifics. The **Maliki** school of law is strongest in North Africa and considers the living *sunna* as more reliable than human reason. The **Hanbali** school is strongest in Saudi Arabia and favors the literal interpretation of written texts such as the *Hadith* for determining the law. The **Shafi'i** and **Hanafi** schools account for the majority of Sunni Muslims, and since the sixteenth century, the Hanafi school has become the most influential legal school among Sunni Muslims. Both the Shafi'i and Hanafi schools favor a much greater use of *ijtihad* (reason and consensus) than the Maliki or Hanbali schools.

The first selection is by Ibn Idris al-Shafi'i (767–820), who was the foremost scholar of early Islamic law. He is best known for his analysis of the Principles of Jurisprudence (*Usul al-fiqh*), which his disciples made the foundation of the Shafi'ite school.

Ibn Abi Zayd al-Quayrawani (922–996), who is the author of the second selection on **salat,** or prayer, is a leading scholar of the Maliki school. He was born in Nafza, Spain, where Maliki was the leading law school until the Moors were driven out.

The selections on marriage and divorce are from the *Hidaya* by Burhan al-Din al-Marghinani (d. 1197), which is one of the authoritative works of the Hanafi school. The final sample of *shari'a* is on the Caliphate and comes from the Shafi'i legalist al-Mawardi (d. 1058). Al-Mawardi uses the term *Imamate* for Caliphate since the *caliph* (successor of Muhammad) is also an *imam* (leader) of the community.

AL-SHAFI'I

Consensus and Analogy

READING QUESTIONS

1. What is the "proof" for accepting the consensus of the public as binding?
2. What is reasoning by analogy, and how does it relate to personal reasoning?
3. Why do you think such detailed instructions for the performance of *salat* (prayer) developed?
4. What are your reactions to the regulations concerning marriage and divorce?
5. What are some political consequences of al-Mawardi's views on the Imamate or Caliphate?

CHAPTER 11, ON CONSENSUS (*IJMA*)

480. Shafi'i said: Some asked me: I have understood your doctrine concerning God's commands and His Apostle's orders that he who obeys God obeys His Apostle, [for] God has imposed [on men] the duty of obeying His Apostle, and that the proof for what you held has been established that it would be unlawful for a Muslim who has known the Book [of God] and the sunna [i.e., Hadith tradition of the Prophet] to give an opinion at variance with either one, for I know that this [i.e., acceptance of the Book and the sunna] is a duty imposed by God. But what is your proof for accepting the consensus of the public [on matters] concerning which no explicit command of God nor any [sunna] related on the authority of the Prophet is to be found? Do you assert, with others, that the consensus of the public should always be based on an established sunna even if it were not related [on the authority of the Prophet]?

481. [Shafi'i] replied: That on which the public are agreed and which, as they assert, was related from the Apostle, that is so. As to that which the public do not relate [from the Prophet], which they may or may not relate as a tradition from the Prophet, we cannot consider it as related on the authority of the Prophet—because one may relate only what he has heard, for no one is permitted to relate [on the authority of the Prophet] infor-

From *Islamic Jurisprudence: Shafi'i's Risala*, translated by Majid Khadduri (Baltimore, Md.: Johns Hopkins University Press, 1961), pp. 285–290, 295–296. Copyright © 1961 by Johns Hopkins University Press. Reprinted by permission.

mation which may or may not be true. So we accept the decision of the public because we have to obey their authority, and we know that wherever there are sunnas of the Prophet, the public cannot be ignorant of them, although it is possible that some are, and we know that the public can neither agree on anything contrary to the sunna of the Prophet nor on an error.

484. He asked: What is the meaning of the Prophet's order to follow the community?

487. [Shafi'i replied: When the community spread in the lands [of Islam], nobody was able to follow its members who had been dispersed and mixed with other believers and unbelievers, pious and impious. So it was meaningless to follow the community [as a whole], because it was impossible [to do so], except for what the [entire] community regarded as lawful or unlawful [orders] and [the duty] to obey these [orders].

He who holds what the Muslim community holds shall be regarded as following the community, and he who holds differently shall be regarded as opposing the community he was ordered to follow. So the error comes from separation: but in the community as a whole there is no error concerning the meaning of the Qur'an, the sunna, and analogy.

CHAPTER 12,
ON ANALOGY (QIYAS)

488. He asked: On what ground do you hold that [on matters] concerning which no text is to be found in the Book, nor a sunna or consensus, recourse should be had to analogy? Is there any binding text for analogical deduction?

489. [Shafi'i replied: If analogy were [stated] in the text of the Book or the sunna, such a text should be called either God's command or the Apostle's order rather than analogy.

490. He asked: What is analogy? Is it personal reasoning [ijtihad], or are the two different?

491. [Shafi'i replied: They are two terms with the same meaning. . . .

493. On all matters touching the [life of a] Muslim there is either a bonding decision or an indication as to the right answer. If there is a decision, it should be followed; if there is no indication as to the right answer, it should be sought by personal reasoning, and personal reasoning is analogy [qiyas].

496. [He asked]: If [legal] knowledge is derived through analogy—provided it is rightly applied—should [the scholars] who apply analogy agree on most

[of the decision], although we may find them disagreeing on some?

497. [Shafi'i replied]: Analogy is on two kinds: the first, if the case in question is similar to the original meaning [of the precedent], no disagreement on this kind [is permitted]. The second, if the case in question is similar to several precedents, analogy must be applied to the precedent nearest in resemblance and most appropriate. But those who apply analogy are likely to disagree [in their answers].

CHAPTER 13, ON PERSONAL
REASONING (IJTIHAD)

534. He asked: On what ground do you hold that [the exercise of] personal reasoning [ijtihad] is permitted in addition to what you have already explained?

535. [Shafi'i replied: It is on the basis of God's saying: "from whatever place thou issuest, turn thy face in the direction of the Sacred Mosque; and wherever you may be, turn your faces in its direction" [Koran. II. 145]. Regarding him who [wishes to] face the Sacred Mosque [in prayer] and whose residence is at a distance from it, [legal] knowledge instructs [us] that he can seek the right direction through ijtihad on the basis of certain indications [guiding] toward it. For he who is under an obligation to face the Sacred House and does not know whether he is facing the right or wrong direction may be able to face the right one through certain indications known to him [which helps him] to face it as accurately as he can, just as another person may know other indications which help to orient him [in the right direction], although the direction sought by each person may be different from that sought by the other.

❦

AL-QUAYRAWANI

Ritual Prayer (Salat)

The consecrating act in prayer is to say *Allāhu akbar* [God is greater]! No other expression is permissible. You should raise your hands as high as your shoulders or

From *The Word of Islam*, edited by John Alden Williams (Austin, Tex.: University of Texas Press, 1994), pp. 72–75. Copyright © 1994 by the University of Texas Press. Reprinted by permission.

less, and then recite from the Qur'ān. If you are in the morning-prayer, recite the opening *sūra* of the Qur'ān. Do not start with the formula "In the name of God, the Merciful, the Compassionate," either in this *sūra* or in the one which you recite after it. When you have said "nor of those who go astray," say "Amen," whether you are alone or praying behind a leader [imam], in a low voice. The imam also should not say it as loudly as the rest of the prayer, but in a low voice, though there is a difference of opinion about this.

Then recite a *sūra* from the last part of the Qur'ān [where the shortest *sūras* occur]. If it is longer than that, there is no harm in it, but it should not exceed the space of time allotted for that prayer. Recite it in an audible voice.

When the *sūra* is finished, repeat "God is greater!" while leaning forward to begin the inclination [*rukū'*]. Place your hands on your knees, and keep your back straight, without arching it, not lifting your head up or ducking it. Be sure to preserve sincere humility in both the inclination and the prostration which follows. Do not pray while making the inclination: if you wish, say "Praise to my Lord, the Great! Glorified be He!" There is no fixed time for that, nor for the length of the inclination.

After this raise your head, saying "God hears those who praise Him." Then say "My God, our Lord, to You be praise!" if you are alone. An imam does not repeat these formulas. Those who pray behind an imam also do not say "God hears those who praise Him," but they do say "My God, our Lord, to You be praise!"

You should then stand erect serenely and quietly. Then begin the prostration, not sitting back on the heels but going directly into a prostration. Say "God is greater!" while leaning forward in the prostration and touch your forehead and nose to the ground, placing your palms spread flat on the ground and pointing toward Mecca, placing them near the ears, or somewhat to the rear of them. All of this is prescribed in a general manner, not strictly. Do not spread the forearms on the ground or clasp the upper arms to your sides, but hold them slightly away. Your feet should be perpendicular to the ground in the prostration, with the ends of the big toes touching it.

You may say in your prostration "Glory be to You, my Lord! I have wronged myself and done wrong. Forgive me!" or something similar. You may utter a private prayer in the prostration if you wish, and there is no set time for this, but at the least your members should remain still in a fixed position.

Then you should raise your head, saying "God is greater!" and sit back, folding the left foot in the time

between the two prostrations and putting the right foot vertical to the ground with the bottoms of your toes touching the ground. Lift your hands from the earth and place them on your knees, and then make a second prostration as you did the first. Then rise from the ground as you are, supporting yourself on both hands, not returning to the sitting position before rising, but directly, as mentioned. While rising, say "God is greater!"

Then recite a part of the Qur'ān as you did at first, or a little less, doing it just as you did before, but add the invocation [*qunūt*] after the inclination, or if you prefer before performing it, after the end of your recitation. The invocation is as follows: "O God, I ask Your aid and pardon. We truly put our faith in You, we put our trust in You, we submit humbly to You, we confide in You, and we forsake all who repudiate You. O God, You only do we serve, to You we pray and prostrate ourselves, for You we strive. We put our hope in Your mercy, and fear Your grave chastisements. Surely Your chastisements shall attain those who repudiate You!"

Then make the prostration and sit back as has been described before. If you sit back after the two prostrations, place the right foot vertical to the ground with the bottoms of your toes touching it and place the left foot flat, letting your posterior come in contact with the ground. Do not sit on your left foot, and if you wish let the right foot incline from a vertical position until the side of the big toe touches the ground: this permits some latitude.

After this, you recite the *tashahhud*, as follows: "Unto God be all salutations, all things good, all things pleasing, all benedictions. Peace be upon you, O Prophet, and the mercy of God and His blessings! Peace be upon us all, and all righteous servants of God. I witness that there is no god but God, the Unique, without partner. I witness that Muhammad is His servant and messenger." If after this you utter the final salutation, it is fitting and permissible, or you may add other formulas.

Then say "Peace be upon you" one time only, looking straight ahead in the direction of Mecca and turning the head slightly to the right. It is thus that an imam or one alone does; one praying behind an imam utters the salutation once, turning slightly to the right, and utters it again in response to the salutation of the man on the left. If there is no one there, he does not say anything to the left.

While reciting the *tashahhud* one puts one's hand in the lap and closes the fingers of the right hand, pointing with the index finger, the side of which is toward one's face. Opinions differ on whether it should move. Some hold that the believer with this gesture indicates his faith that God is one God; those who move it explain it as rebuking Satan. I myself believe one must explain it as a way of warning oneself of the things which in prayer might importune and distract the attention. The left hand should be left open on the right thigh, and one should not move it or point with it.

It is recommended to make two inclinations at dawn, before the regular dawn-prayer which follows the dawn. At each of these inclinations, one should recite the *Fātiḥa*, the opening *sūra* of the Qur'ān, in a low voice.

Recitation at the noon-prayer should be as long as that at the dawn-prayer or a little shorter, and nothing should be recited loudly. One should recite the *Fātiḥa* in both the first and the second inclinations as well as another *sūra*, in a low voice. In the last two inclinations of the noon-prayer, one should recite the *Fātiḥa* alone, in a low voice.

After this, one should perform supererogatory prayers. It is recommended to add four inclinations, saying the final salutation after each group of two. The same supererogatory prayers are recommended before the afternoon-prayer.

At the afternoon-prayer, one does as we have prescribed for the noon-prayer.

For the evening-prayer, one should recite audibly in the first two inclinations and recite the *Fātiḥa* with each inclination as well as one of the shorter *sūra*s. In the third, one should recite the *Fātiḥa* only, and the *tashah-hud* and the salutation. It is reprovable to sleep before the night-prayer, or to converse after it, except for good reason.

"Reciting softly" in the ritual prayer means moving the tongue to form the words in the recitation. "Reciting audibly" is for one to hear oneself and be heard by a person standing next to one, if one is not acting as an imam. A woman should speak more softly than a man.

[Friday is the Muslim day of congregational prayer. Friday does not have to be observed as a day of rest, though it often is. Noon-prayers are recited in congregation, led by an imam, and a public address or *khuṭba* is given.]

AL-MARGHINANI

Marriage and Divorce

Nikāḥ or Marriage: Nikāḥ in its primitive sense means carnal conjunction. . . . In the language of the Law it implies a particular contract used for the purpose of legalizing generation.

Marriage is contracted—that is to say, is effected and legally confirmed—by means of declaration and consent. . . . Where both the parties are Muslims it cannot be contracted but in the presence of two male witnesses or of one man and two women, who are sane, adult, and Muslim . . . evidence is an essential condition of marriage . . . against Mālik, who maintains that in marriage general knowledge is a condition and not positive evidence. It is necessary that the witnesses be free, the evidence of slaves being in no wise valid. . . . If a Muslim marries a woman of the People of the Book in the presence of two men of her kind it is lawful, according to Abū Yūsuf and Abū Ḥanīfa. Muhammad and Zufar hold it is not legal, because their testimony . . . amounts to evidence and the evidence of unbelievers regarding Muslims is illegal . . . the argument of the two elders in reply to this objection is that evidence is necessary . . . merely in order to establish the husband's right of cohabitation, which is in this case the object. . . .

It is not lawful for a man to marry his foster-mother or his foster-sister, the Almighty having commanded "Marry not your mothers who have suckled you or your sisters by fosterage," and the Prophet also declared "Everything is prohibited by reason of fosterage which is so by reason of kindred."

It is not lawful to marry and cohabit with two women being sisters, neither is it lawful for a man to cohabit with two sisters in virtue of a right of possession (as being his slaves) because the Almighty has declared that such cohabitation with sisters is unlawful.

A master may not marry his own slavewoman (except he set her free) or a mistress her bondsman, for marriage was instituted with a view that the fruit might belong equally to the father and the mother, and marriage and servitude are contradictory to each other. . . .

From Burhan al-Din al-Marghinani, *Al-Hidaya*, 2nd ed., translated by Charles Hamilton. London, 1870.

Marriage with Women of the Book is legal. . . . It is unlawful to marry a Zoroastrian woman or a polytheist (until she becomes a Muslim). . . .

It is lawful for a Muslim who is free to marry a female slave, whether a Muslim or Woman of the Book (if she is not his own); his seed is born then in bondage. . . . It is unlawful for a man already married to a free woman to marry a slave; the Prophet (said): "Do not marry a slave after a free woman." Shāfi'ī says the marriage of a slave after a free woman is lawful to a man who is a slave, and Mālik likewise maintains it is lawful, providing it is with the free woman's consent. The above ḥadīth however is an answer to both as it is general and unconditional.

Moreover the legal marriage is a blessing to men and women equally, but the enjoyment of it is by bondage restricted to one half, inasmuch as slaves can have only two wives whereas free men may legally have four. . . .

A temporary marriage, where a man marries a woman (for a contract of) ten days (for instance), is null. . . .

A woman who is adult and of sound mind may be married by virtue of her own consent although the contract may not have been made or acceded to by her guardians, and this whether she be a virgin or otherwise. (Though) Abū Yūsuf says her marriage cannot be contracted except through her guardian. Mālik and Shāfi'ī assert that a woman can by no means contract herself whether with or without the consent of her guardians (it is they who must do the contracting) nor is she competent to act as a matrimonial agent for anyone . . . if the performance of this contract were in any respect committed to women its end might be defeated (they argue), women being of weak reason and open to flattery and deceit. . . . But an adult virgin may not be forced into marriage against her will.

The marriage of a boy or girl under age by the authority of their paternal kindred is lawful, the Prophet having declared "Marriage is committed to the paternal kindred. . . ."

Marriage without a dower [mahr: given to the bride by the groom] is valid . . . but this is contrary to the teaching of Mālik. . . . If a man marry a woman without specifying any dower . . . she is thereby entitled to the (minimum legal dower) mahr mathl . . . it shall not consist of less than ten dirhams [silver coins]. . . .

If a man have two or more wives, all free women (he must cohabit equally with them) because the Prophet has said "The man who has two wives and who inclines particularly to one of them shall on the day of judgement be paralyzed on one side," and it is recorded by 'A'isha that he made such equal partition of cohabitation among his wives, saying, "O God, I thus make equal partition as to that which is in my power; do not therefore bring me to account for that which is not in my

power," (by which he means the affections, these not being optional). . . .

Divorce: The most laudable divorce is where the husband repudiates his wife by a single formula with her term of ritual purity (not during the menstrual period) and leaves her (untouched) to the observance of the 'idda (period of waiting to ascertain she is not with child). This is held to be most laudable for two reasons: (1) The Companions of the Prophet held this to be a more excellent method. . . . (2) In pursuing this method the husband leaves it within his power to recover his wife without shame by reversing the divorce during her 'idda (it is final only after three pronouncements); the method is moreover least injurious to the woman, as she remains (married to her husband until after the expiration of the 'idda). . . . Express divorce is where a husband delivers the sentence in direct and unequivocal terms, as "I have divorced you," or "you are divorced." (To be final, the divorce must be pronounced three times.) This effects a reversible divorce such as leaves it in his power to take her back before the expiration of the 'idda.

<hr>

᪖᪗᪖

AL-MAWARDI

Caliphate

The Imamate is placed on earth to succeed the Prophet in safeguarding the Religion and governing the world. It is a religious obligation to contract it with that person in the *umma* who will perform these duties, according to the consensus [of Sunnī *'ulamā*], even though al-Aṣamm [who held that a model community should not require a leader] stands against them on this.

Opinions differ on whether this duty is necessitated by reason or by the Law. One party holds that reason necessitates it, since it pertains to intelligent beings to submit themselves to a leader who will keep them from wronging one another and will judge between them in their contentions and disputes, so that, if there were no supremacy, there would be anarchy and the human race

<hr>

From *The Word of Islam*, edited by John Alden Williams (Austin, Tex.: University of Texas Press, 1994), pp. 93–95. Copyright © 1994 by the University of Texas Press. Reprinted by permission.

would be a confused rabble. As al-Afwā al-Awdī the pre-Islamic poet says,

> Ill for Mankind is chaos, with no chiefs their own,
> and no chiefs there are, when the ignorant lord it.

According to another party, it is necessitated by the Law, which goes beyond reason, since the Imam has to carry out prescriptions of the Law which reason might not perceive that God's service demands.

Reason therefore (they say) does not necessitate it: reason only demands that intelligent people forbid themselves to commit wrongs against each other or cut relations with one another, and act in accord with justice in equality and friendly conduct, and thus follow their own reason, not that of another. As it is, the Law has come down to give jurisdiction to its delegate in the Religion, for God the Mighty and Glorious has said, "O you who have faith, obey God and obey the Messenger, and those set in authority among you" [Qur'ān 4:58], so that He has made it obligatory for us to obey the ones set in authority, the Imams reigning over us.

The obligatory nature of the Imamate is thus established, but it is only an obligation for those necessary to perform it, like jihād or the seeking of religious knowledge. If no one takes it on, two groups of people emerge:

1. The people suited to choose, until they select an Imam for the umma, and
2. The people suited to be Imam, until one of them is invested with the office.

Those who do not belong to these categories commit no crime or sin if they delay in choosing an Imam. The qualifications of those suited to choose are three:

1. **Rectitude,** with all its qualifications.
2. **Religious knowledge** sufficient to arrive at knowledge of who deserves to be the Imam.
3. **Judgment and wisdom** to select the best man suited for it.

As for those fitted for the Imamate, there are seven qualifications:

1. **Rectitude,** with all its qualifications.
2. **Religious knowledge** necessary to interpret the Law in revealed and religious matters.
3. **Soundness of the senses** of hearing, sight and speech so that these function normally.
4. **Soundness of limb** from any defect which would prevent freedom of movement and agility.
5. **Judgment** for governing and administration.
6. **Courage and bravery** to protect his flock and wage jihād.
7. **Nasab** [correct genealogy]. He must be of the Quraysh. The Prophet, may God bless him and give him peace, said, "Give precedence to the Quraysh and do not go before them." There is no pretext for any disagreement about this, and no word one may raise against it.

There are ten things the Caliph must do in public affairs:

1. **Maintain religion** according to its established principles.
2. **Apply legal judgments** for litigants so that equity reigns, without aiding the oppressor or weakening the oppressed.
3. **Protect the flock** and keep the wolf from the fold, so that people may gain their living and move from place to place securely.
4. **Apply the ḥudūd** or punishments of the Law, so as to secure God's prohibitions from violation.
5. **Fortify the marches** so that the enemy will not appear due to neglect, shedding the blood of any Muslim or protected person.
6. **Wage jihād** against those who reject Islam so that they become either Muslims or protected people.
7. **Collect the zakāt and the taxes** on conquered territory in conformity with the Law, without fear or oppression.
8. **Administer treasury expenditures.**
9. **Delegate loyal and trustworthy people.**
10. **Directly oversee** matters and not delegate his authority seeking to occupy himself either with pleasure or devotion.

12.3.2 Theology (*Kalam*)

The word commonly used for Islamic theology is **kalam,** which means "speech." This indicates that theology emerged as Muslims talked about and debated religious issues. Some of the earliest debates arose out of the assassinations of the caliphs Umar, Uthman, and Ali and the civil wars that resulted in the division between the **Sunni** and **Shi'i** branches. Given these circumstances, questions about who had the right to rule the community, and whether a believer who committed a serious sin (the assassins of the early caliphs were Muslims) could be readmitted into the community or be saved, arose and were fiercely debated.

By the end of the eighth century, distinct theological schools had emerged, one of the most famous of which is the **Mu'tazila.** This school became the official theological school of the Sunni world in the mid-ninth century, but when official patronage was lost, it was declared heretical and its members persecuted. The Mu'tazila was largely replaced by the Ash'aria school, named for the theologian **al-Ash'ari.**

These two schools, the Mu'tazila and the **Ash'aria,** differ on a wide range of issues, among them the role that reason can and should play in the interpretation of revelation. The Mu'tazilites rely more heavily on reason than the Ash'arites. Thus, they are willing to interpret the Qur'an allegorically in those places where it speaks anthropomorphically of Allah. Allah is divine, not human, and hence cannot literally have such things as hands or a face. The Ash'arites agree that Allah is divine, not human, yet Allah's revelation says he has such things as hands and a face. Therefore, it must be true, although the hands and face of Allah are unlike human hands and face since his are divine.

The first selection is attributed to Abu Mansur al-Maturidi (d. 944) who was a leader of the Hanafi law school, but it probably was written a generation after his death by his students as a kind of creed for the school. When the Mu'tazila introduced the use of reason to critically analyze revelation, the Traditionalists, or Old Believers, objected to any use of reason in theological matters. We must, they argued, rely exclusively on Qur'an and *Hadith*. Eventually, however, the traditionalists discovered that reason and argumentation could be used by them to refute the theological positions of the Mu'tazila and others with whom they disagreed. Hence they developed arguments borrowed from Greek and Persian philosophers to support their usually conservative positions.

The second selection is by al-Ash'ari (d. 935), who had once been a member of the rationalistic Mu'tazila school of theology. He became convinced, however, that many sayings of the Prophet could not be reconciled with the teachings of the Mu'tazila so he left the school. Eventually the school he founded, Ash'aria, replaced the Mu'tazila as the official theological school of Sunni Islam. However, Mu'tazilite tendencies lived on among the Shi'ite sects as the last selection, by Hasan ibn Yusuf Hallama al-Hilli (d. 1326), shows.

Among the various sects of Shi'a Islam are the **Twelvers,** so called because they believe that the twelfth in the line of **imams,** or rightly guided caliphs, did not die but was taken by God into occulta-

tion (a state of hidden suspension). Someday he will return as the **Mahdi,** a kind of messianic figure who will herald the last judgment and signal the triumph of Islam. While the Mahdi is mentioned in certain *hadiths,* Sunni scholars question the authenticity of these *hadiths.* The Twelvers are the largest Shi'ite sect and are the official state religion of Iran.

AL-MATURIDI

God and the World

READING QUESTIONS

1. How does al-Maturidi reach the conclusion that there is One Maker of the world who is eternal?
2. What is al-Maturidi's position on the Qur'an as the word of God, and how does it differ from the Mu'tazila and the Ash'aria positions?
3. Why do you think al-Ash'ari denies free will in the matter of belief and that whatever God commands is good?
4. Why, according to al-Hilli, does reason require humans to be "free agents," and why is it not possible for God to do evil?

1. There are three things in which knowledge [*'ilm*] occurs: sound perceptions, right intelligence, and information coming from truthful servants of God. The Sophists held that it does not occur at all, since the data furnished by these sources are self-contradicting: in perception, one who is squint-eyed will see one thing as two; reason's activity may hit or miss, and information may be true or false. We reply: we are dealing here with sound perception, so what you argue is not sound. By reason, we mean right reason, and by information we mean that of the infallible messengers of God, related by consecutive testimony.

2. The cosmos is originated [*muḥdath*], because it is divided into substances and accidents, and accidents are

This selection and the two that follow are from *The Word of Islam,* edited by John Alden Williams (Austin, Tex.: University of Texas Press, 1994), pp. 146–147, 153, 196–198. Copyright © 1994 by the University of Texas Press. Reprinted by permission.

originated, since this is a name given to something that was not and then came to be. Cloud is such an occurrence. Substances are never free from accident, so they also are originated, due to their participation in existence with things that are originated. If it is established that the cosmos is originated, then it is clear that it is occasioned by the action of another than itself. If it is established that it has a maker, then the maker is eternal, since if he were not he would also have to have an originator, and similarly with the second and third events in a regressive causal series, and the causal series cannot be infinite.

According to the materialists, the world is originated from Primeval Stuff, that is to say from an eternal source which is matter, for they hold that creation from nothing is impossible.

3. The Maker must be one, since if there were two they would necessarily either concur or not concur in their creating. Agreement would be evidence of the weakness of both or either of them, since a free agent does not agree except by compulsion, and if they differed, then either both of them would attain their desire, which is absurd, or they would not attain it, which would mean their impotence, and a weakling is not suitable as a Lord. This is also taken from God's Word, exalted be He: "if there were other gods than God in heaven or on earth, they would both go to ruin" [Qur'an 21:22]. The Zoroastrians have held that the cosmos had two creators: one was good and created good things; he is Yazdan. The other was evil and created evil things; he is Ahriman. This creator of evil is purposeless and not to be connected with Yazdan. We reply: the Creator of evil would only be purposeless if there was no wisdom in His creation of it, but there is; the least of it is that it brings down tyrants. . . .

8. The Qur'an, the Word of God, is an eternal attribute, subsisting in God's essence, though not in the form of letters and sounds, as one; not divided into sections and neither Arabic nor Syriac. Rather, His creatures express that one attribute with varying expressions as they do with the essence of God, exalted be He. In the same way, life, will, and eternal existence, among His eternal attributes, are expressed in varying ways. The Mu'tazila have held that the word of God is other than these expressions and that it is originated, for if it were eternal then God would eternally have been a Commander, a Prohibiter, and an Informer about things which did not exist, and that would be pointless.

We reply: it would only be pointless if when a command is given there had to be an immediate response, for priority and posteriority are dependent on time and space, and the Word of God is dependent on neither of these.

If it should be said that God, be He exalted, has said, "We have *made* it an Arabic Qur'an" [43:3], and that making is creating, we reply that His Word, "They *make* the angels, the servants of the Merciful One, females" [43:19] does not support them.

The Ash'ari [theologians] have said that what is in the text is not the Word of God, but is only an expression of the Word of God, which is an attribute, and the attribute is not to be separated from that to which it is attributed. We say, it *is* the Word of God, but the letters and sounds are created, for we do not say that the Word of God inheres in the text so that there can be any talk of separation, for when a thing is known by God's knowledge, the attribute of knowledge is not thereby separated from Him.

AL-ASH'ARI

Whatever God Wills Is Right

Question: Would you hold that evil is from God?
Answer: Some of our associates say that all things are from God, in totality, without specifically saying that evil is from God. This is like saying that all things belong to God. However, I hold that evil is from God in that He creates it for others, not for Himself.

There were twins in a desert, and it occurred to the heart of one of them that God is one: who cast it into his heart? God. Was what God cast into his heart true? Yes. It occurred to the heart of the other of them that God is the third of three: who cast it into his heart? God. Was what God cast into his heart false? Yes. Did God lie to him? It is wrong to say that God told him the truth, because the veracity of the Creator is one of His essential attributes, and He cannot lie. But it is not necessary when He creates falsehood for another, or creates falsehood in the heart of another, that He be lying.
Question: Has God not charged the rejecter with the duty of faith?
Answer: Yes.
Question: Then the rejecter is capable of faith.
Answer: If one were capable of faith, one would have it.
Question: Then God charges one with what one cannot do.

Answer: This is a statement which involves two matters. If you want to say one is incapable of faith because of inability to have it, then no. But if you mean one is incapable of faith because one is preoccupied with its contrary, then yes.

Question: Is God free to inflict pain on infants in the world to come?

Answer: God is free to do that, and in doing it would be just. In the same way, whenever He inflicts an infinite punishment for a finite sin, and subjects some living beings to others, and is gracious to some and not to others, and creates some knowing well that they will reject faith—all that is justice on His part. It would not be wrong on His part to create them in painful torments and make these everlasting. Nor would it be wrong on His part to punish the faithful and cause the rejecter to enter Paradise. We only say He will not do it because He has informed us that He will punish rejecters; and He cannot lie when He gives information. He is the Overwhelming Monarch, subject to no one. That being so, nothing can be wrong on God's part. For a thing is wrong on our part only when we go beyond the limit set for us and do what we have no right to do. But since the Creator is subject to no one, nothing can be wrong on His part.

Question: Then lying is wrong only because God has declared it to be wrong.

Answer: Quite so. And if He declared it good, it would be good; and if He commanded it, there could be no opposition to it.

AL-HILLI

Twelver Shi'ite Theology

Our learned men agree in considering as a legal duty the knowledge of God, what is proper for Him and impossible for Him, and Prophecy, the Imamate, and the Return.

Knowledge of God: God Most High is a Speaker [*mutakallim*], as all agree. By speech [*kalām*] we mean audible and orderly letters and sounds. The meaning of His being a Speaker is that He brings speech into existence in some sort of body [*jism*]. The explanation of the Ash'arīs is contrary to reason. They say that God's speech inheres in the divine essence [hence is uncreated]. The Ḥanbalīs and the Karrāmīs also say it inheres

in His essence. The Mu'tazila and the Imāmī Shī'īs say the reality: it inheres in something else, for example, the burning bush of Moses, not in His essence. The meaning of His being a Speaker is that He makes speech, not that He is One in whom speech inheres. As to the priority of His speech, the Ash'arīs have said that the idea was prior, and the Ḥanbalīs said that the letters were prior. The Mu'tazila have said that speech was an originated thing, and that is the reality, for several reasons.

On the Nature of God: God is truthful, for a lie is necessarily evil, and He is far removed from evil, since it is impossible for Him to have any imperfections.

It is not possible for Him to be in a place, for then He would have need of it, nor in a direction, for then He would have need of it. *These are both negative qualities. Contrary to the Christians and some Ṣūfīs, He is not in a place [e.g., the person of Jesus]. What is understood by Incarnation is the inhering of one entity in another, and if they intend this, then it is false, for then the Necessary would have to be in need, which cannot be.*

Pleasure and pain are not valid attributes for Him, since it is not possible for God to have a constitution.

Ocular vision of God is impossible, because what can be seen has direction. Then He would be a body, and that is impossible. There is also the word of God to Moses, "You shall never see me" [Qur'ān 7:139]. *On the Day of Resurrection, perfect knowledge will be necessary, but it will be without ocular vision.*

Our acts occur by free choice, and reason requires this. *The doctrine of the Ash'arīs is that all actions take place by the power of the Most High, and no action whatever belongs to the creature. But if the creature did not bring its actions into being, then the Creator would be most unjust to punish it, and all agree that God does punish [sin].*

Evil is not possible for God, because He has what deters Him from it, the knowledge of evil. Also He has no motive, for the motive would be either the need or the wisdom of evil, both of which are ruled out.

The will to do evil is impossible for Him, for that will is evil.

Kindness, *lutf,* is necessary in God Most High. *Lutf* is what brings the creature near to obedience and keeps it far from disobedience. If God wills that humankind perform the Law, and gives it no possibility of attainment without His assistance, then not to give it would frustrate His own aim—and reason knows that it would be repugnant behavior. God is far above that.

On the Imamate:

1. The Imamate is a general authority in religious and worldly matters for a specific person, *derived from the Prophet.* It is necessary [*wājib*], according to reason. For the Imamate is a kindness from God, and we know

beyond question that when people have a chief who avenges the oppressed and restrains the oppressor, they come closer to sound behavior and are further from corruption.

2. It is necessary that the Imam be *ma'ṣūm*, divinely preserved from sin and error, otherwise, he would need an Imam himself. Also, if he committed sin, he would lose his place in people's hearts. Also, he is the guardian of the Law, so he must be immune from sin to preserve it from addition or loss. Finally there is the Word of God: "My Covenant embraces not the doers of evil" [Qur'ān 2:118].

3. It is necessary that the Imam be specified [*manṣūṣ*] for the office, for immunity from sin is one of the hidden matters. Thus there is no escaping a specification made by one who knows that he has immunity [i.e., the Prophet or the previous Imam]. *All agree that the Imam may be designated by a prophet or previous Imam, but the Sunnīs go on to say that he is established by the acknowledgment of "those with power to loose and bind," and some of the righteous Zaydī Mu'tazila have agreed with them. The Jā-rūdī Zaydīs add that any learned courageous Fāṭimī [from the line of Ḥasan or Ḥusayn] who rises with the sword to summon people to right becomes the Imam. The objection to this is that then there would be contention among those fitted for the Imamate.*

4. It is necessary for the Imam to be better than any of his subjects. *Otherwise the worse would take precedence over the better.*

5. The Imam after the Messenger of God is 'Alī b. Abī Ṭālib, and then his eleven [named] descendants. *The Twelfth Imam, the lord of our age, Muḥammad b. al-Ḥasan al-'Askarī, is alive and existent since the time of his birth in 870 (A.H. 256), for there must be an Imam in every age, so long as there are people to obey the Law. The cause of his staying absent is the strength of his opponents and the weakness of his helpers, or a benefit on which the faithful depend, or wisdom known to God alone. O God, let advent shine upon us, and enlighten our eyes with his beauty, for the sake of Mu-ḥammad, his following and his family!*

12.3.3 Sufism

Sufism is an umbrella term for a variety of Islamic literary, social, and philosophical phenomena generally sharing a mystical or spiritual tendency. In a narrow sense, it refers to a number of mystical orders and practices as well as popular shrine cults found throughout the Islamic world.

The earliest Sufis emphasized asceticism, devotion, and withdrawal from a corrupt and materialisti-

cally oriented society. The term *suf* ("wool") may derive from the practice of wearing wool robes, and some of the early practices, including dress, may have been influenced by Christian monks living in the Arabian desert.

One of the goals of a Sufi is an intense spiritual experience of God. This experience, sometimes called *fana* (annihilation), is often compared to the ecstasy of falling madly in love or of being intoxicated with wine. Some view *fana* as the loss of one's individuality in an experience of union with the divine like a drop of water merging with the ocean, whereas others think of it as more like a mirror reflecting light. The Sufi polishes his or her heart with prayer until it reflects nothing but the light of God.

Women, who were not allowed official roles in traditional Islamic practice, were particularly attracted to Sufism because it allowed them to express their spirituality. One of the earliest and most revered female Sufis is Rabi'a al-'Adawiya (717–801), who emphasized the unconditional love of Allah (see the first selection).

Even though most Sufis claim the peak mystical experience of Allah is inexpressible, metaphors like love, intoxication, merging, and annihilation made many Muslim legalists and theologians uncomfortable. Sufism appeared to compromise the transcendence of Allah and blur the distinction between the human and the divine. It was dangerously close to that "corruption" of monotheism known as Christianity, and when a popular ecstatic Husayn ibn Mansur al-Hallaj (d. 922), who had chosen Jesus as his spiritual model, proclaimed "I am the Truth" (see John 14:6), he was charged with blasphemy. Refusing to recant, he was publicly scourged and, like Jesus, crucified. He became, for the later Sufis, a holy martyr for the truth.

Abu Hamid al-Ghazali (1058–1111) was a genius who mastered most of the knowledge of his day—science, medicine, mathematics, theology, philosophy—and became a brilliant professor. However, he became unsatisfied with his learning, sought instructions from Sufis, and followed the Sufi path of repentance, renunciation, and special meditative prayer techniques called *dhikr* (or *zikr*)—the remembrance of God by repetition of the divine names. Painfully aware of what happened to al-Hallaj, al-Ghazali argued that *fana* did not amount to identity, however temporary, with God although it constituted the most intimate "nearness" to God possible for humans (see the second selection).

Al-Ghazali's caution about *fana* was not shared by Farid al-Din Attar (1120–1230) a Persian Sufi poet of great power devoted to the memory of al-Hallaj. Like many Sufis, he was a gifted storyteller and helped perfect the Sufi teaching tale. These stories, many of which have become famous worldwide, transmit a spiritual message in a humble and often humorous form.

Our third selection is from the climax of Attar's famous mystical epic, *Mantiq Ut-Tair* or *The Conference of the Birds*. Birds from all the world have been guided by the Hoopoe (a bird famous in Islamic lore) in search of their king, the Simurgh (a great bird of myth and legend that has the gift of speech and whose feathers possess magical properties). They have traveled through many valleys, faced great hardships, and now face the Valley of Death.

By the thirteenth century, Islamic educational and legal institutions had been formalized and Sufism soon followed suit. Sufi orders made up of disciples and masters began to appear. Many of these orders were important in the evolution and expansion of Islam. For example, the Naqshbandi order, founded by a Sufi scholar named Baha al-Din Naqshband (d. 1389), supports the notion that Sufis should pursue spiritual goals while fulfilling social responsibilities of service to the larger community. Several figures from this order were important in eighteenth- and nineteenth-century reform movements in India and Central Asia. This order teaches eight principles: awareness of breathing, watching one's steps, journeying within, solitude within society, recollection, restraining one's thoughts, watching one's thoughts, and concentration on God.

Another order, called the Chisti order, is famous for its particular kind of musical performance called *qawwali*, in which religious songs set to a rhythmic beat are sung. Perhaps the most famous order is the Mevlevi order, known in Europe and the United States as the "Whirling Dervishes" because their distinctive *dhikr* ritual involves a dance called the ***sama***. While turning counterclockwise with the right palm facing up and the left down, the *sama* symbolizes the receipt and transmission of divine grace. This order traces its origin to the Sufi poet Jalal al-Din Rumi (d. 1273), called the Mevlana ("Our Master") in Turkish (see the last selection).

Before we look at the writings of some Sufis, something should be said about the role of saints in Islam. There are two types of saints: the first are the members of Muhammad's family whose shrines are visited by both Shi'is and Sunnis, and the second are important Sufi masters, or *shaykhs*, whose shrines have become important pilgrimage sites. Miracles are attributed to these saints because they are thought to possess a miraculous power called *baraka*. **Baraka** gives its possessors curative powers as well as enables them to intercede with God. Veneration of saints and belief in *baraka* are often discouraged by legal and theological scholars because they believe it not only amounts to superstition but also encourages people to devote themselves to humans and not God.

༄

RABI'A

Love of God

READING QUESTIONS

1. How would you characterize Rabi'a's spirituality?
2. What, for al-Ghazali, is the most distinctive thing about mysticism?
3. How does al-Ghazali describe the mystic way?
4. Why do you think al-Ghazali interprets *fana* as "nearness" to Allah but rejects other interpretations such as "inherence," "union," and "connection"?
5. What do you think the stories of the moths and the Prince and the Beggar mean?
6. What do you think is meant by "Annihilate . . . yourselves . . . in me, and in me you shall find yourselves"?
7. What most impresses you about Rumi's poetry?

Abd Allah b. Isa said: I entered Rabi'a's presence and I saw the light on her face, and she used to weep much, and a man related of her that at every mention of fire (representing the punishment of the unrepentant sinner), she swooned, and I heard the falling of her tears on the ground like the sound of water filling a vessel. . . . I came into Rabi'a's presence and she was worshipping, and when I reached my place, she raised her head, and lo, the place of her worship was like a marsh from her tears and I saluted her. Then she received me and said, "O my son, do you need anything?" and I said, "I came to you to greet you," and she wept and said, "May God

From Margaret Smith, *Rabi'a: The Mystic and Her Fellow Saints in Islam* (Lahore, Pakistan: Kazi Publications, [n.d.]), pp. 56, 58, 83, 97, 102. Reprinted by permission.

censure thee!" Then she rose up for the ritual prayer and said, "I ask forgiveness of God for my lack of sincerity when I say those words 'I ask forgiveness of God.'

[*Siyar al-Salihat*, 26a]

It is related that at one time she saw someone who had a bandage bound about his head. She said, "Why is this bandage bound round your head?" He said, "My head is paining me." Rabi'a asked him how old he was. "Thirty years old," he replied. She asked him, "Were you in pain and trouble for the greater part of your life?" "No," he answered. Then she said, "For thirty years (God) has kept your body fit and you have never bound upon it the bandage of gratitude, but for one night of pain in your head you bind it with the bandage of complaint."

[Attar, *Tadhkirat al-Awliya*]

They told us that Rabi'a al-'Adawiyya once said: I praised God one night with the praises of dawn, then I slept and I saw a bright green tree, indescribable in its size and beauty, and lo, upon it were three kinds of fruit, unknown to me among the fruits of this world, like virgins' breasts, white, red and yellow, and they shone like spheres and suns in the green spaces of the tree, and I admired them and said, "Whose is this?" and one said to me, "This is yours, for your praises aforetime." Then I began to walk round it, and lo, under it were eighteen fruits on the ground, of the color of gold, and I said, "If only these fruits were with the fruits on the tree, it would surely be better." That personage said to me: "They would have been there, but that you, when you offered your praises, were thinking, 'Is the dough leavened or not?' and this fruit fell off."

[*Qut al-Qulub*, I, p. 103]

Some people were speaking in Rabi'a's presence of a devotee, who was known to be holy and in the favor of God, and who lived on what he collected from the refuse-heap of one of our kings, and a man said in her hearing, "What harm would there be in this, if he is in favor with God, and he should ask of him to provide him with food by some other means?" and Rabi'a said to him, "Be silent, O worthless one, have you not realized that the saints of God are satisfied with Him, that they accept his will even if he takes from them their means of livelihood, so long as it is he who chooses this for them?"

[Abu Talib, *Qut al-Qulub*, p. 40]

I have loved you with two loves, a selfish love and a love that is worthy of you. As for the love which is selfish, I occupy myself therein with remembrance of you to the exclusion of all others. As for that which is worthy of you, therein you raise the veil that I may see you. Yet is there no praise to me in this or that, but the praise is to you, whether in that or this.

[*Rawd Al-Fa'iq*, p. 213]

AL-GHAZALI

Deliverance from Error

When God by His grace and abundant generosity cured me of this disease, I came to regard the various seekers (sc. after truth) as comprising four groups: (1) the *Theologians* (*mutakallimun*), who claim that they are the exponents of thought and intellectual speculation; (2) the *Batiniyah*, who consider that they, as the party of "authoritative instruction" (*ta'lim*), alone derive truth from the infallible *imam*; (3) the *Philosophers*, who regard themselves as the exponents of logic and demonstration; (4) the *Sufis or Mystics*, who claim that they alone enter into the "presence" [of God], and possess vision and intuitive understanding....

When I had finished with these sciences [of the philosophers], I next turned with set purpose to the method of mysticism (or Sufism). I know that the complete mystic "way" includes both intellectual belief and practical activity; the latter consists in getting rid of the obstacles in the self and in stripping off its base characteristics and vicious morals, so that the heart may attain to freedom from what is not God and to constant recollection of Him.

The Intellectual belief was easier to me than the practical activity. I began to acquaint myself with their belief by reading their books. . . . I thus comprehended their fundamental teachings on the intellectual side, and progressed, as far as is possible by study and oral instruction, in the knowledge of mysticism. It became clear to me, however, that what is most distinctive of mysticism is something which cannot be apprehended by study, but only by immediate experience (*dhawq*—literally "tasting"), by ecstasy and by a moral change. What a difference there is between *knowing* the definition of health

From *The Faith and Practice of al-Ghazali*, translated by W. Montgomery Watt (London: George Allen and Unwin, 1953), pp. 26–27, 54–62. Copyright © 1953 by George Allen and Unwin. Reprinted by permission of HarperCollins Publishers, Ltd.

and satiety, together with their causes and presuppositions, and *being* healthy and satisfied! . . .

In general, then, how is a mystic "way" (*tariqah*) described? The purity which is the first condition of it [as bodily purity is the proper condition of formal Worship for Muslims] is the purification of the heart completely from what is other than God most high; the key to it, which corresponds to the opening act of adoration in prayer, is the sinking of the heart completely in the recollection of God; and the end of it is complete absorption (*fana'*) in God. At least this is its end relatively to those first steps which almost come within the sphere of choice and personal responsibility; but in reality in the actual mystic "way" it is the first step, what comes before it being, as it were, the antechamber for those who are journeying towards it.

With this first stage of the "way" there begin the revelations and visions. The mystics in their waking state now behold angels and spirits of the prophets; they hear these speaking to them and are instructed by them. Later, a higher state is reached; instead of beholding forms and figures, they come to stages in the "way" which it is hard to describe in language; if a man attempts to express these, his words inevitably contain what is clearly erroneous.

In general what they manage to achieve is nearness to God; some, however, would conceive of this as "inherence" (*hulul*), some as "union" (*itthad*), and some as "connection" (*wusul*). All that is erroneous. . . .

In general the man to whom He has granted no immediate experience at all, apprehends no more of what prophetic revelation really is than the name. The miraculous graces given to the saints are in truth the beginnings of the prophets; and that was the first "state" of the Messenger of God (peace be upon him) when he went out to Mount Hira, and was given up entirely to his Lord, and worshipped, so that the bedouin said, "Muhammad loves his Lord passionately."

Now this is the mystical "state" which is realized in immediate experience by those who walk in the way leading to it. Those to whom it is not granted to have immediate experience can become assured of it by trial [i.e., contact with mystics or observation of them] and by hearsay, if they have sufficiently numerous opportunities of associating with mystics to understand that [ecstasy] with certainty by means of what accompanies the "states." Whoever sits in their company derives from them this faith; and none who sits in their company is painted.

[Sections 78, 122–125, 132–135]

ATTAR

The Conference of the Birds

THE SEVENTH VALLEY OR THE VALLEY OF DEPRIVATION AND DEATH

The Hoopoe continued: "Last of all comes the Valley of Deprivation and Death, which it is almost impossible to describe. The essence of this Valley is forgetfulness, dumbness, deafness and distraction; the thousand shadows which surround you disappear in a single ray of the celestial sun. When the ocean of immensity begins to heave, the pattern of its surface loses its form; and this pattern is no other than the world present and the world to come. Whoever declares that he does not exist acquires great merit. The drop that becomes part of this great ocean abides there for ever and in peace. In this calm sea, a man, at first, experiences only humiliation and overthrow; but when he emerges from this state he will understand it as creation, and many secrets will be revealed to him.

"Many beings have missed taking the first step and so have not been able to take the second—they can only be compared to minerals. When aloe wood and thorns are reduced to ashes they both look alike—but their quality is different. An impure object dropped into rose-water remains impure because of its innate qualities; but a pure object dropped in the ocean will lose its specific existence and will participate in the ocean and in its movement. In ceasing to exist separately it retains its beauty. It exists and non-exists. How can this be? The mind cannot conceive it." . . .

STORY OF THE MOTHS

One night, the moths met together tormented by a desire to be united to the candle. They said: "We must send someone who will bring us information about the object of our amorous quest." So one of them set off and came

From Farid Ud-Din Attar, *The Conference of the Birds: Mantiq Ut-Tair*, translated by C. S. Nott (Boulder, Colo.: Shambhala Publications, 1954), pp. 123–132. © 1954 by C. S. Nott. Reprinted by arrangement with Shambhala Publications, Inc., Boston.

to a castle, and inside he saw the light of a candle. He returned, and according to his understanding, reported what he had seen. But the wise moth who presided over the gathering expressed the opinion that he understood nothing about the candle. So another moth went there. He touched the flame with the tip of his wings, but the heat drove him off. His report being no more satisfying than that of the first, a third went out. This one, intoxicated with love, threw himself on the flame; with his forelegs he took hold of the flame and united himself joyously with her. He embraced her completely and his body became as red as fire. The wise moth, who was watching from far off, saw that the flame and moth appeared to be one, and he said: "He has learnt what he wished to know; but only he understands, and one can say no more." . . .

THE PRINCE AND THE BEGGAR

There was once a king who had a son as charming as Joseph, full of grace and beauty. He was loved by everyone, and all who saw him would gladly have been the dust under his feet. If he went out at night, it was as if a new sun had risen over the desert. His eyes were the black narcissus, and when they glanced they set a world on fire. His smile scattered sugar, and wherever he walked a thousand roses bloomed, not waiting for the spring.

Now there was a simple dervish who had lost his heart to this young prince. Day and night he sat near the prince's palace, neither eating nor sleeping. His face became like yellow gold, and his eyes shed tears of silver, for his heart was cut in two. He would have died, but that from time to time he caught a glimpse of the young prince when he appeared in the bazaar. But how could such a prince comfort a poor dervish in this state? Yet the simple man, who was a shadow, a particle of an atom, wished to take the radiant sun on his breast.

One day when the prince was riding at the head of his attendants the dervish stood up and gave a cry and said: "My reason has left me, my heart is consumed, I no longer have patience or strength to suffer," and he beat his head on the ground in front of the prince. One of the courtiers wanted to have him killed, and went to the king. "Sire," he said, "a libertine has fallen in love with your son." The king was very angry: "Have this audacious scoundrel impaled," he said. "Bind him hand and foot and put his head on a stake." The courtier went at once to do his bidding. They put a running noose on the neck of the beggar and dragged him to the stake. No one knew what it was about and no one interceded for

him. When the wazir had had him brought under the gibbet, the dervish gave a cry of grief and said: "For the love of God, give me a respite, so that at least I can say a prayer under the gibbet." This was allowed, and the dervish prostrated himself and prayed: "O God, since the king has given orders for my death—I, who am innocent—grant me, your ignorant servant, before I die, the good fortune to see only once the face of this young man, so that I may offer myself as a sacrifice. O God, my King, you who give ear to a thousand prayers, grant this last wish of mine."

No sooner had the dervish uttered this prayer than the arrow of his desire reached its mark. The wazir divined his secret and took pity on him. He went to the king and explained the true state of things. At this the king became thoughtful; then compassion filled his heart and he pardoned the dervish, and said to the prince: "Go and fetch this poor man from under the gibbet. Be gentle with him and drink with him, for he has tasted of your poison. Take him to your garden and then bring him to me."

The young prince, another Joseph, went at once— the sun with a face of fire came face to face with an atom. This ocean of beautiful pearls went to seek a drop of water. Beat your head for joy, set your feet dancing, clap your hands! But the dervish was in despair; his tears turned the dust to mud and the world became heavy with his sighs. Even the prince himself could not help but weep. When the dervish saw his tears he said: "O Prince, now you may take my life." And so saying, he gave up the ghost and died. When he knew that he was united to his beloved no other desires were left.

O you, who at once exist and are yet a non-entity, whose happiness is mingled with unhappiness, if you have never experienced unrest, how will you appreciate tranquillity? You stretch out your hand towards the lightning and are stopped by swept-up heaps of snow. Strive valiantly, burn reason, and give yourself up to folly. If you wish to use this alchemy reflect a little and, by my example, renounce yourself; withdraw from your wandering thoughts into your soul so that you may come to spiritual poverty. As for me, who am neither I nor not-I, I have strayed from myself, and I find no other remedy than despair.

QUESTION OF A DISCIPLE
TO HIS SHAIKH

A man who was striving to overcome his weaknesses asked Nuri one day: "How shall I ever be able to arrive at union with God?" Nuri replied: "For this you must cross seven oceans of light and seven of fire, and travel a very long road. When you have crossed these twice seven oceans, a fish will draw you to him, such a fish that when he breathes he draws into his breast the first and the last. This marvellous fish has neither head nor tail; he holds himself in the middle of the ocean, quiet and detached; he sweeps away the two worlds, and he draws to himself all creatures without exception."

ATTITUDE OF THE BIRDS

When the birds had listened to this discourse of the Hoopoe their heads drooped down, and sorrow pierced their hearts. Now they understood how difficult it would be for a handful of dust like themselves to bend such a bow. So great was their agitation that numbers of them died then and there. But others, in spite of their distress, decided to set out on the long road. For years they travelled over mountains and valleys, and a great part of their life flowed past on this journey. But how is it possible to relate all that happened to them? It would be necessary to go with them and see their difficulties for oneself, and to follow the wandering of this long road. Only then could one realize what the birds suffered.

In the end, only a small number of all this great company arrived at the sublime place to which the Hoopoe had led them. . . .

"We have come," they said, "to acknowledge the Simurgh as our king. Through love and desire for him we have lost our reason and our peace of mind. Very long ago, when we started on this journey, we were thousands, and now only thirty of us have arrived at this sublime court. We cannot believe that the King will scorn us after all the sufferings we have gone through. Ah, no! He cannot but look on us with the eye of benevolence!"

The Chamberlain replied: "O you whose minds and hearts are troubled, whether you exist or do not exist in the universe, the King has his being always and eternally. Thousands of worlds of creatures are no more than an ant at his gate. You bring nothing but moans and lamentations. Return then to whence you came, O vile handful of earth!"

At this, the birds were petrified with astonishment. Nevertheless, when they came to themselves a little, they said: "Will this great king reject us so ignominiously? And if he really has this attitude to us may he not

change it to one of honour? Remember Majnun who said, 'If all the people who dwell on earth wished to sing my praises, I would not accept them; I would rather have the insults of Laila. One of her insults is more to me a hundred compliments from another woman!'"

"The lightning of his glory manifests itself," said the Chamberlain, "and it lifts up the reason of all souls. What benefit is there if the soul be consumed by a hundred sorrows? What benefit is there at this moment in either greatness or littleness?"

The birds, on fire with love, said: "How can the moth save itself from the flame when it wishes to be one with the flame? The friend we seek will content us by allowing us to be united to him. If now we are refused, what is there left for us to do? We are like the moth who wished for union with the flame of the candle. They begged him not to sacrifice himself so foolishly and for such an impossible aim, but he thanked them for their advice and told them that since his heart was given to the flame for ever, nothing else mattered."

Then the Chamberlain, having tested them, opened the door; and as he drew aside a hundred curtains, one after the other, a new world beyond the veil was revealed. Now was the light of lights manifested, and all of them sat down on the masnad, the seat of the Majesty and Glory. They were given a writing which they were told to read through; and reading this, and pondering, they were able to understand their state. When they were completely at peace and detached from all things they became aware that the Simurgh was there with them, and a new life began for them in the Simurgh. All that they had done previously was washed away. The sun of majesty sent forth his rays, and in the reflection of each other's faces these thirty birds (si-murgh) of the outer world, contemplated the face of the Simurgh of the inner world. This so astonished them that they did not know if they were still themselves or if they had become the Simurgh. At last, in a state of contemplation, they realized that they were the Simurgh and that the Simurgh was the thirty birds. When they gazed at the Simurgh they saw that it was truly the Simurgh who was there, and when they turned their eyes towards themselves they saw that they themselves were the Simurgh. And perceiving both at once, themselves and Him, they realized that they and the Simurgh were one and the same being. No one in the world has ever heard of anything to equal it. . . .

RUMI

Union and Separation

Only the imagination that has contemplated
Unification, and then, after direct vision, has
undergone separation;

Not a definitive separation, but one for a good
purpose, since that station is secure from all
separation;

In order to preserve the spiritualized body, the
Sun pulls back from the snow for a moment.

[*Masnawi* 6:4012–15]

At the time of union, only God knows what that
Moon is! For even during separation, what
incredible joy and expansion of spirit!

[*Diwan* 30321]

Separation and parting from Thee is difficult, oh
Beloved, especially after Thy embrace!

[*Diwan* 13901]

If man should see himself at all, if he should see that
his wound is deadly and gangrenous,

Then from such looking within, pain would
arise, and pain would bring him out from behind
the veil.

Until mothers feel the pain of childbirth, the
child finds no way to be born.

The trust is within the heart and the heart is
pregnant; all the exhortations of the saints act as a
midwife.

The midwife says, "The woman has no pain. Pain
is necessary, for it will open a way for the child."

He that is without pain is a brigand, for to be
without pain is to say "I am God."

To say "I" at the wrong time is a curse, but to
say it at the right time is a mercy.

[*Masnawi* 2:2516–22]

The body is pregnant with the spirit, the body's
suffering is the pain of childbirth—the coming of
the embryo brings pain and torment for the woman.

Look not at the wine's bitterness, look at the joy
of drunkards! Look not at the woman's affliction,
look at the hope of the midwife!

[*Diwan* 5990]

How much the Beloved made me suffer before this
work settled into the eye's water and the liver's
blood!

A thousand fires and smokes and heartaches—
and its name is Love! A thousand pains and regrets
and afflictions—and its name is Beloved!

Let every enemy of his own spirit set out to
work! Welcome to the spirit's sacrifice and a pitiful
death!

My heart keeps saying, "I suffer because of
Him," and I keep laughing at its weak hypocrisy.

[*Masnawi* 1:1773–82]

Union with this world is separation from that world.
The health of this body is the sickness of the spirit.

It is hard to be separated from this
caravanserai—so know that separation from that
permanent abode is harder!

Since it is hard for you to be separated from the
painting, think what it will be to be parted from the
Painter!

Oh you who cannot bear to be without this
despicable world! How can you bear to be without
God, oh friend, how?

Since you cannot bear to be without this black
water, how can you bear to be without God's
fountain? . . .

If you should see the Beauty of the Loving God
for one instant and throw your soul and existence
into the fire,

Then having seen the glory and splendor of His
proximity, you would see these sweet beverages as
carrion. . . .

Strive quickly to find Self in selflessness—and
God knows best the right course.

[*Masnawi* 4:3209–13, 15–16, 18]

12.4 ISLAM IN THE MODERN AGE

For nearly fourteen centuries Islam provided a coherent worldview, which gave meaning and direction
to the lives of millions of people. It provided a divine
sanction for various political and social orders, and
even though the political fortunes of various parts of
the Islamic world waxed and waned, there was this

sense Muslims had of belonging to the house of Islam. Muslims could look to a glorious past when the truth was revealed to Muhammad—a divine and decisive moment in human history. They could take comfort in the miraculously rapid expansion of Islam through Allah's merciful guidance of their early leaders. Then came the marvelous and mystical flourishing of a rich spiritual and intellectual culture when the Christian West was struggling through the Dark Ages. True, the great Abbasid Empire was destroyed by the Mongols in 1258, but Allah saw fit to convert the invaders and eventually three great Muslim empires—the Ottoman in the Middle East, the Safavid in Persia, and the Mughal on the India subcontinent—emerged to make strong the house of Islam. Then things changed.

From the seventeenth century on, gradual but steady Western intervention has resulted in one of the most serious challenges the Islamic world has ever encountered. As the Western colonial system slowly but surely subjugated the Muslim world, Muslims found themselves ruled by foreign unbelievers whose missionaries tried to convert them and more than hinted that Western rule was due to the superiority of the Christian civilization of the West.

The colonial experience raised profound and serious questions of identity and faith. What had gone wrong in Islam? What had happened to the divine guidance Allah had promised? How could one be a good Muslim in a state ruled by non-Muslims whose laws were not the laws of the *shari'a*? Every aspect of the traditional way of life seemed to be challenged by the modernity colonialism brought with it. Modernity—its science, technology, economics, thought—all led to asking new questions and wondering about new answers.

In the twentieth century, Muslim political fortunes started to change as various independence movements forced an end to colonialism and separate independent nation-states emerged throughout the Muslim world. Islamic religious leaders and Islamic religious values had played a major role in these liberation movements, but the role Islam should play in these newly established modern states was hotly debated. Should Islam be the state religion? What is the place of the *shari'a* in the state's legal system? Should family law be reformed?

With the rejection of purely secular states in Pakistan and Iran, and with the more general call in recent years throughout the Muslim world for governments more supportive of a distinctively Muslim way of life, the issue of Islamic resurgence has emerged. Sometimes it is called the Islamic renaissance, sometimes (usually by a Western media that wishes viewers to draw a negative picture) it is called Islamic fundamentalism.

12.4.1 Pan-Islam

Sayyid Jamal al-Din al-Afghani (1838–1897) was a journalist, activist, orator, and philosopher. He traveled widely from India and Afghanistan to Cairo, Paris, and London exhorting the Muslim community to be strong in the face of imperialistic colonialism. He is the father of both modern Muslim nationalism and pan-Islamism as well as the main inspiration of many different Islamic reform movements.

Al-Afghani argued that authentic Islam was ultimately founded on reason, which is also the basis of the success of Western societies. Thus, Muslims have no good reason to see either their religion or their moral values as somehow inferior to those of the West. There is, he said, no incompatibility between Islam and science. Muslims should use modern technology to improve their standard of living. He called on Sunnis and Shi'is to reconcile their differences and, like some Protestant reformers, argued that anyone with a sound mind and appropriate knowledge could interpret the Qur'an. Thus, he agitated against a privileged and elite clerical class of religious scholars that wished to remain in total control of the religious tradition and Qur'anic interpretation.

Below we sample some of Al-Afghani's thinking on Islamic solidarity.

AL-AFGHANI

Islamic Solidarity

READING QUESTIONS

1. What is the basis of Islamic solidarity?
2. How, according to Al-Afghani, does a Muslim ruler retain authority?

From *The Emergence of the Modern Middle East: Selected Readings*, translated and edited by Robert G. Landen (New York: Van Nostrand Reinhold Company, 1970), pp. 105–110. Reprinted by permission.

A study of the particular identity which characterizes some nations and an examination of their beliefs prove to anyone blessed with a clear and accurate sense of observation that in most nations there is a spirit of ethnic solidarity which in turn produces a sense of pride. Those whom this spirit animates are proud of the glorious deeds of their ethnic brothers. They become angry with any misfortunate which touches them to the point where, in order to combat it, they kill without thinking about the reasons or the causes of the sentiment which pushes them to act. This is why many who are seeking for truth have come to the conclusion that a strong feeling of ethnic identity must be counted as integral to human nature. Yet their opinion is not correct, as we can ascertain by the behavior of a child who, born in one country subsequently is taken before he reaches the age of conscious thinking into the territories of another nation; if he grows up and reaches the age of reason in that place, he will not mention his birthplace or display any natural partiality for it. He will have no idea about his birthplace. Indeed, perhaps he will be more attached to the place where he grew up. Yet, that which is truly natural does not change.

Therefore, we do not think that such a feeling is natural to man, but rather that it is composed of a number of accidental attributes which necessity stamps upon the feelings. Actually, wherever he is, the human being has many wants. Individuals have a tendency to set themselves apart and to seek profit for themselves when they have not been properly taught. Also, they have a tendency to have numerous selfish desires which, when united with power, gives them an aggressive character. That is why some men find themselves struggling against the aggression of others. After fighting troubles for long years they were constrained to band together according to their parentage and in various ways until they formed ethnic units. That is how they became divided into nations such as the Indians, the Russians, the Turkomans, etc. Each of these groups, thanks to the combined strength of its members, was able to preserve its interests and to safeguard its rights from any encroachment by another group. Moreover, they have gone even farther than necessary as is common in the evolution of man: they have reached the point where each group is bitter if it falls under the rule of another. It believes that domination will be oppressive even if it is just. . . .

However, if necessity has created this sort of individualistic racial solidarity, there is no doubt that such solidarity can disappear just as it can arise. Such can take place when an arbiter is accepted and the contending forces are brought together. . . . This arbiter is the Prince of all things, the Conqueror of heaven and earth. . . .

When men recognize the existence of the Supreme Judge . . . they will leave it entirely to the possessor of sacred power to safeguard good and repel evil. No longer will they have any need for an ethnic sentiment which has lost its purpose and whose memory has been erased from their souls; judgments belongs to Allah, the Sublime, the Magnificent.

That is the secret of the aversion which Muslims have for manifestations of ethnic origin in every country where they live. That is why they reject all clan loyalty with the exception of Islamic sentiment and religious solidarity. The believers in Islam are preoccupied neither with their ethnic origins nor with the people of which they are a part because they are loyal to their faith; they have given up a narrow bond in favor of a universal bond: the bond of faith.

Actually, the principles of the Islamic religion are not restricted to calling man to the truth or to considering the soul only in a spiritual context which is concerned with the relationship between this world and the one to come. . . . There is more besides: Islamic principles are concerned with relationships among the believers, they explain the law in general and in detail, they define the executive power which administers the law, they determine sentences and limit their conditions; also, they are concerned with the unique goal that the holder of power ought to be the most submissive of men to the rules regulating that power which he gains neither by heritage, nor inheritance, nor by virtue of his race, tribe, material strength, or wealth. On the contrary, he acquires it only if he submits to the stipulations of the sacred law, if he has the strength to apply it, and if he judges with the concurrence of the community. Thus, in truth, the ruler of the Muslims will be their religious, holy, and divine law which makes no distinction among peoples. This will also be the summary of the ideas of the nation. A Muslim ruler has no other privilege than that of being the most ardent of all in safeguarding the sacred law and defending it.

In safeguarding the rights and the protection of people, of property, and of reputations, the lawgiver has not taken any account of lineage, nor of ancestral privilege. Moreover, any bond, with the exception of the bond of Islamic law, was disapproved by Him. Whoever relies upon such bonds is subject to blame and whoever advocates them deserves criticism. The Prophet said, in this matter: "Tribal solidarity should not exist among us; it does not exist among those of us who are bound by religion; it does not exist among those of us who die believers." The *hadīths* (tradition) of the Prophet all agree upon this point. In summary, whoever surpasses all men in piety, that is to say, in the practice of Islamic law, will be distinguished by the respect and veneration accorded to him: *The noblest among you in the eyes of God, is the most pious* (Qur'ān 49:13). It has followed, down through many ages, and in spite of the differences in generations, that power has been wielded by men who are not noble in their race, nor especially privileged in their tribe; who do not hold sovereignty because of hereditary royalty, or do not claim it by virtue of their noble descent or highborn antecedents; they are raised to power only because of their obedience to the law and to the intense zeal they display in observing it.

The amount of power given to Muslim rulers is a product of their observance of divine regulations, of the way in which they follow the good directions which these prescribe, and of the absence of all personal ambition in them. Each time a ruler tries to distinguish himself by surpassing all others in luxury or the magnificence of his mode of life, or each time that he tries to assume a greater dignity than his people, then the people return to their tribal loyalties, differences arise, and the ruler's power declines.

Such is the lesson which one can learn from the history of the Muslims from the day their religion was revealed up to our own time. They set little value on either ethnic ties or racial sentiment but take only religious ties into consideration. That is why one can say that an Arab has no aversion to domination by Turks, why the Persian accepts the sovereignty of Arab, and why the Indian obeys the laws of the Afghan without any bitterness or hesitancy among them. That is why one also can assert that the Muslim does not revolt or protest against either the regimes which impose themselves over him or against the transfer of power from one tribe to another so long as the possessor of authority maintains religious law and follows its precepts. But if these regimes stray in their conduct and unjustly deviate from the laws' teachings and attempt to execute that which is not right, then the hearts of the Muslims are detached from them and they become the object of disaffection, and even if they are a Muslim people's own blood brothers, they will appear more odious than foreigners in the people's eyes.

One can also say that Muslims are different from the adherents to other religions because of the emotion and regret they feel if one piece of Muslim territory is cut off from an Islamic government, whatever may be the ethnic origin of the inhabitants of this territory or the group which has taken it over.

If among the Muslims one found a minor ruler of whatever racial origin, who followed the divine commandments, was zealous in applying them, compelled the people to apply the punishments which they ordain, obeyed the law himself like his subjects, and gave up trying to distinguish himself through vain pomp, it would be possible for this ruler to enjoy widespread power and great influence. He could assume great authority in Muslim-inhabited countries. He would not encounter great difficulty in doing this, for he would not have to spend money, or build up his army, or conclude alliances with the great powers, or seek the assistance of partisans of civilization and freedom. . . . He could accomplish all this by following the example of the orthodox caliphs [the early caliphs of Islam in the seventh century A.D., Ed.] and by returning to the original sources of Islamic religious law. His conduct would bring a revival of strength and a renewal of the prerequisites of power.

Let me repeat for you, reader, one more time, that unlike other religions, Islam is concerned not only with the life to come. Islam is more: it is concerned with its believers' interests in the world here below and with allowing them to realize success in this life as well as peace in the next life. It seeks "good fortune in two worlds." In its teachings it decrees equality among different peoples and nations.

The times have been so cruel and life so hard and confusing that some Muslims—they are rare—have lost patience and assert with difficulty that Islamic principles are their oppressors and they give up using religious principles of justice in their actions. They resort, even, to the protection of a foreign power but are filled with regret at the things that result from that course of action. . . . Actually, the schisms and divisions which have occurred in Muslim states originate only from the failure of rulers who deviate from the solid principles upon which the Islamic faith is built and stray from the road followed by their early ancestors. Certainly, opposition to solidly based precepts and wandering away from customary ways are the very actions that are most damaging to power. When those who rule Islam return to the rules of their law and model their conduct upon that practiced by early generations of Muslims, it will not be long before God gives them extensive power and bestows strength upon them comparable to that wielded by the orthodox caliphs, who were leaders of the faith. God give us the will to act with justice and lead us upon the road to integrity.

12.4.2 Authentic Islam

The repeated call, almost like the call to prayer, that one hears in Islam today is the call for Islamic authenticity. However, exactly what is authentically Islamic and how that, whatever it is, might be realized in the modern world remain questions of intense debate. Most agree that there are two forms of authenticity: individual and communal. Individually, each true Muslim should seek to perfect himself or herself as a servant of God, learning over and over again in daily life how to overcome self-will and submit to the divine will. Many argue that authenticity on a communal level involves creating a community that lives up to the full human potential ordained by God. Such a community would be a community of peace, unity, and justice for all.

We can read the writings of the philosophers, theologians, political theorists, and activists to gather ideas about how an authentic Islamic community should be created and what it might be like. However, in order to understand individual authenticity, in order to find authentic Islam on the streets and in the alleys among everyday Muslims, we have to go to literature—to the writers of poetry and of fiction.

One writer to whom we can turn for a taste of Islam on the street, as it were, is the Egyptian Nobel laureate Naguib Mahfouz (b. 1911). He is a prolific writer and, in a book titled *Midaq Alley*, writes of the ordinary people who live, work, and die in one of the hustling, teeming back alleys of Cairo. These people are quite ordinary. They are motivated by greed, love, lust, anger, and all the other human passions. Some of them are also motivated by piety and faith. One of these people is Radwan Hussainy to whom many come for advice because of his renown in the alley for piety and wisdom. In the excerpt that follows, Hussainy is about to leave on the pilgrimage to Mecca.

NAGUIB MAHFOUZ

Preparing for Hajj

READING QUESTION

1. How would you characterize the faith of Radwan Hussainy?

CHAPTER 33

It was a day of joyful leave-taking. Radwan Hussainy was loved and respected by everyone in the alley. Hussainy had hoped God would choose him to make the holy pilgrimage to Mecca and Medina this year and so He had. Everyone knew this was the day Radwan Hussainy would leave for Suez on his way to those holy lands, and his house was filled with well-wishers, lifelong friends and devout Muslims.

They clustered in his modest room, which had so often echoed with their pious and friendly discussions. They chatted about the pilgrimage and their reminiscences of it, their voices rising from every corner of the room and mixing with a trail of smoke billowing up from the brazier. They told tales of the modern pilgrimage and those of bygone days and related holy traditions and beautiful verses concerning it. One man, with a melodious voice, chanted verses from the Holy Qur'an, and then they all listened to a long and eloquent speech by Radwan Hussainy that expressed his heart's goodness.

A pious friend wished him: "A happy journey and safe return."

Hussainy beamed and replied in his most gentle manner, "Please, my friend, don't remind me of my return. Anyone who visits God's house with a longing for home deserves to have God deny him reward, ignore his prayers, and destroy his happiness. I will think of returning only when I have left the scene of the revelations on my way back to Egypt. And by 'returning' I mean going back on the pilgrimage again, with the help and permission of the All Merciful. If only I could spend the rest of my life in the Holy Land, seeing the ground which once was trod by the Prophet, the sky once filled with the angels singing, and listening to the divine revelation coming down to earth and rising to the skies again with souls from the earth. There one's mind is filled only with the revelations of eternity. One throbs with love for God. There are the remedy and the cure. Oh, my brother, I long for Mecca and its bright heavens. I long to hear the whispering of time at every corner, to walk down its streets and lose myself in its holy places. How I long to drink from the well of Zamzam and take the road of the Messenger on his Flight, followed by the multitudes of thirteen hundred years ago and those of today, too. I long to feel my heart grow chill when I visit the grave of the Prophet and pray in the Holy Garden. I can see myself now, my brothers, walking through the lanes of Mecca reciting verses from the Qur'an just as they were first revealed, as if I were listening to a lesson given by the Almighty Being. What joy! I can see myself kneeling in the garden imagining the beloved face of the Prophet before me, just as it appears to me in my sleep. What joy! I can see myself prostrated low before the edifice and pleading for forgiveness. What peace I'll have! I see myself going to the well of Zamzam, saturating with water those wounds of passion and crying out for a cure—what divine peace! My brother, speak not of my return, but pray with me to God to fulfill my hopes. . . ."

His friend replied, "May God fulfill your hopes and give you a long and happy life."

Radwan Hussainy lifted his outstretched palm to his beard, his eyes glistening with joy and passion, and continued: "A fine prayer! My love for the afterlife does not turn me toward asceticism or make me dissatisfied with life. You all know of my love for life, and why not? It is a part of the creation of the All Merciful, who filled it with tears and with joys. Let, then, he who will give thought and thanks. I love life in all its colors and sounds, its nights and days, joys and sorrows, beginnings and ends. I love all things living and moving and still. It is all pure goodness. Evil is no more than the inability of the sick to see the good concealed in the crevices. The weak and sick suspect God's world. I believe that love of life is half of worshipping and love of the afterlife is the other half. Therefore, too, I am shocked by the tears and suffering, rage and anger, spite and malice which weigh down the world, and the criticism with which, as well as all these, the weak and sick afflict it. Would they prefer their lives had not been created? Would they ever have loved if they had not been created from nonexistence? Are they really tempted to deny divine wisdom? I do not declare myself innocent. Once sorrow overcame me too and it ate away a piece of my heart. In the throes of my pain and sorrow I asked myself: Why did God not leave my child to enjoy his share of life and happiness? Did not He, the Glorious and Almighty, create the child? Why, then, should He not take him back when He wished? If God had wanted him to have life, then the child would have remained on earth until His will was done. But He reclaimed my child in all the wisdom His will decreed. God does nothing that is not wise, and wisdom is good. My Lord wished well of both me and the child. A feeling of joy overcame me when I realized that His wisdom was greater than my sorrow. I told myself: O God, You brought affliction upon me and put me to the test. I have come through the test with my faith still firm, certain of Your wisdom. Thank You, O God.

"It has since been my practice that whenever anything afflicts me, I express my joyful thanks from the bottom of my heart. Why should I not do so?"

"Whenever I pass over some test to the shores of peace and faith, I become more and more convinced of the wisdom with which He uses His power. In this way

my afflictions always keep me in touch with His wisdom. Why, you could even imagine me as a child playing in his own little world. God treated me severely to rebuke me, frightening me with His mock sternness to double my delight in His real and everlasting kindness. Lovers often put their loved ones to a test, and if they only realized that test is merely a trick and not serious, then their delight in their lovers would be increased. I have always believed that those afflicted on earth are the closest favorites of God. He lavishes love on them in secret, lying in wait for them not far off, to see whether they are really worthy of His love and mercy. All praise to God, for because of his generosity I have been able to comfort those who thought me in need of consolation."

He drew his hand happily over his broad chest, feeling, in so expressing himself, much the same contentment as a singer lost in the rhythm of a melody and elated with the power of his art. He continued with firm conviction: "Some consider that such tragedies afflicting apparently blameless people are signs of a revengeful justice, the wisdom of which is beyond the understanding of most people. So you will hear them say that if the bereaved father, for example, thought deeply, he would realize his loss was a just punishment for some sin either he or his forebears committed. Yet surely God is more just and merciful than to treat the innocent as the guilty. Yet you hear these people justify their opinion by God's Qur'anic description of Himself as 'mighty and revengeful.' But I tell you, gentlemen, that Almighty God has no need of revenge and only adopted this attribute to advise man to practice it. God had already stated that the affairs of this life should be settled only on the basis of reward and punishment. Dear and Almighty God's own essential attributes are wisdom and mercy."

"If I saw in the loss of my children a punishment or penalty I merit, then I would agree with that philosophy and be censured. But I would still be depressed and dissatisfied and no doubt protest that an innocent child died for a weak man's sins. And is that forgiveness and mercy? And where is the tragedy in what reveals wisdom, goodness, and joy?"

Radwan Hussainy's opinions drew objections based on both the literal texts and the scholastic interpretations of Islam. Some present insisted that what seemed revenge was in fact mercy. Many of the older men were both more eloquent and erudite than Radwan, but he had not really been inviting argument. He had merely been expressing the love and joy welling up within him. He smiled, as innocent as a child, his face flushed and his eyes beaming, and went on: "Please forgive me, gentlemen. Permit me to disclose a hidden secret. Do you know what has prompted me to make the pilgrimage this year?"

Radwan Hussainy was silent a moment, his clear eyes glistening with a brilliant light. Then he spoke, in reply to the interested looks in his direction: "I don't deny that I always longed to make the pilgrimage, but each time it was God's will that I put the matter off. Then, as you know, certain things happened here in the alley. The devil managed to ensnare three of our neighbors—a girl and two men. He led the two men to rob a tomb and then left them in prison. As for the girl, the devil led her to the well of sensuality and plunged her into the slime of depravity. All this nearly broke my heart. And I don't wish to disguise from you, gentlemen, my feelings of guilt, for one of the two men lived by mere crumbs of food. He ransacked the graves and decayed bones seeking something of value like a stray dog scratching for food from a garbage heap. His hunger made me think of my own well-fed body and I was overcome with shame and humility. I asked myself what I had done, after all God's goodness to me, to prevent his tragic plight. Had I not simply let the devil amuse himself with my neighbors while I remained lost in my own complacent joy? Cannot a good man unknowingly be an accomplice of the devil by keeping to himself? My conscience told me that I should seek forgiveness in the land of repentance and stay there as long as God wills. I will return with a pure heart and I will put my all to good works in God's kingdom. . . ."

The holy men said prayers for him and happily continued their conversation. . . .

CONTEMPORARY SCHOLARSHIP

There is much debate today about Islamic fundamentalism and the issues surrounding women and Islam. Both of these issues are addressed in this section. The essays model careful scholarship by people educated in the social sciences. The authors have detailed and firsthand knowledge of Islam, and they are sensitive to the important role religion plays in the modern resurgence.

12.5 ISLAMIC REVIVAL

Khurshid Ahmad, author of the following selection, is a leader in the Jamaat-i-Islami, a movement founded by Sayyid Abu'l-A'la Mawdudi. Mawdudi initially op-

posed the formation of a national state in Pakistan on the grounds that it was incompatible with the view that all Muslims formed one community (**umma**). However, once Pakistan was created in 1947, Mawdudi and his organization agitated for a fully Islamic state based on the Qur'an and the *sunna*.

Professor Ahmad was educated in economics and is a former minister of Planning and Development in Pakistan. He writes as both a scholar and someone who has been intimately involved in the Islamic revival in Pakistan. He believes that labeling Islamic resurgence movements "fundamentalist" is misleading and inappropriate. He also argues that religion is vitally important to these movements, which is something Western secularists have had difficulty comprehending.

～⛬～

KHURSHID AHMAD

The Nature of Islamic Resurgence

READING QUESTIONS

1. What has been the impact of colonial rule?
2. What were the strategies for revival?
3. What is one of the most important aspects of Islamic revivalistic movements?
4. What is the relationship between the Islamic revivalist movement and the division between modernists and conservatives?
5. Why is it misleading to call Islamic revivalism "fundamentalism"?
6. What does the West need to understand about Islamic revivalism?
7. Do you think it is possible for the West to have friendly relations with the Muslim world? Why or why not?

Four important consequences directly related to the impact of colonial rule are relevant to an understanding of the contemporary Islamic resurgence in general and the

From *Voices of Resurgent Islam*, edited by John L. Esposito, pp. 218–229. Copyright © 1983 Oxford University Press, Inc. Reprinted by permission of Oxford University Press, Inc. Endnotes omitted.

emergence of the Islamic movement in Pakistan and all of the subcontinent in particular.

MUSLIM PREDICAMENT: THE IMPACT OF COLONIAL RULE

The first is secularization: secularization of the state, its political, economic and social institutions. Secularism tried to introduce and "impose" a new social ethics deriving inspiration from a worldview and a policy perspective diametrically opposed to the basis on which a Muslim society is founded. In a Muslim society individual morality and social ethics are both derived from the same divine source: the Quran and Sunnah. In secularism divine guidance becomes irrelevant and man's roots in the divine scheme of creation and his destiny in the life beyond physical existence are denied. This produces a unique set of parameters for socio-political life, fundamentally different from the ones on which a faith-based society is established. This major change produced catastrophic consequences for Muslim society. The very moral fiber of the society was undermined.

Second is a new pattern of Western dominance, not merely by virtue of its political rule but through basic institutional changes within the colonized countries and their structural relationships with the outside world, particularly the colonizing countries. The result was a pattern of dependence upon the West, institutionalizing the dominance of the West.

Third, and a logical consequence of both the factors cited above, has been the bifurcation of education into two parallel mainstreams of secular and modern education, and religious and traditional education, resulting in the division of the society into two groups: the modern secular elites and the traditional leadership. The members of the new secular leadership, who were carefully groomed into power in different walks of life, are looked upon by the masses of Muslim people as mercenaries—as people who have taken the values and lifestyle of the colonial rulers and who would be prepared to act at the behest of a foreign power, or at least as people who identified themselves with Western culture and its values and became voluntary or involuntary instruments for the Westernization of the society. This has acted as a divisive force in society.

This led to the fourth consequence, a crisis of leadership. The traditional leadership of the Muslim society was systematically destroyed. A foreign political leadership was imposed and in its wake came the imposition of a foreign-oriented local leadership, a leadership which held the reins of political and economic power but which did not enjoy the trust and confidence of the people, a leadership alienated from its own people and identified with the alien rulers and their life-style.

STRATEGIES FOR REVIVAL

These were among the more important consequences of Western dominance and the whole of this scenario made the Muslims ask a very pertinent question: "Why has this happened—this situation of political dominance as well as the decay and deprivation of our past heritage?"

One group tried to answer this question by suggesting that the times have changed and that we must take to the values, the technology, and the institutions of the dominant power. This would be the way to rise up again. This was the strategy of modernism.

Another said that we have reached this stage because we are not true to our original position. We are not truly Muslim. Islam is not responsible for our present predicament; it is the departure from and non-abidance with Islam which is responsible.

This latter answer again produced two further responses—one which tried to fall back upon the Islamic tradition and grasp it tightly, which I will describe as a traditionalist position, which believed that any change would be a change for the worse. Therefore, hold fast to our tradition and its legacy, remain tied to our roots and history. The two aspects of this strategy were: (1) isolation and withdrawal from the process of Westernization; and (2) concentration on preservation and protection of the Muslim legacy, cultural, intellectual, and institutional. This can also be described as a strategy of protective resistance, waiting for an opportunity to reassert itself for the achievement of some positive objectives.

There has also been a second response which emphasized that the preservation of the past was not enough if we are to face the challenge that is knocking at our doors. We have to put up a creative, positive response to this situation by trying to understand the nature of the Western challenge and offer an alternative to that. The challenge from the West was not confined to political domination. It was a challenge from a new civilization, having its own worldview and socio-economic institutions, seeking political domination over the entire world. As such, the response has to be more positive and comprehensive: to prepare for an all-out confrontation with the challenging power and offer Islam as the alternate basis for culture and civilization. This response called for the emergence of Islam as a socio-political movement which sought to go back to the original message of Islam; to discover its relevance to our own times and to strive to change the status quo; to rebuild the society and its institutions in the light of the Islamic milieu; and to inspire the individual with a new vision and a new destiny.

This response has been described as *tajdid* (renewal and reconstruction), a perennial phenomenon in Islamic history and therefore not particularly new or modern. Yet it is distinct in its contemporary manifestation to face the challenge of the twentieth century.

THE ISLAMIC MOVEMENT: ITS ORIGINS AND CHARACTER

The contemporary Islamic resurgence, and particularly the Islamic movements that constitute the sheet-anchor of this resurgence, must be understood not merely by examining them as reactions to colonial rule but in the context of the positive aspirations of the Islamic *ummah* to regain the position it lost because of the Western domination. As such, the contemporary Islamic upsurge deserves to be seen as a positive and creative response to the challenge of modernity. In this respect, in the subcontinent the very establishment of Pakistan, in a way, is symbolic of the Islamic resurgence. The Pakistan movement derived its inspiration from the idea that Islam has to be the decisive factor in building our individual and social life. This was not possible under foreign dominance or under the dominance of the Hindu majority and therefore, the need for an independent country where Islam is free, where Islam is able to determine the course of events. This was the thinking behind the Pakistan movement. That is why the establishment of Pakistan, somehow, constitutes a watershed in contemporary Muslim history; it not only represents the beginning of the end of the colonial rule in Muslim lands but also heralds the beginning of a new era in the ideological life of the Muslim people. Their search for a future assumed a new dimension, an effort to rediscover their ideological personality and to seek for a new social order based on the ideals and values of Islam.

This urge has been articulating itself ever since the mid-forties, despite all the obstacles and deterrents within and without. This creative urge was never looked upon with sympathy in the non-Muslim world in general, and the West in particular. There were genuine difficulties and impediments within Muslim society, particularly the ones generated by the impact of colonial rule on Muslim lands, but the situation was aggravated by the continuing efforts of the Western powers to "Westernize" the liberated Muslim countries and keep them tied to the politico-economic system of the West, to perpetuate some kind of center-periphery relationship between the West and the rest.

This is the background for the contemporary movement of Islamic resurgence. That such an upsurge is there at almost all levels of Muslim existence, intellectual, moral, social, cultural, literary, political and economic, is undeniable. But it would be too simplistic to assume that the movement is heading toward global success. The state of the contemporary Muslim society can at best be described as one of "creative tension." There are certain clear pointers toward the people's positive identification with Islam as a source for personal ethics and the dominant inspiration for the socio-economic order they want to establish in their lands, but the institutional obstacles and selective resistance from certain power-elites are also a reality. A new process has been inaugurated in most of the Muslim countries, but the process has yet to unfold itself fully. It is, therefore, important to identify some of the major factors and forces that are shaping the future of the Muslim world.

RESISTANCE AND RESURGENCE

The major forces of resistance to Islamic resurgence are, somehow, related to the four factors we have identified earlier as aspects of the impact of Western rule in the Muslim World. The forces that lie at the root of Islamic resurgence can be identified as two—first a general urge in the entire Islamic *ummah*, the Muslim people and particularly Muslim youth thrilled by an urge to carve out a new future and seek a place of respect and honour in the world. This is an all-embracing movement which cannot be classified in organization stereotypes. It can only be seen and felt and followed. It is made of two major strands, one negative and the other positive. The negative strand represents strong dissatisfaction with the experiments with secularism and secular ideologies of nationalism, capitalism and socialism in the Muslim World. The positive strand is represented by a rediscovery of Islam as an all-embracing system of life—as a faith as well as an ideology and a programme of life.

Contemporary Islamic resurgence is symbolized as much as it has been strengthened and fortified by the political liberation of the Muslim lands and some significant shifts in the balance of economic power in favour of some of the Muslim countries. But the most decisive influence in producing this upsurge has come from the contribution of the religious leadership of the Muslim countries, the Ulama and the Sufiah in general, and more specifically the Islamic revivalist movements.

ISLAMIC REVIVALIST MOVEMENTS

Islamic revivalist movements have their roots deep in the history of the Muslim people, medieval as well as modern. It would be naive to assume that these movements have emerged out of the blue. There is an almost continuous chain of Islamic movements operating amongst the Muslim people in all parts of the world. These movements have mostly been conveniently ignored by the Western observers of the Islamic scene, who have confined their gaze to the ripples on the surface of the water, never caring to understand the currents and crosscurrents beneath the surface. Those who have tried to touch upon this phenomenon have done greater injustice by misrepresenting these movements as manifestations of militant Islam. The labels put upon them bear no relevance to the nature of these movements; they represent the bias or the fears of the vested interests. Therefore it is very important that the nature of these movements be understood in the light of their own perceptions of their role.

The Islamic movements, despite some local features and indigenous accents, have stood for similar objectives and displayed common characteristics. They have shown unwavering commitment to Islam and great capabilities to face the challenge of modernity creatively. Their intellectual contribution is matched only by their moral fervour and political consciousness.

The most important aspect of the mission of these Islamic movements has been their emphasis on Islam, not just as a set of beliefs and rituals, but as a moral and social movement to establish the Islamic order. And by emphasizing this, they have identified themselves with all the *tajdid* and jihad movements of history. The works of Dr. Muhammad Iqbal, and Mawlana Sayyid Abul Ala Mawdudi (Indo-Pak subcontinent), of Imam Hasan al-Banna Shahid and Sayyid Qutb Shahid (Egypt), of Malik bin Nabi and Shaikh Ibrahim al-Jazairi (Algeria), of Dr. Ali Shariati and Imam Kohmeini (Iran), of Said Nursi (Turkey), and others together constitute the most important influence in producing the contemporary revivalist movements in Islam. Only a close look at the mind and thought of these leaders and the movements they inspired can reveal the true nature of this phenomenon of *tajdid*, an effort to relate Islam to the contemporary reality of the Muslim life and society.

It also deserves to be noted that these Islamic movements seek for comprehensive reform, that is, changing all aspects of life, making faith the centre point. The relationship between the eternal and the temporal, the moral truth and the contemporary socio-political reality, is then a central issue. Mawlana Mawdudi and others have addressed themselves to this issue. They have shown the relevance of faith for individual morality as well as for social ethics, for political life, for economic relationships and for the establishment of a just social order. This all-embracing comprehensiveness of the Islamic movement is integral to the Jamaat-i-Islami Pakistan, the Muslim Brotherhood, as well as to other Islamic movements of the twentieth century. This comprehensiveness of Islam as an integrative principle is something which contrasts sharply with the West for it is not in keeping with the contemporary Western approach to human life and its problems, under whose influence problems are studied piecemeal and in isolation because they are not seen as interrelated and grounded in an integrated worldview.

Another important aspect of Islamic resurgence is that although socio-political struggles have taken place in the context of national situations, even highlighting local interests and problems, the thrust of the Islamic revivalist movement is not nationalistic in character. It is an ideological movement. Even if it is confined or its impact is confined to a particular territory, its approach is not nationalistic or parochial. It is ideological and then by definition international. Islam is a universal religion and all Muslims, regardless of regional or national ties, belong to a single community of brotherhood (*ummah*).

Yet, another important aspect of this movement is that it is non-sectarian. And this is very important in the context of Muslim history. This movement has tried to bring all sects, all the schools of Muslim thought to common ground. It is moving, neither on the pattern of the "ecumenical movement" in the Christian world, nor of that of a religious trade union. Its basic emphasis is that the essential area of agreement amongst all Muslim schools of thought is far greater than its fringe differences. When the basic laws and regulations of Islam are being threatened, we must concentrate upon the essentials in the areas of agreement, allowing for the freedom of each individual and each group to follow his or her own interpretation. Thus, the works of some of the Shia scholars, for example, the late Ayatollah Muhammad Baqir Sadr, Imam Khoumeini, and Dr. Ali Shariati have been published by predominantly Sunni organizations such as Mawlana Mawdudi's Jamaat-i-Islami in Pakistan, the Muslim Brotherhood in Egypt and other Arab countries. On the other hand, the works of Mawlana Mawdudi, Sayyid Qutb, Hasan al-Banna and others have been published by the Shia communities of Qum. The Islamic revolution of Iran has been welcomed by all Islamic revivalist movements, and even when there are differences on many a point of strategy or tactics, the universalistic Islamic current is easily discernable in a world which had unfortunately taken to sectarian and group affiliations.

Finally, an important aspect which deserves to be kept in view is the division in Muslim society between modern and conservative, between the new and the old, the westernizing and the traditional. This Islamic movement represents a third alternative force. Without condemning any of these, it acts as a bridge between these two and derives its strength from both of them. Instead of expanding the distance between these, it seeks to reach a point of convergence and join together all their resources. In the Jamaat-i-Islami Pakistan we find people from the old school, the ulama and the Sufiya (mystics) as well as highly educated people, students, professionals, and the working classes. The movement works among the labour force, among farmers, among all the various segments of society.

On the international plane too, the approach of the Islamic movement is to draw on the modern civilization as well as the original sources of Islam and to seek to modernize without compromising on Islamic principles and values. The movement clearly differentiates between development and modernization on the one hand and westernization and secularization on the other. It says "yes" to modernization but "no" to blind westernization. The Islamic movement seeks to provide a new leadership to society, a leadership which, although culled from the modern and the traditional hinterland of the society is not identified with any one of these two extreme groups but nonetheless preserves the best in both.

THE FAILURE OF THE WESTERN MODEL

This, I think, is extremely significant because a very important dimension of the present-day crisis in the Muslim world is that the westernizing model as well as the westernizing elite have failed. The two classic examples of westernization in Muslim countries are Turkey and Iran. Whether we judge on the basis of the material results these experiments have produced or the moral havoc, the social ills and the psychological shock that have come in their wake, it is the profound feeling of the Muslim people that the Westernization experiment has decisively failed. Both its variants, the capitalistic as well as the socialistic, have been tried and found wanting.

The whole of the Muslim *ummah* has somehow passed through a trauma, becoming more and more conscious that the westernizing model cannot deliver the goods. They want to make a fresh start. They do not want to cut themselves off from the rest of the world. But they also do not want to be dependent on the non-Muslim world. They want freedom with strength; friendship with honour; cooperation without dependence. If the westernizing experiment has failed to achieve this, what next? The Islamic movement represents one such alternative.

If you look at the Islamic movements over the last two centuries, you will find in the first phase the predominant challenge that the Islamic movement faced was invasion by foreign powers. It tried to resist threats to the freedom and political sovereignty of Dar al-Islam (Islamic territory) but it could not succeed. Nonetheless it made its impact. A second phase occurred when western dominance had consolidated itself. Again, the challenge to colonialism came from Islamic sources which informed the people of their Islamic identity and inspired resistance movements against foreign rule. The Islamic movement was the chief source of the independence movement, seeking liberation from the political dominance of foreign powers. And it succeeded. But in its success, there also was a failure. The new system that was established by the new regimes in most of the Muslim countries was not Islamic. It was still cast in the likeness of Western models. The new political, economic, and intellectual leadership of the Muslim countries was just a replica, a transplant implanted by Western powers. Now we have a third phase that Muslim countries are passing through. The third phase is the Islamic resurgence. The westernizing model has failed and now Islamic movements want to reconstruct society. They are in search of a new social order. They want new answers to the questions which have been agitating them. The Islamic movements have given Muslims a new outlook, a new hope, a new possibility. It is the restructuring of their society, individual and collective life and rebuilding socio-economic life on the foundations of Islam. They are not averse to the technology of the West; but are not prepared to have it at the cost of their own identity and ideology.

THE SPECTER OF FUNDAMENTALISM!

The West has failed to see the strength and potential of the Islamic movement. It has chosen to dub it as fundamentalist, as fanatic, as anti-Western, as anachronistic, as what not. Nothing could be farther from the truth. It appears that the West is once again committing the fatal mistake of looking upon others belonging to a different paradigm, from the prism of its own distorted categories of thought and history.

Efforts to put the cap of "fundamentalism" on Islamic movements is one such example. Fundamentalism was a unique phenomenon produced in certain periods of Western Christian history. It tried to impose a literalist interpretation on a Book which claimed divine inspiration but was not the word of God, pure and simple. The fundamentalist groups in Christian history came up with many new interpretations and strange religio-political positions and are generally regarded as reactionary and unrealistic. By clamping the same term on Islamic movements great violence is being done to history. It is also bound to misinform the western people and policy-makers about the true nature of Islamic resurgence, as they are being forced to see them in the light of a particular unhappy chapter of their own history. Islamic resurgence is a future-oriented movement and has nothing in common with the fundamentalist approach of the Christian groups. it has shown great awareness of the problems of modernity and the challenges of technology, and its emphasis on the original sources of Islam, the Quran and Sunna, imparts to its approach a flexibility and a capability to innovate which is conspicuous by its absence in the approach of the conservatives who stick to a particular school of *fiqh* (law). All these possibilities are ignored by analysts who try to see the contemporary Islamic world in categories which are not relevant to it.

The present Muslim mind cannot be understood properly unless we realize that it is deeper than just a political anguish. Unfortunately, efforts to understand the Islamic resurgence are often simplistic. The theory that the Islamic resurgence is just a result of rapid developmental efforts, particularly in the case of Iran, is overly simplistic. Yes, the development syndrome has its own problems, but it would be an oversimplification to assume that the Muslim peoples' overwhelming response to forces of resurgence is simply due to the tensions that have been produced by efforts to achieve quick economic development through technology transfer. Such diagnosis betrays abysmal ignorance of the ethos of the Muslim society.

Similarly, reducing the resurgence to just an angry reaction of people against Western imperialism is equally misleading. There is a reaction against imperialism; there is no doubt about that. However, more than a political fury is being expressed or articulated. A much deeper cause is dissatisfaction with the ideals and values, the institutions and the system of government exported from the West and imposed upon them. It is a dissatisfaction with their leadership which they associate with Western interests and believe has been instrumental in imposing Western models of development on the Muslim society. It is a multidimensional phenomenon. On the one hand, it is an historical expression of the concerns as well as the aspirations of the people, based primarily upon internal indigenous factors. On the other hand, it is also a response to an external challenge, the challenge of post-colonial impacts on Muslim society.

The movement of Islamic resurgence is a critique of the Muslim status quo. It is also a critique of the dominant culture of our times—the Western culture and civilization which is prevalent in many of the Muslim countries. And it is a critique from a different base, from a different point of reference; and that point of reference is Islam, the original sources of Islam—the Quran and Sunna of the Prophet Muhammad (peace be upon him).

It represents a reawakening of faith. This dimension is neglected in most of the Western writings; they assume that it is just a question of political and social rearrangements. The social order is definitely important but the starting point is reawakening and strengthening of faith, and rebuilding of the moral personality and the character of the individual. There is an upsurge of spirituality and idealism, generating a new sense of direction and a commitment to reconstruct their world, whatever be the sacrifice.

The model of leadership during the period of colonial domination and of post-colonial manipulation has been one which just looked after personal interests. That is why Muslim society has become so devoid of moral values and become rife with corruption. Corruption and exploitation have become a way of life in our part of the world. Muslims have their own weaknesses and they had faced many reverses as part of the global situation. But the explosion of corruption which is so visible in the present day Muslim World is a new phenomenon. We relate it to the impact of secularization and westernization resulting in loss of individual morality and of social ethics, which had historically been based upon *tawhid* (the unity of God) and loyalty to the Sunna of the Prophet (peace be upon him), and which were weakened under these alien influences. Muslim modernism which has been the secularizing spearhead of westernization in Muslim lands tried to superimpose the values of western liberalism on Muslim society with the result that the grip of traditional values was weakened; but no new morality could be developed to fill the gap. It is in this moral vacuum that personal aggrandizement and socio-economic exploitation have become rampant, mostly in the name of economic development and material progress. Islamic resurgence represents a rebellion against this state of affairs. It stands for a reaffirmation of Islamic morality and a rededication of the resources of the *ummah*—material as well as human—to the achievement of social justice and self-reliance. Muslim youth have been inspired by a new vision to rebuild their individual and social life in accordance with the ideals and principles given by Islam and to strive to establish a new social order, not only within their own countries but to see that a new world order is established ensuring peace, dignity and justice to the oppressed of the world.

ISLAM AND THE WEST

In conclusion, I would suggest that the Islamic resurgence is primarily an internal, indigenous, positive and ideological movement within Muslim society. It is bound to come into contact, even clash with forces in the international arena. The close contact of the West, particularly through colonial rule is relevant but not the most decisive factor in producing the Islamic response.

Muslims constitute one-fifth of the human race, around 900–1000 million in all parts of the world. There are forty-nine independent Muslim states. If they want to reconstruct their socio-economic order according to the values of Islam, it is bound to come into conflict with the international status quo. So conflict is there. And to that extent, I would like to invite my western colleagues to understand that Muslim criticism of Western civilization is not primarily an exercise in political confrontation. The real competition would be at the level of two cultures and civilizations, one based upon Islamic values and the other on the values of materialism and nationalism. Had western culture been based on Christianity, on morality, on faith, the language and *modus operandi* of the contact and conflict would have been different. But that is not the case. The choice is between the Divine Principle and a secular materialist culture. And there is no reason to believe that this competition should be seen by all well-meaning human beings merely in terms of the geo-politic boundaries of the West and the East. In fact all those human beings who are concerned over the spiritual and moral crisis of our times should heave a sign of relief over Islamic resurgence, and not be put off or scared by it.

Once the nature of the conflict is taking place on the level of values and culture is clarified, I want to underscore that there is a political dimension to the situation that we must not ignore. There is nothing pathologically anti-western in the Muslim resurgence. It is neither pro- nor anti-West regarding the political relationship between Western countries and the Muslim world,

despite the loathsome legacy of colonialism which has the potential to mar these relationships. If China and the United States and Russia and India can have friendly relations without sharing common culture and politico-economic system, why not the West and the Muslim World? *Much depends upon how the West looks upon this phenomenon of Islamic resurgence and wants to come to terms with it.* If in the Muslim mind and the Muslim viewpoint, Western powers remain associated with efforts to perpetuate the Western model in Muslim society, keeping Muslims tied to the system of Western domination at national and international levels and thus destabilizing Muslim culture and society directly or indirectly, then, of course, the tension will increase. Differences are bound to multiply. And if things are not resolved peacefully through dialogue and understanding, through respect for each other's rights and genuine concerns, they are destined to be resolved otherwise. But if, on the other hand, we can acknowledge and accept that this world is a pluralistic world, that Western culture can co-exist with other cultures and civilizations without expecting to dominate over them, that others need not necessarily be looked upon as enemies or foes but as potential friends, then there is a genuine possibility that we can learn to live with our differences. If we are prepared to follow this approach, then we would be able to discover many a common ground and many a common challenge. Otherwise, I am afraid we are heading for hard times.

12.6 WOMEN AND ISLAM

The issues surrounding the status of women in Muslim cultures are both serious and urgent. Women are abused and oppressed as they are elsewhere in the world. What is at issue is what action will improve the situation and whether or not there is something essential in Islam that contributes to the abuse.

Many Muslim women, who are interested in liberation, claim that if one returns to the "authentic Islam" revealed in the Qur'an and associated with the life of the Prophet, one will find a much less oppressive Islam than found today. The Qur'an teaches that men and women are equal in Allah's eyes. It is the Islamic traditions developed by males after the time of the Prophet that teach and promote gender inequality.

Nevertheless, serious questions remain about hierarchical social structures that many Muslims root in a spiritual hierarchy of submission. Submission to the will of Allah is at the heart of Islam. Both males and females are to submit to God's will. Does this also imply that females must submit to the will of males?

Fatima Mernissi, a sociologist working at the University of Rabat in Morocco, thinks that the Islamic demand for submission results in a double standard. Males face a single submission, the submission to Allah. Females face a double submission, the submission to God and to males. In the article that follows, Mernissi explores the sociological reasons for this and its implications for women and for the feminist movement in Islamic countries.

FATIMA MERNISSI

Femininity as Subversion

READING QUESTIONS

1. What does **nushuz** mean?
2. What is Fatma Sabbah's argument?
3. What is Fatima Mernissi's thesis?
4. What is **bid'a,** and what is its relationship to *nushuz?*
5. Who is Sakina, and what does she symbolize?
6. What do each of the three modern instances of "women's rebellion" illustrate?
7. What do you think about Mernissi's claim that some Muslims see the battle between men and women as one aspect of the cosmological battle between good and evil?
8. What does Mernissi conclude?

Nushūz is a Koranic concept; it means the rebellion of the wife against her Muslim husband's authority. The Koran only refers to *nushūz* in order to describe the punishment a husband must inflict upon the wife in case she rebels. Ghazali defines the *nashiz* (the woman who rebels; plural, *nawashiz* or *nashizat*) as a wife who confronts her husband either in act or word. He explains that the word *nashz* means "that which tries to elevate itself above ground."

From Fatima Mernissi, "Femininity as Subversion: Reflections on the Muslim Concept of *Nuzhuz*," in *Speaking of Faith: Global Perspectives on Women, Religion and Social Change*, edited by Diana L. Eck and Devaki Jain (Philadelphia, Pa.: New Society Publishers, 1987), pp. 95–108. Copyright © 1987 Committee on Women, Religion and Social Change. Reprinted by permission. Endnotes omitted.

In this paper, I do not want to elaborate a theory of the concept of surrender in Islamic thought. Fatna Sabbah has convincingly done that in *The Woman in the Muslim Unconscious* (1984). She argues, and I agree with her, that "the ideal of female beauty in Islam is obedience, silence and immobility, that is inertia and passivity. These are far from being trivial characteristics, nor are they limited to women. In fact, these three attributes of female beauty are the three qualities of the believer vis-a-vis his God. The believer must dedicate his life to obeying and worshipping God and abiding by his will." Fatna Sabbah explains that the woman's obedience to the husband is not just a marginal device in Islam; she demonstrates that it is a central element and a key law for the viability of the system. "In the sacred universe," she states, after having analyzed the orthodox Sunni Islamic discourse, "the believer is fashioned in the image of woman, deprived of speech and will and committed to obedience to another (God). The female condition and the male condition are not different in the end to which they are directed, but in the pole around which they orbit. The lives of beings of the male sex revolve around the divine will. The lives of beings of the female sex revolve around the will of believers of the male sex. And in both cases the human element, in terms of multiple, unforeseeable potentialities, must be liquidated in order to bring about the triumph of the sacred, the triumph of the divine, the non-human."

I want to suggest in this paper that women's disobedience is so feared in the Muslim world because its implications are enormous. They refer to the most dreaded danger to Islam as a group psychology: individualism. I want here to suggest that Muslim societies resist women's claim to changing their status, that they repress feminist trends which are actually evident all over the Muslim world, and that they condemn them as western imports, not simply because these societies fear women, but because they fear individualism.

Individualism, the person's claim to have legitimate interests, views and opinions different from those of the group, is an alien concept and fatal to heavily collectivist Islam. Islam, like any theocracy, is group-oriented, and individual wishes are put down as impious, whimsical, egotistical passions. I would suggest, however, that the woman, identified in the Muslim order as the embodiment of uncontrolled desires and undisciplined passions, is precisely the symbol of heavily suppressed individualistic trends. I believe that if the issues of the veil and of women's rights are so central to Muslim fundamentalist movements today, it is because these movements can be interpreted as strong visceral reactions against individualism. The primary issue being debated in the Muslim world today is democracy—the individual right to choose society's rulers. The right of each citizen to choose those who rule, through clear voting procedures, is a total reversal of the idea of personhood in Islam. It is the world upside-down. Democracy indicates clearly that it is the individual who is the sacred source of political authority, and not the group. Islam, like all theocracies, puts the emphasis on the *umma* as a mythically homogeneous group, which is the legitimate source of authority. The objective of Muslim society is the survival of the *umma*, not the happiness of the individual. The latter is totally submissive to the religious law which binds his/her acts and thought in all spheres of human experience, from the most public to the most intimate.

In these few pages I want to indicate that we will not understand the resistance of Muslim societies to the change in women's status and rights if we do not take into account the symbolic function of women as the embodiment of dangerous individualism. It is this individualism that society has chosen to repress in order to safeguard a collective orientation. Therefore we will see, in the first part of this paper, the notion of *nushūz* (rebellion or subversion) as it is linked to one of the most individualistic concepts of Islam, the concept of *bid'a*, that is, innovation; in the second part of the paper, we will see women's rebellion through the historical profiles of dissenting women; and in the final part, we will see the implications of women's dissent in the present situation, namely in the integral relatedness of three phenomena: women's claim to change, the disintegration of traditional society, and the invasion of western, capitalist, consumerist individualism. In this last part, I want to clarify why most feminists in the Muslim world are faced with the threat of being labelled as western agents, traitors or enemies of the community. The western hedonist and consumerist invasion of Muslim societies is, of course, seen as a disruption of the social fabric, and women who claim change—and therefore claim their own individuality—are viewed as agents of such disruption.

This paper will be impressionistic and suggestive in approach. I will not attempt, in this context, to prove each argument with precise scholarly elaboration. . . .

INDIVIDUALISM AS A CRIME AGAINST THE SACRED LAW: THE CONCEPT OF *BID'A* AND ITS PROXIMITY TO THE CONCEPT OF *NUSHŪZ*

Bid'a is "innovation." It is the capacity of the individual to change his or her fate, life and thoughts about people and things, and to act critically in accordance with one's own assessment of the situation. *Bid'a* is considered a deadly sin in Islamic orthodoxy. *Bid'a* is not only error, it is a crime, in that one steps out of the "right path" traced out and organized by the sacred law of the group. It is deviating from the straight paths, the *tariq al mustaqim*, and is dangerous not only because innovators dissent from the community, but because in doing so they challenge the very existence of order based on consensus. In Islamic cosmogony, the sexes play an important role in symbolizing obedience and authority. One sex can be the masters of women and the slaves of God, and that is the male sex; the other can be slaves only, and that is the female sex. In no way can women take the initiative. If they do, the whole order is in jeopardy, since their function and duty is to obey.

It is of real significance that Arabic has a special word for "women's rebellion"—*nushūz*. What happens, then, when *nushūz* occurs? What happens when women rebel and seize their own authority, refuse to obey the sacred laws in a theocracy? Did this ever happen? And if it did what was society's response? It was strong and immediate. Why? As we shall see, the resistance to women's rebellion does not concern women alone—it concerns men as well. If the women, the embodiment of duty, rebel, then what about the men who have the double role of master and slave? They are likely to be faced with the fact that their "slaves" rebel "better" than they do, and that their "slaves" exercise power and take the initiative. This, as one can imagine, undermines the whole hierarchical order.

I want to suggest through several examples that the notion of equality between men and women is profoundly threatening to the Muslim hierarchical order. The notion of a strong bond between a man and a woman, expressed in English by the word "couple," does not exist in Arabic. Arabic has fifty words for "love," but no word for "couple." This linguistic lapse, far from being a random event, is as I see it a crystal clear symbolic message in societies where rigid sex-role stereotyping is so fundamental to hierarchical order, that when women challenge the status quo they threaten not only patriarchal power (their relation to the husband), but the very existence of the entire system (and more specifically God's claim to obedience). The inflation of words for love is, in my view, a mystification, an attempt to hide the absence of the couple in the Muslim family, which is made institutionally unstable by the practices of repudiation and polygamy.

In recent years, the threat of *nushūz*, women's rebellion, has been activated in Islam by the rise of women's consciousness regarding gender issues and by writings about women's liberation in the Muslim world. It is rooted, however, in the fears the *umma*, the Muslim community, has had for many centuries: the fear of dissent. The fear of the individual standing up to claim his or her private interests as a legitimate source of social organization; the fear of change and innovation; the fear of division and dispersion within Islam; the fear of atomization of the centuries-old myth of group solidarity and collective spirit. The struggle of the Muslim community to maintain the myth of unity came from centuries of fighting heterogeneity and dissent, starting with the huge still-unsolved problem of who should head that community. The authoritarian tradition of Islam came precisely from its expansion, its success in very different lands and cultures in Asia, Africa and Europe —all of which strengthened the authoritarian claim for unity. A claim which imperialistic interest nurtured precisely because dissent, from the start, was tearing that community apart.

In the 1980s, the fear within the *umma* is stronger than ever before, because there are threats to consensus not only from without (the West as a deadly enemy with an invading culture), but from within as well. The increasing access of the poor to education, the incredibly high social mobility, the polarization of classes around economic issues, the emergence of women as salaried workers—all these pose a threat to the Muslim community as it traditionally viewed itself, a homogeneous group.

Submission, in the Muslim tradition, has also come to include submission to God's interpreters here on earth: *khalīfs*, *imāms* and their empowered staff in private spheres, i.e. husbands. In the Islamic vision of human society based upon "submission" or "surrender" to God, authority flows from the top to the bottom. Every individual is integrated into a flawless order, with duties and rights clearly defined. A strong sense of belonging stems from integration into this pyramidal order, in which roles and ways of conduct are minutely defined according to age, sex and access to wealth and knowledge.

Access to knowledge is not a human right but a privilege bestowed by God upon believers. It is thus a key factor in the ordering of society. Islam is the religion of knowledge. Intelligence (*aql*) is an instrument of knowing God; with it one penetrates the meaning of the "signs" (*āyāt*) which only the elect can decode. In Islam there is no conflict between God and scientific inquiry, for the decoding of the "signs" of the universe expands our knowledge of God's might and his bewildering creation. But not all Muslims as individuals are equal in their ability to decode the signs of God, to know God, and to transcend sense and gross material involvement. Hence the necessity to rely on the group.

Submission, obedience to divine law, is for both sexes

and is the duty of every Muslim who wants to strengthen the *umma*. Islam, submission, means to acknowledge the authority of the laws, not to make them. Making the law is the unique privilege of God. God makes his will known through his prophets and through signs available in our surroundings; the prophets' task is precisely to help make them accessible. There is no clergy in Islam as we are repeatedly told, but that does not mean that there is no male hierarchy controlling the understanding of the Koran's meaning. These are the elite male interpreters of the sacred laws, and when we are debating, let us say the veil issue, we are not debating how women feel about it, but what Abu hureira or Abu hanifa or Bukhari said, we are debating which male authority's opinion is the prevailing one. Not what women are feeling or desiring.

SAKINA AND AISHA: FEMINISTS OF THE FIRST CENTURY OF ISLAM

The ideal model of femininity upheld by orthodox Sunni Islam is that of an obedient woman, one who is physically modest. Such a woman does not challenge laws and orders. She veils her body and keeps it available for the husband only. Veiling goes together with a key attribute, modesty, and is the expression of the spatial confinement of women. Spatial confinement is the physical expression of women's exclusion from the public sphere, the sphere precisely of knowledge and power. This explains why Muslim conservative activists, manipulating Islam as a disciplinary framework for their claim to guide and decide for their supporters, will insist on women's modesty. Women's modesty has a wider symbolic function: it refers to the need for the believer to curb his initiative and critical judgement.

Muslim history, from the first century to the present, has had to struggle with women's refusal to conform to such models. Each century had to find a response to *nushūz*, from the time of Sakina, a rebel of the 7th century (first Muslim century), to those women who presently rebel, such as those in Egypt, Algeria, Morocco and elsewhere. Women always struggled against the passive models of femininity but they never were as threatening as they are now, because women's dissent expresses itself through writing. Before, women's resistance to patriarchy was not recorded, it was oral, it confined itself to tales, proverbs or acts. A look at several instances of *nushūz* across the centuries will give us a sense of the continuing threat women rebels pose to the public realm.

SAKINA'S REBELLION:
THE FIRST CENTURY

Starting with the first century, *qādis* and *imāms* seem to have faced the refusal of some women to accept the Muslim laws relating to veiling, seclusion, polygamy and obedience to the husband. These women refused to veil, and insisted on the right to go about freely without asking the husband's permission. They insisted on keeping the right to entertain relations with men other than their husbands, often poets with whom they could engage in intellectual exchange outside the house.

These women also refused the basic principle of Muslim marriage: the husband's authority over the wife and his right to polygamy and repudiation. They insisted on putting conditions which preserved their freedom in the marriage act, and deprived the husband of the right to change residence at will, to have many wives, or to divorce by repudiation. They therefore secured for themselves the right Islam denies a woman: the right to leave her husband when she pleases.

Muslim theologians could not prevent this first wave of women "feminists" from subverting the law because they had three assets which gave them incredible power over the *qādis* and *khalīfs* in charge of enforcing law and order. The three assets were beauty, intelligence and aristocracy. This combination was enough to justify a woman's claim to *nushūz*—rebellion against the prevailing models of femininity.

The conditions Sakina put in her marriage act with one of her husbands, Zayd, made of her a celebrity and a *nashiz*, a rebellious wife. She stipulated that he would have no right to another wife, that he could never prevent her from acting according to her own will, that he would let her elect to live near her woman friend, Ummu Manshuz, and that he would never try to go against her desires. (*Agānī* XIV, pp. 168, 169. Mada'īnī, *Kitāb al Murādafāt*, p. 66.) When the husband once decided to go against Sakina's will and went one weekend to his concubines, she took him to court, and in front of the Medina judge she shouted at him, "Look as much as you can at me today, because you will never see me again!" (*Agānī* XVI, p. 155.)

Sakina was described by al-Zubairi, a historian who, like many others, was full of admiration for her, in these words: "She radiates like an ardent fire. Sakina was a delicate beauty, never veiled, who attended the Quraish Nobility Council. Poets gathered in her house. She was refined [*zarīfa*] and playful."

Sakina, extravagantly elegant, set the tone of fashion in the then economically thriving Hijāz, Arabia felix, where happiness and the good life were possible thanks to Islam's conquering power. The power of the Muslim empire had shifted by then from Mecca to the north, to Syria and Iraq. Rich Quraish families whose wealth had been enhanced by the triumph of Islam lived lavishly and peacefully in the increasingly politically marginal Arabia. One example of this lavish, relaxed and hedonistic Arabian life is that not only did women copy Sakina's hairdo, but men did too! The pious Khalif 'Umar ibn 'Abd al-'Aziz felt in time, the need to intervene and ordered his "police" to punish and shave the heads of those men who insisted on adopting Sakina's hairstyle.

Another *nashiz* of this century was 'A'isha bint Talha, the daughter of Khalif Abu Bakr through her mother. She refused to veil, and when asked why said, "God the mighty distinguished me by my beauty. I want people to see that, and acknowledge my superiority over them. I will not veil. No one can force me to do something." (*Agānī* XI, p. 176.)

These *nashiz* who defied openly the Muslim model of female modesty and obedience were, because of their social rank, very prominent women and were, therefore, a threat to the pattern of religious authority. The theologians decided to fight back and to put a stop to *nushūz*. In law, *nushūz* is addressed as a social problem. For example, al-Muwatta (II, p. 6) states that a man has the right to take his wife where he wishes, regardless of what *nashiz* women put in their marriage contracts. Another example in al-Muwatta (II, p. 14) tries to discourage *nushūz* by stating that the husband is not bound by marriage contract conditions depriving him of his right to polygamy.

FEMINISM AS AN INTERNAL
THREAT TO MUSLIM ORDER:
IMPLICATIONS OF WOMEN'S
NUSHŪZ

Although women have had access to education only in the last few decades, they have gained an incredibly high visibility in the public sphere. In most Arab countries for example, one-fourth of the university teachers are women. Although women are barred from important political posts, they have gained substantial access to middle-level positions in national administrations and do strive to get a more and more important share of the salaries distributed in both private and public sectors.

Moreover, they have now started to use writing to express their desire for changing their status and the society around them. Nineteen eighty-three witnessed the appearance in Arabic of a feminist magazine in Morocco, *The Eighth of March*, which started selling 20,000 copies within the first few months. Nineteen eighty-five witnessed the publication of another "popular" magazine in Tunisia called *Nissa* (women). These examples are perceived as extremely dangerous by many conservatives, since they do not try to proselytize among elites or in university settings, but try to recruit followers from among lay persons. Feminism is no more limited to a few women's salon-like discussions; it has become identified by many women as the ground for voicing economic and political discontent which is impossible to push through trade unions and political parties. Let me simply cite three instances of women's rebellion in the present century, primarily to give a sense of the ways in which *nushūz* continues to be a threat in the Muslim world.

The first was in Algeria during the Revolution. The renowned historian Harbi, an important political figure of revolutionary Algeria, in exile since 1973, gave an interview in *Revoltes logiques* called "Women in the Algerian Revolution." It is perhaps the most discrediting documented statement on the ambiguities and hesitations of the Algerian revolution when it comes to the issue of women in relation to equality and democracy. Harbi explains that the revolutionary "brothers" were totally traditional in their contacts and encounters with women in the Maquis, the guerilla camps. They did everything they could to prevent women from escaping traditional roles; they used women for both traditional needs, such as sex and cooking, and modern needs, such as logistics and carrying arms.

This I mention in order to explain that one of the most important modern revolutions the twentieth century has witnessed, the Algerian revolution, showed that Arab society, even as it was forced to make many sacrifices and to adopt radical change, resisted violently the idea of sacrificing sexual inequality. Algerian revolutionaries hoped to keep women in their proper place, even as they fought for radical change in almost everything else.

A second example is from Tunisia. In March of 1983, the monthly journal for "democracy and socialism," *L'Avenir*, one of the voices of opposition to Bourgiba, published an interview with a Muslim feminist entitled "I am a Rebel." Only those who knew the story behind that title could appreciate the challenge it posed.

The Muslim woman about whom the article was written was Nawal el Saadawi, the Egyptian writer, doctor and feminist. President Bourgiba, who listened to the interview on television, was furious when he realized that she never mentioned his name when talking about liberation movements among Arab women. Bourgiba then gave orders to dismiss the person responsible in Tunisian television, since he had let an Arab woman talk about liberation without mentioning Bourgiba, the "Great Warrior" (al-Mujāhid al-Akbar).

For Bourgiba, a man who is one of the most advanced on the women's question, women's liberation is a man's affair. And it is true that, until the last two decades, the liberation of women was a man's prerogative. The Arab woman, according to modern Muslim thought, is a simple instrument: she will obey, when told to liberate herself according to orders. Now, for *L'Avenir* to repeat that Nawal proclaims herself a rebel is to tell Bourgiba that women rebel, sometimes even without being told to do so!

The third example is from March 1983 in Rabat. In the crowded room of the Human Rights Association, Rue Soussa, which is also the Headquarters of the Moroccan Branch of the Arab Writers' Federation, two hundred people gathered. The group became sharply divided when a number of women, most of them wives of political prisoners, started to talk about their experiences as women in an authoritarian state. They began to analyze their own daily struggle with their husbands, with the prison administration, and with the justice ministry. But all said that these latter struggles were minor compared to those with their own "revolutionary" husbands: the struggle to get their own men to rise higher than the prerogatives of husbands and the privileges of patriarchy to become real persons in relation to their militant wives. To be a political militant, they said, does not automatically liberate a man from oppressive attitudes and actions toward his wife.

The reaction in the room was very strong. Male "militants" screamed that the women were serving a conservative state and police apparatus, which tried to degrade and find fault with revolutionaries. And now women, the very wives of political prisoners, were becoming critics, enemies of the revolution!

These women decided that, for them, there is no difference between men unless that difference is materialized in action, in conduct. A leftist militant is different from a feudal lord not when he says so, but when he actually treats women differently. A woman's experience of a revolutionary man, in his intimate behavior, is a determining criterion and guarantee of the truthfulness of his claim to be a true revolutionary. The private sphere of a political man has not only to be integrated in practice, but has to be considered one of the key determinants of his revolutionary life.

When this was said, chaos set in. The session continued for five hours, with interruptions and insults. Dialogue finally became impossible.

Conclusion: The *Umma* and the Challenge of Individualism(s)

Let me return, now, to the initial question: What happens when a woman disobeys her husband, who is the representative and embodiment of sacred authority, and of the Islamic hierarchy? A danger bell rings in the mind, for when one element of the whole structure of polarities is threatened, the entire system is threatened. A woman who rebels against her husband, for instance, is also rebelling against the *umma*, against reason, order and, indeed, God. The rebellion of a woman is linked to individualism, not community (*umma*); passion, not reason; disorder, not order; lawlessness (*fitna*), not law.

The battle between men and women is an aspect of the battle between good and evil, which is a fundamental form of cosmological conceptualization not only in Islam, but in the Jewish and Christian traditions as well. The world is not only the scene of competition, but of polarization between two great competitors. And the polarization implies a hierarchy. One side of the hierarchy —that aligned with God—is destined to win over the devil and his allies.

THE GOOD	THE EVIL
God	Devil (*Iblis, Satan*)
Men, Husband	Women, Wife, Desire (*as-sahwa*)
Reason	Passion (*al-hawa*)
Order	Disorder
Law	Lawlessness (*fitna*)
Obedience, Consensus	Rebellion (*nushūz*), Dissent
Pre-defined Sacred, Eternal Plan	Innovation, Freedom
The Collective Interest (*umma*)	Individualism

Recent studies have supported this dualistic way of thinking in Sunni Islam. On the parallels to the Devil, Iblis in Muslim thought, Galal ad Adm's *Critique of Religious Thought* (*Dār al-Tālia Beyrouth*, 1980) is a concise analysis of the reason-desire dualism. Fatna Ait Sabbah's *The Woman in the Muslim Unconscious* is probably one of the most recent restatements of that analogy.

Sensual involvement with the gross, material world of earthly pleasures is in the private sphere. It takes place in the domestic realm, in the women's world. In this world, access to knowledge is limited. The private sphere is at the bottom of the pyramidal hierarchy. To be a woman is to be excluded from authority (*al-Sultah*) and knowledge (*'ilm*), both being God's attributes. This is precisely what womanhood is about: to be excluded

from the sphere of sacred ritualized and collective knowledge, the sphere in which decisions are made according to the divine code, orders formulated, laws promulgated. And yet the authority and knowledge of the masculine would be inconceivable without the obedience and submission of the feminine, of women.

In principle, one might say that everything in the public sphere is male. The public sphere of prophets, *imāms* and *khalīfs* is monosex and homogeneous. The private sphere of women is duosex and heterogeneous; its heterogeneity comes from the existence of women. The public sphere is characterized by orders and laws; the private sphere is under the control of the representative of the public sphere, the husband. He embodies the interests of the Divine and the law. In relation to women, the man is not in the posture of "submission," but in command.

To be a man, then, is to be *both* an obedient submitter, in the public realm, to God and his earthly surrogates, who are all males, *and* a master to whom submission is made, in the private realm, where men master women. This is the pyramidal structure of the hierarchy. And it is in this structure that *nushīz*, innovation or women's rebellion, is a threat. Innovation alters the laws, the sacred order, the privilege and hierarchy—all of which are eternal. The believer can only reinterpret; he cannot create for creation is the monopoly of God.

Thus, women's rebellion raises the entire complex of questions relating to individualism. Individual freedom, which women's rebellion represents, challenges the entire notion of community as primary. However, it is also because individualism is encroaching from another quarter that it poses such a threat when expressed by women as well. That other quarter is capitalism, which is based upon the profitability of individualistic innovation. Capitalism is seen as ferociously aggressive and fiercely individualistic. Arab countries have also become dumping grounds for capitalistic goods: western arms, films and consumer goods constitute a virtual invasion. Innovation—the freedom to doubt—is precisely what makes scientific inquiry and the western ideology of capitalism so strong and successful! And innovation is what makes women's rebellion so subversive from within.

In the struggle for survival in the Muslim world today, the Muslim community finds itself squeezed between individualistic, innovative western capitalism on the one hand, and individualistic, rebellious political oppositions within, among which the most symbolically "loaded" is that of rebellious women. The common denominator between capitalism and new models of femininity is individualism and self-affirmation. Initiative is power. Women are claiming power—corroding and ultimately destroying the foundation of Muslim hierarchy; whence the violence of the reaction and the rigidity of the response. Femininity as a symbol of surrender has to be resisted violently if women intend to change its meaning into energy, initiative and creative criticism.

PRONUNCIATION GUIDE

Letters are pronounced in the usual English manner unless indicated otherwise in the following list. The symbol indicates the Arabic letter "ayn," which is pronounced in English by lengthening the preceding vowel.

a	fl*a*t	o	n*o*t
ah	f*a*ther	oo	f*oo*d
ay	p*ay*	ōō	f*oo*t
ee	s*ee*	ow	h*ow*
e	l*e*t	u	b*u*t
ī	h*i*gh	ă	*a*bout
i	p*i*ty	izm	tribal*ism*
ō	n*o*	j	*j*et

Some Examples

caliphs (KAY lifs)   salat (sa LAHT)
dhikr (DHI kar)   Qur'an (kor AN)
faqih (fa KEE)   Shi'i (SHEE ee)
hadith (ha DEETH)   tawhid (tow HEED)

KEY TERMS AND CONCEPTS

Abbasids The name of the second dynasty that ruled much of the Islamic world during the Golden Age of Islam (750–1258).

Abu Bakr The name of Muhammad's friend, advisor, father-in-law, and the first **caliph.**

A'isha Abu Bakr's daughter, one of Muhammad's wives, and an important historical source of information about the early years of Islam.

al-Ash'ari (d. 935) Influential Muslim theologian and founder of the **Ash'aria** school of theology. This school opposed the rationalistic tendencies of the Mu'tazilite theologians.

Ali Muhammad's cousin and son-in-law recognized as the first **imam** by **Shi'i** Muslims.

Allah Arabic word meaning "the god" and used as a proper name for God.

Ash'aria The name of the most influential Muslim theological school.

Baraka A miraculous power bestowed on **Sufi** saints by God.

bid'a Means "innovation" and, in Islamic orthodoxy, refers to the sin of religious innovation.

caliphs Means "deputies" and refers to leaders of the Muslim community after Muhammad.

dhikr Literally means "remembrance" or "repetition" and is used for **Sufi** meditation exercises.

fana The mystical experience of annihilation sought by **Sufis.**

faqaha Scholars of Islamic jurisprudence (*fiqh*).

Fatima Muhammad's daughter and wife of Ali.

fatwa A legal opinion or decree.

fiqh Islamic jurisprudence.

hadith Stories about and sayings attributed to Muhammad. Hadith judged authentic are second only to the **Qur'an** in authority.

hajj A pilgrimage to the **Kaaba** in Mecca. It is one of the Five Pillars of Islam.

Hanafi One of the four **Sunni** law schools and, at present, the most influential.

Hanbali A **Sunni** legal school that is most influential in Saudi Arabia.

hijra The migration of Muhammad and his followers from Mecca to Medina in 622.

ijma Consensus of the community and one of the sources of Islamic law.

ijtihad Independent reasoning by a qualified legal scholar.

Imam A term used for anyone who leads prayers in a **mosque** as well as a title for the rightful leader of the **Shi'i** sect.

Iman Arabic word for "faith."

Islam Means "surrender" or "submission" and is used to name the monotheistic religion that recognizes Muhammad as the last messenger of God.

jihad Arabic word that refers to personal or individual striving to follow the path of God and, on a collective level, to any action defending Islam or furthering its cause. Sometimes translated as "holy war."

jinn Sentient beings with supernatural qualities. The English word *genie* is derived from *jinn*.

Kaaba A cubic building in Mecca believed to have been built by Abraham and the focus of the **hajj** and of Muslim prayer.

kalam Refers to Islamic theology and literally means "speech."

Khadija The name of Muhammad's first wife, who is honored as the first convert to Islam.

Mahdi An eschatological figure in Shi'ite Islam who is the appearance of the twelfth **imam** now in occultation.

Maliki One of the Sunni legal schools that has been traditionally strong in North Africa.

mosque A Muslim place of prayer and worship (from the Arabic *masjid*, or "place of prostration").

mufti An expert in law, or *shari'a.*

Muhammad The primary prophet of Islam.

Muslim (fem. **muslima**) A person who professes Islam.

Mu'tazila The name for a Muslim theological school that favors rationalistic methods of interpretation.

nushuz Rebellion of a wife against her husband's authority.

qiyas Reasoning by analogy. One of the four sources of jurisprudence.

Qur'an The holy scripture of Islam. It means "recitation."

Ramadan The ninth month of the Islamic lunar calendar during which Muslims fast. It commemorates the *hijra,* or migration from Mecca to Medina.

Rasul A messenger of God and title for Muhammad.

salat Ritual prayer.

sama The distinctive whirling dance of the Sufi dervishes.

Shafi'i A name for one of the legal schools of the **Sunnis.**

shahada The Islamic profession of faith and the first Pillar of Islam: "There is no god, but God (Allah), and Muhammad is the messenger (*rasul*) of God."

shari'a Islamic law as a whole.

Shi'i The name for a number of Muslim sects who separated from the Sunnis over the status of Ali as the successor to Muhammad.

Sufism A mystical movement in Islam.

sunna The custom or practice of the Prophet that is used as a source of Islamic law.

Sunnis The majority sect of Islam.

surah The name for chapters in the **Qur'an.**

Tawhid The concept of the divine unity.

Twelver Shi'is An important **Shi'i** sect dominant in Iran.

Umayyads The first dynasty to rule the Islamic world.

umma The community of believers made up of Muslims all over the world.

Usul al-fiqh The basic principles of jurisprudence: **Qur'an,** *sunna, qiyas,* and *ijma.*

zakat The obligation to give alms.

SUGGESTIONS FOR FURTHER READING

Elias, Jamal J. *Islam.* Upper Saddle River, N.J.: Prentice-Hall, 1999. Clearly and briefly explains Islamic history, belief, and practice at a beginning level.

Esposito, John L. *Islam: The Straight Path.* 3rd ed. New York: Oxford University Press, 1998. A readable and reliable introduction that is especially good in its treatment of modern Islam.

Renard, John. *Seven Doors to Islam: Spirituality and the Religious Life of Muslims.* Berkeley: University of California Press, 1998. An excellent introduction to Islam.

Renard, John, ed. *Windows on the House of Islam: Muslim Sources on Spirituality and Religious Life.* Berkeley: University of California Press, 1998. One of the best anthologies now available with a wide range of sources.

Sidahmed, Abdel Salam, and Anoushiravan Ehteshami, eds. *Islamic Fundamentalism.* Boulder, Colo.: Westview Press, 1996. A collection of essays covering the wide variety of Islamist movements today.

RESEARCH PROJECTS

1. If you are not a Muslim, and if there are Muslim students on your campus, arrange an interview with two or three of them. Politely ask questions about their religious, social, and political views. Do not argue with them, but seek to elicit as much information as you can. Use this information as a basis for a paper on the views of younger Muslims.

2. Research and write a paper comparing Islamic, Christian, and Jewish views of God. State precisely how they are the same and how they are different. Account for the differences in your paper.

3. Find and read major stories done on Islam in the leading newsmagazines (*Time, Newsweek, US News and World Report*) over the past five years. Critically analyze these stories (pay particular attention to the terminology they use), and check

them for accuracy. Write a report on what you discover.

4. Do a review of two or three Web sites on Islam that you discover. Describe the information available on these sites, and evaluate them for accuracy and usefulness.

5. Select any two articles from *Liberal Islam: A Sourcebook*, edited by Charles Kurzman (New York: Oxford University Press, 1998) and write a critical review. Summarize the articles and evaluate them.

Appendix

Religion on the Web

The resources on the World Wide Web are both fleeting and untrustworthy. The addresses I have annotated below will aid the student who wishes to explore religion in cyberspace. However, some will have changed or no longer exist by the time this book reaches publication. Those seeking more information should consult Patrick Durusau's *High Places in Cyberspace: A Guide to Biblical and Religious Studies, Classics, and Archaeological Resources on the Internet*, 2nd ed. (Atlanta, Ga.: Scholars Press, 1998) for information on searching the internet, browsers, creating Web resources, E-mail discussion lists, and URLs. See **http://schemesh.scholar.emory.edu/scripts/high places.html** for updates.

GENERAL RESOURCES

http://religion.rutgers.edu/vir
"Virtual Religion Index: Links for Research on Religion" is a tool providing hyperlinks to homepages, major subsites, documents, and directories in religion. It is a good starting point for resources relating to the academic study of religion available on the Web.

http://www.freenet.edmonton.ab.ca/~cstier/religion/toc.htm
"A Guide to the Best Religious Studies Resources on the Internet" provides links to resources that the creators regard as the most useful sources for undergraduates seeking more information on the major religions of the world including Buddhism, Christianity, Hinduism, Islam, Judaism, Confucianism, Taoism, and others.

http://www.wlu.ca/~wwwrandc/internet_links.html
"Religious Studies Internet Links" is a well-organized listing that provides not only directories for the major religions but also course syllabi, multimedia resources, departments, societies, and current religious news.

http://scholar.cc.emory.edu/
"TELA" (Scholars Press) is the official Web site for the Scholars Press and sponsoring societies such as the American Academy of Religion, the Society of Biblical Literature, the American Philological Association, the American Schools of Oriental Research, and the American Society of Papyrologists. This is an important and essential site for students of religion.

http://www/academicinfo.net/religindex.html
"Religion: A Directory of Internet Resources for the Study of Religion" provides a good list with hundreds of links to directories, historical studies, bibliographies, sacred texts, and other documents on religions. It is particularly useful for interdisciplinary topics such as "Women and Religion" or "Art and Religion."

http://www.arda.tm
"American Religion Data Archive" lists dozen of influential studies on American religion and allows you to view, print, or download important data files. This project is supported by the Lilly Endowment.

http://www.human.toyogakuen-u.ac.jp/~acmuller/
This site, maintained by Charles Muller of Toyo Gakuen University, provides a listing of many of the most important resources for Buddhism, Confucianism, and Taoism.

BUDDHISM

http://ciolek.com/WWWVC-Buddhism.html
This is an outstanding database with electronic texts, information, and links on nearly every aspect of Buddhism.

http://www.human.toyogakuen-u.ac.jp/
~acmuller/ebti.htm
This site allows access to the Electronic Buddhist Text Initiative (EBTI), a collection of major Buddhist online text projects organized by Lewis Lancaster of the University of California at Berkeley.

http://kaladarshan.arts.ohio-state.edu
"John C. and Susan L. Huntington Archive of Buddhist and Related Art" is an image-intensive site containing almost 300,000 original color slides and black-and-white photographs of Asian art and architecture drawn from the Huntington Archive.

CHRISTIANITY

http://www.iclnet.org/pub/resources/christian-history.html
"Early Christian Texts" is an excellent site for the study of Christianity in its early and medieval periods. It provides full-text versions of creeds and the writings of early theologians.

http://goon.stg.brown.edu/bible_browser/
pbeasy.shtml
This search tool allows users to locate words or phrases in any of eight versions of the Bible.

http://www.hti.umich.edu/relig/mormon.html
This is a searchable electronic version of the Book of Mormon that allows users to browse specific sections.

http://www.vpm.com/thawes
"Theology on the Web" is a useful collection of links relating to Christianity.

CONFUCIANISM AND TAOISM

http://www-personal.monash.edu.au/~sab/
index.html
"Chinese Philosophy Page" seeks to provide all the information available on the internet about Chinese philosophy and related subjects.

http://www.clas.ufl.edu/users/gthursby/taosim
"Taoism WWW Virtual Library" may well be the most comprehensive source of information on Taoism on the Web.

HINDUISM

http://www.hindunet.org
A general directory with links to information on many facets of Hinduism including art, temples, and organizations.

http://rbhatnagar.csm.uc.edu:8080/scriptures.
html
"The Hindu Electronic Scriptures Reference Center" provides the full texts in English translation of several Hindu scriptures including the *Ramayana* and *Mahabharata*. The Hindu Students Council, an international, nonprofit religious organization, produces part of this site (called the Hindu Universe).

ISLAM

http://goon.stg.brown.edu/quran_browser
"Qur'an Browser" is a searchable database of the Qur'an with a choice of translations.

http://www.princeton.edu/~humcomp/alkhaz.
html
"Al-Khazina: The Treasury" is an educational Web site with links to information on the Qur'an, *Hadith*, and *Hajj* databases, along with historical charts, maps, and photographs.

http://wings.buffalo.edu/student-life/sa/
muslim/isl/texts.html
A number of different links to the hypertext version of the Qur'an along with sound files of the recitations of the Qur'an.

JUDAISM

http://www.shamash.org/trb/judaism.html
The most complete directory of links to Jewish resources, both academic and general, on the Web.

http://world.std.com/~alevin/jewishfeminist.html

For those with a specific interest in Jewish feminism, this site provides a wealth of resources and information.

NATIVE AMERICAN

http://www.academicinfo.net/nativeam.html#religions

This connection through the directory of the study of religions will link you to a variety of useful sources on Native American religions.